ANDERSON'S
Law School Publications

Administrative Law Anthology
Thomas O. Sargentich

Administrative Law: Cases and Materials
Daniel J. Gifford

An Admiralty Law Anthology
Robert M. Jarvis

Alternative Dispute Resolution: Strategies for Law and Business
E. Wendy Trachte-Huber and Stephen K. Huber

The American Constitutional Order: History, Cases, and Philosophy
Douglas W. Kmiec and Stephen B. Presser

American Legal Systems: A Resource and Reference Guide
Toni M. Fine

Analytic Jurisprudence Anthology
Anthony D'Amato

An Antitrust Anthology
Andrew I. Gavil

Appellate Advocacy: Principles and Practice, *Third Edition*
Ursula Bentele and Eve Cary

Arbitration: Cases and Materials
Stephen K. Huber and E. Wendy Trachte-Huber

Bankruptcy Anthology
Charles J. Tabb

Basic Accounting Principles for Lawyers: With Present Value and Expected Value
C. Steven Bradford and Gary A. Ames

Basic Themes in Law and Jurisprudence
Charles W. Collier

The Best-Kept Secrets of Evidence Law: 101 Principles, Practices, and Pitfalls
Paul R. Rice

A Capital Punishment Anthology (and Electronic Caselaw Appendix)
Victor L. Streib

Cases and Materials in Juvenile Law
J. Eric Smithburn

Cases and Materials on Corporations
Thomas R. Hurst and William A. Gregory

Cases and Materials on the Law Governing Lawyers
James E. Moliterno

Cases and Problems in California Criminal Law
Myron Moskovitz

Cases and Problems in Criminal Law, *Fourth Edition*
Myron Moskovitz

The Citation Workbook: How to Beat the Citation Blues, *Second Edition*
Maria L. Ciampi, Rivka Widerman, and Vicki Lutz

Civil Procedure Anthology
David I. Levine, Donald L. Doernberg, and Melissa L. Nelken

Civil Procedure: Cases, Materials, and Questions, *Third Edition*
Richard D. Freer and Wendy Collins Perdue

Civil Procedure for Federal and State Courts
Jeffrey A. Parness

Clinical Anthology: Readings for Live-Client Clinics
Alex J. Hurder, Frank S. Bloch, Susan L. Brooks, and Susan L. Kay

Commercial Transactions Series: Problems and Materials
Louis F. Del Duca, Egon Guttman, Alphonse M. Squillante, Fred H. Miller, Linda Rusch, and Peter Winship
    Vol. 1: Secured Transactions Under the UCC
    Vol. 2: Sales Under the UCC and the CISG
    Vol. 3: Negotiable Instruments Under the UCC and the CIBN

Communications Law: Media, Entertainment, and Regulation
Donald E. Lively, Allen S. Hammond, Blake D. Morant, and Russell L. Weaver

A Conflict-of-Laws Anthology
Gene R. Shreve

Constitutional Conflicts
Derrick A. Bell, Jr.

A Constitutional Law Anthology, *Second Edition*
Michael J. Glennon, Donald E. Lively, Phoebe A. Haddon, Dorothy E. Roberts, and Russell L. Weaver

Constitutional Law: Cases, History, and Dialogues, *Second Edition*
Donald E. Lively, Phoebe A. Haddon, Dorothy E. Roberts, Russell L. Weaver, and William D. Araiza

The Constitutional Law of the European Union
James D. Dinnage and John F. Murphy

The Constitutional Law of the European Union: Documentary Supplement
James D. Dinnage and John F. Murphy

Constitutional Torts
Sheldon H. Nahmod, Michael L. Wells, and Thomas A. Eaton

A Contracts Anthology, *Second Edition*
Peter Linzer

Contract Law and Practice
Gerald E. Berendt, Michael L. Closen, Doris Estelle Long, Marie A. Monahan, Robert J. Nye, and John H. Scheid

Contracts: Contemporary Cases, Comments, and Problems
Michael L. Closen, Richard M. Perlmutter, and Jeffrey D. Wittenberg

A Copyright Anthology: The Technology Frontier
Richard H. Chused

Corporate Law Anthology
Franklin A. Gevurtz

Corporate and White Collar Crime: An Anthology
Leonard Orland

Criminal Law: Cases and Materials, *Second Edition*
Arnold H. Loewy

Criminal Procedure: Cases, Materials, and Questions
Arnold H. Loewy

Criminal Procedure: Arrest and Investigation
Arnold H. Loewy and Arthur B. LaFrance

Criminal Procedure: Trial and Sentencing
Arthur B. LaFrance and Arnold H. Loewy

Economic Regulation: Cases and Materials
Richard J. Pierce, Jr.

Elder Law: Readings, Cases, and Materials
Thomas P. Gallanis, A. Kimberley Dayton, and Molly M. Wood

Elder Law: Statutes and Regulations
Thomas P. Gallanis, A. Kimberley Dayton, and Molly M. Wood

Elements of Law
Eva H. Hanks, Michael E. Herz, and Steven S. Nemerson

Ending It: Dispute Resolution in America
  Descriptions, Examples, Cases and Questions
Susan M. Leeson and Bryan M. Johnston

An Environmental Law Anthology
Robert L. Fischman, Maxine I. Lipeles, and Mark S. Squillace

Environmental Law Series
  Environmental Decisionmaking, *Third Edition*
  Robert L. Fischman and Mark S. Squillace

  Water Pollution, *Third Edition*
  Jackson B. Battle and Maxine I. Lipeles

  Air Pollution, *Third Edition*
  Mark S. Squillace and David R. Wooley

  Hazardous Waste, *Third Edition*
  Maxine I. Lipeles

Environmental Protection and Justice
  Readings and Commentary on Environmental Law and Practice, *Second Edition*
Kenneth A. Manaster

European Union Law Anthology
Karen V. Kole and Anthony D'Amato

An Evidence Anthology
Edward J. Imwinkelried and Glen Weissenberger

Family Law in Action: A Reader
Margaret F. Brinig, Carl E. Schneider, and Lee E. Teitelbaum

Federal Antitrust Law: Cases and Materials, *Second Edition*
Daniel J. Gifford and Leo J. Raskind

Federal Income Tax Anthology
Paul L. Caron, Karen C. Burke, and Grayson M.P. McCouch

Federal Rules of Civil Procedure
Publisher's Staff

Federal Rules of Evidence Handbook
Publisher's Staff

Federal Rules of Evidence: Rules, Legislative History, Commentary and Authority
Glen Weissenberger and James J. Duane

Federal and State Civil Procedure Handbook, *Second Edition*
Jeffrey A. Parness

Federal Wealth Transfer Tax Anthology
Paul L. Caron, Grayson M.P. McCouch, Karen C. Burke

First Amendment Anthology
Donald E. Lively, Dorothy E. Roberts, and Russell L. Weaver

The History, Philosophy, and Structure of the American Constitution
Douglas W. Kmiec and Stephen B. Presser

Individual Rights and the American Constitution
Douglas W. Kmiec and Stephen B. Presser

International Human Rights: Law, Policy, and Process, *Third Edition*
David Weissbrodt, Joan Fitzpatrick, and Frank Newman

Selected International Human Rights Instruments and
   Bibliography for Research on International Human Rights Law, *Third Edition*
David Weissbrodt, Joan Fitzpatrick, Frank Newman, Marci Hoffman, and Mary Rumsey

International Intellectual Property Anthology
Anthony D'Amato and Doris Estelle Long

International Law Anthology
Anthony D'Amato

International Taxation: Cases, Materials, and Problems
Philip F. Postlewaite

Introduction to the Study of Law: Cases and Materials, *Second Edition*
John Makdisi

Judicial Externships: The Clinic Inside the Courthouse, *Second Edition*
Rebecca A. Cochran

A Land Use Anthology
Jon W. Bruce

A Section 1983 Civil Rights Anthology
Sheldon H. Nahmod

Sports Law: Cases and Materials, *Fourth Edition*
Ray L. Yasser, James R. McCurdy, C. Peter Goplerud, and Maureen A. Weston

State and Local Government Law: A Transactional Approach
John Martinez and Michael E. Libonati

A Torts Anthology, *Second Edition*
Julie A. Davies, Lawrence C. Levine, and Edward J. Kionka

Trial Practice
Lawrence A. Dubin and Thomas F. Guernsey

Understanding Negotiation
Melissa L. Nelken

Unincorporated Business Entities, *Second Edition*
Larry E. Ribstein

FORTHCOMING PUBLICATIONS

The Art and Science of Trial Advocacy
L. Timothy Perrin, H. Mitchell Caldwell, and Carol A. Chase

Cases and Materials on Comparative Military Justice
Eugene R. Fidel, Michael F. Noone, and Elizabeth Lutes Hillman

Clinical Legal Education–A Textbook for Law School Clinical Programs
David F. Chavkin

First Amendment Law: Cases, Comparative Perspectives, and Dialogues
Donald E. Lively, William D. Araiza, Phoebe A. Haddon, John C. Knechtle, and Dorothy E. Roberts

Taxation: A Skills Approach
Michael A. Livingston and Nancy C. Staudt

BANKRUPTCY ANTHOLOGY

BANKRUPTCY ANTHOLOGY

CHARLES J. TABB
Alice C. Campbell Professor of Law
University of Illinois College of Law

ANDERSON PUBLISHING CO.
CINCINNATI, OHIO

BANKRUPTCY ANTHOLOGY
CHARLES J. TABB

© 2002 by Anderson Publishing Co.

Anderson Publishing Co.
2035 Reading Road / Cincinnati, Ohio 45202
800-582-7295 / e-mail lawschool@andersonpublishing.com / Fax 513-562-5430
www.andersonpublishing.com

ISBN: 0-87084-844-5

Dedication

This book is dedicated to my mother, Jeanne Jordan Tabb,
and to the memory of my father, William Herschel Tabb.

Table of Contents

Acknowledgments

I would like to acknowledge the outstanding scholarship of my colleagues across the nation. In effect, they wrote this book. My only regret is that I could not include more of their fine works. It has been a privilege, an honor, and the education of a lifetime to have the opportunity to read and edit the brilliant bankruptcy scholarship contained in this anthology and that referenced for additional reading. Over the past few years I have read over 500 books and articles on bankruptcy law. What a rich and fascinating study it has been! I also want to thank the many professors who offered their advice and suggestions on what works to include.

I could not have done this book without the able assistance of the staff at the University of Illinois. In particular, my secretary, Sally Cook, is simply the best. She has been invaluable. Thank you. Bonnie Anderson, my prior secretary, also provided excellent support in the early stages of this project.

I thank the University of Illinois for generous research support.

Many students provided superb help in every stage of the production of this anthology. I especially want to acknowledge the following Illinois law students:

William Seitz; Joanna Grama; Sonya Pasquini; Jeffrey Weiland; Gary Wells; Michael Strohmeier; John Chamberlin; Alan Brown; Matthew Kuenning; and Erin Ziaja.

My daughter, Becca Tabb, provided valuable editorial assistance. The rest of my family—my wife Linda, and my other children, Natalie, Charles, and John—enabled me to finish this book with their patience and encouragement.

Finally, my thanks go to the fine people at Anderson Publishing, especially Keith Moore and Sean Caldwell. They are outstanding.

Charles Tabb
November 2001

Index of Authors

Index of Articles and Books

Chapter 1
The History of Bankruptcy

A. Prologue

Bankruptcy has been with us always. Where there is debt, bankruptcy is sure to follow. From the earliest times, societies have puzzled over what to do in the annoyingly recurring instance in which a debtor is unable or unwilling to pay his creditors in full. All sorts of remedies have been attempted, most of them miserable failures.

In the following passage, noted English author Daniel Defoe (of ROBINSON CRUSOE fame) laments the sorry state of the English bankruptcy law in the waning days of the seventeenth century. The reader probably will not be surprised to learn that Defoe himself suffered the ignominy of bankruptcy. It is worth noting that the English law was amended just eight years after Defoe wrote, to inject at least a modicum of leniency for honest and cooperative debtors in the form of the first discharge of debts in bankruptcy proceedings. Statute of 4 Anne, ch. 17, § 7 (1705). But that same act concomitantly introduced the ultimate penalty for fraudulent bankrupts, prescribing that such a criminal should "suffer as a felon, without benefit of clergy"—namely, should be put to death. *Id.* §§ 1, 18. As you read the plaints of Defoe, note the enduring nature of his descriptions of the character of debtors and creditors (the "four Sorts of People"), and of the intractable problem of "how to make a Law to suit all these." If the language were modernized, readers might think they were reading a speech from today in the Congressional Record. Note also Defoe's "Two Points" that make the bankruptcy law "a Publick Grievance." Has much changed?

Daniel Defoe
AN ESSAY UPON PROJECTS (1697)
"Of Bankrupts"

This Chapter has some right to stand next to that of Fools; for besides the common acceptation of late, which makes *every Unfortunate Man a Fool,* I think no man so much made a Fool as a *Bankrupt.* If I may be allow'd so much liberty with our Laws, which are generally good, and above all things are temper'd with Mercy, Lenity, and Freedom, This has something in it of Barbarity; it gives a loose to the Malice and Revenge of the Creditor, as well as a Power to right himself, while it leaves the Debtor no way to show himself honest: It contrives all the ways possible to drive the Debtor to despair, and encourages no new Industry, for it makes him perfectly incapable of anything but *starving.*

This Law, especially as it is now frequently executed, tends wholly to the Destruction of the Debtor, and yet very little to the Advantage of the Creditor.

The Severities to the Debtor are unreasonable, and, if I may so say, a little inhuman; for it not only strips him of all in a moment, but renders him for ever incapable of helping himself, or relieving his Family by future Industry. If he 'scapes from Prison, which is hardly done too, if he has nothing left, he must starve, or live on Charity; if he goes to work, no man dare pay him his Wages, but he shall pay it again to the Creditors. . . .

All people know, who remember any thing of the Times when that Law was made, that the Evil it was pointed at, was grown very rank, and Breaking to Defraud Creditors so much a Trade, that the Parliament had good reason to set up a Fury to deal with it; and I am far from reflecting on the Makers of that Law, who, no question, saw 'twas necessary at that time: But as Laws, tho' in themselves good, are more or less so, as they are more or less reasonable, squar'd, and adapted to the Circumstances and Time of the Evil they were made against; so 'twere worth while (with Submission) for the same Authority to examine:

(1) Whether the Length of Time since that Act was made, has not given opportunity to Debtors,

1.   To evade the Force of the Act by Ways and Shifts to avoid the Power of it, and secure their Estates out of the reach of it?

2.   To turn the Point of it against those whom it was made to relieve?

. . .

(2) Whether the Extremities of this Law are not often carried on beyond the true Intent and Meaning of the Act itself, by Persons, who besides being Creditors, are also Malicious, and gratify their private Revenge, by prosecuting the Offender, to the Ruin of his Family.

If these Two Points are to be prov'd, then I am sure 'twill follow, That this Act is now a Publick Grievance to the Nation. . . .

Time and Experience has furnished the Debtors with Ways and Means to evade the Force of this Statute, and to secure their Estates against the reach of it; which renders it often insignificant, and consequently, the Knave, against whom the Law was particularly bent, gets off; while he only who fails of mere necessity, and whose honest Principle will not permit him to practice those Methods, is expos'd to the Fury of this Act. . . .

The next Enquiry is, Whether the Extremities of this Law are not often carried on beyond the true Intent and Meaning of the act itself, for Malicious and Private Ends, to gratify Passion and Revenge?

I remember the Answer a Person gave me, who had taken out Statutes against several Persons, and some his near relations, who had fail'd in his Debt; and when I was one time dissuading him from prosecuting a man who ow'd me Money as well as him, I used this Argument with him; *You know the man has nothing left to pay. That's true,* says he, *I know that well enough. To what purpose, then*, said I, *will you prosecute him? Why, Revenge is sweet,* said he.—Now a man that will prosecute a Debtor, not as a Debtor, but by way of Revenge, such a man is, I think not intentionally within the benefit of our Law.

In order to state the Case right, there are four Sorts of People to be consider'd in this Discourse; and the true Case is how to distinguish them.

(1) There is the Honest Debtor, who fails by visible Necessity, Losses, Sickness, Decay of Trade, or the like.

(2) The Knavish, Designing, or Idle, Extravagant Debtor, who fails because either he has run out his Estate in Excesses, or on purpose to cheat and abuse his Creditors.

(3) There is the moderate Creditor, who seeks but his own, but will omit no lawful Means to gain it, and yet will hear reasonable and just Arguments and Proposals.

(4) There is the Rigorous Severe Creditor, that values not whether the Debtor be Honest Man or Knave, Able, or Unable; but will have his Debt, *whether it be to be had or no*; without Mercy, without Compassion, full of Ill Language, Passion, and Revenge.

How to make a Law to suit to all these, is the Case: *That a necessary favour might be shown to the first*, in Pity and Compassion to the Unfortunate, in Commiseration of Casualty and Poverty, which no man is exempt from the danger of. *That a due Rigor and Restraint be laid upon the second,* that Villany and Knavery might not be encourag'd by a Law. *That a due Care be taken of the third*, that men's Estates may, as far as can be, secur'd to them. *And due limits set to the last*, that no man may have an unlimited Power over his Fellow-Subjects, to the Ruin of both Life and Estate.

B.   Early History

Bankruptcy has existed as long as there has been debt—which is a very long time indeed. Two of the following passages examine the early development of bankruptcy law. One is from an article by Professor Louis Levinthal of the University of Pennsylvania Law School, published in 1918. Professor Levinthal was the preeminent historian of bankruptcy law in the early part of the twentieth century. The other excerpt is from a book published the very next year, in 1919, by F. Regis Noel, a member of the District of Columbia bar.

Before turning to the Levinthal and Noel works, however, consider the following accounts of debtor-creditor relations found in the Holy Bible. There was no practice in biblical times precisely akin to modern notions of "bankruptcy," but the treatment of debts and debtors was very much of concern. In Leviticus we learn of the practice of the Hebrew "Jubilee" every fifty years, which as a "proclamation of liberty" decreed the unconditional release and return of a person "to his property" and "to his family." Deuteronomy demonstrates the operation of the sabbatical every seventh year, in which debts were released. Note God's cautionary note that creditors should not tighten credit in anticipation of the impending release! In the final selections, taken from both the Old (II Kings and Isaiah) and New (St. Matthew) Testaments, we observe the harsh reality of imprisonment (or sale) for debt, which could be tempered only by the creditor's mercy. Even in God's kingdom, apparently, some of the tensions identified centuries later by Defoe were inescapable.

THE HOLY BIBLE

Leviticus
Chapter 25, Verses 8-10, 25-28, 35-37, 39-41

And you shall count seven weeks of years, seven times seven years, so that the time of the seven weeks of years shall be to you forty-nine years. Then you shall send abroad the loud trumpet on the tenth day of the seventh month; on the day of atonement you shall send abroad the trumpet throughout all your land. And you shall hallow the fiftieth year, and proclaim liberty throughout the land to all its inhabitants; it shall be a jubilee for you, when each of you shall return to his property and each of you shall return to his family. . . .

If your brother becomes poor, and sells part of his property, then his next of kin shall come and redeem what his brother has sold. If a man has no one to redeem it, and then himself becomes prosperous and finds sufficient means to redeem it, let him reckon the years since he sold it and pay back the overpayment to the man to whom he sold it; and he shall return to his property. But if he has not sufficient means to get it back for himself, then what he sold shall remain in the hand of him who bought it until the year of the jubilee; in the jubilee it shall be released, and he shall return to his property. . . .

And if your brother becomes poor, and cannot maintain himself with you, you shall maintain him; as a stranger and a sojourner he shall live with you. Take no interest from him or increase, but fear your God; that your brother may live beside you. You shall not lend him your money at interest, nor give him your food for profit. . . . And if your brother becomes poor beside you, and sells himself to you, you shall not make him serve as a slave: he shall be with you as a hired servant and as a sojourner. He shall serve with you until the year of the jubilee; then he shall go out from you, he and his children with him, and go back to his family, and return to the possessions of his fathers.

Deuteronomy
Chapter 15, Verses 1-11

At the end of every seven years you shall grant a release. And this is the manner of the release: every creditor shall release what he has lent to his neighbor; he shall not exact it of his neighbor, his brother, because the Lord's release has been proclaimed. Of a foreigner you may exact it; but whatever of yours is with your brother your hand shall release. . . .

If there is among you a poor man, one of your brethren, in any of your towns within your land which the Lord your God gives you, you shall not harden your heart or shut your hand against your poor brother, but you shall open your hand to him, and lend him sufficient for his need, whatever it may be. Take heed lest there be a base thought in your heart, and you say, 'The seventh year, the year of release is near," and your eye be hostile to your poor brother, and you give him nothing, and he cry to the Lord against you, and it be sin in you. You shall give to him freely, and your heart shall not be grudging when you give to him; because for this the Lord your God will bless you in all your work and in all that you undertake. For the poor will never cease out of the land; therefore I command you, You shall open wide your hand to your brother, to the needy and to the poor, in the land.

II Kings
Chapter 4, Verse 1

Now the wife of one of the sons of the prophets cried to Elisha, "Your servant my husband is dead; and you know that your servant feared the lord, but the creditor has come to take my two children to be his slaves."

Isaiah
Chapter 50, Verse 1

Thus says the Lord: . . . Or which of my creditors is it to whom I have sold you? Behold, for your iniquities you were sold. . . .

St. Matthew
Chapter 18, Verses 23-35

Therefore the kingdom of heaven may be compared to a king who wished to settle accounts with his servants. When he began the reckoning, one was brought to him who owed him ten thousand talents [*editor's note: this was more than fifteen year's wages*]; and as he could not pay, his lord ordered him to be sold, with his wife and his children and all that he had, and payment to be made. So the servant fell on his knees, imploring him, "lord, have patience with me, and I will pay you everything." And out of pity for him the lord of that servant released him and forgave him the debt. But that same servant, as he went out, came upon one of his fellow servants, who owed him a hundred denarii [*editor's note: the denarius was about a day's wage*]; and seizing him by the throat he said, "pay what you owe." So his fellow servant fell down and besought him, saying, "Have patience with me, and I will pay you." He refused and went and put him in prison till he should pay the debt. When his fellow servants saw what had taken place, they were greatly distressed, and they went and reported to their lord all that had taken place. The his lord summoned him and said to him, "You wicked servant! I forgave you all that debt because you besought me; and should not you have had mercy on your fellow servant, as I had mercy on you?" And in his anger his lord delivered him to the jailers, till he should pay all his debt. So also my heavenly Father will do to every one of you, if you do not forgive your brother from your heart.

Following is Professor Levinthal's classic work on early bankruptcy history. As you read it, consider the following questions.

1. What are the "two general objects" of "all bankruptcy law"?

2. What "third object" is found in some systems but not others, leading the author to conclude that it is not "a fundamental feature of the law"?

3. What are the essential characteristics of a bankruptcy system, necessary to carry out the general objects of a bankruptcy law?

4. In primitive societies, what two principal types of sanctions were utilized to compel the payment of debts?

5. As primitive economies evolved, what was the most significant change in the nature of execution for debt?

6. What two systems of proprietary execution evolved? How did they operate?

7. How did ancient laws attempt to prevent fraud by debtors?

8. In what ways did debtor-creditor laws in the early Middle Ages revert to the primitive model?

Louis Levinthal
The Early History of Bankruptcy Law
66 U. PA. L. REV. 223 (1918)

All bankruptcy law, however, no matter when or where devised and enacted, has at least two general objects in view. It aims, first, to secure an equitable division of the insolvent debtor's property among all his creditors, and, in the second place, to prevent on the part of the insolvent debtor conduct detrimental to the interests of his creditors. In other words, bankruptcy law seeks to protect the creditors, first, from one another and, secondly, from their debtor. A third object, the protection of the honest debtor from his creditors, by means of the discharge, is sought to be attained in some of the systems of bankruptcy, but this is by no means a fundamental feature of the law.

(1) COLLECTIVE EXECUTION.

The laws that have for their object the protection of the creditors from one another seek to prevent any one of the creditors from obtaining more than his proportionate share of the debtor's assets. A special process of collective execution is devised, a process directed against all of the property of the debtor, resorted to for the common benefit and at the common expense of all the creditors.

There are two necessary antecedents before this special procedure of collective execution need be invoked: (a) insolvency, actual or apparent, of the debtor, and (b) plurality, actual or potential, of creditors. . . . If a debtor has enough assets to meet all his debts, there is no need to seek special regulation to protect the creditors from one another. . . . If a creditor be alone in the field, there is obviously no need of regulations to protect the claimant from himself. . . .

(2) FRAUD ON CREDITORS.

The laws that seek to protect the creditors from their debtor by preventing fraud on his part are frequently independent of those seeking to protect the creditors from one another by making an equitable distribution of the debtor's property. . . . It is immaterial, however, whether there be only one creditor or many creditors; in either case, laws must vitiate fraudulent transfers and punish the defrauders.

(3) MANAGEMENT OF ESTATE.

In order to work out the two general objects of bankruptcy, it is necessary to devise and establish a systematic method of managing the debtor's estate during the pendency of the process. Some agency must be given control over all the property of the debtor, . . . and must be given authority to prevent and set aside fraudulent transfers of property, and to collect, manage, and distribute all the assets. . . . [There are] two theories as to the management of the bankrupt estate,—private management or management by the creditors, and diametrically opposed to it, public management or management by the state. . . .

DEBTOR AND CREDITOR IN PRIMITIVE SOCIETY

In very primitive society there are no laws preventing fraud of debtors or regulating the distribution of a debtor's estate among his several creditors, for the reason that, generally speaking, debtors and creditors are unknown in the early stages of social evolution. Credit is an institution that lives by virtue of man's confidence in his fellow-man's good faith, and good faith and the primitive man are strangers. . . .

By force of economic necessity, suspension of payment was gradually introduced; but for a very long time, indebtedness was regarded as an anomaly, as a special privilege, as a perversion of the traditional and customary method of dealing. . . . Public opinion provided two sanctions, each of them extremely powerful, by which the debtor was compelled to perform his part of the contract, which the ancients thought ought never to have been postponed. One sanction was religious in character; the other was the peculiarly severe form of the primitive procedure of execution.

Typical illustrations of the religious sanction are the practice of "sitting d'harna," the usual procedure throughout India of old and still in vogue in Nepaul, and the similar practice of "fasting on" a person resorted to in ancient Ireland. In both, the creditor placed himself before the debtor's doorway, there to remain until the debt was paid. The expected payment was seldom delayed, for public opinion would have punished instantly and severely the debtor who allowed his creditor to become exhausted or to die of starvation before his door. In Egypt, another species of spiritual sanction compelled payment by the debtor. From the earliest time, it seems to have been almost a universal custom for the debtor to pledge the body of his nearest deceased relative, specially that of his father. In case of default of payment, the creditor was given the right to remove the mummy, and the tomb was closed against any interment by the debtor. . . .

A more direct means of compelling payment in ancient days was the extremely severe treatment accorded defaulting debtors, whether fraudulent or honest. In Hindu law, for instance, execution in civil cases was a matter simply of self-help. The creditor could seize the person of his debtor and compel him to labor for him. Actual violence might also be resorted to by the creditor; he could kill or maim the debtor, confine his wife, sons or cattle, or besiege him in his home. This is typical of primitive law generally.

We find in the Code of Hammurabi that the insolvent debtor was regularly sold into slavery. It also frequently happened that the debtor's kinsmen would be sold into bondage in order to pay off his obligations. . . .

Whether slavery for simple debt was known among the ancient Hebrews is mooted. On the one hand, a number of Biblical references are cited to prove that slavery for debt did exist. On the other hand, it is probable that at least from the time when the Israelites came in contact with Egypt, personal servitude for debt was unknown. In the land of the Pharaohs, from the days of Bocchoris certainly (772-729 B. C.), and perhaps much earlier, it was established that in the case of debt, the debtor's property, and not his person, might be attached. The Egyptians regarded the claim of the state to the debtor's person as superior to that of the creditor, for the state might at any time require the debtor's service, in peace as an official or laborer, in war as a soldier. . . .

In the law of Rome, as set forth in the Twelve Tables (B. C. 451-450), the borrower was said to be *nexus* to his creditor, *i.e.*, his own person was pledged for the repayment of the loan. If the borrower failed to fulfill his obligation, the creditor might arrest him by *manus injectio*, by the "laying on of hands," a mode of execution which proceeded directly and with inexorable rigor against the person of the debtor. After having thrice publicly invited some one to come forward and pay the debt, the creditor might, in default of any one appearing, and after the lapse of sixty days, regard the debtor as his slave, and might either kill him or sell him into a foreign country. The old proverb, "He who cannot pay with his purse pays with his skin," was literally applied in Roman law. Not only freedom and honor, but life itself was at the mercy of the creditor. The earliest provision dealing with collective execution is found in the Twelve Tables; it is there decreed that if several creditors have claims upon the same debtor, they might cut the debtor's body into pieces.

So long as execution was directed against the person, rather than the property, of the debtor, and so long as the religious and primitive sanctions prevailed, there was obviously little need for the introduction of bankruptcy as a distinct system of jurisprudence.

TRANSITION FROM EXECUTION AGAINST THE PERSON TO EXECUTION AGAINST PROPERTY

In course of time, execution for debt came to be directed against the property of the debtor rather than his person. . . . The change from the one form of execution to the other, slow and gradual as it was, is an instance of the general evolution of legal process from the stage where retaliation is the end in view to the stage where compensation is the chief desideratum.

In most systems of jurisprudence, the development of proprietary execution was a natural one. The ancient Jewish and Germanic notion, for instance, of the execution against the person was that the body of the debtor was a pledge or security for the payment of the debt. It is perfectly natural that in course of time the Jewish and Germanic people should come to look upon each portion of the debtor's property as a pledge or security for the debt. . . .

Thus, there were evolved two systems of proprietary execution: individual proprietary execution, and collective or entire proprietary execution.

INDIVIDUAL PROPRIETARY EXECUTION

Where execution is directed by individual creditors against specific portions of the debtor's estate, the problem that arises when there are several creditors and an estate that is insolvent was solved, at first, by having the creditors paid in a definite and specified order. . . .

Where there are several creditors of the same rank, the most natural rule would be to divide the property *pro rata* among all the creditors. . . .

Where . . . the individual creditor had general mortgage liens depending upon the date of their obligations, thanks to which they escaped any principle of contribution, they had little interest in organizing a real *concursus creditorum*. . . .

Where, on the other hand, the principle of priority of execution prevailed, which, in the case of the insolvent debtor, made payment the prize of a race of diligence and fostered fraud and collusion, a system of bankruptcy became a pressing necessity. Selfish individualism which impelled each creditor to anticipate and outwit his fellows, and to rescue whatever he could for himself alone, gave way, by force of an enlightened sense of justice, to co-operation and contribution among all the creditors.

GENERAL PROPRIETARY EXECUTION

The process of general execution against the debtor's property introduced into Roman law by Rutilius was called *bonorum emptio* or *venditio*. Whether the debtor was solvent or insolvent, whether there were many creditors or there was but one creditor, the proceeding was the same, leading to a sale of the entire estate of the debtor for the benefit of his creditors. The *bonorum venditio* was only granted when the debtor had committed one of several acts. These acts, which might be termed acts of bankruptcy, were (a) absconding (*latitans*) or hiding from creditors, (b) leaving a judgment unsatisfied for thirty days, and (c) admitting, without discharging, a debt, and taking no steps to pay it. . . .

. . . [W]e find that the *bonorum venditio* was gradually superseded by the *bonorum distractio*. . . . The creditors, or some of them, applied to the magistrate for a *missio in bona*, as in the *venditio*, but the estate was not sold by a *magister* chosen by the creditors, but by a *curator*, chosen by the Praetor, whose duty it was to dispose of, not the universal succession of the debtor, but the several objects of which his estate was composed, and to pay the creditors *pro rata* out of the proceeds.

The *venditio* and the *distractio*, and not the *cessio bonorum*, constituted the Roman system of bankruptcy process, a system that is in fact the origin and fountain-head of all bankruptcy systems. . . .

PREVENTION OF FRAUD IN ANCIENT LAW

In ancient systems of law, insolvency *per se* was looked upon as something irregular and fraudulent, whether the debtor was actually honest or dishonest. Gradually public opinion came to discriminate between the unfortunate insolvent and the felonious bankrupt. . . .

The Romans clung tenaciously to the conception that infamy attached to the debtor whose estate had been sold to the *bonorum emptor*. . . . [T]he debtor whose insolvency was not due to his own fault was permitted to make a *cessio bonorum*. This was more in the nature of a voluntary composition with creditors. By adopting this course, the debtor escaped liability to arrest and imprisonment, which bankrupts properly incurred if the *missio in bona* produced no results. . . .

These alternative processes were available to the innocent insolvent only. In this way Roman law indirectly punished the fraudulent debtor, for he could not have the privilege granted to the honest insolvent.

Religious fears and scruples were often employed as preventives of fraud. Excommunication was the means resorted to by the Assyrians thousands of years before the Common Era. In Jewish law, the execution process commenced with a writ issued by the court, which was in the nature of a ban of excommunication against the debtor, and the creditors also had the right to demand the proclamation of the ban of excommunication against all who knew and did not inform them of any fraudulent conduct on the part of the debtor. . . .

BANKRUPTCY IN THE MIDDLE AGES

In Europe during the early Middle Ages we find the laws relating to the relation of debtor and creditor to have been peculiarly similar to those of the most primitive period. Execution directed against the person of the debtor became prevalent once more; credit trade again became unusual, and the religious sanctions wielded their pristine force and potency. . . .

The Italian bankrupt was usually treated very severely. . . . Insulting and reviling procedures were ordinary. . . . Occasionally the bankrupt who had absconded was given a safe conduct if he were needed back, but more frequently the insolvent debtor was tortured in order to force him to expose his property. These statutes were not penal in their nature; they were simply inquisitorial. . . .

The first legislation in Holland dealing specifically with bankruptcy was enacted in 1531 by Charles V of Spain; and the Perpetual Edict of the 4th of October, 1540 . . . . The preamble went on to point out the great impulse trade had received, and that, in order to guard and foster that trade, debtors must be compelled to pay their debts and must be prevented from evading their liabilities by flight. The ordinance then provided that all persons who absented themselves from their ordinary residences with the object of defrauding their creditors were to be regarded as common thieves, and if caught might be summarily dealt with and publicly hanged. . . . [B]ankruptcy was not regarded as a private matter of concern to the creditors exclusively, but as something of vital importance to the entire community, a matter in which the public interest transcended the interest of the creditors. . . .

. . . [In Spanish law,] if a person became insolvent, he was imprisoned until he made a *cessio*. As a corollary of the decree that a *cessio* could be coerced through imprisonment, it became universally accepted that until the bankrupt's case was all cleared up, the person who made *cessio* should languish in jail.

. . . In Jewish law, . . . [a]ll execution commenced . . . on petition of a creditor. This writ was in the nature of a ban of excommunication on the debtor for ninety days. The debtor could avoid the effect of the ban and the other proceedings by coming forward and surrendering all his property, taking for himself his exemptions. In order to make this assignment or *cessio*, he had to take a rabbinical oath that he had no other property, that he had made no fraudulent transfers, and that he would apply his future earnings, beyond what was necessary for his simple needs, to the payment of his debts.

Another insight into early bankruptcy history is provided in the following excerpts from Regis Noel's 1919 book on the history of the bankruptcy law. Think about the answers to the following questions as you read Noel's work.

1. Where did the term "bankrupt" come from?

2. How have primitive societies dealt with debtors?

3. Whom does Noel credit with instituting the "modern" system of dealing with debts? What was that system? Who ameliorated that approach to debtors?

4. What was the nature of the Roman system? How did it evolve?

F. Regis Noel
HISTORY OF THE BANKRUPTCY LAW (1919)

There are differences of opinion as to the origin as well as the meaning of the term *bankrupt*. . . . The explanation most generally accepted is that the word is a compound formed from a Latin noun, *bancus*, meaning a table or counter, and the perfect passive participle of a Latin verb, *ruptus*, meaning broken. The usual account is that a trader in the days of Rome's supremacy being disgusted and discouraged, broke his table where he kept his coins and plied his trade, thus demonstrating his emotions and his intention to discontinue business. Sometimes his creditors finding that he had fled and left nothing else on the premises destroyed the table. . . . Still another derivation strongly urged is that from the French, *banque*, a bench, and *route*, a trace or track; that is, one who has removed his bench leaving only a trace behind. . . .

The most likely explanation of the origin of the term to be gained from an historical view of available opinions is that the practice of Rome was directly adopted by the English, while the name came indirectly from Rome through the medium of the French language, but was afterwards modified and finally reduced to the original Latin form by a subsequently acquired knowledge of its relation to the primary Latin or Italian words. . . .

During twenty-five centuries the lawgivers of the world have periodically legislated on this human relation. In primitive communities a formulated practice was unknown, but it is reasonable to suppose that satisfaction for a hopeless debt was secured by labor or some personally inflicted punishment. In harmony with the spirit of those ages we can be certain that it was cruel. In semi-civilized parts of the earth harsh treatment of debtors persists. It is well established that in Pegu and the adjacent countries of East India a creditor is given full sanction in disposing of a debtor, his wife and children. Extreme cases are recorded in which a debt was satisfied by the creditor violating with impunity the chastity of the debtor's wife. . . .

The Athenian Draco is believed to have been responsible for the institution of the modern system of treating debt. It is recorded that, in his criminal code of B.C. 623, he was unusually harsh in his treatment of debtors. The purpose was to stimulate industry. He classified debt with murder and laziness as a capital crime. . . . This rigor was somewhat abated when, instead of death as a penalty for debt, the unfortunates were compelled to cultivate and remain on the land the same as cattle and fixtures and to surrender their children to be exported as slaves. To abscond was the alternative, and, as later in England, this became an extensive abuse.

Solon, in revising the tyrannical tablets of Draco, considered debt a misfortune rather than a crime, and mitigated the punishment of debtors. By his decrees, . . . he abolished servitude for debt and forbade anyone to lend or borrow money on the security of the person of the debtor. He ordained that what debts remained should be forgiven, and for the future, no man should engage the body of his debtor for security; but the bankrupt and his heirs forfeited Greek citizenship, a penalty more deeply felt than the loss of life or liberty. For these wise laws, enacted bout 594 B.C., the ages have accorded him the title, "Benefactor of Men." . . .

The Roman *Laws of the Twelve Tables*, alleged to have been "more Draconic than Draco," were engraved on tablets of brass and promulgated by the Decemvirs in 451 or 450 B.C., and are described as having been "written in blood," especially the terrible section *de debitore in partes secando*. This section empowered the creditors, as a final resort, to cut the debtor's body into proportionate shares. The effect of the laws was that a debtor who was unable to discharge his obligations, upon judicial proof or confession of the debt, was allowed thirty days grace during which time he could in every way endeavor to satisfy the account. If no means of relief were found or the debtor made no effort to change his condition by some adjustment, he was delivered into the custody of his creditors. While thus privately imprisoned his daily food allowance was twelve ounces of rice. He might be bound with a chain not exceeding fifteen pounds in weight, and to arouse the compassion of his relatives and friends he was exposed trice daily in the market-place. . . . In case of fraud or obstinate refusal the death penalty was inflicted. There are authorities who maintain that the stigma was extended by the Romans to the debtor's family and that they were sometimes compelled to accompany him into slavery. . . . Authorities differ, however, as to whether they were ever enforced. . . . The opinion of most commentators is that the laws were interpreted to mean only the division of the money arising from the sale of the debtor into slavery. . . .

Caesar is credited with having promulgated the law *Cessio Bonorum*, a leading principle of modern bankruptcy laws. . . . [H]e relates that when dictator he permitted debtors to yield their lands in payment to their creditors at the valuation at which they were assessed before the war. . . . Under it all citizens were exempt from imprisonment, but it did not discharge the debt or exempt future acquisitions.

At this period in the history of Rome the doctrine of discharge originated and it was gradually extended. . . . As is usually the case with emergency measures, it was inadequate, was misapplied, and not affording permanent relief, we find that its provisions were not long observed. There followed great oppression of debtors . . . .

The codifiers, headed by the illustrious Tribonian, under the direction of the Christian emperor Justinian, in the year 533 embodied in their treatises the first purely charitable treatment of debtors. This code, *Corpus Juris Civilis*, which has come down to us, provided that if a debtor yielded up all his property to his creditors, he should not be continued in prison. . . . By swearing that he was unable to pay his debts, the debtor was relieved from the payment of them, an indulgence which encouraged fraud and perjury. . . . [A]s Roman splendor declined, and its earlier customs crumbled, the laws on the subject of debt fell into the general decay. They were re-established in the commercial republics of Italy, but before that time the principles of that legislation had been carried to England, the next country in which an earlier form of the present American system is discernible.

C. English Bankruptcy Laws

The original conception of "bankruptcy" in the United States came directly from mother England. The first excerpt that follows, a modern recapitulation by Professor Charles Tabb of the University of Illinois (and editor of this anthology), reviews the origins of English bankruptcy law in the Middle Ages and explains the character of that law. Tabb also shows how the English law changed over the centuries, up to the time of the American Revolution. Thereafter, American and English bankruptcy laws evolved along somewhat divergent paths.

The second piece is from the source himself: Sir William Blackstone. In the course of his monumental review of English law in the mid-eighteenth century, Blackstone cast his gaze upon the bankruptcy law. Blackstone addressed four components of the law: who can be a bankruptcy debtor; what acts trigger a bankruptcy proceeding; the conduct of the proceedings; and the means of transferring property in bankruptcy. Perhaps the most intriguing aspect of Blackstone's work for us today is the general *attitude* his writing reflects on the nature and treatment of debt. Do you agree with his justification for limiting the bankruptcy laws to "traders"? Blackstone viewed England as "steering in the middle" between extremes in its normative policies on the accommodation of debtor and creditor interests. Note the echoes of Defoe in Blackstone's description of the extremes in types of creditors and debtors. Finally, what did Blackstone see as the fundamental tensions, problems, and goals of the bankruptcy laws? To what extent are his insights pertinent to the modern condition?

Charles Jordan Tabb
The History of the Bankruptcy Laws in the United States
3 AM. BANKR. INST. L. REV. 5 (1995)[*]

A. English Antecedents

1. Origins

The framers of the United States Constitution had the English bankruptcy system in mind when they included the power to enact "uniform laws on the subject of bankruptcies" in the Article I powers of the legislative branch. The first United States bankruptcy law, passed in 1800, virtually copied the existing English law. United States bankruptcy laws thus have their conceptual origins in English bankruptcy law prior to 1800. . . .

Early English law had a distinctly pro-creditor orientation, and was noteworthy for its harsh treatment of defaulting debtors. Imprisonment for debt was the order of the day, from the time of the Statute of Merchants in 1285, until Dickens' time in the mid-nineteenth century. . . .

English law was not unique in its lack of solicitude for debtors. History's annals are replete with tales of draconian treatment of debtors. Punishments inflicted upon debtors included forfeiture of all property, relinquishment of the consortium of a spouse, imprisonment, and death. In Rome, creditors were apparently authorized to carve up the body of the debtor, although scholars debate the extent to which the letter of that law was actually enforced.

As commerce expanded, the need for a collective procedure to collect debts became evident. Individual collection remedies, such as the common law execution writs of fieri facias, elegit, and levari facias, did not address the distinct problems presented by a debtor's multiple defaults. Creditors needed protection from defaulting debtors and from each other.

2. First Bankruptcy Laws: 1542 and 1570

In 1542, during the reign of Henry VIII, the first bankruptcy law was passed in England, entitled "An act against such persons as do make bankrupts." This law viewed debtors as quasi-criminals (they were called "offenders"), and placed additional remedies in the hands of creditors. A more comprehensive bankruptcy law was passed in 1570 during the reign of Queen Elizabeth I. That law filled out the basic parameters of the English bankruptcy system, lacking only the discharge provisions added in the early eighteenth century. . . .

Only creditors could commence a bankruptcy proceeding. This limitation, which persisted for three centuries, was indicative of the law's overriding purpose, namely, to aid creditors in the collection of debts. Relief was not for debtors, but from debtors. Debtors could be imprisoned for committing fraudulent acts of bankruptcy. A discharge of debts was unheard of, and indeed would have been at odds with the entire premise of the law. The ground for commencing a bankruptcy proceeding by the creditor was the commission of an "act of bankruptcy" by the debtor. An act of bankruptcy was a form of conduct that indicated that the debtor was attempting to prevent creditors from recovering on debts justly owed them. For example, one act of bankruptcy was "keeping house," whereby the debtor would hole up in their home, immune from the reach of creditors. . . .

Upon the occurrence of an act of bankruptcy, creditors could petition the Lord Chancellor to convene a bankruptcy proceeding. The Chancellor would appoint bankruptcy "commissioners" to

---

    *   Charles Jordan Tabb: "The History of the Bankruptcy Laws in the United States," *American Bankruptcy Institute Law Review*, Spring 1995, Vol. 3, No. 1. Copyright © 1995 by the American Bankruptcy Institute. Reprinted by permission.

supervise the process. In broad form, the process mirrored a modern straight liquidation case. The bankrupt's assets were seized, appraised, and sold, and the proceeds distributed pro rata to creditors. . . . Since there was no discharge, creditors were free after bankruptcy to continue to pursue individual collection remedies against the debtor. . . .

The bankruptcy law only applied to "traders," *i.e.*, to merchant debtors. This limitation remained until the nineteenth century. Non-merchants were relegated to the separate "insolvency" laws, which sporadically allowed for release from prison in certain circumstances and occasional relief from debt. . . . [A]t that time, the bankruptcy laws were viewed as a necessary concomitant to the exigencies of commerce, but no more. Credit generally was viewed as immoral and almost fraudulent. . . .

In commerce, however, credit became recognized as a necessary evil. And once credit is used, things can go wrong. Defaults happen, and in the instance of multiple defaults, a collective remedy such as bankruptcy is needed. Bankruptcy was limited to traders because it was believed that they had "peculiar facilities for delaying and defrauding creditors." Non-traders, in short, simply lacked the wherewithal to commit a wrong sufficient to need the bankruptcy remedy.

Over the next two centuries, Parliament periodically amended the bankruptcy laws. In many instances, especially in the seventeenth century, Parliament sought: (1) to enhance the power of the bankruptcy commissioners to reach more of the debtor's assets; and (2) to increase the penalties against noncompliant debtors. For example, the commissioner was empowered to break into the debtor's house or shop to seize the debtor's property, thus eliminating the effectiveness of "keeping house." A debtor could be pilloried and have his ear cut off. . . .

3. Discharge Introduced in 1705

The English bankruptcy law of this era became complete with the passage of the Statute of Anne in 1705. That law introduced the discharge of debts for the benefit of a debtor who cooperated in the bankruptcy proceeding. A cooperative debtor also was granted a monetary allowance out of the bankruptcy estate, the amount of which depended on the percentage dividend that was paid to creditors. At the same time, however, the Statute of Anne raised the stakes even higher for uncooperative debtors by providing for the death penalty for fraudulent bankrupts. While the quasi-criminal nature of bankruptcy remained, the Statute of Anne first established the roots of a more humanitarian legislative treatment of honest but unfortunate debtors.

It is unlikely, however, that humanitarian concerns for debtors primarily motivated the legislators of 1705. Rather, the main focus was on assisting creditors; the title and preamble to the act reflect as much. Indeed, the fact that only creditors could file a bankruptcy petition negates any serious argument that the 1705 law was intended as a debtor relief measure. Furthermore, non-traders remained ineligible for bankruptcy. Nor was a discharge an automatic entitlement. The commissioners had to certify that the debtor had "conformed" to the requirements of the act, meaning in essence that the debtor cooperated in the bankruptcy proceeding. . . .

More evidence of the predominantly pro-creditor orientation of even the discharge provision is the fact that during the very next year, 1706, creditor consent was added as a prerequisite to the granting of a discharge. In various forms creditors retained some voice in whether the debtor received a discharge until the late nineteenth century. . . .

While obviously quite dramatic, the importance of the death penalty for fraudulent bankrupts should not be overstated (except for the few unfortunate souls who suffered that punishment). . . . [I]n fact at most five executions occurred in the 115 years that the death penalty for fraudulent bankruptcy was on the books. It also should be remembered that bankruptcy was no different from most property crimes of that era, which also provided for the possible imposition of the death penalty.

Although on the books the laws remained strongly pro-creditor, by the middle of the eighteenth century a somewhat more enlightened attitude toward bankruptcy had taken hold. Attitudes about credit and commerce were changing as the Industrial Revolution took hold. . . .

The 1732 Statute of George II was the English bankruptcy law in effect at the time of the ratification of the United States Constitution and the passage of the first United States bankruptcy law in 1800. That English law served in many respects as the model for the American 1800 Act. . . .

Bankruptcy throughout remained an involuntary proceeding available only against traders. A separate set of "insolvency" laws addressed the concerns of debtor relief more directly. These laws dealt with relief from debts and, more commonly, release from imprisonment. In this early English period, such laws were only infrequently in force, and were often ineffective. Discharge from debts was rare. The Privy Council had intervened directly on behalf of debtors with greater effect, but the Council's jurisdiction was abolished in 1641. Debtor relief laws became more common, and effective, in the nineteenth century.

Sir William Blackstone
COMMENTARIES ON THE LAWS OF ENGLAND

Chapter 31: Of Things
OF TITLE BY BANKRUPTCY.

BANKRUPTCY; . . . Let us therefore first of all consider, 1. *Who* may become a bankrupt: 2. What *acts* make a bankrupt: 3. The *proceedings* on a commission of bankrupt: and 4. In what manner an estate in goods and chattels may be *transferred* by bankruptcy.

1. Who may become a bankrupt. A bankrupt was before defined to be "a trader, who secretes himself, or does certain "other acts, tending to defraud his creditors." He was formerly considered merely in the light of a criminal or offender; and in this spirit we are told by Sir Edward Coke, that we have fetched as well the name, as the wickedness, of bankrupts from foreign nations. But at present the laws of bankruptcy are considered as laws calculated for the benefit of trade, and founded on the principles of humanity as well as justice: and to that end they confer some privileges, not only on the creditors, but also on the bankrupt or debtor himself. On the creditors, by compelling the bankrupt to give up all his effects to their use, without any fraudulent concealment: on the debtor, by exempting him from the rigour of the general law, whereby his person might be confined at the discretion of his creditor, though in reality he has nothing to satisfy the debt: whereas the law of bankrupts, taking into consideration the sudden and unavoidable accidents to which men in trade are liable, has given them the liberty of their persons, and some pecuniary emoluments, upon condition they surrender up their whole estate to be divided among their creditors.

In this respect our legislature seems to have attended to the example of the Roman law. I mean not the terrible law of the twelve tables; whereby the creditors might cut the debtor's body in pieces, and each of them take his proportionable share: if indeed that law, *de debitore in partes secando*, is to be understood in so very butcherly a light; which many learned men have with reason doubted. Nor do I mean those less inhuman laws . . . of imprisoning the debtor's person in chains; subjecting him to stripes and hard labour, at the mercy of his rigid creditors; and sometimes selling him, his wife and children, to perpetual foreign slavery. . . . But I mean the law of *cession*, introduced by the christian emperors; whereby if a debtor *ceded*, or yielded up all his fortune to his creditors, he was secured from being dragged to a gaol. . . . Thus far was just and reasonable: but, as the departing from one extreme is apt to produce its opposite, we find it afterwards enacted, that if the debtor by any unforeseen accident was reduced to low circumstances, and would *swear* that he had not sufficient left to pay his debts, he should not be compelled to cede or give up even that which he had in his possession: a law, which under a false notion of humanity, seems to be fertile of perjury, injustice, and absurdity.

The laws of England, more wisely, have steered in the middle between both extremes: providing at once against the inhumanity of the creditor, who is not suffered to confine an honest bankrupt after his effects are delivered up; and at the same time taking care that all his just debts shall be paid, so far as the effects will extend. But still they are cautious of encouraging prodigality and extravagance by this indulgence to debtors; and therefore they allow the benefit of the laws of bankruptcy to none but actual *traders*; since that set of men are, generally speaking, the only persons liable to accidental losses, and to an inability of paying their debts, without any fault of their own. If persons in other situations of life run in debt without the power of payment, they must take the consequences of their own indiscretion, even though they meet with sudden accidents that may reduce their fortunes: for the law holds it to be an unjustifiable practice, for any person but a trader to encumber himself with debts of any considerable value. If a gentleman, or one in a liberal profession, at the time of contracting his debts, has a sufficient fund to pay them, the delay of payment is a species of dishonesty, and a temporary injustice to his creditor: and if, at such time, he has no sufficient fund, the dishonesty and injustice is the greater. . . . But in mercantile transactions the case is far otherwise. Trade cannot be carried on without mutual credit on both sides: the contracting of debts is therefore here not only justifiable but necessary. And if by accidental calamities, as by the loss of a ship in a tempest, the failure of brother traders, or by the non-payment of persons out of trade, a merchant or trader becomes incapable of discharging his own debts, it is his misfortune and not his fault. . . .

The first statute made concerning any English bankrupts was 34 Hen. VIII. c. 4., when trade began first to be properly cultivated in England: which has been almost totally altered by statute 13 Eliz. c. 7., whereby bankruptcy is confined to such persons only as have *used the trade of merchandize*, in gross or by retail, by way of bargaining, exchange, rechange, bartering, chevisance, or otherwise; or have *sought their living by buying and selling*. . . . But no *farmer, grazier,* or *drover*, shall (as such) be liable to be deemed a bankrupt: for, though they buy and sell corn, and hay, and beasts, in the course of husbandry, yet trade is not their principal, but only a collateral, object; their chief concern being to manure and till the ground, and make the best advantage of its produce. . . .

Having thus considered who may, and who may not, be made a bankrupt, we are to inquire, secondly, by what *acts* a man may become a bankrupt. A bankrupt is a trader, who "secretes himself, or does certain other acts, tending to defraud his creditors." . . . And, in general, whenever such a trader, as is before described, hath endeavoured to avoid his creditors, or evade their just demands, this hath been declared by the legislature to be an act of bankruptcy, upon which a commission may be sued out. For in this extrajudicial method of proceedings, which is allowed merely for the benefit of commerce, the law is extremely watchful to detect a man, whose circumstances are declining, in the first instance, or at least as early as possible: that the creditors may receive as large proportion of their debts as may be; and that a man may not go on wantonly wasting his substance, and then claim the benefit of the statutes when he has nothing left to distribute.

To learn what the particular acts of bankruptcy are, which render a man a bankrupt, we must consult the several statutes . . . . Among these may therefore be reckoned, 1. Departing from the realm, whereby a man withdraws himself from the jurisdiction and coercion of the law, with intent to defraud his creditors. 2. Departing from his own house, with intent to secrete himself, and avoid his creditors. 3. Keeping in his own house, privately, so as not to be seen or spoken with by his creditors, except for just and necessary cause . . . . 4. Procuring or suffering himself willingly to be arrested, or outlawed, or imprisoned, without just and lawful cause . . . . 5. Procuring his money, goods, chattels, and effects, to be attached or sequestered by any legal process . . . . 6. Making any fraudulent conveyance to a friend, or secret trustee, of his lands, tenements, goods, or chattels . . . . 7. Procuring any protection, not being himself privileged by parliament, in order to screen his person from arrests . . . . 8. Endeavouring or desiring, by any petition to the king, or bill exhibited in any of the king's courts against any creditors, to compel them to take less than their just debts . . . . 9. Lying in prison for two months, or more, upon arrest or other detention for debt, without finding bail, in order to obtain his liberty. For the inability to procure bail argues a strong deficiency in his credit, owing either to his suspected poverty, or ill character; and his neglect to do it, if able, can arise only from a fraudulent intention; in either of which cases it is high time for his creditors to look to themselves, and compel a distribution of his effects. 10. Escaping from prison after an arrest for a just debt of 100£ or upwards. For no man would break prison that was able and desirous to procure bail . . . . 11. Neglecting to make satisfaction for any just debt to the amount of 100£ within two months after service of legal process, for such debt, upon any trader having privilege of parliament. . . . Let us next consider,

    3. The *proceedings* on a commission of bankrupt; so far as they affect the bankrupt himself. . . . And, first, there must be a *petition* to the lord chancellor by one creditor to the amount of 100£, or by two to the amount of 150£, or by three or more to the amount of 200£; which debts must be proved by *affidavit*: upon which he grants a *commission* to such discreet persons as to him shall seem good, who are then styled commissioners of bankrupt. . . .

    When the commissioners have received their commission, they are first to receive proof of the person's being a trader, and having committed some act of bankruptcy; and then to declare him a bankrupt, if proved so; and to give notice thereof in the gazette, and at the same time to appoint three meetings. At one of these meetings an election must be made of assignees, or persons to whom the bankrupt's estate shall be assigned, and in whom it shall be vested for the benefit of the creditors. . . . And at the third meeting, . . . the bankrupt, upon notice also personally served upon him, or left at his usual place of abode, must surrender himself personally to the commissioners; which surrender (if voluntary) protects him from all arrests till his final examination is past: and he must thenceforth in all respects conform to the directions of the statutes of bankruptcy; or, in default of either surrender or conformity, shall be guilty of felony without benefit of clergy, and shall suffer death, and his goods and estate shall be distributed among his creditors. . . .

    When the bankrupt appears, the commissioners are to examine him touching all matters relating to his trade and effects. They may also summon before them, and examine, the bankrupt's wife, and any other person whatsoever, as to all matters relating to the bankrupt's affairs. And in case any of them shall refuse to answer, or shall not answer fully, to any lawful question, or shall refuse to subscribe such their examination, the commissioners may commit them to prison without bail, till they submit themselves, and make and sign a full answer. . . .

    The bankrupt, upon this examination, is bound upon pain of death to make a full discovery of all his estate and effects, as well in expectancy as possession, and how he has disposed of the same; together with all books and writings relating thereto: and is to deliver up all in his own power to the commissioners (except the necessary apparel of himself, his wife, and his children). . . . And unless it shall appear that his inability to pay his debts arose from some casual loss, he may, upon conviction by indictment of such gross misconduct and negligence, be sent upon the pillory for two hours, and have one of his ears nailed to the same and cut off. . . .

    Hitherto every thing is in favor of the creditors; and the law seems to be pretty rigid and severe against the bankrupt; but, in case he proves honest, it makes him full amends for all this rigour and severity. For if the bankrupt hath made an ingenuous discovery (of the truth and sufficiency of which there remains no reason to doubt), and hath conformed in all points to the directions of the law; and if, in consequence thereof, the creditors, or four parts in five of them in number and value . . ., will sign a certificate to that purport; the commissioners are then to authenticate such certificate under their hands and seals, and to transmit it to the lord chancellor; and he, or two of the judges whom he shall appoint, on oath made by the bankrupt that such certificate was obtained without fraud, may allow the same, or disallow it, upon cause shown by any of the creditors of the bankrupt.

If no cause be shown to the contrary, the certificate is allowed of course; and then the bankrupt is entitled to a decent and reasonable allowance out of his effects, for his future support and maintenance, and to put him in a way of honest industry. . . .

Besides this allowance, he has also an indemnity granted him, of being free and discharged for ever from all debts owing by him at the time he became a bankrupt; even though judgement shall have been obtained against him, and he lies in prison upon execution for such debts. . . . Thus the bankrupt becomes a clear man again; and, by the assistance of his allowance and his own industry, may become a useful member of the commonwealth: which is the rather to be expected, as he cannot be entitled to these benefits, unless his failures have been owing to misfortunes, rather than to misconduct and extravagance.

For no allowance or indemnity shall be given to a bankrupt, unless his certificate be signed and allowed, as before mentioned. . . . Neither can he claim them, if he has given with any of his children above 100£ for a marriage portion, unless he had at that time sufficient left to pay all his debts; or if he has lost at any one time 5£ or in the whole 100£ within a twelve-month before he became bankrupt, by any manner of gaming or wagering whatsoever. . . . Also, to prevent the too common practice of frequent and fraudulent or careless breaking, a mark is set upon such as have been once cleared by a commission of bankrupt, or have compounded with their creditors, or have been delivered by an act of insolvency. . . . Let us next consider,

. . . How such proceedings affect or transfer the *estate* and *property* of the bankrupt. . . .

By virtue of the statutes before mentioned all the personal estate and effects of the bankrupt are considered as vested, by the act of bankruptcy, in the future assignees of his commissioners, whether they be goods in actual *possession*, or debts, contracts, and other choses in *action*; and the commissioners by their warrant may cause any house or tenement of the bankrupt to be broken open, in order to enter upon and seize the same. And when the assignees are chosen or approved by the creditors, the commissioners are to assign every thing over to them; and the property of every part of the estate is thereby as fully vested in them, as it was in the bankrupt himself, and they have the same remedies to recover it.

The property vested in the assignees is the whole that the bankrupt had in himself at the time he committed the first act of bankruptcy, or that has been vested in him since, before his debts are satisfied or agreed for. Therefore it is usually said, that once a bankrupt and always a bankrupt; by which is meant, that a plain direct act of bankruptcy once committed cannot be purged, or explained away, by any subsequent conduct, . . . but that, if a commission is afterwards awarded, the commission and the property of the assignees shall have a relation, or reference, back to the first and original act of bankruptcy. Insomuch that all transactions of the bankrupt are from that time absolutely null and void, . . . for they are no longer his property, or his debts, but those of the future assignees. . . . In France this doctrine of relation is carried to a very great length; for there every act of a merchant, for ten days *precedent* to the act of bankruptcy, is presumed to be fraudulent, and is therefore void. But with us the law stands upon a more reasonable footing: for, as these acts of bankruptcy may sometimes be secret to all but a few, and it would be prejudicial to trade to carry this notion to its utmost length, it is provided . . . that no money paid by a bankrupt to a *bona fide* or real creditor in a course of trade, even after an act of bankruptcy done, shall be liable to be refunded. Nor . . . shall any debtor of a bankrupt, that pays him his debt without knowing of his bankruptcy, be liable to account for it again. The intention of this relative power being only to reach fraudulent transactions, and not to distress the fair trader. . . .

When they have got in all the effects they can reasonably hope for, and reduced them to ready money, the assignees must . . . give one-and-twenty days' notice to the creditors of a meeting for a dividend or distribution; at which time they must produce their accounts, and verify them upon oath if required. And then the commissioners shall direct a dividend to be made, at so much in the pound, to all creditors who have before proved, or shall then prove, their debts. This dividend must be made equally, and in a rateable proportion, to all the creditors, according to the *quantity* of their debts; no regard being had to the *quality* of them. Mortgages indeed, for which the creditor has a real security in his own hands, are entirely safe; for the commission of bankrupt reaches only the equity of redemption. . . . And, . . . the landlord shall be allowed his arrears of rent to the same amount, in preference to other creditors, even though he hath neglected to distrain, while the goods remained on the premises . . . . But, otherwise, judgements and recognizances, . . . and also bonds and obligations by deed or special instrument, . . . these are all put on a level with debts by mere simply contract, and all paid *pari passu*. . . . And if any surplus remains, after selling his estates and paying every creditor his full debt, it shall be restored to the bankrupt. . . . And therefore, though the usual rule is, that all interest on debts carrying interest shall cease from the time of issuing the commission, yet, in case of a surplus left after payment of every debt, such interest shall again revive, and be chargeable on the bankrupt, or his representatives.

D.   The Constitution and the Bankruptcy Clause

In the powers given to the federal Congress, the United States Constitution includes the Bankruptcy Clause in Article I, § 8, clause 4: "The Congress shall have power . . . To establish . . . uniform Laws on the subject of Bankruptcies throughout the United States." What does that Clause mean? The Bankruptcy Clause was adopted by the framers after little debate. The conception of bankruptcy was certainly not an unfamiliar one to the framers. England had bankruptcy laws in place for almost a quarter of a millennium by the time our Constitution was adopted, and many of the drafters were quite familiar with the English law. Furthermore, for a long time the individual colonies had in place a wide spectrum of laws on bankruptcy, insolvency, debt collection, and imprisonment for debt. For an excellent treatment of the colonial period, see Peter J. Coleman, DEBTORS AND CREDITORS IN AMERICA: INSOLVENCY, IMPRISONMENT FOR DEBT, AND BANKRUPTCY, 1607-1900 (1974). But the historical record of the constitutional convention itself sheds little light on the original meaning of the Bankruptcy Clause.

For a fuller understanding of (1) how the Bankruptcy Clause came to be included in the Constitution, and (2) what evils the drafters were seeking to redress, three sources are included. An additional excellent study is by Professor Thomas Plank, *The Constitutional Limits of Bankruptcy*, 63 TENN. L. REV. 487 (1996). First we hear from a near contemporary of the constitutional event, the illustrious Justice Joseph Story, writing in 1833 in his COMMENTARIES ON THE CONSTITUTION OF THE UNITED STATES. Justice Story is worth listening to, not only because he lived close to the time of the Constitution itself, but also because he was considered to be a leading authority on bankruptcy law. Indeed, he is reputed to have written most of the Bankruptcy Act of 1841. The passages from Story reveal much, not only about the intendment of the Bankruptcy Clause itself, but also about bankruptcy history and the normative underpinnings of a bankruptcy law.

Next, over a century later, Professor Kurt Nadelmann gives the most recent, and probably the most authoritative, account of the origins of the Bankruptcy Clause. He concludes that the drafters sought to deal with actual problems of interstate cooperation facing the states in dealing with insolvency issues, "not with a doctrinaire proposition," and thus the reach of the Bankruptcy Clause should not be confined to the parameters of the then-extant English model. If Nadelmann is right, then the Supreme Court likewise has been right in giving a broad and permissive construction in the past two centuries to that clause.

Finally, Professor Tabb's 1995 history article briefly looks at the constitutional origins of the Bankruptcy Clause.

Joseph Story
COMMENTARIES ON THE CONSTITUTION OF THE UNITED STATES (1833)

§ 1100. The power to pass laws on the subject of bankruptcies was not in the original draft of the constitution. . . . The committee subsequently made a report in favor of incorporating the clause on the subject of bankruptcies into the constitution; and it was adopted by a vote of nine states against one. The brevity, with which this subject is treated by the Federalist, is quite remarkable. The only passage in that elaborate commentary, in which the subject is treated, is as follows: "The power of establishing uniform laws of bankruptcy is so intimately connected with the regulation of commerce, and will prevent so many frauds, where the parties or their property may lie, or be removed into different states, that the expediency of it seems not likely to be drawn in question."

§ 1101. The subject, however, deserves a more exact consideration. Before the adoption of the constitution the states severally possessed the exclusive right, as matter belonging to their general sovereignty, to pass laws upon the subject of bankruptcy and insolvency. . . . [T]he general object of all bankrupt and insolvent laws is, on the one hand, to secure to creditors an appropriation of the property of their debtors *pro tanto* to the discharge of their debts, whenever the latter are unable to discharge the whole amount; and, on the other hand, to relieve unfortunate and honest debtors from perpetual bondage to their creditors, either in the shape of unlimited imprisonment to coerce payment of their debts, or of an absolute right to appropriate and monopolize all their future earnings. The latter course obviously destroys all encouragement to industry and enterprise on the part of the unfortunate debtor, by taking from him all the just rewards of his labour, and leaving him with a miserable pittance, dependent upon the bounty of forbearance of his creditors. The former is, if possible, more harsh, severe, and indefensible. . . . [W]hen the debtors have no property, or have yielded up the whole to their creditors, to allow the latter at their mere pleasure to imprison them, is a refinement in cruelty, and an indulgence of private passions, which could hardly find apology in an enlightened despotism; and are utterly at war with all the rights and duties of free government. Such a system of legislation is as unjust, as it is unfeeling. . . . One of the first duties of legislation, while it provides amply for the sacred obligation of contracts, and the remedies to enforce them, certainly is, *pari passu*, to relieve the unfortunate and meritorious debtor from a slavery of mind and body, which cuts him off from a fair enjoyment of the common benefits of society, and robs his family of the fruits of his labour, and the benefits of his paternal superintendence. A national government, which did not possess this power of legislation, would be little worthy of the exalted functions of guarding the happiness, and supporting the rights of a free people. . . .

§ 1102. But there are peculiar reasons, independent of these general considerations, why the government of the United States should be entrusted with this power. They result from the importance of preserving harmony, promoting justice, and securing equality of rights and remedies among the citizens of all the states. It is obvious, that if the power is exclusively vested in the states, each one will be at liberty to frame such a system of legislation upon the subject of bankruptcy and insolvency, as best suits its own local interests, and pursuits. Under such circumstances no uniformity of system or operations can be expected. . . . [D]iversities of almost infinite variety and object may be introduced into the local system, which may work gross injustice and inequality, and nourish feuds and discontents in neighbouring states. What is here stated, is not purely speculative. It has occurred among the American states in the most offensive forms . . . . There will always be found in every state a large mass of politicians, who will deem it more safe to consult their own temporary interests and popularity, by a narrow system of preferences, than to enlarge the boundaries, so as to give to distant creditors a fair share of the fortune of a ruined debtor. There can be no other adequate remedy, than giving a power to the general government, to introduce and perpetuate a uniform system.

§ 1103. In the next place it is clear, that no state can introduce any system, which shall extend beyond its own territorial limits, and the persons, who are subject to its jurisdiction. Creditors residing in other states cannot be bound by its laws; and debts contracted in other states are beyond the reach of its legislation. It can neither discharge the obligation of such contracts, nor touch the remedies, which relate to them in any other jurisdiction. . . . Among a people, whose general and commercial intercourse must be so great, and so constantly increasing, as in the United States, this alone would be a most enormous evil, and bear with peculiar severity upon all the commercial states. Very few persons engaged in active business will be without debtors or creditors in many states in the Union. The evil is incapable of being redressed by the states. It can be adequately redressed only by the power of the Union. . . .

§ 1104. In the next place, the power is important in regard to foreign countries, and to our commercial credits and intercourse with them. . . .

§ 1105. It cannot but be matter of regret, that a power so salutary should have hitherto remained . . . a mere dead letter. It is extraordinary, that a commercial nation, spreading its enterprise through the whole world, and possessing such an infinitely varied, internal trade, reaching almost to every cottage in the most distant states, should voluntarily surrender up a system, which has elsewhere enjoyed such general favour, as the best security of creditors against fraud and the best protection of debtors against oppression.

§ 1106. What laws are to be deemed bankrupt laws within the meaning of the constitution has been a matter of much forensic discussion and argument. Attempts have been made to distinguish between bankrupt laws and insolvent laws. For example, it has been said, that laws, which merely liberate the person of the debtor, are insolvent laws, and those, which discharge the contract, are bankrupt laws. But it would be very difficulty to sustain this distinction by any uniformity of laws at home or abroad. . . . Again; it has been said, that insolvent laws act on imprisoned debtors only at their own instance; and bankrupt laws only at the instance of creditors. But, however true this may have been in past times, as the actual courses of English legislation, it is not true, and never was true, as a distinction in colonial legislation. . . . And if an act of congress should be passed, which should authorize a commission of bankruptcy to issue at the instance of the debtor, no court would on this account be warranted in saying, that the act was unconstitutional, and the commission a nullity. . . . And an historical review of the colonial and state legislation will abundantly show, that a bankrupt law may contain those regulations, which are generally found in insolvent laws; and that an insolvent law may contain those, which are common to bankrupt laws.

§ 1107. The truth is, that the English system of bankruptcy, as well as the name, was borrowed from the continental jurisprudence, and derivatively from the Roman law. . . .

§ 1108. The system of discharging persons, who were unable to pay their debts, was transferred from the Roman law into continental jurisprudence at an early period. . . . [T]he law of cession (*cessio bonorum*) was introduced by the Christian emperors of Rome, whereby, if a debtor ceded, or yielded up all his property to his creditors, he was secured from being dragged to gaol . . . . Neither by the Roman, nor the continental law, was the *cessio bonorum* confined to traders, but it extended to all persons. It may be added, that the *cessio bonorum* of the Roman law, and that, which at present prevails in most parts of the continent of Europe, only exempted the debtor from imprisonment. It did not release or discharge the debt, or exempt te future acquisitions of the debtor from execution for the debt. The English statute . . . went no farther, than to discharge the debtor's person. . . . But with a view to the advancement of commerce, and the benefit of creditors, the systems, now commonly known by the name of "bankrupt laws," were introduced; and allowed a proceeding to be had at the instance of the creditors against an unwilling debtor, when he did not choose to yield up his property . . . . In the English system the bankrupt laws are limited to persons, who are traders, or connected with matters of trade and commerce, as such persons are peculiarly liable to accidental losses, and to an inability of paying their debts without any fault of their own. But this is a mere matter of policy, and by no means enters into the nature of such laws. There is nothing in the nature, or reason of such laws to prevent their being applied to any other class of unfortunate and meritorious debtors.

§ 1109. How far the power of congress to pass uniform laws on the subject of bankruptcies supersedes the authority of state legislation on the same subject, has been a matter of much elaborate forensic discussion. It has been strenuously maintained by some learned minds, that the power in congress is exclusive of that of the states; and, whether exerted or not, it supersedes state legislation. On the other hand, it has been maintained, that the power in congress is not exclusive; that when congress has acted upon the subject, to the extent of the national legislation the power of the states is controlled and limited; but when unexerted, the states are at liberty to exercise the power in its full extent, unless so far as they are controlled by other constitutional provisions. . . .

§ 1110. It is, however, to be understood, that although the states still retain the power to pass insolvent and bankrupt laws, that power is not unlimited, as it was before the constitution. It does not, as will be presently seen, extend to the passing of insolvent or bankrupt acts, which shall discharge the obligation of antecedent contracts. It can discharge such contracts only, as are made subsequently to the passing of such acts, and such, as are made within the state between citizens of the same state. It does not extend to contracts made with a citizen of another state within the state, nor to any contracts made in other states.

Kurt H. Nadelmann
On the Origin of the Bankruptcy Clause
1 AM. J. LEGAL HIST. 215 (1957)[*]

On the origin of the Bankruptcy Clause in our Constitution little is known. . . .

At the time of [Story's] writing, in 1833, the only source material available was the *Journal of the Federal Convention. . . .* The *Journal* itself had not been published until 1819 . . . . The other source material on the Constitutional Convention, Madison's *Notes of Debates in the Federal Convention,* only appeared in 1840 . . . .

Madison's *Notes of Debates* are more explicit than the *Journal.* On the basis of the Notes, Charles Warren, in his *Bankruptcy in the United States History,* has related that "On August 29 [1787], Charles Pinckney of South Carolina moved to commit the Full Faith and Credit Clause (Article XVI of John Rutledge's report of the Committee of Detail of August 6) with an addition 'to establish uniform laws upon the subject of bankruptcies and respecting the damages arising on the protest of foreign bills of exchange.'" And he is more specific also on what followed, namely, that, on September 1, Rutledge reported a recommendation that, in the article relating to the Legislative Department, there be added after the power "to establish an uniform rule of naturalization throughout the United States", a power "to establish uniform laws on the subject of bankruptcies"; that, on September 3, this clause was adopted with practically no debate, the State of Connecticut alone vot-

---

ing nay; and that in the report of the Committee on Style and in the final draft, this power was inserted immediately after the power to regulate commerce as Clause 4 of Section 8 of Article I.

What moved Pinckney to make the proposal? . . . Pinckney was not a bankruptcy law specialist, and nothing in the conditions in South Carolina would seem to have suggested special attention to this question. . . .

Closer examination of Madison's *Notes of Debates*, however, furnishes additional information—information of great interest. . . .

The entry in Madison's *Notes of Debates* under "Wednesday, August 29th. 1787. In Convention" begins as follows: "Art. XVI taken up." . . .

Article XVI was essentially a copy of the Full Faith and Credit clause of the Articles of Confederation, but with an alteration. Full faith was to be given not only to the records and judicial proceedings of the courts but also to acts of the legislature. . . .

The next entry after: "Art. XVI taken up", is:

> Mr. Williamson [of North Carolina] moved to substitute in place of it, the words of the Articles of Confederation on the same subject. He did (not) understand precisely the meaning of the article.
>
> Mr. Wilson [of Pennsylvania] & Docr. Johnson [of Connecticut] supposed the meaning to be that judgments in one state should be the ground of actions in other states, & that acts of the legislatures should be included, *as they sometimes serve the like purpose as act*—for the sake of acts of insolvency, etc.
>
> Mr. Pinkney moved to commit Art. XVI, with the following proposal—"To establish uniform laws upon the subject of bankruptcies, and respecting the damages arising on the protest of foreign bills of exchange."

This is all that is of interest to our discussion. After Pinckney, three more delegates spoke on Article XVI . . . and Article XVI was committed, together with Pinckney's motion, to a committee. . . .

The important fact is that the bankruptcy power was proposed at one stage of the discussion of the Full Faith and Credit Clause—more concretely, after Wilson and Johnson had stated, in answer to a question, that they supposed the meaning of the clause to be that judgments in one state should be the ground of actions in other states and that acts of the legislature should be included . . . "for the sake of Acts of insolvency etc." . . .

William Samuel Johnson, of Connecticut, the second to speak, was not on the Committee of Detail, but the Committee had a member from Connecticut in the person of Judge Ellsworth. If Wilson had made a remark about acts of the legislature sometimes serving a like purpose as court decisions or had referred to "Acts of insolvency", the delegate from Connecticut was the proper person to intervene and give further explanations.

Connecticut, at the time of the Constitutional Convention, had no general bankruptcy or insolvency law. . . . [I]nsolvent debtors desiring to obtain a discharge from their debts and be protected from imprisonment had to petition the legislature for what was called a special act of insolvency and, sometimes, a special act of bankruptcy. . . . Such acts embodied the principal features of general bankruptcy or insolvency legislation, provision for assignment of the estate to a trustee, designation of a trustee or trustees, provision for distribution of the assets, discharge from debts, and so forth. . . .

The practice of special acts of the legislature for the relief of individual debtors was not limited to Connecticut. . . .

Imprisonment for debt, an institution inherited from the mother country, had become one of the great plagues of the time. Insolvent debtors, victims of the consequences of the war and, in particular, of the monetary disorders, filled the prisons to capacity. Legislation, different in each state, was inadequate to cope with the situation. . . . The great question remained whether action in one state could protect the debtor if he ventured into another state. . . .

What had happened in the Committee of Detail, when "acts of the legislature" was added to the old form of the Full Faith and Credit Clause, we shall probably never know. But in as much as Ellsworth was on the Committee of Detail and the Connecticut practice was to achieve by acts of insolvency of the legislature what elsewhere was done by court decrees, it would not have been surprising if the member from Connecticut, in a discussion of the Full Faith and Credit clause, had suggested extension of the command of full faith to cover also acts of the legislature, like acts of insolvency, serving the like purpose as court decisions. But this is in the realm of speculation.

The fact, which we have, and which cannot be overlooked, is that Pinckney moved committal of Article XVI, together with the proposition "to establish uniform laws upon the subject of bankruptcies," immediately after whatever discussion there was of "acts of the legislature" and "acts of insolvency etc." The discussion must have brought out, and recalled, the difficulties resulting from the differences in state legislation on the subject. And this may well have sufficed to produce in the mind of a constitution builder like Pinckney the thought that Congress should receive power to establish uniform laws upon the subject of bankruptcies.

Linking the Pinckney proposal for a bankruptcy power with the discussion of full faith problems in matters of insolvency finds some collateral support in the treatment given these subjects by Madison in *The Federalist*. Although the Bankruptcy Clause and the Full Faith and Credit Clause are in different parts of the Constitution, in *The Federalist* Madison chose to take up the congressional power under the Full Faith and Credit clause immediately after discussing the bankruptcy power. . . .

It is true that we have the reference to the regulation of commerce and that Madison showed more concern about prevention of fraud than about the solution of problems of debtor relief, but the fact of the successive and somewhat parallel treatment remains, reflecting—possibly reflecting—the sequence of events in the Constitutional Convention five months before. . . . The insertion, by the Committee on Style, of the Bankruptcy Clause immediately after the power to regulate commerce, of course makes a reference to that clause almost unavoidable.

May conclusions of a permanent value be drawn from a finding that Pinckney's motion for a bankruptcy power was in consequence of a discussion of interstate conflicts problems in the field on insolvency? We think so. From such a finding it would follow that the Constitutional Convention sought to deal with live problems of the American states, problems well known to all delegates, and not with a doctrinaire proposition. This would exclude once and for all the argument many times made that the clause must be read against the background of the conception of "bankruptcy" in the English law at the time of the Convention. . . .

It is true that, in some of the American States, the English System had been copied; it is no less true that it had been completely disregarded in other states, including Connecticut. And it is no accident, we think, that the Bankruptcy Clause speaks of "uniform laws," rather than one "uniform law," which Congress may pass on the subject of bankruptcies, thus leaving Congress a free hand in adopting, if it so desired, different laws for different types of debtors. Contemporaries of the drafters of the Constitution had no doubt as to the broad reading to be given to the Bankruptcy Clause.

Charles Jordan Tabb
The History of the Bankruptcy Laws in the United States
3 AM. BANKR. INST. L. REV. 5 (1995)[*]

1. The Constitution

In the colonial era, many of the states had comprehensive laws regulating debtor-creditor relations. Some of these were bankruptcy laws, and others were insolvency laws. Imprisonment for debt was commonplace in the colonies and then in the states, until the mid-nineteenth century. Some states had more liberal debtor relief measures than did England. Since no provision was made for federal bankruptcy legislation in the Articles of Confederation, state regulation continued.

The subject of bankruptcy received only passing attention from the framers at the Constitutional Convention of 1787. A bankruptcy law was apparently believed to be a necessary subject of federal legislation because of the problems that varying and discriminatory state laws caused for nonresident creditors and interstate commerce in general. James Madison described the perceived purpose of the Bankruptcy Clause:

> The power of establishing uniform laws of bankruptcy is so intimately connected with the regulation of commerce, and will prevent so many frauds where the parties or their property may lie or be removed into different states that the expediency of it seems not likely to be drawn into question.

The Bankruptcy Clause, empowering Congress to "pass uniform laws on the subject of bankruptcies," was added late in the proceedings of the Constitutional Convention, after very little debate. Charles Pinckney of South Carolina is generally credited with first drafting the Bankruptcy Clause. The only vote against was by Connecticut, with Roger Sherman expressing concern that bankruptcies could be punished by death, as was still the law in England. An unsuccessful attempt was made to extend the prohibition against impairing the obligation of contracts from the states to the federal government, which if successful would have undermined the utility of any federal bankruptcy legislation.

E.   American Bankruptcy Law Prior to 1978

The current bankruptcy law in the United States was enacted in 1978, in the Bankruptcy Reform Act of 1978, Pub. L. No. 95-598, together with several amendatory acts, most notably in 1984 and 1994. This law is called the "Code" by bankruptcy aficionados. Much water had gone under the bankruptcy bridge before that time, however. One must know what went before to more fully understand the current bankruptcy law.

Two different sources illuminate the historical landscape. The first is from a continuation of Professor Tabb's article that was excerpted earlier. Tabb takes us from the passage of the first Bankruptcy Act in 1800 to the cusp of the reform movement of the 1970s. As you read Tabb's article, note the political tensions that pervaded the nineteenth century struggle to develop a federal bankruptcy

---

law. Sectional and philosophical differences motivated momentous debates over what the nature of a federal bankruptcy law should be, and what role state law should have. The four federal laws enacted in that century changed dramatically in character and purpose, and marked the transition from the early conception of bankruptcy as a creditors' remedy to bankruptcy as a debtor relief measure. The landscape changed forever in 1898, with the passage of permanent federal legislation. The most critical bankruptcy point in the twentieth century, unsurprisingly, came in the Great Depression of the 1930s. As with so many other areas of the law, that cataclysmic decade marked the point at which federal law became pervasively entwined in the bankruptcy arena.

The second reading in this section is from the late Professor Lawrence King, of New York University Law School. Professor King was one of the giants of bankruptcy law in the second half of the twentieth century. He served for many years as a linchpin of the Bankruptcy Rules Committee, and was chief editor of COLLIER ON BANKRUPTCY, the leading multi-volume treatise in the field. As Professor King shows in his delightful piece *An Ode to the Bankruptcy Law*, a poetic retelling of United States bankruptcy history up to the 1970s, he has a creative and whimsical side as well. A companion article well worth reading in that same issue of the Commercial Law Journal is *A History of American Bankruptcy Law*, 81 COM. L.J. 226 (1976), by late Professor Vern Countryman, of Harvard Law School. Professor Countryman's article tells a similar story, albeit not in verse. Professor Countryman is another of the bankruptcy legends.

Charles Jordan Tabb
The History of the Bankruptcy Laws in the United States
3 AM. BANKR. INST. L. REV. 5 (1995)[*]

For over a century after the Constitution, however, the Bankruptcy Clause remained largely unexercised by Congress. During this period, many states stepped into the void and passed their own bankruptcy legislation. A federal bankruptcy law was in existence only from 1800 to 1803, from 1841 to 1843, and from 1867 to 1878. Permanent federal bankruptcy legislation did not go into effect until 1898. Thus, states were free to act in bankruptcy matters for all but 16 of the first 109 years after the Constitution was ratified. Each instance of federal legislation followed a major financial disaster: the Act of 1800 followed the Panic of 1797; the Act of 1841 came after the Panic of 1837; the 1867 Act followed the Panic of 1857 and the Civil War; and finally the 1898 Act was passed in the wake of the Panic of 1893.

2. Bankruptcy Act of 1800

The first federal bankruptcy law was passed on April 4, 1800, eleven years after the ratification of the Constitution. Pressure had been brought for a national bankruptcy law by a crash in 1792, but nothing was done until 1797, when another panic caused widespread ruin and the imprisonment of thousands of debtors. Robert Morris, one of the main financiers of the Revolution, spent three years in debtor's prison owing $12 million, and Supreme Court Justice James Wilson fled from Pennsylvania to avoid a like fate. The 1800 Act finally was passed, carrying by but a single vote in the House. Federalist representatives of commercial interests pushed the bill, while the law was

---

[*]   Charles Jordan Tabb: "The History of the Bankruptcy Laws in the United States," *American Bankruptcy Institute Law Review,* Spring 1995, Vol. 3, No. 1. Copyright © 1995 by the American Bankruptcy Institute. Reprinted by permission.

opposed by anti-Federalist southerners and agricultural sympathizers. The 1800 Act was designed as a temporary measure, to sunset in five years, but actually was repealed after only three.

The 1800 Act was very similar to the 1732 English act, and also had many of the features of the Pennsylvania statute. It was purely a creditors' remedy. Only creditors, upon proof of the debtor's commission of an act of bankruptcy, could initiate a bankruptcy. Debtors, however, apparently were often able to persuade a friendly creditor to bring a case. Only merchants were eligible debtors. Fraudulent bankruptcy was a criminal offense, but was not punishable by death. Commissioners appointed by the district court supervised the process, and had powers very similar to the English commissioners. The commissioners would appoint assignees to effect the liquidation and distribution.

A discharge of the debts and the person of a cooperative debtor was allowed. Before a discharge could be granted, the bankruptcy commissioners had to certify to the federal district judge that the debtor had cooperated, and two-thirds of the creditors, by number and by value of claims, had to consent to the discharge. The debtor received a graduated allowance out of the estate, depending on the size of the dividend to creditors. Modest exemptions were also permitted. The 1800 Act did provide a discharge for some of the prominent financiers, including Robert Morris, who had been ruined in 1797.

By 1803, the sentiment for repeal of the 1800 Act was overwhelming. Some of the objections ring familiar. Small dividends were paid, and many of the discharged debtors were high-rolling speculators who went through bankruptcy and then started their operations anew. In addition, travel to the distant federal courts was difficult. Finally, agricultural interests were outraged at the perceived favoritism of mercantile groups.

3. State Law in Nineteenth Century

The states picked up part of the slack and continued to regulate relations between debtors and creditors, bankruptcy, and insolvency during the lengthy era of federal inaction after the 1803 repeal. In some important respects state relief was limited. In 1819, the Supreme Court, in *Sturges v. Crowninshield*, [17 U.S. (4 Wheat.) 122 (1819),] held that states could not constitutionally discharge preexisting debts. In 1827, the Court, in *Ogden v. Saunders*, [25 U.S. (12 Wheat.) 213 (1827),] held that states could not discharge the debts due a citizen of another state. *Ogden* did hold, however, that states could discharge future debts against citizens of the same state. The *Sturges* decision in particular caused considerable consternation, because the period around 1819-1820 was one of extreme economic depression. During this depression there was no federal bankruptcy law by which debtors could be relieved, and because of *Sturges,* state relief was not possible as to preexisting debts.

In the meantime, the lengthy era of widespread use of imprisonment for debt was coming to an end. The practice was abolished at the federal level in 1833, and many states followed suit in the 1830s and 1840s. In England, general abolition of the practice did not come until 1869. . . .

Even though debtors eventually no longer went to prison, they lacked any means to discharge preexisting debts during the first four decades of the nineteenth century after 1803. At times, especially in the 1830s, states did give partial relief through the enactment of stay laws or moratoria on debt collection. These laws presaged the stay laws to follow a century later.

4. Bankruptcy Act of 1841

Throughout the 1820s attempts were made to pass a bill permitting voluntary bankruptcy for the direct relief of debtors, merchant and non-merchant alike. Yet throughout that period all such efforts were rebuffed by an alliance of southerners, who opposed any federal bankruptcy bill, and others who believed that voluntary bankruptcy was unconstitutional. John Calhoun, for example, heatedly fought off federal intervention. Daniel Webster, conversely, was a leading advocate of a national bankruptcy law, and often fronted for Joseph Story, who wrote a number of bankruptcy bills. Even those who favored a bankruptcy bill differed on whether involuntary bankruptcy should be permitted and whether corporations should be eligible debtors. Finally, the devastating Panic of 1837, coupled with the victory by the Whigs over the Democrats in the 1840 election, turned the tide. In a very close vote, the Bankruptcy Act of 1841 was passed. Again a major national financial crisis had forced Congress's hand. The legislative background to the passage of the 1841 Act is a fascinating story in itself, demonstrating how strange bedfellows and apt logrolling can sometimes work to accomplish seemingly impossible legislative goals. The final compromise allowed both involuntary and voluntary bankruptcy, did not limit eligibility to merchant debtors, but did exclude corporations from eligibility.

While the 1800 Act was nothing more than a reprise of the old English bankruptcy model, the 1841 Act, because of its establishment of voluntary bankruptcy, was a watershed event in bankruptcy history. For the first time, a financially troubled debtor could file for bankruptcy and receive a discharge. Nor was relief limited to merchant debtors; eligibility was extended to "all persons whatsoever . . . owing debts . . . ." Considerable debate focused on whether such a law even fell within the "subject of bankruptcies" specified by the Constitution as one of Congress's enumerated powers. Ultimately Congress's power was upheld, although never directly by the Supreme Court.

The 1841 Act was a coordinated, simple, and short act of only seventeen sections. It was reputedly written in large part by Story and modeled after the Massachusetts insolvency law of 1838. The act provided that "[a]ll persons whatsoever . . . owing debts" who did petition "for the benefit of this act, and therein declare themselves to be unable to meet their debts . . . shall be deemed bankrupts within the purview of this act." Involuntary bankruptcy was permitted against merchants. Jurisdiction was vested in the district court, "in the nature of summary proceedings in equity." Assignees effected the liquidation and distribution, thus replacing the commissioners featured in previous bankruptcy laws.

The debtor was allowed basic exemptions, but was not permitted to invoke state exemption laws. This restriction became a point of considerable contention during the consideration of later federal bankruptcy acts. The discharge extended to "every bankrupt, who shall bona fide surrender all his property [except that made exempt], and shall fully comply with . . . and conform to . . . this act." Creditors still could block the discharge, but only through a written dissent filed by a majority in number and value of creditors. Even then the debtor could demand a trial by jury or appeal to the circuit court on the issue of whether the debtor had conformed. Unlike the 1800 Act, a number of grounds for denying discharge were included. Like the 1800 Act, very few debts were excepted from the discharge. Special emphasis in the new law was placed on halting preferences. The giving of preferences was made a ground for denial of discharge. A hearing on the discharge was held in the district court. The old practice of commissioners certifying the discharge to the court was abandoned. The discharge was enforced as an affirmative defense raised by the debtor in subsequent collection efforts. This practice did not change until 1970.

Even though in operation the law worked well, from the viewpoint of creditors, the 1841 Act, like its 1800 predecessor, was a dismal failure. Many thousands of debtors were discharged, minimal dividends were paid to creditors, and administrative fees were high. Control was in the hands of the courts and the assignees, not creditors. With the immediate goal of relieving the plight of the mass of insolvent debtors accomplished, and with little continuing political capital to be gained from the law, the 1841 Act was repealed in early 1843 after little more than a year of operation. Nonetheless, the 1841 Act established the fact of voluntary bankruptcy for all debtors. Voluntary proceedings have been a feature of all subsequent bankruptcy laws. Never again was the constitutionality of voluntary bankruptcy seriously questioned. The 1841 Act, with its marriage of the concepts of "bankruptcy" and "insolvency," could be called the first modern bankruptcy law.

5. Bankruptcy Act of 1867

The years after the 1843 repeal of the 1841 Act were finally times of prosperity for the United States, and consequently, no push was made for a federal bankruptcy law. To the Whigs, considering the political harm done to them by the 1841 Act, a bankruptcy law was anathema. Determined to stave off any more disastrous federal laws, states experimented even more with stay and insolvency laws. . . .

After the Panic of 1857 and the financial cataclysm caused by the American Civil War, overwhelming pressure for another federal bankruptcy law led to the enactment of the Bankruptcy Act of 1867. The inability of state laws to discharge preexisting debts or debts of nonresident creditors contributed to the need for a federal law. Northern creditors pushed hard for the bankruptcy bill, viewing such a law as essential to their ability to collect anything from southern debtors. The compromise bill that eventually passed was described as "unwieldy because of too great attention to details."

The 1867 Act included both voluntary and involuntary bankruptcy. The constitutionality of voluntary bankruptcy was now taken for granted. Unlike the 1841 Act, corporations were permitted to take advantage of the act. In keeping with the times, an oath of allegiance to the United States had to be taken by a petitioning bankrupt. The 1841 Act's restriction of involuntary bankruptcy to merchants was dropped. Now "any person" was subject to the threat of involuntary bankruptcy. The list of "acts of bankruptcy" that would support an involuntary petition was greatly extended as well.

The judicial machinery for dealing with bankruptcy cases was much closer to the system in place today. The district courts were given original jurisdiction as "courts of bankruptcy." The district courts were directed, however, to appoint one or more "registers in bankruptcy, to assist the judge of the district court in the performance of his duties." These registers thus were the predecessors of the twentieth century referee and bankruptcy judge. Assignees superintended the liquidation itself.

In time, this law too proved to be a failure and was eventually repealed in 1878. As with the prior federal bankruptcy acts, criticisms levied by creditors included small dividends, high fees and expenses, and lengthy delays. Northern creditors who had hoped to use the bankruptcy law to facilitate collection from southern debtors were disappointed. Indeed, most of the pressure for repeal came from creditors.

Nor did debtors do very well under the 1867 law. Due to the inclusion of numerous grounds for denying discharge, only about one-third of the debtors received a discharge. Procedurally, the discharge was obtained after application by the debtor, upon notice to creditors and a court hearing. The discharge still had to be raised as an affirmative defense to subsequent collection efforts.

The issues of creditor consent to the discharge and the need for a minimum dividend were very hotly debated, and produced an odd history. In the 1867 Act itself, creditors seemingly carried the day; unless a majority of creditors consented, the law required a fifty percent dividend as a prerequisite to the granting of a discharge. However, the effective date of this provision was postponed for a year, which of course allowed debtors to file before that time and discharge their debts. Later amendments denuded the provision of what little vitality it still had. Later laws completely abandoned the creditor consent restriction.

An important benefit of the 1867 Act to debtors, however, was that it allowed debtors to elect the benefit of generous state exemption laws as an alternative to the federal scheme. The constitutionality of this provision was contested, on the ground that it violated the uniformity requirement of the Bankruptcy Clause. In 1902, while construing the 1898 Act, the Supreme Court finally held that the uniformity requirement was satisfied notwithstanding the incorporation of state exemptions. The utilization of state exemption laws in federal bankruptcy cases has continued to the present.

A major innovation, the composition agreement, was introduced into the bankruptcy law in 1874. England had taken a similar step in 1869. Congressional action had been hastened by the Panic of 1873. The composition agreement, the forerunner of modern reorganization provisions, allowed the debtor to propose payment of a certain percentage of his debts over time in full discharge of those debts, while also keeping his property. If the proposed composition was accepted by a majority in number and three-fourths in value of the creditors, it was binding on all creditors named in the composition. Dissenters were protected by a "best interests" test, which required that creditors be paid as much as they would receive in a liquidation.

The new composition law also was held to be within the "subject of bankruptcies," thus complying with the Bankruptcy Clause. Indeed, as a proceeding in bankruptcy, compositions were governed by other provisions of the bankruptcy law. . . . Of course, the composition law died with the rest of the bankruptcy law upon its repeal in 1878. By all accounts, the sentiment for repeal was overwhelming.

The twenty years following the repeal of the bankruptcy act in 1878 marked the final period during which there was no federal bankruptcy law. One last attempt was made to solve bankruptcy and insolvency problems at the state level, and again these efforts did not succeed. The Panics of 1884 and 1893 highlighted the inability of the states to deal with national financial problems.

6. Equity Receiverships

Federal courts entered the reorganization business with the advent of the equity receivership. Use of this device blossomed in the late nineteenth century as a means to keep the railroads running. At a time when railroads were of great economic importance, but in dire financial straits, there was no federal bankruptcy law or composition provision on the books to deal with their problems. Given the interstate nature of virtually all of the railroads, state remedies were entirely inadequate. The creative solution achieved was to invoke the power of the federal courts to supervise the restructuring of troubled railroads. Court-supervised receiverships remained the predominant means of corporate reorganization for about a half century, until federal reorganization laws were enacted during the Great Depression. . . .

In practice, the equity receivership came to be dominated by insiders, and was subject to much abuse. In form, the receivership resulted in the sale of the debtor's assets, with the proceeds distributed to creditors. In substance, however, the entire elaborate proceeding often resulted in old management retaining control of the enterprise, and dictating the terms of the sale. . . .

A number of judicial doctrines were developed to curb insider abuses. The most important was the "absolute priority rule," which precluded shareholders from retaining their interests unless all creditors were paid. Another was the use of an "upset price," to ensure that an adequate price was paid at the foreclosure sale. . . .

Vestiges of many of the judicial doctrines developed in the receivership cases remain in present-day corporate reorganizations. Furthermore, many of the issues confronted in the receivership cases—notably, how to protect dissenting creditors and ensure that the sale price is fair—are still sources of considerable controversy in the current debate over the merits of Chapter 11.

C. Bankruptcy Act of 1898 and Amendments

1. Bankruptcy Act of 1898

The Bankruptcy Act of 1898 marked the beginning of the era of permanent federal bankruptcy legislation. The 1898 Act remained in effect for eighty years, until being replaced by the Bankruptcy Reform Act of 1978. During the course of its existence, the 1898 Act was amended numerous time, most radically in 1938 by the Chandler Act.

The road to the passage of the 1898 Act was anything but smooth. Enormous hostility against a federal bankruptcy law of any sort had been generated by the 1867 law. However, the panics of 1884 and 1893 clearly exposed the need for some form of federal bankruptcy law. State laws were simply incapable of dealing with the financial problems created by these widespread calamities.

As had been true throughout much of the nineteenth century, southern and western congressmen, in particular, opposed a national bankruptcy bill. Their opposition focused on the use of involuntary bankruptcy as a means of collection by northern and eastern creditors. An alternative bill, introduced by Bailey of Texas, provided only for voluntary bankruptcy. In 1894, it actually was passed by the House. Ironically, in half a century the debate had come full circle; bankruptcy was now being urged only as a relief measure for debtors. . . .

A leading advocate and draftsman of a bankruptcy bill during the 1880s was Judge Lowell of Massachusetts. His bill proposed striking revisions to bankruptcy administration, anticipating some of the changes to come many decades later. Although at one point the Lowell bill did pass the Senate, his efforts did not bear fruit. More successful was the bill drafted by Jay Torrey, a St. Louis lawyer. The "Torrey Bill" originally was inspired by commercial creditor interests. First introduced in 1889, the Torrey Bill eventually became the Bankruptcy Act of 1898. . . .

Notwithstanding its origins with the credit industry, the 1898 Act ushered in the modern era of liberal debtor treatment in United States bankruptcy laws. While the earlier laws had allowed a debtor a discharge, many restrictions qualified that privilege. In particular, the 1867 Act, containing numerous grounds for denial of the discharge, had made discharge hard to obtain. All prior bankruptcy laws had conditioned discharge upon the consent (or at least failure to object) of a specified percentage of creditors and a minimum dividend payment to creditors. The 1898 Act abolished those restrictions, and also severely limited the number of grounds for denial of discharge. Furthermore, very few debts were excepted from the discharge. . . .

The exemption question, so divisive under the 1867 Act, was resolved in favor of allowing the debtor to claim only state exemptions. No separate federal exemptions were permitted. In 1902, the Supreme Court held that this delegation to the states did not run afoul of the Bankruptcy Clause mandate for uniform laws.

Much of the 1898 Act was directed not at debtor relief, but rather at facilitating the equitable and efficient administration and distribution of the debtor's property to creditors. Considerable attention was devoted to the details of estate administration. . . . Creditors exercised significant control over the bankruptcy process through the power to elect the trustee (no longer called an assignee) and creditors' committees.

The federal district courts sat as "courts of bankruptcy," but the bulk of the judicial and administrative work was done by "referees in bankruptcy" appointed by the district courts. Referees were compensated on a fee basis, which did not change until 1946, when a salary based compensation scheme was substituted. Referees became "bankruptcy judges" in 1973. . . . State courts retained concurrent jurisdiction of many bankruptcy-related issues. Litigation over which court had jurisdiction was frequent. The distinction between "summary" jurisdiction and "plenary" jurisdiction became a point of enormous contention. . . .

Provisions were made in the 1898 Act for both voluntary and involuntary bankruptcy. Acts of bankruptcy were retained as the basis for submitting a debtor to involuntary bankruptcy . . . .

The 1898 Act gave the trustee important powers to avoid preferential and fraudulent transfers and to recapture their value for the bankruptcy estate. In addition, such transfers constituted an act of bankruptcy that could subject the debtor to involuntary bankruptcy. The need to unwind preferential transfers was viewed as a primary justification for the passage of the national bankruptcy law.

Compositions in lieu of liquidation were authorized much along the lines of the 1874 law. . . .

2. Legislation Between 1898 and the Depression

The enactment of the Bankruptcy Act of 1898 did not end Congressional infatuation with the bankruptcy law. To the contrary, this century has witnessed an unending parade of bankruptcy legislation. During the period between the passage of the 1898 Act and the onset of the Depression, Congress made a number of changes. . . . Periodic attempts were made to ameliorate the perceived extreme pro-debtor orientation of the 1898 Act. Several of the acts added grounds for denial of discharge or added debts excepted from the discharge, and the number of acts of bankruptcy was increased. . . . Corporations were made eligible for voluntary bankruptcy in 1910. . . .

Not all congressmen were enamored of the permanent bankruptcy law. Concerted efforts were made to repeal the law in 1902, 1903, 1909, and 1910. Those efforts failed. The main objections were raised by southern congressmen who believed that bankruptcy should only be used to relieve debtors, not as a collection law.

By the time of the Hoover administration, the credit industry had come to question the wisdom of the still generous discharge provisions. In efforts similar to those launched by the credit industry in the 1960s, 1980s and 1990s, a serious attempt was made in the late 1920s and early 1930s to change the basic premise of the discharge. The credit industry wanted to impose a form of payment requirement upon those debtors with some ability to pay as a condition to receiving a discharge. The idea of a suspended or conditional discharge along the lines of the English system was suggested. However, the creditors' timing was bad. With the Depression deepening daily, their concerns over debtor abuse of the bankruptcy discharge were hard to sell to Congress. The creditors' attempts were rebuffed. With the coming of the New Deal and its militant pro-debtor attitude, the credit industry could do little in Congress but fight a rear-guard action, then take their fight to the Supreme Court.

3. Depression-Era Legislation: Congress Versus the Court and the Chandler Act

After the Depression came crashing down in 1929, Congress passed several pro-debtor amendments that facilitated rehabilitation through bankruptcy. Severe restraints were laid upon the ability of creditors to collect, even upon their collateral. The Supreme Court that infuriated President Roosevelt so much held some of these acts to be unconstitutional. Ultimately, however, Congress was able to enact revised versions that passed constitutional muster. The pro-reorganization sentiment in Congress became cemented during these trying times. With the passage of these amendments, federal equity receiverships fell into disuse.

The legislative onslaught began in 1933 with a law that made compositions more readily and widely available, authorized agricultural compositions, and permitted railroads to reorganize. Corporate reorganizations were sanctioned just a year later. Also in 1934, Congress introduced a reorganization law for municipalities. The Supreme Court overturned this law in 1936. Congress passed yet another version in 1937, which then was upheld by the Court. The Frazier-Lemke Act was passed in 1934, giving farmers greater ability to keep their farms. In 1935, the Supreme Court struck down this act on the ground that it violated the Fifth Amendment property rights of mortgagees. In just a few weeks Congress responded by passing a revised amendment, which then survived judicial review. The railroad reorganization law was amended in 1935, as was the corporate reorganization section. In a crucial decision, the Supreme Court upheld the constitutionality of § 77, the railroad reorganization section. . . .

The fury of bankruptcy legislation in the 1930s came to a head in 1938 with the passage of the comprehensive Chandler Act. The Chandler Act followed a lengthy period of careful study of the bankruptcy law, although not by a formal commission. At the instance of President Hoover, Congress published the Donovan Report in 1931, and the Thacher-Garrison Report in 1932. . . . The bill finally was enacted in the summer of 1938, forty years after the 1898 Act had become law, and forty years before the 1978 Code was enacted.

The Chandler Act substantially revised virtually all of the provisions of the 1898 Act. The substantive law and procedural workings of liquidation cases were thoroughly updated. A serious attempt was made to improve bankruptcy administration. Perhaps most significant, however, was its reworking of the recently enacted reorganization provisions into the form that prevailed for the next forty years: Chapter X governed corporate reorganizations; Chapter XI dealt with arrangements; Chapter XII applied to real property arrangements; and Chapter XIII provided for wage earners' plans.

Another important development at the time was the investigation of protective and reorganization committees by the Securities and Exchange Commission under the leadership of William Douglas. The end result was a monumental eight-part study, published between 1937 and 1940. The essential conclusion of the report was that public investors needed protection from insiders in reorganization cases.

4. Legislation After 1938

Over the next forty years, Congress amended the bankruptcy laws dozens of times, but only as to specific and discrete issues. . . .

Bankruptcy procedure was governed in substantial part by many sections of the 1898 Act. Under the authority of section 30 of the 1898 Act, the Supreme Court periodically passed General Orders in Bankruptcy to further govern procedure. In 1960, an Advisory Committee on Bankruptcy Rules was established. In 1964, Congress authorized the promulgation of rules of bankruptcy procedure by the Supreme Court. After years of effort by the Rules Committee, the bankruptcy rules took effect in 1973. Special rules for the various rehabilitation chapters came into being in the years following. The rules superseded inconsistent statutory provisions, which was quite important under the Act, given its detailed procedural provisions. Today the situation is reversed; rules cannot supersede a statute. However, since the current Bankruptcy Code has very few procedural provisions, the rules still actually have a fairly unfettered field in which to operate.

In 1970, Congress enacted a new dischargeability law, strongly enhancing the debtor's ability to protect and enforce the discharge. The law made the discharge self-executing rather than just an affirmative defense. It also gave the bankruptcy court exclusive jurisdiction over some common types of dischargeability litigation. The principal features of that reform of the discharge provisions were continued in the 1978 Code.

5. The Commission

In 1970, Congress created the Commission on the Bankruptcy Laws of the United States to study and report on the existing law. The Commission filed its two-part report in 1973. Five years later, almost a decade of study and debate about bankruptcy reform culminated when the Bankruptcy Reform Act of 1978 replaced the 1898 Act with the Bankruptcy Code.

Lawrence P. King
An Ode to the Bankruptcy Lawr
81 COM. L.J. 234 (1976)[*]

Prior to fourteen hundred ninety-two
Bankruptcy cases were very few
The testament decreed a seven year bar
And Collier was not yet a star.

Before the States became United
There was no Act to help the plighted.
But 1800 saw an answer
To help the merchant and financer.

Its five-year term, temporary;
Filings were involuntary.
Debtors still remained in jail,
With no tax refunds (to help make bail).

Repealed in eighteen hundred three
Til '41 no Act had we.
This new Act had no creditor control,
But had a discharge and could be voluntary,
though.

Just two years did that "New Act" last,
Twas 26 more before end of fast.
The Civil War brought us back to heaven,
It caused the Act of '67.

People on their own volitions,
Now could file their petitions.
To succeed in their proceedings
Owe three hundred in the pleadings.

Re discharge, a court would laugh
Lest a bankrupt offered half.
One could only offer less,
If his creditors first said "yes."

Compositions, we first saw,
In eighteen hundred seventy-four.
Not to liquidate, a change.
Don't close up—instead arrange.

Only four years did this last,
Though the future die was cast.
Twenty years then passed without,
Any Act for us to tout.

Now the Act of '98!
Pretty much our present state.
Venture to the State of Mass,
Judge named Lowell, quite upper class.

What a bill he put in draft.
Many must have thought him daft.
He was mostly contemplative
Of changes administrative.

Salaries instead of fees
Would be paid to referees.
While a trustee's supervisor
Doubled as the ref's advisor.

Many years ahead of time,
Lowell's bill met hostile clime.
In the current pending Act
Are ideas from Judge Lowell's tract.

For a more successful story
Let's turn to a Colonel Torrey.
While at Lowell so many laughed,
Torrey handed in *his* draft.

Then the Texan Bailey's bill,
Made its way up to the Hill.
Once compared with Torrey's tome
Bailey's bill was soon sent home.

Now 7/1 in '98,
Is quite an auspicious date.
McKinley signed the Torrey bill
An enactment with us still.

Loopholes Congress tried to fix
In sixteen, seventeen, twenties two & six.
This despite the prior fixing,
In '03, '06 and '10 and '15.

By '33 and four years next,
Additions made to Torrey's text.
Gave a debtor more decisions
With the debtor-relief provisions.

Added first in '33,
Railroads, farmers could agree
To join non-corp debtor's heaven,
Sections seventy-three to seven.

In May of 1934
Cities had relief in store,
When their debt was out of line,
They found relief in Chapter IX.

Still in '34, in June
Come a corporation boon.
To reorg., a corp. could plea,
Seventy-seven, A or B.

Chapter IX in '36
Our highest court did nix.
It was re-passed in '37
Just before Chapter XI.

Now to 1938.
Chandler, from Atlanta's state,
Said to Congress "this is mine,"
"H.R. 12889."

Congress number seventy-four
Was assisted by an expert core.
Aiding it make sense from nonsense,
Called the National Bankruptcy Conference.

Though no commission studied it,
Chandler's Act was quite a hit.
Inexpensive, changes great,
Act of 1938.
. . .
From 'three-eight to 'seven-oh,
Piecemeal changes were made though,
'Three-nine, 'four-six, and 'five-two—
'Five-oh, 'seven-oh and we're through.

We come to times we all remember,
Even we of ages tender.
Ironic that we've come so far—
With a tax refund and car.

A 1960 Rules Committee,
Here first mentioned in this ditty,
Sent a message sweet and short,
"Judicial Conference: Our Report."

Congress gave the nod, you see
To the Court for Rules to be.
How the bankrupt should proceed.
These new Rules sure filled a need.

Substance, our new Rules don't touch,
Well, I should say not as much.
Pointing the Committee's way
Was the foreman: Forman, J.

The Reporter whom we thank,
Was a Kennedy, name of Frank.
Frank, quite frankly was magnificent.
(He teaches at the U. of Michigent.)

After 13 years these Rules
Came in as procedure's tools.
With XIII, they were effective,
Although one was held defective.

The XI Rules, we saw,
In Nineteen Hundred and Seventy Four,
X and XII Rules came alive,
One year later—'75.

. . .

'Fore their work had reached completion
Some advanced our Act's deletion.
Revise! Revise! the new refrain,
All this change was quite a pain.

A 1970 Commission
As it is in our tradition
Drawn from many different factions.
With a single thought—take actions.

. . .

Kennedy directed staff,
Asked for money, they got half.
Time was short to do their work,
From their task they did not shirk.

Concepts added, needs to cater
Even an administrator.
End at last the summary fiction,
With a broadened jurisdiction.

In went change and in suggestion,
One gave judges indigestion:
"Fewer judges, stress ability"
They replied with facility.

With a strength and with a will,
Judges wrote another bill,
Keeping jurisdiction's load in,
But added (you might guess), a fold-in.

These two bills are much the same
'Cept the personal bankruptcy game.
Yet once more do they diverge,
Should we let three chapters merge?

Merging X, XI, XII,
In some depth we now will delve.
Should there be one Chapter chief,
For the businessman's relief?

The Commission, into VII,
Would put XII, X, and XI.
With the lawyers it must spar,
Some like things the way they are.

Re XI, should we vary
It? Allow involuntary?
Can the court touch debt secured?
(It's done now, please rest assured).

Chapter XII, unlike Iago
Came from the midwest—Chicago.
Quoth the words straight from the bard:
"Merging XII is not so hard."

Lest to litigate conversion
Is a hobby, not aversion.
I won't now sit on the fence,
Merging chapters here makes sense.
. . .
The Commission's Bill preempts
State laws as to what's exempt.
A decision which will grate
Those in Texas (Lone Star State).
. . .
Look! In forma pauperis,
For those without a pot in which to
. . . (hiss!).
Waive the fifty dollar bite,
Switch the privilege to a right.

Overall, despite some gripes,
Both protect consumer types.
Small loan companies have objected.
Hope their views will be rejected.

Lawyers fear a holocaust,
Saying fees will thus be lost.
What they argue's clearly wrong,
But they always sing that song.

Re: administrators: who is right?
Arguments seem black and white.
Should a judge waste time as clerk?
Don't they now have too much work?

Also, is there something sinister
To adjudge and then administer?
Why should they still chair first meetings,
Look at claims, then judge re cheatings?

All are reaching for one goal.
Help the court perform its role.
Thus, the robe and pay and pension,
(And the district court don't mention).
. . .
Even our good bankrupt judgery,
Want the help with seeming drudgery.
They're in some form for administrators.
But Congress may be anti-innovators.

The judges' stance is borne of fears,
Of their treatment in past years.
Now's the time to make the change.
Judicial system, at last rearrange.
. . .

Epilogue

Throughout hist'ry one thought's clear.
The main purpose doth appear.
There for all who care, to see—
To increase the attorney's fee.
I, for one, am much opposed,
To results gained such as those;
Increased fees I much abhor,
Unless they include (ahem!), the Law Professor.

F.   The Bankruptcy Reform Act of 1978

The current bankruptcy law in the United States was enacted in 1978, as the Bankruptcy Reform Act of 1978, Pub. L. No. 95-598. Even though that law has been amended numerous times since its initial adoption, the basic structure and tenets of that law generally remain intact. Accordingly, it is worth pausing to look more closely at the process by which that law came to be. As one engages in this enterprise, Bismarck's famous comment about laws and sausages (*i.e.*, that it is better not to look too closely at how either is made) may spring to mind.

Two accounts are presented. The first is by Kenneth Klee, a professor at UCLA Law School and a prominent bankruptcy attorney in Los Angeles. Klee's recounting of the *Legislative History of the New Bankruptcy Law* was written in 1979, right after the passage of the Act. Klee is able to bring the perspective of an insider to the telling of the enactment story: he served on the House staff that helped write the 1978 Act, and thus was a direct participant in the events he shares.

Professor Klee gives a careful, factual chronological recapitulation of the long and winding road leading up to the final passage of the Act. That process took a full decade. As you read Klee's tale, trace each step along the way. At each critical juncture, what had to happen to keep the legislation moving forward? Note the many hurdles that had to be overcome for the bill to become a reality, and how each hurdle was surmounted.

In the second excerpt, Professor Eric Posner of the University of Chicago Law School paints a somewhat different sort of portrait of the enactment of the Bankruptcy Reform Act of 1978. He first offers a convenient "three-stage" grouping of legislative events. That portion of Professor Posner's article is presented in this chapter. In the remainder of the article Posner focuses on the "political economy" of certain key aspects of the Act: administrative structure, exemptions, and business reorganizations. These were three of the most controversial issues in the legislative battles of the 1970's. Posner's discussion of the treatment of administrative structure is presented in Chapter 4 and his analysis of exemptions in Chapter 11. On each issue, Posner examines in detail who the interested parties were, what the nature of their interest was, what influence they had, and how Congress resolved the conflicts. From Posner's story we see clearly how dominating and controlling the political forces can be in the enactment of a major piece of federal legislation, and what machinations may be required to bring about desired results. Remember sausages.

Kenneth N. Klee
Legislative History of the New Bankruptcy Law
28 DePaul L. Rev. 941 (1979)[*]

On November 6, 1978, the fifth bankruptcy law of the United States, promulgated under Congress' power to enact uniform laws on the subject of bankruptcies, was signed by the President. . . . Pub. L. No. 95-598 became effective, for the most part, on October 1, 1979, the date on which the former Bankruptcy Act was officially repealed. . . .

Courts and legal scholars often look to the legislative history of the statute in order to determine the precise meaning of certain words of provisions. Consistent with such a process of interpretation, this Article will examine the legislative procedures followed in enacting Pub. L. No. 95-598. . . .

Making the New Law

Like each of the previous bankruptcy laws of the United States, the legislative history of Pub. L. No. 95-598 is surrounded by controversy and intrigue. The new law is unique, however, in that it is the only bankruptcy law of the United States adopted absent the impetus of a severe economic depression or panic. Pub. L. No. 95-598 is the culmination of ten years of effort involving hundreds of participants.

The legislative history of Pub. L. No. 95-598 began in 1968 when Senator Quentin Burdick chaired hearings conducted by a subcommittee of the Senate Judiciary Committee to determine whether a commission to review the bankruptcy laws of the United States should be formed. Those hearings prompted congressional action, and two years later the commission on the Bankruptcy Laws of the United States was formed to study, analyze, evaluate, and recommend changes in the substance and administration of the bankruptcy laws of the United States. . . . Finally, a two-part report was filed with Congress on July 30, 1973. The first part of the report contained the recommendations and findings of the Commissions, while the second part embodied a proposed statute complete with explanatory notes.

After submission of the Commission's report, it became Congress' responsibility to continue the process of formulating a new bankruptcy law. The Commission's statutory proposal was introduced as a bill in the House of Representatives by Congressmen Don Edwards and Charles Wiggins in 1973. A comparable bill was also introduced in the Senate by Senator Quentin Burdick, supported by Senator Marlow Cook. In 1974, Congressmen Edwards and Wiggins introduced in the House a competing bill proposed by the National Conference of Bankruptcy Judges. The only formal legislative action taken during the 93rd Congress was one day of hearings. . . . This relative inactivity was due to the Judiciary Committee's preoccupation with the possible impeachment proceedings of Richard M. Nixon.

In contrast, intensive study of the bankruptcy legislation in both the House and Senate occurred during the 94th Congress. Congressmen Edwards and Wiggins reintroduced both the statutory proposal of the Commission in the House of Representatives as H.R. 31 and the competing proposal of the bankruptcy judges in the Senate as H.R. 32. Senator Burdick reintroduced in the Senate the Commission's proposal as S. 236 and the alternative drafted by the National Conference of Bankruptcy Judges as S. 235. Between May of 1975 and May of 1976, Congressman Edwards presided over thirty-five days of hearings on H.R. 31 and H.R. 32 as Chairman of the Subcommittee on Civil and Constitutional Rights. By his side in this bipartisan process was Congressman M. Caldwell Butler, the new ranking minority member of the subcommittee. The extensive House hearing produced over 2,700 pages of testimony from more that 100 witnesses. Senator Burdick pursued an ambitious schedule, presiding over the Subcommittee on Improvements in Judicial Machinery of the Senate Committee on the Judiciary during twenty-one days of hearings on S. 235 and S. 236 between February and November of 1975. . . .

As the House hearings drew to a close, one witness questioned the constitutionality of the commission's bill and the judges' bill insofar as they both provided for bankruptcy judges who would not have the "life tenure" guarantee of serving during good behavior under Article III of the Constitution. This testimony prompted Congressman Rodino, Chairman of the House Judiciary Committee, to consult several constitutional experts concerning the constitutionality of these two bills. Nine distinguished experts responded to Chairman Rodino's written request with several different conclusions.

Congressman Edwards then requested the staff of the Subcommittee on Civil and Constitutional Rights to research and report on the issue of constitutionality. In addition, he instructed the staff, in consultation with various bankruptcy experts, to formulate a proposal resolving the hundreds of differences between the commissions' bill and judges' bill. The staff then prepared a subcommittee print dated November 10, 1976, which served as a discussion draft for meetings with bankruptcy experts which took place from November 6, 1976, through February 25, 1977. Before the conclusion of these meetings, the discussion draft was further refined and formulated into a bill which was then offered to the subcommittee for introduction in the 95th Congress.

On January 4, 1977, Congressmen Don Edwards and M. Caldwell Butler introduced this bill as H.R. 6 in the House of Representatives. This bill was a *congressional* product representing a conglomeration of ideas proposed in the commission's bill, the judges' bill, House hearings, and various meetings. Among the provisions included in the legislation was one which required the establishment of an independent tenured bankruptcy court. H.R. 6 was then circulated to the bench, the bar, and academicians who forwarded numerous comments to the subcommittee. From these and other sources, the staff of the Subcommittee on Civil and Constitutional Rights assembled extensive briefing materials in preparation for "markup," the legislative procedure during which a subcommittee holds business meetings to consider legislation and offer amendments.

On March 21, 1977, the Subcommittee on Civil and Constitutional Rights of the House Committee on the Judiciary commenced marking up H.R. 6. . . . [A]n amendment in the nature of a substitute to H.R. 6 was formulated. The amendment was offered by Congressman Robert F. Drinan, a member of the subcommittee, on March 21, 1977, and became the legislative template for the balance of the markup sessions. By the time markup was concluded on May 16, 1977, the subcommittee has convened in twenty-two separate meetings and heard forty-two hours of debate examining the Drinan substitute line by line. Over 120 amendments were considered and more than 100 were adopted. Before markup concluded, the staff had prepared over thirty memoranda including a draft report entitled *Constitutional Bankruptcy Courts* dated May 16, 1977. On that day, the subcommittee also voted 7-0 to report out a clean bill incorporating the Drinan substitute into H.R. 6, as amended. One week later, on May 23, 1977, the clean bill was introduced as H.R. 7330. . . . Thereafter, H.R. 7330 was further improved as a result of technical comments received from the bench, the bar, and academicians. The result was that a new clean bill, H.R. 8200, superseded H.R. 7330 and was introduced by the members of the subcommittee on July 11, 1977, for consideration by the full House Judiciary Committee.

Meanwhile, in the latter part of May, 1977, Congressmen Edwards and Butler directed their subcommittee staff to prepare briefing materials for the full committee. A 700-page briefing notebook was circulated to all members of the House Judiciary Committee in preparation for full committee markup. . . . On June 13, 1977, the staff of the Subcommittee on Civil and Constitutional Rights also completed its report entitled *Constitutional Bankruptcy Courts*. This report concluded that because the bankruptcy court contemplated by the subcommittee's bill would be exercising the judicial power of the United States, the constitution required that the bankruptcy judges serve during good behavior. . . . Two issues, the independence of bankruptcy courts and the status of bankruptcy judges, dominated the debate concerning the bankruptcy legislation for the balance of the 95th Congress.

The House Judiciary Committee commenced markup of H.R. 8200 on July 14, 1977. . . . On July 19, 1977 H.R. 8200, as amended, was ordered reported by a roll call vote of 26-3, with one member voting present.

On the same day, Congressman Al Ullman, Chairman of the powerful House Ways and Means Committee, wrote a letter to Chairman Peter W. Rodino, Jr., of the House Judiciary Committee informing him of a potential jurisdictional conflict with Ullman's committee relating to certain tax provisions in the bankruptcy legislation. . . . Therefore, on September 8, 1977, the House Judiciary Committee voted to reconsider its vote of July 19, 1977, ordering H.R. 8200 reported, and adopted an amendment in the nature of a substitute to the bill which contained limited special tax provisions. H.R. 8200, as amended, was then ordered reported by a roll call vote of 23-8, and Congressman Don Edwards immediately filed his 535-page committee report to accompany the bill.

Once the jurisdictional problem with the Ways and Means Committee was resolved and H.R. 8200 was reported out by the House Judiciary Committee, the bankruptcy legislation was ripe for floor action in the House of Representatives. Like most legislation, however, H.R. 8200 was sent to the House Rules Committee as a prerequisite to floor consideration. A rule regulating the procedure under which H.R. 8200 would be considered was granted the House Rules Committee on October 12, 1977.

Congressmen Edwards and Butler were hopeful that floor consideration of H.R. 8200 would be conducted in the middle of the week; the greatest number of congressmen usually are present and voting at that time. . . . Congressman Edwards approached the Speaker of the House concerning floor time and was verbally assured by the Speaker that efforts would be made to arrange a mid-week consideration. H.R. 8200 was called up for debate, however, late the afternoon of Thursday, October 27, 1977, with the crucial amendments not to be decided until Friday, October 28, 1977.

The House debate revealed no surprises and the stage for the amendment process was set. . . . Congressman Danielson offered an amendment commonly known as the "Danielson-Railsback Amendment." The amendment was designed to eliminate the Article III status of bankruptcy courts and to reinstitute their original position as adjuncts to the United States District Courts. . . . The Danielson-Railsback Amendment was debated and passed on a roll call vote by a margin of 183-128. Congressman Don Edwards then successfully employed a parliamentary device whereby H.R. 8200 was temporarily withdrawn from further floor consideration.

With proceedings in the House at impasse, the focus shifted to the Senate. . . . On October 31, 1977, Senator DeConcini introduced S. 2266, cosponsored by Senator Malcolm Wallop, ranking minority member of the subcommittee. S. 2266 was essentially the analogue of H.R. 8200, although there were substantial differences between the two bills. In late November and early December, 1977, Senator DeConcini presided over three days of hearings on S. 2266 by the Subcommittee on Improvements in Judicial Machinery. . . .

Meanwhile in the House, Congressman Don Edwards conducted an investigation of alternative court and administrative systems. He presided over hearings on this aspect of H.R. 8200 . . . . After the hearings concluded, the subcommittee published a report reflecting its unanimous and continued belief that Article III bankruptcy courts were constitutionally required.

Buoyed by the tenacity of the Subcommittee on Civil and Constitutional Rights on the issue of Article III courts, several groups who had testified in opposition to the Danielson-Railsback Amendment commenced a spontaneous educational effort with various congressmen. . . . Congressman Edwards decided to employ a parliamentary device that would entitle him to request another vote on the Danielson-Railsback Amendment when H.R. 8200 was again considered by the House.

On Wednesday, February 1, 1978, the House of Representatives resumed consideration of H.R. 8200. . . . Immediately before the vote on final passage of the bill, Congressman Don Edwards asked for a separate vote on the Danielson-Railsback Amendment. In a dramatic reversal of the vote of October 28, 1977, the House defeated the amendment by a record vote of 146 for and 262 against. The House then passed H.R. 8200, as amended, by the voice vote, and the bill was engrossed and sent to the Senate on February 8, 1978.

Passage of H.R. 8200 by the House of Representatives spurred action in the Senate. The Subcommittee on Improvements in Judicial Machinery synthesized both the results of the hearings it held on S. 2266 in November and December of 1977 and comments made after those hearings into an amendment in the nature of a substitute to S. 2266. On May 17, 1978, the subcommittee reported out the amendment to S. 2266 by a vote of 3-0 with one member not voting. The full Senate Judiciary Committee met and considered S. 2266, as amended, on July 12, 1978. After adopting and incorporating three of its own amendments, the Senate Judiciary Committee voted unanimously in favor of the amendment in the nature of a substitute to S. 2266. Senator Deconcini promptly filed his report to accompany S. 2266 on July 14, 1978.

Supporters of the bankruptcy legislation waited nervously as S. 2266 was sent to the Senate Finance Committee on a thirty-day sequential referral to review certain specified provisions. There was legitimate doubt whether the bill could be passed by the Senate, and resolved in a conference with the House before adjournment of the 95th Congress. If new bankruptcy legislation was not enacted during the 95th Congress, the entire process would have to start afresh in the 96th Congress in 1979.

Congressman Don Edwards recognized that if the Senate did act on the bankruptcy legislation in August or September of 1978, there would be very little time to resolve the differences between the two houses of Congress. Accordingly, as soon as S. 2266 passed the Senate Judiciary Committee, he instructed his subcommittee staff to prepare a memorandum comparing H.R. 8200 as passed by the House, and S. 2266 as reported by the Senate Judiciary Committee. . . . The full Senate Finance Committee considered S. 2266 on August 8, 1978, and adopted several committee amendments to S. 2266. The Senate Finance Committee then reported S. 2266 as amended, and Senator Russell B. Long, Chairman of the Finance Committee, filed his committee's report on August 10, 1978.

The Senate proceeded to consider S. 2266 on September 7, 1978. . . . [A]ccording to normal Senate procedure, the Senate tabled S. 2266, took up H.R. 8200, struck out all of the text appearing after the enacting clause, and instead inserted the text of S. 2266, as amended. H.R. 8200, as revised by the Senate amendment in the nature of a substitute, was then passed by voice vote. The Senate immediately insisted on its amendment and requested a conference with the House, but no Senate conferees were appointed.

The Senate amendment in the nature of a substitute to H.R. 8200 differed substantially from the House version. The principal difference involved the court and administrative systems. Under the House bill, independent Article III bankruptcy courts were established, while supervision of the administration of cases was entrusted to United States trustees monitored by the Department of Justice. Under the Senate amendment to H.R. 8200, bankruptcy courts would remain adjuncts to the United States District Courts eliminating United States trustees. There were significant differences in the substantive law as well, including issues such as exemptions, reaffirmation, and the treatment of public companies in reorganization cases.

For the moment, all of these differences were dwarfed by a seemingly insignificant amendment to the Internal Revenue Code which was originally adopted by the Senate Finance Committee and passed by the Senate. . . . This amendment originated in the Senate and reduced revenues, and, since the bankruptcy bill was not a revenue-raising bill, the amendment violated the Constitution. Therefore, the engrossed copy of the Senate amendment would not be accepted by the Speaker of the House. . . . On September 22, 1978, passage of H.R. 8200 was vitiated by unanimous consent of the Senate, and, after an appropriate amendment in the nature of a substitute was adopted, the bill was passed again by unanimous consent.

On September 26, 1978, the Senate insisted on its version of H.R. 8200, requested a conference with the House, and appointed conferees. On that same day, Congressmen Edwards, Butler, Drinan, Volkmer, and McClory met with Senators DeConcini and Wallop at a public meeting to discuss the procedure for resolving the differences between the House and Senate versions of H.R. 8200. It was readily apparent that a House-Senate conference would not be fruitful because the crucial compromises to be reached would not be within the scope of the differences between the House and Senate versions of the bill. Accordingly, the managers of the legislation in the House and Senate agreed to resolve the differences between the two versions of the bill without a formal conference. . . . An amended version of H.R. 8200 was then passed by unanimous consent. . . . Immediately thereafter, the new House amendment was engrossed and sent to the Senate, where it would have been considered and probably passed on the evening of September 28, 1978.

At that point, however, the Chief Justice of the United States personally intervened in an attempt to thwart passage of the bankruptcy legislation. As a compromise between the House bill and the Senate amendment, the new House amendment provided for non-tenured bankruptcy judges to serve on independent bankruptcy courts as adjuncts to the United States Courts of Appeals, with a pilot program of United States trustees in eighteen judicial districts. The Chief Justice objected to the proposed elevation in status of bankruptcy judges. He first voiced his objection to Senator

DeConcini during a telephone conversation. The Chief Justice then telephoned Senators Wallop and Thurmond, at which time Senator Thurmond immediately placed a "hold" on the legislation, effectively preventing its consideration by the Senate.

The next week witnessed intense confrontations at several levels. The most important of which was a meeting of the Attorney General with the House and Senate managers of the bankruptcy legislation, called in order to forge a compromise. Efforts by the Chief Justice to meet with congressional principals were rebuffed. With varying success, special interest groups lobbied senators to place additional "holds" on the legislation unless Senator DeConcini would accept their amendments. Prospects for final passage diminished as negotiations continued. As soon as one problem was solved, a different special interest group would make additional demands. With every passing day adjournment of the 95th Congress, set for October 14, 1978, drew closer.

Thus, it was no small matter that on October 5, 1978, Senator DeConcini arranged a time agreement with Senator Thurmond which facilitated consideration of the bankruptcy legislation. The Senate Majority Leader asked the Chair to lay before the Senate the House of Representatives' amendment to H.R. 8200. Shortly thereafter, Senator DeConcini moved to concur in the House amendment with a series of unprinted Senate amendments offered en bloc. The motion was agreed to by voice vote, and the Senate amendment was returned to the House.

On the morning of Friday, October 6, 1978, Congressman Don Edwards had to make an immediate decision regarding the bankruptcy legislation. Senator DeConcini had telephoned to say that the Senate would not act on the legislation again during the 95th Congress and that the bill was in a "take it or leave it" posture. Congressman Edwards urged acceptance of certain controversial provisions included by the Senate "because of the lateness of the session and our concern with insuring passage of this much-needed legislation."

Passage of H.R. 8200 by the House, however, was far from insured. Because of the lateness of the session, Congressman Edwards could not obtain a rule from the House Rules Committee to gain access to the House floor for consideration of H.R. 8200. Since the bill did not go through the procedure of a conference, consideration was not privileged under the rules of the House and an alternative approach was needed. Therefore, on the afternoon of October 6, 1978, Congressman Edwards asked the House of Representatives to unanimously consent to take H.R. 8200, as amended, from the desk, and to unanimously concur in the latest Senate amendment. . . .

Unanimous consent is seldom obtained during the final days of a session when the power of dissenting congressmen becomes enormous. . . . Late on the afternoon of October 6, 1978, Congressman Herbert E. Harris II renewed the request for unanimous consent to concur in the Senate amendment. . . . [T]he motion to concur in the latest Senate amendment carried without objection.

Normally when a bill passes both houses of Congress, enrollment is swift and transmission to the White House for presidential action is rapid. Nothing was normal, however, in the history of H.R. 8200. Days passed. . . . Whatever the reason for or source of the delay, the enrolled bill was not transmitted to the White House until October 25, 1978.

Once the enrolled copy of H.R. 8200 arrived at the White House, it was officially circulated through the Executive Branch. It was rumored that although most recommendations were positive, the Securities and Exchange Commission and the Chief Justice urged the President to veto the bill. . . . [I]t is public record that the President signed H.R. 8200 into law at Camp David, Maryland, late on the night of November 6, 1978, the last day on which the bill could have been signed into law. Thus, the legislative history of the fifth bankruptcy law of the United States was concluded successfully.

Using Legislative History to Interpret the Law

Recounting the legislative history of the new bankruptcy law is of practical importance to practicing lawyers as well as to legal scholars. To some extent, the legislative history is useful in inter-

preting the statute whether the purpose is to gain academic insight or to advocate a legal proposition.
. . .

The best method of using the legislative history to aid in interpretation is to begin with the most recent statement of authority and delve backward through the legislative process. Thus the following authorities should be consulted in this order:

1. floor statement of Congressman Don Edwards, October 6, 1978, on final passage of H.R. 8200;

2. floor statement of Senator DeConcini, October 5, 1978, on passage of the final Senate amendment in the nature of a substitute to H.R. 8200;

3. floor statement of Congressman Don Edwards, September 28, 1978, on passage of the House amendment to the Senate amendment in the nature of a substitute to H.R. 8200;

4. floor statement of Senator DeConcini, September 7, 1978, on initial passage of the Senate amendment in the nature of a substitute to H.R. 8200;

5. Senate Report of the Finance Committee to accompany S. 2266 filed by Senator Long on August 10, 1978;

6. Senate Report of the Judiciary Committee to accompany S. 2266 filed by Senator DeConcini on July 14, 1978;

7. floor statement of Congressman Don Edwards, February 1, 1978, on passage of H.R. 8200, as amended;

8. floor statement of Congressman Don Edwards, October 27, 1977, on consideration of H.R. 8200; and

9. House Report of the Judiciary Committee to accompany H.R. 8200 as reported filed by Congressman Don Edwards, September 8, 1977.

. . . [I]t is important to remember that only the statements listed in items one and two above refer to the new bankruptcy law as enacted. Every other source, items three through nine, interprets an earlier version of the final legislative product. Accordingly, each source must be correlated with the appropriate piece of legislation. . . .

Thus, when step one or two of the legislative history contains an explanation, it is a mistake to rely unquestioningly on legislative history from step eight or nine because the language of the statute may have been amended. Stated in a different way, the more recent legislative history is usually more accurate than the older history in describing the code.

Often there will be no legislative history derived from step one, two, or three. Then it is necessary to dig deeper. . . .

Sometimes the legislative history found in one step will expressly incorporate the legislative history from another step. In that event, the legislative history from intervening steps should be ignored in preference to the history that is specifically incorporated by reference. . . .

The foregoing method should assist legal scholars, advocates, and judges in accurately evaluating "congressional intent" in relation to Pub. L. No. 95-598. While the method may seem cumbersome or opaque the first few times it is used, eventually it will become as routine as "shepardizing" cases.

Eric A. Posner
The Political Economy of the Bankruptcy Reform Act of 1978
96 MICH. L. REV. 47 (1997)[*]

IV. Legal Background of the 1978 Act

A. The 1898 Act as Amended

On the eve of the passage of the 1978 Act, bankruptcy law was a complicated and arcane field. The complexity was due to many factors. The 1898 Act was itself complicated and vague, and it reflected needs produced by economic and social conditions, including a severe depression, that no longer existed in the second half of the twentieth century. . . .

B. Legislative History of the 1978 Act

The legislative history of the Bankruptcy Reform Act is complex. It consists of thousands of pages of hearings, reports, and debates spanning a decade. To simplify the analysis, we divide the legislative history into three stages. The first stage extends from the enactment of the law creating a bankruptcy commission in 1968 to the commission's release of a report and proposed bill in 1973. The second stage extends from the House and Senate hearings on the commission's bill and on an alternative proposed by a group of bankruptcy judges, mainly in 1975 and 1976, to the passage of House Bill 8200 and Senate Bill 2266 in 1978. The third stage covers the resolution of the conflicts between House Bill 8200 and Senate Bill 2266, leading to enactment of the Bankruptcy Reform Act in November, 1978. A brief description of these events sets the stage for the analysis and foreshadows many of its themes.

1. Stage 1

Growing dissatisfaction with the bankruptcy laws in the 1960s persuaded first a subcommittee of the Senate Judiciary Committee and then the full Congress to create a commission to evaluate the bankruptcy laws. The original Senate bill provided that the commission would consist of representatives from the House and Senate, three bankruptcy judges, and three businessmen. Apparently in response to objections from the federal judiciary to the presence of bankruptcy judges and the absence of Article III judges, the House version of the bill provided for three presidential appointees, two representatives from the House, two representatives from the Senate, and two appointees of the Chief Justice of the Supreme Court. This version passed the full Congress in 1968.

The Commission on the Bankruptcy Laws of the United States was formed in 1971 and met over the next two years. In 1973 the Commission issued a report criticizing the existing bankruptcy laws and proposing a legislative replacement known as the Commission's Bill, or CB. The Commission listed the following complaints about the bankruptcy laws:

1.   The rapid increase of bankruptcies from 10,196 in 1946 to 208,329 in 1967, and especially of consumer bankruptcies.
2.   Administrative waste. For example, in 1972 $6.7 million of the $17 million spent on the operation of bankruptcy courts was spent on no-asset cases.

---

3. Insufficiently generous fresh start for debtors, and inadequate incentives for creditors to collect in bankruptcy.

4. Lack of uniformity in the treatment of debtors.

5. Abusive or negligent practices by bankruptcy judges, trustees, and bankruptcy lawyers.

The CB contained many modifications of the bankruptcy system, but three stood out. First, it provided for a sharper distinction between bankruptcy judges and trustees, elevating the status of the bankruptcy judges and placing the trustees in a new, centralized bankruptcy agency in the executive branch. Second, it provided for a system of uniform federal exemptions. Third, its reorganization provisions consolidated Chapters X, XI, and XII and modified the procedural and substantive rules of confirmation.

Infuriated by their exclusion from the Commission and suspicious of its capacity to produce an adequate bill, the bankruptcy judges created their own bill, known as the Judges' Bill, or JB. The CB and the JB had many similarities but several important differences. The bankruptcy judge under the JB was to have more power and status than the bankruptcy judge under the CB, and the JB did not provide for a bankruptcy agency. The JB provided for minimum, rather than uniform, federal exemptions. Although both bills had special provisions for publicly held corporations, the JB, unlike the CB, would have maintained separate tracks for close corporations and public corporations.

2. Stage 2

Representatives Don Edwards and Charles Wiggins introduced the CB in 1973, but little was accomplished that year. In 1974 Edwards and Wiggins reintroduced the CB as House Bill 31 and the JB as House Bill 32 and during 1975 and 1976 held lengthy and detailed hearings on them before the Judiciary Committee's Subcommittee on Civil and Constitutional Rights. These hearings culminated in House Bill 6, which was introduced in 1977. The Subcommittee held meetings on House Bill 6, which resulted in a new version, House Bill 7330, and after further discussions yet another version, House Bill 8200. The Judiciary Committee amended House Bill 8200 and issued a new version, along with a committee report. Meanwhile, the Subcommittee also prepared a report on the constitutionality of the proposed bankruptcy courts. The House debated and amended House Bill 8200 in October 1977, but because the legislative managers did not approve of this amendment— a similar one had been rejected by the Subcommittee—they removed the bill from the calendar. The Subcommittee held further hearings and released a new report. The House debated House Bill 8200 again in February 1978, reversed the earlier amendment, and passed the bill by a voice vote.

The 1977 House Report identified three major problems with the bankruptcy system: (1) impaired adjudication of cases resulting from judges' lack of independence and low status; (2) insufficient relief to consumer debtors; and (3) excessive vagueness. To address these and other problems, House Bill 8200 proposed the following changes to the law.

Administrative structure. House Bill 8200 would have abolished the old referee system. It would have given the new bankruptcy judges full powers of law, equity, and admiralty, including injunctive powers, the power to hold jury trials, contempt power, and jurisdiction over all matters arising in connection with a bankruptcy case, with appeal to the circuit courts. . . . Bankruptcy judges would have become Article III judges, with full tenure and advice-and-consent presidential appointment. In addition, the bill would have created a system of U.S. Trustees, modeled on the U.S. Attorney system. Trustees would have been autonomous but under the loose supervision of the Department of Justice. They would have had administrative authority over bankruptcy cases.

Exemptions. House Bill 8200 provided for a $10,000 exemption for the homestead and $5,000 for personal property, among other things, but would have given the debtor the right to choose between the federal and state exemptions—effectively making the federal exemptions a floor. . . .

Business reorganizations. House Bill 8200 provided for the consolidation of the old Chapters X and XI, and it chose as the standard for approval of confirmations a substantially more liberal rule than the one that prevailed under Chapter X. The debtor would have had an exclusive 120-day right to propose a plan. The management would presumptively have retained control as the debtor in possession. The CB, in contrast, made the trustee presumptive for large, public corporations. . . .

Meanwhile, in the Senate the CB and the JB had been introduced as Senate Bill 236 and Senate Bill 235 in 1975. The Senate Judiciary Committee's Subcommittee on Improvements in Judicial Machinery conducted hearings. No further activity occurred until 1977, when a new bill, Senate Bill 2266, was proposed and hearings were held. After the House passed House Bill 8200, the Subcommittee revised Senate Bill 2266 and reported it out to the Judiciary Committee. The Judiciary Committee voted in favor of the new Senate Bill 2266 after amending it, and a report was filed. After Senate Bill 2266 traveled through several committees, it came before the full Senate, which amended it and passed it by a voice vote as an amendment in the nature of a substitute to House Bill 8200. Senate Bill 2266 included the following provisions.

Administrative structure. Senate Bill 2266 would have created less powerful and prestigious bankruptcy judges than House Bill 8200. Bankruptcy judges would have continued as adjuncts of the district courts. Bankruptcy judges would have been appointed by the court of appeals for each circuit, rather than by the President, and would have had a twelve-year term. Senate Bill 2266 also would not have created a bankruptcy agency in the executive branch, instead keeping the trustee system in the judicial branch.

Exemptions. Senate Bill 2266 followed old law and provided for the incorporation of state exemptions.

Business reorganization. Senate Bill 2266 would have consolidated Chapters X, XI, and XII, but it left a separate track for public corporations. Among other things, it provided for mandatory appointment of a trustee in the case of public corporations. It would have retained the old, strict standard for reorganization of public corporations, while providing for a standard similar to the House's for the reorganization of private corporations. . . .

3. Stage 3

Stage 3 began with an impasse. Congress faced two bills, House Bill 8200 as originally passed by the House and Senate Bill 2266, though the latter was now known as House Bill 8200 as amended by the Senate ("first Senate amendment"). Instead of holding a joint conference, the managers of the legislation conducted negotiations and hammered out a deal. The compromise was reflected in the House's amendment to House Bill 8200, passed in September 1978. In October the Senate passed the House amendment by a voice vote after adding several of its own amendments ("second Senate amendment"). The House concurred, also by a voice vote, and the President signed the bill in early November.

The House amendment split the differences between House Bill 8200 and Senate Bill 2266 in several ways. The House prevailed on the transfer of new powers to the bankruptcy judge, but the bankruptcy judge would not be an Article III judge. The Senate prevailed in its efforts to prevent the creation of a bankruptcy agency in the executive branch, but agreed to a limited pilot program to test the idea. The compromise created a uniform system of federal exemptions—for example, a $7,500 homestead exemption—but gave the states the right to opt out. It adopted the House's version of reorganization law, with two concessions to the Senate: it included vague provisions designed to create some special protections for cases involving public corporations, and it provided for the automatic appointment of an examiner in such cases, though not of an independent trustee as the Senate had preferred. Reaffirmations were to be permitted, but they had to meet disclosure and related requirements. Numerous other compromises occurred, but we need not detail them.

The provisions of the second Senate amendment are strikingly trivial. . . . Because of the lateness of the date, the House passed the second Senate amendment without making further changes.

The second Senate amendment is surprising not only because its provisions were trivial, but also because it seems to have violated the deal made between the House and the Senate. As we shall see, the evidence suggests that Senator DeConcini unilaterally made these changes and told the House that they were non-negotiable. Rep. Edwards was distressed about these changes but could not oppose them at the late date. The House passed the second Senate amendment in early October; the President signed the bill in early November. . . .

Some readers might take this political history of the 1978 Act as an indication of the futility of legislative reform. If politics determines legislative outcomes, what is the purpose of reform? But such pessimism is unjustified. The lessons of the analysis are concrete and practical. Because of the indeterminacy of the normative arguments for and against various kinds of bankruptcy reform, one must rely on experience and history. The experience of lawyers and courts tells us which parts of the law create practical difficulties. History tells us which parts of the law reflect political compromises rather than normative goals. Because the political forces that led to unsatisfactory compromises in 1978 have changed, there is hope that proper amendments can now be made.

Additional suggested readings

Douglass G. Boshkoff, *Limited, Conditional, and Suspended Discharges in Anglo-American Bankruptcy Proceedings,* 131 U. PA. L. REV. 69 (1982)

Jay Cohen, *The History of Imprisonment for Debt and its Relation to the Development of Discharge in Bankruptcy*, 3 J. LEGAL HIST. 153 (1982)

Peter J. Coleman, DEBTORS AND CREDITORS IN AMERICA: INSOLVENCY, IMPRISONMENT FOR DEBT, AND BANKRUPTCY 1607-1900 (1974)

Vern Countryman, *A History of American Bankruptcy Law*, 81 COM. L.J. 226 (1976)

Ian P.H. Duffy, *English Bankrupts: 1571-1861*, 24 AM. J. LEGAL HIST. 283 (1980)

Karen Gross, *Ladies in Red: Learning from America's First Female Bankrupts*, 40 AM. J. LEGAL HIST. 1 (1996)

Frank R. Kennedy, *Bankruptcy and the Constitution*, U. MICH. LAW. QUAD. 40 (Spring 1989)

Judith S. Koffler, *The Bankruptcy Clause and Exemption Laws: A Reexamination of the Doctrine of Geographic Uniformity*, 58 N.Y.U. L. REV. 22 (1983)

Louis Levinthal, *The Early History of English Bankruptcy,* 67 U. PA. L. REV. 1 (1919)

John C. McCoid, II, *Discharge: The Most Important Development in Bankruptcy History*, 70 AM. BANKR. L.J. 163 (1996)

John C. McCoid, II, *The Origins of Voluntary Bankruptcy*, 5 BANKR. DEV. J. 362 (1988)

Thomas Plank, *The Constitutional Limits of Bankruptcy*, 63 TENN. L. REV. 487 (1996)

Stefan Riesenfeld, *The Evolution of Modern Bankruptcy Law*, 31 MINN. L. REV. 401 (1947)

Peter Rodino & Alan A. Parker, *The Simplest Solution*, 7 BANKR. DEV. J. 329 (1990)

James S. Rogers, *The Impairment of Secured Creditors' Rights in Reorganization: A Study of the Relationship Between the Fifth Amendment and the Bankruptcy Clause*, 96 HARV. L. REV. 973 (1983)

David A. Skeel, Jr., DEBT'S DOMINION: A HISTORY OF BANKRUPTCY LAW IN AMERICA (Princeton 2001)

David A. Skeel, Jr., *The Genius of the 1898 Bankruptcy Act,* 15 BANKR. DEV. J. 321 (1999)

David A. Skeel, Jr., *Bankruptcy Lawyers and the Shape of American Bankruptcy Law*, 67 FORDHAM L. REV. 497 (1998)

Charles Jordan Tabb, *A Century of Regress or Progress?: A Political History of Bankruptcy Legislation in 1898 and 1998*, 15 BANKR. DEV. J. 343 (1999)

Charles Jordan Tabb, *The Historical Evolution of the Bankruptcy Discharge*, 65 AM. BANKR. L.J. 325 (1991)

Charles Warren, BANKRUPTCY IN THE UNITED STATES HISTORY (1935)

Robert Weisberg, *Commercial Morality, the Merchant Character, and the History of the Voidable Preference*, 39 STAN. L. REV. 3 (1986)

Chapter 2

The Nature and Theory of Bankruptcy Law

A. Early Views

Why have a bankruptcy law at all? After all, every state has a veritable cornucopia of laws regulating the collection of debts—execution, attachment, garnishment, exemptions, fraudulent conveyances, and so on. Is yet another layer of debtor-creditor laws really necessary or wise? For almost half a millennium, Anglo-American lawgivers have thought so. But to what end? This chapter highlights the never-ending search for the "essence" of bankruptcy (if there even is such a creature). A later chapter (Chapter 15) will revisit the issue of whether a bankruptcy *reorganization* law is a good idea, and if so, in what shape. In the waning years of the twentieth century, the intellectual fires prompting the search for the first principles of bankruptcy burned with a consuming passion. But, contrary to popular belief, bankruptcy theory was not invented in 1982 when Thomas Jackson (then a law professor at Stanford, and later at Harvard and Virginia, and now President of the University of Rochester) published his seminal article in the YALE LAW JOURNAL, entitled *Bankruptcy, Non-Bankruptcy Entitlements, and the Creditors' Bargain.* In the first section, we begin with "early views" of bankruptcy.

Three articles are included in this opening part. The first, written by James Olmstead in 1902, shortly after the passage of the Bankruptcy Act of 1898, argues that bankruptcy is primarily a "commercial regulation." The core functions of that regulation, he proposes, are administration of debtor's estates and distribution to creditors. Olmstead apparently was upset at the excessive generosity of that Act to debtors. According to Olmstead, it is the necessities of commerce that drive the need for a bankruptcy salve. The debtor-relief aspect of a bankruptcy law is seen as little more than incidental to the primary purpose.

Professor Garrard Glenn of the University of Virginia Law School wrote the second article, published in 1937, in the depths of the Great Depression and as Congress was in the process of considering the legislative reforms that culminated in the Chandler Act of 1938. Professor Glenn is still well-known today for his monumental work on fraudulent conveyances. Apparently attuned to, or perhaps obsessed by, what he saw as the pervasiveness of fraud (Glenn did not seem to hold a particularly favorable view of the fellow members of his species), he argued that the "essentials of bankruptcy" were two: the prevention of fraud, and the control of the debtor. Glenn's viewpoint would resonate well with the prophets of the modern consumer credit industry, who trumpet the message of debtor abuse and seek to tailor the bankruptcy laws to address that concern. They might find attractive the "repulsive ceremonies" a medieval debtor had to suffer in penance for his debts.

The final selection is from the eclectic Professor Max Radin of the University of California, writing in 1940, just after passage of the Chandler Act. Radin, one of the leading judicial philosophers of his time, and a bit of an academic radical, presages many of Jackson's ideas. Radin recognizes that remedies apart from a bankruptcy law already exist to rectify debtor fraud and to facilitate collection of debts by individual creditors. Bankruptcy must add something, he posits. That extra something is the conception of bankruptcy as a *collective* action, necessitated by a *plurality* of creditors, which binds all creditors, assenting or not. The core function of bankruptcy, by which its true nature must be measured, is to coerce recalcitrant creditors. Everything else, he asserts, including relief of distressed debtors, is incidental.

In the ensuing sections we move to "modern" theory, which must be dated from Professor Jackson's controversial master work. His focus on the "creditors' bargain" brought notions from the burgeoning field of "law and economics" to bear on bankruptcy theory. Jackson brought together the many threads of his theoretical writing on bankruptcy into a brilliant book, THE LOGIC AND LIMITS OF BANKRUPTCY LAW, published in 1986 by Harvard University Press. While this anthology does not contain excerpts directly from that book, many of the original articles that helped comprise the book are individually excerpted in connection with the appropriate subject area. Following Jackson's original "creditors' bargain" article are a variety of responses to Jackson and his frequent co-author, Professor Douglas Baird of the University of Chicago Law School. Much of the leading bankruptcy scholarship in the late twentieth century can be seen as a pitched battle over the merits of Jackson's and Baird's work. Pieces from some of the leading critics of the law and economics school, such as Professor Elizabeth Warren of Harvard Law School, Professor David Carlson of the Benjamin N. Cardozo School of Law, Professor Donald Korobkin of Rutgers Law School, and Professor Karen Gross of New York Law School, are included. Even within the law and economics ranks some dissent is noted, from Professor James Bowers of LSU Law Center, Professor Barry Adler of NYU Law School, and Professor Randal Picker of the University of Chicago. Even Jackson himself reformulated some of his ideas, in cahoots with Professor Robert Scott of the University of Virginia Law School.

Now let us turn to the "early views" on bankruptcy theory.

James M. Olmstead
Bankruptcy a Commercial Regulation
15 HARV. L. REV. 829 (1902)[*]

It may therefore be truly said that . . . commerce proved to be one of the corner-stones of the Constitution. To be sure the framers of the Constitution . . . may have had in mind the regulation of the relation between debtor and creditor. At the same time, inasmuch as bankruptcy was known to be a measure primarily for the benefit of creditors, its origin is undoubtedly to be traced rather to commercial reasons than to those for the relief of the debtor class. . . .

An examination of the origin of the bankruptcy clause in the Constitution will show that this subject was akin to or closely related to commerce. . . .

In this connection a brief glance at the English origin and history of the bankruptcy system . . . will also show its intimate relationship to trade and commerce. . . . It is a historical fact that there also existed in England, concurrently with bankruptcy legislation, insolvent laws . . . for the benefit of non-traders . . . .

Professor Richard Brown, in an excellent article . . . in . . . August, 1900, . . . asserts that three theories have been advanced as to the objects of bankruptcy legislation:

(1) The punishment of the fraudulent debtor; (2) the reinstatement of the unfortunate but innocent debtor; or (3) the equitable distribution of the insufficient assets among all the creditors.

Both in England and the United States there has been a great departure from the primitive theory. . . . In England the theory—one which, it is submitted, is the only sound theory—still prevails that the true functions of bankruptcy are administration and distribution. . . .

In America, unfortunately, bankruptcy has come to be regarded as a sort of poor-debtor law, as a species of clearing house for the liquidation of debt, or, as some have expressed it, a "Hebrew Jubilee," whereby the people at intermittent periods receive emancipation from their debts, are rehabilitated, and the "dead wood" of the community is thereby eliminated. That the rehabilitation theory was farthest from the minds of the framers of the Constitution, it has heretofore been attempted to be shown.

It is now proposed to demonstrate that the true functions of bankruptcy are administration and distribution, and that sound statesmen and legislators in Congress have ascribed to the regulation of commerce the true reason for bankruptcy legislation. . . . [C]ommerce and its regulation have been among the foremost arguments advanced by statesmen for the enactment of a system which means to the creditors administration, to the merchants a uniform system of law, and incidentally to the debtor a release from his obligations. . . .

James A. Bayard of Delaware . . . was an ardent champion of bankruptcy legislation, and . . . on January 2, 1799, Mr. Bayard spoke in the House as follows:—

The necessity of a bankrupt law results wherever a nation is in any considerable degree commercial. No commercial people can be well governed without it. Wherever there is an extensive commerce, extensive credits must be necessarily given.

He further spoke of the fact that such legislation prevented fraudulent speculation, and that it would be a great hardship for a merchant, losing his ships in trade, to be so situated that he could not compromise his creditors. . . .

On May 26, 1824, . . . Daniel Webster . . . spoke as follows:—

He remained fully of the opinion that, in a country so commercial, with so many States, . . . true policy and just views of public utility required that so important a branch of commercial regulation as bankruptcy, ought to be uniform throughout all the states . . . .

. . . [In 1878] Senator Ingalls said:—

It is an anomaly in civilization that a great commercial country like ours . . . should remit to the conflicting decisions of State insolvent courts the question whether or not a debtor shall be relieved from the payment of his debts upon the surrender of his assets.

. . . President Harrison, . . . in his second annual message of December 1, 1890, observed:—

The inconveniences resulting from the occasional and temporary exercise of this power by Congress, and from the conflicting State codes of insolvency which come into force intermediately should be removed by the enactment of a simple, inexpensive, and *permanent* national bankrupt law. . . .

From the foregoing consideration of the historical and constitutional origin of bankruptcy laws, and from this view of contemporaneous congressional debates, an endeavor has been made to prove that bankruptcy . . . is essentially a *commercial regulation*, and that its main objects are administration or distribution, rather than the relief of the debtor. . . .

It is perfectly apparent, however, that there exists among some judges, on the floors of Congress and in the community, a fallacious and superficial view that bankruptcy legislation should partake of the nature of a "Hebrew Jubilee," and that at intermittent periods the country should have such a law for the purpose of relieving the unfortunate debtor from his burden of debt. While the humanitarian or relief features are meritorious, it should be constantly borne in mind that this principle of the law is merely an incident to its main purpose.

Garrard Glenn

Essentials of Bankruptcy: Prevention of Fraud, and Control of the Debtor
23 VA. L. REV. 373 (1937)

Relief of the distressed debtor was an outstanding object of the reforms that have featured the last three years; but just as it was with other efforts to attain the millennium overnight, our lawmakers ignored human nature, and therefore they paid little attention to history. . . . [A] careful study of bankruptcy involves several well worn propositions. First, there is always the fraudulent debtor; and never yet, so far as human experience goes, has it been proper to legislate in bankruptcy matters without providing for his case. Next, the idea of bankruptcy includes the concept of a debtor who is within the control of the court. And finally there is the point, so helpful in the presentation of the other two, that bankruptcy reforms are by no means a matter of late dispensation or twentieth century rhetoric; but on the contrary, all our ideas trace back to English legislation of two centuries ago and more. . . .

There is always the fraudulent debtor; and, to meet his case, bankruptcy requires a controllable debtor. Hence the bankrupt must do two things. He must give full discovery, that is, he must tell the truth about his estate and his doings; and, in order to insure this, the debtor must surrender to the court, not only his estate if he has any, but also himself. Such is the method by which fraud can be detected and creditors will get their due.

. . . Let me see, then, if the story of John Perrot, who was executed at Smithfield in 1761, will not touch responsive chords of memory in the breasts of many a referee in bankruptcy.

Now, *Perrot's* case embodied all these propositions, in that he bought goods on credit, sold them through fences for cash, and kept lady friends, to whom some of the money went, the rest being hid away. Finally,—inevitably, I would be inclined to say,—the debtor committed perjury upon his examination. . . . Perrot was convicted of "concealing his effects under a commission of bankruptcy, with a view to defraud his creditors", and hanged therefor at Smithfield. The creditors were doubtless edified by the fact that their debtor, on the morning of his execution, "confessed that he had been justly condemned."

For our purposes we can now leave this eighteenth century crook at peace. . . . [B]ut it remains true . . . that all the things Perrot did have been repeated in modern times. In fact, his story so clearly demonstrates that the fraudulent bankrupt is perennial. . . .

. . . [T]here is always danger of fraud, and the safeguard is to require full submission on the part of the debtor, with its attendant duties of discovery, and truthful answers upon examination.

That, indeed, has been the idea throughout all history. . . . [I]n the earlier days such a trader had a way out of his troubles by means of going through a process of voluntary bankruptcy at any of the great fairs that were a feature of the Middle Ages. In short, long before Parliament had enacted a general bankruptcy law, the merchant could resort to a practice which, roughly corresponding to the *cessio bonorum* of Roman law, had become a part of the Law Merchant; and it furnished a fairly complete model of bankruptcy.

. . . [T]he merchant who thus placed himself in the hands of his creditors at the fair, had to do the very things that are required today of all bankrupts. In the first place, he must render a true and perfect account of his assets, something that was required in Roman law, and also by the mediaeval custom of merchants. To that end, he had to remain at the disposal of his creditors. . . . By way of emphasis, the insolvent was required to make a public act of submission at the fair. This, a modern scholar tells us, was often accompanied by "repulsive ceremonies". But it was really a public act of penance which, not being tied down by churchly sanctions, had in it, naturally enough, something that would appeal to the rough sense of humor in which the mediaeval mind delighted. The trader, by certain acts that savoured of nursery wit, signalized his regret that he had failed to meet his debts, and his submission to the will of his brothers in commerce. . . . Hence bankruptcy after the fashion of the law merchant was demonstrated by acts that denoted regret, but also showed submission.

Our ancestors, then, were right when they affirmed . . . that frauds abound always, and that each generation is wiser in its wickedness than those which preceded it. . . . Yet never, in all this process, was fraud to be overlooked or go unpunished; and to that end no bankruptcy process was conceivable without a controllable debtor. And there, I submit, is a test of bankruptcy.

Max Radin
The Nature of Bankruptcy
89 U. PA. L. REV. 1 (1940)[*]

The word bankrupt is a good English word deliberately Latinized from the French. It was used in ordinary speech and writing almost as early as it was used in the law merchant, where, of course, it properly belonged. . . .

When the phrase "on the subject of bankruptcies" was used in the Constitution, it had an aura of suggestion and emotion about it. But it had at least one definite implication. This was that a law on the subject of bankruptcies was a law similar to the statutes which had been passed on this subject in England and the colonies since the time of Henry VIII.

There was no reason why the process of development should have ceased—indeed there was no way in which it could have ceased—on the adoption of the Constitution. Bankruptcy as a need of commercial life was bound to gather further experience and so to enlarge its tangible limits and would also necessarily intensify its emotional suggestiveness, since the background of new bankruptcy legislation or of new expansion of bankruptcy by decisions was almost certain to be that of commercial crisis. . . .

We are concerned with a legal process that is meant to perform an important commercial function.

What function? That of enabling creditors to get their debts paid after they have reduced them to judgment? Clearly not, since that is the function of the ordinary writs of execution and the many writs in aid of execution, both legal and equitable. May the function then be described as the attempt to prevent debtors from overreaching their creditors by concealing or disposing of their assets? This again is performed by processes, originally equitable in their nature but now generally gathered

---

[*]   Copyright © 1940 by the University of Pennsylvania. Reprinted with permission. All rights reserved.

under statutes that seek to prevent fraud on creditors. Bankruptcy must add something new to these two types of process or else it would never have come into existence.

. . . [I]f we follow the history of bankruptcy back into the experience of England, we shall find that . . . the interest of the creditor was almost exclusively kept in view, until under Anne a more or less qualified discharge of the debtor was made possible.

How was the interest of the creditor served? After all, with *fieri facias, capias* and, later, with the Statute of Elizabeth at his command, what need did a creditor—so long as he was a single creditor—have of any new method of controlling an evasive debtor, the *decoctor* of the Roman law? That is, of course, just the point. A single creditor could have got along without a bankruptcy procedure. But if there were many creditors, any one stood in great danger of being left in the lurch by the greater good-fortune, insistence, harshness or skill in intrigue of some of his fellow-creditors. Equity could do something for him in the single case of collusion or fraud. But that was obviously not sufficient.

It will be well to keep in mind, therefore, that bankruptcy posits a plurality of creditors, although once established its process may well be used by a single creditor. If we follow the course of bankruptcy from the earliest statute—that of Henry VIII in 1542—to the Chandler Act, we shall find that whatever else was present or absent, there was always some method by which *all* the creditors were compelled to accept some arrangement or some disposition of their claims against the bankrupt's property, whether they all agreed to it or not.

Everything else is clearly incidental. The bankrupt might be stripped of all his property and thrown into prison. He might be allowed certain exemptions. He might be relieved of his debts or have them scaled down or postponed. All these are stages of increasing humanity toward an unsuccessful member of the commercial community. He might even be helped to reconstruct and carry on his business, and this, with a view to maintaining an economic unit that involved a great many persons who are not properly creditors.

But whatever happens to the debtor, in every case the creditors have been assembled in some formal way, their claims examined and classified, and assigned for satisfaction in definite proportions to an existing or prospective fund. The extent of the participation of the creditors in reaching a final disposition is also irrelevant. Whoever initiates the process and however it is done, the important thing is that the bankruptcy court or commission rounds up the creditors and compels them to adjust or discharge their claims in a particular way. . . .

The essence of bankruptcy, accordingly, is not that the debtor's property is impounded nor that the creditors are affected, nor even that all of them are affected. Something additional is required. Unless we intend to bring the creditors into one large group, and adjust their common claims to a fund consisting of a single debtor's property, there is no reason to have recourse to bankruptcy. . . .

It is stated frequently in the discussion of the nature of bankruptcy that a bankruptcy law has certain definite purposes and that the relief of distressed debtors may well be called the most important of them. Certainly this fact was most prominently mentioned in the agitation for bankruptcy laws in the United States. . . . It is equally a fact that bankruptcy is . . . one of many examples in which the general welfare of the community is achieved by mutual sacrifices of various groups in it.

But while the purposes of a statute are of paramount importance in interpreting its provisions, we cannot merely by knowing these purposes learn what a bankruptcy system is. History and semantics may perhaps be snubbed but we hardly dare snub functionalism. And the function of a legal system is not to be separated from the way in which it works. Whatever purposes bankruptcy attempts to carry out, it does by working on the creditors primarily, by compelling them to reorganize their relations to the debtor or to each other in regard to the debtor's property. No extension of the bankruptcy power has in fact attempted anything else, whatever the words used may have been. In the course of this process, bankruptcy can adopt whatever incidental device may serve the economic and social ends so often brought out in discussion of the subject. But we need not lose ourselves in large generalities which might bring the entire law merchant within the range of Congressional power.

B.   Modern Theory

The Creditors' Bargain

Bankruptcy theory moved to a position of prominence in the academic and legal world with the occurrence of one event: the 1982 publication of Professor Thomas Jackson's article in the YALE LAW JOURNAL entitled *Bankruptcy, Non-Bankruptcy Entitlements, and the Creditors' Bargain.* This foundational article was followed four years later by the publication of Jackson's brilliant and provocative book, THE LOGIC AND LIMITS OF BANKRUPTCY LAW. During the 1980's Jackson and his co-author, Professor Douglas Baird of the University of Chicago, attacked many of bankruptcy's canards and sacred cows with a cool, incisive logic like a surgical knife. It is difficult for one to appreciate today the vehemence of the reactions to the propositions put forward by the "Baird & Jackson" team, which ranged from fawning mimicry to petulant outrage.

The linchpin of Jackson's and Baird's normative theory of bankruptcy was the famous (or infamous?) "creditors' bargain." In his 1982 Yale article, Jackson presented the bargain postulate. He attacked the question of "why bankruptcy?" by creating a model that asked what sort of system and rules a debtor and its creditors would agree to, if they could, in a hypothetical bargain made before the onset of insolvency. As you read the following excerpt from that article, try to answer the following questions.

1. How is the concept of the "creditors' bargain" in bankruptcy informed by the "prisoner's dilemma"?
2. What three principal reasons might prompt a debtor's unsecured creditors to bargain for a collective proceeding such as bankruptcy?
3. Why would it be beneficial for that bargain to be negotiated *ex ante, i.e.,* before the need for the collective proceeding arises, rather than *ex post*?
4. Why does the collective proceeding need to be compulsory?
5. Why can't the hypothetical creditors' bargain *actually* be implemented in the real world on a regular basis, and what ramifications follow from that difficulty?
6. How does the existence of statutory rules governing a collective proceeding shape the out-of-court negotiations between a debtor and its creditors that are able to be carried out in practice?
7. Does the creditors' bargain model for a compulsory collective proceeding still work when one or more creditors has a property right, such as a secured claim, in the debtor's assets?
8. Why does Jackson assert that the "non-bankruptcy entitlements" of a secured creditor should be respected in a bankruptcy collective proceeding?
9. What assumptions underlie Jackson's core arguments regarding (i) the creditors' bargain and (ii) the need to respect non-bankruptcy entitlements? Are these assumptions realistic? Does it matter whether those assumptions are realistic?

Thomas H. Jackson
Bankruptcy, Non-Bankruptcy Entitlements, and the Creditors' Bargain
91 YALE L.J. 857 (1982)[*]

Bankruptcy, at first glance, may be thought of as a procedure geared principally toward relieving an overburdened debtor from "oppressive" debt. Yet this discharge-centered view of bankruptcy is correct neither from an historical perspective nor from a realistic appraisal of the presence and operation of most of the provisions in the federal bankruptcy laws over the years. For although discharge of the debtor (and such related issues as "exemptions" that enable an individual debtor to keep assets out of the bankruptcy pool) may well be the motivating *cause* of a majority of bankruptcy cases, most of the bankruptcy *process* is in fact concerned with creditor-distribution questions. Assets are marshalled so that they can be allocated among those holding claims against the debtor or the debtor's property. Claims are determined so that participants in the allocation process may be assembled. And the rules governing priorities determine who, among the claimants, will get what and in what order. Although the Bankruptcy Code specifies some of these priority rules, the claimants who fare best in the bankruptcy process hold special entitlements under applicable non-bankruptcy law. The priorities enunciated in the Bankruptcy Code itself deal largely with the allocation of rights among persons not entitled to preferential treatment outside of bankruptcy.

Despite the importance and durability of such distributional rules, no normative theory has been developed against which these inter-creditor bankruptcy rules could be examined. This Article will attempt to supply that theoretical analysis by exploring the role bankruptcy should play in shaping rules for distributions among creditors, and then testing certain existing rules against the resulting model. First, the Article provides a justification for the time-honored proposition that non-bankruptcy entitlements, such as security interests, should be recognized in bankruptcy. This justification is developed by using a hypothetical model that I call the "creditors' bargain" in a simple setting where all debts are assumed to be already due and owing. Second, the Article applies that model by considering the role bankruptcy should play in dealing with debts that are not yet due and owing. I call this the phenomenon of "temporal" concerns in bankruptcy. . . .

I. Individual Rights in a Collective Proceeding:
An Initial Examination of Bankruptcy as a Creditors' Bargain

A longstanding slogan is often used in discussing the non-discharge-related rules of bankruptcy law: "equality is equity." But this phrase explains little. It fails to deal, even roughly, with the plain fact that all bankruptcy laws to date accord substantial respect to non-bankruptcy entitlements. The slogan "equality is equity" similarly fails to explain satisfactorily why bankruptcy would ever be an occasion for altering the non-bankruptcy allocation of assets among creditors. Bankruptcy law's beguiling slogan has been little more than a banal reminder that equals are to be treated equally in bankruptcy: the important determination of who those "equals" are is often not resolved under bankruptcy law.

A more profitable line of pursuit might be to view bankruptcy as a system designed to mirror the agreement one would expect the creditors to form among themselves were they able to negotiate such an agreement from an *ex ante* position. It is this approach that I characterize as the "creditors' bargain." This view provides an illuminating vantage point from which to analyze bankruptcy

---

    *   Reprinted by permission of The Yale Law Journal Company and Fred B. Rothman & Company from *The Yale Law Journal*, Vol. 91, pages 857-907.

law's treatment of many non-bankruptcy entitlements, and a focus from which to examine the deviations made in the name of bankruptcy policy.

A. The Creditors' Bargain and Unsecured Creditors

First, consider a world in which a debtor could consensually create only one class of claimants, called "unsecured creditors." These unsecured creditors would enjoy typical state-law collection rights of attachment, execution, and so forth, but would not (at least prior to the time such collection rights are pursued) have the sort of property interests in or priority rights to any of their debtor's collateral that are enjoyed by secured creditors. . . . Are there any reasons to believe that this unitary group of creditors would favor the existence of a government-imposed system providing for the collective treatment of claims against a common debtor?

To examine this, it is worth considering a simple hypothetical. D has a small printing business. Potential creditors estimate that there is a twenty percent chance that D will become insolvent. At the point of insolvency, the business is expected to be worth $80,000 as an operating entity and $60,000 if sold piecemeal. D borrows $50,000 from each of two creditors, $C1$ and $C2$. $C1$ and $C2$ expect to spend $2,000 each in pursuit of individual creditor remedies should D become insolvent and fail to repay them. Are there any reasons to believe that under these circumstances D, $C1$, and $C2$ would jointly agree to contract for a collective liquidation system to deal with the twenty percent chance that D will not be able to pay $C1$ and $C2$ in full? From the creditors' point of view (and ultimately from D's, since inefficiencies in a non-collective system will be charged back to D—either wholly or in part—in the form of higher credit costs), three reasons suggest themselves: reduction of strategic costs; increased aggregate pool of assets; and administrative efficiencies.

1. Reduction of Strategic Costs

A collective system that treats all claimants standing in the same relationship to the debtor alike has the virtue of substituting a sum "certain" for the uncertain amount that might be realized under an individualistic creditors' remedy system. This has two advantages, even in a case where the assets will inevitably be sold on a piecemeal basis. First, it eliminates strategic costs that would otherwise be associated with a race to the courthouse. Second, even if no such race would occur, the collective proceeding reduces variance in recoveries—which is itself a virtue to risk-averse creditors.

Consider, first, the incentives for a race and the associated strategic costs. $C1$ and $C2$, in our hypothetical, have each loaned D $50,000. Each of $C1$ and $C2$ knows, however, that if the other creditor gets to the courthouse first (or to D first, to persuade D to pay voluntarily), that other creditor will collect $50,000, leaving only $10,000 for the "slower" creditor. Absent a prior agreement, this situation presents a classic example of the game theorists' "prisoner's dilemma." The central feature of a prisoner's dilemma is rational individual behavior that, in the absence of cooperation with other individuals, leads to a sub-optimal decision when viewed collectively. This occurs whenever certain rules are in the interest of an entire class of persons but, because of an inability to reach a collective solution, each class member acts out of immediate self interest in such a way that a less efficient solution results. This is precisely what occurs in our hypothetical. Each creditor, unless assured of the other's cooperation, has an incentive to take advantage of individual collection remedies, and to do so before the other creditor acts. Unless each creditor individually attempts to "beat out" the other, that creditor will fare worse than the other. Yet this race not only creates costs for the individual creditors (such as frequent checking of the courthouse records for evidence of actions against the debtor by other creditors), it is also likely to lead to a premature termination of a debtor's business, because each creditor will consider only that creditor's own advantage from racing, instead of the disadvantages imposed on creditors collectively. Thus, each creditor must participate in collectively non-optimal "advantage-taking" simply to avoid being taken advantage of. This creates a race to use individualistic remedies, even though it is not in the creditors' collective interest to use them at all.

An assumption of creditor risk-aversion facilitates the exposition of the logic of collective action. If both $C1$ and $C2$ have a fifty percent chance of winning through the use of individualistic remedies, then each faces a fifty percent chance of being paid in full ($50,000) and a fifty percent chance of being paid only $10,000. But if $C1$ and $C2$ agree to share equally in the event of D's misfortune, each could be assured of $30,000. If $C1$ and $C2$ are risk-averse, one would expect them, prior to extending credit to D, to agree on a distributional system in the event of D's insolvency in which each would receive this partial, but certain, payment of $30,000. The reduction of uncertainty would itself be viewed as a virtue by $C1$ and $C2$ and, therefore, by D as well, who would get lower aggregate credit costs. . . .

2. Increased Aggregate Pool of Assets

The use of individualistic remedies may lead to a piecemeal dismantling of a debtor's business by the untimely removal of necessary operating assets. To the extent that a non-piecemeal bankruptcy process (whether in the form of liquidation or reorganization) is likely to increase the aggregate pool of assets, its substitution for individualistic remedies may be advantageous to the creditors as a group. In the above hypothetical, for example, keeping D's printing business in one piece increases the pool of assets available to D's creditors by $20,000. Whether or not D's printing business should be sold to a third party as a going concern (*i.e.*, "liquidation" at its highest value use), or "reorganized," it is obviously to the joint advantage of $C1$ and $C2$ to keep the entity alive. Again, however, $C1$ and $C2$ face a classic prisoner's dilemma: they are jointly better off if they act collectively, but if they are unable to act collectively, rational individual behavior will require collectively non-optimal advantage-taking on the part of each. It is true that an agreement to act collectively could theoretically be negotiated after a precipitating event (*i.e*, after $C1$ has taken the steps necessary to acquire a judicial lien). By acquiring a judicial lien, $C1$ has assured herself of $50,000 prior to the advent of these negotiations. $C2$, however, is faced with losing the difference between $30,000 and $10,000 if he cannot convince $C1$ to keep the entity together. This provides a $20,000 bargaining chip for $C1$ and $C2$ to allocate among themselves through negotiations carried out after $C1$'s attachment but before the ultimate foreclosure.

The bargaining, however, will be costly. This bargaining with $C1$ could be avoided if the remaining creditors were able to act collectively and repurchase the asset at the foreclosure rate of $50,000, or replace it for $50,000. In any case in which there is a large number of such creditors, not only would free-rider problems make any collective agreement after one creditor has attached almost impossible, but subsequent creditors would still have incentives to "beat out" the remaining creditors by using their individual remedies and collecting first on the remaining assets. For these reasons, *ex post* deals capable of preserving the debtor's "going concern" value, while possible, would not be very likely in a large number of cases. Such an agreement would be much more likely *ex ante*. Neither $C1$ nor $C2$ would know at that time which one will be the first to attach. They do know, however, that the total pool of assets available to satisfy their claims may be increased through collective action. For those reasons, one would expect them to agree to a collective system that deterred the sub-optimal behavior of the prisoner's dilemma, and allowed $C1$ and $C2$ to capture and share the "going concern" value of D's business—the difference between the worth of D's assets in a piecemeal sale and the worth of those assets as a continuing business.

3. Administrative Efficiencies

Issues such as the precise amount of the debtor's assets and the nature and extent of secured claims must be resolved in virtually every collection proceeding. We have posited that $C1$ and $C2$ would each spend $2,000 in an individual collection proceeding. In a number of cases, it is likely that *C1* and *C2* will attempt to collect their claims at roughly the same time. . . . A single inquiry into recurring collection questions is likely to be less expensive than the multiple inquiries necessary in an individualistic remedies system. If a collective proceeding costs *C1* and *C2* a total of $3,000, for example, its use would save *C1* and *C2* $500 each. At the time of negotiating the creditors' bargain, this reduced cost would be viewed as a clear advantage of a collective process. Consequently, in the event of *D*'s insolvency, we would expect to see *D*, *C1*, and *C2* prefer a collective system, and therefore agree to the inclusion of a procedure for implementing such a system in their *ex ante* bargain.

The three considerations I have described above make it likely that a general unsecured creditor will agree to a collective system in lieu of a scheme of individualistic remedies. No single creditor, however, would agree to be bound to this collective system unless it were a compulsory system binding all other creditors: to allow the debtor to contract with other creditors on an opt-out basis would destroy the advantages of a collective proceeding.

Although we would expect to see a mandatory collective proceeding as a standard feature of the creditors' bargain, no *ex ante* meeting of the creditors will, realistically, take place. A debtor's pool of creditors changes over time and even the debtor is unlikely to know who the creditors of the business will be at any point in the future. As a result, the creditors themselves cannot be expected to negotiate this agreement, even though it would be in their joint interest to do so. A federal bankruptcy rule solves this problem by making available a mandatory collective system after insolvency has occurred.

It is important, however, not to overstate the role of the collective system imposed by the government. The *presence* of a bankruptcy system does not mandate its *use*. The realization that a creditor could always initiate the bankruptcy process would deter attempts in any non-bankruptcy collective proceeding to provide any creditor with less than the minimum obtainable in a bankruptcy proceeding. The availability of a mandatory collective system in which distributions are governed by a set of statutory rules is, therefore, important because it stipulates a minimum set of entitlements for claimants that, in turn, provides a framework for implementing a consensual collective proceeding outside of the bankruptcy process. One would normally expect to see consensual deals among creditors outside of the bankruptcy process attempted first, at least to the extent that there are potential cost savings in remaining outside of the formal bankruptcy process, since those savings could be consensually allocated. The formal bankruptcy process would presumably be used only when individualistic "advantage-taking" in the setting of multi-party negotiations makes a consensual deal too costly to strike—which may occur frequently as the number of creditors increases.

But because the bankruptcy rules set the stage against which consensual collective proceedings will be negotiated outside of bankruptcy, it is important that those rules be drawn in a fashion that is likely to minimize incentives for inefficient recourse to a collective proceeding. These rules should be clear and determinable, so as to be ascertainable at low cost in any negotiated non-bankruptcy collective process. . . .

B. Property Claimants and the Creditors' Bargain

To this point, we have assumed that all creditors were similarly situated in that they all held unsecured claims. Our scope will now be expanded to include creditors whose contracts afford them superior rights vis-á-vis other creditors.

Consider, for purposes of this discussion, the utility of the creditors' bargain model in dealing with consensually secured claimants. In this discussion, it is a key assumption that consensually negotiated security interests have aggregate efficiencies . . . . Consequently, from an *ex ante* position, the debtor and the creditors would view it as in their joint interest to behave in a fashion that will keep the efficiencies of such consensually negotiated security interests.

Assuming that other creditors would consent to the existence of secured creditors, we can now turn to the question of whether those secured creditors would consent to be bound by a collective proceeding. Fully secured creditors are not direct beneficiaries of either the "reduction of strategic costs" or the "increased aggregate pool of assets" advantages of a collective proceeding previously explored. Moreover, fully secured creditors are less likely to view "administrative efficiencies" as a reason to support a collective proceeding because at least some of these administratively difficult issues, such as the availability of assets and the priorities of competing claimants, have previously been negotiated away.

These observations ignore, however, the aggregate advantages that will accrue to the debtor and all the creditors from minimizing the debtor's total credit costs. Unsecured creditors have several reasons for desiring a collective proceeding. Consider first the "increased aggregate pool of assets." If a secured creditor could remove collateral from the debtor's estate and remain outside of any collective proceeding this advantage would be diminished or lost. One would expect, therefore, that the unsecured creditors would be willing to pay a secured creditor at least something to agree to join in the collective proceeding. Moreover, while a secured creditor might otherwise be indifferent to the administrative efficiencies associated with a collective proceeding (because a secured creditor's costs of collection are often contractually allocated to the debtor), the debtor and the creditors as a group will benefit as a result of *ex ante* adjustments for the elimination of such costs. Since costs passed on to the debtor by a secured creditor would increase the secured creditor's claim, they would, *pro tanto*, reduce the pool of assets available for the unsecured creditors and thereby increase their costs of credit. As a result, the unsecured creditors would in fact be sensitive to these costs. The introduction of secured creditors into the model, accordingly, should not make a difference: we would still expect the debtor and the creditors (including secured creditors) to select a system in which the aggregate collection costs would be minimized.

The system in which collection costs are best minimized remains the collective proceeding. Since the advantages of secured credit would be weakened to the point of being lost if a secured creditor could be forced to participate on a *pro rata* basis with unsecured creditors in any bankruptcy proceeding, maintaining these advantages requires respecting a secured creditor's ability to be paid first from the assets constituting the secured creditor's collateral. But this is not inconsistent with a mandatory collective system: the unsecured creditors, for the reasons we have just explored, would view a secured creditor's ability to ignore the collective proceeding as a cost of credit. It is, therefore, in the joint interest of the unsecured creditors (and hence in the debtor's interest as well) to have a secured creditor included in the collective proceeding. A secured creditor, on the other hand, would have no reason to object to such an inclusion *if* left as well off as before. Thus, the mandatory inclusion of a secured creditor in the collective asset-disbursement process, even if that creditor's preferential entitlements were respected, would produce a net benefit: the secured creditor would be no worse off than before and the unsecured creditors could be made better off.

Consider the hypothetical examined earlier, except allow *C1* to be a creditor with a security interest in *D*'s printing press, the principal piece of *D*'s business equipment. This press could be sold for $50,000 on the open market. By virtue of this security interest, *C1* is "assured" of receiving $50,000, the amount of *C1*'s loan. If *C1* is to proceed independently of *C2*, however, thereby forcing a piecemeal liquidation, *C2* will receive only $10,000. If *C1* and *C2* proceed collectively (and sell *D*'s business as a going concern), *C2* would receive $30,000. Thus, at the time *C1* attempted to collect by foreclosing on *D*'s printing press, we would expect *C1* and *C2* to negotiate an agreement to proceed collectively, with *C2* paying *C1* between $0 and $20,000 to agree to this. Exactly as before, however . . ., the uncertainties of these negotiations, plus the inevitable "free rider" problems that would arise if there were multiple unsecured creditors, make an *ex ante* agreement preferable.

. . .

This suggests that there is nothing "unfair" about recognizing a secured creditor's prior entitlements in bankruptcy. Instead, it is exactly the sort of agreement we would expect to see negotiated voluntarily once the issue of the *existence* of secured credit were decided. To the extent there are advantages to secured financing, respecting the non-bankruptcy priority of secured creditors is a necessary corollary of protecting those advantages. Moreover, a secured creditor has already "paid" for this prior entitlement—really a higher probability of being repaid—through receipt of a lower return. Conversely, the unsecured creditors have already been "paid" for allowing this prior entitlement and they receive a higher rate of return because of their lower priority position. The creditors' bargain model, then, provides a satisfying theoretical explanation of why bankruptcy law should make a fundamental decision to honor negotiated non-bankruptcy entitlements. . . .

Conclusion

. . . Bankruptcy law has, for too long, been molded and interpreted without any systematic questioning or understanding of its normative role in a larger legal, economic, and social world. This Article asserts that not only is there a coherent normative theory justifying a bankruptcy system that deals with inter-creditor questions, but also that we would be better able to formulate and apply principled bankruptcy rules if we would give systematic and critical attention to the impact of those rules on non-bankruptcy entitlements. That the answers to creditor-allocation questions posed by the bankruptcy process will often be difficult does not excuse the failure of the statutory drafters, bankruptcy judges, and the bankruptcy bar from even identifying the questions they purport to be answering. Greater attention to the relevance of the creditors' bargain model in formulating the non-discharge related rules of the bankruptcy process appears to be a promising, and necessary, beginning to a principled development of our bankruptcy laws.

Responses to the Creditors' Bargain Theory

Professor Jackson's "creditor's bargain" model prompted numerous and varied reactions in the groves of academe. The opening slot in the response column is accorded to the late Professor Vern Countryman of Harvard Law School. His sarcastic critique of the creditors' bargain is found in a masterful 1985 article on preferences in the VANDERBILT LAW REVIEW (see Chapter 6), and focuses on the preference-law ramifications of the creditors' bargain. His basic premises, though, are equally applicable to any aspect of the creditors' bargain.

A more detailed critique of the Jackson's model is presented by Professor David Gray Carlson of the Benjamin N. Cardozo School of Law. Professor Carlson, an extraordinarily prolific, thoughtful, and never bashful commentator on the bankruptcy scene, seemingly has focused his career on two aims: assessing the law of secured transactions as impacted by bankruptcy, and challenging the legions of law and economics apostles. In his review of Jackson's LOGIC AND LIMITS book, published in 1987 in the MICHIGAN LAW REVIEW's annual survey of books relating to the law, Professor Carlson takes on Jackson. He minces no words in expressing his disdain for Jackson's grand theory, an undertaking which he believes was doomed from the outset.

As you read Carlson's scathing attack, assess all of the reasons why he argues (1) that the creditors' bargain "contractarian" construct should be abandoned, and (2) that bankruptcy cannot and should not always respect and enforce "non-bankruptcy entitlements." In this passage, Carlson questions Jackson's creditors' bargain model as a justification for creditor equality. In an excerpt in Chapter 11, Carlson turns his critic's eye to Jackson's analysis of the bankruptcy discharge. Who has the better of the argument, Jackson or Carlson? Which prongs of Carlson's attack are more telling?

Vern Countryman
The Concept of a Voidable Preference in Bankruptcy
38 Vand. L. Rev. 713 (1985)[*]

. . . [R]ecently, Professor Jackson . . . came up with a new analysis. Bankruptcy rules, including rules about preferences, should be viewed as based on a new "creditors' bargain" theory for the cases in which not enough assets are present to pay off all creditors—"an attempt to implement the type of collective and compulsory system that rational creditors would privately agree to if they could bargain together before the fact." Professor Jackson reasons: "From the perspective of the creditors' bargain theory, bankruptcy exists at its core to maximize the value of assets in the face of individualized pressures to ignore the common weal for individual gain." Of course, creditors do not bargain on such matters "before the fact," and there is in fact no creditors' bargain. Nevertheless, Professor Jackson can intuit what that bargain would be and tell us how preference law can "bind them to their presumptive [*i.e.*, fictitious] ex ante agreement and . . . foil the attempts of each creditor to welsh on the agreement for individual gain."

. . . But at this point Professor Jackson, who began by intuiting a fictitious agreement for all creditors, seems to have narrowed his constituency to intuit a separate fictitious agreement for secured creditors only, since he suggests no reason why unsecured creditors would agree to recognize the sanctity of the "advance grab" of an after-acquired property clause.

. . . I am not prepared to say that Professors Kronman, Jackson, Eisenberg, and Baird are 100% wrong in their views on preferences. I will leave that assertion to Professor Alan Schwartz when and if he gets around to it. And I will admit that their approach leaves them free from the burden of scrutinizing the vast judicial output that reveals how the current preference law is being administered—a subject in which they evince little interest.

But I do not find their approach helpful. They assume that every creditor—apparently including asbestos victims and other tort claimants ("nonconsensual creditors" like the IRS), the most unsophisticated customer or supplier of goods and services, and the lowliest employee—will have full information and competent legal advice in dealing with the debtor. They assume further that every creditor will make the same assumptions they do and bring to bear the same highly skilled free market economic analysis—which also assumes that everyone acts solely on the basis of pure and fully informed greed—in fixing his price and other terms. I confess to sharing the reaction of Professor Richard Markovitz after he had listened to another preacher of the true gospel. He suggested that the answer to the question, "How many Chicago economists does it take to change a light bulb?" was: "None. If it needed changing, the market would have changed it already."

With all their assumptions, it is not even presumptuous for some of the young turks to proceed to invent fictitious "agreements" among all creditors concerned with what the law of preferences should be. But, since their assumptions are wrong to such a large extent, the authority some of them assume to concoct fictitious agreements is left without foundation, as are their proposals for a preference law to implement such "agreements." For this reason, I do not find their approach helpful either in drafting a preference law or in interpreting it.

David Gray Carlson
Philosophy in Bankruptcy
85 MICH. L. REV. 1341 (1987)[*]

In *The Logic and Limits of Bankruptcy Law*, Thomas Jackson reworks his recent law review articles into a book that attempts to be a coherent jurisprudence of federal bankruptcy law. Undoubtedly, the book will find some admirers among people who think that bad law-and-economics is better than no law-and-economics, but virtually all other audiences will find the book badly wanting. The book is unhelpful in solving hard interpretive problems. No important sociological issues are discussed or even mentioned. On its own chosen level of generality, Jackson's vision of the rationality in bankruptcy law is internally inconsistent and hopelessly ad hoc.

Jackson's basic technique is to filter bankruptcy law through a "creditor's bargain" model. In this model, anyone who loses his or her entitlements in bankruptcy is shown to have consented in advance to the loss. Somewhat separately, Jackson believes that bankruptcy should be totally neutral about property entitlements created by state law. Otherwise, "incentives" are created.

In this essay, I will present some criticisms of these two propositions. My conclusion will be that, at his best, Jackson rises to mere tautology. Beyond that, Jackson entangles himself in unreconciled contradictions and depends upon factual assertions that no one could accept as true. Almost never does he present an insight that can survive serious scrutiny.

I. JACKSON'S CONTRACTARIAN METHODOLOGY

Jackson joins a distinguished coterie in pursuing contractarian theory. Hobbes, Locke, and Rousseau also find in hypothetical contracts a means by which the postulate of individual sovereignty may be reconciled with coercive government power. The practice of contractarian theorists is not to argue that any real human being has actually manifested consent. Instead, they present an *essence* of the human personality in the abstract, devoid of historic characteristics. These personalities are defined by a very limited number of attributes that the theorist perceives to be universal among humans. Defined by these limited attributes, such personalities, it is argued, would consent to socializing institutions that involve coercion and pain.

Contractarians are often persuasive in arguing that humans (as *they* reconstitute them) *would* pursue the rationality dictated by the attributes and needs assigned to them and would indeed agree to future coercion. The controversial aspect of contractarian rhetoric is whether the theorist has introduced a plausible account of personality. If you don't agree that human beings have been abstracted fairly in the contractarian model, then the model fails to have any rhetorical value. . . .

. . . [C]ontractarianism is not a very effective technique to pursue economic efficiency. Unlike basic institutional questions, which depend upon very abstract assertions of human desire, efficiency requires a close analysis of precise historical attributes of human beings. Identifying the *ex ante* state in which a loser would have consented to a disadvantageous-but-efficient law almost always requires an ad hoc attribution of historic qualities to the person who would agree to take the loss. However, in spite of the utilitarian's heavy reliance on historical attributes of persons, Archimedean contractarianism has attracted some law-and-economics professors precisely because it answers a very difficult ethical question about cost-benefit analysis: why should a person incur costs just so some other people can benefit? . . .

Usually, the bargain posed by efficiency contractarians goes like this:

Contractarians:

We have here a proposal for an efficient rule that enriches investment bankers at the expense of widows and orphans. Between you people, none of you now knows who will be the investment banker and who will be the widow. . . .

Abstracted Persons:

We are risk-neutral wealth maximizers. We are willing to risk a loss in the hope of achieving even greater wealth. . . . The efficient rule, however, increases the value of our chances for a good life. Therefore, we consent to the rule that favors investment bankers over widows.

Such arguments, I think, are ineffective. One cannot really fathom a time when people are so disembodied from their histories that they have no idea whether they are more likely to be investment bankers or widows. . . .

I therefore come to Jackson's scholarship with a great deal of skepticism . . . . But beyond challenging the persuasiveness of the technique, I have two other complaints about the way Jackson practices his contractarianism. First, in pursuit of efficiency, Jackson uses the model ineptly. His models don't show what he claims they do. Second, Jackson, without warning, maintains the facade of contractarianism while dropping utilitarianism as the basic normative goal. . . .

My critique of the efficiency version of his contractarianism will center on his allegation that all or most creditors would bargain to get equal priority in bankruptcy. My critique of his nonefficiency contractarianism will focus on Jackson's explanation of bankruptcy discharges. . . .

A. *Creditor Priorities*

A central claim of Jackson's book is that all creditors would agree to equal priority in bankruptcy. This is the so-called "creditor's bargain." The logical steps to this conclusion are as follows: (a) Nonbankruptcy law is the "state of nature" out of which the creditor's bargain emerges. (b) The essence of nonbankruptcy debtor-creditor law is "first in time, first in right," a concept that preexists creditor equality. (c) Creditor equality is in turn the essence of bankruptcy. (d) Creditors have a precisely equal perception of their chance of winning a priority collection in case the debtor becomes insolvent. (e) Creditors care only about maximizing their recovery; they have no altruism about their fellow creditors and no particular animus toward them either. (f) If the creditors act together, they can gain, either by (i) capturing the "going concern" value of an enterprise, or at least by (ii) reducing the administrative cost of recovering from the debtor.

Unfortunately, each and every assumption in Jackson's model is open to challenge. As a result, this model proves nothing about the institution of creditor equality in bankruptcy. In fact, even on his assumptions, Jackson does not prove that equality is the *only* agreement the creditors could possibly reach. Not only would these creditors agree to bankruptcy equality, but they would agree to bankruptcy inequality as well, if Jackson asked them to.

Let's go over Jackson's logical steps one by one. . . .

1. *Essences and Exceptions*

In attempting to show that the status quo is fueled by rational normative principles, Jackson must, of course, describe what he takes the status quo to be. According to Jackson, the essence of state debtor-creditor law is a race of creditors to grab what they can. In contrast, the essence of federal bankruptcy law forces creditors to be treated equally. . . . The following paragraphs will argue that Jackson has no good justification for his essentialism.

a. *The essence of state law.* State (or nonbankruptcy) law does give rise to a race among creditors to obtain judicial liens, of course, but it also contains norms of creditor equality. These equality norms are found in state receiverships and assignments for the benefit of creditors. . . .

If "first in time" is the essence of state debtor-creditor law, it is only a twentieth-century essence. This development is itself surely the product of federal bankruptcy law. That is, once Congress enacted a federal bankruptcy law, the use of creditor equality systems in state law became subject to competition from the federal system. This does not necessarily mean that state legislatures no longer cared about or would oppose creditor equality. . . .

b. *The essence of bankruptcy.* Not only is Jackson's account of the essence of state debtor-creditor law open to challenge, but his account of bankruptcy's essence is also dubious. Jackson claims that the essence of bankruptcy is creditor equality. This claim is not borne out by examining the content of the bankruptcy statute, which contains all sorts of creditor priorities, nor is it borne out by empirical investigation. Bankruptcy statistics show that the vast majority of dollars produced by bankruptcy trustees go to administrative expenses and priority creditors. On the basis of practice, the numbers strongly suggest that creditor *in*equality is the essence of bankruptcy. . . .

The fact that state law already contains norms of communitarian sharing implies that Jackson has presented a false choice to the hypothetical creditors in his bargaining model. As state-law creditors, they already can force each other to share. Their consent to a communitarian federal bankruptcy proceeding is therefore unrelated to maximizing profits by capturing the enhanced value of the estate in bankruptcy. Federalization of state debtor-creditor law has to be justified by principles that are closer to the logic of diversity jurisdiction than to the logic of profit maximization.

To summarize, Jackson claims that he can decode the essences of state and federal debtor-creditor law, but he doesn't say where these essences come from. . . . The false assertion of the essences of the law is not a minor flaw. . . .

2. Equally Powerful Creditors

In order for Jackson's contractarian justification of creditor equality to work, it is necessary for Jackson's abstract creditors to be equal to all other creditors in their ability to collect. Therefore, at the core of Jackson's model is the notion that creditors are already deemed to be equal. Equal creditors are then shown to agree upon equality.

Isn't this smuggling the rabbit into the hat? It shouldn't take any empirical study to convince you that creditors are *not* equal in their ability to collect. Historic creditors differ in their leverage and knowledge, their skill in obtaining payment or liens, and their opportunity costs of litigating. Profit maximizing creditors who are powerful vis-á-vis other creditors would not agree to give up power to weaklings unless they were compensated for it. Creditors who are weak would love to take power from stronger creditors, if they could. . . .

. . . A rule that ignores the differences of creditors has the distinct *dis*advantage of producing the very false impression that Jackson's contractarian model has a modicum of validity. . . .

3. Equals Agreeing Upon Equality

Ironically, even though it is natural to assume that a priori equal creditors agree to be equal, it turns out that not even this pitiful thesis is justified under the assumptions Jackson gives us! In fact, depending on what question they are asked, equal creditors might also agree on unequal priorities. Furthermore, *unequal* creditors can be made to consent to *equal* priorities. . . .

. . . Under these premises, so long as each profit-maximizing creditor makes a gain in bankruptcy, Jackson could win consent from the creditors to a variety of propositions. All that is required to produce creditor consent is that each creditor get more from bankruptcy than from state law.

The reason that Jackson's contract model is so indeterminate is that Jackson has erroneously connected the existence of bankruptcy efficiencies with the institution of creditor equality. The two have no logical connection whatsoever. They are non sequiturs.[29] Stipulating the existence of a wealth gain does not prove that profit-maximizing creditors *must* as a consequence agree to divide up the gain equally. In fact, . . . equal *or* unequal creditors will agree on any distribution that gives them more than they would have received under state law.

. . . If creditors do not feel equal, there is no guarantee that equality would emerge from such a pot-splitting session. Creditors who would do better under state law will simply veto any proposal that does not recognize the value of their state law entitlements.

4. *Profit Maximization and the Ideology of Equality*

The creditor's bargain assumes (a) that creditors have equal power under state law, and (b) that creditors desire to maximize profits (to the exclusion of all other human desire). . . .

Profit maximization (among equals) therefore displaces all other forms of ideology and allows the illusion that the norm of equality is produced by self-interest. But this illusion is the product of extremely unrealistic assumptions about human nature. Not only are real-life creditors unequal in power, but they certainly do not care only about maximizing profit.

The addition of other conflicting ideologies may produce a "creditor's bargain" for inequality. For instance, suppose that the creditors are workers who face major displacement costs, separate from their claims for back wages, because their employer has gone bankrupt. . . . These creditors might not agree to creditor equality and might insist on a bankruptcy priority for wage claims.

. . . The truth of the matter is that efficiency-based contractarians like Jackson aren't utilitarians at all. Rather, they are conservatives who like the status quo and (in this status quo and none other) find the language of utilitarianism a fancy way for them to sound neutral and scientific. . . .

5. *Enhanced Value of the Bankruptcy Estate*

Suppose Jackson is right in claiming that all creditors are equal in collecting power and are greedy to the exclusion of all other human attributes. Jackson's contractarian justification of equal priorities in bankruptcy still requires a belief that communitarian bankruptcy enhances the value of the debtor's property while selfish state-law systems do not.

If such an assumption is valid, it is true by definition that equally powerful creditors as a whole would prefer to share equally in a larger pie than to share equally in a lesser pie. This is merely the same as saying that creditors prefer the bigger pie over the smaller pie. . . .

Even this modest conclusion presupposes one of two facts: either (a) bankruptcy produces more value from assets than do state enforcement systems, or (b) bankruptcy law saves more enforcement costs than nonbankruptcy law. These factual assertions are not self-evident. . . .

In fact, Jackson identifies only one kind of value enhancement in bankruptcy: the capture of going-concern value. I find this confusing, since bankruptcy liquidations do not depend on capturing going-concern value. For cases in which going-concern value is absent, Jackson gives no clue as to why or whether bankruptcy liquidations can enhance the value of the estate better than state-law liquidation systems. In any case, we don't inevitably need a bankruptcy system to capture going-concern value. State receiverships could do the same.

The allegation that state law produces more enforcement costs than bankruptcy is also not proven. One can imagine all sorts of extra legal costs in bankruptcy that might not exist in state law. . . .

This is a good place to invoke the Coase Theorem, which holds that the background legal regime does not matter; profit maximizing people will maneuver to maximize profit whether in or

---

[29]   That entitlements are non sequiturs to the maximization of a joint venture was a central insight of Coase.

out of bankruptcy. Jackson presents no clear picture of why state law inevitably sacrifices going-concern value and bankruptcy does not.

6. *Summary*

Jackson's "creditors' bargain" is even less than a hollow tautology. It is based on a false picture of legal doctrine. The bargain is the product of creditors being totally equal in all aspects and completely apathetic to status and prestige between themselves, a highly unbelievable portrait of historically situated human beings. Finally, the bargain for equality ends up being a non sequitur. Profit-maximizing creditors would agree to *anything* so long as they get more in bankruptcy than out of it. For these reasons, Jackson's contractarianism fails to justify the institution of federal bankruptcy.[43] . . .

[*Editor's note: In the next section of the article, Professor Carlson challenges Professor Jackson's explanation of the bankruptcy discharge. We pick up Carlson's article as he critically examines Jackson's assertion that bankruptcy should be a neutral forum and should normally enforce nonbankruptcy entitlements.*]

II. BANKRUPTCY AS NEUTRAL FORUM

In addition to contractarianism, Jackson has another major normative principle to push. According to Jackson, bankruptcy should always be neutral toward creditor rights in state law. Otherwise, "incentives" are created whereby firms that should not be in bankruptcy are pushed into it, and vice versa. . . . Although it hardly seems possible, the idea of bankruptcy neutrality is even less satisfactory than Jackson's contractarian claims. This section will sketch out some of the major failures in the bankruptcy neutrality idea.

A. *There Can Be No Such Thing as Neutrality Between State Law and Bankruptcy*

In order for a totally neutral environment to exist whereby creditors can choose between bankruptcy and nonbankruptcy liquidation systems, the following formula must hold for each and every creditor:

$$C_s/E_s = C_b/E_b$$

where C_s is the creditor's expected return under state (or nonbankruptcy) liquidation systems, C_b is the creditor's expected return from a bankruptcy proceeding, while E_s and E_b are the value of the entire estate in a state-law and in a bankruptcy-law proceeding. If (and only if) the above formula is true for each and every creditor, then (and only then) will creditors choose between state law and bankruptcy law based solely on the efficiency of the competing collection systems. . . .

---

[43] It might be fair to ask if I have any better suggestions than Jackson for attributing "meaning" to the equal priority in bankruptcy. I do. My interpretation does not go to the phenomenon of federal bankruptcy, but rather to the idea of creditor equality in any kind of collective proceeding. . . .

. . . [A] creditor's "job" is not to maximize recovery through a non-consensual grab. Rather, the creditor is expected to share when the debtor is insolvent in a sort of anti-feudal gesture toward a market ideology. . . . Bankruptcy, then, becomes the primary (but not the only) institution designed to force creditors to share with other creditors. It is a communitarian, rather than a self-interested, regime. It tells the creditor that he is going to share equally with his fellows whether he likes it or not.

. . . I only wish to suggest that equal priority may be a normative idea put in place to confirm desired creditor conduct, rather than the product of what creditors really want separate from law.

Where bankruptcy treats general creditors as equal, while state law permits creditors to be paid or to obtain judicial liens, the above formula never holds. The implication of this observation is that bankruptcy equality (the essence of bankruptcy, says Jackson) is itself non-neutral in relation to state law. Therefore, the suggestion that bankruptcy should have no substantive content is inherently impossible. . . .

B. *Debtor-Creditor Federalism As a Value More Important Than Efficiency*

. . . Nonbankruptcy law may well be inefficient or even unfair, but Jackson still thinks that bankruptcy must never erode any state-law entitlements. Indeed, efficiency and bankruptcy neutrality are contradictory principles. . . .

Jackson, then, privileges a vague sort of debtor-creditor federalism over efficiency. If this debtor-creditor federalism is more important than efficient law, then Jackson really ought to have explained what values debtor-creditor federalism serves. . . .

. . . Why does it follow that bankruptcy courts must be neutral, when state courts and state legislatures have the power to neutralize a bankruptcy rule by conforming state law to it? In short, bankruptcy neutrality seems anti-reform, anti-efficiency, anti-fairness. . . .

C. *The Ad Hoc Nature of Debtor-Creditor Federalism*

. . . [S]ometimes federalism is asserted over efficiency, and sometimes efficiency is asserted over federalism. This leaves Jackson's book deeply contradictory on whether bankruptcy should be neutral or whether bankruptcy should be efficient. . . .

Jackson does attempt a calculus to tell us when efficiency should or should not be asserted as the most important value. According to Jackson, bankruptcy should be non-neutral whenever such interference furthers the "goal" of bankruptcy. The "goal" of bankruptcy is the efficient maximization of value in the debtor's estate. In particular, Jackson imagines that bankruptcy equality among unsecured creditors is necessary to justify the maximization of the estate that bankruptcy supposedly achieves. . . .

It can be seen that, even though Jackson opposes efficiency when it contradicts bankruptcy neutrality, efficiency is nevertheless at the heart of bankruptcy neutrality after all. Therefore, Jackson favors some non-neutral bankruptcy rules because they are efficient. He opposes other non-neutral rules even though the rules are efficient. Sometimes efficiency is good and sometimes it is bad.
. . .

Having admitted that bankruptcy law cannot always be neutral (because sometimes neutrality is too expensive), it is incumbent upon Jackson to explain how much neutrality is worth (assuming for the sake of argument that it is worth anything at all). . . .

D. *An Inconsistent View of the Efficiency of Bankruptcy*

Although Jackson sometimes claims that bankruptcy neutrality is different from and privileged over wealth maximization, Jackson asserts (inconsistently) that the purpose of bankruptcy is wealth maximization. But if bankruptcy were always efficient in comparison to the nonbankruptcy liquidation procedure, wouldn't incentives leading creditors toward bankruptcy be a good thing?

Jackson repeats again and again that he hates such incentives, however. His stated reason: even though bankruptcy exists because it is more efficient than nonbankruptcy liquidation alternatives, nevertheless there are *inefficient* bankruptcies that could occur if creditors have non-neutral bankruptcy rights. . . .

. . . Jackson must think that in some bankruptcies aggregate creditor enforcement costs would be lower if the firm were liquidated under nonbankruptcy law. . . . Bankruptcy neutrality therefore seems aimed at guaranteeing that the choice made by creditors (bankruptcy or no bankruptcy) will be efficient.

If this is what Jackson means when he denounces disincentives, I find several things wrong with the account. First, if bankruptcy is efficient *most* of the time, then aren't non-neutral incentives good most of the time as well? . . .

Second, Jackson assumes that every non-neutral law produces a result in society. It could be, however, that the cost to the creditor of precipitating an involuntary (inefficient) bankruptcy far outweighs the benefit received from the non-neutral bankruptcy rule. . . . [B]ankruptcy law might be irrelevant to the conduct of creditors much of the time. . . . [C]reditors do not seem to be reacting in the way Jackson predicts. It seems that debtors are practically the only people deciding whether bankruptcy is a good thing. . . .

E. *The Theory of the Second Best*

Jackson's neutrality position has a further problem which he does not acknowledge—the problem of the "second best." The second-best problem raises whenever there is more than one evil tendency in the world. . . . The theory of the second best, then, tells us that it is never enough to proclaim a tendency nonoptimal. The analyst must also demonstrate that the tendency is not needed to counteract some other, more serious counter-tendency.

The implication of the theory of the second best for Jackson's book is that Jackson cannot pick out disincentives and urge their repeal in the abstract. To do so could produce just the opposite effect from what Jackson intends. . . .

Before bankruptcy neutrality can even begin to make sense, Jackson has to assure us that he has succeeded in removing every non-neutral bankruptcy rule. If he allows even one non-neutral rule to survive, removing any countervailing incentive is inefficient. Yet Jackson explicitly endorses lots of non-neutral rules (such as avoiding preferences). . . .

F. *The Indeterminacy of State Law and the Impossibility of Neutrality*

According to Jackson, bankruptcy courts should find out precisely what rights creditors have at state law and then guarantee them at least that much in bankruptcy. This view presupposes that state law is determinate and yields an answer. In making this assertion, Jackson ignores almost eighty years of legal realism and (more recently) critical legal theory. . . .

Equity courts in particular have always been heavily involved in debt collection. . . . Indeed, it is safe to say that the whole purpose of equity is to render the law indeterminate.

If it is true that the law is indeterminate, not just some of the time, but all of the time, then Jackson's neutrality principle is useless. Inevitably, the bankruptcy judge must mediate between conflicting state-law norms. This mediation can be accomplished only through the use of some theory or intuition that is not part of the neutrality principle.

In short, Jackson's neutrality principle reduces to atavistic formalism—the idea that neutral judges can simply consult the law and find the answer, without ever having to exercise judgment. Formalist legal theory has not been respectable since Roscoe Pound demolished it way back in the Roosevelt administration. Yet if there is any difference between Jackson's bankruptcy neutrality theory and the "mechanical jurisprudence" Pound denounced, it is not a difference that I can discern.

III. CONCLUSION

Thomas Jackson has written an unremittingly dreadful book. Let me quickly summarize the reasons why.

Jackson's project is to find the essences of bankruptcy law, prove that those essences are rational, usually by a contractarian claim, and use those essences to club to death the numerous exceptions he finds that render bankruptcy law nonsystematic. But system alone, aside from its aesthetic appeal, is worthless. Jackson must explain to us the ethical norms that fuel these systems. Much of the time, Jackson does not bother to do so, leaving it to the reader to guess why his principles are indeed worth following. . . .

Meanwhile, contractarianism pervades Jackson's work and gives the appearance of a coherent deep structure, but it is a sham. Sometimes Jackson makes up contracts in pursuit of efficiency and sometimes he makes up contracts in pursuit of protecting the individual against the ruthless logic of contracts. . . .

The whole idea of finding a deep structure in a complicated, historic artifact such as the Bankruptcy Code was doomed from the start. Considering the tens of thousands of congressmen, judges and lawyers who have contributed to the content of bankruptcy law, it would have been a miracle if all of them were driven by the same ethical impulse every time a legislative decision was made. Legal texts are situated in history, and just as historical explanation is infinitely complex, so should we expect jurisprudential explanations to be infinitely complex, based on entropy, anomie, conflict, and confusion, as well as the dictates of logic and reason.

The Warren-Baird Debate

Perhaps the most famous and enduring staging of the whole "creditors' bargain" debate came in a pair of dueling articles in the UNIVERSITY OF CHICAGO LAW REVIEW in 1987. As one participant joked, the debate was designed to be conducted in the fashion of the "Point-Counterpoint" skit then in vogue on the *Saturday Night Live* television comedy show. Dan Aykroyd and Jane Curtin (the comedians on the show) did not take part in this bankruptcy-policy analogue; in their stead were two of the leading bankruptcy scholars of the age, Elizabeth Warren and Douglas Baird. Baird and Warren focused their debate on business bankruptcies, which conveniently eliminated troublesome and complicating issues of the "fresh start" for individual debtors. It is fair to say that Warren and Baird hardly could have disagreed more about what the core functions and purposes of bankruptcy should be or even how one should go about trying to divine the answer.

Challenging the "Jacksonian" creditors' bargain view was Professor Elizabeth Warren, then a professor at the University of Texas, now at Harvard. Professor Warren served most recently as the Chief Reporter for the second National Bankruptcy Review Commission, which issued its 1300-page report in 1997. In her article *Bankruptcy Policy*, Professor Warren challenges the premises of the theoretical construct of the law-and-economics-inspired creditors' bargain model and the implications that follow, including the insistence that bankruptcy must respect non-bankruptcy entitlements. Even more fundamentally, though, she questions whether it even makes sense to try to explain bankruptcy by resort to a normative academic construct. She comes down more on the side of a pragmatic realism; she holds a "dirty, complex, elastic, interconnected view of bankruptcy," and cannot blithely predict answers to the very difficult real-world problem of how to allocate the losses caused by a debtor's multiple defaults.

Standing up for his mentor, teacher and frequent co-author Thomas Jackson, and championing the creditors' bargain model, is Professor (later Dean) Douglas Baird of the University of Chicago Law School. Baird has been eloquently espousing the economic approach to legal analysis for many years. His path-breaking book GAME THEORY AND THE LAW, written with Professors Randal Picker and Robert Gertner and published in 1994, is considered the "Bible" for that area of scholarship. In *Loss Distribution, Forum Shopping, and Bankruptcy: A Reply to Warren*, Professor Baird asserts (as the title suggests) that forum shopping is a serious concern when a bankruptcy system is superimposed on other priority and collection regimes. The default rule insisting on conformity in bankruptcy with "non-bankruptcy entitlements" serves to minimize the risk of harmful forum shopping. Baird asserts (echoing Max Radin) that "the challenge facing anyone who wants to write about bankruptcy policy is to explain why a distinct bankruptcy law exists at all." He offers the normative justification of the creditors' bargain model as a tool for allocating losses in recognition of the collective action problem.

In reading the Warren and Baird articles, which today remain as prototypes of the polar positions taken by dueling camps of bankruptcy scholars, think about the following issues:

1. By what methodology do Warren and Baird believe bankruptcy policy should be derived?
2. By what authority?
3. What fundamental issues must a bankruptcy law attempt to address and resolve?
4. Of what relevance is it that substantive rights are created by non-bankruptcy law, and that substantive law and collection law are distinct?
5. How do bankruptcy law and state collection law differ?
6. What are the justifications for having a bankruptcy law separate from state collection law?
7. What are the problems and risks inherent in having a separate bankruptcy law?
8. How should a bankruptcy law respond to the fundamental issues that justify the system's existence? What "answers," if any, are there to those issues?
9. What values should bankruptcy law take into account?
10. What are the most fundamental bases of each author's disagreement with the other?
11. What aspect of each author's analysis do you find most telling? Most dubious?
12. Who wins? Why? And, finally—does it matter?

Elizabeth Warren
Bankruptcy Policy
54 U. CHI. L. REV. 775 (1987)[*]

. . . [T]here is a quiet but persistent question: what function does bankruptcy serve? . . .

In order to join issue more clearly and to narrow the focus of the debate somewhat, Professor Baird and I have agreed to debate the basis of bankruptcy policy in the context of business bankruptcies. While we both believe that the principles we discuss have significance in a consumer setting as well, we recognize that additional issues should be a part of a discussion about consumer bankruptcy policy and that those issues would make the discussion even more complex.

Professor Baird and I hold very different views of the purpose bankruptcy law serves. I see bankruptcy as an attempt to reckon with a debtor's multiple defaults and to distribute the consequences among a number of different actors. Bankruptcy encompasses a number of competing—and sometimes conflicting—values in this distribution. As I see it, no one value dominates, so that bankruptcy policy becomes a composite of factors that bear on a better answer to the question, "How shall the losses be distributed?"

By contrast, Baird has developed a coherent, unified view of bankruptcy that revolves around a single economic construct. According to Baird, the only goal of bankruptcy is to enhance the collection efforts of creditors with state-defined property rights. He explains that all bankruptcy laws are to be tested by a single measure: whether they enhance or diminish the creditors' collective ben-

---

efits. With that construct, Baird purports to answer a host of wide-ranging questions and translate his policy into specific statutory recommendations.

As Baird and I begin this debate, I am acutely aware that we disagree not only about what bankruptcy policy should be, but also about how that policy should be derived. Baird begins with hypothetical behavior and ends with firmly fixed answers. I begin with a historical observation about legal structures, I surmise the concerns of the drafters, and I end only with tentative conclusions and more complex questions. Baird presumes that there can be a simple answer to explain all of bankruptcy, and that the relationship between statutory law and modification of the behavior of debtors and creditors is known and can be predicted in new circumstances. I see bankruptcy as a more complex and ultimately less confined process than does Baird. . . .

I. The Central Policy Justification of Bankruptcy: Coping with Default in an Integrated System

A. Default and Contract Enforcement

The debtor-creditor system is itself part of a larger, integrated order of public enforcement of promises between individuals. An analysis of promise enforcement should begin with contract law—the laws enforcing private promises—and come full circle with bankruptcy law—the laws sanctioning default on private promises. Each element of this system balances against the other. . . .

A contract is not a legally enforceable obligation to do a promised thing. . . . [A] contract requires a party to do the thing promised or to pay the money equivalent *or* to discharge the promise through the bankruptcy system. That is a positive description—a statement of the law as it is, with contract enforcement and bankruptcy default. I am willing to argue that it is also a normative description—a statement of precisely what the law should do to create a coherent system of contract enforcement. . . .

[I]t is useful to pause occasionally to reflect that a system of enforceable promises necessarily involves an escape valve—a way to avoid the enforcement of those promises when sufficiently compelling circumstances arise. . . .

Default—or nonpayment—of debt has long been an essential feature of a system of promise enforcement. Centuries before bankruptcy law became an integrated part of the collection scheme, default existed. Biblical jubilees, medieval English debtor sanctuaries, and poorhouses are evidence of society's past attempts to balance rightful demands for payment with some possibility of escape. When organized forgiveness has been unavailing, debtors have devised their own nonpayment plans. Debtors have been known to flee the jurisdiction, to threaten their creditors, or—as an extreme measure—to die. Even today, with corporate debtors and risk-spreading creditors, a significant feature of the debt collection system is the possibility of escape from payment through a variety of maneuvers, both legal and extralegal. Anyone who ever extends credit faces the possibility that repayment will not be forthcoming. . . .

B. Default and the Collection System

The current debt collection system has two primary responses to a debtor's default: state collection law and federal bankruptcy law. When discussing the two collection schemes, it is important to bear in mind that property and contract rights are not synonymous with collection rights. Bankruptcy is only a collection scheme; it necessarily depends on other legal rules for the determination of substantive rights underlying bankruptcy claims. . . . Similarly, state collection law is different from the underlying substantive law. . . . The state system and the bankruptcy system are both only collection systems.

The real issue . . . is whether the state collection and distribution scheme presumptively should be the federal scheme. That bankruptcy builds on state substantive law does not require it to build on state collection law.

It would, of course, be possible to create a single, fully integrated debt collection scheme rather than the separate state and federal schemes now in effect. But even a unified scheme would have to consider two prototypes of default: first, the single default where only one creditor complains about repayment and the remaining creditors are evidently (even if only temporarily) content with their repayment prospects; and second, the debtor's widespread default and collapse in which every creditor's prospects for repayment are sharply diminished. . . . [T]he policy issues involved in the two exemplary circumstances differ importantly, and they must be addressed separately whether they are part of one collection system or two.

The current debt collection system treats these issues in different fora: state collection laws cope with a wide spectrum of limited defaults, while the bankruptcy scheme concentrates on default in the context of the debtor's imminent collapse. . . . The different factual contexts change the focus of the policymaking decisions of state collection law and bankruptcy.

C. Default and State Collection Law

A central purpose of state debt collection law is to provide a means for collection of a single unpaid debt. State collection law swings into action on the complaint of a single creditor, and it provides that creditor an avenue to pursue payment of the obligation owed to it. In enforcing the rights of one creditor, state collection law does not address the possible consequence that the collection will render the debtor unable to pay its remaining creditors. . . .

. . . [P]aying one creditor may affect the debtor's ability to repay other creditors. In the race of the diligent, the slower creditor always runs the risk that by the time it arrives, the assets will be depleted. . . . Article 9 of the Uniform Commercial Code (UCC) and the state law of liens create priority arrangements that permit a creditor to isolate certain property and to ensure that it will be used to pay that creditor before it is sold or seized to profit anyone else. These state law priority systems create what sometimes turn out to be effective rank-orderings of collection rights.

In some cases, then, state collection laws will resolve the relative collection rights of parties when a debtor collapses. But it does not follow that the state system is well-suited to the circumstances of debtor collapse. I submit that the state law system is *not* well-suited to those circumstances precisely because it necessarily must consider too broad a range of possible debtor-creditor relationships and follow collection principles inconsistent with those raised in the circumstances of complete collapse. . . .

State collection law and bankruptcy law also differ in their central policy considerations because they rest on fundamentally different collective premises. The two systems make very different adjustments for the survival of creditors' unpaid claims. . . . [I]t is worth noting that the premise of state law rank-ordering is that no claim is extinguished. Nothing in state law discharges the lawful claim of a creditor who is unable to collect. . . .

To structure collection rules and priorities in the context of inextinguishable claims is to create one kind of system. To graft that set of collection rules and priorities onto a system that discharges debt is to create a very different collection system. . . .

D. Default and Bankruptcy

By contrast with state law, which sees only one default, bankruptcy begins with a presumption of default on every obligation the debtor owes. . . . Bankruptcy law aims first to conserve and divide an estate that cannot meet all its obligations, and second to terminate the rights of unpaid creditors. Unlike state law, which considers innumerable circumstances of default, bankruptcy law is sharply focused on the consequences of a debtor's imminent collapse.

The difference from state collection law is fundamental. Bankruptcy disputes do not share the debtor-versus-creditor orientation of state collection law. In bankruptcy, with an inadequate pie to divide and the looming discharge of unpaid debts, the disputes center on who is entitled to shares of the debtor's assets and how these shares are to be divided. Distribution among creditors is not incidental to other concerns; it is the center of the bankruptcy scheme. Accordingly, bankruptcy disputes are better characterized as creditor-versus-creditor, with competing creditors struggling to push the losses of default onto others. . . . These are choices about distribution and redistribution, and they are not controlled by state law. . . .

Congress intended bankruptcy law to address concerns broader than the immediate problems of debtors and their identified creditors; they indicate clear recognition of the larger implications of a debtor's widespread default and the consequences of permitting a few creditors to force a business to close. These comments are also a reminder that, while the broader effects of business failure can be elusive to measure, they are nonetheless very real. Congress—whether out of a crass concern about reelection or a superior view of the deeper social implications of business failure in a highly integrated society—accepted the idea that bankruptcy serves to protect interests that have no other protection . . ., regardless of whether they have rights recognized at state law.

E. Distributive Rationales in Bankruptcy

By definition, the distributional issues arising in bankruptcy involve costs to some and benefits to others. Enforcing the state law collection rights of secured creditors often comes at the cost of defeating the state law collection rights of unsecured creditors whose claims are discharged without payment. A priority payment to one unsecured creditor necessarily leaves less for the remaining creditors. . . .

It might be reasonable to ask about the legitimacy of forcing losses on those with lawful expectations of repayment. The difficulty with this question, however, is that it posits that bankruptcy is the "cause" of the cost. Bankruptcy is not the cause of the cost—it is merely the distributor of the cost. The cost of default is occasioned by the debtor's inability to repay.

Without a bankruptcy system, someone would still bear the costs of default. . . . But speculation on what would happen at state law is nothing more than the substitution of a different distributional scheme—one created indirectly by focus on the collection of a single debt rather than one created deliberately with an overriding attention to widespread default.

Even if there were no legal scheme to distribute the costs of default, the losses would be distributed by some method. The distribution of losses might be determined by creditor speed (who first backs up to the warehouse with big trucks) or strength (who can carry away the most while others look on) or by debtor favoritism (who gets the first call when the debtor decides to give up). Indeed, outside bankruptcy, it is not clear as an empirical matter whether losses are distributed according to the state law scheme or according to creditor strength, debtor favoritism, or some other factor. But the point is that the costs must be distributed in some manner. Bankruptcy is simply a federal scheme designed to distribute the costs among those at risk.

On what basis does bankruptcy law distribute these costs? . . .

1.   *Relative ability to bear the costs of default.* . . .
2.   *Incentive effects on pre-bankruptcy transactions.* . . .
3.   *Similarities among creditors.* . . .
4.   *Owners bear the loss when a business fails.* . . .
5.   *Benefit to the bankruptcy estate.* . . .

F. Sorting Cases in a Dual System

A process such as bankruptcy, designed to consider the rights of more than two parties and to distribute the losses occasioned by the debtor's failure, is necessarily expensive. It requires more detailed factual inquiries into both the circumstances of the debtor and the conflicting claims of many creditors than does state collection law. The expense of this process is justified by a normative conclusion that spreading the losses of default by an organized scheme, developed by Congress and supervised by the courts, is superior to an unmonitored distribution by powerful creditors or self-interested debtors.

No law requires that firms defaulting on all their obligations do so only in bankruptcy. Instead, the scheme permits an efficient self-selection by the affected parties. The cheaper, less comprehensive state law system operates until a party can show that the bankruptcy system is required. . . . But once a party appropriately petitions for bankruptcy, the resolution is in bankruptcy without further dispute. . . .

G. Preliminary Conclusions: A Premise That Raises More Questions

. . . [I]t may be more valuable to examine what I have not done. I have not offered a single-rationale policy that compels solutions in particular cases. I have not given any answers to specific statutory issues. I have only identified normative considerations that may drive legislative and judicial decisions.

For a hard-nosed commercial lawyer (once again, I aspire to be among the chosen), the obvious question is: what good is it to identify the premises of bankruptcy law if they won't yield any specific answers? Aside from the fact that debating these issues is good, clean fun, what does it accomplish?

Even if it does not compel specific answers to hard questions, identifying the premise of bankruptcy has a very real impact on how those questions are answered. If the central policy justification is nothing more than a single economic construct, specific conclusions with systemwide impact follow neatly from an abstract principle. But if the justification for bankruptcy is also distributional, the relevant inquiry is necessarily larger: what are the values to be protected in the distributional scheme, and is the implementation scheme effective? The questions become more difficult, and the answers, while less certain, take into account many more of the considerations important to a reasonable decision.

A policy that focuses on the values to be protected in a bankruptcy distribution scheme and on the effective implementation of these values assists the decision-making process even if it does not dictate specific answers. This approach illuminates the critical questions. . . .

Bankruptcy policy has always rested on an unarticulated blend of empirical assumptions and normative conclusions. The approach I describe denies that the uncomfortable normative issues can be avoided by playing a narrow game of logic. My approach also exposes and highlights the empirical assumptions underlying specific bankruptcy policy decisions. . . .

The difficulty of the process does not mean that the considerations amount to fuzzy "do equity" preachments of the hopelessly confused, who leave good results to good people and assume that ideas and analysis have no content. Instead, the questions are tough and specific. The distributional premise of bankruptcy is implemented through a difficult and complex tapestry of empirical presumptions interwoven with normative concerns, some of which I have tried to identify here. The process yields better, but never complete, answers to specific bankruptcy questions. There are easier solutions and easier solutions are seductive. A focus on the difficulty of the appropriate questions helps stiffen the spine against easy answers and makes the task of imperfect search for the illusive answer a little more tolerable.

II. Baird's Approach: Collectivism Alone

Professor Baird's view of the bankruptcy world is much neater than mine. He explains that there is a single justification for bankruptcy: enhancing the collective return to the creditors. He also explains that there is only one interest to be protected: the interest of those "who, outside of bankruptcy, have property rights in the assets of the firm filing a petition." Baird has rejected the notion that any values other than collectivism may be important in fashioning bankruptcy policy. . . .

Baird also considers the role of other distributional issues in bankruptcy and concludes that they should play none. . . . Thus, the distributional issues involved in determining the creditors' legal pecking order are, according to Baird, the same whether the debtor is in default on a single obligation or in a state of complete collapse.

Having dispensed with any other policy considerations, Baird is ready to turn to his single justification for bankruptcy: enhancing the collective return for creditors who have identified property rights. Here Baird purports to use only careful logic to answer some of the most intractable bankruptcy problems, all the while avoiding any discussion of the distributional consequences of his work. The difficulty with Baird's approach is that collectivism alone won't get him where he is going. He necessarily uses—even if he does not discuss—distributional principles. Moreover, Baird endorses the wholesale use of the state law distributional scheme, but he does not defend the distributional rationale of that scheme, nor does he address the possibility that the state scheme was designed to resolve questions significantly different from those to which he applies it.

Baird is engaged in a game of pulling rabbits from other hats. . . . Baird purports to avoid distributional concerns—and the attendant normative and empirical issues—by discussing only the "neutral" principle of collectivism. I believe Baird only diverts the debate from the central issues.

A. Collectivism: The Test that Isn't

Collectivism provides a useful way to examine some bankruptcy problems. Baird shows how the need for collectivism can explain why the bankruptcy system substitutes a single, lower-cost action for expensive, multiple individual ones. . . .

My dispute with Baird centers instead upon his attempts to use collectivism not only to explain significant features of the bankruptcy system, but also to justify the entire system and to provide answers to specific, complex questions. . . .

Ultimately Baird's argument is not one of collectivism so much as one of economic rationality: the aim of bankruptcy policy is to make certain that assets go to their highest-valued use. Baird is at pains to avoid the economic lingo, but he cannot escape the conclusion that the only value he protects is economic wealth maximization for the bankrupt estate. As Baird has used it . . ., collectivism is nothing but a veil to conceal his relentless push for single-value economic rationality, an excuse to impose a distributional scheme without justifying it, and, incidentally, a way to work in a damn good deal for secured creditors. By focusing on an economic rationale—without defending this exclusive focus—Baird eliminates without discussion or proof any other values that may be served by bankruptcy.

Even if that single value were accepted, Baird isn't home free. He quietly works distributional elements into his economic example, all the while denying a distributional consequence. . . . [I]t is simply not possible to avoid a distributional decision. To destroy the special, pre-bankruptcy rights of some creditors is to make a distributional decision. To enforce those rights is to make a different distributional decision. Baird does not want to discuss distributional objectives, but he cannot avoid them by pretending they are not there. . . .

Ultimately, Baird rounds out collectivism with additional objectives. . . . The implications of strategic planning pose yet another debate Baird and I might have, but my point here is made: collectivism alone doesn't go so far as Baird always claims. He needs to incorporate other values into his tight, "neutral" scheme in order to justify adoption of a specific plan. . . .

C. Collectivism and State Law

In discussing bankruptcy policy, Baird assumes away the very thing I think we should discuss: how to distribute the losses occasioned by the debtor's widespread default. It is important to understand exactly how he avoids this central issue. To Baird, distributional issues are the same in and out of bankruptcy. Baird seems to believe that this presumption not only permits him to support a single-issue bankruptcy policy, but that it also permits him to ignore any distributional consequences of the policies he embraces. By announcing that he is merely enforcing nonbankruptcy rights, and declaring, in effect, that he is changing nothing, Baird seeks to build a presumption into bankruptcy—a presumption that it will always follow the state-determined collection scheme—without ever defending that scheme. State law, as Baird explains it, is merely "our baseline," from which any bankruptcy "modification" must be justified.

Baird cannot assert that he is offering no distributional scheme simply because he accepts the scheme that exists in state collection law. Any scheme distributes, whether Baird chooses to discuss it or not. If he proposes to adopt state collection law as the baseline for federal bankruptcy, he is obligated to offer some rationale for this choice and to make some examination of the consequences of using state distribution within the very specialized context of bankruptcy.

Baird ignores the fact that the way state collection law operates outside of bankruptcy is fundamentally different from the way it operates when grafted onto a bankruptcy system. There is in this respect a delicious irony in Baird's relentless defense of the secured creditor's demand for its "nonbankruptcy rights." At state law, the secured creditor was promised repossession rights if the debtor defaulted on its loan obligations. But, as anyone who has practiced a little collections law will readily acknowledge, there is many a slip twixt default and cash from the sale of collateral. . . .

Life is no bed of roses for the secured creditor drawn into a bankruptcy: the bankrupt debtor may still resist payment, and for some creditors the delays of bankruptcy simply follow the delays of the state court process. But a few things may improve in bankruptcy. In one stroke, all the lawsuits are in a single forum. The bankruptcy court, unlike many state courts, recognizes the importance of time and the likelihood that the debtor will use court processes for delay. Several critical bankruptcy rules require that the court act quickly, often within thirty days. . . . The creditor gets nationwide service of process regardless of where the collateral is located. The court monitors the debtor's behavior, restricting the debtor's control over the disposition of assets. No other creditor may slip away with the debtor's assets. . . . And, perhaps most importantly for the secured creditor, the debtor in bankruptcy is the one that didn't close up in the middle of the night, shipping out its assets in a rented truck.

Without giving up any of these benefits, the creditor whose debtor has filed bankruptcy pleads unblushingly that it "just wants what was promised at state law." The secured creditors want all the court supervision and control, national jurisdiction, protection against other creditors, and speedy trials of bankruptcy. Then they want the foreclosure rights (or the equivalent interest value) of state law. Baird may find that cry moving; I find it disingenuous.

In short, once the debtor is in bankruptcy, no one gets "just what was promised at state law"— neither secured nor unsecured creditors. The sort of "forum shopping" Baird claims he wants to avoid may lead secured creditors as well as unsecured creditors to conclude that bankruptcy is a better deal than state collection proceedings. With its debtor in bankruptcy, every creditor gets something more by way of control over the debtor and the competing creditors, and something less by way of curtailed collection rights. The secured creditor can claim it has given up too much, and we can debate that issue. But the simple claim that the secured creditor wants only what it had at state law adds nothing to the debate. Once the debtor is in bankruptcy, it is no longer possible to give any party to the dispute its state law rights.

Whether the "baseline" for creditor rights in bankruptcy is state collection law or some other collection scheme, once the dispute enters the federal bankruptcy forum changes are made and a new collection system is created. . . . The distributional issues of bankruptcy must be resolved at every step in determining bankruptcy policy. There is no way to escape them.

My view is that the central job of bankruptcy is to apportion the losses of the debtor's default, and that a variety of factors impinge on the difficult policy decision of where to let those losses fall.

... [L]et's not hammer out the appropriate system balances in a debate by proxy over collectivism.
. . .

Conclusion

I have offered a dirty, complex, elastic, interconnected view of bankruptcy from which I can neither predict outcomes nor even necessarily fully articulate all the factors relevant to a policy decision. Baird has offered a rational, clean approach in which he claims few factors are relevant and solitary conclusions are always compelled. Baird's view of bankruptcy is more chic than mine, but I believe my view is more realistic and more likely to yield useful analysis.

Baird and I disagree about the fundamental purpose of bankruptcy law. But the differences Baird and I nurture run deeper. Baird believes in a method of policymaking that will ineluctably yield a single right answer. I believe in an approach that only asks better questions, focuses on better evidence, yields closer approximations, and offers increasingly better, but still tentative, answers.
. . .

The attractions of an abstract economic analysis such as Baird's are many. A simple economic analysis of bankruptcy is clear, straightforward, and always promises to yield firm answers to hard questions. . . . The economic analysis Baird practices is seductive.

Mine is not an entertaining (or, I suspect, popular) position for an academic. I cannot claim that bankruptcy, at its heart, is an intellectual construct or that I can reason to a meaningful conclusion by doing nothing more than thinking hard about logical consequences derived from a handful of untested assumptions. I would like to endorse something that requires only library time and yellow legal pads to uncover ideal solutions to legal problems. The trouble is that I can't do it.

But I do not think Baird can do it either. The certainty of Baird's position is a fiction. Although he purports to avoid difficult normative questions and he ignores empirical issues, Baird's conclusions are nonetheless driven by normative values and empirical assumptions. By hiding these values and assumptions, Baird simply makes the debate a shadow game that offers little real illumination.

Ultimately, I disagree not so much with what Baird argues as with how he argues. . . . But Baird uses his economic analysis to limit the inquiry—and there is the final rub.

. . . Baird begins with an artificial construct of behavior, applies a few immutable principles, and jumps directly to specific statutory recommendations. Nowhere is there room to consider other factors that should be part of the decision-making process, or to make empirical observations that will indicate whether the model conforms sufficiently to reality to be useful. If Baird wants to add his questions to all the others that should be considered in making distributional decisions, then I will readily endorse his work. But so long as he explains his analysis in terms of the sole issue involved, the single question to be answered, and the only parties to be protected, I contend that his approach gives answers that are both illusory and dangerous.

I readily admit that I do not offer a single rule that will resolve all disputes. Instead, I call attention to the difficult distributional issues in bankruptcy, and I identify factors that influence how those distributional issues are resolved. Perhaps more importantly, I advocate a process of framing and refining questions, considering both their normative and empirical elements, to give content to the bankruptcy debate. Slick economic analyses give quick answers, but only by sliding past the troublesome issues that pervade the resolution of real problems.

Baird's single, unified theory of bankruptcy is more fun for academic games than is a complex view of bankruptcy that constantly reminds the player how little she knows about the empirical assumptions that underlie the game or whether other elusive values influence the balance among competing interests. His theory also runs an extraordinary risk of providing answers that are quite sensible within a confined, abstract scheme but that will not work in a complex reality. If the only test for acceptance of a specific statutory rule of law is whether the rule conforms to a logical—but possibly incomplete—concept, then grievous mistakes will go unchecked.

And in this corner . . .

Douglas G. Baird
Loss Distribution, Forum Shopping, and Bankruptcy: A Reply to Warren
54 U. CHI. L. REV. 815 (1987)*

Elizabeth Warren has presented a view of bankruptcy that, while rarely as well articulated, is widely shared. . . .

Warren's attack on the theory of bankruptcy that I have developed with Thomas Jackson goes to methodology. Jackson and I claim that we can isolate bankruptcy issues . . . from the question of how losses should be borne in the event that a firm fails. . . . Warren insists that we cannot do this. The issue, it must be noted, is not *how* losses from a firm failure should be distributed, but whether this question (however hard it may be to answer) is a question of the law generally (as Jackson and I would argue) or one peculiar to bankruptcy law (as Warren would argue). . . .

I. The Traditional View of Bankruptcy Policy

Warren admits that her own view of bankruptcy policy is "dirty, complex, elastic, [and] interconnected." But like most traditional views of bankruptcy policy, it rests on a number of fairly simple propositions: (1) bankruptcy law has a special role to play in determining how losses from a business failure should be borne; (2) creditors as well as others may sometimes be required to give up some of their ultimate rights to the assets of the firm so that the firm will have a better chance of surviving; (3) entrusting a bankruptcy judge with equitable discretion is a useful and unobjectionable way to balance the conflicting and competing interests of the parties; and (4) creditors in bankruptcy have no cause to complain when they lose some rights they had outside of bankruptcy, because bankruptcy is an entirely new game that deals with different kinds of problems. These propositions sound innocuous enough, but none of them can withstand close scrutiny, and adhering to them invites analysis that is unfocused and misguided.

Warren asserts that the law must distribute losses that flow from a business failure and that distributing such losses should be the central concern of bankruptcy law. The second observation, however, does not follow from the first. As long as many firms close or fail outside of bankruptcy, treating the question of how to distribute the losses that flow from a business failure as a bankruptcy question ignores much of the problem and creates perverse incentives. . . .

Warren thinks that the benefits of bankruptcy justify additional burdens on creditors. But the issue is not whether the burdens on creditors in bankruptcy are just, but whether the burdens should exist only in bankruptcy. . . . [T]axing creditors differently depending on which enforcement mechanism they use invites troublesome forum shopping. But Warren does not take the problem of forum shopping seriously. . . .

Warren, however, never explains the link that she and many others see between multiple default and firm failure; she never explains why the presence of a dispute among creditors requires a special set of rules governing the distribution of losses from the closing or failure of a firm.

Warren and others seem to think that a glance at history and situation sense make the link self-evident. Jackson and I, however, have made two points that should give pause to those who find it hard to put aside the lay intuition that a firm that fails is a firm that "goes bankrupt." First, we raise the problem of forum shopping. . . .

The second point is deeper. To argue that a special set of distributional concerns arises when a debtor defaults to many creditors at the same time it fails or closes is to assume a link exists between who has rights to the assets of a firm and how those assets are used. . . . Whether a firm continues to manufacture a particular product or even stays in business is an issue utterly distinct from the question of who owns the firm's assets. Thus, in a world in which all assertions of ownership rights are stayed (as they are in bankruptcy), how much a particular owner gets should have *nothing* to do with how a firm's assets are used or whether it stays in business. . . .

II. Loss Distribution and Nonbankruptcy Priority Rules

My basic disagreement with Warren is not with the distributional schemes she embraces, but with whether a single set of rules should distribute losses that flow from a business failure. Many laws, from UCC Article 9 to ERISA, concern themselves with distributing such losses. Nonbankruptcy priority rules distribute losses and will continue to do so regardless of whether a special set of bankruptcy priority rules exists. A coherent approach to the question of how losses from failed firms should be distributed cannot ignore the distributional effects many legal rules have on firms that are not in bankruptcy. Legal rights should turn as little as possible on the forum in which one person or another seeks to vindicate them. Whenever we must have a legal rule to distribute losses in bankruptcy, we must also have a legal rule that distributes the same loss outside of bankruptcy. All Jackson and I advocate is that these two rules be the same. . . .

To say that bankruptcy and nonbankruptcy priorities should be the same does not say anything about what those priorities should be. Despite Warren's assertions to the contrary, Jackson and I in our work on bankruptcy do not say who should bear the loss when a firm fails; we do not conceive this as a bankruptcy question. In our work on bankruptcy, we have talked only about the issues that remain after one decides how losses should be distributed because we regard only these issues as distinct *bankruptcy* issues. To respond to us in a normative debate about bankruptcy policy, Warren has to challenge our assertion that fixing priorities among creditors is not a bankruptcy problem. . . . Even if Warren has some reason for rejecting the idea of parity, she must still explain why the problem of forum shopping is unimportant. . . .

III. Bankruptcy and the Problem of Forum Shopping

As a definitional matter, one can make bankruptcy mean anything at all. But my notion of bankruptcy law is, I think, largely uncontroversial. As far as corporations are concerned, bankruptcy law is a procedure in which the actions of those with rights to the assets of a firm are stayed and the affairs of the firm are sorted out in an orderly way. Two characteristics of this procedure are crucial for present purposes: (1) it is an alternative avenue for vindicating legal rights, in the sense that those with rights to the debtor's assets could, in the absence of the stay, vindicate them elsewhere (albeit perhaps less effectively); and (2) it involves the rights of more than a single player.

The challenge facing anyone who wants to write about bankruptcy policy is to explain why a distinct bankruptcy law exists at all. Introducing multiple avenues of enforcement is costly. To say that existing bankruptcy law does good hardly suffices. Other things being equal, one would want to transplant what good things are done in bankruptcy to ordinary avenues of rights enforcement and do away with bankruptcy law. . . .

A. The Costs of Forum Shopping

. . . We live in a world in which there are multiple avenues of enforcement for every substantive right. One avenue is provided under ordinary rules of debt collection; another, under the aegis of bankruptcy law. To justify this state of affairs, one must explain why more than one avenue of enforcement is called for. An additional avenue of enforcement creates special costs and, accordingly, deserves close scrutiny. . . . The differences in the avenues should stem from the reason for having separate avenues and not from anything else.

It is possible to criticize worlds with multiple avenues of enforcement without taking a position on the wisdom of the substantive rights of any of the players. . . .

B. Priority Rules and Forum Shopping

I do not think that I have said anything terribly controversial. There is no virtue in giving parties an incentive to engage in forum shopping for its own sake. Yet the premise upon which Jackson and I have built our theory of bankruptcy law is not much more complicated than that. Bankruptcy law creates another avenue of enforcement. It represents a parallel system of debt collection. . . .

When we talk about bankruptcy policy, Jackson and I do treat nonbankruptcy rules as a baseline; but we do this only because, by and large, existing bankruptcy law does not set substantive rights and its procedural rights can be understood only against the background of nonbankruptcy procedural rights. . . .

. . . Jackson and I have asked *why* a parallel debt collection system is desirable at all. The answer, we assert, is the collective action problem. But we then suggest that *this* reason for a second avenue of enforcement provides no reason for reassessing relative entitlements. Workers should not have a different place in line simply because someone has been able to start a bankruptcy proceeding. All that Jackson and I require is that the differences in the two avenues follow from the reasons for having the two avenues in the first place. We have no objection to differences in multiple avenues of enforcement. We object only to *unnecessary* differences. . . .

IV. "Rehabilitation," Noncognizable Injuries, and Bankruptcy Policy

Warren suggests that bankruptcy law should be designed to keep businesses from closing even when those with legally cognizable interests in the business want it to close. She does not, however, explain why special rules in bankruptcy are necessary to achieve this goal. One could, for example, have a federal statute that prevented any business from ceasing operations without making a showing in court that the business was unprofitable, destined to fail, or whatever. One cannot say that bankruptcy is necessary to protect those without legally cognizable interests without first answering the question of why these individuals cannot be given such interests. Similarly, one should not assert that bankruptcy law is necessary to prevent the owners of firms from taking actions that injure third parties without explaining why some other kind of legal rule cannot prevent these injuries without encouraging forum shopping.

The law by omission or commission affects who bears the losses from a failed business, but one must explain why placing the solution in bankruptcy law is the preferred course of action. Business "failure" is not necessarily connected with default. . . .

As I noted earlier, one should not link default and bankruptcy. Default is not necessarily connected with a collective action problem. Indeed, it is because default does not *always* raise a collective problem that there are two avenues of enforcement: the existence of bankruptcy's avenue of enforcement springs from the collective action problem. . . .

The challenge of entering a normative debate about bankruptcy policy is to isolate what is distinctive about bankruptcy. If one does not, one simply talks about social policy generally.

V. Secured Creditors in Bankruptcy

Few would advocate trimming back the rights of secured creditors outside of bankruptcy merely by asserting that misery loves company. Opponents of secured credit would feel obliged to discuss what the benefits and costs of secured credit were. . . . But when the virtues and vices of secured credit are mixed with any number of other issues in bankruptcy, vague notions about equity can replace hard thinking. . . .

Whatever adjustments should be made to the rights of secured creditors should be made outside of bankruptcy law. In bankruptcy, whatever rights the secured creditors have under nonbankruptcy law should be respected. The idea is not to give them a *good* deal, but rather to approximate the *same* deal that they had outside of bankruptcy so that no one has an incentive to begin a bankruptcy proceeding simply because its distributional rule is different. For purposes of this debate, I can stipulate to any set of rights for secured creditors Warren chooses—including the abolition of priority rights for secured creditors altogether. Warren must do more than assert that Jackson and I look too kindly on secured creditors. She must show why giving secured creditors a *different* deal in bankruptcy is a good idea, given the costs of forum shopping. Warren must explain why she thinks that for any level of priority protection accorded secured creditors outside of bankruptcy, the appropriate level in bankruptcy is something less. . . .

Conclusion

The belief that nonbankruptcy law does not take sufficient account of many whose interests deserve the protection of the law in hard times colors the view Warren and many others have of bankruptcy policy. Legal rights, however, are formed (for better or for worse) with bad times in mind. Legal rights matter least when times are good. If a legal rule is wrong or unjust, it must be changed. The incantation of "bankruptcy policy" will not make it disappear. Hard times are themselves not invariably or even typically associated with default, let alone bankruptcy. That our laws seem to leave too many unprotected may be a telling criticism of our lawmakers, our laws, and our society, but not of our Bankruptcy Code.

The world is a messy and complicated place, where justice is often hard to find. But it does not follow that bankruptcy policy should be vague and mysterious and that nothing more can be said other than that bankruptcy judges have a general mandate to do equity, but not too much equity. Bankruptcy law has its own contours and the key to understanding it lies in recognizing its limitations. Warren and I disagree so dramatically in our view of bankruptcy law not because of politics or ideology. Much of what she would like to see as a part of bankruptcy are things I would like to see as part of our substantive law more generally. We differ because we approach the job of understanding and reforming the law in opposing ways. I believe that one can talk intelligently about bankruptcy without at the same time developing an all-encompassing view of social policy.

The theory of bankruptcy law that Jackson and I have developed is an inviting target. It is not so vague that it can never be right or wrong. It generates falsifiable hypotheses. But Warren has not faced our theory squarely. Warren must do more than assert that having a good bankruptcy judge balance everything is preferable to a bankruptcy law built on the theory Jackson and I have developed. Such an assertion does not focus on our theory or even on bankruptcy. It applies equally to any legal theory that suggests that rules are sometimes preferable to vaguely restrained judicial discretion. One cannot begin to understand the existing state of affairs or comprehend the possibility of reform without first searching for the principles that underlie the law. A panegyric on the virtues of equitable jurisprudence is neither a theory nor an adequate substitute for a theory.

Revising the "Bargain": Risk Sharing

Just a few years after pronouncing the "creditors' bargain" theory, Professor Jackson, writing with his then fellow colleague at the University of Virginia, Professor Robert Scott, modified (or "enhanced") his theory. The updated Jacksonian theory embraced a somewhat broader view of bankruptcy policy and theory, recognizing the importance of the sharing of risk between interested parties. As you read the following article, consider (1) how the risk-sharing theory differs from the pure creditors' bargain and (2) how it is similar. Which (if either) is more persuasive? Does the "expansion" of the creditors' bargain undermine the very premise of the model? Would it be fair to conclude that by expanding the model Jackson has tacitly acknowledged much of Carlson and Warren's arguments?

Following the Jackson and Scott article is an article by Professor Barry Adler, *Bankruptcy and Risk Allocation,* in which he challenges their vision of risk sharing. Adler's attack is all the more intriguing because he does not reject the basic premise that economic analysis can be a useful tool to dissect bankruptcy theory. Professor Adler has written many thoughtful articles on bankruptcy theory, notably including *Finance's Theoretical Divide and the Proper Role of Insolvency Rules*, 68 S. CAL. L. REV. 401 (1994). In this article, what are Adler's principal bases for rejecting Jackson's and Scott's risk-sharing theory? Do you agree?

For a more complete assessment of risk sharing and the expanded creditors' bargain model, the careful reader also should examine Professor Carlson's work, *Bankruptcy Theory and the Creditors' Bargain*, 61 U. CIN. L. REV. 453 (1992), as well as Mark Roe, *Commentary on "On the Nature of Bankruptcy": Bankruptcy, Priority, and Economics*, 75 VA. L. REV. 219 (1989), and Theodore Eisenberg, *Commentary on "On the Nature of Bankruptcy": Bankruptcy and Bargaining,* 75 VA. L. REV. 205 (1989).

Thomas H. Jackson & Robert E. Scott
On the Nature of Bankruptcy:
An Essay on Bankruptcy Sharing and the Creditors' Bargain
75 VA. L. REV. 155 (1989)[*]

. . . One of us has developed over the past several years a conceptual paradigm, based on a hypothetical bargain among creditors, as a normative criterion for evaluating the bankruptcy system. The cornerstone of the creditors' bargain is the normative claim that prebankruptcy entitlements should be impaired in bankruptcy only when necessary to maximize net asset distributions to the creditors as a group and never to accomplish purely distributional goals.

The strength of the creditors' bargain conceptualization is also its limitation. The hypothetical bargain metaphor focuses on the key bankruptcy objective of maximizing the welfare of the group though collectivization. This single-minded focus on maximizing group welfare helps to identify the underlying patterns in what appear to be unrelated aspects of the bankruptcy process. It also implies that other normative goals should be seen as competing costs of the collectivization process. Yet this

---

claim uncovers a further puzzle. Despite the centrality of the maximization norm, persistent and systematic redistributional impulses are apparent in bankruptcy. Is redistribution in bankruptcy simply attributable to random errors or misperceptions by courts and legislators? Or are other forces present in the bankruptcy process as well?

In this Article we undertake to examine the "other forces" that may be at work in bankruptcy. Many bankruptcy rules require sharing of assets with other creditors, shareholders, and third parties. Too often these distributional effects are grouped together under general references to equity, wealth redistribution, or appeals to communitarian values. These labels are unhelpful. They disguise the fact, for instance, that the justification and impact of consensual risk sharing among creditors is entirely different in character from the rationale for using bankruptcy to redistribute wealth to nonconsensual third parties. Understanding these diverse effects requires, therefore, a method of discriminating among the different motivations that impel redistributions in bankruptcy.

In Part I, we reconstruct and embellish the original creditors' bargain model by relaxing several of the implicit assumptions underlying the ex ante bargain. Within this framework, we examine more precisely the contours of the original creditors' bargain to see if any purportedly redistributional concerns of bankruptcy law reflect a part of the ex ante agreement. To the extent that they do, it is then incorrect to say as a matter of theory that there is a conflict between bankruptcy's distributional goals and the creditors' bargain.

This expanded framework illuminates an important distributional principle that underlies a richer version of the creditors' bargain. Under this principle, all participants share (at least in part) the risks of business failure attributable to certain "common disasters." We argue that those distributional effects premised on the anticipation of these common disasters would be explicitly included in an ex ante bargain, so long as the costs of implementation did not outweigh the benefits in enhancing the creditors' wealth. . . .

The theoretical appeal of the expanded model is dampened, however, by its significant limitations once implementation costs are reintroduced. . . . [T]he impulse for redistribution in bankruptcy seems to founder on an inability of the system to distinguish between favored and disfavored distributions. Indeed, the problem is basic. Absent a refined selection mechanism that permits such distinctions, distributional considerations that differ from those used outside of bankruptcy will inevitably impair the realization of bankruptcy's collective goals.

We conclude, therefore, that to the extent that the bankruptcy process embraces diverse distributional goals, it inevitably generates significant offsetting costs, even when those goals are consistent with implementing a common disaster component in the ex ante bargain. . . . Whether the benefits of reflecting the expanded bargain model in the rules of bankruptcy are worth the implementation costs ultimately is an empirical question. That the tradeoff exists, however, invites renewed attention as well to the question of selection rules that aid in distinguishing the uses of bankruptcy that further the ex ante bargain from those that further the interests of only one group, at the expense of the whole.

I. An Expanded Model of the Creditors' Bargain

A. *Reconstructing the Creditors' Bargain*

1. *Background Assumptions and Starting Points*

A primary objective of any bankruptcy process is to regulate the inherent conflicts among different groups having separate claims against a debtor's assets and income stream. . . .

. . . Whichever course the law encourages parties to take, maximizing the total welfare of the group will necessarily be the central objective. The dilemma, however, is that the law cannot ensure that the interests of any particular group of claimants will coincide with this interest of the whole.

Thus, allocation of decisionmaking power in bankruptcy is likely to be difficult and to reflect only imperfectly the group goal, even if that group goal is easy to articulate.

2. *The Bargain Redux*

In seeking to understand how bankruptcy law implements a general objective of maximizing group welfare, one can usefully imagine "bankruptcy as a system designed to mirror the agreement one would expect the creditors to form among themselves were they to negotiate such an agreement from an ex ante position." A central premise underlying this creditors' bargain conceptualization is that a system of state law entitlements (including priorities among secured and unsecured creditors) is already in place and that parties know what their priority positions will be so long as state law continues to govern their rights. Given these background conditions, the question is whether the parties would nevertheless agree to a collective scheme of distribution, and, if so, what form would it take?
. . .

The creditors come to the bargain, then, with their individual state law entitlements intact. It is logical, therefore, to begin by assuming that insolvency is a foreseeable risk—one that will be borne individually by the various claimants. The calculation of this risk will have influenced individual creditors' decisions as to whether a security interest should be taken and, if so, on what terms. . . . The participants in the bankruptcy bargain could thus be expected to honor this relationship by maintaining the secured creditors' nonbankruptcy entitlements and by preventing redistribution in bankruptcy from secured creditors to unsecured creditors and the debtor.

This basis argument is supported by two further observations. First, unless the rules regulating bankruptcy access were perfectly drawn, the recognition that bankruptcy provides a method of distributing entitlements that differs from state law would create incentives that would motivate parties to use the bankruptcy process strategically. . . .

The second reason to believe that the parties to an ex ante bargain would preserve prebankruptcy entitlements in bankruptcy is that secured creditors would otherwise be unwilling to join in a bankruptcy process from which they derive no advantage. . . .

3. *The Problem of Distributional Effects*

This simple creditors' bargain conception focuses on maximizing group welfare through collectivization. It is concerned with distribution only insofar as bankruptcy distributions either undermine the sharing rules of the ex ante bargain or promote inefficiencies through strategic forum shopping. Yet the distinction between maximization of group welfare and distribution within the group is not so clear. Any collectivization procedure necessarily has both a redistributive and an allocative effect. In order to implement a collective system of distribution, individual creditors must be restrained from exercising entitlements that they would otherwise enjoy under state law. There will obviously be an interference with prebankruptcy *rights*; there will also, however, almost inevitably be a change in the *relative value* of those prebankruptcy rights. It is too costly to determine and respect relative values in full in a collective proceeding. . . .

B. *Bankruptcy Sharing and the Common Disaster*

A central premise of the simple creditors' bargain is that redistribution in bankruptcy is inconsistent with the maximizing objectives of the collective. Insolvency is seen as a foreseeable risk that is borne individually by the various claimants of any business enterprise. Thus, the model assumes, *inter alia,* that none of the risks of business failure will be shared among claimants of different classes, except as otherwise explicitly agreed.

As a starting point for reexamination, we focus critically on this assumption. Consider the possibility that the bankruptcy process reflects a normatively satisfactory accommodation between the objective of asset maximization and a complementary distributional norm: that all participants should share (at least in part) in the "common" risks of business failure. Common risks include those contingencies whose probabilities or effects cannot be influenced by the actions of individual parties, contingencies that are, in consequence, common to the affected group of claimants. Common risks are thus distinct from the individual or particular risks of business failure that can be attributed to a single group, such as risks arising out of incompetent or dishonest management for which the shareholders as a group are "responsible." Perhaps certain redistributions in bankruptcy can be understood as a response to the effects of such common disasters on business enterprises.

1. *Allocating Insolvency Risks Under Uncertainty*

a. *Strategies for Reducing Insolvency Risks*

The risks of business failure do not all arise from the same source, nor would claimants necessarily treat all of them in the same way. Some risks of insolvency arise from contingencies whose probabilities or effects can be influenced by the actions of particular parties or groups. In these cases, one party or another can act in a way that will alter the objective amount of risk that is created. When such precautionary actions are cost-beneficial, all parties will gain from agreement on a binary strategy of *risk control*: assigning the *entire* risk of a particular contingency to the party (or group) best able to influence the amount of the risk.

. . . Under some circumstances, parties to a creditors' bargain might also be motivated to pursue a complementary strategy: transferring risks to others who have greater tolerance for the consequences of a risk. This strategy of *risk transfer* would be sensible if various creditors attached different subjective values to the same risk.

Risk control and risk transfer are complementary, binary strategies that reduce risk by allocating the entire risk to individual parties. As such, these binary strategies fit comfortably into the original creditors' bargain conception. . . . Not all risks, however, are best borne by one group as opposed to another. Allocating the risks of insolvency is considerably more complex if the parties also consider alternative, noncomplementary strategies. One possibility is risk sharing. By sharing the risk of events that are not especially in the control of one party or another, the parties can reduce the amount of uncertainty and thus potentially reduce the cost of the risk for some if not for all. . . .

Risk-sharing agreements, however, are costly to negotiate ex ante, because the parties must settle vexing distributional questions. . . .

One strong implication follows from this analysis. We might well predict, contrary to the assumptions of the simple creditors' bargain model, that parties to a creditor's bargain would adopt a mixed strategy for bearing risk. Individualized strategies designed to reduce risk would generally be preferred, but some form of risk sharing would be adopted for those common perils that are too uncertain and interactive to make individual action meaningful.

b. *Risk Sharing as a Means of Diversifying Common Risks*

The assumption that creditors in an ex ante bargain might well include a risk-sharing component in their distribution scheme complicates, to some extent, the claim that the value of nonbankruptcy entitlements should be fully respected. . . . [I]f default or insolvency could be causally linked to a common disaster, a pro rata sharing rule would be the optimal arrangement. Thus, it can no longer be fairly assumed that the ex ante bargain would grant secured creditors 100% of the value of their security in bankruptcy, for such an outcome assumes a binary risk assignment. Moreover, it can no longer be assumed that unsecured creditors were paid to assume *all* of the risks of business failure in the initial extension of credit. This, too, assumes a binary risk assignment. . . .

. . . Begin by visualizing the risk-sharing agreement between secured and unsecured creditors as a form of prepaid insurance in which secured creditors would be paid in advance to potentially share a part of their assets in the future. Secured creditors would agree that whenever insolvency is triggered by common risks . . . they would share with unsecured creditors and equity some of the asset pool otherwise reserved to them.

. . . Once implementation costs are reintroduced into the analysis, the question recurs: How would the parties structure a risk-sharing scheme within the constraints of a broader system of individual risk bearing? Here again the relationship between bankruptcy and nonbankruptcy responses to business failure comes into sharper focus. Risk-sharing impulses are not peculiar to bankruptcy, but they may well be impossible to implement outside of bankruptcy. There are formidable operational difficulties in distinguishing common risks from those that have been assigned to individual claimants. An attempt to do so on a case-by-case basis, whether inside or outside of bankruptcy, is likely to be excessively cumbersome. Thus, the absence of contractual mechanisms to do this sorting does not imply that the sorting is undesirable as a matter of theory. A prepaid insurance scheme that effects a partial across the board reduction in the returns to secured creditors may be the only feasible implementation option. As long as the parties to the creditors' bargain are repeat players, such an insurance device is a simple form of risk spreading more efficient than a case-by-case attempt to distinguish between contingencies that trigger either individualized or risk-sharing arrangements.

From this follows an important point about bankruptcy's distributional rules. The fact that bankruptcy's distributional rules are distinct from those outside of bankruptcy does not justify the conclusion that bankruptcy's collective regime violates the creditors' bargain. . . .

2. *Eve of Bankruptcy Conflicts of Interest*

The problem of perverse incentives (or forum shopping) provides a powerful argument for preserving the value of prebankruptcy entitlements in bankruptcy. It is important to remember, however, that perverse incentives are an inevitable consequence of any bankruptcy process. . . .

Thus, any collectivization process generates inevitable conflicts of interest among claimants. These conflicts are especially severe on the eve of bankruptcy. As the risk of business failure increases, an individual creditor is motivated to coerce the debtor to pay a greater share of its claim than that creditor would be able to recover in bankruptcy. This familiar problem underlies the preference rules of bankruptcy. . . .

An additional conflict arises as a product of a general agency problem: those who have some control over a debtor's decisionmaking will have an incentive to make decisions that favor them, even if those decisions are harmful to the interests of the claimants as a group. . . . The problem appears again in the bankruptcy timing decision. As previously noted, residual owners (such as equity) are likely to respond to insolvency by using delay tactics, even though delay may not be in the interest of the claimants as a group. . . .

a. *The Analogy to General Average Contribution*

The phenomenon of eve of bankruptcy conflicts finds an analogue in the law of admiralty and the problem of general average contribution, which attempts to minimize agency problems associated with diverse ownership. The basic principle underlying general averaging is that if a ship loaded with valuable cargo should founder at sea, the captain may make whatever sacrifices are necessary to prevent the ship and cargo from sinking altogether. All owners involved in the sail will contribute thereafter to the general average expense according to their percentage of ownership.

Agency theory offers a persuasive justification for such a general average rule. The captain is the agent of all of the parties participating in the venture. When a perilous situation arises, it is in the interest of all participants that the captain take all interests equally into account, affecting whatever sacrifice is necessary to promote the *joint interests* of all participants in the voyage. One method of approximating the cooperative result is to encourage the captain to act *as if* there were only one owner in the enterprise. If the ownership interests were integrated, it would not matter whose property were sacrificed, because all participants would bear the loss as joint venturers.

. . . Claimants in the creditors' bargain can predict that analogous events may occur on the eve of bankruptcy. The threat of a business failure owing to complex and interactive contingencies . . . may be seen as a common risk that, *despite individual efforts*, will inevitably occur unless creditors agree to sacrifice a portion of their claim in order to save the enterprise. On the other hand, the normal risks of business failure are not common risks, and the interests that sustain the loss must bear it alone. . . . [E]ve of bankruptcy contribution requires both a common peril and a sacrifice of individual rights in order to rehabilitate the enterprise.

Anticipating these conditions, the parties to the creditors' bargain would seek to avoid self-interested bias whenever such "jettison" decisions must be made. In the bankruptcy analogue to general average contribution, a dominant secured creditor—such as a general financing bank—is equivalent to the ship's captain struggling to save the vessel in high seas. The dominant secured creditor is peculiarly able to influence the course of events prior to insolvency in such a way that its ultimate self-interest may be advanced. The interests of the owners as a group (secured creditors, unsecured creditors, and equity) are advanced, however, only if the dominant secured creditor acts as if it were the sole owner. Some form of sharing rule may promote that cooperative behavior.

b. *Risk Sharing as a Means of Bankruptcy Contribution*

The preceding analysis suggests that participants in the ex ante bargain would agree to contribution *in bankruptcy* so as to encourage an optimal *prebankruptcy* jettison of some of the debtor's assets and liabilities. . . . [T]he right to a general average-type contribution if bankruptcy results is a necessary inducement to secure the cooperation of all creditors.

. . . [T]o the extent that the creditors in the ex ante bargain determine to collectivize in order to solve a central problem of noncooperation, they would necessarily agree to a contribution arrangement in order to restrain eve of bankruptcy conflicts. . . .

III. Conclusion: Normative Implications

. . . The preceding analysis suggests that substantial difficulties will attend attempts to accommodate maximization and distributional goals in bankruptcy. Several key normative implications follow from this analysis. First, these operational problems should not obscure the fact that a single-minded focus on preserving the value of prebankruptcy entitlements is not necessarily the optimal means of mirroring a hypothetical ex ante bargain among the creditors. The expanded bargain model offers instead an alternative benchmark for evaluating the goals of the current bankruptcy system. Our model suggests that various distributional objectives shape the bankruptcy process and that these objectives are entirely congruent with the goal of maximizing expected group welfare. . . .

The central challenge, therefore, is to devise bankruptcy rules that better reflect both maximization and distributional norms. At this level, the analysis offers specific prescriptive guidance as well. Rules that attempt to redistribute bankruptcy assets in particular cases are peculiarly susceptible to exploitation. Case-by-case analyses simply do not screen effectively between desired and disfavored redistributions. . . .

A preferable strategy for achieving bankruptcy's distributional goals would be to visualize the various distributional effects as a kind of "bankruptcy tax." If the distributional tax is certain and fixed, the parties have the capacity to adjust to the distributional rules. Furthermore, the more the tax is made certain and horizontally equitable, the less individual parties will be motivated to escape their share of the distributional burden. . . .

Where this all leads remains, predictably, an empirical question. In theory, incorporating a common disaster perspective into the creditors' bargain approach offers a richer vision of the bankruptcy process because it rationalizes some of the distributional impulses that are unambiguously present in bankruptcy. Unhappily, the model also reveals the significant strains that bankruptcy sharing imposes on the bankruptcy process. . . .

We have suggested that the distributional effects of bankruptcy are a bankruptcy tax imposed on the participants in the collective proceeding. To the extent that the tax revenues are used to support the welfare of the claimants as a group, one can visualize the parties agreeing to so burden themselves in an ex ante bargain.

Barry E. Adler
Bankruptcy and Risk Allocation
77 CORNELL L. REV. 439 (1992)[*]

INTRODUCTION

Bankrupt business firms distribute property to low-priority investors even though the firms do not fully repay high-priority investors. That bankruptcy in this way alters contractual priorities effectively reallocates among investors the risk of business insolvency. Commentators have roundly criticized such reallocation as an impediment to efficient business practice. Recently, however, a "risk-sharing" defense of bankruptcy reallocation has appeared in both the law and finance literature. Risk-sharing theorists argue that all investors in a business debtor—equity investors and creditors alike—would choose to share the risk of loss from the debtor's insolvency. These theorists surmise that investors cannot agree to share such risk, because a risk-sharing agreement is prohibitively expensive to negotiate. Therefore, the theorists conclude, bankruptcy reallocation furnishes a mutually beneficial hypothetical bargain to which investors would expressly agree but for transaction difficulties.

Though ostensibly plausible, risk-sharing theory must overcome a formidable obstacle: the *actual* bargain among investors is not silent on how to allocate insolvency risk. That bargain, in the form of equity and creditor contracts, expressly allocates insolvency risk to the low-priority, or "junior" investors, *i.e.*, to equity investors and general unsecured creditors. Thus bankruptcy reallocation appears to conflict with the parties' express intent.

Moreover, one cannot properly attribute contractual priority to transaction costs. . . .

Risk-sharing theory, to succeed, must explain how bankruptcy reallocation offers investors a better bargain than the carefully integrated actual bargain that reallocation alters. This paper refutes the possibility that risk-sharing theory can offer a successful explanation under any set of reasonable assumptions. . . .

Thus the Article concludes that bankruptcy's reallocative provisions, including bankruptcy reorganization, its most pernicious reallocation vehicle, lack justification and that Congress should abolish them. The abolition of bankruptcy reorganization and kindred provisions would greatly simplify and reduce the price of the insolvency process. Alternatively, courts properly sympathetic to contractual priorities should interpret extant law to remove bankruptcy's reallocative bias. . . .

III. A CRITIQUE OF RISK-SHARING THEORY

Risk-sharing theorists argue that bankruptcy's reallocative provisions may truly reflect an efficient bargain among investors, a bargain investors would reach but for difficulties of negotiation. If this is correct, then risk-sharing theory may justify bankruptcy's reallocation of contractual pri-

---

orities. Whether bankruptcy reallocation is justified, in turn, depends on whether "the costs of implementation . . . outweigh the benefits in enhancing the creditors' wealth."

The benefits of bankruptcy reallocation, however, *cannot* outweigh its costs, risk-sharing arguments to the contrary notwithstanding. The reasons fall into two classes. First, the costs of bankruptcy's reallocative provisions are potentially far greater than traditionally understood. Second, the benefits from those provisions are illusory, both because the class of beneficiaries is small, and because alternatives provide any risk-sharing benefit at lower cost.

A. Bankruptcy Reallocation Costs

. . . [T]he central theme of the discussion that follows is that these [bankruptcy reallocation] costs are large and indefensible. . . .

1. Reorganization Costs

Reorganizations are expensive because claimants suffer from a lack of perfect information and from incentives for strategic behavior. A reorganized debtor would emerge quickly and cheaply from bankruptcy if every creditor and equity claimant knew the true value of the debtor's assets, the true amount of its own claim, the relative priority of its own claim, and accepted that relative priority. In practice, however, claimants often battle over these factors, and have incentives to bargain strategically even if they clearly understand their legal entitlements. These reorganization battles and bargains impose both direct and indirect costs on a debtor. And while not all these costs are properly attributable to bankruptcy reallocation, most probably are.

a. *Direct and Indirect Costs*

Estimates of reorganization's direct costs, in the form of legal fees and administrative expenses, range from 3% to 25% of a debtor's value. These costs are necessary to reorder the complex network of contracts that comprises a firm. Estimates of direct costs, however, do not represent total costs. In addition to direct costs, reorganization costs include opportunity and uncertainty costs. The opportunity costs stem from the distraction of management. With its energies devoted to reorganization, management may have few resources to expend on the debtor's business operations. The uncertainty costs emerge from the doubts reorganization raises about the firm's ultimate survival. . . . [O]pportunity and uncertainty costs both flow from reorganization's "disruption" of the debtor's affairs.

Disruption costs can be more than important; they can be enormous. For example, in the Texaco-Pennzoil dispute, Pennzoil won a multibillion dollar judgment against Texaco, which entered bankruptcy reorganization to seek protection from its judgment creditor. Soon after, the parties settled the claim and terminated the bankruptcy action. Almost immediately after the settlement announcements, the combined value of Texaco and Pennzoil stock rose $2.3 billion. The market price of a firm's publicly traded securities provides an unbiased estimate of the firm's value. One can estimate, therefore, that the news of settlement coincided with a $2.3 billion increase in the combined values of Pennzoil and Texaco. Any unanticipated wealth transfer to Pennzoil from the settlement, though, ought to have been exactly offset by an unanticipated wealth transfer from Texaco, and vice versa. The explanation for the combined gain must be nondistributional. A sound explanation is that the settlement avoided what investors anticipated would be a protracted and costly bankruptcy reorganization process, one with an expected cost of an additional $2.3 billion. . . .

b. *Attribution to Bankruptcy Reallocation*

Not all costs of reorganization are necessarily attributable to bankruptcy reallocation. . . . The difference in cost between current bankruptcy law and the alternative is properly attributable to bankruptcy reallocation and *does* offset any risk-sharing benefit.

This alternative and less costly version of bankruptcy can be found in a Douglas Baird proposal. He asks why we should not simply do away with bankruptcy reorganization [and] sell the firm at a public auction, free from all prebankruptcy claims. . . . [T]he proposal would eliminate one set of bankruptcy's most onerous costs: the costs of a protracted reorganization process. . . .

All that is lost in Baird's proposal is bankruptcy's reallocation function. . . . If risk-sharing theory is to defend bankruptcy reallocation, it must at a minimum justify that portion of bankruptcy reorganization costs that exceed the expense of a simple auction. Although excess expense may not always attach to bankruptcy reorganization, given the potentially enormous disruption costs of a reorganization protracted by the bankruptcy process, bankruptcy reallocation's burden is considerable.

2. Forum Shopping Costs

Forum shopping imposes costs on any dispute resolution system that provides different entitlements within the system than those provided outside the system. Accordingly, if a manager-equity investor has an advantage inside bankruptcy and creditors have an advantage outside, the manager could waste the debtor's resources in an attempt to use the bankruptcy process, even if a nonbankruptcy resolution would be less costly. This is also true of incentives for strategic behavior in a conflict between general and secured creditors, with the former as bankruptcy's proponents and the latter its opponents.

In theory, bankruptcy need not entail forum shopping costs. . . .

3. Perverse Investment Incentives

Bankruptcy's reallocative provisions create two types of perverse incentives for managers whose interests are aligned with those of equity: perverse risk incentives and perverse diligence incentives.

a. Risk Incentives

As risk-sharing theorists contend, bankruptcy's reallocative provisions probably reduce management's incentive to take undue risks with the debtor's assets, on equity's behalf, when the debtor is insolvent, on or after the eve of bankruptcy. But the effect these provisions have on incentives is not limited to the period immediately before bankruptcy. The provisions also provide incentives to management and equity in periods of debtor solvency. And in certain instances of debtor solvency, bankruptcy reallocation *increases* management's incentive to take undue risks with the debtor's assets on equity's behalf.

. . . If the debtor is substantially solvent, however, the prospect of reallocation only *exacerbates* management's equity incentive to invest the debtor's assets in a risky project. Bankruptcy reallocation provides equity with a stake in an insolvent debtor regardless of insolvency's cause. In effect, bankruptcy reallocation forces the creditors to compensate equity for any of its losses from risky investment of the debtor's assets. This compensation both subsidizes and encourages such investment. Thus, bankruptcy reallocation's effect on management's equity risk incentive serves to discourage risky investment *only* when the debtor is insolvent or nearly insolvent at the time of a prospective investment. . . .

When viewed from the whole-life perspective of a debtor, then, bankruptcy's reallocative provisions may provide risk incentive costs that outweigh the risk incentive benefits of insolvency. . . .

b. Diligence Incentives

. . . All nonmanager claimants also have an interest in management's incentive to find and manage the debtor's investments diligently. . . . Recall from risk-sharing theory that, once insolvency mutes the discipline of debt, bankruptcy reallocation provides management with a substitute disciplinary incentive. Viewed at a time when the debtor is solvent, however, bankruptcy reallocation softens the blow of insolvency to any manager who owns an equity interest in the debtor. . . . In short, the less insolvency hurts, the less personal expense and effort managers will devote to its avoidance. . . .

4. Compulsory Contract Term Inefficiencies

Viewed properly, from the time of equity or creditor investment, bankruptcy's reallocation of contractual priority constitutes an imposition of compulsory contract terms. This imposition carries two related costs: costs from inefficiencies in the expectation of bankruptcy and costs from inefficiencies in the avoidance of bankruptcy.

a. In Expectation of Bankruptcy

Bankruptcy reallocates broadly. . . . There is a potentially large cost: even direct reallocation interferes with the operation of investment markets. . . .

[The] inefficient incentive to monitor can be characterized as a general cost of bankruptcy reallocation. Because of reallocation, no creditor will rely fully on its priority position over equity. As a result, creditors may generally waste resources in an attempt to monitor the debtor's activity to an extent that would have been unnecessary had they been able to rely on contractual priority. Put simply, bankruptcy reallocation coaxes creditors toward a position of eternal vigilance because by the time the debtor is on the brink of insolvency, the creditors may have already lost a significant portion of their investment. . . .

b. In Avoidance of Bankruptcy

Just as compulsory contract terms prevent efficient contractual arrangements, rules that increase the expense of an efficient contractual arrangement discourage that arrangement and sacrifice net benefit. To address exclusively those costs that arise in bankruptcy would, therefore, underestimate bankruptcy reallocation costs. A proper account includes the efficiency losses to firms that never enter bankruptcy but operate inefficiently so as to avoid the risk of costs that result from bankruptcy's reallocative provisions.

B. Bankruptcy Reallocation's Illusory Benefits

To critique risk-sharing theory, one might now speculate whether the purported benefits of risk-sharing outweigh the costs of bankruptcy reallocation. Ultimately, however, such speculation is unnecessary because bankruptcy reallocation as a vehicle for risk-sharing furnishes only illusory benefits. First, risk-sharing theory's misapplication of risk aversion analysis overstates risk-sharing's potential benefits. Second, one should not compare the benefits of risk-sharing to the costs of bankruptcy's reallocative provisions. Only the actual benefit *from those provisions* matters. This important distinction draws attention to reallocation alternatives that provide the same benefits at a lower cost. . . .

1. Limited Benefits

Bankruptcy's reallocative provisions provide benefits, if at all, to a strictly limited class of investors, because the benefits from risk-sharing accrue exclusively to those investors who bear undiversified risk. Only manager-equity investors are likely to bear a heavy burden of undiversified risk. . . . Moreover, even under circumstances in which risk-sharing can plausibly provide benefits to undiversified investors, bankruptcy's reallocative provisions are as likely to harm as to help such investors.

a. *Firm-Specific Risk*

Ordinary investors garner little benefit from risk-sharing. . . . The risk disappears—is "diversified"—because an investor can purchase interests in or make loans to a large number of firms and thus insulate itself from the failure of any one in particular. So insulated, the investor will not benefit from sharing risk that is unique to any particular firm.

. . . From the investor's perspective, bankruptcy reallocation alters contractual priority to the benefit of junior claims and may, therefore, increase the likelihood that the investor will get a return from each firm in which it invests. The investor, however, must pay a higher price for its interest in each firm in exchange for that higher expected return. . . . In an efficient market, the price of the insurance will offset the present value of the increased expected returns. This offset ensures that the net value of the investor's portfolio is no higher with a risk-sharing regime than it is without one. . . .

This conclusion is unaltered by the probability that the investor is risk averse, because the total expected return on the diversified investor's portfolio remains unchanged regardless of the insurance afforded by bankruptcy reallocation. . . . Consequently, with respect to firm-specific risk, even risk-averse, well-diversified, equity investors and general creditors would abjure a risk-sharing regime with some expense, no matter how little, because such investors garner no benefit from the regime. All costs of bankruptcy's reallocative provisions are wasted to the extent they serve to limit firm-specific risk.

. . . The flaw in the Jackson and Scott analysis is subtle but important. Their conclusion blurs the distinction between risk aversion and risk diversification. Even fully diversified investors are risk-averse. Those investors, however, are fully diversified with respect to a particular outcome, and no longer bear the risk of that outcome. Because the investors spread the expected cost across a number of investments, they gain a fixed rate of return.

b. *Interdependent Risk*

Ordinary investors can shed not only firm-specific risk, but, in theory, all risk that is uncorrelated with general trends in the economy. An investor could, for example, purchase a portfolio of diversified equity interests in and debt obligations of firms in all industries. Such an investor would be indifferent to even a costless risk-sharing regime *regardless* of the insolvency risk's source. . . .

Not all investors, however, can afford full diversification and some may benefit from risk-sharing. . . .

Bankruptcy's reallocative provisions would generate beneficial risk-sharing, even for such a creditor, however, only by mere chance. Bankruptcy reallocation provides the supplier with relief from risk only through the imposition of risk on other creditors, such as secured creditors denied pendency reimbursement. There is no reason to believe that the secured creditor can bear the risk any more efficiently than the supplier. . . .

In sum, a large number of investors, relatively well equipped to bear risk, receive no benefit from bankruptcy reallocations. Bankruptcy reallocation, moreover, often interferes with deliberate contractual risk allocation. Thus even if bankruptcy reallocation does provide some benefit to manager-equity investors, risk-sharing theorists overestimate reallocation's total benefit. . . . But such a discussion becomes unnecessary on closer analysis, which reveals that all purported beneefits are illusory.

2. *Contractual Risk-Sharing*

Bankruptcy reallocation benefits no one, because a bankruptcy process that abandons reorganization and honors absolute priority would allow *investors* to accomplish risk-sharing at a fraction of the cost that bankruptcy reallocation imposes. . . . However, the elimination of bankruptcy's reallocation function would not foreclose the possibility of any risk-sharing advantage. Investors can accomplish risk-sharing with a simple set of contracts. . . .

Contractual risk-sharing is not merely an alternative to bankruptcy's reallocative provisions, it is the superior alternative. Unlike bankruptcy's reallocative provisions, a capital structure that includes managers as creditors provides insurance against failure and any beneficial eve-of-bankruptcy incentive without the costs of uncertainty, delay, contract abrogation, and strategic behavior. Moreover, such a capital structure does not suffer from bankruptcy reallocation's tendency to exacerbate endogenous risk in preinsolvency time periods. . . .

If risk-sharing establishes benefits, then, contractual risk-sharing is the most efficient means to achieve them. Recall, however, that risk-sharing theorists assume contractual risk-sharing is impractical. One account of the impracticality stems from the "formidable operational difficulties in distinguishing common risks from those that have been assigned to individual claimants." . . . But bankruptcy's reallocative provisions suffer the same inability to distinguish between endogenous risk, for which creditors would not endorse insurance, and exogenous risk, for which they might. . . .

Thus bankruptcy's reallocative provisions appear to be no more than a complex and costly way to accomplish that which investors can achieve more cheaply on their own. . . .

3. Proceeds Reallocation

Finally, assume for the sake of argument that *some* bankruptcy reallocative provisions are necessary to accomplish risk-sharing, and that bankruptcy-imposed risk-sharing is worth its costs of inefficiency in compulsory contract terms. Not even these ill-supported assumptions justify bankruptcy's actual reallocative provisions, most significantly, bankruptcy reorganization.

As an alternative to reorganization and its substantial costs, bankruptcy could impose risk-sharing features on the distribution of sale proceeds after the court auctioned a debtor free of all prebankruptcy claims. . . .

CONCLUSION AND IMPLICATIONS

There is no good reason for bankruptcy to alter nonbankruptcy contractual priorities. Although risk-sharing theory proposes that bankruptcy reallocation of contractual entitlement from high-priority to low-priority investors mitigates equity's prebankruptcy incentive to risk the debtor's assets and serves a valuable insurance function for low-priority investors, bankruptcy reallocation may well exacerbate, not temper, the problems of prebankruptcy behavior and uninsured risk. Contract, not mandatory rules, can most effectively provide any conceivable benefit that bankruptcy reallocation now provides, if at all, only at substantial cost to investors.

An important consequence of this conclusion is that there is no need for bankruptcy reorganization, which serves no purpose other than reallocation. Congress should repeal bankruptcy's reorganization provisions. As a result of reorganization's exorcism, bankruptcy could provide an easier and less costly resolution of business insolvency. . . .

In sum, a bankruptcy system that respects contractual priority is equitable, more certain, and promotes greater economic efficiency, than a system that gives free reign to the crude and costly tools of compulsory risk-sharing.

Flankruptcy and Murphy's Law

One of the most interesting, thoughtful, original, and enjoyable articles on bankruptcy theory came from the clever pen of Professor James Bowers of the LSU Law Center in 1990. Published in the *Michigan Law Review*, Professor Bowers's article, *Groping and Coping in the Shadow of Murphy's Law: Bankruptcy Theory and the Elementary Economics of Failure*, took a carefully aimed shot at the "creditors' bargain" and the whole "common pool" notion of bankruptcy ideology trumpeted by Thomas Jackson. What made Bowers's challenge so intriguing was that, like Adler, he favors the "law and economics" approach to legal analysis. The crucial insight put forward by Professor Bowers was elegant in its simplicity: don't forget about the *debtor*! As Bowers demonstrates through careful economic analysis, the debtor is the most efficient liquidator of her own assets, and any *creditors'* bankruptcy bargain that leaves the debtor out of the picture is doomed. As Bowers explains, the creditors' bargain model simply does not reflect reality, and the reason is its failure to factor in the actions and obvious self-interest of the person most affected, the debtor.

James W. Bowers
Groping and Coping in the Shadow of Murphy's Law: Bankruptcy Theory and the Elementary Economics of Failure
88 MICH. L. REV. 2097 (1990)[*]

Edsel Murphy is the only philosopher ever to have metaphysically accounted for the occurrence of bankruptcies. Admittedly, his famous First Law[1] is nonspecific. It covers *all* of life's misunderstandings, misfortunes and failures. Murphian thinkers have nevertheless always recognized that bankruptcies were among the distinct disasters Murphy had implicitly predicted and explained. . . .

Murphy taught that if we fail to understand failure, we fail to understand. Our profession has ignored his teaching and fallen into that trap. Bankruptcy scholars lack any systematic theory which explains the behavior of people in trouble. . . . We don't even have any empirical information about how failing debtors behave.

All we do know is that bankruptcy is not working as a creditors' remedy. General creditors don't get paid by bankrupts. Murphy's Law foretells that neither theoretical voids nor lack of information will inhibit experts from expressing opinions. Predictably, bankruptcy scholars assume that the "problem" of zero collections in bankruptcies can somehow be cured by clever tinkering with bankruptcy law.

This study departs from that tinkering tradition. One of its conclusions springs directly from an early corollary of Murphy's Law, Seamus O'Reilly's Irrelevance of Repair Rule ("Attempts to fix things are not only doomed but also meaningless"). The logic linking Murphy's Law to O'Reilly's Rule is straightforward: if things cannot ever be made to perform as they were intended to, it is futile to try to repair them. I show below why bankruptcy law can never be made to work as it is supposed to and can never be fixed. It follows that tinkering is a waste of time.

---

[1]   Murphy's Law is so well known that it seems pedantic to footnote its content. Nevertheless, the Law itself suggests that if it is important for a person to know it, that person might not. I will, therefore, restate it here. Murphy's Law (in its weaker formulation) holds that *Whatever can go wrong, will.* A stronger version has been derived from Sullivan's Co-Proposition which states that "Murphy was an optimist." This has been taken to mean, when restated in rigorous form, that the basic law is subject to the condition that *Nearly everything can go wrong* yielding the so-called strong version of the law which can be simplified as "Nearly everything *will* go wrong." This paper takes no position on whether the weaker or stronger version best reflects empirical reality.

The Murphian argument does not stop there, however. Another corollary, O'Shaunessy's Irony, holds, "It is *good* that remedies don't succeed." Attempted repairs are often worse than wasteful. They can also be retrogressive. Bankruptcy law is itself an attempt to correct previous conditions that made unpaid creditors unhappy. If it worked, we would all be worse off. I also show that the best bankruptcy estates are the empty ones. The people who don't get paid are the very ones who shouldn't get paid. . . .

I. THE POVERTY OF PARITY POLICY: WHAT EQUALITY THEORY DOESN'T TELL US

The first theorem derived from Murphy's Law was developed by Murphy himself, and came to be known as Edsel's Edict. It states: "The better you think you understand what's going on, the less likely it is that you really do." This study begins by showing that bankruptcy scholarship proves the validity of the Edict.

Classic bankruptcy law, as I will use that term, is a collective creditors' remedy with one defining feature: the procedure provides in advance just how the proceeds recovered by the collective will be distributed among its members. The fundamental policy of bankruptcy law, goes the ritual incantation, is to obtain equal treatment for creditors of the same class (at least in "straight" bankruptcies). That at least, is surely Congress' intent. . . . The troubling thing about that conclusion is, however, that there seems to be no good reason why Congress should care. . . .

Moreover, if Congress thought bankruptcy law was needed to achieve "equality," either its conclusion was superfluous or its reasoning morally and logically incoherent. If creditors were in fact "equal," there is no reason to believe that they would not be treated accordingly. . . . Consequently, the problem must be that creditors are not in fact "equal" to each other, in which case we are left to wonder why Congress wants unequal people to be treated equally.

It is no answer to say that "equal" treatment of different people is nevertheless a normative standard worth pursuing for itself. . . . [B]ankruptcy's pro rata formula cannot be explained by a desire for simple "equality." The formula must instead be justified by a wish to foster some other unarticulated underlying norm, but we are left in the dark about what that norm is. While we remain in the dark, bankruptcy policy is incomprehensible. If, on conventional grounds, we do not know why it exists or how it can be justified, it is difficult to know whether or not bankruptcy law is working. It is also difficult to justify any proposals to change it.

II. POOLS, PRISONERS AND PIES: THE PERILOUS PARABLES OF BANKRUPTCY LAW

Anti-Murphian scholars believe there is an underlying normative criterion which justifies bankruptcy equality, to wit: wealth maximization. They argue that pro rata distribution of debtors' estates tends to encourage efficient behavior. Murphian theory implies that nonequality is the only distributional standard which is wealth maximizing, which suggests that those scholars' attempts to justify bankruptcy are misguided. . . .

No one proposes that all creditors' remedies be collective proceedings. Understanding bankruptcy law thus means understanding why and when collective proceedings are appropriate. Anti-Murphians have attempted to explain bankruptcy law by likening the insolvent-debtor/creditors relationship to a "common pool" or "prisoner's dilemma." . . . This essay does not challenge the usefulness of those heuristics. It does question whether they apply to bankruptcy.

My argument begins by recasting the Anti-Murphian pool, prisoner and pie images into an appropriate Murphian form. In Murphian poetics the vulture symbolizes the force which regulates reality. Pictures of pools and pies elicit unrealistically pleasurable, possibly optimistic images. Even the prisoner metaphor evokes notions that disasters are voluntarily avoidable. Rigorous Murphian analysis requires a root of appropriately hopeless hue, which is why the vulture, and not fishing, pastry, or even plea-bargains must constitute our starting point.

A. *The Parable of the Vultures—Reflections on Common Pools*

Once upon a time, a vulture cruised the desert observing critters plodding over the sand. It ignored several fat ones. When meaty critters die, there is enough food for everyone and thus no reason to linger and watch them. Eventually, however, the vulture saw a dying critter which didn't have enough flesh on its bones to feed the entire flock. That discovery led the vulture to begin circling to ensure that when death came, it would be first in line to chomp on the carcass. Other vultures saw the first one circling. Guessing what was afoot and not wishing to miss an impending feast, they too joined the circle. Soon, the entire flock was going round and round.

Each vulture noted that as other members joined the circling flock, prospects of getting a full meal diminished. Skittish vultures became overeager and were tempted to sneak in and snarf up some sirloin even while there was life left in the failing critter. As a result, the critter was prematurely dismembered. Many unfed vultures wondered whether, had the critter been able to reach a water hole, it might have put on enough meat to feed the entire flock. Worse, the carcass was not butchered as part of a plan to yield rib-eyes and roasts. Torn up in a free-for-all, valuable cuts became chopped meat.

The moral of the story is simple: Murphy's Law primes Pareto Optimality.[25] Nature, in all of its disastrous manifestations, is always necessitating interactions which make someone worse off. Despite the time and energy vultures spend circling, watching to see whether other vultures are circling, and disguising their own activity, their diet consists of little hamburger and almost no T-Bone.

The Anti-Murphians, unfortunately, have not been content merely to replicate the proof of this essential Murphian insight. They claim an ideal bankruptcy-type act could ameliorate the vultures' problems. The claim that Congress could repeal Murphy's Law is transparently preposterous. Only Murphy's Law itself could explain why anybody would take such a claim seriously. Nevertheless, to establish the superiority of the Murphian Model, it will be useful to clear the underbrush first. The mistakes of the Anti-Murphians are best exposed by considering the scenario envisioned by their prescriptions.

B. *The Fable of Flankruptcy—Cures for the Common Pool*

The vultures realized the flock would prosper if they all agreed to schedule the banquet at the optimal moment, butcher the carrion into choice cuts and distribute portions equally. Flock members could then engage in productive activity (like cruising for new carrion or sleeping) instead of spying on each other and circling, and yet eat flank steak instead of scraps. Holdout and free-rider problems prevented them from agreeing, however. Fortunately, Congress realized the vultures needed to be saved from themselves and enacted an optimal collective scavenging law, adopting the terms that the vultures would have bargained for had they been able to agree—a Flankruptcy Act.

Murphians observed that the carcass was a conspicuous nonparty to the Vultures' Bargain. Cynics agreed that the Flankruptcy Act had been predicted by Mulligan's Mandate for Multi-Party Conflicts ("Let's you and me agree before the fight to gang up and clean him out"). The Vultures' Bargain proponents implicitly assume that carcasses do not care if they are ganged up on or not, and assert, "What's good for vultures is good for carcasses."

Whatever its motivation, The Flankruptcy Act had predictable features. There was an automatic "King's-X" on the death of the carrion to prevent any vulture from sneaking bites before the

---

[25]   Pareto Optimality . . . is a normative welfare criterion used by economists to evaluate varying states of economic affairs. A situation is said to be "Pareto Optimal" when it is impossible to effect a change benefiting one individual without harming someone else.

others arrived. To discourage the overeager from trying to evade the King's-X rule, premature biters were required to regurgitate any chunks eaten *pre-mortem*. Butchers were appointed to cut up carcasses which, by replacing frenzied *ad hoc* carving committees, lowered butchering expenses. Butchers were charged with distributing the carved carrion to members of the flock in equal portions.

The fable makes interesting literature. Anti-Murphians, however, argue it shows vultures can live happily ever after, a conclusion that does not follow. The notion that anybody could live happily ever after violates every known Murphian principle.

If we enact a bankruptcy law it should be engineered to do as little damage as is possible. My disagreements with the Anti-Murphians on engineering questions only amount to quibbles. The point of the parable for the Anti-Murphians, however, is not that bankruptcy could and should be made better but that a world *with* a bankruptcy law is better than a world *without* one. *That* Murphian theory denies. The denial is credible. Vultures' Bargains do not seem to be very profitable.

1. *The Factual Flaws of Flankruptcy*

Even within the logic of the parable, a Flankruptcy system has costs. Whether we ought to have Flankruptcy is not a question of metaphor or theory, but rather of numbers. Do the benefits exceed the costs? Efficiency, even using a weak measure, is after all potentially an empirical concept. The existing numbers do not suggest the ending of the vulture story is a happy one. Although better data might discourage us less, it is difficult to believe that the point of the Vultures' Bargain was to adopt a regime in which vultures end up with little or nothing. Maybe the failure of the existing mandate for collective behavior to produce any apparent benefits for the cooperating actors results from small defects in the present terms of the mandatory charter. That is the tinkerer's basic hope. If the Vultures' Bargain theory has in fact been largely implemented, but the predicted benefits to the vultures do not materialize, it is equally possible that something is wrong with the theory.

The Anti-Murphians acknowledge that replacing an array of individualized remedies with a mandatory collective process imposes costs on the community of vultures which result from either the inability or failure to engineer perfectly a Flankruptcy system. . . .

There are other costs of Flankruptcy, however, which the Anti-Murphians do not explicitly acknowledge. Flankruptcy requires the formation of a "firm" with appointment of "management" (a trustee vulture or butcher) and conflicts of interest among its "owners." The creation of firms can be explained on efficiency grounds when transaction costs of organizing productive activity using market contracts are high, but conducting business in that form never comes free. Administering a firm, even one with the narrow mission of scavenging a single carcass, spawns agency costs as the management tries to expropriate the gains the owners hoped to obtain by forming the firm, and the owners struggle with each other for control. Conflict doesn't go away in firms. It merely takes a different form.

The inability to engineer an appropriate division of any carcass under the collective system imposed serious social costs on the community of vultures. The Flankruptcy Act regulated only salvaging of carcasses that had already been found. It did not coordinate the butchering and distributing of dead carcasses with other vulture activity (like cruising in search of new carrion) which remained unregulated, but it affected that behavior nonetheless. In the pre-Flankruptcy state of nature, there was some greater-than-pro-rata pay-off to vultures for being strong, swift, or clever. The prospect of larger rewards for finding carrion which might not have to be shared tended to induce the most efficient scavengers to cruise, looking for dying critters. The pro rata outcome under Flankruptcy, which promised the weak and lazy vultures a free ride from the activity of their stronger brothers and sisters, diminished the incentive for the strong, swift, and clever to search for new carrion. The Act thus tended to eliminate the gains (even if they were only in the form of scraps) to the flock from the extra carcasses which might have been found by the strong had they the former, larger incentive to search. As a consequence, by the time carrion was found by the flock, much if not all of the meat had rotted off the bones. The corpses with meat on them seemed to have fewer pounds of it. That led to proposals to pay a bounty to any vulture discovering a corpse.

There is an analogous potential social cost of bankruptcy. To the extent it works, it eliminates part of the competitive advantage of creditors who are master monitors and capable collectors, raising the cost of credit to the level charged by less efficient creditors. Whether our lower credit costs gained by eliminating common pools outweigh our losses from having to borrow at rates which protect less effective lenders is a question to which we have no direct answer. At present, creditors actually get very little out of bankruptcy so the savings we obtain from a supposedly superior salvage technique look small. Since most bankruptcy estates are empty ones, it may be that the superior collectors already do get paid, so we may not be paying extra. The free riders may be getting nothing. In that case, of course, bankruptcy is a pure waste, since it costs us to undertake the proceedings, but we do not really get anything for it. (The butchers, however, may live happily ever after.)

A pro rata formula can be justified only as the best we can do *lacking more information* (at the time the statute is being drafted). Real vultures, like real debtors and creditors, in real cases know which vultures are strong and which are weak. The pro rata requirement is intended to force them to behave as though they were ignorant. The information they have (but must disregard) as parties to a legislated pro rata creditors' or vultures' bargain, is socially valuable. Making life run as though people are ignorant wastes the value of their information which is likely to be substantial. Real creditors striking real, presumably optimal bargains would arrive at distributional terms shaped by that information. The "Bankruptcy Bargain" is thus, even in theory, suboptimal. . . . I suggest below that debtors are likely to make distributions of their diminishing assets using real, not hypothetical, information and, by doing so, tend to optimize the value of the distributions to the debtor and creditors as a group. For now I conclude only that bankruptcy is not delivering what the theory promises and that the case for an Act improved by any sort of tinkering is, at best, unproved.

2. The Logical Problems with the Parable

One reason why the benefits predicted by the parable seldom materialize is that the logic of the parable is flawed. Debtor-creditor games are different from vulture-carrion games. Since the Anti-Murphian logic assumes the games are alike, its foundations are faulty. Even brilliant engineering cannot save a structure erected on that assumption. The Bargain Theory errs by ignoring the economics of failure in our real Murphian world.

Common pools have unowned, nonreactive resources in the pool. The fish in the sea, the oil and gas in the ground, and the soil and grass in the tragic feudal commons do not care who captures them. In our fable, the forlorn critter caught dying in the desert is likewise a purely passive character in the plot. Dead, he does not care how his carcass is butchered or which vulture gets the stew meat and which gets the soup bones. In real debtor-creditor relationships, debtors are not passive. For that reason, such relationships do not generate common pools. Moreover, the classical prescription for solving a common pool problem is to create property rights in the assets in the pool. In the real Murphian world, the pool consisting of the debtor's assets is already "owned" by someone— the debtor. Bankruptcy law cannot, therefore, be justified as an efficient solution for a common pool.

To adapt the parable to reality, assume that critters are in herds owned by debtors and replace the vultures in the story with a number of equally hungry creditors. If the owner-debtors can be forced by any nonbankruptcy creditors' remedy to dole out the value of the critters to creditors, those debtors have every interest in butchering the critters at the moment they achieve optimum weight into optimal proportions of steak and hamburger. In other words, once a property right is granted to a debtor over her own assets she will maximize their value for her own benefit. In doing so, she will take into account the costs to her creditors as well.

For the logic of the pool argument to hold, incentives for the owner of pool assets to react must somehow disappear. That allegedly happens on "'insolvency." If all the benefits from feeding and carefully butchering the critters will inevitably be captured by creditors, the debtor allegedly no longer has any incentive to maximize asset value. Hence, the argument goes, control should pass to the creditors who do have the incentive, if they are forced to act cooperatively.

The insolvency argument is both factually and theoretically in error. Insolvency is not the point at which the maximization motive shifts from debtors to creditors if insolvency is measured by the market. Market value is an imperfect measure of the value of the assets to their owners who ordinarily value them for their infra-marginal rents (consumer or producer surpluses) and their marginal quasi rents. Thus market-insolvent debtors have incentives to maximize the value of the assets in their portfolios to retain as much of the rents as possible.

Not only is the "insolvency" assumption unjustifiable, but also in the real Murphian world the market-insolvent debtor can gain by choosing which creditors to pay. The available data indicate that insolvent debtors do liquidate and distribute their own estates until they have no distributable value to any remaining creditors. That is far beyond the point of market insolvency (the level at which the market value of the debtor's assets is just under the aggregate of the creditors' claims). Such observed behavior provides strong indication that the debtor passivity implicitly assumed in the Creditors' Bargain model exists in theory but not in the real world. What we need is either a new world which actually suffers from the defect of debtor docility or a new theory which explains the behavior of failing debtors. Inasmuch as revising the world to make it match the theory is the more difficult choice, I will take the easy route and explore the principles of failure.

III. INTRODUCTION TO MURPHIAN ECONOMICS: ASSET MANAGEMENT IN THE FACE OF FAILURE

. . . The data suggest that debtors are not passive, but instead react to creditors or vultures with the result that bankruptcy estates are mostly empty. . . .

This model illustrates two simple but very general points about the dynamics of failure. First, as losses in wealth occur, Victims will attempt to minimize them by making portfolio adjustments in efforts to reach optimal holdings. Second, because assets are indivisible, the portfolio will not be liquidated proportionately. Portfolio adjustments start with the liquidation of assets whose surplus, idiosyncratic, or specialized values to their owners are lowest relative to their market values. The assets that remain in portfolios after adjustment, accordingly, tend to be those with the highest relative idiosyncratic or specialized values to their owners. The more portfolios have been diminished by disaster, the less their market value explains why their owners prize them. That is one reason why debtors who are insolvent by a market measure are likely to be highly motivated to preserve the assets they have left and thus unlikely to be passive when facing risks of continuing losses. . . .

E. *Optimal Coping in Environments of Advanced Failure, in the Absence of Markets*

. . . To restate the significance of this differential in Victim/vulture incentives, the absence of costless markets creates a strong desire in the Victim to control rather than leave to chance the order in which vultures consume his indivisible assets. Vultures are generally indifferent to the order. . . .

The intensity of the Victim's incentives to maximize the value of his portfolio is a continuous rather than binary function of two variables: the probability that the last asset will be seized, and the expected timing of the seizure. Utter passivity occurs only in the extreme case of *certainty of immediate seizure* when there is no possible action that can be taken by the Victim to affect either the order, timing or the probability of the seizure losses. If the probability of seizure is less than total, or if the order or timing of the seizure is uncertain, Victims have incentives to maximize their asset values. The Common Pool justification for bankruptcy legislation is built on the extreme case of absolute debtor certainty of immediate seizure of his last asset. Until that point is reached, victims still have incentives to react. While such incentives exist, there is no common pool problem.

There is some logic to the notion that the probability of seizure of one's last asset by creditors is very low until the point of market insolvency is reached. At the insolvency point, however, it remains low. Debtors would become certain that post-insolvency reactions cease to be worthwhile only in a world which possesses a number of very unreal, non-Murphian features. Among them, at minimum, are: that all creditors can costlessly determine exactly when the point of insolvency is reached, that the odds of the insolvency being permanent are 100%, and that creditors can costlessly and immediately exercise their right to seizure. Because those assumptions fly in the face of Murphy's Law, we can dismiss them. . . .

G. *Loss Minimization in a World with Creditors*

. . . [I]n a world with creditors having legal remedies, debtors are likely to retain the right to liquidate when it is efficient for them to do so, and to convey that right to *individual* creditors when it is not. Given the power to liquidate and distribute a portion of their estate, they are not likely to remain passive in the face of losses but instead are likely to exercise the power they bargained for. Left in their bankruptcy estates will be the encumbered assets which they had no power to liquidate and distribute, but those assets will benefit the secured parties and not the general creditors. So long as debtors are the superior liquidators of certain assets in their own estates they will liquidate those assets themselves rather than turn the task over to a process which is less efficient. Since bankruptcy law is unlikely to affect the superior liquidating abilities of debtors, except in the occasional accidental case, it is never likely to produce anything but empty bankruptcy estates.

IV. THE MORAL OF THE MURPHIAN MANDATE: BANKRUPTCY IS SUBJECT TO MURPHY'S LAW

The purpose of this study has been to demonstrate that we lack any persuasive theory for why we have or ought to have bankruptcy legislation. Legal explanations for bankruptcy policy are simply unexplanatory. The only systematic attempts to justify bankruptcy law which go beneath the conclusory legal explanations are also unconvincing. They implicitly ignore the possibility that debtors will react to losses. They predict that creditors will make recoveries in bankruptcies when we can easily observe that creditors do not.

The reason why bankruptcy estates will be empty, and why the "Creditors' Bargain" theorists were mistaken, is basically the same. Debtors, as we have demonstrated, *will* react to threats of loss so long as they have any power and opportunity to do so. The theory developed here explains just how they can be expected to react. That, in turn, explains the ways in which the character of debtors' portfolios changes as losses continue, and, eventually, why debtors' estates are likely to be valueless to creditors by the time bankruptcy occurs.

The source of debtors' powers to react resides in the property rights they have in their assets. So long as we permit private property, which includes entitling property owners to transact with their property, the power exists for them to react to the threat of losses in the ways described above. The theory developed in this study demonstrates the utility of permitting such transactions: debtors will use that entitlement either to minimize the impact of losses, without harming their creditors, or to pay creditors in advance for any harm creditors may suffer by the exercise of that power. In that sense, the private property system tends to induce optimal loss minimization in a world which contains risks that losses might occur. It also follows that if we wish to change the behavior of debtors in ways which better ensure that creditors will always get paid in full in bankruptcies, tinkering with the bankruptcy act itself is likely to be unproductive. What would be required to achieve such an ideal is, instead, a drastic constriction of the number and scope of the rights which we grant owners under our law of property.

Even when permitting debtors to self-liquidate generates welfare conflicts between debtors and creditors, there is no theoretical point at which we can say overall welfare would be enhanced by making a change to collective control. Because those welfare conflicts potentially exist, a bargain theory which justifies bankruptcy law must posit a bargain to which the debtor is a party. Real debtors, however, are parties to real credit contracts with real creditors. If there are potential welfare conflicts between debtors and creditors, there is no reason to believe that the existing credit contracts do not resolve them. Creditors might agree to take the risk that the debtor will liquidate her own property and adjust the price of credit accordingly, or they may eliminate the debtor's ability to control her affairs by taking real rights in the debtor's assets and thus prohibit the debtor from transacting in those assets. In short, there are good theoretical reasons, grounded in conventional economic assumptions, for believing that debtors are apt to be efficient liquidators when they are facing failure. Their creditors have been paid for the risk that losses will result from the contract term that permits debtors to liquidate their unencumbered assets, and debtors, in turn, have taken the risk that their encumbered assets will be unavailable for use in making portfolio adjustments when losses occur.

Indeed, the efficiency of permitting the debtor to control the liquidation of her own affairs even explains the shape of the common creditor's remedy, which permits the debtor to foresee the time at which seizure may occur and to employ any of her assets to satisfy or refinance maturing obligations. The secured transaction, which limits the ability of the debtor to deal with the assets which collateralize the debt without first paying off or obtaining consent of the creditor, is the unusual credit term. Debtors usually want as much discretion as possible in dealing with their assets and are presumably willing to pay many of their creditors to give them that discretion. That is the import of being unsecured. So long as Victims will bargain for the right to liquidate themselves and our law of property permits them to make such bargains, it is likely that empty bankruptcy estates will always be a feature of bankruptcy. No amount of tinkering is likely to change that fact.

A. *Whither Murphian Economic Theory: An Introduction to Murphian Bankruptcy Distributions*

. . . A complete Murphian theory would show that non-pro rata distributions of debtors' assets that occur in the real Murphian world tend to approach the loss minimizing ideal. There are certainly impressionistic reasons for believing that permitting debtors to control the distribution of their assets would tend toward the optimal. . . . It is obvious, however, that pro rata distribution of the sort envisioned by classic bankruptcy law would achieve none of those distributional gains. That may further explain why actual distributions occur outside of bankruptcy leaving nothing to be distributed when the proceedings occur. If there were anything left to be distributed pro rata, the world would be worse off if it were done under the classic pro rata scheme.

B. *Principles of Murphian Politics—An Afterword*

Murphian theory proves that collective control over the liquidation and distribution of debtors' assets is unnecessary if we are interested in optimal liquidations. The question remains: Why then do we have bankruptcy law? Why do we wish to entrust liquidation and distribution decisions to those who will make them in ways which harm rather than enhance aggregate welfare? The interests of those who get to make the decisions (the butchers and their helpers) are of course clear enough, but why would those they are supposed to serve (who generally get nothing from the services being provided) ever agree to hire them? Not surprisingly, Murphian theory has an answer to those questions as well.

The impulse to have bankruptcy law and to tinker with it after we have it comes not from notions of "equality" or "efficiency" but rather from wishful thinking. We are doomed because we harbor hope, a specific belief in alchemy: that if we are only clever enough, gold can be squeezed from turnips. Our fatal wish is for a world in which disasters don't occur. We don't really care if anybody gets paid "equally" or paid "efficiently." What we really want is a world in which they get paid. Period.

Our commitment to the proposition that everybody should get paid grows from our belief that their claims are worthy. We are offended if promises upon which we rely aren't performed, if injuries go uncompensated. At least since the abolition of debtors' prisons, however, we have also adopted a regime in which our commitment to enforce worthy claims is limited to extractions of money. Laws which enforce contract, tort, and property obligations are effective only against those who have monetizable wealth. The poor are free to commit their torts, breach their contracts, ignore their duties. Among those poor are our bankrupts.

When someone doesn't get paid, we are forced to confront just how weak the law really is. . . .

Bankruptcy law is a symbol of our faith that wealth can be created by voting, lobbying, and litigating. We sometimes overlook the Murphian possibility that wealth can also be destroyed by the same means. What is hardest to accept, however, is that sometimes law is likely neither to create nor to destroy much wealth. The core insight of Murphy's Law is not that the world is necessarily an inevitably unhappy place. Murphy's point was actually both more potent and more subtle. Expending the effort required to make the world happier tends to make us unhappier. We can credit ourselves with the happiness that results from honest effort in trying to improve the world by tinkering with bankruptcy law and, fortunately, we can't do much damage. Until we are ready to abandon the institution of private property, however, we won't accomplish much either.

Professor Randal Picker of the University of Chicago learned his bankruptcy theory from Baird, who in turn learned from Jackson. Picker shares the view of his mentors that economic theory can inform bankruptcy theory. But in the following article, Picker calls into question the starting premise that there even is a common-pool problem in bankruptcy cases. Furthermore, Picker demonstrates that the core problem of creditor misbehavior can be ably solved by the use of security interests.

Randal C. Picker
Security Interests, Misbehavior, and Common Pools
59 U. Chi. L. Rev. 645 (1992)[*]

Just as the debtor is capable of misbehaving, so too are the creditors. A creditor may seize assets and sell them piecemeal, even if a sole owner would keep the assets together. If no single creditor enjoyed priority over another, each creditor might have an incentive to spend resources monitoring both the debtor and the other creditors to ensure that it was paid if the debtor failed.

. . . I suggest that secured credit is a sensible response to the problem of creditor misbehavior. In doing so, I offer a new view of perhaps the central premise of recent bankruptcy scholarship. The same scholars who have not seen a link between secured credit and creditor misbehavior have nevertheless argued that bankruptcy law exists primarily to overcome the problems that arise when too

---

many creditors chase too few assets. By failing to see that secured credit is a response to creditor misbehavior, these scholars misunderstand the institution of secured credit and, more importantly, structure their analysis of bankruptcy law upon an unsound premise.[6]

These scholars assume that creditors who face a troubled debtor face a common pool problem, and that bankruptcy law exists to overcome it. The common pool problem, however, is typically within the domain of property law. It arises among strangers who have had no established relationships with each other or with any common third party. The setting is an English pasture in the fifteenth century, a Texas oil field at the turn of the century or a fishery in Malaysia today. The common pool problem arises in these situations from an overlapping distribution of rights where acquisition or capture means an absolute priority in ownership. When each person has the same right to graze, drill or fish and no one has the right to exclude the others, the dominant strategy for each person is to graze, drill, or fish, without regard to the common interest in assuring that the resource is put to its best use.

Those who enjoy these rights to a common resource acquire them independently. There are no prior dealings among them. By contrast, the relationships among the debtor and its creditors are largely contractual. The parties themselves can structure their relationships with each other to minimize the common pool problem. Many firms have both secured and unsecured creditors; others grant no secured debt but still have senior and subordinated unsecured creditors. By the initial allocation of priority rights, many firms can avoid the common pool problem altogether. For example, if the firm would owe a single secured creditor more than the firm would be worth if it failed, no common pool problem would arise.

The debtor will also seek ways to minimize the harms of the common pool. The creditors can anticipate the common pool problem and will therefore charge interest rates to cover the anticipated losses that will result. Because the debtor bears these interest costs directly, it will internalize the cost of the common pool and will therefore search for mechanisms to minimize the costs. Security interests and other priority devices play this role. . . .

CONCLUSION

During the 1980s, two separate strands of academic work in commercial law attempted to explain the pervasive existence of secured credit and to provide a theoretical basis for the bankruptcy laws. This work tried to explain secured credit by focusing narrowly on the problem of the misbehaving debtor. At the same time, bankruptcy law scholarship was premised on the idea that bankruptcy law solved a common pool problem. The common pool problem arises from an overlapping distribution of rights among the unsecured creditors of the failing firm. No creditor has the right to exclude another, and therefore the dominant strategy for each creditor may be to monitor the debtor

---

[6]   This scholarship also suffers from a more basic defect. It begins the inquiry in the wrong place. It starts with the notion that the underlying debt-collection rules are fixed and that bankruptcy law should be designed around them. An issue I expect to pursue in further research is whether first accepting state law baselines and then asking how to best respect those baselines in a collective bankruptcy proceeding fundamentally misconceives the appropriate nature of the inquiry. We might be better served by focusing directly on the form of a set of optimal insolvency rules. In particular, the current bankruptcy law is now designed to solve the common pool problem, but that problem arises only because levying on assets and establishing priority to those assets are treated as one. If they were separated—if seizing assets left unchanged the unsecured creditor's right to only a pro rata share of the assets if the debtor were insolvent at the time of seizure—the traditional common pool problems would be minimized, if not completely eliminated. We need to weigh carefully the advantages and disadvantages of linking seizure and priority. By looking only at bankruptcy law with debt-collection rules as a given, we have ignored these fundamental questions.

in an attempt to defeat the pro rata distribution scheme of bankruptcy. The possible relationship between security interests and common pools was ignored.

This Article presents an integrated treatment of these issues in a standard game-theoretic context. . . .

Consequently, security interests do play an important role in the efficient allocation of capital; most of their benefits derive from eliminating the duplicative monitoring of possible creditor misbehavior that defines the common pool. Moreover, we must reconsider the common pool construct that currently forms the basis for our understanding of the bankruptcy laws. The existence or nonexistence of the unsecured common pool at the end of the firm's life depends on the design of the firm's capital structure at its inception. The common pool need not arise, and we must therefore reconsider the mission of the bankruptcy laws since the parties themselves can and do keep this problem from arising in the first place.

Should Non-Economic Factors Be Taken Into Account?

A central premise of the creditors' bargain, whether in its pure form or modified to encompass risk sharing, is that economic factors are the key touchstone of bankruptcy policy. In the following selections, we see bankruptcy scholars debating that premise. Professor Donald Korobkin, in his important article *Rehabilitating Values: A Jurisprudence of Bankruptcy,* urges that other values should be factored into the bankruptcy policy equation. What are the essential aspects of Korobkin's "value-based account"? What are his criticisms of the "economic account"? Professor Korobkin has written numerous other articles about bankruptcy theory, including *Contractarianism and the Normative Foundations of Bankruptcy Law*, 71 TEX. L. REV. 541 (1993), and *Value and Rationality in Bankruptcy Decisionmaking*, 33 WM. & MARY L. REV. 333 (1992).

As the next selection shows, Professor Bowers is not persuaded by Korobkin. In *Whither What Hits the Fan?: Murphy's Law, Bankruptcy Theory, and the Elementary Economics of Loss Distribution*, Bowers's sequel to his *Groping and Coping* MICHIGAN LAW REVIEW article, he sharply questions Korobkin's views. Who has the better of the debate?

In the third selection, *The Need to Take Community Interests into Account in Bankruptcy: An Essay*, Professor Karen Gross urges that community interests must be taken into account in formulating bankruptcy policy. Gross elaborated in depth on those views in an excellent book, FAILURE AND FORGIVENESS: REBALANCING THE BANKRUPTCY SYSTEM, published by Yale University Press in 1997. Along with Korobkin, Professor Gross may be the most ardent advocate of the idea that economic factors cannot provide the sole key to unlocking the bankruptcy puzzle.

Professor Robert Rasmussen takes the next turn. In *An Essay on Optimal Bankruptcy Rules and Social Justice*, he looks at bankruptcy policy (specifically chapter 11) from the viewpoint of Rawlsian philosophy. In so doing, Rasmussen ultimately sides with the economists. Their approach better promotes social justice, he argues. Why do the "nonutilitarian" arguments fail, according to Rasmussen?

Next, in his own inimitable style, Professor John Ayer asks in *Bankruptcy as an Essentially Contested Concept: The Case of the One-Asset Case* whether there is *any* purpose to a bankruptcy law. What does he conclude? If bankruptcy law has no purpose, what are the consequences?

The final space is given to Professor Christopher Frost. In *Bankruptcy Redistributive Policies and the Limits of the Judicial Process*, Frost brings a critical issue to the table: is the judiciary even capable of taking non-economic factors into account in implementing a bankruptcy law? If not he asserts, the whole academic debate over bankruptcy theory may be just that.

Donald R. Korobkin
Rehabilitating Values: A Jurisprudence of Bankruptcy
91 COLUM. L. REV. 717 (1991)*

As of late, bankruptcy law has rocketed to a kind of celebrity status. The number of bankruptcy cases has been climbing, and the importance of these cases has increased with their notoriety. Yet in the midst of all this fame and glory, bankruptcy law has been struggling through a kind of existential crisis. Certain scholars, most notably Dean Thomas Jackson and Professor Douglas Baird, have questioned the underlying reasons for bankruptcy law's existence. Inspired by the law and economics movement, they have presented what they view as a comprehensive theoretical explanation and critique of bankruptcy law. According to this "economic account," bankruptcy law responds to the problem of collecting debt and exists to address one specific concern: to solve the "common pool problem" arising from diverse claims to limited assets. In so narrowing their explanation of bankruptcy law, they have questioned or repudiated much of bankruptcy law as it now exists, including the provisions for corporate reorganization under Chapter 11 of the Bankruptcy Code. . . .

This Article will directly challenge the economic account and its efforts to define bankruptcy law's "distinct function" as a mechanism to "collectivize" debt collection and thereby maximize economic returns to creditors as a group. The economic account is deeply flawed, and its view of what makes bankruptcy law "distinct" is misguided. Indeed, that account leaves unexplained why bankruptcy law has the contours and dimensions that it does.

As an alternative to the economic account, the Article offers a competing normative explanation of bankruptcy law, which I shall call the "value-based account." . . .

Part III presents the value-based account, rejecting the economic account's principal contention that bankruptcy law is merely a response to the problem of collecting debt understood in purely economic terms. On the contrary, bankruptcy law is a response to the many aspects of financial distress—moral, political, personal, social, and economic—and, in particular, to the grievances of those who are affected by financial distress. Because the participants' varied grievances typically reflect conflicting and fundamentally incommensurable values, bankruptcy law provides a forum for an ongoing debate in which these diverse values can be expressed and sometimes recognized.

The focus of this ongoing debate is the bankruptcy estate, a legal entity removed from the historical business in distress. The estate should be seen not as merely a pool of assets; instead, the estate should be viewed as an evolving and dynamic enterprise, capable of having diverse aims.

Under the value-based account, bankruptcy law creates conditions for a discourse in which the aims of the estate as enterprise are defined and redefined. Loosely speaking, it accomplishes a kind of "group therapy": the values of the participants in financial distress are rehabilitated into a coherent and informed vision of what the estate as enterprise shall exist to do. The value-based account thus explains bankruptcy law as a system with varied contours and dimensions, having the distinct function of facilitating the expression and recognition of those diverse values important in dealing with financial distress.

I. THE LOGIC AND LIMITS OF THE ECONOMIC ACCOUNT

A. *An Economic Picture of the Problem of Collecting Debt*

. . . Bankruptcy law . . . is perceived by the economic account as a system uniquely designed to capture . . . additional value. Like nonbankruptcy collection law, bankruptcy law includes a mechanism by which creditors exchange their rights against a common pool of assets. But bankruptcy law does more: it regulates the creation of collective wealth. Bankruptcy law is designed to maximize the economic outcome for creditors as a group by maximizing the value of the pool against which creditor rights are exchanged.

Bankruptcy law accomplishes the creation of this collective wealth in two steps. First, it stays individual creditor actions so as to prevent an immediate dismemberment of the common pool. Second, it allows for a process in which the "best use" of the common pool can be determined. . . .

The economic account identifies this aspect of the bankruptcy process—maximizing the economic value of the common pool by optimizing its deployment—as what makes bankruptcy law "distinct." In contrast to nonbankruptcy "grab law," bankruptcy law "collectivizes" decision making regarding asset deployment, forcing diverse "co-owners" of the common pool to act as if they were a sole owner. . . .

There is reverse side to this normative coin. From the proposition that bankruptcy law should concern itself with optimizing asset deployment, the economic account contends that bankruptcy law should do nothing that might interfere with optimal asset deployment. Most importantly, as a general rule, bankruptcy law should not include rules that alter the rights of parties under substantive nonbankruptcy law. . . . The economic account thus insists that the "deployment question" must be clearly separated from the "distributional question." . . .

B. *The Failings of the Economic Account*

According to the economic account, then, bankruptcy law exists to maximize economic returns. . . . In other words, the reason that we have bankruptcy law—to maximize economic returns—lends support for our continuing to have a system of this kind. Yet this causal explanation would leave unvindicated—indeed, would undermine—much of existing bankruptcy law.

1. *The Distinctness of Bankruptcy Law Under the Economic Account.*—The economic account purports to have discovered the "essence" of bankruptcy law, thereby locating what makes that law distinct: it provides a mechanism for preserving and maximizing the economic value of the common pool. . . .

Upon closer examination, however, the economic account does not show bankruptcy law to be distinct . . . . Notably, at various periods in our history, nonbankruptcy collection law has contained mechanisms that may be seen, in economic terms, as paralleling bankruptcy law in pursuing a wealth-maximizing function—in particular, state and federal receiverships and assignments for the benefit of creditors. . . . There is nothing about the structure of nonbankruptcy collection law, as such, that prevents it from achieving economic outcomes comparable to those under bankruptcy law. . . .

These historical ties between bankruptcy and nonbankruptcy collection law underscore their structural similarities in performing the function of preserving and maximizing the value of the common pool. Considered purely as a vehicle for performing an economic function, then, bankruptcy law is not structurally distinct from nonbankruptcy collection law.

2. *Equality of Distribution and the Creditors' Bargain Model.*—Assume that we were to grant the economic account's claim that, by its very structure, bankruptcy law is capable of achieving economic returns superior to those under nonbankruptcy collection law, thus accomplishing a "distinct function" not performed by any other legal system. The economic account still disappoints us. At best, the economic account reveals bankruptcy law as "distinct" in purely quantitative terms. We might have expected that a system as complex and rich as bankruptcy law would be qualitatively distinct from nonbankruptcy law. An explanation that treats bankruptcy law as merely quantitatively distinct raises serious puzzles about matters that the economic account cannot explain.

For example, the economic account is unable to explain why we are loathe to abandon parts of bankruptcy law that seem in no way to further its supposedly distinct function. Consider one of the most pervasive doctrines in bankruptcy law: the rule of equality of distribution among similarly situated creditors. . . . How can the economic account, based solely on its economic model, explain this rule?

. . . The economic account . . . seeks to offer a vindicating explanation of the rule of creditor equality, but one that is based on a separate model. In this as well as other contexts, it uses what it refers to as the "creditors' bargain model." . . .

According to the economic account, these creditors would agree to the rule of equality. . . .

The use of the creditors' bargain model, however, does not solve the puzzle. As Professor David Carlson has pointed out, the creditors' bargain model is able to explain the rule of creditor equality only by presupposing what it is to prove. . . .

Ultimately, the creditors' bargain model suffers from the same disability as the economic model itself: its explanation is limited by the economic account's vision of bankruptcy law as a mechanism for achieving superior economic returns. . . . At best, a model based on these economic assumptions can produce only explanations vindicating rules that achieve certain economic outcomes.

That continues to leave unexplained the most important puzzle of all: if the essence of bankruptcy law is simply to maximize economic outcomes, why did bankruptcy law emerge as a system with the varied contours and dimensions that it has? . . .

II. Corporate Reorganization and the Reactionary Character of the Economic Account

A. *The Economic Account's Critique of Corporate Reorganization*

The economic account is like the stereotypical ugly American abroad. "The Eiffel Tower," he complains, "is not tall enough to be the Empire State Building and not expensive enough to be the Trump Tower." . . .

The economic account views corporate reorganization law exclusively as a mechanism for collecting debt and promoting certain economic outcomes. . . .

The economic account thus reduces the essence of corporate reorganization, like that of liquidation, to a sale of the common pool for the highest return. . . . In converting corporate reorganization entirely to these terms, the economic account implicitly bars the possibility that corporate reorganization may have a distinct role that involves its achieving not only economic, but also noneconomic outcomes.

After so reducing the possible role of corporate reorganization, the economic account proceeds to question whether such a process can be justified. . . .

Because bankruptcy law's distinct function is to maximize the value of the common pool, and because corporate reorganization does not yield better numbers than liquidation, corporate reorganization should be abolished.

The ugly American might sum up its views on the Eiffel Tower in these terms: "If they aren't going to build it up higher, they might as well tear it down." That is a hard claim to dispute on its own terms. It would be like trying to convince the ugly American to appreciate the Eiffel Tower by asking him to check its height again. The mistakes are not in his capacity to measure, but in what he has chosen to value.

The economic account translates corporate reorganization into a local instance of its own economic model. If corporate reorganization does not measure up to the economic account's standards, it can do nothing of value. By viewing the corporate reorganization process as involving essentially the sale of a pool, the economic account bases its normative position on an impoverished picture of corporate reorganization. More profoundly, it reflects the very perspective as to which the law of corporate reorganization has served as a corrective. It is thus a reactionary position. If taken seriously, it affirms a view of corporate bankruptcy that would carry the law back to a stage before corporate reorganization ever developed.

B. *The Development of Corporate Reorganization Law: Toward a New Vision of the Bankruptcy Process*

The economic account repudiates corporate reorganization law based on the very vision that, as a matter of history, corporate reorganization law itself has repudiated. In particular, corporate reorganization law has emerged, over the past century, by questioning and revising the two ideas implicit in the vision of the bankruptcy process as a sale of a pool: it has developed in reaction to the limits of viewing the corporation in bankruptcy as merely "a pool of assets," and of viewing the bankruptcy process as reducible to a "sale." . . .

1. *The Corporation in Bankruptcy as a Pool of Assets.*— . . . [C]orporate bankruptcy may appear to involve only property. . . .

But this view overlooks an essential aspect: a corporation is also an enterprise; it has personality. Unlike mere property, a corporation, whether in or out of bankruptcy, has potential. . . . In this sense, a corporation is not merely acted upon; it is, like an individual debtor, a moral, political, and social actor.

. . . The law of corporate reorganization developed as a corrective to a bankruptcy jurisprudence that would have ignored a financially distressed corporation's dynamic potential. It reflected a means of bringing the corporation's dynamic personality into public view and regulating not merely its economic division, but the playing out of its moral, political, and social values.

. . . While the equity receivership generally included a foreclosure of corporate assets, this sale was maintained as a mere ritual. By design and in substance, the receivership accomplished a quite different end—the continuation of the business. . . .

The equity receivership moved beyond corporate liquidation as the exclusive form of corporate bankruptcy and thus away from the concept of the corporation in bankruptcy as merely a pool of assets to be gathered and distributed. It was a move toward recognizing the corporation, even in bankruptcy, as a source of continuation and evolution. In bankruptcy, the corporation rediscovered its essential character as an enterprise with the potential to adjust and change.

After the equity receivership, the law of corporate bankruptcy has never been the same. In an essential way, the question whether the corporation should be treated as merely a pool of assets, or as a potentiality, had become obsolete. . . .

2. *The Bankruptcy Process as a "Sale."*— . . . [W]hile the equity receivership incorporated the ritual of sale, it also included rules and procedures that evidenced an appreciation of the inadequacy of viewing the corporate bankruptcy process as merely a "sale." Instead, in an important sense, the bankruptcy process consisted of the struggles for power, the ethical tensions, and the competition among diverse values that characterized insider negotiations about the terms of the corporation's continuation. . . .

Ultimately, the equity receivership was judged a failure not as a procedure for conducting a "sale," but as a mechanism for realizing the potentialities of the enterprise—of promoting rehabilitation through a fair, open process. . . .

The equity receivership had already undermined the concept of the corporation as merely a pool of assets and had relegated the concept of the bankruptcy process as a sale to ritualistic status. The equity receivership had established that, in bankruptcy, the corporation has potential—it may continue. . . .

Modern corporate reorganization law, including Chapters X and XI of the Bankruptcy Act and Chapter 11 of the Bankruptcy Code, is best understood as creating conditions for the realization of both economic and noneconomic aspects of the personality of the financially distressed corporation. It regulates the changes in personality that occur in this rehabilitative process. Its central metaphor is not the sale of the pool, but the reinvention of an enterprise. . . .

III. A VALUE-BASED ACCOUNT OF BANKRUPTCY LAW

The economic account has so neglected the dimensions and contours of bankruptcy law that it has misidentified what makes bankruptcy law distinct. At best, the economic account offers an undermining explanation of a bankruptcy system that recognizes noneconomic outcomes as independent values. At worst, the economic account does not explain "bankruptcy law" at all, but merely restates its own economic assumptions.

This Part will sketch an alternative, value-based account that will provide a vindicating explanation of bankruptcy law, one that explains why this "bankruptcy law" system has emerged with the contours and dimensions that it has. The value-based account thereby will enable itself to identify what makes bankruptcy law "distinct."

The economic account has misidentified the distinct function of bankruptcy law because, fundamentally, it has tracked the wrong problem from the start. The economic account views bankruptcy law as a response to the economic problem of collecting debt. In contrast, the value-based account is founded on a deeper understanding of the concern to which bankruptcy law is addressed. Bankruptcy law is a response to the problem of financial distress—not only as an economic, but as a moral, political, personal, and social problem that affects its participants. . . .

A. A Concept of "Financial Distress"

. . . As a first move toward defining a concept of "financial distress," we might say that a corporation is in financial distress when it faces actual or anticipated payment demands to which its own response is or is likely to be inadequate. . . .

Financial distress implicates a complex array of human values, only some of which can be measured in dollars. With the impairment of its capacities to adjust, the corporation flounders in direction and may struggle to explain itself to those affected by its distress—management, employees, shareholders, creditors, and the public. As the corporation struggles to define its current position and its aims, participants in the struggles to define its current position and its aims, participants in the financial distress, from management to the public, seek recognition of their individual demands—economic and noneconomic alike. As the situation worsens, they press their individual demands more urgently.

In this emergency, the participants in financial distress have conflicting interests. Some of these conflicts are economic. . . .

By no means, however, are the conflicts confined to a competition of economic interests. More realistically and profoundly, economic conflicts between participants of financial distress are occasions for the expression of their more fundamental moral, political, personal, and social values. . . .

These conflicts do not only exist between one participant and another; in their individual decision making as well, participants each face difficult choices between conflicting values. . . .

Financial distress forces its participants into these difficult choices. The chaos of financial distress is the chaos created by these individual, unorchestrated choices. Some employees or members of management stay, others leave; some work less, some work harder; some creditors sue, others do not. Financial distress feeds off of economic distress, but it is broader and more profound. What undermines a corporation is not merely a crisis of dollars, but a crisis of values experienced in individual ways by those who have contributed to and are affected by the enterprise.

. . . In financial distress, however, the corporation's capacity for meeting demands is seriously impaired. Financial distress works to reopen, among its participants, the questions of what the enterprise shall exist to do. . . . [B]ankruptcy law has the distinct function of providing a context in which that question can be addressed and answered.

B. *The Distinctness of Bankruptcy Law Under the Value-Based Account*

Bankruptcy law is a distinct system for responding to the problem of financial distress, understood as involving a crisis in values. It is "distinct" in two senses: no other legal system responds to the problem of financial distress understood in this special sense and, concomitantly, bankruptcy law provides a structure to perform this unique function. . . .

Bankruptcy law provides a forum in which competing and various interests and values accompanying financial distress may be expressed and sometimes recognized. Through the bankruptcy process, these competing interests are transformed, over time, into a renewed vision of the corporation as a moral, political, social, and economic actor. Bankruptcy law creates conditions for a special kind of discourse, one that is fundamentally rehabilitative in character. . . .

According to this view, bankruptcy law is not merely a form of collection law; unlike nonbankruptcy collection law, it is not simply a response to the problem of collecting debt. . . .

Bankruptcy law, however, is a legal system distinct from that of substantive nonbankruptcy law because it responds to a different problem—not the problem of rights per se, but the problem of financial distress. In responding to financial distress, bankruptcy law sometimes should and must alter rights recognized under substantive nonbankruptcy law. This is not a forbidden act, as the economic account suggests; it is an essential and inevitable part of a full response to the problem of financial distress.

Indeed, bankruptcy law is distinct precisely because it allows for a discourse in which the question of how financial distress should affect nonbankruptcy rights may be asked and ultimately answered. This question is complicated, and requires serious discussion among all those who will be affected by the outcome. . . . Bankruptcy law creates conditions for a discourse in which the problem of financial distress may be confronted on its own moral, political, personal, social, and economic terms.

Bankruptcy discourse is, fundamentally, open and open-ended. As participants confront the difficult questions that arise in financial distress, they begin to define a future for the enterprise. . . .

C. *The Basic Structure of Bankruptcy Discourse*

. . . Unlike mere property, a corporation has potential as an enterprise: it can continue to evolve and even change its personality. Whether and how long it continues and how it changes its personality affects people in ways that are not merely economic. The corporation is a moral, political, and social agent. The development of corporate reorganization law represents a move toward a view of the corporation in bankruptcy that accounts for this potential. . . .

. . . [B]ankruptcy discourse is radical and far-reaching. Once the estate is viewed as a dynamic and evolving enterprise, the fundamental question for bankruptcy discourse is altered. The question is no longer "what to do with the estate," as the model of the estate as a static pool might suggest. Rather, the question becomes: "what shall the estate exist to do." The estate is not merely an economic pie to be deployed and distributed. It is a medium by which the enterprise's moral, political, social, and economic aims are defined and redefined. By debating the aims of the estate as enterprise, participants express and explore the incommensurable values that accompany financial distress.

Modern corporate bankruptcy law allows for realization of the potential of the corporation, whatever form that potential ultimately takes. . . . Bankruptcy law creates conditions for an ongoing debate in which, by expressing these conflicting and incommensurable values, participants work toward defining and redefining the fundamental aims of the enterprise. Through the medium of bankruptcy discourse, the enterprise realizes its potential as a fully dimensional personality. . . .

CONCLUSION

. . . Ultimately, then, bankruptcy law must be explained not as a maximizer of economic outcomes, but as a system for rendering richer, more informed decisions in response to financial distress.

. . . [B]ankruptcy law frames decision making in a way that allows a full response to the problem of financial distress. Historically situated participants express conflicting and fundamentally incommensurable values; they make decisions based on the possible visions of the enterprise that exist—or that may be invented—at a particular moment in the case. Out of these debates, the enterprise is reconstructed as an expression of the concerns and values of those affected by the corporation's financial distress.

In an important sense, the progress of the estate may be compared with that of a human life. How does a person determine what is "good" for her? It is not a decision that can be made once and for all. Nor does the answer exist in any fixed, packaged form, like ingredients in a recipe. Instead a person makes frequent, historically situated decisions; and out of those decisions, a "new" person emerges. What is "good" for this new person may not be the same as for the original person. The answers change with the questions. The value-based account explains how, through answering changing questions in historically situated contexts, the participants in financial distress shape the process by which the "good" of the enterprise is realized.

"The challenge facing anyone who wants to write about bankruptcy policy," Professor Baird has stated, "is to explain why a distinct bankruptcy law exists at all." The value-based account explains bankruptcy law as existing to address the problem of financial distress and as creating conditions for a discourse in which values of participants may be rehabilitated into a coherent and informed vision of what the enterprise shall exist to do.

James W. Bowers
Whither What Hits the Fan?
Murphy's Law, Bankruptcy Theory,
and the Elementary Economics of Loss Distribution
26 GA. L. REV. 27 (1991)[*]

IV. WHY BANKRUPTCY

. . .

A. CUDDLES, KISSES, AND "COMMUNITY"

I contend that there is an economic justification for a form of bankruptcy law. Having concluded, however, not only that nonbankruptcy law is economically justified but also that bankruptcy law in its current form is not, I first must deal with the argument that there may be some "noneconomic" excuse for having bankruptcy law.

Bankruptcy law is concerned mostly with phenomena such as lending, borrowing, financial losses, stocks, bonds, contracts, payments, and security interests. Surely most people would grant that these can easily be classed as economic. Skepticism whether economic theory has anything to

---

    *   This Article was originally published at 26 Ga. L. Rev. 27 (1991) and is reprinted with permission.

contribute to the understanding of legal policies regulating these concededly "economic" activities thus seems misplaced when bankruptcy or collection law is the subject of concern. . . .

It is nevertheless demonstrable that the existing Bankruptcy Code has adopted overtly redistributive provisions. Economic theory in general has little to say about distributive questions. It does tend to address troublesome questions, however, to those with strong redistributive preferences.

. . . [W]hat may pass as criticism of economic analysis of collection and bankruptcy law is the assertion that the analysis, by its very nature, simply omits highly desired "other" values that are noneconomic. The argument goes something like this:

> Except at charity bazaar kissing booths and selected New Orleans street corners, Love is not bought and sold. Therefore the value of Love is not adequately accounted for in economic arguments. Since it is possible, for example, that bankruptcy law is designed to foster the development of a more loving, caring world, an economic justification (or critique) of bankruptcy law is fatally underinclusive because it does not account for this noneconomic value.

> Economists reject that argument. . . .

All of this discussion is relevant because academia, at least, is in a considerable state of doubt about whether and how the Bankruptcy Code can be justified. Dean Jackson and Professor Baird . . . have urged that an ideal bankruptcy law could be justified on economic grounds, at the same time demonstrating that the current Code deviates substantially from the ideal. Recently, Professor Korobkin has found a way to vindicate our current Code while at the same time explaining why Jackson and Baird failed to find any persuasive justification of Chapter 11 or reorganization law generally. His solution to the mystery, of course, is that Baird and Jackson overlooked noneconomic values in their analysis. They overlooked, he claims, the need for a distinctive system that fosters "rehabilitative discourse" (which, I suppose, is poststructuralist for "talk that makes somebody feel better") as therapy for "financial distress." We need Chapter 11, Korobkin explains, with all its specific redistributional features, so that folks in financial crises can have an opportunity to chat, after which everybody will feel a lot better about what Murphy's Law hath wrought. The result is known in advance—none of the talkers is going to get paid much, if anything. Thus Korobkin's attachment to talking is explainable only under Murphian premises. . . .

Murphians have always felt that those who think things could be made a whole lot better just by talking have failed to understand what Murphy said. . . . I doubt, however, that either Baird or Jackson has anything against talking (or even "discourse"), and they might even harbor the hope that talking can sometimes be therapeutic. Their objection to a regime in which people must talk would be based on the notion that talk is not necessarily cheap. They would ask, who should pay the costs of talking, and why them instead of the people being healed by it all? One objection to Chapter 11 is captured in the following story:

> You took my container of silver dollars. In a Chapter 11, I come to you and ask for my dollars back. Your response is : "The judge has enjoined you from asking for the dollars, but I'll tell you what. While I stand here plugging them into the slot machine, let's talk."

It is obvious that the gambler may feel better for the discourse so long as it forestalls paying. Murphians would ask how the owner of the carton of dollars feels, too, and might be skeptical, if not cynical, about how much better he feels for the little chat. . . .

If talk is so helpful and healing to everybody, the wonder of it is that more of it does not happen except in bankruptcy court. The reason, even Korobkin admits, is that most bankruptcy claimants do not value talk enough to do it without being compelled to. What is more, even if talk can be compelled, it might not do any good unless it is appropriately "orchestrated." I take that to mean what we need bankruptcy for is not only to compel people to talk but also to make them say what appeals to the bankruptcy judge's values. He listens to the conversations and then decides what to do based not on law but rather on noneconomic moral, political, and social values. It follows that any judge-made decision must be justified by these values, but we never need to know what they are. . . . All we need to know is that bankruptcy reorganization law is justified because it fosters (judges'?) undefended moral values.

In order, I presume, to distinguish his argument from the standard self-justifications of despots, Korobkin finally addresses the problem of inducing people to cooperate when doing so might make them all better off. It takes legal intervention, he asserts. At the end, however, his argument is almost identical to that of Baird and Jackson, who began by asking how to solve a particular type of perverse incentive problem (called the common pool problem by economists) and ended up advocating a law that forces a collective regime. It is odd how all those noneconomic values lead to the same place as those economic ones.

Karen Gross
The Need to Take Community Interests into Account in Bankruptcy: An Essay
72 Wash. U. L.Q. 1031 (1994)[*]

I. Introduction and Caveats

. . . I believe that community interests must be taken into account in both the corporate and personal bankruptcy systems. My belief that communities matter is obviously just a conclusory statement that masks numerous complex questions. For example, what is meant by "community"? What justifies taking the interests of "community" into account? How can we measure the value of community interests, and what are we valuing? How important are the interests of community in the context of the other interests that bankruptcy law must balance? Lastly, why should we depart (are we really departing?) so far from existing bankruptcy law, which is already having trouble doing that which it is supposed to do? . . .

II. Common Misperceptions

Before I begin, I want to be very clear about what I am *not* saying. . . . [I]t is easy to misunderstand and mischaracterize what it means to say that community matters. First, saying that community interests are important and must be taken into account in the bankruptcy process does *not* mean that the other interests that bankruptcy seeks to protect, such as those of creditors and equityholders, are forgotten. Thus, recognizing the import of community does not mean, *a fortiori*, that community interests trump other interests. Second, consideration of community is *not* necessarily a noneconomic decision and is also not, per se, economically inefficient. Taking community interests seriously is *not* synonymous with rejecting all economic modeling; what it reflects is a desire for a different, more expansive economic model. Such a model would account for (value) things not currently considered by the narrow economic paradigm. Finally, considering community does *not* mean that we should always save the buggy whip maker, the euphemism used . . . for the company whose need to exist has apparently obsolesced and whose prolonged existence through a Chapter 11 reorganization is a waste of both time and money. . . .

III. Underlying Assumptions and Theoretical Frameworks

. . . [I]t appears that two premises underlie the conclusion that community interests are not a necessary part of the bankruptcy debate. The first is that community interests are extremely difficult to quantify, and this difficulty accounts for, indeed justifies, their absence from an economic model of bankruptcy. The second premise is that community welfare and well-being are not appropriate concerns for bankruptcy. Instead, bankruptcy is all about repaying creditors in an efficient manner. Indeed, in many ways, a law and economics approach to bankruptcy can be described as "bankruptcy Darwinism"—only the fittest companies should survive. I refer to these two premises collectively as the "L & E Premises."

The L & E Premises, it seems to me, are seriously flawed. If the L & E Premises are flawed, it necessarily follows that the conclusions based on these premises are also flawed. Stated conversely, community is irrelevant only if one accepts the above two premises as true. . . .

V. The L & E Premises: Resting on Still Other Assumptions

Both the focus on quantification and the narrow approach to bankruptcy's scope in the L & E Premises demonstrate reliance on a traditional economic model that itself rests on certain underlying assumptions. . . . The assumptions that I believe underlie the L & E Premises are: (1) individuals are selfish and nonaltruistic (and hence disinterested in community concerns); (2) tastes and choices are unchanging and exogenous (and thus easily addressed through ex ante decisionmaking, usually in the form of a contract); and (3) interpersonal utility comparisons are impossible and that which we value can be expressed only in monetary terms. For reasons that I will explain, I disagree with these three assumptions on both feminist and communitarian grounds. And, if these assumptions fall, so do the L & E Premises. Furthermore, as previously noted, if the L & E Premises fall, so too does the position that community interests have no place in bankruptcy. . . .

A. *Human Nature*

Unlike the assumption in the traditional economic model, I do not believe that people are inherently self-interested and nonaltruistic. I have an optimistic view of human nature and believe that there is room and desire for altruism. . . .

A belief in the goodness of human nature leads to another conclusion. In defining the scope of corporate and personal bankruptcy, we should care about the universe beyond the debtor and its immediate creditors. Communitarian thinking is helpful in this regard. As the communitarian movement has pointed out, a rights-centered conceptualization of the world ignores the fact that individuals live in society. And, with rights also come responsibilities. Unlike law and economics. communitarianism rejects a contractarian model of the world. Instead, it suggests a model in which we are challenged to act as our brother's and sister's keeper. . . .

The application of communitarian concepts to the world of bankruptcy suggests that the welfare of the community should be very much a part of corporate bankruptcy. While it may not be evident to those with a different conceptualization of rights and responsibilities, community *does and should* matter to those addressing both corporate and personal bankruptcy. . . .

This is a very different vision of the world than that which would grow out of the L & E Premises. It is not surprising that this vision of community would produce a different set of issues to consider in the context of developing a bankruptcy system.

B. *Contracting Everything Away*

Turning to the second assumption, I believe that people do change and that life's exigencies and the passage of time do call for us to rethink personal decisions that we have made. . . . The recognition that our decisions may change and that such changes are not bad makes us uncomfortable because it disturbs our need for certainty. It makes planning difficult, although far from impossible. On the positive side, it permits flexibility and malleability, concepts with singular importance in bankruptcy.

In terms of the L & E Premises, this means that basing a legal theory on ex ante decisionmaking (default rules) is problematic at its core. Creating a legal system based on how we believe people will act, essentially conjecturing, and then binding them to those conjectures (generally by contract) is certain to create problems. Not only may the initial conjectures be wrong, but the choices among the conjectures may change as well. . . .

Indeed, in this context, we would be well-served to reflect on how contract law addresses unforeseen events. Despite the efforts of parties to contract for all future events, they frequently fail to foresee everything that can happen. . . . So, courts have had to interject their own view of what should transpire between the parties. Indeed, there is a growing tendency in contract law to move beyond the paradigm of a voluntary, private relationship between two parties. . . .

My concerns about ex ante decisionmaking are based on feminist theory. It has (until quite recently) been assumed that everyone approaches decisionmaking in the same way (utilizing what could be termed "male dominated" thinking). That is far from the truth. Decisionmaking is extremely complex. For example, some people are more goal-directed than others. Some are more concerned about the effect of decisions on others. Moreover, decisions are frequently not as freely made as some people believe. What we decide may be based on issues over which we have no control. Indeed, were we armed with knowledge, power, and money, many of our decisions would be altered. Life experience tells me that we respond to day-to-day issues differently than we might expect and that change is not necessarily so bad. Similarly, crises (such as illness or financial distress) evoke different conclusions when we view them in the concrete as opposed to the abstract.

. . . Indeed, what is best may change when one actually confronts a real situation. And, if we have trouble keeping promises with ourselves, it is no wonder that we have trouble keeping them with others.

C. Measuring: What and How

Turning to the third assumption, I do not believe that personal utility comparisons are unquantifiable. I agree with the L & E Premises that they cannot easily be quantified under existing economic models. They do not easily lend themselves to a wealth maximization formula because wealth maximization is directed to individual enhancement rather than enrichment (monetary or nonmonetary) realized through another's enrichment or the enrichment of a community. . . . However, it is possible to develop other ways of measuring utilities. We should be able to account for altruism in some way. . . . I have confidence in the ability to measure seemingly amorphous concepts (which could be termed externalities in economic parlance) if we set about trying to do so rather than assuming it cannot be done.

Perhaps more importantly, even if some community interests could never be measured in economic terms, that does not mean, a fortiori, that they lack value. It is certainly possible that there are things of value that we cannot quantify. For me, their nonquantification does not make them unimportant to our world. The inability to translate the interests of community into money . . . does not mean that they lack worth. Instead, it means that we have to consider "worth" in both economic and noneconomic terms.

This leads me to conclude that the third assumption, like the first two, is flawed. It does not necessarily follow that community should not be considered because it cannot be quantified. It may be that there are other reasons for which community interests should be discarded in the bankruptcy context but nonquantification is not among them.

VI. GETTING OUT FROM BEING UNDER: FOOTNOTES, SILENCE AND BEYOND

. . . The heart of the debate about bankruptcy policy involves a determination of who and what the system is designed to protect. That is a question that we need to address. And, we need to address it where everyone can see it and engage in the debate. We do not need to be wed to the law as it is; we do not even need to justify change based on what was. But, we do need to discuss the fundamental issues, informed by what is currently happening in the bankruptcy system to the extent that we have that information or can gather it based on new empirical work. It is my hope that . . . all of us [will] bring issues to the table. Indeed, in that regard, we would do well prospectively to include anthropology, sociology, and psychology on our list of disciplines that can enrich our thinking on bankruptcy. Then, we can all sit down at the table and discuss what the bankruptcy buffet currently has to offer, what new foods (ideas and data) need to be added, developed, or created, and then what we will each choose to eat and why.

Robert K. Rasmussen
An Essay on Optimal Bankruptcy Rules and Social Justice
1994 U. ILL. L. REV. 1[*]

This essay responds to the nonutilitarian attack on the economic conception of bankruptcy law. I argue that the conception of bankruptcy law produced by the economic theorists better comports with a nonutilitarian perspective of social justice. In doing so, I rely heavily on John Rawls's seminal work, *A Theory of Justice*. Rawls's celebrated work offers a comprehensive alternative to an economic vision of social justice. Indeed, Rawls conceived his work as an alternative to utilitarian thought in general. Rather than viewing justice as maximization of utility, Rawls defined justice as fairness.

Those who endorse the traditional understanding of bankruptcy law appear to share this focus on fairness. Concerns with fairness run throughout their work. Despite this mutual emphasis on fairness, however, Rawls's compelling work does not lead to an endorsement of the ideas advanced by traditional bankruptcy theorists. Instead, a Rawlsian approach to bankruptcy law is much more attuned with the concerns of economic theorists. Rawls differs from traditional bankruptcy theorists, not so much in the goals sought to be achieved, but rather in the perspective that he takes. Rawls begins his inquiry from the "original position." . . .

Rawls proposes that those in the original position would attempt to maximize the position of the least advantaged members of society. This "difference principle" . . . contains a highly redistributive element: Inequalities are allowed only to the extent that they improve the lot of the least fortunate. When Rawls's difference principle is applied to the competing bankruptcy theories, the economic approach proves itself more capable of protecting the interests of the least advantaged. . . . [A]ll groups which might possibly qualify as the least fortunate fare better under the economic approach to bankruptcy law than under the traditional theory.

The importance of this conclusion cannot be overstated. John Rawls is the architect of modern social-justice theory, and the fact that his views of social justice comport with an economic approach to bankruptcy law completely undermines arguments which reject, solely on fairness grounds, the economic approach. . . .

I. Bankruptcy from the Original Position
A. Why Rawls?

. . . Rawls's project shares the premises and values espoused by those who embrace the traditional approach to bankruptcy law. If Rawls's conception of social justice nevertheless supports the economic approach to bankruptcy law, the assertion that such an approach slights important values would be seriously undermined. . . .

Rawls's work contains a strong redistributive element. . . . Rawls's preference for redistribution tracks one of the main themes in traditional bankruptcy scholarship. Indeed, some scholars defend current bankruptcy law because of its redistributive element. Thus, one might think that if any theory of social justice could supply a philosophical foundation for the traditional approach to bankruptcy, it would be that of Rawls.

B. Rawls's A Theory of Justice *and Bankruptcy Law*

Rawls's *A Theory of Justice* offers a theory which attempts to establish standards under which a society can be considered just. This theory focuses on what Rawls terms the *basic structure* of society, and the way in which this structure distributes *primary goods*. . . .

Bankruptcy law . . . is an appropriate subject for the application of Rawls's theory of justice. The operation of a private property, market-based economy, such as the current American system, directly implicates bankruptcy law. . . .

The structure of the economy clearly falls within Rawls's definition of the basic structure of society. The economic system is the central way by which a society creates wealth and decides which goods are to be created. Wealth and income, two of Rawls's primary goods, are created and distributed by a country's economic system. . . .

Rawls posits that a society is just when the basic structure by which it distributes primary goods is "fair." Indeed, Rawls describes his entire project as "Justice as Fairness." Fairness, for Rawls, is a procedural fairness. In other words, fairness occurs when the principles governing society have been selected according to the proper procedures; there is no external constraint on the *content* of these principles.

The appropriate procedures, for Rawls, begin from the "original position," which asks what political system people would prospectively choose if they did not know what their place in society would be. This approach prevents the status quo from serving as a justification for itself, and also prevents individual members of a society from denoting a system as "just" solely because it allows them to retain or obtain a favored place in that system. Under Rawls's approach, those in the original position are unaware of their current amount of societal wealth and the nature and extent of their natural abilities. Rawls thus treats wealth and natural abilities as societal, rather than individual, assets.

Thus, persons in the original position evaluate competing societal institutions from behind a thick veil of ignorance. They do not know whether they are rich or poor, smart or dumb, female or male. These individuals are, however, moral persons in the sense that they can understand and act according to the selected principles of justice and that they can form judgments and act according to their own sense of the good. . . .

. . . The parties are not altruistic, however, in using this knowledge to choose a just society. Rather, each person—or one person chosen at random—seeks to further her own ends as best she can determine them in the absence of complete self-knowledge.

Applying Rawls's theory to bankruptcy involves evaluating the form of bankruptcy law from the original position, behind the veil of ignorance. . . .

Bankruptcy law affects firms both inside and outside of bankruptcy. For example, bankruptcy law can affect a debtor's competitors. . . .

Moreover, the consequences of bankruptcy law extend well beyond the firm's competitors. Bankruptcy law affects interest rates that all firms must pay, regardless of whether they eventually end up in bankruptcy. . . .

If a bankruptcy regime causes a rise in interest rates, fewer business ventures will be undertaken in the first instance, and existing businesses will have a harder time servicing debt payments, driving more firms into financial distress. Both of these effects will in turn reduce the number of jobs available in the economy. When a bankruptcy regime protects certain persons who have dealt with a bankrupt firm, this protection may come at the expense of others in society who would have obtained jobs but for the rise in interest rates caused by the bankruptcy regime. In comparing competing bankruptcy regimes, it is important to use a scheme which will assess the effect on those firms which file for bankruptcy *and* those entities which, although they might not file for bankruptcy, are nonetheless affected by the governing bankruptcy law. . . .

Rawls argues that behind the veil of ignorance, parties would first select two principles of justice by which they evaluate competing societal structures. The first principle of justice is that "each person is to have an equal right to the most extensive basic liberty compatible with a similar liberty for others." This principle addresses the dispensation of society's basic rights and liberties. The second principle of justice is that "social and economic inequalities are to be arranged so that they are both . . . reasonably expected to be to everyone's advantage, and . . . attached to positions and offices open to all." Rawls defines this second principle of justice as the *difference principle*. This principle governs the dispensation of the remainder of society's primary goods.

Application of the difference principle in assessing competing societal structures requires a lexical ordering of such structures. Such a process compares the position of the worst-off class of individuals under the competing regimes. If these individuals are treated better in one regime than the other, the former regime is chosen. . . . In other words, parties in the original position select among competing institutions based on the "maximin" principle. This principle, as its name implies, seeks to maximize the utility of the class in the minimum position, *i.e.*, the class which has the smallest amount of primary goods. The baseline is thus equal distribution of the primary goods which remain after the first principle of justice has been implemented. . . .

. . . By accepting the difference principle as a criterion of analysis, I endeavor to meet the traditionalists' objections on their own terms. I am thus willing to assume, for the purposes of this essay, that bankruptcy law should be primarily concerned with the status of the least-advantaged members of society. It remains to be determined, nevertheless, which conception of bankruptcy, the economic or the traditional approach, comports with the difference principle.

II. Selection of a Socially Just Bankruptcy Regime
A. Application of Rawls's First Principle

. . . [C]onstitutional implementation of the first principle of justice has no effect on the contours of bankruptcy law. . . .

B. Application of the Difference Principle

. . . [L]aws established by the legislature implement the second principle of justice, the difference principle. Legislators thus seek to enact "social and economic policies . . . aimed at maximizing the long-term expectations of the least advantaged . . . ."

. . . [W]e can conclude that the Rawlsian legislature would select the economic vision of bankruptcy law over that proposed by the traditionalists. . . .

C. The Difference Principle and Modern Economic Bankruptcy Theories:
General Considerations

. . . The modern economic conception of bankruptcy law comports with the goal of maximizing societal wealth. The basic insight supporting this conclusion is that the payoff which debt collection law gives to a consensual creditor is part of the initial contract between a creditor and the firm. The more a creditor expects to receive upon default, the lower the interest rate it will charge.
. . .

The question remains whether legislators behind the veil of ignorance would enact an economically-derived bankruptcy regime when faced with the choice between it and current law. In Rawlsian terms, the hypothetical legislature must choose which of the competing conceptions of bankruptcy better comports with the difference principle. . . .

The problem of determining who counts as the least advantaged remains. . . . I have selected groupings based on the standard distinctions found in the bankruptcy literature. These include employees, tort victims, shareholders, consensual creditors, and members of the firm's community.

. . . As each type of party is analyzed, I assume that party to be in fact the least advantaged. I then examine whether the treatment of that party under an economic account of bankruptcy law, as opposed to current law, violates the difference principle, and would thus cause those in the original position to reject the economic regime. . . .

III. CLASSES OF CREDITORS AFFECTED BY BANKRUPTCY
A. Consensual Creditors

The group least likely to be composed of society's most-disadvantaged members is the firm's consensual creditors. Nevertheless, engaging in the contrary assumption, the economic vision of bankruptcy law clearly prevails over the traditional view when measured from the original position.
. . .

It is . . . reasonable to conclude that redistribution away from consensual creditors will cause them to raise their interest rates. Given this situation, those in the original position would, to the extent they considered relevant the treatment of consensual creditors under the difference principle, select the economic approach to bankruptcy law over the current system.

B. Shareholders

A second group of individuals that bankruptcy law affects is the firm's shareholders. As with consensual creditors, it is unlikely that this class of persons would be the least advantaged in a bankruptcy proceeding. . . . Nevertheless, if shareholders are the least advantaged, the difference principle requires that those behind the veil of ignorance reject the current form of Chapter 11 in favor of the economic approach to corporate bankruptcy law. . . . [E]mpirical analysis reveals that shareholders consistently receive distributions from a firm under federal bankruptcy law despite the fact that the firm's unsecured creditors are not paid in full.

. . . Shareholder protection, to the extent that it does not come at the expense of nonconsensual creditors, must come at the expense of consensual creditors. . . . Consensual creditors, however, will charge shareholders higher interest rates for the protection provided. Viewed in this light, to the extent that bankruptcy law protects shareholder interests, it acts as a form of financial distress insurance. . . .

Some shareholders might very well want such insolvency insurance if given the choice. It is unlikely, however, that *all* shareholders would find the protections offered by current bankruptcy law worth the price of higher interest rates. The economic vision of bankruptcy permits shareholders to decide whether such insurance is desirable. . . . Thus, if shareholders are the persons least advantaged in bankruptcy, the difference principle's concern with maximizing their welfare would ensure that the economic view of bankruptcy prevails over the traditional approach.

C. The Surrounding Community

The third group of persons affected when a firm enters bankruptcy is those individuals who live in the surrounding community. Supporters of the present form of Chapter 11 often invoke community interests in justifying the pro-reorganization bias of current law. When a firm fails, especially a large one, those in the community are made worse off. . . . The strength of this argument depends on how many firms are saved under the current law that would otherwise be lost under a bankruptcy regime based on the economic theory of bankruptcy law. The consequences of a bankruptcy regime for any given community will never be completely positive or negative. Some communities will suffer greatly when a firm located in that community files for bankruptcy. Protecting these communities by encouraging reorganization at all costs, however, will harm other communities. . . .

Faced with this state of affairs, those in the original position would have to make an educated guess about the competing effects of the economic and traditional approaches to bankruptcy law. Behind the veil of ignorance, legislators do not know the type of community in which they live. The first matter the legislature must decide is the relevant benchmark by which to measure these effects. To the extent that by encouraging reorganization, bankruptcy law raises interest rates, and this increase causes another firm to fail, the comparison is straightforward. The legislators in the original position simply compare the number of firms which are saved to the number which are lost. . . .

In the end, it is necessary to compare the effects of the competing bankruptcy approaches on corporate formation and survival. The question is not whether Chapter 11 saves some firms—there is no question that it does. Rather, the inquiry for those in the original position is whether, as a comparative matter, the traditional approach saves more firms than does the economic approach, and if so, whether there are sufficient benefits from the economic approach in terms of encouraging new firms, and allowing existing firms to service their debt, which offset the advantage that the current form of Chapter 11 has in terms of maintaining existing firms.

It is difficult to imagine that Chapter 11 saves significantly more firms than would the economic approach to bankruptcy law. . . .

Moreover, to the extent that an efficient bankruptcy regime would lower the interest rate that all firms pay for credit, one would expect that fewer firms would face financial distress in the first instance. . . . [A]n economic conception of bankruptcy law promises to have a beneficial indirect effect of decreasing the number of firms facing financial distress. This conclusion, coupled with that regarding firm formation, implies that those in the original position would, if they viewed members of the surrounding community as the least advantaged, select an economic conception of bankruptcy over the traditional one.

D. Tort Creditors

Tort creditors are the fourth group of persons affected by a bankruptcy regime. The group for which perhaps most traditional bankruptcy scholars express the greatest sympathy consists of those persons injured in some fashion by the operations of the firm. Such sympathy is hardly surprising. Existing nonbankruptcy law contains two features which disadvantage these individuals. These features are limited shareholder liability and according tort claimants priority status equal to that of general unsecured creditors. Taken together, these rules tend to result in tort creditors receiving minimal payouts from insolvent firms. This shabby treatment of tort creditors has prompted traditional bankruptcy scholars to advocate an increased ability for such persons to recover on their claims.
. . .

The difference principle suggests that the Rawlsian legislature would adopt . . . priority for tort creditors coupled with unlimited liability. From the perspective of the original position, this proposal better serves the interest of the least advantaged than the competing proposals. . . .

In sum, if those in the original position considered tort victims to be the least-advantaged members of society affected by the bankruptcy regime, they would, applying the difference principle, adopt the economic approach to bankruptcy law over current law. Moreover, a Rawlsian legislature would probably select a tort system which gives tort creditors a priority to the firm's assets, and makes the firm's shareholders individually liable on a pro rata basis if the firm's assets are insufficient to fully compensate all tort victims.

E. Employees

The final class of individuals affected by bankruptcy law is the firm's employees. Bankruptcy courts and academics often justify Chapter 11 by invoking the need to save jobs. Indeed, my sense is that workers are most likely to be the least-advantaged group in any given bankruptcy proceeding. . . . But, does the prospect of being an employee, who may be the least advantaged of those affected by financial distress, suggest that those in the original position would endorse current law? Again, the focus must not be on whether current law or the economic theory of bankruptcy increases the welfare of employees of firms that have already filed for bankruptcy, but instead on which vision of bankruptcy law increases the welfare of workers as a group. . . .

The present form of bankruptcy law may very well be superior to a regime based on economic theory for those less-skilled employees able to actually secure employment under current conditions. These employees receive benefits under the present form of Chapter 11 from two potential sources: redistributions from firms which ultimately fail, and the ability to keep their jobs in those firms which successfully reorganize under Chapter 11. . . .

The present form of bankruptcy law thus benefits some employees, but those in the original position would ascribe little weight to such a gain. At most, this type of bankruptcy redistribution provides a short-term increase in employee income. . . .

Supporters of Chapter 11 argue that the present form of bankruptcy law not only saves jobs in the short term, . . . but in the long term as well. . . . Evaluating this claim from the original position turns on the number of jobs current law is likely to save as compared to the economic approach. If current law does save a more significant number of jobs than the economic approach would, this fact would be a strong argument in favor of its adoption by those in the original position. Indeed, it would probably be compelling.

There is little evidence, however, that these savings exist. First, the number of successful reorganizations tends to be small. . . . Moreover, many successful reorganizations which do result in job retention, such as those of large publicly-held companies . . ., would not end up as piecemeal liquidations under the economic approach. . . . Thus, there is little reason to suggest that the economic approach would result in fewer jobs being saved than are saved under current law.

Nevertheless, I am willing to assume for the sake of argument that present bankruptcy law saves some jobs in firms which experience financial distress that would be lost under an economic approach. This does not mean, however, that legislators behind the veil of ignorance would reject the economic approach in favor of current law based on the possibility that each legislator might end up being an employee who has little choice in selecting her employer. The choice of bankruptcy regimes affects not only those who work for firms in financial distress, but also other actual and potential workers. In particular, if a bankruptcy regime redistributes wealth to workers, this redistribution will result in increased interest rates which consensual creditors charge the firm. This increase in interest rates in turn causes additional firms to fail—thus losing those jobs—and other firms not to form in the first instance—causing a loss of potential jobs. Behind the veil of ignorance, the legislators do not know whether they will be workers favored by a bankruptcy redistribution, or instead an employee whose job prospects are lessened by bankruptcy's redistributive element.

Faced with this uncertainty, a Rawlsian legislature would attempt to compare the number of jobs saved and lost under the competing bankruptcy regimes. Thus, the inquiry boils down to whether the economic account of bankruptcy law would create significantly many more jobs than it destroys. All available evidence suggests that it favors job creation. . . . [T]he subsequent increase in interest rates will ultimately exceed the benefits to employees. For these reasons, bankruptcy redistributions favoring employees do not maximize the position of the worst off. Instead, workers are, as an overall group, negatively impacted under a traditional approach. The chance of being a worker would thus lead those in the original position to select an economic bankruptcy regime.

F. Further Considerations

The Rawlsian analysis does not conclude with the application of the difference principle. After the principles of justice are implemented, the resulting institutions are compared with our intuition. Rawls terms this comparison "reflective equilibrium." . . .

The economic theory of bankruptcy easily passes this test. American society is by no means wedded to the current form of reorganization law. . . .

In summary, the conclusions from applying Rawls's analysis to the ongoing bankruptcy debate is that those in the original position would enact an economically-derived bankruptcy regime rather than current law. Furthermore, the economic approach also meets Rawls's requirement of reflective equilibrium. Thus, *A Theory of Justice*, fairly considered, endorses the justness of a social institution which handles the problems of financial distress from an economic perspective. . . .

V. CONCLUSION

. . . In considering bankruptcy law, arguments for wealth-maximization and justice-enhancement actually coincide to support the adoption of an economic approach to such law. A bankruptcy regime designed to promote efficiency ensures that the least-fortunate members of society, whoever they may be, are treated better than they are under current bankruptcy law. . . .

This overlap between the demands of efficiency and the requirements of social justice should not be surprising. Rawls, unlike some bankruptcy law scholars, is not hostile to efficiency. . . . To be sure, social justice at times demands redistribution from the more affluent to those who are less well off. There is little reason to suggest, however, that bankruptcy law, broadly defined, should be the vehicle for this reallocation.

John D. Ayer
*Bankruptcy as an Essentially Contested Concept:
The Case of the One-Asset Case*
44 S.C. L. REV. 863 (1993)[*]

Bedenk: Man liebt den kase wohl, indessen man deckt ihn zu. (Consider: We like cheese well enough, but we still cover it up.)

—WILHELM BUSCH

There has been an explosion of good academic work recently about bankruptcy. Some of it has attempted to identify a sort of essence or unifying core of bankruptcy. I call this "mainline scholarship," for lack of a better name. Alongside it stands a genre of scholarship that seems to sidestep the austere parsimony of the "unifying core" material, seeking instead to take account of the refractory complexity of bankruptcy practice. As much as I admire some of the mainline work, I have perhaps a greater temperamental affinity for this "revisionist" material because it seems to do a better job of keeping in touch with the irreducible indeterminacy of bankruptcy as a theater for human greed and betrayal, with all the attendant hopes and disappointments.

Yet much of this revisionist scholarship, admirable though it may be, seems in an important sense less radical than it may appear at first glance. For the revisionist scholarship shares with its more elegant predecessor the fundamental assumption that there is a core of some sort in bankruptcy law. Thus, mainline scholarship seeks to articulate the core of bankruptcy law in ideas such as asset allocation, efficiency, and so forth—the standard jargon of economics. Revisionist scholarship, to its great credit, tries to show how bankruptcy, for all its dynamism and fluidity, serves recognizable social goals (even if dynamism and fluidity are the goals that it serves). Both mainline and revisionist scholarship are thus seen as irenic, in the theological sense of the term.

In this Article, I take a somewhat different spin on the problem by suggesting that bankruptcy may harbor no purpose at all, except in the most attenuated sense. Specifically, I suggest that the "purpose," if you can call it that, of bankruptcy law may be to serve no purpose at all, other than to take highly divisive conflicts over public policy and dispose of them under the pretense that they have been resolved, while in fact not resolving them at all. In effect, I attempt to exhibit bankruptcy as an "essentially contested concept"—a mechanism that, by its nature and not by accident or inadequacy, harbors irreconcilable conflicts. The idea, then, would be to use the rhetoric of the law as a rallying-point for some kind of social solidarity, while leaving important conflicts intentionally (and perhaps mercifully?) unresolved.

It is obvious how this idea differs from standard "unifying core" scholarship. Perhaps less obvious is how the idea differs from what I have called revisionist work, but I think the difference is important and should be emphasized. The standard revisionist texts seem to suggest that the arena of conflict in bankruptcy law is structured as it is to serve as a kind of therapeutic exercise in which "justice" will emerge from "combat," on the metaphor, perhaps, of a trial.

My view is somewhat more skeptical (I do not say cynical). I tend to view the matter as one of not so much solving a problem as getting rid of it—putting it out of harm's way while keeping the books straight and general principles intact. This idea, of course, is a kind of "purpose," just as the number "one" is a kind of "prime number," in the sense that a prime is any number that cannot be divided except by itself or one. But this is a somewhat attenuated view of the term, and I will not let it me detain me here.

As the reader may surmise, I believe that this view of things is a helpful way of approaching a great many areas of the law. The principle could be demonstrated in any of a number of facets of bankruptcy law. . . .

V. SUMMARY: AGAINST PYRRHONISM

The point of this exercise has been to suggest that in one arena, at least, there is no pattern or predictability to bankruptcy cases. . . .

I do not mean to deprecate the value of abstraction. Certainly if we did not abstract and simplify, we could never speak or think at all, because no two things are precisely alike; everything is unique. The reader can be assured that there is indeed a category called "bankruptcy" and that useful generalizations can be made about it. But unifying principles come in many forms. And while I deny that there is any "core idea" to govern the one-asset bankruptcy case, I do suggest that there is an intelligible reason for the lack of a core idea; and this intelligible reason may perfectly well constitute a "core idea" all its own. The difficulty, if there is one, is only that we have moved to a separate logical plane.

In an earlier draft, the title of this Article was "Bankruptcy as an Evasion." But I do not wish to be misunderstood. As a concept, evasion needs a press agent. To impute evasion to bankruptcy might be understood as accusing bankruptcy of having failed to meet some obligation that it should serve. This is not at all what I mean. Rather, let me make clear that I have no particular hostility to evasions: I think they can serve a useful purpose in the law, and in society. If each of us knew what the rest of us were thinking—really thinking—at any given moment, we would probably be at war all the time.

There are good reasons for shoving problems under the table and for making the rally 'round symbols of unity. You pay a price for this sort of thing, of course, but I am not so sure the price is always as high as we suppose it is. For example, it is probably true that the world is a somewhat less predictable place than it would be if the rules were neater. But from the standpoint of litigation, I suspect that good lawyers probably exercise a palpable (and marketable) skill in narrowing the bounds of uncertainty, whatever the stated general rules. . . .

Finally, there is good reason to believe that "clear" rules are never as clear as they seem. The more precise and specific, the more energy the parties expend in developing means of coping with the resulting inconvenience.

"What is truth? said jesting Pilate, and would not stay for an answer." Bacon's jibe is understood to reflect badly on Pilate, but perhaps he knew more than we give him credit for. Holmes said that it is the genius of the common law to decide the case first and think of the reason afterwards. Justice is not only blind; at times she seems developmentally disabled as well. In a perfect world, you might want more. But in a perfect world, you would not need justice at all.

Christopher W. Frost
Bankruptcy Redistributive Policies and the Limits of the Judicial Process
74 N.C. L. Rev. 75 (1995)[*]

INTRODUCTION

. . . This Article examines the problem of determining the incidence of redistributive cost in the bankruptcy system. . . . [T]he focus here is on the practical problem of fitting means to ends. Concluding that non-investors should be afforded some relief from the most devastating effects of financial failure is only the beginning of the inquiry. A rational bankruptcy policy must ensure both that such relief goes to those in need and that its costs are not borne by those least able to pay. This Article demonstrates that the bankruptcy process specifically and the judicial process generally are poorly designed to render informed and rational judgments on these questions. . . .

I. BANKRUPTCY THEORY AND THE INCLUSION OF NON-INVESTOR INTERESTS

. . . A justification for limiting bankruptcy law to the enforcement of investor claims is possible. Treating bankruptcy as a broadly inclusive device intended to protect the interests of investors and non-investors alike requires close scrutiny of the capabilities of the process to achieve those goals. It is not enough simply to point to problems in need of resolution. We must further assess the fit between our normative goals and the institutions designed to achieve them. As this Article will demonstrate, bankruptcy in particular and the judicial process generally are poorly designed to achieve redistributive goals. . . .

II. Non-Investor Protection Under Chapter 11

One of the primary grounds for criticism of the creditor wealth-maximization criterion is that it is not an accurate description of the current bankruptcy system. The bankruptcy process departs from non-bankruptcy priorities in ways that cannot be justified under the economic criterion. Thus, critics argue, bankruptcy can only be explained fully in terms that include loss allocation and the protection of non-investor interests as a fundamental policy. . . .

. . . [N]on-investor protection in the bankruptcy process may have economy-wide effects that are poorly considered due to the indirect nature of the protection. Bankruptcy judges and lawyers speak in economic and legal terms rather than social terms. Under its current design, the reorganization process pushes social policy concerns into the background where they lurk unspoken. Facts essential to determining the social costs of failure find no means of expression. As a consequence, while it is possible that the process serves some broad social function, we cannot be sure of the level of such concern, its cost, or who bears that cost. As a matter of institutional design, the current bankruptcy regime seems ill-suited to undertake an analysis of the difficult policy choices implicated by distributive goals.

III. Distributive Justifications for a Protective Bankruptcy Regime

Of course, the fact that the existing bankruptcy process does not provide a coherent means of distributing the social costs of business failure does not provide a normative justification for excluding non-investor interests from its reach. It may simply point out the need for reform. It might be possible to craft a bankruptcy scheme that explicitly considers the costs and benefits of non-investor protection in particular cases. . . .

The observation that the specific managerial and representational difficulties involved in the protection of non-investor interests might be resolved places us at a crossroads. Should corporate bankruptcy reform take us in the direction of creating a broad, inclusive regime designed to balance all of the competing interests affected by business failure? Or should we instead limit the reorganization process so that it focuses solely on investor claims, and leave the alleviation of the hardship associated with business failure to other institutions?

The practical and normative dimensions of such questions are interwoven. What we should be looking for in choosing a direction is the fit between the practical capabilities of the process and the normative policies chosen. . . .

A. The Normative Dimension:
Departures from Explicit Contracting Based on Distributive Aims

. . . [E]fficiency concerns point in the direction of a bankruptcy regime that focuses solely on creditor wealth maximization. This baseline leaves non-investors the ability to bargain for protection individually or in groups, ensuring maximum flexibility in the structure of default risk relationships. The alternative would likely result in mandated protection of non-investor interests because contracting for a complete waiver of such protections would be prohibitively expensive.

Of course, this efficiency-oriented analysis implicates some fairly strong moral arguments. . . .

A bankruptcy regime protective of the interests of non-investor constituencies would impose a redistributive device . . . . Under such a regime, credit contracts would include a mandatory term alleviating the harshness of strict enforcement in the event of general financial failure. Such a term would create rights benefitting non-investors beyond those created by their contractual or tort-based relationship with the firm. Against an existing social and legal regime that grants primacy to the notion of freedom of contract, such a mandatory term finds its justification in the desire to call off freedom of contract to serve distributional aims.

B. The Practical Dimension:
Achieving Distributional Ends Through Bankruptcy Policy

It is pointless to debate the desired ends of a legal institution without developing a sense of whether the institution under study is capable of achieving those ends. It is not my aim to make the definitive case for or against redistributive urgings. For purposes of this Article, we may assume that these goals are desirable. The importance of understanding the moral justifications for a redistributive bankruptcy policy lies principally in the practical questions such justifications generate.

A decision to redistribute entitlements through the bankruptcy process raises two principal concerns. Initially, because the redistributive policy is likely to result in allocational inefficiencies, the process must enable the decisionmaker to understand and control the level of redistribution. . . .

An equally serious problem raised by redistributive policies is defining the group that will ultimately bear the cost of the redistributions. . . . It is this problem that most clearly illustrates the inadequacies of the bankruptcy process. . . .

An analysis of distributional goals cannot end with moral arguments regarding the desirability of wealth redistributions. Once the desirability of such transfers is established, the analysis must consider whether the institution under study is capable of realizing such goals. As illustrated earlier, our current bankruptcy process is ill-suited to the task. The remainder of the Article demonstrates the inability of any judicial process to come to grips with the questions raised by bankruptcy redistributional policies.

IV. PROBLEMS IN DETERMINING THE INCIDENCE OF REDISTRIBUTIVE COST

Determining who would bear the cost of protecting non-investor interests in the bankruptcy process is likely to be an extremely complex, if not impossible, task. The cost of allocative inefficiency created by a redistributive bankruptcy system will be spread in at least two ways. First, the cost will be spread through increases in the cost of capital as investors adjust their required returns in response to the possible redistributions. Second, some of the cost may be borne by industry competitors as the bankruptcy process maintains businesses in industries suffering from overcapacity. The results of both types of loss spreading are difficult to predict. . . .

V. BANKRUPTCY REDISTRIBUTIONS AND THE LIMITS OF THE JUDICIAL PROCESS

Regardless of the strength of our commitment to achieving a just distribution of wealth in society, we must pay close attention to the abilities and limitations of the institutions chosen to reach such goals. The information problems accompanying bankruptcy redistributions present a practical obstacle to the realization of redistributive goals in the process. This section examines the institutional features of the bankruptcy judicial process that limit its ability to accomplish such redistributions in a rational way. . . .

A. Polycentric Problems and the Practical Limits of the Judicial Process

Of more interest here are the insights of the legal process theorists who focus on the pragmatic capabilities of the process to effect social change. Fuller described problems such as those involved in spreading the social costs of financial failure as polycentric, involving many possible outcomes, each affecting different actors. . . .

A number of limitations on the judicial process render it less capable than other institutions of responding to highly polycentric problems. The judicial process is designed to elicit information regarding past acts or relationships. It focuses on what has occurred between the parties before it rather than on what might occur in the future. This limitation is captured in the oft-noted distinction between legislative and adjudicative facts. . . .

In addition to the problem of limited fact gathering capabilities, the judicial process suffers from other procedural and remedial limitations. Judicial decisionmaking focuses on resolving disputes regarding rights of parties before the court. One implication of this seemingly benign statement is the limit that such focus places on remedial possibilities. . . . Another implication of the focus on "rights" is that it provides conceptual barriers to experimentation and monitoring of result by the judiciary. . . .

B. Redistributive Policies and the Limits of the Bankruptcy Process.

Bankruptcy is, in the main, a judicial process much like any other. . . . The presence of Chapter 11 adds another dimension to the judges' task, however. The continued operation of the business during a Chapter 11 coupled with the need to provide some control over the negotiation process implicate numerous administrative issues that, in turn, lead to fact-soaked inquiries involving data that are subject to a wide range of interpretations.

1. The Judicial Character of Bankruptcy Redistributive Policies

These two dimensions to the bankruptcy judicial process again illustrate the two possible methods through which redistributive goals might be pursued. First, Congress could legislate direct changes in entitlements. . . .

What is lost in this approach to redistribution, however, is an ability to individually tailor redistributive decisions to the needs of the parties involved in the actual cases. An alternative method of accomplishing redistributive goals is to change the process in ways that have the effect of skewing asset deployment decisions toward reorganization in marginal cases. While this method avoids the tailoring problems inherent in more direct redistributive enactments, it directly implicates the judicial process concerns that follow. . . .

The indirect nature of such redistributive policies requires us to consider the bankruptcy process on the level of the individual bankruptcy court and bankruptcy case. Because redistributions occur in the context of administering an individual case, decisions that arise are likely to have little precedential effect. . . . The need to tailor outcomes to specific cases is also likely to reduce redistribution-oriented legislative changes to the bankruptcy process to a fairly vague authorization for the judiciary to consider the interests of the non-investor constituencies. Statutes intended to alter the balance of power between competing constituencies in the process are unlikely to be self-executing. They will continue to leave vast discretion in the bankruptcy judge because of the fact-specific nature of bankruptcy cases. Thus, in large part the burden of determining the amount of redistribution and who will bear the cost of non-investor protection will fall on bankruptcy judges.

In some ways the bankruptcy judicial process might appear to be a uniquely qualified institution to pursue such policies. The bankruptcy process differs from other judicial proceedings in that it is intended to effect a global settlement of all of the controversies surrounding a failed business. The process provides voice to a wide range of affected persons . . . .

These attributes of the bankruptcy process might appear to alleviate some of the concerns regarding institutional competence. . . . The flaw in such an optimistic view of the capabilities of the bankruptcy process lies in its assumption that because judges in the process are capable of resolving the complex issues raised by the parties to the case, they can also account for the secondary effects of their decisions. A close examination of the decisionmaking structure of the process renders that assumption unwarranted.

2. The Intractable Problem of Representation

An obvious requirement for any redistributive process is that it provides a voice to those who stand to lose. Not only is representation of such interests required to ensure due process and fundamental fairness, it is also necessary to the formation of rational policy. Policymakers are not omniscient. They can only respond to the interests of those asserting injury in the policy-making process. Only by ensuring adequate representation can the process reach sensible redistributive outcomes.

. . . The problem . . . lies in identifying who is affected by business failure. . . . Bankruptcy does not operate in an economic vacuum. The decision to liquidate or to reorganize the operations of a failed firm implicates allocative concerns on an economy-wide basis. While liquidation may harm the community served by the closed enterprise, it may benefit a distant community served by a competing enterprise.

While it may be theoretically possible to consider the interests of such communities, practical difficulties would abound. Assuming that such communities could be identified, their inclusion in the bankruptcy process would increase administrative cost. More importantly, however, such communities would be impossible to identify fully. . . .

. . . Assuming that the bankruptcy process allows or requires the court to consider the redistributive justification, the process should also require the court to consider the incidence of the redistributive cost. This consideration in turn requires some means to ensure the representation of parties who stand to lose from the decision.

Who should have standing to press their claims in such a process? . . .

Standing is only one part of the problem. An equally important question is how the court should balance the interests of the potential claimants. . . .

The inquiry cannot logically stop even here, however. . . . [C]an [the court] conclude that the community in which the debtor is operating is the most deserving? . . .

. . . [T]he bankruptcy process is ill-equipped even to begin to sort through cases to determine whether the effect of the process on the well-being of some far-flung community is deserving of consideration. Furthermore, any limit on the potential range of the interests presented will be as artificial as the limits imposed by the creditor wealth-maximization criterion.

3. The Uncoordinated Nature of Bankruptcy Decisionmaking

The tenuous nature of the causal links between a given bankruptcy decision and the well-being of distant communities provides further support for an investor-focused bankruptcy regime. A second institutional feature of the bankruptcy process that limits its competence to resolve distributional questions is that bankruptcy courts act on an uncoordinated basis. The economic effect of redistributive decisions made by any one bankruptcy judge may be small in comparison to the aggregate, economy-wide effect of decisions made by all judges. . . . [T]he way redistributions occur in bankruptcy is indirect. . . . In this environment, the uncoordinated decision-making structure of the bankruptcy process renders it unlikely to yield informed, rational answers to redistributive issues. . . .

The net effect of judges' uncoordinated decisions may be redistributions that none of them desired. Consider the plight of a bankruptcy judge with a vision of the world that incorporates a balance of wealth and power that favors non-investor interests more than does the current state of affairs. . . . How should such a judge approach cases he believes implicate redistributive goals?

The judge could simply ignore the economy-wide effects of his decision and take care of the people and organizations that appear before him. In limiting his focus, our judge must simply hope that his colleagues share his vision. . . .

Because of the number and diversity of bankruptcy judges, however, it is likely that his colleagues do not share his exact vision. Perhaps some are more investor-focused. . . . The complexity of the problem is further compounded when one realizes that when our judge assesses the views of his colleagues he must understand that each is also assessing the views of all of the others. . . .

Developing a redistributive bankruptcy system thus requires that we bracket the broad redistributive effects of the regime. The ideal of representation of all affected persons requires somewhat artificial limitations based upon our ability to discern the groups affected by the redistribution. The notion of redistribution must exclude the aggregate economic effects of the system's outcomes. But the very justification for such a regime requires that the system account for these redistributive effects. . . .

. . . The attack here is on the use of the bankruptcy system to achieve redistributive ends—not on the ends themselves. Not all institutions are capable of accomplishing distributional equity. Some touch too many people in radically unpredictable ways. Bankruptcy is an example. . . .

CONCLUSION

. . . The institutional structure of the bankruptcy process renders it unable to develop the kind of detailed understanding necessary to formulate a rational redistributive policy or to act on that information in a uniform manner.

Admittedly, the arguments presented here raise empirical questions regarding the effect of bankruptcy decisions on an economy-wide basis. It is possible that the effects of a redistributive bankruptcy policy may be susceptible to falsification by empirical data. But it is also possible that many of the redistributions occurring under such a regime may be too subtle to admit of rigorous scientific analysis. At the very least, we must view with skepticism conclusions drawn from empirical studies that ignore the effect of the regime on constituencies beyond those connected with the firms under study. While they may tell of the beneficial or detrimental effects of the process on those immediately affected, they can say little regarding the overall distributional effect of the regime.

Normative analysis, of course, occupies a critical place in policy debates. Economic theory alone cannot provide a complete answer to those who question its normative underpinnings. As the development of the bankruptcy debate illustrates, we will continue to debate the normative trade-off between equality and efficiency. Policymakers must deal with the art of the possible, however. Given the practical limitations of the bankruptcy process, we should engage the normative debate in the context of other institutions.

Additional suggested readings

Barry E. Adler, *Finance's Theoretical Divide and the Proper Role of Insolvency Rules*, 68 S. CAL. L. REV. 401 (1994)

Barry E. Adler, *A World Without Debt*, 72 WASH. U. L.Q. 811 (1994)

John D. Ayer, *The Role of Finance Theory in Shaping Bankruptcy Policy*, 3 AM. BANKR. INST. L. REV. 53 (1995)

John D. Ayer, *So Near to Cleveland, So Far From God: An Essay on the Ethnography of Bankruptcy*, 61 U. CIN. L. REV. 407 (1992)

Douglas G. Baird, *Bankruptcy's Uncontested Axioms*, 108 YALE L.J. 573 (1999)

Douglas G. Baird, *A World Without Bankruptcy*, LAW & CONTEMP. PROBS., Spring 1987, at 173

David Gray Carlson, *Bankruptcy Theory and the Creditors' Bargain*, 61 U. CIN. L. REV. 453 (1992)

Theodore Eisenberg, *A Bankruptcy Machine That Would Go of Itself*, 39 STAN. L. REV. 1519 (1987)

Karen Gross, FAILURE AND FORGIVENESS: REBALANCING THE BANKRUPTCY SYSTEM (Yale 1997)

Thomas H. Jackson, *The Two Roles of Bankruptcy Law*, 1-6, and Ch. 1, *The Role of Bankruptcy Law and Collective Action in Debt Collection* 7-19, *in* THE LOGIC AND LIMITS OF BANKRUPTCY LAW (Harvard 1986)

Thomas H. Jackson, *Of Liquidation, Continuation and Delay: An Analysis of Bankruptcy Policy and Nonbankruptcy Rules*, 60 AM. BANKR. L.J. 399 (1986)

Donald R. Korobkin, *The Role of Normative Theory in Bankruptcy Debates*, 82 IOWA L. REV. 75 (1996)

Donald R. Korobkin, *Contractarianism and the Normative Foundations of Bankruptcy Law,* 71 TEX. L. REV. 541 (1993)

Donald R. Korobkin, *Value and Rationality in Bankruptcy Decisionmaking*, 33 WM. & MARY L. REV. 333 (1992)

Lynn M. LoPucki, *A General Theory of the Dynamics of the State Remedies/Bankruptcy System*, 1982 WIS. L. REV. 311

Mary Josephine Newborn, *The New Rawlsian Theory of Bankruptcy Ethics*, 16 CARDOZO L. REV. 111 (1994)

Mark Roe, *Commentary on "On the Nature of Bankruptcy": Bankruptcy, Priority, and Economics*, 75 VA. L. REV. 219 (1989)

Robert E. Scott, *Through Bankruptcy With the Creditors' Bargain Heuristic*, 53 U. CHI. L. REV. 690 (1986)

Morris G. Shanker, *The Abuse and Use of Federal Bankruptcy Power*, 26 CASE W. RES. L. REV. 3 (1975)

Morris G. Shanker, *Why the Bankruptcy Course Ought to Be Mandatory*, 39 J. LEGAL EDUC. 299 (1989)

Philip Shuchman, *An Attempt at a "Philosophy of Bankruptcy,"* 21 UCLA L. REV. 403 (1973)

David Stanley & Marjorie Girth, BANKRUPTCY: PROBLEMS, PROCESS, REFORM (Brookings 1971)

Elizabeth Warren, *Bankruptcy Policymaking in an Imperfect World*, 92 MICH. L. REV. 336 (1993)

Chapter 3
Initiation of a Bankruptcy Case

A. Overview

Chapter Two explored some of the many justifications offered for having a bankruptcy law. Well and good. But a bankruptcy case does not just happen. There are no benevolent and omniscient genies patrolling the country waiting to magically file a bankruptcy case at precisely the right instant and in precisely the proper cases. As it happens, deciding the twin questions of (1) *who* should have the power, privilege and duty to file bankruptcy and (2) *on what grounds* is not at all easy or self-evident. This "gatekeeping" problem is extremely important, but often overlooked. The materials in this Chapter seek to unravel some of the mysteries of the initiation question.

The first section addresses the general issue of commencing a bankruptcy case. Later sections focus in turn on voluntary and then on involuntary bankruptcy. The selection presented in this first part is by Professor and later Dean Douglas Baird of the University of Chicago. Baird tackles the "initiation problem" in the context of corporate bankruptcies, and seeks to provide a more general theory of "who" and "why" regarding initiation issues.

Douglas G. Baird
The Initiation Problem in Bankruptcy
11 INT'L. REV. L. & ECON. 223 (1991)[*]

American bankruptcy law provides creditors of a corporate debtor with an alternative way of sorting out their claims to the debtor's assets. Bankruptcy differs from ordinary avenues of debt collection in that all claims against a common debtor are determined at one time and in one place. Creditors are forced to give up their right to seek repayment on their own. Each creditor must stay its hand while decisions are made about what to do with the firm's assets and how to recognize the different claims against it. Some creditors who might have been paid in full if bankruptcy had not intervened are worse off. Others, who might have been unaware of the debtor's financial straits, may be better off. The premise of American bankruptcy law is that sometimes the creditors and others who contributed capital to the firm are better off as a group than they would be if this avenue of debt collection did not exist and creditors had to depend upon their individual remedies under nonbankruptcy law.

This premise—that the collective interests of the group can be put at risk when individual creditors exercise their rights—brings with it a problem that other legal regimes do not face. Ordinarily, one can depend upon the party that benefits from a particular legal rule to invoke it. Bankruptcy is

---

different. The beneficiaries of bankruptcy law are the creditors as a whole, not individual creditors within the group. One wants a bankruptcy proceeding to begin when it is in the collective interest of the group, but one must still depend upon someone to initiate it. One must somehow ensure that when a bankruptcy proceeding is in the collective interest of the creditors, it is also in someone's individual interest as well.

Existing bankruptcy law allows creditors to trigger the collective proceeding when three of them with unsecured claims totaling more than $5,000 join in a bankruptcy petition. This trigger is so easy for a creditor to pull that it might seem likely that bankruptcy would begin too early rather than too late. Only a few creditors need to get together to invoke the scrutiny of the bankruptcy court and ask if the debtor has a future. Cases do exist in which a creditor finds bankruptcy in its interest. A creditor with a security interest in all of the debtor's assets may discover that the assets are being dissipated at an alarming rate, but that its ability to foreclose on the assets under nonbankruptcy law may be so limited that it is better off starting the collective proceeding. Its individual benefits from bringing the debtor under control may offset the costs of bringing the other creditors into the picture. The creditor may be better off with a smaller share of a larger pie.

Cases in which the creditor begins the bankruptcy proceeding, however, are the exception.[4] For the most part, any particular general creditor is unlikely to find it in its interest to trigger a bankruptcy petition. A creditor that joins a bankruptcy petition brings down upon it and all the other creditors a pro rata sharing rule. The attentive and aggressive creditor who is most likely to start the bankruptcy proceeding may be the one most likely to be paid in full if it pursues its individual remedies. The creditor shares the benefits of bankruptcy with all the other creditors, but bears a disproportionate share of the costs (including sanctions if a court later finds that the creditor began a bankruptcy proceeding inappropriately). A creditor that is pursuing an individual creditor remedy may have little to gain by forcing the debtor to sort out its affairs in a collective proceeding, even though that course might be in everyone's interest. Because creditors largely lack the incentive to begin the bankruptcy proceeding, American bankruptcy law depends upon those who control the corporate debtor under nonbankruptcy law to start it. In the case of the closely held firm, these are typically the managers of the firm who are also its sole shareholders.

On its face, putting the burden of starting a bankruptcy proceeding on the managers seems unlikely to ensure that a bankruptcy proceeding will begin when, but only when, it is in the collective interest of the creditors as a group. Managers will sometimes keep a firm outside of bankruptcy even though it belongs inside. Other times, they will put a firm in bankruptcy even though the creditors as a group would be better served if everyone used the nonbankruptcy avenue of debt collection. In this paper, I seek to explain why entrusting the managers of a firm with the task of starting the bankruptcy proceeding makes more sense than it might at first seem.

In the first part of this article, I explain why the managers of a firm should be the ones who start a bankruptcy proceeding when the firm is liquidating. In the next two parts, I explore the more complicated case of the reorganizing debtor. Part II looks at the extent to which the existing rules

---

[4]   The number is less than one percent for all bankruptcy cases. *See* Federal Judicial Workload Statistics for 1980. Creditors are unlikely to bring an involuntary petition against individuals, given that they have a substantive right of discharge in bankruptcy that they do not have elsewhere. Bankruptcy's fresh start policy reduces the substantive nonbankruptcy rights of creditors and makes creditors less likely to bring a bankruptcy petition against individual debtors. Hence, most involuntary petitions are against corporations, and the number for involuntary petitions against corporations in Chapter 7 liquidations is much higher than one percent. The number, however, is still less than 10 percent of all corporate bankruptcy filings.

leave outside of bankruptcy some firms that belong there, and Part III looks at the extent to which these rules put firms into bankruptcy that should remain outside.

I. The Liquidating Firm

There are many cases in which a debtor corporation has no hope of continuing as a going concern and may in fact have little in the way of unencumbered assets. The rules governing the commencement of the case are easiest to explain in the context of these cases. Bankruptcy began as an additional device that creditors could use to collect what they were owed. . . .

The nineteenth century gave rise to the limited liability corporation. Because the liability of the individuals who invested in these firms was already limited, they had no need of bankruptcy's fresh start. Nevertheless, bankruptcy remains a means of sorting out the affairs of a failed firm and bringing things to a close. When a debtor fails and can no longer meet its obligations, either a creditor of the debtor or the managers of the debtor itself can begin a bankruptcy proceeding. The affairs of the debtor are exposed to scrutiny, what assets exist are divided among the creditors, and the life of the firm is brought to an end. The creditors turn to other things, knowing there is nothing more to fight over.

Chapter 7 does not provide a discharge to the corporation. There is no pretense that the bankruptcy proceeding will give the debtor corporation a "fresh start." In the typical case, the firm has ceased its operations or will cease them in short order. To the extent that there are any assets after the secured creditors have taken what they can, they most frequently go to the tax collector. Nor does Chapter 7 have much to do with ensuring that the general creditors receive as much of the value of the assets as possible. In most cases, the firm has no unencumbered assets. The purpose is not so much to give creditors assets as it is to assure them that no assets are there.

The collective action problem that the creditors face is largely an informational one. Each creditor individually has no way of knowing that the debtor has no assets and cannot meet its obligations. The bankruptcy petition is a way of surrendering. It tells the creditors to stop their pursuit. A Chapter 7 petition is the easiest way for the managers who are being constantly harassed to convince the creditors of the firm that the firm has no assets and that their lawsuits are pointless. The filing of a Chapter 7 petition sends creditors an effective signal. To use bankruptcy to assert that creditors should stop their pursuit, the debtor must give up control of its assets and subject itself to the scrutiny of a court.

Firms should be able to fail. Those who start them should be able to abandon them when they do not succeed and go on to start new ventures or return to their old line of work. It follows naturally from this idea that we should have firms with limited liability that we should have some mechanism for wrapping up the affairs of a firm, even if the firm has no assets. Even if there are no assets for the general creditors in the typical Chapter 7 case, bankruptcy does serve to overcome a collective action problem. The bankruptcy process can offer scrutiny of the debtor's overall health that no individual creditor can match. Chapter 7's promise may lie not so much in making it easy for creditors to reach assets as in making it easy for creditors to satisfy themselves that there are no assets.

If this signalling function is the proper purpose of Chapter 7, we may want to change the way we compensate the trustee. In many cases, those in which there are no assets, the trustee is paid only the statutory minimum of $45. To be sure, if the trustee's role is envisioned as one of distributing assets, it makes little sense to pay more when there are no assets on hand. But if the trustee's job is to ensure that all is as it appears to be and that the debtor is not hiding anything, it may be in the interests of the creditors as a group to pay more. The trustee that undertakes what appears to be a no-asset case, however, has an expected recovery that is more than $45. If on investigation there is a voidable preference or a fraudulent conveyance, the trustee can bring the action. Although a fee of $45 gives the trustee little incentive to scrutinize a debtor that has no assets, the possibility that there is a voidable transfer in each case may make it worthwhile for the trustee to give each case greater scrutiny because the trustee can hire himself or his law firm to bring the action and in the process earn a substantial fee. Even in what appears to be a no-asset case, there are two elements to the trustee's compensation. There is a small flat fee and a contingent fee that is much larger. If there is work to be done because of a fraudulent conveyance or a voidable preference, the trustee has an incentive to do it. The trustee's pay is geared to how successful he is at deciding whether actions can be brought successfully.

What is sometimes thought to be a vice—the trustee bringing an avoiding action only because he is interested in the fee a successful recovery will bring—may in fact be a virtue. There is no direct way to monitor the trustee and tell how much effort he has given to finding suspicious transactions. To overcome this agency problem, it may make sense to give the trustee what is in effect a contingent fee. The creditors as a group cannot sift through the record to find out if any transactions can be avoided, but they may be able to count on the trustee. The trustee has the same incentives as any agent whose compensation is tied to performance. . . .

In the typical no-asset case, however, monitoring may come not from the trustee, but from the debtor itself. To a large extent, Chapter 7 relies upon self-monitoring, in the same way that the American income tax system relies upon self-reporting. In a world in which a trustee is rarely going to be paid more than a thousand dollars, the trustee must rely on what the debtor itself reports. Most of the information about possible fraudulent conveyances and voidable preferences comes from the schedules that the managers of the debtor must fill out.

Under the current state of affairs, the debtor typically pays $1,000 to $3,000 to a lawyer to file a simple Chapter 7 petition. The lawyer earns the fee in large part by ensuring that schedules that list assets and creditors are filled out correctly. Moreover, the largest cost of bankruptcy for the debtor is not the filing fee, but rather the cost of assembling all the information that the schedules accompanying the petition require. A debtor that fills out schedules incorrectly faces substantial penalties. It may be that the relative reliability of the information in these schedules makes the bankruptcy signal a strong one. A debtor who claims that it cannot pay may not, outside of bankruptcy, be able to convince its creditors to give up their efforts to be paid. By contrast, they are likely to give up when the debtor files a bankruptcy petition, gives up all its assets, and provides extensive information about all its assets and liabilities. If this view of Chapter 7 holds, we may want to do more to ensure that the information in the schedules covers the relevant questions and that the sanctions for providing incomplete or inaccurate information are sufficiently strong.

II. The Incentives of the Managers to Stay Out of Bankruptcy

I now turn to the case of the firm that is reorganizing. Here too, existing law gives creditors the power to begin a Chapter 11 reorganization proceeding, but in practice we depend largely upon the managers to begin it. A corporate reorganization brings with it substantial costs. Creditors become unable to pursue their individual remedies, managers find many of their decisions subject to court scrutiny, and outsiders from suppliers to customers rightly or wrongly view firms in bankruptcy fundamentally differently from firms that are not in bankruptcy. These costs have to be balanced against the costs of remaining in the nonbankruptcy world of debt collection, a world in which individual creditors can threaten the survival of the firm as a going concern by threatening to seize its assets. Determining when the latter costs exceed the former requires knowledge of the condition in which the firm finds itself, knowledge that the managers of the firm are most apt to have.

Those best positioned to know both the financial condition of the firm and the likelihood that creditors will assert their nonbankruptcy default rights are the managers of the firm. Individual creditors lack a sense of the overall, day-to-day health of the firm. . . .

The managers of a firm are charged with looking out for the welfare of all contributors of capital when they make decisions, quite apart from those matters that are the subject of specific loan covenants. Trusting the managers when the firm is solvent is relatively easy to justify. When a firm is solvent, the managers need pay attention only to the interests of the shareholders. The shareholders are the residual owners of the firm, and they stand to gain or lose from the managers' decisions. The duty of the managers of a firm shifts from the shareholders to the creditors when the firm becomes insolvent. More precisely, a firm's managers should use the assets the way a sole owner would who was acting on her own account. The managers' loyalty needs to change when there is a change in the residual owner, the person who gains or loses from any change in the fortune of the firm. Such a change takes place when the firm becomes insolvent and creditors cannot be paid in full.

This general principle appears to give the managers a duty to bring a bankruptcy petition when to do so would be in the collective interest of creditors. Few reported decisions, however, fault managers for favoring the interests of shareholders at the expense of the contributors of capital as a group on any matter, and there is nothing in the law that suggests that the managers have a legal duty to begin a bankruptcy petition when it is in the creditors' interest. The absence of litigation over such a legal duty is easy to explain. Imposing a legal duty on the managers to begin a bankruptcy proceeding is likely to have little effect because there would be no effective sanction for a failure to meet it. . . .

Moreover, imposing a general duty on the managers to file a bankruptcy petition will fail to the extent the managers are unable to take full advantage of what they know. After all, the firm may find itself in financial difficulty because the managers are incompetent. Being well positioned to know what course the firm should take is not the same as being able to exercise good judgment with the information available. Even if the managers are able, they are not likely to make the transition from the nonbankruptcy world to a collective regime. Moreover, the managers may not behave completely rationally and may suffer from excessive optimism. . . .

Finally, imposing a duty on the managers of a firm to bring a bankruptcy proceeding at the appropriate time would be all but impossible to enforce. The moment at which a collective proceeding becomes in everyone's interest is hard to identify even for someone intimately familiar with a firm and its financial condition; a judge has neither knowledge of the condition of the firm nor the skills needed to use this knowledge. Even after the fact, no one has a way to determine precisely the "right" time to file a bankruptcy petition. . . .

It makes sense to rely upon the managers to file a bankruptcy petition only if the moment at which it is in the collective interest to file a bankruptcy petition frequently corresponds with the moment it is in the managers' own self-interest to file. In the typical case, the managers file a bankruptcy petition because a number of creditors threaten to seize assets of the firm and the managers cannot make peace with all of them. We need to ask if this threat is likely to exist if, but only if, the firm should be in bankruptcy.

Creditors can demand payment of their loans in full whenever the debtor is in default, and "default" in a typical bank loan is ordinarily defined extremely broadly. . . . If the firm is solvent and a collective proceeding is unnecessary, the managers will be able to pay off any loan that becomes due or is in default. Even if they do not have the necessary cash on hand, they can find another investor who is willing to lend them the necessary money. If the firm is insolvent, they will likely not be able to find such an investor. In such a case, however, there is a good chance that a collective proceeding is desirable.

Defaults and an inability to raise new capital to cure them is likely to occur at the same time that it makes sense for the firm to be in a collective proceeding. At this moment, the managers may face a Hobson's choice. Their only alternative to filing a bankruptcy petition is to sit back and watch creditors dismember the firm. Relying upon the managers to file a bankruptcy petition makes sense because, at the time that the bankruptcy petition needs to be filed, the managers are likely to see a bankruptcy proceeding as the only way in which they can keep their jobs, at least for a time. Managers act out of self-interest when they file bankruptcy petitions, but their self-interest in putting a halt to a destructive race to the assets may correspond with the collective interest of the creditors.

This system, however, can work effectively only if a number of creditors can declare a default when the firm becomes insolvent. If only one loan is in default, the managers of a firm may try to strike a deal with that one lender. The managers may give up needed assets as they play for time. As the firm becomes more insolvent, the managers may engage in risky behavior that is not in the interests of the creditors as a group and that would not be possible in bankruptcy. . . .

The correct time to start a bankruptcy proceeding may not be the moment before a number of creditors levy on the assets, but much earlier. Much depends on the ability of creditors to draft broad events of default and to monitor the debtor closely enough to know when these events have occurred. The individual creditors may not have the incentive to begin a bankruptcy proceeding rather than exercise their individual nonbankruptcy rights, but once they attempt to exercise these rights, the managers have the incentive to begin the collective proceeding.

If the mechanism for beginning the collective proceeding relies upon the managers responding to multiple efforts to levy, we may want to make it easier for creditors to monitor their debtors and discover when the firm is insolvent. The weakness of the existing rules may lie not in the ability of creditors to move against the firm when they discover that it is insolvent, but rather in their inability to discover a firm's true financial condition. . . .

An alternative to rewarding the managers by allowing them to keep their jobs if they file a bankruptcy petition would be to compensate them explicitly for starting the bankruptcy petition at the appropriate time. The weakness of giving a cash bounty to the managers (or indeed to a creditor or anyone who starts a bankruptcy proceeding at the optimum time) may lie in the inability of the court to determine after the fact when the bankruptcy petition should have been brought and how much difference bringing the proceeding at the right time makes. One could not, of course, give the managers a flat fee. The amount they receive must turn on how much of the value of the firm they preserved by bringing the bankruptcy petition at the appropriate time.

III. The Costs of Retaining Control

Many firms that need to be reorganized also need new managers. The restaurant failed not because of its location, but because the owner-chef's vision of food that people want to eat (British dim sum—small plates with minuscule portions of Beef Wellington, Yorkshire pudding, and cold scones) is wanting. The first thing a sole owner of the assets would do would be to fire the chef. There are, of course, cases in which the problems of the firm have nothing to do with the ability of the managers to run it, but the presumption in the Bankruptcy Code that the old managers should stay on to run the firm may seem hard to justify.

Bankruptcy law, however, keeps the managers in place only for as long as it takes to sort out the problems of the firm. Once a plan of reorganization is confirmed, the new owners of the restaurant can fire the chef. If the managers are sufficiently bad, the creditors can ask for the appointment of a trustee. Before either event takes place, however, it may make sense to keep the old managers around. The old managers, however bad they may be, know where the books are kept and where the light switches are.

To ensure that the managers are not using bankruptcy only to delay the inevitable, a set of rules must be created that allows courts to dismiss cases that do not belong in bankruptcy. The court could also be given the power to displace existing management. Here the problem may not lie with the way the Bankruptcy Code is written, but rather with the way in which it is applied. The bankruptcy judge has the power to dismiss a bankruptcy case when it is not in the interests of everyone as a group. Judges routinely dismiss bankruptcy cases in which it appears that there is only a single creditor. (A debtor with a single creditor cannot, by definition, confront a collective action problem with its creditors.) Judges also are apt to take a dark view of bankruptcy filings that are brought only because bankruptcy offers a different substantive rule than nonbankruptcy law, not because the creditors of the debtor face any collective action problem. In addition, secured creditors can remove their collateral (and as a practical matter end the bankruptcy case) if they can show that they are owed more than their collateral is worth and that "an effective reorganization is not in prospect."

It might seem that if the court effectively replaced bad managers in bankruptcy, bad managers would tend not to start bankruptcy proceedings in the first instance. As long as the managers survive longer in bankruptcy than they would outside of bankruptcy, however, they will choose to enter bankruptcy even if their prospects for survival there are not good. Those most apt to keep their jobs are also likely to be ones who should keep them. Under existing law, a court is likely to allow the managers to remain in place in cases in which a sale of the assets to a third party (either piecemeal or as a going concern) is not likely. The less practicable a sale of the firm to a third party, the longer the managers will stay in place, but the more likely the value of the firm will turn on the firm-specific skills of the managers.

IV. CONCLUSION

At first blush, a bankruptcy regime that relies upon the managers of the debtor to begin it seems anomalous with bankruptcy's origins and purposes. Bankruptcy began as a means of helping creditors recover what they were owed, and it still primarily serves that function in the case of the corporate debtor. It exists primarily to sort out the rights of creditors when the firm's condition has taken a turn for the worse. For this reason, it might seem that it is inappropriate to rely on the managers to start a bankruptcy proceeding. They cannot be counted upon to make a decision that is in the creditors' interest but not in their own. In this article, however, I have argued that the managers may be better able than any individual creditor to begin a bankruptcy proceeding that is in the interest of all the creditors as a group.

The typical Chapter 7 liquidation of a corporation has little to do with dividing assets pro rata among the general creditors. More frequently, it is a proceeding that ensures that there is nothing more to the debtor's financial affairs than meets the eye and that the creditors should all go their separate ways. In such a case, the managers are as anxious as the creditors to bring a stop to debt collection efforts that are fruitless.

A bankruptcy reorganization tries to keep intact firms that might not survive if all creditors resorted to individual avenues of debt collection. Here again there is a correspondence of interest between the creditors as a group and the managers. The managers have a desire to keep their jobs, and it is usually in everyone's interest that the managers stay around, at least for a while. By allowing the managers to continue, if only for a time, bankruptcy law ensures that the managers will not let creditors exercise nonbankruptcy rights of debt collection that will shut down a firm that should survive. To the extent that keeping the managers in place postpones the inevitable, bankruptcy law imposes some costs on creditors. But given how often even the worst managers need to stay in place for a time and the ability that creditors have to bring a halt to the reorganization process when it is not in their interest, this cost may be less than is commonly recognized, at least if the bankruptcy judge is willing to exercise a firm hand.

B.   Voluntary Cases

A bankruptcy case can be commenced either by the debtor (Bankruptcy Code § 301) or by creditors (Bankruptcy Code § 303). A case commenced by the debtor is called "voluntary," whereas a creditor-initiated case is termed "involuntary." Today, the vast majority of cases are voluntary. Involuntary cases, by comparison, are fairly rare. Without the benefit of history, a modern observer might think that the modern condition is the historic norm. Nothing could be farther from the truth. Indeed, for several centuries in Anglo-American bankruptcy jurisprudence, there was no such concept as "voluntary" bankruptcy. Bankruptcy was by definition a creditors' remedy. Part of the essence of a "bankruptcy" case, as any lawyer knew, was that it was initiated by creditors against a debtor. To speak of "voluntary bankruptcy" would have been to speak nonsense. To be sure, it was not unheard of for a debtor to persuade a cooperative creditor to file a bankruptcy petition against him; thus in a loose sense a debtor could "voluntarily" seek relief, but the creditor was still a necessary party. Debtor petitions for relief from their debts were possible, but only under the separate concept of an "insolvency" proceeding.

One of the most fascinating tales in the development of bankruptcy jurisprudence concerns the monumental transformation by which the unthinkable—voluntary bankruptcy—became commonplace. To tell that tale, we could ask for no better a story-teller and historian than John C. McCoid, II, Vicars Professor of Law at the University of Virginia Law School. In his lengthy career at Virginia, spanning from 1957 until his retirement in 1994, Professor McCoid wrote many scholarly articles on civil procedure and on bankruptcy law; many of the latter are excerpted in this anthology. In the first article, Professor McCoid tries to discover who came up with the idea of voluntary bankruptcy that became law in 1841.

The second article is by Professor Randal Picker. In *Voluntary Petitions and the Creditors' Bargain*, 61 U. CIN. L. REV. 519 (1992), Picker asks why, in the context of business debtors, we allow voluntary petitions *at all*, and given that we do, how the governing legal rules should be structured. According to Picker, the initiation rules need to respond to a monitoring problem. What does he perceive the appropriate resolution to be?

Let us turn to the story of how voluntary bankruptcy came to be a part of the Bankruptcy Act of 1841.

John C. McCoid, II
The Origins of Voluntary Bankruptcy
5 BANKR. DEV. J. 361 (1988)[*]

Debtors resort to voluntary bankruptcy far more often than creditors institute involuntary proceedings against them. . . . Yet involuntary bankruptcy is by far the older institution. Not until 1841 did our national bankruptcy law depart from English precedent which had limited bankruptcy to involuntary proceedings against traders and merchants following an act of bankruptcy. In that year, our second bankruptcy act included provision for petitions by "all persons whatsoever" who would "declare themselves unable to meet their debts and engagements." By extending bankruptcy beyond traders and merchants and by allowing debtors to initiate proceedings, Congress seemingly broke new ground. Bankruptcy was no longer a creditor's remedy against a narrow class of debtors thought to be peculiarly dependent on credit.

Most of the literature attributes this development to Justice Joseph Story. There seems to be little doubt that he was the draftsman of the 1841 bill sponsored by Daniel Webster. That the first formal proposal of voluntary bankruptcy to the Congress came from Senator Nicholas Van Dyke of Delaware twenty years earlier is less frequently acknowledged. Regardless of when the idea was first advanced at the federal level, it may well have been borrowed from colonial or state bankruptcy (more often called insolvency) laws which were debtor-invoked and which occasionally called for discharge of debts as well as for the usual release from imprisonment. More recently, the conception has been attributed to a late 17th Century essay written by Daniel Defoe when he was financially entangled.

My own research has yielded no neat "solution" to the puzzle of the source of voluntary bankruptcy. . . . What I can provide is a fuller account of what transpired, particularly in the early part of the 19th Century. Doing so, I hope, will reinforce the idea that the law develops in small, uncertain, and incremental steps.

I. DANIEL DEFOE

Without question, Defoe proposed bankruptcy upon the request of the debtor in the essay titled *Of Bankrupts* which is a part of his *An Essay upon Projects*. . . .

Defoe wrote from personal experience. He was a merchant before he was a writer, dealing in the stocking trade, wine, tobacco and other items, as well as engaging in marine insurance and speculating in diving machines and civet cats. He was more successful with his pen, however, than in pursuit of these other trades. There is general agreement that he failed in 1692, with debts approaching seventeen thousand pounds, and that a statute of bankruptcy (today an involuntary petition) was taken against him. He was temporarily imprisoned at the demand of some creditors. When released, he may have repaired to a debtors' sanctuary, to the Mint at Southwark or to Bristol. Certainly he sought to stay clear of his creditors until he could make a proposal to them. *An Essay upon Projects*, published in 1697, is said no have been written during this period. . . . At the time of his essay, bankruptcy offered no fresh start; composition was the debtor's only refuge. While Defoe compounded with some of his creditors, he could not emerge completely from his debilitating debt. . . .

In succeeding years he was to say a good deal more about bankruptcy, however. Early in 1706, in his newspaper, *Review of the State of the English Nation*, he wrote elaborately on the subject. . . . He wrote, he said, while a bill was pending before the House of Commons, but what he had to say seemed to deal with 4 Anne, ch. 17 (1705), which had introduced into the law the discharge concept for which Defoe had previously argued in his essay, and he was fulsome in his praise of the bill. . . . Nevertheless, the act did not provide for voluntary petitions, and not a word about the subject appeared in his editorializing. . . .

With the discharge law in effect, Defoe in 1706 revived his earlier bankruptcy with the apparent aim of obtaining a discharge. He was examined several times by the commissioners, but opposition by creditors and a necessary trip to Scotland on Crown business apparently delayed his obtaining a certificate, the requirement of which he had previously opposed. By the time he returned, the law had been amended to require the consent of four-fifths of his creditors as a precondition of discharge. This he could not manage, and he was haunted for many years by old debts.

Still later, in *The Complete English Tradesman* (1726), Defoe turned once again to the subject of bankruptcy. That volume is filled with counsel to the merchant to "break," that is, to stop business in timely fashion before inadequate assets are entirely dissipated. But *The Complete English Tradesman,* like his earlier work, is devoid of further suggestions regarding voluntary bankruptcy (or of a law that goes beyond merchants and traders for that matter).

What inference should be drawn from this? There is room to conclude, of course, that Defoe had deliberately planted a seed that was only to bear fruit across the ocean more than one hundred year later. . . . [I]t is clear that *An Essay Upon Projects* was read by many Americans. Benjamin Franklin, for example, reported its influence on him. It must have been familiar to many colonial, state, and national legislators.

Yet it seems equally plausible to conclude that the idea of a debtor-petitioner was something tossed out almost casually in "On Bankrupts." The idea, after all, may have seemed less central to the protection on honest debtors than was the concept of discharge, at least so long as a debtor could find a friendly creditor to initiate proceedings. . . .

One can credit him with having the idea without necessarily conceding to him full recognition of its worth. . . .

II. COLONIAL AND EARLY STATE LAWS

In *Debtors and Creditors in America*, Peter J. Coleman . . . fully described colonial and early state laws dealing with insolvency, imprisonment for debt, and bankruptcy. . . . While most of the state and colonial laws described therein provided simply for release of debtors from imprisonment, a few went further and discharged debts on petition of the debtor as well.

Coleman tells us that only four colonies—New York, North Carolina, Rhode Island, and South Carolina—had "bankruptcy" laws at the time of the Revolution. Others, notably Massachusetts and Connecticut, had experimented only briefly in the area.

The first colony to adopt a bankruptcy law was South Carolina, which in 1721 authorized discharge from debt. . . . Somewhat limited as to eligibility, this nevertheless was a voluntary scheme. . . .

North Carolina passed legislation in 1749 which allowed a discharge from debts to prisoners who took an oath of poverty. . . . Discharge of debts was abolished in 1793 because of concern about fraudulent transfers; only jail delivery, good against imprisoning creditors, remained. . . .

New York's first legislation providing for discharge of debts of a debtor willing to give up his property appeared in 1755, but only on petition of three-fourths in amount of the creditors. In other words, the statute required a kind of collaboration between the debtor and his creditors. . . . This was changed in 1811 to allow a petition by the debtor without the assent of any creditors, and it was the validity of discharge under this law that was before the Supreme Court in 1819 in *Sturges v. Crowninshield*. . . .

In 1757, Massachusetts, which had had legislation based on English law, briefly allowed merchant debtors to petition and be granted a discharge if a majority of creditors assented. The Crown rejected the law in 1758. . . . Renewed efforts between 1811 and 1813 came to naught.

Rhode Island's first statute, in 1756, legislatively discharged the debts of all inhabitants, who on June 1st of that year, were imprisoned or had absconded or hidden themselves on account of debts in exchange for the debtors' yielding up real and personal property. The benefits of this law were soon extended to later failures who petitioned the legislature. This system remained in operation until 1828. . . .

Following the Seven Years War, Connecticut passed bankruptcy legislation in 1763. It allowed imprisoned debtors to petition and discharged debts but was in force for only eight months. . . .

Maryland's proprietary government enacted a relief law in 1774, but its discharge was limited. . . . This law was not repealed until 1817. . . .

Pennsylvania passed a temporary bankruptcy law in 1812. It . . . allowed any person believing himself insolvent to petition. The statute was later held invalid in 1814 by Bushrod Washington in *Golden v. Prince*.

Louisiana, in 1808, passed an insolvent debtors' act which provided for discharge of debts on the petition of the debtor. . . .

I have found no direct link between this legislation and Defoe's essay. That the earliest of these provisions—in South Carolina and North Carolina—begin with imprisoned debtors suggests, rather, an insolvency law source, joined to a concept borrowed from bankruptcy: the discharge. In some measure this interpretation of events is confirmed by the fact that few of these statutes were limited, as was bankruptcy of the period, to traders and merchants. If jail delivery and discharge were English ideas, their marriage seems to have been an American improvement.

III. In Congress (1820-1841)

The first formal proposal of voluntary proceedings was put before Congress in 1820. Before the end of the decade three variations were considered in one house or the other or in both. None of the proposals became law, for Congress was unable to pass a bill in any form. But the ultimate concept had emerged. Voluntary bankruptcy awaited only the Panic of 1837 for enactment. . . .

In the aftermath of the War of 1812, inflation, caused by virtue of currency issued by state banks, and land speculation created renewed interest in a national bankruptcy law. . . . [T]he Supreme Court's decision in *Sturges v. Crowninshield* in 1819, casting doubt on the ability of states to discharge debts, provided further impetus. . . .

A. *Nicholas Van Dyke*

In the first session of the 16th Congress another traditional bankruptcy bill, providing for involuntary petitions against merchants and traders, was reported from the Judiciary Committee. In the course of debate on the bill, Senator Nicholas Van Dyke of Delaware promised on March 20, 1820, an amendment "to extend its provisions to the voluntary acceptance of other classes, not now comprehended in the bill." On the very next day he offered such an amendment. . . .

Nicholas Van Dyke was the scion of an illustrious family. His father, also Nicholas, had been a member of the Continental Congress during the Revolution and President of Delaware, the title then given to the state's chief executive. The younger Nicholas was graduated from Princeton and read law. . . . In 1817 he was elected to the United States Senate where he served until his death in 1826. . . .

Van Dyke's voluntary bankruptcy amendment was apparently a bombshell and aroused immediate opposition. Senator Burrill, a familiar antagonist, suggested that the amendment did not even deal with the subject of bankruptcy because it was voluntary and applied to nonmerchants. Consideration was postponed because of the significance of the proposal. The subject of bankruptcy because it was voluntary and applied to nonmerchants. Consideration was postponed because of the significance of the proposal. The subject was hotly debated the following day. Senator King argued that the amendment was unconstitutional because bankruptcy was, by definition, limited to traders. Senator Hunter noted that, although he shared this view, the Supreme Court felt differently, an obvious reference to dictum in *Sturges v. Crowninshield*. Hunter, however, approved of the idea if not of its legitimacy. Others were opposed. Van Dyke's argument . . . that it was constitutional, expedient, and equitable, prevailed, at least for the moment. The amendment was adopted by the Senate, sitting in committee, by a 25-13 vote. . . .

On Thursday, March 30th, Senator Otis moved to recommit the bill, and Senator Barbour sought to postpone consideration of it until the next session. Both maneuvers failed, but the Senate rejected the bill by a 23-15 vote. The *National Intelligencer*, in reporting the outcome, suggested that the amendment had been adopted by virtue of a coalition of its supporters and those who opposed any legislation on the subject. According to the newspaper, the amended bill was defeated when the latter group combined with those who wished only a traditional law. . . .

In the Second Session, in 1821, a bill limited to involuntary proceedings against traders and merchants was again reported. Van Dyke gave this bill his support even when he was chided by Senator Roberts for abandoning his earlier stance. This change of position became even more obvious when Senator John Holmes of Maine sought, on February 8th, to amend the bill to add a provision extending bankruptcy to any nonmerchant who consented to a commission for which a creditor had petitioned. Van Dyke opposed the amendment, and the Senate rejected it. It was, therefore, a traditional, limited bill, supported by Van Dyke, that passed the Senate on February 19th. And it was this bill, not voluntary bankruptcy, that Henry Clay seemed to have supported in the House on the 28th before it was tabled on March 1st.

Van Dyke's advocacy of voluntary bankruptcy, followed by his opposition to its cousin, as proposed by Holmes, strongly suggests that the Delaware senator was not so much committed to the concept as he was anxious to obtain passage of some bankruptcy law. I have not been able to uncover a certain course for his 1820 proposal. Nevertheless, he was aware of state legislation on the subject. . . . More immediately, the *National Intelligencer* had reported on February 28, 1820, the existence of a "bankruptcy system . . . digested by a judicial character whose experience has been not a little" which proposed voluntary bankruptcy for all persons as well as involuntary bankruptcy for merchants and traders. It seems likely that the senator would have seen this column in Washington's only newspaper of the day.

B. "*A Judicial Character*"

The *National Intelligencer* gave no further clues as to the identity of "a judicial character whose experience has been not a little," and my attempts to penetrate that Delphic phrase have met with very little success. Five men, however, come to mind: Joseph Story, Daniel Webster, John Marshall, Bushrod Washington, and Henry Wheaton. Story and Webster, of course, are natural prospects because of their long identification with the 1841 Act, although Webster was not a judge. Marshall is perhaps a somewhat less obvious candidate, but his judicial opinions and brief legislative career firmly suggest his name. Washington, too, is suggested because of his judicial opinions. Wheaton seems least likely. His connection to the judiciary, like Webster's is thin for the appellation "judicial character." Nonetheless, examination of the question can usefully begin with him.

1. *Henry Wheaton*

Henry Wheaton is perhaps best known to 20th Century lawyers as reporter for the Supreme Court from 1816 to 1827. But he was also a prolific author and skilled advocate. In 1824 and 1827 he joined Daniel Webster in arguing, ultimately without success, in *Ogden v. Saunders* against the validity of a New York law discharging debts. His biographer, Elizabeth Baker, tells us that he had urged a national bankruptcy law as early as 1815. . . . [He] argued that the Bankruptcy Clause of the Constitution was not intended to restrict Congress to the English model and urged enactment of a uniform act. . . .

A copy of the 1815 bill with Story's annotations . . . reveals that neither the bill nor Story's suggestions included voluntary bankruptcy. . . . I have found nothing beyond Wheaton's expressed view that Congress was not limited to the English model to support the conclusions that he was the "judicial character," but the possibility cannot be entirely excluded.

2. *Bushrod Washington*

The argument could be made that Bushrod Washington, nephew of our first president and Supreme Court justice from 1798 to 1829, was the "judicial character." The case for Washington is derived entirely from his position on the legitimacy of state bankruptcy laws and is, therefore, exceedingly thin.

Washington, writing for the circuit court in the 1814 case, *Golden v. Prince*, held that the Pennsylvania bankruptcy law was invalid. The basis of that decision was Washington's view that the Bankruptcy Clause preempted the field for the national government. Washington believed in this federal preemption even in the absence of the federal government taking any action on the subject. . . .

If the states' inability to provide relief argued for national action, nothing on the record suggests that Washington himself urged it. There is no evidence that Washington favored debtor relief. And there is no indication that he was ever disposed to move beyond his judicial role. . . .

3. *John Marshall*

The case for John Marshall as the "judicial character" is stronger. This position is primarily based on Marshall's judicial opinions. In *Sturges v. Crowninshield*, . . . Marshall wrote that a state insolvency statute, under which debts contracted before enactment of the statute were discharged on the debtor's petition, impaired the obligation of contract. In the course of the opinion, Marshall addressed the distinction between bankruptcy and insolvency laws and indicated that Congress could authorize voluntary petitions. . . .

Moreover, the thesis of Marshall's 1827 dissent in *Ogden v. Saunders*, arguing that a state law could not impair contracts entered subsequently to the law's enactment, would also seem to invite a federal law that allowed a debtor to petition. . . .

It is one thing to say what Congress may do and what states may not. It is, of course, quite another to say what Congress should do. Marshall had experience on both scores, for he had served in the Sixth Congress which enacted the first bankruptcy act in 1800. Indeed, Marshall was a member of the House committee which crafted the bill. . . .

There is nothing to suggest that voluntary bankruptcy was then considered. . . .

Thus, apart from Marshall's judicial recognition of the constitutional legitimacy of voluntary bankruptcy there is very little to connect him to Van Dyke's proposal. Yet, Marshall's *Sturges* dictum could well have planted the seed of voluntary bankruptcy in mind of the senator.

4. *Joseph Story and Daniel Webster*

Joseph Story was among the first to raise the possibility that the bankruptcy power given to Congress by the Constitution and the Impairment Clause might restrict discharge by state insolvent laws. . . . The 1827 decision in *Ogden v. Saunders*, which allowed a state discharge of a post-enactment obligation against a local creditor, where no bankruptcy statute was in conflict, found Story joining Marshall in dissent. This view of the allocation of power between the national and state governments, aggrandizing the power of the former, surely would be consistent with the idea of voluntary proceedings in federal bankruptcy. No other protection of debtors would be available.

William Story . . . said that in 1816 his father "drew another bankrupt act, more in conformity with his views, which formed the basis of the bankrupt act of 1827." The younger Story apparently referred to a bill reported by the Judiciary Committee in the First Session of the Nineteenth Congress. . . . Hayne added that the bill was:

[s]ubmitted to one of the ablest judges of that bench [the Supreme Court], who, after a careful examination, suggested several amendments, but made no objection to this clause. I hold in my hand a printed sketch of a bankruptcy bill prepared a few years since by another able member of that bench . . . in which he himself proposes a system of voluntary bankruptcy similar to this.

This bill was tabled on May 1826, but resurrected in the Second Session. Section 93, the "voluntary" provision, came under immediate attack but on January 25th the provision survived a motion to strike. . . . [T]he bill itself was rejected on the 29th. . . .

One plausible reading of this evidence would identify Story as the "judicial character" whose work was described by the *National Intelligencer*, the "printed sketch" being his draft of 1816. If that was the case, Story's form of voluntary bankruptcy, introduced to Congress through Senator Holmes in 1821 and again by Senator Hayne in 1826, was a hybrid requiring the cooperation of the debtor and the creditor, with the creditor as petitioner. And if this was so, Van Dyke's 1820 proposal had another source. . . .

There is, moreover, further and possibly conflicting evidence. In December, 1816, Daniel Webster, then representing New Hampshire in the House of Representatives, wrote to Story asking for "any suggestions that may occur to you, for altering any part of the Bill as reported last year."

No reply has been found. . . . In April 1824, Webster again asked Story for "ideas of an outline" of a bankruptcy law. There is no known response from Story. In November, 1925, Webster asked for a draft bill and urged brevity. And in December of the same year Webster sought Story's view of a draft resolution. . . .

Again, no reply by Story has been found. . . . In the 1826-1827 session Webster offered his own verion of voluntary bankruptcy in the House. Somewhat like his earlier draft resolution, it combined a debtor's declaration of insolvency or inability to pay debts with the petition of a single creditor owed $300 (amended to $500) or of two or more creditors owed $1,000. The concept resembled concerted bankruptcy, authorized in England in 1825. No action was taken in the House on this bill.

All of this suggests that Webster moved toward the idea of voluntary bankruptcy between 1816 and 1827 without much help from Story. . . .

C. *Variations*

In fact, there had been still another form of "voluntary" bankruptcy before Congress, in the House of Representatives during the Seventeenth Congress. A committee bill limited to "adversary" proceedings against traders was reported. On January 22, 182, Samuel Woodson of Kentucky offered an amendment allowing a debtor to petition if he had the consent of the majority, in value, of his creditors. . . . On March 9th Albert Tracy of New York offered an amendment allowing any non-trader to petition even without creditor consent. This, of course, was very nearly the Van Dyke proposal of 1820. . . . It was rejected, however, by the House sitting in committee. . . . Tracy's amendment was defeated, but Woodson's passed 86-78. However the amended bill was rejected 99-72.

D. *A Law At Last*

After 1827, Congress did not address bankruptcy in a serious fashion until after the Panic of 1837. . . . When further financial difficulties arose in 1839, the Twenty-Sixth Congress acted. At the First Session, Daniel Webster introduced a bill, said to have been drafted with Story's aid, which included a voluntary provision for "all persons whatsoever owing debts"—the Van Dyke-Tracy-Webster approach rather than the Holmes or Woodson models—and provided as well for involuntary proceedings against traders only. . . . The committee divided the matter into three issues: voluntary bankruptcy, involuntary bankruptcy, and corporate bankruptcy; and it reported a bill limited to the first of these. Senator Wall of New Jersey offered a substitute which included involuntary proceedings and corporate bankruptcy but was limited to merchants, traders, and banks. The Wall substitute was enlarged to include all classes of debtors. It survived a motion by Henry Clay to strike the compulsory provisions. . . . After a sharp fight, in which John Calhoun argued that voluntary bankruptcy would be unconstitutional and Hubbard of New Hampshire worried that voluntary proceedings for *all* debtors would lead to involuntary bankruptcy against farmers, the Senate passed a bill on June 25, 1840, which included bankruptcy on petition of the debtor. Discharge was to be denied if a majority, in number and value, of creditors objected, but a creditor voice on discharge was already a familiar feature.

The bill had to be reenacted by the Senate in the Second Session where Calhoun again attacked the voluntary provision. The House, at first, tabled the bill but subsequently passed it in political maneuvering involving two other bills on different subjects. The Senate accepted the House version, and voluntary bankruptcy for all debtors became law.

CONCLUSION

. . . [A] bankruptcy process which includes discharge but no voluntary proceedings lies comfortably within the range of contemplation. But it is hardly possible to conceive of the opposite, voluntary bankruptcy without a right of discharge. . . . Consequently, voluntary bankruptcy could not appear unless it was combined with or followed the creation of a right of discharge. And, that is exactly what happened. . . .

If the order of appearance is clear, so also is the linkage of the two concepts. The natural, if not the necessary, consequence of creation of the right of discharge was a desire on the part of debtors to initiate the process. . . .

It may seem strange, as well, that it took from 1697 until 1841 to make an idea into a law. The course was slow and tortuous. There are a number of reasons for the delay. Agitation for bankruptcy legislation tends to come only in hard times. Moreover, . . . there were differences as to the form that voluntary proceedings should take. . . . Finally, there was frontal opposition to the very idea of voluntary proceedings.

Such opposition was often mixed or obscured by other battles. There were those who opposed bankruptcy altogether. Its extension to voluntary proceedings only aggravated that opposition. For these opponents, the issue was a moral one; failure to meet obligations was unforgivable. For others there was a definitional problem; bankruptcy by its terms was limited to involuntary proceedings against traders and merchants. . . . Still others feared that adoption of voluntary proceedings would lead to extension of the involuntary process to debtors then immune from bankruptcy at the instance of creditors. These divisions were regional, pitting the Northeast against the South and West. They were also occupational, industrial against agricultural.

Yet it seems to me that the central issue posed by voluntary bankruptcy was concern about possible debtor abuse of the process. . . . The principal fear at the time covered by this account was that debtors, who by tightening their belts would be able to repay their creditors in substantial measure, would seize on bankruptcy as a means of avoiding the repayment obligation. . . .

But there are countervailing arguments. One of Defoe's insights was that, better than anyone else, the debtor knows when relief is needed. The process should not await some debtor "act of bankruptcy" or the slower recognition of insolvency by creditors. Even more important, in my view, was Defoe's recognition that bankruptcy could be a benefit to honest debtors as well as to creditors. If bankruptcy has sometimes been the resort of scoundrels, it far more often has provided unfortunate-but-honest debtors a second chance to bring order to their troubled financial affairs. Remedying abuse, however difficult, should be confined to cases where there is in fact abuse.

The linkage of the discharge and voluntary petition was ultimately necessary to make bankruptcy truly a remedy for debtors as well as creditors. The many contributors to that linkage would have reason to be proud of their contrivance.

Randal C. Picker
Voluntary Petitions and the Creditors' Bargain
61 U. Cin. L. Rev. 519 (1992)[*]

One of the most notable features of United States bankruptcy law is the relative ease with which a debtor can invoke the protection of the bankruptcy court. Typically, the debtor need do no more than pay the appropriate filing fee and sign the petition. The debtor need not be insolvent, and in fact, there has been substantial doubt on this issue in some of our best-known bankruptcies. Nor must the debtor make the substantive showing that creditors filing an involuntary petition typically must make—that the debtor is not paying its debts as they become due or perhaps that the debtor cannot pay its debts as they become due, given how readily manipulable a "not paying" requirement would be for voluntary filings. This is not to say that debtors file casually. The consequences of filing for the debtor and its managers are often substantial and there is every reason to believe that most filings are made only after much deliberation. My point is only that once the debtor has concluded that filing is sensible, very little stands in the way. . . .

This is somewhat surprising given its consequences. We have a rich nonbankruptcy insolvency law. . . . State law may, through statute or judicial creation, provide an assortment of winding-up devices. . . . Yet, filing for bankruptcy largely displaces state insolvency law. . . .

Given all of this, a fundamental, but surprisingly, largely unexplored question is presented: Why should we allow voluntary petitions? Assuming we should, how should we structure our legal rules to induce filings by the right firms at the right times? In pursuing these questions, I want to separate flesh-and-blood human beings from entities that exist by the grace of the state. . . . The idea of the fresh start gives content to much of the jurisprudence for individual debtors in bankruptcy. This idea is largely, if not completely, irrelevant for corporations and other business entities . . . . Given this basic difference between individuals and other entities, I will put to one side the merits of allowing individuals to file voluntarily and will instead consider this question for other entities. I will usually call these "firms."

The idea that firms should not be allowed to file voluntary petitions may sound odd, but of course it harkens to the early days of bankruptcy in England and this country. The idea of voluntary bankruptcy was not introduced in England until 1825. The first federal bankruptcy statute in the United States, the Bankruptcy Act of 1800, allowed only involuntary bankruptcy, and it was not until 1910 that corporations could be brought before the bankruptcy court, voluntarily or involuntarily. Thus, the notion that a firm might be denied the right to file voluntarily, or perhaps to be denied access to a federal proceeding in its entirety, is one worth considering. . . .

I will focus on the relationships among the creditors of a typical business firm. I suggest that the stylized deal defined by the relevant United States bankruptcy and debtor-creditor statutes has two central characteristics. First, secured creditors are entitled to first priority to the debtor's assets to the full extent of their security interest (subject, of course, to no more than payment in full) prior to any payment to unsecured creditors. Second, unsecured creditors are entitled to any value in excess of that necessary to pay secured creditors—again subject to no more than payment in full—and this value is to be divided among the unsecured creditors on a pro rata basis.

Unfortunately, this deal is not self-enforcing. In particular, a real risk exists that the secured creditor might cheat on the deal and grab the extra incremental value when it goes to enforce its

---

security interests. As a group, the unsecured creditors face standard collective action problems in enforcing their rights. Enforcing the deal with the secured creditor redounds to the benefit of all of the unsecured creditors, but each unsecured creditor might seek to free ride on the efforts of other unsecured creditors. These collective action problems would be daunting alone, but they are compounded by informational problems. Enforcing the deal between the secured creditors and the unsecured creditors turns on knowing whether the value of the assets subject to the security interest exceeds the size of the loan. To put this in the economic jargon of the day, the unsecured creditors face a state verification problem: they don't know which state of the world has occurred. Consider a firm with a secured debt of $100 and unsecured debts totaling $100. The assets may be worth less than the amount of the secured debt, say, $80, or they may be worth more, say, $150. In both cases, the firm would be insolvent, but the unsecured creditors would be ignorant of the relevant state. The unsecured creditors may be able to acquire that information, but that will be costly, and there is a substantial risk that unsecured creditors will duplicate each other's efforts if they proceed separately.

The debtor may know this value. The debtor will often, though not necessarily always, have better information than the creditors about the value of the assets. Given the debtor's informational advantage and the possibility of duplicative information expenditures, the creditors as a group would want to enlist the services of the debtor in helping to enforce the bargains among the creditors. Unfortunately, unless payoffs to the debtor are specifically tied to providing the relevant information, there is good reason to think that the debtor will be indifferent about doing so. In the situations relevant to bankruptcy law, the debtor will be insolvent and will not care about whether the deal between secured and unsecured creditors is enforced.

We can make the debtor care, even when its equity interest has ceased to be valuable. The debtor must be induced to provide the critical information about the state of the firm (or, equivalently, be allowed to sell the information in the marketplace). This could be done through a penalty scheme, as occurs in the United Kingdom and Germany, or through a bonus scheme.

The United States has chosen the latter. The Bankruptcy Code contains a powerful mechanism that should induce the debtor to enforce the creditors' bargain. The debtor's right to file a voluntary petition and to invoke the holdup power conferred on the debtor by the automatic stay and the exclusivity period operates as a mechanism for compensating the debtor for filing a voluntary petition. The right of the secured creditor under § 362(d) of the Bankruptcy Code to seek to lift the stay can be used to sort out appropriate cases that should and should not be in bankruptcy. The petition has the effect of resulting in better enforcement of the creditors' bargain than would be possible in a world in which only involuntary petitions were permitted.

. . . [T]he automatic stay and the exclusivity period transfer value to shareholders. . . . This article suggests that the transfer of value to the debtor effectuated by the stay provides an appropriate inducement for the debtor to commence voluntary proceedings when it would otherwise not do so. . . .

II. VOLUNTARY PETITIONS AS AN ENFORCEMENT MECHANISM

. . . Consider a corporation, ACorp, Inc. ACorp has a single widget project and the project has three possible outcomes. In the good state, S1, the project is a great success and is worth $300. This is expected to happen 50% of the time. Of course, the project may fail, too. In the first bad state, state S2, the project is worth $120. This happens 25% of the time. Finally, in the second failure outcome, state S3, the project is a complete bust and is worth only $100. This happens 25% of the time.

In addition to the single project, ACorp has a very simple debt structure. It has a single secured creditor owed $100 with a perfected, prior security interest in the firm's sole asset, the widget project. In addition, the firm has unsecured debts totaling $100 comprised of ten separate debts of $10. The firm therefore has total debts of $200 matched with the project. For the given probabilities and the associated values, the project's expected value is $205. Based on these figures, prior to running the project and determining the outcome, the firm is solvent.

Consider how this situation plays out in a world of perfect information. If the project is a success—meaning that state S1 occurs—the creditors will be paid in full. The firm will be worth enough to pay the creditors and the creditors will know this. The equity holders of the firm will then hold stock worth $100. If the project fails completely—meaning that state S3 occurs—the contractual priority of the secured creditor would be enforced. The secured creditor would simply get the full $100 in value, and none of the unsecured creditors would receive anything. Again, given the assumption of perfect information, there is no difficulty reaching this outcome. And, if the project fails but not completely—meaning S2 occurs—the secured creditor would still receive payment in full, but each unsecured creditor would get its pro rata portion—recall § 726(b) of the Bankruptcy Code—of the remaining $20, or $2.

All of this is simple and straightforward. With full information about the firm's value, the agreed upon division of value among the equity holders, the unsecured creditors, and the secured creditors is implemented as per the agreement. No one can deviate from the prearranged split, as it is costless to enforce it.

Reality, though, is uncertainty. The creditors do not know, without more, which state of the world has occurred, but in some situations, the debtor may convey some information about the status of the project. If the project is a success, the creditors will probably get checks in the mail on time, and therefore a simple signal by the debtor—payment in full, on time—makes it easy for the creditors to distinguish state S1 from states S2 and S3. But if one of states S2 or S3 occurs, no check may arrive. The debtor will be insolvent, and without more, will have no stake in how its assets are divvied up among its creditors. The debtor may pay particular creditors or it may simply abandon ship. It will not necessarily send any signal that will inform the creditors of the relevant state of the world.

The consequences of not knowing whether state S2 or S3 has occurred are substantial. The most likely course is that the secured creditor will take action against the project under its state law default rights. The secured creditor knows that, regardless of whether bad state S2 or S3 occurred, it is entitled to first crack at the assets. In this situation, the concern should be that the secured creditor will breach its agreement with the unsecured creditor group. It may do that by selling the assets for $100 when they are actually worth $120. Since the secured creditor must remit to the debtor any excess sale price, it may not exert any efforts to receive full value for the sold property, if that value exceeds the amount of the debt.

The secured creditor also might behave opportunistically and seek to pocket the excess value. . . . The debtor may be indifferent to all of this. These issues influence how the insolvent firm's assets are divided among its many creditors, but these issues do not result in value being made available to the debtor. . . .

Given all of this, to return to the example, the unsecured creditors can have little assurance that they will receive, without some effort, the $20 to which they are entitled if state S2 rather than S3 occurred. How will the unsecured creditors respond to the uncertainty over which bad state has occurred? As a group, they have as much as $20 at stake, though the expected amount at stake is only $10. If we assume (for now) that the unsecured creditors could perfectly enforce their deal with the secured creditor once they had learned the debtor's status, they would be willing to spend up to $10 to acquire that information.

The unsecured creditors, though, do not proceed as a group, and the real question is how the individual unsecured creditors will proceed. To answer this question, focus on how the benefits and burdens of the information acquisition—the monitoring, for short—will be divided. It seems that both undermonitoring and overmonitoring are possible. First consider rules that provide for each unsecured creditor to bear its own costs of monitoring and that further provide for the benefits of monitoring to be divided pro rata. For example, if the cost of monitoring is $k and only one unsecured creditor monitors and none of the others do, all of the non-monitoring unsecured creditors receive $2, and the monitoring creditor nets $2-k, if state S2 has occurred, and $0 and -$k respectively if state S1 has occurred.

Two points should be apparent. First, the creditor will not monitor if the cost of monitoring exceeds its expected payoff from monitoring, or if k > $1. Second, each unsecured creditor would rather free ride on the monitoring efforts of another creditor than monitor. Under this regime, if the monitoring costs exceeded the individual creditor's pro rata share of the recovery for each creditor, no creditor would monitor and the secured creditor would be able to capture the value in excess of the amount owed to it. In our simple example, that would occur if k > $1, since that is the expected pro rata benefit from monitoring for each creditor.

Nevertheless, it is very unlikely that this would happen this way. The benefits of monitoring for the unsecured creditors would be divided pro rata only if the monitoring creditor chose to file an involuntary bankruptcy petition. Pro rata division is the rule of § 726(b) of the Code and thus only applies after a proceeding has been commenced. Pro rata division is not the rule that would otherwise be applicable under state law. State law is grab law. The monitoring unsecured creditor will seek payment in full of its debt and may even seek to split some of the excess remaining value with the secured creditor. To return to the example, if the creditor monitors and learns that there is $20 generally available for the unsecured creditors, the creditor will demand $10 in payment in full. He may also seek a share of the remaining $10 by threatening to inform one (and only one) fellow unsecured creditor about the extra money.

Where does this put the unsecured creditors? Individual monitoring is relatively unattractive if the benefit of monitoring is divided pro rata, but that will not happen unless the monitor files a petition in bankruptcy. Since the monitor will not file, monitoring could be profitable and more than one unsecured creditor could wind up monitoring the secured creditor's behavior. . . .

Both undermonitoring and overmonitoring seem possible. In any event, the lowest cost monitor will not be monitoring: the debtor would be the lowest cost monitor of the secured creditor's behavior. As a general matter, the debtor may have the best information about the value of the firm. . . . [T]he debtor will surely have the best information about the secured creditor's actions. Given this, the best possible result for the creditors as a group would be to pay the debtor a fee to inform them of whether S2 or S3 has taken place. Recall that that knowledge is essential to enforcing the upfront deals of the creditors. The debtor is the lowest cost monitor of this, but in the absence of a device for channeling value to the debtor (or for penalizing the debtor), the debtor will not care about seeing that the upfront deal is enforced between the secured and the unsecured creditors.

The Bankruptcy Code does this through the debtor's right to file a voluntary petition and through the automatic stay/exclusivity rules. As already noted, §§ 109 and 301 of the Bankruptcy Code give the debtor a virtually limitless right to file a voluntary petition. The debtor's control over the property is created by the automatic stay of § 362, which generally prevents creditors from seizing the debtor's property. It is further enhanced by § 1121 of the Code, which gives the debtor the exclusive right to file a reorganization plan for 120 days, a period which is often extended.

The unsecured creditors want the debtor to file when the value of the project exceeds the amount of the secured creditor's claim, or, to put this in the language of the Bankruptcy Code, when the debtor has equity in the property. In a world where judges value property and businesses accurately, the debtor will do just that. If there is no value available for the unsecured creditors, the debtor will not file. No value available means that the secured creditor's claim exceeds the value of the project, or to put it the other way, that the debtor has no equity in the property. The secured creditor would win its lift stay motion, and the debtor will lose its ability to holdup the creditors for value. The debtor will not file. If there is value available to the unsecured creditors—meaning there is an equity in the property—the debtor will survive the secured creditor's lift stay motion, and will therefore file as it will be able to exercise the holdup powers conferred on it through the automatic stay and the exclusivity rule.

This scheme sorts the cases precisely along the dividing line of cases in which value in excess of the debt owed to the secured creditor exists and those in which it does not. If there is no value for the unsecured creditors, the debtor will not file, as it will lose the lift stay motion and will therefore receive nothing through the exclusivity holdup. If there is value for the unsecured creditors, the debtor will win the lift stay motion, and can therefore maintain the exclusivity period. The creditors will buy off the debtor, and therefore the debtor will receive the value that will induce it to file in the first place. This sorting is precisely what is required to enforce the split agreed to between the secured creditor and the unsecured creditors.

This suggests that in many cases deviations from absolute priority can be justified as a bonus for bringing the case in the first place. The bonus is a contingent bonus, and thus avoids the overfiling problem that would be associated with a flat fee or any other mechanism not directly tied to the value of the assets. On this view, the automatic stay operates as a non-waivable means of channeling value to the manager-shareholders that induces them to file voluntary petitions in those situations in which there is value to be distributed to the unsecured creditors. In effect, the unsecured creditors appoint the manager-shareholders as their agent for enforcing the original deal between the secured creditor and the group of unsecured creditors. And the problems with verifying the state of the world—are the assets worth $80 or $150?—that put the deal between the secured and unsecured creditors at risk are squarely presented and answered by coupling the voluntary petition with the lift stay motion. . . .

III. Criticisms and Comments

There are a number of open items. Consider these one-by-one. First, a standard problem still exists: who monitors the monitor? . . .

Finally, we might try sticks instead of carrots; many countries do. In Germany, directors of an insolvent joint stock company or limited liability company have a duty to initiate insolvency proceedings. Failure to comply may result in liability for damages, fines, or imprisonment. In the United Kingdom, the Insolvency Act of 1986 added the concept of wrongful trading. A director that knows or should have known that the company could not avoid going into liquidation and allowed it to continue to operate may be forced to contribute to the debtor's assets. And, under the Company Directors Disqualification Act of 1986, such a director may also be disqualified for a period of years from the management of other companies.

The choice between carrots and sticks should be guided by the ex ante consequences of the different rules. Penalties that do not run to the direct benefit of creditors, such as fines, imprisonment, or disqualification going forward, may just dampen entrepreneurial initiative. Unless we think too many projects are started, we might be better served by a bonus scheme that had the same effect on inducing petition filings. Penalties that do run in favor of the creditors may also be less efficient than bonuses if manager-shareholders are systematically more risk averse than creditors. A bonus scheme acts as insurance, while a penalty scheme exacerbates the substantial losses already suffered by poorly diversified insiders. Monetary penalties also may be meaningless if the manager is insolvent herself. Another benefit of carrots is that managers seek carrots; they run from sticks. Someone will have to play policeman—quite literally in Germany—to enforce penalties and that adds an extra layer of costs.

IV. Conclusion

The two key elements of the implicit bargain between secured and unsecured creditors are priority for secured creditors to the extent of their debts and pro rata division of the balance among unsecured creditors. Collective action and information problems put this deal at risk.

Most typically, the secured creditor may cheat on the deal by keeping the excess amount. The unsecured creditors will not know whether the secured creditor's failure to turn over money reflects the true state of the world—the unsecured creditors were entitled to nothing—or cheating by the second creditor given the actual state of the world.

The party best situated to know is the debtor. The debtor receives notice from the secured creditor of its intentions under the relevant statutes and also has the most particular knowledge of the property. With the firm insolvent, the debtor may pay too little attention to the secured creditor. To make the debtor pay attention, we must change its incentives. This can be done through penalties, though this has problems, or through bonuses. The current Bankruptcy Code allows the debtor to select a bonus by filing for bankruptcy. The procedural holdup the Code allows translates into an ability to extract value from the creditors. This leads to the systematic deviations from absolute priority found in practice. These are tempered by the right of the secured creditor to seek relief from the stay. In a pristine system, the stay hearing would seek to determine the relevant state of the world, to identify whether there was value available for unsecured creditors. It is that question which must be answered if we are to implement fully the implicit bargain struck between secured and unsecured creditors.

The Good Faith Filing Debate

One of the major lingering issues regarding the commencement of bankruptcy cases is whether a chapter 11 debtor is constrained by an implied "good faith" requirement. The issue has arisen often, albeit not exclusively, in single asset real estate cases, in which the court believes that the debtor is using chapter 11 solely as a tactical stalling device to the detriment of the secured creditor. Numerous courts of appeals have held that there is such a limitation, notwithstanding the absence of any specific statutory support in the Code.

The good faith filing question is addressed in *The Implied Good Faith Filing Requirement: Sentinel of an Evolving Bankruptcy Policy*, 85 Nw. U. L. Rev. 919 (1991), by Professors Stephen Knippenberg and Lawrence Ponoroff. They examine the good faith filing issue in the larger context of the nature, scope, and evolution of bankruptcy policy and its implementation by the courts. What is their ultimate assessment of the problem and its appropriate resolution?

Lawrence Ponoroff & F. Stephen Knippenberg
The Implied Good Faith Filing Requirement: Sentinel of an Evolving Bankruptcy Policy
85 Nw. U. L. Rev. 919 (1991)[*]

Introduction

. . . In this Article, we propose that the bankruptcy courts' adaptation of the good faith doctrine presents an excellent example of the law in evolution, a process we believe to be describable in meaningful terms from the positive law of the cases. With this as our working assumption, good faith

---

is transformed from a tired cliché, invoked in suspicious response to an array of novel filings, to a useful instrument pressed into service by the courts to bring order and standards to the business of assuring that bankruptcy policy and purposes evolve in a sensible, purposeful way. . . .

I. THE GOOD FAITH FILING REQUIREMENT IN THE CASE LAW

. . .

B. Categories of Good Faith Cases

Three broad patterns of conduct implicate good faith concerns in Chapter 11 filings: (1) the one-asset (usually real estate) debtor case; (2) resort to bankruptcy court protection in order to make strategic use of a specific bankruptcy law right or power; and (3) use of bankruptcy to secure a tactical litigation advantage. . . .

III. TOWARD AN ALTERNATIVE UNDERSTANDING OF THE GOOD FATH DOCTRINE IN BANKRUPTCY

A. Role of Bankruptcy and the Bankruptcy Courts

. . . For better or worse, bankruptcy has evolved into a legal institution to which commercial concerns, both large and small, have turned to resolve basic business and economic problems that are not satisfactorily addressed elsewhere. In many instances, these problems are related only incidentally, if at all, to the problems of default and immediate financial ruin.

. . . [W]hether by default or caprice, the institution of bankruptcy has become a medium for relieving the pressure which inevitably builds in a commercial economy for solutions to new and unprecedented societal problems.

. . . If, as we have argued, the parameters of the bankruptcy process are yet to be determined and perhaps are even indeterminable, the courts need an instrumentality to assure controlled expansion or contraction of the fixed body of substantive bankruptcy law to accommodate ever-changing views about what the process should include. Good faith, we suggest, is that instrumentality. Implicit in this proposition, of course, is the basic jurisprudential assumption that the courts and the judiciary are the appropriate political agency for making these scope determinations. . . .

For two essential reasons, we believe, the judiciary is the appropriate repository of power to decide issues of bankruptcy's scope. First, the decisions of courts, endlessly memorialized in a continuous stream of published opinions, are subject to both immediate and reflective scrutiny. This presents the opportunity for an indirect discourse to develop . . . . The resultant dialectic minimizes the potential for random or inconsistent decision making.

The second reason that the judiciary is the appropriate entity to regulate bankruptcy access is the very conclusion that the role of the bankruptcy process is continually changing. This critical fact places a premium on an agency which is at once tolerant of a dynamic process and naturally resistant to sweeping and abrupt change. Limited to deciding specific disputes between specific litigants, courts are by and large incapable of implementing change other than at a molecular level. In sharp contrast to a legislative body, which acts broadly, abstractly, and episodically, courts can only react in a relatively measured and incremental fashion. This ensures that the evolution of bankruptcy policy will proceed at a similar pace.

B. The Good Faith Calculus

These principles are strikingly illustrated in the courts' use of the good faith doctrine to analyze issues of bankruptcy access. The term "good faith" has a long and storied history in the law. . . . Good faith has been called upon in radically disparate contexts to establish the outer boundaries of acceptable behavior. . . . Indeed, in large part, the term "good faith" has become little more than a convenient way to refer to a set of criteria by which conduct is tested. . . . [T]he one constant has been this murky but persistent idea of a moral imperative.

The malleability of the doctrine, the result of a rich history of varied applications, together with its capacity to call to mind certain familiar referents of honesty and dishonesty, make good faith a singularly useful instrument to aid the development of the contours of the bankruptcy process. Application of an implied good faith requirement in bankruptcy thus functions less as a substantive rule of standing or eligibility to file, and more as an enabling convention allowing the bankruptcy courts to systematically test their performance in guarding the portal into bankruptcy. In other words, a good faith filing requirement is inevitable once it is acknowledged that the system accommodates an evolving reality of social, political, and economic challenges. . . .

We believe, however, that it is possible by studying the cases to understand a great deal about the evolutionary process. The cases not only enable us to identify and critique the present contours of bankruptcy policy, but they also suggest the normative inclinations which might be expected to influence the outcome of future decisions—decisions that will play a significant part in shaping the contours of future bankruptcy policy.

On assembling the good faith cases into the three loose categories we earlier suggested, we were at once struck by an easily observable pattern: one-asset/one-creditor cases are frequently dismissed for want of good faith; the public company filing is never dismissed on bad faith grounds; and filings by economically viable companies making tactical use of the bankruptcy system are occasionally dismissed on this basis. . . . [I]t is important to go beyond mechanical division of the cases in favor of a more demanding and policy-sensitive analysis. . . .

In keeping with our thesis that bankruptcy policy continually evolves, principally at the hands of courts employing the mediating device of good faith, our analysis dictates that we return to the case law to identify the broad, recurring themes that delineate the evolutionary process. . . . It is important, however, to disclose the limits of an analytical approach, such as ours, that derives largely from positive law. Since propositions abstracted from cases can no more be expected to conform to any logical ideal than the cases from which they proceed, it would be nonsense to suppose that the derivative propositions themselves reflect a unified system capable of formulaic expression in absolute terms. Our end, therefore, is to propose a calculus, not an equation.

As observed earlier, the courts, particularly in the one-asset debtor cases, are inclined to articulate and then apply a laundry list of illuminating factors to decide whether a filing was undertaken in good faith. Our study and synthesis of the cases leads us to believe, however, that there is more at work here than the mere juggling and reconstitution of those factors. We discern in this exercise an unexpressed intermediate step in the process that is apparent only with the recognition that the so-called factors or indicia of good faith are not actually themselves proof of good or bad faith; rather, they serve to identify a category or type of case which has been earmarked by courts as suspect. What type of case is suspect? In our view, it is the case that manifestly fails to present the pattern which everyone, Collectivists and Traditionalists alike, agrees invokes the core function of bankruptcy—namely, to resolve the problem of multiple defaults and limited assets. . . .

A case may also be identified as suspect when, from the surrounding circumstances, it can reasonably be inferred that the filing, voluntary or involuntary, was precipitated by an exigency other than the problem of multiple defaults. . . .

From our reading of the cases, then, we infer a two-step analysis at work beneath the routine discussion of motive, badges of bad faith, and ability to reorganize. The first step, again, is identification of the case as suspect. The second step involves a calculus that can be expressed in terms of two pivotal considerations, which we have termed intent and impact. Although simple in its formulation, this calculus can become quite complex in operation due to the varying attention these two considerations receive from one case to the next.

Preliminarily, it is necessary to give substantive content to the terms "intent" and "impact" for our purposes. The courts that address the implied good faith filing issue frequently speak in terms of intent. In that context, we believe intent most often means the sum of the motives inferred from objective facts that prompted the filing.

. . . Where it is evident that the dominant motive is debt collection relief in the traditional sense of adjusting the rights of multiple claimants, courts have had little trouble concluding that the case before them belongs in bankruptcy, based on the intent consideration alone. The more complex the debtor's organizational structure, however, and the more complicated its financial affairs, the more difficult and less meaningful it becomes to talk about subjective motivation. . . . In these instances, the appropriateness of the case for bankruptcy turns largely on what we call impact. In any given case, impact takes into account: (1) the size of the community affected by the debtor's filing, which frequently is a function of the size of the debtor enterprise; (2) the immediacy of the effects of the filing upon that community; and (3) whether the particular adversities that prompted the filing are adequately addressed elsewhere.

With these definitions of intent and impact in mind, we turn our attention to their interaction since it is that interaction which forms the basis for determining bankruptcy purposes. . . . [W]e conclude that the relationship between intent and impact is one of interactive and mutual dependence. Consequently, the relationship can easily be described and understood with the help of a Cartesian graph, the axes of which are established by our two elemental considerations.

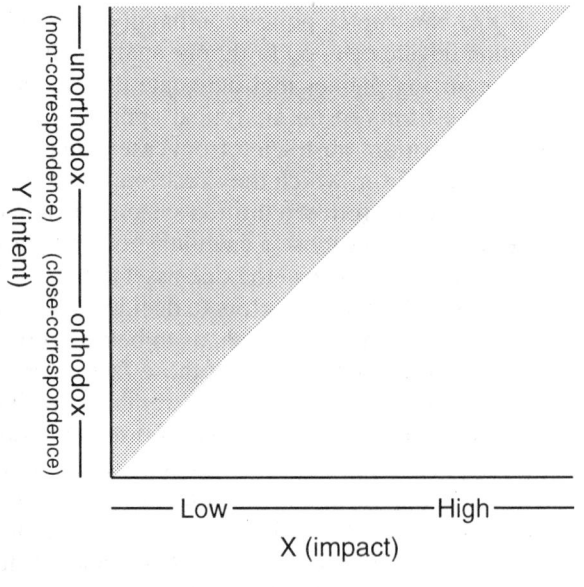

Fig. 1

The intent consideration is plotted along the vertical or "Y" axis. At the base of this axis we find the case where there is a complete correspondence of the filer's intent with the historic and still foundational function of bankruptcy. For the sake of convenience, we refer to this point as "orthodox intent." At the apex of the axis is the case having no correspondence of intention with that historic function, what we refer to as "unorthodox intent." This case represents the filing with none of the characteristics of cases presenting the archetype common pool problem.

The impact consideration is plotted along the horizontal or "X" axis. At the point where the "X" axis intersects the "Y" axis is the case of least impact. The farther one proceeds along the "X" axis away from that intersection, the greater the impact of the case.

Drawing a line at a 45-degree angle from the intersection of the "X" and "Y" axes illustrates the relationship we believe exists between the intent and impact variables. Cases plotted into the shaded area of the graph on the basis of the good faith calculus would be subject to dismissal. Conversely, cases plotted into the unshaded area of the graph would survive a threshold good faith challenge.

. . . [W]hat we hope to display by use of this graph are the boundaries that currently circumscribe the permissible scope of bankruptcy. . . . In our analysis, the object is not to define good faith, an exercise without purpose once the concept of good faith is recognized to be nothing more than the instrumentality used by the courts to control the evolution of the bankruptcy process. Instead, we consider it important to talk about good faith only insofar as it facilitates discussion of the unfolding of bankruptcy policy.

C. The Good Faith Cases Reconsidered

Having elaborated an abstract, analytical calculus, we arrive at the point of its concrete application. . . .

In giving content and dimension to the good faith calculus, it is helpful to begin with the one-asset debtor case . . . . On their face, these primary facts indicate an intent so remote from orthodox intent and a level of impact so idiosyncratic as to make the one-asset debtor case the prototype for dismissal on bad faith grounds. Accordingly, the one-asset debtor case establishes points along the impact and intent axes amounting to the current reported extremes of low impact and unorthodox intent alike. . . .

In the case of a large public company filing, it is usually the ability to derive strategic advantages in bankruptcy not available outside of a Chapter 11 proceeding which invites good faith challenges. In these cases, the preliminary inquiry into the debtor's intent (as we use that term) will almost always lead to close scrutiny for two reasons. First, the infrastructure that forms the operating framework of the large debtor enterprise is nearly always complex and extensive, having the potential to spawn a dizzying array of motivational impulses. . . .

Second, resolution of the intent question is complicated by the fact that in the mega-reorganization case there is seldom a clear answer to the question whether the case presents a common pool problem. . . .

For the two reasons stated above, courts are likely to have difficulty in determining the existence of orthodox intent. Thus, we believe the next step, which involves the balancing of intent and impact, will almost invariably be taken, if only implicitly, in the large reorganization case. However, the impact quotient in the public company reorganization is frequently so enormous that it can be expected in most cases to carry the day for the debtor. Certainly this is the teaching of the *Continental Airlines* and *Manville* decisions. . . .

Of all the cases discussed so far, the bankruptcy filing of Texaco, Inc. presents the most serious question of whether a major business filing was a proper use of Chapter 11. Parenthetically, we note that discussion of Texaco's reorganization proceeding also presents the occasion to apply our analysis to the third type of good faith case, the tactical filing. . . .

Another area where we believe our proposed analysis would prove useful is in connection with environmental cleanup obligations . . . .

What, then, should be the response to a debtor that files a Chapter 11 bankruptcy petition in reaction to an order from a state or federal environmental regulatory agency to clean up property contaminated with hazardous waste? The answer depends on where the case falls along the intent and impact axes we have described. As in most other contexts, an enterprise that is not only solvent but also relatively stable financially should not find a receptive host in the bankruptcy court. Orthodoxy of intent remains an important threshold consideration. When the extent or uncertainty over the extent of cleanup costs threatens a company's continued survival, however, the next step must be taken. Recalling that the impact quotient takes into account the breadth of interests directly affected by the filing, the immediacy of those effects, and the existence of non-bankruptcy institutions to respond to the particular crisis inducing the bankruptcy filing, we conclude that in most environmental cases impact would be considerable.

Thus . . . it becomes necessary to look beyond the fact that the filing was prompted by a dispute between two parties and to inquire into the effects, actual and potential, of that dispute and its possible resolution on both the debtor's financial condition and the condition of the community in which the debtor exists and interacts. It is precisely that inquiry which is forced by the calculus we have put forth. . . . [W]hen a new decision is rendered, whether or not its outcome comports with prior prediction, we are able to detect and observe the dynamic of the good faith doctrine at work.

This is not to assert that every case that departs from current thinking about the scope of bankruptcy policy rises to the dignity of a working example of the evolutionary process. We do not believe that every decision is right by definition. Rather, each decision that signals a departure invites close study. A case that runs counter to the result predicted by the calculus must offer a reasoned basis for its outcome. If it does not, it is a random departure and of no value insofar as the evolution of bankruptcy policy is concerned.

CONCLUSION

. . . [B]y proceeding from the assumption that the scope of bankruptcy is determinate but evolving as a result of exogenous demands upon it, we have been able to formulate a calculus by which to describe the current state of bankruptcy policy and with which to speculate on possible future directions. In the course of this endeavor we found that questions concerning the role of the courts and the function of the good faith requirement in the evolutionary process presented themselves naturally and obviously for consideration. So perceived, the good faith doctrine was transformed from a stale platitude called upon in despair of a clear rule to "do equity," to a flexible instrument providing standards in an environment where the boundaries of bankruptcy policy are constantly tested. . . .

Finally, we have been led to assert that the evolution of bankruptcy policy and purposes is observable and describable from the positive law. It is from this assertion that we were challenged to construct a simple calculus with a dynamic component to accommodate the dynamic system it seeks to describe.

C.   Involuntary Cases

"Involuntary" bankruptcy means that creditors initiate the proceeding, not the debtor. Thus, the bankruptcy case is said to be "involuntary" from the debtor's perspective. The critical task in involuntary bankruptcy is defining the grounds upon which the creditors' petition for bankruptcy should be granted. What should the creditors be required to show? Until 1978, creditors had to prove that the debtor committed an "act of bankruptcy," which was an act that indirectly signaled that the debtor posed a collection risk to its creditors as a group or to creditors *inter se*. In 1978, Congress finally abandoned the act-of-bankruptcy model, adopting instead the requirement that the creditors show that the debtor is generally not paying its debts as they come due. This test is a modified version of the "equity" insolvency test. It focuses on the actuality of ongoing payment. Interestingly, the Code eschews a "balance-sheet" (debts greater than assets) insolvency test as a criterion for involuntary bankruptcy. Indeed, proof by a debtor of balance-sheet *solvency*—which would by definition mean that all creditors could be paid in full—would not even be sufficient to rebut an involuntary petition if the creditors established the debtor's failure to pay debts as they came due.

In the first two articles, Professor McCoid, in *The Occasion for Involuntary Bankruptcy*, 61 AM. BANKR. L.J. 195 (1987), and Professor Susan Block-Lieb, in *Why Creditors File So Few Involuntary Petitions and Why the Number is Not Too Small*, 57 BROOKLYN L. REV. 803 (1991), examine carefully the question of what grounds should trigger involuntary bankruptcy. Each couches their analysis in terms of what they view the goals of bankruptcy to be. How are McCoid's and Block-Lieb's visions alike? How are they different? Each author determines that proof of actual "balance-sheet" insolvency should suffice as a basis for involuntary bankruptcy. What are their justifications for proposing this change? Professor McCoid also includes a very interesting historical exegesis of the development of the standard.

In the final article, *Involuntary Bankruptcy and the Bona Fides of a Bona Fide Dispute*, 65 IND. L.J. 315 (1990), Professor Lawrence Ponoroff examines a different problem that arises in involuntary filings: what constitutes a "bona fide dispute" that will serve both to disqualify a creditor as a petitioning creditor and disqualify a debt from counting against the debtor under the "generally-not-paying" test? Congress in 1978 did not initially exclude debts subject to a bona fide dispute in either situation, but then in 1984 Congress did an about-face and added the exclusion. The trick is to balance the legitimate interests of creditors and debtors and minimize the risk of strategic gamesmanship by either group. How would Ponoroff define "bona fide dispute" in the two situations?

John C. McCoid, II
The Occasion for Involuntary Bankruptcy
61 AM. BANKR. L.J. 195 (1987)[*]

Precisely what event, behavior, or condition should provide the occasion for involuntary bankruptcy proceedings is a question about which much has been written without the emergence of any clear statement of theory. The Anglo-American tradition called for an act of bankruptcy with ideas of what constituted such an act changing over time, usually in expansive fashion. In most other countries cessation of payments, or its equivalent, warrants such proceedings. Reform in 1978 brought the United States' position close to the prevailing view. Section 303(h) of the Bankruptcy Code calls for an order for relief when an involuntary petition is controverted in two circumstances: when the debtor is generally not paying such debtor's debts as such debts become due and where within 120 days before the date of the filing of the petition, a custodian . . . was appointed or took possession. The former provision, surely the dominant ground of involuntary proceedings, is often termed equity insolvency. Its adoption for this purpose thus largely replaced balance-sheet insolvency—assets exceeded by liabilities—which was a component of most, but not all, of the acts of bankruptcy specified by the 1898 Act. . . .

Intuitively, one might conclude that the balance-sheet test is the more appropriate circumstance for involuntary proceedings. Insufficiency of assets to pay all creditors in full creates a need for ratable distribution that is the hallmark of bankruptcy law. It may be thought to call as well for discharge of the balance, the debtor's fresh start. Yet balance-sheet insolvency was only temporarily central to initiation of involuntary proceedings. Any appraisal of the basis for such a process thus may well begin with an account of the rise and fall of that standard.

I. HISTORY

A. IN THE COURTS

Neither the 1867 Act nor its predecessors had defined insolvency. This is not surprising. Involuntary proceedings under those statutes were triggered by acts of bankruptcy in which insolvency was only rarely a stated element. The quasi-criminal origins of involuntary bankruptcy doubtless account for this. . . . [T]he need for a test of insolvency emerged.

In *Toof v. Martin* the Supreme Court provided such a test. Rejecting the appellants' argument for a balance-sheet measure, the Court ruled that insolvency was inability of a party to pay his debts, as they become due in the ordinary course of business. . . . [N]oteworthy was the Court's acknowledgement that its definition was not the general and popular meaning of the term. . . .

B. IN THE CONGRESS

. . . [T]*oof v. Martin* was not a popular decision. Indeed, President Grant seemed to make that ruling one ground for the repeal of the Bankruptcy Act he sought in his December 1, 1873 message to Congress. . . . Repeal was not immediately forthcoming. It was prefaced in 1874 by revision, which did not touch the insolvency issue. Not until 1878 was the statute withdrawn.

Hardly had the ink dried on repeal when agitation for a new act began. . . . [I]n the first session of the Forty-Seventh Congress from that body came the Equity Bill, so called because its simple provisions, creating bankruptcy jurisdiction in federal equity courts, committed most of the content of bankruptcy law to judicial decision. One matter, however, was reserved to the legislature. The bill defined insolvency, and it did so by the balance-sheet test.

That definition was immediately attacked by Senator Hoar of Massachusetts who had offered as a substitute the Lowell Bill, named for its drafter, Judge Lowell of Massachusetts. That bill did not define insolvency and thus accepted the judicial definition. Hoar's argument was practical and anticipated most of what was to be said later in opposition to the balance-sheet measure:

> The next difference between these two schemes is in their definition of insolvency. The Lowell Bill adopts the only definition which is practicable and which has proved itself to the experience of mankind, and that is the inability to pay debts in the course of business. The committee's bill on the other hand provides that the man is only to be deemed insolvent, to be a subject for bankruptcy jurisdiction, where the entire value of all his property, whether it is capable of being realized within one year or within ten years, exceeds the amount of his indebtedness.
>
> Consider, in the first place, how impossible of practical ascertainment is the fact you propose as your test. You require at the threshold of every application in bankruptcy that the court shall go into an investigation of the value of every debt, bad debt or good debt, the value of every interest, contingent or absolute, in property, the value of all expectations of every sort which are the property of the debtor, and if that value seems to exceed the amount of the indebtedness, the debtor can have no relief in bankruptcy, and each attaching creditor may, in his turn seize the property by attachment and get a preference or the debtor is at liberty to prefer creditors without liability to bankruptcy.
>
> In the case of two-thirds of the mercantile or manufacturing failures in this country such an inquiry would take weeks, perhaps months. It involves not merely an inquiry into the business condition of every debtor, but into the business condition of every debtor of that debtor.

The senator's objections, thus, were to the difficulty of the test and to the delay that it would engender. . . .

Defense of the balance-sheet test came principally from Senator Garland of Arkansas. His position was hardly a surprise; he had argued and lost *Toof v. Martin* in the Supreme Court. Garland's argument had an empirical ring: in agricultural communities men perfectly solvent by the balance-sheet test could not and did not pay their debts as they matured. . . .

. . . Thus began a long process of debate and compromise between proponents of the Lowell Bill and others, some of whom opposed any law on the subject, some of whom wanted voluntary bankruptcy only, and some of whom wished to confine involuntary proceedings to cases of fraud. Ultimately neither the Equity Bill, endorsed in 1887 by the American Bar Association, nor the Lowell Bill was adopted. Rather it was the Torrey Bill, named for its draftsman, a St. Louis attorney, which was finally passed in 1898.

As originally designed and introduced in 1890, the Torrey Bill, which borrowed liberally from the Lowell Bill, did not define insolvency. . . . In succeeding sessions it was modified. . . .

Finally, in the 55th Congress a bankruptcy act was passed. In the Senate the Torrey Bill was introduced by Senator Lindsay of Kentucky, but a substitute introduced by Nelson of Minnesota passed. Nelson's bill provided for involuntary bankruptcy only of noncorporate bankers, brokers, merchants, traders, or manufacturers and only in cases of actual fraud. The House, however, passed the Torrey Bill. A compromise worked out by a subcommittee was passed by both the Senate and the House in June and signed into law by President McKinley on July 1, 1898. A unitary rule, the balance-sheet test, defined insolvency. The flexible, inability-to-pay standard of *Toof v. Martin* had finally been overridden.

In the Congressional process of nearly twenty years the test of insolvency was not often the focus of debate. It is clear, however, that the change from the courts' inability-to-pay test to the balance-sheet measure was an important ingredient of establishing a permanent law which included involuntary proceedings. It was, perhaps, a triumph of the political argument over the practical one. Theory played no real part in the matter. . . .

D. THE FALL

Organized opposition to the balance-sheet standard was almost immediately forthcoming. In 1907 the Committee on Commercial Law of the American Bar Association described the test as practically embarrassing in matter of proof and as operating to put creditors at the debtor's mercy. They sought to enlarge the definition and also proposed that insolvency be provable by specified circumstantial evidence. "[I]nability to pay debts in due course of business as they mature. (This to be limited to commercial classes.)" was one such circumstance. The Committee was explicit in seeking to reinstate the *Toof v. Martin* approach. . . .

Further criticism emerged in a classic article by Bonbright and Pickett in 1929. Those authors focused primarily on the absence of any settled basis of valuation of assets, but they found additional difficulties in deciding what property should be included in aggregate of the debtor's property and in ascertaining the meaning of sufficient to pay his debts. . . .

At about the same time the direction of the movement for change shifted. Commentators began to challenge the Anglo-American tradition that an act of bankruptcy was required to trigger involuntary proceedings. These reformers wanted to replace an act of bankruptcy with insolvency as the basis for action. . . .

In 1938 Professor Israel Treiman vividly stated the case for eliminating acts of bankruptcy and redefining insolvency in what was to become the most influential article on the subject. The acts, he argued, had no place in a system designed to protect honest debtors as well as creditors. Redefinition of insolvency, he believed, was essential because the balance-sheet test at once necessitated retention of acts of bankruptcy and presented the practical difficulties of delay and access to information. Balance-sheet insolvency, he argued, described an internal condition which could be ascertained only by a comprehensive examination of the debtor's affairs. Inability to pay current obligations, on the other hand, described both the internal financial condition and its external man-ifestation. He cited continental reliance on cessation of payment as fixing similarly and satisfacto-rily the requisite *condition* of bankruptcy. . . .

Professor MacLachlan added his influential voice in his 1956 treatise. He argued that the bal-ance-sheet test produced delay and increased creditor losses as well as causing jockeying for posi-tion by creditors. . . . For MacLachlan early disclosure allowing intelligent creditor choice between adjustment and liquidation was indispensable.

The companion ideas that bankruptcy should be triggered by the condition of insolvency rather than by specified acts and that insolvency was better measured by cessation of payments than by a balance-sheet test were persuasive to a Canadian study commission which reported in 1970. . . .

That report along with the views of Treiman and MacLachlan persuaded the Commission on the Bankruptcy Laws of the United States which issued a report and recommendations, including a proposed statute, in 1973 after a two-year study. . . . [T]he Commission proposal provided for involuntary proceedings when the debtor was generally unable to pay his current liabilities as they become due or has generally failed to pay his debts as they become due.

. . . The final version, however, read is generally not paying such debtor's debts as such debts become due. . . . [T]he final wording might have been thought to focus more on debtor behavior than condition and thus be easier to establish without examination of the debtor's records.

In effect, then, equity insolvency became the basis of involuntary proceedings. The acts of bankruptcy were eliminated. Insofar as balance-sheet insolvency had been a component of an act of bankruptcy, it too was displaced as defining the occasion for bankruptcy. . . .

II. THEORY

. . . If the issue is approached from a theoretical perspective, it is well to begin by considering the essence of bankruptcy. . . . Since 1940 we have had an elegant distillation of the concept. Writing then, Professor Max Radin described bankruptcy as a method by which *all* the creditors were com-pelled to accept some arrangement or some disposition of their claims against the bankrupt's prop-erty, whether they all agreed to it or not. That simple formulation of the nature of bankruptcy . . . gives bankruptcy three elements. It is a (1) *coercive* and (2) *collective* judicial *process* the purpose of which is (3) *to settle creditors' claims between each creditor and the debtor and among creditors themselves*. It is thus a process with two characteristics and a single aim.

None of these three components is peculiar to bankruptcy. . . .

There is, however, a logical explanation for bankruptcy's particular combination of compo-nents, an explanation which may point as well to what the occasion *for* bankruptcy should be. Bankruptcy's process components, that it is coercive and collective, essentially are those of manda-tory joinder of parties. . . . [B]ankruptcy is a procedure by which the debtor (voluntary) or another creditor (involuntary) may act in anticipation of or response to such a suit or some other collection effort. And the bankruptcy proceeding, once instituted, displaces or prevents further individual col-lection effort, by suit or otherwise. It is in this sense that bankruptcy can be viewed as a device for mandatory party joinder.

That being so, it ought to be possible to identify the occasion for bankruptcy by asking why a proceeding with bankruptcy's purpose component, settlement of claims between creditor and debtor and between creditors, necessitates joinder, the collective-coercive components. Rule 19 of the Federal Rules of Civil Procedure . . . lists three such factors: (1) inability of the court to provide com-plete relief to those already parties; (2) a practical threat to the interest of an absentee; or (3) the risk to a party of incurring double, multiple or otherwise inconsistent obligations by virtue of the claimed interest of a nonparty. . . .

It seems clear that balance-sheet insolvency of a debtor would produce the need for mandatory joinder. If the debtor's assets are insufficient to meet the claims of his creditors, any settlement between one of them and the debtor may prejudice others by committing more than a pro-rata share of assets to the collecting creditor's claim. The case of a limited fund inadequate to satisfy fully all claims against it is a paradigm of a mandatory joinder situation which encompasses bankruptcy.

One could argue further that other circumstances, including the various acts of bankruptcy and failure to pay debts as they mature, may be material as evidence, circumstantial or presumptive, of that condition. The practical problems of delay and creditor access to information, perhaps coupled with the difficulties of valuation bases, provide further justification for allowing proof of such circumstances to trigger involuntary bankruptcy. . . . Yet one taking this position presumably would have to accept proof of balance-sheet solvency as a bar to going forward with bankruptcy. . . . The question remains whether these other circumstances, equity insolvency or acts of bankruptcy, might warrant mandatory joinder in their own right.

In the debates leading to adoption of the 1898 Act the statement that bankruptcy was appropriate when there was fraud or insolvency was common. It is difficult, however, to see why fraud in the absence of insolvency necessitates joinder under the functional tests stated by Federal Rule 19. A creditor-victim of fraud may proceed against the debtor and/or the debtor's transferees and obtain complete relief without joining other creditors. So long as the debtor is solvent that creditor's recovery presents no threat to others who may satisfy their claims from other assets. . . . The fraud basis of involuntary bankruptcy finds its justification in the quasi-criminal origins of the process. As a matter of theory, fraud is no longer a satisfactory basis for involuntary proceedings. . . .

Precisely the same question should be asked about inability, or failure, to pay debts as they mature. Does that fact in and of itself present the need for mandatory joinder? If one thinks of bankruptcy solely in terms of its traditional liquidation function, it is difficult to see why equity insolvency requires joinder. A collecting creditor, perhaps the very one not paid at maturity, can receive complete relief by getting a judgment and execution against the debtor's assets. Other creditors would not be injured thereby. Neither does unilateral collection expose the debtor to inconsistent or multiple obligations of the right sort. . . .

. . . [C]ontemporary evaluation of equity insolvency as a circumstance warranting mandatory joinder of creditors must take reorganization into account. Reorganization is designed for business debtors, individual or corporate. It presupposes that the going concern value of a debtor's assets exceeds their liquidation value, and its goal is to preserve that excess. . . .

The key to successful reorganization is prevention of piecemeal dismemberment which would deprive the debtor of assets essential to continued operation. The principal risk of such dismemberment comes from creditors using the judicial debt-collection processes of prejudgment attachment and post-judgment execution because, in the main, such creditors' selection of target property is unregulated. . . . This risk of unilateral creditor action crippling a going concern materializes when the creditor is not paid at maturity, i.e., at the point of equity insolvency. Bankruptcy provides protection against this threat to other creditors (and to the debtor) by the automatic stay. Filing of the petition, whether voluntary or involuntary, prevents further individual creditor action which might destroy a going concern and thus prevent reorganization. Thus equity insolvency, in addition to being an indicator of balance-sheet insolvency, can itself be occasion for the collective and coercive proceeding that bankruptcy is.

III. CONCLUSION

This analysis, proceeding from the mandatory joinder perspective, suggests that the circumstances warranting involuntary bankruptcy arise from the need to protect creditors generally from the efforts of individual creditors to collect from the debtor. Creditors need protection when individual collection efforts would interfere with ratable distribution of the debtor's assets, i.e., where the debtor is insolvent in the balance-sheet sense. This is so regardless of the nature of the debtor. Creditors also need protection when the debtor is a business enterprise and individual collection efforts interfere with maintaining the debtor as a going concern where reorganization would yield more than liquidation. This threat materializes when the debtor does not pay his debts as they mature, *i.e.*, when there is equity insolvency.

The implication of the analysis is that as a matter of theory only balance-sheet insolvency presents a case for involuntary proceedings against consumers. Use of another standard such as equity insolvency reflects either departure from the theory or the belief that equity insolvency constitutes circumstantial or presumptive evidence of balance-sheet insolvency which is itself too difficult a standard for use in judicial proceedings. But debtor proof of solvency by a balance-sheet measure ought to provide a defense to involuntary proceedings in a consumer case.

For the business debtor, however, the analysis indicates that the threat to creditors depends on the outcome of bankruptcy proceedings. If liquidation is the appropriate outcome, the business debtor is no different from the consumer debtor: the threat to creditors is interference with ratable distribution posed only in cases of balance-sheet insolvency. If reorganization is the appropriate result, because going-concern value exceeds liquidation value, then equity insolvency creates the risk that individual creditor action will destroy the going concern by judicial or other collection proceedings against an essential asset. Of course, it is not always possible to ascertain at the beginning of bankruptcy whether liquidation or reorganization is the appropriate outcome for the business debtor. That uncertainty argues for making balance-sheet and equity insolvency alternative bases for involuntary proceedings in business cases. Here equity insolvency is itself a legitimate basis for collective action as long as reorganization is a possible outcome. . . . It seems sensible . . . in light of the difficulties presented in establishing balance-sheet insolvency, to have allowed creditors to commence involuntary proceedings on proof of equity insolvency. In my view it would have been wise to cabin the concept, however. Where distribution is the issue, equity insolvency as proof of balance-sheet insolvency should be merely a rebuttable presumption. Only where protection of going-concern value is at stake should equity insolvency be recognized as a justification in its own right for involuntary proceedings.

Susan Block-Lieb
Why Creditors File So Few Involuntary Petitions and Why the Number is Not Too Small
57 Brooklyn L. Rev. 803 (1991)[*]

With its enactment of the Bankruptcy Reform Act of 1978 Congress abolished the "acts of bankruptcy" as the standard for commencement of involuntary bankruptcy cases, and replaced it with the "general failure to pay" test. It adopted the "general failure to pay" standard at the suggestion of the Commission on Bankruptcy Laws, in part, because it was viewed as an easier standard for creditors to prove. By liberalizing the standard, Congress hoped to encourage creditors to file involuntary petitions against a debtor before the situation becomes "hopeless" and "the assets are largely depleted." Despite this change in the applicable standard for commencement of an involuntary case, the vast majority of bankruptcy petitions are, as they historically have been, brought voluntarily by debtors rather than involuntarily by creditors.

Of course, these statistics do not present a clear picture of the extent to which debtors are coerced into bankruptcy. The line between voluntary and involuntary filings is an ambiguous one because debtors often file voluntary petitions in reaction to creditors' collection efforts. . . .

. . . [A] surprisingly small number of involuntary petitions are filed each year. This article attempts to explain why creditors have not taken up Congress's invitation to file more involuntary petitions against their debtors, and suggests some possible reforms. . . .

I. CHANGES TO THE STANDARDS FOR COMMENCEMENT OF AN INVOLUNTARY BANKRUPTCY CASE: CONGRESS'S MIXED MESSAGES

Under the former Bankruptcy Act of 1898, as amended in 1938, three petitioning creditors whose provable claims, fixed as to liability and liquidated as to amount, aggregated $500 or more in excess of the value of liens held by them, could file an involuntary petition against an eligible debtor. If the debtor contested the filing, petitioning creditors were required to show that the debtor had committed an "act of bankruptcy" within four months prior to the filing of the petition before the debtor would be adjudicated a bankrupt and a Chapter VII liquidation case would be commenced. . . .

The 1898 Act identified six different "acts of bankruptcy":

(a) fraudulent transfers . . .;
(b) preferential transfers . . .;
(c) the failure to vacate a judicial lien in a timely manner . . . if the debtor was insolvent during ths period;
(d) making a state law assignment for the benefit of creditors;
(e) the appointment under state law of a receiver of property when the debtor was insolvent or unable to pay its debts; and
(f) the admission in writing of an inability to pay debts and a willingness to be adjudicated bankrupt.

Although it was widely assumed by practitioners, courts and commentators alike that only an insolvent debtor could be thrust into bankruptcy involuntarily, the debtor's solvency was a defense only to an involuntary petition grounded on the first act of bankruptcy (concealment or fraudulent transfer). This misconception arose because . . . many of the acts of bankruptcy implicitly required a showing of the debtor's insolvency as an element of their proof. . . .

There were several problems of proof associated with establishing a debtor's insolvency as that term was defined under the Act. . . .

Because of these ambiguities, trials on contested involuntary petitions often dragged on for long periods of time at considerable expense to petitioning creditors and others. . . .

The legal community nearly uniformly criticized the "acts of bankruptcy" as an anachronism that impeded the smooth workings of the modern credit economy either by delaying resolution of a contested involuntary petition or by deterring creditors from bringing an involuntary case. . . .

In 1973 the Commission on Bankruptcy Laws recommended in its report to Congress that the area of involuntary bankruptcy be reformed so that "[t]he concept of 'an act of bankruptcy' be abolished and the debtor be made amenable to involuntary proceedings when he has [generally] ceased to pay his debts or will be generally unable to pay his current liabilities." The primary reason for the Commission's recommendation that the "concept of an act of bankruptcy be abolished" was a practical one:

> It is time to abandon the complex, litigation-producing constraints and substitute the test of inability or failure to pay debts as the basis for initiating involuntary bankruptcy.
>
> . . .

The Commission sought to encourage creditors to bring an involuntary case by changing the standard for commencement from the "acts of bankruptcy" to the "general failure to pay" standard, in part because they understood that creditors were more likely to have access to the sorts of information necessary to prove the debtor's general default than the debtor's insolvency, which often was an element of the debtor's act of bankruptcy. They accepted the view that a debtor's general default is an external event, that the debtor's insolvency is an internal financial condition, and that an external event is more readily determinable by creditors than an internal condition. In addition, the Commission viewed a liberal standard for bringing an involuntary case as good policy because it encourages creditors to file an involuntary petition at an earlier stage in the debtor's financial difficulty—early enough either to rehabilitate the debtor's business, or to prevent the debtor from becoming "more insolvent" as a result of the continued devaluation of its assets. In doing so the Commission hoped to increase dividends distributed to creditors in bankruptcy cases, which had been abysmally low.

Although Congress did not incorporate all of the Commission's suggestions on this topic when it enacted the Bankruptcy Reform Act of 1978, it removed the "acts of bankruptcy" as the standard for commencement of an involuntary case and replaced it with a standard that considered, among other things, the debtor's general failure to pay its debts as they came due. . . .

Under the first and more commonly cited avenue for bringing an involuntary case creditors must allege that the debtor is "generally not paying [its] debts as [they] come due," excluding contingent and certain disputed obligations. The Code does not define this "general failure to pay" standard, and courts have found the standard "woefully lacking in clarity." Legislative history indicates that Congress intended to give courts considerable discretion in making this determination. Courts have rejected the contention that the term "generally" means a majority of the time, and have declined to apply an invariable mathematical formula; instead they have applied a flexible standard that "look[s] to the totality of the circumstances." In doing so they consider both the number and amount of unpaid claims as of the filing of the petition, and also may consider other related and unrelated factors such as the manner in which the debtor has conducted its financial affairs. Absent special circumstances, the majority of courts do not find that the debtor's failure to pay a single debt constitutes a failure generally to pay its debts as they come due. . . .

The second standard for commencing an involuntary case—involving the appointment of a custodian or the custodian's possession of the debtor's property—is less often relied upon by creditors. . . . [C]ourts have limited its application to instances in which the debtor has given up both possession and ownership of its property. . . .

In addition to modifying the grounds available to creditors desiring to file an involuntary petition, Congress also reformed the law to minimize the costly loss in value that may result from lengthy contested hearings. . . .

Congress sought to balance competing interests by repealing the "litigation-producing" acts of bankruptcy as the grounds for initiating an involuntary case. When it reformed the requirements for involuntary bankruptcy, Congress was concerned, not only with encouraging creditors' petitions, but also with minimizing the leverage that this liberalized standard might create. . . .

Finally, it provided debtors redress for improvidently filed involuntary petitions. . . .

Congress also sought to encourage negotiation among a debtor and its creditors. Section 305 empowers a bankruptcy court to abstain from a liquidation or reorganization case in "the interests of creditors and [if] the debtor would be better served by such dismissal." Legislative history explains that abstention would be appropriate under this section, for example, if an arrangement is being worked out by creditors and the debtor out of court, there is no prejudice to the results of creditors in that arrangement, and an involuntary case has been commenced by a few recalcitrant creditors to provide a basis for future threats to extract full payment. The less expensive out-of-court work-out may better serve the interests in the case. . . .

II. Creditors' Disincentives to Commence an Involuntary Bankruptcy case

When Congress abolished "acts of bankruptcy" as the standard for commencement of an involuntary bankruptcy case, it did so for two different but related reasons. First, it recognized that petitioning creditors had difficulty establishing their debtor's insolvency, which often was an element under the "acts of bankruptcy." . . . Congress also intended "to encourage and facilitate earlier resort to [bankruptcy] relief" and, as a result, to increase dividends to creditors. . . .

There is no empirical evidence to show that this statutory reform has had any impact on distributions to creditors. Nor are there statistics to determine whether creditors now file involuntary petitions at an earlier stage in their debtor's financial troubles than they did under the former Act. Statistics do show, however, that the number of involuntary petitions has increased very little, if at all, since enactment of the "general failure to pay" standard. Whether the consistently small numbers of involuntary filings mean that Congress's reform of the standard for commencement of an involuntary case was unsuccessful depends upon which of Congress's purposes is considered.

When its goal of easing creditors' difficulties in proving the standard for commencement of an involuntary case is considered, clearly Congress did not succeed. Creditors continue to have difficulties obtaining access to the information necessary to commence a bankruptcy case against a debtor's will. But this failure is fairly easily remedied by further reform to the standard. When its intent to increase dividends to creditors, by inviting earlier or more frequent involuntary petitions, is considered, Congress's failure is less easily remedied but perhaps less troublesome. It is harder to get creditors to file sooner or more often, not because the standard requires tinkering, but because creditors prefer nonjudicial resolution of payment disputes for many reasons. . . . Congress's invitation to creditors' petitions was inconsistent, not merely competitive, with its intent to encourage creditors to pursue these nonbankruptcy solutions to debtor/creditor problems. Thus Congress succeeded in its goal to encourage creditors to pursue nonbankruptcy options for resolution of a debtor's difficulties, although this success is moderated by Congress's failure to get creditors to file petitions earlier and more often.

A. *Informational Disadvantages*

The "general failure to pay" standard is not an easy one for creditors to satisfy. . . . Proof of this requires not only general information about the debtor's cash disbursements, but also about the due dates of its obligations, whether the debtor's nonpayment of a past due obligation is the result of an inability or an unwillingness to pay, and, if the latter, whether the debtor's dispute involves a substantial issue of fact or law. . . . Creditors often do not have ready access to information from which to determine whether the debtor is generally unable to pay its debts as they come due.

Until the news spreads by word of mouth, a creditor may be unaware of a debtor's general default . . . . In addition, creditors will have a difficult time assessing which of the debtor's unpaid debts are disputed and whether a dispute is bona fide. . . .

Even if creditors theoretically have access to information about the occurrence, regularity and nature of a debtor's defaults and disputes, the cost of acquiring this information may be so great as to deter creditors from making the effort. Because access to information may be costly, creditors with small claims—especially small claims that arise out of a single, discrete transaction—will have little incentive to acquire information about the debtor's financial condition. They may choose to rely on other creditors or the debtor to commence a bankruptcy case, even though the benefits of a collective proceeding may outweigh the costs associated with making an informed decision about the need for bankruptcy. . . .

. . . Congress sought to encourage creditors to bring involuntary cases, but it also feared the unwarranted filing of involuntary petitions. To prevent the filing of an involuntary petition against financially sound debtors, the Bankruptcy Code permits courts to require creditors to compensate debtors for all out-of-pocket expenses incurred in successfully defending an involuntary petition, as well as additional damages if they can show that the petitioning creditors acted in bad faith. The threat of a sanction that creditors are certain to face if an involuntary petition is dismissed for any reason, and the possibility of actual and punitive damages should the court question their motives in filing, undoubtedly chills creditors from filing involuntary petitions based upon even well-founded suspicion.

By contrast, creditors are able to establish the second standard for commencement of an involuntary case—the appointment of a custodian or the custodian's possession of the debtor's property—by referring to publicly available information, since the appointment of an assignee for the benefit of creditors or an equitable receiver generally is a matter of public record. . . .

B. *Preferences for Non-Judicial Resolutions*

Creditors may decide not to force their debtor into bankruptcy for reasons other than that they are unable to gain access to the information necessary to establish that their debtor "generally is not paying [its] debts as [they] come due." Creditors may decide not to file an involuntary petition because, for one reason or another, they prefer not to seek the aid of the courts in collecting the debtor's unpaid debt. General creditors need not, and often do not, seek the aid of the courts and their officers to coerce repayment of delinquent debts. Debtors may be persuaded to pay simply by force of moral suasion or use of the forceful negotiating leverage creditors can marshall.

Creditors may prefer not to pursue their coercive collection remedies because they stand to gain little from litigation with the debtor. Because all coercive remedies involve repayment from the proceeds of the forced sale of unencumbered, nonexempt property, creditors may determine that coercion would be fruitless because their debtor's assets are mostly exempt or subject to liens.

Even when creditors are able to identify nonexempt, unencumbered assets, they may be reluctant to rely on repayment from the receipts of a forced sale of these assets. Repayment from the proceeds of a forced sale will be a less efficient and effective collection device than a method that relies on repayment out of liquid funds, because forced sales of assets generally result in a loss of value. . . .

Creditors' preference for extralegal solutions to the debtor's nonpayment also follows from the simple fact that there often is little to lose from pursuit of nonjudicial collection efforts. It is cheaper and easier to collect a debt by dunning the debtor with telephone calls and letters than to sue the debtor in court. And, in some cases, creditors may write off the bad debt as a loss and take the tax deduction rather than litigate the claim in the hope of collecting a small portion of its entirety.

Moreover, the threat of coercive collection remedies can be far more effective than implementation of the remedies themselves. . . .

Perhaps more than the creditors who pursue their individual collection remedies, debtors also suffer from the loss of value that inevitably results from pursuit of the state law remedies of attachment, levy and garnishment. . . . Creditors know this and often threaten to pursue these remedies solely to intimidate the debtor into payment. . . .

In addition, forceful requests may be all that a creditor needs to persuade the debtor to repay. Studies show that a common cause for the delinquency of an individual debtor is a temporary interruption in disposable income, either as a result of the loss of a job or the occurrence of an unusual major expense. Although there is no single empirical explanation for business failures, seasonal cash flow problems presumably account for a fair percentage of business debtors' financial difficulties. If only some of a debtor's creditors press for payment, the debtor is likely to pay those few creditors who squawk until finances improve . . . .

C. *Interest in Preservation of Long-Term Relationships*

Creditors' preferences for extrajudicial resolution of their payment disputes also may be explained by the relationships between debtors and creditors. When a creditor and debtor enjoy a complex, uncertain or long-standing relationship, the parties will tend to resolve their disputes through negotiation, mediation or some other informal dispute resolution mechanism, rather than through litigation.

This preference for informal resolution of disputes involving relational contracts should be just as strong, if not stronger, in the context of coerced repayment of delinquent obligations. All collection remedies are likely to harm the profitability of the debtor's firm and . . . often result, at least by the conclusion of the proceeding, in the cessation of the business. . . . Thus a creditor with a long-term, or otherwise important, relationship with the debtor, contractual or otherwise, is less likely to coerce repayment through a collective rather than an individual remedy, and is less likely to coerce repayment through a court-sanctioned collection remedy than through negotiation.

While creditor inhibitions may disappear as the creditor determines that the debtor's earning capacity is no longer viable, the relationship between a creditor and debtor may cause the creditor to delay bringing a collective proceeding until the debtor's financial failure is certain, rather than feared. . . .

Finally, if a relational creditor determines that the debtor should file a reorganization petition in order to preserve its business or financial affairs, the relational creditor may be in a position to prevail upon the debtor to initiate its own reorganization case, rather than force the debtor into reorganization by filing an involuntary petition. . . .

III. Some Proposed Reforms

Congress intended for petitioning creditors to be able to prove the standard for commencement of an involuntary case with the sorts of evidence available to the general public, to discourage creditors from filing involuntary petitions in bad faith, and to promote a negotiated resolution of a debtor's financial difficulties. The current standard falls short of realizing these goals and could be improved. First, the 1984 amendment to section 303(h) should be repealed, although the companion amendment to section 303(b) should be retained. In addition, creditors' grounds for commencement of an involuntary case should be expanded to include external indicators of the debtor's financial distress other than a debtor's general default and the appointment of a custodian for the debtor's property.

A. *Repeal of the 1984 Amendment to Section 303(h)*

The current standard for commencement of an involuntary case excludes disputed debts from the calculation of whether the debtor is in general default if the debtor shows that its dispute involves either a genuine issue of material fact or a substantial question of law. . . . Congress asks petitioning creditors to prove a standard that, in part, is based on information to which they generally will not have access.

The bona fide dispute part of the "general failure to pay" standard was added with the 1984 amendments to the Code to quell suspicions that creditors were filing involuntary petitions against their debtors solely to gain negotiating leverage in settlement discussions. But this concern could be addressed simply with an initial inquiry into the bona fides of disputed obligations held by the petitioning creditors. . . .

The standard for commencement of an involuntary bankruptcy case should minimize undue negotiating leverage. Under the current "bona fide dispute" standard financially distressed debtors may feel it is in their best interest to litigate disputed claims . . . in order to support their claim that the dispute is bona fide should an involuntary petition later be commenced because courts are more likely to find that a bona fide dispute exists if litigation is pending. In addition, the current standard may compel debtors to "pay off" all creditors whose claims they only partially dispute. . . .

B. *Adding To the Grounds for Involuntary Bankruptcy*

The standard for commencement of an involuntary bankruptcy case should be expanded. Creditors may have difficulty proving the "general failure to pay" standard because proof may require information to which creditors do not have access. Expanding upon the external indications of a debtor's financial distress is one easy solution to creditors' problems of proof. Thus, the 120 day limitation should be removed from section 303(h)(2). Unpaid debts that remain following (i) a corporate or partnership debtor's dissolution under state law, (ii) a business debtor's cessation of business, or (iii) an individual debtor's unexplained disappearance, should be added as rebuttable grounds for involuntary relief. In addition, a debtor's admitted inability to pay its debts as they come due should be rebuttable grounds for the commencement of an involuntary case. Petitioning creditors' allegations of these external events could be rebutted by the involuntary debtor's proof that it is paying its debts as they come due.

Creditors' problems of proof also could be resolved by adding insolvency as a rebuttable grounds for bringing an involuntary bankruptcy case, providing insolvency is defined in a way that permits proof with reference to publicly available facts. As with the other proposed grounds for relief, petitioning creditors' proof of insolvency should be rebuttable by the debtor's proof of its general payment of debts as they come due. . . .

How should "insolvency" be defined under the Code if it were to be added to the grounds for commencement of an involuntary bankruptcy case? The current balance sheet definition of insolvency should be retained under the Code, with some refinements, including the improvements made to the definition under the UFTA. . . .

This definition of insolvency addresses creditors' problem of proof because insolvency is defined in a way to permit creditors to establish their debtor's insolvency based upon readily available information. . . .

CONCLUSION

From July 1, 1987 to June 30, 1988, creditors filed 1,409 involuntary bankruptcy petitions against their debtors. Whether this number is viewed as too small depends upon which of Congress's purposes in amending the statute governing involuntary bankruptcy is considered. The number might have been greater had Congress succeeded in its effort to make proof of the standard for commencement of an involuntary case dependent solely upon publicly available information. In addition, more creditors might have filed involuntary petitions had Congress sought to encourage creditors to file earlier in a debtor's financial crisis through a more effective means than liberalization of the standard for commencement, such as through a bounty system that rewards petitioning creditors for successfully obtaining the entry of an order for relief against their debtor. By contrast, the number can be viewed as about right when considered in light of Congress's goal to encourage creditors to resolve a debtor's financial difficulties outside of bankruptcy when a nonbankruptcy solution can be accomplished more quickly, less expensively and with less disruption than would have occurred in an involuntary case.

The difficulty in assessing whether creditors file too few involuntary petitions is that two of these three goals are inconsistent. It is possible to streamline proof of the standard for commencement of an involuntary case and encourage creditors to file petitions earlier in a debtor's financial troubles, but realization of these goals is inconsistent with the notion that nonbankruptcy options should be exhausted before an involuntary petition is filed. . . .

Creditors' preferences for resolution of their debtor's financial troubles without litigation are both strong and appropriate. As a result, it would be undesirable to change the statute governing commencement of an involuntary bankruptcy case to encourage creditors to shortcut these consensual efforts. Congress should seek to increase dividends to creditors from bankruptcy estates in some other way.

Lawrence Ponoroff
Involuntary Bankruptcy and the Bona Fides of a Bona Fide Dispute
65 IND. L.J. 315 (1990)[*]

INTRODUCTION

. . . In 1984, . . . Congress amended the Reform Act's requirements for involuntary bankruptcy by inserting identical language in sections 303(b) and 303(h)(1) which excludes for both purposes claims and debts subject to a "bona fide dispute." . . .

The legislative history of the 1984 Act makes clear that, in amending section 303, Congress was reacting to a concern that the threat of involuntary bankruptcy might be used as a tool to bludgeon a debtor into payment of dubious claims or satisfaction of obligations open to legitimate question. . . .

IV. THE 1984 AMENDMENTS

In 1984 Congress attempted to end the judicial disagreement over the treatment of disputed debts in involuntary proceedings . . . by: 1) disqualifying under subsection (b) any entity holding a claim subject to a bona fide dispute from validly joining in an involuntary petition; and 2) purging from the category of unpaid debts which might count against the debtor under subsection (h)(1) debts subject to a bona fide dispute. Thus, in one fell swoop, Congress seemed to eliminate the debate over the exclusion of disputed debts under section 303 in favor of debtors' interests. . . .

VI. ASSESSING THE IMPACT AND WISDOM OF THE 1984 AMENDMENTS TO SECTION 303

. . . [I]t is worthwhile to appraise how effectively the 1984 amendments directed to section 303 have responded to the articulated concerns and objectives which prompted their adoption. Certainly, there can be no doubt that the mandatory exclusion under section 303 of claims and debts subject to a bona fide dispute has "upped the ante" for creditors considering resort to the involuntary bankruptcy remedy. Statistical information . . . indicates that the number of involuntary filings has dropped steadily in recent years. This reduction in the volume of involuntary cases, which shows every sign of continuing, should come as no surprise. Under the original 1978 version of section 303, petitioning creditors in involuntary cases already pulled the laboring oar in what amounted to a demanding and potentially expensive piece of litigation. In most cases, debtors had every incentive to vigorously resist the petition. On top of that, petitioning creditors have always been subject to the risk of affirmative liability in the event that the debtor is successful in obtaining a dismissal of the petition. On the other hand, notwithstanding the added burden and risk assumed, petitioning creditors receive no favored treatment or other special advantage in the bankruptcy administration which follows entry of an order for relief on an involuntary petition.

The 1984 amendments have now further discouraged involuntary filings. By complicating the petitioners' proof, and adding to the statutory bases upon which a debtor might controvert and defend a petition, Congress has made the prosecution of involuntary filings an even more difficult and perilous affair. While there is no question that the 1984 amendments have reduced the number of involuntary filings, that the placement of these additional obstacles in the path of involuntary relief was warranted, or that they represent a necessary or inevitable price to be paid to achieve other important policy objectives, is a far more debatable proposition.

As a starting place, it is revealing to recall the reasons which first prompted reform of the law and procedure governing involuntary bankruptcy in 1978. It is interesting, if not ironic, to note that it was the perceived need to simplify the issues in involuntary cases, and thereby promote their prompt and effective disposition, that persuaded the drafters of the Bankruptcy Code to lower the barriers which had frustrated creditors' access to bankruptcy relief under the 1898 Act. . . .

VII. EXISTENCE OF A BONA FIDE DISPUTE: AN ALTERNATIVE FRAMEWORK FOR ANALYSIS

. . . [B]y lumping together the analysis of the bona fide dispute issue in two very different contexts, the 1984 Act amendments have precipitated a harmful judicial overreaction to what, at most, amounted to a few aberrant cases and an alleged but unsubstantiated pattern of creditor "misuse" of the bankruptcy system. The subsequent reduction in the percentage of filings under amended section 303, a phenomenon very likely attributable to the more inflexible judicial posture toward involuntary bankruptcies bred by the new statutory language, loudly signals a return to the pre-1978 days of "creditor dissatisfaction and lack of interest" in the bankruptcy system. By interpreting the statute in a manner which vastly complicates creditors' difficulties of proof and, therefore, increases the costs and risks associated with seeking bankruptcy relief, courts have largely neutralized any benefits that creditors might have otherwise gained by resort to the involuntary bankruptcy remedy.

It is submitted that such a result is wrong and that the 1984 amendments to section 303 should be interpreted and applied with attention to the prior history and experience of involuntary bankruptcy under the Act and the early Code. . . .

Prior to the 1984 Act, courts generally recognized the existence of jurisdiction over petitions filed by creditors holding disputed claims, but then took the existence of such disputes into account in ruling on the merits of the petition. This system . . . "proved to be both workable and fair in practice." Thus, it is logical to construe the amendments as refashioning the existing practice to the least extent possible consistent with their aim, thereby avoiding the mistake of fixing something which wasn't broken.

A. Determining a Bona Fide Dispute Under Section 303(b)

Given the clear and direct language of amended section 303(b), it is difficult to dispute that by virtue of the 1984 Act Congress overruled the practice established in *In re All Media Properties, Inc.* of including nearly all disputed claimholders in the category of creditors eligible to invoke the bankruptcy court's jurisdiction under section 303(b). However, . . . a debtor's primary protection against a non-meritorious petition is and properly should be found in the assessment of whether or not proper grounds for relief exist under section 303(h). . . . There is simply no compelling reason why a creditor should be required to shoulder the heavy burden of proving the absence of any material issue of fact or law bearing on the debtor's liability solely as a condition to having the merits of an involuntary petition heard.

The underlying question of the debtor's ultimate liability on any particular creditor's claim, whether disputed or not, is never the matter directly at issue at the trial of an involuntary petition. Therefore, it is puzzling that the petitioning creditors have been required at any point in the process of obtaining an order for relief to establish the absence of all factual or legal barriers to the debtor's liability on their claims. . . .

Viewed from that perspective, it would be consistent with both conventional civil practice and the original legislative history of section 303 to treat the debtor's contradiction of a petitioning creditor's claim as an affirmative legal defense to that creditor's entitlement to maintain suit for involuntary relief. As such, the debtor would ordinarily be responsible not only for challenging the validity of the claim, but would also bear the ultimate burden of showing the existence of a bona fide dispute. . . .

Establishing how the issue is joined and on whom the evidentiary burdens rest does not complete the analysis of the proper standard for identifying a bona fide dispute under section 303(b). The fact still remains that the trial on an involuntary petition is not the proper forum for extensive litigation over individual claims and defenses. Therefore, as the courts have long appreciated, a more mechanical test than adjudication on the merits must be found for evaluating a debtor's challenge to a petitioning creditor's standing which is based on the existence of alleged counterclaims and defenses to the creditor's claim. Happily, such a test is readily and easily available. . . .

A debtor should not be able to avoid bankruptcy and defeat the objectives served by the federal bankruptcy system simply by raising unsubstantiated theories of law, or by averring the minimum factual allegations necessary to avoid summary judgment. Instead, bearing in mind that federal bankruptcy legislation is not designed solely or even primarily to serve the needs and protect the interests of debtors alone, the debtor challenging a petition on this ground should be required to make an extraordinary showing to justify denying a creditor's access to involuntary relief.

Accordingly, under a better interpretation of the amendment to section 303(b), the term "bona fide dispute" would be narrowly construed. Unless the debtor's defenses would be sufficient to entitle the debtor to summary judgment dismissing the creditor's claim as a matter of law, . . . the petition would be heard on its merits. In other words, the summary judgment analysis would be transposed from a plaintiff's to a defendant's motion. Furthermore, even when the facts entitling the debtor to such relief are undisputed, the petitioning claimholder should not be rendered ineligible from seeking involuntary relief if that creditor can demonstrate a serious contention as to the application of the governing legal principles to undisputed facts. . . .

Thus, several benefits result from reversing the parties' positions under the existing judicial standards. . . .

B. Determining a Bona Fide Dispute Under Section 303(h)(1)

In contrast to some of the past approaches for dealing with disputed debts under section 303(b), the courts evaluating the merits of involuntary petitions have always given some weight to the debtor's allegations that its unpaid debts were the subject of a good faith dispute. Thus, to a degree not true with respect to section 303(b), the inclusion of the "unless subject to a bona fide dispute" language in section 303(h)(1) can defensively be viewed as codifying, rather than refashioning, prior case law and practice. . . .

In practice, this approach would mean that a creditor with standing under section 303(b) would still be required to allege and, if contested, establish that as of the filing date the debtor was generally not paying its non-disputed debts as they came due. However, satisfaction of the petitioning creditors' burden would be measured under a flexible and liberal standard. In this regard, "non-disputed" would certainly include debts contested only as to amount, as well as debts to which liability could be established on a summary basis. In addition, departing from most of the recent judicially-developed standards, a debt as to which colorable but non-dispositive defenses of fact or law had been raised could be included in the "generally not paying" analysis as well. . . .

In a case where the debtor challenges the validity of a matured debt upon which the creditor relies for relief, there would be no absolute rule of inclusion or exclusion, or even a bias one way or the other. Instead, the judgment would be made on a case-by-case basis in which the court would be principally guided by the underlying policies of bankruptcy law. Rather than considering the merits of the competing claims or defenses, courts would take into account the inherent tension between an innocent debtor's interest in being free from the havoc wreaked by a non-meritorious petition and the creditors' equally compelling interest in obtaining the protections and safeguards afforded by bankruptcy relief before the debtor's assets have been irretrievably dissipated.

. . . Unlike the more expansive judicial interpretations, this reading of amended section 303(h)(1) avoids the potential for a debtor to frustrate both its creditors and bankruptcy policies simply by raising unproven allegations disputing the existence or validity of its unpaid claims.

On the other hand, there is much more at stake in including disputed debts for purposes of section 303(h)(1) than is true under section 303(b). The finding that the debtor is generally not paying his debts ordinarily means that he will be placed in an involuntary bankruptcy proceeding. Therefore, for the purposes of this inquiry, unlike under section 303(b), no distinction should be made between defenses, and setoffs or counterclaims. . . .

Finally, because the appropriateness of bankruptcy relief is at issue, rather than simply the objective merits of the claims and defenses, the court should be able to factor into the balance the consideration of whether the debtor's claims and defenses are being asserted in good faith. A "bona fide" assertion is commonly defined as one made with honest, genuine and earnest intent. . . .

. . . [U]nder this approach courts could sustain jurisdiction over a petition when it appeared that the debtor's defenses, while facially of substance, were interposed merely for purposes of delay or to unfairly favor one creditor over others. . . .

To be sure, a rule which requires balancing of competing interests based upon consideration of a wide range of factors lacks the certainty and predictability which a more mechanical rule would provide. However, it would be wrong to read the new statutory language to section 303(h)(1) as providing any such specific guidance. . . .

CONCLUSION

A fair and evenhanded system of involuntary bankruptcy would result from untying the standards for defining a bona fide dispute under sections 303(b) and 303(h)(1) and reformulating the test for each in a manner sensitive to the particular inquiry being made. . . . [A]pplication of these standards for determining when a debtor's dispute to a particular claim or debt will be regarded as a bona fide dispute under section 303 would not necessitate the dismantling of a basic statutory system which was deliberately and carefully crafted to strike a fair balance between the interests of debtors and their creditors.

Additional suggested readings

Susan Block-Lieb, *Fishing in Muddy Waters: Clarifying the Common Pool Analogy as Applied to the Standard for Commencement of a Bankruptcy Case*, 42 AM. U. L. REV. 337 (1993)

Janet Flaccus, *Have Eight Circuits Shorted? Good Faith and Chapter 11 Petitions*, 67 AM. BANKR. L.J. 401 (1993)

John Hansberger, *Failure to Pay One's Debts Generally as They Become Due: The Experience of France and Canada*, 54 AM. BANKR. L.J. 153 (1980)

Thomas H. Jackson, Chapter 8, *Timing the Bankruptcy Proceeding: The Problems of Proper Commencement, in* THE LOGIC AND LIMITS OF BANKRUPTCY LAW 193-208 (Harvard 1986)

Frank R. Kennedy, *The Commencement of a Case Under the New Bankruptcy Code*, 36 WASH. & LEE L. REV. 977 (1979)

Lawrence Ponoroff, *The Limits of Good Faith Analyses: Unraveling and Redefining Bad Faith Involuntary Bankruptcy Proceedings*, 71 NEB. L. REV. 209 (1992)

Linda J. Rusch, *Bankruptcy as a Revolutionary Concept: Good Faith Filing and a Theory of Obligation*, 57 MONT. L. REV. 49 (1996)

Israel Treiman, *Acts of Bankruptcy: A Medieval Concept in Modern Bankruptcy Law*, 52 HARV. L. REV. 189 (1938)

Chapter 4
Jurisdiction and Procedure

A. Creating a Modern Bankruptcy Court and its Jurisdiction

One of the most interesting and important bankruptcy stories in recent times concerns the efforts to create a modern bankruptcy court with an appropriately broad jurisdiction. Under the old Bankruptcy Act, the shortcomings of the bankruptcy court system and its splintered jurisdiction had become manifest. Indeed, one of the primary driving forces for reform circa 1970 was the widely-held perception that the bankruptcy system was broken and needed to be fixed. Also widely held was the view that the most effective reform would be to create a unified jurisdiction encompassing all bankruptcy matters under the umbrella of a single specialized court. Alas, what was *not* agreed on was what the status of that court should (or must) be. The battle was over whether the specialized court should be established under Article III of the Constitution. The outcome was that Congress decided to create a broad and unified jurisdiction but under a bankruptcy court that lacked Article III status. This decision proved disastrous when the Supreme Court held in *Northern Pipeline Construction Co. v. Marathon Pipe Line Co.*, 458 U.S. 50 (1982), that it was unconstitutional for the non-Article III bankruptcy court to exercise that broad jurisdiction. In 1984, Congress responded to that decision by retaining a non-Article III bankruptcy court with a slightly reduced jurisdiction—rather than keeping the comprehensive jurisdiction under the auspices of an Article III bankruptcy court.

The following selections tell this story. The first three excerpts from the legislative history describe the congressional compromise in the 1978 Act. Following that is Professor Eric Posner's recounting of the political economy that led to that compromise. Next are Professor Lawrence King's comments on the 1984 amendments that created the current bankruptcy and jurisdictional system. King's account is followed by Professor Vern Countryman's tale of the political machinations that led to the 1984 legislation. Finally, the 1997 National Bankruptcy Review Commission Report recommends—yet again—just such a move to an Article III bankruptcy system. For a dissenting view, see Thomas E. Plank, *Why Bankruptcy Judges Need Not and Should Not Be Article III Judges*, 72 AM. BANKR. L.J. 567 (1998).

As you read these various selections, try to assess (1) why a unified jurisdiction is important; (2) who has constituted the opposition to giving bankruptcy judges Article III status, and on what grounds; (3) why Congress has refused, at every turn, to take the Article III step; and (4) whether such a step is ever likely to be taken.

H.R. Rep. No. 95-595
95th Cong., 1st Sess. (1977)

Chapter 1. Constitutional Bankruptcy Courts

INTRODUCTION

A major feature of H.R. 8200 is the change of the present bankruptcy system. The bill establishes bankruptcy courts that are independent of the United States district courts. The judges of the proposed bankruptcy courts are granted full constitutional tenure. The present referee system, under which the bankruptcy courts are subordinate adjuncts of the district courts, is abolished.

The historical development of the treatment of bankruptcy cases under the present Bankruptcy Act has demonstrated the need for an independent bankruptcy court. Sound bankruptcy and judicial policy dictate the creation of those courts with the full grant of powers and protections provided under Article III of the Constitution. Constitutional principles governing the Federal courts also establish a strong presumption in favor of a life-tenured Federal judiciary. A full grant to the bankruptcy courts of the jurisdiction and powers necessary to the proper functioning of a bankruptcy system raises serious constitutional doubts of that presumption is avoided.

S. Rep. No. 95-989
95th Cong., 2d Sess. (1978)

ESTABLISHMENT OF BANKRUPTCY COURT

The need for a functionally independent bankruptcy court has been demonstrated beyond question . . . .

. . . It is the view of the subcommittee that the establishment of the new bankruptcy court as an adjunct of the U.S. district court offers several important advantages:

(1) The presently established U.S. district courts can serve as article III repositories for the broadened jurisdiction essential to efficient judicial administration in bankruptcy cases.

(2) The expanded jurisdiction vested in the U.S. district courts may be delegated by statute for exercise exclusively by bankruptcy judges, subject always to review, as under present law, by the district courts. Certain perceived constitutional impediments to the exercise of the judicial power of the United States by non-tenured judges are thus eliminated.

(3) The dislocations associated with continued evolution of the present referee system into a functionally independent adjunct of the district court are minimal in comparison to those attendant upon the establishment of a separate bankruptcy court system.

(4) The fragmentation of Federal court jurisdiction envisioned by some is thus avoided.

(5) The convenience and economy of district court appeals are preserved. . . .

124 CONGRESSIONAL RECORD S17404 (October 6, 1978)

Mr. Deconcini: The Senate prevailed in the concept that the new courts will not have article III judges. While the new judges will not have life tenure they will be elevated to a status far above that of the present day referee. The new courts will be adjuncts of the district courts.

Eric A. Posner
The Political Economy of the Bankruptcy Reform Act of 1978
96 MICH. L. REV. 47 (1997)*

1. Administrative Structure

The two main players under the old bankruptcy law were the bankruptcy judge and the trustee. The bankruptcy judge—prior to 1973 officially known as the "referee" and sometimes unofficially so called up until 1978—decided the disputes that arose in connection with bankruptcy cases. . . . The bankruptcy judge was appointed by panels of district judges for six-year terms. Originally, the bankruptcy judge had been considered to be a kind of clerk or "adjunct" of the district court. The district court had jurisdiction over the bankruptcy case, and although it delegated most of the decisionmaking functions to the bankruptcy judge, appeal from the bankruptcy judge's order was to the district court. In practice, the bankruptcy judge had a great deal of power over the day-to-day operation of the bankruptcy proceeding. The district courts would rarely conduct bankruptcy hearings themselves. The bankruptcy judge made routine decisions regarding the property in the bankruptcy estate (summary jurisdiction) and made decisions regarding property in the possession of third parties when all consented (plenary jurisdiction). Some commentators argued that the bankruptcy judges did not have sufficient jurisdictional and remedial powers to decide cases in an expeditious way--they would have to refer issues outside their power to the supervising district court—and that bankruptcy judges' subordinate status weakened their authority with litigants.

The trustee was a private individual, usually a lawyer, who would represent and administer the debtor's estate. When, as frequently happened, the creditors did not elect the trustee, the trustee would be appointed by the bankruptcy judge. The trustee performed many of the functions associated with the trustee today. . . . However, the pre-1978 bankruptcy judge often engaged in activities within the domain of the post-1978 trustee. The bankruptcy judge would, along with the trustee, attend the first creditor's meetings. As a result, the judge would hear evidence that would not be admissible at trial. The bankruptcy judge and the trustee would have frequent ex parte contact. Sometimes a bankruptcy judge would persuade a trustee to pursue a particular course of action, such as going after property, then rule on the trustee's behavior at a later hearing. Sometimes, a bankruptcy judge would actually negotiate contracts with interested parties—such as between union and management—and give business advice to a debtor in possession. The close contact between the bankruptcy judge and the trustee raised concerns that bankruptcy judges biased their decisions in favor of trustees. . . .

V. Administrative Structure

Participants in the hearings came into conflict over two major issues of administrative structure. The first issue concerned the power and status of the bankruptcy court. Some participants believed that bankruptcy judges should have broader powers than those they enjoyed under the old law and that they should have greater status; other participants preferred the old law. Because the status of a judge depends in part on the extent of his powers, the questions of power and status were intertwined. The second issue concerned the nature of the administrative apparatus that would con-

---

trol the appointment of trustees. Some participants wanted to create a "bankruptcy agency" in the executive branch; other participants wanted to keep the appointment of trustees in the judicial branch.

... [T]he federal judiciary's most passionate concern about bankruptcy reform was that the status of federal judges would be diluted by an increase in the power of bankruptcy judges. ...

... The Commission argued that bankruptcy judges' low status hampered their efforts to adjudicate bankruptcy disputes in a fair and expeditious manner. The solution to this problem was "to enhance the real and apparent judicial independence of bankruptcy judges." One route to enhancement would occur through modification of appointment, tenure, and compensation. The CB [Commission Bill] would have made bankruptcy judges subject to presidential appointment with the advice and consent of the Senate, increased their tenure from six to fifteen years, and increased their compensation. The other route to enhancement of status would occur through modification of the role of the bankruptcy judge, so that the judge would have fewer "administrative" and more "judicial" responsibilities—the theory being that administrative actions dissipated the cloud of impartiality that otherwise enhanced the prestige of the judge. ...

Why did the majority of the Commission support the enhancement of the independence and prestige of the bankruptcy courts, while Judge Weinfeld opposed it? Why did the Commission support the creation of a bankruptcy agency while the bankruptcy judges opposed it? Looking beyond the parties' statements and at their interests, it appears that the proposed administrative structure reflected concerns about maintaining and expanding power, especially the power of patronage.

Seven of the nine members of the Commission came from the executive and legislative branches, both of which had an interest in creating new patronage opportunities. ...

The federal judges opposed the creation of more independent bankruptcy courts, because (1) they would lose their appointment power over bankruptcy judges, and thus one of their main patronage opportunities, and (2) their status would be diluted through the vast increase in the number of federal judicial positions. The federal judges also opposed the creation of the bankruptcy agency, because to the extent that the agency would deprive bankruptcy judges of the power to appoint trustees and to the extent to which the bankruptcy judges were within the control of the federal judges, the creation of the bankruptcy agency would reduce the power and independence of the judiciary.

The bankruptcy judges supported the enhancement of the power and prestige of the bankruptcy courts, because they would gain power, status, and possibly pecuniary compensation. Bankruptcy judges had for a long time complained about what they saw as their low status, and they saw bankruptcy reform as an opportunity to solve this problem. ...

The bankruptcy judges, however, opposed the creation of the bankruptcy agency. ...

A ... plausible explanation for the bankruptcy judges' opposition to the bankruptcy agency is that the latter would have deprived them of their main source of patronage—the power to appoint trustees from their acquaintances in the local bankruptcy bar. ...

If the patronage motives were half hidden in the Commission Report and related documents, they became clearer during the hearings in Stage 2. The federal judges, who had earlier resisted the bankruptcy judges' efforts to have their title changed from "referee" to "bankruptcy judge," apparently on the grounds that such a change would dilute the prestige of the title "judge," reiterated their opposition to elevation of the bankruptcy judges and to the creation of a bankruptcy agency. Again, the federal judges could not admit that their motive was a fear of a loss of prestige ....

In addition to the evidence that the judges feared losing status, there emerged evidence that they feared losing the patronage power to appoint bankruptcy judges. One must admit the possibility that the federal judges were right on policy grounds, but if they had been, one would have expected some support for their views from outside the judicial branch. Almost no one—creditors, debtors, or lawyers—expressed such support.

Stage 2 also saw the bankruptcy judges reiterating their support for higher status bankruptcy courts and their opposition to the creation of a federal bankruptcy agency. Evidence of the bankruptcy judges' practice of appointing cronies to the position of trustee supports the hypothesis that the bankruptcy judges opposed the bankruptcy agency because they feared losing their patronage power. Some observers suggested the existence of a "bankruptcy ring," consisting of the local bankruptcy bar and bankruptcy judges who favored each other over outsiders. . . .

Lawyers, as noted, generally supported the creation of the higher status bankruptcy courts and opposed the creation of a bankruptcy agency, but they were divided in some respects. Commercial lawyers and bankruptcy lawyers strongly supported the creation of independent bankruptcy courts. One reason for their support was that in districts where the bankruptcy judge did not use the trustee position as a source of patronage, the bankruptcy lawyers used it as a source of profit . . . .

By electing each other as the trustee and hiring each other as the trustee's counsel, bankruptcy lawyers assured themselves a steady source of business and a steady source of profit.

Another reason that commercial and bankruptcy lawyers supported the enhancement of the status of bankruptcy courts is that lawyers, like bankruptcy judges, care about prestige; just as it is more prestigious to argue in front of federal courts than to argue in front of state courts, so would it be more prestigious to argue in front of high-status bankruptcy courts than to argue in front of low-status bankruptcy courts. . . .

Lawyers as a class were less enthusiastic about the proposed administrative changes but were generally supportive. . . .

The creditors generally supported increasing the independence of bankruptcy courts, just because they hoped that higher-status courts would attract better judges and that more powerful bankruptcy courts would be less vulnerable to reversal by higher courts and attendant delays. They opposed the creation of the bankruptcy agency, at least partly because they feared that such an agency would encourage consumers to enter bankruptcy.

The Department of Justice opposed the creation of independent bankruptcy judges and a bankruptcy agency. . . .

The House Hearings led to a bill that greatly expanded the patronage powers of the executive and legislative branches of the federal government. House Bill 8200 endorsed the idea of the stronger bankruptcy courts . . . . Most significant, House Bill 8200 would have created Article III bankruptcy judges, with life tenure. The House Report argued that it was necessary as a matter of policy to increase the power and status of bankruptcy judges, but this could not be done under Article III of the Constitution unless the judges were given life tenure. . . . In addition, House Bill 8200 gave the bankruptcy judges broad jurisdictional and remedial powers and provided that appeal from a bankruptcy order would be to the circuit court. This last provision was particularly unattractive to the federal judges, because it seemed to put the bankruptcy courts on par with the district courts. House Bill 8200 also followed the Commission's recommendation and created a federal bankruptcy agency, but put the agency in the Department of Justice. . . .

Although Senate Bill 2266 gave bankruptcy judges new powers, duties, and privileges (including the right to appoint their own clerks), it did not go so far as the House bill. Senate Bill 2266 did not turn bankruptcy judges into Article III judges, but it did increase their terms from six to twelve years. The power to appoint bankruptcy judges was transferred from district courts to courts of appeal. Administrative functions remained in the judicial branch. No federal bankruptcy agency was to be created. The overall effect was to raise the independence and status of the bankruptcy judges slightly, but not by nearly as much as under House Bill 8200, and to prevent the shift of patronage power from the judiciary to the legislative and executive branches and from the local level to the national level.

. . . The crucial points are that Congress shifted the appointment power to the executive and legislative branches, and it increased the desirability of the positions, making them more valuable as currency for paying off political debts. . . . Recall that the Commission members other than the judges sought to create Article III positions. . . .

But given that expansion of patronage served the interests of Democrats in both chambers, it is no surprise that a compromise was hammered out. The bankruptcy judges would acquire significant new powers and independence, but they would become Article I judges rather than Article III judges. They would become presidential appointments, but their terms were limited to fourteen years, and appeal from their orders would be to district courts. Constitutional concerns were met with assurances from the Chief Justice that the Supreme Court would uphold the new bankruptcy positions. The bankruptcy agency would be put on a hold, but a pilot program would be initiated. The Democratic Party as a whole would benefit from the elevation of the status of bankruptcy judges, and because the party controlled the Senate, the Senate Democrats could be expected to consent as long as suitably compensated for any political disadvantage.

But one problem remained. The compromise may have satisfied the Senate Democrats' fear that they would lose patronage power vis-á-vis the House Democrats. It did not, however, address the federal judges' own desire not to lose any status at all. Hence, the dramatic intervention of Chief Justice Burger. Burger, who had earlier opposed the elevation of bankruptcy judges in a letter to Senator DeConcini and through the Administrative Office of the United States Courts, telephoned DeConcini and other senators, after the House passed the compromise bill, and complained about presidential appointment of bankruptcy judges, their retirement benefits, and their status as adjuncts to the circuit courts. "Burger 'not only lobbied, but pressured and attempted to be intimidating,' DeConcini said. He said the Chief Justice was 'very, very irate and rude.'" Nevertheless, the second Senate amendment threw some crumbs to Burger in the form of remarkably petty reductions in the independence and status of the bankruptcy judges. . . .

Why did DeConcini make these concessions to Burger? . . . First, the vehemence of the federal judges' protest may have led DeConcini to reconsider his judgment that under the compromise bill the Senate would not lose too much patronage power. If federal judges were upset about the bill, that must mean that they expected to lose a great deal of status. If that was so and the position of federal judge would therefore become less attractive, the Senate had lost more patronage power than it had first thought. Second, DeConcini may have worried that the Supreme Court would undo the legislative deal, either by interpreting the statute in a strict way or even by striking down the already constitutionally suspect provisions dealing with bankruptcy judges. The House, in going along with the Senate's unilateral amendment, may have shared this concern. . . .

Although our story ends in 1978, the reader may be interested in subsequent events. In 1982 the Supreme Court struck down the provisions in the 1978 Act relating to the position of bankruptcy judges. The Court held that the Act violated the Constitution by giving Article III powers to judges who do not have lifetime tenure and independent salaries. Justice Burger joined the dissent, which argued that the bankruptcy courts could be considered limited Article I courts. House members felt that Burger had broken a promise to deliver Supreme Court approval of the 1978 Act.

The 1984 Amendments

Lawrence P. King
Jurisdiction and Procedure Under the Bankruptcy Amendments of 1984
38 VAND. L. REV. 675 (1985)[*]

On July 10, 1984, the President signed into law the Bankruptcy Amendments and Federal Judgeship Act of 1984. This legislation was the long-awaited congressional response to the Supreme Court's invalidation on constitutional grounds of provisions of the Bankruptcy Reform Act of 1978. The Supreme Court found unconstitutional a basic jurisdictional provision in the Bankruptcy Reform Act of 1978 and held that the jurisdiction given to a bankruptcy court under the 1978 Act was too broad for a nonarticle III court.

The 1984 amendments could have eliminated the constitutional defects of the 1978 Act by converting the bankruptcy courts to article III courts. But faced with the well-organized opposition of the rest of the federal judiciary, which adamantly had refused to accept life tenure for bankruptcy judges since it was first proposed in 1977, Congress did not adopt this simple solution to the jurisdiction problem. . . .

III. REFERENCE TO THE UNITED STATES BANKRUPTCY COURT

The real issue addressed by the 1984 amendments is the jurisdiction of the bankruptcy court. The 1984 amendments do not require the district courts to refer bankruptcy cases to the bankruptcy courts but allows them to do so. . . . The authority to refer cases and proceedings under section 157(a) has been exercised by local rule or order in all federal judicial districts. Accordingly, bankruptcy judges continue to handle most, if not all, bankruptcy cases.

Two basic considerations appear to have motivated the 1984 legislation. The first was the congressional attempt to cure the unconstitutional jurisdictional defects. . . . The second consideration was the district courts' already ample workload and the evident lack of desire and inability of the district court judges to take on more work. . . .

A. Jurisdiction of the Bankruptcy Court

. . . Section 157 spells out the role of the bankruptcy judge in some detail. . . . First, the section creates a dichotomy between "core" and "noncore" proceedings. Second, section 157 specifies the ultimate judicial authority of the bankruptcy judge regarding both core and noncore proceedings. . . .

Since the statute provides that the bankruptcy judge may enter final orders in core proceedings, noncore proceedings must have a different authority. Section 157(c)(1) is the counterpart to section 157(b)(1) and concerns noncore proceedings. Theoretically, the 1984 amendments have rendered the bankruptcy judge's role much more limited and the district judge's role more broad. In noncore proceedings, section 157(c)(1) specifies that the bankruptcy judge is to "submit proposed findings of fact and conclusions of law to the district court." Any final order is to be entered by the district judge after "considering" the proposed findings and conclusions, or after "reviewing de novo" any matter in the proposed findings and conclusions to which a party has "timely and specifically" objected.

Section 157(c)(1) is rife with problems and temptations. The major temptation is for the district judge to rubber-stamp the proposed findings and conclusions of the bankruptcy judge. . . .

The purpose of section 157(c)(1) is to make the legislative scheme appear constitutional in any case that may come before the Supreme Court. Congress provided that, except for core matters and

---

absent consent of the parties, the article III court is the final arbiter at the trial level. Thus, excessive jurisdiction is not given to the nonarticle III court. . . . In practical terms, however, the nonarticle III court's proposed findings and conclusions will be *the* findings and conclusions. "Consider" and "review" will disintegrate into rubber-stamped acceptances of the bankruptcy court's findings and conclusions. The constitutional protection for article III judges to adjudicate noncore proceedings has been accomplished semantically and cosmetically. But actually little or no change will occur.

One effect of section 157 is the added opportunity for counsel to employ delaying tactics. A built-in litigation ploy now is available for one side of a disputed matter to assert that the proceeding is noncore. . . .

IV. CONCLUSION

The complexity and possible invalidity of the 1984 amendments arise from Congress' refusal to constitute the bankruptcy courts as article III courts. The only group, if any, that this refusal has aided is the district court bench, by keeping their numbers small (except to the extent that additional bankruptcy duties require additions to their numbers) and their status elite. The congressional action works against the needs of all parties involved in the functioning of the Bankruptcy Code and the judicial system itself. Debtors in Bankruptcy Code cases are left uncertain as to the authority of the bankruptcy courts adjudicating proceedings in their cases. New layers of potential litigation tactics have been added, which will further burden the bankruptcy court system and the district court system, both of which have sufficient real and legitimate work to perform. Aside from the merits of the arguments opposing the bankruptcy system instituted pursuant to the 1984 amendments, in view of the Supreme Court's pronouncements in *Northern Pipeline*, it is irresponsible for Congress to have enacted legislation containing such inherent risks of constitutional invalidity when the lives of so many financially troubled persons and companies look to the federal bankruptcy laws for a fresh start and reorganized future.

Vern Countryman
Scrambling to Define Bankruptcy Jurisdiction:
The Chief Justice, the Judicial Conference, and the Legislative Process
22 HARV. J. LEGIS. 1 (1985)[*]

In the arcane world of federal bankruptcy law, nothing is more arcane than the jurisdiction of the bankruptcy court. That was true under the old Bankruptcy Act of 1898, as frequently amended, and was even more true when that Act was replaced by the new Bankruptcy Code of 1978, effective October 1, 1979. The situation became still worse in 1982, when the Supreme Court found at least some part of the 1978 effort unconstitutional. The Ninety-Eighth Congress responded to the Court's ruling by amending the Code in 1984. The best that can be said of the 1984 amendments to the new Code is that a hitherto unacceptable situation has now been rendered intolerable by a process that reflects no credit on any branch of the federal government. . . .

II. The Bankruptcy Code of 1978

The federal commission that produced the first draft of what became the new Bankruptcy Code recommended that the jurisdictional problems under the old Act be eliminated by giving the bankruptcy courts jurisdiction over "all controversies that arise out of a [bankruptcy] case" without regard to possession of property or the consent of the defendant. The commission further recommended that the bankruptcy court be established as a court independent of the district court. It also recommended that bankruptcy judges be appointed by the President with the advice and consent of the Senate for fifteen-year terms, with salary subject to adjustment, and with the bankruptcy judges removable by a commission of three judges for incapacity, misconduct, or neglect of duty.

Essentially, Congress adopted the recommendation on bankruptcy jurisdiction. The House Judiciary Committee, however, concluded that the bankruptcy courts should be Article III courts. On policy grounds, the Committee contended that the enhanced status would attract better-qualified judges. It also concluded, after consultation with a number of mostly academic experts, that there was "substantial doubt" whether a non-Article III court would be constitutional. . . .

In an agreed compromise measure, which passed the House on September 28, 1978, the bankruptcy judges lost Article III status. They were to be appointed as "adjuncts" of the circuit courts by the President with the advice and consent of the Senate for fourteen-year terms. . . .

A few days after the House action, Chief Justice Warren Burger reportedly called Senator Strom Thurmond (R-S.C.), ranking minority member of the Senate Judiciary Committee, and Senator Malcolm Wallop (R-Wyo.), a minority sponsor of the bill, to delay a vote in the Senate because of his dissatisfaction with the new bankruptcy court provisions. The Chief Justice was particularly unhappy with those provisions calling for presidential appointment, making the bankruptcy courts "adjuncts" of the circuit courts of appeals rather than the lower level district courts, and adding bankruptcy judges to the Judicial Conference. The Supreme Court's public information officer reportedly confirmed the Chief Justice's call to Thurmond. He explained this "unusual action" by saying that the Chief Justice was acting in his role as Chairman of the Judicial Conference, "which by law is authorized to tell Congress what it thinks of bills affecting the court system." . . .

The press also reported that Senator DeConcini had said that there would be no further negotiations between Congress and the Chief Justice, because DeConcini considered dealing with the third branch of government to be a violation of the doctrine of separation of powers. A few days later, however, Senator DeConcini was reported as saying that the Chief Justice had called him on September 28 and "yelled at me that I was irresponsible" and that the Chief Justice was "going to go to the president and get him to veto this."

The Chief Justice's efforts were apparently not entirely without effect. An amended compromise measure passed the Senate on October 5 . . . . The bill made the bankruptcy courts "adjuncts" of the district courts rather than the courts of appeals. The expanded bankruptcy jurisdiction was vested in the district courts, but "all" of it was to be exercised by the bankruptcy courts. . . . The House accepted the Senate amendments and, despite a reported letter from the Chief Justice to the President urging veto, President Carter signed the bill on November 6, 1978.

III. The *Northern Pipeline* Decision

Incumbent bankruptcy judges were acting under this interim scheme when the Supreme Court decided the *Northern Pipeline* case in June 1982. Debtor, Northern Pipeline, had filed a voluntary petition for reorganization under new Chapter 11 . . . .

Northern Pipeline asserted a prepetition cause of action for breach of contract against Marathon Pipe Line, which became property of the estate . . . . Northern Pipeline filed an action in the bankruptcy court against Marathon for breach of contract. Marathon moved to dismiss that action on the ground that the new jurisdictional provision conferred Article III judicial power on non-Article III courts in violation of the separation of powers doctrine. A majority of the Court sustained Marathon's contention, with the Chief Justice among the three dissenters.

The *Northern Pipeline* opinion was one of Justice William Brennan's most ambitious excursions . . . . The holding of six justices in *Northern Pipeline* is fairly well encapsulated in a footnote to the plurality opinion:

> [A]t the least, the new bankruptcy judges cannot constitutionally be vested with jurisdiction to decide this state-law contract claim against Marathon. . . . [W]e cannot conclude that if Congress were aware that the grant of jurisdiction could not constitutionally encompass this and similar claims, it would simply remove the jurisdiction of the bankruptcy court over these matters . . . . We think that it is for Congress to determine the proper manner of restructuring the Bankruptcy Act of 1978 to conform to the requirements of Art. III. . . .

Justices Rehnquist and O'Connor concurred . . . .

IV. THE EMERGENCY RULE

Congress did not act to resolve the jurisdictional controversy for more than two years after the *Northern Pipeline* decision. In September 1982, however, the Judicial Conference stepped into the breach by adopting a resolution requiring the Director of the Administrative Office of United States Courts to "provide each circuit with a proposed rule," which was to take effect in the absence of congressional action. The resolution was intended "to permit the bankruptcy system to continue without disruption in reliance on jurisdictional grants remaining in the law as limited by" the *Northern Pipeline* decision. This resolution was a remarkable position for the Judicial Conference, a group of Article III judges, to take. For one thing, its assumption that there were "jurisdictional grants remaining" after the *Northern Pipeline* decision ignored a holding of a majority of the Court that the "single statutory grant of jurisdiction" in bankruptcy was nonseverable. Second, it assumed that allocation of this remaining jurisdiction between district courts and bankruptcy courts was a proper function of court rules . . . . Third, . . . the Judicial Conference is given no bankruptcy rulemaking authority. . . .

Director William E. Foley nonetheless prepared and dispatched to all circuit, district, and bankruptcy court judges an Emergency Rule. An accompanying memorandum of September 27, 1982, explained that "the Administrative Office concludes that [*Northern Pipeline*] did not invalidate" section 1471(a) and (b) of the Judicial Code, which vested the bankruptcy jurisdiction in the district courts. The unstated assumption was that *Northern Pipeline* had only invalidated section 1471(c), which directed the bankruptcy courts to exercise "all" of that jurisdiction. Accordingly, the Emergency Rule was "an interim measure by which district courts may delegate many of their bankruptcy powers to bankruptcy judges." . . .

The Emergency Rule was, by its own terms, effective only until Congress acted or until March 31, 1984, whichever occurred first. It provided for reference of all civil proceedings covered by section 1471(a) and (b) to the bankruptcy courts, although (1) the reference could be withdrawn in whole or in part by the district court and (2) the bankruptcy judges were forbidden to conduct jury trials.

But the rule then undertook to separate "related proceedings," defined in the rule as "those civil proceedings that, in the absence of a petition in bankruptcy, could have been brought in a district court or a state court," from all other cases and proceedings. It also undertook to treat the two groups differently. In "related proceedings," the bankruptcy court could not "enter a judgment or dispositive order" unless the parties consented, but, like a special master, was to "submit findings, conclusions, and a proposed judgment or order to the district judge." All such proposed judgments and orders were to be reviewed by the district court. In other cases and proceedings, the orders and judgments of bankruptcy judges were made effective upon entry unless stayed by the bankruptcy judge or a district judge. The district judge was to review such orders and judgments only if an appeal was taken or if the bankruptcy judge "certifie[d] that circumstances required that the order or judgment be approved by a district judge."

In an apparent effort to show that the final decisionmaking authority remained with the district court, the rule also provided that, in reviewing orders or judgments of either type, the district court could hold a hearing and "receive such evidence as is appropriate" and "need give no deference to the findings of the bankruptcy judge." Apparently, then Bankruptcy Rule 810, prescribing the "clearly erroneous" standard for review of bankruptcy courts' findings, was to be disposed of by a provision in the Emergency Rule . . . . It may be even more difficult to reconcile with the rubber-stamp mentality suggested by a statement made in the Foley memorandum of September 27, and repeated in his memorandum of December 3, that "where the bankruptcy judge certifies that circumstances require, an order or judgment entered by a bankruptcy judge will be confirmed by a district judge even if no objection is filed."

All circuit councils and, with minor local variations, district courts followed directions. Thus, after Christmas Eve, 1982, there was in place, as a matter of form at least, a rule allocating bankruptcy jurisdiction between bankruptcy and district court judges. And all of this was accomplished with no participation by the Supreme Court, except as the Chief Justice might be thought to have had some hand in it.

In an effort to keep their cases moving, counsel did not, in most instances, challenge the allocation of jurisdiction to the bankruptcy courts by the Emergency Rule. They relied instead on the ancient doctrine that federal courts, while courts of limited jurisdiction, have jurisdiction to decide whether they have subject matter jurisdiction. According to this doctrine, absent a direct attack, those judgments are res judicata on the jurisdictional issue and not subject to collateral attack.

. . . Even if this same jurisdictional doctrine applies to non-Article III courts, however, does it apply to such a court that has no other jurisdiction whatsoever? That would be the situation of the bankruptcy courts after December 24, 1982, if the promulgators of the Emergency Rule were wrong on any one of their four assumptions: (1) that bankruptcy jurisdiction remained in the district courts after *Northern Pipeline*; (2) that the promulgators of the rules had rulemaking authority; (3) that jurisdiction could be allocated by rule; or (4) that the Emergency Rule's allocation of jurisdiction was valid under *Northern Pipeline*.

Those who have challenged the validity of the Emergency Rule have met with little success beyond the bankruptcy court level. The Supreme Court has three times denied petitions for original writs of mandamus or prohibition attacking the rule. Each of the eight courts of appeals that have considered the question have held the rule valid. . . .

The provision in the Emergency Rule permitting bankruptcy courts to entertain and to dispose of "related proceedings" with the consent of the parties was doubtlessly inspired not only by the practice under the former Bankruptcy Act, but also by a 1979 amendment to the Federal Magistrates Act. . . .

V. CONGRESSIONAL ACTION

During this time Congress approached the problem with nothing like the near unanimity exhibited by the Article III judges. After the district court decision in *Northern Pipeline*, which had also held the bankruptcy jurisdictional grant unconstitutional, and two months before the Supreme Court decision in *Northern Pipeline*, Chairman Peter Rodino (D-N.J.) of the House Judiciary Committee introduced a bill to make bankruptcy judges Article III judges. During hearings that were held on this bill, a spokesman for the Justice Department testified that there were three possible solutions to the problem created by the Supreme Court's decision in *Northern Pipeline*. The first was a return to the pre-1978 referee system. The second possibility was the creation of "Article I bankruptcy courts with limited original jurisdiction but with powers to act as adjuncts of the district court in other matters." Finally, "[i]f it [was] thought to be important to retain all of the procedural reforms of the 1978 . Act, . . . the easiest and safest course [was] to grant Article III status to the bankruptcy judges." Thereafter, the House Committee reported out a revised bill, which retained the proposal that bankruptcy judges be made Article III judges. . . . [T]he Judicial Conference opposed the House Committee's bill and proposed instead that bankruptcy judges should remain Article I judges and exercise "all" of the bankruptcy jurisdiction. . . .

. . . In early 1983, the Senate and the House held further hearings on the matter, during which spokesmen for the Justice Department expressed the Department's doubts that the Emergency Rule then in effect would "be found consistent with the requirements of the *Northern Pipeline* decision." . . . The spokesmen reported that the Department could not recommend "any Article I solution that is either workable as a practical matter or sufficiently free of Constitutional doubt." . . . .

. . . District Judge Spencer Williams appeared at the Senate Hearings as President of the "newly formed" Federal Judges Association, a group of 280 circuit and district court judges. The Association "urgently" sought "disapproval of any solution that would authorize more than one Article III court," and Judge Williams rejected as "unwarranted and unfair" any suggestion that opposition to Article III bankruptcy courts was attributable to "the egocentricity of existing Article III judges." . . .

Following these hearings, the House Judiciary Committee again reported out a bill that would have created 227 Article III bankruptcy judgeships. But Representative Kastenmeier . . . reintroduced the Judicial Conference bill . . . . Shortly thereafter, Kastenmeier issued a "Dear Colleague" letter, presumably circulated only to Democratic colleagues, in which he urged them not to "act to give President Reagan power to appoint 227 life tenure judges."

On the Senate side, Senator Robert Dole . . . introduced another bill . . . . Senator Strom Thurmond introduced a bill that would retain the bankruptcy courts as Article I courts. Both of these bills passed the Senate in April 1983. But with Chairman Rodino and a majority of the House Judiciary Committee insisting that there should be no action on substantive amendments to the Bankruptcy Code until the court problem had been settled, there was no action in the House in that year.

Subsequently, in February 1984, the Supreme Court held that a collective bargaining contract was an "executory contract," which could be rejected with the approval of the bankruptcy court. It also prescribed some standards for the bankruptcy court to apply in approving or disapproving rejection, and held that the National Labor Relations Board could not base an unfair labor practice charge on an employer's unilateral modification or rejection of a collective bargaining contract, without awaiting bankruptcy court approval. . . . The day that the Court's decision was announced, Representative Rodino introduced a bill to amend the Bankruptcy Code to impose a stricter standard for rejection of labor contracts and to forbid unilateral modification or rejection by the employer prior to court approval of rejection. He later introduced a bill that combined his proposal for Article III bankruptcy judges with his substantive proposal for labor contracts. . . .

The latter bill passed the House in March, but only after its provisions for Article III bankruptcy courts had been replaced by the Kastenmeier-Kindness bill's provisions for non-Article III bankruptcy courts. After the addition of many substantive amendments, the bill passed the Senate in June. Finally, on June 29, both Houses agreed on a conference committee report reconciling their differences, and the bill was sent to the President for his signature.

Before this compromise was reached, some stop-gap amendments had been necessary. . . .

VI. The Bankruptcy Amendments and Federal Judgeship Act of 1984

The bill took effect as the Bankruptcy Amendments and Federal Judgeship Act of 1984 upon the President's signature on July 10, 1984. . . .

The entire bankruptcy jurisdiction is again conferred on the district courts by language identical to that employed in section 1471(a) and (b) of the Judicial Code of 1978, but there is no provision similar to old section 1471(c) directing the bankruptcy court to exercise "all" of that jurisdiction. Instead, new section 157 of the Judicial Code authorizes each district court to provide that "any or all cases" or "proceedings" within that jurisdiction shall be referred to the bankruptcy judges.

The balance of new section 157 is similar to the Emergency Rule, although there is some change in terminology, and the emphasis is placed on when the bankruptcy judge can act as a judge rather than on when he acts only as a special master. . . .

With a statute replacing the Emergency Rule in the allocation of bankruptcy jurisdiction between bankruptcy and district courts, three of the four issues raised by the Emergency Rule have disappeared. There remains, however, the considerable question whether the statutory allocation meets constitutional requirements under the separation of powers doctrine. Because the 1984 statute carries this feature over from the Emergency Rule, there also remains the question of whether the parties can, by their consent, confer on the bankruptcy courts subject matter jurisdiction that the courts could not otherwise exercise because of either statutory or constitutional limitations.

Constitutional questions apart, the 1984 legislation dealing with the bankruptcy courts must establish a record for inept performance by Congress. . . .

VII. Conclusion

For the year ending June 30, 1983, the number of bankruptcy cases filed exceeded all civil and criminal cases filed in the federal district courts. . . . To carry such a caseload, we need a better system than that given us by the 1984 congressional action. . . .

Many of the 1984 defects are doubtlessly due to the fact that too many special interest cooks were stirring the broth, each concerned with adding its own ingredient but without much knowledge of or interest in the impact on the overall end product. Nothing more is to be expected of lobbyists for the consumer credit industry or other private interests. But it is most disturbing that the special interest lobbyists in this case included the Chief Justice of the United States and the Judicial Conference of the United States. It is also most disturbing that the one ingredient essential to them in any solution was that bankruptcy judges not be given Article III status. It seems appropriate, therefore, to conclude by suggesting some questions for consideration for many of our Article III judges as they reflect on their roles as part of our government.

First, does the separation of powers doctrine function only to protect the judicial branch from intrusion by the executive and legislative branches and to protect the executive and legislative branches from intrusions by each other, or does it function also to protect the executive and legislative branches from intrusions by the judiciary? . . .

Second, are the further tenure and compensation protections in Article III designed to give Article III judges protection not only from other branches but also from other Article III judges within the judicial branch? . . . The Emergency Rule was adopted by the district courts at the direction of the circuit judges in their capacities as members of the Judicial Councils, who were in turn acting at the direction of the Chief Justice and many circuit and district judges in their capacities as members of the Judicial Conference. Is it reassuringly apparent that, of the many Article III circuit and district judges who have ruled on the validity of the Emergency Rule, it was the "total and absolute independence" of those judges that led all but three of them to find no question about the validity of that Rule?

NATIONAL BANKRUPTCY REVIEW COMMISSION
FINAL REPORT
BANKRUPTCY: THE NEXT TWENTY YEARS
(October 20, 1997)

CHAPTER 3: JURISDICTION, PROCEDURE AND ADMINISTRATION

INTRODUCTION

Since the inception of a comprehensive bankruptcy system in the United States nearly a hundred years ago, there has been a constant search for the best way to supervise the progress of cases and to resolve the inevitable procedural disputes that arise during the course of a bankruptcy case. Bankruptcy differs from all other forms of litigation in the federal courts, and it always has. Bankruptcy, essentially, is an *in rem* proceeding as distinguished from a simple (even complex) dispute between two parties. Rather than being a legal action in which one person sues another, with a plaintiff seeking a judgment of liability against a defendant, bankruptcy is a collective proceeding to determine the status of a number of obligations affecting several or many diverse parties. . . .

Bankruptcy courts are required to resolve a number of competing issues with a myriad of affected parties. They must do so under sharp constraints on both time and resources. . . . Bankruptcy is a little like Ginger Rogers dancing with Fred Astaire: these courts have to do everything the other courts do, only backwards and in high heels.

Working out the disputes, whatever their nature, is time consuming; yet, the very essence of a bankruptcy case requires prompt resolution. The time value of money is of particular importance in a bankruptcy setting . . . . Therefore, the more smoothly a case proceeds, the more efficient the judicial process and the less money lost all around even by those not involved in the particular dispute. The recommendations of the Commission are based, in large part, on this critical factor of time. . . .

JURISDICTION AND STRUCTURE OF THE BANKRUPTCY COURT

. . . All of the Commission's Recommendations on the structure of the bankruptcy court are designed to reduce the cost, delay, and redundancy that is inherent in the current system. . . .

DISCUSSION

. . . Bankruptcy courts are not established under Article III of the Constitution. Instead, bankruptcy courts operate as "units" of the district court. As non-Article III courts, bankruptcy courts cannot exercise the "judicial power" of the United States.

The Supreme Court has recognized that not every adjudication constitutes an exercise of the "judicial power" of the United States. At what point a bankruptcy judge exercises the "judicial power" of the United States and is thus in violation of Article III is not easily discerned. The Supreme Court in *Marathon* held that a non-Article III bankruptcy judge "cannot constitutionally be vested with jurisdiction to decide [a] state-law contract claim." Because bankruptcy judges had jurisdiction to hear and determine this type of claim, the Supreme Court held unconstitutional the broad grant of jurisdiction in the 1978 Reform Act.

In response to *Marathon*, Congress divided proceedings in bankruptcy cases into those over which a bankruptcy judge could preside and enter a final order (*i.e.*, those where the bankruptcy judge arguably was not exercising the "judicial power" of the United States, referred to in the judicial code as "core" proceedings) and those in which the bankruptcy judge could submit findings of fact and conclusions of law to the district court judge for entry of a final order (*i.e.*, those where the bankruptcy judge would be exercising the "judicial power" of the United States, commonly referred to as "noncore" proceedings). The resulting bifurcation of bankruptcy jurisdiction between these two types of proceedings has led to a great deal of needless cost, confusion and delay because the authority of the bankruptcy judge to enter a final order can often be disputed.

The Commission's Recommendation on the authority of the bankruptcy court would create a constitutionally sound structure and eliminate costly litigation over bankruptcy court authority. . . .

3.1.1 *Establishing the Bankruptcy Court under Article III of the Constitution*

The bankruptcy court should be established under Article III of the Constitution.

The evolution of the bankruptcy court has not kept pace with the system's need for the efficient and final determination of bankruptcy and bankruptcy-related issues. How best to structure the bankruptcy court system in order to accomplish these goals has been debated twice since the 1970 Commission recommended the creation of an independent bankruptcy court with pervasive jurisdiction over all bankruptcy and bankruptcy-related matters. Both sides of the debate agreed that the bankruptcy court must have pervasive jurisdiction over all bankruptcy and bankruptcy-related matters in order to effectively and efficiently adjudicate bankruptcy cases and proceedings. The difference lay in what each side of this debate believed was necessary to achieve efficient and effective bankruptcy courts. During the congressional deliberations culminating in the 1978 Bankruptcy Reform Act, the House determined that expansive jurisdiction could only be granted to an Article III bankruptcy court. The Senate determined that expansive jurisdiction could be granted to a non-Article III court and therefore Article III status was unnecessary. The Senate view prevailed and Article III status was not granted to the bankruptcy courts under the 1978 Bankruptcy Reform Act.

. . . The present bankruptcy system comes into contact with more individuals and entities and handles more money than the rest of the federal court system combined. The soundness and efficiency of the bankruptcy system is therefore paramount. Two reforms will greatly enhance the efficiency and reliability of the present system. These reforms are (1) granting bankruptcy judges Article III status, and (2) giving the bankruptcy court unfettered, pervasive jurisdiction over any matter related to a case filed under the Bankruptcy Code.

These two reforms are inextricably intertwined. The Supreme Court has ruled that a grant by Congress of pervasive jurisdiction to a non-Article III court is unconstitutional. Thus, Article III status is a *sine qua non* for accomplishing the jurisdictional goal. . . .

Article III status will also eliminate the need for procedural complexities and devices such as the core/noncore distinction that add a great deal of delay and expense to the current system. It will also eliminate the need for other jurisdictional requirements that have no bearing on the constitutionality of the current bankruptcy court such as mandatory withdrawal, mandatory abstention, and liquidation of personal injury claims. . . .

The key to efficiency in bankruptcy is speed and finality. Resources in bankruptcy are limited and creditors bear the costs of administration. Under the current core/noncore system, disputes over the jurisdiction of the court can take years. Extended litigation over the jurisdiction of the court with no determination on the merits of a dispute diminish the creditors' recovery. Resources that would otherwise be available to pay unsecured creditors and fund the debtor's ongoing operation are instead used to litigate the boundaries of bankruptcy court jurisdiction. The jurisdictional inefficiency of the system thus threatens two bedrock principles of bankruptcy: maximizing recovery for creditors and providing debtors with the ability to reorganize or obtain a fresh start.

The cost of uncertainty in the present system will also be eliminated if bankruptcy courts are established under Article III. . . .

Article III status will also, in synergy with these reforms, promote the goal of achieving a high quality judicial system. Critics of the current system argue that bankruptcy judges are too debtor-oriented and as a result the system is too insular and self-referential. Article III status may address some of these concerns. Lifetime appointment may encourage and provide an incentive for high quality generalists who will bring a generalist perspective to the whole system to seek bankruptcy judge appointments.

The net result would be a more prestigious, more efficient court authorized to resolve quickly and completely all in a single setting the proceedings that come before it. . . .

D. The Need for an Article III Bankruptcy Court

1. Elimination of Jurisdictional Litigation

The core/noncore distinction has created a judicial system first by necessity and second by design, that is time consuming, unnecessarily expensive, and inefficient. It produces procedural routes that require court and attorney time for purposes having nothing to do with resolving the substantive merits of the controversy. Article III status would clearly eliminate the need for withdrawal provisions, special jury provisions, special abstention provisions, core vs. noncore distinctions, a double layer of litigation at the trial level through the present need for proposed findings by one judge which are given to another judge who can retry the same matter, and the like.

Opponents of the Recommendation argue that disputes over jurisdiction do not arise very often and therefore, no change to the structure of the bankruptcy court system is necessary. But the numbers do not tell the important part of the story. The important fact is that in any single case the parties—the actual debtors, creditors, trustees, employees, etc.—are forced to spend money and time in a fruitless endeavor. That is, they are required to incur litigation expense over nonsubstantive issues. . . .

2. Alternatives to Article III

Article III status was not the only solution the Commission considered to resolve the current jurisdiction quagmire. The Commission also considered a number of alternative "stream-lining" proposals. Extensive discussions were held, but the Commission did not make any recommendation with regard to these proposals. The following discussion is included to illuminate why the streamlining proposals will not solve the fundamental jurisdictional problems in the current system.

As discussed above, the jurisdiction provisions of BAFJA were enacted in response to *Marathon* in an effort to reconstitute a constitutional bankruptcy court. A number of provisions were added under BAFJA, however, that have no effect on the constitutionality of the bankruptcy court. For example, mandatory withdrawal, mandatory abstention, and the forum for liquidating personal injury claims are all provisions that increase the cost and delay of bankruptcy-related litigation but neither improve nor impair the constitutionality of the current system.

Under *Marathon* a non-Article III court may not be given pervasive jurisdiction nor may it finally decide a proceeding involving a purely state law cause of action brought by the estate representative against a third party. If bankruptcy courts do not have Article III status, the core/noncore provisions in section 157(c) must be retained. All of the unanswered questions, such as, whether all counterclaims are core proceedings even if so listed in section 157(b)(2)(C) and whether implied consent is constitutionally tolerated under section 157(c)(2), remain as the system continues to struggle with this dichotomy.

All other provisions of a procedural nature affecting trials in the bankruptcy court may be eliminated in order to remove strategic delay-causing devices from the arsenal of litigators. The delay caused by these provisions is funded by the unsecured creditors who must bear the costs of administration. Because these provisions do not buttress the constitutional nature of the current system they only serve to add further delay and expense to an already lengthy and costly core/noncore procedure. . . .

The net effect of these streamlining proposals would be to assist in reducing cost and increasing efficiency. The delays caused by provisions that do not buttress the constitutionality of the bankruptcy system under BAFJA only serve to exacerbate the problems that already inhere in the core/noncore distinction. The system would only become marginally more efficient by amending these provisions. The same dichotomy between core and noncore proceedings would still have to be maintained . . . .

Conclusion

The procedural morass of the bankruptcy judicial system is extraordinarily costly and inefficient. The cost is borne by creditors, debtors, and the court and its administration. Article III status is not a panacea, but it is a miracle cure for the majority of jurisdictional ills that currently afflict the bankruptcy court. It would not relieve the system of a motion raising the basic jurisdiction issue, *i.e.*, "related to" jurisdiction. It would, however, relieve it of all of the other jurisdictional motions which would eliminate a great deal of expense for the estate, the creditors, interested third parties, and the system itself in terms of court and administration time.

B. The Nature and Limits of Bankruptcy Jurisdiction

The preceding section focused on the creation and structure of the bankruptcy court system that was designed to exercise bankruptcy jurisdiction. But what, exactly, *is* the nature of bankruptcy jurisdiction? Unfortunately, for a jurisdiction that governs more cases than any other type in federal court, bankruptcy jurisdiction is little understood, and is indeed probably misunderstood more often than not. The following excerpts from articles by Professor Ralph Brubaker of Emory Law School seek to allay that confusion. Professor Brubaker has established himself as the leading authority on the nature of federal bankruptcy jurisdiction.

In the first article, *One Hundred Years of Federal Bankruptcy Law and Still Clinging to an* In Rem *Model of Bankruptcy Jurisdiction*, 15 BANKR. DEV. J. 261 (1999), Brubaker examines the historical vacillation between two models of bankruptcy jurisdiction—an in rem model and an in personam model. He concludes that the in rem model persists today—causing significant (and unnecessary) difficulties—even though Congress has sought to establish an in personam model. In the second work, *On the Nature of Federal Bankruptcy Jurisdiction: A General Statutory and Constitutional Theory*, 41 WM. & MARY L. REV. 743 (2000), Brubaker expands on his prior study and takes on an even more ambitious challenge—explaining the fundamental nature of bankruptcy jurisdiction. In particular, he seeks to ascertain and explain the outer limits of federal "related to" jurisdiction in bankruptcy—and demonstrates why the current "received wisdom" on that question is deeply flawed. Brubaker reconceptualizes the federal bankruptcy jurisdictional grant in a clear, workable manner. He also demonstrates why the furor over the exercise of supplemental jurisdiction in bankruptcy is misguided and unnecessary. This article is surely destined to become the definitive analysis on bankruptcy jurisdiction.

Ralph Brubaker
One Hundred Years of Federal Bankruptcy Law and Still Clinging to an In Rem *Model of Bankruptcy Jurisdiction*
15 BANKR. DEV. J. 261 (1999)*

I. INTRODUCTION

. . . Perhaps no other aspect of bankruptcy law remains as steeped in historical esoterica as does jurisdiction. Historical concepts retain a very heavy influence on bankruptcy jurisdiction. . . .

. . . [F]ederal bankruptcy jurisdiction is, very much, a product of its history. In fact, for most purposes the only meaningful way to explain bankruptcy jurisdiction is to explain the history of bankruptcy jurisdiction.

This essay sketches the historical development of bankruptcy jurisdiction . . . . This historical lens reveals an anomalous *in rem* slant that persists in federal bankruptcy jurisdiction, despite both clear congressional intent to rid bankruptcy jurisdiction of *in rem* strictures and significant deleterious consequences for the efficacy of federal bankruptcy litigation.

II. THE ENGLISH *IN REM* MODEL OF BANKRUPTCY JURISDICTION

American bankruptcy jurisdiction, of course, developed from an English system, which itself had quite a history. The English model of a jurisdiction in bankruptcy was, very explicitly, an *in rem*, property-based jurisdiction—centered around the construct of a bankrupt's "estate." The English bankruptcy commissioners, who exercised bankruptcy jurisdiction under the supervision of the Lord Chancellor in Equity, had jurisdiction over administration of the bankrupt's estate, for ultimate distribution to the bankrupt's creditors. As part of the administration of the estate, the commissioners could, inter alia, pass on the validity of creditors' claims.

This English version of bankruptcy jurisdiction, however, was limited to jurisdiction over a debtor's property that actually found its way into the hands of the commissioners and the estate's representative, the assignee in bankruptcy . . . . Thus, if a determination was required to ascertain whether property belonged in the bankrupt's estate, there was no "bankruptcy" jurisdiction, as such, over the matter. . . .

So we see in the English model a bifurcation of jurisdiction. There was *in rem* jurisdiction over property rightfully in the possession of the estate, and bankruptcy jurisdiction extended to administration of that property for the benefit of the bankrupt's creditors. If an assignee were required to sue someone to recover money or property *for* the estate, however, there was no "bankruptcy" jurisdiction at all; such an action required an ordinary formal suit in the appropriate court.

III. THE EARLY AMERICAN MODEL OF A GENERAL FEDERAL BANKRUPTCY JURISDICTION

In establishing federal bankruptcy law, early American bankruptcy statutes (prior to the 1898 Act) also conferred bankruptcy jurisdiction on the federal courts. Operative language in both the Bankruptcy Act of 1841 and the Bankruptcy Act of 1867 contained nearly identical grants of federal jurisdiction over "all matters and proceedings in bankruptcy." Of course, if that statutory reference to "bankruptcy proceedings" were limited to the English notion of "bankruptcy proceedings," it would exclude an assignee's suits to recover money or property *for* the estate. But determining the scope of *federal* bankruptcy jurisdiction (vis-á-vis the jurisdiction of the state courts) implicates an issue of judicial federalism that was unknown to the English system. And Justice Story placed a uniquely American spin on the idea of a *federal* jurisdiction over "bankruptcy proceedings" in a couple of early opinions construing the 1841 Act—one while riding circuit in his capacity as a Circuit Justice, and the second in the Supreme Court case of *Ex parte Christy*.

For Justice Story, the construct of the bankrupt's "estate" remained central to bankruptcy jurisdiction, just as it had in England. But Story's concept of *federal* bankruptcy jurisdiction was not the equivalent of English bankruptcy jurisdiction. . . . Justice Story construed *federal* jurisdiction over "proceedings in bankruptcy" to encompass "all cases where the rights, claims, and property of the bankrupt, or those of his assignee, are concerned, since they are matters arising under the act, and are necessarily involved in the due administration and settlement of the bankrupt's estate." According to Justice Story, then, *federal* jurisdiction over "bankruptcy proceedings" extends to "the ascertainment and adjustment of all claims and rights in favor of or against the bankrupt's estate."

Thus, in our federal system of dual sovereigns with both state and federal courts, the American model of "bankruptcy" jurisdiction was established, through the early American bankruptcy statutes, as that of a general *federal* bankruptcy jurisdiction over any claim to which a bankruptcy estate is a party, whether that claim is made by or against the estate.

IV. THE 1898 ACT'S REVIVAL OF THE *IN REM* MODEL OF BANKRUPTCY JURISDICTION

The more expansive model of a general federal bankruptcy jurisdiction over all claims by and against a bankruptcy estate, under the 1841 and 1867 Acts, was seen as a concomitant to effectual and efficient administration of bankruptcy estates. This jurisdictional scheme, however, produced a persistent tension between the federal interest in estate administration and the localized interests of particular litigants, witnesses, and attorneys, who often found the federal forum inconvenient as compared with state courts. . . . And in the making of the first bankruptcy statute in the era of "permanent" bankruptcy law, the 1898 Act, there were widely-held "states' rights" misgivings about conferring too much power on the federal courts, especially amongst Southerners, who deeply disdained the "carpetbagging" federal judges. The 1898 Act, therefore, responded to this animosity toward a general federal jurisdiction over "all matters and proceedings in bankruptcy" by narrowing the compass of federal bankruptcy jurisdiction.

The 1898 Act reduced the sweep of federal bankruptcy jurisdiction essentially through a return to the English *in rem* model of bankruptcy jurisdiction, in the now-infamous summary/plenary jurisdictional dichotomy erected by the 1898 Act. Under the 1898 Act, there was summary *in rem* jurisdiction in the federal courts to adjudicate all disputes incident to administration of property in the actual or constructive possession of the court (through its officer, the bankruptcy trustee), and this summary *in rem* jurisdiction included adjudication of all creditors' claims against the estate. There was no summary *in rem* jurisdiction, however, over trustees' suits to recover money or property for the estate—so-called plenary suits against "adverse claimants"—and that is the means by which the 1898 Act curtailed federal bankruptcy jurisdiction. The 1898 Act restricted federal jurisdiction over a trustee's plenary *in personam* suits.

In our federal system, then, absence of federal jurisdiction over a trustee's plenary *in personam* suits meant, for the most part, that the trustee had to bring such suits in state court. That was not universally true, though, because in limited instances the 1898 Act expressly granted the federal courts bankruptcy jurisdiction over a trustee's plenary *in personam* suits. . . . And in corporate reorganization proceedings, *any* plenary suit . . . could be pursued in federal court as part of the "bankruptcy proceedings." In fact, it was in that very context, a corporate reorganization case, that the Supreme Court, in the momentous decision in *Williams v. Austrian*, reaffirmed Justice Story's broad view of the concept of federal "bankruptcy proceedings." The concept of a federal jurisdiction in "bankruptcy proceedings" endured as a general federal jurisdiction over all claims by and against the bankruptcy estate, including a trustee's plenary suit to recover money or property from an adverse claimant . . . .

The legacy of the 1898 Act's jurisdictional scheme, therefore, is a rather complicated amalgam of both the English *in rem* model of bankruptcy jurisdiction and Justice Story's conception of a general federal bankruptcy jurisdiction over all claims by and against a bankruptcy estate. The 1898 Act is probably most well-known for its *in rem* jurisdiction, but the 1898 Act clearly contained elements of a broader *in personam* rationale for federal bankruptcy jurisdiction.

V. Our Current System: Pervasive Federal Bankruptcy Jurisdiction?

One of the primary targets of the bankruptcy reform efforts of the 1970s, of course, was the 1898 Act's *in rem* jurisdictional scheme. The federalism concerns that motivated the 1898 Act's restrictive federal bankruptcy jurisdiction had subsided considerably and, consequently, were dwarfed by the manifest inefficiencies and inequities produced by the summary/plenary dichotomy and its splintering of bankruptcy jurisdiction. The jurisdictional provisions of the resulting Bankruptcy Reform Act of 1978 were variously characterized in Congress as: "pervasive," "complete," "comprehensive," "as broad [a] jurisdiction as possible," and "as broad as can be conceived." This pervasive federal bankruptcy jurisdiction was explicitly designed to eliminate the summary/plenary dichotomy and its *in rem* confines, permitting the federal courts to "exercise in personam as well as *in rem* jurisdiction in order that they may handle everything that arises in a bankruptcy case."

Unfortunately, however, we are yet to fully realize this vision of complete, unrestricted *in personam* federal bankruptcy jurisdiction. A significant stumbling block standing in the way of full *in personam* bankruptcy jurisdiction is Congress's decision to not make the bankruptcy courts Article III courts. After the *Marathon* case and the ensuing Bankruptcy Amendments and Federal Judgeship Act (BAFJA) of 1984, we are left with federal bankruptcy jurisdiction that is divided between the non-Article III bankruptcy courts and the federal district courts, and that division predominately follows the lines of the 1898 Act's summary/plenary dichotomy which, of course, itself originated in the English *in rem* model of bankruptcy jurisdiction. That is an *in rem* aspect of bankruptcy jurisdiction with which we must suffer, however, at least until it becomes politically feasible to elevate the bankruptcy courts to Article III status. The objective of this essay, though, is to explore a less obvious realm of bankruptcy jurisdiction that remains haunted by *in rem* ghosts: the outermost limits of federal bankruptcy jurisdiction.

Marathon and the 1984 BAFJA amendments were concerned with an issue of separation of powers, and *Marathon*'s proscription, at its most basic level, was that the entirety of the 1978 Reform Act's pervasive federal bankruptcy jurisdiction cannot be assigned to non-Article III bankruptcy courts. That separation-of-powers holding speaks solely to the proper allocation of federal bankruptcy jurisdiction as between Article III and non-Article III federal tribunals. *Marathon* and BAFJA, however, say nothing about the issue traced in this essay's historical overview, which pertains to the *scope* of federal bankruptcy jurisdiction. Irrespective of the type of federal judicial officer that will exercise it (Article III or non-Article III), what is the full extent of federal bankruptcy jurisdiction?

The scope of federal bankruptcy jurisdiction is, of course, a judicial federalism issue going to the allocation of judicial power as between the federal courts and the state courts. What disputes can we essentially take from the state courts and place before the federal courts through our pervasive federal bankruptcy jurisdiction? This essay . . . suggest[s] that the scope of federal bankruptcy jurisdiction has been unnecessarily constricted by lingering *in rem* jurisdictional notions. . . .

B. *Constructing an* In Personam *Model of "Related To" Bankruptcy Jurisdiction*

A true *in personam* approach to bankruptcy jurisdiction would comprehend the bankruptcy estate as more than a mere jurisdictional res; such an *in personam* model would view the bankruptcy estate as a jurisdictional person, in the same manner that a corporation is considered a jurisdictional person. . . . Constructing the juridical person simplifies Byzantine relationships, including jurisdictional and joinder complexities, and to that end, the Bankruptcy Code expressly authorizes the bankruptcy estate to sue and be sued as an entity.

If we regard the bankruptcy estate as a federally created legal entity, rather than a jurisdictional *res*, then Justice Story's conception of a general federal bankruptcy jurisdiction over all claims by and against a bankruptcy estate is not an *in rem* jurisdiction over claims connected to the *res*; general federal bankruptcy jurisdiction is *in personam* jurisdiction over all claims by and against our jurisdictional person—the "bankruptcy estate." When we think about federal bankruptcy jurisdiction in those terms, "related to" jurisdiction over third-party claims is simply a grant of conventional supplemental jurisdiction. . . .

C. *Defending the Constitutionality of an* In Personam *Model of Federal Bankruptcy Jurisdiction*

. . . The *in rem* model also pervades popular theory of the constitutionality of federal bankruptcy jurisdiction. An *in personam* model of federal bankruptcy jurisdiction, however, finds support in the most orthodox and established of constitutional theories of federal jurisdiction. . . .

When we envisage the bankruptcy estate as a federally created entity, rather than a mere jurisdictional *res*, a very different constitutional theory of federal bankruptcy jurisdiction emerges. Mr. Chief Justice Marshall's venerable opinion in *Osborn v. Bank of the United States* teaches that federal law is an "original ingredient" in any claim by or against a juridical person created by federal law. Consequently, any such claim by or against a federally created entity is one "arising under . . . the Laws of the United States" within the meaning of Article III and, therefore, has an independent constitutional basis for federal jurisdiction as a constitutional federal question.

General federal bankruptcy jurisdiction, then, as originally articulated by Justice Story—a power to hear all claims by and against the bankruptcy estate—is nothing more than an *Osborn* federal entity approach to bankruptcy jurisdiction. . . .

An *in personam* model of federal bankruptcy jurisdiction, thus, demarcates the constitutional bounds of federal bankruptcy jurisdiction by attributing a general federal bankruptcy jurisdiction over all claims by and against a bankruptcy estate to Article III's federal question category. This general federal bankruptcy jurisdiction then sustains federal jurisdiction over any third-party claim "related to" a claim by or against the estate—with that relationship measured by a conventional supplemental jurisdictional nexus.

VI. CONCLUSION

History provides us with two models of bankruptcy jurisdiction—an *in rem* model and an *in personam* model—and much of the history of federal bankruptcy jurisdiction can be understood as vacillation between those two models. If we now truly lived in a world of full *in personam* bankruptcy jurisdiction, as Congress evidently intended in granting the federal courts pervasive bankruptcy jurisdiction, then our third-party "related to" bankruptcy jurisdiction would be considered a grant of conventional supplemental jurisdiction. . . . At the same time, construing third-party "related to" bankruptcy jurisdiction as supplemental jurisdiction would fully effectuate Congress's design for a fair and efficient, pervasive federal bankruptcy jurisdiction.

Ralph Brubaker
On the Nature of Federal Bankruptcy Jurisdiction:
A General Statutory and Constitutional Theory
41 WM. & MARY L. REV. 743 (2000)[*]

INTRODUCTION

. . . Bankruptcy . . . is a substantial and significant component of the charge of the federal courts. Yet, the jurisdiction in bankruptcy remains one of the most enduring puzzles of our federal court system. Congress, of course, has plenary legislative power "on the subject of Bankruptcies." For the most part, however, creditors' and debtors' rights and obligations in bankruptcy are governed by state law, not federal law. For example, a creditor may assert a right to payment from a debtor founded upon a disputed state-law cause of action. Likewise, among the debtor's assets, to which the creditors lay claim, may be similar state-law causes of the debtor against others. Bankruptcy brings all such state-law disputes into federal court, but without any diversity-of-citizenship requisite, and thus, the constitutional source of this federal "judicial Power" is not at all self-evident. The Supreme Court consistently has confirmed the propriety of the federal jurisdiction in bankruptcy, but has been cryptic, parsimonious, and inconsistent in its explanations of this judicial province.

The Supreme Court's abstruseness is, of course, fuel for the scholarly engine, and bankruptcy has become the seemingly inscrutable crucible of federal jurisdiction theory. In fact, because it is not easily explained by traditional theory, most scholars rely upon bankruptcy to buttress novel and unconventional departures that would accommodate the apparent anomaly of federal bankruptcy jurisdiction. These efforts, however, have not grappled with the parallel and equally bedeviling problem of charting the outermost bounds of the statutory grant of federal bankruptcy jurisdiction, which contemplates a federal forum for any proceeding "related to" a bankruptcy case. This provision for pervasive federal bankruptcy jurisdiction is the most extensive in our history, and indeed, was designed to be as broad as the Constitution permits. The extant jurisdictional structure, therefore, provides a contextual framework that proves critical for testing constitutional theories of federal bankruptcy jurisdiction.

In the absence of clear constitutional guidance, jurisprudential demarcation of the content of the statutory grant, not surprisingly, has been chaotic. In fact, the case law has developed in a vacuum-like separation from constitutional principles that would define the reach of federal bankruptcy jurisdiction. This disconnect is aggravated by the literal breadth of the statute itself, which on its face extends to any dispute, even one wholly between third parties and not directly involving the debtor nor the debtor's bankruptcy estate, but that nonetheless is in some manner "related to" the debtor's bankruptcy case. The dominant test for "related to" bankruptcy jurisdiction in such a third-party dispute, the so-called *Pacor* test, merely asks "whether the outcome of that [third-party] proceeding could conceivably have any effect on the estate being administered in bankruptcy."

. . . *Pacor* is manifestly inadequate, as it simply provides no principled limits for third-party "related to" bankruptcy jurisdiction. . . . In fact, *Pacor* has produced a state of affairs in which jurisdictional determinations are essentially arbitrary—with countless instances of identical factual and procedural postures producing diametrically disparate results on nominal application of the same "test."

The daunting disarray of the case law cries out for a new approach, and this Article proffers a comprehensive, unifying statutory and constitutional theory that would vastly simplify and bring principled limits to third-party "related to" bankruptcy jurisdiction. Given the intended expanse of that provision, the limits of "related to" bankruptcy jurisdiction are constitutional limits. The search for a sensible solution to the statutory conundrum of federal bankruptcy jurisdiction, therefore, becomes meaningful only if it is explicitly coupled with a coherent constitutional explanation for our federal bankruptcy jurisdiction—an explanation that has eluded both courts and scholars. . . .

. . .This Article . . . approaches interpretation of the grant of federal bankruptcy jurisdiction as a multifaceted historical inquiry that must begin by exploring statutory antecedents. From this historical understanding, we then can fashion a reconciliation with the Constitution's provisions for federal judicial power and comparable congressional conferrals of the same. The result is a comprehensive theory of federal bankruptcy jurisdiction that integrates constitutional theory with an interpretive theory for the bankruptcy jurisdiction statute. . . .

III. A STATUTORY THEORY OF FEDERAL BANKRUPTCY JURISDICTION

If we combine [our] constitutional theory of federal bankruptcy jurisdiction . . . with the history of American bankruptcy jurisdiction . . ., a theory for interpreting the current jurisdictional statute emerges. Only through this historical, constitutional prism can we compensate for the skew that the *Marathon* case has placed upon the meaning of the jurisdictional statute, recognize the serious errors of the *Pacor* opinion and its seemingly indelible imprint upon "related to" bankruptcy jurisdiction, account for the glaring contradictions in the case law of third-party "related to" bankruptcy jurisdiction, and understand the impetus behind and senselessness of the raging debate over so-called supplemental bankruptcy jurisdiction. . . .

A. Deconstructing the Bankruptcy Jurisdiction Statute

Consistent with the premise . . . that the conceptual jurisdictional unit in bankruptcy is an individual "proceeding" rather than the bankruptcy "case," the methodology employed in this Part III.A utilizes the three nexuses contained in the bankruptcy jurisdiction statute—"arising under," "arising in," and "related to"—to identify those "claims" that each type of proceeding was designed to envelop. This approach, of course, also proceeds from the assumption that the bankruptcy jurisdiction statute operates in the same fashion as all other federal jurisdiction statutes: "[O]riginal jurisdiction attaches on a claim-by-claim or 'claim-specific' basis." This Article departs from the prevailing analysis of bankruptcy's jurisdictional nexuses, though, because it is employed for a very different purpose.

The statute's jurisdictional nexuses have evolved into catachrestic compartments that mark the boundaries between the limited jurisdiction of non-Article III bankruptcy judges and the residual authority of the Article III district courts. The nexuses could not have been designed for such a purpose, however, as their original function was to vest the entirety of this federal jurisdiction in non-Article III bankruptcy judges, and the ex post separation of powers gloss impedes the task at hand, which is delineating the outer bounds of federal bankruptcy jurisdiction—implicating principles of judicial federalism rather than separation of powers. In particular, we seek to capture the elusive meaning of the statutory grant of "related to" jurisdiction in third-party disputes. For that purpose, then, we must reinvent bankruptcy's jurisdictional nexuses, through an experimental interpretive exercise. . . .

1. Marathon's Transmogrification of "Related to" Jurisdiction

A statutory theory of federal bankruptcy jurisdiction for purposes of exploring the outermost limits of federal jurisdiction (vis-á-vis that of the state courts) must begin with a recognition that the basic grant of federal jurisdiction over "arising under," "arising in," and "related to" proceedings was constructed in the 1978 Reform Act, long before the *Marathon* holding necessitated the complicated allocation of that jurisdiction between the district courts and their adjunct bankruptcy courts in the 1984 BAFJA amendments. Although *Marathon* and BAFJA contemplated no change whatsoever in the sum total of federal bankruptcy jurisdiction, they have nonetheless converted the statute's three jurisdictional nexuses into terms of art that draw a divide in this federal bankruptcy jurisdiction between: (1) "core" proceedings "arising under" or "arising in," in which a bankruptcy judge can enter final orders, and (2) noncore "related to" proceedings, in which only a district court can enter final orders absent consent of the parties to a bankruptcy court adjudication. This separation of powers function of the jurisdictional nexuses has yielded the unwitting, unnatural, and unnoticed side effect of obfuscating the intended reach and supplemental nature of "related to" bankruptcy jurisdiction.

Marathon declared the bankruptcy estate's suits on a debtor's state-law actions to be beyond the constitutional capacity for final adjudication by a limited tenure, non-Article III bankruptcy judge. In so doing, Justice Brennan's plurality opinion repeatedly depicted such an action by the bankruptcy estate as falling within the "related to" jurisdictional grant of the 1978 Reform Act. Subsequently, then, "related to" became the jurisdictional category in which the 1984 BAFJA amendments restricted the powers of the non-Article III bankruptcy judges. Accordingly, the Court recently characterized "related to" bankruptcy jurisdiction as including two types of actions: (1) *Marathon*-like "causes of action owned by the debtor which become property of the estate . . . and (2) suits between third parties which have an effect on the bankruptcy estate."

When viewed in historical context, however, the all-encompassing, pervasive "related to" bankruptcy jurisdiction was not necessary to authorize the bankruptcy estate to pursue a *Marathon*-like action in federal court. . . . [A] general federal bankruptcy jurisdiction over all claims by and against the bankruptcy estate under both the 1841 and 1867 Acts was established with "arising under" and "in bankruptcy" terminology, alone, and nothing that even resembled "related" jurisdiction. Likewise, under the 1898 Act such a general federal bankruptcy jurisdiction in corporate reorganization cases was accomplished with a simple reference to "bankruptcy proceedings" and "proceedings under this [1898] Act." The broader "related" language of section 2a(7) of the 1898 Act, in conjunction with and as constrained by section 2a(6), were the vehicles for the narrow "necessity" jurisdiction of certain third-party disputes.

As recognized in the 1978 Reform Act's legislative process, then, the primary significance of the "related to" grant was to bring "related" *third-party* disputes into federal court. Although it was unnecessary to specify the precise jurisdictional nexus for an estate's suits before *Marathon*, the estate's action in *Marathon*, nevertheless, could easily be characterized as a proceeding "arising in" the debtor's bankruptcy case, since an action by the bankruptcy estate itself is, in the words of Justice Story, "necessarily involved in the due administration and settlement of the bankrupt's estate." Thus, if we put aside the separation of powers concerns of *Marathon* and BAFJA and, for the moment, read bankruptcy's jurisdictional nexuses solely through our historical lens of judicial federalism, a *Marathon* action by a bankruptcy estate is an "arising in" proceeding, *not* a "related to" proceeding.

2. Reconstructing Bankruptcy's Jurisdictional Nexuses

Placing Marathon actions in the "arising in" category, rather than the "related to" category, means that "arising under" and "arising in" proceedings are synonymous with all constitutional federal questions in bankruptcy, and "related to" bankruptcy jurisdiction is conventional supplemental jurisdiction over third-party disputes "related to" these constitutional federal questions.

a. "Arising Under" and "Arising in" Proceedings: Constitutional Federal Questions

If a *Marathon* action is an "arising in" proceeding, as suggested by the history of American bankruptcy jurisdiction, then federal jurisdiction over all proceedings "arising in" a bankruptcy case equates nicely with the historical and constitutional concept of a general federal bankruptcy jurisdiction over all claims by and against a bankruptcy estate. Our constitutional theory tells us that this general federal bankruptcy jurisdiction of claims by and against the estate is *constitutional* federal question jurisdiction under an *Osborn* federal entity theory.

Under this view, then, the bankruptcy version of *statutory* federal question jurisdiction—jurisdiction over proceedings "arising under" the Bankruptcy Code—assures a federal bankruptcy forum for federally created, conventional federal question claims that do *not* directly involve the estate, such as those concerning an individual debtor's discharge of indebtedness. . . .

Thus, if we remove the separation of powers influence from the bankruptcy jurisdiction statute, "arising under" and "arising in" bankruptcy jurisdiction can be seen as grants of federal jurisdiction over all constitutional federal question claims that arise during a bankruptcy case—those involving bankruptcy causes of action and those involving the bankruptcy estate. The most revealing aspect of this exercise, however, is its effect upon construction of the broadest of bankruptcy's jurisdictional categories—"related to" bankruptcy proceedings.

b. "Related to" Proceedings: Supplemental Jurisdiction over Third-Party Disputes

If "arising under" proceedings account for all claims under bankruptcy causes of action and "arising in" proceedings subsume all claims to which a bankruptcy estate is party, then the unique role of bankruptcy's "related to" jurisdiction is in the realm of claims that do *not* "arise under" the Bankruptcy Code, such as state-law claims, and to which the bankruptcy estate is *not* a party. Our constitutional theory tells us that federal bankruptcy jurisdiction over such third-party state-law claims is a species of supplemental jurisdiction.

This interpretation of "related to" proceedings not only finds support in the 1978 Reform Act's legislative history, it also accords with common usage of the jurisdictional nomenclature of "related" proceedings. In the isolated instances in which Congress has sought to expressly create supplemental jurisdiction, it has used the "related" terminology, and to the extent that a grant of "related" jurisdiction has a plain or ordinary meaning, it is recognized as connoting supplemental jurisdiction. Furthermore, the symbiosis between pervasive "related to" bankruptcy jurisdiction and bankruptcy's discretionary, permissive abstention "in the interest of justice, or in the interest of comity with State courts or respect for State law" replicates that of supplemental jurisdiction, which likewise "is a doctrine of discretion" informed by "the values of judicial economy, convenience, fairness, and comity in order to decide whether to exercise jurisdiction." Indeed, Professor Kennedy, who served as Executive Director of the 1973 Commission and who was an active participant in the congressional process for the 1978 Reform Act, contemporaneously opined that "related to" jurisdiction of third-party disputes "requires a consideration of the potential reach of a concept or doctrine of ancillary jurisdiction."

This revisionist version of bankruptcy's jurisdictional nexuses, thus, views (1) "arising under" jurisdiction as including federally created bankruptcy claims, whether or not the estate is a party, (2) "arising in" jurisdiction as all claims to which the bankruptcy estate is a party, and (3) "related to" jurisdiction as supplemental jurisdiction over third-party claims. Of course, this view differs significantly from the popular version of the jurisdictional nexuses only insofar as it casts a *Marathon* action as an "arising in" rather than a "related to" proceeding. The object of this exercise, however, is *not* an attempt to relabel *Marathon* actions, which now will be forever coupled with "related to" bankruptcy jurisdiction as codified by BAFJA. For purposes of determining those core proceedings that can be finally adjudicated by a non-Article III bankruptcy court, a *Marathon* action cannot be considered a core "arising in" proceeding and must be characterized as a noncore "related to" proceeding; nothing in this analysis is meant to suggest otherwise. Again, though, that separation of powers concern is not the focus of this Article, which addresses only the judicial federalism dimension of "related to" jurisdiction, regarding the reach of *federal* bankruptcy jurisdiction. The troublesome aspect of "related to" jurisdiction in determining the scope of federal bankruptcy jurisdiction is *third-party* "related to" jurisdiction, *not Marathon* jurisdiction. *Marathon* actions are unquestionably a component of federal bankruptcy jurisdiction, whether categorized as "arising in" or "related to" proceedings. The modest ambition of this analytical deconstruction, that hypothetically recharacterizes Marathon actions as "arising in" proceedings, is merely to correct widely held misconceptions regarding the supplemental nature of "related to" bankruptcy jurisdiction, *solely* in an effort to properly construe the parameters of *third-party* "related to" jurisdiction.

From the standpoint of judicial federalism and the scope of federal bankruptcy jurisdiction, classifying a *Marathon* action as a "related to" proceeding is misleading only when combined with the proposition that "related to" jurisdiction is a form of supplemental jurisdiction. As our constitutional theory demonstrates, *Marathon* claims are *not* supplemental claims; a *Marathon* claim is a freestanding constitutional federal question claim. The insinuation of *Marathon* claims into the "related to" category, to the extent this carries the implication that *Marathon* claims are supplemental claims, actually perpetuates the misplaced in rem receivership model of supplemental bankruptcy jurisdiction, and Part III.D of this Article demonstrates how this has confounded analysis of "supplemental" bankruptcy jurisdiction. The *only* "related to" claims that are properly considered supplemental are *third-party* "related to" claims.

The other virtue of this alternative, experimental rendering of bankruptcy's jurisdictional nexuses is that it clarifies the appropriate relationship necessary for an exercise of third-party "related to" jurisdiction. The statutory grant affords "jurisdiction of all civil proceedings . . . related to [bankruptcy] cases," which of course, requires some conception of the bankruptcy "case" and how the proceeding is "related to" the bankruptcy case. If a *Marathon* claim is "related to" a bankruptcy case, then it must be because the claim has the potential to enhance the bankruptcy estate—a formulation very much in accord with an in rem jurisdictional model and the dominant outcome-oriented, functional test for third-party "related to" bankruptcy jurisdiction. A bankruptcy "case" within the meaning of the jurisdictional statute, however, is merely a collective reference to all of the civil "proceedings" associated with a particular debtor's bankruptcy filing. A proceeding "related to" the "case," then, is one that is "related to" another proceeding in the case, and supplemental jurisdiction theory tells us that both our (1) "arising under" bankruptcy claims and (2) "arising in" estate-as-a-party claims are freestanding constitutional federal questions that will sustain supplemental jurisdiction over (3) "related" third-party claims. Thus, rethinking the jurisdictional nexuses, freed from BAFJA's separation of powers taint, replaces the outcome-oriented, functional test for third-party "related to" bankruptcy jurisdiction, which has proven so unmanageable, with a conventional supplemental jurisdiction test.

Hence, the key interpretive insight that springs from this Article's comprehensive, unifying constitutional and statutory theory of federal bankruptcy jurisdiction is *not* in regard to *Marathon* actions; rather, it is in the solution this theory yields for the statutory interpretation quandary presented by the seemingly limitless "related to" bankruptcy jurisdiction over third-party disputes. Stripped of the hypothetical, revisionist nexus labels used in its derivation, the interpretive theory propounded by this Article is that a third-party claim should be considered "related to" a debtor's bankruptcy case if it shares a conventional supplemental linkage with either (1) a claim asserted under a cause of action created by the Bankruptcy Code, or (2) a claim asserted by or against the debtor's bankruptcy estate. Equipped with this more accurate understanding of the supplemental nature of federal bankruptcy jurisdiction in third-party disputes, one can readily appreciate how and why the extant jurisprudence of third-party "related to" bankruptcy jurisdiction has gone awry. This

Article's interpretive theory also brings a thoroughly illuminating perspective to the cognate struggle with so-called supplemental bankruptcy jurisdiction.

B. Pacor's *Mutilation of Third-Party "Related to" Jurisdiction*

One of the first circuit-level cases to grapple with "related to" bankruptcy jurisdiction in a third-party dispute was the Third Circuit's opinion in *Pacor, Inc. v. Higgins*. Although the *Pacor* court boldly announced what would become the almost universally accepted standard for third-party "related to" bankruptcy jurisdiction, its opinion transparently displays the contradictory impulses that portend the ensuing havoc that the *Pacor* test has wrought.

Pacor is fundamentally at odds with the interpretive theory developed in this Article. The thesis of this Article is that third-party "related to" bankruptcy jurisdiction *is* supplemental jurisdiction; *Pacor* says that third-party "related to" bankruptcy jurisdiction is *not* supplemental jurisdiction. *Pacor*, though, has been widely influential in the courts and commentary as the unquestioned, eminent authority on third-party "related to" bankruptcy jurisdiction. Thus, the remainder of this Article will take great pains to discredit *Pacor* and demonstrate not only that its test should be abandoned, but for all practical purposes, that has already occurred. Given the disheartening disorder of the decisions, the real issue is formulating a suitable replacement test that accommodates all of the underlying tensions in the case law, which is the object of the interpretive theory proposed in this Article.

. . . *Pacor* recognized but did not deal with the constitutional implications of third-party "related to" bankruptcy jurisdiction. In fact, *Pacor*'s functional "conceivable effect" test has such conceptual vastness that it is almost certainly unconstitutionally overreaching. *Pacor* expressly rejected principles of supplemental jurisdiction as a curb on third-party "related to" bankruptcy jurisdiction. *Pacor*'s hostility to supplemental jurisdiction, though, can be attributed to both a fundamental misunderstanding of bankruptcy law and a misreading of the Supreme Court's misgivings about general supplemental jurisdiction doctrine. Thus, while *Pacor* also recognized the adjudicative efficiency goals of "related to" bankruptcy jurisdiction, it needlessly ignored the contributions that supplemental jurisdiction holds in that regard, opting instead for an outcome-oriented, functional test that is not designed to facilitate such efficiencies. *Pacor* attempted to confine the expanse of third-party "related to" jurisdiction with an ill-conceived "automatic liability" principle that has fertilized jurisdictional litigation and that is inconsistent with the flexibility built into the jurisdictional structure through the abstention provisions.

The ultimate contradiction in *Pacor* . . . is that its test *is* a supplemental jurisdiction test, but an anachronistic in rem test that precludes modern in personam principles of supplemental jurisdiction. Furthermore, the *Pacor* test is a gauche in rem test that negates some of the most basic in rem functions of bankruptcy jurisdiction. In the end, then, *Pacor* discredits itself; third-party "related to" bankruptcy jurisdiction *is* supplemental jurisdiction even under the *Pacor* test, and there is no legitimate basis on which to restrict it to an in rem supplemental relationship. Third-party "related to" bankruptcy jurisdiction must be recognized as a form of both in rem and in personam supplemental jurisdiction. . . .

D. *Erasing the Line Between "Related to" and "Supplemental" Bankruptcy Jurisdiction*

Subsequent case law has tacitly refused to follow *Pacor*'s disavowal of third-party "related to" bankruptcy jurisdiction as a grant of supplemental jurisdiction. The migration of third-party "related to" bankruptcy jurisdiction toward both in rem and in personam versions of supplemental jurisdiction seems clear. Nonetheless, the courts' failure to challenge the *Pacor* opinion outright, and indeed their unthinking repetition of *Pacor*'s platitudes, has produced a third-party "related to" bankruptcy jurisdiction that is, at best, only a crude and incomplete form of supplemental jurisdiction. The jurisdictional frictions lying in *Pacor*'s wake have also manifested in what is now cast as a distinct doctrine of "supplemental" bankruptcy jurisdiction, which has stirred quite a controversy with considerable aid from Professor Block-Lieb's critical commentary.

So-called supplemental bankruptcy jurisdiction is a direct outgrowth of *Pacor*'s declaration that third-party "related to" bankruptcy jurisdiction is *not* supplemental jurisdiction. That conclusion, of course, leads to the further inquiry as to whether bankruptcy courts nonetheless can exercise supplemental jurisdiction as an incident to their statutory bankruptcy jurisdiction. Thus, when confronted with third-party disputes to which *Pacor* affords no "related to" bankruptcy jurisdiction, but that arise in contexts in which federal courts have routinely resorted to supplemental jurisdiction, many bankruptcy courts have done the same.

Take, for example, a suit commenced in bankruptcy court by a bankruptcy trustee or debtor-in-possession against several codefendants. . . . The propriety of federal bankruptcy jurisdiction over the estate's claims against the defendants is, of course, beyond doubt. Claims under bankruptcy causes of action would come within the bankruptcy court's "arising under" bankruptcy jurisdiction, and state-law claims could be entertained through either "arising in" or "related to" bankruptcy jurisdiction.

If a defendant in the estate's adversary proceeding were to make a state-law cross-claim against a codefendant for contribution or indemnification, joinder of such a cross-claim in the same action would be permissible under the transactional joinder standard of Rule 13(g). Unlike the estate's claims against the defendants, however, this cross-claim would be a third-party dispute that is *not* within "related to" bankruptcy jurisdiction under the *Pacor* test.

Consider also a defendant's third-party impleader of a state-law contribution or indemnification claim against a new third-party defendant under Rule 14(a). Nearly one hundred years ago, in *Bryan v. Bernheimer*, the Supreme Court intimated that there ought to be room for federal bankruptcy jurisdiction over such a third-party impleader claim, even under the 1898 Act's more restrictive third-party "related" jurisdiction, as a matter of simple fairness to the defendant haled into federal court. Nevertheless, according to the *Pacor* test, such a third-party impleader claim finds itself outside the bounds of the current statute's unqualified third-party "related to" bankruptcy jurisdiction, because the possibility of a defendant recouping sums paid to the estate from a codefendant or a third party has no bearing at all on the estate's anterior claim against the defendant. In fact, such a third-party claim for contribution or indemnification presupposes that the bankruptcy estate has already successfully recovered from the defendant, and the third-party claim merely reallocates ultimate responsibility for that recovery.

Rule 13 cross-claims and Rule 14 impleader claims, though, are a common context for the invocation of supplemental jurisdiction, because the federal courts have tended to equate the *Gibbs* "common nucleus of operative fact" supplemental nexus with the Federal Rules' "same transaction or occurrence" joinder standard. Thus, there is considerable authority holding that federal bankruptcy courts, likewise, can exercise supplemental jurisdiction over properly joined third-party claims in such an adversary proceeding, as an incident to their federal bankruptcy jurisdiction over the claims asserted by the bankruptcy estate. As stated by one court, "[w]e can perceive no reason why a bankruptcy court cannot exercise pendent jurisdiction and hear non-federal claims raised in a proceeding before it, in the same fashion as any other federal court."

Aldinger v. Howard, Finley v. United States, and the subsequent 1990 supplemental jurisdiction statute, however, point up the need to find statutory approbation for supplemental jurisdiction over such third-party claims, and . . . a host of both statutory and constitutional objections to this "supplemental" bankruptcy jurisdiction have now appeared. The tussle over so-called supplemental bankruptcy jurisdiction, however, actually reinforces the true supplemental nature of third-party "related to" bankruptcy jurisdiction and punctuates the remarkably misguided ferment of *Pacor*'s reign. When the illusive divide between "related to" and "supplemental" bankruptcy jurisdiction is destroyed, statutory and constitutional clouds over supplemental bankruptcy jurisdiction vanish, revealing a self-contained bankruptcy jurisdiction statute, for which resort to any auxiliary source of "supplemental" bankruptcy jurisdiction is entirely unnecessary and counterproductive.

1. The Irrelevance of the Supplemental Jurisdiction Statute

Relying upon the supplemental jurisdiction statute for "supplemental" bankruptcy jurisdiction is troublesome, because that statute gives no jurisdictional authority to the non-Article III bankruptcy courts in which all bankruptcy litigation originates. It is not necessary, however, to resort to the supplemental jurisdiction statute, because the bankruptcy courts' third-party "related to" bankruptcy jurisdiction is itself a grant of supplemental jurisdiction. Moreover, those who object to "supplemental" bankruptcy jurisdiction, in an unknowing indictment of *Pacor*, actually advance that proposition very forcefully.

If third-party "related to" bankruptcy jurisdiction is not supplemental jurisdiction, as *Pacor* propounds, then the only alternative statutory receptacle for supplemental bankruptcy jurisdiction is the 1990 supplemental jurisdiction statute, which provides the federal district courts with supplemental jurisdiction "in any civil action of which the district courts have original jurisdiction." Federal bankruptcy jurisdiction is a source of original jurisdiction for the district courts. Thus, the bankruptcy jurisdiction statute and the supplemental jurisdiction statute, in combination, would appear to give the federal *district courts* supplemental bankruptcy jurisdiction. Indeed, several courts have so held.

Original bankruptcy jurisdiction, though, is seldom exercised by the district courts. The Judicial Code permits a district court to refer *all* of its bankruptcy jurisdiction to the non-Article III bankruptcy court for the district, and the district courts have done so through standing orders of reference in effect in every district. . . .

Given the fact that bankruptcy litigation, as a practical matter, occurs in the bankruptcy courts and not in the district courts, supplemental bankruptcy jurisdiction will be an effective jurisdictional medium only to the extent that it can be employed in the bankruptcy courts. Moreover, it is in the bankruptcy courts, not the district courts, where "supplemental" bankruptcy jurisdiction has encountered the strongest resistance. . . .

. . . There is no statutory sanction, however, for bankruptcy courts to hear any claims other than those within the district courts' statutory bankruptcy jurisdiction over "arising under," "arising in," and "related to" bankruptcy proceedings.

Thus, even if the supplemental jurisdiction statute enhances the bankruptcy jurisdiction of the *district courts*, by appending "supplemental" jurisdiction to the district courts' statutory bankruptcy jurisdiction, nothing in the Judicial Code seems to permit the district courts to refer this "supplemental" bankruptcy jurisdiction to the *bankruptcy courts*. Consequently, many courts have concluded more recently that bankruptcy courts have no "supplemental" bankruptcy jurisdiction whatsoever, not even for purposes of entry of proposed findings and conclusions with respect to "supplemental" third-party claims. . . .

The statutory gap identified by these courts, of course, is wholly dependent upon the assumption that third-party "related to" bankruptcy jurisdiction—unquestionably within the province of the bankruptcy courts—is *not* a grant of supplemental jurisdiction. As this Article maintains, though, this is a wholly unwarranted assumption, carelessly asserted in *Pacor* and never openly or critically questioned since. When third-party "related to" bankruptcy jurisdiction is properly recognized as a grant of supplemental bankruptcy jurisdiction, in its own right, the interaction between the bankruptcy jurisdiction statute, the supplemental jurisdiction statute, and the bankruptcy referral statute is simply immaterial. The bankruptcy courts derive their supplemental jurisdiction from the bankruptcy jurisdiction statute, *not* the supplemental jurisdiction statute; the noncore third-party "related to" jurisdiction of the bankruptcy courts *is* supplemental jurisdiction. Moreover, the irony in the attacks on "supplemental" bankruptcy jurisdiction is that they actually acknowledge that "related to" bankruptcy jurisdiction is, indeed, a grant of supplemental bankruptcy jurisdiction. . . .

Supplemental bankruptcy jurisdiction . . . finds itself in the proverbial "Catch 22" of blind adherence to mutually inconsistent rules. Efforts to imbue third-party "related to" bankruptcy jurisdiction with principles of supplemental jurisdiction are met with the edict of *Pacor* that third-party "related to" bankruptcy jurisdiction is *not* supplemental jurisdiction, while those who resort to the supplemental jurisdiction statute are told they must look to "related to" bankruptcy jurisdiction for such principles. The absurdity of this jurisdictional predicament is visible in courts' frequent expressions of regret and exasperation when jurisdiction is found lacking on third-party claims that beg for an exercise of supplemental jurisdiction. . . .

The supplemental jurisdiction statute, therefore, is inapplicable in the bankruptcy context, but not because of the negative implication of a more limited statutory bankruptcy jurisdiction that could be rendered superfluous by the supplemental jurisdiction statute. When third-party "related to" bankruptcy jurisdiction is properly construed as an unqualified grant of supplemental jurisdiction, the supplemental jurisdiction statute simply becomes redundant.

2. Braving the Chill of Indeterminate Constitutional Theory

Constitutional anxiety abounds in the resistance to supplemental bankruptcy jurisdiction over third-party disputes. Constitutional concerns about supplemental bankruptcy jurisdiction, though, are rooted in the inapposite separation of powers influence of *Marathon* and an antiquated in rem constitutional theory of federal bankruptcy jurisdiction that must not be permitted to impose such a substantial burden upon Congress's design of an all-encompassing in personam federal bankruptcy jurisdiction.

The advantageous features of in personam transactional supplemental jurisdiction will not be fully available in bankruptcy litigation until the uncertainties surrounding third-party "related to" bankruptcy jurisdiction and the validity of "supplemental" bankruptcy jurisdiction are resolved. The unfairness of subjecting parties to suit without an ability to assert third-party mitigating claims, the risks of inconsistent adjudications and preclusion pratfalls when multiple courts address common occurrences, and the duplication of effort and delay occasioned by fracturing of disputes are all as prevalent in the bankruptcy context as in nonbankruptcy litigation. Even more importantly, though, bankruptcy can amplify the most pernicious aspects of incomplete joinder—multiplicative litigation and dilution of the federal forum. . . .

The vision and benefits of a complete, pervasive federal bankruptcy jurisdiction cannot be realized without universal acceptance of unrestricted supplemental bankruptcy jurisdiction in third-party disputes. . . .

The most intimidating obstacle for supplemental bankruptcy jurisdiction is constitutional diffidence. Indeed, the most visible critic, Professor Block-Lieb, acknowledges the many advantages supplemental jurisdiction holds for bankruptcy litigation, yet concludes that "[s]till, constitutional concerns may cause courts to question the wisdom of such an exercise." Moreover, the *Pacor* court's disfavor of supplemental jurisdiction precepts also seemed to be an outgrowth of constitutional trepidations. The scope of pervasive "related to" bankruptcy jurisdiction, though, was designed to be as broad as the Constitution permits. A proper interpretation of the exterior perimeter of third-party "related to" jurisdiction, then, requires an active search for those constitutional limits, rather than a rule of construction that attempts to sidestep constitutional complications. And as we've seen, the *Pacor* test does not successfully avert constitutional imbroglios; quite to the contrary, *Pacor*'s literal breadth perpetuates the constitutional quandary inherent in pervasive "related to" bankruptcy jurisdiction. . . .

To illustrate the constitutional apprehensions surrounding supplemental bankruptcy jurisdiction, return to our example of a *Marathon* state-law action in which a trustee or debtor-in-possession sues multiple codefendants in an adversary proceeding in the bankruptcy court, and one of the defendants wishes to assert both a transactionally related state-law (1) cross-claim against another defendant and (2) an impleader claim against a new third-party defendant. It is the thesis of this Article that the defendant's third-party claims are properly entertained in the bankruptcy court as "related to" proceedings. Those third-party claims are "related to" the bankruptcy case within the meaning of the bankruptcy jurisdiction statute, because they share a transactional, in personam supplemental relationship with the bankruptcy estate's claims against the defendants.

The constitutional challenge to supplemental bankruptcy jurisdiction over the defendant's third-party claims, like the statutory challenge (and again, somewhat ironically), also proceeds from the assumption that "related to" bankruptcy jurisdiction is itself a grant of supplemental jurisdiction. Of course, the *Marathon* actions against the defendants are now regarded as "related to" proceedings. If the defendant's third-party supplemental claims are also "related to" claims, as this Article asserts, then it is because they are "related to" the estate's "related to" claims. Detractors cast this as an unconstitutionally attenuated related-to related-to relationship, twice removed from the core federal element of the debtor's bankruptcy case and inviting a potentially limitless number of links in a "related to" chain.

We now discover the damage wrought by the hapless pigeonholing of *Marathon* actions as "related to" proceedings and an indiscriminate mixing of statutory and constitutional apples, oranges, and bananas. The content of "related to" bankruptcy jurisdiction has been defined more by separation of powers concerns surrounding our non-Article III bankruptcy judges than it has by principles of supplemental jurisdiction, and inclusion of *Marathon* actions as "related to" proceedings is attributable to the former rather than the latter. With *Marathon* claims now permanently ensconced in the "related to" category, though, the afterthought that "related to" bankruptcy jurisdiction may, indeed, be a grant of supplemental jurisdiction leads to a reflexive adoption of the misplaced in rem receivership model of supplemental bankruptcy jurisdiction, which fallaciously characterizes a *Marathon* action as a supplemental claim. The related-to related-to argument, then, is founded upon an anachronistic, beguiling in rem constitutional theory.

If Justice Story believed that he was freeing the scope of federal bankruptcy jurisdiction and American principles of judicial federalism from the English notion of bankruptcy jurisdiction in *Ex parte Christy*, he was mistaken. Of course, the struggle with the idea of federal "bankruptcy proceedings" under the 1898 Act . . . ultimately vindicated Justice Story. Nevertheless, now we see that another subtle influence of the more limited English concept of bankruptcy jurisdiction continues to linger. The bifurcated English, in rem model of bankruptcy jurisdiction, revived in the 1898 Act, also became the separation of powers model for *Marathon*. English ideas of bankruptcy jurisdiction, thus, obliquely encumber the scope of federal bankruptcy jurisdiction once more, through *Marathon*'s seepage into "related to" bankruptcy jurisdiction and the resulting insinuation of an in rem constitutional theory of federal bankruptcy jurisdiction.

Of course, it is not at all surprising that such an in rem constitutional theory will not sustain federal jurisdiction over the defendant's third-party claims in our example. The constitutional theory developed in this Article has already revealed the inadequacy of such an in rem theory for third-party state-law claims, just as *Pacor*'s in rem approach to "related to" bankruptcy jurisdiction cannot reach these third-party claims. Federal jurisdiction of the defendant's third-party claims simply is not based upon a functional, in rem relationship to a jurisdictional res; it is dependent upon an in personam, transactional nexus to the estate's claims against the defendants.

An in personam approach to supplemental bankruptcy jurisdiction requires an in personam model of federal bankruptcy jurisdiction—as a matter of both statutory and constitutional theory. . . .

CONCLUSION

Widespread confusion among scholars and the courts has made federal bankruptcy jurisdiction one of the most mysterious and perplexing facets of federal jurisdiction. Consequently, the development of the scope of federal bankruptcy jurisdiction has been retarded and remains shackled to outmoded ideas of in rem jurisdiction. Thus, as we stand on the cusp of a new millennium, federal bankruptcy jurisdiction seems hopelessly mired in the nineteenth century. This Article, though, has constructed a comprehensive, unifying theory that can not only rationalize both the constitutional and statutory nature and extent of federal bankruptcy jurisdiction, but greatly simplify and modernize federal bankruptcy jurisdiction. We need not modify our accumulated understanding of federal jurisdiction to accommodate bankruptcy. Indeed, just the opposite is true. We must alter the prevailing conception of bankruptcy in order to assimilate the wisdom of accepted principles of federal jurisdiction.

C. Jury Trials in Bankruptcy

A problem that starkly tests the nature, status and power of the bankruptcy courts concerns the right to a jury trial in a bankruptcy-related matter. Under the Seventh Amendment, of course, a party is guaranteed a jury trial in "[s]uits at common law, where the value in controversy shall exceed twenty dollars." In bankruptcy, two important issues have been raised: first, does the jury trial right apply in a bankruptcy proceeding; second, assuming there is a jury trial right, may the non-Article III bankruptcy court conduct that trial? In the wake of the Supreme Court's 1982 decision in *Marathon Pipe Line*, doubts about the constitutional legitimacy of a non-Article III court engaging in such a classically judicial function as supervising a jury trial are inescapable. Yet, ancient Supreme Court dictum suggests that the bankruptcy court, as a court of "equity," might lie outside the ambit of the Seventh Amendment.

Professor Elizabeth Gibson assayed the jury trial dilemma in a superb 1988 article, *Jury Trials in Bankruptcy: Obeying the Commands of Article III and the Seventh Amendment*, 72 MINN. L. REV. 967 (1988), which is the first selection. She concluded that the Seventh Amendment does apply to a number of bankruptcy proceedings, and that allowing the bankruptcy court to conduct jury trials raised a serious constitutional conflict between Article III and the Seventh Amendment. One or the other must give. Her recommendation was for the Article III district court to conduct jury trials in bankruptcy proceedings.

Professor Gibson proved prescient as to the first issue when the Supreme Court held the very next year in *Granfinanciera, S.A. v. Nordberg*, 492 U.S. 33 (1989), that the right to a jury trial does persist in a bankruptcy matter. The Court decided that the trustee's right to recover a fraudulent conveyance, even though denominated a core proceeding in bankruptcy, retains its common law nature and is not transformed into an equitable matter by the bankruptcy court's superintendence. The Court did not, however, decide whether a bankruptcy judge could conduct the constitutionally mandated jury trial. Indeed, the Court has not yet decided that issue. The Court also gave consideration in *Granfinanciera* to Professor Ray Warner's fine article, G. Ray Warner, *Katchen Up in Bankruptcy: The New Jury Trial Right*, 63 AM. BANKR. L.J. 1 (1989).

The next article, by Professor John McCoid, was published in 1991 in the *American Bankruptcy Law Journal* in the wake of the Court's *Granfinanciera* decision. Other articles in that volume worth reading are Douglas G. Baird, *Jury Trials After* Granfinanciera, 65 AM. BANKR. L.J. 1 (1991), and John E. Mathews, *The Right to Jury Trial in Bankruptcy Courts: Constitutional Impli-*

cations in the Wake of Granfinanciera, S.A. v. Nordberg, 65 AM. BANKR. L.J. 43 (1991). McCoid analyzes the Court's decision as well as prior Supreme Court precedents, and assesses the implications of *Granfinanciera*. McCoid's article in particular contains a very informative historical review. He echoes Gibson and expresses doubt as to whether the non-Article III bankruptcy judge can entertain jury trials concerning matters such as preferences and fraudulent conveyances, which are not historically core bankruptcy issues. As of the present writing, the statute has been amended to assign jury trials to bankruptcy judges only on a consent basis, altering somewhat the constitutional calculus and permitting the Court to more easily dodge the complex constitutional issues.

S. Elizabeth Gibson
Jury Trials in Bankruptcy:
Obeying the Commands of Article III and the Seventh Amendment
72 MINN. L. REV. 967 (1988)[*]

INTRODUCTION

In 1978 Congress comprehensively revised federal bankruptcy laws for the first time in forty years. . . . [T]he Bankruptcy Reform Act (1978 Act) also expanded the jurisdiction and enhanced the status of bankruptcy courts. . . . To ensure that litigants' rights to a jury trial would not be lost as a result of this jurisdictional expansion, Congress provided for the preservation of preexisting jury trial rights.

In 1982, however, the Supreme Court upset Congress's restructured bankruptcy system. In *Northern Pipeline Construction Co. v. Marathon Pipe Line Co.*, the United States Supreme Court held that the provision of the 1978 Act expanding the bankruptcy courts' jurisdiction violated article III and thus was unconstitutional. . . . When Congress eventually responded to the Court's decision, it retained the non-article III status of bankruptcy judges but reduced their authority over judicial proceedings to comply with article III's apparent requirement that the essential attributes of judicial power be vested only in article III courts. Simultaneously, and without explanation, Congress replaced the 1978 Act's jury trial provision with a provision narrowly focused on specific categories of cases.

In the wake of these developments, the constitutional status of jury trials in bankruptcy is confused. Lower courts and legal scholars are divided over the existence of a statutory or constitutional right to a jury trial in bankruptcy and the circumstances under which a bankruptcy judge is authorized to conduct a jury trial. . . .

The complex statutory and constitutional questions underlying these disagreements about jury trials in bankruptcy are the subject of this Article. . . .

The Article concludes that the seventh amendment requires a jury trial for certain matters currently adjudicated in the bankruptcy courts. In many of the cases in which such rights exist, however, authorizing a non-article III bankruptcy judge to preside over the jury trial produces a serious constitutional conflict. Article III's requirement that the decisions of non-article III courts be subject to de novo review cannot be reconciled with the seventh amendment's prohibition against the reexamination of jury verdicts. To avoid this conflict and to assure compliance with both constitutional provisions, the Article proposes that jury trials of such matters be conducted only by article III district judges. . . .

III. THE SEVENTH AMENDMENT'S PROTECTION OF JURY TRIALS IN BANKRUPTCY

Until recently the question of the right to a jury trial in bankruptcy matters seemed relatively simple. Under the 1898 Act, it was assumed that the seventh amendment was inapplicable to bankruptcy courts because they were courts of equity. The Supreme Court's 1966 decision in *Katchen v. Landy* appeared to confirm this view. The 1978 Act expanded the bankruptcy courts' jurisdiction, however, to include matters previously encompassed by the seventh amendment's jury trial guarantee. With that expansion, the consensus of opinion disappeared. . . . Many of these diverse opinions result from disagreement over the meaning and current effect of *Katchen*.

A. *KATCHEN V. LANDY*

. . . At the time, it was well established that there was no right to a jury trial for matters falling within the bankruptcy court's summary jurisdiction. The creditor, who sought a jury trial, therefore argued that a finding in favor of summary jurisdiction was precluded by the seventh amendment. The Supreme Court rejected this argument, holding that the bankruptcy court had summary jurisdiction over the preference counterclaim. In reaching its decision, the Court concluded that there was no constitutional right to a jury trial of a preference claim asserted as an objection to a claim against the bankruptcy estate. . . .

The Supreme Court recognized the dilemma posed by this situation. On the one hand, . . . bankruptcy courts are "essentially courts of equity, . . . and they characteristically proceed in summary fashion to deal with the assets of the bankrupt they are administering." On the other hand, if Katchen had not filed his claims in the bankruptcy proceeding, the trustee would have been forced to bring "a plenary action . . . in the federal courts where the creditor could have demanded a jury trial." Thus the Court analyzed whether an equitable bankruptcy court could determine this otherwise legal claim without violating the seventh amendment.

The Court first determined that the trustee's preference counterclaim fell within the bankruptcy court's summary jurisdiction. Such jurisdiction included the power to allow and disallow claims, which necessarily encompassed the power to determine the validity of debts alleged to underlie the claim. . . .

The Court then considered whether the bankruptcy court's summary jurisdiction extended to the judgment entered against Katchen for the payments on the notes. Rejecting the argument that such affirmative relief was only obtainable in a plenary suit, the Court reasoned that in ruling on the claim objection, the bankruptcy court could decide all other essential issues. . . .

In response to Katchen's seventh amendment objection to the finding of jurisdiction, the Court held that there was no constitutional right to a jury trial of the preference claim in this particular context. The Court reasoned that the preference claim was presented as part of the essentially equitable process of adjudicating claims against the bankruptcy estate. Underlying the Court's rejection of the seventh amendment argument was the concept of transforming a legal claim into an equitable one. According to the Court, the 1898 Act "converts the *creditor's legal claim* into an equitable claim to a pro rata share of the *res* . . . ." The trustee's preference counterclaim, which would be viewed as an action at law if asserted by way of plenary action, was now part of the equitable claim allowance-disallowance proceeding and thus was not triable by a jury. . . .

B. CONFLICTING VIEWS OVER *KATCHEN'S* CURRENT EFFECT

The implications of the *Katchen* decision, uncertain under the bankruptcy statute then in effect, are even less certain under current law. Since the case was decided, Congress has expanded bankruptcy court jurisdiction to include matters previously litigated only in nonbankruptcy courts. This jurisdictional expansion raises questions about the current applicability, validity, and meaning of *Katchen*.

Some authorities interpret *Katchen* broadly by taking the position that under current law there is no constitutional right to jury trial in any bankruptcy matters. They accept *Katchen*'s description of bankruptcy courts as essentially courts of equity and conclude that the seventh amendment's guarantee of jury trial rights is inapplicable to all matters coming within bankruptcy jurisdiction . . . .

At the other end of the spectrum are decisions that either ignore *Katchen* or consider it irrelevant to analyzing whether jury trial rights exist in current bankruptcy courts. These courts take the view that bankruptcy courts should determine jury trial rights according to the same seventh amendment analysis applied by district courts in nonbankruptcy cases. . . . [I]f the case is equitable in nature, these courts rule that there is no right to a jury trial. If legal in nature, however, they grant the jury trial demand. . . .

The greatest number of cases take an approach between the two extremes. . . .

Courts that adopt a middle position on the issue of jury trial rights base their approach on the statutory distinction between core and noncore proceedings. Attempting to translate *Katchen* into the current terminology, these courts hold that there is no constitutional right to a jury trial in core proceedings. . . .

C. Jurisdictional Dichotomy Under the 1898 Act

To resolve the uncertainty *Katchen* poses for the current structure of bankruptcy courts, it is necessary to reconsider the jurisdictional context in which *Katchen* was decided. This inquiry helps to explain how bankruptcy courts under the 1898 Act were viewed as courts of equity. With that understanding it is possible to analyze the effects caused by the subsequent expansion of bankruptcy jurisdiction. . . .

At the time the Supreme Court decided *Katchen*, the bankruptcy courts' work was limited to matters falling within their summary jurisdiction. . . .

It was in the context of administering a res that bankruptcy courts were essentially courts of equity. At the same time, however, other matters essential to the administration of the bankruptcy case were carried out by nonbankruptcy courts. Collecting assets from third parties, for example, generally was pursued by a plenary suit in a state or federal district court. This aspect of the bankruptcy case, which helped determine the size of the res to be distributed, was not necessarily equitable in nature. Instead, a plenary action was governed either by legal or equitable principles depending upon the nature of the claim asserted and the relief sought.

For example, when a trustee sued to enforce a breach of contract claim held by the bankrupt prior to bankruptcy, the plenary action was of a legal nature and thus triable to a jury. Likewise, in *Schoenthal v. Irving Trust Co.*, the Supreme Court held that the defendants to a preference action brought by a bankruptcy trustee were entitled to have the action tried at law by a jury. . . .

Thus, under the bifurcated jurisdictional scheme of the 1898 Act, some bankruptcy matters, particularly those relating to the administration and distribution of the bankruptcy estate, were resolved in the bankruptcy court acting as a court of equity. Other bankruptcy matters, usually those involving efforts by the trustee to bring assets into the bankruptcy estate, were resolved in nonbankruptcy courts, where litigants might be constitutionally entitled to a jury trial. The 1978 Act, however, expanded bankruptcy jurisdiction to encompass all of these matters. The effect of this jurisdictional expansion on pre-existing jury trial rights depends upon whether the seventh amendment permits Congress to eliminate jury trial rights by means of its forum assignment.

D. Restrictions on Congressional Elimination of Jury Trial Rights

Some courts have concluded that *Katchen* permits Congress to convert legal claims arising out of bankruptcy into equitable ones, thereby "displacing any Seventh Amendment right of trial by jury." . . .

The *Katchen* Court appeared to endorse the view that Congress could transform actions at law into equitable proceedings, and thereby eliminate jury trial rights, merely by assigning adjudication of the actions to the equitable bankruptcy court. . . . To determine the limits on this congressional circumvention of the seventh amendment, the context of the Court's statements in *Katchen* must be carefully considered.

When the *Katchen* Court spoke of converting legal claims into equitable ones, it was referring specifically to claims belonging to a creditor of the bankrupt. In *Barton v. Barbour,* the Court discussed the same transformation in a similar context. That context was one in which the event of bankruptcy had transformed the nature of the claim. When a defendant or potential defendant to an action at law files for bankruptcy, the nature of the plaintiff's claim is automatically changed by these circumstances. The plaintiff no longer is asserting a claim against a solvent defendant, which might have enabled the plaintiff to obtain a judgment against the defendant's nonexempt assets. Instead, the intervening bankruptcy means that the plaintiff becomes one of many creditors seeking to share a limited fund. The plaintiff's recovery, if any, will be governed by equitable principles applied by the bankruptcy court in administering the res within its exclusive control. The transformation of the plaintiff's legal claim for a money judgment into an equitable claim to a portion of the res is thus brought about, not by a mere change in forums, but by a change in factual circumstances.

The expansion of bankruptcy jurisdiction to include matters previously pursued only by plenary suit, however, works no such factual transformation. . . . [A] trustee under the present Act is permitted to sue third parties to recover assets for the estate. As discussed earlier, a trustee formerly could proceed by an action at law, in which case the seventh amendment provided a right to a jury trial. The same result should still obtain despite the expansion of bankruptcy jurisdiction . . . . Neither the nature of the claim nor the relief sought is in any way altered by the bankruptcy filing or by the bankruptcy courts' jurisdictional expansion.

. . . [A] legal claim is not magically transformed into an equitable one merely because it is asserted in what traditionally has been viewed as a court of equity. Unless the claim has been factually transformed, such as in *Katchen* and *Barton*, the right to a jury trial remains. If . . . a jury trial is unavailable in the equity court, then the court cannot hear the legal claim because doing so would deprive the parties of their jury trial rights. If, however, . . . the claim is presented in a merged court of law and equity, then the court can hear the claim and grant the jury trial demand. Under this analysis, actions by a bankruptcy trustee once pursued by plenary actions at law in state or district courts retain their legal nature even though they now may be maintained in the bankruptcy court. Therefore, the seventh amendment applies, entitling the parties to a jury trial. . . .

It might be argued that the foregoing conclusion cannot be reconciled with the Supreme Court's decision in *Atlas Roofing Co. v. Occupational Safety & Health Review Commission*. The *Atlas Roofing* Court rejected a seventh amendment challenge to a federal statute authorizing the government to sue for civil penalties in an administrative proceeding. The Court explicitly recognized that Congress's choice of a forum for particular litigation could eliminate jury trial rights that might have existed had another forum been chosen. The decision may suggest therefore that Congress, by assigning the litigation of legal actions to the bankruptcy court, can eliminate previously existing jury trial rights.

Although *Atlas Roofing* does give Congress some latitude to escape the seventh amendment's requirements, the limits the Court placed on its holding render it inapplicable to the present bankruptcy situation. Throughout the opinion, for instance, the Court stressed that the decision was applicable only to congressionally created *public rights*. . . . [T]he concept of public rights . . . is not broad enough under any viable definition to encompass most of the estate-enhancing actions pursued by bankruptcy trustees. The bulk of such actions are between private individuals or entities and are based on state common law . . . .

Among the actions added to the bankruptcy courts' jurisdiction, however, are a few that are congressionally created. Preference and fraudulent conveyance actions, once pursued by plenary actions and now classified as core proceedings, are created by federal statute. Despite their federal statutory origin, however, they do not fit within *Atlas Roofing*'s description of public rights cases. . . . [A]ctions by a bankruptcy trustee to recover property for the bankruptcy estate can hardly be characterized as involving anything other than private rights. Moreover, preference and fraudulent conveyance actions, traditionally authorized by bankruptcy law, are unlike the newly created cause of action in *Atlas Roofing*. . . .

The nature of the forums involved also distinguishes *Atlas Roofing* from the bankruptcy situation. In *Atlas Roofing* the Court was concerned with "an administrative forum with which the jury would be incompatible." A similar conclusion of incompatibility cannot be reached about the federal bankruptcy courts, however. . . . [J]ury trials, even if not welcome in the bankruptcy courts, are not incompatible with these courts. . . . [B]ankruptcy courts possess the procedural mechanisms to summon and impanel jurors, and jury trials have in fact been conducted there.

Neither *Katchen* nor *Atlas Roofing* supports the view that the seventh amendment permits Congress to eliminate jury trial rights by expanding the jurisdiction of the bankruptcy courts. Instead, matters previously pursued by actions at law in nonbankruptcy courts retain their legal nature when pursued in the bankruptcy courts, and the seventh amendment guarantees litigants jury trial rights in these actions.

E. BANKRUPTCY COURTS AS COURTS OF LAW AND EQUITY

. . . Now that bankruptcy jurisdiction has been expanded to include matters of a legal nature, . . . bankruptcy courts are properly viewed as merged courts of law and equity, like federal district courts. Accordingly, the seventh amendment requires examination of the nature of claims asserted and relief sought to determine the existence of jury trial rights.

The foregoing approach does not categorically reject jury trials in all matters now classified as core proceedings. . . . [S]ome matters now expressly classified by Congress as core, such as preference and fraudulent conveyance actions, previously were pursued only by plenary actions in which jury trials were sometimes available. This Article contends that plenary actions at law retain their legal nature even though they now may be pursued in the bankruptcy courts and that Congress lacks authority to override the seventh amendment's command with regard to them. This approach thus recognizes the continuation of jury trial rights in such core proceedings in the bankruptcy courts.

This approach does not suggest, however, that jury trial rights be determined in the bankruptcy courts just as they would be in the district courts. . . . *Katchen* continues to require that bankruptcy's factual transformation of legal causes of action into equitable claims to a share of the estate be considered. . . . [T]he bankruptcy context in which the claim is asserted must be taken into account. It is not sufficient to look only to whether compensatory damages are sought. If damages are sought from the bankruptcy estate or in connection with an objection to a claim against the estate, *Katchen* teaches that the claim has been transformed by bankruptcy into an equitable claim triable without a jury.

What this approach requires, then, is that jury trial rights be preserved for actions that retain their legal nature despite their assertion in the bankruptcy courts. Matters viewed as equitable because of the nature of the relief sought will not be triable by jury; nor will matters involving the equitable administration of the bankruptcy estate. . . .

. . . [N]otwithstanding Congress's failure to provide for the right to jury trial in bankruptcy except in a narrow category of cases, jury trials continue to be available in both core and noncore bankruptcy proceedings pursuant to the seventh amendment.

IV. AUTHORITY OF BANKRUPTCY JUDGES TO CONDUCT JURY TRIALS

A. CONFLICTING VIEWS

If the seventh amendment guarantees litigants the right to a jury in certain bankruptcy matters, it must be determined who may conduct the jury trial. The logical choice is a bankruptcy judge. . . .

The following sections of the Article accordingly examine whether a jury trial before a bankruptcy judge is both constitutionally sufficient and constitutionally permissible. Because the jury trial rights under discussion are mandated by the seventh amendment, it must be determined whether a trial before a non-article III bankruptcy judge satisfies the seventh amendment's requirements for a trial by jury. Secondly, even if the seventh amendment would be satisfied by such a trial, the requirements of article III of the Constitution must be explored to determine whether it is permissible for bankruptcy judges to exercise this judicial power.

B. THE SEVENTH AMENDMENT'S REQUIREMENTS

An issue raised briefly during the hearings leading up to the 1978 Act, but addressed infrequently by the courts, is whether a trial before a non-article III judge constitutes a "trial by jury" within the meaning of the seventh amendment. . . .

The most extensive judicial consideration of the issue occurred in a nineteenth century Supreme Court decision, *Capital Traction Co. v. Hof*. . . . [T]he Court held that the trial before the justice of the peace did not constitute a trial by jury within the meaning of the seventh amendment. The Court emphasized that District of Columbia justices of the peace performed only the ministerial tasks of impaneling the jury and entering judgment on the jury's verdict. They did not possess the power to instruct jurors on the law, to advise them on the facts, or to set aside verdicts in appropriate cases. The Court thus concluded that a jury trial in such a forum did not satisfy the seventh amendment's trial by jury requirements.

Hof's description of the characteristics required of a judge conducting a seventh amendment jury trial remains valid. . . .

The Supreme Court's description of the vital characteristics of a trial by jury emphasize the court's procedures and the exercise of legal discretion by the judge. They contain no suggestion that the seventh amendment requires the presiding judge to be appointed pursuant to article III of the Constitution. Instead, the characteristics necessary to satisfy constitutional requirements are ones potentially possessed by many types of federal judges, including those serving pursuant to authority other than article III.

The District of Columbia courts illustrate most persuasively that the seventh amendment does not require that only article III judges preside over jury trials. Each day jury trials required by the seventh amendment are conducted in these non-article III courts before judges appointed for fifteen-year terms. The Supreme Court has sanctioned this practice without questioning its constitutionality. . . .

If the seventh amendment is satisfied by jury trials conducted by District of Columbia judges, the same conclusion should follow with respect to bankruptcy judges. Bankruptcy judges . . . are judges presiding over courts of record. They possess the legal training and ability to instruct jurors on the law, advise them concerning the facts, and set aside inappropriate verdicts. The seventh amendment thus appears to pose no constitutional obstacle to jury trials conducted by bankruptcy judges.

C. ARTICLE III's REQUIREMENTS

Even though a jury trial before a bankruptcy judge may satisfy the seventh amendment's requirements, some courts conclude that article III of the Constitution prohibits bankruptcy judges from exercising such authority. These courts believe that presiding at jury trials is a judicial power reserved exclusively for judges possessing the protections mandated by article III. . . .

The conclusion reached by these courts is not compelled by *Northern Pipeline*. Its plurality opinion referred to jury trials conducted by bankruptcy judges only to illustrate the bankruptcy courts' independence from district courts. Because of this independence, the Court held that bankruptcy courts were not constitutionally permissible "adjuncts" to the article III courts. The Court did not suggest, however, that article III would always be violated if bankruptcy judges conducted jury trials.

Jury trials conducted by other non-article III judges suggest that the practice is not absolutely prohibited by article III. As the *Pernell* case illustrates, District of Columbia judges preside over jury trials despite their lack of article III status, and the Supreme Court has acknowledged their right to do so. In addition, United States magistrates, also non-article III judges, are statutorily authorized to preside over jury trials with the consent of the parties. . . .

Affirming the constitutionality of jury trials conducted by some non-article III judges, however, does not settle the question with respect to bankruptcy judges. . . . The specific circumstances in which bankruptcy judges might be asked to preside over jury trials must therefore be analyzed in the light of article III's requirements.

1. Core Proceedings

. . . [B]ankruptcy judges are authorized to "hear and determine" all core proceedings . . . . When presiding over these matters, bankruptcy judges are essentially independent of the district courts.

Assuming that it is constitutional to permit bankruptcy judges to hear and enter final judgments in core proceedings, it remains to be determined whether conducting jury trials is a power uniquely reserved for article III judges. In other words is article III so protective of jury trials that it precludes bankruptcy judges from conducting them even though it permits those judges to conduct bench trials and to enter final judgments?

The policies underlying article III provide no basis for concluding that jury trials were intended to be singled out for special treatment. It is well accepted that the tenure and salary requirements of article III were included to ensure the independence of federal judges from the other branches of government. . . . The potential for domination of the federal judiciary, however, is greater in the case of a bench trial . . . . If there is a difference between the status of bench and jury trials under article III, it is the bench trial that may require more protection.

Moreover, insofar as core proceedings are concerned, bankruptcy courts are comparable to the District of Columbia courts. The Supreme Court has recognized Congress's power under article I to establish the District of Columbia courts and to permit them to operate outside the constraints of article III. District of Columbia courts are permitted to conduct jury trials with no apparent offense to article III. If granting authority to bankruptcy judges over core matters is also upheld as a permissible exercise of Congress's article I powers, then these judges should similarly be able to exercise all powers in such proceedings, including presiding over jury trials.

2. Noncore Proceedings

The issue of jury trials in noncore proceedings is more complicated. . . . The district judge is required to review de novo any matter to which a party objects before entering a final judgment. . . .

Assuming the consent provision is valid under article III, the authority of bankruptcy judges to enter final judgments in noncore matters with the parties' consent does not differ significantly from the authority they possess in core proceedings. Because the bankruptcy judge is authorized to take final action, subject only to normal appellate review, it should not matter for article III purposes that the facts are found by a jury rather than a judge.

A similar situation is presented by a provision of the Federal Magistrates Act authorizing magistrates, with the parties' consent, to conduct proceedings and to enter judgments in jury or non-jury civil matters. Nine courts of appeal have upheld this provision . . . . It seems reasonable to conclude, therefore, that article III poses no obstacle to the conduct of jury trials by bankruptcy judges in noncore proceedings in which the parties consent to the entry of judgment by the bankruptcy judge.

A different problem is raised by noncore proceedings in which the parties do not consent to the entry of judgment by the bankruptcy judge. Under article III, is a bankruptcy judge permitted to conduct a jury trial here as well? . . . [A] statutory obstacle is the requirement of de novo review, and possibly a second jury trial, by the district judge. A number of courts have concluded that this requirement makes it impractical for bankruptcy judges to conduct jury trials in noncore proceedings . . . .

The difficulty posed by the de novo review requirement, however, is more fundamental. Subjecting the factual findings of a bankruptcy court jury to de novo review by a district court would violate the reexamination clause of the seventh amendment. Under that provision the district court's ability to review the results of the bankruptcy court jury trial would be limited. It could only review the bankruptcy jury's findings according to ordinary principles of appellate review. This limited review, however, would not satisfy the review de novo required by the statute. . . . Because the reexamination clause requires that deference be given to the facts found by a jury, allowing bankruptcy judges to conduct jury trials in noncore, nonconsensual proceedings would preclude the district court from complying with its statutorily mandated scope of review.

. . . [E]ven if it is permissible for bankruptcy judges to conduct hearings in noncore proceedings without the parties' consent, that authority should not be interpreted to embrace the power to conduct jury trials. Although such a trial would satisfy the seventh amendment's requirement of a "trial by jury," the subsequent de novo review required by the statute would violate the seventh amendment's reexamination clause. To avoid this conflict, jury trials of noncore matters must take place in the district court, unless the parties consent to the entry of judgment by the bankruptcy judge.

3. May Congress Eliminate the De Novo Requirement?

. . . If the problem under the current scheme is the requirement for de novo review, could Congress, consistent with article III, eliminate that requirement?

An argument can be made that article III does not require a district judge to review de novo facts found by a bankruptcy court jury. Instead, the bankruptcy judge could conduct a jury trial of a noncore matter and submit the verdict and proposed judgment to the district court. The district court could then review de novo all of the bankruptcy judge's rulings to which an objection was made, according them no deference. The jury's factual findings, however, would not be reexamined except according to principles normally governing appellate review of jury verdicts. In this manner the article III district judge would ultimately decide all questions on the law and enter the judgment. The jury's factual findings, however, would not be reexamined in violation of the seventh amendment.

The strongest support for this argument comes from the Supreme Court's decision in *Crowell v. Benson*. The Court there held that permitting an administrative agency to make conclusive factual findings did not violate article III, so long as the district court retained authority to review de novo all questions of law and those jurisdictional facts upon which the agency's authority to act depended. . . . If article III permits non-article III officers to make final determinations of fact because they are acting in a manner analogous to jurors, does it not necessarily permit those officers to utilize jurors to accomplish the same task? And is it really constitutionally significant whether a jury sits in a bankruptcy courtroom rather than in a district courtroom, so long as the district judge retains authority to review all questions of law?

Although some support can be found for the argument that article III is not violated if a bankruptcy judge or a magistrate conducts a jury trial under circumstances in which adjudication by an article III judge is ultimately required, the argument is flawed. It assumes that a litigant's constitutional rights are fully vindicated by the district judge's nondeferential review of questions of law. The plurality in *Northern Pipeline* rejected such an assumption. It stated that "the constitutional requirements for the exercise of the judicial power must be met at all stages of adjudication, and not only on appeal. . . ." [T]he Court's concern appears to involve the many discretionary rulings inevitably made by a presiding judge that are simply not amenable to appellate review.

. . . In bankruptcy cases, even if review is de novo, the deference necessarily given the jury's verdict would, in effect, insulate from review the bankruptcy judge's discretionary rulings. Thus the district judge's de novo review of legal rulings, with only limited review of the jury's factual findings, would not serve as the constitutional equivalent of a jury trial conducted by the district judge.

. . .

Perhaps the most fundamental problem caused by authorizing bankruptcy judges to conduct jury trials in cases requiring an article III judge is that, in exercising this power, the bankruptcy judge crosses the hazy line separating adjunct and judge. No longer is the bankruptcy judge just an assistant acting under the close supervision of the district judge. Instead, the bankruptcy judge in effect exercises final, unreviewable authority over matters that may significantly affect the outcome of the case.

The premise of article III . . . is "that it matters that final decisions are made by specially empowered actors." If this is an accurate conclusion, then even if bankruptcy judges are constitutionally valid adjuncts to the district court, they should not be permitted to conduct jury trials of noncore matters without the parties' consent. Allowing them to do so vests too much authority in these unprotected actors.

CONCLUSION

. . . [T]he seventh amendment remains a vital part of the Constitution. Its commands may not be ignored just because a matter happens to fall within the jurisdiction of the bankruptcy court. Viewing bankruptcy courts as courts of equity operating outside the scope of the seventh amendment is no longer accurate. Instead, bankruptcy courts are courts of law and equity authorized to hear matters retaining their legal nature even though asserted in bankruptcy proceedings. Consequently, the Constitution requires that jury trial rights in these cases be recognized, whether or not Congress statutorily acknowledges the existence of such rights.

. . . The present procedural structure of the bankruptcy courts is poorly suited for the efficient conduct of jury trials. . . . Without the parties' consent to entry of judgment by the bankruptcy judge, jury trials in noncore cases must be conducted by a district judge to avoid an unconstitutional de novo review of the jury's verdict.

. . . Congress wisely decided in 1978 to consolidate all bankruptcy-related matters in the bankruptcy court. It should not undercut that policy by retaining a clumsy and inefficient court structure that requires some matters to be tried in the district court and forces the bankruptcy proceeding into abeyance while awaiting the district court's decision. Instead, in recognition of the need to execute the seventh amendment's requirements efficiently, Congress should reconstitute the bankruptcy courts as article III courts with full powers to conduct jury trials in all types of bankruptcy proceedings.

John C. McCoid, II
Right to Jury Trial in Bankruptcy: Granfinanciera, S.A. v. Nordberg
65 AM. BANKR. L.J. 15 (1991)*

I. INTRODUCTION

Determining whether there is a right to jury trial in federal court under the Seventh Amendment is a difficult task. That provision states that "the right of trial by jury shall be preserved . . .," and the verb "preserved" has always been thought to require a historical inquiry into English practice at the end of the Eighteenth Century. As American law has changed over the years, the job of matching history has become increasingly complex. Not only must courts consider new substance, but reform of practice as well makes "preservation" a mind-boggling effort . . . .

Nowhere is the difficulty more apparent than in bankruptcy cases. The problem had been troublesome even under the 1898 Act, particularly in the context of preference recapture by the trustee. The 1978 reform exacerbated matters by creating as an adjunct to the district court a non-Article III bankruptcy court having jurisdiction over all cases and "civil proceedings arising under title 11, or arising in or related to cases under title 11." The Supreme Court's decision in *Northern Pipeline Construction Co. v. Marathon Pipe Line Co.* invalidated this jurisdiction to an uncertain extent . . . on Article III grounds. Congress' 1984 effort to cure the defect continued in part the enlarged jurisdiction of the bankruptcy court over "core proceedings" and thus set the stage for *Granfinanciera, S.A. v. Nordberg*, which is the focus of this article.

In *Granfinanciera*, Nordberg, the trustee of Chase & Sanborn Corporation in a Chapter 11 reorganization, instituted a proceeding to set aside an allegedly fraudulent conveyance of $1.7 million by the debtor to Granfinanciera and Medex. The defendants, denying fraud, demanded a jury trial. Ruling that such actions were historically brought in equity, the bankruptcy judge denied a jury. . . .

The Supreme Court reversed. Writing for the Court, Justice Brennan sought to overcome both of the obstacles to jury trial raised by the court below. First, following the analytical pattern recently adopted by the Court, he concluded that the trustee's claim was a legal one. As he saw it, the action was analogous to Eighteenth Century actions instituted by bankruptcy assignees to recover fraudulent preferences which were brought at law. In addition and more important from his perspective, the money remedy sought was legal. Secondly, he ruled that Congress could not defeat the right by assigning it to a tribunal in which the mode of trial was nonjury on the theory that the right asserted by the trustee was "private" rather than "public." . . . [H]e reasoned only in terms of what Congress could or could not do under the Seventh Amendment. Thus, he avoided determining whether the bankruptcy judge could entertain such a proceeding and, if so, whether he could preside over a jury trial. Whether "core proceeding" jurisdiction legitimately extends to preference and fraudulent conveyance recapture from a defendant who asserts no claim against the debtor has been doubted. Since *Granfinanciera*, a circuit split has already developed concerning whether a bankruptcy judge can conduct a jury trial in core proceedings. It seems inevitable that the Court ultimately must face both the issues it escaped in *Granfinanciera*. . . .

Justice White dissented. The decision, he believed, was contrary to, rather than supported by, his own opinion for the Court in *Katchen v. Landy*, which had sustained nonjury trial of a preference counterclaim by the trustee in summary proceedings before a referee under the 1898 Act. Moreover, he thought Justice Brennan's historical analysis was inaccurate, and he believed that a bankruptcy court was a court of equity entitled to proceed without a jury on that account.

Justices Blackmun and O'Connor also dissented, but on the narrower ground that Congress was entitled to assign the controversy to a nonjury tribunal to effectively implement a bankruptcy system in the public interest. . . .

Where the issue is legal, whether Congress could defeat jury trial by assigning the proceeding to a specialized court of equity poses a more difficult problem, I believe. So long as bankruptcy judges are not given Article III status, it seems to be tied inextricably to the question of Congress' power to allocate jurisdiction to non-Article III tribunals. Indeed, this much was acknowledged by Justice Brennan who said that the test, "public" or "private" right, was the same for both the jurisdiction (Article III) and jury-trial (Seventh Amendment) issues. . . . But it is far from clear that a "bankruptcy court," whether or not constituted as an Article III court, should be thought of solely as a court of equity. On this point, I believe, the historical evidence indicates that such courts, formally coming into existence only in the Nineteenth Century, have always had jurisdiction both at law and in equity. Thus, if the bankruptcy court's "core proceeding" jurisdiction is found to pass Article III muster, jury trial there is appropriate so long as it is legitimate for the bankruptcy judge to preside.

If this conclusion is correct, then it seems to me that, given classification of the issue as legal, the Court would have done better to address the Article III issue and, if it found the bankruptcy court's jurisdiction legitimate in that sense, decide whether a bankruptcy judge can conduct a jury trial. . . .

III. A COURT OF BANKRUPTCY

The idea that a court of bankruptcy is a court of equity has been repeated so often that it is difficult to entertain the notion that it might be mistaken. I believe, however, that the history of bankruptcy courts, both in England and the United States, is to the contrary and that a bankruptcy court should be understood to exercise both legal and equitable powers. If that is so, the right to jury trial in bankruptcy does not automatically follow from characterization of an issue as legal; legal issues arising in the course of administering the bankrupt's estate, such as the validity of a claim, were generally tried in bankruptcy without a jury. More important for our purposes, because committing a matter to the jurisdiction of a bankruptcy court does not direct it to an exclusively equity tribunal, no Seventh Amendment problem arises simply from lodging a matter there. Jury trial in a bankruptcy court may be perfectly legitimate.

A. In England

Until 1831 there was not, in any formal sense, a court of bankruptcy. The first bankruptcy statute, passed in 1541, gave to the Lord Chancellor, the Lord Treasurer, the Lord President, the Lord Privy Seal, other members of the Privy Council, and the chief justices of either bench the power themselves to seize the estate of a bankrupt and arrange for its ratable distribution, as well as to imprison the bankrupt. . . . The entire process was "summary" at best. . . .

In 1571, the Elizabethan statute modified the scheme. It vested bankruptcy jurisdiction exclusively in the Lord Chancellor who was expressly authorized on written complaint of an act of bankruptcy to appoint commissioners under the Great Seal. It was the commissioners who took the bankrupt's property, assigned it, and distributed the proceeds to creditors who had proved their claims. This power was said to combine legal and equitable jurisdiction. Necessarily making determinations of law and fact as they carried out these duties, the commissioners clearly functioned in a judicial fashion, and colloquially, at least, they could be labeled a court. In many respects, however, their work perhaps more nearly resembled the activities of our present-day administrative agencies. . . .

It seems to have been recognized that this bankruptcy jurisdiction of the Lord Chancellor was separate from the authority of the Court of Chancery and that a commission of bankruptcy was not a proceeding in that court . . . . While the whole administration of property of the bankrupt fell under this jurisdiction, it did not extend to determining what was the bankrupt's estate. That had to be done at law or in equity, and the reports show actions at law and suits in equity. . . .

Ultimately, this system proved unsatisfactory. At the beginning of the Nineteenth Century the bankruptcy process was widely considered to be a scandal in several respects. It was slow, expensive, and nonuniform. . . .

Finally, in 1831, Parliament authorized creation of "The Court of Bankruptcy," a court of record which was expressly said to be a court of law and equity, an authorization on which the Crown acted the following year. It consisted of four judges, one of whom was designated Chief Judge, and six commissioners. . . .

The Bankruptcy Act of 1849 continued this structure of bankruptcy jurisdiction. . . .

This account, I believe, traces English law as far as necessary. The English model was pretty constant. From the outset, bankruptcy decisions were regarded as both legal and equitable. The commissioners' power was dual. When formally constituted, a bankruptcy court had law and equity power which it exercised, by a procedure resembling equity procedure, in administration of the estate and even beyond on consent of a party who submitted to jurisdiction.

B. In the United States

1. The Legislation and its Construction

Our first bankruptcy legislation, the Bankruptcy Act of 1800, said nothing about a bankruptcy court. Parroting in most respects the Elizabethan statute then in force in England, it authorized a judge of the district court to appoint commissioners, who were sworn to execute the powers conferred by the statute, and largely left administration of the law to them. . . . [T]here was no indication of a "bankruptcy" jurisdiction in a federal court to recapture either preferences or property fraudulently conveyed, although there was some recapture in nonbankruptcy courts. The act contained extensive provision for jury trial, to be presided over by the district judge. One charged with bankruptcy was entitled to have a jury decide whether a commission should issue. Either the bankrupt or a creditor could demand a jury determination of "any material fact" arising "in the commencement or progress of the said proceedings, or in the allowance of the certificate (of discharge)." Whether it was afforded, however, rested in the discretion of the judge. Finally, either the creditor or the assignees were entitled to a jury trial on the validity of a claim. . . . Most commentary views the right to jury trial thus conferred as statutory only.

The 1841 Act also seems to have borrowed from the English model, which by then provided expressly for a bankruptcy court. Without labelling the district court a "court of bankruptcy," the 1841 Act in section 6 gave the district court jurisdiction in "all matters and proceedings in bankruptcy arising under this act, and any other act which may hereafter be passed on the subject of bankruptcy." . . . Section 6 also provided that this jurisdiction was to "be exercised summarily, in the nature of summary proceedings in equity." It seems likely that it was this last provision, more than anything else, which led to later statements that a bankruptcy court is a court of equity. Only in an entirely different provision, section 8, was concurrent jurisdiction conferred on the circuit and district courts over suits at law and in equity involving controversies between the assignee and a person claiming an adverse interest touching property or rights in property of the bankrupt. A right to jury trial was again provided the debtor on the fact of bankruptcy, and to a creditor or the assignee on the validity and amount of a claim. A bankrupt also could have a jury on the right to a discharge. The broad provision of the earlier act for discretionary jury trial was abandoned.

This structure seemed to preserve the distinction established in English law between bankruptcy jurisdiction covering administration of the estate and nonbankruptcy jurisdiction covering claims by and against strangers to the bankruptcy. Justice Story, however, gave the statute a different reading. In *Ex parte Christy*, the assignee filed a summary petition to set aside a mortgage given by the bankrupt to secure a loan. The creditor, who had filed no bankruptcy claim, objected on that ground to a summary proceeding. Story ruled that the district court's summary jurisdiction extended to a party claiming adversely. . . . [H]e added the policy argument that the design of the act was "to secure a prompt and effectual administration and settlement of the estate of all bankrupts within a limited period" and to do so "independently of all aid and assistance from any other tribunals over which it could exercise no effectual control." These goals could be accomplished, he concluded, only by "clothing the courts of the United States sitting in bankruptcy with the most ample power to accomplish them." Story firmly believed that Congress had given the district courts an enlarged bankruptcy jurisdiction. And he held to this though the proceedings were summary and no appeal was provided. If ever there was a precedent for the legitimacy of a bankruptcy court with a broad jurisdiction, it is *Ex parte Christy*.

Section 1 of the 1867 Act constituted the district courts "courts of bankruptcy" in precisely those words. It gave them jurisdiction "in all matters and proceedings in bankruptcy." It lacked, however, the language of the 1841 Act on which Story had relied in *Ex parte Christy*. Section 2 gave the circuit and district courts concurrent jurisdiction "of all suits at law or in equity which may or shall be brought by the assignee in bankruptcy against any person claiming an adverse interest, or by such person against such assignee, touching any property or rights of property of said bankrupt transferable to, or vested in such assignee." Subsequent sections authorized the use of "registers in bankruptcy" to assist the district judges. The registers, however, were required to refer disputed issues of fact or law to the district judge for resolution. Explicit grant of the right to jury trial was narrowed to the debtor's insolvency and whether he had committed an act warranting an involuntary petition. However, section 24, providing for appeal to the circuit court of the disallowance of a claim, stated that where an appeal was taken "like proceedings shall thereupon be had in the pleadings, trial, and determination of the cause, as in an action at law commenced and prosecuted, in the usual manner, in courts of the United States." This language would seem to have called for jury trial on demand of either party and thus to have preserved the right provided in the earlier American laws.

. . . The jurisdictional range which Justice Story had found under the 1841 Act thus was narrowed under the 1867 Act.

Unlike their English counterparts after 1831, neither the 1841 or 1867 Acts expressly described the bankruptcy jurisdiction conferred on the district court as including both legal and equitable powers. The provision in the 1841 Act that jurisdiction "be exercised summarily, in the nature of summary proceedings in equity," however, was not to the contrary. Matching the English approach to bankruptcy procedure, it spoke to *how* the jurisdiction was to be asserted rather than to *what* the nature of that jurisdiction was. Moreover, the subject matter covered by the statutes of the two countries so nearly matched in this period that it seems likely that the American omission was not deliberate. Of course, Parliament did not operate under the stricture of the Seventh Amendment. Congressional reluctance to confer jurisdiction at law arguably might have been prompted by an unwillingness to complicate bankruptcy proceedings with jury trials. . . .

In any event, the gap was repaired in the Act of 1898. Section 2 made the district courts "courts of bankruptcy" and invested them "with such jurisdiction at law and in equity as will enable them to exercise original jurisdiction in bankruptcy proceedings." The statute provided for jury trial only as to insolvency and whether an act of bankruptcy had been committed. The statute was interpreted to allow the exercise of summary jurisdiction by the referee whenever the dispute was about property in the actual or constructive possession of the bankruptcy court; otherwise a plenary action at law or in equity was required.

The 1978 reform gave the district courts exclusive jurisdiction over cases under Title 11 and original but not exclusive jurisdiction over all civil proceedings arising under Title 11 or arising in or related to cases under Title 11. . . . The Act also created a bankruptcy court in each district "as an adjunct to the district court," gave it law, equity, and admiralty powers, and directed that this court exercise the jurisdiction conferred on the district court. It provided for nonjury trial on whether an involuntary petition was appropriate but otherwise left jury trial unaffected.

After *Marathon,* the 1984 amendments continued the district court's jurisdiction and made the bankruptcy court staffed by bankruptcy judges a "unit" of the district court. . . . In a puzzling provision, nonjury trial as to involuntary bankruptcy was continued, and the right in personal injury and wrongful death cases was said to be left unaffected.

It seems to me that it is fair to read what Congress has done, beginning in 1800 and extending through 1984, as perpetuating the English concept of a bankruptcy court with legal as well as equitable jurisdiction. Whether constituted of commissioners, district judges, referees, or bankruptcy judges, the essence of the enterprise has remained the same, a durable example of the merger of law and equity. The idea that a bankruptcy court is a court of equity seems to have originated with the Supreme Court.

2. Transforming the Bankruptcy Court

The Supreme Court's references to bankruptcy courts as courts of equity began with a somewhat casual analogy in *Barton v. Barbour.* That case was not a bankruptcy matter at all. . . . Likening a receivership to a bankruptcy, Justice Woods noted that in bankruptcy claims for damages against the bankrupt were "investigated by chancery methods" because "the bankruptcy court, which acts as a court of equity, exercises exclusive control."

In *Bardes v. Hawarden Bank,* the Supreme Court held that a trustee's bill in equity to set aside a fraudulent conveyance could not be maintained in the district court sitting in bankruptcy but required a plenary suit. . . . [I]n the course of his opinion Justice Gray gratuitously said "[p]roceedings in bankruptcy generally are in the nature of proceedings in equity" . . . .

The statements in these two cases can be read only to describe how the bankruptcy court functioned, but *Local Loan v. Hunt* went further, albeit again without need. There the issue was whether the bankruptcy court had power to enforce a discharge by enjoining a subsequent suit brought against the debtor. Writing for the Court, Justice Sutherland upheld the injunction. In the course of sustaining the bankruptcy court's exercise of equity power and after laying aside its jurisdiction at law by reference to *Bardes,* he said "otherwise courts of bankruptcy are essentially courts of equity, and their proceedings inherently proceedings in equity."

Justice Douglas repeated the dictum in *Pepper v. Litton* in the course of sustaining bankruptcy court jurisdiction to disallow a claim on equitable grounds. Once again it was not necessary to deny the legal jurisdiction of a bankruptcy court to sustain its use of equity power. Yet it was *Local Loan* and *Pepper* that the Court cited in *Katchen v. Landy* when it classified the exercise of summary jurisdiction as equitable.

C. Justification and Consequence

Why were bankruptcy courts thought from the beginning to have legal jurisdiction? It seems to me that the reason probably was derived from the fact that most claims of most creditors against a debtor in bankruptcy are legal in nature. In passing on the right of a creditor to a share of the debtor's estate the court is adjudicating a legal issue just as in allocating insufficient assets among creditors it may be acting in equity.

Jury trial did not follow from this legal component in England when the "judges" were great officers of state or when they were commissioners. Neither was it a matter of right when a bankruptcy court was created. The Seventh Amendment could have been thought to make the question more difficult in the American context. That could explain why Congress insisted on the right to a jury trial on claim validity under our first three bankruptcy acts. The disappearance of that insistence without explanation in the 1898 legislation might have stemmed from the Supreme Court's dicta about bankruptcy jurisdiction.

The conjunction of constitutional right to jury trial and bankruptcy jurisdiction was not presented squarely in the Supreme Court until it surfaced in *Katchen v. Landy*, where the referee had ordered a claiming creditor to return a preference at the instance of a counterclaiming trustee. The creditor contended that this violated his Seventh Amendment right to jury trial. The Court's determination that it did not was based on a finding that there was summary bankruptcy jurisdiction over the creditor's claim. . . . Central to this was the Justice White's assumption, based on the earlier statements of the Court, that bankruptcy jurisdiction was exclusively equitable, so that there was no right to a jury on the question of allowance.

. . . History seems to have defined bankruptcy jurisdiction differently, as embracing law as well as equity power. Had the *Katchen* Court recognized this, I believe it would have required a jury trial of the preference issues. . . . It contained a nonjury claim, the creditor's, and a jury counterclaim, the trustee's, with the preference issues common to both before a court (the district court) with both legal and equitable power. . . . The district judge sitting in bankruptcy should have presided over a jury trial of the common issues in *Katchen*.

What follows from recognition that a bankruptcy court is a court of law and equity? It seems to me that the kinds of issues, though legal, which the bankruptcy court traditionally resolved without a jury should continue to be resolved in that fashion. . . .

IV. Remaining Issues

Two important problems remain. It has not been settled whether under Article III the bankruptcy court can exercise jurisdiction over core proceedings which involve the recapture of preferences and fraudulent conveyances. Neither has it been established whether a bankruptcy judge can preside over a jury trial. . . .

It is difficult for me to see a material difference between the bankruptcy trustee's assertion of a right to recover a preference or a fraudulent conveyance on the one hand and his suing on an alleged cause of action which, before bankruptcy, belonged to the debtor, the situation in *Marathon*, on the other. . . . [I]n both the trustee simply is seeking to augment the estate for the benefit of creditors.

Both preferences and fraudulent conveyances are matters outside the traditional scope of bankruptcy jurisdiction, in England as well as here. Except under the brief regime of the 1841 Act and *Ex parte Christy*, the trustee until recently would have brought suit in another court, of law or equity depending on the nature of the claim. Of course, it was not the absence of bankruptcy jurisdiction that produced the *Marathon* decision. Rather, it was the fact that the bankruptcy judge lacked Article III status. There is no reason why the district judge who has that status could not entertain either a *Granfinanciera* or a *Marathon* type of proceeding under the explicitly expanded bankruptcy jurisdiction conferred on the district court in 1978 and 1984.

It could be argued that preferences and fraudulent conveyances are distinctive because they are the peculiar subjects of federal bankruptcy law as the debtor's breach of contract action in *Marathon* was not. This argument perhaps has somewhat more force as to preferences which are generally valid outside bankruptcy. The contours of avoidable preferences are peculiarly the subject of bankruptcy law. Bankruptcy law also has a provision, section 548, giving a special, federal definition of fraudulent conveyances. That section, however, largely tracks the Uniform Fraudulent Conveyance Act. . . . [I]t seems probable to me that under the *Marathon* precedent Article III would prevent the bankruptcy judge from entertaining preference and fraudulent conveyance recapture proceedings too.

Should the court hold otherwise, I would not expect it to hold that the Constitution stands in the way of a bankruptcy judge presiding over a jury trial. Nontenured state court judges have done so for years in federal question cases. Federal legislative judges in the District of Columbia have done so as well. It is clear that the English gave bankruptcy judges authority to conduct jury trials when courts of bankruptcy were created in 1831. Because bankruptcy jurisdiction was lodged in district courts, no additional grant was necessary in this country. While no bankruptcy tradition stands in the way of bankruptcy judges presiding over a jury trial, it may be that the Court will find a lack of statutory authority for this procedure under the existing statute. . . .

D. Sovereign Immunity

States are important players in bankruptcy cases. A state government may be implicated in bankruptcy in myriad ways, especially as a creditor. The thought long had been that the State as a creditor had to play, for the most part, by the same rules as all other creditors. That basic assumption was rudely destroyed and the bankruptcy landscape inalterably changed by a momentous 1996 Supreme Court decision, *Seminole Tribe of Florida v. Florida*, 517 U.S. 44 (1996)—ironically, a case that did not even involve bankruptcy. There the Court held that Congress lacked the authority under its Article I powers (in that case, the Indian Commerce Clause) to abrogate the States' Eleventh Amendment immunity. The Court's rationale applied with equal force to Congress's Article I powers under the Bankruptcy Clause—a point that the Court acknowledged—meaning that Congress could no longer could blithely waive a States' immunity in bankruptcy cases as it had purported to do in § 106 of the Bankruptcy Code. The implications were, and are, staggering. To date the Court has not visited the State sovereign immunity problem in the bankruptcy context; it has, however, issued several more decisions (especially a 1999 trilogy of cases) that have taken away a variety of options that had been thought to be possible ways to skirt *Seminole Tribe*.

Two selections are included here. The first is from Professor Gibson again, writing in 1996 immediately after the *Seminole Tribe* decision. She analyzes that opinion, assesses its impact on the bankruptcy scheme, and suggests possible ways to circumvent the sovereign immunity problem. The next is from the 1997 National Bankruptcy Review Commission Final Report. That Report, like Gibson's piece, notes a number of possible ways that bankruptcy proceedings can be maintained against States notwithstanding *Seminole Tribe*. The Supreme Court's further retrenchment in 1999 must be borne in mind, though. Other articles worth reading on the subject include Laura B. Bartell, *Getting to Waiver—A Legislative Solution to State Sovereign Immunity in Bankruptcy After* Seminole Tribe, 17 BANKR. DEV. J. 17 (2000), and Kenneth N. Klee et al., *State Defiance of Bankruptcy Law*, 52 VAND. L. REV. 1527 (1999). Also, be looking for a forthcoming article on sovereign immunity from Professor Brubaker.

S. Elizabeth Gibson
Sovereign Immunity in Bankruptcy: The Next Chapter
70 AM. BANKR. L.J. 195 (1996)[*]

In *Seminole Tribe v. Florida*, . . . the Supreme Court decisively answered the questions that had been raised about its adherence to [*Pennsylvania v.*] *Union Gas* by announcing that the decision "was wrongly decided and that it should be, and now is, overruled." While not a bankruptcy case itself, *Seminole* embraced a view of the Eleventh Amendment that has direct implications for the congressional effort in the Bankruptcy Code to abrogate the sovereign immunity of states. Part I of this Article examines the *Seminole* decision. Part II analyzes the impact of the decision on § 106 and concludes that the congressional abrogation of the states' Eleventh Amendment immunity in bankruptcy is invalid, but points out that the 1994 amendment of § 106 was not all in vain. Substantial portions of § 106 are unaffected by *Seminole*. In Part III, the Article concludes that the clarity of expression with which Congress subjected states to suit may serve to permit state court remedies for claims barred from litigation in federal court. . . .

I. THE *SEMINOLE* DECISION

The federal statute at issue in *Seminole* was the Indian Gaming Regulatory Act, which permits an Indian tribe to conduct certain gaming activities within a state only if the tribe and the state first enter into a compact prescribing the conditions under which such activities will be conducted. The statute imposes on states a duty to negotiate with tribes in good faith in an attempt to form such compacts, and it provides for judicial enforcement of that duty. . . .

Pursuant to this statutory scheme, the Seminole Tribe brought suit in federal district court against the State of Florida and its governor, alleging a failure to negotiate a gaming compact in good faith. The defendants moved to dismiss the suit on the ground of sovereign immunity. The motion was denied. . . . [T]he Court of Appeals reversed, holding that suit against both defendants was barred by the Eleventh Amendment.

The Supreme Court affirmed the dismissal in a 5-4 decision. The Court held that the Eleventh Amendment prevents Congress, acting pursuant to its Article I powers, from subjecting unconsenting states to suits brought by private parties in federal court. In so concluding, the Court overruled its 1989 decision in *Pennsylvania v. Union Gas Co.* . . .

. . . In overruling *Union Gas*, the majority embraced a broad view of the Eleventh Amendment, reading it as going beyond its express terms and imposing state sovereign immunity as a limitation on the entirety of the federal judicial power under Article III. Having defined state sovereign immunity in federal question cases as a constitutionally compelled doctrine, . . . the Court held that Congress could not statutorily abrogate this protection for the states in the exercise of its Article I powers—even as to matters within the exclusive control of the federal government. Thus, the Court held that the Gaming Act's provision, permitting tribes to sue unconsenting states in federal district court, was unconstitutional.

II. *SEMINOLE*'S IMPACT ON SECTION 106

Although *Seminole* directly addressed only the validity of the judicial enforcement provision of the Gaming Act, the majority's language and rationale were broad, encompassing all congressional attempts to abrogate the states' sovereign immunity by legislation enacted pursuant to Article I of the Constitution. Accordingly, the decision must be examined to determine the extent to which it renders invalid the abrogation of sovereign immunity in § 106 of the Bankruptcy Code.

A. Parts of Section 106 Unaffected by *Seminole*

An analysis of *Seminole*'s effect on § 106 might best begin by taking stock of those parts of the bankruptcy provision that are undisturbed by the decision. . . . [T]he bankruptcy sovereign immunity provision remains valid in much of its application. Only the states and their agencies are protected by the Eleventh Amendment, and thus only they are the beneficiaries of *Seminole*. The other governmental units covered by § 106 remain subject to suit according to its terms. . . .

Pursuant to § 106(a), therefore, the United States and federal agencies can still be sued in bankruptcy courts to recover preferences, to impose sanctions for violations of the automatic stay or the discharge injunction, or for any of the other bankruptcy causes of action specified in that subsection.

The same is also true for foreign governments and for cities, counties, and municipal agencies . . . . Likewise, these non-state governmental parties remain subject to counterclaims and setoffs under § 106(b) and (c).

B. PARTS OF SECTION 106 RENDERED UNCONSTITUTIONAL BY *SEMINOLE*

To the extent that § 106 purports to abrogate the sovereign immunity of states and state agencies and permits them to be sued without their consent in bankruptcy court by private parties, it is directly contrary to *Seminole*. . . . [T]he basis for the decision was the majority's understanding of the Eleventh Amendment as imposing state sovereign immunity as a constitutional limitation on the federal judicial power conferred in Article III. Thus, the Court in *Seminole* held that Congress cannot subject an unconsenting state to suit by a private party in federal court by enacting legislation pursuant to its Article I powers. . . . It . . . applies without regard for the identity of the Article I power being exercised by Congress.

Such a sweeping rationale leaves no room for § 106 to operate against the states in federal court. Enacted pursuant to the Bankruptcy Clause of Article I, § 106(a) is invalid in authorizing the enumerated bankruptcy proceedings to be brought in federal court against state governmental units "[n]otwithstanding an assertion of sovereign immunity." Likewise, except to the extent that a state's filing of a proof of claim in a bankruptcy case can be deemed to constitute waiver of its Eleventh Amendment immunity, Congress exceeded its authority in authorizing counterclaims and setoffs to be asserted against states in bankruptcy court.

From a bankruptcy perspective, the unfortunate result of this partial invalidation of § 106 is the asymmetry it creates. Of all the parties who might be involved in a bankruptcy case, only state governments are given the special shield of immunity. . . .

. . . [T]he precise scope of the protection afforded by the Eleventh Amendment should be carefully noted. *First*, the Eleventh Amendment shields states from suits in federal court only; state court litigation is not proscribed by the amendment. *Second*, the Eleventh Amendment prohibits suits against unconsenting states only; if a state is found to have consented to such litigation in federal court, the suit may proceed. *Finally*, the protection of the Eleventh Amendment extends to the states and their instrumentalities, but not always to state officials; therefore, some suits against state officials in their official capacity may be brought in federal court to challenge the legality under federal law of actions taken by the state. . . .

III. REMEDIES IN BANKRUPTCY STILL AVAILABLE AGAINST STATES

A. STATE COURT LITIGATION

Proceedings arising in connection with a bankruptcy case are usually brought in or removed to a federal bankruptcy or district court. . . . But the federal forum is not the only one available for such proceedings. In conferring jurisdiction on the bankruptcy courts over "all civil proceedings arising under title 11, or arising in or related to cases under title 11," Congress expressly declared such jurisdiction to be "not exclusive," meaning that state courts of general jurisdiction have concurrent jurisdiction over such suits. . . .

If a trustee should sue a state agency in state court to recover, for example, a preference, may the state seek dismissal on the ground of sovereign immunity derived either from the Constitution or from state law? Stated differently, must it be shown that the state has consented to such state court litigation before the preference suit will be allowed to proceed? The Chief Justice's opinion in *Seminole* gives that impression, yet recent Supreme Court decisions more directly on point suggest otherwise. . . .

A more intriguing question is the possibility of pursing federal remedies in state courts against states that have *not* consented to suit in their courts. Although the *Seminole* majority seemed to assume that the state had to have consented to being sued in its own courts, the Court has in other recent cases held that, if Congress makes its intent sufficiently clear, it may create a federal remedy against the states that is enforceable in state court, notwithstanding any assertion of sovereign immunity, and that the state courts have a duty to entertain such suits in the absence of a valid excuse for declining to do so. In effect, the Supremacy Clause might be used to finesse the Eleventh Amendment by requiring state courts to implement federal remedies against nonconsenting states. . . .

In the case of § 106, Congress has *clearly* articulated the determination that states and state agencies should be subject to recovery in bankruptcy proceedings to the extent specified therein. Except for those proceedings over which a bankruptcy court has exclusive jurisdiction, the state courts have a coordinate duty to enforce the federal rights against state defendants, notwithstanding any doctrine of sovereign immunity that would otherwise apply in their courts.

B. FEDERAL COURT LITIGATION WITH THE STATE'S CONSENT

Despite *Seminole*'s view of state sovereign immunity as a limitation on "'the grant of judicial authority in Article III'" that cannot be overcome by congressional enactment, the Supreme Court continues to recognize the legitimacy of state consent to suit in federal court. . . . [T]he Eleventh Amendment permits states to consent to federal suits that would otherwise be outside the courts' jurisdiction. . . .

A bankruptcy plaintiff desiring to pursue a state defendant in the bankruptcy court, therefore, might inquire whether the state has consented to such suit. Such consent is not easily found, however. The Supreme Court has held that it will find a waiver by the state "only where stated 'by the most express language or by such overwhelming implications from the text as [will] leave no room for any other reasonable construction.'" Furthermore, it is not sufficient to find a general waiver of immunity or consent to suit in state courts because, according to the Supreme Court, "a State does not waive Eleventh Amendment immunity in federal courts merely by waiving sovereign immunity in its own courts."

If a state has not expressly consented to suit in federal bankruptcy court by statute, a would-be plaintiff must consider whether the state may give its consent by any other means. Inaction on the part of the state is clearly not enough. . . . [S]ome affirmative action indicating consent on the part of the state is required, at the very least.

A number of lower court decisions and commentators have concluded, on the basis of rather limited Supreme Court authority, that a state that brings a claim in federal court waives its Eleventh Amendment immunity from suit with respect to any recoupment claim that the defendant may assert against it. . . . Under this theory of waiver, no affirmative recovery against the state is permitted; the defendant may recover only up to the amount of the state's recovery against it.

Section 106(b) and (c) therefore can be constitutionally applied to some counterclaims and setoffs asserted against state entities that file proofs of claim in bankruptcy cases. Neither subsection is constitutionally valid in its entirety, however, under this doctrine. Subsection (b) permits affirmative recoveries exceeding the amount of the state's claim and thus goes beyond recoupment; and subsection (c) is not limited to setoffs arising out of the same transaction or occurrence as the state's claim. Nevertheless, to the extent that a bankruptcy estate seeks to set-off against a state's claim a claim arising out of the same transaction or occurrence, as permitted by § 106(b) and (c), the recoupment doctrine supports the bankruptcy court's authority to entertain such a counterclaim notwithstanding the Eleventh Amendment.

Whether the filing of a proof of claim by a state may give rise to a waiver of Eleventh Amendment immunity on a broader scale is more doubtful. . . .

. . . [E]ven if a majority of the Court is willing to find a waiver by a state that chooses to proceed in the face of a clear warning of potential federal court liability, it might be questioned whether the filing of a proof of claim in bankruptcy is a sufficiently voluntary act on the part of the state to trigger such a finding. As the Court pointed out in *Granfinanciera, S.A. v. Nordberg*, "creditors lack an alternative forum to the bankruptcy court in which to pursue their claims." Thus, despite the clear language in § 106(b) and (c), the Supreme Court might be unwilling to find a waiver on the part of a state that merely pursues the only option it has for collecting its claim against a bankruptcy debtor.

. . . It remains to be seen, however, whether the Court that decided *Seminole* and rejected congressional authority to abrogate the states' Eleventh Amendment immunity in the exercise of its Article I powers will be willing to uphold a congressional enactment that requires the state to waive that same immunity in order to engage in a federally regulated activity.

C. FEDERAL COURT LITIGATION AGAINST STATE OFFICIALS

When a state has not consented to suit in federal court, a bankruptcy plaintiff desiring to adjudicate an issue involving that state in the bankruptcy court needs to consider the extent to which the Eleventh Amendment's bar can be circumvented by means of a suit against appropriate state officials rather than against the state governmental entity itself. In a series of cases prior to *Seminole*, the Supreme Court developed an intricate body of law governing the circumstances under which a private suit in federal court against state officials will be allowed to proceed and when, on the other hand, such a suit will be viewed as being against the state and thus barred by the Eleventh Amendment. . . . The Court's *Ex parte Young* decision . . . recognized an important limitation on the rule that a suit against state officials will be deemed to be a suit against the state. As the Court later explained, "[i]n an injunctive or declaratory action grounded on federal law, the State's immunity *can* be overcome by naming state officials as defendants. Monetary relief that is 'ancillary' to the injunctive relief also is not barred by the Eleventh Amendment." In other words, suits against state officials for prospective relief are permitted; suits against state officials seeking retroactive relief— that is, relief seeking to compensate the plaintiff for past wrongs with funds from the state treasury— are barred.

The *Seminole* decision unfortunately introduces further confusion into this body of law. The Court's holding that the suit by the *Seminole* tribe against the governor for injunctive relief was barred by the Eleventh Amendment seems inconsistent with the just summarized case law. . . .

While this part of the *Seminole* decision might be questioned on a number of grounds, the immediate issue is the impact it has on the ability of a bankruptcy plaintiff to seek injunctive or declaratory relief in the bankruptcy court against a state official. For example, does *Seminole* permit a trustee to seek an injunction in the bankruptcy court against a state tax official to prevent continued efforts to collect a discharged tax debt, or would such a suit be barred by the Eleventh Amendment? It appears that, notwithstanding *Seminole*, such a suit still constitutes a permissible means of enforcing the bankruptcy laws against state governments. . . . Moreover, the statutory scheme before the Court in *Seminole*, on which it so heavily relied, is distinguishable from the bankruptcy provision in which Congress authorized relief against the states. The Supreme Court itself has previously noted the importance of making declaratory and injunctive relief available against governmental parties in the bankruptcy court. Accordingly, although the waters may have been muddied a bit, it appears to continue to be permissible to sue state officials in the bankruptcy court in their official capacities to prevent future violations of the bankruptcy laws.

CONCLUSION

The congressional attempt to subject state governmental entities to most of the bankruptcy courts' remedial powers—just like any other creditor or party affected by a bankruptcy—has been thwarted once again by the Supreme Court. By overruling *Union Gas*, the Court in *Seminole* has withdrawn the constitutional underpinning of § 106's abrogation of the states' Eleventh Amendment immunity. As a result, state governmental entities can no longer be sued in the bankruptcy court for any type of relief unless they give their consent to such proceedings.

It is important, however, that the Supreme Court's decision in *Seminole* not be read for more than it in fact holds. Governments other than states are not affected by the decision, and as a result § 106 remains valid with respect to federal, municipal, and foreign governmental entities. Moreover, suits against states can still be maintained in state courts, where the Eleventh Amendment is inapplicable, and, with the states' consent, bankruptcy proceedings may be brought against them in federal court. If a state governmental entity files a proof of claim in a bankruptcy case, it should be found to have consented to at least the bringing of any recoupment counterclaims the estate might have against it. Finally, state government officials remain subject to suit in the bankruptcy court for injunctive and declaratory relief requiring their prospective compliance with the bankruptcy laws.

While bankruptcy plaintiffs may still be able to find ways of obtaining some relief from state governments, from a bankruptcy perspective this resolution is not ideal, for it undermines the evenhanded and efficient application of the bankruptcy laws. It is but one illustration of the cost of the Supreme Court's insistence upon a broad reading of the Eleventh Amendment that goes beyond its express terms and imposes state sovereign immunity as a constitutional limitation on the complete scope of the federal judicial power.

NATIONAL BANKRUPTCY REVIEW COMMISSION
FINAL REPORT
BANKRUPTCY: THE NEXT TWENTY YEARS
(October 20, 1997)

Chapter 3: Jurisdiction, Procedure and Administration

STATE SOVEREIGN IMMUNITY IN BANKRUPTCY AFTER *SEMINOLE TRIBE OF FLORIDA V. FLORIDA*

A recent Supreme Court decision—in a case not involving bankruptcy—will continue to have a significant impact on the role states play in bankruptcy cases. In *Seminole,* the Supreme Court held that the Eleventh Amendment prevents Congress, acting pursuant to its Article I powers, from abrogating a state's sovereign immunity by subjecting it to suit in federal court without its consent. . . . Congress has plenary power to enact "uniform laws of bankruptcy" under the Bankruptcy Clause in Article I of the Constitution. Accordingly, *Seminole* calls into question whether Congress may abrogate a state's sovereign immunity under its Article I plenary bankruptcy powers. The Court briefly mentioned the potential impact of its opinion on bankruptcy cases, noting in a footnote that "[a]lthough the copyright and bankruptcy laws have existed practically since our nation's inception . . . , there is no established tradition in the lower federal courts of allowing enforcement of those federal statutes against the States." . . .

In the 1994 amendments to the Bankruptcy Code, Congress substantially revised the sovereign immunity provisions in 11 U.S.C. § 106. As amended, section 106(a)(1) explicitly abrogates a state's sovereign immunity with respect to a wide variety of Bankruptcy Code protections including the automatic stay, avoidance, and turnover proceedings. Now in the wake of *Seminole*, lower courts have held that section 106(a)(1) is invalid because it purports to abrogate a nonconsenting state's sovereign immunity by subjecting it to the jurisdiction of the bankruptcy court under a variety of substantive Bankruptcy Code provisions. The conflict between the holding in *Seminole* and the language of section 106(a) has almost uniformly been resolved in favor of *Seminole* and Eleventh Amendment sovereign immunity.

Prior to *Seminole,* it was widely believed that Congress was empowered by the Fourteenth Amendment and by Article I to abrogate expressly a state's sovereign immunity to suit in federal court as provided by the Eleventh Amendment. Following *Seminole,* however, Eleventh Amendment sovereign immunity arguably insulates a state from bankruptcy court jurisdiction. Thus, *Seminole* may well have invalidated Congress' express abrogation of the sovereign immunity of states and state agencies, which otherwise permitted private parties to engage states without their consent in bankruptcy court.

A. Bankruptcy Policy Before and After *Seminole*

Bankruptcy is a collective proceeding, providing a single forum for the resolution of claims against a debtor's property "wherever located." Accordingly, all creditors who seek to assert a claim against property of the estate must assert their claims in the bankruptcy court where the debtor's case is pending. By providing a single forum governed by a single set of procedural rules, the bankruptcy process ensures uniform procedural treatment for every type of claimant . . . . A single bankruptcy forum also advances a variety of fundamental policy goals, including, equal distribution and treatment for similarly-situated creditors, promotion of a cost-effective and speedy process to minimize the cost to creditors, and the rehabilitation of individuals as well as business entities. Determining creditors' rights in the debtor's estate is a fundamental role of the bankruptcy court. A single forum for the resolution of claims against a bankruptcy estate is a critical component of the court's responsibility for a number of reasons.

First, multiple proceedings in different courts may result in conflicting determinations of rights in a debtor's estate. . . . Moreover, separate treatment in multiple courts may also result in unequal treatment of similarly-situated creditors. . . .

Second, the ability of a bankruptcy court to quickly restructure a debtor's obligations enhances the likelihood of saving a business or giving a family a fresh start and increasing the distribution to creditors. . . .

Third, a single forum reduces the cost of collection for creditors. . . .

Fourth, Chapter 11 of the Bankruptcy Code favors the reorganization of debtors in an effort to preserve going-concern value, retain jobs, and promote the efficient use of capital. . . .

Because the Eleventh Amendment protects *only* the states, the ability to bring actions against federal and municipal agencies remains unaffected by the *Seminole* decision. . . . As a result, states must be treated differently from all other creditors and parties in interest (including the federal government) in the bankruptcy process.

States play an important role in the bankruptcy process, appearing in many bankruptcy cases in a myriad of roles—as priority tax creditor, secured creditor, unsecured creditor, police and regulatory authority, environmental creditor, landlord, guarantor, bondholder, leaseholder, and equity interest holder. Similarly, a debtor may have a number of potential actions against a state, including a stay violation, preferences, turnover of property, and lien avoidance. The different treatment accorded states under *Seminole* may result in fewer proceedings against them within the bankruptcy process due to the increased costs required to seek a recovery against a state, including sanctions for violation of the automatic stay. Different treatment of state entities will alter the statutory equilibrium struck in the Bankruptcy Code that balances the rights of creditors against each other as well as against the rights of the debtor.

The Bankruptcy Code carefully balances the rights of the debtor and all creditors, including states. . . . *Seminole's* interpretation of the Eleventh Amendment, as applied by the lower courts, has begun to alter this delicate balance by removing states from the jurisdiction of the bankruptcy court unless they consent to that jurisdiction.

B. Bankruptcy Litigation Involving States After *Seminole*

Given the fundamental need for a single binding bankruptcy proceeding, there are a number of possible alternatives to an action against a state in bankruptcy court. Assuming that a nonconsenting state is not subject to suit in the bankruptcy court, a debtor may be able to seek an *Ex parte Young* injunction against an individual state official (not the state itself) in federal court. Alternatively, the debtor could bring a suit against the state in state court. If the state has filed a proof of claim, the debtor may be able to show that the state waived its sovereign immunity under section 106(b) . . . . In addition, a debtor may be able to assert an *in rem* action to recover property of the estate. While a few courts have upheld section 106(a) in light of *Seminole,* finding that section 106 was enacted as a proper exercise of Congressional power under section 5 of the Fourteenth Amendment, this argument has been undercut recently by the Supreme Court. Finally, the U.S. trustee could be empowered to sue states on behalf of debtors in federal court to enforce states' compliance with the Bankruptcy Code.

1. *Ex parte Young* Injunction

While a state may be immune under the Eleventh Amendment, individual state officials nonetheless may still be subject to federal injunctive relief from ongoing Bankruptcy Code violations. Before a state official actually has completed an act of wrongfully obtaining property, a debtor may be able to use an *Ex parte Young* injunction to enjoin the state official from completing the seizure. An *Ex parte Young* injunction operates on the theory that an individual state official who is about to act or is acting in violation of federal law is not protected by the state's sovereign immunity. Once the state has obtained the property, the federal violation may no longer be ongoing and this option would no longer be available. . . .

2. State Court Action

A state's Eleventh Amendment immunity only protects it from suit in federal court. As a result, a state court action may be brought to enforce a state's compliance with the Bankruptcy Code. In the event of a wrongful seizure by a state of property of the estate, for example, the debtor may be able to commence a state court action to recover the property. State civil litigation, with its concomitant delays, might not provide an adequate substitute for the expedited hearing that otherwise would have been available in the bankruptcy court. There is also some question, in light of the comprehensive federal bankruptcy scheme, whether a state court would enforce federal relief. . . .

3. State Waiver of Eleventh Amendment Sovereign Immunity

Eleventh Amendment immunity is not absolute; a state may waive its own immunity. A state's Eleventh Amendment waiver must be specific and must be "stated by the most express language." The Bankruptcy Code also provides for a waiver of sovereign immunity under certain circumstances. Section 106(b) provides that a "governmental unit" that has filed a proof of claim has waived its sovereign immunity with respect "to a claim . . . that is property of the estate and that arose out of the same transaction or occurrence" in which the government's claim arose. The same principle is applied more generally outside the Eleventh Amendment context; creditors who file proofs of claim against a debtor's estate are subject to the equitable jurisdiction of the bankruptcy court. . . .

At least one commentator has suggested that the Bankruptcy Code could condition a state's very participation in the bankruptcy process on its waiver of sovereign immunity. "For example, [Congress] may condition state claim tax priority on a state's voluntary waiver of its immunity." Whether a waiver of this type would withstand Supreme Court scrutiny remains in some doubt, however, state action in order to participate in a related federal program has been upheld in other circumstances.

5. *In Rem* Proceeding in Bankruptcy Court

Another possible post-*Seminole* alternative is to frame a debtor's claim against a state as an *in rem* proceeding against property of the estate. Since *Seminole,* one court has found that a trustee's turnover action was an *in rem* proceeding against the property and not a "suit" against the state in violation of the Eleventh Amendment. . . .

An admiralty action is a close common law analogy to this type of *in rem* proceeding. The Supreme Court has held that actual title to property may not be affected in an *in rem* proceeding consistent with the Eleventh Amendment. Only *possession* of the property at issue but not the *title* to the property may be resolved by a federal court. In the bankruptcy context, an *in rem* proceeding to recover a critical piece of the debtor's property from a state may be sufficient to enable a debtor to continue operations (to the benefit of all creditors) pending a state court determination of the title to the property.

6. Congress' Power Under the Fourteenth Amendment

Seminole does not necessarily eliminate all avenues of congressional power to abrogate a state's Eleventh Amendment immunity. The *Seminole* Court recognized a valid exercise of congressional abrogation of Eleventh Amendment immunity under Section 5 of the Fourteenth Amendment. . . .

In upholding congressional abrogation power, the Court relied on the fact that the Fourteenth Amendment "expand[ed] federal power at the expense of state autonomy, [and] fundamentally altered the balance of state and federal power struck by the Constitution." A few courts now have used the *Seminole* rationale to find that section 106 was enacted as a "valid exercise of power under the Fourteenth Amendment." . . .

The Supreme Court, however, has questioned nonremedial legislation under the Fourteenth Amendment. In *City of Boerne*, the Court held that the Religious Freedom Restoration Act of 1993 ("RFRA") exceeded Congress' power under Section 5 of the Fourteenth Amendment. Specifically, the Court found . . . that its Section 5 power "to enforce" the Fourteenth Amendment is only preventative or remedial in nature. The RFRA was not a remedial statute because it was not enacted in response to offensive state statutes. Similarly, section 106 was not revised to remedy an inequity under state law . . . . Re-enactment of section 106(a) under Section 5 of the Fourteenth Amendment may, however, exceed the Section 5 bounds set by the Court in *City of Boerne*.

7. Empowering the U.S. Trustee to Sue States in Bankruptcy Court

The Eleventh Amendment does not bar suits against states in federal court as long as those suits are commenced by the federal government rather than private parties. Under the Bankruptcy Code, the U.S. trustee has standing to raise, appear, and be heard on any issue in any case or proceeding in bankruptcy with certain limitations. As a consequence, the U.S. trustee could be empowered to commence suits in the bankruptcy court against states to enforce compliance with the Bankruptcy Code. . . . [T]his alternative would be more expeditious if the U.S. trustee acted as the case trustee. . . .

C. Repercussions of *Seminole* on Other Bankruptcy Policy Decisions

The Bankruptcy Code strikes a delicate balance between the rights of creditors to collect debts and the rights of debtors to restructure or discharge those debts. By exempting states from the jurisdiction of the bankruptcy court, *Seminole* arguably places states and state agencies outside this delicate balance regardless of what role they play in the case. This exclusion is detrimental to both debtors and creditors. Bankruptcy works in large measure because it provides a single forum with a binding determination of all of the competing rights in the debtor's property. Exempting even one party from this process invariably reduces its effectiveness for the remaining parties. . . .

Altering the power of any of the possible roles that states play in bankruptcy will magnify the results under *Seminole.* . . . A "uniform" system of bankruptcy may be unattainable if bankruptcy courts no longer provide a single forum for the resolution of claims by and against a bankruptcy estate.

In the context of bankruptcy legislation, the inability of a bankruptcy court to enforce a state's compliance with the Bankruptcy Code increases the power already exercised by states in bankruptcy cases. . . .

As both a creditor and a regulator of debtors, states benefit from the collective, binding procedures under the Bankruptcy Code. Creditors bear the cost of administering the estate and, as discussed previously, duplicative litigation costs will be borne by creditors. Similarly, states (as both creditor and regulator) benefit from the fresh start to the extent that individual debtors become productive members of society after bankruptcy. An expeditious and binding bankruptcy process advances these policies under the Bankruptcy Code. As a result, it may be in the state's best interest to waive some or all of its Eleventh Amendment sovereign immunity and participate in bankruptcy cases to achieve these beneficial goals. If the waiver decision is left up to the state's litigation attorneys on a case-by-case basis, however, it is doubtful that they will give up an absolute defense to the federal suit.

E.   Other Procedural and Administrative Issues

The final section of this Chapter deals with a variety of additional procedural and administrative issues. The first article, *Towards a Model of Bankruptcy Administration*, 44 S.C. L. REV. 963 (1993), is by Richard Levin, a noted bankruptcy attorney who served on the legislative staff that drafted the 1978 Act. In this work, Levin explores the nature of the peculiar beast that is the bankruptcy system, with its unique mix of judicial and administrative tasks. In doing so he notes the differences between "forensic" and "nonforensic" decisions and between disputed and undisputed decisions, and the significance of those distinctions for the effective administration of the bankruptcy system. Levin develops a model of bankruptcy administration that would account for these differences and allocate decision-making responsibility efficiently and effectively. He also explains the importance of supervision of estate representatives. Levin recommends the establishment of a new position for an "Administrative Officer" who would undertake many of the administrative functions that a judge cannot handle as readily. This is an important article, worthy of serious consideration by Congress.

The second work is from Professor Robert Lawless of the University of Missouri. In *Realigning the Theory and Practice of Notice in Bankruptcy Cases*, 29 WAKE FOREST L. REV. 1215 (1994), Lawless tackles the knotty problems surrounding notice in bankruptcy cases and proceedings. As he explains, there are a wide variety of bankruptcy matters requiring differing sorts of notice. The present system, unfortunately, reflects inconsistent, ad hoc approaches to these different situations. Professor Lawless proposes a "Restatement of Notice," which can be applied to some of the most common and important bankruptcy proceedings. The Advisory Committee on the Bankruptcy Rules as well as bankruptcy judges would do well to study Lawless's proposals carefully.

Third up is Professor John P. Hennigan, Jr. of St. John's University. He takes on another bankruptcy procedural nightmare—the problems involving the appealability of decisions in bankruptcy proceedings. In *Toward Regularizing Appealability in Bankruptcy*, 12 BANKR. DEV. J. 583 (1996), Hennigan assesses the current confused state of affairs in bankruptcy appeals, showing how the modified view of "finality" in bankruptcy has caused innumerable problems. Hennigan suggests that courts adhere more faithfully to non-bankruptcy federal law on appealability, with only very slight accommodation of to the demands of the bankruptcy system. Following Hennigan's article are the 1997 Review Commission recommendations on bankruptcy appeals.

Richard B. Levin
Towards a Model of Bankruptcy Administration
44 S.C. L. Rev. 963 (1993)[*]

I. Introduction

Two of the principal goals of the 1978 Bankruptcy Reform Act were to separate the administrative and judicial functions of bankruptcy judges and to establish a strong administrative system to fill the void left by the removal of bankruptcy judges from administrative and supervisory tasks. The United States trustee system was supposed to fill that void. The 1978 Act, however, provided only a framework for the role of the United States trustees. Congress established policy and form, but not mechanics or procedures for bankruptcy administration. . . . Congress failed to define adequately a theoretical basis for, or a model of, bankruptcy administration that would give guidance to those charged with implementing the program. . . . In addition, the statute provides no policy guidance on the proper roles of the bankruptcy judges and the United States Trustees.

This Article attempts to develop an appropriate model for bankruptcy administration. In addition, it strives to refine the distinction between "administrative" and "judicial" functions that precipitated the establishment of the United States trustee system in the 1978 bankruptcy legislation. . . . [I]t is a conceptual piece, designed to explore the nature of decisions in bankruptcy cases—both liquidations and reorganizations—as well as the appropriateness of the decision-making institution and the decision-making process to the task at hand.

II. Towards a Model of Bankruptcy Administration

. . .

B. The Historical Model

Historically, bankruptcy has been considered a judicial proceeding. This view seems more a result of the assignment of bankruptcy cases to the courts for the adjudication of bankruptcy and for the supervision of case administration from the earliest times rather than a result of anything inherent in the nature of the process, or of any conscious decision based on an analysis of the functions performed by the process. To the contrary, after the declaration or adjudication of bankruptcy, the process appears to be one more of administration than dispute resolution, despite the placement of the function in the courts. Indeed, both the statutes and the courts have so treated the bankruptcy process. . . . The judge's role after adjudication has been more of a supervisory role in reviewing the administration of the case. Disputes often arose in the course of settling the affairs of a bankrupt. Therefore, it was convenient to have the court (or its adjunct, the referee) at hand for summary resolution of those disputes. Still, the case itself was more of an administrative process of liquidating or reorganizing assets and reviewing claims than one of adjudicating disputes. By its nature, the overall case was not a dispute suitable for judicial resolution.

C. The Model Under the 1978 Bankruptcy Reform Act

The "separation of administrative and judicial functions currently performed by bankruptcy judges" was one of the principal goals of the 1978 legislation. . . . The simple manner in which the problem was stated, however, defined the simple model for the solution. As a result, the solution failed to comprehend the underlying nature of the functions involved.

The 1978 Bankruptcy Reform Act attempted to address the problem by recharacterizing the proceeding and emphasizing its administrative nature. It removed many of the bankruptcy courts' "administrative" responsibilities and lodged them with the United States trustees. This administrative structure established under the Reform Act was based on a simple model of bankruptcy administration. It divided functions into two categories, judicial and administrative, based solely on whether there was a dispute about a particular issue. If a dispute existed, the matter was considered proper for judicial attention and was directed to the bankruptcy court for decision. If there was no dispute, then the court was not supposed to become involved, regardless of the subject matter of the dispute or whether the dispute was appropriate for judicial resolution.

Nevertheless, long history and established practice created heavy chains. Thus, despite the apparently simple and absolute bifurcation of functions, the Code requires or permits court involvement in certain matters, either for historical reasons or because some matters were felt to be too "important" to escape court supervision or intervention. . . .

As a result, many bankruptcy judges continue to view themselves as responsible for the overall management and supervision of the cases on their dockets. . . .

Thus, the Bankruptcy Code's simple administrative model, which bifurcated disputed (judicial) from nondisputed (administrative) matters, was implemented imperfectly. Despite its simplicity, the model could have been implemented strictly and consistently. Although any such implementation would have improved the plan Congress actually enacted, the model still would have been inadequate, primarily because it was incomplete. In allocating responsibility in the system, the Code fails to acknowledge that, in most of the kinds of matters described above, decisions are and must be made even when there is no dispute. Moreover, the Code does not address the nature of the decisions that must be made or the suitability of the decision-maker to the particular kind of decision. Therefore, an additional concept is needed to describe the kind of decisions being made and the suitability of both the decision-maker and the decision-making process to the decisions that must be made.

D. A Better Model of Judicial/Administrative Bifurcation

1. Defining the Nature of the Decision

Any parent with more than one child is well schooled in the dual roles of judicial and administrative decision-maker. . . . On the one hand, the parent assumes a judicial role when asking and then deciding "what happened?" and "what are the consequences?" following a sibling conflict. On the other hand, the parent acts a administrator when asking and deciding "what should we do today?" following expressions of differing interests for the day's activities. . . .

Unlike ordinary civil or criminal litigation, which focuses almost solely on "what happened?" and "what are the consequences?," bankruptcy cases involve both judicial and administrative decisions. A bankruptcy case must accomplish a complete settlement of all of the debtor's affairs and existing legal relationships, many of which may involve disputes akin to ordinary civil litigation. However, the case must also manage the business of the estate, whether the business is liquidation or operation.

Thus, a concept that distinguishes between decisions based on past events (who did what, when, how, and to whom?) and decisions based on judgments about the future (what should be done?) might better describe the kinds of decisions that must be made in the course of a bankruptcy case. Such a concept can better define the distinction between the judicial and administrative functions that the Bankruptcy Code sought to implement. This concept is useful because it recognizes the differences in the kinds of decisions to be made, the information they require, and the remedies that must be fashioned. A more complete model of the bankruptcy system should clearly define this distinction and allocate responsibility based on these factors.

2. Forensic Decisions

Decisions based on past events are the kinds of questions involved in a typical, classic civil action. These decisions require proof of existing facts and events that have already occurred and the application of governing law to those facts. The decision-maker in a civil case decides "what happened?," determines the substantive rights of the parties to the action at a particular time ("what are the consequences?"), and enforces those rights. . . . These decisions will be referred to as "forensic decisions" in this Article . . . .

Forensic decisions . . . are typically suitable for resolution by judicial forms and procedures, such as the introduction of disputed evidence to permit the court to find facts. Forensic disputes arise in bankruptcy cases over such things as the allowability of claims, the validity and priority of liens, entitlements to property of the estate (*i.e.*, "who is the owner?"), exemptions, discharge, and dischargeability. Indeed, the Bankruptcy Rules require that adversary proceedings be brought to resolve all of these kinds of disputes except disputes over claims and exemptions.

3. Nonforensic Decisions

The other kind of decisions are those about the future. They require an exercise of judgment as to the course of action that should be taken. The decision-maker may rely heavily on historical facts and the existing substantive rights of the parties in order to set the context for the decision. . . . However, the critical bases for these decisions are primarily predictions of future events (how will a decision one way or the other affect the course of administration or obtain a desired result?). These decisions require an evaluation of risks and a balancing of competing risk/reward preferences among those involved in the case. Decisions of this kind relate more to administration, either of the case or of an operating business, and will be referred to in this Article as "nonforensic decisions."

In administering a case, the trustee must make a variety of nonforensic decisions that are influenced very little by the past . . . .

Many of the daily, ordinary-course decisions are routine and made without much thought. Many of the decisions out of the ordinary course are also clear and easily reached without much controversy or debate. As the cases get bigger and more complex, however, decisions on many of these issues can have serious implications for the values to be realized and the time required for administration of the case. When these decisions may have a significant effect on the amount that creditors or equity holders will recover in the case, disputes can and do arise. Whether or not there is a dispute, however, a decision must still be made by someone.

Moreover, even if there is a dispute, nonforensic decisions are fundamentally different from forensic decisions. Nonforensic decisions do not involve determining what the facts were at a particular time in the past and applying the law to those facts to determine the rights and entitlements of the parties. Rather, they involve the exercise of considered judgment, typically business judgment, about a future course of action. As a result, disputes over these decisions often involve disagreement about a prediction of the future—events both within and beyond the control of the participants in the administrative process—and about what constitutes an acceptable level of risk and reward. . . .

There is no standard in the Bankruptcy Code, nor would it be easy to create one, that could be applied in an adversarial setting to answer these kinds of questions. Moreover, the solution may be a synthesis of various nonlegal factors, such as devising means to reduce the risk or limit the exposure of the estate if the venture is unsuccessful. These approaches require constructive business strategies. No amount of evidence can enable the decision-maker to "find facts" about the future. In fact, because the objective facts are rarely in dispute, litigation over these matters often involves the testimony of managers and consultants concerning why a particular proposed course of action is likely to succeed or fail.

4. Disputed vs. Nondisputed Decisions

Many decisions in bankruptcy cases, both forensic and nonforensic, simply do not involve disputes at all. In some situations, the parties are simply in agreement or have been brought to an agreement by a party with an ability to influence others in the case. For many decisions, the amounts involved are too small relative to the bankruptcy case, or the parties' investment in it, to warrant the necessary time and attention for a dispute. . . . Often, creditors refrain from reviewing decisions because they have confidence in the decision-maker (trustee or debtor-in-possession). Thus, the identity of the initial decision-maker may heavily influence the decision and whether it is challenged or disputed.

Not all decisions in bankruptcy cases can be neatly categorized as forensic or nonforensic. The disputed-undisputed categorization is much simpler and easier to apply. Nevertheless, bifurcating decision-making, as the Bankruptcy Code does, based solely or primarily on whether the matter is disputed or undisputed, without regard to whether the decision is forensic or nonforensic, does not address who is best qualified to make the initial decision, to review the decision, or to supervise the decision-maker. The disputed-undisputed bifurcation also fails to address what effect the nature of the review has on the decision itself. . . . Thus, the forensic-nonforensic dichotomy can help to determine the function of the decision-maker, assist in the development of a model, and allocate tasks among bankruptcy officials.

However, categorizing decisions does not complete the model. A bankruptcy case is not just forensic dispute resolution; it is a process. Each activity in the process requires an *authoritative* decision. . . .

E. Allocation of Decision-Making Responsibility

Determining the nature of the decisions that must be and are made daily in the bankruptcy system is only the first step. To develop the model further requires an allocation of the responsibility for decision making and a brief examination of the suitability of the decision-maker to the decision. The task of allocating decision-making responsibility in the bankruptcy system is the determination of who can make the first authoritative decision about a particular matter.

Responsibility should be allocated, in part, based upon the effect the allocation will have on advancing the progress of the case. That effect is defined by the authority the decision will carry in the process. The critical issue of the applicable standard of review to be used by higher (second or third) level decision-makers in reviewing a first-level authoritative decision both determines and is determined by how much authority is or should be vested in the first-level decision-maker.

. . . [T]he model bifurcates decision-making responsibility along forensic-nonforensic lines.

1. Forensic Decisions

Authoritative forensic decisions in bankruptcy cases are the kind of decisions that are typically delegated to the court system, and they have long been placed there. The responsibility for making authoritative forensic decisions should be allocated, however, only when a dispute exists. . . .

When there is a dispute, making a fully authoritative forensic decision involves evaluating adverse parties' disputed views of the facts or the law. . . . The formal, adversarial process is appropriate for this kind of fact finding and resolution of disputed legal issues.

Thus, for purposes of the model, authoritative decisions about disputed forensic matters in bankruptcy cases should be made in the judicial system. That is, when a disputed forensic decision must be made, one of the disputants should bring an action in court, where a judge having full authority to resolve the dispute can resolve the issue, uninfluenced by the decision either disputant made before bringing the issue to the court for resolution. These decisions should be reviewed by ordinary appeals, as they are now.

2. Nonforensic Decisions

Authoritative nonforensic decisions in bankruptcy cases are, by their nature, more often made unilaterally. . . . [S]omeone has to be responsible for managing the case and the estate's business and making the nonforensic decisions necessary to move the process forward. The allocation of nonforensic decision-making responsibility involves selecting an officer or institution to perform that managerial job.

Historically, the allocation of managerial responsibilities has been governed by a different policy choice, based on an unrelated principle. The bankruptcy system adopted the concept of private, as opposed to governmental, control in conducting the business and management of bankruptcy estates. . . .

There is no reason to change this principle or the resulting system for purposes of the model. The principle is well ingrained, and there are independent reasons for leaving it in place. . . . Thus, first-level nonforensic decisions have generally rested with the representative of the estate (trustee or debtor-in-possession), who is a private (nongovernmental) party. The model retains this approach.

F. Supervision of Estate Representatives

1. The Need for External Supervision

A system of checks and balances ensures that ordinary business people and fiduciaries act with the interests of their businesses or trusts ahead of their own personal interests. . . .

Some form of deterrent or a system of checks and balances is equally necessary in regulating the conduct of decision-makers in the bankruptcy system. There is reason to suspect, however, that the imposition of personal liability as a deterrent does not work effectively in bankruptcy.

External supervision is not, however, essential to the bankruptcy system. . . . [T]he imposition of personal liability on fiduciaries might not be as effective a deterrent to misconduct in bankruptcy cases. . . . Accordingly, bankruptcy has developed a system of direct external supervision of the actions of trustees and debtors-in-possession, in addition to the ordinary deterrents.

The model accepts the premise of the existing system of bankruptcy administration that external supervision of nonforensic decisions is the best way to deter misconduct and keep the bankruptcy fiduciary true to his trust. The need for supervision is especially strong in business reorganizations, because it is often a lack of strong business acumen on management's part that caused the business to fail in the first place. To allow management to continue unsupervised could easily invite the same problems to recur.

2. Governmental Supervision of Estate Representatives

External supervision can be governmental or private. Private supervision can be accomplished through general creditor supervision of the activities of the estate's representative or through use of a private supervisor, such as a receiver. Neither method is likely to be successful. At one time, the law assumed that creditors would exert sufficient supervision and control over estate administration to maintain honesty, care, and sound business judgment. However, active creditor control has proven to be a myth in all but a few of the largest bankruptcies or reorganizations.

Use of private supervisors (such as the receivership system under the Bankruptcy Act) has the advantage of providing the incentive of compensation for good work. However, compensating private supervisors from estate assets creates an equal incentive for misconduct, which in turn requires supervision of the estate representative. Thus, private supervisors would themselves need to be supervised, requiring the creation of a governmental supervision system in any event. . . . Thus, although private administration of cases appears to be appropriate, supervision of the private administration should be governmental.

3. The Governmental Supervisory Officer

The Bankruptcy Act vested courts with direct supervisory responsibility. Under the Bankruptcy Code, courts retain some general supervisory authority over undisputed nonforensic decisions, many administrative functions, and some tools for taking charge of bankruptcy cases. Moreover, bankruptcy judges, many of whom served as judges or lawyers under the former regime, feel obligated to fill any voids in administrative supervision, lest the bankruptcy system, especially operating Chapter 11 cases, run amok. As a result, bankruptcy judges actually take an active role in the administration and supervision of bankruptcy cases. There are at least four reasons why using courts for supervision of these matters is not ideal.

First, courts are not designed to make decisions in the absence of a dispute. . . . They do not have independent investigatory arms. . . . [T]hey cannot and do not conduct independent factual research. Nonforensic decisions about the conduct of a bankruptcy case or the operation of a business are heavily fact based. . . . In the absence of a dispute, courts are ill-equipped to become fully informed. There is no check or balance on the information that is being presented to the court. . . .

Second, even when a dispute arises, the adversary system is not a particularly satisfactory way to make, or supervise the making of, nonforensic decisions. The adversary system is, by nature, formal. The system does not encourage the disputing parties to cooperate in developing solutions to nonforensic problems. Also, the adversary system does not promote collegiality or the exchange of ideas in developing solutions. . . .

Third, courts have no particular expertise in the substance of nonforensic decisions, nor do they have the ability to become sufficiently involved in the particular estate or business to make sensible decisions. . . .

Based on this reasoning, most courts approve transactions by a trustee that involve "a business judgment made in good faith, upon a reasonable basis, and within the scope of his authority under the Code." . . .

Finally, no legal standards exist to guide courts in making nonforensic decisions. There is neither a fixed set of rights to protect nor a right or wrong answer to the issues presented in a nonforensic decision.

If the court is not an appropriate or adequate supervisor for the representative of the estate, then an alternative must be found. To be effective, the supervisory function must be performed by an independent official who is able to investigate facts on his own. . . . The supervisory officer must be familiar with the administration of the estate, including the operation of any business, in order to have a context in which to evaluate decisions about proposed courses of action. Also, the supervisory officer must be able to follow the bankruptcy from beginning to end in order to understand and properly evaluate the context in which decisions are being made. This Article will refer to this proposed governmental supervisory official as the Administrative Officer.

4. Matters Subject to the Administrative Officer's Review

This model assumes private administration of cases and estates. Such a system is more susceptible to breaches of the duties of care and loyalty than is a governmentally administered system. Therefore, there is a greater need for "professional" supervision. As such, the Administrative Officer should be authorized to supervise or review all nonforensic decisions of the estate representative, with only minor exceptions. . . .

This system does not suggest, however, that the Administrative Officer should be involved in the day-to-day administration of the estate or the operation of a reorganizing business. The Administrative Officer should realistically be able to monitor decisions in the ordinary course of administration of the estate or the operation of a business from regular reports, periodic reviews, and assessments of the estate representative's ability. The estate representative should be required to notify the Administrative Officer in advance of decisions that do not arise in the ordinary course of business because, by definition, these decisions would not be anticipated. . . .

G. Review of Decisions

1. Standard of Review of the Estate Representative's Decisions

Because the model relies on private administration through trustees or debtors-in-possession, the initial decisions for nonforensic matters should remain with the private representatives. The Administrative Officer's role should be limited to reviewing those decisions. Consequently, how much discretion should the estate's private representative have in making nonforensic decisions, and what standard of review should the Administrative Officer apply to these decisions?

. . . [T]he estate representative should be responsible for nonforensic decisions, but also should be subject to some form of review by the Administrative Officer in order to give some weight to the representative's decision. The standard of review should be stringent enough to avert the dangers of an unsupervised bankruptcy system—lack of adequate care and breach of fiduciary duty; but the standard should not be so stringent as to remove the decision-making authority from the estate representative.

A standard of review such as "abuse of discretion" would probably provide far too much latitude to the estate representative. The standard of "sound exercise of business judgment," however, should serve the stated goals. First, a breach of trust would not constitute a sound exercise of business judgment. Second, sound exercise of business judgment would require due care by the estate representative in the administration of the estate and the operation of the business. . . . The representative would not be overruled if the decision were supportable. This standard would provide the estate representative the control and authority necessary for sound administration of the estate, without permitting conduct outside of the bankruptcy system's stated goals. . . .

2. Review of the Administrative Officer's Decisions

The Administrative Officer's decisions should be reviewable by the bankruptcy court. The level of review should meet the goals stated above—that the Administrative Officer be primarily responsible for administration and review of nonforensic decisions, and that the office play a meaningful role, not a subservient role to the court, in the areas of its responsibilities.

. . . [T]he court might consider whether the Administrative Officer abused his discretion or applied an incorrect legal standard in evaluating the nonforensic decision of the estate representative. This is a familiar standard . . . . This standard affords proper weight to both the Administrative Officer's decisions and the estate representative's decisions. . . . To assist the court in deciding what standard the Officer used in evaluating the estate representative's decision, the Officer should be required to state why he objects to the decision.

H. Form of Proceedings

Currently, many disagreements over nonforensic matters could be resolved by negotiation among the parties. However, the Code and the Bankruptcy Rules effectively require a court-based procedure, under which notices of nonforensic matters are filed with the court whether or not they are likely to be disputed. Objections to these matters are filed with the court, even when the objector is the United States trustee. Consequently, the court's process is set in motion, even when a dispute is and could be resolved by negotiation. If the trustee, debtor-in-possession, or other proponent of an action, the Administrative Officer, and other parties in interest were to . . . consult with each other before a proposed administrative action they would often obviate any objections.

Therefore, the Administrative Officer's decision-making should be informal and interactive with the estate representative and other interested parties. The Administrative Officer should review or consult on proposed transactions before a "proposal" or "objection" is finalized and formalized. . . .

When the Administrative Officer disapproves of proposed action by an estate representative, he should be able to prevent such action by filing a written notation of disapproval in the case file (with a copy mailed to the estate representative), rather than by filing an objection with the court.. The estate representative will have to meet a high standard, described above, to overturn the Administrative Officer's recommendation in court. That burden, coupled with prior informal consultation, will likely result in the estate representative's acquiescing in the Administrative Officer's decision or reaching an accommodation with the Officer before the matter ever gets to court. . . .

When the estate representative disagrees with the Administrative Officer's decision, the estate representative should seek affirmative authority from the court to proceed. . . .

The nature of the Administrative Officer system, which promotes informal consultation and communication prior to any "formal" objection to an estate representative's actions, should result in similar consultation prior to the Administrative Officer's attempting to require action by the estate representative. . . .

III. CONCLUSION

The nature of a model is to attempt to describe the ideal. Whether the model suggested in this Article in fact describes an ideal administrative system may well be open to question. Undoubtedly, a significant criticism of this model will be that the existing administrative system, the United States trustee system, is bureaucratic, inflexible, cumbersome, expensive, and staffed by people whose competence is less than desirable. Another criticism will likely be that bankruptcy practitioners would never willingly cede such authority to an Administrative Officer; it is, after all, the person in the black robe who is really in charge. To these potential criticisms, I offer the following response.

These criticisms are not of the model itself, as an ideal, but of bankruptcy administration and of the feasibility of the model. . . . The ability, integrity, and dedication of personnel is the key to success in any system . . . . This model assumes that persons equal to the task—both as administrators and as practitioners—will administer it in the spirit in which it was designed.

The model is intended to provide flexibility rather than bureaucratic rules that would stifle case administration with countless diverse facts and challenges. It is intended to impose a structure that permits supervision of bankruptcy cases, and of the bankruptcy system, by experienced individuals with the tools and authority to become knowledgeable about the matters that come before them, without reliance on the adversary system for education. . . . [S]omething was lost in the transition to the United States trustee system under the Bankruptcy Code. Something other than an adversary system is necessary to replace it and to protect the functioning of the bankruptcy system.

Robert M. Lawless
Realigning the Theory and Practice of Notice in Bankruptcy Cases
29 WAKE FOREST L. REV. 1215 (1994)[*]

INTRODUCTION

A bankruptcy case typically involves a wide variety and large number of competing interests. In this sense, a bankruptcy case differs substantially from the normal adversarial model of plaintiff versus defendant. For a bankruptcy case to be successful, the bankruptcy court must have the power to bind the disparate interests appearing before it. Without appropriate notice, a party is not bound by judgments of the court. But who has a right to notice of which proceedings in a bankruptcy case? For example, do the thousands of trade creditors in a multimillion dollar corporate bankruptcy have a right to notice of every event in the case? Do holders of underwater equity claims have a right to notice?

Although notice is fundamental to the success of a bankruptcy case, defining the parameters of when and to whom notice must be given has not received the attention that it deserves. The Bankruptcy Code, procedural rules, and reported bankruptcy decisions leave no consistent answers. Caught up in the enormous practical task of administering many complex cases, few bankruptcy courts have time to wax poetic about the theoretical niceties of notice and due process. . . . As a result, the law of due process and notice in bankruptcy cases strikes the reader as arbitrary and irrational, undermining confidence in its application.

This article aims to replace inconsistencies with clarity, working toward an overarching theoretical ground for notice in bankruptcy cases. Primarily, this article answers the question of which parties in a bankruptcy case are entitled to notice of the various proceedings within the case. . . .

I. THE GENERAL FRAMEWORK FOR PROCEDURAL DUE PROCESS AND NOTICE

Many bankruptcy courts and commentators have relied heavily on one sentence from *Mullane v. Central Hanover Bank & Trust Co.* as the theoretical foundation for notice in bankruptcy cases: "An elementary and fundamental requirement of due process in any proceeding which is to be accorded finality is notice reasonably calculated, under all the circumstances, to apprise interested parties of the pendency of the action and afford them an opportunity to present their objections." Emphasis on this language leads to a "strong" reading of *Mullane*—all actual, known parties always must have individual notice of all proceedings. But when one takes into account the breadth of procedural due process analysis, the "strong" reading of *Mullane* is not accurate. . . .

B. Threshold Inquiries

Two threshold inquiries arise when making the transition from theory to doctrine. Before a bankruptcy claimant can raise an issue of due process, there must be (1) governmental action that (2) deprives a person of life, liberty, or property.

1. Governmental action

Discharge or reduction of claims through an adjudicatory bankruptcy process undoubtedly constitutes governmental action. Thus, as governmental actors, the federal bankruptcy courts readily fulfill the first condition. . . .

---

2. Property interests

a. Defining property interests. Next, one must consider the interests protected by due process. . . . [A]re the claims of bankruptcy litigants properly characterized as "property" for due process purposes?

Fortunately, the Supreme Court has answered this question for the most common bankruptcy claimants. The Court has held that due process protects the chose in action of an unsecured creditor and the lien of a secured creditor. . . . [D]ue process also should protect shareholders from the caprices of a bankruptcy court. Thus, unsecured creditors, secured creditors, and equity security holders all have a "property interest" protected by the Fifth Amendment. . . .

C. The Balancing Test for Notice

Providing notice to bankruptcy claimants is a type of procedure, but is it a procedure that due process always requires? . . . [T]he answer of many bankruptcy scholars and courts has been an inflexible "yes"—a surprising conclusion given that the flexibility of due process is so well established that the principle needs no citation.

The starting point for due process analysis is the three-part balancing test of *Mathews v. Eldridge*, in which the Supreme Court held that due process did not require an evidentiary hearing before termination of Social Security disability benefits. In *Mathews*, the Court announced its prior decisions required consideration of three distinct factors: (1) the private interest at stake, (2) the risk of erroneous deprivation and the possibility of minimizing that risk, and (3) the government's interest. Essentially, this test represents the classic utilitarian balancing of societal costs of providing notice against benefits to the individual. . . .

D. A Proposal for a Restatement of Notice

Based on principles of due process and notice that the Supreme Court has enunciated and applied, a short restatement of the law of notice for bankruptcy proceedings is proposed here. . . .

§ 1. SOURCE OF LAW. Notice is an issue of procedural due process . . . .

§ 2. GOVERNMENTAL ACTION. In a bankruptcy case, the bankruptcy court's involvement is governmental action sufficient to trigger due process protections.

§ 3. PROPERTY INTEREST. In the bankruptcy context, procedural due process protects against arbitrary deprivations of "property." The property requirement ensures that the claimant has a sufficient stake in the bankruptcy case to justify due process protections.

(a) Traditional claimants in a bankruptcy case, such as unsecured creditors, secured creditors, and equity holders, hold a "property interest" for purposes of due process.

(b) As the likelihood of a claimant receiving any distribution from a bankruptcy estate decreases, the claimant's property interest in the bankruptcy case also decreases. In the event of a deeply insolvent debtor, some claimants' property interests may be too attenuated to justify due process protection.

§ 4. BALANCING TEST. In deciding whether a claimant is entitled to the procedural safeguard of notice, a bankruptcy court should balance the costs of providing notice to that party and similarly situated parties against the benefits to be derived therefrom. In applying this balancing test, a bankruptcy court should use the following guidelines:

(a) Notice of bankruptcy proceedings are important to claimants' dignity and their perception of the bankruptcy system's fairness. In the usual case, notice will greatly benefit the claimants who receive the notice.

(b) The strength of a claimant's property interest in the bankruptcy case, as discussed in section 3(b), may be considered in determining the benefit of giving that party notice.

(c) The mails are usually an inexpensive and efficient means of providing service.

(d) The federal government has a legitimate interest in the efficacious and expeditious administration of a debtor's estate. A bankruptcy court may consider how providing notice will affect that interest.

(e) Group representation of common interests mitigates the harm suffered when a claimant does not receive notice. The greater the identity of interests among the group, the more effective the group representation will be.

Application of this "Restatement" must heed the Supreme Court's lead of integrating both the utilitarian and dignity theories of due process. The cost-benefit balancing reflects the Court's predominately utilitarian thinking. At the same time, the Restatement framework captures the dignity theory by attaching extreme importance to the individual benefit of receiving notice.

John P. Hennigan, Jr.
Toward Regularizing Appealability in Bankruptcy
12 BANKR. DEV. J. 583 (1996)*

I. INTRODUCTION

Under 28 U.S.C.A. § 158, the special statute for bankruptcy appeals, "final" decisions are appealable as of right, initially from the bankruptcy court to the district court or bankruptcy appellate panel and thereafter to the court of appeals. Of course, finality is generally required for any kind of appeal in the federal courts. That requirement has given rise to both interpretive problems and significant exceptions. But why should it be any different, or any murkier, in bankruptcy cases?

One difference is clear in principle, though sometimes obscure in application. A single bankruptcy case commonly encompasses a number of distinct litigated proceedings . . . . It has long been established that a decision fully resolving at least some kinds of proceedings is final and appealable, even if others remain pending; the individual proceeding is the relevant "judicial unit" for assessing finality. In contrast, a civil action ordinarily reaches finality only when every claim has been fully concluded as to every party.

However, many bankruptcy decisions have gone beyond that distinctive definition of the judicial unit to introduce a more fundamental departure, "flexible finality." While ostensibly requiring a final decision, these decisions modify the conventional process of assessing the completeness of the relevant unit. Instead, or in addition, they focus upon factors commonly associated with interlocutory appeals, especially the impact of immediate or delayed review on the parties and on the litigation yet to be completed in the trial court. . . .

Because flexible finality rests upon highly case-specific considerations, it often produces uncertainty and confusion. . . .

Such puzzlement entails both practical and systemic problems. It is black-letter law that if a completely final order is not promptly appealed, it cannot be challenged later. When finality is unclear, litigants routinely must choose between immediately attempting a jurisdictionally questionable appeal or else risking forfeiture of their arguments on the merits. Jurisdictional litigation also burdens the courts: even if the appeal is ultimately dismissed, flexible finality will first immerse them in factual specifics as they struggle to explain how that amorphous standard could go unsatisfied. . . .

While endorsing relatively modest adaptations required by the fact that numerous disparate proceedings may occur within a single bankruptcy case, this article otherwise advocates adherence to non-bankruptcy federal law on appealability. Compared to flexible finality, that body of statutes, judicial decisions, and rules is well-developed and widely understood. At the same time, it offers analytical resources sufficient to address pertinently and reasonably the recurring bankruptcy contexts which have fueled flexibility.

Under the proposed approach, a bankruptcy decision is final if it is both procedurally complete and determinative of substantive rights. Procedural completeness is achieved upon the resolution of all non-ministerial litigation within a unit. An order determines substantive rights when it decides the sorts of entitlements at issue in civil litigation outside bankruptcy, that is, rights to money damages, property, or injunctions. . . .

There's got to be a better way.

IV. TOWARD REGULARIZING APPEALABILITY IN BANKRUPTCY

A. *The Proposed Approach*

The murkiness surrounding appellate jurisdiction in bankruptcy would be considerably dispelled with the adoption of one simple rule: adhere as closely as practicable to the general law of appealability.

Under the proposed approach, a bankruptcy decision is final if it determines substantive rights and qualifies as procedurally complete. The requirement of substantiality is developed below. Procedural completeness is reached upon the resolution of an individual proceeding, such as an adversary proceeding or contested matter contemplated by the Federal Rules of Bankruptcy Procedure, as opposed to the entire case.

The long-established focus on individual proceedings promotes prompt resolution of the entire bankruptcy-case puzzle by placing some of its pieces conclusively, subject to displacement only by immediate appeal. Perhaps less obviously, that focus also comports with the non-bankruptcy finality principles proposed here as the governing standard, as can be seen from analysis of the only plausible alternative.

If the appealable unit consisted of the entire bankruptcy case, the only truly final order would be the one closing the estate. But then review of earlier decisions would present a theoretical problem. The bar on immediate appeal of interlocutory orders is generally balanced by the losing party's right to challenge them on appeal from the final judgment, in which they are said to be "merged," the idea being that those earlier rulings contributed to the final judgment. . . . However, a closing order has nothing to do with the merits of significant conclusions reached earlier in the case. . . . It would therefore make no sense to treat those conclusions as merged in the closing order.

At the same time, they would arguably be appealable as collateral orders. They would be non-tentative and sufficiently separate from the merits of the closing order that reviewing them on appeal from that order would be problematic and unreasonable, if not "ineffective." If those previous decisions comprised immediately enforceable orders for the delivery of property, such as a turnover order or denial of a claimed exemption for property in the debtor's possession, they would independently be appealable under *Forgay*.

Conventional finality doctrine is therefore consonant with the established rule treating the proceeding as the relevant judicial unit. . . .

. . . As a mechanism for enforcing the finality requirement, the court should expressly identify the unit in each bankruptcy appeal.

That exercise might itself produce some clarification. . . .

Once the relevant unit has been identified, it must be determined whether it has reached the requisite point of resolution. In fixing that point, the courts have broadly applied conventional doctrine, including that developed from *Cohen* and *Forgay-Conrad*, except in such problematic areas as those described in Part III of this article. The proposed approach would adhere to convention in those areas as well. The only fundamental departure would be the modest and necessary one developed in *Saco*: given a proper litigative unit, a disposition is procedurally complete when it effects the most conclusive resolution possible within the confines of the unit. . . .

VI. Conclusion

In enacting a final judgment rule, Congress brought appellate jurisdiction in bankruptcy into closer conformity with general federal practice. The courts have universally modified conventional finality doctrine in response to the possibility of numerous disparate proceedings within each bankruptcy case. Beyond those necessary adaptations, however, some of the circuits have taken such a flexible approach to finality that neither they nor prospective litigants can assess with any confidence. To dispel that murkiness and give effect to the apparent legislative design, courts faced with a bankruptcy appeal should adhere as closely as practicable to non-bankruptcy law in assessing their jurisdiction.

National Bankruptcy Review Commission
Final Report
Bankruptcy: The Next Twenty Years
(October 20, 1997)

Chapter 3: Jurisdiction, Procedure and Administration

Introduction

Another major flaw in the bankruptcy system that results in unnecessary cost is the current appellate process. Appeals from bankruptcy courts go to district courts—or, in some circuits, bankruptcy appellate panels—and then to the courts of appeals before they are eligible for hearing by the U.S. Supreme Court. This two-tiered appeal system is found nowhere else in the federal judicial system. There should be no need for an appeal from one trial judge (the bankruptcy court) to another trial judge (the district court). Moreover, and most importantly, neither the appeal to the district court nor to the bankruptcy appellate panel, if one has been established in the particular circuit and district, settles anything except the dispute between the parties in their particular matter. No precedent is established for future cases in the judicial district and certainly not in the judicial circuit. One appeal should be all that is necessary. In time, the rulings of the courts of appeals will settle basic issues of bankruptcy law, ridding the system of repeated appeals involving the same matters.

To further expedite litigation in bankruptcy cases, the Commission recommends that a greater variety of appeals be permissible. Again, it is worth noting that a bankruptcy case differs from the ordinary civil action. In the appellate process, there are many orders that would be considered interlocutory and not subject to appeal—at least, as of right. Necessarily, however, in the bankruptcy context, many of these orders may be of such importance to the of the liquidation or reorganization case that an immediate appeal should be allowed. The Judicial Code should be amended to provide for the appeal of some interlocutory orders. The Recommendation gives the courts of appeal the authority to permit the appeal of any interlocutory order by consent, which permits the courts of appeal to control the process.

RECOMMENDATIONS TO CONGRESS

Chapter 3: Jurisdiction

3.1.3 *Bankruptcy Appellate Process*
The current system which provides two appeals, the first either to a district court or a bankruptcy appellate panel and the second to the U.S. Court of Appeals, as of right from final orders in bankruptcy cases should be changed to eliminate the first layer of review.

3.1.4 *Interlocutory Appeals of Bankruptcy Orders*
28 U.S.C. § 1293 should be added to provide, in addition to the appeal of final bankruptcy orders, for the appeal to the courts of appeals of interlocutory bankruptcy court orders under the following circumstances: (1) an order to increase or reduce the time to file a plan under section 1121(d); (2) an order granting, modifying, or refusing to grant an injunction or an order modifying or refusing to modify the automatic stay; (3) an order appointing or refusing to appoint a trustee, or authorizing the sale or other disposition of property of the estate; (4) where an order is certified by the bankruptcy judge that (x) it involves a controlling issue of law to which there is a substantial difference of opinion, and (y) immediate appeal of the order may materially advance resolution of the litigation, and leave to appeal is granted by the court of appeals; and (5) with leave from the court of appeals.

Additional suggested readings

Douglas G. Baird, *Jury Trials After* Granfinanciera, 65 AM. BANKR. L.J. 1 (1991)

Douglas G. Baird, *Bankruptcy Procedure and State-Created Rights: The Lessons of* Gibbons *and* Marathon, 1982 SUP. CT. REV. 25

Laura B. Bartell, *Getting to Waiver—A Legislative Solution to State Sovereign Immunity in Bankruptcy After* Seminole Tribe, 17 BANKR. DEV. J. 17 (2000)

Laura B. Bartell, *Contempt of the Bankruptcy Court—A New Look*, 1996 U. ILL. L. REV. 1

Susan Block-Lieb, *Permissive Bankruptcy Abstention*, 76 WASH. U. L.Q.781 (1998)

Susan Block-Lieb, *The Case Against Supplemental Bankruptcy Jurisdiction: A Constitutional, Statutory, and Policy Analysis*, 62 FORDHAM L. REV. 721 (1994)

Ralph Brubaker, *Nondebtor Releases and Injunctions in Chapter 11: Revisiting Jurisdictional Precepts and the Forgotten* Callaway v. Benton *Case*, 72 AM. BANKR. L.J. 1 (1998).

Daniel J. Bussel, *Power, Authority and Precedent in Interpreting the Bankruptcy Code*, 41 UCLA L. REV. 1063 (1994)

Erwin Chemerinsky, *It is Time to Overrule Northern Pipeline*, 65 AM. BANKR. L.J. 311 (1991)

Vern Countryman, *The Use of State Law in Bankruptcy Cases* (pts. I & II), 47 N.Y.U. L. REV. 407, 632 (1972)

John T. Cross, *Congressional Power to Extend Federal Jurisdiction to Disputes Outside Article III: A Critical Analysis from the Perspective of Bankruptcy*, 87 NW. U. L. REV. 1188 (1993)

John T. Cross, *State Choice of Law Rules in Bankruptcy*, 42 OKLA. L. REV. 531 (1989)

David P. Currie, *Bankruptcy Judges and the Independent Judiciary*, 16 CREIGHTON L. REV. 441 (1983)

Jeffrey T. Ferriell, *The Perils of Nationwide Service of Process in a Bankruptcy Context*, 48 WASH. & LEE L. REV. 1199 (1991)

S. Elizabeth Gibson, *Removal of Claims Related to Bankruptcy Cases: What is a "Claim or Cause of Action"?*, 34 UCLA L. REV. 1 (1986)

Alfred Hill, *The Erie Doctrine in Bankruptcy*, 66 HARV. L. REV. 1013 (1953)

Frank R. Kennedy, *The Bankruptcy Court Under the New Bankruptcy Law: Its Structure, Jurisdiction, Venue, and Procedure*, 11 ST. MARY'S L. REV. 251 (1979)

Lawrence P. King, *The History and Development of the Bankruptcy Rules*, 70 AM. BANKR. L.J. 217 (1996)

Kenneth N. Klee et al., *State Defiance of Bankruptcy Law*, 52 VAND. L. REV. 1527 (1999)

Kenneth N. Klee, *The Future of the Bankruptcy Rules*, 70 AM. BANKR. L.J. 277 (1996)

Hon. Christopher M. Klein, *Bankruptcy Rules Made Easy: A Guide to the Federal Rules of Civil Procedure that Apply in Bankruptcy,* 70 AM. BANKR. L.J. (1996)

Thomas Krattenmaker, *Article III and Judicial Independence: Why the New Bankruptcy Courts Are Unconstitutional*, 70 GEO. L.J. 297 (1981)

James Lowell, *Conflict of Laws as Applied to Assignments for Creditors*, 1 HARV. L. REV. 259 (1888)

Ralph R. Mabey et al., *Evaluating the Reach of Alternative Dispute Resolution in Bankruptcy: The Legal and Practical Bases for the Use of Mediation and Other Forms of ADR*, 46 S.C. L. REV. 1259 (1995)

John E. Mathews, *The Right to Jury Trial in Bankruptcy Courts: Constitutional Implications in the Wake of* Granfinanciera, S.A. v. Nordberg, 65 AM. BANKR. L.J. 43 (1991)

Kurt H. Nadelmann, *The National Bankruptcy Act and the Conflict of Laws*, 59 HARV. L. REV. 1025 (1946)

Thomas E. Plank, *Why Bankruptcy Judges Need Not and Should Not Be Article III Judges*, 72 AM. BANKR. L.J. 567 (1998)

Martin Redish, *Legislative Courts, Administrative Agencies, and the* Northern Pipeline *Decision*, 1983 DUKE L.J. 197

Alan N. Resnick, *The Bankruptcy Rulemaking Process*, 70 AM. BANKR. L.J. 245 (1996)

Peter Rodino & Alan A. Parker, *The Simplest Solution*, 7 BANKR. DEV. J. 329 (1990)

Charles J. Tabb, *Lender Preference Clauses and the Destruction of Appealability and Finality: Resolving a Chapter 11 Dilemma*, 50 OHIO ST. L.J. 109 (1989)

Chapter 5

Avoiding Powers:
The Strong Arm Power,
Constructive Trusts, and Statutory Liens

A. The Strong Arm Power

One of the most amazing facets of bankruptcy law to the uninitiated observer is that the trustee in bankruptcy has the power to set aside—or avoid—certain settled transactions and recover money or property for the bankruptcy estate, thereby benefitting the residual claimants of the estate. Many of the transactions subject to avoidance and recovery would be perfectly legal and valid outside of bankruptcy. While there are numerous avoiding powers, three tower over the bankruptcy landscape: the "strong arm power," discussed in this Chapter; preferences, which are dealt with in Chapter 6; and fraudulent transfers, which are covered in Chapter 7.

Under § 544(a) of the Code, the trustee is given the powers of a hypothetical lien creditor and the powers of a hypothetical bona fide purchaser of real estate, as of the time of the commencement of the case. In practice, the strong arm power enables the bankruptcy trustee to avoid unperfected security interests and unrecorded real property interests. The first section of this Chapter focuses specifically on the justifications for and parameters of the strong arm power. Two of the giants of bankruptcy scholarship lend their interpretive aid. First is Thomas H. Jackson, who essentially reinvented and reinvigorated bankruptcy scholarship in the 1980s. He weighs in with a brilliant overview in the article *Avoiding Powers in Bankruptcy*, 36 STAN. L. REV. 725 (1984). Here Jackson explains what it is about bankruptcy's collectivizing function that necessitates the strong arm clause. In doing so, he draws a distinction between the trustee's power to set aside unperfected security interests and the power to set aside unrecorded real estate interests, based on the non-bankruptcy entitlements and powers of unsecured creditors generally.

Following Jackson is his former colleague at the University of Virginia, John C. McCoid, II, who delves into the mystery of *Bankruptcy, the Avoiding Powers, and Unperfected Security Interests*, 59 AM. BANKR. L.J. 175 (1985). McCoid, as is his wont, examines carefully both the historical evolution of the strong-arm power and the possible policy justifications for that power. He finds two primary explanations offered: a policy against secret liens peculiar to bankruptcy and a notion that the trustee must have lien creditor status as a representative of unsecured creditors. McCoid asserts, though, that neither argument is persuasive, calling into question the long-assumed legitimacy of the strong-arm clause. The only defense of the power that McCoid finds plausibly defensible is a general non-bankruptcy policy against secret liens, implemented indirectly through bankruptcy avoidance. McCoid also questions the accuracy of Jackson's description of the relative entitlements of unperfected secured creditors versus general unsecured creditors outside of bankruptcy.

A superb article that surveys in depth the many mysteries of the strong-arm power is by David Gray Carlson of Cardozo, *The Trustee's Strong Arm Power Under the Bankruptcy Code*, 43 S.C. L. REV. 841 (1992). Carlson exposes many of the logical defects in the trustee's power, attributable both to inconsistencies and incoherence in defining the underpinnings of the power and to the difficulties in application that are inevitable when one plays in the realm of imagination. He stresses the unfairness that can sometimes result when secured creditors make innocent and harmless mistakes.

Thomas H. Jackson
Avoiding Powers in Bankruptcy
36 STAN. L. REV. 725 (1984)[*]

Avoiding powers, like much of bankruptcy law, have "grow'd" like Topsy. No critical systematic theory of bankruptcy law has existed within which to explore the precise role of avoiding powers. . . .

This article asserts that the role of, and the limitations on, avoiding powers can be understood and systematically examined only by focusing on the goals of the bankruptcy process. After offering a general account of what these goals should be, this article uses the framework of this account to divide the so-called avoiding powers into two separate groups, only one of which relates to the proper normative concerns of the bankruptcy process itself.

The first group, which comprises those powers that preserve the advantages associated with the collective nature of the bankruptcy proceeding, may best be thought of as arranging rights among the creditors *inter se*. These avoiding powers, most notably the "strong-arm" power of the trustee under section 544(a) of the Bankruptcy Code and the preference power embodied in section 547, are integral to bankruptcy because they allow it to preserve the benefits of a compulsory and collective proceeding that justify the process' creditor-oriented rules in the first place.

The second group of powers generally considered to be avoiding powers—those represented by fraudulent conveyance law—is of substantially different origin. Laws that strike down actions designed (or presumed designed) to hinder, delay, or defraud creditors are not an offspring of, nor particularly related to, the bankruptcy process itself. Whereas the avoiding powers in the first group adjust the rights of creditors vis-à-vis other creditors, fraudulent conveyance law adjusts the rights of creditors vis-à-vis the debtor. That the second group of avoiding powers does not spring from a need to implement bankruptcy's collective proceeding becomes evident when one observes that the fraudulent conveyance principle not only resides in Bankruptcy Code section 548, but also operates dehors bankruptcy, as it has done for more than four hundred years, and retains its force in bankruptcy, as do other nonbankruptcy rights, through section 544(b). While no harm comes from calling fraudulent conveyance law an "avoiding power" of the trustee in bankruptcy, one must recognize its distinct, and less collectivist justification.

These two conceptually distinct categories provide a framework for examining the contours of avoiding powers, as well as for discovering their inherent limitations. . . . [A] number of longstanding problems associated with bankruptcy avoiding powers stem from a simple failure to identify the underlying purpose of each particular avoiding power in the context of bankruptcy's collective proceeding. . . .

I. THE BANKRUPTCY FRAMEWORK FOR ANALYSIS

Much of the bankruptcy process and most provisions of the Bankruptcy Code sort out rights among creditors. These creditor-oriented distributional rules, which fulfill the primary aims of the bankruptcy process itself, have little to do with creditor rights vis-à-vis a debtor. The principal advantage to creditors of bankruptcy is to substitute a collective process of paying claims for the system of individualized remedies that exists outside of bankruptcy. . . . [C]reditors generally share in assets of the estate ratably in accordance with the value of their nonbankruptcy entitlements.

When a debtor does not have enough to pay everyone in full (and we would say the debtor is insolvent), this "collectivist" method of allocating assets is in the interest of the creditors as a group. Bankruptcy, then, exists to constrain creditors (and others) from attempting to promote their individual interests when doing so would be detrimental to the group of claimants. . . .

Bankruptcy's rules therefore can be seen as an attempt to implement the type of collective and compulsory system that rational creditors would privately agree to if they could bargain together before the fact. This creditor-oriented justification for bankruptcy—the "creditors' bargain" theory—rests on the notion that with any given set of entitlements creditors would prefer a system that kept the size of the pool of assets as large as possible. In the face of known insolvency, and in light of that goal, the creditors' bargain would require that creditors not resort to individual advantage taking. Bankruptcy imposes such a scheme.

Whereas slicing the asset "pie" according to the size of claims when creditors hold the same set of entitlements is a proper bankruptcy concern, assigning (or ordering) the substantive entitlements ab initio is *not* inherently a proper bankruptcy function. Changing the relative entitlements of creditors does not serve to constrain individualistic actions that are collectively destructive within an initial set of entitlements. . . . Much of bankruptcy law and analysis is flawed by the failure to separate the question of how the process can maximize the value of a given pool of assets from the question of how the law should divide entitlements to whatever pool exists. . . .

From the perspective of the creditors' bargain theory, bankruptcy exists at its core to maximize the value of assets in the face of individualized pressures to ignore the collective weal for individual gain. . . . Because the collective damage to adhering to a right may sometimes exceed any benefit, a bankruptcy statute sometimes *must* replace nonbankruptcy rights with bankruptcy rules. They justifications for the existence of a bankruptcy system, however, only carry the replacement as far as the collectivist principle. . . . [I]f the preempting rule does not spring from the necessity of replacing an individual remedies system with a collective system, that preemption, however desirable in the abstract, is not justified by the concerns that inform a *bankruptcy* process. . . .

. . . Creating a different relative set of entitlements in bankruptcy from those that exist outside of bankruptcy is actually counterproductive. Fashioning a distinct bankruptcy rule that is not justified by the creditors' bargain theory for a collective proceeding or by notions relating to a "fresh start" for individuals creates a perverse set of incentives for the creditors advantaged by the distinct bankruptcy rule to use the bankruptcy process when it is not in the collective interest of the creditors as a group to do so. It is this problem that makes such rule changes normatively undesirable.

. . . Even though a nonbankruptcy rule may suffer from infirmities such as inefficiency or unfairness, if the nonbankruptcy rule does not undermine the advantages of a collective proceeding (or sabotage the individual's "fresh start"), imposing a different bankruptcy rule is a second best, and perhaps a counterproductive, solution. At bottom, bankruptcy overrides nonbankruptcy rights *because* those rights interfere with the group advantages associated with creditors acting in concert.

. . .

II. THE TRUSTEE AS HYPOTHETICAL LIEN CREDITOR OR PURCHASER

Within this theoretical framework, the principal rationale for the trustee's avoiding powers, other than the power to upset fraudulent conveyances, comes into focus. The basis of those avoiding powers is to protect the advantages of bankruptcy's collective proceeding. Consider the trustee's power to assert the rights of a "hypothetical" lien creditor—the so-called "strong-arm" power. The creditors' bargain rationale for bankruptcy's collective and compulsory proceeding clearly explains the basic role of that power. At its core, this power simply implements the collective proceeding. The trustee is able to "avoid" interests that creditors hold in property of the estate if such interests would be subordinate to an execution lien creditor's interest outside bankruptcy. This enables the trustee to preserve the equality in value that existed among these creditors' rights at the moment before bankruptcy. Instead of changing relative entitlements, the lien creditor power does just the opposite: It provides that those similarly situated *outside* of bankruptcy will be treated equally *in* bankruptcy.

The best illustration of this preservation of the value of the creditor status quo is the ability of the trustee to avoid unperfected security interests, surely the property right most frequently avoided under the strong-arm power. . . .

. . . [I]f one were to take a conceptual snapshot at the moment before bankruptcy, the picture might not appear to reflect presumptive equality between unsecured creditors and unperfected secured creditors. The unperfected secured creditor would, after all, prevail over the unsecured creditor if the "race" were to end right then and there. Why then should the trustee have the power to strike down, on behalf of the unsecured creditors, an unperfected security interest that none of them could defeat at that time?

The reason that the unperfected secured creditor loses his apparent priority relates to bankruptcy's notion of a collective proceeding. The relative position of the two classes of creditors is only partially, and misleadingly, depicted by a snapshot of their respective positions at the moment before bankruptcy. While the unperfected secured party is, to be sure, entitled to prevail over the unsecured party if *no* further action is taken, the more relevant point is that neither party has in fact taken the step that assures ultimate victory. Which party would have taken that final step first is unknown the moment before bankruptcy. Had he acted first, the secured creditor could have prevailed by taking possession of the collateral or by filing a notice of his interest. The unsecured creditor, conversely, could have assured himself of priority by acting first, either by taking and perfecting a consensual security interest in the property or by obtaining a nonconsensual attachment or execution lien on the property.

. . . If any one of the unsecured creditors obtains a lien or perfected security interest first, the unperfected secured creditor loses his priority. . . . Evaluating the outcome of the unfinished race thus becomes problematic. Because, prior to the debtor's bankruptcy, neither the unperfected secured creditor nor any of his unsecured counterparts have in fact taken the ultimate step that assures priority, they stand at that moment, for purposes of valuation, in relative positions of equality . . . . In "avoiding" the secured party's unperfected interest, the trustee does not confer victory upon the unsecured creditors; rather, he assures a tie. This tie reflects the position one would expect the parties to have reached if they were able to bargain with each other before the race began because it spares them an unproductive or destructive race.

The trustee, then, wields the power of a hypothetical lien creditor to assure that creditors who generally have an equal chance to win the hypothetical race at the moment of bankruptcy will be treated as equals once the collective proceeding commences. Yet that rationale also indicates the limits on that avoiding power. The trustee's power as a hypothetical lien creditor ultimately rests on nonbankruptcy entitlements—the state law definitions of lien creditor rights; it measures the values of the relative rights of competing claimants to the debtor's property by the yardstick of nonbankruptcy rights existing the moment before bankruptcy. Once those rights are fixed outside bankruptcy, however, nothing in the collectivizing nature of bankruptcy calls for the reallocation of their value inside bankruptcy.

This point, although simple, has a number of implications respecting the shape and direction of Bankruptcy Code section 544(a). Consider first section 544(a)(3), which permits the trustee to avoid any transfer of property of the debtor that is "voidable by . . . a bona fide purchaser of real property from the debtor, against whom applicable law permits such transfer to be perfected, that obtains the status of a bona fide purchaser and has perfected such transfer at the time of the commencement of the case, whether or not such a purchaser exists." The syllogism that presumably resulted in the promulgation of this section is understandable but, under a creditors' bargain analysis, wrong.

. . . [S]ection 544(a)(3) almost certainly reflects the straightforward observation that the trustee's hypothetical lien creditor power principally served to avoid rights in property (such as security interests) with uncured ostensible ownership problems. Not surprisingly, . . . the drafters of the Bankruptcy Code concluded that the trustee's strong-arm power principally addressed the evil of property interests with ostensible ownership problems that remained despite available curative measures under nonbankruptcy law. The problem was—or seemed—obvious: A lien creditor power alone would not enable the trustee to trump all interests with uncured ostensible ownership problems. But this limitation was susceptible to a simple correction. Where applicable law prescribed a form of notoriety as a condition for "full" protection against competing claims, and where such notoriety of a particular interest had not been given prior to bankruptcy, that interest should be invalid against the trustee.

. . . To overcome these unrecorded interests and to cure the attendant ostensible ownership problem, the drafters found that they had to give the trustee the power of a bona fide purchaser in order to give him the same power against interests in realty, under the laws of many states, that the lien creditor power gave him against interests in personal property.

That syllogism, as simple as it may seem, fundamentally misconceives the reason that bankruptcy policy calls for a strong-arm avoiding power. From the perspective of creditors as a group, the reasons for a bankruptcy process do not justify revaluing rights among creditors unless that readjustment serves to preserve the advantages of a collective proceeding. Ostensible ownership may—and often does—create problems, but it does not do so in any way that harms a collective proceeding relative to a system of individual remedies. Accordingly, no bankruptcy-related reason requires an "anti-secret-lien" principle in bankruptcy where nonbankruptcy law says that general unsecured creditors can do nothing about it.

Deciding the issue of whether section 544(a)(3) correctly furthers bankruptcy's collectivizing goal requires an examination of the values of various creditors' rights the moment before bankruptcy instead of an incantation about the generalized evils of secret liens. In short, to the extent that they based the enactment of section 544(a)(3) on an anti-secret-lien principle, the drafters misperceived the inquiry, for they ignored the vitally important fact that real property law often *is* different from personal property law. It is the value of those differences among creditors that should be the focus of bankruptcy law. At first glance, this comparison is unfavorable to the existence of section 544(a)(3). In states that have a bona fide purchaser rule, unsecured creditors are unable, outside of bankruptcy, to defeat the holder of an unrecorded real estate interest directly. . . .

Whether or not section 544(a)(3) is desirable, in short, still depends on the relative attributes of unrecorded real estate mortgagees and unsecured creditors under state law. Focusing on ostensible ownership itself is, as a matter of bankruptcy law, a red herring; the issue derives instead from state law and requires, in the first instance, fact, Congress left untouched many of entitlements under state law. . . .

This point is related to a more fundamental insight about the relationship between the avoiding powers of the trustee and the rights of creditors under nonbankruptcy law. In a creditors' bargain model of bankruptcy, the trustee acts simply as an agent charged with implementing a collective proceeding for the benefit of all similarly-situated unsecured creditors. If none of the unsecured creditors could have upset a transfer outside bankruptcy, the trustee as their agent should not be able to upset that transfer inside bankruptcy. Enabling him to do so would shift the expected distribution of assets among creditors upon the commencement of bankruptcy. The concern here, however, is not simply distributional—that some creditors would win and some would lose—but that the creditors as a group would suffer a net loss because the incentives for strategic use of bankruptcy by individual creditors would increase. . . .

CONCLUSION

Approached individually, the avoiding powers of the trustee in bankruptcy appear technical and confusing. But when armed with a theory as to why bankruptcy's collective process should exist, one can develop the concepts to explain what the role of avoiding powers should be. So viewed, avoiding powers of the trustee are of two separate types. On the one hand, there are those that act to implement the collective proceeding by preserving the reasons for the existence of the collective proceeding in the first place. As such, these powers inherently diverge from nonbankruptcy rights, for they are part and parcel of the substitution of a collective set of rights for the individualized rights that exist outside of bankruptcy. On the other hand, as represented by fraudulent conveyance law, there are those that act to protect against forms of misbehavior by a debtor against his creditors. In this form, they are but a part of a system of rights that exists—or should exist—both inside and outside bankruptcy. Here, unlike the situation presented by the other avoiding powers, the role of *bankruptcy* policy is virtually nonexistent.

. . . When appropriately limited to the bankruptcy-related justifications from whence they come, avoiding powers are an integral part of the bankruptcy process. When they depart from those justifications, however, so as to favor, relative to nonbankruptcy rights, one class of claimants over another, their use interferes with the collective bankruptcy proceeding that is the core reason for their existence.

John C. McCoid, II
Bankruptcy, the Avoiding Powers, and Unperfected Security Interests
59 AM. BANKR. L.J. 175 (1985)*

Today it is almost commonplace to rank the bankruptcy trustee's power to avoid security interests unperfected at bankruptcy or belatedly perfected before bankruptcy with his right to set aside preferential transfers and fraudulent conveyances. When these attacks succeed, the debtor's unsecured creditors whom the trustee represents are the beneficiaries. Yet under nonbankruptcy law unperfected security interests in real or personal property are, for the most part, valid against unsecured creditors. Moreover, the trustee's attacks on perfection failures, unlike those on preferences and fraudulent conveyances, are indirect in the sense that they require resort either to preference provisions or to other provisions of bankruptcy legislation referring to nonbankruptcy law. . . .

I. HISTORY

A. REPRESENTATIVE POWERS

The Bankruptcy Acts of 1800, 1841, and 1867 had contained provisions invalidating fraudulent conveyances; and the 1841 and 1867 Acts included anti-preference provisions. To these the 1898 Act added two provisions new to American bankruptcy law. Section 67a, under the heading "liens," allowed invalidation of "(c)laims, which for want of record or other reasons, would not have been valid liens as against the claims of creditors of the bankrupt." At the same time section 70e provided for avoidance of "any transfer by the bankrupt of his property which any creditor of such bankrupt might have avoided." . . . [T]he words "for want of record" in section 67a seem to identify clearly the unperfected security interest as a specific target. . . . Not every unrecorded security interest was vulnerable, however; only those invalid against creditors could be set aside, as could claims invalid against them for "other reasons." . . .

. . . [A]n important issue under the 1841 and 1867 Acts was the status of the assignee in bankruptcy. Whether the assignment conferred on him the rights of the creditors whose interests he represented or he was merely the successor of the bankrupt was a question that divided federal courts.

The decisions arising under the 1841 Act seem uniformly to have adopted the successor-to-the-bankrupt view. The few opinions were dominated by Justice Story. . . .

While no language in the 1867 Act surely warranted a different view of the status issue, the competing position, that the assignee as representative of the creditors had their rights as well as those of the debtor, was taken almost immediately. . . .

The Supreme Court itself seemed to vacillate. . . . The question was squarely presented, however, in 1879 in *Stewart v. Platt*, where a chattel mortgage was not filed in the proper office and therefore was void against creditors. Nonetheless, . . . Justice Harlan held for the mortgagee against the assignee on the express ground that the mortgage was valid as between the mortgagee and the mortgagor-bankrupt. Thereafter and until 1898 the assignee's limited status was clear. Then Congress overruled *Stewart* by enacting sections 67a and 70e.

. . . Whatever the power of the bankruptcy assignee under the assignments required by the 1841 and 1867 Acts, he could be given greater power if the legislature so desired. Congress did so desire; hence sections 67a and 70e. It is important, however, to see that Congress enacted those provisions, not so surely from its own view that unrecorded security interests were evil, as, because the trustee represented creditors who often had such invalidating power under nonbankruptcy law until bankruptcy intervened, from the purpose of allowing the trustee to represent creditors effectively.

B. HYPOTHETICAL LIEN CREDITOR STATUS

Ultimately Congress went much further. In 1910 it enacted as section 47a(2) a provision giving the trustee the power of a creditor who had obtained a judicial lien on the date of the bankruptcy petition. Sometimes called the "strong-arm clause," this section conferred hypothetical lien creditor status, that is, the trustee had the power of a judicial lien creditor as of bankruptcy though no actual creditor had obtained such a lien. . . . [T]his power of the trustee was dramatically enlarged as to real estate when, in 1978, a successor subsection gave the trustee the power of a bona fide purchaser who had perfected at bankruptcy.

. . . [T]here had been a further division. . . . [S]ome of the state statutes invalidating unrecorded security interests did so only as to judgment, or judicial lien, creditors and not as to general, unsecured creditors. For some judges that did not include the bankruptcy assignee, unless some actual creditor had obtained a judgment or lien. Others, however, thought that the assignee ought to be able to do what creditors not interrupted in their collection efforts by bankruptcy could have done. . . . .

After the 1898 Act was adopted, some had thought that the question was resolved in the trustee's favor by section 70(a)(5) which vested in the trustee title to property "which might have been levied upon and sold under judicial process against him." . . . But the Supreme Court soon held otherwise. In *York v. Cassel* the unfiled security interest was invalid under state law as to judicial lien creditors but not as to general, unsecured creditors or the debtor. . . . The Supreme Court, however, held for the secured party. . . . Section 47(a)(2) was expressly designed to overcome the *York* decision. . . .

Some of the pre-1898 and pre-*York* decisions permit the inference that here, too, what was intended was not so much an attack on unrecorded security interests as a recognition of the trustee's representative role. But there is language in the Senate and House reports accompanying the 1910 addition that would support the argument that sanctioning secret liens was the basis of the enactment. . . . "Thus the evil of secret liens has continued. It is this evil and the injustice worked upon creditors who rely upon the debtors' apparent ownership against which the bankruptcy law has set its face." . . .

If there is room for debate about the purpose of the 1910 expansion, there can be no doubt about the bona fide purchaser status granted as to real property in 1978. Such power cannot be rationalized on any theory of representation of creditors. The reports accompanying the bill cryptically announce that the provision is "new," and there is a further indication that the provision is intended to coerce perfection.

C. ANTI-PREFERENCE POWER

Because individual preference avoidance would only replace one preference with another, preference avoidance to achieve equal treatment of creditors is the exclusive province of a collective proceeding. Consequently, it is, essentially, peculiar to bankruptcy and confers on unsecured creditors benefits unavailable in nonbankruptcy proceedings. Accordingly, its structure cannot be explained rationally in terms of giving the trustee as the creditors' representative the rights they enjoyed outside bankruptcy.

Under the 1867 Act the Supreme Court had taken the position that, for the purpose of determining whether the elements of a preference existed and, if so, whether it occurred sufficiently close in time to bankruptcy, a transfer of a security interest to a creditor by a debtor occurred when it was effective between those parties.

To deal with the problem of withholding from the record the Act was amended in 1903. . . .

The House and Senate reports accompanying the 1910 amendments make it clear, by their citations, that the expansive view of the power to avoid preferences was to prevail and the restrictive view was to be overruled. Section 60 was amended in a way designed to make perfection the measuring point for all aspects of preference law. Professor Morris, arguing that the effect of this is distortion of preferences, has concluded that Congress had as its target secret liens . . . . There is strong supporting evidence. The House and Senate reports accompanying the bills both state that "[t]he object of this amendment is further to protect against the evil of secret liens" and that "secret liens are still being held good in many jurisdictions." These reports already had used the same phrase, "evil of secret liens," as well as noting "the injustice worked upon creditors who rely upon the debtors' apparent ownership" in justifying the strong-arm clause.

The author has suggested that the latter provision arguably can be defended as giving the creditors' representative power that the creditors themselves might have had absent bankruptcy. There is some indication that similar thinking might have supported the changes in preference law. . . .

Thinking about the trustee as the creditor's representative rather than the debtor's successor, of course, makes sense in the context of conferring status which allows exercise of nonbankruptcy avoidance power. It would seem to have little bearing, however, in the context of structuring an avoiding power peculiar to bankruptcy. In understanding the 1910 preference amendments one is left with two other possibilities: 1) Congress intended to sanction secret liens. Alternatively, 2) the drafters did not think through the implications of the preference changes . . . .

In sum, the history of the power to avoid unperfected or belatedly perfected security interests is muddy. There is substantial indication that its evolution was based, at least initially, on making the trustee an effective representative of creditors with whatever power that entailed. But there was also antipathy for secret liens which were thought to be instruments of fraud and deception. That basis for avoiding power had an ancient lineage and seemed a powerful influence in 1910.

II. CONTEMPORARY ASSESSMENT

Both history and logic argue that defense of the power of the trustee in bankruptcy to avoid unperfected or belatedly perfected security interests must rest either on a policy against secret liens or on the trustee's role as representative of unsecured creditors. A policy against secret liens might be peculiar to bankruptcy. Alternatively, it might have a more general, or nonbankruptcy, foundation with bankruptcy avoidance simply a special tool of its implementation. A policy against secret liens, whether peculiar to bankruptcy or more general, is founded on the belief that others, principally creditors, rely to their prejudice on the debtor's apparently unencumbered ownership of assets in the absence of perfection which publicizes the secured party's interest.

A. Bankruptcy Policy Against Secret Liens

Professor Thomas Jackson has suggested that it is useful to differentiate bankruptcy avoiding powers which effect the goals of bankruptcy process and those which implement nonbankruptcy policies. As examples of the former he lists provisions outlawing preferences and conferring hypothetical lien creditor status on the trustee. . . .

While Professor Jackson's perception is most useful, the author disagrees with his classification of hypothetical lien creditor status. What distinguishes bankruptcy, and then not perfectly, is not the fact that it deals with creditor-creditor relationships but its collective character. . . . [A] process designed to deal at once with the claims of all creditors is the essence of bankruptcy. Considered in that light, bankruptcy does not present a special case for avoidance of secret liens. Their vice is as severe for other creditors individually as it is for them collectively. In this respect secret liens and preferences are very different. The latter are said to frustrate equality, a goal that can only be regarded as material in a collective proceeding. Except as secrecy may conceal a true preference, it is not germane to bankruptcy's equality principle or to any other special goal of that process that the author can identify.

This may explain why, outside preference rules, bankruptcy law strikes at secret liens only indirectly, by reference to nonbankruptcy law. Sections 544(a) and (b) do not declare, as does section 547, what is avoidable. They simply confer a status the utility of which can be determined only by looking to nonbankruptcy provisions. In the case of secret liens these may or may not provide avoidance. . . . If there were reasons for targeting secret liens arising from the collective character of bankruptcy proceedings, those reasons would be defeated by a system leaving avoidance to depend on nonbankruptcy law under which the result may vary.

One may surmise that Professor Jackson classifies hypothetical lien creditor status as a bankruptcy power because he views it as necessary to the process where creditors themselves are stayed from obtaining liens. In that sense the power is derived from the trustee's representation, a matter dealt with in Part II.C. of this article.

B. Implementing Nonbankruptcy Policy With A Bankruptcy Avoiding Power

It is possible that the threat of invalidation of secret liens in bankruptcy is a club used to coerce timely perfection desired for reasons not confined to bankruptcy. This would account for why provision for avoidance in bankruptcy is, in the main, indirect. It would be consistent as well with the legislative history behind the 1910 amendments of the 1898 Act with its recurring reference to the evil of secret liens. . . .

The same kind of argument, of course, can be used to condemn bankruptcy avoidance by the trustee. . . .

There remains the possibility of a collusive scheme to withhold from the record. . . . One might well conclude that these nonbankruptcy threats to the secret lienor are sufficient deterrents to secrecy and that no special bankruptcy power is necessary.

To so argue is not to say that Congress did not intend at one time to provide a bankruptcy means of achieving nonbankruptcy ends. Neither could lack of necessity surely establish that it is unsound to use avoiding powers as a deterrent. There is reason, however, to doubt the wisdom of a general policy against secret liens.

Whether the collateral should be redistributed from the secured party who bargained for its protection to the unsecured creditors (including, after avoidance, the secured party) who did not would seem to depend on a weighing of the benefits and harmful consequences of avoidance. Such redistribution would make sense if the secured party's fault harmed the unsecured creditors. . . . Even among those who believe that recording systems are useful—and that has been questioned—it is regularly concluded that unsecured creditors do not consult the record before extending credit but rely instead on the debtor's financial statements, the reports of credit reporting agencies, and personal judgments about the creditworthiness of the borrower. And there is logic behind that behavior. The unsecured creditor does not rely on the record concerning particular property of the debtor because he cannot. He is always subordinate to subsequently created security interests which are timely perfected.

Thus invalidation of unperfected security interests by the bankruptcy trustee takes from innocent secured parties to give to unsecured creditors who are not prejudiced by the failure to perfect. Even if avoidance did not take time and effort, one might seriously question this structure which requires those who meant no harm to compensate those who have not been injured, particularly when both bargained for the extension of credit on a different assumption.

C. Representation

Finally, there is the argument that the bankruptcy trustee should have the power to avoid unperfected or belatedly perfected security interests because of his role as representative of unsecured creditors. At first blush that argument might seem flawed for the reason elaborated in Part II B. If unsecured creditors are not prejudiced by nonperfection, they should not receive the benefits of avoidance. That point may undercut a policy against secret liens. But the representation argument . . . as a bankruptcy policy is quite different from a policy against secret liens. It stands simply for the proposition that the trustee should be able to do whatever the unsecured creditors whose interest he represents could have done in the absence of bankruptcy. If they had priority over an unperfected security interest, the trustee should enjoy the same advantage.

No one today contests this proposition nor can the author find any principled basis for doing so. The bankruptcy process is, in part, a remedy for creditors. Absent a reason based on bankruptcy policy for restricting their substantive rights, as discharge does, the same rights that are available outside bankruptcy should be enjoyed in the course of provision of bankruptcy remedies. The difficult question in this context is not whether the trustee should have representative status, but how far that status should carry him. More specifically, the problem is the legitimacy of hypothetical judicial lien creditor status . . . .

The most compelling argument in favor of that status, first advanced by the Nineteenth Century judges, has been that commencement of bankruptcy proceedings bars unsecured creditors from judicial proceedings that would result in judicial liens and that to give the trustee judicial lien status is therefor only to preserve nonbankruptcy rights. Professor Jackson apparently makes the same point, but sharpens the issue by describing the problem in terms of a race for priority. . . .

A different view of the race is possible and, perhaps, more compelling. It is derived in part from the fact that under the Uniform Commercial Code and most real estate recording statutes the secured party has priority over the unsecured creditor without perfection. When bankruptcy stops the race, these parties are not equals because the secured party is ahead. Hypothetical lien creditor status does not just preserve the status quo; it reverses the order of priority and thus does more than substitute the trustee for unsecured creditors.

Perhaps that made a kind of sense in the Nineteenth Century and even in 1910. Then commencement of bankruptcy did not end the race for both parties as it does today. While bankruptcy prevented subsequent judicial proceedings by unsecured creditors, it did not bar postbankruptcy perfection. Indeed, that was not clearly prohibited until the 1978 Act. With the secured party still "running," something was required if the trustee was to have meaningful representative status. Under the present structure which stops the race for both parties, however, hypothetical lien creditor status provides more than mere representation. It gives unsecured creditors what they did not have outside bankruptcy and, perhaps, something they could not quickly have obtained. Indeed, it may provide, as does hypothetical bona fide purchaser status in connection with real estate, an incentive to initiate bankruptcy to obtain an otherwise unavailable advantage.

III. CONCLUSION

The historical basis of the trustee's sometime power to avoid unperfected or belatedly perfected security interests is ambiguous, although there is little doubt that concern about fraud on creditors lies at its base.

Treatment in bankruptcy of unperfected or belatedly perfected liens as avoidable either under preference provisions or hypothetical lien creditor power is indefensible in terms of trustee representation of unsecured creditors or a policy against secret liens peculiar to bankruptcy. Using bankruptcy avoiding powers to implement a nonbankruptcy policy against secret liens makes greater sense. Whether avoidance in bankruptcy is necessary to implement such a policy and, indeed, whether such a policy is itself sound are matters as to which there is room for disagreement. It is far from clear, however, that Congress gave thought to either question in setting the contours of the 1978 Act.

B. Constructive Trusts and Statutory Liens

One of the most intractable sets of issues afflicting the bankruptcy avoiding powers concerns the treatment of statutory liens and constructive trusts. While nominally distinct, the two types of claims are conceptually quite similar, as Thomas Jackson points out in the first article, *Statutory Liens and Constructive Trusts in Bankruptcy: Undoing the Confusion*, 61 AM. BANKR. L.J. 287 (1987). In each case, if honored in bankruptcy, the lien or trust would allocate a share of the property in the bankruptcy estate to the recognized lienholder or constructive trust beneficiary. Doing so, of course, would mean that proportionately fewer assets would be available for other claimants. What has befuddled the courts and Congress is how these sorts of property-based claims should be analyzed. What are the first principles that apply? Jackson argues (as the attentive reader now might be able to predict) that the problem is amenable to a simple solution: track the non-bankruptcy treatment. If the lien or trust would be effective against competing claimants outside of bankruptcy, then nothing about the pendency of bankruptcy warrants a different result.

Professor McCoid returns with an incisive analysis of the problem of statutory liens in *Statutory Liens in Bankruptcy*, 68 AM. BANKR. L.J. 269 (1994). His approach differs from that of Professor Jackson. Where Jackson would simply follow non-bankruptcy entitlements, McCoid is less sanguine: he demonstrates that in effect statutory liens in bankruptcy are just a form of *priority*; as such, the relevant questions are (1) whether that priority should be established by state law or bankruptcy law?, and (2) to the extent the priority outcome should be dictated by bankruptcy law, to whom should priority be accorded? McCoid proposes a test that would turn on whether the claimant had any other sources of protection from the risk of nonpayment. Only those lacking such alternative means of protection should be accorded protection via the bankruptcy statute.

The final two articles focus on the problems raised by application of constructive trust law in bankruptcy. Assertion of a "constructive trust" has been a common savings mechanism propounded by claimants distressed at having been bilked or misled by a nefarious debtor. Many courts purport to find a "conflict" between the strong-arm power and constructive trusts, and then resolve the conflict one way or the other. Neither Professor Emily Sherwin, in *Constructive Trusts in Bankruptcy*, 1989 U. ILL. L. REV. 297, nor Professor Andrew Kull, in *Restitution in Bankruptcy: Reclamation and Constructive Trust*, 72 AM. BANKR. L.J. 265 (1998), finds such an approach productive. Both think it preferable to look at the nature and substance of constructive trust claims and then to assess how those claims should be filtered through the bankruptcy lens. In the final analysis, though, Sherwin ends up being much more skeptical about the enforceability of constructive trust claims in bankruptcy than Kull.

For Sherwin, a constructive trust is nothing more or less than a "a remedy for prevention of unjust enrichment," and she insists that in bankruptcy the unjust enrichment focus should be placed on the body of general creditors, rather than the debtor. Under that remedial approach, few constructive trust claimants will fare well in bankruptcy. Professor Kull, by contrast, views constructive trust claims based on non-bankruptcy restitutionary principles as a species of *property* right that should be honored in bankruptcy if, indeed, the non-bankruptcy law of restitution would recognize a property right in the claimant. Having established that baseline principle, Kull then demonstrates how the Bankruptcy Code—which he shows does not really speak to the basic problem at all—can be read to support his interpretation.

Thomas H. Jackson
Statutory Liens and Constructive Trusts in Bankruptcy: Undoing the Confusion
61 AM. BANKR. L.J. 287 (1987)*

Analysis of statutory liens and constructive trusts alike should start and stop with an examination of whether the priority thereby granted has force and effect outside of, as well as inside of, bankruptcy's collective proceeding, in the sense of providing the protected group with priority over levying creditors on the relevant assets irrespective of the commencement of a bankruptcy proceeding (or similar event). Simple analysis suggests it is time for courts and scholars to stop obfuscation in this area by returning to first principles of bankruptcy analysis. . . .

I. THE GOALS OF THE BANKRUPTCY PROCESS AND THE RELATIONSHIP BETWEEN ASSETS AND LIABILITIES

Bankruptcy provides a collective forum for sorting out the rights of "owners" (creditors and others with rights against a debtor's assets) and can be justified in providing protections against the destructive effects of an individual remedies system when there are not enough assets to go around. This makes the basic process one of determining *who* gets *what*, in *what order*. "Who" is fundamentally a question of "claims," or what is often referred to outside the bankruptcy arena as "liabilities." "What" is fundamentally a question of "property of the estate," or what is often thought of outside the bankruptcy arena as "assets." At one level, there is nothing magical about these basic building blocks. A "liability" is something that makes you less valuable—that you would pay to get rid of. An "asset," on the other hand, is something that makes you more valuable—that someone would pay you for.

In looking at all of this, bankruptcy law is procedural more than it is substantive. It is a collective debt-collection device imposed to supplement traditional "first-come" rules of nonbankruptcy law because of deficiencies with those "grab-race" procedures. As such, it represents a parallel system of debt collection, whose distinguishing feature is that it is collective. Because it imposes a collective structure on a system of individual entitlements, it is helpful to think of bankruptcy as follows. What bankruptcy should be doing, in the abstract, is asking how much someone would pay for the assets of a debtor, assuming they could be sold free of liabilities. The resulting money is then taken and distributed to the holders of the liabilities according to their nonbankruptcy entitlements. Such a system solves the deficiencies of individualistic "grab" remedies without interfering with the value of the underlying entitlements or leading to undue forum shopping.

One cannot, however, successfully approach bankruptcy law under this view without a realization that the question of what is an "asset" and what is a "claim" are integrally related in bankruptcy. One can say, for example, that the asset is "Debtor's" (in the sense that title to the property is located in Debtor) but that Smith has an unavoided perfected security interest in that property. The consequence of this determination is that, in a bankruptcy proceeding, Smith has first call on the asset to get paid, and the asset has value to the residual claimants (generally the unsecured creditors) only net of Smith's claim to the asset. . . . One, alternatively, could say that the asset is "Smith's" (in the sense that title to the property is located in Smith), even though Debtor has possession of the property, such as exists in the cases of bailments, leases, and trusts. But seen as a matter of who gets what, this characterization really has not changed matters very much: Smith still gets first dibs to the asset in question and Debtor's unsecured creditors get nothing (except rid, once again, of Smith as someone they have to worry about sharing the remaining assets with).

This point can be put another way. At first blush, the questions what are assets and what are liabilities appear to be at opposite poles. Nonetheless there is a close, indeed symbiotic, relationship between the two issues. One must focus on *who* benefits from having something declared an asset. From the perspective of the residual claimants, it is only possible to determine what is an asset after the priority interests of the various claimants are first set out. This point is obviously true when one contemplates the rights of a bailor to have goods returned to it: its property interest is respected in full and the debtor's residual claimants get nothing. . . . In these cases, nonbankruptcy law is clear in its determination: all claimants derive their rights to assert claims against assets through the debtor, and accordingly must take the assets as they come into the hands of the debtor. Creditors of a dry cleaner, for example, cannot lay claim to all the clothes being cleaned at the time the dry cleaner files a bankruptcy petition. . . .

The point is equally true, however, where the estate can claim for the benefit of unsecured creditors only the equity interest in land or chattels that are subject to either statutory liens or security interests. General creditors have only residual rights to property that is subject to a properly perfected security interest. The security interest is itself a property right giving a particular creditor rights superior to the debtor and the other creditors in certain assets. Unlike the case of clothes at the dry cleaner, we tend to think of these as ways of "ordering" claimants against property "owned" by the debtor, because nonbankruptcy law would locate "title" in the debtor. But location of title is a label, and bankruptcy law is, and should be, concerned with attributes. Thus, similar results can either be cast as one of determining relative orderings of liabilities or one of determining the extent of the debtor's rights in property.

II. MIRROR IMAGES: STATUTORY LIENS AND CONSTRUCTIVE TRUSTS

When examining statutory priorities or liens, governed by section 545, the question clearly posed . . . is whether the interest is effective against competing claimants outside of a bankruptcy proceeding (or its surrogates). In these cases, one determines rankings of claimants against property of the estate, because the way nonbankruptcy law had framed ownership of the asset, the affected property was property that nonbankruptcy law said the debtor "owned."

The exact same outcome could be, and often is, decided by *reversing* the way nonbankruptcy law frames the issue. Consider the case of statutory trusts. A statutory trust is a device that locates nominal ownership other than in the hands of the debtor. . . . Analytically, of course, this way of characterizing such things is no different, from the perspective of relevant attributes (*i.e.*, rights among claimants), than a state statute giving the subcontractor a true statutory lien on the funds. In the one case (the trust), nominal ownership of the funds is lodged in the subcontractor, and hence the asset is not viewed as "belonging" to the contractor in the first instance; in the other case (the lien), nominal ownership of the funds is lodged in the contractor, and the asset is viewed as the contractor's, subject, however, to the rights of subcontractors to get paid first from it. From the perspective of bankruptcy policy, there is no relevant difference. As long as the statutory trust is effective against competing claimants outside of bankruptcy, its relative value should be respected in bankruptcy as well. . . .

. . . The important issue is picking the relevant "function" for purposes of bankruptcy, which surely is the question of relative entitlements. . . .

The point, moreover, also applies to myriad other types of rights. . . . The analytical structure is the same no matter whether the doctrinal question is posed as one of identifying the property of the estate or as one of determining the relative value of a particular claim.

The current tests under bankruptcy law for determining property of the estate, then, have been needlessly complicated by a failure to observe the close linkages between assets and liabilities outside bankruptcy law. Certain assets that might appear to an outside observer to be the debtor's, and hence available to the debtor's claimants, for example, are really assets that nonbankruptcy law says belong to someone else. This can be rephrased to say that the person who claims to own the property in question is entitled to prevail over the other claimants of the debtor. However the inquiry is phrased, the outcome should be the same.

The proper approach, therefore, is to examine any concrete situation from the vantage point of an unsecured creditor attempting to execute on a particular asset or to assert a security interest in it. . . . If unsecured creditors cannot execute against that property as a matter of nonbankruptcy law, then that property has no value to them and should not be considered to be (to that extent, at least) property of the estate. And, even if the property can be executed on, if execution by an unsecured creditor would take a back seat to some other entity's rights, then only that residual value is an asset from the perspective of the unsecured creditors.

III. ANALYZING THE VALIDITY OF NONBANKRUPTCY ENTITLEMENTS

Thus, from a policy perspective, there is no reason to approach statutory lien issues differently from constructive trust issues. They locate nominal title in different parties, but their effect on the relevant class—residual claimants—is really the same. As a matter of the Bankruptcy Code, there is no reason to do so either. No section, other than the possible application of section 545, suggests that the decision of nonbankruptcy law to treat something as a constructive trust should be treated with any different respect than the decision of nonbankruptcy law to treat something as a statutory lien.

. . . Bankruptcy is a response to a problem of diverse creditors acting in self-interest and making things worse for the group. It does so by imposing a compulsory, collective system of debt collection on them. Nothing in the process of moving from an individual to a collective regime, however, calls for redistributing entitlements. . . .

. . . [I]n order to advocate that recognizing constructive trusts on commingled funds violates bankruptcy policy, one *must* rely on more than the fact that their recognition permits some claimants to do better than others. One must point so something in the concept of commingling that is itself in conflict with some identified bankruptcy policy. It is plain, however, that no such conflict exists.
. . .

Instead, the validity of constructive trusts, as with other nonbankruptcy claims of preferred status, should be analyzed by considering whether they in fact fixed a place in line vis-à-vis the relevant competing interests: general creditors. That examination is whether a general creditor could trump these competing interests by acquiring a lien. Because of the extension made by section 545(2), one must also look at whether such interests would survive the attack, under nonbankruptcy law, of a bona fide purchaser. But such examinations, not any other, establish whether the nonbankruptcy rule in question "in fact has force and effect independent of the bankruptcy proceeding." These tests resort ultimately to the effect of such rules against competing claimants under nonbankruptcy law, not to any ratable distribution principle inherent in bankruptcy law itself.

To be sure, when a statutory lien or a constructive trust exists on a large pool of assets, the answer given by nonbankruptcy law may be difficult to discern. . . . As long as they do not have effect solely in bankruptcy, one still has to turn to nonbankruptcy law before declaring these interests invalid. Nothing in bankruptcy law or logic suggests that constructive trusts should be analyzed distinctly.

CONCLUSION

It is time to stop creating distinctions without support and traps for the unwary. Whatever the nonbankruptcy label for the claimed status in issue—whether security interest, statutory lien, constructive trust, or general "priority"—bankruptcy analysis should be the same. It is a matter of substance, not labels. The test is sensible and easy to apply. If the interest is effective against competing claimants outside of bankruptcy (or similar event), nothing in bankruptcy law or policy suggests it should not be effective inside of bankruptcy as well. Before one runs to a bankruptcy policy of "ratable distribution," one has to decide if the claimants are similarly situated under nonbankruptcy law. That courts have gotten this point wrong so frequently . . . says less about a failure of bankruptcy law than it does about a failure of bankruptcy analysis to start with first principles, and to recognize obvious analogies.

John C. McCoid, II
Statutory Liens in Bankruptcy
68 AM. BANKR. L.J. 269 (1994)[*]

V. ANOTHER PERSPECTIVE

Bankruptcy's general principle of equal treatment of creditors is qualified by the conferral of lien or unsecured priority status on specified claimants. In general, those with lien status are entitled to be paid before those with unsecured priority, and claimants with unsecured priority, in turn, enjoy like advantage over holders of general unsecured claims. The right to lien status is by and large determined by nonbankruptcy law, while the right to unsecured priority is regulated solely by bankruptcy law. The puzzle is why lien and unsecured priority status are fixed by different sources of law. The question is most interesting when *statutory* liens are compared with priorities. Judicial liens are available to any creditor who successfully resorts to the judicial collection process, and consensual liens are the subject of bargain between almost any debtor and creditor in a consensual relationship. Statutory liens and priorities, on the other hand, are assessments of the relative desert of competing claimants.

If there were basic differences between statutory liens and unsecured priorities, an explanation of the present structure might be found there. It is sometimes said that a lienor has a property right while a claimant with a priority does not. Without explanation of how a right of property differently affects a creditor's position, this distinction is an empty statement. . . .

The remaining function of statutory liens is the ranking of claimants where a debtor's assets are insufficient to satisfy all claimants in full, *i.e.*, distributional priority. This function is performed by both statutory liens and unsecured priorities. . . . The basic job is one of ranking claims, and the question remains why part of that ranking function should be performed by one body of law and part by another.

At first blush, the present structure seems a recipe for chaos. State-created priorities are eliminated on the ground that there are too many of them consuming too large a portion of debtors' estates. At the same time, the states are left free to create liens having an even greater distributional impact (because liens in the main rank ahead of all priorities) so long as these are not just "hidden priorities." Yet in bankruptcy the only significant function performed by a lien is to fix priority. That such a system could work almost defies logic. If it can be said to work, I believe it is because of the threat that Congress will expand its control over priority should the states abuse their power by creating too many advantaged categories. . . .

But why is priority based on relative desert not regulated in its entirety by one law source? It is true that both statutory liens and unsecured priorities could be established entirely by nonbankruptcy law. But it is probably unthinkable to consider such a regime so long as a bankruptcy law is in effect. It is unlikely that Congress could be persuaded to give up the power, exercised in all American bankruptcy legislation, to establish some unsecured priorities in addition to, if not instead of, those of state-law origin. At most, one might imagine a return to the 1898 structure under which state-created unsecured priorities were honored alongside nonbankruptcy statutory liens and bankruptcy priority categories. . . .

It is equally possible to conceive a system in which bankruptcy law is the exclusive determinant of priority, at least as it is measured by relative desert. Arguably, vertical uniformity is no

---

longer as vital as has been suggested. Now that a national bankruptcy law is apparently a permanent fixture and, just as important, the vehicle of choice in the vast majority of cases where formal proceedings are instituted as well as the shadow under which more informal bargains resolving an insolvency are usually struck, concern about vertical uniformity may be misplaced. We might have reached the point where "practical preemption" has taken place, so that whatever bankruptcy law might say about priority would be taken into account by those who plan with an eye to the law. In fact, the greater danger could lie in a regime governed by nonbankruptcy law. If there is flexibility about the state in which bankruptcy case is begun, a flexibility currently provided, especially in business cases, by a venue provision with domicile, residence, and principal place of business as options, vertical uniformity could lead to a different form of forum shopping, one seeking priority rules on the basis of geography.

An all-bankruptcy determination of priorities based on desert, however, would pose a major problem. Congress would have to create a suitable structure of statutory liens as well as unsecured priorities, so that the creditors to be preferred would not be uniformly junior to consensual and judicial lienholders, who still presumably would acquire their rights under nonbankruptcy law. . . .

The more likely prospect, then, is that priority based on desert will continue to be regulated by a mixed regime of bankruptcy and nonbankruptcy law. The latter law will provide the basic structure, but will be occasionally overridden or even supplanted by the former. Perhaps such a system has advantages. In addition to the convenience of adopting the nonbankruptcy system as a starting point, this approach also provides, for lien status at least, double scrutiny of a claim of entitlement to priority.

But there is a major defect in the present structure as well. It lies in the absence of a principle or set of principles explaining the bankruptcy law regulation of priority outcomes. State law priorities and what are perceived to be priorities have been eliminated across the board and without regard to the nature of the underlying claims. . . .

My approach would differ substantially from the Commission's and from existing law as well, if I were to undertake to fix a bankruptcy standard of insolvency priority. My principle is quite simple. I believe that priority ought to be reserved for those who have no other source of protection from the risk of nonpayment of their claims. The sources of payment, of course, are limited. A creditor can be paid from the assets of debtor's estate or from the assets of others. If the debtor is insolvent, payment from the estate's assets depends on having priority. That can come by virtue of bargaining for security or by legislative grant thereof. If the creditor, rather, would look to the assets of others, it must be in one of two ways. The creditor can fix an interest rate for, or price to, those with whom it deals high enough so that the payments of other debtors will cover losses from nonpayment by the insolvent debtor. By diversifying the risk, the creditor becomes a kind of self-insurer. Alternatively, the creditor may seek indemnification from a third party, whether an insurer, a guarantor, or the like. It is only when the creditor cannot meet the risk of non-payment by bargaining with the debtor for security, by fixing the rate or price to others, or by contracting for indemnity that the legislature should provide a statutory priority. If one or more of the other options is available to the creditor, it should be expected to take care of the risk of nonpayment itself without legislative help.

Thus, I would exclude statutory priority in cases where there is a consensual relationship between debtor and creditor *and* the latter has the ability to bargain. In such a case, where the cost of credit reflects the existence of priority or the lack of it, I would leave the question of priority to the agreement of the parties. The creditor can deal with the risk by rate/price or by demanding security, and hence priority. It may be that some statutory liens presently serve in such cases as default rules of priority, and thus eliminate the need for a contractual provision. But I think we would be better served if the default rule were one of no security, because the instances where that is the appropriate solution substantially outnumber the cases where priority makes sense under my principle.

As indicated, I also would exclude statutory priority where the creditor, though unable to bargain with the debtor for security, can readily cover the risk of nonpayment by its dealings with others either in terms of rate/price in contracts with other debtors or by contracting for indemnity. Some creditors probably cannot do this, and the legislature should step in on their behalf. The debtor's employees and some tort victims may be among this group. . . . No government claim for priority based on revenue need would be honored: governments can always avoid the risk of nonpayment by charging other debtors more. . . .

Where a statutory priority should be conferred under this principle, it should be a general lien applied ratably to all the debtor's property and, as to consensually encumbered property, senior to the highest bargained-for security. Holders of consensual security, whether senior or junior, presumably would adjust to the demotion either by demanding more security or by raising the rate charged for credit. The holder of statutory priority has no like mechanism with which to respond to the possibility of inadequate assets. To give it a lesser advantage would be to ignore the reason for giving any advantage at all.

Conferring lien status on disabled creditors means that there should be no occasion for unsecured priority other than the administrative expenses of bankruptcy. . . .

The principle should also lead to nonrecognition of judicial liens in bankruptcy. Those liens are available to any and every creditor. It seems to me that no creditor, however, can properly be said to have relied on such a lien to protect it against the risk of nonpayment. . . . [T]he risk of nonpayment would or should have been addressed earlier by bargained-for security, rate-price, indemnity, or a statutory priority. The judicial lien, therefore, adds nothing to the bankruptcy priority calculus, even though it has leverage, collection and priority values in the nonbankruptcy race for creditors.

Finally, the principle would justify the immunity from preference recapture now enjoyed by statutory liens. A statutory priority, after all, is a preference intended by the legislature. It is not clear to me that perfection of such a lien need be required. Were it to be required, however, there is no reason to object to that taking place after a bankruptcy petition is filed.

I must confess that it is far easier to state the principle of protecting only those creditors who have no other means of protection from the risk of nonpayment than it is to craft implementing bankruptcy legislation. . . . It seems likely, however, that legislation in this form would lead to considerable litigation of the question, perhaps exceeding what is desirable. Yet how could one define in a statute when the ability to bargain is an unrealistic assumption? Similarly, how can one describe legislatively when it is that a creditor can diversify the risk among many debtors or shift it to a third party so that disputes about these possibilities do not unduly complicate bankruptcy cases?

Another way to approach the issue would be to assemble lists of the various statutory liens found under nonbankruptcy law and then attempt to classify them according to the principle. Thus, employees might be given a statutory lien for wages. . . . Because of the difficulty in its implementation, if not for substantive reasons, then, the principle may be misconceived.

Yet it seems to me that deciding what principle or principles of relative desert should govern statutory priority in cases of insolvency remains an important and still-unfinished task. No sound bankruptcy scheme of priorities can be formulated without such a determination. The current mix of bankruptcy and nonbankruptcy law is far from satisfying in these terms. Surely we can do better.

Emily Sherwin
Constructive Trusts in Bankruptcy
1989 U. ILL. L. REV. 297[*]

I. INTRODUCTION

A constructive trust is a restitutionary remedy developed in equity to give relief against unjust enrichment. It has been called "the formula by which the conscience of equity finds expression." The purpose of this article is to consider whether and how the conscience of equity should express itself in a bankruptcy proceeding.

The constructive trust remedy applies to all forms of unjust enrichment, whenever the enrichment is represented in specific property. The substantive basis for the trust may be misappropriation, fraud, mistake, breach of fiduciary duty, or abuse of confidential relations. A constructive trust allows the injured party to claim restitution of specific property traceable to her claim, either in its original form or as the product of exchange. The right to specific restitution has important consequences if the defendant is in bankruptcy, because it places the constructive trust claimant ahead of other creditors with respect to the property at issue.

Most bankruptcy courts have enforced constructive trust claims as a form of state law entitlement: if the state court would impose a constructive trust on certain property in an action between the claimant and the debtor, the bankruptcy court treats the claimant as the equitable owner of the property and allows her to recover it in bankruptcy, to the exclusion of other creditors. . . .

The following article . . . moves to the more difficult question of why a constructive trust claimant is given priority over other creditors: what justifies a remedy that allows one creditor—the constructive trust claimant—to bypass others and receive payment in full? Excluding formal explanations, the only acceptable answer is that other creditors will be unjustly enriched if they are allowed to share in the assets at issue.

. . . [T]he article traces three elements of a constructive trust claim that favor the constructive trust claimant in relation to other creditors. The case for priority depends on (1) the special appeal of a claim based on unjust enrichment, (2) identification of assets that represent the debtor's unjust enrichment in the bankruptcy estate, and (3) claimant's position as an involuntary creditor. When all of these elements are present, a constructive trust may be appropriate to prevent unjust enrichment of general creditors at the claimant's expense.

Assuming the reasons identified . . . are sufficient to justify a constructive trust and elevate the claimant above other tort or contract creditors, several additional conclusions (and problems) follow. First, the three elements . . . are not common to all constructive trust claims. When one or more are absent, a constructive trust might be appropriate in a state court action between the claimant and the debtor, but not in a bankruptcy contest between the claimant and other creditors. . . .

Second, application of the constructive trust remedy in bankruptcy cases requires further consideration of the respective roles of federal and state law in bankruptcy proceedings. Characterization of constructive trusts claims as state law entitlements that bankruptcy courts must accept without question leads to unsatisfactory results. State courts seldom consider the special problem of unjust enrichment among creditors in a collective proceeding. Practically, a federal bankruptcy court cannot bring the constructive trust remedy into line with the principle of unjust enrichment unless is assumes control of the decision and allocates priority as each case demands. As long as

---

bankruptcy courts treat constructive trust claims as fixed entitlements based on state law precedent, the remedy will continue to miss the mark and produce disturbing decisions. . . .

II. CONSTRUCTIVE TRUSTS

A. Unjust Enrichment

The substantive basis for imposing a constructive trust is unjust enrichment represented by property. . . .

C. Operation of the Constructive Trust Remedy

1. Incidents of the Remedy

. . . The *Restatement of Restitution* treats the priority associated with a constructive trust as an inevitable incident of the claimant's restitutionary rights against the defendant. . . .

The article rejects the *Restatement's* position on creditors' rights. According to the analysis proposed here, priority over general creditors should not follow automatically from the plaintiff's right to a constructive trust against the defendant's property. Instead, the priority of a restitution claimant in bankruptcy (or a similar collective creditor proceeding) should be based on the strength of her claim in relation to the claims of competing parties who will bear the burden of the remedy. Put another way, the right to a constructive trust in bankruptcy should depend on whether *creditors* would be unjustly enriched by sharing in the property the plaintiff claims. . . .

3. The Remedial Character of a Constructive Trust

Nearly all literature on constructive trusts makes the point that a constructive trust is a remedy, rather than a substantive property right. It is not a trust, but an analogy to a trust employed to correct unjust enrichment. . . .

Equating constructive trust claims with equitable ownership is misleading. . . . When the concept of equitable ownership is confused with the reasons for granting the remedy, it obscures the function of the constructive trust as a means of preventing unjust enrichment. . . .

The *Restatement's* view of a constructive trust as a legal institution separate from its enforcement is an illusion by which the drafters explained away the impact of the remedy on creditors. A constructive trust arises only when the court decides to grant relief between the parties. Before that time, the defendant has property, and the plaintiff has a restitutionary claim based on principles of unjust enrichment. When the court imposes a constructive trust, it is making a decision to give the plaintiff a prior right to certain property, ahead of the defendant's creditors. . . .

IV. JUSTIFICATIONS FOR A CONSTRUCTIVE TRUST REMEDY IN BANKRUPTCY

The first step in defining a role for constructive trusts in bankruptcy is to identify the reasons for the constructive trust remedy. . . . [T]he purpose is to determine when restitution of specific property or its products, to the exclusion of general creditors, is necessary to prevent unjust enrichment. In other words, why is the constructive trust claimant placed ahead of a claimant who was severely injured by the defendant's negligent or willful acts, or a claimant who sold goods to the defendant and has not been paid? . . .

A. The Equation of Gain and Loss

The special feature of restitutionary claims is that they arise (in most cases) from the enrichment of one person at the expense of another. . . . In most restitution cases—for example, when the defendant acquires property from the plaintiff by theft or fraud—there is both a loss to the plaintiff and a corresponding gain to the defendant. This correlation of gain and loss gives the restitutionary claim strong appeal in terms of fairness and corrective justice.

. . . [T]he correspondence of defendant's gain and plaintiff's loss does not provide a full explanation for constructive trusts and their incident of priority over general creditors. The equation of gain and loss is the foundation of a constructive trust claim, but something more is needed to understand and justify the constructive trust claimant's priority.

B. Unjust Enrichment Represented by Property

Prevailing constructive trust rules hold that the claimant must establish a connection between her claim of unjust enrichment and specific property in the hands of the defendant at the time of suit. . . .

1. Gain Manifested in Assets

The main reason why a connection to specific property advances the case for priority over general creditors is that this connection makes it possible to say that the constructive trust will prevent unjust enrichment of creditors. Tracing the claim to particular assets demonstrates that the unjust enrichment is still present among the assets to be divided among competing parties. The constructive trust remedy avoids unjust enrichment of other creditors by denying them a share of property that would not be available for distribution but for the debtor's unjust gain at the constructive trust claimant's expense. . . .

C. The Claimant as an Involuntary Creditor

. . . The final element in favor of the constructive trust claim, which separates it from ordinary contract claims, is that the claimant did not extend credit voluntarily to the debtor. . . .

Under the present system of priorities in bankruptcy, the claimant's position as an involuntary creditor is not enough, in itself, to place her ahead of other creditors. . . .

Nevertheless, the involuntary nature of a constructive trust claim is a circumstance to be considered in combination with the others identified above. . . .

D. Deterrence

Outside bankruptcy, one of the principal justifications for constructive trusts and tracing is their role in policing misconduct: the defendant must not be permitted to profit from a wrong. . . .

In bankruptcy, the deterrent reasons for constructive trusts and tracing disappear. Profit from wrongdoing is not an incentive unless the wrongdoer will realize the profit. When the contest for assets is between the restitution claimant and other creditors, a remedy that allocates property to one claimant in favor of others has no deterrent effect on the wrongdoer (their debtor).

It follows that any instance or incident of the constructive trust remedy based solely on deterrence should be eliminated in bankruptcy, no matter how egregious the debtor's conduct. Conversely, the innocence of the debtor in obtaining the gain should not weigh against the constructive trust claimant if sharing the gain would result in an unjust enrichment of creditors. . . .

E. Summary

It is wrong to begin analysis of a constructive trust claim in bankruptcy, as bankruptcy courts often do, with the assumption that the claimant is entitled to priority as the equitable owner of the property she claims. The claimant does not own the property unless the court grants the remedy. If the court places her ahead of general creditors, it must be because general creditors would be unjustly enriched by sharing in the property.

In a contest between the constructive trust claimant and other creditors, the claim of unjust enrichment depends on three facts: (1) the debtor obtained an unjust gain at the claimant's expense; (2) the claimant can identify the gain among the assets claimed by creditors; and (3) the claimant did not voluntarily extend credit to the debtor. These three elements of a constructive trust claim provide the basis for priority in bankruptcy. . . .

The intent of the present discussion is not to prove conclusively that a constructive trust claim should have priority over the claims of other creditors. The point is that the reasons identified above in support of constructive trust claims are the only justifications for priority. Equitable ownership justifies nothing, because it means nothing. Deterrence may be a justification for tracing remedies between the claimant and the defendant but not between the claimant and other creditors. . . .

VI. THE PROBLEM OF STATE AND FEDERAL LAW

Defining the respective contributions of state and federal law to the resolution of disputes among creditors is a persistent problem in bankruptcy. . . .

The constructive trust problem illustrates the weakness of the narrow view of bankruptcy policy proposed by Professors Baird and Jackson: it denies bankruptcy courts the power to tailor remedial decisions to the cases before them. The decision to impose a constructive trust in bankruptcy is a distributional decision, because it affects the relative values of the parties' nonbankruptcy rights. But it is also a remedial decision that should not be separated from the facts and parties before the court. . . .

Thus if bankruptcy courts treat constructive trust claims as questions of state law entitlement, as Professors Baird and Jackson suggest, their decisions will be based on state law precedents set in disputes between the claimant and the wrongdoer. Importing those precedents into bankruptcy defeats the purpose of the constructive trust remedy by distorting the determination of unjust enrichment. In bankruptcy, the relevant question is unjust enrichment of creditors. The constructive trust remedy will be more consistent with the substantive nonbankruptcy principle it enforces—the principle of unjust enrichment—if the bankruptcy court is willing to make a distributional decision between the constructive trust claimant and other creditors. . . .

VII. CONCLUSION

Properly understood, a constructive trust is a remedy for prevention of unjust enrichment. In the area of creditors' rights, courts often have lost sight of the essential purpose of the remedy. Traditional constructive trust doctrine assumes that if the claimant is entitled to recover unjust gains from the defendant, she also is entitled to priority over the defendant's general creditors. . . .

In bankruptcy, where the burden of a constructive trust falls on general creditors, the court should not impose a constructive trust unless it concludes that without it, general creditors would be unjustly enriched at the claimant's expense. This article has identified three reasons why a restitution claim traceable to specific assets of a debtor may have special appeal in relation to the claims of other creditors. These are the correspondence of an unjust gain to the defendant with a loss to the claimant, the presence of the gain among the assets to be divided among creditors, and the position of the claimant as an involuntary creditor. Assuming these reasons (in combination) can justify priority, they also should define the limits of a restitution claimant's priority in bankruptcy. When they are not present and the motives for the constructive trust are primarily deterrent, bankruptcy courts should refuse specific restitution and leave the claimant to share pro rata with other creditors.

In federal bankruptcy proceedings, constructive trusts also raise questions about the relation of state and federal law. The prevailing approach treats the constructive trust remedy as a state law entitlement. The result is to transpose a state law remedy designed to correct unjust enrichment of the individual debtor to a contest between the constructive trust claimant and the debtor's creditors. This is not a principled solution, because it separates the remedy from its purpose. Instead, bankruptcy courts should address constructive trust claims as remedial issues and grant or deny relief according to the relative equities of the claimant and creditors.

Perhaps a remedial application of constructive trusts in bankruptcy is not feasible, because the litigation required is too costly to justify its results. If so, the answer must be to exclude all constructive trust claims from bankruptcy, rather than to avoid difficult decisions by referring to equitable ownership and state law entitlement.

Andrew Kull

Restitution in Bankruptcy: Reclamation and Constructive Trust
72 AM. BANKR. L.J. 265 (1998) *

"The Bankruptcy Act simply does not authorize a trustee to distribute other people's property among a bankrupt's creditors."

—Justice Black in *Pearlman v. Reliance Insurance Co.*

The characteristic problem of restitution in bankruptcy results from a voidable transfer from the restitution claimant to the debtor. Typically, the claimant can show that identifiable property in the hands of the debtor was obtained from the claimant in consequence of the debtor's fraud or the claimant's mistake. A valid restitution claim under such circumstances—in essence, the right to recover title and possession of the property in question—is a state-law property right of a kind traditionally known as an "equitable interest" or simply an "equity." The bankruptcy question is whether this form of equitable ownership is valid against the general creditors. . . .

The contemporary treatment of restitution in bankruptcy has become confused and haphazard because the subject is not addressed by the Bankruptcy Code. This only means that a restitution claim of this kind is like other species of property, a creation of state law; with the difference, however, that the common law of restitutionary rights and remedies has itself become unfamiliar to most lawyers and judges. The attempt to find a Code answer to questions the Code does not address has led to a long-standing but misplaced emphasis on § 541(d) (referring to the secondary mortgage market) and § 544(a) (the strong-arm clause), two provisions having essentially nothing to say about the problem. Judicial frustration came to a head in *XL/Datacomp, Inc. v. Wilson (In re Omegas Group, Inc.)*, where a Sixth Circuit panel—declaring that constructive trusts were "anathema to the equities of bankruptcy"—decided in effect that a restitution claim should no longer be cognizable in bankruptcy at all.

I. THE BACKGROUND RECEDES

Scarcely anyone in the United States understands what restitution is about, to begin with, and the particular role of restitution in bankruptcy is further obscured by the way in which American commercial law has been codified. Unlike the comprehensive framework of a continental legal code, the Uniform Commercial Code and the Bankruptcy Code were drafted as common-law statutes. In theory, at least, they displace the preexisting common law only to the extent they alter it, and they presume the continued existence of this background law to govern every question not otherwise resolved. In practice it does not work quite like that. Lawyers and judges who deal regularly with commercial materials come to expect that any problem worth arguing about has been made the subject of an express statutory provision, their usual task being to locate and explicate the relevant statutory language. In consequence, the neglected background law recedes still further—until we reach a point at which the most orthodox legal proposition, if not tied to a specific code section, may actually be challenged as spurious. So it came about that a panel of the Sixth Circuit could begin its 1994 opinion in *Omegas Group* with the observation that "Nowhere in the Bankruptcy Code does it say, 'property held by the debtor subject to a constructive trust is excluded from the debtor's estate.'"

Restitution in a commercial setting is the law of fraud, of mistakes, and of transactions that miscarry; its function is to sort out rights in property after transfers that are attacked as void or voidable for one reason or another. . . . Most law schools gave up teaching restitution a generation ago, and many judges and practitioners are not familiar with its general principles. Lack of familiarity with the restitutionary elements of the background rules results in a predictable distortion of commercial law. . . .

. . . [E]ven the most elementary and compelling claims to restitution in bankruptcy may now be met with judicial incomprehension.

II. *OMEGAS GROUP* AND OTHER HERESIES

For the last twenty years, the controversy surrounding constructive trust in bankruptcy has involved a debate over the application of Code provisions to a subject the draftsmen did not squarely address. The usual way of framing the question is whether property of the debtor that is subject (under relevant state law) to a constructive trust in favor of a given claimant is within or without the bankruptcy estate under § 541, particularly in light of § 541(d). . . . [T]his proves to be essentially a nonissue. A more significant aspect of the standard debate is whether the avoidance powers under the strong-arm clause (§ 544(a)) permit the trustee to take property for the estate free of what would otherwise be a valid restitutionary claim—a claim that will ordinarily be described using the language of constructive trust. Prior to 1978 this, too, was essentially a nonissue: The Bankruptcy Act gave the trustee the status of an ideal lien creditor, but a creditor (as opposed to a bona fide purchaser) cannot ordinarily reach property that is subject to a valid claim of constructive trust. The Bankruptcy Code raised the stakes significantly, by adding to the trustee's strong-arm powers certain attributes of a bona fide purchaser of real property. Because good faith purchase is one of the principal defenses to restitution, this new hypothetical attribute is one that potentially makes a difference to the fate of the restitution claim. . . .

. . . A more recent development—the unrestrained decision of the Sixth Circuit in *Omegas Group*—moved the debate over restitution in bankruptcy to the more stimulating terrain of first principles. *Omegas Group* rejected a restitution claim that probably deserved to fail anyway, but it did so on the ground that a restitution claim that takes the common form of a claim to constructive trust is not cognizable in bankruptcy at all.

Datacomp, the claimant in *Omegas Group*, paid the debtor in advance for computers that the debtor was to purchase from IBM on behalf of Datacomp. Bankruptcy intervened. Asserting that its prepayments were induced by the debtor's fraudulent assurances about its intentions and ability to perform, Datacomp claimed the whole amount of its payments to the debtor (some $1.1 million) in constructive trust. . . . The Sixth Circuit reversed:

> We think that § 541(d) simply does not permit a claimant in the position of Datacomp to persuade the bankruptcy court to impose the remedy of constructive trust for alleged fraud committed against it by the debtor in the course of their business dealings, and thus to take ahead of all creditors, and indeed, ahead of the trustee.

In the view of the *Omegas* court, a fraud victim who asserts a restitution claim against the debtor is merely another creditor attempting to push to the head of the line. . . . In short, "Constructive trusts are anathema to the equities of bankruptcy since they take from the estate, and thus directly from competing creditors, not from the offending debtor." Because constructive trust is the remedy usually sought by a restitution claimant in bankruptcy . . ., the Sixth Circuit was saying, in effect, that its conception of bankruptcy law foreclosed even a meritorious restitution claim against the estate.

. . . The Sixth Circuit's announcement that constructive trust was "anathema to the equities of bankruptcy" contradicted a century of bankruptcy law, including Supreme Court authority, legislative history, and the standard commentary. These radical conclusions were wholly unnecessary because *Omegas Group* denied a restitution claim that could easily have been denied on the most orthodox view. . . .

Omegas Group takes it as axiomatic that the "equities of bankruptcy" and the equities of restitution—in other words, the usual equities of ownership outside bankruptcy—are somehow at odds. . . . All this is error. Properly understood, restitution is not a source of competing equities that bankruptcy must either accommodate or resist. On the contrary, at those points where issues of restitution and issues of bankruptcy coincide, their actuating principles are precisely congruent. The point of overlap, seen from the bankruptcy side, involves the placement of assets inside or outside the bankruptcy estate. From the restitution perspective, the problem is to distinguish between nonconsensual transfers that should and should not be given effect to alter property rights.

III. NONCONSENSUAL TRANSFERS

Restitution and its remedies are inadequately explained even by the canonical authorities. Judge Cardozo's celebrated observation that "constructive trust is the formula through which the conscience of equity finds expression" happens to be both meaningful and accurate; so is the more pedestrian remark that restitution is concerned with "liability based in unjust enrichment." But such statements are meaningful only to someone who has previously inferred a good deal about the underlying relationships that constitute the material of restitution. To describe the liability in Lord Mansfield's terms, as a duty owed by the defendant to a claimant *ex aequo et bono*, poses the question of what equity and good conscience require.

What they ordinarily require, so far as the law of restitution is concerned, is that the recipient of certain nonconsensual transfers return (or pay for) the advantage obtained at the expense of the transferor. A transfer creating a right to restitution is a transfer without an adequate legal basis, meaning a transfer that the law treats as ineffective to shift property rights in the thing transferred. . . . The law of restitution is in this sense an appendix, though a very substantial one, to the law of property. Its chief concern is to define the obligations of the recipient with respect to benefits obtained under circumstances that are legally anomalous, in that the transfer from the claimant to the recipient was neither a gift nor the product of a voluntary exchange.

. . . [O]f the three broad divisions of restitution, each is concerned with transfers that are nonconsensual in a different sense:

1. A nonconsensual transfer effected by the transferee may be the result of taking without asking. This is the part of restitution that requires the disgorgement of profits realized by conscious wrongdoing—typically conversion, trespass, or infringement. . . .

2. A transfer that is voluntary on the part of the transferor may nevertheless be nonconsensual because the transferee has not agreed to pay. This heading of liability in restitution comprises transfers that are both nongratuitous and noncontractual; . . . the law permits someone to confer a benefit, not pursuant to contract, and then demand payment from the recipient. Familiar examples include claims for services provided in an emergency; claims between co-owners of property to contribute to taxes or mortgage payments; and typical cases of insurance subrogation.

3.   Finally, a transfer may be nonconsensual because it is insufficiently voluntary on the part of the transferor. A transfer of property induced by fraud, mistake, coercion, or undue influence is for that reason subject to avoidance.

A nonconsensual transfer falling into any of these categories yields a potential claim in restitution against the transferee. If the transferee becomes insolvent, the restitution claim may be asserted against the bankruptcy estate. But the characteristic and difficult issues associated with "restitution in bankruptcy" all stem from nonconsensual transfers of the third type, in which the debtor has obtained money or other property from the claimant in a transfer the claimant seeks to avoid. In such cases, the claim in restitution is not (or not simply) that the debtor owes the claimant money, but that the debtor has possession and legal title of identifiable property that in equity belongs to the claimant.

A restitution claim of the first type is hard to get wrong. If the claimant can prove that the debtor picked his pocket on the steps of the bankruptcy court, and now identifies his wallet in the hands of the trustee . . ., it is hard to imagine even the Sixth Circuit denying the claim. . . . Conversely, a restitution claim of the second type, in which the plaintiff seeks compensation for benefits conferred without request, is unlikely to pose a bankruptcy problem at all. Such a claim, if successful, results in a money judgment against the person benefitted, but it does not yield rights *in rem* against specific property in the hands of the recipient. Unless he can present himself as the owner, legal or equitable, of property that the trustee holds for the bankruptcy estate, even the plaintiff whose restitution claim is good against the debtor will fail to state a claim in restitution as against the general creditors.

It is this vital difference between a claim against the recipient and a claim against the recipient's creditors that is the distinguishing feature of restitution in the bankruptcy context. Restitution in bankruptcy involves a kind of "second-order" restitution, meaning that the transfer at issue is once removed from the transfer in which the restitution claim originates. The transaction begins with a nonconsensual transfer from the claimant to the debtor. With the debtor's insolvency, however, the transfer at issue—alias the potential unjust enrichment, should the restitution claim be denied—is no longer between the claimant and the debtor, but between the claimant and the creditors of the debtor. It is on an analysis of the potential transfer from the claimant to the creditors that the claim in restitution is either allowed or disallowed.

This shift in focus from one nonconsensual transfer (claimant/debtor) to another (claimant/creditors) alters the restitution analysis in important respects. . . .

[Consider] a restitution claim of the second type, one in which a claimant is permitted to recover the value of benefits conferred voluntarily, notwithstanding the lack of a prior promise to pay for them on the part of the recipient. . . . [T]he effect of granting the claim in restitution is literally quasi-contractual: it allows the claimant to recover on the basis of the hypothetical bargain that the law presumes would in other circumstances have been struck. Against a solvent recipient, in other words, the successful restitution claimant . . . is put into the position of a contract creditor.

What is the effect of the recipient's bankruptcy on such a claim? A successful restitution claim makes the claimant a creditor of the debtor, but the other creditors are already creditors. . . . There is thus no identifiable transfer from the restitution claimant to the rival creditors; and restitution accordingly remains a first-order claim (against the debtor), rather than a second-order claim (against the creditors). In short, there is no reason why the surgeon's claim should not be allowable in bankruptcy; but by establishing his claim in restitution, the surgeon (or any other successful claimant in this category) merely becomes another creditor like the others.

Consider finally a restitution claim in the third category, one in which the claimant attacks a transfer on the grounds that it was induced by fraud or mistake. . . . [U]nlike the victim of simple conversion, the victim of fraud or mistake needs the law of restitution—in this aspect, the law of rescission and avoidance—to reestablish rights of ownership. It is this claim to ownership of property, as opposed to a simple money claim against the debtor, that yields the conditions for second-order restitution, because it allows the claimant to assert that the trustee is attempting "to distribute other people's property among a bankrupt's creditors."

Against a solvent transferee the restitution claim in such cases is straightforward. Fraud or mistake makes a transfer subject to rescission. . . . [T]his equity in the transferor is a power to rescind the transfer, reclaiming title and possession of what has been transferred.

Bankruptcy makes any such nonconsensual transfer a problem in second-order restitution. Property in which the claimant has an equitable interest—a claim to restitution that is valid at state law—is now in the hands of the trustee. By asserting the restitution claim in bankruptcy . . ., the claimant seeks legal confirmation of his equitable title. Denial of the restitution claim means that the claimant's equitable title is destroyed; what had been the debtor's voidable title becomes good title in the hands of the trustee. The result is a transfer of property from the claimant to the creditors. Such a result is impermissible in a bankruptcy scheme that takes property rights as it finds them.

. . . The restitution claimant in this third category prevails over the creditors because, unlike them, he has not consented to be a creditor of the debtor. Property obtained by fraud or mistake, like property obtained by theft, has not come into possession of the debtor by a voluntary transaction. To distribute it to creditors would therefore result in an involuntary transfer, accomplished in two stages, from claimant to creditors.

To recapitulate, the logic of restitution in a bankruptcy context starts as a matter of preserving the claimant's ownership of property that has come into the hands of the debtor by means of a nonconsensual transfer. Because restitution in bankruptcy is second-order restitution—because the relevant contest is no longer between the claimant and the debtor, but between the claimant and the creditors—the claimant must establish, not merely that there was a nonconsensual transfer from claimant to debtor, but that the alternative to restitution in bankruptcy will be a nonconsensual transfer from the claimant to the creditors. To make this showing a successful claim of restitution in bankruptcy must satisfy two further tests . . . . One of these is the requirement of tracing. The other is the need for a clear distinction in the respective positions of claimant and creditors vis-à-vis the debtor. The two limiting conditions are imposed, not by bankruptcy law, but by the theory of the restitution claim itself.

A. TRACING

. . . The issue is one of identification and causation. The problem is that the fungibility of money blurs the issue as soon as an asset is reduced to cash in the bank. . . . Where the claimant cannot point to an identifiable fund—where he cannot say "this is my money" about any particular money in the hands of the debtor/trustee—he can no longer exclude the possibility that the funds in question have been dissipated by the debtor. If the claimant's funds have been dissipated, we can no longer say with any assurance that the fraud of the debtor (or the claimant's mistaken payment) has increased the assets available for distribution, resulting to this extent in a transfer from claimant to creditors.

The overriding causation problem, in other words, is the question of the extent, if any, to which the initial nonconsensual transfer from claimant to debtor has increased the net assets available for distribution in bankruptcy, thereby threatening a second nonconsensual transfer from claimant to creditors. . . . The tracing rules are simply rules of thumb, based on rough but common-sense assumptions, designed to split the difference between claimants and creditors where a more precise accounting is unattainable. The claimant is conceded ownership of what he can trace; he loses ownership, becoming instead merely a creditor, with respect to anything he cannot trace.

B. Owners Versus Creditors

Tracing is a necessary but not sufficient condition of the restitution claim in bankruptcy. To be able to object that the trustee is trying to rob Peter to pay Paul, Peter must be able to insist on the distinction between himself as an owner and Paul as a mere creditor. . . .

In short, the restitution claimant who succeeds in bankruptcy prevails over the general creditors because he is not himself merely a creditor, but an owner. He is an owner because the law allows him to avoid the transfer by which the assets in question got into the debtor's hands. . . .

Consider now a bankruptcy scenario in which the debtor (call him "Ponzi") has been running a fraudulent investment scheme. Peter and Paul have both been victims of the fraud. Because he remitted funds to Ponzi just before the swindle was exposed, Peter is able to trace his money into Ponzi's bank account; Paul's funds were remitted earlier and are untraceable. Ponzi is now in bankruptcy and Peter wants restitution of the traceable funds from the bankrupt estate. . . . But Ponzi's creditors are defrauded investors just like Peter. Because Peter cannot properly differentiate his claim against Ponzi from that of the other creditors, his claim to priority fails. . . .

Restitution is denied in the Ponzi scenario because the conditions for second-order restitution no longer exist. The viable claim to restitution in bankruptcy opposes an owner of property in the hands of the debtor and a creditor of the debtor; in other words, a property claim against the debtor *vs.* a contract claim against the debtor. The owner defeats the creditor because the law of property does not permit us to pay our debts with the property of others. But in the Ponzi scenario, neither Peter nor Paul has voluntarily extended credit to the debtor. Both were defrauded; each asserts a right to rescind. . . . [T]he contest is between conflicting claims of ownership—that is to say, between competing restitution claims. Between claimants similarly situated, the equities of restitution (like the equities of bankruptcy) favor ratable distribution.

IV. HOW CONSTRUCTIVE TRUST WORKS

"Constructive trusts are anathema to the equities of bankruptcy because they take from the estate, and thus directly from competing creditors, not from the offending debtor." This much of the basic misconception of *Omegas Group* should now be clear. Restitution, which in a given case may or may not employ the language of constructive trust, does not take from the estate anything that properly belongs to it. . . . A court must decide the restitution claim in order to identify those legal or equitable interests that are or are not available, as a matter of state law, to satisfy the debtor's obligations. . . .

This misunderstanding of the role of restitution is due in large part to a failure to understand the role of constructive trust. . . . In the view of the Sixth Circuit and the courts that have followed it, a constructive trust is merely "a remedy," and a remedy of a peculiarly amorphous kind: an "equitable panacea" for special burdens occasioned by a debtor's bad faith or bad acts. The equitable panacea operates by granting one creditor an effective priority over the other creditors. . . . It follows that constructive trust is "fundamentally at odds with the general goals of the Bankruptcy Code." Moreover, because constructive trust is not a real trust but "a remedy," it does not "exist" before it is judicially declared; so that the beneficial interest under a constructive trust cannot be something that is excluded from the bankrupt estate unless the constructive trust is judicially declared prepetition.

There is one half-truth in the foregoing account. Constructive trust is indeed a remedy, so there is a sense in which we could say—if it mattered, which it doesn't—that a constructive trust, like an award of damages, does not "exist" until it is judicially declared. Such an approach, however, ignores the wrong that the remedy serves to redress. . . . A decree that certain assets are held in constructive trust for the benefit of a claimant means that, in the judgment of the court, the claimant has a right of ownership in those assets superior to that of the person with possession and legal title. The claimant's property right necessarily antedates its judicial acknowledgment . . . .

"Constructive trust" is a declaratory judgment about property out of place. The necessary condition of constructive trust, and the legal wrong to which the remedy responds, is that ownership, possession, and title to property have been improperly separated. The restitution claimant complains of an involuntary transfer, typically one resulting from fraud, mistake, or coercion: a transfer, in short, that is legally insufficient to bring about a conclusive alteration of property rights. . . . [T]he involuntary transferor retains residual rights in the asset. . . . Property rights of this character are asserted by means of a claim in restitution.. . .

Omegas Group challenges this account directly in the statement just quoted: that "a creditor's claim of entitlement to a constructive trust is not an 'equitable interest' in the debtor's estate existing prepetition" . . . .

This seems clearly wrong. "Equitable interest" . . . describes a real relationship, fundamental to the law of property, between the claimant and the debtor. The legal proposition is that a transfer that is involuntary, because of fraud, duress, or mistake, conveys less than complete ownership. "Voidable title" is what is conveyed; "equitable interest" is the common name for what remains. . . .

The usual remedy for a liability in restitution is a money judgment. By contrast, constructive trust is a "proprietary" remedy yielding rights *in rem*: a declaration that the claimant is the owner of specific property as against the titleholder. The fact that constructive trust is declarative of property rights marks the characteristic feature of the remedy . . . . The same characteristic explains why . . . the indispensable attributes of constructive trust become apparent only when the restitution defendant is or becomes insolvent. The truth about constructive trust and bankruptcy is that only in bankruptcy does constructive trust really matter.

Insolvency transforms the restitution claim in the manner we have seen, shifting the focus to a potential involuntary transfer between the claimant and the general creditors. . . . What the claimant needs is a judgment that recognizes his ownership interest in identifiable (*i.e.*, traceable) assets, to support a claim in what has become second-order restitution: that the debtor's obligations are being paid with the claimant's property. . . .

V. NEGOTIATING THE STATUTORY MAZE

A. PROPERTY OF THE ESTATE

The most frequent argument about restitution in bankruptcy—whether "constructive trust property" is within or without the estate under § 541(d)—is essentially a red herring. The answer is that it depends on how you look at it, and that the two ways of looking at it bring you out in about the same place.

Observe first that § 541(d) of the Code does not actually say anything. . . . [T]he statement is pure tautology. . . .

More to the point, § 541(d) is entirely redundant: It is no more than a labored paraphrase, with gratuitous examples, of the basic definition of "property of the estate" set forth in § 541(a)(1). . . . If the debtor holds Blackacre subject to a third party's equitable interest—including an equitable interest, namely a restitution claim, of a kind that would entitle the third party to recover title and possession of the property under applicable state law—the estate takes Blackacre subject to the same equitable interest. The conclusion is compelled by the proposition that bankruptcy does not alter state-law property entitlements. Whether the strong-arm clause empowers the trustee to avoid the mortgage or the equitable interest is the next phase of the question, to which we turn in a moment.

This is why the usual debate over § 541(d) is essentially a waste of time. . . .

B. THE STRONG-ARM POWER

There is, however, a second avenue through which the trustee might theoretically prevail over the constructive trust claimant . . . . The real argument about the fate of restitution claims in bankruptcy is accordingly whether the trustee's avoidance powers permit him to take free of this kind of claim. Those who believe the trustee has this power find it in the "strong-arm clause," § 544(a).

. . . [I]t appears most unlikely that § 544(a) was intended to have any bearing on the status of restitution claims—competing equitable interests—asserted against property to which the debtor holds legal title. . . . [T]he language of the provisions seemingly points to other concerns. . . .

. . . [I]f the addition of subsection 544(a)(3) gave the trustee the power to destroy competing equitable interests, it added to the strong-arm clause a power that was radically new; that overturned the settled understanding of the status of equitable interests in bankruptcy; and, that was unrelated to the existing objects of the provision. The change was made, if such was the intent, with no announcement of its purpose, in language that virtually defies comprehension, and in a manner so arbitrary as to invite ridicule. . . .

Actually we know why subsection 544(a)(3) was added to the Code, and the reason had nothing to do with the fate of restitution claims in bankruptcy. . . . Subsection 544(a)(3) was added to the strong-arm power to ensure its uniform application in avoiding unperfected transfers, not to make it into a weapon for the destruction of equitable interests in real, though not personal, property.

Last but not least among the threshold objections to this purported use of the strong-arm power is the difficulty of identifying a suitable rationale. The transactions that are the acknowledged focus of § 544(a) bear no relation to the transactions giving rise to a restitution claim against property in the hands of the debtor. The former consist of voluntary, but unperfected, transfers *by* the debtor; the latter consist of involuntary transfers *to* the debtor, transfers that may or may not be perfected or perfectible. To the extent the concern of the strong-arm clause is with "secret liens" and ostensible ownership, it cannot be directed at involuntary transferors. To the extent the rationale is that of bankruptcy as a collective proceeding, it has no application where the power asserted on behalf of all the creditors—to take property free of a restitution claim—is one that no creditor *qua* creditor could assert outside bankruptcy. A distinct rationale would be needed, therefore, and it is difficult to identify an appropriate one. . . .

The foregoing objections . . . might well be compelling enough to decline to read § 544(a)(3) as giving the trustee a power to destroy competing equitable interests in real property, even if a literal reading of the provision appeared to yield that unintended result. The final irony of this controversy, however, is that a literal reading of § 544(a) does not confer any such power. On the contrary: § 544(a)(3), read literally, can only refer to the trustee's power to avoid an unperfected transfer of property by the debtor. . . .

1. Section 544(a) in Isolation

It is impossible to read § 544(a)(3) literally as conferring on the trustee "the rights and powers of . . . a bona fide purchaser of real property . . . from the debtor," because the language simply will not parse. . . .

The introductory clauses of § 544(a) identify three potential elements of the strong-arm power . . . . Subsections 544(a)(1) and (2) . . . are easily read in conjunction with each of these three elements. Subsection (3), adding the status of bona fide purchaser, is different because of the succeeding phrase referring to "such transfer" . . . . The presence of this limiting phrase reveals that the status of bona fide purchaser conferred in § 544(a)(3) relates only to the trustee's power to "avoid any transfer of property of the debtor."

This is so for two reasons. The first is purely a question of syntax . . . .

The second is a matter of sense. The words "against whom applicable law permits such transfer to be perfected" qualify the trustee's hypothetical status of bona fide purchaser in an intelligible fashion. . . .

. . . If we attempt to squeeze out of § 544(a)(3) a right to exercise the broader "rights and powers" of some other bona fide purchasers, specifically the right to take real property of the debtor free of the competing equities of third-party claimants, the words "against whom applicable law permits such transfer to be perfected" can yield no coherent meaning. . . .

In short, a literal interpretation of the strong-arm clause as currently written limits the applicability of subsection 544(a)(3) to the trustee's power to "avoid any transfer of property by the debtor." The avoidance of certain unperfected transfers by the debtor is manifestly the principal object of the strong-arm power; this is why Congress could add subsection 544(a)(3) in terms which, read literally, can only be construed in connection with the power to "avoid any transfer." As already noted, however, the power to "avoid any transfer of property of the debtor" cannot be read as a power to avoid a restitution claim against property in the possession of the debtor. Such claims arise from transfers *to* the debtor, not transfers *by* the debtor, and the "avoidance" of an equitable interest is not in any event the avoidance of a transfer. The conclusion is that § 544(a)(3) has not even a literal applicability to the characteristic problem of restitution in bankruptcy.

2. Section 544(a) in Context

If we bear in mind that the whole controversy is ultimately a matter of identifying the property of the estate, there is a final objection to any interpretation of § 544(a) that would allow the trustee to distribute constructive trust property to creditors, even when such property takes the form of real estate. Recall the starting hypothesis about any constructive trust claim, which is that the property interests in a particular asset have been disaggregated: the debtor has possession and voidable title, while the claimant has equitable ownership. This equitable interest is the piece of property the parties are fighting over. Does it ever become part of the bankruptcy estate, and if so, by what statutory route?

Our starting point is that it does not come in under § 541(a)(1): at the commencement of the case, this interest belongs to somebody else. The response is made, by Circuit Judge Easterbrook and others, that there is no anomaly in bringing into the estate assets that were not the property of the debtor at the commencement of the case: "allowing the estate to 'benefit from property that the debtor did not own' is exactly what the strong-arm powers are about." This is true within limits. . . . [S]ome property interests of persons other than the debtor are drawn into the bankruptcy estate: among others, the interest of a purchaser or a mortgagee from the debtor, where the transfer has not been perfected.

By contrast, the power to appropriate for the estate the equitable interest represented by a claim of constructive trust cannot be described either as the recovery of property or as the avoidance of a transfer. The claimant's equitable interest cannot, therefore, come into the bankruptcy estate by the literal terms of §§ 550(a) and 541(a)(3). Nor is there any other statutory route by which such property becomes part of the bankruptcy estate. Viewed from the standpoint of first principles, the omission is not surprising. What is surprising is the notion that bankruptcy should ever seek to pay creditors with the property of others, where such property has only come into the hands of the debtor by fraud or mistake.

CONCLUSION

Omegas Group protests that "[t]he equities of bankruptcy are not the equities of the common law," but on a clear view of the matter the supposed divergence disappears. Ratable distribution, whether inside or outside bankruptcy, can only mean ratable distribution to claimants similarly situated; otherwise bankruptcy could not distinguish between secured and unsecured creditors, between creditors and mere bystanders. Bankruptcy and the common law of property share the objective of determining what is the property of the debtor, and therefore of the estate, and what is the property of others. Bankruptcy respects the common-law determination of property rights—because the courts have said so, and because any failure to do so would either deprive the creditors of assets properly subject to their claims, or else satisfy those claims with assets belonging to someone else.

The problem of restitution in bankruptcy derives from the divisibility of property interests: a debtor may have less than complete ownership of property in his possession, even of property to which he holds legal title. If property is held by the debtor subject to an express trust, the distinct interest of the trust beneficiary is readily recognizable. If the debtor has title to property that he has obtained from its owner by fraud or mistake or coercion, the relation of legal and equitable interests is essentially the same though inevitably harder to establish. . . . Unfortunately for claimants, the law that regulates nonconsensual transfers of property—the law of restitution—has become the least familiar region of present-day commercial law.

The solution to the "constructive trust in bankruptcy" puzzle does not actually lie in § 541(d) of the Bankruptcy Code, but the very existence of the provision reveals something of the broader problem: namely, a decline in the dependability of the uncodified part of our commercial law.

Additional suggested readings

David G. Carlson, *The Trustee's Strong Arm Power Under the Bankruptcy Code*, 43 S.C. L. REV. 841 (1992)

Carlos J. Cuevas, *Bankruptcy Code Section 544(a) and Constructive Trusts: The Trustee's Strong Arm Powers Should Prevail*, 21 SETON HALL L. REV. 678 (1991)

Jeffrey Davis, *Equitable Liens and Constructive Trusts in Bankruptcy: Judicial Values and the Limits of Bankruptcy Distribution Policy*, 41 FLA. L. REV. 1 (1989)

Thomas H. Jackson, Ch. 3, *Refining Liabilities: The Basic Trustee Avoiding Powers of Section 544*, *in* THE LOGIC AND LIMITS OF BANKRUPTCY LAW 68-88 (Harvard 1986)

Thomas H. Jackson, *Translating Assets and Liabilities to the Bankruptcy Forum*, 14 J. LEGAL STUD. 73 (1985)

Frank R. Kennedy, *Statutory Liens in Bankruptcy,* 39 MINN. L. REV. 697 (1955)

Harold Marsh, Jr., *Triumph or Tragedy? The Bankruptcy Act Amendments of 1966*, 42 WASH. L. REV. 681 (1967)

Chapter 6
Avoiding Powers: Preferences

The avoiding power that spawns the most bankruptcy litigation and that is the most uniquely dependent on the collective nature of a bankruptcy case is the power to set aside preferences. This avoiding power is dramatic in its consequence: it permits the trustee to set aside and recover a transfer that was made prior to bankruptcy *and* that may have been perfectly legal when made. Preference avoidance has been part and parcel of bankruptcy law virtually from the beginning, many hundreds of years ago. But what exactly *is* a "preference," and what justifies the avoidance and recapture of a preference, whatever it may be? The selections in this Chapter are included to illuminate the nature, scope, and evolution of preference theory and practice. At the core of the whole debate lies the fundamental question of whether a preference law is designed principally to protect equality as between similarly situated creditors in the ensuing bankruptcy proceeding or whether that law seeks primarily to deter bad behavior of some sort (by the debtor, creditors, or both) motivated by the looming onset of bankruptcy.

First is an excerpt from the House of Representatives Report that accompanied the bill that later became the 1978 Code. According to that Report: (1) what is a preference?; (2) what are the two purposes of preference law?; and (3) which purpose predominates, and why?

The second work presented is a masterful article by Professor Robert Weisberg of the Stanford Law School, *Commercial Morality, the Merchant Character, and the History of the Voidable Preference*, 39 STAN. L. REV. 3 (1986). Weisberg tracks the historical development of preference law, and demonstrates convincingly "that the actual history of preference law has been, not a progression from standards to rules, but a nervous oscillation between these two approaches." He shows how preference law has been shaped by moral views, and highlights the "inherent instability of rule-making in a world where norms are intensely embraced, yet are elusive and controversial." After reading Weisberg, is there any reason to think that the pattern of oscillation is ever likely to change?

Professor Vern Countryman's monumental 1985 survey of preference law, *The Concept of a Voidable Preference in Bankruptcy*, 38 VAND. L. REV. 713 (1985), follows Weisberg. Countryman's work, as is typical of many of his efforts, is an encyclopedic recapitulation and analysis of the whole field. If there is something a reader wants to know about the meaning, origin, or application of almost any point of preference law, Countryman should be the first place to turn. As one reads his article, the many tensions and undercurrents—and accidents!—swirling around and through preference law become painfully apparent. In the excerpt presented, emphasis is placed on Countryman's discussion of the exceptions to preference liability in § 547(c).

Another bankruptcy masterpiece follows: Professor John McCoid's famous work, *Bankruptcy, Preferences, and Efficiency: An Expression of Doubt*, 67 VA. L. REV. 249 (1981). McCoid performs his usual historical study as a means of divining the goals of preference law, which he shows have been far from constant. He then examines the efficacy and efficiency of preference law in achieving its purported goals, and finds the shortfall to be severe indeed. McCoid concludes that "at least in the absence of fraud, the most efficient response to preferential transfers may be to abolish preference law." Why does Professor McCoid make this seemingly radical suggestion?

The review of preference law then returns to an excerpt from Thomas Jackson's article, *Avoiding Powers in Bankruptcy,* 36 STAN. L. REV. 725 (1984), other parts of which are included in Chapters 5 and 7. Many of the thoughts expressed in Jackson's article are restated and expanded in his book, THE LOGIC AND LIMITS OF BANKRUPTCY LAW, in Chapter 6, *Prebankruptcy Opt-Out Activity and the Role of Preference Law,* 122-150 (Harvard 1986). Jackson sees preference law primarily as a means of redressing the efforts of the debtor or creditors to "opt out" of the bankruptcy distributional scheme by means of preferential activity once they see bankruptcy coming.

Professor Charles Tabb weighs in next with *Rethinking Preferences,* 43 S.C. L. REV. 981 (1992). Tabb examines the historically fault-based nature of preference law, embodied today by the "ordinary course" exception of § 547(c)(2). Equality after the onset of insolvency as a goal may be given lip service but is given short shrift in implementation. Tabb argues that fault-based preference criteria make little sense and asserts that equality should be dominant. To accomplish that end he proposes the repeal of the ordinary course exception.

The small changes in preference law recommended by the 1997 Review Commission are then included. Most notable of these would be the creation of an absolute safe harbor from preference liability for transfers of less than $5000. The rationale for this recommendation, which grew out of a national preference survey by the American Bankruptcy Institute (for which Professor Tabb served as Reporter), essentially is that for such small claims it is not cost-effective for creditors to defend.

The final excerpt is from Professor Peter Alces' article, *Clearer Conceptions of Insider Preferences,* 71 WASH. U. L.Q. 1107 (1993). This piece is the culmination of a running debate between Professor Alces and Professor Jay Westbrook. Westbrook started with *Two Thoughts About Insider Preferences,* 76 MINN. L. REV. 73 (1991); Alces responded with *Rethinking Professor Westbrook's Two Thoughts About Insider Preferences,* 77 MINN. L. REV. 605 (1993); Westbrook volleyed back with *Clear Thinking About Insider Preferences: A Reply,* 77 MINN. L. REV. 1393 (1993), and then the final shot was the Alces work included here. All of these articles make for excellent and thoughtful reading, and one would profit from reviewing them as a group. Space constraints simply prevent including the whole debate. Alces' final flurry was excerpted because it ably provides a short summary of the contours of the debate.

H.R. Rep. No. 95-595
95th Cong., 1st Sess. (1977)

III. AVOIDING POWERS

A. PREFERENCES

A preference is a transfer that enables a creditor to receive payment of a greater percentage of his claim against the debtor than he would have received if the transfer had not been made and he had participated in the distribution of the assets of the bankrupt estate. The purpose of the preference section is two-fold. First, by permitting the trustee to avoid prebankruptcy transfers that occur within a short period before bankruptcy, creditors are discouraged from racing to the courthouse to dismember the debtor during his slide into bankruptcy. The protection thus afforded the debtor often enables him to work his way out of a difficult financial situation through cooperation with all of his creditors. Second, and more important, the preference provisions facilitate the prime bankruptcy policy of equality of distribution among creditors of the debtor. Any creditor that received a greater payment than others of his class is required to disgorge so that all may share equally. The operation of the preference section to deter "the race of diligence" of creditors to dismember the debtor before bankruptcy furthers the second goal of the preference section—that of equality of distribution.

The current preference section contains several impediments to the proper functioning of these two policies. . . . [T]he trustee must show that the creditor for whose benefit the preferential transfer was made had "reasonable cause to believe the debtor was insolvent at the time of the transfer." This provision was designed when the primary purpose of the preference section was to prevent the race of diligence. Whether or not a creditor knows or believes that his debtor is sliding into bankruptcy is important if the only purpose of the preference section is to deter the race. However, a creditor's state of mind has nothing whatsoever to do with the policy of equality of distribution, and whether or not he knows of the debtor's insolvency does little to comfort other creditors similarly situated who will receive that much less from the debtor's estate as a result of the pre-bankruptcy transfer to the preferred creditor. To argue that the creditor's state of mind is an important element of a preference and that creditors should not be required to disgorge what they took in supposed innocence is to ignore the strong bankruptcy policy of equality among creditors.

Robert Weisberg
Commercial Morality, the Merchant Character,
and the History of the Voidable Preference
39 STAN. L. REV. 3 (1986)[*]

American bankruptcy law has never decided what to do about the crucial but elusive concept of the voidable preference. . . . Preference doctrine would seem to be a central part of bankruptcy law. . . .

Preference law, however, reflects a kind of insecurity about the formal process of bankruptcy. . . . Bankruptcy law empowers the trustee and the court to enforce ratable distribution as a matter of public power; preference law implies that the debtor and creditor have a private duty to save the bankruptcy process from becoming moot before it has a chance to start. It places on the debtor and individual creditor a social or moral responsibility to respect the interests of the general class of the debtor's creditors, presumably in the name of the larger social goal of enhancing the efficient sale of credit.

Despite apparent consensus about the purpose of preference law, the conditions under which debtor and creditor owe this duty have been heavily contested for several centuries. A common historical observation is that preference law has followed a line of progress from somewhat vague ethical edicts to modern, systematic, technical rules. In its English origins, the idea of the voidable preference took shape in a sort of criminal law, full of complicated mens rea notions, that condemned devious transfers or payments by debtors who purposely tried to subvert the bankruptcy process. Preference law therefore adopted a moralistic posture by imposing on debtors a duty toward creditors in the abstract, rather than to individual creditors on the basis of individual commercial relationships. As American bankruptcy law evolved from the English model at the start of the nine-

---

teenth century, the law of preferential transfers shifted its concern from the culpability of the debtor to the culpability of the favored creditor. It thus sought to discourage, if not punish, aggressive self-interested economic behavior by imposing on individual creditors a social or moral duty to their fellow creditors.

By the end of the nineteenth century, however, American preference law had lost most of its express moral content. The theory of twentieth century preference legislation has been that we need not engage in any intense moral scrutiny of the behavior of debtors and creditors as commercial citizens. Rather, the theory—or pretense—is that we have achieved some scientific, economic consensus that certain transactions undermine the trustee's power of ratable distribution and obstruct the efficient production of commercial credit, and that we can therefore draw very technical statutory rules that focus impersonally on classes of transactions. This notion of a rational progression in preference law is essentially a Whiggish myth. Preference law has remained one of the most unstable categories of bankruptcy jurisprudence. Indeed, its instability is obvious in the most recent, and perhaps most scientifically pretentious, efforts at legislating an American preference law, efforts that have been quickly undermined by the courts and then by Congress itself.

The perennial—and continuing—debate over preferences has usually taken the form of a choice between formal mechanical rules and open-ended normative standards. . . . I will argue that the rules/standards debate about preference law reflects a very deep division in a capitalist culture about the supposed goal of enhancing credit, and suppresses important questions about moral values in a mercantile credit economy. Moreover, I will argue that the actual history of preference law has been, not a progression from standards to rules, but a nervous oscillation between these two approaches to lawmaking. In this regard, the tortured life-cycle of the law of preferences is an emblem of the morally ambivalent history of bankruptcy law and of commercial law in general.

I. INTRODUCTION: RULES, STANDARDS, AND MORALS IN THE CREDIT MARKET

Bankruptcy law has been playing out a ritualized dance between formal legislative rules and normative commercial and moral standards for 500 years. And for 500 years, there has been a ritualized pattern of criticism of bankruptcy law: rules-proponents attacking standard-based bankruptcy laws, standards-proponents attacking overly formalistic bankruptcy laws, or sometimes a single critic trying to patch together both rules and standards as if combination were resolution. The ritual will continue so long as we waffle over the "essential" purposes of bankruptcy law, and so long as we conceive, and erratically suppress, deep-rooted moral and philosophical questions about the phenomena of trade and credit. . . .

A. *The Themes of Preference Law*

. . . The assumption of preference law is that we can establish a category of prebankruptcy payments by debtor to creditor that are economically, and perhaps morally, subversive. But preference law thereby assumes that the debtor and creditor owe a general duty to the abstract class of the debtor's creditors, a duty that is itself deeply controversial. . . .

Throughout the history of preference law, legislators and commentators have ritually claimed that they have designed a precise legal instrument to single out just those prepetition transactions between debtor and creditor that wrongly threaten the process of ratable distribution. Lawmakers thus proclaim that there is some consensus in our commercial culture about which commercial actors or transactions merit legal sanction. Moreover, a common, if unstated, assumption of preference law has been that legislation can create harmony between our moral concern for sanctioning antisocial conduct by debtors or creditors and our purely instrumental concerns with enhancing the flow of credit in commerce.

Historically, we can associate this optimistic view of preference law with calls for more inclusive preference-avoiding rules. This view assumes that the credit system is fundamentally morally sound, but that we can identify a few clear abuses, and can thereby create clear rules to regulate them. Commercial actors will then be able to rely on predictable preference rules in planning and executing their credit transactions.

B. *The Rituals of Preference Lawmaking*

Yet the historical ritual has been that, shortly after such scientific, morally uncontroversial preference rules are passed, they are quickly undone. The causes of the ritual breakdown seem to be several. On the simplest level, preference legislation breaks down due to mere instrumental uncertainty. . . .

On another level, the instability of preference legislation lies with judges who deny that precise legislative rules are ever sensitive enough to capture the nuances of commercial behavior and the norms of the marketplace. The one dominant historical ritual in twentieth century American preference law has been for Congress to enact a new and supposedly clear and broad preference rule, and for judges then to ignore or shamelessly manipulate statutory rules to preserve transactions against a preference attack. In short, judges transform rigid statutory rules into flexible discretionary norms, and turn preference law into a matter of "I know it when I see it." . . .

But commercial custom has strong and complex moral roots, and when judges act this way, they suggest deeper reasons why preference rules get undone. When judges nullify clear preference-avoiding rules, they imply that the legislature has failed to establish a consensus about proper commercial behavior and about the goals of commercial law. . . .

The undoing of clear and broad preference legislation has not been the work of the courts alone. As another part of the historical ritual, the frequent reconsiderations of bankruptcy law in Congress have become occasions for an explicit debate by legislators and scholars over the purpose and feasibility of preference law. . . . The language of the statute may reflect an elephantine compromise as a result of clumsy legislative efforts to accommodate conflicting views.

As a result of judicial or legislative subversion, preference laws have inadvertently become symptoms of the instability of our commercial norms. On the other hand, as we have seen very recently, the instability of preference law has resulted from very deliberate economic or political attacks on the very concept of systematic preference rules. The oscillation from rule to standard often reflects a belief that, because there can be no clear moral confidence about what are good and what are bad transactions, we must abjure any attempt at scientific legislation and should simply accept the necessity of somewhat indeterminate legal standards.

C. *The Contemporary Effort*

Perhaps no aspect of the landmark 1978 Bankruptcy Code has displayed such a pretense to scientific formalism as section 547, which purported to be the final scientific word on preferences, a radically systematic scheme of definition and exception. Yet shortly after its enactment, federal judges began reviving the grand old style of ignoring or manipulating the clear language of preference legislation to uphold transactions that appeared to accord with intuited norms of the credit market. And just six years later, we encounter an "Improvements" Act that further tinkers with section 547. The new law undermines the scientific formalism of the statute by indirectly incorporating a "customary norm" into the definition of preferential behavior, undoing the new formal rules with a standard thinly masked as a mild amendment to a subrule. . . .

This article is an interpretive history of preference law as it reflects the general debate over rules and standards in bankruptcy law. . . .

II. ENGLISH BANKRUPTCY LAW AND THE ADVENT OF THE PREFERENCE

A. *English Mercantile Culture*

Renaissance and Restoration English culture developed a morally complex image of the merchant character, an image that helps explain the ambivalence of English bankruptcy law in regulating, punishing, and rewarding merchant behavior. The image is actually a pair of images. The dominant image in the eighteenth century is the merchant as a noble but vulnerable statesman of international trade, always the helpless victim to the vagaries of elusive credit, reputation, and fortune. But the earlier and ever-persisting image is the viciously ugly picture of the cheat, the evil magician who manipulates intangible credit and property, who devours the store of others, and who literally and figuratively absconds.

1. *The merchant as villain.*

The imagery of the merchant derives from English culture's perception of, or troubled attempt to comprehend, the new phenomenon of capitalist credit. Credit is essentially a form of property or money, an intangible wealth that depends on trust, reputation, and rumor. Like the merchant, it has its good and its bad images. Credit can be a noble bond or solvent trust among merchants and indeed among nations, and a means to leverage great wealth out of limited natural resources. Yet credit instruments are also a false wealth, an illusion, a design of smoke and mirrors manipulated by merchants to devour the property of others. . . .

The moral ambivalence of the Renaissance view of the merchant debtor appears in imagery of reality and illusion, of manipulation of appearance. The image thereby reflects a kind of social paranoia about a new economic phenomenon that is perceptually and conceptually elusive, and for that same reason morally suspect. . . .

Commercial capital struck the English mind as discomfortingly unmoored from the solid reality of land . . . .

The merchant class moved up, and somewhat unsettled, the landbased social hierarchy. While the landed used their status to create wealth, the merchants used their wealth to create status. . . . Ironically, the very evanescence of the merchant class was part of its threat to English culture: The fragile contingency of the merchant world became the fragile contingency of the economy generally, or so some perceived.

The conservative political response to the discomforting rise of commercial exchange was to legislate restrictions. The harsh bankruptcy laws of the seventeenth century were only part of the statutory effort to control the morally and perceptually elusive forms of trade that the common law and law merchant had little power to constrain. The statutes were, in effect, atavistic attempts to maintain a world based on land status and duty.

2. *The merchant as hero.*

The counter-response in this political battle over the role of commerce in English culture was an intellectual project by a great number of seventeenth century writers—an affirmative ideology of credit and trade. The emerging sympathetic imagery of the contingent life of the merchant, and of credit as the solvent of social relations, began to cohere into a political vision.

The new ideology demanded a redefinition of money itself as a sort of symbolic force of nature, not an object of devious manipulation. Money was imagined in ideal terms as the pure passive medium, the proxy for all things of value. Mercantile credit was not only desirable, but historically inevitable. . . . The specific political conclusion from this ideology, of course, was that the statutory restrictions on credit were either counterproductive or futile, since they fought with human nature itself. . . .

Of course, a counter-ideology persisted, but the argument remained that trade, if not morally admirable, was nevertheless socially inevitable, and that the elusiveness of its phenomena, though raising moral doubts, nevertheless made trade regulation futile. . . .

Moreover, the new ideology of trade succeeded by inventing a more specific ideology of the merchant character. If the moral problem lay with the image of the merchant as a creature of pure interest, unconstrained by any traditional standards of religious virtue or social responsibility, the solution had to lie in the justifying ideology of mercantile self-interest as potentially restraining and socially responsible itself. It was natural, and thus predictable, for people to act according to measurable economic self-interest, rather than variable or volatile heroic aspirations. Thus, despite their subtlety and invisibility, commercial transactions were socially desirable. Because mercantile self-interest ensured the predictability of private economic transactions, it created reliance interests among commercial actors, and so commerce became a form of ethical bonding. . . .

. . . [T]he merchant figure became an unheroic hero, praised for his benignity and not for his nobility. . . .

Credit is the symbolic currency through which society expresses its moral and economic health. Credit is a civilizing influence and can lead to a mercantile utopia. It is also potentially a corrupting influence because it is based on the passions of fantasy and opinion. To prevent corruption, society had to engineer these passions. The first two centuries of English bankruptcy law, and of preference law in particular, show a revealing form of this engineering. . . .

C. *The Origins of English Preference Law*

. . . Early English law barely apprehended the concept of the preferential transfer. Unlike the fraudulent conveyance, the preference was not illegal at common law. And because it benefitted at least one creditor, it did not seem the sort of antisocial act that inspired the original criminal form of bankruptcy. Once English law evolved toward viewing bankruptcy as a debtor's condition, rather than his crime, the preferential transfer became more visible: English law came to view the bankruptcy process more as a fair settlement or adjustment of claims among worried parties than as a crime or a tort. But the fault-based view of the debtor has never really disappeared from English law. . . .

1. *The advent of the "relation-back" doctrine.*

. . . [B]y 1584, the courts had come to recognize what might loosely be called a preferential transfer. . . . [T]he question was whether the "preference period," or, more strictly, whether the Commissioners' title to the bankrupt's property, related back to the original act of bankruptcy that had precipitated the commission. Lord Coke, in dictum in *The Case of Bankrupts*, said that the bankruptcy law imported a distrust of a bankrupt's handling of his own assets and a principle of equal division among creditors that justified the voiding of the transfer. . . .

Parliament thereby created a new bona fide creditor law [in 1746], protecting such payments from avoidance where the payment was to an innocent creditor "in the usual and ordinary course of trade," where the creditor neither knew nor had reason to know that the debtor was insolvent or faced bankruptcy. The relation-back doctrine was an overbroad rule, insensitive to the commercial reality that many creditors in the ordinary course of business accepted payments without knowing their debtors were bankrupt. . . . Thus, Parliament had to soften the relation-back rule with a normative standard.

The standard looks ahead to American law in two important ways: It tests a suspect payment against some intuited sense of the ordinary course of commerce, and it looks to the mental state of the creditor to discern the commercial morality of the payment. . . .

2. *The mens rea of the preference.*

. . . It is one thing to impose a duty on debtors after they commit acts of bankruptcy but before the commission is sued out. But it is another thing to engage in moral scrutiny of the debtor's mens rea before he commits what is in any event a "constructive" action.

If the key to bankruptcy law is some sort of statutory certainty, it faces a problem of infinite regress in controlling transactions outside the rules. Yet something in commercial reality put a counterstrain on bankruptcy law to create just that duty. . . .

. . . [T]he problem English culture faced in perceiving and apprehending elusive forms of credit and tying them to formal rules is inseparable from the moral issue. If people in commerce cannot always discern the subtle indicia of credit and insolvency, who is to blame, and who is the victim? Once widespread credit combined with abstract credit instruments to create an epidemic of "invisible commerce," the question arose as to who is the exploiter and who is the victim of the invisibility. Once English law and literature began to accept the ideology and imagery of the merchant as a respectable and sympathetic figure, and indeed an important strand in the national and international community, preference law might have become the means of securing the bond of intermerchant moral duty. Yet the concept of commercial interdependence seems to have remained a sentiment, and one that the law could adopt only slowly and unsystematically.

On the other hand, if bankruptcy law is seen chiefly as punishing or regulating the debtor's behavior, it is not intuitively clear why a preferring debtor has violated the norm. A preferring debtor hurts some creditors individually, but does not necessarily hurt creditors in the aggregate. So to "blame" him for a preference, which is exactly what the still morally-bound English law did, is to assume an established principle of intercreditor equity based on some moral theory of a duty of a debtor to the general class of his creditors, or some economic theory that, moral concerns aside, preferences encourage wasteful extensions of credit or cause an inefficient dismemberment of the estate. . . .

As Lord Mansfield ultimately developed the idea, the debtor commits a preferential transfer before he commits an act of bankruptcy only if he exhibits a very strange sort of moral will. If the creditor puts great pressure on the debtor, the transfer does not meet that test. Rather, it is only a preferential transfer when, in effect, the debtor tries to create his own scheme of distribution. The sin of the debtor to violate a norm of commercial fellowship is captured in the idea of ratable distribution . . . . Yet the obligation of loyalty to this commercial fellowship remains in the debtor, not the creditor. . . . Lord Mansfield thereby sets in motion a historical confusion about states of mind in preference law which later vexes American bankruptcy law.

Worsely v. DeMattos, in 1758, the first Mansfield case to explicitly address the legality of a preferential transfer in the modern sense, sets the moral form of early bankruptcy law in its two aspects: Though it is hard to imagine any illegality in merely paying off a bona fide debt, a preference is void where it reflects some deliberate effort by the debtor to undo the concept of political and economic community imagined by modern bankruptcy law. . . .

3. *The complex ethics of the preference.*

The themes Lord Mansfield introduces in the *Worsley* opinion illuminate all of English preference law. Ten years later, in *Alderson v. Temple*, he defined the mens rea of a preferential transfer more explicitly. A payment on a debt is a preference only when it lies outside the normal course of trade: It is still a *fraudulent* preference. But Mansfield defines the fraudulent intent in a somewhat circular fashion: The debtor must "intend to give a preference." Thus begins the concept of mens rea with respect to preferences, but it is a very curious mens rea. . . . The focus on the debtor's state of mind might, of course, be an indirect way of getting at creditor misbehavior. But Mansfield seems curiously hesitant to recognize any intercreditor moral responsibility. Indeed, quite the opposite: His doctrine rewards the nasty creditor who put pressure on the debtor, because then the transfer would not be a preference. . . .

Though Lord Mansfield, ironically, invites treatment of the preference under a broad moral norm, he retreats to the purported rule-boundedness of the bankruptcy scheme of distribution and the assumed implicit rules of ordinary course trade to govern these transactions. Lord Mansfield is then forced to acknowledge that his effort at rule-making begins to look like arbitrary formalism. . . .

III. THE DEVELOPMENT OF AMERICAN PREFERENCE LAW: THE NINETEENTH CENTURY

A. *The New American Commercial Ideology*

1. Ideology and the need for a bankruptcy law.

The early American ideologists of commerce inherited the British ambivalence about the ethics, ontology, and politics of credit. But probably the major intellectual strategy of American and European writers who played a role in American ideology was to invert the moral and perceptual elusiveness of credit that characterized much of the earlier British thinking. The emerging bourgeois ideology conceded that commerce was an expression of self-interest, but argued that though self-interest might seem a vice in private, it could become a public virtue in the aggregate. . . . The commercial republic created a more solid, if duller, form of public virtue rooted in private interest. Men pursuing raw economic self-interest achieved benign peace, if not grandiloquent heroism. . . .

. . . [T]he merchant became the model for all modern citizens. . . .

Thus, underlying bankruptcy law is a deep cultural division over the moral worth of a credit economy as well as more fundamental questions about reality and illusion in which money and credit become epistemological symbols. By the beginning of the nineteenth century, the issue of whether to have a national bankruptcy law became one of the major questions in the general division over the moral validity of a commercial culture. . . .

The trade ideologists saw the need for a rationalized bankruptcy system in uniform, predictable, market-serving terms. Bankruptcy would facilitate credit and limit liability. The argument for the new bankruptcy law is an argument for the historical necessity of expanded capitalism and credit and for recognizing that the merchant, as a crucial participant in this historical progress, merits protection from the risks he takes in its name . . . .

The argument opposing bankruptcy took a number of forms. Some conceded that a bankruptcy law is necessary in a modern trading nation, but denied that the United States had reached that stage of capitalist development or that it had actually developed a special class of professional merchants as had England. Others argued that bankruptcy was a bad thing in itself. . . . Yet other opponents of a new bankruptcy law managed to make a dramatically different argument at the same time: that bankruptcy was an inherently corrupting force in society because it only exacerbated the corrupting effects of commerce. . . .

2. The rhetoric of the new bankruptcy debate.

The wild struggles over the bankruptcy law reflect a conceptual confusion about the essential purposes of bankruptcy law, which in turn reflects the wonderful plasticity of bankruptcy as a medium for debate over a wide variety of moral and political issues in a changing economy. . . .

B. *Credit, Morals, and Preferences in America*

I have argued that the history of bankruptcy law reveals a persistent debate over a few fundamental moral and political issues about commercial culture . . . .

Assuming that one major purpose of any bankruptcy law is to restrict preferences, opponents of a bankruptcy bill viewed the preferential payment as a healthful expression of local trust, family ties, and personal moral commitment. For the proponents of a modern bankruptcy law, preferences might be evil in at least two polar ways . . . . If the image was one of the small-time local tradesman, then preferences were bad because they were at best inefficient, provincial, and perhaps sentimental anachronisms that blocked the development of an efficient national machine of credit and commerce. If one's image of the preferring debtor was that of the devious speculator and absconder . . ., then the preference was one of the most nefarious, fraudulent leveraging tricks of the corrupt speculator. It was not an expression of homespun (if inefficient) trust and honor, but a horrible distortion of the whole concept of trust and honor. . . .

1. *Some early views on mercantile morals and the need for a preference law.*

Examination of a few documents from the nineteenth century helps capture the complexity of the moral and cultural problems of credit and bankruptcy and the pretense of their resolution. One of the most revealing is Samuel Sewall's article in the 1829 *American Jurist*, an article which represents the pretenses of the "scientific" approach to credit and bankruptcy associated with the proponents of a uniform national bankruptcy law. Once again, the arguments over bankruptcy in general, and about preferences in particular, reflect deeper concerns about the relationship between a credit society and moral and political virtue. The argument for a national bill generally viewed bankruptcy law as a robust, economical, and scientific instrument of commercial efficiency. Yet the documents also reveal, if not acknowledge, a murky, persistent moral anxiety about the credit culture they purport to celebrate. . . .

The general stance is one of highly rational moral enlightenment. . . .

Sewall then describes his worst vision: Pressured by the absence of discharge, the debtor makes a side-deal with one or a few of his creditors in depreciated paper. The quiet settlement between debtor and creditor is not a laudable act of trust and humanity, but a crooked and coercive form of preference, violating an assumed moral duty the debtor bears to the general class of his creditors. . . .

The scientific view of preferences thus takes a moralistic tone, rejecting the argument that what seems to be an illegal preference may indeed be an admirable gesture of personal trust and confidence that should be sustained against the pressures of impersonal, rationalized commerce. . . .

Hence the more scientific argument against preferences takes the familiar form of an abstract choice between rules and standards. It recognizes that a preference may be an expression of moral honor, but laments that matters of moral honor are not wholly susceptible to modern rational predictable regulation. . . .

2. *The advent of a formalist American preference law.*

The early history of American preference law reflects the general effort of American bankruptcy and commercial law to achieve formality, abstraction, and scientific precision. But that movement nevertheless is marked by a continuing struggle with the underlying moral questions about preferences. . . .

State law. During the long battle over federal bankruptcy legislation, the states had the power to regulate preferences under their insolvency laws. . . . [T]he state cases reveal a flexible tolerance of favorable arrangements between debtors and particular creditors. Underlying this tolerance is an odd mixture of moral confusion and sophisticated moral agnosticism about the feasibility or wisdom of highly formal legislative regulation of preferences. . . .

Congress and preferences. The 1800 Bankruptcy Act, a rather close imitation of the English law, did not mention preferences, but the courts did infer, from the mere passage of a national bankruptcy bill, a vigorous principle of ratable distribution. They articulated an aggressive preference doctrine, firmly condemning eve-of-bankruptcy transfers that constituted bona fide payments of bona fide debts. The courts thus ignored the rhetoric of the English cases that required some suspicion of fraudulent collusion, and embarked on a more categorical, objective preference theory. . . .

The 1841 statute was boldly original in its breadth. It created the concept of voluntary bankruptcy and, as if following the commercial ideologues' vision of the merchant as the Everyman of American democracy, it extended the new privilege to nontraders as well as traders. The 1841 Act was also the first bankruptcy statute in English or American history to expressly forbid preferences, and the first great legislative expression of a broad, formal policy of ratable distribution according to objective rules. It introduced to Anglo-American bankruptcy law the notion of a determinate time period for measuring the legality of a payment. The statute did include pregnant language about the debtor's mens rea. . . . A preference was illegal where the debtor created one "for the purpose of giving . . . preference or priority" to a creditor, "in contemplation of bankruptcy." But during the brief life of the 1841 Act, the courts aggressively renewed their campaign to remove from American preference law the vestiges of the subtle parsing of mental states that had characterized English law and American state law.

Judicial development of a formalist preference law. The key designer of the new formal, objective American preference doctrine was Justice Story, who, in a rather ironic way, worked within and inverted the mens rea approach to preference law. Even if the trustee or general creditors had to prove that the debtor intended to give a preference, the courts could finesse the issue by using a doctrinal trope developed in the criminal law, and in the law of homicide in particular: the rebuttable, or even conclusive, presumption that a person intends the natural and probable consequences of his acts. If a debtor pays a particular creditor shortly before bankruptcy, the natural and probable consequence is a preference that depletes the entitlement of the general creditors. . . .

Thus the vague normative standard of Mansfield was twisted to become a virtual rule forbidding the payment. . . . Henceforth, the bankruptcy courts were to examine the objective situation of the debtor, not the elusive facts of his motive or the subtleties of Mansfield's "pressure" doctrine. The new American preference law thus purported to remove some of the moralistic intensity of English law: Relying on what is almost an automatic rule to establish the debtor's "fault," it diluted the very concept of culpability in the preference. . . .

The 1867 Act was the next erratic step in establishing formal categorical rules for bankruptcy process in general. . . . [I]t took another step toward the formal rationalization of preference doctrine, expressly establishing the preference as an act of bankruptcy and fixing the time period for the danger zone of preferences in its technical modern form. In defining the debtor's mental state in a preference, it offered yet another verbal formula, declaring a preference where "any person, being insolvent, or in contemplation of insolvency, within four months before the filing of the petition [makes payment to a creditor] with a view to give a preference" . . . .

Borrowing from state law to replace "in contemplation of bankruptcy" with the fact or contemplation of insolvency, the 1867 statute avoided the conceptual muddle that Story had to solve earlier, and thus represented a further step toward objectifying the mental state of the preferring debtor. . . . [T]he courts took the occasion of a new short-lived bankruptcy act to reinforce the notion that the intent to prefer was a legal vestige, to be almost automatically presumed from the mere fact of the debtor's insolvency. . . .

Finally, the Supreme Court in 1871 [in *Toof v. Martin*] firmly adopted Justice Story's objective rule that the debtor's culpable intention inheres in the natural and probable consequences of his conduct. Holding that payment would remain with the favored creditor only if the insolvent debtor could bear the rather overwhelming burden of proving he was wholly ignorant of his insolvency, the Court essentially removed the principle of debtor culpability from American preference law.

The pretense of formal rationality of American preference law was thus well established in the preference cases decided during the erratic life of the national bankruptcy act, in the latter half of the nineteenth century. Yet a strong undercurrent of legal agnosticism persisted, sustaining the view of preferences established under the English bankruptcy law and the American insolvency laws. The old skepticism about the ability of lawmakers to draw sharp and categorical moral distinctions among debtor-creditor transactions continued to appear in the form of the imperious opinion that essentially ignored the categorical rules about preferences where the transaction did not match the judge's negative moral imagery of the collusive preference. Some judges claimed simply to know illegal preferences when they saw them. . . .

IV. THE SCIENTIFIC TRIUMPH OF 1898

The scientific pretenses of the 1898 Act were manifest in its elaborate scheme for regulating preferences. As if to emphasize that preference law had become an amoral, nonpunitive regulatory scheme, the statute no longer made the giving of a preference grounds for denying the debtor a discharge, and, as if to underscore the formalist spirit of the new national law, it replaced the old and controversial equitable insolvency test for bankruptcy with the new balance sheet test, supposedly more mathematically determinate, but in the end equally controversial. . . . The formal rationality of the scheme, however, quickly proved an almost comic failure. . . .

A. *The New Rational Preference Law*

There was one near-certain thing about the statute: It confirmed the theme of nineteenth century preference law that subjective questions about the debtor's mental state were virtually irrelevant to the definition of an illegal preference. Indeed, the crucial provisions about preferences did not directly mention the debtor's state of mind. Thus, the deeply-rooted English concept of the debtor's commercial or moral culpability for making a preference disappeared from American law—at least as a visible and distinct concept. . . . [T]he old cultural debate over guilt and innocence in preferential transfers had mostly moved to another arena—the mind of the creditor.

1. *The new rules of creditor behavior.*

The 1898 statute illuminates a slow but dramatic shift in American law, from the notion of the debtor's moral duty to his creditors, to the notion, essentially irrelevant under English doctrine, of the preferred creditor's moral duty to his fellow creditors.

The first American preference statute, enacted in 1841, contained an obscure provision suggesting that the good faith of the favored creditor might render a preferential payment legal. . . . The more elaborate preference scheme in the 1867 statute reintroduced a form of creditor mens rea as an element of the voidable preference. . . .

In any event, the 1898 Act sustained the principle of requiring some culpable mental state in the creditor. . . . The trustee could now avoid a payment only if the favored creditor had "reasonable cause to believe that it was intended . . . to give a preference." A 1910 amendment tinkered further to remove this debtor-focused vestige, and the question became whether the favored creditor had reasonable cause to believe the payment "would effect a preference." . . .

2. *The agnostic view reappears.*

This statutory gap soon caused a great deal of lower court division and is the basis for one of the most remarkable judicial opinions in the entire history of bankruptcy law. Referee Hotchkiss' 1901 opinion in *In re Hall* is justly famous for containing perhaps the best scholarly summary of the twisted history of Anglo-American preference law. What has escaped attention, however, is that the Hotchkiss opinion also contains one of the most illuminating episodes in the long moral and intellectual battle over the conflict between technical rules and normative standards in bankruptcy.

As Hotchkiss sets up the morality play, the victim-protagonist is the ordinary course trade creditor of the debtor, who has been extending rather conventional credit for supplies and accepting regularly scheduled and modest payments. . . . Hotchkiss uncovers in the scientific scheme of the 1898 Act a destabilizing problem: the fate of the "ordinary course" creditor. . . .

. . . Hotchkiss concedes that any mental state requirement will impinge on perfectly ratable distribution, but views this fact with Burkean tolerance: "Creditors will insist that their receipts were in due course—this they have been doing ever since there was a bankruptcy law, and some guilty creditors will escape with more than their share."

The alternative is far worse. The categorical reading would mean that no creditor who innocently receives a payment would know for four months whether he could keep it. . . .

Hotchkiss expresses bitter cynicism about the shibboleth that "equality is equity" and outrage at the notion of creditors suffering any sanction from payments on legitimate debts when the payments evince no aspects of moral culpability: "Innocent of guile, they are guilty." From "time immemorial" the preference had been a moral as well as a legal wrong. . . .

A final footnote to the early twentieth century history of the preferred creditor's mens rea comes from Judge Learned Hand. . . . Judge Hand invoked the parallel traditional theme in preference law—that of the admittedly *extraordinary* creditor who was fully aware of the dismal facts of the debtor's financial state, but who deserves to escape the preference prohibition because of his honorable effort to help the debtor survive. . . .

. . . The creditor certainly knew of the debtor's miserable condition and of the latter's frantic efforts to buy time. But the creditor had sincere, if quixotic, faith in some unfinished contracts of the debtor, and shared the debtor's guarded optimism. . . . But Judge Hand refused to believe that the statute could be so strict. He wrote that the statute did not

> compel creditors to overturn all shaken debtors while they have an honest hope of regaining a firm foundation. That creditor only the statute proscribes who dips his hand in a pot which he knows will not go round. . . . The only test is the honesty of his purpose. . . .

. . . [I]n the 1938 Chandler Act, Congress made yet another effort to take the subjectivity out of the creditor's mental state. It purported to take the absolutely final step in 1978 when it removed the very language of reasonable cause to believe from the key part of the Bankruptcy Code. But the spirit of Hand's and Hotchkiss' legal agnosticism persists.

B. *The Breakdown of the Scientific Bankruptcy Law*

. . . [T]he legislative discussion in 1910 turned out to be far more than a debate over the timing of mortgage recording. It was an almost scripted, ritualized reenactment of the historical debate over the legality and morality of preferences, and indeed over all the fundamental questions about the need for a bankruptcy law in our culture. Once again, the technicalities of rule-making for voidable preferences reawakened deep moral ambivalence over the role of credit in our culture. . . .

The 1910 amendment purported to be the final step in the scientific regulation of the secret lien. But it solved the secret lien problem only incompletely, and, as the opponents warned, the amendment proved to be merely the next minor stage in the historical ritual. Like the preference rules before and after it, the 1910 amendment faced undoing by the imagination of judges who would not strike down a transaction as a preference unless it violated some intuitive norm of commercial conduct. . . .

C. *The Chandler Act*

1. *The new pretense, and the cure of the 1898 Act.*

The Chandler Act of 1938 is the next great episode in the history of the scientific pretense in American bankruptcy law. As some of the contemporary commentary shows, its supporters were not too shy to call it "one of the most 'scientifically' created pieces of legislation ever penned by the hand of man.". . .

The new preference rule was the key element in the new progressive reform. Its advocates happily received it as recognition of the clearheaded modern view that the quintessence of bankruptcy is ratable equity among creditors. The encrusted, sentimental historical view of bankruptcy had wrongly focused on its sources in economic distress, and thus had misconceived the role of bankruptcy law as debtor relief. . . .

2. *The downside of the cycle again: the "equitable lien."*

The persistence of the equitable lien. To appreciate why the scientific pretensions of the Chandler Bill suffered the ritual fate of preference legislation, we must take a step back to see another major preference issue that had been relatively dormant for a century—the equitable lien. . . .

But the Supreme Court's tolerance of equitable liens culminated in the famous case of *Sexton v. Kessler*, where Justice Holmes acknowledged that the "equitable lien may not carry the reasoning further or do much more than express the opinion of the court that the facts give a priority to the party said to have it." *Sexton* confirmed a long Supreme Court effort to enhance personal property security, but it was quickly denounced and followed by decades of controversy in the commentary and the courts. . . .

Congressional backfire. The Chandler Act of 1938 was supposed to kill *Sexton* by making the transfer good as of the time when a bona fide purchaser could defeat the lienholder. . . .

But Congress' effort to create a formal rule quickly proved a disaster, and, ironically, prompted calls for a legislative standard more sensitive to commercial custom. In *Corn Exchange Bank v. Klauder*, the Supreme Court, for once, construed the preference statute in favor of the trustee, and against a creditor bank that had loaned money on accounts receivable. Though it is not clear that the drafters of the Chandler Act had even contemplated this possibility, everyone immediately recognized that the result was brutal for non-notification financers, who were lending nearly a billion dollars a year. Thus, a new line of commentary appeared, denouncing the Chandler Act as mindless overkill. . . .

Even the strongest supporters of the Chandler Act's bona fide purchaser test had to acknowledge that, at least as construed, the Chandler Act bludgeoned a wide variety of state-ratified financing schemes. . . .

The tinkering recurs. The solution, of course, was to propose yet another very mild adjustment in the statute. . . .

In 1950 Congress did replace the powerful bona fide creditor test with the more moderate lien creditor test. . . . [T]he result was an incomprehensible, elephantine law, a perfectly ambivalent statute that incoherently mixed supposedly sensitive new formal rules with hopelessly vague normative standards. . . .

. . . But, of course, this ultimate refinement quickly proved to be just the next episode. . . .

V. THE MODERN PHASE

A. *The Infamy of the Floating Lien*

Despite some confidence that the 1950 Act had solved the problem of the equitable lien, there still lurked anxiety that one variant, the floating lien in after-acquired property, might remain troublesome. . . . But no one anticipated that the floating lien would become the subject of perhaps the most famous episode in the ritualized conflict between confident mechanical rules and agnostic normative standards in bankruptcy law.

The unbelievably complex debate over this narrow point of commercial law suggests that larger questions are at stake. Preference law was again to be used and abused as an instrument to reflect various ill-articulated views of virtue in the marketplace, and to reconcile the principle of debtor or creditor self-interest with the duties of these actors to the abstracted community of creditors. The history of the floating lien, in a sense a microcosm of the history of bankruptcy generally in the last four decades, is yet again a history of legal attempts to fashion formal rules on the pretense that we have drawn the relevant moral distinctions about debtor-creditor behavior. It is also a history of the undoing of those rules by judges who find them unharmonious with their standards of commercial custom and ethics, by political forces that see large issues of power ill-resolved by these rules, and by commentators who are skeptical of the feasibility of such rulemaking in the face of the moral indeterminacy of commercial behavior. . . .

B. *The Bankruptcy Reform Act of 1978*

1. *The new scientific pretense.*

What followed was another decade of legislative and scholarly tinkering, grounded in the hope of drawing firmer lines in a modern scientific statute that would draw all the relevant distinctions in preference law. But, as always, that effort in section 547 of the 1978 Bankruptcy Reform Act quickly proved a failure if measured against its pretenses. . . . Courts continued to find play in the statutory joints to uphold transfers that seemed morally unassailable, and political critics found its resolution of debtor-creditor politics prejudicial to those they perceived as the underclass of the credit markets. . . .

[B]y 1973, the Commission assisting Congress in drafting the 1978 Act clearly stated its guiding philosophy: Preference law is designed to capture secret liens and eve-of-bankruptcy grabs . . . . The new law would afford clean rationality. It had three goals—to lessen the scramble among creditors, to promote equality, and to eliminate any incentive for debtors and creditors to arrange unwise loans.

The drafters of the new statute seemed to enjoy considerable moral clarity in their vision of the credit market, and that vision contained one prototypical villain: the undercollateralized financer who increases his collateral in the preference period and thus commits a "classic preference." . . .

2. *The elegant subtleties of section 547.*

. . . The 1978 Act was drafted in a spirit of confidence that "the new structure should herald a tighter, more literal construction of the familiar definitional language." The goal of interpretation should be "a more efficient, mechanical integration." This integration would emphasize equality of distribution and provide a "more efficient system of recapture.". . .

Yet soon after this confidently scientific scheme became the law, it drew attack as a classically failed, quixotic effort to prescribe formal rules in an area that could only sensibly be left to the more modest regulation of flexible norms. . . .

In the face of philosophical and empirical indeterminacy, the only clear effect of adding an extra set of rules is a wasteful increase in litigation over the gaps in the pretentious new statutory scheme. Normative standards might seem to invite more litigation than rules, but rules that threaten to treat many transactions as preferences increase litigation the most. . . .

C. *The Unraveling of Section 547*

1. *The case law.*

The skeptical position quickly found confirmation in the new case law, which both deliberately expressed and inadvertently confirmed the futility of preference rulemaking. . . .

Some courts read the statute with ceremonial respect, paying fealty to the new categorically formal spirit of the Code. But several others followed Judge Friendly's approach [in *In re Riddervold*] (if not with his arch, insouciant disdain for the statute) allowing state law labels to define away the preference problem, thus committing the Bankruptcy Act to a role of policing commercial ethics, rather than imposing abstract redistributional theory. And in other situations, courts managed to manipulate the amorphous definition of the debtor's property, in order to protect a favored creditor who did not meet the imagery of the aggressive manipulator, at times even invoking the old spirituality of the equitable lien.

But the judicial subversion of the new statute was not limited to floating liens. It was equally evident in the application of what is perhaps the most revealing subsection of the statute in the context of the rules-standards conflict. Subsection 547(c)(2) was the drafters' effort to capture the norm of protecting innocuous, like-cash, ordinary course payments to garden-variety trade creditors. The drafters loaded up the provision with the rhetoric of ordinariness to ensure that the normative goal was clear. Purely normative or customary language would have created an inherent instability in a preference law that had purported to make moral innocence irrelevant. But it seemed a political necessity when so many threatened creditors were holders of small, regular debts whose billing cycles made most payment antecedent, but who were not aggressive creditors in any intuitive, normative sense of the term. The drafters then sought to avoid this instability by constraining the normative language with a clear-cut rule: If, and only if, payment were within 45 days of the incurrence of the debt, it could be treated as if it were an exchange for present consideration. . . .

. . . [T]he sudden eruption of case law showed how unstable this mixed rule-standard was. . . .

The norm underlying section 547(c)(2) can be characterized as a mens rea standard: The creditor should be protected for his nonculpable mental state, even if the reasonable cause standard has been eliminated, where the situation suggests he engaged in no true creditor grabbing at all, but has received payment simply resulting from an automatic schedule. This norm would, of course, reflect the American inversion of the old English pressure rule. But the notion of simultaneity offers another way to view that norm. If the creditor put something into the estate essentially at the same time that he took something out, his payment is really a wash, and so it does not truly diminish the estate. Like the equitable lien, "diminution of the estate" is, in a sense, a very vague moral theme that runs through much of the antipreference case law. . . .

2. *Reform and instant re-reform.*

If section 547 was designed as a scientific and precise new rule that would condemn all undeserving transfers as manipulative and that would enhance the estate for the general creditors, then it was quickly denounced as a failure in both premise and execution. Indeed, the convergence of several different and contradictory criticisms of the new law suggest that it only revived fundamental political and moral conflicts about credit and bankruptcy in our political economy.

One criticism was that the elimination of the "reasonable cause" mens rea test for creditors has resulted in preference-finding overkill for creditors as a class. The argument is that the new statute unfairly shifts the burden of preference litigation from debtor to creditor. . . .

A more striking criticism was that . . . the statute proved immediately impotent against secured inventory and accounts receivable financers, yet was used cruelly against nonculpable general creditors. . . . It has essentially worked to the detriment of unsecured creditors, who have received no trickle-down in preference redistribution, yet have suffered the avoidance of their own payments, which are important to them but are trivial to the estate as a whole.

The instant re-reform movement thus aimed either directly at restoring the reasonable-cause-to-believe standard or more broadly at using the statute to express a flexible moral norm. But any effort to restore some moral flexibility on behalf of creditors was quickly denounced as a conspiracy against debtors by those who saw the 1978 statute as a victory in a Manichean class struggle. In that struggle, the virtuous victors had been consumer debtors and small-time good faith creditors, and the temporarily thwarted enemy had been consumer finance lenders. Now the preference debate absorbed moral energy from the parallel battle over debtor's rights.

But restoration of a creditor culpability test, or deregulation of the statutory scheme, was attacked on another ground as well. Critics charged that re-reform would revive, if anything, insuperable proof problems for the trustee or lead to vastly increased wasteful litigation where the section 547 rules had spoken clearly and categorically, essentially validating the worst forms of aggressive creditor behavior. . . .

But when the 1984 Bankruptcy Amendments and Federal Judgeship Act was finally enacted, it did not restore the reasonable-cause-to-believe test at all. Instead, it undermined the formality of the 1978 statute and restored normative flexibility in an unforeseen way. It focused on the very formal 45-day rule in the ordinary course trade-credit exception under section 547(c)(2). In an amusing new permutation of the rules and standards conflict, the 1984 Act eliminated the 45-day rule altogether, so that the narrow formal exception now became a potentially huge normative standard capable of turning the entire section 547 into an antiformal statute. . . .

The next great statutory episode in preference law may then, ironically enough, be an essentially common law effort to create some criteria for determining when credit transactions meet the norm of "the ordinary course.". . .

VI. Conclusion

The effort to develop rational criteria for applying the "ordinary course" principle in preference law is not quixotic. If we are indeed destined to recur to this norm, there are some rational guidelines available, though they are likely to find expression in economic, not moral, terms. . . .

But of course both common law and legislative efforts at such subtle moral and economic distinctions have ritually proved futile. Indeed, the contemporary thinking about preferences reveals two extreme tendencies that reflect the inherent instability of rulemaking in a world where norms are intensely embraced, yet are elusive and controversial. One solution might be described as the super-rule. The premise of a super-rule is that rulemaking efforts in preference law fail when they try to draw subtle moral distinctions. . . . Scientific rulemaking fails when it is less than totally committed to its mission of eliminating all fault-based distinctions. . . .

A super-rule would almost categorically prohibit transfers from debtor to creditor during the entire period of time, readily discernible to all, that the transfer can cause any of the harms traditionally conceived by preference law. Its premise would be an almost absolute principle of ratable equality. It would have no mens rea test, because it would not purport to encompass questions of culpability at all, and it would thereby enormously reduce the trustee's burden of proof. . . .

The super-rule may seem unjust in its categorical extremity, sweeping away most of the distinctions among creditors and credit schemes with which preference law has tinkered. But the benefits might be considerable: Preference law would be wholly loosed from its moral, stigmatic moorings. The gain in certainty would be considerable . . . . It would, in short, be the ultimate in codifications of the long-imagined abstract duty of a creditor—or debtor—to the entire class of creditors.

The alternative consequence of disbelief in the effectiveness of subtle rulemaking distinctions is the abolitionist position. Under this view, the costs of rulemaking are too great, in political controversy, legal uncertainty, and the expense of litigation. Moreover, any preference law that tries to protect transactions that have any strong political constituency is doomed to produce trivial economic benefits. . . .

In the abolitionist view, no effort at refinement is worth the costs. For the abolitionist, deregulation would eliminate uncertainty costs, as well as the unfair retroactive effects of bankruptcy—effects that are especially unfair under modern preference law, which captures many nonfraudulent transfers. . . .

Both the super-rule and abolitionist positions remain, however, no more than whimsical academic speculations. Preference law seems destined to continue in its cycles of regulatory pretense. . . . The cycles seem inevitable in a world in which the phenomena of debt and credit seem to defy clear moral categories, stump economic theorists, and trouble empirical observers.

This is a world where the creditor warding off mechanical application of preference rules to "ordinary course" payments may be the small local trade supplier, interruption of whose regular collection may throw him into bankruptcy, or may be AT&T; the "creditor class" may include workers thrown into unemployment as well as manipulative secret lienors. This is a world where the "debtor" may turn out to be the poor consumer needing federal relief from the cruel finance company, the foolish wastrel, or the manipulator absconding from just debts under an overly generous bankruptcy law; the honest fragile new enterprise needing protective encouragement, or the asbestos or contraceptive manufacturer escaping liability for homicidal recklessness, or the oil and gas speculator whose debts consist of artificial inflated currency that can bring down billion-dollar banks. In this world, we cannot readily tell the virtuous from the villainous, and the various temporary constituencies of debtor and creditor interests never seem to align themselves for very long with any more familiar categories of political or economic interest, or with any consistent moral view of our credit culture.

Vern Countryman
The Concept of a Voidable Preference in Bankruptcy
38 Vand. L. Rev. 713 (1985)[*]

I. Introduction

A bankruptcy trustee is armed by statute with a number of powers to avoid prebankruptcy transfers made by the now bankrupt debtor. Probably none of these powers is of more concern to prebankruptcy transferees than the trustee's power to avoid preferential transfers. . . .

We inherited the notion of the preferential transfer from England; but, as elsewhere, we frequently have concluded that we could improve on the English model. Substantial differences exist, therefore, between the English law of voidable preferences and the American approach. . . .

IV. The Reform Act and Later Amendments

A. *The Basic Concept*

The draftsmen of the Bankruptcy Reform Act of 1978 addressed the difference in treatment of the two kinds of preferential transfers by almost entirely eliminating any requirement that the creditor have reasonable cause to believe the debtor insolvent. The federal Commission that drafted the first version of the Reform Act identified the following three goals for the preference section of the Act: "First, it lessens the possibility of a scramble among creditors for advantage; second, it promotes equality [among classes]; and third, it eliminates the incentive to make unwise loans in order to obtain a preferential payment or security." The Commission proposed a new preference section, which eliminated the requirement that the creditor have reasonable cause to believe the debtor insolvent. The section provided that the debtor was presumed to be insolvent during the period of preference vulnerability, which was reduced from four to three months as a rough trade-off for easing the trustee's evidentiary burden. . . .

During congressional hearings on the Commission proposals, no one stated opposition, and for that reason, the proposals received little attention. The National Bankruptcy Conference fully endorsed the proposals. . . . [T]he Conference's spokesman addressed elimination of the requirement that the creditor have reasonable cause to believe the debtor insolvent:

Logically and theoretically, the knowledge of the recipient of the preference has nothing to do with equality of distribution. Equality is determined by the fact that all creditors are being treated reasonably alike. So, if two creditors received a payment . . . and one had knowledge and one did not of the insolvency of the debtor, that has really no relevance to equality of treatment.

Second, this element has been a constant source of litigation. It has been used by creditors more or less as a shield. There are a great many cases where the creditor was well aware of the financial difficulties of the debtor but managed to escape the recovery of a preference because the trustee just was not able to meet the burden of proof.[98]

Congress accepted the Commission's proposals in the definition of a voidable preference in new section 547(b) and in the presumption of insolvency in section 547(f), and defined the "transfer" to which section 547(b) applies to include involuntary transfers such as judicial liens. . . .

. . . [W]e have finally come, in part by accident, to a voidable preference concept that abandons the English requirement of the debtor's culpability and our own former requirement of the creditor-defendant's culpability. Lord Mansfield's concern about transfers "in contemplation of bankruptcy" has long been replaced with a definite time period preceding bankruptcy, and no one has voiced criticism of this change. Probably all would prefer the certainty afforded by this change, although others might pick, as England has picked, a different period than ninety days. All that the trustee need show to avoid transfers within the ninety day period is that the debtor was insolvent at the time of the transfer, with the presumption of section 547(f) usually carrying the day for the trustee on this issue; that the transfer was to or for the benefit of a creditor, for or on account of antecedent debt; and that the transfer had a preferential effect as heretofore explained.

This result seems consistent with the purpose of the preference concept, although the purpose never has been explained very accurately. Even though statements in the legislative history discuss deterring creditors from scrambling for advantage, it seems ridiculous to expect deterrence for two reasons. First, a preferred creditor can retain his preference if the ninety day period elapses before the bankruptcy petition is filed. Second, if the petition is filed within the ninety day period, the preferred creditor can escape all consequences of having been preferred by simply surrendering his preference . . . . Given these alternatives, few creditors will be deterred from seeking or accepting a preference.

Statements in the legislative history also mention preserving the bankruptcy policy of "equality" of distribution. But, with creditors classified for distribution purposes on the basis of liens and priorities, no bankruptcy policy of "equality" exists. A policy of preserving classes and of preserving equality within classes does exist, however, and the preference concept is designed to preserve this policy. The function of the preference concept is to avoid prebankruptcy transfers that distort the bankruptcy policy of distribution. Transfers that do distort this policy do so without regard to the state of mind of either the debtor or the preferred creditor. . . .

C. *The Exceptions from Preference*

Even though the trustee . . . proves his entire case under section 547(b), he may recover nothing. Section 547(c) contains seven exceptions from section 547(b), and the creditor-defendant may prevent avoidance of his transfer "to the extent that" he can bring it within one or more of these exceptions. No picture of the current American concept of a voidable preference would be complete without an examination of these exceptions.

---

[98] . . . As another experienced but less diplomatic witness later put it, the requirement "put a premium on lying, because if the recipient simply said: 'I know nothing,' how could the trustee get around that denial of knowledge?" . . .

1. The Contemporaneous Exchange Exception

In *National City Bank v. Hotchkiss*, a bank made an unsecured day loan to a stockbroker at 10:00 a.m., the stock market broke before noon, and the New York Stock Exchange suspended the broker at noon. When the bank learned of these facts, it demanded a pledge of securities from the broker, and got it between 2:00 and 3:00 p.m. the same day, although the broker advised the bank that a bankruptcy petition would be filed against it (as it was at 4:00 p.m.) and that the pledge would be a preference. In one of Justice Holmes' cryptic opinions, the Court held that the pledge was a voidable preference.

Four years after *Hotchkiss*, the Court decided *Dean v. Davis*, a case much better known for holding that a mortgage was a fraudulent conveyance when knowingly given to secure a loan that enabled a debtor to give another creditor a preferential payment. But the Court also held that, since the parties intended a secured loan at the outset, the fact that the mortgage was not executed until seven days, or recorded until eight days, after the loan did not convert the mortgage into a voidable preference, because it "was given to secure . . . a substantially contemporary advance."

The Commission that drafted the first version of the Reform Act proposed to define antecedent debt for preference purposes as a debt incurred more than five days before a transfer paying or securing the debt. This proposal was made for the express purpose of overruling *Hotchkiss*. This author pointed out to Congress that this provision would overrule both *Hotchkiss* and *Dean v. Davis* and suggested that the two cases demonstrated that "this matter is much better left to the courts." The House and Senate staff dropped the proposed definition of antecedent debt and substituted the language now in section 547(c)(1) . . . . Apparently, the more demanding requirement of (A) came from *Hotchkiss* and the less demanding requirement of (B) from *Dean v. Davis*. . . .

2. The "Current Expenses" Exception—And How It Grew

Formerly, establishing the debtor's intent to prefer was essential before a preferential transfer would be considered an act of bankruptcy. During that time, a number of cases held that creditors who filed involuntary petitions did not establish the debtor's intent to prefer in payments usually, but not invariably, for current expenses made within four months of bankruptcy. Usually, the payments were described as "necessary" to the continuance of the business or made in the "ordinary course of business." And, with no help from, or regard for, the language of the statute, a smattering of cases held that such payments were also exempt from avoidance under old section 60. Based on these cases, the leading bankruptcy treatise advised that "payments on account of current expenses . . . are generally not within the category of preferential transfers." . . .

The House and Senate draftsmen instead supplied section 547(c)(2) as enacted in 1978 . . . . Clearly, Congress intended to limit the exception to the payment of current expenses. . . .

. . . [A] 1984 amendment to that section eliminated the forty-five day limit.

The 1984 amendment has long roots. One of the first groups to seek any amendment to section 547 were issuers of commercial paper backed by an irrevocable letter of credit from a bank . . . . Their concern was with the market for this paper in the light of the horrible possibility that the issuer might pay at maturity but then go into bankruptcy within ninety days. . . . The only possibly available exception was section 547(c)(2), but frequently the exception would not apply because the commercial paper involved had more than a forty-five day maturity. . . .

In explaining the Conference Report before its adoption in the Senate, Senator Dole blanketed the amendment of section 547(c)(2) in with "a host of technical matters." Senators Dole and DeConcini explained only that the elimination of the forty-five day period would "relieve buyers of commercial paper with maturities in excess of 45 days of the concern that repayments of such paper at maturity might be considered as preferential transfers." But the elimination does much more than that. Elimination of the forty-five day period creates a gaping hole in the preference policy by protecting every creditor who receives a payment otherwise avoidable under section 547(b) who can persuade the court that the debt was incurred and the payment was made "in the ordinary course of business or financial affairs" of debtor and creditor and that the payment was made "according to ordinary business terms." . . .

. . . [S]ection 547(c)(2) in its present form (which I am unable to characterize as another "legislative accident") seems doubly indefensible. The exception creates a huge gap in the policy underlying section 547. First, that a debt was "ordinarily" incurred and paid has no more relevance to whether the debt repayment distorts the bankruptcy distribution scheme than does the purpose of the debtor in making the payment, and of the creditor in receiving it. Second, the present section 547(c)(2) immunizes the ordinary "payment," whether in cash or property, but does not immunize ordinary transfers by way of security. No rational explanation for this distinction is conceivable. . . .

The only apparent justification for section 547(c)(2) as enacted in 1978 (I have not yet heard, but would like to hear, a plausible justification for it in its present form) is the following: If a debtor selectively can meet debts currently coming due in order to continue functioning outside of bankruptcy, creditors should be encouraged to accept these payments, even though preferential. Consequently, creditors may continue doing business with the debtor because they will not be penalized if the debtor's attempt to function outside of bankruptcy fails. This justification is not compelling because it is contrary to the entire concept of preference. . . .

In view of the feeble inspiration for this exception, and because the exception is completely at war with the concept of a preference and has no rational confining limits, the best future for present section 547(c)(2) is repeal. . . .

4. The Subsequent Advance Exception

. . . The House and Senate staff cast the subsequent advance proposal in section 547(c)(4) in its present form. . . . The requirements of old section 60c that the new credit be given in good faith and the express requirement that the new credit remain unpaid at bankruptcy were deleted. Furthermore, in place of the requirement of old section 60c that the credit be given "without security of any kind," section 547(c)(4) requires only that an otherwise nonvoidable transfer not secure or be made on account of the credit extension. The House and Senate reports do not explain clearly any of these changes; rather, they state only:

> The fourth exception codifies the net result rule in § 60c of current law. If the creditor and debtor have more than one exchange during the 90-day period, the exchanges are netted out according to the formula in paragraph (4). . . .

In fact, no "net result" rule has existed since 1903, and the rule never was applicable to old section 60c. . . .

Fortunately, the misleading legislative history of section 547(c)(4) has caused less damage than the similarly misleading history of section 547(c)(1) and (2). Most courts have agreed . . . that, in light of the clear requirement that the new value be given "after" the voidable preference, section 547(c)(4) "has transformed the judicially created net result rule into . . . a subsequent advance rule." . . .

. . . [T]he courts consistently have held that, for the purposes of section 547(c)(4), a transfer occurs when the debtor's check is delivered to the creditor, at least when the drawee later honors the check. Thus, the creditor who is encouraged by receipt of the check to extend new unsecured credit without waiting for the check to clear may invoke section 547(c)(4) to apply the credit against the trustee's recovery of an earlier preference.

The creditor, however, must give the new value *after* the preferential transfer. . . .

Section 547(c)(4) does not expressly require, unlike old section 60c, that the new unsecured credit remain unpaid at bankruptcy. Most courts nonetheless agree . . . that when the debtor has paid for the new credit, the requirement is preserved by section 547(c)(4)(B), which directs that the debtor make no other unavoidable transfer on account of the new value. . . .

The prevailing interpretation seems to be the correct one. If the debtor has made payments for goods or services that the creditor supplied on unsecured credit after an earlier preference, and if these subsequent payments are themselves voidable as preferences (or on any other ground), then under section 547(c)(4)(B) the creditor should be able to invoke those unsecured credit extensions as a defense to the recovery of the earlier voidable preference. On the other hand, the debtor's subsequent payments might not be voidable . . . . In this situation, the creditor may keep his payments but has no section 547(c)(4) defense to the trustee's action to recover the earlier preference. In either event, the creditor gets credit only once for goods and services later supplied. . . .

5. The No-Improvement-in-Position Exception

The Gilmore committee's chief concern was reconciling the after-acquired property clause, legitimated and made effective by section 9-204 of the U.C.C., and the preference concept of bankruptcy law. Suppose a creditor makes an advance to the debtor, takes and perfects a security interest in the debtor's presently owned and after-acquired inventory or receivables more than ninety days . . . before bankruptcy, and makes no further advances to the debtor. Section 9-203 of the U.C.C. . . . also provides that a security interest cannot attach until, among other requirements, the debtor acquires rights in the collateral. . . . If the debtor enters bankruptcy and the secured party claims a security interest in inventory that the debtor acquired, or in accounts that arose, within ninety days of bankruptcy, then isn't the secured party claiming under a transfer that occurred within ninety days of bankruptcy to secure antecedent debt?

The substitution of collateral doctrine offers little comfort. Inventory generally declines over a period of time as the debtor makes sales and then increases abruptly as the debtor replenishes inventory. To conclude that most of the increase would be substantially contemporaneous with the decrease is difficult. . . .

While the Gilmore committee was grappling with the after-acquired collateral problem, two circuit courts of appeals ruled on cases concerning accounts receivable. In *DuBay v. Williams,* the Ninth Circuit concluded under the 1962 version of the U.C.C. that the bankruptcy trustee could not recover after-acquired accounts receivable arising within the then four month preference period because the transfer occurred more than four months before bankruptcy and, thus, by the same token was not for antecedent debt. . . . The court read section 60 to say that the transfer was "deemed" made when it was perfected against levying creditors. Because by state law no levying creditor could have defeated the secured party's security interest from the time a financing statement was filed more than four months before bankruptcy, the transfer was made when the statement was filed. . . .

In the other case concerning accounts receivable, *Grain Merchants v. Union Bank*, the Seventh Circuit also decided the case under the 1962 version of the U.C.C., . . . and reached the same conclusion as *DuBay*. The Seventh Circuit embraced what I have called the *DuBay* court's "Abracadabra, or The Transfer Occurred Before It Occurred" theory.

In addition, *Grain Merchants* advanced two alternative theories. One theory was the "Entity" or "Mississippi River" theory. An ancient metaphysician, Heraclitus, once said, "You can't step twice in the same river," and I believe we can understand what he meant. But a more recent metaphysician, Professor Raymond Henson, argued, "You can step twice into the Mississippi River, and that is good enough." . . . Don't think about individual accounts or about individual items of inventory; think about only an "entity" called "accounts" or "inventory" without regard to its composition at any given time. If a person can expand his thoughts to that extent, he can persuade himself that the only transfer occurs when the original security agreement was made and perfected. The

Seventh Circuit was able to expand its thoughts to that extent. The second alternative theory in *Grain Merchants* was a "Relaxed Substitution" theory. . . .

DuBay and *Grain Merchants* established that, subject to any prior valid liens on the accounts concerned, the secured party defendants in those cases could take all the accounts they could find at bankruptcy to the extent needed to pay their claims. . . .

The Gilmore committee recommended an exception from section 60 that was a compromise between these two positions. . . .

The Committee Reports explain that section 547(c)(5) "codifies the improvement of position test, and thereby overrules such cases as *DuBay v. Williams* and *Grain Merchants of Indiana v. Union Bank* . . .," although the reports also add that section 547(e)(3), "more than any other in [section 547], overrules" those cases. The reports further note

> that the test of section 547(c)(5) is a two point test, and requires determination of the secured creditor's position 90 days before the petition and on the date of the petition. . . .

So far, section 547(c)(5) has proved to be of as little importance as many supposed it would be. As the Gilmore committee pointed out, "[u]nless there is a deficiency . . . on the first date, there can be no preference" under section 547(c)(5) from the acquisition of more collateral through an after-acquired property clause. . . .

7. The Consumer's Small Preference Exception

The 1984 amendments added section 547(c)(7), excepting from section 547 a transfer by "an individual debtor whose debts are primarily consumer debts" if "the aggregate of all property that constitutes and is affected by such transfer is less than $600." The Bankruptcy Commission had proposed a similar exception for all transfers of less than $1000, not made to insiders, and not confined to consumer debtors or individuals. The Commission explained, in support of its proposal, that the exception of "relatively small" preferences would not "seriously impinge" on the preference policy; that the "expense of recovery [of small preferences] is often disproportionate to the benefit to creditors"; and that the exception "is also intended to soften the impact of the Commission's recommendation to abandon the reasonable cause to believe requirement and to impose a presumption of insolvency." The National Bankruptcy Conference recommended that the maximum exempt transfer be reduced to $500. . . .

The congressional draftsmen did not incorporate any "small preference" exception, and none appeared in the Reform Act of 1978. The new section 547(c)(7), with a $750 limit, originated as one of many amendments to the Reform Act sponsored by the consumer credit industry. . . .

It still seems to me that the small preference exception is unjustifiable. . . .

. . . [I]t seems to me indefensible to give each preferred creditor of a consumer a $600 immunity from section 547 . . . .

V. CONCLUSION

As previously indicated, it seems to me that the basic concept of a preference, as defined in section 547(b), is in satisfactory form . . . .

The large area of disarray and disagreement has occurred in the exceptions from section 547 contained in section 547(c). In part, I suppose it was predictable that the very idea of a substantial list of exceptions to the preference policy was bound to produce efforts for legislative change. . . .

In the exception expansion process, the 1984 amendment deleting the forty-five day limit in what I have called the "current expense" exception of section 547(c)(2) has torn the bankruptcy preference policy asunder in a completely indefensible way. Because this exception was originally ill-conceived and, as amended in 1984, indefensibly at war with the bankruptcy preference policy, my solution for this exception would be to repeal it. Repeal is also the solution for the new exception of section 547(c)(7) for consumer preferences of less than $600. Although section 547(c)(7) does less damage to the bankruptcy preference policy than present section 547(c)(2), it is nonetheless at war with preference policy. . . .

The remaining exceptions . . . seem to me to be either consistent with the preference policy or . . . to represent a tolerable compromise with the preference policy which does little damage to it.

John C. McCoid, II
Bankruptcy, Preferences, and Efficiency: An Expression of Doubt
67 VA. L. REV. 249 (1981)*

On the eve of bankruptcy an insolvent frequently transfers his property to pay or secure an existing creditor. Upon bankruptcy, the consequence of the transfer is that such a creditor fares better than his fellows. What, if anything, should be done about this preference? The simplest answer is to let the transfer stand. That is often said to have been the rule at common law, although in some respects the history recounted below suggests otherwise. Another response is to recapture the transferred property and distribute it with the rest of the debtor's estate—the general approach of the Bankruptcy Reform Act of 1978. Other intermediate approaches either permit or deny recapture depending on the debtor's intent, the creditor's knowledge of the debtor's insolvency, or some combination of the two.

This article explores the history of preference law to provide a background for choosing between the competing approaches to preferential transfers. It then discusses the goals of preference law and assesses the law's efficiency in achieving those goals. Concluding that contemporary preference law may not be the most efficient response to preferential transfers, the article tentatively suggests that, at least in the absence of fraud, the most efficient response to preferential transfers may be to abolish preference law.

I. HISTORY OF PREFERENCE LAW

A. *English Law*

Although preferences and fraudulent conveyances are distinct concepts, the emergence of preference law was closely tied to the concept of fraud, no doubt because early English bankruptcy law regarded bankrupts as fraudulent. Although preference law depends on the existence of legislation creating a bankruptcy process and, thus, has a statutory foundation, the early development of preference law was decisional. Two strands, separated by more than one hundred years, run through these decisions.

The first strand was the premise that all transfers by the debtor following an act of bankruptcy were invalid against the commissioners, the administrators appointed by the Chancellor on petition by the creditors to take and distribute the debtor's assets. In *The Case of Bankrupts*, as reported by Sir Edward Coke, the court so interpreted the then current statute. . . . Lord Coke, however, went beyond the case to state the broader rule, which he based on the statutory language and on the principle of equal distribution: "[B]ut if, after, the debtor becomes a bankrupt, he may prefer one (who peradventure hath least need), and defeat and defraud many other poor men of their true debts, it would be unequal and unconscionable, and a great defect in the law." . . .

The second strand related to property transferred preferentially before an act of bankruptcy. Although statutes made such transfers criminal, property so transferred apparently was not subject to recapture until 1768. In *Alderson v. Temple,* Lord Mansfield labeled such a transfer made outside the course of trade as a fraud. . . . In *Alderson,* however, Mansfield expressly declined to declare all preferences invalid: "A general question has been started, whether a man may or may not, at the eve of a bankruptcy, give a preference to a particular creditor." That, Mansfield held, would depend upon the act: "If [the creditor] demands it first, or sues [the debtor] or threatens him, without fraud, the preference is good. But where it is manifestly to defeat the law, it is bad.". . .

The distinction between a deliberate preference that may be recaptured and other transfers with preferential effect that are invulnerable does not mesh neatly with the announced purpose of bankruptcy law to provide equal distribution among creditors. . . .

B. American Law

1. Debtor's Intent

The first American bankruptcy legislation, the Bankruptcy Act of 1800, neither defined nor prohibited preferences. Preferences were sometimes recaptured, however, on principles drawn from the English decisions. By contrast, the 1841 Act, which also introduced voluntary bankruptcy, expressly defined preferences, called for their avoidance, and provided that one who granted an unlawful preference could receive no discharge. Section 2 of the Act required, among other elements, that the transfer be "in contemplation of bankruptcy" and "for the purpose of giving any creditor . . . any preference or priority over the general creditors of such bankrupts." . . . Story ruled . . . that one who was aware of his insolvency and gave a mortgage to secure an antecedent debt necessarily contemplated bankruptcy. . . .

Similar developments regarding the debtor's intent occurred under the preference provision in the Massachusetts insolvency law, the model for the federal bankruptcy provision on preferences in the Act of 1867. . . . Intent to prefer *could* be inferred from a transfer by one who knew he was insolvent because it was presumed that he intended the natural and probable consequence of his acts. . . .

After Congress, following the Massachusetts lead, adopted insolvency or the contemplation of insolvency and a "view to give a preference" as the standards of the 1867 Act, the Supreme Court held that a debtor who was aware of his insolvency and who made a transfer to a creditor did so with a view to giving a preference. The decision was justified by the presumption that the debtor intended the necessary consequence of his act. The result was a shift in the burden of going forward. The transfer now had to be justified to avoid recapture. This decision set the stage for the Act of 1898, which did not require an intent to effect a preference as a condition of recapture. The Supreme Court held that the statute meant just that: no intent on the debtor's part was required. Thus, a steady progression of small steps had eliminated the debtor's state of mind as a factor: First an inference as to intent was permitted; then the burden of going forward was shifted; finally the element of the debtor's intent ceased to be material.

2. Creditor's Knowledge

The Act of 1841 had provided that bona fide transactions more than two months before a bankruptcy petition was filed were immune from recapture if the other party had no notice of a prior act of bankruptcy or of the debtor's intent to enter bankruptcy. . . . The Massachusetts Insolvency Act of 1838, as amended in 1841, had required that "the creditor, when accepting such preference, [have] reasonable cause to believe such debtor was insolvent.". . . This language is almost identical to the language of the Bankruptcy Act of 1867. The 1898 Act required that "the person receiving the transfer, or to be benefitted thereby, or his agent acting therein, shall have had reasonable cause to believe that it was intended thereby to give a preference." In 1910 that language was revised to require only "reasonable cause to believe that the enforcement of such judgment or transfer would effect a preference." Knowledge of preferential result rather than knowledge of the debtor's intention became the key. In 1938 Congress reverted to the simpler "reasonable cause to believe that the debtor is insolvent." This requirement was deleted in 1978. Its removal was justified on the ground that the difficulty in proving it sometimes allowed unworthy creditors to prevail or forced parties to devote too much time to an issue that did not implicate the policies underlying preference law.

. . . It seems clear . . . that the creditor's knowledge became material before the debtor's intent ceased to be so. It is possible, moreover, for the debtor to have an intent to prefer and for the creditor still to be innocent.

3. Period of Vulnerability

Mansfield had confined himself to transfers on the eve of bankruptcy. The 1841 Act had no such time limit, although it did protect bona fide payments made more than two months before filing of the petition. The Massachusetts statute, as amended in 1841, had a six-month limitation, which the Act of 1867 reduced to four months. The 1898 Act made the four-month limit applicable to avoidance, but not to surrender. . . . The 1978 Act reduced the period of vulnerability from four months to ninety days. Apparently that reduction was a tradeoff for elimination of the creditor's reasonable-cause-to-believe-the-debtor-insolvent requirement and for creation of a presumption of insolvency during the shorter period.

Preference law has thus moved from a notion of debtor fraud to a standard of absolute liability for a limited period for preferred creditors. The gradual, evolutionary character of the change suggests that contemporary preference law has not been assessed carefully on its own terms. . . .

II. GOALS OF PREFERENCE LAW

So long as a debtor is solvent, every creditor can expect to be paid in full, and each may act independently without affecting others. There is generally no occasion for collective action. Once the debtor is insolvent, however, payment of one creditor necessarily prejudices others because there are insufficient assets to satisfy all. Bankruptcy, a collective claim enforcement proceeding, appears in the law in response to this kind of potential prejudice. From the creditor's standpoint, bankruptcy's principal theme is equality, or ratable distribution of the debtor's assets, among unsecured creditors. Once proceedings have been initiated, independent collection efforts are forbidden because they run counter to that theme. Because the law leaves initiation of bankruptcy to the parties, however, there may be an interval between the beginning of insolvency and the commencement of bankruptcy proceedings. Although preference law comes into play only after bankruptcy proceedings have been instituted, its focus is on the period between the onset of insolvency and bankruptcy, and its target is a transfer to one creditor during that period.

Equal treatment of creditors is the oldest and most frequently advanced goal of preference law. Preference law tries to impose equality on prebankruptcy behavior so that that behavior will not make the principle of equality in bankruptcy distribution meaningless. An infrequently stated companion goal is to maximize the estate from which equal distribution is to be made. . . . Preferential transfers may result in dismemberment of the debtor's estate and prevent decisions that would achieve maximization.

. . . [T]his article assumes that the real goals of preference law are to equalize distribution and to maximize estate value.

III. EFFICIENCY OF PREFERENCE LAW

One way to judge the soundness of contemporary preference law is to consider whether it efficiently achieves its goals. Conducting such an examination requires inquiries into both the effectiveness and the costs of preference law.

A. *Effectiveness*

Preference law operates through recapture and deterrence. . . . [R]ecapture takes two forms. First, the trustee can initiate proceedings to recover preferentially transferred property or its value. . . . Second, the claim of a creditor who received an avoidable preference is disallowed unless he surrenders the preferentially transferred property or its value. . . .

There is little information regarding the extent of recapture. . . . There are some indications that recapture is not very substantial. . . .

To the extent preferential transfers are recaptured, inequalities between preferred creditors and others are eliminated, and the size of the debtor's estate is increased. Recapture, however, is only minimally useful in ensuring that all of the options for maximizing estate value will be available. The very necessity of resorting to recapture usually indicates that a breakup, making rehabilitation difficult, has already occurred.

Deterrence, on the other hand, serves both the equality and maximization goals. If creditors are restrained from independent, piecemeal dismemberment of the debtor's estate, the optimum choice for maximization purposes between liquidation and support of the debtor at least becomes possible. Equality necessarily follows from bankruptcy's scheme of distribution if the estate is protected from preferences. . . .

There are reasons to be skeptical of preference law's deterrent effect. First, only a creditor aware of the debtor's insolvency, or at least of his financial difficulty, would be deterred by preference law from accepting or seeking payment. . . . Moreover, existing law may not dissuade even a knowledgeable creditor from engaging in "preference behavior." Assuming that such a creditor acts out of self-interest, he will seek to maximize his own recovery, even at the expense of his fellows. For the creditor who is willing, apart from preference law, to engage in a preference transaction, there may seem to be much to gain and little to lose by doing so. There is a good chance that one who receives a preference will be able to keep it. Bankruptcy may never be filed. Even if it is, the petition may not be filed within ninety days of the transfer. . . . Finally, even if bankruptcy is filed soon enough, the trustee may find it inexpedient to initiate recapture proceedings.

The creditor must balance the probability of successfully retaining a preference against the costs of failure. The only sanction for unsuccessful preference behavior is recapture plus payment of interest from the time of the demand for return or from the commencement of proceedings to recover the property. At worst, return of the property simply restores the status quo. . . . If a creditor may be able to keep the payment and at worst only has to return it, he has every incentive to accept it. . . .

Unsuccessful preference behavior, on the other hand, may entail real costs. If the creditor must incur expenses, such as litigation costs, to acquire the preference, those expenses will be lost if the preference is recaptured. . . . Moreover, to the extent that preference behavior has prevented maximization of the estate, the preferred creditor will lose along with other creditors. . . .

. . . It seems fair to anticipate, however, that a creditor frequently will conclude that the sensible course is to accept the preference and to hope for success. To the extent that this is true, preference law is not an effective deterrent, and achievement of equality and maximum estate value will be limited to the results of recapture. Moreover, if there is an incentive to accept or seek a preference because the chance of success is good and the cost of failure is low or nonexistent, there is a companion incentive to act as early as possible and increase the odds of effecting the transfer outside the ninety-day period of vulnerability. . . . This incentive to act early undermines the estate maximization goal because it encourages independent dismemberment of the debtor's estate.

Thus, it appears that preference law is not a very effective means of achieving equality and maximum estate value. Although some success in achieving these goals must be acknowledged, its value depends on its incidence and costs.

1. Incidence of Success

If preference law deters preference behavior in some, but not all, cases, it is likely that this limited success is not random, but regularly works to the advantage of some creditors and to the disadvantage of others. . . .

The limited success of preference law thus may give rise to a kind of inequality among creditors. . . . [B]ecause it stems from manipulation of the law, it seems to be an undesirable byproduct of preference law. . . . The likelihood of successful preference behavior in many instances, however, remains a substantial source for generating this inequality, and it should be taken into account.

2. Costs

The expense of the recapture process is the most obvious cost of preference law. Whether that cost is simply administrative or entails litigation expense will depend on the particular case. . . . The trustee's costs, whether a contest is involved or not, become administrative expenses that have first priority in distribution of the estate. Taken off the top, they reduce dividends and, apart from other priorities, are borne ratably. . . .

At least some creditors incur costs in monitoring the debtor's situation as they guard against preference activity by others and consider preference behavior for themselves. . . .

There is another cost that grows solely out of preference law. Any creditor who receives a transfer that might be recaptured faces a period when he is not sure whether the transfer will stand or be invalidated. This period of uncertainty has cost significance because it affects the creditor's ability to commit resources to other transactions. That this "uncertainty cost" may be bearable does not detract from its importance. . . .

Many creditors can pass on process and uncertainty costs to their debtor-customers by increasing the cost of credit. . . . Equality among creditors, however, affects only the distribution of resources among them without enlarging the estate and thus produces no benefits to pass on to debtors. Accordingly, from the debtor's standpoint, there may be cost without corresponding benefit.

IV. OTHER APPROACHES

. . . [O]ther approaches ought to be considered. . . .

A. Increasing the Effectiveness of Preference Law

One possibility is to increase the effectiveness of preference law. Doing so would also reduce maldistribution of its benefits. By eliminating the reasonable-cause-to-believe-the-debtor-insolvent requirement, and by creating a presumption of insolvency during the ninety days immediately preceding bankruptcy, the 1978 Act moved in this direction. By shortening the period of vulnerability from four months to ninety days, . . . however, the Act moved in the other direction as well.

The way to increase effectiveness is to reduce a creditor's incentive to accept or seek a preferential transfer either by limiting his chance of success or by increasing the sanction for failure. It has been suggested that elimination of the ninety-day time limit would be a significant step in reducing the creditor's chance of success. All transfers during the period of insolvency would thus be vulnerable. The hope that more than ninety days would pass before bankruptcy, a major escape hatch under existing law, would no longer encourage a creditor. This proposal is similar to Lord Coke's proposition in *The Case of Bankrupts*. . . .

In considering the consequences of such a step, it seems fair to assume that some creditors would continue to seek an advantage and that some debtors would try to confer it by attempting to anticipate insolvency. The result might be more dismemberment of the debtor's estate at the expense of maximization. . . . [T]he change would eliminate a major source of creditor incentive. The principal difficulty with the proposal is its cost. Its adoption would dramatically increase uncertainty costs because it would eliminate the time limit on uncertainty. The ninety-day limit functions essentially as a statute of limitations. . . . The brevity of the preference law period suggests that repose rather than stale evidence is the principal concern. Indeed, this brevity is rather clear evidence of the importance attached to certainty in payment of obligations. The short period reflects a judgment that finality of transfers is more important than the achievement of equality and maximum estate value in dealing with insolvent debtors. That judgment is based partially on the fact that the uncertainty created by preference law also affects transactions not involving insolvent debtors.

Increasing the sanction for accepting avoidable transfers would also reduce the creditor's incentive. Requiring the preferred creditor to return two or three times the amount of the preference would certainly deter knowing preference behavior. Unless imposition of the penalty were confined to knowing creditors, however, it would fall on innocent ones as well. Imposing a penalty on innocent creditors surely would be unacceptable. Distinguishing between knowing and innocent creditors, however, would resurrect the problems of proof . . . .

B. Abolition of Preference Law

An alternative to more regulation is less of it. What would be the consequences of "deregulation" or the abolition of preference law?

Abolition of preference law would eliminate uncertainty costs. Creditors could rely on transfers made to pay or secure antecedent debts, at least in the absence of fraud. The argument that preference law is "unfair" because it retroactively changes the rules of the game for creditors also makes abolition attractive. Nonbankruptcy law tells a creditor that he is in a race with other creditors. Receiving payment first or getting a prior lien is the creditor's only protection against the possibility that a debtor's assets will prove inadequate to satisfy all claims against him. Bankruptcy stops the race for priority and replaces it with the principle of equality. Preference law makes that change retroactive by applying the equality principle to the period immediately preceding bankruptcy. Although creditors are on notice that this may occur, a transfer that was perfectly legitimate when made may nevertheless be invalidated. Ordinarily, setting aside a transaction implies that it never should have occurred. . . . By contrast, contemporary preference law is indifferent to the propriety of the transfer when it is made.

The unfairness of retroactively changing the rules of behavior can only be justified on the ground that it is necessary to achieve fairness of another sort—equality among creditors. Without preference law, the argument runs, there would be nothing left to distribute equally. Although abolition would eliminate recapture and deterrence, these are not the only avenues to distributional equality and to maximization of estate value. In theory, at least, those goals may also be achieved by filing a bankruptcy petition promptly on the debtor's insolvency. . . .

The efficacy of filing would depend on the willingness of creditors to file and on their ability to do so promptly. Desire for equality in distribution and maximization of estate value would seem to argue for filing. The individual creditor, however, acting out of self-interest, might elect instead to accept or seek a preference where one is available and file only when it is not and when there is a danger of others receiving preferences. Thus, the same considerations that prevent effective deterrence under current law would seemingly inhibit willingness to file. Presumably, those considerations would also grant undue advantage to the knowledgeable creditor. . . . The need to file promptly would require knowledge of the debtor's situation. The new standard for filing makes that easier, but there might still be some delay and thus room for prefiling preference transfers. In sum, were preference law abolished, prompt filing, although an avenue to equality and maximum estate value, would not lead to greater efficacy.

Additionally, dependence on filing would entail the costs of proceeding formally in cases that creditors currently handle informally. Informal collective action has its own costs, but it seems clear that the expenses of a formal proceeding are greater. . . .

The increased cost of formal proceedings seems to provide the most powerful argument against abolition because abolition would require prompt filing to achieve distributional equality and maximization of estate value. It seems impossible to quantify that increase, and in any event, to be instructive, that increase would have to be compared with the uncertainty costs of preference law.

V. CONCLUSION

The goals of preference law are equality of distribution and maximization of estate value. Preference law is not fully effective in achieving these goals because individual creditors have an incentive to ignore or even to evade it. Its limited efficacy favors more knowledgeable creditors, and its operation creates substantial uncertainty costs. Making preference law more effective·by eliminating the ninety-day limit on vulnerability would unacceptably increase those costs. Abolition of preference law, on the other hand, would eliminate them. Although it would not require abandonment of the goals of preference law, abolition does not promise to be more effective in achieving them, and it would require dependence on prompt filing. Increased filing would have costs, although it seems likely that, for debtors and creditors as a whole, the costs of increased filings would be less than the uncertainty costs of preference law. Perhaps those more familiar with the world of commerce would arrive at a different view of relative costs or of effectiveness. It is not clear, however, that existing preference law is derived from such an assessment. Instead, it seems to be the product of a gradual evolution originating in the law of fraud. From the standpoint of professed goals, current preference law appears to be a nervous compromise between effectiveness and cost. It deserves reappraisal in those terms.

Thomas H. Jackson
Avoiding Powers in Bankruptcy
36 STAN. L. REV. 725 (1984)[*]

V. PREFERENCES: THE TRANSITIONAL AVOIDING POWER

Preference law, which has long captured the fancy of the bankruptcy world, is reasonably well understood at its core. Its exact scope is less well understood, however, because preference law's integral relation to bankruptcy's core functions has not been completely explored.

In their simplest form, preferences are transfers that favor one existing creditor over another. Debtor prefers Creditor *A* to Creditor *B* if Debtor pays Creditor *A* before he pays Creditor *B*. Such behavior is not conventionally thought to be a fraudulent conveyance—assuming Debtor is not motivated by an actual desire to delay, hinder, or defraud Creditor *B*—because Debtor's antecedent debt to Creditor *A* is considered fair consideration for the transfer (presumably of cash) that Debtor makes to him. . . .

. . . Preference law, unlike fraudulent conveyance law, is not a part of the arsenal of rights and remedies between a *debtor* and his *creditors*. Rather, preferences differ from fraudulent conveyances precisely because preference law focuses on relationships *among creditors* in light of the advantages of a collective proceeding, not on relationships *between creditors and their debtor*. So stated, it is easy to see that preferences generally are permitted outside bankruptcy because the relationships of creditors among themselves are inherently collective in nature; preferences are a source of concern only when the creditors perceive there may not be enough to go around. Not surprisingly, no conflict exists among creditors absent that worry.

. . . Any system that prevented preferences, therefore, would necessarily be a collective system in which creditors could not recover from their debtor without accounting for the interests of other creditors. For this reason, preferences do not seem inherently objectionable outside bankruptcy (or other collective proceeding). Preference law is part and parcel of the substitution of collective remedies for individual remedies.

The essence of a collective proceeding such as bankruptcy is ratable distribution among those similarly situated. . . . Creditors view this as desirable ex ante because collectivizing the disbursement of assets after insolvency brings gains to the creditors as a group.

Yet while the creditors would agree to this system before they lent money, they face the usual problems of policing a deal after it is struck. Each creditor has incentives to advance his individual interests, even though doing so might work against the greater collective benefit. Once his debtor becomes insolvent, and without collective enforcement of the creditors' bargain, each creditor must race for assets, not necessarily just to grab more than his share but also simply to avoid being left with nothing. Accordingly, creditors need a mechanism to bind them to their presumptive ex ante agreement and to foil the attempts of each creditor to welsh on the agreement for individual gain.

Providing such an enforcement mechanism would not be a problem if a debtor's insolvency became manifest at a single, unanticipated point in time, followed immediately by a collective proceeding. In practice, of course, the point of insolvency almost never can be identified with precision. Moreover, creditors usually can see a debtor's insolvency—or, more accurately, a collective proceeding—coming, some before others. Some of the creditors who know that the collective proceeding is imminent predictably will attempt to satisfy their own claims and thereby to opt out of the collective proceeding altogether. Also, debtors, knowing that bankruptcy is imminent, may pay first the creditors whom they like or whom they think they will need in the future. By the time a bankruptcy petition is actually filed, and without reach-back provisions, those creditors that remained would have to share equally in "tag ends and remnants" of assets.

Such eve-of-bankruptcy asset-grabbing may be detrimental to the collective interest of the creditors. By reaching back to undo the actions of individual creditors, preference law deters such potential grabbing, thereby protecting the creditors' bargain. Therefore, preference law essentially prevents individual creditors from opting out of the collective proceeding during the transitional period before bankruptcy. It enforces the hypothetical creditors' bargain that justifies a collective proceeding in the first place. . . .

Creditors' attempts to opt out of the collective proceeding take two ostensibly different forms, both of which modern preference law addresses. The first is the last-minute grab that preference law reaches by what can be denominated the "anti-last-minute-grab" policy. . . .

The second form of opt-out behavior is to provide prescribed public notice of property interests that a claimant had previously taken "in secret." This is reached by a second policy contained in modern preference law that may be labeled, somewhat misleadingly, as we shall see, the "anti-secret-lien" policy. . . .

Are both the "anti-last-minute-grab" and the "anti-secret-lien" policies appropriately related to the goals of a preference section? According to common wisdom, the first is. Most commentators recognize that by striking down "last-minute grabs" by individual creditors the preference section preserves the advantages of a collective proceeding. . . .

Few people have ever had much problem with the basic thrust of the anti-last-minute-grab policy. The anti-secret-lien policy, however, is commonly viewed as unrelated to preference law. The reason for this is that, at first glance, the anti-secret-lien policy has little to do with the anti-last-minute-grab policy. . . . [A]s noted earlier, ostensible ownership itself is not a problem particularly related to bankruptcy.

The bifurcation of the two policies is unwarranted, however, at least insofar as the anti-secret-lien policy serves to upset property interests that, although invulnerable to attack on the date of bankruptcy, were vulnerable to attack by unsecured creditors—perhaps through the obtaining of a lien—sometime during the preference period. Both the anti-last-minute-grab policy and the anti-secret-lien policy, as limited, function to substitute a collective procedure for individual remedies in allocating assets among creditors. At bottom, both are designed to deter opt-out behavior that interferes with the goals of bankruptcy. The anti-secret-lien policy accordingly displaces the applicable nonbankruptcy rule to protect the collective proceeding. For during the time that the anti-last-minute-grab policy prevents the general creditors from upping themselves to lien creditors, the anti-secret-lien policy restricts unperfected *secured* creditors from improving their positions vis-à-vis general creditors by imposing a similar limitation.

Properly understood and limited, therefore, both polices grow out of the reasons for a bankruptcy process in the first place. . . .

To fulfill this underlying role, what should an optimal preference section look like? And how well does the current preference provision, section 547 of the Bankruptcy Code, compare with an optimal section? In principle, a bankruptcy statute's section on voidable preferences should read something like this:

> If a creditor tries to change his position after the extension of credit in order to improve his lot in an anticipated bankruptcy (or other collective) proceeding, or if the debtor, at the behest of such creditor, so tries to change the position of such creditor in order to improve such creditor's lot in an anticipated bankruptcy (or other collective) proceeding, the creditor must return any advantage so obtained.

Such a section may perhaps express the underlying policies behind a preference section most accurately.

But to fit an underlying set of policies perfectly is not the only goal of statutes. Sometimes, a clear, easy-to-administer rule that does not perfectly fit the underlying policies better serves society than a less precise standard that fits the underlying policy perfectly. The costs of a bright-line rule . . . may be less than the administrative costs of a better fitting, but fuzzier, standard. . . . [T]he Bankruptcy Code leans toward per se rules rather than loose standards in defining preferences. The idea of these rules is to pick up most of the transfers that are objectionable (*i.e.*, creditors taking special action with respect to an insolvent debtor's property in anticipation of a collective proceeding) and to leave untouched most of the transactions that are unobjectionable. . . .

VI. PREFERENCE LAW AND SECURED CREDITORS

Focusing on the role of preference law as it relates to the goals of bankruptcy illuminates the relationship between preference law and secured creditors. It is a commonplace that preference law exempts fully-secured creditors from its grasp. Accordingly, payments to such creditors are not considered preferential. In light of the underlying role of preference law in preventing "opt-out" behavior designed to benefit the individual creditor, such an exclusion is entirely proper in normative bankruptcy theory. Under this theory, bankruptcy law should say nothing about the value of relative allocations to the extent those allocational rights were fixed before bankruptcy. And to the extent that judges fully respect the *value* of a secured creditor's entitlements in bankruptcy, there is no reason to believe that opt-out motives underlie a fully-secured creditor's receipt of payment on the eve of bankruptcy.

Charles J. Tabb
Rethinking Preferences
43 S.C. L. Rev. 981 (1992)[*]

I. INTRODUCTION

The conventional wisdom is, and long has been, that there are good preferences and bad preferences, with only the latter subject to avoidance and recapture. Over two hundred years ago Lord Mansfield observed, "A general question has been stated, whether a man may or may not, at the eve of a bankruptcy, give a preference to a particular creditor? *I think he may, and he may not.*" . . .

The bankruptcy law in the United States today follows the conventional wisdom and permits only the avoidance of preferences of the bad variety. A preference neutered from the adjoining denomination of good or bad refers simply to the transfer of property of an insolvent debtor to one of its creditors shortly before the debtor goes into bankruptcy, thus enabling that creditor to receive more than it would have otherwise. The essential attribute of such a transfer is that one creditor gets paid and others do not. Creditors are treated unequally, at a time when the debtor was insolvent.

Under the conventional wisdom, however, this fact standing alone is not enough to cast the transaction into the ultimate categories of good or bad—or, more specifically, to determine whether the transaction is avoidable. What, then, is the decisive factor that determines the avoidability of the transaction, whether that transfer falls on the good or bad side of the line? One answer, which has been expressed and implemented in a variety of ways over the past two and one-half centuries, is that payments made to creditors in the ordinary course of business and trade are permitted. Payments made outside of that ordinary course of business, on the other hand, are much more likely to be avoided.

This Article challenges the conventional wisdom. My thesis is that many of the currently protected good preferences should be made subject to avoidance and recapture. Specifically, I advocate the repeal of the ordinary course of business exception in section 547(c)(2) of the Bankruptcy Code. That section undercuts the proper basis of preference liability. As long as section 547(c)(2) remains on the books in its current form, it is difficult to justify having a preference law at all. . . .

II. PURPOSES OF PREFERENCE LAW:
THE PRIMACY OF EQUALITY OVER DETERRENCE

To set the stage, consider a simple example. Assume that there is a debtor D who has three trade creditors, imaginatively named A, B, and C. Assume further that D owes each creditor $600 and that each debt was incurred in the ordinary course of business. D, however, only has $900 in assets. D therefore is insolvent within the meaning of the Bankruptcy Code. The day before D files a Chapter 11 case, D pays creditor A in full, on ordinary business terms and during the normal trade cycle (assume thirty days). D retains the other $300 to use in the Chapter 11 case. Neither creditor B nor C is paid anything. Assume that the Chapter 11 case fails (having consumed the last $300 of the debtor's assets) and that the case is converted to Chapter 7. The trustee then sues creditor A to recover the preferential payment.

Two ultimate results are possible. One is to let A keep the money. This means that A would receive $600, and B and C would receive nothing. The second is to make A give the money back. Then, the $600 would be distributed equally to A, B, and C, or $200 each. Preference law is about

---

making a choice between these two alternatives. To make that choice requires the identification of the purposes that underlie preference law.

Two rationales for preference law predominate: equality and deterrence. The latter is sometimes cast in terms of the result supposedly achieved by deterrence—namely maximization of the value of the debtor's assets. These two policy goals conflict at times—as in the case of an ordinary course transfer shortly before bankruptcy. The distinction between good and bad preferences follows naturally from the identification of deterrence as the predominant purpose of preference law. I assert that equality instead should be given ascendancy, and that doing so leads to the conclusion that section 547(c)(2) should be repealed.

Equality in this context means the pro rata treatment of creditors who share the same priority claim to the debtor's assets. . . .

Outside of bankruptcy, unsecured creditors do not have a right to an aliquot share of the debtor's unencumbered assets. Rather, the defining characteristic of nonbankruptcy collection law is the race of diligence—"first in time is first in right." The creditor who first obtains a writ of execution and has the sheriff levy on the debtor's assets, or who first garnishes the debtor's bank account, wins and gets paid before less diligent creditors. Outside of a collective proceeding, then, a preference is not considered inherently evil.

This view is predicated, however, on the implicit assumption that the debtor is solvent, *i.e.*, that all creditors eventually will be paid in full. If that assumption fails and the debtor is instead insolvent, the fairness of a preference becomes much more questionable. In the event of insolvency the payment of one creditor necessarily means not only that other creditors will not get paid in full, but also that they will not even receive a pro rata share of the debtor's already insufficient assets.

This result by itself does not necessarily require the conclusion that a preference is a bad thing, even following insolvency. In theory, in advance of anyone being paid, all creditors have an equal shot at winning the race of diligence. Rewarding the more diligent creditors by permitting them to keep the assets that they obtained might be justified as economically efficient, or under the equitable maxim that equity rewards the vigilant.

One problem with this view is that the underlying assumption that all creditors have an equal shot at winning the race is flawed. . . .

Another basic problem exists with the argument that favors upholding preferences made after the onset of insolvency. Doing so is inconsistent with the fundamental tenet of equality of distribution that undergirds a bankruptcy or other collective proceeding that deals with an insolvent debtor. In a collective proceeding equality replaces the nonbankruptcy law premise of race as the defining principle. . . .

Saying that equality prevails in a collective proceeding does not necessarily demand the conclusion that a like premise should be extended into the time period before the collective proceeding begins. Many of the problems in casting preference law stem from the difficulty of making the transition from the nonbankruptcy race paradigm to the bankruptcy equality model. If insolvency and the collective proceeding (*e.g.*, bankruptcy) occurred at the same instant, preference law would be unnecessary. The race model, which may be justifiable for a solvent debtor, would continue until insolvency occurred. At that juncture equality would take over in the context of the collective proceeding.

However, this convenient theoretical ordering of things does not exist in real life. Insolvency almost always occurs before the collective proceeding is commenced. Some creditors are paid during this transition period. Once the existence of a transition period between the onset of insolvency and the commencement of a collective proceeding is recognized, the need for choosing between the race and equality paradigms arises.

The opt out theory, which is advanced primarily by Professors Baird and Jackson, suggests a means for making that choice. This theory assumes that some creditors may see the collective proceeding coming before it actually occurs. Given this window of opportunity, when the race model is still apparently in effect, but with equality looming, it is only natural that those who see what is coming should try to avoid its consequences and obtain a personal advantage. The personal advantage obtained is, however, contrary to the interests of the creditor group as a whole. Thus, a way to restrain individual pursuit of self-interest is needed.

The deterrence rationale therefore becomes important. The argument is that if preference law reaches back to recapture payments made during this transition period, in which insolvency has occurred but the collective proceeding has not yet been commenced, creditors will be deterred from taking advantage of their superior knowledge. . . .

Deterrence is effective, however, only against parties who are aware of the debtor's financial distress and who therefore see the collective proceeding coming. Innocent parties by definition will not be deterred; the state of the preference law will have no impact on their behavior. The logical leap that is then made is that recapture should not be extended to these innocent parties because they would not be deterred anyway. Apparently, for those lucky innocent creditors the race model continues to apply until the actual commencement of the collective proceeding.

I submit that the operative paradigm during the transition period between the advent of insolvency and the filing of the bankruptcy proceeding should be equality, not race. Whether preferred creditors knowingly opted out or were just lucky should not be relevant to whether they get to keep the preferential payment. . . .

The foregoing argument for making deterrence the operative premise of preference law must withstand the initial criticism that deterrence does not work. . . .

Even more fundamentally, however, the unstated premise of the deterrence rationale is that culpability somehow matters and that innocence should therefore be rewarded. More than anything else, preference theory needs to shake off this antiquated morality notion and embrace instead the equality principle. . . .

A preference rule favoring equality would be simpler and easier to administer. Difficult issues regarding what is in the ordinary course and the like, which promote so much costly litigation, would be eliminated. Furthermore, and somewhat paradoxically, adopting a more absolute equality rule would further deterrence by increasing the likelihood of recapture. . . .

III. HISTORICAL DEVELOPMENT OF THE ORDINARY COURSE SAFE HARBOR

A. Early English Bankruptcy Preference Law

The distinction between good and bad preferences appears to have originated in the middle of the eighteenth century in England. . . .

One cornerstone of the distinction between good and bad preferences was laid in 1746 in the statute of 19 George 2. . . . The statute created a safe harbor for creditors who the debtor paid in the ordinary course of trade *after* the commission of an act of bankruptcy but *before* the issuing of a bankruptcy commission. . . .

. . . [I]n *Alderson v. Temple*, . . . Lord Mansfield struck down a prebankruptcy preferential transfer as void. At the same time, he made clear that not all such transfers are vulnerable. Two strands of a preference safe harbor appear. First . . ., he initiated the idea—still followed in England, but abandoned in the United States—that a preference given in response to creditor pressure is valid. Thus, a bad preference required an intent on the part of the debtor to prefer the creditor to the wrong of other creditors. Second, following the lead of the 1746 Statute . . ., he recognized by negative inference an exception for prebankruptcy transfers made in the ordinary course of business. . . .

B. United States Preference Law in the Nineteenth Century Prior to the 1898 Act

1. Prior to the Bankruptcy Act of 1841

. . . The first United States bankruptcy law, the Bankruptcy Act of 1800, did not speak to the question of preferences made prior to the commission of the act of bankruptcy. . . . However, the same section of the law contained a safe harbor derived in spirit from the 1746 English statute. . . .

Some judicial decisions followed the English cases and permitted the recapture of preferences. Justice Marshall in *Harrison v. Sterry* voided an assignment that the debtor made shortly before bankruptcy. . . .

Here again the debtor's intent ("in contemplation"), which was derived from the circumstances, appears to be determinative. . . .

2. The Bankruptcy Act of 1841

The first federal bankruptcy statute that directly addressed the question of preferences was the Bankruptcy Act of 1841. . . .

. . . [T]he critical element of a voidable preference under the 1841 Act was the intention of the *debtor*. Section 2 required proof that the debtor acted "in contemplation of bankruptcy, and for the purpose of giving [a] preference.". . .

3. The Bankruptcy Act of 1867

. . . In the 1867 Act a number of threads of preference law are brought together. In a sense, that Act serves as the bridge between the earliest notions of preference law and those obtaining in more recent times. First, consistent with all prior preference rules, legislative or judicial, a wrongful intent on the part of the debtor was required. Section 35 required the debtor to have acted "with a view to give a preference." . . .

Section 35 also required that the debtor either actually *be* insolvent, *or* act "in contemplation of insolvency." This formulation dispensed with the mens rea relating to insolvency entirely if the debtor in fact was in that state, thus beginning a transition completed in the 1898 Act. . . .

The Bankruptcy Act of 1867 added another component to the preference equation, . . .: the requirement that the creditor recipient of the preference have reasonable cause to believe that the debtor was insolvent at the time of the transfer, *and* that the payment was "made in fraud of the provisions of this act." Creditor knowledge had never before been considered a factor in defining a preference . . . Indeed, the English view, adhered to unfailingly ever since *Alderson v. Temple* in 1768, was that a preference given in response to creditor pressure was not voluntary on the part of the debtor and thus not fraudulent.

The introduction in 1867 of the requirement that the creditor have reasonable cause to believe that the debtor was insolvent perhaps more than any other event led to the direct consideration by judges of the issue of whether the payment had occurred in the ordinary course of business as relevant to the preference determination.

C. The Bankruptcy Act of 1898 and Amendments

The preference avoidance and recovery provisions in section 60 of the Bankruptcy Act of 1898 completed and carried forward many of the transitional ideas and innovations introduced in the 1867 Act. First, the requirement that the debtor have an intent to prefer the creditor, present but often almost meaningless in the 1867 Act, was finally and formally abandoned in section 60 . . . .

The 1898 Act further limited recovery to situations in which the debtor in fact was "insolvent" at the time of the transfer. The alternative proof available under the 1867 Act, that the debtor acted "in contemplation of insolvency," was discarded. Thus the "contemplation" provision finally passed out of the bankruptcy law.

At the same time, two prerequisites to recovery of a preference that were first introduced in 1867 were continued in section 60b of the 1898 Act: the requirement of a bad state of mind on the part of the recipient creditor, and a four month limit on the preference reachback. . . .

. . . [O]rdinary course transactions still tended to escape recapture, on several theories.

One way that ordinary course payments were protected was through the operation of the reasonable cause to believe test of section 60b. . . .

Another justification for excluding certain ordinary course transfers from the reach of the preference section was on the ground that the payment was for a "current expense" and that in essence no depletion or diminution of the debtor's estate was accomplished thereby. . . .

D. The Bankruptcy Commission Report

. . . The Commission filed its report in 1973. . . . The Commission recommended a "substantial revision" of the preference section.

Most notably, the Commission proposed that the reasonable cause to believe test be abolished. Congress made this significant change in the 1978 Code. Abolition of the reasonable cause test, however, which had provided safety to many creditors under the Act, was thought to require some countervailing measures to ameliorate the impact of that action. . . .

E. The Bankruptcy Reform Act of 1978

The recommendation of the Bankruptcy Commission was not followed precisely in the Bankruptcy Reform Act of 1978. The proposal to repeal the reasonable cause to believe test for transfers within the three month period was adopted. That test was seen as antithetical to the overriding preference purpose of promoting equality.

However, the shape of the protection for short-term ordinary course transfers was different. Congress in 1978 settled on the ordinary course exception of section 547(c)(2), which . . . imposed the limitations of "ordinary course" and that payment be within forty-five days after the debt was incurred. . . . [T]he principal concern . . . still was with protecting the payment of ordinary trade debts that were "'not truly antecedent.'" . . .

F. The 1984 Amendments and Wolas

Trouble developed fairly quickly with the ordinary course exception under the Bankruptcy Code, on two fronts. First, the courts ran into considerable difficulty in applying the forty-five day limitation. . . . Second, the limitation was assailed as unfairly discriminatory against creditors with a trade cycle longer than forty-five days and as undermining the market for short-term commercial paper.

After considering a wide variety of alternatives, Congress ultimately responded to these various complaints in 1984 by repealing the forty-five day limitation in section 547(c)(2)(B). . . . In one ill-considered stroke of the legislative pen, Congress effectively undercut the major premise of the preference reform effected in 1978—that of making equality of distribution the paramount policy. . . .

IV. NORMATIVE JUSTIFICATIONS FOR THE ORDINARY COURSE EXCEPTION AND CRITIQUES THEREOF

A. Introduction

The nagging question remains whether this assumed need for protecting ordinary course transfers stands up to close scrutiny. . . .

Three explanations nonetheless may be offered. The first, insulating payment of current expenses, is drawn from the possible genesis of section 547(c)(2) in the judicial doctrine under the Act that protected those payments. I have categorized the second as value maximization or the

incentive effect. The final rationale that supports the ordinary course exception is furthering repose.
. . .

B. Current Expenses

A number of commentators and courts have asserted that section 547(c)(2) is derived from the judicially developed current expense rule. . . . [T]he current expense doctrine was predicated largely on the idea that payment of a current account does not diminish the debtor's estate and is not really for an antecedent debt when one looks at the entire transaction—the credit extension and the payment—as a unit. . . .

I suggest here that protecting the payment of current expenses cannot logically be justified on the no-diminution, no-antecedent debt ground. To begin with the obvious, the debtor's estate is diminished by the payment, and the debt being paid was antecedent to the payment. . . .

The fundamental problem with the suggestion that the creditor who is paid for current expenses somehow deserves to be paid is that it ignores the whole idea of preference law. By definition all contractual unsecured creditors of the debtor gave value to the debtor. At least part of that value may still be in the debtor's estate, even if extended long before the bankruptcy. However, because of the debtor's insolvency, all of these creditors cannot be repaid in full. The question is why this current expense creditor should be treated better than those other creditors. . . .

C. Value Maximization and the Incentive Effect

1. The Argument in Favor

The second justification for the ordinary course exception focuses on the possibility of benefitting the body of creditors as a whole by increasing the total value of the debtor's assets. The argument is something along the following lines. If ordinary course transfers were made subject to avoidance, then creditors would be even more reluctant than they presently are to do business on a credit basis with a financially distressed debtor. The withholding of credit from questionable debtors would inevitably drive more debtors out of business and into bankruptcy.

If, on the other hand, ordinary course transfers are protected, then creditors can safely continue to do business with financially troubled debtors without having to worry that payments received now may have to be disgorged later if the debtor subsequently files bankruptcy. In essence, the ordinary course safe harbor can be characterized as creating or preserving an incentive for creditors to extend credit to distressed debtors. The positive results that supposedly flow from this incentive effect may keep the debtor out of bankruptcy entirely, thus making everybody better off. . . . [T]he basic notion is that even though some creditors are paid a larger percentage share of their claim than others, every creditor ultimately recovers more total dollars because the total asset pie is larger. . . .

2. Critique of the Incentive Effect Justification

. . . Let us now consider the broader issue of the validity of the incentive effect justification. The first criticism that can be levied against this justification for the ordinary course exception is that the preference issue comes up only if the debtor in fact goes bankrupt. Thus, by definition the ultimate objective of the incentive effect argument, which is keeping the debtor out of bankruptcy, has not been realized. Outside of bankruptcy a debtor is free to make preferences.

Second, the argument assumes that the legal rule chosen actually will influence the decision of creditors whether to do business on a credit basis with a distressed debtor. I find that assumption extremely questionable. As discussed above, the argument that the preference law deters last-minute grabs has been subjected to severe criticism.

I likewise question the converse proposition—the supposed incentive effect of the ordinary course safe harbor of preference law. . . . [T]he creditor's estimation of the likelihood of the debtor's payment on a timely basis dwarfs all other considerations. . . .

Third, even if there is an incentive effect, the model described above is fatally deficient because it assumes that an ordinary course of business exception creates only positive incentives to do business with the debtor. The paradigm ignores negative incentives—namely that a creditor might take into account the possibility that another creditor might get paid in preference to itself and therefore decide not to lend. If all creditors were rational economic actors, they would realize that payments by an insolvent debtor to a group of creditors is a zero-sum game. . . . Economically, the percentage of negative incentives should exactly balance out the positive incentives, resulting in no net gain to the debtor in terms of credit made available. . . .

Fourth, the standard recitation of the incentive effect assumes that section 547(c)(2) creates a greater incentive for creditors to do business with the debtor and thereby keep the debtor out of bankruptcy than would be true if section 547(c)(2) did not exist. On the contrary, exactly the opposite may be true. Creditors may accept or demand a payment within the preference period in the ordinary course of business and then refuse to conduct further business with the debtor, driving the debtor into bankruptcy. Given section 547(c)(2), those creditors do not have to fear recapture of the payment in bankruptcy. . . . If section 547(c)(2) were repealed, however, and a stricter recovery standard implemented, then creditors would have every incentive to keep the debtor out of bankruptcy. Only by doing so would the creditors be able to keep their payments.

Fifth, even if the incentive effect really exists and even if it magically results in a positive increment in the amount of credit made available to the debtor, the exception in section 547(c)(4) for subsequent new value already provides for an adequate incentive effect. . . . The ordinary course of business exception in section 547(c)(2) therefore is important only for creditors who do not extend any further credit after being paid off during the preference period. The need to protect these creditors in order to keep the debtor's business going is far from obvious. . . .

D. Repose

1. The Argument in Favor

The final normative justification for the ordinary course of business exception approaches the whole issue from a completely different orientation than the current expense and incentive effect justifications. Those rationales attempt to explain as a positive matter why section 547(c)(2) effects a beneficent result. The repose justification operates, however, from the premise that there is nothing to explain. Under this argument those who advocate upsetting settled transactions should bear the affirmative burden of justification.

The baseline assumption is that all prebankruptcy transfers should be left undisturbed. The important policy of finality in commercial transactions is preserved. Economically, this is the lowest cost alternative. Recovering preferences entails administrative and litigation costs for the estate and for the creditor defendant. . . .

A second cost of preference vulnerability is the uncertainty cost that is inflicted on the creditors. For some potentially extended time period they cannot know whether they will or will not be able to keep payments that they have received from the debtor. This possible exposure to recapture limits the creditor's ability to use the potentially recoverable funds. . . .

The repose theory then would assert that no suitable argument can be made for avoiding ordinary course transactions. By definition, the creditor recipients of an ordinary course transfer have done nothing wrong. . . .

Some advocates of the repose argument make the further assertion that recognizing and protecting all preferential transfers before bankruptcy is desirable. According to this view, the premise of similarly situated creditors, or of creditor equality, is a myth. Advocates of this view argue that some creditors have more leverage in getting paid than others—a point with which I would agree. They also argue that the fruits of this leverage should, as a matter of economic efficiency, be honored—a point with which I disagree.

2. Critique of the Repose Justification

Repose is a potentially legitimate basis for allowing ordinary course transfers to stand. No one would seriously deny that the policy of finality in commercial transactions is important. Parties need to and do rely on the finality of these transactions. Costs are implicated if repose is ignored. . . .

Having said that finality is important, however, one runs the risk of proving too much. If repose really is so critical, then how can we rationalize permitting the recapture of *any* preferential transfers? The most logical conclusion to be drawn from a sincere belief in the importance of finality is that section 547 should be repealed in its entirety. . . .

An alternative step, which recognizes the importance of repose but stops short of complete abolition of preference law, is to establish an absolute cutoff date prior to the commencement of bankruptcy proceedings beyond which transactions will be secure. . . .

The current embodiment of the policy of repose in the ninety day exposure rule does not explain why repose *also* should be applied to protect transactions that occur *within* the short preference period preceding the bankruptcy case. . . . Once one admits, however, that *any* preferential transfers should be recaptured (here within the ninety days) and that repose in and of itself therefore is not the ultimate trump card, the difficulty of establishing a logical and workable premise upon which to sort good from bad preferences arises. The issue is not really about finality anymore.

Instead, the argument has again shifted back to equality versus deterrence. Here the fundamental misconception is that the deterrence rationale is the essence of preference law. . . . The assumption that the current preference law deters even blatant opt-out behavior probably is erroneous. My conclusion was that the defining premise of preference law should be equality of distribution between unsecured creditors after the debtor becomes insolvent. The policy favoring repose does not change that conclusion, unless one is willing to do away with preference law altogether.

V. RAMIFICATIONS OF REPEALING SECTION 547(c)(2)

. . . The most immediate ramification would be that what should be the primary preference policy—equality of distribution between creditors after the debtor becomes insolvent—would be furthered greatly. Under the current scheme, section 547(c)(2) undercuts equality to such a degree that it cannot rationally be asserted that the preference law substantially furthers that goal. . . .

To the extent one believes that deterrence works, that policy too arguably would be furthered if section 547(c)(2) were repealed. If creditors know that it is more likely that they will have to give back payments received if the debtor goes into bankruptcy within a short time period . . . , then those creditors may be deterred from expending resources to try to obtain those payments.

Perhaps more significantly, the transfer of some of the debtor's assets to a few creditors after the debtor becomes insolvent is less likely to trigger a wild scramble for the remainder of the debtor's assets if the remaining creditors are secure in the knowledge that they can instead file an involuntary bankruptcy case and then compel the preferred creditors to give back what they took. Under the current system, however, in which the preferred creditors have a good chance of keeping what they receive because of section 547(c)(2), a mad race to dismember the debtor is more likely to occur.

What are the potential negative consequences of repeal? . . .

The more substantial concern to be addressed if Congress repeals section 547(c)(2) is the deleterious effect on finality and repose. . . . [W]hile repose certainly is a matter of valid concern, that policy is furthered primarily by the establishment of the absolute (except for insiders) ninety day limitation on the preference reachback. Within the ninety day period, it makes less sense to focus on finality, in terms of justifying the ordinary course exception itself, or in debating the effects of its repeal.

The chief practical ramification of repealing section 547(c)(2) that must be considered is the cost, which is mentioned above as part of the rationale supporting the repose policy. These costs can be subdivided into litigation costs and uncertainty costs. Litigation costs will be increased in one respect if section 547(c)(2) is repealed for the simple reason that many more transfers will be subject to avoidance. . . .

However, the argument that the ordinary course exception should not be repealed because of increased litigation costs can be rebutted on two levels. First, and most fundamentally, as is true with the repose argument in general, it proves too much. The logical and ultimate conclusion reached if avoidance of litigation costs is identified as the paramount policy determinant is that section 547 should be repealed in its entirety. . . .

. . . [H]owever, . . . [i]f preference law is retained in general, thus indicating that cost savings has not been embraced as the controlling policy, arguing against repeal of section 547(c)(2) on the ground that an incremental savings in litigation cost will be realized loses much of its persuasive force. Drawing a line that allows some transfers to be retained, so that some costs will be saved, but thus undermining equality, smacks of an arbitrary compromise.

Furthermore, I am not even willing to concede that the repeal of section 547(c)(2) will lead to a net increase in litigation costs. . . .

. . . The main issue in almost every preference case involving trade creditors is the application of section 547(c)(2). . . . Any semicompetent creditor's lawyer should be able to present at least a colorable ordinary course defense. The prospect of daunting litigation costs in having to counter an ordinary course argument undoubtedly deters trustees from bringing many potentially meritorious preference actions and influences them to settle many more. If section 547(c)(2) were repealed, however, a very large number of preference cases would be greatly simplified; the creditor would not have even an arguable defense.

If potential litigation and administrative costs in permitting the recapture of every payment made within the ninety days preceding bankruptcy are viewed as simply unacceptable, much less radical alternatives than current section 547(c)(2) are available. One is to reduce the preference period, which is discussed below. By reducing the period of vulnerability, the number of exposed transactions likewise would be reduced.

A second way to reduce unacceptable litigation and administrative costs would be to extend the small preference exception of section 547(c)(7) to business debts as well. . . .

. . . I would prefer on the whole to repeal section 547(c)(7) and defer to the discretion of the trustee in individual cases. If, however, cost concerns concomitant with a repeal of section 547(c)(2) are simply too horrifying to contemplate, then I would suggest a comprehensive (*i.e.*, for all types of debts) small preference exception. . . .

The uncertainty costs involved in allowing preference recapture, also discussed as part of the repose argument, must be dealt with as well in considering the repeal of the ordinary course exception. Abolishing section 547(c)(2) arguably will increase these uncertainty costs because of the increased likelihood of preference recapture. . . .

If the uncertainty cost nevertheless is determined to be unbearable, that cost could be reduced substantially by shortening the ninety day preference period, say to forty-five days. . . . The forty-five day period is used elsewhere in commercial law as an indicator of a reasonable exposure period. The uncertainty cost could be further reduced if a comprehensive small preference exception were enacted. Adoption of a forty-five day preference period also would reduce litigation costs by decreasing the number of exposed transactions, as pointed out above. At the same time, the increased certainty in and simplicity of preference lawsuits actually brought (and thus reduced costs) stemming from repeal of section 547(c)(2) would be preserved. . . .

VI. CONCLUSION

In this Article I have suggested that the true nature of preference law should be seen as akin to strict liability. The discriminatory result is the important fact. After the debtor becomes insolvent, one creditor gets paid, and others do not. Fault-based criteria make little sense. . . .

Any attempt to differentiate between preferences in this context is, I believe, largely doomed to failure. Identifying the proper criteria for sorting between good and bad preferences, and then fairly implementing those criteria, has proven an elusive task at best for over two centuries. . . .

Ultimately, one policy of preference law must predominate. Equality after insolvency as a model is fairest to all creditors, economically most efficient, and logically most convincing. . . .

In *The Spirit of Laws* Montesquieu wrote, "The freedom of commerce is not a power granted to the merchants to do what they please; this would be more properly its slavery. The constraint of the merchant is not the constraint of commerce." So too we should not by section 547(c)(2) of our preference law give merchants virtual carte blanche to aggrandize themselves at the expense of others. The guiding principle of the preference law should be the spirit of equality.

NATIONAL BANKRUPTCY REVIEW COMMISSION FINAL REPORT BANKRUPTCY: THE NEXT TWENTY YEARS October 20, 1997

Chapter 3: Procedure

Procedural Changes to the Bankruptcy Code. The procedural section of this chapter focuses on two types of claims: preference actions brought by the estate and tax claims asserted against the estate. Preference actions seek to recover all transfers of property (except under certain circumstances) made within 90 days of the debtor's filing date. By recapturing all transfers made within this time frame, the preference power prevents one creditor from being "preferred" over other creditors on the eve of bankruptcy. The complaints voiced to the Commission focused on preference actions against small trade creditors that cost more for the creditors to defend than to settle, regardless of the merits of the action. The Commission concluded that the preference policy of equality of distribution to creditors was sound but agreed that certain of preference recovery procedures discriminated against small trade creditors. The Recommendation in this area is designed to reduce the number of actions that cost more for small trade creditors to defend than they do to settle. In addition, the Commission proposes to clarify the ordinary course of business exception to the preference power in the hope of expediting the litigation in this area.

Recommendations

3.2.1 *Minimum Amount to Commence a Preference Action under 11 U.S.C. § 547*
11 U.S.C. § 547 should provide that $5,000 is the minimum aggregate transfer to a noninsider creditor that must be sought in a nonconsumer debt preference avoidance action.

3.2.2 *Venue of Preference Actions under 28 U.S.C. § 1409*
28 U.S.C. § 1409 should be amended to require that a preference recovery action against a noninsider seeking less than $10,000 must be brought in the bankruptcy court in the district where the creditor has its principal place of business. The Recommendation applies to nonconsumer debts only.

3.2.3 *Ordinary Course of Business Exception Under 11 U.S.C. § 547(c)(2)(B)*

11 U.S.C. § 547(c)(2)(B) should be amended to provide a disjunctive test for whether a payment is made in the ordinary course of the debtor's business if it is made according to ordinary business terms. The ordinary course of business defense to a preference recovery action under section 547(c)(2) should provide as follows:

(2) to the extent that such transfer was in payment of a debt incurred by the debtor in the ordinary course of business or financial affairs of the debtor and the transferee and such transfer was—
  (A) made in the ordinary course of business or financial affairs of the debtor and the transferee; or
  (B) made according to ordinary business terms[.]

Peter A. Alces
Clearer Conceptions of Insider Preferences
71 WASH. U. L.Q. 1107 (1993)[*]

It is axiomatic in the general debtor-creditor law that an impecunious debtor may pay her creditors in the order she chooses, preferring some over others with impunity. It is axiomatic in the bankruptcy law, however, that a creditor accepts a preference at its peril . . . .

The creditor in a position to exact a preference may impose pressure on the debtor, or the principals of the debtor, that is inimical to the interests of the debtor and its other creditors. . . .

. . . The Bankruptcy Code provides for the avoidance of transfers that benefit an insider, someone in the position to control or manipulate the debtor, even if the same transfer would not have been avoidable had it benefitted a creditor not in the position to manipulate. . . .

Because it is not feasible to determine the bona or mala fides of all preferential transferees before deciding whether to subject transactions between them and the debtor to heightened scrutiny, the Code's preference provision relies on an ostensibly certain proscription: transfers that benefit insider-*creditors* made by an insolvent debtor within one-year prior to bankruptcy are avoidable to the extent that they are preferential.

If *ABC Co.* makes a preferential transfer to its president, Jane Roe, an insider, within ninety days of bankruptcy, the trustee may recover that transfer as a section 547 preference. Indeed, that would be the case whether or not Roe was president of *ABC*. If the same transfer were made to Roe six months prior to bankruptcy, however, the trustee might be able to recover it from Roe even though the trustee could not recover a transfer in the same amount from an ordinary, non-insider, trade creditor of *ABC*. Curiously, though, if *ABC* makes a transfer to Roe who is president of the company, but who is not a creditor of *ABC* and holds no claim against the company, the trustee would not be able to recover the amount of the transfer on a preference theory. Creditor status has nothing to do with control, but is determinative of the insider's preference exposure.

The reason supporting enhanced scrutiny of relations between a debtor and its insiders is the persistent concern that those in a position to manipulate the debtor at the expense of those not so positioned are more likely to manipulate. . . .

From the foregoing premises, how should the preference law treat a transfer made more than ninety days but less than one-year before the debtor-corporation's bankruptcy that is not made directly to the insider but, instead, *benefits* the insider? Consider the case of a loan made by Bank to *ABC Co.* that is guaranteed by Jane Roe, the president of *ABC*. When the financial fortunes of *ABC* begin to flounder, a circumstance of which Bank is well aware because Bank maintains the accounts of *ABC* and periodically requires an audit of *ABC*'s finances, Roe realizes that she will be liable for the debt of *ABC* to Bank if *ABC* fails to pay Bank. More potentially alarming, Roe's guaranty of the *ABC* indebtedness is secured by a mortgage on Roe's personal residence, not an atypical arrangement. Thus, if *ABC* fails to pay Bank, Bank will proceed against Roe, perhaps foreclosing its mortgage on Roe's residence to the disappointment of Roe and her family.

Certainly, one reason that Bank required Roe's guaranty and the mortgage on Roe's residence to secure her performance of the guaranty was to ensure that Roe, an insider of *ABC*, took very seriously the indebtedness of *ABC* to Bank, as seriously as any "homeowner" would take the mortgage on her own home. . . . [T]he secured guaranty agreement is a way for lenders to circumvent the realities of limited liability provided by the corporate form. . . . Bank will be in the position to bring to bear the pressure that an insider can assert against *ABC* because Bank controls the person who controls *ABC*.

Enter *Levit v. Ingersoll Rand Financial Corp.* Writing for a panel of the United States Court of Appeals for the Seventh Circuit, Judge Frank Easterbrook confronted an issue that had confounded the lower courts in the Seventh and the other circuits: whether a trustee in bankruptcy can recover a preferential transfer made to a lender that benefitted an insider of the debtor who had guaranteed the indebtedness and as a consequence of the payment to the lender had its exposure on the guaranty reduced or eliminated. Counsel for creditors argued that the transferee, the lender, was not itself an insider. Thus, the fact that the transfer benefitted the lender should not be sufficient to support recovery from the lender.

Judge Easterbrook saw the issue differently and I believe more clearly. For Judge Easterbrook, resolution of the issue required no more than a straightforward application of Code sections 547 and 550. Under section 547 the preferential transfer benefitted an insider, a creditor of the debtor, by virtue of the common-law reimbursement right of all guarantors. Section 550 provides for the recovery of such transfers from "the initial transferee [Bank] of such transfer or the entity for whose benefit such transfer was made [Roe]." That is, the trustee could recover the amount of the transfer from either the lender, the initial transferee, or the insider, the "entity" benefitted by the transfer. The lender, in turn, if the trustee recovered the preference from the lender, could proceed against the insider-guarantor according to the terms of the guaranty. . . .

Counsel for lenders were nevertheless aghast at the *Levit* result and have gone to some lengths to describe their outrage in various law journals. In the midst of the falling sky, Professor Jay Westbrook offered a qualified defense of *Levit*. His defense was provocative, but seriously flawed. I wrote a Response to the Westbrook Article . . . which identified deficiencies in his analysis and suggested that a much better case could be made for *Levit*. Westbrook then wrote a passionate Reply that was sharply critical of my Response. This essay-rejoinder will put *Levit*, the Westbrook/Alces differences, and the consequences of our differences in perspective.

I. CONTOURS OF THE CONTROVERSY

Levit sanctions recovery from a lender that has benefitted at the expense of the debtor's other creditors by utilizing *control* obtained through the lender's having taken an insider's personal guaranty of the debtor's obligation to the lender. Westbrook argued that the rule of *Levit* works because it effectively, albeit serendipitously, distinguishes some guaranties (and guarantors) from other guaranties (and guarantors). In addition, Westbrook contended that the limit imposed on *Levit* by the section 547 "creditor" requirement is logical, or at least operates as though it were.

The two types of guaranties described by Westbrook are the "true" guaranty and the "pure leverage" guaranty:

A true guarantor is one who gives personal security (for example, stocks and bonds) to support the guaranty or one who is financially able to respond to a judgment on the guaranty (for example, a person with other substantial business interests). By contrast, a leverage guarantor is one who puts up no security for the guaranty and is unlikely to be able to pay any judgment on the guaranty.

According to Westbrook, a lender would not be inclined to take the leverage guaranty after *Levit* because doing so would only extend the preference period from ninety days to one year without affording the lender the financial protection provided by the true guaranty.

My Response to Westbrook demonstrated that, where preference law is concerned, it is facile to understand the incentives that operate on a lender only in terms of the financial condition of the guarantor *at the time that the guarantor executes the guaranty* in favor of the lender. The financial condition of the guarantor may either improve or deteriorate between the time the guaranty is executed and the time the lender would want to impose pressure on the guarantor to cause the debtor to prefer the lender over the debtor's other creditors.

Even more curious, however, is Westbrook's conclusion . . . that the impecunious insider, the insider who granted a leverage guaranty, would be more inclined to succumb to the lender's pressure to effect the type of preference avoidable per *Levit*. My Response demonstrated that there was no reason to believe that the pure-leverage guarantor would be any more predisposed to prefer the lender than a true guarantor; indeed, I established that there was good reason to believe that the true, solvent guarantor, with more to lose than the insolvent guarantor, would be more inclined to succumb to the lender's pressure.

The second portion of Westbrook's Article was devoted to a defense of the "creditor" requirement. Recall that given the formulation of Code sections 547 and 550, a transfer is only avoidable as a preference if it is made to or for the benefit of a creditor of the debtor. If the insider is a guarantor of the debtor's obligation to the lender, the insider would be a creditor of the debtor because upon the insider's payment of the guaranteed indebtedness, the guarantor would have a right to reimbursement from the debtor. Of course, if the insider-guarantor were to waive that right to reimbursement, creditor status might be denied and the transfer to the lender would then not have been for the benefit of a *creditor* and thus not avoidable as a preference.

Westbrook concluded that the creditor requirement is worthwhile because it provides a nice limitation on the scope of preference avoidance. Westbrook argued that boilerplate waivers of the right to reimbursement should not be enforceable. However, he determined that benefit to a non-guarantor insider, an insider who is not a creditor of the debtor, should not provide the basis for preference avoidance, even in cases in which a lender had imposed pressure on the insider to exact a preferential payment. Westbrook concluded that other bankruptcy policing mechanisms provide the basis to avoid the consequences of pressure that result in such indirect benefit to an insider.

My Response took issue with Westbrook's defense of the creditor requirement. Westbrook distinguished between the direct benefit realized by an insider-guarantor who is a creditor of the debtor by virtue of the reimbursement right and the indirect benefit realized by an insider who was not a creditor, either because she was not a guarantor or because she had waived the right to reimbursement. He supported that distinction by opining that the value of the benefit realized by the insider would be the measure of the avoidable preference and it would be too difficult to accurately value that indirect benefit in terms that would accommodate application of the preference law. My Response demonstrated that nothing in the preferential transfer provisions of the Code contemplates avoidance based on the benefit realized by the transferee; the focus is, instead, on the amount of the *transfer*.

In sum, I believe the *Levit* case is sound, but not for the reasons Westbrook posited. The rule of the case works precisely because it overcomes the insubstantial (and dubious) bases of distinguishing among guaranties posited by Westbrook. Further, I would refine the doctrine by eliminating the creditor requirement. The foundation of Westbrook's and my disagreement is the control concept, particularly, and the nature of preference liability more generally. . . .

II. LENDER ACTION AND GUARANTOR REACTION

In the Reply, Westbrook explains that his first Article was *primarily* about lender's actions and incentives and only *secondarily* about insider-guarantor's reactions to the lender's demands. He says that I ignored his assertion of that important distinction. However, one of the primary arguments of my Response was that Westbrook's failure to appreciate the symbiotic relationship between the lender's actions and guarantor's reactions is fatal to his thesis.

To deny that relationship, the coincidence of interest that is the very object of the lender when the lender takes the insider guaranty, is to fail to appreciate the force of Judge Easterbrook's opinion in *Levit*. The opinion is preoccupied with control; it concerns the lender's ability to exert control over the debtor by putting pressure on the individual that controls the debtor. . . . Thus, a great deal is at stake in deciding to ignore the control concept by denying the conceptual basis of Judge Easterbrook's opinion in *Levit*: the lender takes an insider guaranty to gain control at the ultimate expense of the other creditors of the debtor. . . .

Westbrook would find a "true" (and unassailable) guaranty when the lender takes a mortgage on the personal residence of the guarantor (so long as the value of the house exceeds the amount of the loan guaranteed). I am sure that such a guaranty would yield the very type of improper leverage that preference proscriptions are designed to police. Any candid counsel for a lender will acknowledge that the lender gets a mortgage on the guarantor's house in order to focus the guarantor's attention on its loan; rarely would the lender want to foreclose such a mortgage to realize the market value of the residence. Its greatest value is as a lever. . . .

More startling, however, is Westbrook's failure to respond to the argument that comprised a full third of my Response: the observation that the lender-guarantor relationship is dynamic and that, even were Westbrook's conceptions of incentives accurate, the incentives evolve over the course of the guaranteed loan. . . .

Westbrook either fails to recognize the relational dynamic of guaranty agreements or denies that relational contract principles inform the lender-guarantor (insider) relationship. My critique of his model recognized the consequences and incidents of that relationship over the course of the guaranteed indebtedness; his conclusions rest on a static conception of the control relationship. I would have a bankruptcy reform commission take into account the control that a lender could impose on the debtor through the lender's imposition of leverage on an insider *during the preference period*; Westbrook would freeze the frame at the time the loan officer decides to take the guaranty, perhaps long before the preference period, and long before the loan becomes a problem for the lender.

III. THE FORCE OF CONTRACT

Because the insider-guarantor would have a right to reimbursement from the debtor in the event the guarantor pays the guaranteed indebtedness, the guarantor is a "creditor" of the debtor, and the premise of section 547(b)(1) is satisfied. If the insider-guarantor contractually waives that right, Westbrook is correct that such a waiver is tantamount to a waiver of *Levit*. He and I agree that such waivers should not be enforceable . . . .

. . . Westbrook again separates a fact, the existence of a waiver of a right to reimbursement, from its consequences, avoidance of *Levit* by denying the guarantor creditor status. While he argues that waivers are unenforceable, he defends the creditor requirement as providing the means to limit *Levit* to "core" preference cases. On the one hand, preferential transfers effected at the instance of insider-*guarantors* would be recoverable from either the lender-transferee or the benefitted insider-guarantor. Preferential transfers effected at the instance of mere non-guarantor insiders, on the other hand, would not be recoverable from *either* the preferred lender *or* the insider. The first type of preferential transfer would be "core" and the second "non-core" because such transfers would not benefit a creditor.

The only reason avoidance of the waiver is relevant is because of the waiver's effect on the creditor status of the insider. To acknowledge one, waiver unenforceability, and deny the consequences, effective abrogation of the creditor requirement, is to obscure the very interrelation that animates *Levit*. Moreover, it is this interrelation that fixes the scope of preference law and the operation of contract principles in the more tort-than-contract-like ambiance of the bankruptcy fraudulent disposition dynamic. . . .

. . . [T]hough *Levit* preference policies may be implicated when an insider succumbs to pressure brought by the lender, *Levit* is inapposite unless the insider is a creditor of the debtor. Westbrook apparently endorses this conclusion. . . . Westbrook then represents that he has thereby discovered and pulled the golden thread that would unravel the Response. In fact, he discovered only pyrite: my Response proceeded from the *assumption* that Westbrook *was* correct concerning the operation of the creditor requirement . . . .

I agree with Westbrook that Judge Easterbrook's opinion in *Levit* is a correct reading of the Code and that if the insider is not a creditor of the debtor, no basis exists for *Levit* avoidance. However, I am considerably less comfortable with that conclusion than is Westbrook. . . .

The difference between Westbrook and me is clear on this point. Westbrook believes that, in what he considers non-core cases, there should not be preference recovery against lender or insider. The creditor requirement accomplishes this result. I would abrogate the creditor requirement and permit recovery from the lender, the insider, or both, as the trustee deems appropriate. There is no middle ground, given the clumsy nature of the creditor requirement: the trustee either can recover the preference under section 547 from both lender and insider or cannot recover it from either of them.

Ultimately, the source of Westbrook's and my disagreement is our differing conceptions of the jurisprudence of fraudulent disposition law. I would extend the preference rules to reach the indirect benefit cases such as those posited by Westbrook. We both recognize that the issue would persist notwithstanding congressional abrogation of *Levit*. . . .

IV. "TRANSFER" AND "BENEFIT"

. . . *Levit*, whatever its destiny in the hands of a Congress subject to the pressures of special interests, is something of a litmus test: we can tell a good deal about what one thinks of creditor-debtor relations by how one reacts to Judge Easterbrook's opinion. From that reaction we can tell a good deal about one's understanding of specific preference principles as well as general bankruptcy fraudulent disposition principles. There is that much at stake.

What matters for the insider preference law, even after *Levit*, is the nature of preference liability, a topic I treated at the beginning of my Response. Westbrook does not take issue with my constructive fraud formulation of the preference law. It is the premise from which my conclusions necessarily flow. Due to time and space limitations, neither of us has comprehensively confronted the other's views on fundamental preference doctrine, although I am sure that is the source of our differences.

V. CONCLUSION

. . . *Levit* has caused many individuals and groups concerned with bankruptcy jurisprudence to come to terms with the issue of insider preferences. For the most part, most who have thought and written about the case have found reason to urge the decision's abrogation. Jay Westbrook and I, for very different reasons, have found a good deal to commend Judge Easterbrook's opinion. However, when we compare our conclusions, we find that what distinguishes our analyses may be more substantial than what distinguishes the anti-*Levit* forces from either of us. Westbrook and I do not understand the preference law in the same way; indeed, we probably do not understand debtor-creditor law in the same way.

This Essay has endeavored to formulate the terms of our disagreement and to suggest that if Westbrook and I can think carefully about a challenge facing the preference law and reach such diametrically opposed conclusions about the most fundamental fraudulent disposition issues, then there might be good reason for the keepers of the bankruptcy law flame to come to terms with the interests to be balanced in the control calculus. When an insider uses her position to realize benefits not available to creditors of the debtor, how does the bankruptcy law respond? By application of preference principles, or otherwise, or not at all? It should be clear that, correctly understood, *Levit* provides the means to police manipulation by insiders *as well as those who control the insiders.*

Levit is only one means to that end and maybe an imperfect one at that. If the decision and the logic supporting it are to operate effectively, then the creditor requirement should be abrogated. Short of that extreme and rather unlikely development, bankruptcy courts should deem the requirement satisfied whenever an insider is a guarantor of the debtor's liability to the lender that receives a preferential transfer.

Additional suggested readings

Barry E. Adler, *A Re-Examination of Near-Bankruptcy Investment Incentives*, 62 U. Chi. L. Rev. 575 (1995)

Peter A. Alces, *Rethinking Professor Westbrook's Two Thoughts About Insider Preferences*, 77 Minn. L. Rev. 605 (1993)

James W. Bowers, *Whither What Hits the Fan?: Murphy's Law, Bankruptcy Theory, and the Elementary Economics of Loss Distribution*, 26 Ga. L. Rev. 27 (1991)

Irving A. Breitowitz, *Article 9 Security Interests as Voidable Preferences*, 3 Cardozo L. Rev. 357 (1982)

Irving A. Breitowitz, *Article 9 Security Interests as Voidable Preferences: Part II: The Floating Lien*, 4 Cardozo L. Rev. 1 (1982)

Lissa L. Broome, *Payments on Long-Term Debt as Voidable Preferences: The Impact of the 1984 Bankruptcy Amendments*, 1987 Duke L.J. 78

David Gray Carlson, *The Earmarking Defense to Voidable Preference Liability: A Reconceptualization*, 73 Am. Bankr. L.J. 591 (1999)

David Gray Carlson, *Security Interests in the Crucible of Voidable Preference Law*, 1995 U. Ill. L. Rev. 211

David Gray Carlson, *Tripartite Voidable Preferences*, 11 Bankr. Dev. J. 219 (1995)

Neil B. Cohen, *"Value" Judgments: Account Receivable Financing and Voidable Preferences Under the New Bankruptcy Code*, 66 Minn. L. Rev. 639 (1982)

Garrard Glenn, *The Diversities of the Preferential Transfer: A Study in Bankruptcy History*, 15 Cornell L.Q. 521 (1930)

Michael J. Herbert, *The Trustee Versus the Trade Creditor: A Critique of Section 547(c)(1), (2) and (4) of the Bankruptcy Code*, 17 U. Rich. L. Rev. 667 (1983)

Thomas H. Jackson, Ch. 6, *Prebankruptcy Opt-Out Activity and the Role of Preference Law*, *in* THE LOGIC AND LIMITS OF BANKRUPTCY LAW 122-150 (Harvard 1986)

Thomas H. Jackson & Anthony T. Kronman, *Voidable Preferences and Protection of the Expectation Interest*, 60 MINN. L. REV. 971 (1976)

F. Stephen Knippenberg, *Future Nonadvance Obligations: Preferences Lost in Metaphor*, 72 WASH. U. L.Q. 1537 (1994)

Robert R. Kraus, *Preferential Transfers and the Value of the Insolvent Firm*, 87 YALE L.J. 1449 (1978)

John C. McCoid, II, *Corporate Preferences to Insiders*, 43 S.C. L. REV. 805 (1992)

James A. McLaughlin, *Defining a Preference in Bankruptcy*, 60 HARV. L. REV. 233 (1946)

C. Robert Morris, Jr., *Bankruptcy Law Reform: Preferences, Secret Liens, and Floating Liens*, 54 MINN. L. REV. 737 (1970)

Lawrence Ponoroff & Julie C. Ashby, *Desperate Times and Desperate Measures: The Troubled State of the Ordinary Course of Business Defense—And What to Do About It*, 72 WASH. L. REV. 5 (1997)

Lawrence Ponoroff, *Now You See It, Now You Don't: An Unceremonious Encore for Two-Transfer Thinking in the Analysis of Indirect Preferences*, 69 AM. BANKR. L.J. 203 (1995)

Lawrence Ponoroff, *Evil Intentions and an Irresolute Endorsement for Scientific Rationalism: Bankruptcy Preferences One More Time*, 1993 WIS. L. REV. 1439

Charles Seligson, *Preferences Under the Bankruptcy Act*, 15 VAND. L. REV. 115 (1961)

Morris G. Shanker, Ch. 13, *The American Bankruptcy Preference Law: Perceptions of the Past, the Transition to the Present, and Ideas for the Future*, *in* CURRENT DEVELOPMENTS IN INTERNATIONAL AND COMPARATIVE INSOLVENCY LAW (Ziegel ed. Oxford 1994)

Charles Jordan Tabb, *Panglossian Preference Paradigm?*, 5 AM. BANKR. INST. L. REV. 407 (1997)

Thomas M. Ward & Jay A. Shulman, *In Defense of the Bankruptcy Code's Radical Integration of the Preference Rules Affecting Commercial Financing*, 61 WASH. U. L.Q. 1 (1983)

Jay Lawrence Westbrook, *Clear Thinking About Insider Preferences: A Reply*, 77 MINN. L. REV. 1393 (1993)

Jay Lawrence Westbrook, *Two Thoughts About Insider Preferences*, 76 MINN. L. REV. 73 (1991)

Chapter 7
Avoiding Powers: Fraudulent Transfers

Fraudulent transfer law seeks to protect creditors from the adverse effects of transfers that unfairly impede their ability to collect from their debtor. Unlike preference law, which deals with inter-creditor distributional squabbles (and thus applies only in a collective proceeding), fraudulent transfer law focuses on the rights of creditors versus the debtor, and applies in *and* out of bankruptcy. The fountainhead of fraudulent transfer law was the Statute of 13 Elizabeth in 1570. Today fraudulent transfers are dealt with by state law (often a version of the Uniform Fraudulent Transfer Law, or, more rarely, the much older Uniform Fraudulent Conveyance Act), and, in the event of bankruptcy, also by the Bankruptcy Code. The Code has its own fraudulent transfer section (548) and incorporates state law via § 544(b).

The writing in the field of fraudulent conveyances or transfers is rich indeed. Many of the luminaries of bankruptcy and commercial law scholarship for a very long time have been preeminent authorities in the realm of fraudulent transfers—Orlando Bump, Garrard Glenn, Frank Kennedy, and Peter Alces, to name a few. In this Chapter, I have drawn from a number of noted modern scholars, who address a variety of issues.

The first article is from Professor and Dean Robert Clark of Harvard, *The Duties of the Corporate Debtor to its Creditors*, 90 HARV. L. REV. 505 (1977). Clark identifies the few distinct normative ideals that underlie fraudulent conveyance law: Truth; Respect; and Evenhandedness; in turn, these three ideals constitute particularizations of the general norm of Nonhindrance. As is evident from the labels, Dean Clark views fraudulent conveyance law as profoundly moral in nature. Clark goes on in his article to demonstrate how these ideals drive legal doctrines other than fraudulent conveyances.

Thomas Jackson's seminal article, *Avoiding Powers in Bankruptcy*, 36 STAN. L. REV. 725 (1984), is excerpted for the third time in this anthology, this time with his thoughts on the foundations of fraudulent conveyance law. With his trusty sidekick and coauthor, Douglas Baird, Jackson elaborates his views in *Fraudulent Conveyance Law and Its Proper Domain*, 38 VAND. L. REV. 829 (1985). In those articles, Jackson and Baird identify the protection of creditors against debtor misbehavior as the core principle of fraudulent conveyance law. They attempt to fit this realm of debtor-creditor law into the broader scheme of the "creditors' bargain." With debtor naughtiness the prevailing worry, the inability of creditors to opt out of fraudulent conveyance law—that is, the mandatory nature of the law—suggests to Jackson and Baird that fraudulent conveyance law should be limited in scope. It should not be applied to arms' length transactions, they assert. This restriction would have serious implications for several commonly contested fraudulent conveyance issues, such as foreclosure sales and leveraged buyouts, each of which Baird and Jackson analyze.

The late Professor Barry Zaretsky, who served as an examiner in assessing the likelihood of fraudulent transfer liability due to a failed leveraged buyout in the mammoth bankruptcy of *In re Revco Drugstores,* also looks for a unifying principle in constructive fraud cases. In *Fraudulent*

Transfer Law as the Arbiter of Unreasonable Risk, 46 S.C. L. REV. 1165 (1995), Zaretsky argues that fraudulent transfer law should be used to protect creditors as a group against a range of transactions undertaken by their debtor that create unreasonable collection risks for the creditors. He then applies his paradigm to leveraged buyouts and corporate guarantees.

The issue of applying a constructive fraud analysis to mortgage foreclosure sales is analyzed in the next article, Robert M. Lawless & Stephen P. Ferris, *Economics and the Rhetoric of Valuation*, 5 J. BANKR. L. & PRAC. (1995). Professors Lawless and Ferris, frequent collaborators who nicely combine expertise in law and finance, present a fine article that explodes a number of fallacies about valuation issues. In this excerpt, they challenge the Supreme Court's premises in *BFP v. Resolution Trust Co.*, 511 U.S. 531 (1994), in which the Court held that a noncollusive foreclosure sale price conclusively establishes "reasonably equivalent value" for fraudulent conveyance purposes. Lawless and Ferris explain how the Court's analysis misses the point: in the context of a pervasive market failure, sales price cannot be determinative of value. The question that needs to be asked, they assert, is whether the governing legal rules should allow such a bargain purchase to be made and to then be immune from attack.

The final spot in the Chapter is reserved for Professor David Gray Carlson, who asks: *Is Fraudulent Conveyance Law Efficient?*, in 9 CARDOZO L. REV. 643 (1987). His conclusion, as the suspicious reader might guess, is "no." Thus, he doubts seriously whether the "law and economics" camp (typified by the writings of Jackson and Baird) legitimately can claim to know *the* right solutions to the mysteries of fraudulent transfer law. As Carlson observes, "ultimately, science has nothing to tell us about ethical choice. We have to develop our own notions of good and right." And on that score, he posits, the economists "have no more idea of right and wrong than we ordinary shmoes have"!

Robert Clark
The Duties of the Corporate Debtor to its Creditors
90 HARV. L. REV. 505 (1977)[*]

INTRODUCTION

The initial thesis of this articles is that the law of fraudulent conveyances contains a few simple but potent moral principles governing the conduct of debtors toward their creditors. . . .

I. THE NORMATIVE IDEALS OF FRAUDULENT CONVEYANCE LAW

The law of fraudulent conveyances, of which the Uniform Fraudulent Conveyance Act (UFCA) is the principal but not exclusive embodiment, allows creditors to set aside certain transfers by debtors. Fraudulent conveyance law has a broad applicability, restricted neither to conveyances—since virtually all transfers of property, and, under the UFCA and under the Bankruptcy Act, the incurrence of obligations, are covered—nor to fraud—since unfair transfers made without deceptive intent are included. Court opinions involving allegedly fraudulent transfers have not infrequently sounded muddled and uncertain notes because of a failure to discriminate among the various distinct ideals that this body of law seeks to implement. Although more than one of these distinct ideals are

---

usually involved in the cases, what these ideals are, and how closely they are related to the ideal underlying the law of preferential transfers, can be seen through an examination of four simple situations.

1. Debtor grants Friend a mortgage on his small factory in return for a loan of $160,000, which Friend actually makes to Debtor. Debtor, wishing to discourage unpaid trade creditors having $30,000 of claims from litigating them to judgment and seeking execution against the factory, prevails upon Friend to have the recorded mortgage recite that it is a debt for $200,000, which equals the well-known market value of the factory. The trade creditor's attorneys search the real estate records, discover and give credence to the false mortgage, and, knowing that Debtor has few assets other than the factory, become discouraged and cease pursuing Debtor.

Here, then, is a case of Ur-Fraud, that primeval fraud on creditors than which no greater can be thought. The transfer of the mortgage interest to Friend was known to be false, was intended to thwart legitimate creditors, and actually did so. The keynote of the evil is the *actual deception* or falsehood practiced on the trade creditors to their detriment. By hypothesis, Friend gave full and fair consideration for the extent of the mortgage interest that he could enforce against Debtor. Further, the mortgage interest that he obtained did not actually render Debtor incapable of satisfying the remaining creditors. The ideal offended is simply that of Truth: in connection with transfers of property rights to others, a debtor is forbidden to tell lies to his creditors that will lead to the non-satisfaction of their claims.

2. Debtor has reached the point where $100,000 of her debts are due and payable, and her entire assets have a fair market value of the same dollar amount. Thinking that she would prefer that her husband and sister rather than her creditors get the benefits of her assets, she makes a deed of gift of all her possessions to those two fortunate relatives, and immediately delivers full and exclusive actual possession of the property to them, relinquishing any use or benefit from the transferred property. She makes no secret of the transactions or of her intentions: she reports the deed of gift in every conceivable recording office, and mails a copy by certified mail to each and every creditor, together with a detailed and psychologically accurate account of her motivations, purposes, and feelings toward her creditors. In this case, Debtor has made a transfer which would clearly be voidable since it was made without fair and full consideration and she was insolvent immediately after the transfer.

The ideal offended by Debtor in the above example is not that of truthful conduct toward creditors. Debtor has been completely open with her creditors and has never tried to deceive them, unless one wants to overstretch the notion of fraud by saying that, when she originally borrowed from her creditors, she "implicitly" promised to satisfy her legal obligations before her moral obligations and personal allegiances, that she has now failed to fulfill this promise, and that the failure is conclusive evidence that the promise was falsely and deceptively given. Instead, it is much simpler, and intellectually more honest, to recognize that another ideal is served by fraudulent conveyance law. The ideal can be captured by a cliche: be just before you are generous. The debtor has a moral duty[17] in transferring his property to give *primacy* to so-called legal obligations, which are usually

---

[17]   I describe the duties inherent in fraudulent conveyance law as "moral" for at least two reasons. First, they are standards of right and wrong in debtor-creditor relationships, both commercial and personal, that have endured over many centuries and have governed extremely common transactions. The relation between debtors and creditors is as old as civilization, is only slightly less significant than relations among family members, social classes, and races, has always occupied a substantial portion of the resources of legal systems, and has always been regulated in the commercial context by attitudes and emotion of a decidedly moral sort. Second, these duties are, I think, not really perceived as *imposed* by the statutes and cases which reflect them—as are many modern legal obligations—but are perceived to be part of normative custom.

the legitimate, conventional claims of standard contract and tort creditors, as opposed to the interests of self, family, friends, shareholders, and shrewder or more powerful bargaining parties. I will somewhat hesitantly refer to this as the normative ideal of Respect.

3. Pierce is indebted to Twyne for $400 and to C for $200. Pierce's nonexempt assets are worth only $300. Suppose that Pierce, simply because Twyne is the first to ask that he do so and because he dislikes C, and for no other reason, transfers all of his property to Twyne. Suppose, contrary to the apparent facts in a similar, well-known case, that Pierce makes the transfer openly and with much publicity and fanfare, so that no deception of any sort is practiced on C, and that Pierce does not intend to and never does get a kickback of part of the transferred property or its use or any other kind of benefit from Twyne. Assume also that Twyne's claim is a completely valid, unobjectionable, due and payable, legal obligation of the most conventional sort.

Pierce's transfer to Twyne does not run afoul of the normative ideals of Truth and Respect toward creditors because Pierce has fully and truthfully described the transaction and has given primacy to his legal obligations. It is, however, objectionable for a debtor to satisfy the claims of just one creditor at a time when he lacks sufficient assets to meet his other legitimate and conventional legal obligations. A preferential payment of this sort hinders pro tanto the interest of all the other creditors. In such a situation, a debtor should deal equally with all his creditors. I will dub this principle the ideal of Evenhandedness toward creditors, with the understanding that in using this term the connotation is of equality of treatment of legal obligations in connection with liquidation proceedings. Evenhandedness, in its fullest expression, has two attributes. Whenever a debtor is or is about to become insolvent and thus unable to satisfy all his creditors in full, the debtor should refrain from preferring one creditor over another. Similarly, in such cases creditors should refrain from seeking such a preference. In either instance, transfers resulting in better than equal treatment on the eve of liquidation proceedings should be undone—and may actually be undone in bankruptcy proceedings as voidable preferential transfers.

4. Debtor, who owns 250 shares of stock, sold those shares to her husband for full value in illiquid assets. She was not insolvent at the time of the sale but the stock had been her only liquid asset and as a result of the transaction she had no assets which creditors could easily reach. She made the transfer for the purpose of hindering her creditors but did not deceive them. This transaction would be avoided under the open-ended language of the UFCA, which covers transactions made with actual intent to hinder or delay creditors.

Although the debtor intends and accomplishes a transfer leading to a hindering of her creditors, this case does not strictly offend the ideals of Truth, Respect or Evenhandedness as developed above. The scheme involves no actual deception, for she has truthfully informed all her creditors of the transaction. Moreover, the transfer of the shares is not for less than their fair value, nor does the transfer leave the debtor insolvent, so the transfer does not violate the ideal of Respect. Finally, the scheme results in no preference of any preexisting creditor over the others. Hence, one could say that there may be transactions which are not offensive of the above ideals in their normal applications, but which are yet fraudulent conveyances because they violate the more general expression of the ideal of which all three of the subsumed ideals are specifications. The general ideal might be described as that of Nonhindrance of the enforcement of valid legal obligation against oneself, in connection with transfers of one's property.

In summary, then, fraudulent conveyance law embodies a general ideal, in connection with a debtors's transfers of property rights and incurrences of new obligations, of Nonhindrance of creditors. This vague ideal is made operational through the effectuation of the more specific ideals of Truth, Respect, and Evenhandedness as well as a general, residual prohibition of conduct which hinders creditors in attempting to satisfy their claims.

Thus far, Evenhandedness has been conceived of as one of three particular duties derived from the general duty of Nonhindrance, because a violation of the duty of Evenhandedness operates to hinder the nonpreferred creditors. It is also possible, however, to view Evenhandedness as a policy independent of, and on a par with, a general ideal of Nonhindrance, and this aspect of the policy has led to its development as a separate topic. While like the other two ideals Evenhandedness specifies the moral duties of a debtor to his creditor, Evenhandedness is also the ideal behind what is referred to as the law of voidable preferences and many cases assume or state explicitly that a preference is not a fraudulent conveyance. However, the fact situations in many fraudulent conveyance cases suggest that those cases might have been treated equally as well as instances of voidable preferences.

For example, one of the great ironies of legal history is that *Twyne's Case,* which is widely regarded as the fountainhead of the modern Anglo-American law of fraudulent conveyances, does not, as presented in the reports, clearly involve anything more than a preference. The transaction offended the ideal of Evenhandedness, which was not then an ideal that the common law of individual collection efforts respected, but it is not clear that it offended the ideals of Truth and Respect in any relevant way. The facts, which are roughly similar to those in the third example discussed above, do appear to include the circumstance that Pierce's transfer to Twyne was a secret. But why a transaction which would be a mere nonvoidable preference if done openly should become a voidable fraudulent conveyance because done secretly is not at all clear, either from the report of the case or in logic. Perhaps the secrecy led *C* to pursue his collection effort longer than he would have had he known of the preference, and thus to waste money. The possibility it seems, could have been covered quite adequately by letting *C* recover the pointless expenses, rather than condemning the whole transfer to Twyne as a criminal act. It might conceivably be that the key to the case was that Pierce was satisfying some moral obligation to Twyne, for the report is full of apparently irrelevant remarks concerning that theme. More likely, and supported by inferences from the report, is the hypothesis that Pierce violated the ideal of Truth because he did not really transfer the entire amount of his property, but under a kickback agreement with Twyne (who was apparently too slow of foot at that point to win his race against *C* via the use of judicial process) kept the use and benefit of certain property. Pierce was to keep some of his assets, though insolvent: Twyne was to obtain a larger percentage of his claim than if he resorted to legitimate collection procedures; and both were to defraud *C* in his collection efforts by pretending that Pierce no longer had any assets. The case may actually be understandable, then, as a case similar to the first example above, which involved actual, detrimental deception.

Despite their essential kinship, the fact that fraudulent conveyances and voidable preferences have emerged as distinct legal doctrines has significant consequences. While both fraudulent conveyances and preferences are voidable in bankruptcy, preferences can be avoided only by the bankruptcy trustee while fraudulent conveyances are voidable under state law at the behest of individual creditors. . . .

Perhaps the key to the existence of the two great, "separate" branches of the law concerning the debtor's moral duties to his creditors is that the ideal of Evenhandedness has never been considered as important to the functioning of the commercial system, which constitutes the essence of our culture, as the ideals of Truth and Respect. Evenhandedness, therefore, has been relegated in part to a separate doctrinal category, where it can be diluted and adjusted by limited implementing rules, without affecting the other two ideals. This strategy is reflected in such tired, and not entirely accurate or meaningful, saws as the one that there is nothing morally or legally "wrong" with giving or seeking a preference, though fraudulent conveyances should not be counselled by the debtor's or the creditors' attorneys. It is also reflected, of course, in the enormous number of exceptions made to the principle of equal treatment of creditors in bankruptcy—exceptions ranging from security interests through statutory priorities to contractual and other forms of subordination among creditors.

The ideals of Nonhindrance, including the special evolution of Evenhandedness in the void-able preference doctrine, have been presented above in a rather tidy and purified form. In actual implementation, the ideals are often balanced against other objectives of the legal system, especially that of the fairness toward the debtor's transferee. . . . [T]he good faith or absence of actual fraudulent intent of the transferee may have a bearing on the extent of the creditor's recovery. . . .

In addition, the legal system, in implementing the ideals of Nonhindrance, has had to go beyond the fraudulent conveyance doctrine, embedding Nonhindrance principles in other branches of the law. In theory, the norms of Nonhindrance could be effectuated through three radically different modes. First, the ideals could be expressed as a system of transactional rules; decision of cases under the rules would necessitate examination of specific transactions and proof of a violation of an ideal in each transaction. Fraudulent conveyance law fits this mode. The second mode of implementation is the gestalt approach: when transactions are complex or involve elements that are not normally covered under the transactional mode, this approach would permit a court to apply a remedy, albeit a crude one, to correct a pattern of fraudulent transfers of obligations that may reasonably be inferred. This mode of implementation is . . . exemplified by the doctrine of equitable subordination. Finally, the ideals could be embodied in a system of preventive rules.

Thomas H. Jackson
Avoiding Powers in Bankruptcy
36 STAN. L. REV. 725 (1984)[*]

VII. FRAUDULENT CONVEYANCES: PROTECTIONS AGAINST DEBTOR MISBEHAVIOR

Fraudulent conveyance law, unlike preference law, applies both inside and outside a collective proceeding such as bankruptcy. This nonbankruptcy application expresses a great deal about the conceptual difference between the roles of preference law and of fraudulent conveyance law in sorting out legal rights. While preference law enforces the bargain among the creditors themselves, fraudulent conveyance law enforces the bargain between the *debtor* and his creditors. That is to say, preference law, like most other trustee avoiding powers, is designed to preserve the ability of creditors as a group to resort to a collective proceeding when it is advantageous to them. Conversely, fraudulent conveyance law protects creditors against misbehavior by their debtor. As such, it is a debtor/creditor misbehavior rule, not a creditor/creditor misbehavior rule, and accordingly, it is not related to the creditor-oriented collective justification for a bankruptcy proceeding.

Many of the difficulties associated with fraudulent conveyance law arise from the failure to distinguish the general role of fraudulent conveyance law from the bankruptcy-oriented role of preference law. . . .

The rough contours of fraudulent conveyance law are easy to establish. Classic fraudulent conveyance law is concerned with a debtor who manipulates his assets so as to keep them from his creditors. . . . These types of action form the core behavior that classic fraudulent conveyance law is designed to prevent. Actions taken to "hinder, delay, or defraud" one's creditors are, therefore, fraudulent.

Since here, as elsewhere, proving intent is difficult, fraudulent conveyance law not surprisingly contains an objective element in the form of a rule to supplement the standard: Actions taken by a debtor while insolvent (and hence while having little to lose) are presumed to be fraudulently motivated, unless those actions substitute one asset for another of equal value. Fraudulent conveyance law thus attacks these transactions without inquiry into intent through the alternative, and objectivized, approach of deeming fraudulent those transactions for less than fair consideration made while the debtor was insolvent.

Fraudulent conveyance law generally comes into play only if a debtor becomes insolvent and is unable to pay all his creditors. . . . Though fraudulent conveyance law is generally necessary only if a debtor becomes insolvent, that does not mean that it is essentially related to the justifications for a bankruptcy process. . . . [T]he justification for fraudulent conveyance law is fundamentally broader than are the reasons for a bankruptcy proceeding.

Fraudulent conveyance law, then, is distinctly less collectivist in its justification. Moreover, both the fact-specific and the rule-oriented branches of fraudulent conveyance law focus, at their core, on activities by a debtor that harm his creditors. The essence of fraudulent conveyance law, therefore, is to prevent manipulative activities by the debtor. If the activity in question is, at best, a manipulation by a *creditor* vis-à-vis other creditors, then it should succumb, if at all, to a preference-type rationale rather than a fraudulent-conveyance-type rationale.

One of the more perplexing recent additions to fraudulent conveyance case law poses this distinction in the context of the trustee's attack on a mortgage foreclosure sale. . . .

The facts of these cases do not support a presumption of debtor-induced misbehavior. Indeed, to the extent that misbehavior appears, the cases suggest the possibility of misbehavior by the creditor against the debtor. . . .

. . . While the debtor may offer insufficient resistance to a creditor's attempt to buy the asset at the foreclosure sale for less than market value, this transaction does not bear the *presumptive* elements of fraud by the *debtor* against his creditors. The presumption, if any, is of debtor-passivity, not of active debtor concealment or dissipation of assets. The activity's impetus comes from the creditor, not from the debtor. . . . This description, however, depicts the paradigmatic violation of preference principles—creditor misbehavior directed against other creditors when a debtor is insolvent—*not* a violation of fraudulent conveyance principles.

Foreclosure sales therefore seem better analyzed, presumptively at least, as a part of preference law, not fraudulent conveyance law. . . .

Whatever the proper resolution of this point may be, foreclosure sales seem more a problem of creditor misbehavior than of debtor misbehavior. As such, they should be regulated either by nonbankruptcy foreclosure rules or by preference-like rules in bankruptcy. The preference approach would be justified by a presumption of debtor passivity that occurs upon insolvency and that allows a creditor to grab assets from the pool, leaving less for the others. Thus conceived, the misbehavior threatens the bankruptcy process and enters the domain of preference law. Neither nonbankruptcy foreclosure rules nor preference rules, however, suggest misbehavior by the debtor; application of the rule-oriented provisions of fraudulent conveyance law, in or out of bankruptcy, therefore, appears unwarranted.

Douglas G. Baird & Thomas H. Jackson
Fraudulent Conveyance Law and Its Proper Domain
38 VAND. L. REV. 829 (1985)*

I. INTRODUCTION

In 1571 Parliament passed a statute making illegal and void any transfer made for the purpose of hindering, delaying, or defrauding creditors. This law, commonly known as the Statute of 13 Elizabeth, was intended to curb what was thought to be a widespread abuse. Until the seventeenth century, England had certain sanctuaries into which the King's writ could not enter. A sanctuary was not merely the interior of a church, but certain precincts defined by custom or royal grant. Debtors could take sanctuary in one of these precincts, live in relative comfort, and be immune from execution by their creditors. It was thought that debtors usually removed themselves to one of these precincts only after selling their property to friends and relatives for a nominal sum with the tacit understanding that the debtors would reclaim their property after their creditors gave up or compromised their claims. The Statute of 13 Elizabeth limited this practice.

The basic prohibition of this statute, which prevents debtors from making transfers that hinder, delay, or defraud their creditors, has survived for over four centuries. A debtor cannot manipulate his affairs in order to shortchange his creditors and pocket the difference. Those who collude with a debtor in these transactions are not protected either. An individual creditor who discovers his debtor's assets have been fraudulently conveyed can reduce his claim to judgment and have the sheriff levy on the property that is now no longer in the debtor's hands (as long as the property is not in the hands of a bona fide purchaser for value).

The difficulty that courts and legislatures have faced for hundreds of years has been one of trying to define what kinds of transactions hinder, delay, or defraud creditors. From very early on, common law judges developed per se rules, known as "badges of fraud," that would allow the courts to treat a transaction as a fraudulent conveyance even though no specific evidence suggested that the debtor tried to profit at his creditors' expense. . . .

Over the past hundred years, there has been an increasing tendency to treat transfers of property of insolvent debtors in which the debtor received nothing or too little in return as fraudulent conveyances. The Uniform Fraudulent Conveyance Act, for example, contains a separate section that deems a transfer by an insolvent debtor made for less than "fair consideration" to be a fraudulent conveyance. The most straightforward justification for this provision is the same as the justification for the Statute of 13 Elizabeth: it is a rule designed to set aside transfers by an insolvent debtor that are intended to hinder, delay, or defraud his creditors. This approach presumes mischief when an insolvent debtor voluntarily transferred property and got nothing or clearly too little in return unless the debtor simply was paying off an antecedent debt. Because it is a per se rule, it may treat some transactions in which a debtor was not trying to hinder, delay, or defraud his creditors as fraudulent conveyances. The number of cases in which an insolvent debtor gives away something for nothing but is not trying to hinder, delay, or defraud his creditors, however, may be sufficiently small that it is preferable to treat all these cases as fraudulent conveyances. . . .

If one begins with the premise that the provision covering transactions made without fair consideration is simply a per se rule that embodies the more general standard that a debtor cannot transfer property if his purpose is to hinder, delay, or defraud his creditors, the provision carries with it the limits imposed by its origins. . . .

This view of section 4 of the Uniform Fraudulent Conveyance Act, however, is incomplete. The drafters of that act intended to reach some transactions—such as gifts by insolvent debtors—quite apart from whether the debtor could be thought to have harbored any fraudulent intent. . . . The drafters deemed these fraudulent not because the transfers were too costly to distinguish from gifts by insolvents made with an intent to defraud, but rather because they found them inherently objectionable. . . .

If fraudulent conveyance law is not limited simply to cases in which the debtor intended—or could be presumed to have intended—to hinder, delay, or defraud his creditors, what are its limits? . . .

. . . Identifying the precise reach of fraudulent conveyance law is the crucial inquiry in several important legal disputes, such as whether a foreclosure of a debtor's equity of redemption or a leveraged buyout is a fraudulent conveyance. These cases are strikingly different from gratuitous transfers or transfers intended to defraud. It is not clear that permitting the debtor to engage in a leveraged buyout, for instance, is against the long-term interests of the creditors as a group. . . . [A] view has recently gained currency that suggests the core principle of fraudulent conveyance law is that creditors should be able to set aside transfers by insolvent debtors that harm the creditors as a group. . . . But, just as a view of section 4 that treats it as a surrogate of section 7's intentional fraud standard is too narrow, we believe this competing principle is too broad.

To establish this, we start from a simple, but important, proposition. After a debtor has borrowed money, his interests conflict with those of his creditors. A debtor has an incentive to take risks that he did not have before he borrowed. He enjoys all the benefits if a risky venture proves successful, but he does not incur all the costs if the venture fails. . . .

Fraudulent conveyance law is a restraint that the law imposes upon debtors for the benefit of creditors by giving creditors the power to void transactions. The power of creditors to set aside transactions after the fact limits the ability of debtors to engage in the transactions in the first instance. This power is unobjectionable if the transaction—such as a gift by an insolvent debtor—always injuries creditors. But often the transaction—such as a leveraged buyout—might or might not injure creditors. . . .

Treating transfers by a debtor that make creditors as a group worse off as fraudulent conveyances is overbroad because many ordinary transfers that a debtor makes do this. . . . [I]n considering a legal rule such as fraudulent conveyance law, overbroad rules may be more pernicious than underbroad rules. It is easier for creditors to contract into prohibitions on conduct by a debtor than it is to contract out. . . . Myriad restrictions in loan agreements, for example, perform this function. . . . Yet, contracting *out* of a rule that prohibits conduct, such as fraudulent conveyance law, is much harder. . . .

Thus, we believe, one must be careful in deciding where to place the reach of fraudulent conveyance law. In establishing its limits, one must recognize that the debtor-creditor relationship is essentially contractual. . . . Not all the rights that the creditor wants, or that the debtor would agree to give it, however, can be bargained for explicitly. Sometimes these rights (such as priority rights with respect to a debtor's assets) affect third parties as well and should be subject to legal constraints. The ambition of the law governing the debtor-creditor relationship, including fraudulent conveyance law, should provide all the parties with the type of contract that they would have agreed to if they had had the time and money to bargain over all aspects of their deal. Fraudulent conveyance law, in other words, should be viewed as a species of contract law, representing one kind of control that creditors generally would want to impose and that debtors generally would agree to accept.

II. DEBTOR MISBEHAVIOR AND THE CREDITORS' BARGAIN

Hundreds of different mechanisms have evolved—from net worth and accounting requirements to security interests and default clauses—that also guard against the risk of unacceptable debtor behavior. These contract provisions have evolved in the context of a tension between debtor freedom and creditor protection. . . . The function of legal rules in this area should be either to constrain deals between debtors and creditors that affect third parties or to provide preformulated provisions that the parties usually would contract for anyway.

It is in this context, we believe, that one must approach fraudulent conveyance law. It should not be construed to reach all transfers that benefit a debtor at the creditors' expense because such a principle is unlimitable and conflicts with the general notion that the debtor should make investment decisions. Any time that a creditor lends his debtor 100 dollars and the debtor converts the cash into an asset the value of which is less certain, then the creditor is worse off, in the same way it would be worse off if the debtor used the 100 dollars to buy a lottery ticket that has a one-in-ten chance of paying 1000 dollars. . . . If the investment does return more than 100 dollars, the debtor enjoys the benefit; if it returns less, the creditors bear most of the loss. Thus, one should not construe a prohibition on transfers for less than "fair consideration" by asking simply whether the investment leaves the creditors with as much as they had before. At a minimum, the concept of "fair consideration" needs to be analyzed from the perspective of the debtor and creditors taken as a unit.

What, then, of an argument about investments that simply are bad? . . . [O]ne might choose to justify these statutes not on the overly broad ground that creditors should be able to set aside all transfers that make them worse off, but rather on the narrower ground that creditors should be able to set aside transfers that are bad even if there were no conflicts between the debtor and his creditors. . . . One can argue that a creditor should be able to set aside its insolvent debtor's deal only if it is bad from a neutral perspective. An insolvent debtor might choose to go beyond merely taking risks—he might take unwise ones.

Using the fraudulent conveyance remedy to undo bad deals, however, can be justified only if its benefits are greater than the costs of the uncertainty such a rule brings. Often one cannot determine with any certainty whether a debtor was insolvent at a particular time or whether a particular transaction at that time was a good deal or a bad deal. Even if a definite determination could be made, creditors still might not bargain for the right to set such transfers aside after the fact because of the effects such a right would have on third parties and, ultimately, on the debtor's investment decisions. . . . Only by giving the debtor discretion can the creditor hope to profit. Giving a debtor discretion, however, necessarily gives him the ability not only to make good decisions, but bad ones as well.

Of course, creditors do place limits on a debtor's ability to make bad decisions. . . .

Creditors can expect their debtor to enter into favorable deals with others only if they expose themselves to the risk that the debtor will enter into unfavorable deals. That is part and parcel of the reason for making the investment in the first place—to use the debtor's comparative advantage in entrepreneurial or investment skills. A fraudulent conveyance law that protects creditors from all bad deals a debtor enters into gives the creditors too much. Such creditor protection is unlikely to be a right that all interested parties would agree to if they were able to bargain explicitly. The effect of such protection is to reduce risky investments. But risk-taking may be in the best interests of all the parties concerned. Therefore, a preformulated rule should not protect creditors from bad investments. . . .

A broad fraudulent conveyance rule does not provide an incentive for creditors to do the monitoring they are capable of doing. If creditors always can undo transactions afterwards, they have every incentive to wait and upset only those transactions that turn out unfavorably for their perspective. . . .

Extending fraudulent conveyance law beyond preventing sham transactions and gratuitous transfers by insolvents is a step that should be taken only with caution.

These problems are all in addition to the enormous practical problem of determining whether a debtor is insolvent at any given time. . . .

. . . [V]aluations necessarily involve uncertainty. How much a piece of property is worth depends both on when the valuation is made and on how much is known by the person making the valuation. . . .

Monday morning quarterbacking is easy. . . . Even if judges do not have the bias that usually accompanies valuations after the fact, the process of valuing assets is an uncertain one. This uncertainty imposes costs on the parties, which somehow must be offset by the gains from reexamining closed deals.

As we have seen, however, that principle itself is suspect. The fallacy of imposing a general duty on those who transact with a debtor who is later determined to have been insolvent to pay fair consideration or be at risk for the difference stems from the notion that a rule permitting creditors to overturn bad deals is needed when the debtor is insolvent to prevent him from acting against the interests of the creditors. But this proves too much. A debtor's incentives almost never parallel his creditors' interests. . . .

III. FORECLOSURE SALES

All debtors have an incentive to take risks that are not in the interest of either the creditors or the creditors and debtor collectively. . . . Fraudulent conveyance law can be understood as a response to the incentives for advantage-taking that exist whenever a debtor-creditor relationship arises. It is only a partial response, however. . . .

The inconsistency between an expansive ban on transfers of property of insolvent debtors for less than fair consideration, whether voluntary or involuntary, and the rules governing creditors' remedies is apparent from the recent controversy over whether to treat some foreclosure sales as fraudulent conveyances. . . .

If one adopts the view that the prohibition on transfers for less than fair consideration . . . merely implements, in rule fashion, the principle embodied in the prohibition on transfers intended to hinder, delay, or defraud creditors, then the problem of whether to treat foreclosure of a debtor's equity of redemption as a fraudulent conveyance is quite straightforward. Such foreclosure cannot be a fraudulent conveyance. Bank has given the world notice of its interest and merely is exercising rights that every other creditor knows Bank already has. . . .

But section 4 does more than function as a per se rule derived from section 7. Therefore, deciding whether a foreclosure sale can be a fraudulent conveyance when there has been only debtor-passivity requires identifying the principles underlying fraudulent conveyance law. It might be argued, as it increasingly has been, that debtor-passivity alone should be enough to trigger the provision. . . . Before the foreclosure sale, Debtor had an asset that was worth 50,000 dollars to him. . . . After the sale, the asset vanished and Debtor gained nothing in return. The injury to the creditors is the same regardless whether Debtor actively colluded with Bank or whether he simply did nothing while the foreclosure sale was taking place. Under this view, the foreclosure sale should be set aside because the extinguishing of the debtor's right of redemption . . . is a "transfer" of property that disadvantages the creditors as a group. . . . Hence the total amount received by the creditors as a group diminishes.

Yet this approach suffers from several problems. As we have shown, a rule that looks simply to whether the creditors are as well off after a transfer as before is, as a principle, overbroad and must be articulated in some narrower fashion. Moreover, this transaction historically was not considered a fraudulent conveyance in the absence of collusion between Bank and Debtor. Section 4 of the Uniform Fraudulent Conveyance Act and the analogous provisions of the Bankruptcy Code are subject to the interpretation that foreclosure of a debtor's equity of redemption might be a fraudulent conveyance, but one easily can argue that that would be an incorrect interpretation. . . . Under both section 4 and section 548 of the Bankruptcy Code, one can argue that the price realized at a properly conducted foreclosure sale is always for "fair consideration" or "reasonably equivalent value."

Choosing between the two possible interpretations . . . should begin with an inquiry into why a foreclosure sale ever should be subject to judicial scrutiny after the fact. . . . [P]rotecting the rights of the debtor in a foreclosure sale through fraudulent conveyance law may be counterproductive. One effect of a rule that subjects all foreclosure sales to the possibility of being set aside at some later time may be to depress the price realized at these sales still further. . . .

Rules governing the sale of collateral area compromise between facilitating secured credit and protecting the interests of the debtor and those who have claims against him. . . .

. . . [I]t seems unlikely that fraudulent conveyance statutes ever were intended to be a part of this balance between a secured creditor on the one hand and the debtor and his other creditors on the other. Hence, it seems unwise to conscript those laws for this purpose now. They are not part of the off-the-rack terms that govern the problem. Most fraudulent conveyance statutes were passed long before rules governing the sale of collateral were created, and the statutes never applied to noncollusive foreclosure sales until decades after the sale-of-collateral rules were adopted. There is no evidence in the interim that creditors thought this kind of problem warranted the fraudulent conveyance remedy. There is no evidence of a need for such a preformulated rule. Introducing a broad prohibition on transfers for less than fair consideration in this case extends a general standard into an area in which a specific rule already has been promulgated without any evidence that creditors think such a prohibition is worth its costs. A careful balance already has been struck that is designed to address exactly the same problems it is now argued should be attacked through fraudulent conveyance laws.

To be sure, the costs that foreclosure sales impose on creditors of an insolvent (and often passive) debtor might be substantial. These costs are of two sorts. First, a foreclosure sale, like any other action that repays a particular creditor, results in fewer assets being available for others. . . . Preferring one creditor over another, without more, however, is not a fraudulent conveyance.

. . . A simple preference makes some creditors worse off, but it does not make the debtor better off nor does it necessarily disadvantage the creditors as a group. Preferences do undermine collective proceedings, and, accordingly, it is clear why preferences generally are prohibited only in bankruptcy or other collective proceedings.

Individual creditor remedies, however, make other creditors worse off for another reason besides the fact that money which might have gone to them is transferred to someone else. This second and frequently neglected cost is the expense and wastefulness of the individual creditor remedies themselves. . . .

These costs exist whether Debtor actively cooperates or is completely passive. When these costs are large enough, a bankruptcy proceeding is in order. Indeed, these costs justify the bulk of bankruptcy laws. But the imposition of these costs on a debtor and his other creditors is part and parcel of a legal regime in which individual creditors are permitted to and, indeed, must safeguard their own interests. In this regime, other creditors are exposed to two types of risks: the risk that others will be preferred and the risk that the act of preferring another will increase their costs. The fraudulent conveyance remedy—voiding the transaction—is not the appropriate one for this problem. If either cost looms too high, the remedy of the creditors is to file a bankruptcy petition and collectivize the process.

Foreclosure of a debtor's equity of redemption and the sale of property at a sheriff's sale following levy and execution impose identical costs on an insolvent debtor's other creditors. Neither transaction is a fraudulent conveyance because the preference cost and the collection cost they impose are necessary when individual creditors must pursue their own remedies. If the conditions are ripe for a collective proceeding when the foreclosure sale is to take place, the debtor should be put into bankruptcy. But if the conditions are not ripe, the transactions that take place under an individual debt-collection regime should be respected as long as they are properly conducted under the specific rules that govern them. In a world such as this, general creditors have a greater burden of monitoring their debtor so that they can act (either by pursuing individual remedies or by joining with other creditors in a bankruptcy petition) than they would if a general standard protected them and put others at risk of a debtor dissipating his assets. But monitoring a debtor and his general financial condition is precisely what general creditors are able to do effectively. Those that cannot monitor effectively have other alternatives available to them, such as taking a security interest.

IV. THE LEVERAGED BUYOUT

. . . Even under the narrowest view of fraudulent conveyance law, the leveraged buyout may be a fraudulent conveyance. The managers and the old shareholders are made better off (by virtue of having a highly leveraged investment) and the general creditors are made worse off. The transaction "hinders" the creditors in the sense that it leaves them with fewer assets than before, and this may be the intent behind the transaction. . . . There are two sections containing per se rules that might lead to the characterization of the leveraged buyout as a fraudulent conveyance. One, embodied in section 4 of the Uniform Fraudulent Conveyance Act, provides that any transfer made by a debtor while insolvent without receiving fair consideration is a fraudulent conveyance. In a better world, a leveraged buyout never would run afoul of this provision. . . .

In a world in which information is imperfect, however, it may not be clear whether Firm is solvent. Indeed, even if liabilities exceed assets at fair valuation, the stock still might trade for a positive price because of the possibility that the value of the assets might prove larger than expected or the liabilities less. If the managers are mistaken and buy out the shareholders of Firm when it is insolvent, the leveraged buyout seems to fall within section 4.

Another per se rule, embodied in section 5 of the Uniform Fraudulent Conveyance Act, may reach the leveraged buyout, even when the transaction does not render Firm insolvent but simply leaves it with "an unreasonably small capital.". . .

As a matter of sound practice, lawyers must ensure that a firm acquired in a leveraged buyout is not insolvent or rendered insolvent and that managers and others put up enough capital so that the firm is not too thinly capitalized. An important conceptual question is whether a leveraged buyout in fact presents fraudulent conveyance problems or comes under a per se rule that turns out to be overbroad as applied to this particular case. A firm that incurs obligations in the course of a buyout does not seem at all like the Elizabethan deadbeat who sells his sheep to his brother for a pittance.

The question, in other words, is whether a corporate debtor that incurs additional debt in a leveraged buyout can be presumed either to be engaging in a manipulation by which it (or its shareholders) will profit at its creditors' expense or in some other transfer that its creditors would almost always want to ban. At one level, the answer to this question is straightforward. This transaction does hinder the general creditors of Firm. After the transaction, the general creditors are less likely to be paid. . . .

Moreover, Firm, or more precisely, its owners (the old and new shareholders), benefit to the extent that the general creditors are disadvantaged. . . .

It thus might seem a good thing that these transactions appear to trigger sections of existing fraudulent conveyance statutes. But we doubt this is the case. These transactions do not seem to be clearly to the detriment of creditors, nor did we always see creditors treating such transactions as events of default in their loan agreements, even before the issue was moved to the domain of fraudulent conveyance law. With the buyout may come more streamlined and more effective management. Among other things, a going-private transaction may save the costs of complying with relevant federal securities statutes.

. . . If in a particular case those creditors who were in a position to control this conduct did not, one might conclude that these creditors should not be able to set this transaction aside. If they had the knowledge and the sophistication to control such conduct, but did not, there seems to be little reason for fraudulent conveyance law to control it for them. . . .

. . . [O]ne might argue that the fraudulent conveyance remedy is an appropriate off-the-rack term that creditors should presumptively have. A difficulty with this approach, however, is that the fraudulent conveyance remedy is very hard to contract out of. Even if it were in the interests of everyone that the leveraged buyout take place, a debtor would not be able to ensure that the transaction would be immune to a fraudulent conveyance attack. In bankruptcy, the trustee has the power to set aside the entire transaction, even if at the time of the actual transaction every existing creditor waived its right to set the transaction aside. . . . Nevertheless, the inability of creditors to contract around the fraudulent conveyance remedy when it is in their interest may suggest that fraudulent conveyance law should be applied in bankruptcy to a narrow range of cases in which there is little chance that creditors would find the transfer in their interest. In those cases in which it is not clear whether creditors would want to prevent the activity, all the creditors may be protected if a single one prohibits the transaction. The fraudulent conveyance remedy is far easier to contract into than it is to contract out of.

V. CONCLUSION

Ultimately, it is the inability of parties to opt out of fraudulent conveyance law that leads us to think that its reach should be limited. Fraudulent conveyance law should never apply to arms-length transactions, even if it appears after the fact that the debtor's actions injured the creditors. A broader rule than this one might pick up more cases of fraudulent behavior by debtors and might allow fewer transactions that creditors would want to prohibit, but it would do so only at the cost of preventing some desirable transactions from taking place. A broader rule subjects parties who bargain noncollusively and in good faith to the risk that a court later will find that the buyer paid too little. The uncertainty such a rule imposes makes debtors and creditors as a group worse off. When an individual engages in a financial transaction with multiple parties (as in the case of an insider guarantee or a leveraged buyout), the transaction generally should not be viewed as a fraudulent conveyance provided that the transferee parted with value when he entered into the transaction and that the transaction was entered in the ordinary course.

Barry L. Zaretsky
Fraudulent Transfer Law as the Arbiter of Unreasonable Risk
46 S.C. L. Rev. 1165 (1995)[*]

Fraudulent transfer law is hot. A body of law that originated to prevent deadbeat debtors from putting their property beyond the reach of creditors has, in recent years, been applied to a wide range of modern business transactions that do not appear to reflect the motivation of the original fraudulent transfer laws. . . .

. . . In this Article, I embark upon the first stage of an exploration of the purpose of fraudulent transfer law and, in particular, the purpose of the constructive fraud tests, by considering the role of fraudulent transfer law in regulating the level of risk taken by debtors. I suggest that fraudulent transfer law addresses a range of transactions that, although not engaged in with any malevolent intent, necessarily have the effect of improperly or unfairly interfering with creditors' abilities to collect on their claims by unreasonably increasing the risk faced by creditors. By monitoring the level of risk undertaken by debtors, application of the constructive fraud provisions to modern transactions may

---

serve an important purpose not explicitly contemplated when these provisions were initially promulgated. . . .

PART II

REGULATION OF RISK

In general, the constructive fraud provisions are intended to address transfers that, although perhaps not made with any malevolent intent, necessarily have the effect of improperly and adversely affecting creditors. . . .

What does it mean, then, to characterize a transaction as improperly or unfairly interfering with creditors? I suspect that there is a range of improper and unfair interferences. The mere diminution (at least unjustified) of the debtor's estate when the debtor is financially impaired, depriving creditors of the ability to collect on their claims, suggests impropriety or, at least, unfairness, at least when there is no justification for the diminution. . . .

The traditional cases did not consider some of the situations that arise in modern cases, where the transfer or obligation is part of a larger investment transaction. These involve not merely transfers of property, but the undertaking of business risks that, in some cases, may not be entirely unusual or improper.

. . . Creditors expect their debtors to take risks and should not be heard to complain when risks are taken.

Thus, fraudulent transfer law does not bar debtors from taking risks with their creditors' funds. It does, however, regulate the permissible degree of risk. Under this view, the improper and unfair interference with creditors' rights that is addressed by fraudulent transfer law occurs when a debtor takes not merely risks, but unreasonable risks, with assets that would otherwise be available to satisfy creditors' claims.

This approach assures that analysis of a transaction through the prism of fraudulent transfer law need not lead necessarily to avoidance of a transaction. A court may find that a risky transaction ultimately depriving creditors of satisfaction of their claims was not unreasonably risky when it occurred. If the constructive fraud tests adequately reflect the policy of addressing only unreasonable risk, then a transaction that is not unreasonably risky would not be avoidable under fraudulent transfer law.

By addressing unreasonable risks, fraudulent transfer law can be viewed as providing credit transactions and agreements with an off-the-rack term requiring the debtor to limit itself to reasonable business or financial risks. This limitation is very likely consistent with the terms that creditors and a debtor would negotiate were they sufficiently prescient and sophisticated to do so. . . .

This implied term represents an important creditor protection. When creditors extend credit to debtors, they expect the debtors to take risks with their money. To the extent that the parties can predict the types of risks that might be taken, the parties may limit the debtor's ability to take risks through the use of covenants in a loan agreement. In some cases, however, such limitations may be commercially or practically unrealistic. . . .

Additionally, a term implied through fraudulent transfer law yields remedies that would be unavailable in a debtor-creditor agreement. A debtor-creditor agreement would enable creditors to declare a default and enforce their remedies against the debtor if the debtor violated the agreement. However, if the debtor transferred property to a good faith purchaser, unsecured creditors could not recover it merely because the credit agreement was violated. The agreement risks creating a wrong without a remedy. Fraudulent transfer law seeks to identify the wrong and to provide a meaningful remedy.

Thus, . . . fraudulent transfer law may be viewed as implying a requirement that a debtor taking risks with its creditor's funds limit itself to reasonable risks. It may also provide the meaningful remedy that would otherwise be unavailable to the injured parties.

The constructive fraud standards attempt to describe these unreasonably risky transactions. Notice what transactions are included in the constructive fraud provisions: transfers for which the debtor fails to receive reasonably equivalent value and after which the debtor (1) is insolvent; (2) is left with unreasonably small assets to continue its business; or (3) intends or expects to incur debts beyond its ability to pay as the debts become due. A transaction fitting any of these tests is not simply risky, it is unreasonably risky because there is a high probability that the transaction will inhibit the debtor's ability to pay its creditors. . . .

The unreasonable risk flows from the substantial impairment of the debtor's ability to service its debt after the transaction. . . . The constructive fraud provisions suggest that when a debtor puts at unreasonable risk the property needed to satisfy its creditors, the transaction in which it does so may be avoided by the adversely affected creditors. Viewed in this light, it is possible to reconcile the application of fraudulent transfer law to a wide range of corporate as well as individual transactions. . . .

PART III

APPLICATION OF CONSTRUCTIVE FRAUD STANDARDS

. . . Many transactions that have been examined through the lens of fraudulent transfer law have not involved actual fraudulent intent nor were they, by their generic nature, necessarily doomed to fail and consequently to harm creditors. Some of these transactions may have been so unobjectionable in theory that, if asked in advance if a debtor should be permitted to engage in the type of transaction at issue, creditors might have been expected to say yes.

In some cases, however, the financial condition of the debtor may have made these transactions not merely risky, but so unreasonably risky as to become objectionable even to creditors who recognize that their debtor will take risks with their funds. A review of the application of fraudulent transfer law to leveraged buyouts and intercorporate guarantees illustrates how it can be applied to transactions in a manner that permits risky transactions to proceed without objection, but also protects creditors against truly unreasonable risks.

a. Leveraged Buyouts

One of the most controversial extensions of fraudulent transfer law beyond actually fraudulent transactions involves leveraged buyouts (LBOs). In an LBO, a target company's stock is purchased and paid for by a third-party acquiror, primarily using financing secured by the assets of the target. . . .

The common theme in these transactions is that the old shareholders are cashed out, the new shareholders put up little of their own funds, and the target's assets secure the claims of the lenders who supplied the funds for the purchase. By securing with its assets the LBO debt and using the proceeds primarily to cash out the old shareholders, the target reduces the unsecured creditors, who previously were senior to the shareholders, to a position that is junior to the financier of the transaction and, in effect, to the old shareholders who have been satisfied ahead of the creditors. The priority positions of the old shareholders and the creditors thus are reversed.

An LBO offers several potential benefits for parties to the transaction. . . . [I]f the LBO works as planned, the LBO may not adversely affect creditors and others who deal with the target because they may eventually face a stronger debtor or customer.

However, a transaction involving substantial leverage is inherently risky. High leverage ratios increase the possibility of business failure. If the business does fail, the non-LBO creditors, some of whom may have unsecured claims against the target predating the LBO, are likely to share the cost of failure.

Although an LBO imposes risk on creditors, creditors who lend on an unsecured basis must recognize that the debtor will take risks that may affect them adversely. One potential risk is that the debtor will use assets otherwise available to creditors generally to secure new obligations and that the debtor will more highly leverage itself. This alone is not objectionable; leverage is not unusual in business and may, under appropriate circumstances, enable a business to increase its return on equity. Thus, some commentators have concluded that LBOs, which take advantage of high leverage ratios, are simply not a type of transaction that, absent actual fraud, should be subject to attack under fraudulent transfer law.

This conclusion, however, flows from a narrow view of fraudulent transfer law that would limit its scope to transactions involving fraudulent intent. Under this view, the constructive fraud provisions primarily provide the evidence of fraudulent intent that was sought under early fraudulent transfer law. . . .

. . . Under this approach if the constructive fraud provisions applied at all, it would be only when the transaction already appeared suspicious.

This narrow originalist view of fraudulent transfer law also seems to have been based on an assumption that application of fraudulent transfer law to LBOs would lead to invalidation of all LBOs. . . .

Instead of this narrow view of fraudulent transfer law, limiting its reach to transactions actually or constructively intended to hinder, delay, or defraud creditors, a broader purpose may be recognized. Fraudulent transfer law may represent a useful means of distinguishing between those legitimate business transactions that present reasonable, acceptable risks and those that present an unreasonable level of risk. . . .

Under this approach, high leverage ratios caused by an LBO would not render an LBO transaction avoidable per se. However, unreasonably high leverage is another matter. Unreasonably high leverage shifts virtually all of the risk of failure to creditors, instead of the sharing of risk between creditors and equity that exists in more reasonable transactions. . . . [F]raudulent transfer law seems to suggest that there is a level of unreasonable risk to which creditors should not be subjected.

This rationale may not be far from the original purposes of fraudulent transfer law. Early law proscribed not only transactions intended to defraud, but those intended to hinder or delay creditors. A transaction with unreasonably high leverage, or one that imposes unreasonable risk, may be viewed as one that was intentionally done and, because of its unreasonable level of risk, one that hinders, delays, or perhaps, defrauds creditors. Certainly, there is a level of leverage or risk that virtually assures that creditors will be unlikely to recover in a timely fashion.

Cases considering the application of fraudulent transfer law to LBOs seem to have begun to recognize that fraudulent transfer law provides a standard for distinguishing between transactions that are so risky as to be objectionable from the perspective of creditors and those that represent reasonable business risk. . . .

One might argue that in modern arms-length transactions, the parties would never take unreasonable risks in the absence of some fraud. After all, those who acquire companies in LBOs often invest at least some of their own funds. They project substantial profits if the transaction succeeds and understand that they will lose their investment if the transaction fails. Similarly, lenders part with real value in financing these transactions and face the risk that they will not be repaid or will at least face substantial delay and expense if the transaction fails. It seems unlikely that investors or lenders would knowingly and intentionally place their funds at unreasonable risk. This suggests that although these transactions may be subjected to fraudulent transfer analysis if the business ultimately fails, many should pass the fraudulent transfer test.

Yet the cases suggest that even in the absence of actual fraudulent intent, sophisticated commercial parties may sometimes induce a debtor to take unreasonable risk. In some transactions the parties may simply fail adequately to analyze the transaction and the debtor's financial condition in order to appreciate the level of risk that they are undertaking. This may result from a failure to use sufficient care in evaluating the transaction. In some cases the deal may be so far along and have so much invested already that by the time warning signs appear the parties choose to ignore the warnings and proceed with the deal. Other institutional interests also may propel a deal forward even after it no longer seems well advised. . . .

As the examiner in *In re Revco D.S., Inc.*, I found evidence of a similar failure to take account of a debtor's inability to meet targeted performance just prior to an LBO and reliance on projections developed without attention to this failure. These types of situations, in which parties, without fraudulent intent, fail to heed warning signs in their zeal to complete the deal, may be exactly the situations in which fraudulent transfer law can regulate the risk imposed on creditors by these failures.

Even when the parties accurately evaluate a transaction, there is incentive for investors to engage in a transaction that may be unreasonably risky. This is because the risk-reward ratio faced by LBO investors may be more favorable than that faced by non-LBO creditors. An equity investor in an LBO will typically invest few if any of its own assets. That is the nature of leverage. If the deal fails, the investor loses relatively little. Yet if the deal succeeds the investor may reap substantial profits. Similarly, an LBO lender will often receive collateral as well as a high interest rate and substantial fees. The risk that this senior collateralized lender will not be repaid is relatively small while the potential profits are large. Thus, these investors may pursue a transaction even if there is a relatively high risk of failure if the expected return for them is significantly higher than the cost of investing.

However, from the perspective of non-LBO creditors, the loss upon failure of the enterprise is likely to be substantial while the potential reward from success is small. Prior to the LBO these creditors stood to be repaid in full by a healthy debtor. After the LBO they could receive no more than full payment but face greater risk of non-payment. If this increased risk, the probability that the enterprise might fail, is unreasonably high, fraudulent transfer law may provide some remedy.

b. Corporate Guarantees

An approach to fraudulent transfer law that seeks to distinguish between reasonably and unreasonably risky transactions can also aid in the analysis of intercorporate guarantees. Lenders to members of a corporate group often require credit support, or guarantees, from other members of the group. . . .

An approach to fraudulent transfer law that seeks to determine whether a transaction was unreasonably risky provides a useful framework for analysis of these intercorporate guarantees. When the loan at issue is a working capital loan to a group that historically has operated as a corporate group, upstream or cross-stream guarantees normally will not be the unexpected, unreasonably risky type of transaction that is objectionable under fraudulent transfer law. Creditors of individual subsidiaries should not be surprised to learn that their debtor also is responsible jointly for some relatively normal business debts of the other members of the corporate group. This arrangement is common for a modern corporate group and is valuable for all of the members. All may find additional credit availability, resources, and synergies as a result of their group membership, making the risk more reasonable from the perspective of creditors of each of the subsidiaries. . . .

Another way to analyze these guarantees is to consider whether they are a type of obligation that is reasonably expected by creditors, one to which creditors likely would agree if they were asked when they extended credit to the debtor. If the guaranty is part of a transaction that is ordinary and reasonably expectable and that strengthens the corporate group as a whole, then it should not normally be objectionable from the perspective of creditors. Nevertheless, even though the guaranty transaction may be reasonably expectable and should normally be unobjectionable, the transaction may become unreasonable and objectionable if the financial structure of the corporate group is such that unreasonable risk is imposed on creditors of particular members of the group. In terms used by fraudulent transfer law, if certain corporate group members receive no reasonably equivalent benefit and the new liability renders them financially impaired, the guaranty may create the type of unreasonable risk to creditors of those members that is proscribed by fraudulent transfer law. This might result, for example, if the financial strength of some subsidiaries was being diverted to prop up other subsidiaries with seriously troubled finances.

Intragroup guarantees of loans that are not for working capital may be less expectable and may have to satisfy a higher financial standard to be found to involve reasonable risk. When the obligation guaranteed is not a working capital loan for the group, but is a more unusual transaction, the additional obligation may not be reasonably expectable by creditors and, therefore, may require a more careful showing that the guarantor received actual value reasonably equivalent to the obligation undertaken or that the guarantor was financially sound after the transaction. . . .

Of course, courts have recognized that this analysis must consider the actual nature of the obligation undertaken by the guarantor in determining the degree of risk and whether any value it received was reasonably equivalent to the obligation assumed. This requires an analysis, as of the time that the transaction was entered into, of the likelihood that the debt will be repaid by the principal debtor and the availability of contribution from other members of the corporate group. . . .

One factor in determining whether the guarantor received reasonably equivalent value is the economic viability of the corporate group. If no viable enterprise exists, so that the ultimate effect of the guaranty is simply to shift assets from creditors of the guarantor to creditors of the principal debtor, then it will be difficult to find that the guarantor received value in exchange for undertaking an obligation and, perhaps, transferring property to secure that obligation. . . .

The thrust of this analysis is that normally a parent corporation receives value from the guaranty of a subsidiary's debt because the funds borrowed by the subsidiary increase the value of the parent's equity interest in the subsidiary. If the subsidiary is insolvent, the additional funds cannot add to the parent's equity interest an amount equal to the obligation assumed by the parent because the funds borrowed by the subsidiary must first be applied to satisfy the claims of creditors of the subsidiary before the parent-equity holder can receive any benefit. . . .

. . . [I]f the investment is obviously a loser from the start, the guaranty represents an unreasonable risk because there is little or no potential benefit for the parent in assuming the guaranty liability. Alternatively, if the investment had some reasonable prospect of success, then the parent might still have received value in the form of the opportunity to make the investment and take the risk in the first place even if the venture later failed without ultimate benefit to the parent. . . .

PART IV
LIMITATIONS OF UNREASONABLE RISK ANALYSIS

Recognition that fraudulent transfer law is intended to regulate unreasonable risk but to permit reasonable risk-taking by debtors ameliorates some of the problems with applying fraudulent transfer law to modern transactions. However, this does not eliminate all problems created by this body of law. In particular, the application of fraudulent transfer law to relatively normal business transactions may increase the cost or inhibit the completion of some of those transactions by forcing a lender to increase its price for a loan to account for the increased risk imposed by fraudulent transfer law. . . . Consequently, otherwise beneficial transactions may be deterred because of the increased risk imposed by fraudulent transfer law.

The risk of fraudulent transfer avoidance is particularly difficult for parties to quantify because fraudulent transfer law permits an after-the-fact re-evaluation of the value given and of the debtor's financial standing, both of which may be colored by hindsight. . . .

Even if some level of regulation seems appropriate, it will be necessary to analyze whether the constructive fraud standards are the optimal measure of unreasonable risk. Moreover, more careful analysis is needed to determine whether fraudulent transfer costs are imposed on the correct parties and whether the remedies provided by fraudulent transfer law effectively implement its policies. At this point, it may be of some value simply to recognize why fraudulent transfer law considers some transactions "unfair" and authorizes attacks on them.

Robert M. Lawless & Stephen P. Ferris
Economics and the Rhetoric of Valuation
5 J. BANKR. L. & PRAC. 3 (1995)[*]

An asset ultimately has only one value—its market value. To be sure, an asset may bring different prices in different types of sales, but these different prices do not arise because the asset has different values. Rather, the pricing differences result from the circumstances surrounding the sale or the varying expectations of market participants. Price and value are different concepts, which the confusing rhetoric of valuation mistakenly intermingles in an unduly formalistic inquiry that Section 506(a) does not mandate. Valuation issues require subjective, normative judgments to resolve.
. . .

. . . [A]s presently formulated, the valuation inquiry is a two-step mental process. In addition to the evidentiary questions, the bankruptcy court also selects a legal standard by which to measure value (*e.g.*, liquidation value, replacement value, or retail value). The court will apply the evidence presented at the valuation hearing to the legal standard selected and arrive at an appropriate valuation. It is the quest for a legal standard at which we take aim and fire. The quest is chimerical, nothing more than the confusing rhetoric of valuation. As we discuss later, the idea that the same asset can have different values simultaneously is economic nonsense. Courts would do better to focus only on the evidentiary question of what compromises an asset's value.

Value, Markets, and Prices

The Concept of Valuation

Beginning with the first principles, one must distinguish between an asset's value and its price. The value of an asset is simply the present value of its future cash flows. The price of an asset is the amount of money that the asset will obtain in an open market transaction. . . .

. . . The observed transaction price associated with the transfer of an asset's ownership thus will represent a market consensus resulting from negotiation between various individuals. To further refine this concept, one must ask how each individual establishes his own estimate of an asset's value. An individual will require estimates of the timing, amount, and riskiness of the asset's cash flows to calculate the asset's value, because these elements are the necessary inputs into the calculation of present value. Thus, an asset's value is originally investor specific, because judgments regarding the elements of present value will be subjective and vary across individuals. Once an investor has estimated an asset's value, the investor must compare this estimate to the asset's market price.

If the marketplace for an asset is efficient, it ultimately will force a convergence between the market price and the value estimated by investors. What do we mean by an "efficient market?" An efficient market addresses the availability and timeliness of information. In an efficient market, information flows freely and is widely available to interested parties. Prices are publicly quoted and free to change in response to the public release of relevant information. There are no monopolies or regulatory agencies that restrict or delay the dissemination of information that is relevant to an

---

    *   Reprinted by permission of the copyright holder, West Group, and the Journal of Bankruptcy Law & Practice.

evaluation of an asset's risk and return. Likewise, informational asymmetries between buyers and sellers do not exist.

If an investor's estimate of value differs from market value, then competition between investors will force their alignment. . . . Thus, in equilibrium, the market price will equal the investor's estimate of value.

When Markets Fail

Although an extensive economics literature discusses market failure, our interest is restricted to an analysis of how that failure can effect asset valuation. More specifically, we are interested in the conditions that prevent market prices from serving as an unbiased measure of an asset's value. An asset's true worth always remains hidden. In estimating an asset's value, bankruptcy courts must work with market prices as estimates of true worth. But to what extent can observable market prices serve as reliable estimates of true worth?

The preceding section developed how an efficient market causes market prices to converge to the best measure of true worth. For the market mechanism to function effectively and for the resulting observed prices to be true measures of an asset's worth, we observed that the market must be "efficient."

To start with, the marketplace must be characterized by an adequate number of participants. . . .

There also must be freedom in the mobility of financial resources if market prices are to be true indications of an asset's value. . . .

Perhaps most importantly, an efficient market mechanism requires the widespread dispersion of relevant knowledge. . . .

Related to these preceding factors is the length of time an asset has exposure in the marketplace. In many ways, this is not a distinct requirement for market prices to allocate resources efficiently but rather incorporates consideration of information adequacy and the extent of participation. . . .

Applying the Basic Principles to Some Common Fact Patterns

The principles developed in the previous text are of interest to bankruptcy lawyers and judges only if these principles help to illuminate the issue of bankruptcy valuation. The following text applies these economic ideas to several situations that often arise in bankruptcy court. . . .

Real Estate Foreclosures and Fraudulent Transfers

Then there is the issue presented by *BFP v. Resolution Trust Corp.* Suppose Thomas Real Estate Corp. owns real property subject to a first mortgage held by Lender. The mortgage secures Thomas's obligation to Lender. Thomas defaults on the obligation, and Lender commences state-law foreclosure proceedings. At this foreclosure sale, the real estate is sold either to Lender, or to a third party for $430,000. Now insolvent, Thomas files a bankruptcy petition within one year of the foreclosure sale. Section 548 now allows the bankruptcy trustee (or Thomas if it is a debtor-in-possession) to bring a fraudulent transfer action to avoid any transfer if it was made for "less than a reasonably equivalent value." The bankruptcy trustee asserts that the actual "value" of the property is $725,000, and therefore the $430,000 sales price at the foreclosure sale is not a reasonably equivalent value for the real estate.

BFP bars such an action. In *BFP* the Supreme Court ruled that the foreclosure sales price is deemed to be the property's value. . . . Because the Supreme Court has spoken, our most prudent course of action would be to move on, but we will imp(r)udently charge ahead. . . . The analysis suggested in the preceding pages exposes its false logic.

As noted before, sales prices represent investors' or purchasers' best estimates of an asset's true, hidden worth. As humans with limited knowledge, we cannot know true worth with any certainty, and we must rely on observable market prices as estimates of true worth. Even Justice Scalia, *BFP*'s author, recognizes that the foreclosure sale market is relatively inefficient.

A foreclosure sale exhibits several of the characteristics of a failed market. Most significantly, the real estate to be sold has limited exposure in the marketplace. . . . Another cause of market failure for the foreclosure market is the inadequate number of participants. . . .

Returning to the issue in *BFP*, we need to ask ourselves whether the foreclosure sales price can be interpreted as a reliable, investor estimate of the real estate's true worth. Because Justice Scalia recognizes the pervasive market failure present in a foreclosure sale, one would expect him to answer this question with an appropriately negative response. But Justice Scalia departs from the line of inquiry by mistaking sales price for value; he misinterprets the foreclosure sales price as a market consensus of value.

To illustrate our point, suppose that the law provided your authors the exclusive right, for their own personal use, to purchase any Barry Manilow record offered for sale. Now, your authors would not pay more than five cents for a Barry Manilow record that they could not immediately resell. Nevertheless, your authors would have a legal entitlement to purchase all Barry Manilow records, and because the entitlement is exclusive, no one could sell a Barry Manilow record for more than five cents. Because the market for such records would be characterized by pervasive market failure, it would not be accurate to say that five cents is a good estimate of these records' true worth. In our example, the legal regime would not allow the market for Barry Manilow records to operate efficiently.

The *BFP* case presents the same problem. Legal rules may insulate the foreclosure sale from attack and give a foreclosure sale purchaser the ability to make bargain purchases. It begs the question, however, to take Justice Scalia's position that because the legal rules result in bargain prices at foreclosure sales, the purchaser therefore has a right to purchase at the bargain price. The better question is to ask whether the rules should allow the bargain price to begin with. The relevant statute dictates no clear answer, a point Justice Scalia concedes, leaving it the judiciary to develop the best rule.

As a normative matter, the answer to the question posed should be no. We can think of no reason of distributive or corrective justice that would give a secured lender or a third party the right to use the foreclosure sales as their own "bargain basement." Indeed, because most foreclosure sale gains would come at the expense of the mortgagor (or the mortgagor's other creditors), it seems substantively unfair to allow such bargain purchases. Also, in the specific context of fraudulent transfer liability, it does not further federal bankruptcy policies to insulate foreclosure sales from attack. Fraudulent transfer liability helps to prevent strategic debtor and creditor behavior that could harm the interests of unsecured creditors as a class. Foreclosure sales present an opportunity for such strategic behavior. There is no reason to place them beyond fraudulent transfer attack.

The best reasons for insulating an foreclosure sale from attack are pragmatic ones. . . .

The pragmatic reasons ultimately devolve into an empirical question. Do the social gains from maximizing foreclosure sales prices outweigh the social costs of the injustice done in individual cases when bargains are realized at foreclosure sales?

David Gray Carlson
Is Fraudulent Conveyance Law Efficient?
9 CARDOZO L. REV. 643 (1987)[*]

This article will not attack the legal status quo . . . . But it will attack the assumption that the norm of efficiency can explain or justify fraudulent conveyance law. The end result of my study is to show that we can never know whether fraudulent conveyance law is efficient. . . . The efficiency justification for fraudulent conveyance law is too contingent upon assumptions of human wants and desires, which change from society to society, from year to year, and even from week to week. . . .

By maintaining that efficiency norms do not explain fraudulent conveyance law, I do not mean to suggest in any way that fraudulent conveyance law is therefore without normative justification. On the contrary, fraudulent conveyance law redistributes power from positionally strong debtors to positionally weak creditors on the principle that repayment of debt is privileged over the debtor's freedom to alienate his property. These values are important in any society where it is felt that a person should live up to her word of honor. . . .

I. UTILITY AND EFFICIENCY

. . . If the proposed change produces a net gain to society, then the change is "efficient.". . .

Cost-benefit comparisons of the sort we are about to indulge in are merely one of two traditional elements of efficiency. The first one—which shall not be used here—is the Pareto definition: An allocation is efficient if and only if there are no losers and only winners. . . .

Instead, we shall use the Kaldor-Hicks definition of efficiency: A move is efficient if gains exceed losses. Such a definition presupposes that society benefits when resources are moved to higher valuing users from lower valuing users. Whether the loser is compensated is beside the point. . . .

In my efficiency model, I assume that any loss that is offset by an even larger gain is justifiable. . . .

II. A DESCRIPTION OF FRAUDULENT CONVEYANCE LAW
A. *The Remedy*

The normative command of fraudulent conveyance law is that insolvent debtors should not make gifts, nor should they launder gifts or other corrupt deals through co-conspiring third parties (bulk sales). A chief element in my claim that no good efficiency case for fraudulent conveyance law exists is that creditors cannot easily predict that they will benefit from a remedy currently supplied by the law. Hence, if we were to repeal fraudulent conveyance law, there would be no great rise in the cost of unsecured credit. . . .

To summarize my comments on the fraudulent conveyance remedy, the debtor bears no liability for making fraudulent conveyances because the debtor is already liable to his creditors in the first place. The creditor gets an advantage from the fraudulent conveyance remedy when (a) the debtor makes a gift or a bulk sale to a bad faith purchaser for value or donee who can be located; (b) that purchaser still retains the property (or (i) does not retain the property and is solvent, or (ii) is insolvent but has transferred the property to a non-BFP); (c) the creditor is in a position to obtain a judicial lien, *i.e.*, she has a judgment against the debtor or the advantage of a prejudgment lien; (d)

---

   *   This article originally appeared in 9 Cardozo L. Rev. 643 (1987). Reprinted with permission of the Cardozo Law Review.

no other creditor of the debtor has obtained a lien before the creditor in question; (e) the debtor has not filed for bankruptcy or been forced into an involuntary proceeding or their state law equivalents; and (f) the debtor will not file for or will not be placed in bankruptcy for at least ninety days after the judicial lien attaches to the fraudulently conveyed property. . . .

B. *The Substantive Standards of Liability*

It is often observed that fraudulent conveyances are misnamed if they lead people to think that the creditors have somehow been misled or tricked. In fact, as the law currently stands, creditors who were not misled in the least have as many rights as creditors who were fooled by the fraudulent conveyance. . . .

The only requirements for fraudulent conveyance liability in the third party are that (a) the debtor must have intended to defraud creditors generally by making the conveyance, or (b) the debtor made a transfer without fair consideration at a time when the debtor was insolvent or in poor financial condition. . . .

III. THE NECESSARY CONDITIONS FOR FRAUDULENT CONVEYANCE LAW TO BE EFFICIENT
A. *Fraudulent Conveyances in a Perfect Market*

In the forthcoming model, my goal is to identify the costs and benefits of fraudulent conveyance, as it has been defined above. I will attempt to identify the costs and benefits by comparing our current world in which the fraudulent conveyance remedy is part of debtor-creditor law ("the fraudulent conveyance world") to a world in which creditors are not permitted to pursue property in the hands of any third party ("the no-fraudulent conveyance world"). We will speculate on the amount creditors will demand from debtors and donees to dispense with fraudulent conveyance law and compare that amount to what donees and debtors would offer creditors to give up their fraudulent conveyance rights.

A few preliminary assumption should be set forth with regard to the frictionless, near-perfect market with no transaction costs.

The players don't lie. In such a utopia, creditors, debtors and donees tell each other the precise truth about their utilities. . . .

The moral hazard is known. Another feature of this perfect market is that the odds of debtor misbehavior are precisely known. . . .

Everyone is solvent. There are no process costs or insolvency costs in this universe, except the risk of the debtor's insolvency. . . .

Perfect markets for property. All markets are perfect, so that property will end up in the hands of the highest valuing user ("HVU") . . . .

All people are equal. All people in the world have identical utility curves for wealth. . . .

No taxes. . . .

The public is apathetic and self-involved. . . .

It is time to open the auction. How much will creditors (and perhaps debtors) require to allow insolvent debtors to make gifts? How much will donees (and perhaps debtors) bid?

Before answering that question, I want to elaborate further on the distinction between utilities derived from the wealth transfer itself and utilities derived from the acts of giving and receiving in the abstract (apart from the utilities of the wealth itself).

As a matter of probability, the hopes of donees for receiving gifts precisely equals the creditor's fear that such gifts will be given. . . .

If it is true that donee-hopes precisely equal creditor-fears in a perfect market, and if we also stipulate that no utility gains or losses . . . by pure redistribution are possible in a perfect market, then it does *not* follow that a donee's (and debtor's) utilities in a no-fraudulent conveyance world will precisely equal the creditor's (and debtor's) disutilities in a fraudulent conveyance world. It is important to distinguish between the utilities derived from the wealth transfer itself and the utilities arising from the acts of giving and receiving. Presumably, gifts are given because the act of giving produces pleasure in the giver. Similarly, the hope of receiving produces a warm glow of anticipation which is separate from the utilities to extracted from the material goods themselves. . . .

Because gift giving and gift receiving has utilitarian significance apart from the wealth transfer itself . . ., it cannot be said with certainty that, in a perfect market, the parties would always prefer fraudulent conveyance law. Remember that the creditors are indifferent to charging more interest up front (together with the creditor's waiver of fraudulent conveyance rights) or charging less (with a fully enforceable covenant against fraudulent conveyances). Remember also that the donees are the only parties who lose out because of fraudulent conveyance law.

Now surely . . . the debtor will sometimes prefer to pay higher interest . . . today and will gladly sacrifice her bankruptcy discharge (which is contingent on not making fraudulent conveyances) . . ., rather than surrender the pleasure of giving later . . . . In this situation, the debtor will bribe the creditors to give up their fraudulent conveyance rights by paying higher interest today. . . . But suppose (as most of you will) that the debtor prefers wealth today and in the future over the opportunity to make gifts later. This implies that the debtor has a potential surplus (s_r) defined as the utility from the saved interest expense . . . today and creditor-free wealth later following a bankruptcy discharge . . ., minus the pleasure of giving later . . . . Meanwhile, the donee, who knows the precise chance of receiving a serendipitous wealth transfer later, feels the warm glow of anticipation from such a possibility (g_e), a utility that is separate from the utilities extractable from the thing itself. In a perfect market—where the donee must protect these hopes by bribing the debtor into paying more interest instead of preserving the gift power—the donee can obtain a repeal of fraudulent conveyance law *only* if:

$$s_r < g_e$$

The implications of my discovery could not be more profound! What I have proved is that in a fraudulent conveyance world, the debtor *or* the donee might have sufficient utilities to justify an economic argument for the repeal of fraudulent conveyance law. . . .

Hence, by no means can we assume that fraudulent conveyance law would *always* be preferred in a perfect market. The efficiency of fraudulent conveyance law is contingent on a comparison between the debtor's surplus utility of present and future wealth over future gifting (s_r) and the donee's pleasure from anticipating gifts (g_e).

B. *The Circularity of Law-and-Economics*

So far, I have proved that a utilitarian assessment of fraudulent conveyance law must inevitably amount to measuring debtor-donee gains in moving to a non-fraudulent conveyance world against debtor losses (if any) in moving to a no-fraudulent conveyance world. Many of you may respond, "Big deal. I am confident as a general matter that $s_r > g_e$ almost all of the time."

This may or may not be right. But I counter with an observation about whether law can ever be efficient. Efficiency is a study of what other people want and expect. What people want and expect, however, is in very large part produced by law itself. Therefore, we reach a kind of circularity, whereby the product of law itself is used to justify the law. . . .

In any case, before you stop reading this Article and sign on with the view that fraudulent conveyance law must always be efficient, please remember (as many economists sometimes forget) that we do not live in a world of perfect markets. Whether fraudulent conveyance law is efficient in our "second best" world is the subject of the next part of this Article.

C. *Relaxing the Assumptions of a Perfect Market*

The time has come to relax the assumptions of perfect information and no transaction costs. We must now assume that neither creditors, nor donees, nor the debtor himself know the odds of debtor misbehavior. Creditor fears may exceed donee hopes or vice versa. In addition, any attempt to firm up an expectation or reduce a fear is costly. Once we make such assumptions, the contingent nature of an efficiency argument for fraudulent conveyance law makes itself even more visible than it was in a perfect credit market.

1. Benefits

When markets are not perfect and one moves from a fraudulent conveyance world to a no-fraudulent conveyance world, the conditions of fraudulent conveyance efficiency are radically transformed, compared to what they were in a perfect market. Here are some of the transformations . . . .

Creditors may take upstream and cross-stream guarantees. . . .
The status of gifts is clarified. . . .
It is easy to hide the assets from the sheriff. . . .
Repeal means more gifts. . . .

This concludes a rough summary of how market defects affect the benefits of giving and receiving. What follows is a look at the transfiguration in costs.

2. Costs

In a perfect market, the cost of moving to a no-fraudulent conveyance world was limited by the disutility in having to pay creditors higher interest. In a perfect market, creditors were indifferent between the debtor's freedom to give gifts . . ., and receiving an interest premium plus the right to post-bankruptcy income . . . . Creditor indifference will still be the case, but the premium the debtor must pay for the privilege of making fraudulent conveyances will be much transformed by the fact that the creditor information and creditor remedies are extremely imperfect.

Fraudulent conveyance law is not reflected in prices. . . . In the real world, . . . [c]reditors will have different assessments of the "moral hazard" they face from debtor misbehavior. I wish to emphasize here that the risk premium (i) a creditor is willing to charge is not very high.

First and foremost, there are relatively cheap alternatives to a large amount of (i). Suretyship from someone dear to the debtor may be an effective deterrent to fraudulent conveyances, such that if the fraudulent conveyance remedy disappears, no great loss to the creditor will occur. The creditor is also free to demand a security interest in specific assets. . . .

Similarly, recall that debtors making fraudulent conveyances lose their bankruptcy discharge in the no-fraudulent conveyance world, just as they did in the fraudulent conveyance world . . . . Because this is so, an important deterrent continues to exist which might help prevent debtor misbehavior. This continuing disincentive also helps to minimize the risk that the debtor will make fraudulent conveyances. . . .

Even in a reduced risk state, the risk premium (i) must now be discounted by the creditor's fear that, in the fraudulent conveyance world, fraudulent conveyances cannot be recovered anyway (c_{fc}). This fear cannot be dissipated by the fraudulent conveyance remedies as they now exist. . . . This might be so for several reasons. . . . [T]here are numerous obstacles in front of the creditor in obtaining any benefit from the right to pursue property in the hands of donees. . . . All these contingencies to recover drastically reduce the value of the remedy to a creditor who is about to offer credit terms to a debtor. . . .

Finally there is a cross-elasticity between modes of debtor misbehavior. . . .

. . . All of these factors suggest that (c_{fc}) is very high. High (c_{fc}) militates against the efficiency of fraudulent conveyance law.

To summarize, when credit is the result of consensual bargaining, the losses imposed on creditors by fraudulent conveyances can be passed right back to the debtors via higher ex ante interest rates. But these losses may not be very large. Because the perceived benefits of the fraudulent conveyance remedy will probably be trivial and because cheap methods of deterrence are available, creditor losses . . . , which are charged to the debtor, are likely to be low if fraudulent conveyance law were to be repealed.

Macroeconomic effects. If there is any increase in the riskiness of general credit, some external harms might result. . . .

External Preferences. In a complete equilibrium model, the public's existing feelings toward the legal change in question is an important—usually determinative—factor. By external preferences, I simply mean that the pleasure and pain felt by each member of the public in contemplating the harms and benefits that people may do to each other in the new legal regime.

With regard to fraudulent conveyances, the public might plausibly feel that debtors should pay their debts as a moral matter. The increased ability of debtors to flee or to make gifts on the eve of bankruptcy might strike people as unjust. . . .

On the other hand, the public might be highly pro-debtor. People may feel, in the aggregate, that creditors tend to be rich and debtors tend to be poor. A move to the no-fraudulent conveyance world might have at least the short-term effect of rendering the poor slightly more powerful. The public may actually wish to see the move to the no-fraudulent conveyance world . . . .

Now the ultimate question: Would there be an efficiency loss in the move from a fraudulent conveyance world to a no-fraudulent conveyance world? In order to answer that question, we must compare the gains to debtors and donees against the losses to creditors and debtors. If losses are greater than the gains, the move would be inefficient.

What follows is a formula expressing the conditions of the efficiency of moving to a no-fraudulent conveyance world. On the left side of the inequality sign are all the costs of making the move. On the right side are all the benefits of the move:

$$i' + p(d') + m + h_e > (wb) + (g_e - g_{fce}) + (g_r - g_{fcr}) + f_r + f_e + b_e{}^{73}$$

Most of you are now gazing at the above formula, thinking: "If all those factors are relevant to whether fraudulent conveyance law is efficient, how can we know the utilitarian status of fraudulent conveyance law?"

---

[73]   To remind the reader what the formula means, the following are the costs I could think of in doing away with fraudulent conveyance law:

i' = increased risk premium (although I maintain the increase will be trivial);

$p(d')$ = the debtor's sacrifice of the bankruptcy discharge because the debtor made a fraudulent conveyance, discounted by the probability perceived by the creditor who is setting an interest rate that the same creditor will benefit from such an increase in entitlements . . . ;

m = macroeconomic harms because the loans are (trivially) more risky;

h_e = the public's external preference for continued fraudulent conveyance law.

The benefits I can think of are:

wb = the increased security available to creditors because cross-stream guaranties are not possible;

$g_e - g_{fce}$ = increased donor pleasure in giving unrestricted gifts while insolvent, discounted by the fact that the donor had some of these utilities anyway in the fraudulent conveyance world;

$g_r - g_{fcr}$ = increased donee pleasure in giving unrestricted gifts while insolvent, discounted by the fact that the donee had some of these utilities anyway in the fraudulent conveyance world;

$f_r + f_e$ = donor and donee fears that valid gifts will be mistaken for fraudulent conveyances, a fear that is eliminated in the no-fraudulent conveyance world;

b_e = the public's external preference for doing away with fraudulent conveyance law, thereby empowering debtors against their creditors.

The answer is, "We can't." I maintain that the data are not clear enough to hazard a guess. Nor can a valid research project be designated to test the matter. We cannot know how large donee utilities or debtor utilities are in remaining free to make gifts. Similarly, we cannot know the extent to which creditors value the fraudulent conveyance remedy at the time they price their loans. Given the contingencies implicit in the remedy, they probably would place minimal value on the remedy itself. Nor can we measure the external benefits accurately. Even if we could, we could not measure them quickly enough to keep up with the changing mood of the public.

I certainly hope this analysis puts an end once and for all to the claim that fraudulent conveyance law is efficient.

IV. An Alternative Mode of Understanding Fraudulent Conveyance Law

Because of the blizzard of contingencies, is does not pay to understand the fraudulent conveyance law in terms of efficiency. A few attractive nonefficiency points can be made in favor of fraudulent conveyance law, however. . . .

First, it should be observed that fraudulent conveyance law shifts power from strong debtors to weak creditors. . . .

. . . The fraudulent conveyance remedy therefore increases creditor power by allowing the creditor to pursue fraudulently conveyed property in the hands of a third party in certain cases. The shift of power from strong debtors to weak creditors has no certain efficiency rationale, but it is consistent with the following norms:

Keeping promises. Debtors have promised to reserve or generate assets in the future for payment to their creditors. To divert assets to other purposes is wrong in the same way that violating any promise is morally wrong.

Protestant desert. Keeping promises seems very closely aligned with the establishment of norms of reason and rationality. Therefore, legal norms, such as those found in fraudulent conveyance law, manifest something very central in maintaining our sense of sanity, our sense of feeling at home in a hostile universe. . . . I am only suggesting that our hatred of defaulting debtors and their relatives (as congealed in fraudulent conveyance law) reverberates deeply with the fundamentals of rational thought itself.

Donees have not generally worked for the largesse of a gift. To some degree, property at the margin should be reserved for those who contribute work to the public welfare. Creditors have contributed their capital by lending. In a capitalist society, this contribution is entitled to important recognition. Their position is preferred over donees who have not worked. . . .

If I am right that fraudulent conveyance law evens out the situational advantages of debtors who have decided they cannot survive financially, then it follows that gifts consistent with financial survival should not be fraudulent conveyances. . . . A debtor has to feed and clothe herself and her family. As long as these expenditures are duly modest, they ought not to be fraudulent conveyances. . . . Which estate-decreasing acts are abuses of positional advantage by the debtor will have to be decided on a case-by-case basis and are not conducive to a more precise description than this.

These are important norms that make sense to me. Fraudulent conveyance law helps strengthen a set of norms that favors work over idleness, self-determination over grabbing sustenance from others, and honor over deceit. We do not need efficiency norms to justify fraudulent conveyance law.

V. Current Efficiency Theories

. . . The academic treatment of fraudulent conveyance law and efficiency can be divided into two camps. First, there is a contractarian group that asserts fraudulent conveyance law is an "off-the-rack" term signifying principles that most debtors and creditors would agree on anyway. Second, there is a half-hearted externality theory. . . .

A. *"Off the Rack"*

The contractarian account of fraudulent conveyance law and efficiency holds that most debtors and creditors would agree upon fraudulent conveyance provisions in a loan agreement anyway. Therefore, providing it as a suppletive principle is efficient because it saves negotiation costs. . . .

. . . [B]y viewing fraudulent conveyance law as a bargain solely between creditors and debtors, the fraudulent conveyance law of Baird and Jackson itself becomes a kind of externality, in that the debtor and creditor are agreeing that third parties should have no right to retain gifts or assets sold in bulk. This is a deprivation for which donees and bulk buyer are not being hypothetically compensated.

Even if the Baird and Jackson bargain were extended to include donees and bulk buyers, there exists the serious question of why such persons should ever agree to a fraudulent conveyance bargain. . . .

Furthermore, Baird and Jackson do not even have any justification for believing that *debtors* would universally agree to give up their right to alienate property. This power has a positive value . . . .

At a minimum, Clark, Baird and Jackson must show why donees would agree to give up their gifts without receiving anything in return. . . .

The contractarian model completely fails. It cannot even be rehabilitated by adding in the parties who really hold the fraudulent conveyance invoice. . . .

CONCLUSION

As elsewhere in law-and-economics, the stakes in the efficiency debate on fraudulent conveyance law are low. No one is proposing to do away with fraudulent conveyance law on the basis of efficiency, and no one is proposing to extend it on the basis of models either. . . . In the end, we can only say what every law-and-economics article ends up saying: In a world with no transaction costs, no one gives a hoot what the law is. But in a world *with* transaction costs, who the hell knows what is going on!

The revelation that fraudulent conveyance law is probably not justified by norms of efficiency should not cause any great concern. It simply reminds us that, ultimately, science has nothing to tell us about ethical choice. We have to develop our own notions of good and right. We cannot escape our intuitions. If we disagree with the intuitions of economists, we should not back off in awe of false and mysterious expertise. They have no more idea of right and wrong than we ordinary shmoes have.

Additional suggested readings

Peter A. Alces, THE LAW OF FRAUDULENT TRANSACTIONS (1987)

Peter A. Alces & Luther M. Dorr, Jr., *A Critical Analysis of the New Uniform Fraudulent Transfer Act*, 1985 U. ILL. L. REV. 527

Peter A. Alces, *Generic Fraud and the Uniform Fraudulent Transfer Act*, 9 CARDOZO L. REV. 743 (1987)

Philip I. Blumberg, *Intragroup (Upstream, Cross-Stream, and Downstream) Guaranties Under the Uniform Fraudulent Transfer Act*, 9 CARDOZO L. REV. 685 (1987)

David Gray Carlson, *Leveraged Buyouts in Bankruptcy*, 20 GA. L. REV. 73 (1985)

Scott B. Ehrlich, *Avoidance of Foreclosure Sales as Fraudulent Conveyances: Accommodating State and Federal Objectives*, 71 VA. L. REV. 933 (1985)

Garrard Glenn, THE LAW OF FRAUDULENT CONVEYANCES (1931)

William H. Henning, *An Analysis of* Durrett *and Its Impact on Real and Personal Property Foreclosures: Some Proposed Modifications*, 62 N.C. L. REV. 257 (1985)

Daniel Keating, *Bankruptcy, Tithing, and the Pocket Picking Paradigm of Free Exercise*, 1996 U. ILL. L. REV. 1041

Frank R. Kennedy, *Involuntary Fraudulent Transfers*, 9 CARDOZO L. REV. 531 (1987)

Frank R. Kennedy, *Reception of the Uniform Fraudulent Transfer Act*, 43 S.C. L. REV. 655 (1992)

Frank R. Kennedy & Gerald K. Smith, *Fraudulent Transfers and Obligations: Issues of Current Interest*, 43 S.C. L. REV. 709 (1992)

Bruce A. Markell, *Toward True and Plain Dealing: A Theory of Fraudulent Transfers Involving Unreasonably Small Capital*, 21 IND. L. REV. 469 (1988)

John C. McCoid, II, *Constructively Fraudulent Conveyances: Transfers for Inadequate Consideration*, 62 TEX. L. REV. 639 (1983)

James A. McLaughlin, *Application of the Uniform Fraudulent Conveyance Act*, 46 HARV. L. REV. 404 (1933)

James F. Queenan, Jr., *The Collapsed Leveraged Buyout and the Trustee in Bankruptcy*, 11 CARDOZO L. REV. 1 (1989)

Robert J. Rosenberg, *Intercorporate Guaranties and the Law of Fraudulent Conveyances: Lender Beware*, 125 U. PA. L. REV. 235 (1976)

Emily L. Sherwin, *Creditors' Rights Against Participants in a Leveraged Buyout*, 72 MINN. L. REV. 449 (1988)

Paul M. Shupack, *Confusion in Policy and Language in the Uniform Fraudulent Transfer Act*, 9 CARDOZO L. REV. 811 (1987)

Mary Jo Newborn Wiggins, *A Statute of Disbelief? Clashing Ethical Imperatives in Fraudulent Transfer Law*, 48 S.C. L. REV. 771 (1997)

Jack F. Williams, *The Fallacies of Contemporary Fraudulent Transfer Models as Applied to Intercorporate Guaranties: Fraudulent Transfer Law as a Fuzzy System*, 15 CARDOZO L. REV. 1403 (1994)

Jack F. Williams, *Revisiting the Proper Limits of Fraudulent Transfer Law*, 8 BANKR. DEV. J. 55 (1991)

Todd J. Zywicki, *Rewrite the Bankruptcy Laws, Not the Scriptures: Protecting a Bankruptcy Debtor's Right to Tithe*, 1998 WIS. L. REV. 1223

Chapter 8
Secured Claims

A. Prologue

Better secured than unsecured. That simple motto is virtually an article of faith for claimants in bankruptcy. The reason, of course, is that secured claims are honored in full (up to the value of the collateral) while unsecured claims are paid only out of whatever residue remains in the bankruptcy estate after secured claims take their prime cut. This Chapter explores the nature of and justification for the special treatment of secured claims in bankruptcy. The Chapter consists of four parts.

Leading off is the Prologue, in which Professor James Rogers questions the assumed constitutional basis underlying the treatment of secured creditors in bankruptcy, in *The Impairment of Secured Creditors' Rights in Reorganization: A Study of the Relationship Between the Fifth Amendment and the Bankruptcy Clause*, 96 HARV. L. REV. 973 (1983). The assumption is that the Fifth Amendment limits the extent to which secured creditors' rights may be impaired in a bankruptcy case—what he calls the "Unconstitutional Impairment Thesis." This Thesis informs the statutory and judicial handling of secured claims. Rogers, after an exhaustive historical survey, concludes that the Unconstitutional Impairment Thesis is unsound. Instead, his conclusion is that *only* the Bankruptcy Clause in Article I limits the manner in which secured claims may be impaired.

The second part of the Chapter, "Whither Security?," addresses two even more fundamental issues: why does security exist in the first place, and why are secured claims honored ahead of unsecured claims in bankruptcy? The literature in this area is quite rich. The commentators evince considerable disagreement.

Parts three and four move from the realm of the theoretical justifications for security's existence and priority to an examination of the actual manner in which secured claims are dealt with in bankruptcy cases. The third section speaks to the closely related issues of how secured claims are *valued* in bankruptcy and what constitutes "adequate protection" of those secured claims. Part four deals with the further related issue of "strip down," which is the colloquial description of the treatment of undersecured claims—to what extent may an undersecured claim be "stripped down" to the judicially determined value of the collateral?

James S. Rogers
The Impairment of Secured Creditors' Rights in Reorganization: A Study of the Relationship Between the Fifth Amendment and the Bankruptcy Clause
96 HARV. L. REV. 973 (1983)[*]

Article I, section 8 of the Constitution provides that "[t]he Congress shall have Power . . . [t]o establish . . . uniform Laws on the subject of Bankruptcies throughout the United States." As the concept of bankruptcy is now understood and implemented, this clause confers authority on the federal government to adopt far-reaching measures to deal with the problems of insolvent or otherwise financially troubled individuals and enterprises. . . . Other provisions of the Constitution, however, appear to limit the power of government to disrupt private economic rights: "No State shall . . . pass any . . . Law impairing the Obligation of Contracts"; "No person shall . . . be deprived of . . . property, without due process of law"; "nor shall private property be taken for public use, without just compensation."

Because exercise of the bankruptcy power substantially impairs private property and contract rights, some accommodation must be reached between the affirmative grant of power in the bankruptcy clause and the limitations found in the fifth amendment and related provisions. It is the purpose of this Article to consider how these constitutional provisions can be reconciled. Although the subject is, at the most general level, the relationship between the bankruptcy clause and the fifth amendment, much of the discussion centers on a narrower issue—the source and nature of constitutional limits on impairment of secured creditors' rights during the pendency of reorganization proceedings. . . .

I. THE UNCONSTITUTIONAL IMPAIRMENT THESIS

Perhaps more by dint of repetition than by analysis, it seems to have become an accepted proposition of reorganization law that the fifth amendment limits the extent to which secured creditors may be subjected to the risk of loss due to restraint of their foreclosure rights. Virtually every discussion of the problem includes a reference to Justice Brandeis' statement in *Louisville Joint Stock Land Bank v. Radford* that "[t]he bankruptcy power, like the other great substantive powers of Congress, is subject to the Fifth Amendment." The theory that the fifth amendment places substantive limits on the ability of the government to restrain secured creditors' rights in reorganization has crystallized into the following proposition: any impairment of the liquidation value of a secured creditor's collateral attributable to the exercise of powers conferred on the reorganization court by bankruptcy legislation is, in the absence of just compensation, a violation of the takings clause of the fifth amendment. For convenience, this proposition is referred to in this Article as the Unconstitutional Impairment Thesis. . . .

. . . [T]he widespread acceptance of the Thesis seems to have had a substantial impact on the evolution of the present statutory law of reorganization. The new Bankruptcy Code contains detailed provisions specifying the extent to which impairment of secured creditors' rights is permissible during the pendency of bankruptcy proceedings, the key being the concept of adequate protection. . . .

The adequate protection model, therefore, precisely mirrors the supposed constitutional requirements of the Unconstitutional Impairment Thesis.

. . . If, as this Article argues, the Unconstitutional Impairment Thesis is entirely unsound, a major aspect of the new Bankruptcy Code's treatment of reorganization problems may be based, to some extent, on a foundation of sand. . . . [U]nless the flaws of the Thesis are exposed, many possible proposals for amending the present reorganization provisions will be doomed from the outset by the assumption that the proper treatment of secured creditors' rights in reorganization is dictated by constitutional requirements rather than by policy considerations that are within the discretion of Congress.

A. *Precedent for the Unconstitutional Impairment Thesis*

1. *The Frazier-Lemke Act Cases.*—The principal source of authority for the Unconstitutional Impairment Thesis is a series of Supreme Court decisions involving amendments to the Bankruptcy Act that were enacted by the Frazier-Lemke Act of 1934. The Frazier-Lemke Act, which applied only to debts existing at the time of its enactment, was designed to assist farmers who faced the prospect of losing their farms through mortgage foreclosure. The Act affected mortgagees in two major respects. First, it enabled the debtor to obtain a stay of foreclosure proceedings for a period of five years . . . . Second, at any time during the five-year period, the debtor could acquire full title to the mortgaged real estate by paying the mortgagee the appraised value of the real estate. . . .

In *Louisville Joint Stock Land Bank v. Radford*, the Supreme Court, in a unanimous opinion authored by Justice Brandeis, held the Frazier-Lemke Act unconstitutional. Although the precise basis of the ruling is not entirely clear, the case has been widely interpreted to hold that the Frazier-Lemke Act violated the takings clause of the fifth amendment by taking from a mortgagee without compensation rights that he otherwise would have had to the mortgaged premises. In response to the *Radford* decision, Congress amended the Frazier-Lemke Act. Two years after *Radford*, the Supreme Court upheld the revised Act in *Wright v. Vinton Branch of the Mountain Trust Bank*, another unanimous opinion by Justice Brandeis.

It is by no means easy to discern the principle that enabled Justice Brandeis to conclude that the changes made by Congress in response to *Radford* sufficed to overcome the constitutional objections found fatal in that case. Congress' changes in the two key provisions of the Act were, in fact, rather insubstantial. First, with respect to the stay imposed by the original Act, the revised Act simply shortened the period of the stay from five to three years. . . . Second, as it was ultimately interpreted, the revised Act did not change significantly the provision denying the mortgagee the right to acquire the property through a judicial sale. . . .

2. *Relevance of the Frazier-Lemke Act Cases to the Unconstitutional Impairment Thesis.*—The most plausible explanation of the irreconcilability of *Radford* and the subsequent Frazier-Lemke Act cases is that the later cases overrule or substantially undercut the vitality of *Radford*. Courts and commentators, however, have often stated that the subsequent Frazier-Lemke Act cases only refined the principles developed in *Radford* and that certain dicta in *Union Central* express the determinative principle—that the mortgagee is constitutionally entitled to have the value of the property preserved and devoted to the payment of his debt. On this view, the reason that the revised Act was upheld is that it preserved to the mortgagee this constitutional minimum. . . . The Frazier-Lemke Act cases, that is, are taken to establish the validity of the Unconstitutional Impairment Thesis.

Even if *Radford* survives the subsequent Frazier-Lemke Act cases, it is difficult to see how the Frazier-Lemke Act cases support the position of the Unconstitutional Impairment Thesis that preservation of the value of collateral is the key constitutional right of the secured creditor. . . .

Commentators who read the Frazier-Lemke Act cases to have established the Unconstitutional Impairment Thesis seem to rely primarily on the *Union Central* opinion, in which Justice Douglas, in the course of describing the revised Act, stated that "[s]afeguards were provided to protect the rights of secured creditors, throughout the proceedings, to the extent of the value of the property" and that "[t]here is no constitutional claim of the creditor to more than that." Although Justice Douglas' comments are consistent with the proposition that a secured creditor is constitutionally entitled to have the liquidation value of the collateral preserved, there is little reason to suppose that Justice Douglas had such a proposition in mind. . . .

The most fundamental flaw in the suggestion that *Radford* supports the Unconstitutional Impairment Thesis is the irrelevancy of that case to the central assertion of the Thesis, that the fifth amendment imposes definite constitutional limitations on the substance of bankruptcy legislation. It seems to be thought that fifth amendment principles derived from *Radford* impose generally applicable limits on the substantive scope of bankruptcy power of a sort that would apply even to purely prospective bankruptcy legislation. . . .

Radford and its progeny, however, provide no support at all for the assertion of such a broad substantive limit on the powers of Congress under the bankruptcy clause. . . .

In context, Justice Brandeis' comments suggest that the holding of the case is only that the modification of secured creditors' rights effected by the Frazier-Lemke Act was too substantial to permit the Act to be applied retroactively. Thus, the famous statement that the bankruptcy power is subject to the fifth amendment must be taken to mean nothing more than that the fifth amendment, through either the due process or the takings clause, is the constitutional foundation for the proposition that statutes that retroactively disrupt settled expectations may be subject to particularly attentive judicial scrutiny. Hence . . . none of the Frazier-Lemke Act cases provides any support whatsoever for the proposition that fifth amendment property-protection concepts limit the substantive scope of the bankruptcy power.

B. *Theoretical Flaws in the Unconstitutional Impairment Thesis*

Lack of support for the Unconstitutional Impairment Thesis in the Frazier-Lemke Act cases does not, in itself, demonstrate that the Thesis is invalid. It is necessary, therefore, to consider whether there is any independent theoretical support for the Thesis. There are two constitutional provisions that appear to be plausible candidates as textual support for the notion that the bankruptcy power is limited by the requirement of nonimpairment of secured creditors' property rights: the due process clause and the takings clause. The due process clause is, today, hardly an appealing candidate. The contention that the due process clause is the source of the Unconstitutional Impairment Thesis reduces to the claim that rather freewheeling *Lochner*-style economic substantive due process should be revived. In light of the glee with which the Supreme Court seizes every available opportunity to repudiate *Lochner* yet again, few are likely to pursue that route. Accordingly, adherents of the Unconstitutional Impairment Thesis seem to rely on the takings clause. That avenue, however, proves on careful examination to be no less troublesome.

1. *Retroactivity, Prospectivity, and the Takings Clause.*—Much of the intuitive appeal of the Unconstitutional Impairment Thesis probably is traceable to the assumption that the decision made by a reorganization court during bankruptcy proceedings is the "taking" of which the secured creditor complains. . . .

The appeal of this view is entirely illusory. Except in situations in which an amendment to bankruptcy law is applied retroactively . . ., all that happens when a reorganization court stays a secured creditor from foreclosing on his collateral is that the court applies a preexisting rule of law to a specific case. What, one may ask, has been "taken" from the secured creditor? At the time he entered into the security arrangement, he knew or should have known that his rights were circumscribed by the federal legislation. If his property rights are defined by reference to existing law, obviously no taking has occurred. Thus, the proposition that the fifth amendment imposes limitations on even purely prospective restrictions of the rights of secured creditors seems to assume that the property rights held by secured creditors are in some sense anterior to positive law. The implications of that concept are staggering. . . .

2. *The Distinction Between Secured and Unsecured Creditors.*—The Unconstitutional Impairment Thesis cannot be maintained without drawing a sharp distinction between the constitutional rights of secured creditors and those of unsecured creditors. Exercise of the bankruptcy power clearly entails substantial impairments of the rights of unsecured creditors, the clearest instance being the grant of a discharge to the debtor. The constitutionality of such impairments of unsecured creditors' rights, however, has long been settled. Thus, unless some substantial basis exists for distinguishing the constitutional rights of secured creditors from those of unsecured creditors, the ready acceptance of impairments of unsecured creditors' rights in bankruptcy must cast grave doubt on the validity of the Unconstitutional Impairment Thesis.

Although unsecured creditors' rights against the debtor are generally described as contractual rights, this characterization alone cannot explain why impairment of unsecured creditors' rights in bankruptcy has not been viewed to pose substantial constitutional problems. First, the Supreme Court on a number of occasions has explicitly stated that contractual rights are a species of property protected by the due process and takings clauses. Second, modern developments in the area of procedural due process protections of entitlements . . . are hardly consistent with a narrow interpretation of the fifth amendment that would exclude contractual rights from the scope of the term "property." . . .

Even if constitutional protection were limited to "property" rights, it is by no means clear that unsecured creditors' rights against a debtor's estate would fail to qualify as such to the same extent as secured creditors' liens. It is true that, unlike secured creditors, unsecured creditors have no specific interest in any particular portion of the debtor's assets. Unsecured creditors do, however, have legally recognized interests in the debtor's assets as a whole. Through various forms of process specified by state debtor-creditor law, virtually all of a debtor's assets may be reached to satisfy the demands of his creditors. . . .

Reliance on the labels "property" and "contract," therefore, hardly suffices to explain the supposed distinction between the constitutional rights of secured and unsecured creditors. The task thus is to identify more precisely the differences between secured and unsecured creditors' rights and to consider whether these differences warrant the conclusion that different constitutional principles apply in the two fields. . . .

. . . The difference between secured creditors' rights and unsecured creditors' rights lies in the remedy: the secured creditor has identified in advance of default the property to be seized and sold in satisfaction of his claim. . . .

That the secured creditor has preselected the particular property to be devoted to the satisfaction of his claim seems to play a strong role in the contention that secured creditors' "property" rights are a matter of special constitutional significance. Curiously, however, the identity of the specific property involved is perhaps the matter of least importance to the secured creditor. The secured creditor has no concern about the collateral *per se.* Rather, the secured creditor's concerns are only that the collateral have and retain sufficient value to satisfy his claim and that it be readily salable—the same concerns that unsecured creditors have about the debtor's property in general. Indeed, the preselection of the property to be devoted to repayment of his claim is one aspect of the secured creditor's remedial rights that even adherents of the Unconstitutional Impairment Thesis seem to concede may be impaired in bankruptcy. . . .

The specificity of the secured creditor's claim against the debtor's property is therefore a matter of neither practical nor constitutional significance. Rather, the factor that distinguishes secured creditors' rights from those of unsecured creditors is that, as a matter of state law, the secured creditor's claim ranks above those of the unsecured creditors. It is difficult, however, to see why the particular position of the secured creditor in the ranking of claims against the debtor's

property is entitled to constitutional protection not enjoyed by claimants occupying different ranks.
. . .

3. *The Requirement of Preservation of the Value of Collateral.*—Even if the supposed distinction between secured creditors' "property" rights and unsecured creditors' "contractual" claims provided a persuasive reason for distinguishing between the constitutional rights of secured creditors and those of unsecured creditors, that distinction would fail to explain the assumption of the Unconstitutional Impairment Thesis that preservation of the value of the collateral is the key constitutional right of the secured creditor. One who contends that secured creditors' "property" rights are entitled to special constitutional protection might argue that the secured creditor should be protected against any impairment of the rights that he would otherwise enjoy by virtue of his state-created property rights in the collateral. It is, however, quite clear that our present reorganization system does not provide such extensive protection. Yet once one concedes that such full protection is not compelled, one is left without any principled basis for asserting that a specific lesser degree of protection—preservation of the value of the collateral—is required. . . .

Thus, even if one could find a commodious textual or jurisprudential mooring for the notion that fifth amendment principles limit even prospective bankruptcy legislation, one would encounter serious problems in attempting to support the Unconstitutional Impairment Thesis; it is very difficult to find any principled basis for either the Thesis' sharp distinction between the rights of secured and unsecured creditors or the Thesis' emphasis on the preservation of the value of collateral as the matter of critical constitutional significance. Moreover, these problems equally cast doubt on even a limited version of the Thesis—that secured creditors' rights to have the value of their collateral preserved may not constitutionally be impaired by retroactive bankruptcy legislation. . . .

II. THE RELATIONSHIP BETWEEN THE FIFTH AMENDMENT AND THE BANKRUPTCY CLAUSE

The preceding Part demonstrates that the Unconstitutional Impairment Thesis is wholly unsatisfactory. I submit that the fundamental flaw in the Thesis is the assumption that the takings clause or other fifth amendment principles provide an independent source of limitations on the substantive scope of the bankruptcy power. In the balance of this Article, I develop an alternative view of the relationship between the bankruptcy clause and the family of constitutional provisions—including the takings clause, the due process clause, and the contracts clause—that limits the extent to which contractual or property rights may be impaired by governmental action. My thesis is that these constitutional provisions do not impose substantive limitations on congressional exercise of the bankruptcy power. Instead, the principal source of substantive limitations on bankruptcy legislation is the bankruptcy clause itself, and hence the constitutionality of a statute adopted under the bankruptcy clause depends only on whether the measure falls within the scope of the powers conferred by the bankruptcy clause.

. . . I examine the principal nineteenth and early twentieth century decisions that resolved the fundamental issues concerning the constitutionality of bankruptcy legislation, and demonstrate that these decisions support the model of the relationship between the bankruptcy clause and the fifth amendment described above rather than the model implicit in the Unconstitutional Impairment Thesis. . . .

A. *The Historical Development of the Scope of the Bankruptcy Power*

The first step in a satisfactory analysis of the constitutional limits of the bankruptcy power is to consider why the fifth amendment, or analogous constitutional principles, has not been regarded as a significant restraint on the extent to which bankruptcy law may impair *unsecured* creditors' rights. Careful examination of the nineteenth century cases that resolved basic issues concerning the constitutionality of bankruptcy legislation reveals that the courts did not rely on any simplistic notion of the supposed distinction between contractual and property rights. Rather, the substantial impairments of unsecured creditors' rights that are effected by any bankruptcy legislation were upheld against constitutional challenge on the ground that, because such impairments are inevitable in the bankruptcy system, they necessarily must be authorized by the bankruptcy clause.

1. *Scope of the Bankruptcy Power: Voluntary Straight Bankruptcy.*—The first significant case in the evolution of the analysis of the relationship between the bankruptcy clause and the fifth amendment is *In re Klein*, which involved the 1841 Bankruptcy Act. The 1841 Act, in a sharp departure from prior English bankruptcy law and the 1800 federal bankruptcy act, was at least as much a measure for the relief of debtors as it was a creditors' remedy: it provided for voluntary bankruptcies; it applied to any type of debtor rather than being limited to those engaged in trade; and it provided for the discharge of debts without the consent of creditors. In the district court, Judge Wells held the 1841 Act unconstitutional, essentially on the theory that the power conferred on Congress by the bankruptcy clause was only the power to enact bankruptcy legislation substantially as it had been known in English law at the time the Constitution was adopted.

The district court's ruling in *In re Klein* was reversed on appeal in an opinion written by Justice Catron of the Supreme Court, sitting on circuit. Justice Catron rejected the district court's approach of tying the bankruptcy power to prior English practice, and adopted an expansive view of the power conferred by the bankruptcy clause:

> I hold [that the bankruptcy power] extends to all cases where the law causes to be distributed the property of the debtor among his creditors; this is its least limit. Its greatest is a discharge of the debtor from his contracts. And all intermediate legislation, affecting substance and form, but tending to further the great end of the subject—distribution and discharge—are in the competency and discretion of congress. With the policy of a law, letting in all classes, others as well as traders, and permitting the bankrupt to come in voluntarily, and be discharged without the consent of his creditors, the courts have no concern; it belongs to the law makers.

The difference between the approaches of Judge Wells and Justice Catron is quite significant. . . . Thus, Judge Wells' opinion may be interpreted to suggest that creditors' rights to have the debtor's property devoted to satisfaction of their claims are entitled to constitutional protection and that the necessity of protecting such rights operates as an independent limitation on the permissible exercise of the bankruptcy power.

Justice Catron's expansive view of the bankruptcy power cannot be fit within such a model. . . . Justice Catron's response to Judge Wells' contracts clause argument was simply that the bankruptcy clause confers on Congress the authority to enact legislation that has the effect of impairing the obligation of contracts. Under Justice Catron's approach, the contracts clause component of the fifth amendment has no independent significance in the context of bankruptcy legislation. . . . Though the *Klein* decision was not appealed to the Supreme Court, its authority is beyond question; indeed, Justice Catron's opinion has been cited frequently by the Court as the leading statement of the scope of the bankruptcy power. . . .

. . . The early cases such as *In re Klein* determined that exemption and discharge provisions were generally constitutional. Therefore, the substantive power conferred by the bankruptcy clause includes at least the authority to determine the extent to which a debtor's pool of economic values shall be devoted to the satisfaction of the claims of his existing creditors.

2. *Scope of the Bankruptcy Power: Binding Compositions.*—The next significant step in the evolution of the bankruptcy power came in 1874 when Congress, for the first time, adopted a bankruptcy provision permitting a composition arrangement accepted by a majority of creditors to bind dissenting creditors. In the case of *In re Reiman*, the constitutionality of the 1874 Act was challenged

by creditors who had dissented from a composition approved by the necessary majority of the creditors of two partners engaged in a business enterprise. . . .

The Act was upheld in *In re Reiman*, and both the district and circuit courts, following Justice Catron's approach in *In re Klein*, devoted their opinions entirely to the question whether the Act fell within the scope of the powers conferred by the bankruptcy clause. The opinions contain no suggestion that the fifth amendment operates as an independent limitation on the scope of the bankruptcy power.

In re Reiman's approval of the principle of binding compositions marks a significant step in the evolution of the concept of bankruptcy, for the composition principle lies at the heart of the reorganization provisions of modern bankruptcy law. . . .

3. *Scope of the Bankruptcy Power: Reorganization—. . .*

Any question about the force of what may have been dicta in *Canada Southern* was laid to rest in *Continental Illinois National Bank & Trust Co. v. Chicago, Rock Island and Pacific Ry. Rock Island* was the Supreme Court's first decision on the constitutionality of a modern reorganization act, the railroad reorganization provisions of section 77 of the Bankruptcy Act. . . . [T]he Court held that the approval of the composition principle in *In re Reiman* and *Canada Southern* sufficed to demonstrate that section 77 fell within the scope of the bankruptcy power. The Court quoted and explicitly approved the *Canada Southern* discussion of the relationship between the bankruptcy power and the due process clause.

The *Canada Southern* and *Rock Island* cases are significant at two levels. . . . *Canada Southern* and *Rock Island*, however, involved challenges brought by secured creditors. Nonetheless, the constitutional analysis applied was that developed in *Klein* and the other nineteenth century cases dealing with unsecured creditors' rights. Indeed, in *Canada Southern* the Court explicitly referred to the due process clause and made it quite clear that a valid exercise of the bankruptcy power is not open to attack on fifth amendment grounds.

Second, the approval of bankruptcy legislation providing for reorganization of corporate enterprises represents a significant advance in the evolution of the bankruptcy power. . . . Thus, *In re Reiman, Canada Southern*, and *Rock Island* suggest an expansion of the scope of the substantive powers conferred by the bankruptcy clause: the bankruptcy clause confers on the federal government the authority to exercise control over the use of the debtor's existing assets in order to enhance and preserve his earning power.

B. *The Permissibility of Restraint of Secured Creditors' Foreclosure Rights*

. . . In this Section, I use the proposition that the limits on the substantive scope of the bankruptcy power derive from the bankruptcy clause itself to examine the extent to which secured creditors may be restrained from foreclosing on their collateral during the pendency of reorganization proceedings.

The issue of the permissibility of interim stays of secured creditors' foreclosure rights was considered by the Supreme Court in the *Rock Island* case, in which the reorganization court had entered an order restraining a group of secured creditors of the railroad from selling or disposing of their collateral pending the effort to devise a plan of reorganization. It is quite noteworthy that, before addressing the secured creditors' contention that the restraint order violated the fifth amendment, the Supreme Court felt it necessary to consider the constitutionality of the railroad reorganization act in general as an exercise of the bankruptcy power, even though that issue had not been raised by the parties. This approach is precisely what one would expect of a court applying the model of constitutional analysis developed in *In re Klein* and the other nineteenth century cases. Having found that the pursuit of reorganization was a legitimate objective of bankruptcy legislation, the Court readily concluded that the reorganization court had authority to enjoin secured creditors from selling the collateral "if a sale would so hinder, obstruct and delay the preparation and consummation of a plan of reorganization as probably to prevent it." Moreover, as one would expect in light of the constitutional model developed in the nineteenth century cases, when the Court passed from consideration of the constitutionality of section 77 under the bankruptcy clause to the fifth amendment challenge, it found the latter issue entirely unproblematic. Justice Sutherland's remarks are worth setting forth at length:

> We find no substance in the contention of the petitioning banks that § 77, as applied by the court below to permit an injunction restraining the sale of the collateral, violates the Fifth Amendment. . . .
> . . . Speaking generally, it may be said that Congress, while without power to impair the obligation of contracts by laws acting directly and independently to that end, undeniably, has authority to pass legislation pertinent to any of the powers conferred by the Constitution, however it may operate collaterally or incidentally to impair or destroy the obligation of private contracts. And under the express power to pass uniform laws on the subject of bankruptcies, the legislation is valid though drawn with the direct aim and effect of relieving insolvent persons in whole or in part from the payment of their debts. So much necessarily results from the nature of the power, and this must have been within the contemplation of the framers of the Constitution when the power was granted.

This passage is about as clear a statement of the relationship between the fifth amendment and the bankruptcy clause as can be found in the case law.

The significance of *Rock Island* is highlighted by the striking contrast between that decision and *Home Building & Loan Association v. Blaisdell*, decided one year before *Rock Island*. In *Blaisdell*, a contracts clause and due process challenge to the Minnesota Mortgage Moratorium Act, which authorized a stay of foreclosure for no more than two years, was rejected by only a five-to-four decision . . . . The difference between the two cases is only that the federal government possesses a power denied to the states—the bankruptcy power. Thus, the only explanation for the striking difference between the Court's responses in the two cases is the proposition that the bankruptcy clause trumps the fifth amendment.

The *Rock Island* case thus suggests that questions concerning the constitutionality of interim restraints of secured creditors' foreclosure rights should be analyzed in the same manner as is any other issue involving the constitutionality of bankruptcy legislation—solely as a matter of the substantive scope of the bankruptcy power. . . .

. . . [I]n light of the delineation of the scope of the bankruptcy power in *In re Reiman, Canada Southern*, and *Rock Island*, it is quite clear that exercising control over the debtor's existing assets in an effort to preserve the earning power of the debtor is a permissible exercise of the bankruptcy power and hence, on that ground alone, is not vulnerable to fifth amendment challenge.

The possibility that the reorganization system may err in its prediction of the likelihood of successful reorganization does not preclude the exercise of the power to attempt reorganizations. . . .

Some commentators have suggested that the Supreme Court's 1974 decision in the *Regional Rail Reorganization Act Cases (RRRA Cases)* provides substantial support for the view that fifth amendment concepts concerning the protection of secured creditors' property rights impose limitations on the permissible extent of interim restraints of secured creditors' rights during reorganization proceedings. . . .

The suggestion that the *RRRA Cases* support the view that the fifth amendment limits the bankruptcy power does have a surface appeal. To be sure, the Supreme Court did not actually decide that the RRRA would violate the fifth amendment in the absence of compensation. Nonetheless, if the constitutional assertions had been insubstantial, it would have been a simple matter for the

Court to say so . . . . In the *RRRA Cases*, however, it was irrelevant that the parties objecting to continued deficit operations happened to be secured creditors of an enterprise involved in reorganization proceedings.

The real problem in the Penn Central reorganization proceedings was that within a fairly short period after the reorganization proceedings were initiated it became apparent that a traditional reorganization simply was not possible; the railroad had become a financial basket case. No one could plausibly contend that the purpose of continued deficit operations was to maintain a going business in order to devise an effective plan of reorganization. Rather, the only reason for continuing operations was the public interest in continued rail service. In such a situation, legislation requiring continued operations to the detriment of the estate may well exceed the authority conferred by the bankruptcy clause. . . .

. . . In any case involving an impairment of the rights of creditors or other investors in reorganization proceedings, the first issue is that of substantive power under the bankruptcy clause. . . .

IV. CONCLUSION

This Article has considered specific issues concerning the impairment of secured creditors' rights in reorganization proceedings in order to provide a framework for consideration of the more general issue of the relationship between the bankruptcy clause and the due process and takings clauses of the fifth amendment. The conclusion must be that Justice Brandeis' famous statement in the *Radford* case that "[t]he bankruptcy power . . . is subject to the Fifth Amendment," a statement that at first blush seems to be such a truism, is in fact false. The only significant constitutional restraint on the substance of purely prospective bankruptcy legislation is the bankruptcy clause itself. . . .

One of the most intriguing observations to be drawn from a study of the early cases in which the constitutionality of bankruptcy legislation was challenged is the remarkable transformation that has occurred in the style and language of constitutional analysis. No longer does one find challenges to the constitutionality of bankruptcy legislation phrased as contentions that the measure in question is not "a law on the subject of bankruptcy." Rather, since the time of *Radford*, the inquiry has shifted to the question whether the act at issue takes property rights in violation of general principles sought to be deduced from a theory of the takings clause.

Yet the attempt to use general fifth amendment concepts as a source for deriving specific principles limiting the bankruptcy power has led only to arbitrary and unsatisfactory results. Thus, there may have been far more wisdom than is now generally recognized in the concentration of nineteenth century lawyers and judges on specifying the scope of the powers implicit in the constitutional grant to Congress of authority over the subject of bankruptcies.

B.   Whither Security?

In 1981 Professor Alan Schwartz touched off a firestorm of academic debate that rages to this day when he asked (without finding a persuasive answer) what justifies security interests and their priority status in *Security Interests and Bankruptcy Priorities: A Review of Current Theories*, 10 J. LEGAL STUD. 1 (1981). He expanded on an earlier article by Professors Thomas Jackson and Anthony Kronman, *Secured Financing and Priorities Among Creditors*, 88 YALE L.J. 1143 (1979). Schwartz posited that the risk calculus facing creditors as a group is in effect a zero-sum game: any decrease in risk to secured creditors is matched by a corresponding risk to unsecured creditors. Each type of creditor should be expected to adjust their cost of credit accordingly, and thus any decrease in the costs of secured credit should be offset by an increase in unsecured credit costs. With transaction costs thrown into the hopper, the debtor's overall cost of credit may even increase. Thus, secured credit and its accompanying priority cannot be proven to be efficient, Schwartz argued, and the priority accorded secured claims in the event of default cannot be justified. In this Chapter, Professor Schwartz's initial article is not included (although it is highly recommended). Instead, the first excerpt in this section is from Schwartz's follow-up article, *The Continuing Puzzle of Secured Debt*, 37 VAND. L. REV. 1051 (1984). In this piece, Schwartz tidily restates and updates his original thesis.

The principal modern defenders of the institution of secured credit are given the stage next. Professors Steven Harris and Charles Mooney served as co-reporters for the revision of Article 9 in the 1990s, and throughout they staunchly supported security. Indeed, they identified as their "first principle" that "Article 9 should facilitate the creation of security interests." Mooney and Harris provide their most sophisticated formal defense of security and its accompanying priority in *A Property-Based Theory of Security Interests: Taking Debtor's Choices Seriously*, 80 VA. L. REV. 2021 (1994). They reject the premises of the "Efficiency" literature and assert instead that the secured credit puzzle must be viewed as an empirical question. Their own justification for security turns on their view of security as a form of property, which the debtor-owner presumptively should be empowered to alienate as the debtor sees fit, just as for any other type of property. Nor do they find any bankruptcy-specific policy that dictates ignoring the debtor's choices. Professor Schwartz rejoined by questioning the Harris and Mooney hypothesis in Alan Schwartz, *Taking the Analysis of Security Seriously*, 80 VA. L. REV. 2073 (1994).

The Chapter then makes a quantum shift from the arch-defenders of secured credit to its arch-enemies. In a landmark article by Lucian Arye Bebchuk & Jesse M. Fried, *The Uneasy Case for the Priority of Secured Claims in Bankruptcy*, 105 YALE L.J. 857 (1996), the authors challenge the established scheme that accords priority to secured claims. Instead, they assert that "contrary to this conventional view, the efficiency case for full priority is at best problematic." Bebchuk and Fried find "that according full priority to secured claims leads to distortions in the arrangements negotiated between commercial borrowers and their creditors, which in turn generate a number of inefficiencies," and propose "that these inefficiencies could be reduced or eliminated by according only partial priority to secured claims, and that a rule of partial priority therefore may well be superior to the rule of full priority from the perspective of efficiency." What is particularly intriguing about this frontal assault on the priority of secured claims is that it comes from two adherents of the "economic" view; in a sense, one could best characterize this article as a "palace revolt."

Another excellent presentation of the case against full priority for secured claims is by Lynn LoPucki, who in *The Unsecured Creditor's Bargain*, 80 VA. L. REV. 1887 (1994) argues that "Security tends to misallocate resources by imposing on unsecured creditors a bargain to which many, if not most, of them have given no meaningful consent." LoPucki expresses particular concern over the unfairness of the present system to involuntary unsecured creditors, and concludes that such involuntary creditors should be afforded priority over all voluntary creditors, secured and unsecured alike—that is, a "tort-first" regime. LoPucki's second major thesis is that "secured creditors who sought to bind unsecured creditors to a subordinate position would have to take whatever steps were reasonable to communicate their intentions to those unsecured creditors." Insufficient information, in short, undermines the justification for secured priority.

A further defense of security and its priority can be found in Steven L. Schwarcz, *The Easy Case for the Priority of Secured Claims in Bankruptcy*, 47 DUKE L.J. 425 (1997). Professor Schwarcz echoes many of the Harris and Mooney principles regarding the benefits of security.

Schwarcz's main theme is that "New money secured credit appears to be class Pareto efficient because such credit would make the classes of secured creditors and debtors better off, without making unsecured creditors, as a class, worse off. Unsecured creditors as a class are better off under a rule of full priority because the availability of secured credit increases debtor liquidity and therefore increases the expected value of unsecured claims."

Alan Schwartz
The Continuing Puzzle of Secured Debt
37 VAND. L. REV. 1051 (1984)[*]

I. INTRODUCTION

In 1981, I wrote an article showing that no good answer had been given to the question why corporations issue some debt on a secured basis and other debt on an unsecured basis. This showing had normative implications because claims that the institution of personal property security is efficient or otherwise desirable must be impeached if the actual purposes that security serves are unknown. Consequently, the law's favorable treatment of secured debt—for example, giving it first place in bankruptcy distributions—is without plausible support. My article did not advocate repealing the privileges attached to secured debt, however, because then-current knowledge also did not permit very precise predictions about repeal's effects. Rather, I claimed, the appropriate response to ignorance is enlightenment through research. This article caused a stir among lawyers but, for reasons that will become clear, not among economists. A generation of lawyers has been taught that security is a good thing. . . .

II. THE MM HYPOTHESIS AND THE SECURED DEBT PUZZLE

Before 1958, finance economists thought that a corporation could increase its value in two ways—by increasing its income (without taking undue risks) and by issuing the correct mix of debt and equity securities. Therefore, the accepted wisdom was that corporate managers who wanted to maximize profits had the two distinct tasks of choosing appropriate projects for their firms and selecting "optimal capital structures." The MM hypothesis, the first version of which was published in 1958, holds that under certain assumptions there is only one task to perform—to choose appropriate projects. A corporation, Modigliani and Miller proved, could not increase its value by altering its capital structure; firm value is solely a function of the size and risk of the firm's income stream. Consequently, the MM hypothesis concludes that no optimal capital structure exists; any particular structure is as good as any other.

The logic underlying the MM hypothesis is simple. A corporation could increase its value by altering its capital structure only if investors valued particular capital structures and so were willing to pay premiums to firms for adopting them. . . . Under the MM assumptions, investors place a value of zero on any particular corporate form and so will pay no premium to hold shares reflecting it. Consequently, no firm can increase its value by altering its capital structure. . . . In the world of the MM hypothesis, investors can hold unleveraged portfolios, by holding stock only in all equity firms, or they can hold any portion and quality of debt they want by appropriate lending—buying a firm's bonds—or borrowing.

The assumptions that generated the MM result varied in their realism. The MM proof assumed perfect capital markets, which meant that individual investors can borrow and lend on the same terms as firms could. Modigliani and Miller also assumed that all debt is riskless—equivalently, that bankruptcy costs are zero—and that no taxes exist. The first assumption, many believe, is not far wrong but the last two are plainly false. Modigliani and Miller of course knew this. And they also knew that firms act as if capital structure matters . . . . Rather, Modigliani and Miller adopted their assumptions for heuristic purposes. In an "ideal world," capital structure does not matter. The analyst's task is to relax the assumptions selectively; for example, to assume that bankruptcy costs are positive but that the other assumptions hold, and then to ask whether this new model explains what actually is observed. If it does, then, following our example, bankruptcy costs would be the key to capital structure. If not, then the analyst can try something else. . . .

My article was written against this intellectual background. If no one knew why firms issue debt rather than equity, or why they issue preferred rather than common stock, it was unlikely that everyone knew why firms issue secured rather than unsecured debt, or why markets generate the mixture of secured and unsecured debt that is observed. Consequently, I made a series of assumptions much like those of MM and proved that firms cannot increase their value by issuing one form of debt rather than another. If they cannot, security should not be seen because security is costly for firms to issue; firms will not incur costs that are unmatched by corresponding gains. The logic of my proof also was simple. Secured creditors will charge lower interest rates because security reduces their risks, but unsecured creditors will raise their interest rates in response because security reduces the assets on which they can levy, and so *increases* their risks. The interest rate reductions are precisely matched by interest rate increases; hence, the firm makes no net gain from granting security. . . . [T]he conclusions I drew from this fact were unsurprising to economists; in effect, the economists already knew.

The assumptions that underlay my proof also were unrealistic and I knew that much secured debt exists, but I was playing the same game as Modigliani and Miller. Much of my article consisted in relaxing the assumptions on which my proof rested or adding additional factors, to see whether a convincing explanation for the present pattern of secured lending would emerge. None did. This is not to say that none will but . . . none yet has. . . .

V. The MM Hypothesis Revisited: Sources of Possible Explanation

A central problem . . . is . . . why a *variety* of debt instruments is seen. . . . Finance economists have begun to address the "variety" question by focusing on the existence of taxes and bankruptcy costs. . . .

The likelihood of firms to incur bankruptcy costs—*i.e.*, to experience financial distress—rises with the amount of debt in their capital structures; simply, the more a firm borrows the more likely it is to default, other things equal. Thus, the expected costs of financial distress constrain the amount of debt firms will find it optimal to assume. Also, the more risky a firm is, the more likely it is to fail. Since the costs of financial distress rise with the amount of debt that a firm issues, scholars have predicted that high risk firms will issue less debt than low risk firms, but the facts do not strongly support the predictions. These financial distress models ultimately may contribute to understanding the secured debt puzzle, but understanding seems far away. One intuitive reason for the lack of help these models give is that the presence of security seems to correlate positively with risk, yet the presence of risk, at least in theory, seems to correlate negatively with debt; and security cannot be taken if no debt exists.

A promising heuristic that these recent analyses of the MM problem suggest, however, is to ask why *some* debtors find security less costly than other debtors do, and why *some* investors/lenders want it more than others do. Inquiries should focus directly on the possibility of differential preferences among debtors and creditors regarding security. . . . Another possibility is to focus on the differing characteristics of debtors. Retailers that borrow, for example, seemingly are secured more frequently than manufacturers that borrow. . . . This Article's task is not to develop such a theory, but rather to suggest that answers to the secured debt puzzle are less likely to be found in simple notions that "security interests reduce risk" than in careful analyses of the *differing* preferences for security among debtors and creditors.

VI. CONCLUSION

The secured debt puzzle remains: firms issue much debt on a secured basis, yet the causes and effects of this practice are largely unknown. The normative implications of this ignorance are a separate question. Professor White argues that security should not be banned because creditors will substitute more costly ways to achieve the objectives that security now serves. This argument is correct but beside the point. No one has argued, at least not in the last three decades, that security should be banned. The issue concerns the priority position of secured debt in the event of default, and this issue usually entails clashes between equity and efficiency goals. For example, it is one thing to say that employee claims should come behind secured creditor claims in bankruptcy if it is *known* that security as an institution creates important efficiency gains for the economy as a whole. It is another thing to argue for this position on the ground that although security itself may be a bad thing, secured lending will become marginally more costly if poor employees are moved ahead in the line. Calling the efficiency properties of security into question, that is, will and should influence the balancing process usually invoked to solve bankruptcy distribution questions. Indeed, ignorance regarding the true properties of security may underlie the Bankruptcy Code's relatively unfavorable treatment of the secured creditor, which is done to increase the likelihood that insolvent firms will reorganize; and reorganizations are thought to be desirable largely because they save jobs and sometimes salvage something for small equity investors. That ignorance respecting security can have such policy consequences makes research into its actual nature an important matter, both for those to whom recent bankruptcy distributional trends are desirable and for those to whom these trends are undesirable.

Steven L. Harris & Charles Mooney, Jr.
A Property-Based Theory of Security Interests: Taking Debtor's Choices Seriously
80 VA. L. REV. 2021 (1994)[*]

INTRODUCTION

In embarking upon the revision of what many consider the most successful commercial statute ever, we take as our "first principle" that Uniform Commercial Code Article 9 should facilitate the creation of security interests. Stated otherwise, we think the transfer of an effective security interest ought to be as easy, inexpensive, and reliable as possible. . . .

Our position has been controversial. The nineteenth and early twentieth century saw many secured transactions struck down on the ground that they were at least potentially injurious to unsecured creditors. A good deal of the perceived injury stemmed from the distributional consequences of security: property subject to a security interest would be unavailable for distribution to unsecured

---

creditors. If the debtor became insolvent, allocation of particular property to secured creditors would unjustly interfere with, and perhaps eliminate, the recovery by unsecured creditors.

. . . [T]his discomfort persists. Contemporary commentators have continued the tradition of expressing diffuse suspicion about the "favored" treatment the law affords to security interests. The fact that secured creditors appear to recover a larger portion of their claims in bankruptcy than do unsecured creditors has been of particular concern. . . .

In this Article we identify and explain a normative basis for our first principle of secured transactions. . . .

Part II.A. examines the creation of security interests as a subset of the law governing private property. The well-accepted rights of property owners—to use and freely and effectively to alienate their property and to be secure in their ownership—form the basis of our normative theory of secured transactions. Like broader theories of property law, which generally validate the decisions of debtors to transfer their property outright, our theory generally validates the decisions of debtors to transfer their property for collateral purposes. And like the broader theories, our theory respects personal autonomy and freedom of contract. In developing our theory, we seek to put to rest any general skepticism about the value of security interests and biases against the creation and effectiveness of security interests. . . . [T]he property analysis does account for the general proposition that parties are entitled to allocate their resources among their creditors as they see fit. . . .

II. SECURITY INTERESTS AS PROPERTY
A. Free and Effective Alienability of Property and Freedom of Contract: A Normative Theory of Secured Transactions

Our normative theory of security interests is grounded upon the normative theories that justify the institution of private property. The right to own private property is the bedrock of capitalism and an essential component of a market economy. Consider four elements of the ownership of property:

> (i) the right to use an asset (*usus*), (ii) the right to capture benefits from that asset (*usus fructus*), (iii) the right to change its form and substance (*abusus*), and (iv) the right to transfer all or some of the rights specified under (i), (ii), and (iii) to others at a mutually agreed upon price.

Implicit in these elements is an owner's right to exclude others from exercising ownership rights over the owner's property. . . .

According to a well-known economic account, private property promotes efficiency by providing incentives for the allocation of property to those who place the highest value on its use. . . .

A central feature of the economic account of property is the transferability—free alienability—of property rights, without which resources could not find their way to users who value them more. Nevertheless, some restrictions on alienability actually may promote efficiency. . . .

In our legal culture the principle of freedom of contract is closely interrelated with private ownership and free alienation of property. Each concept manifests respect for the autonomy of the persons concerned. . . .

We embrace the baseline principles that underlie current law insofar as it generally respects the free and effective alienation of property rights and the ability of parties to enter into enforceable contracts. We believe that these principles reflect widely shared normative views that favor party autonomy concerning both property and contract. . . . [W]e accept them as sound and consider their implications for the law of secured transactions.

It seems clear enough that security interests, under Article 9 and real estate law alike, are interests in property. The legal regime for security interests reflects property law functionally as well as doctrinally. We believe it follows that the law should honor the transfer or retention of security interests on the same normative grounds on which it respects the alienation of property generally. Because security interests are property, any *general* theory of the law of secured transactions must emanate from theories of property law. The challenges posed . . . derive primarily from the distributive effects of secured credit on unsecured creditors of a debtor who has become insolvent. . . . [I]nsofar as any distributive effects of wealth transfers and any adverse effects on existing and future unsecured creditors are concerned, the transfer of a security interest does not differ fundamentally from other transfers of a property interest in exchange for equivalent value. Thus, to carry the day, those who question secured transactions must attack the generally applicable treatment of party autonomy in property and contract law or must explain why secured transactions differ from other transactions that the law respects.

The legal regime's respect for transfers of property interests . . . is based in large part on the idea that respecting an owner's liberty to freely alienate its property generally promotes social welfare. . . .

The positive value of permitting debtors to give security freely and effectively suggests two important rules of thumb to be followed in the process of revising Article 9. First, the drafters should purge Article 9 of obstacles to the creation of effective security interests. . . . Second, the scope of Article 9 should be expanded. . . .

III. Security Interests and Bankruptcy Policy

. . . [T]he questions and concerns raised [about security] . . . stem primarily from the distributive effects of secured credit when a debtor becomes insolvent. . . . A principal motivation for taking security is the desire to increase the likelihood of payment in the event of bankruptcy. The purposes and benefits of giving and taking security would be undermined considerably if security interests were not generally honored in bankruptcy.

. . . [W]e examine two possible bases for tension between bankruptcy policy and a property-based normative theory of secured transactions that generally gives effect to security interests. First, bankruptcy policy might conflict with honoring a debtor's prebankruptcy transfers of property generally. Second, there might be something special about security interests that gives rise to a conflict with bankruptcy policy. We conclude that there is no conflict of either kind. . . .

Certainly no conflict arises between the Bankruptcy Code's basic policies and either the general respect the Code affords to the debtor's prebankruptcy transfers of property (including security interests) or the corresponding respect the Code shows for the rights of those (including secured parties) who have property interests that do not belong to the debtor. Indeed, respect for nonbankruptcy property interests lies at the heart of the Bankruptcy Code. . . .

We see nothing in the Bankruptcy Code that suggests any animus toward prebankruptcy transfers generally. And, although the Bankruptcy Code explicitly recognizes and makes provision for secured claims, for the most part it does not single out secured transactions. . . .

Say what one will about whether the drafters of Article 9 facilitated the creation of secured credit more than they could have imagined. But the Bankruptcy Code was drafted in the shadow of Article 9. . . . Congress clearly left the door open for secured creditors to take everything in bankruptcy.

Nothing in the Bankruptcy Code instructs the drafters of the new Article 9 to make secured credit less available, more expensive, or more risky. . . . We submit that unsecured creditors of insolvent debtors go unpaid in bankruptcy because their debtors have gone broke. . . . [E]ven if secured creditors were to take everything in every insolvency, that would tell us nothing about whether secured credit is beneficial to unsecured creditors or society generally. . . .

IV. Conclusion

. . . In taking issue with a number of our material points and with our conclusions, Professor Schwartz asserts that we have "fail[ed] to take the analysis of security seriously." Most readers easily will see that by this phrase Schwartz means that we have failed to approach his "puzzle" of secured credit on his terms and in the manner he and some other contributors to the Efficiency Literature previously have chosen to address the subject. Instead, we have based our analysis on two assumptions that we do not believe can be seriously questioned: that something like security interests will continue to be an important feature of our legal landscape, and that much credit would not be extended without security. Given these assumptions, we have explored whether the extension of secured credit to a debtor necessarily is harmful to the debtor's unsecured creditors, as some (including Schwartz) have assumed. Professor Schwartz's critique fails to shake our conclusions. To the contrary, we are gratified that Schwartz apparently has conceded that the question is an empirical one.

We see secured transactions as a subset of property law and secured credit as one species of exchange for value.

Lucian Arye Bebchuk & Jesse M. Fried
The Uneasy Case for the Priority of Secured Claims in Bankruptcy
105 Yale L.J. 857 (1996)[*]

I. Introduction

This Article challenges the desirability of a fundamental and longstanding feature of bankruptcy law: the principle that a secured creditor is entitled to receive the entire amount of its secured claim—the portion of its bankruptcy claim that is fully backed by collateral—before any unsecured claims are paid. There is a widespread consensus among legal scholars and economists that the rule of according full priority to secured claims is desirable because it promotes economic efficiency. The analysis we offer demonstrates that, contrary to this conventional view, the efficiency case for full priority is at best problematic. We find that according full priority to secured claims leads to distortions in the arrangements negotiated between commercial borrowers and their creditors, which in turn generate a number of inefficiencies. Our analysis indicates that these inefficiencies could be reduced or eliminated by according only partial priority to secured claims, and that a rule of partial priority therefore may well be superior to the rule of full priority from the perspective of efficiency. . . .

We will show that a rule according full priority to secured claims in bankruptcy tends to reduce the efficiency of the loan arrangement negotiated between a commercial borrower and a potentially secured creditor. That is, full priority tends to reduce the total value captured by the borrower, the potentially secured creditor, and all other parties affected by the arrangement, which we assume to be the borrower's other creditors.

Our analysis does suggest that the loan arrangement between a commercial borrower and a potentially secured creditor under the rule of full priority would be efficient in a hypothetical world in which the use of a security interest does not have distributional consequences for the borrower's other creditors. . . .

*   Reprinted by permission of The Yale Law Journal Company and Fred B. Rothman & Company from The Yale Law Journal, Vol. 105, pages 857-934.

In the real world, however, the creation of a security interest under the rule of full priority has distributional consequences. In particular, under the rule of full priority, the creation of a security interest diverts value from creditors that do not "adjust" the size of their claims to take into account the effect of the loan transaction that creates the security interest, including the fact that any security interest given to the secured creditor subordinates their unsecured claims.

A firm will have many such "nonadjusting" creditors. The size of the claims of any tort creditors will not take into account the existence of a security interest encumbering the borrower's assets. Similarly, the size of government tax and regulatory claims will be fixed by statute without regard to the possibility that the claims may be subordinated by a secured claim in bankruptcy. There will also be nonadjusting creditors whose claims arise out of voluntary dealings with the borrower. Many creditors will have claims that are simply too small to justify the cost of taking the security interest into account when contracting with the borrower, and will thus be "rationally uninformed" about the borrower's financial structure. Finally, any contractual creditor that extends credit on fixed terms before a decision is made whether to create a particular security interest, and is therefore unable to adjust its claim to take into account the fact that the security interest is created, will be nonadjusting with respect to that security interest.

The fact that security interests may be used to transfer value from nonadjusting creditors under a full-priority rule means that security interests may be used even when they give rise to inefficiencies. . . . [T]he ability to use security interests to divert value from nonadjusting creditors tends to distort the borrower's choice of contractual arrangements with its creditors, giving rise to certain efficiency costs. . . .

Accordingly, we believe that full priority is unlikely to be the most efficient rule for allocating value between secured and unsecured creditors. We therefore will consider as alternatives to the rule of full priority two bankruptcy priority rules that would reduce or eliminate the inefficiencies we identify by according only partial priority to secured claims. The first partial-priority rule presented—the "adjustable priority rule"—would operate like the rule of full priority, except that the bankruptcy share of each nonadjusting creditor would be determined by treating the secured claims to which it could not adjust as unsecured claims. The effect of this rule, which would prevent a secured claim from subordinating the claims of any creditors that could not adjust to it, would be to transfer some bankruptcy value from secured creditors to nonadjusting creditors. The second partial-priority rule would treat a fixed fraction of every secured claim as an unsecured claim, rendering all secured creditors at least partially unsecured. . . .

Neither of the partial-priority rules presented would be superior to the rule of full priority in all respects. Any partial-priority rule would involve certain efficiency costs and create certain enforcement challenges. . . . [T]here may well be a partial-priority rule that is superior to full priority from the standpoint of efficiency.

Our analysis also considers other issues related to the adoption of a mandatory partial-priority rule. We show that, if partial priority is preferable to full priority, the adoption of such a rule should not be left to private ordering. That is, borrowers should not be given the choice to opt into or out of such a rule. We also demonstrate that a mandatory partial-priority regime would be consistent with fundamental principles of contract law. We show that partial priority would give the secured creditor the benefit of its bargain and not be unfair. We also show that since the creation of a security interest in favor of a particular creditor under full priority transfers value from nonconsenting third parties, limiting the priority accorded to secured claims would not violate conventional notions of freedom of contract. . . .

II. Toward Reconsideration of the Priority of Secured Claims in Bankruptcy

The notion that a secured creditor is entitled to recover the full value of its collateral (up to the amount of its claim) whenever a borrower defaults on a secured loan permeates conventional thinking about the treatment of secured creditors in bankruptcy. The first two sections of this part therefore offer a brief and intuitive explanation why giving a secured creditor the full value of its collateral in bankruptcy is problematic. The third and last section then explains why the adoption of an explicit partial-priority rule would not be as radical a move as it might seem at first glance. . . .

A. *The General Prohibition Against Nonconsensual Subordination*

One of the most important purposes of a bankruptcy system is to allocate the value of a bankrupt debtor's assets among its creditors. . . .

A fundamental feature of bankruptcy allocation rules is that they are mandatory. That is, a borrower may not circumvent the distribution rules by subordinating or reducing one creditor's bankruptcy claim in favor of another's. . . .

While the borrower may not give C_1's claim priority over C_2's with a simple contract, under the rule of full priority it may do so in effect merely by creating a security interest in favor of C_1. It is anomalous that, by complying with a few mechanical procedures, the borrower and C_1 may arrange to give C_1's claim priority not only over C_2's claim, but also over the claims of every other ordinary unsecured creditor without any of those creditors' consent, when the general rule is that the borrower may not give C_1's claim priority over that of any other unsecured creditor without the latter's consent.

. . . It . . . might be argued that a security interest and a simple contract giving C_1's claim priority over that of C_2 are not really alike: Since the security interest is publicly registered, creditors whose bankruptcy allocation is affected by the creation of the security interest may learn of the security interest and adjust the terms of their arrangements with the borrower to compensate themselves for the risk of subordination in bankruptcy. . . .

But to the extent that the other creditors of a borrower are unable to adjust the terms of their arrangements when the borrower creates a security interest subordinating their claims, the argument that these creditors implicitly consent to subordination loses its force. And, . . . many of the creditors of a commercial borrower are likely to be nonadjusting with respect to security interests created by the borrower. . . . When these creditors are not able to adjust their claims against the borrower when it creates a security interest subordinating their claims, they cannot be regarded as even implicitly consenting to the subordination of their claims.

It should be clear that the rule of full priority creates a discontinuity between a borrower's general inability to subordinate the claim of one unsecured creditor to that of another and its ability, through the use of a security interest, to transform an unsecured creditor into a secured creditor with a claim that has priority over not one but all of the borrower's unsecured creditors. Full priority is consequently in tension—rather than in harmony—with an important principle of bankruptcy law— that a borrower may not circumvent the statutory allocation scheme by changing the priority rankings of various creditors without their consent.

B. *Value Transfer and Efficiency*

. . . [W]e now turn to the intuition that underlies much of our economic analysis: that, when two parties are able to create a contractual arrangement that transfers value from a nonconsenting third party, they will have an incentive to create such an arrangement even if value is lost as a result. That is, the two parties will have an incentive to transfer value from the nonconsenting party even if doing so reduces the total value that is available to all three parties.

. . . [F]ull priority permits a borrower to subordinate the claims of nonconsenting unsecured creditors. This in turn gives the borrower and the secured creditor an incentive to use even value-reducing arrangements to transfer value from these parties. . . . [A] borrower's ability to transfer value by using security interests may in fact cause the borrower to create a security interest in order to transfer bankruptcy value to the secured creditor, even if use of the security interest would be inefficient. . . . [F]ull priority may also distort the borrower's investment and precaution decisions and reduce the secured creditor's incentive to control inefficient behavior by the borrower after credit is extended.

All of the above inefficiencies result from the ability of a borrower, under full priority, to transfer value from nonconsenting unsecured creditors. To the extent that a borrower is not permitted to transfer value from nonconsenting creditors, it will have less of an incentive to adopt value-reducing arrangements for that purpose, and the severity of the inefficiencies will decrease. For this reason, a rule according only partial priority to secured claims may well be more efficient than the rule of full priority.

C. *Would Adopting a Partial-Priority Rule Be a Radical Change?*

. . . [T]he principle of full priority has a long history in U.S. bankruptcy law, and the notion that a secured creditor is entitled to the full value of the collateral backing its interest is deeply rooted in thinking about the subject. Thus, even if a partial-priority rule appears to be desirable from the standpoint of efficiency, there might be reluctance to adopt such a rule. . . .

But the adoption of a formal rule of partial priority would not in fact be as sweeping a change as it might seem. Notwithstanding the long history of the principle of full priority, certain features of Chapter 11 reorganizations tend either to waste value or to enrich junior claimants at the expense of secured creditors. . . . Thus, the U.S. bankruptcy system already implements a rule of de facto partial priority. . . .

IV. The Incentive to Use Security Interests Under Full Priority

The purpose of this part is to show that, in the presence of nonadjusting creditors, the parties to a loan contract may have an incentive to use an inefficient security interest when secured claims are accorded full priority in bankruptcy. . . .

A. *The Loan Contract Between Firm and Creditor*

The analysis that follows will focus on a hypothetical relationship between Bank, a creditor that is in the business of lending money to commercial borrowers, and Firm, a commercial borrower. . . .

From the standpoint of efficiency, the arrangement will be desirable to the extent that it increases social wealth. Therefore, the optimal arrangement is the one that maximizes the value captured by Firm, Bank, and all other parties affected by the arrangement, which we assume to be Firm's other creditors. However, Bank and Firm will have an incentive to shape the arrangement—which may or may not include a security interest—in the manner that maximizes their private joint gains. As we will see, in the presence of nonadjusting creditors, the arrangement that makes them best off is unlikely to be the socially optimal arrangement. Our aim will be to analyze systematically the ways in which the rule of full priority for secured claims increases the divergence between the socially desirable arrangement and the one Bank and Firm have an incentive to adopt.

B. *The Easy Case for Full Priority in a World with Perfectly Adjusting Creditors*

. . . Consider a world in which the claims of all creditors other than Bank perfectly reflect all elements of the agreement between Bank and Firm. . . .

In such a world, the arrangement between Bank and Firm could not impose a negative externality on these other creditors, meaning that Bank and Firm could not make these creditors worse off. Thus, Bank and Firm would never adopt an inefficient security interest in order to divert value from other creditors. These creditors would simply respond by raising their interest rates to recover the value diverted, leaving Bank and Firm to bear the net efficiency costs associated with the inefficient security interest. Nor in such a world could the arrangement between Bank and Firm confer a positive externality on the other creditors, making them better off, since the other creditors would reduce the size of their claims against Firm to reflect the benefits flowing to them from the arrangement. Thus, Bank and Firm would capture all of the benefits of any contractual term that is desirable, and have an incentive to adopt it.

Since Bank and Firm would bear all of the net efficiency losses and enjoy all of the net efficiency benefits of their arrangement, Bank and Firm would find it in their interest to choose the socially optimal arrangement. The bargain struck between Bank and Firm would therefore tend to be efficient. Thus, according full priority to secured claims in bankruptcy could not give rise to any inefficiencies.

C. *The Presence of Nonadjusting Creditors*

In the real world, in contrast to the world assumed in the previous section, the use of a security interest giving Bank's secured claim full priority may make Bank and Firm better off by transferring bankruptcy value from creditors that cannot adjust the size of their claims against Firm to take into account the existence of the security interest. And . . . every commercial borrower will have many creditors that are unable to make such adjustments.

1. *Private Involuntary Creditors*

. . . [A]ccording full priority to secured claims permits a firm to divert value from its tort creditors. . . . These tort creditors cannot adjust their claims to reflect the existence of a security interest. . . .

2. *Government Tax and Regulatory Claims*

Although tort claims against bankrupt firms may in some cases be substantial, on aggregate they are not as significant as the claims of the second group of involuntary creditors: federal, state, and local government agencies with tax and regulatory claims. . . .

The size of the government's various tax and regulatory claims are set by statute without regard to a firm's capital structure and, in particular, without regard to any security interests the firm may have created that subordinate these claims to those of secured creditors. Thus, the government is nonadjusting with respect to any security interests created by a firm. As a result, when a firm and creditor must decide whether to create a security interest, the firm will treat its tax and regulatory obligations to the government—like its obligations to tort creditors—as fixed.

3. *Voluntary Creditors with Small Claims*

. . . [T]he fact that a creditor voluntarily contracts with a firm does not necessarily make that creditor adjusting with respect to any security interest created by the firm. Many of a firm's voluntary creditors are customers, employees, and trade creditors that have relatively small claims against the firm. Even though these creditors may sometimes, in principle, be able to take the existence of a security interest into account in contracting with the firm, the small size of their claims will generally make it irrational for them to do so. . . .

4. *Prior Voluntary Creditors*

. . . There is another category of voluntary creditors that would be nonadjusting with respect to particular security interests: creditors with unsecured claims—no matter how large—that extend credit on fixed terms before the borrower makes a decision whether or not to create those security interests. To the extent that the terms set by the creditors are fixed, such creditors, no matter how commercially sophisticated, will not be able to adjust with respect to any security interest subsequently created by the borrower. . . .

D. *Full Priority and the Decision to Create a Security Interest*

We are now ready to consider how, under the rule of full priority, the presence of nonadjusting creditors affects the borrower's and a potentially secured creditor's decision about whether to create a security interest.. . . .

The reason Firm is better off inefficiently pledging the . . . asset is that nonadjusting creditors will not raise their interest rates to take into account the effect of encumbering that asset on them. . . .

Whether or not the nonadjusting creditors in this example are compensated for the increased risk of loss due to the creation of the . . . security interests, what these creditors charge Firm will not be affected by the actual arrangement between Firm and Bank—because they are involuntary, or are rationally uninformed about Firm's arrangement with Bank, or had extended credit before the transaction with Bank. Thus, the use of a security interest providing Bank with full priority in some of Firm's assets will transfer value from these creditors. Consequently, Firm and Bank will have an incentive to encumber assets with a security interest, even if this results in a loss of social value.

V. EFFICIENCY COSTS OF FULL PRIORITY

We are now ready to examine systematically five efficiency costs that arise when full priority is accorded to secured claims. The first two efficiency costs are that full priority (1) increases the use of inefficient security interests and (2) increases the use of security interests that are efficient, but less efficient than a set of covenants, and therefore undesirable. Full priority thus causes excessive use of security interests.

The last three costs—(1) distorted investment and precaution decisions of the borrower; (2) suboptimal use of the covenants by the secured creditor; and (3) suboptimal enforcement efforts by the secured creditor—are priority-dependent efficiency costs of security interests. . . .

A. *The Use of Inefficient Security Interests*

As we saw in Part IV, a borrower and a secured creditor may have incentives under full priority to expend resources inefficiently encumbering an asset merely to transfer bankruptcy value from nonadjusting creditors. That is, a borrower and a secured creditor may adopt a security interest that gives the two parties a larger slice of the pie at the expense of nonadjusting creditors even though the security interest at the same time reduces the size of the total pie. This is the first efficiency cost of full priority. . . .

B. *Distorted Choice Between Security Interests and Covenants*

Full priority may also cause commercial borrowers and their sophisticated creditors to use a security interest that is less efficient than a set of covenants in order to control inefficient behavior by the borrower after the loan transaction. . . .

C. *Distorted Investment and Precaution Decisions*

. . . We now turn to a different category of costs that arises from full priority: costs that may arise whenever a security interest is used under full priority. These priority-dependent efficiency costs make the use of any given security interest less efficient or more inefficient than it would be in the absence of priority. Thus, these costs would arise even if full priority did not affect the overall use of security interests.

The first priority-dependent efficiency cost of security interests is that their use under full priority may distort a borrower's choice of investments and level of precaution. . . .

Consider the case in which Firm must decide, prior to contracting with Bank, whether to take certain precautions that will make its products safer and thereby reduce the number of future tort claims against Firm. . . .

Under the rule of full priority, . . . Firm may give Bank a security interest that more or less protects the value of Bank's loan from being diluted by tort claims. To the extent that Bank is given a security interest that insulates its claim from the effect of Firm's activities, it will not charge a higher interest rate if Firm fails to take precautions and additional tort claims against Firm are expected. And, to the extent Firm does not face the prospect of a higher interest rate if it fails to take precautions, Firm will have less incentive to invest in these precautions. . . .

D. *Suboptimal Use of Covenants*

The second priority-dependent efficiency cost of security interests is that their use, under full priority, may cause a secured creditor to use too few covenants. As we explained in Part IV, in a perfect world in which the terms of other creditors' loan agreements fully reflect the consequences to them of the arrangement between a borrower and a creditor, the two parties would have an incentive to adopt any covenant that is efficient because they would capture all of the resulting benefits. In the real world, however, nonadjusting creditors would capture part of the benefits and bear none of the costs of any set of covenants negotiated between the contracting parties. Consequently, even if the set of covenants were socially optimal because its total benefits exceeded its total costs, it would not be privately optimal for the borrower and the creditor if the benefits accruing to the contracting creditor (and any other adjusting creditors) were less than the costs to the borrower. . . .

E. *Suboptimal Enforcement Efforts*

. . . [T]he use of the security interest under full priority will permit the borrower to act more inefficiently following the extension of credit. . . .

Even in the absence of full priority, a creditor will engage in less than the optimal amount of enforcement activity since some of the benefit of this activity will flow to other creditors, while it (and the borrower) will bear all of the costs. But the creditor will have even less of an incentive to engage in enforcement activities to the extent that it is protected from risk of loss by a security interest giving the creditor's claim full priority in bankruptcy . . . . As a result, a borrower may be more likely to violate a covenant and to act inefficiently when its sophisticated creditors have security interests giving them full priority in their collateral. . . . [F]ull priority . . . may . . . lead to efficiency problems—by reducing the creditor's incentive to monitor the borrower's compliance with those covenants. . . .

VI. POSSIBLE ALTERNATIVES TO FULL PRIORITY

. . . In this part we present two rules that would reduce or eliminate these inefficiencies by providing only partial priority to secured claims. The first partial-priority rule presented, the "adjustable priority rule," works by denying secured claims priority over the claims of nonadjusting creditors. This approach, if properly implemented, would eliminate all of the inefficiencies associated with full priority that we identified. Under the second partial-priority rule, the "fixed-fraction priority rule," a fixed fraction of each secured claim would be treated as an unsecured claim. Both rules would have the effect of leaving all secured creditors at least partially unsecured.

Neither of these partial-priority rules would be superior in every respect to the rule of full priority. . . . [T]here would be efficiency costs associated with these rules—or any rule of partial priority—that must be weighed against the benefits these rules would provide. However, three points need to be emphasized before we examine the rules in detail. The first is that neither of these rules would completely eliminate the priority accorded to secured claims over unsecured claims in bankruptcy. The partial-priority rules would affect only the degree to which the secured creditor enjoys priority in its collateral over the claims of unsecured creditors when the debtor enters bankruptcy. Second, a secured creditor would continue to enjoy full priority in bankruptcy over the claims of any junior secured creditors in the same assets. The third and most important point is that neither of these priority rules would have any effect on the secured creditor's "repossessory right" and state-law "priority right" outside of bankruptcy. That is, neither alternative would be inconsistent with Article 9 of the UCC or current state laws governing transactions in real property. Thus, the operation of security interests outside bankruptcy would be completely unaffected by either rule. . . .

VIII. FURTHER CONSIDERATIONS CONCERNING THE DESIRABILITY OF PARTIAL PRIORITY

. . .

B. *Leaving the Priority Rule to Private Ordering*

One might propose that U.S. firms be allowed to choose to be governed by either a full-priority or a partial-priority rule. Such an arrangement would appear to eliminate the need to determine the relative efficiency of the two rules, since each firm would presumably choose the regime that was most efficient given its particular circumstances.

However, if a firm were given the choice between a full-and a partial-priority regime, it is unlikely that it would choose the partial-priority regime even if that regime were more efficient. . . .

Given the expectation that even many voluntary creditors will not adjust the interest rate they charge to reflect the priority regime chosen by firms, allowing firms to choose between partial priority and full priority is unlikely to answer the question of which rule is socially optimal since their choice will be distorted in favor of full priority. This analysis further suggests that since firms may choose a full-priority regime over a partial-priority regime even if the partial-priority regime were more efficient, a partial-priority rule should be made mandatory rather than optional if it is believed to be the most efficient rule.

C. *Fairness and Bargain Considerations*

Our analysis thus far has focused on the rules of full and partial priority primarily from an efficiency perspective. . . . But, before closing, it is worth considering whether some other normative principle can be seen as requiring the rule of full priority.

One might take the position that giving a secured claim less than full priority in bankruptcy is inconsistent with the bargain that the secured creditor makes with the borrower and is thus unfair. . . .

However, the fairness or bargain argument for according full priority to secured claims in bankruptcy is less valid than it may appear at first glance. Under a partial-priority regime, creditors taking security interests would expect partial-priority treatment in bankruptcy (not full priority) and choose their terms accordingly. Providing them with only partial priority in the end would therefore be perfectly consistent with their initial bargain. . . .

Finally, it is worth noting that the transition to an explicit partial-priority rule need not deny secured creditors the benefit of the bargains they entered into before the change of regime. If necessary, the rule could be applied only prospectively. . . .

D. *Freedom of Contract Concerns*

. . . [O]ne might still raise the objection that such a rule constrains freedom of contract. In particular, one might argue that a partial-priority rule denies a borrower the right to grant a creditor a security interest giving the creditor full priority in the collateral under all circumstances. Indeed, the rule of full priority has been defended on just this ground.

However, freedom of contract arguments have force only with respect to arrangements that do not create direct externalities. . . . But when the contract directly impinges on the rights of third parties, there is no prima facie presumption of freedom of contract.

When an insolvent debtor enters bankruptcy, . . . an arrangement between the debtor and a particular creditor that gives the creditor more than its pro rata share of the debtor's bankruptcy assets must therefore reduce, dollar-for-dollar, the amount that will be available to other creditors—that is, such an arrangement creates a direct externality on these other creditors.

Since an arrangement that allows the debtor to increase the bankruptcy share of one party must come at the expense of another, it is only natural that the law imposes restrictions on the ability of a debtor to enter into such arrangements. . . .

IX. CONCLUSION

This Article has reexamined a basic principle of bankruptcy law—that secured claims should be accorded full priority over unsecured claims. We have taken issue with the view widely held by legal scholars and economists that economic efficiency is best served by giving secured claims full priority in bankruptcy. Our analysis has demonstrated that the rule of full priority in fact creates distortions in the contractual arrangements between commercial borrowers and their creditors, producing various efficiency costs. In particular, the Article has shown that full priority causes excessive use of security interests, reduces the incentive of firms to take adequate precautions and choose appropriate investments, and distorts the monitoring arrangements chosen by firms and their creditors.

Having identified the efficiency costs associated with full priority, we also have considered the desirability of a different approach—according only partial priority to secured claims. Our analysis of partial priority has shown that such a rule could eliminate or reduce these efficiency costs—and that such an approach may well be more efficient than the full-priority rule. Therefore, we have put forward two particular partial-priority rules—the adjustable-priority rule and the fixed-fraction priority rule—that should be considered as alternatives to the rule of full priority. Our analysis has also shown that a partial-priority rule should not be left to private ordering, could be feasibly implemented, and would be consistent with considerations of fairness and contractual freedom.

C. Valuation and Adequate Protection of Secured Claims

Whatever the theoretical merits of or justifications for the current scheme that accords full priority to secured claims in bankruptcy, the reality at least for now is that such priority will be accorded. But that does not tell us all that we need to know in order to implement and effectuate the secured claim priority. To say that a secured claim will be paid in full necessitates ascertaining what the value of the secured claim is. And, since a claim is "secured" only to the extent it is backed up by collateral, we cannot simply assume that the face amount of the claim will be the amount treated as secured and thus entitled to full priority. Rather, it is imperative to determine the value of the collateral itself. Determining the value of collateral, and thus of the secured claim, is important in numerous bankruptcy contexts. In the common scenario in which the bankruptcy judge is making a judicial assessment of the collateral's value, rather than exposing the collateral to the marketplace, the valuation challenge becomes all the more daunting. The first three excerpts speak to this most critical of bankruptcy judicial tasks: valuation.

Leading off is an excellent work by common collaborators, Professors Robert Lawless and Stephen Ferris, *Economics and the Rhetoric of Valuation*, 5 J. BANKR. L. & PRAC. 3 (1995). Lawless and Ferris first look at the role of valuation on a bankruptcy case, then turn to the economic question of what constitutes value. They note the important distinction between an asset's value and its market price, and emphasize how the two can diverge in an imperfect market, with critical consequences for bankruptcy practice. Perhaps their most useful insight is that any asset only has one "value." Lawless and Ferris then apply their ideas to three common bankruptcy settings: the valuation of an automobile for purposes of a chapter 13 "cramdown" (an issue also explored below in Part D of this Chapter); foreclosure sales as fraudulent conveyances (excerpted in Chapter 7 previously); and a motion for relief from the automatic stay.

Professor David Gray Carlson, one of the leading scholars in the field of secured claims in bankruptcy, next ruminates on the "eely character" of bankruptcy valuations. Carlson's article, *Secured Creditors and the Eely Character of Bankruptcy Valuations*, 41 AM. U. L. REV. 63 (1991), looks carefully at different theories of valuation and at the bankruptcy contexts in which valuation questions arise. He takes pains to demonstrate the inherently "subjunctive" nature of valuing assets. What does he mean by describing valuation in bankruptcy as "subjunctive," and why is that idea important? Ultimately, where does Professor Carlson come out on questions of valuation and its role in bankruptcy?

Following Carlson is an excerpt from the 1997 Review Commission's recommendations for how to value secured claims in personal property (*viz.*, at wholesale) and in real property (*viz.*, at fair market value minus hypothetical sale costs). Note that the Commission thus agreed with Lawless and Ferris. What reasons does the Commission Report give for recommending the use of those valuation standards? Note that Congress in several reform bills (none enacted as of November 2001) from 1997 to 2001 took exactly the opposite approach, requiring use of retail value when the debtor is retaining the collateral.

The last selection in this section is from the leading advocates of the "economic" approach to bankruptcy policy, Professors Thomas Jackson and Douglas Baird. In striving to elucidate the "first principles" of bankruptcy policy in the 1980s, Jackson and Baird found it imperative to explain how secured claims should be treated in bankruptcy. In one of their most important articles, *Corporate Reorganizations and the Treatment of Diverse Ownership Interests: A Comment on Adequate Protection of Secured Creditors in Bankruptcy*, 51 U. CHI. L. REV. 97 (1984), they announced their general theory. Jackson and Baird emphasize that bankruptcy rules should serve a limited function—preserving the value of the assets for the investor group. In seeking this goal, it is important to keep distinct the questions of how to deploy the debtor's assets and how the value of those assets should be distributed; that is, the answer to the distributional question ideally should not preclude using the assets in the most efficient way. But they caution that when diverse owners are involved, use decisions can affect distribution (and vice versa) because of the competing positions of various claimants. As regards secured creditors, their bottom line is that the non-bankruptcy rights of secured creditors presumptively should be honored in bankruptcy, unless a bankruptcy-specific reason dictates otherwise. That notion impacts the question of what should be afforded as adequate protection to secured creditors by dictating that the risk costs of an attempted reorganization should not be borne by secured creditors but rather by the residual claimants. In other words, unsecured creditors should not be permitted to gamble with the secured creditor's money. In concrete terms, they propose that secured creditors should be compensated for bankruptcy delay.

Robert M. Lawless & Stephen Ferris
Economics and the Rhetoric of Valuation
5 J. Bankr. L. & Prac. 3 (1995)[*]

"True value is an elusive Pimpernel."

Despite its centrality to bankruptcy law, very few commentators have critically examined the concept of valuation. Valuation is pervasive throughout the Code. . . . [T]he courts have experienced extreme difficulty in articulating what it means for an asset to have a "value." Opinions speak of "retail value," "wholesale value," "fair market value," "liquidation value," "going concern value," or "replacement value." The Bankruptcy Code may be the principal culprit behind the confusion. Section 506(a) directs that an asset's value "shall be determined in light of the purpose of valuation and of the proposed disposition or use of such property."

Although such is the confusing rhetoric of valuation, it is nevertheless unnecessary. An asset ultimately has only one value—its market value. To be sure, an asset may bring different prices in different types of sales, but these different prices do not arise because the asset has different values. Rather, the pricing differences result from the circumstances surrounding the sale or the varying expectations of market participants. Price and value are different concepts, which the confusing rhetoric of valuation mistakenly intermingles in an unduly formalistic inquiry that Section 506(a) does not mandate. Valuation issues require subjective, normative judgments to resolve. This essay outlines an economic analysis that makes the normative judgments explicit. . . .

Our goals are modest. This essay represents some preliminary thoughts concerning how the economics of the marketplace can inform the legal question of bankruptcy valuation.

The Role of Valuation in a Bankruptcy Case

Anyone who spends a few minutes in a bankruptcy courtroom will quickly see the importance of asset valuation to a bankruptcy case. The value that a bankruptcy judge assigns to a particular asset can control many issues within a bankruptcy case and often the entire bankruptcy case itself. The valuation inquiry is a factual one, drafting the bankruptcy judge into the role of asset appraiser. . . .

. . . Where parties cannot agree, bankruptcy courts determine valuation as a contested issue of fact. Typically, valuation hearings consist of each side bringing a sufficient number of expert witnesses who disagree with the other side's experts. The bankruptcy judge then will have to choose between the dueling appraisers' estimates of value or perhaps pick a point in between. The evidentiary questions are difficult enough.

But, as presently formulated, the valuation inquiry is a two-step mental process. In addition to the evidentiary questions, the bankruptcy court also selects a legal standard by which to measure value (*e.g.*, liquidation value, replacement value, or retail value). The court will apply the evidence presented at the valuation hearing to the legal standard selected and arrive at an appropriate valuation. It is the quest for a legal standard at which we take aim and fire. The quest is chimerical, nothing more than the confusing rhetoric of valuation. As we discuss later, the idea that the same asset can have different values simultaneously is economic nonsense. Courts would do better to focus only on the evidentiary question of what compromises an asset's value.

Value, Markets, and Prices

The Concept of Valuation

Beginning with the first principles, one must distinguish between an asset's value and its price. The value of an asset is simply the present value of its future cash flows. The price of an asset is the amount of money that the asset will obtain in an open market transaction. Consider a widget-making machine that can produce 2,000 widgets over the course of one year. At the end of the year, the machine will be beyond repair and lack any salvage value. Suppose further we know with absolute certainty that the profit per widget will remain constant at $5. Ignoring any time value of money effects, the widget-making machine will have a value of $10,000, and in a competitive market transaction, widget-making machines would have the same price as their value—$10,000.

Of course, there never will be such absolute certainty in an actual market. Market participants cannot know with absolute certainty how many widgets the machine can produce, the machine's useful life, or perhaps most importantly, the future sales price for widgets. Thus, the true worth of widget-making machines will not be known by market participants. Instead, the market participants will offer a price for the widget-making machine based on their best estimates of those factors that determine the machine's value.

The observed transaction price associated with the transfer of an asset's ownership thus will represent a market consensus resulting from negotiation between various individuals. To further refine this concept, one must ask how each individual establishes his own estimate of an asset's value. An individual will require estimates of the timing, amount, and riskiness of the asset's cash flows to calculate the asset's value, because these elements are the necessary inputs into the calculation of present value. Thus, an asset's value is originally investor specific, because judgments regarding the elements of present value will be subjective and vary across individuals. Once an investor has estimated an asset's value, the investor must compare this estimate to the asset's market price.

If the marketplace for an asset is efficient, it ultimately will force a convergence between the market price and the value estimated by investors. What do we mean by an "efficient market"? An efficient market addresses the availability and timeliness of information. In an efficient market, information flows freely and is widely available to interested parties. Prices are publicly quoted and free to change in response to the public release of relevant information. There are no monopolies or regulatory agencies that restrict or delay the dissemination of information that is relevant to an evaluation of an asset's risk and return. Likewise, informational asymmetries between buyers and sellers do not exist.

If an investor's estimate of value differs from market value, then competition between investors will force their alignment. . . . Thus, in equilibrium, the market price will equal the investor's estimate of value.

When Markets Fail

Although an extensive economics literature discusses market failure, our interest is restricted to an analysis of how that failure can affect asset valuation. More specifically, we are interested in the conditions that prevent market prices from serving as an unbiased measure of an asset's value. An asset's true worth always remains hidden. In estimating an asset's value, bankruptcy courts must work with market prices as estimates of true worth. But to what extent can observable market prices serve as reliable estimates of true worth?

The preceding section developed how an efficient market causes market prices to converge to the best measure of true worth. For the market mechanism to function effectively and for the resulting observed prices to be true measures of an asset's worth, we observed that the market must be "efficient."

To start with, the marketplace must be characterized by an adequate number of participants. . . .

There also must be freedom in the mobility of financial resources if market prices are to be true indications of an asset's value. . . .

Perhaps most importantly, an efficient market mechanism requires the widespread dispersion of relevant knowledge. . . .

Related to these preceding factors is the length of time an asset has exposure in the marketplace. In many ways, this is not a distinct requirement for market prices to allocate resources efficiently but rather incorporates consideration of information adequacy and the extent of participation. . . .

Applying the Basic Principles to Some Common Fact Patterns

The principles developed in the previous text are of interest to bankruptcy lawyers and judges only if these principles help to illuminate the issue of bankruptcy valuation. The following text applies these economic ideas to several situations that often arise in bankruptcy court.

Automobiles and the Chapter 13 Cramdown

The valuation of automobiles for the Chapter 13 cramdown presents itself as an issue repeatedly in the pages of the *Bankruptcy Reporter*. For purposes of illustration, consider a debtor named Sally Segue. Prior to filing her Chapter 13 petition, Sally purchased an automobile for personal use. In exchange for financing the automobile's purchase, Sally granted Dealer's Motor Acceptance Corporation (DMAC) a security interest against the automobile. As Section 1325(a)(5) directs, Sally must pay DMAC the value of its secured claim. Because Section 506(a) bifurcates DMAC's claim into secured and unsecured portions, the value of DMAC's secured claim is the value of its collateral. Sally contends that the value of the automobile is its wholesale price listed in the automobile bluebook. DMAC contends Sally must pay the bluebook's retail price. Thus, the issue is joined: should the bankruptcy court use "retail value" or "wholesale value" for purposes of the Chapter 13 cramdown?

. . . [T]he suggested inquiry misses the point. The automobile has only one value, and a better inquiry would be to ask whether the retail or wholesale market prices provide the best estimate of the automobile's value.

An analogy to a portfolio of securities may help. Suppose an investor holds a portfolio of financial securities (*e.g.*, common stock). What is the value of these securities? The bid quote is the price at which the investor can transact and dispose of the securities. The bid price could be viewed as similar to the wholesale price of an automobile. . . . The dealer is also willing to sell the shares at the ask quote. The ask quote will exceed that of the bid quote, much like the relationship between retail and wholesale prices. The difference between the bid and the ask quotes is referred to as the bid-ask spread.

The bid-ask spread represents a value-added charge by the securities dealer. In other words, it is the result of value added by the dealer to the transaction as well as a return for risk bearing. . . .

The economics of the bid-ask spread are quite pertinent to the issue presented by *In re Sally Segue*. Just like the securities dealer, the automobile retailer adds value to the transaction. The retailer maintains an inventory of automobiles, reducing the number of sites a buyer must visit to complete a transaction and thereby reducing the buyer's search costs. The retailer, like the securities dealer, also stands ready to buy and sell automobiles, thereby providing liquidity to the marketplace. A retailer also may provide explicit or implicit certifications of quality, perhaps through the retailer's reputation in the community. For example, a new automobile sold by a BMW dealership likely would be superior to one sold by a Lawless dealership because BMW automobiles have a reputation for quality but Lawless automobiles are unknown. These observations apply equally to both new and used automobiles.

As explained previously, the market mechanism will cause the retail price for automobiles to converge around purchasers' estimates of true worth. But at the retail level, these estimates will have two components: (1) each purchaser's estimate of the automobile's worth plus (2) each purchaser's estimate of the worth of the value added by the retailer. Thus, it is not accurate to say that the retail price represents, or even provides an estimate of, the automobile's value.

. . . It may be true that, economically speaking, the automobile's retail price is not a good estimate of the automobile's value. Nevertheless, Sally's creditor, DMAC, claims a legal right to be paid in an amount equal to the automobile's full retail price. The law could rationally give DMAC such an entitlement regardless of the relevant economics. The question as to whether DMAC does have an entitlement requires a normative judgment. In other words, the legal issue is quite distinct form the economic one. The Bankruptcy Code's answer to the legal issue is ambiguous, leaving it to the courts to exercise the normative judgment. We merely suggest that consideration of the situation's economics will lead to a better normative judgment.

While reasonable people can differ over the normative question of whether DMAC should have an entitlement to be paid the automobile's full retail price, we have the (computerized) pen in hand and will offer our own answer. We believe that a value that approximates the wholesale price should be the relevant measure of DMAC's claim for purposes of Chapter 13 cramdown. Our economic analysis provides several reasons for our conclusion. Most importantly, the inflated retail price includes value-adding activities by the retailer. Because DMAC is not a retailer of automobiles, it is unable to take advantage of these value-adding activities. There should be no reason why a secured creditor like DMAC should profit from the value-adding activities of others. Because the value of an automobile sold in the market at wholesale level comes almost directly from the manufacturing abilities of the dealer, the wholesale price of the automobile likely comes closest to representing the automobile's true worth.

Also, a consumer debtor like Sally cannot provide any services to the marketplace that would permit her to charge a higher retail (ask) price for her automobile. . . . Therefore, there is no windfall to Sally if she pays DMAC only the wholesale price of the automobile. Concomitantly, when DMAC contracted with Sally, it knowingly contracted with a consumer. If anything, DMAC would recognize a windfall by capturing retail value from a person DMAC knew could not provide value-adding, retail activities.

[*In* Associates Commercial Corp. v. Rash, *520 U.S. 953 (1997), the Supreme Court concluded that a debtor who proposes to retain collateral in a chapter 13 plan must pay "replacement" value to the secured creditor—although the Court's explanation of what comprises replacement value was less than crystalline.*]

[*In the next section of the article Professors Lawless and Ferris discuss the issue of value in the context of a fraudulent conveyance challenge to a foreclosure sale of real estate, a question decided by the Supreme Court in* BFP v. Resolution Trust Corp., *511 U.S. 531 (1994). That discussion was excerpted in Chapter 7 of the anthology.—Ed.*]

. . .

Machinery and Relief From the Stay

Our third example involves Raymond Excavating, a Chapter 11 debtor-in-possession. Raymond Excavating borrowed money from Finance Company to pay for the earthmoving equipment Raymond used in its business. In exchange for extending credit, Finance Company received a security interest in the earthmoving equipment. As of the date of Raymond's bankruptcy petition, Finance Company is owed $100,000. Citing a lack of adequate protection, Finance Company moves for relief from the automatic stay. Finance Company states that the retail price of similar used earthmoving equipment is $85,000 and seeks adequate protection for that amount. Raymond Excavation asserts that the earthmoving equipment would bring only $50,000 at an auction. For which amount must Raymond Excavating provide adequate protection? . . .

To answer the question posed, one need only apply the relevant economic principles to the facts. It seem obvious that Raymond should not have to provide adequate protection for value-adding activities provided by a hypothetical retailer. . . . It would be a windfall to Finance Company to receive adequate protection from these value-adding activities. The price that the equipment manufacturer charges to the retail dealer, which is probably the wholesale price, should be the estimate of the asset's true worth.

We are left, however, with Raymond's assertion that the appropriate level of adequate protection should be determined by the price the equipment would receive at an auction. If the auction would exhibit the characteristics of an efficient market, then Raymond's assertion would probably be accurate. . . . [I]t is more likely that Raymond is contemplating a distress price, a forced auction. As noted before, the typical judicial sale, whether for real or personal property, will represent the antithesis of an efficient market. In these circumstances, there would be no reason to use the hypothetical auction price as the best estimate of the asset's true worth.

When determining the appropriate level of adequate protection for cases like *In re Raymond Excavating*, bankruptcy judges often ask themselves another question we have not posed. What is the debtor's proposed use of the collateral? Section 506(a), which tells the court to value the collateral in light of "proposed disposition or use," suggests the inquiry. Nevertheless, the debtor's proposed use of the collateral is irrelevant to the collateral's true worth. In the concluding portion of this text, we will explain why we believe that a proper interpretation of Section 506(a) does not direct an inquiry into the debtor's proposed use of the collateral. In this instance, we explain why such an inquiry does not accord with economic reasoning.

For example, return to our hypothetical widget-making machine discussed earlier. Becasue the widget-making machine would generate an income stream of $10,000 over a one-year useful life, we said the machine would have a price of $10,000 in an efficient market. Suppose, however, that a debtor proposed not to use the machine in its business to produce widgets but instead decided to sell the machine as part of an auction of its assets. In this circumstance, some courts will distinguish between the value of the machine in place, as part of the debtor's ongoing business ("going-concern value"), and the value of the machine in liquidation ("liquidation value"). Such a distinction makes little economic sense. If the proposed auction will operate in an efficient market, then the machine will bring a $10,000 price — the same value as when the machine is used to produce widgets. If the machine will not bring $10,000 in an auction, then the auction is characterized by market failure, and the auction price is not a reliable market estimate of the machine's true value. When setting the appropriate level of adequate protection, bankruptcy courts should drop the inquiry into whether the debtor proposes continued use of the collateral in the debtor's business.

Some Concluding Thoughts

In these pages, we have advanced a different version of bankruptcy valuation. Our version uses economic analysis to describe valuation in a manner distinct from that currently in vogue. Our approach rests on identifying a distinction between the concepts of price and value. . . .

This essay had its genesis in the authors' frustration experienced while trying to understand the bankruptcy courts' explanation of valuation. The term "value" has permutated into a number of concurrent, yet mutually inconsistent, concepts. Now, a bankruptcy court will point at an asset and declare "liquidation value," "retail value," and so forth. Such an approach is intellectually unsatisfying. These different concepts of value had no meaning until the bankruptcy courts provided one. Giving something the label "liquidation value" or "retail value" is a formalistic legal conclusion, not reasoning toward an answer. Distilled to its essence, this essay asks the bankruptcy courts and commentators to consider both the components of an asset's value and the associated market mechanisms that provide us with the best estimates of this value.

But does the Bankruptcy Code decree the formalistic inquiry about valuation that we abhor? A decent statutory argument can be made that it does. As stated before, Section 506(a) directs that a secured creditor's collateral should be valued "in light of the purpose of the valuation and of the proposed disposition or use of such property." The "purpose of the valuation" could be read to make a formal distinction between "liquidation value," "retail value," and the other permutations of value. At the very least, the language appears to contradict our assertion that the debtor's proposed "use" of collateral should be irrelevant for the valuation inquiry. If Section 506(a) requires courts to make artificial assumptions for valuation, it defies the economics of the marketplace. . . .

For several reasons, we do not think that Section 506(a) rises to the level of a clear legislative direction for bankruptcy courts to ignore the economics of valuation. . . .

Perhaps the most persuasive evidence of the proper interpretation of Section 506(a) is its own text. Read in context, Section 506(a) directs nothing more than a flexible, case-by-case inquiry. . . .

Our own account of valuation is entirely consistent with a case-by-case, proceeding-by-proceeding, issue-by-issue approach. We ask the bankruptcy courts to consider the economics of valuation rather than blindly invoking a magical incantation of "retail value" or "wholesale value." . . . Our analysis even leaves open the possibility that in a particular situation, it may be appropriate for a bankruptcy court to make a normative judgment not to apply the result suggested by economics. Our account of valuation only forces the bankruptcy court to recognize that it is making this normative judgment.

We will end where we began, by observing that the current rhetoric of valuation is sterile, imprecise, and intellectually deficient. This is unfortunate because valuation can play a dispositive role in so many portions of a bankruptcy case. In this essay, we have provided an account of valuation that is more faithful to the economics of the marketplace. By examining the marketplace's mechanisms for valuation our analysis begins with fundamental first principles, and thereby, we humbly suggest, reasons to a more complete, accurate, and persuasive account of bankruptcy valuation. Valuation decisions ultimately rest on normative judgments. This essay outlines an economic analysis that makes these normative judgments explicit.

David Gray Carlson
Secured Creditors and the Eely Character of Bankruptcy Valuations
41 AM. U. L. REV. 63 (1991)[*]

The fallacy in that argument stems largely from lack of recognition of the eely character of the word "value." It is a bewitching word which, for years, has disturbed mental peace and caused numerous useless debates. Perhaps it would be better for the peace of men's minds if the word were abolished. Reams of good paper and volumes of good ink have been wasted by those who have tried to give it a constant and precise meaning.

—Judge Jerome Frank

Throughout the bankruptcy process—and especially in any reorganization process—the secured party's collateral must be valued. Congressional history celebrates the fact that judges are to make the rules for valuation on a case-by-case basis. . . .

Not surprisingly, bankruptcy courts have indeed gratified the wishes of Congress by producing an extremely diverse and contradictory set of valuation theories. These theories share a common element, however. None of them is a verifiable proposition. That is to say, the values derived by bankruptcy courts are not objective or even subjective facts. Rather, they are *subjunctive* facts—facts that can be assessed only contingently in the context of a hypothetical universe which can never be. . . .

II. The Subjunctive Nature of Value

Value is a function of exchange. Since a bankruptcy judge will determine value without the benefit of an historical exchange, the judge is required to hypothesize one. The rules for this speculation have never been spelled out. But this much can be said. Inevitably, valuation must invoke a picture of what a secured party could realize from the collateral if no bankruptcy had occurred. . . . [V]aluation invokes an alternative universe in which the bankruptcy petition was never filed and where no automatic stay exists to prevent repossession and foreclosure.

This hypothetical universe with its alternate history is governed by what one prominent philosopher calls "subjunctive information." "What would have happened if . . . ?" is a natural question—one that is fundamental to human judgment and creativity and to the assignment of meaning itself. Unfortunately, historical claims in universes that never did exist are not verifiable propositions. Therefore, valuations and other subjunctive claims cannot count as objective facts in the rigorous sense of the word. Nor can subjunctive claims disencumber themselves from objective truths. Subjunctive claims are designed to have normative purchase in the ethical marketplace, and this requires that they be plausible. What force they have is rhetorical.

. . . [W]e may ask, "what makes one valuation plausible and the next completely unbelievable?" No answer to this question is currently available. All that can be said is that, if they wish to be upheld on appeal, judges must make their valuation analyses plausible. As Judge Bonney has pointed out, "[t]rue value is an elusive Pimpernel." This is a good observation because, like the Scarlet Pimpernel, value is a fictional character, whose viability, if you can call it that, depends on whether we are persuaded to suspend our disbelief.

Consistent with the above, the customary valuation exercise of bankruptcy judges is, "Well, had there been no bankruptcy, repossession would have occurred promptly, and a sale would have occurred within three months time for X dollars." This scenario is plausible, but it does not logically exclude other equally plausible scenarios, such as: "If there had been no bankruptcy, then the debtor would have prevented foreclosure by deluging the courts with procedural objections and would have ultimately blown up the collateral with dynamite, so that the secured party's security interest has no value whatsoever." Both of these histories depend upon assertions of what creative human beings "would have done," and yet human beings are capable of anything! How can we choose which one is the "true" counterfactual?

One might say, for example, that the first hypothetical history reflects ordinary events and the second reflects extraordinary events. Between the two, pick the most ordinary counterfactual. But a retreat to abstractions of this sort amounts to the substitution of crude rules for contextual speculation. However reasonable the crude rule may seem, it is not the same as finding out what would have happened to the collateral that is actually before the court. This subjunctive exercise is the very soul of valuation.

Alternatively, we can advertise our preferred vision of moral conduct by imagining a value based upon the secured party doing the most socially desirable thing. Thus, Judge Cyr valued inventory in a famous case on the basis of the *most* commercially reasonable sale, not just on a reasonably commercial sale. But in pursuing such visions, it should be noted that high values based on good commercial practice in a *subjunctive* universe enrich secured creditors in our *actual* universe, even if actual creditors cannot meet up to the high subjunctive standards upon which such a valuation is founded. If an undersecured creditor actually would have done a poor job in marketing collateral, then there is an argument for punishing that creditor in the subjunctive universe as well. . . .

If abstract rules are not allowed, and if a court must discover what would have happened in the absence of bankruptcy, then no logical reason impels one alternative history over another. Rather, choices are edited on the basis of non-logical cultural criteria. This implies politics or aesthetics, but not logic and not empirically verifiable claims.

But this does not mean that bankruptcy valuations are unpredictable and subject to no restraints. Quite the contrary. If the law is indeterminate, bankruptcy judges are indeed predictable. They tend to be culturally and temperamentally homogenous and they do succeed in agreeing among themselves on what sorts of counterfactual speculations are acceptable and what sorts are unacceptable. For this reason, it can be said that the law is simultaneously indeterminate and reasonably predictable. Yet even if adequate protection decisions are usually predictable, it is important to recognize that construction of alternative histories is not the province of logic or fact, and therefore, in any given case, there is room for enormous free play.

III. Liquidation Versus Going Concern Value

The above sections have established that valuations are frequently (but not universally) necessary to administer secured claims, and that estimating the value of property is an art, not a science. Art demands some structure, and bankruptcy valuations are no different in this regard. Accordingly, courts seek to govern the counterfactual quality of valuations by means of some aphorisms.

At the highest level of generality, it is often said that a court "should make an informed projection as to the amount recoverable upon conversion of the collateral into cash in a commercially reasonable manner." Or, alternatively, fair market value is frequently defined as "what a willing seller . . . and a willing buyer . . . would agree upon after the property has been exposed to the market for a reasonable amount of time." Such formulations seem almost entirely without content, and so the choice for hypothesizing market exchanges is usually narrowed down to a choice of going concern value and liquidation value. Liquidation value is usually taken to imply what the creditor could realize in a forced sale under the rules of U.C.C. Article 9, real estate mortgage provisions, or, even worse, under the rules of judicial execution. Such sales are notoriously poor in producing cash proceeds, and, if hypothetical liquidation is the standard, a court could easily justify a low figure by way of value.

Going concern value has been used in two senses. First, it might represent what a third party would pay for an entire business. Alternatively, it might represent the selling price of inventory in the ordinary course of business and is therefore synonymous with retail value. Either way, in a reorganization proceeding, going concern value is supposed to exceed liquidation value.

The added content of such aphorisms, however, should not be overrated. Both going concern value and liquidation value can easily collapse into each other. For example, a liquidating secured party might be able to sell the collateral as part of a going concern . . . .

Very frequently, courts choose going concern value in reorganization cases and choose liquidation value in liquidation cases. This rule has the dubious virtue of associational logic. In addition, as courts have recognized, section 506(a) seems to support a switch to going concern value by providing that value should be determined "in light of the . . . *use* of such property . . . ." This sentence contradicts the idea that value must be determined according to what would have happened in a subjunctive no-bankruptcy universe, since how property is used in *reality* does not necessarily affect how property *would have been used* in a non-existent universe.

The cases that routinely associate going concern value with reorganization proceedings are vociferously attacked by Judge Queenan in his learned essay on bankruptcy valuation. His position is simply that judges should always imagine a sale by a secured party . . . . This position would provide a great deal more coherence to the law of valuation, but such a standard is inconsistent with section 506(a) which requires consideration of how the property is being used today. . . .

In the end, the choice between liquidation or going concern value is based on whether you think that secured parties or general creditors should own the bonus that adheres to the idea of a going concern. Who deserves what property is a question on which we can all have intuitions, but logic alone cannot settle such questions in an uncontroversial manner. . . .

VII. Conclusion

While the bankruptcy process absolutely depends on the concept of collateral having a value, the legal and even philosophical status of that concept is far from clear. It is not clear when a court should use a high going concern value or a low liquidation value. It is not even clear what these terms mean in their own right. It is equally unclear whether a bankruptcy court should be allowed to change valuation standards in the middle of the proceeding, depending on the pro- or anti-debtor sentiments of the court. Neither is it clear whether valuations based on creditor bid-ins are allowed when liquidation value is used or whether valuations should be reduced for probable transaction costs.

The answer to these questions profoundly affects substantive bankruptcy rights. Yet, important as the answers are, they will perhaps inevitably be arrived at in an unsystematic manner because of the subjunctive quality of valuations. Subjunctivity is neither subjective nor objective, but is rather a third kind of knowledge constituted by mysterious combinations of subject and object.

The difficulty in dealing with these conditions, however, does not mean valuation in bankruptcy is unreliable or worthless. The subjunctive speculation on which valuations are based is the foundation of judgment itself. We are constantly equating one thing with another, even though to do so is an act of violence to the things being equated. This is what Hegel called our condition of finitude. To condemn valuation as proof of bankruptcy's deficiency is to dismiss communication itself as an impossibility. Fundamental to any thought system, subjunctive speculation cannot be banished from the Bankruptcy Code. Accordingly, it behooves us to understand the nature of this mode of reasoning.

National Bankruptcy Review Commission
Final Report
Bankruptcy: The Next Twenty Years
(October 20, 1997)

Chapter 1: Consumer Bankruptcy—Chapter 13 Repayment Plans

1.5.2 *Valuation of Collateral*
A creditor's secured claim in personal property should be determined by the property's wholesale price.

A creditor's secured claim in real property should be determined by the property's fair market value, minus hypothetical costs of sale.

. . .

2.4.11 *Valuation of Property*

A creditor's secured claim in personal property should be determined by the property's wholesale price.

A creditor's secured claim in real property should be determined by the property's fair market value, minus hypothetical costs of sale.

The need for statutory guidance on the valuation of collateral was a consistent theme throughout the Commission's hearings. . . .

The Bankruptcy Code currently does not define the appropriate method to determine "value" of collateral. Instead, the process for valuation is left to case-by-case determination. . . . Due to the flexibility inherent in [§ 506(a)], the amount of the allowed secured claim may differ depending on the type of bankruptcy case, the kind of property, and the proposed disposition of the collateral. Even in low-dollar-amount cases, therefore, there is no bright-line rule to give the parties quick, inexpensive answers to a valuation question. With the method for determination left completely undefined, courts have applied disparate methods to similar circumstances, yielding results ranging from the highest (*e.g.* retail) to the lowest (e.g., forced sale) possible valuations, with many options in between, including replacement cost, wholesale, and "midpoint" . . . .

The United States Supreme Court released a much-awaited decision on this issue, *Associates Commercial Corp. v. Rash. Rash* was a Chapter 13 case involving a tractor truck used by the debtor in his freight hauling business. In an *en banc* opinion . . ., the United States Court of Appeals for the Fifth Circuit held that . . . the bankruptcy court did not err when it valued the truck at wholesale; this price reflected the secured creditor's yield if it had repossessed and sold the truck.

The Supreme Court reversed and remanded the case. . . . The proper valuation standard if the collateral remained in the hands of the debtor, said the Supreme Court with only one dissenter, was replacement value less certain costs. Although the term "replacement value" is sometimes equated with retail value, the Supreme Court's definition explicitly requires deductions for certain costs, such as warranties, inventory costs, storage, and reconditioning. The application of this standard would entail a fact-intensive analysis, with the actual method of determination to be left to individual judges.

. . . [T]he application of the standard announced by the court is fraught with ambiguity. . . . Variations based on the types of property and the expenses to be deducted make clear that a fact-intensive analysis and multiple valuations would be inevitable.

. . . The Supreme Court's ruling was based on the interpretation of section 506(a) rather than a more comprehensive policy judgment about the appropriate valuation standard. The Commission recommends that Congress provide more guidance in this area to ensure that similar cases would be treated more equally and to reduce unnecessary litigation and transaction costs. The Commission's Recommendation aims at a valuation based on fewer factors to be determined using a standard provable with relatively more ease.

Significance of Establishing a Standard to Determine the Allowed Secured Claim and the Problems with the "Replacement Value Less Certain Costs" Standard. Although the Supreme Court ruled in the context of a Chapter 13 cramdown, the standard for valuing the allowed secured claim has significant implications in all cases under all chapters of the Bankruptcy Code. Issues involving the valuation of property arise in almost every business bankruptcy case. It is not possible to overstate the significance of clarifying the method to determine the allowed secured claim. Valuation is central to adequate protection contests and to the plan confirmation process . . . [T]he Supreme Court's interpretation of section 506(a) calls into question the valuation standards heretofore used in all of these contexts. . . .

This Proposal recommends that the same baseline standards be employed for all valuation purposes. . . . [I]t is not entirely clear why the same piece of property *should* be valued by various standards in multiple proceedings depending on the nature of each proceeding. . . . A clearer standard that does not change from one factual setting to another is warranted to provide certainty and consistency for all valuation determinations.

The variety of applications of valuation standards demonstrate that no particular method can be deemed "pro-debtor" or "pro-creditor." Depending on the circumstances, parties have different stakes in favoring a high or low valuation. . . .

A relatively simple standard would reduce litigation costs while it increases the predictability of outcomes, thereby encouraging parties to settle their differences without always turning to the courts. A clear standard also would promote consistency in application . . . .

Wholesale Price as a Compromise Bright-Line Standard. Among the spectrum of various options for valuation, from retail (highest value) to forced sale (lowest value), the Commission recommends that a price in the middle—wholesale price—be used to determine the allowed secured claim for personal property under section 506(a). This approach is supported by policy considerations and offers several advantages.

Many items of personal property have a readily identifiable wholesale price. Wholesale price satisfies the first fundamental requirement for a bright-line rule—that it be workable—and thus helps to reduce transaction costs in bankruptcy. . . .

Another reason to support a wholesale valuation standard is the importance of developing a "compromise" valuation to reflect the competing interests of debtors and creditors. Wholesale price provides a compromise between the lower valuations, such as the foreclosure price, and the higher valuations, such as retail price. . . .

A wholesale valuation . . . permits the parties to share in the benefits of the reorganization. A compromise approach is consistent with the notion that the chosen valuation standard should not create perverse incentives to use bankruptcy strategically. If creditors can count on property valuations well in excess of the creditors' state law entitlements, then they have an incentive to force bankruptcy filings rather than out-of-court workouts. At the same time, if property valuations in bankruptcy will be far below what the debtor could yield by selling the property, the debtor can use bankruptcy to extract value from creditors in ways that are not consistent with bankruptcy principles. A clear standard pegged at a compromise point is most likely to keep strategic maneuvering by either party to a minimum.

. . . An important policy consideration underlies adoption of a wholesale valuation. Quite significantly, adoption of a wholesale valuation ensures that a creditor's secured claim will cover at least what the creditor would have received under state law. This standard properly defines property rights in the absence of an overriding bankruptcy policy. . . . If the creditor is entitled to a higher replacement cost or retail, the creditor has a larger entitlement than if the debtor surrendered the property, without having to incur the expenses necessary to fetch a retail price. . . .

The wholesale standard also is fair to debtors. A debtor who retains collateral will have to pay more than liquidation value on the allowed secured claim, but the debtor has the opportunity to keep the property, which the debtor could not do outside bankruptcy. Thus the debtor also receives a benefit it would not have if the property had been repossessed under state law.

No valuation standard will be wholly satisfactory to all parties. The zero-sum game of many bankruptcy decisions necessarily reveals itself somewhere in the process. . . .

The wholesale standard should promote overall economic efficiency. . . . If a high valuation prevented retention of collateral, a debtor would forfeit the collateral to a creditor that would realize only the much lower foreclosure price if it repossessed and sold the property or forced a foreclosure sale. Thus, a higher valuation standard would force the transfer of property to a party that would yield a lower return for it. Wholesale valuation may be more economically efficient because the debtor will be able to keep the property in those cases where the debtor values it most. . . .

Fair Market Value Minus Hypothetical Costs of Sale. Fair market value minus hypothetical costs of sale provides a parallel standard of valuation for real property. A number of circuit courts of appeals have adopted the fair market value standard for assessing the allowed secured claim on real property. The proposed approach diverges from some court decisions that have not deducted hypothetical costs of sale. . . .

Competing Considerations. Some would criticize the wholesale and fair market standards as being too high. These standards, it has been argued, provide a windfall to secured creditors that bargained for and would receive only foreclosure value outside bankruptcy, where they also would have to bear the costs and burdens attendant to those collection activities. To the extent that distributions to unsecured creditors depend on valuation of collateral, the interests of unsecured creditors are harmed by these higher valuation standards.

Perhaps reflecting the pitfalls of any compromise approach, the recommended valuation standard has also been criticized for being too low. Some argue that wholesale valuation permits the debtor to obtain a windfall in the event that the debtor resold the property for retail price. The debtor generally will be ill-equipped to take the steps that add the requisite value . . . .

Some have argued that a different policy issue should be reflected in the valuation standard. They argue that property valuation should offset the risk of loss to the creditor. According to this argument, valuation should be high because it may be inaccurate or because the value may decline—in effect, the valuation standard should provide a cushion for secured creditors. The Bankruptcy Code addresses risk issues, but it uses different statutory means. . . . By using these devices, the question of risk is squarely presented, not buried in a broad—and deliberately distorted—rule of valuation. The Code's current approach is more accurate because it is based on actual risk, not some universally-presumed risk incorporated into a valuation standard applicable to all debtors and all situations.

Some have questioned whether the costs of sale should be deducted from the fair market value of real property. It might be improper to allocate the hypothetical costs to the creditor when, outside of bankruptcy, such costs might be added to a debtor's deficiency and not deducted from the first dollar of proceeds from the sale. However, the rule proposed here exactly mirrors the non-bankruptcy rule: in bankruptcy, the claim is simply bifurcated into its secured and unsecured portions. In or out of bankruptcy, the secured creditor bears the costs of its loan plus the costs of resale, and it must seek a deficiency for whatever costs that sale of the collateral will not cover. In bankruptcy, the deficiency remains the same; it merely becomes an unsecured claim. Because creditors bear initial responsibility for the costs of sale outside bankruptcy, deducting these hypothetical costs from the allowed secured claim best comports with reality under state law and prevents a greater burden from being shouldered by the unsecured creditors.

Douglas G. Baird & Thomas H. Jackson
Corporate Reorganizations and the Treatment of Diverse Ownership Interests: A Comment on Adequate Protection of Secured Creditors in Bankruptcy
51 U. Chi. L. Rev. 97 (1984)[*]

Bankruptcy law does not exist in a vacuum, yet one cannot spend much time reading in the field without noting that few judges or scholars have taken this observation to heart. Too many seem to think that a bankruptcy proceeding provides, in the main, an essentially unlimited opportunity to

---

do what appears at the moment to be good, just, or fair without regard to the reasons for having a system of bankruptcy laws in the first place. A close study of the present controversy over the adequate protection of secured creditors illustrates the shallowness of much of the recent discussion of bankruptcy law and the consequences of a failure to view bankruptcy as serving a unique, but limited, function in our society. . . .

. . . [A]n inquiry . . . is whether those who want to limit the rights of secured creditors are correct as a matter of what bankruptcy law *should* be. This normative inquiry must begin with critical questions about why a *bankruptcy* process exists at all—questions that simple statements about the purposes of bankruptcy law do not answer. Consider the "rehabilitation" goal of a Chapter 11 proceeding. No one, to our knowledge, argues that keeping a firm intact is *always* a good thing. Yet as soon as one concedes that a reorganization may not always be desirable, one is faced with the problem of understanding and articulating *why* reorganizations are favored in the first place and *how much* should be given up to facilitate them. . . .

In this article, we suggest that bankruptcy law at its core should be designed to keep individual actions against assets, taken to preserve the position of one investor or another, from interfering with the use of those assets favored by the investors as a group. Arguments over the wisdom of many substantive rules are not arguments about the way to implement this goal, and it misperceives the inquiry to focus on the wisdom of such rules as a matter of bankruptcy policy. Bankruptcy law should change a substantive nonbankruptcy rule only when doing so preserves the value of assets for the group of investors holding rights in them. For this reason, bankruptcy law necessarily overrides the remedies of individual investors outside of bankruptcy, for those "grab" rules undermine the very advantages sought in a collective proceeding. Changes in substantive rules unrelated to preserving assets for the collective good of the investor group, however, run counter to the goals of bankruptcy. Such rule changes in bankruptcy can induce an individual investor to seek bankruptcy merely to gain access to rule changes that offer him benefits, regardless of whether there are any benefits—or indeed costs—to the investor group as a whole.

Based upon this view of bankruptcy law, we examine the protection afforded to secured creditors in bankruptcy, asking, first, what exactly the secured creditors' nonbankruptcy rights are and, second, whether any modification of those rights is necessary in order to preserve or enhance the firm's assets for the general benefit of the investor group. What these nonbankruptcy rights should be is a question that is unrelated to whether they should be followed in bankruptcy. We show that protecting the value of a secured creditor's nonbankruptcy rights—whatever they might be—actually reinforces the bankruptcy policy of putting the firm's assets to their best use by placing the costs of trying to keep the assets of a firm together on those who stand to benefit from such an effort. If these parties do not bear these costs, they will have an incentive to place a firm in bankruptcy and to draw out the proceeding, even though doing so does not work to the advantage of those with rights to the firm's assets when their interests are considered as a group.

I. The Problem of Diverse Ownership Interests

Those who have argued that secured creditors should not be given the full value of their rights under state law in bankruptcy often also argue that a bankruptcy proceeding must respond to the greater social problems that attend a business failure. The failure of a firm affects many who do not, under current law, have cognizable ownership interests in the firm outside of bankruptcy. The economy of an entire town can be disrupted when a large factory closes. Many employees may be put out of work. The failure of one firm may lead to the failure of those who supplied it with raw materials and those who acquired its finished products. Some believe that preventing such consequences is worth the costs of trying to keep the firm running and justifies placing burdens on a firm's secured creditors.

We think that this view is, as a matter of bankruptcy policy, fundamentally wrong. Fashioning remedies for all the harm a failing business may bring is difficult and beyond the competence of a bankruptcy court. The wider effects of the failure of a particular enterprise are not easy to assess. A principal characteristic of a market economy is, after all, that some firms fail, and postponing the inevitable or keeping marginal firms alive may do more harm than good. . . .

But there is a more important reason for denying a bankruptcy judge broad license to protect people in the wake of economic misfortune. The problems brought by business failures are not bankruptcy problems. A bankruptcy proceeding should not be the place to implement a policy that society does not enforce outside of bankruptcy and that is unrelated to the preservation of assets for the firm's investor group. Most businesses fail without a bankruptcy petition ever being filed. If it is a bad policy to protect secured creditors in full while workers remain unpaid, it should not matter whether a bankruptcy petition has been filed. So, too, if a secured creditor should properly share with everyone else in the economic misfortunes of a debtor, he should be required to carry his share of the loss in every instance, not just in the minority of cases in which a bankruptcy petition is filed.

Nonbankruptcy concerns, we believe, should not be addressed by changing bankruptcy policy. Our view derives from two related observations: first, that bankruptcy law is, and should be, concerned with the interests of those (from bondholders to unpaid workers to tort victims to shareholders) who, outside of bankruptcy, have property rights in the assets of the firm filing a petition, and, second, that in analyzing the interests of these parties with property rights, our baseline should be applicable nonbankruptcy law. A collective insolvency proceeding is directed toward reducing the costs associated with diverse ownership interests and encouraging those with interests in a firm's assets to put those assets to the use the group as a whole would favor.

Other problems should be addressed as general problems, not as bankruptcy problems. . . . Such comprehensive reform ensures that like cases are treated alike and makes clearer the rights of all players, who, before the fact, do not know whether a bankruptcy petition will be filed. . . .

Just as the filing of a petition in bankruptcy provides little justification for altering the relative rights of owners and non-owners of the firm, so should it have little effect on the rights of owners *inter se*. Changes in nonbankruptcy rights should be made only if they benefit all those with interests in the firm as a group. . . .

When a firm files a petition in bankruptcy, two questions arise. First, one must decide what to do with the firm's assets, and, second, because of the presence of diverse owners, one must decide who gets them. Our principal proposition is that the answer to the second question should not, ideally, alter the answer to the first. Consider the case where only one person has all the rights to the firm's assets. . . . [T]his sole owner would continually reevaluate his use of the assets. . . . Because a sole owner has no distributional decision to make, his only concern is the best deployment of the assets.

The unique function of a bankruptcy system comes into sharp focus when the situation of the sole owner, who does not need bankruptcy and can ignore its policies, is compared to that of diverse owners. Bankruptcy law is fundamentally a collective proceeding and as such, is needed only when there is no such sole owner of the firm's assets. When the "rights" to the assets are spread among more than one person, as they almost always are, someone must decide not only how best to deploy the assets, but also how to split up the returns from those assets. The answer to this second question, however, should not affect the determination of how to deploy the assets. As a group, these diverse owners—bondholders, tort victims, trade creditors, shareholders, and others—would want to follow the same course as a sole owner. The owners as a *group*, in other words, would want to keep the distributional question from spilling over into the deployment question.

When ownership of a firm is diverse and the individual owners have different packages of rights, however, all have an incentive to take actions that will increase their own share of the assets of an ailing firm, even if in so doing they deploy the assets in a way that a sole owner would not. Bankruptcy law, at bottom, is designed to require these investors to act collectively rather than to take individual actions that are not in the interests of the investors as a group. Individual diverse owners have a particular incentive to act against the collective interest in cases where, under non-bankruptcy law, some owners are entitled to be paid before others and where the available assets are insufficient to satisfy all those with rights to them. A fully secured creditor, for example, has the right to be paid before more junior creditors receive anything. . . . [H]e will tend to favor an immediate liquidation, even in circumstances in which a sole owner would keep the assets together. . . . [H]e has nothing to gain from waiting . . ., but he can do worse if the firm continues and its fortunes decline . . . .

By contrast, junior parties, who, under current law, are typically general creditors and share-holders, often have interests that pull them in the opposite direction. Members of any group of investors that would be eliminated by a present liquidation or sale of assets have nothing to lose by seeking a solution that avoids a final distribution today. A group that would get nothing if the business ceases will resist an immediate liquidation, even if liquidation is best for the owners as a group. If there is any chance, however remote, of an upswing that will bring them value, they will want to take that chance. Waiting for the upswing, however, and trying to preserve the firm's good will and expertise in the meantime, involves a gamble for the owners as a group. . . .

No single group, then, if unconstrained, will necessarily make a decision that is in the best interests of the owners considered together. As a first approximation, therefore, the law governing bankruptcy in general, and corporate reorganizations in particular, should ensure that the disposition of the firm's assets is in the interest of the owners as a group. . . . Bankruptcy law, accordingly, should aim to keep the asset-deployment question separate from the distributional question, and to have the deployment question answered as a single owner would answer it.

The best way to approach this goal is to ensure that the parties who decide how to deploy the assets enjoy all the benefits and incur all the costs of their decisions. Bankruptcy rules that enable classes of investors to gain from any upswing in the firm's fortunes, while avoiding the full costs of an attempt to keep the assets together, create an incentive for those investors to make such an attempt, even if it is not worth making for the investors as a group. That is, they will attempt to reorganize even when an individual who had complete ownership of the assets would liquidate them immediately. Imposing on junior parties the risks of keeping a firm intact removes this incentive. They become like a sole owner in the sense that they suffer the consequences of making the wrong decision and enjoy the benefits of making the right one. Unless the law imposes these burdens on them, junior parties will systematically make decisions that ignore the real costs of keeping a firm together.

II. The Secured Creditor's State-Law Rights

. . . Once one accepts the idea that bankruptcy law is primarily concerned with recognizing nonbankruptcy entitlements and ensuring a deployment of assets that is in the interests of all those with rights to the assets under state law, analysis of adequate protection of secured creditors in bankruptcy is straightforward. Questions about the desirability of secured credit and the wisdom of allowing secured creditors to be paid in full ahead of others are not relevant. These questions, like questions about the rights of employees of failing enterprises, are not bankruptcy questions. If secured credit is undesirable, it is as much so outside of bankruptcy as in. Limiting it indirectly by changing bankruptcy rules is counterproductive to the basic goal of bankruptcy: using a collective forum to preserve the value of assets for the benefit of those who own them. Our argument, then, does not rest on an assumption that secured credit, as it currently exists under state law, is worth having. . . .

We can focus our analysis of the rights of secured creditors in bankruptcy, then, by posing two questions suggested by the view of bankruptcy law set forth in Part I. First, what are the existing nonbankruptcy rights of secured creditors, and second, is any modification of those rights necessary to ensure that the assets of the firm are deployed in a way that is in the interests of the owners of the firm as a group? . . .

A. The Nature of Security: A Form of Ownership Priority

Many analyses of secured credit assume that its characteristic feature is the ability of the secured creditor to seize property of the debtor should the debtor default on a primary obligation. This right, however, is relatively unimportant in distinguishing between secured and unsecured creditors. Virtually all extensions of credit give a creditor a contingent right to take possession of a debtor's property if the debtor should fail to pay his debts when due. . . .

The essence of a secured creditor's rights, therefore, is not captured by focusing on the debtor-creditor relationship. Rather, secured credit is concerned with ensuring that the secured creditor receives priority rights in certain assets over the rights of other owners with claims against the assets of a debtor. The property right, in other words, is principally a means to an end—priority as against third parties with regard to repayment. . . .

This observation about the nature of a secured creditor's property rights suggests something fundamental about secured credit. A secured creditor's property right is limited in its scope by its purpose, which is to implement the secured creditor's priority right. In acquiring a security interest, a secured creditor does not "buy" a right to the asset itself, but, rather, he buys a right to use the asset to gain repayment of the debtor's debt to him. . . .

B. Valuing the Secured Creditor's Rights

. . . [E]ven if the collateral does not depreciate and is stable in value, Investor bears the time value cost of delay. It is not enough to say that Investor has a right to the collateral in priority to other creditors: One has to establish *when* Investor has a right to the collateral. . . .

To insist upon a difference between depreciation and time value is to misunderstand the nature of private property. Ownership of an asset is nothing more than a right to make some use of that asset over time. . . . [O]ne cannot ask simply *how much* the secured creditor would receive under state law. One must also ask *when* he would receive it.

When Investor calculates the rate at which he will be willing to lend Firm money on a secured basis, he must take into account *when* he will be able to foreclose on and sell the collateral just as surely as he must take into account the likelihood of its physical depreciation. Under state law, the filing of the bankruptcy petition usually identifies the "when." . . . [T]he state-law process could be set in motion by the time of filing. If Investor is not given the liquidation value of the asset at the time he would have enjoyed it if a default occurred and a bankruptcy petition had not been filed, his state-law rights are not being protected.

The intrinsic value of Investor's security interest, therefore, is the right it gives him to sell the drill press and thereby to obtain its liquidation value ahead of the rights of other creditors at a particular time. . . .

III. BANKRUPTCY AND THE SECURED CREDITOR

Under existing nonbankruptcy rules, a sole owner of assets may freely decide whether to continue an unsuccessful business venture or to do something else with the assets, depending upon what he thinks is in his interest. A bankruptcy proceeding helps to ensure a comparable freedom where ownership of the ailing firm is diverse. In the absence of a coercive and collective proceeding, the dispersed owners' individual interests will prevent them from acting as a single owner would. In this Part of the article, we ask whether recognizing the rights of a secured creditor to repossess collateral interferes with that goal.

In a world without friction, it would not. If the secured party's collateral is, in fact, worth more to the firm than to a third party, that collateral should end up back in the hands of the firm notwithstanding its repossession by the secured creditor in the interim. As a practical matter, however, to permit a secured creditor the full exercise of his rights may hinder efforts to preserve the going-concern value of the business. It may be in the interests of the owners as a group to stay the repossession rights of the secured creditor and to substitute a requirement that the secured creditor instead accept the asset's liquidation value. Because of the costs repossession and subsequent repurchase may bring, it is consistent with the purposes of bankruptcy to substitute for a secured creditor's actual substantive *rights* under nonbankruptcy law a requirement that the secured creditor accept the equivalent *value* of those rights.

We then must ask if there is anything in the goals of the bankruptcy process that suggests that respecting the *value* of a secured creditor's rights in full also interferes with the goals of bankruptcy. The relevant bankruptcy goal, as we have seen, is not that a firm stay in business, but rather that its assets are deployed in a way that, consistent with applicable nonbankruptcy restrictions, advances the interests of those who have rights in them. . . .

The crucial question we have to face is whether giving the secured creditor the benefit of his bargain is inconsistent with the policy of ensuring that the firm's assets are deployed in a way that brings the most benefits to the owners as a group. . . . If the firm is in fact worth more as a going concern than sold piecemeal, then there must necessarily be enough to pay a secured creditor the full liquidation value of the machine. One follows from the other. . . .

In principle, any firm that is worth more as a going concern than chopped up will be able, then, to give the secured creditor the value of his state-law rights. To be sure, giving the secured creditor the benefit of his bargain does mean that other investors, such as general creditors or shareholders, receive less or perhaps nothing of what is owed to them, but how rights to the assets are divided among the investors is, we have seen, a question distinct from that of how the assets are deployed. It is the difference between the size of the slices and the size of the pie. Only the latter is a bankruptcy question. Giving the secured creditor the benefit of his bargain should not prevent a firm from staying together when a sole owner would keep it together. Indeed, a failure to recognize the secured creditor's rights in full will *undercut* the bankruptcy goal of ensuring that the assets are used to advance the interests of everyone. If those who stand to benefit from delay do not bear its cost (including the costs that secured creditors face), they will have an incentive to keep firms together even when a sole owner would not.

IV. THE SECURED CREDITOR AND THE COSTS OF UNCERTAINTY IN CORPORATE REORGANIZATIONS

Reorganizations take time. In the world as we actually find it, valuations are hard to come by. It may not be clear whether a firm is worth keeping intact. One may need time to decide whether liquidation piece by piece is the only course that is available. . . . But it does not follow that protecting the value of the secured creditor's state-law rights promotes liquidations when the appropriate course is patience. Again, the appropriate focus is one that takes benefits and costs into account.

Waiting for changed conditions or for more information imposes a cost. If a firm's assets would fetch $10,000 on liquidation today, an investor who owned the firm's assets outright would have to weigh the value of obtaining $10,000 immediately against the more uncertain value that waiting would bring. . . . The analysis should be exactly the same if the firm's ownership were dispersed . . . . If, however, the junior parties could force a creditor holding a security interest in the firm's assets to accept $10,000 a year hence in satisfaction of a claim worth $10,000 today only if the firm reorganized, but not if it liquidated, they would have an incentive to keep the firm together in order to reap for themselves the benefit of $1000, even though the creditors as a group would receive less than if the firm were liquidated immediately and they were free to reinvest the proceeds in treasury bills. If the secured creditor receives the time value of his claim, and junior creditors remain the ones who decide whether to try to reorganize, this perverse incentive is removed.

. . . Again, the analysis of the choice between liquidation and reorganization should be no different if the firm has diverse owners. . . . When ownership is diverse, however, this decision will be reached only if the residual class (assuming it can control the decision) bears the costs as well as enjoys the benefits of a decision to continue. . . .

Giving the secured creditor the value of his state-law rights in the face of uncertainty does not impair the effort to keep the assets together. . . .

Unlike a sole owner, dispersed investors, because their relative rights differ, have an incentive to make the wrong decision if unchecked. The secured creditors will rush to liquidate, while the general creditors and shareholders (who often have more to gain than to lose from delay) will be too optimistic and push for a reorganization. Bankruptcy law makes a grave mistake if it assumes that a junior class (or another class) will make the correct decision about the deployment of the assets without a legal rule that forces it to take account of the investors as a group. In the world as we find it, chances of success or failure over time can never be calculated with certainty. But to say that they cannot be calculated with certainty is not to say that they cannot be calculated at all. . . . [T]he best way of ensuring the correct decision—by which we mean the decision that is not distorted by the self-interest of individuals at the expense of the interests of the group—is to create a legal rule that imposes upon the person who makes the decision all the benefits if he decides correctly and all the costs if he guesses wrong. A rule that forces general creditors and shareholders to give secured creditors the full value of their claims (including compensation for the time value of money) puts the cost of a decision to reorganize the firm entirely on the junior classes, who already stand to benefit if the firm succeeds. As a consequence, they have incentives that approximate those of a sole owner, and their decision about how to deploy the firm's assets will not be distorted by self-interest. . . .

Conclusion

Junior classes, be they equity holders or unsecured creditors, resort to reorganization in bankruptcy because they want the opportunity to sort things out for their benefit and to capture any upside potential in giving their firm a future, however uncertain. The precise nature of that uncertainty is irrelevant, but if the choice between liquidation and reorganization of the firm is not to be skewed, the residual classes must pay for the opportunity they seek. Such a requirement does not violate any well-conceived notion of fairness or equity. After all, *someone* must bear the risk that the reorganized firm will fail. To insist that the residual class bear the burden by way of a rule that provides secured creditors with the value of their rights under state law does not prevent desirable reorganizations. To the contrary, it encourages junior owners to put the firm's assets to the use that the owners as a group would prefer.

. . . Nothing in our argument, however, depends in the slightest on showing that secured credit is a good thing, for the argument would apply with equal force to any group given favored treatment under nonbankruptcy law. The desirability of secured credit—or other nonbankruptcy property rights—is ultimately not a bankruptcy question and attempting to transform it into one creates incentives that are perverse and counterproductive.

D. Strip Down

A pervasive problem regarding the bankruptcy treatment of secured claims is what to do with undersecured claims—that is, those claims for which the value of the collateral is less than the amount of the claim. While it is a basic axiom of current bankruptcy law that a claim is considered a "secured" claim only up to the value of the collateral, what are the ramifications of that axiom in terms of how a secured claim is actually handled? In concrete terms, should the debtor be allowed to "strip down" the undersecured claim to the judicially determined value of the collateral? And, should the answer be any different in a liquidation case as compared to a reorganization case? What are the interests of the affected parties and what are the governing policies?

Any discussion of these questions must confront the Supreme Court's decision in *Dewsnup v. Timm*, 502 U.S. 410 (1992). In *Dewsnup*, the Court held that a chapter 7 debtor could not invoke § 506(d) to strip down an undersecured claim to the collateral's value. In so holding, the Court intimated the existence and persistence of a powerful extra-statutory historical pro-secured creditor policy bias, but did not elaborate on the exact parameters of that policy. This part of the Chapter turns first for guidance on the mysteries of strip down to the leading scholar on that subject, Professor Margaret Howard of Washington & Lee. Howard first addressed the problem prior to the Court's decision in *Dewsnup* in her article, *Stripping Down Liens: Section 506(d) and the Theory of Bankruptcy*, 65 AM. BANKR. L.J. 373 (1991). She argued that the Code does and should authorize strip down in chapter 7. What are her key arguments? Alas, the Supreme Court in *Dewsnup* went the other way, mangling (or at least ignoring) the statutory language in the process, and creating numerous uncertainties about the scope of the rights of secured creditors, even in reorganization cases.

Professor Howard assessed the post-*Dewsnup* strip down landscape in two articles, recommended but not included here: *Dewsnupping the Bankruptcy Code*, 1 J. BANKR. L. & PRAC. 513 (1992) and *Secured Claims in Bankruptcy: An Essay on Missing the Point*, 23 CAPITAL U. L. REV. 313 (1994). In those articles she worried especially about the ramifications of *Dewsnup* and its rationale for the treatment of secured creditors in reorganization. She argued that strip down still is and should be permitted in reorganization cases even after *Dewsnup*. Fortunately, Professor Howard's plea to limit *Dewsnup* to chapter 7 has largely been heeded by the lower courts.

Howard is hardly the only critic of *Dewsnup*. In *The Immovable Object Versus the Irresistible Force: Rethinking the Relationship Between Secured Credit and Bankruptcy Policy*, 95 MICH. L. REV. 2234 (1997), Professors Lawrence Ponoroff and Stephen Knippenberg team up once again to offer a sophisticated and devastating critique of *Dewsnup*, and urge Congress to overrule that decision. Significantly, Ponoroff and Knippenberg take issue with the threshold metaphor that drove that decision, the metaphor of security as a conveyance of property. In the bankruptcy setting, they assert that the more accurate view, and the one that best accords with proper bankruptcy policy, is of security as a priority claim. Seen in that light, the case for strip down becomes much easier to sustain.

The avid reader should be aware that there are many excellent articles on strip down. The list of additional suggested readings at the end of this Chapter notes many of those fine works. For a defense of the anti-strip down view, consult Professor Barry Adler's piece, *Creditor Rights After Johnson and Dewsnup*, 10 BANKR. DEV. J. 1 (1993).

Margaret Howard
Stripping Down Liens: Section 506(d) and the Theory of Bankruptcy
65 AM. BANKR. L.J. 373 (1991)[*]

I. INTRODUCTION

. . . "[S]trip down" . . . arises frequently in Chapter 7 cases, because real estate is often over-encumbered at the time bankruptcy is filed. . . . [S]tripping down liens involves fundamental questions about the nature of bankruptcy and the policies implemented in the Bankruptcy Code . . . .

. . . [T]his Article turns to a discussion of the broader policy considerations implicated by strip down. It demonstrates that strip down replicates the results of a foreclosure under state law, without depriving undersecured creditors of appreciation they would otherwise obtain. It argues that the interests of secured creditors are appropriately protected by giving them an opportunity to contest the property's fair market value and by paying them that value in cash. Finally, the Article demonstrates that prohibiting strip down creates inappropriate opportunities for creditor leverage against debtors. . . .

III. POLICY AND PRINCIPLES

The preceding review of statutory provisions relevant to strip down reveals that the Bankruptcy Code permits strip down of liens on real estate in Chapter 7 cases. This conclusion is consistent with the policies implemented in bankruptcy and the normative principles upon which bankruptcy is built.

Two policy issues are central. First is the argument that strip down and foreclosure put creditors in equivalent positions. The force of this argument depends, in turn, upon whether foreclosure gives creditors access to appreciation, either as a practical matter or as a constitutional right, and upon the accuracy of valuation. The second important policy question concerns the opportunity for strategic behavior that denial of strip down offers creditors.

Analysis of these policy questions supports the conclusion that strip down is appropriate.

A. REPLICATING FORECLOSURE

Arguably, permitting debtors to strip down liens in Chapter 7, under sections 506(a) and (d), merely replicates foreclosure, putting creditors in the same position they would enjoy (or suffer) by realizing upon their collateral in the absence of bankruptcy. . . .

1. Access to appreciation

The creditor experiences the same outcome under section 506(d) as under foreclosure only if the property is stable in value. If it is appreciating, the creditor can bid in its debt at the foreclosure sale, hold the property for a while, and then capture the appreciation upon resale. Because lien avoidance deprives the undersecured creditor of this opportunity, section 506(d) arguably does not replicate foreclosure.

This argument contains several assumptions. . . .

A second assumption is that the value of the property fixed under section 506(a) did not take the possibility of appreciation into account. A potential for appreciation, however, is relevant to a determination of value and the creditor should receive compensation for it as part of its secured claim.

A third assumption is that the undersecured creditor can and will hold real estate in order to capture appreciation. In fact, the creditor may not be in a position to do so. . . .

Holding property to capture appreciation makes no economic sense unless the rate of appreciation exceeds lost opportunity costs. If the property had been sold immediately, the proceeds could have been reinvested in the current market, producing some return. . . .

Finally, courts concerned about creditors' access to appreciation seem to assume that property only increases in value. Sometimes it depreciates, of course. The creditor whose lien is stripped down and cashed out does lose later appreciation, but he also avoids later depreciation. A creditor who is certain that the property will appreciate can invest the proceeds in an enterprise having risk factors similar to the debtor's property.

A major legal assumption, made by those who argue that strip down fails to replicate foreclosure because it does not give access to appreciation, is that the creditor has a right to appreciation. This assumption raises a series of complex questions. To begin with, appreciation during the bankruptcy case is distinguishable from appreciation after the case is completed. The creditor might be entitled to one increment of value but not the other.

Appreciation at all stages derives from at least three sources: market forces unrelated to acts or efforts of the debtor; pay-down of senior interests; or investments by the debtor in improvements. . . . [C]ases on both sides of the section 506(d) debate treat all appreciation alike, regardless of its source. Thus, denial of section 506(d) avoidance gives a creditor access to appreciation from all sources. Bidding in a debt at foreclosure and holding the property for later resale, on the other hand, allows the creditor to capture only market appreciation. No one has yet explained why denial of strip down should permit broader access to appreciation than does foreclosure and bid in.

Allowing the creditor to reach appreciation arguably interferes with the debtor's incentives to make productive use of property. This argument gains vigor if the source of appreciation is either the debtor's postpetition investment or pay-down of a senior lien. . . .

Appreciation, regardless of its source, may be categorized as after-acquired property. Allowing the creditor to reach increases in the property's value arguably interferes with the debtor's fresh start. The strength of this argument depends upon the appropriate scope of the fresh start, and invoking it as a talisman is not helpful. . . . [T]he question requires evaluation of the functional role of section 506(a) from the viewpoint of overall bankruptcy policy, balancing the needs of debtors for an unencumbered new beginning against the rights of creditors.

2. Secured creditors' rights and constitutional entitlements

Dispute over an undersecured creditor's right to reach appreciation raises fundamental questions concerning the nature of secured creditors' rights in bankruptcy—what property rights of secured creditors are protected in bankruptcy and how. Bankruptcy alters rights that secured creditors enjoy under state law. The most immediate alteration is the automatic stay's interception of collection efforts. In addition, the secured creditor can be forced to accept a cash payment in the amount of the secured claim if the trustee sells the property, even though the creditor would prefer to take the collateral and sell it himself. Furthermore, in bankruptcy a secured creditor is entitled to postpetition interest only if the collateral has excess value . . . . A secured creditor has no right to compensation from the estate for the lost opportunity to foreclose upon collateral and reinvest the proceeds.

It seems beyond cavil that bankruptcy assures a secured creditor the value of the secured claim, measured by the value of the collateral, and *nothing more*. Although the secured creditor may get more than this in a particular situation, the point is that he cannot compel it under any chapter of the Code. . . .

Notwithstanding that bankruptcy assures a secured creditor only the value of the secured claim, at least two courts have declared that depriving a creditor of the opportunity to bid in at a foreclosure sale and hold property for appreciation is unconstitutional. . . .

This constitutional argument is plainly wrong. The lien avoided under section 506(d) is without current value —"an empty legal right." It is only the expectancy interest in future appreciation that conceivably gives rise to a constitutionally protected property right. That expectancy is extinguished upon a senior lienholder's foreclosure, however, and no constitutional attack upon foreclosure has been mounted on that basis. To extinguish such an expectancy through strip down is equally permissible.

. . . Section 722 prevents a secured creditor from enjoying any appreciation that happens along . . . . If section 722 raises no constitutional problems on that basis, neither does section 506(d). It is much too late in the day to believe that the Constitution protects all of a lien's state law attributes. On the contrary, only the value of the secured claim is constitutionally protected.

. . . Courts finding no inequity in strip down correctly recognize that strip down replicates foreclosure, and that counterarguments based on access to appreciation do not withstand analysis. Recognition of the relationship between fairness and constitutionality resolves the matter.

3. Misvaluation

Stripping down a lien and cashing out the lienholder replicates foreclosure and does no violence to the lienholder's constitutional rights only if the court accurately values the encumbered property. . . .

Valuation is inexact, probably because it is, by definition, hypothetical. If the bankruptcy court undervalues the property, the creditor will indeed do worse upon strip down than in foreclosure. . . .

If valuation errors fall in both directions, the problem is variance and debtors and creditors bear the risk of misvaluation in equal measure. If the problem is consistent bias in the direction of undervaluations, then creditors always pay for it.

Even if consistent bias exists, barring strip down is not good policy. First, a party who has fully litigated an issue—valuation, in this case—should not get a second opportunity to vindicate its position, this time in the market rather than before the bench. . . .

Secondly, denial of strip down is not the appropriate remedy for an undervaluation bias. Since the same risk exists in other contexts, those who would deny strip down because of possible valuation errors must explain why misvaluation is more detrimental in this context than in others. For courts to deny strip down because of valuation errors seems a devastating vote of no-confidence in their own ability to act as fact-finders. The solution is to make bankruptcy valuations as accurate as possible, rather than to target strip down. Denial of strip down that leads to loss of a debtor's home or farm, when the creditor is unlikely to realize any gain, is too lopsided to commend itself as a solution to valuation errors.

B. CREDITOR LEVERAGE

Denial of strip down carries a potential for inappropriate strategic behavior by creditors that runs counter to Congress' demonstrated concern with creditor misbehavior. This concern appears throughout the Code. Bifurcation of an undersecured claim into secured and unsecured portions was itself intended to address creditor leverage that made successful bankruptcies more difficult to accomplish.

None of the courts that have considered strip down has recognized the potential for creditor abuse invited by denial of strip down. . . . One may legitimately expect, however, that the property had a significance to the [debtors] that it would not have to an arms' length third party purchaser. . . . The land may well have had an additional increment of value to the [debtors] over and above its fair market value—call it the "emotional increment" . . . . Denial of strip down puts creditors in a position to extract this emotional increment, giving them inappropriate leverage over debtors.

Here's how it would work. . . . [T]he [creditor] can outbid the [debtors] every time. . . . [T]he [debtors] must bid the amount, above fair market value, representing the additional emotional increment that the property is worth to them. Again, this must be cash. The [creditor], however, can match the [debtors] bid by bidding in . . . its . . . unsecured claim. This is "funny money" . . . . Its actual worth depends upon the dividend being paid to unsecured creditors in the case. . . . Nevertheless, the bid is counted as if its economic value equaled its face value. Debtors . . . can never match such a bid. The [creditor] controls the outcome by deciding how much of its unsecured claim to bid, ratcheting the price up to the outer limit of the [debtors'] emotional increment, and thus leveraging from the [debtors] a price not obtainable at a foreclosure sale from an arms' length purchaser. . . .

Creditors who argue that strip down denies them the benefit of their bargain are on shaky ground. If a creditor bargained for an interest in land at all . . ., he must take a worst-case perspective in order to protect his interests. That worst case is, from the creditor's viewpoint, a lengthy bankruptcy reorganization, even though the debtor ultimately pays the present value of the secured claim. . . . Realistic creditors know that they cannot control the bankruptcy alternative that debtors choose, even though creditors can, by collection pressure or forebearance, influence whether debtors seek the protection of the automatic stay in the first place. Thus, a bargain that includes rights against collateral—a secured transaction or mortgage—cannot realistically offer benefits beyond the value of the collateral, and creditors know it.

It is incumbent on creditors, then, to make sensible lending decisions based on actuarial calculations of risk and to adjust their terms accordingly. To argue that strip down should be denied, so that more than the collateral's current value can be leveraged out of debtors emotionally attached to their homes and farms, is to alter the original bargain, not to enforce it. . . .

IV. CONCLUSION

Part of what is at work in strip down cases is suspicion about where a debtor who is discharging substantial debts in bankruptcy is getting the money to pay the secured claim. . . . If the debtors are able to accumulate enough postpetition property to satisfy the lien, to find a postpetition lender, or to borrow from friends or relatives for this purpose, those funds would not have been available to creditors and nothing is gained for the estate by refusing strip down.

Also at work is concern that debtors are getting in bankruptcy something they could not get outside of it. That focus is misplaced for two reasons. First, it comes from the wrong perspective. The correct question is whether creditors subjected to strip down get less in terms of economic value than they would get outside bankruptcy, and not whether debtors utilizing strip down are doing something they could not do outside bankruptcy. Secondly, it fails to realize that things are different in bankruptcy. The focus should be on whether bankruptcy's purposes are served by strip down, with appropriate protections to creditors. Since debtors must pay the market value of property retained after strip down, the appropriate analogy is to a right of first refusal. No "windfall" exists when debtors pay full and fair market value for property they keep. Courts concluding otherwise are looking at what the debtor gains (which is only what is paid for) rather than at what the creditor loses (which is nothing of value).

Strip down, followed by cashing out the secured creditor, provides an appropriate balance between the debtor's need for an unencumbered new beginning and the creditor's right to realize the value of its secured claim.

The arguments against strip down, once analyzed closely, are not compelling enough to overcome the statute's plain language. One is left to wonder whether the real hurdle for courts asked to strip down liens is the thought that debtors will come out of a bankruptcy liquidation with some of their nonexempt property still in hand. Bankruptcy is supposed to hurt more than that.

Debtors are supposed to sacrifice all of their nonexempt property, not to emerge from bankruptcy as landowners.

Moralistic views such as these, which rely on the normative when only the economic is pertinent, simply have no place in the bankruptcy system. Debtors who seek strip down are guilty of no misbehavior and they do not fall out of the ranks of the "honest but unfortunate." If property is to be retained following strip down, its full and fair market value must be paid to the creditor. That is all a secured creditor has a right to expect or demand.

Lawrence Ponoroff & F. Stephen Knippenberg
The Immovable Object Versus the Irresistible Force: Rethinking the Relationship Between Secured Credit and Bankruptcy Policy
95 MICH. L. REV. 2234 (1997)[*]

INTRODUCTION

. . . The Supreme Court's decision in *Dewsnup v. Timm* . . . has had, and continues to have, a deleterious effect on the ability of many individual debtors to obtain meaningful relief and a truly "fresh start" in bankruptcy.

This article urges Congress . . . to sever the last thread and consign the Supreme Court's 1992 decision to its rightful role as a historical anomaly. . . .

. . . *Dewsnup* must to a considerable degree be understood as the product of certain imaginative conceptions about the nature of secured credit. . . . [S]cholars . . . are increasingly reaching the conclusion that secured credit as an institution, and its derivative rule of full priority for secured claims upon insolvency, does not in fact promote systemic efficiency. Nevertheless, the law in this area continues to be guided by the precepts of freedom of contract and free alienability of property rights. . . .

. . . [W]e examine this "conveyance model" of the security interest in the bankruptcy setting and find that it fails to account adequately for certain unique but fundamental bankruptcy policies, including, in consumer cases, the fresh-start policy. . . . [W]hat is called for in the bankruptcy context is an alternative to the conceptualization of the secured claim as "property." . . .

. . . [W]e critique the metaphor that implicitly dictated the result in *Dewsnup*. We then offer, and consider the practical applications of, an alternative characterization of security interests in bankruptcy that conceptualizes the security interest as a claim *to* property, rather than as an indefeasible right *in* the property itself. . . .

IV. SECURED CLAIMS AND BANKRUPTCY POLICY
A. *The Limits of the Conveyance Model*

Insolvency, of course, is the risk against which a secured creditor has hedged. Harris and Mooney's defense of secured credit is premised, in significant part, on the belief that the distributive effects of secured credit upon insolvency are neither contrary to the wealth maximization norm nor any more prejudicial to unsecured creditors than are other forms of wealth transfers. . . . [W]hen Harris and Mooney test their conveyance model of security interests against bankruptcy policy, and find the two not fundamentally incompatible, they overlook a central tenet of their own normative view of security interests. Specifically, they fail to see that the logical concomitant of a property-based theory would be that a secured creditor's protectible interest is not limited to the value of the property at any given point in time. Rather, it should extend to future as well as to existing equity and to control over the decision of when to realize that value through foreclosure or otherwise. In bankruptcy, however, while there may be general agreement that bankruptcy proceeds from state-law entitlements and priorities, we also begin with the notion that a claim is "secured" only to the extent of the value of the underlying collateral as of the date of filing or confirmation. . . .

. . . Moreover, there are numerous instances in which the Code substantively alters prebankruptcy entitlements and priorities in order to advance a specific bankruptcy policy, whether it be equality, equity, maximization of value, or fresh start. . . .

B. *"Liens Survive Bankruptcy": Eternal Verity or Silly Semantics?*

. . . As useful and as normatively appealing as Harris and Mooney's property metaphor may be for understanding the institution of secured credit within the broader framework of the commercial law, the explanatory prowess of the model breaks down when extended to the bankruptcy milieu. It does so not because this conceptualization of security is flawed necessarily, although the attempt to define a security interest as a property interest has been vigorously resisted in some quarters. Rather, even giving this conceptualization of security its due, the model fails because bankruptcy policy establishes the limits of private property no less than it does the limits of sanctity of contract. *Dewsnup*'s interdiction against lien stripping has been rejected in chapter 11 and 13 cases because it would effectively eviscerate the rehabilitative policy that underlies those chapters. Similarly, *Dewsnup* should be discarded in chapter 7 because it interferes fundamentally with fresh-start policy and is not necessary to protect the secured creditor's interest in the estate's property in a bankruptcy proceeding. To the extent that the property-based characterization of security interests is at odds with this formulation, it too should be rejected once a bankruptcy proceeding has been initiated.

Once we get beyond the false rhetoric in *Dewsnup* that lien stripping implicates constitutional concerns, we can appreciate that Justice Blackmun's analysis was influenced heavily by the implicit conception of a security interest as entailing a *bargain* between the debtor and creditor, a notion that is congruent in many respects with the theoretical underpinnings of Harris and Mooney's conveyance model. This bargain metaphor, perfectly valid and fiercely rational under state law and procedures, conjures up entailments of vested rights and interests that, once internalized, preordain the protection of those rights and interests under virtually any circumstances. The bankruptcy regime, however, changes the rules of the game. Many bargains, fairly struck and fully enforceable in the workaday world, come undone once a bankruptcy petition is filed. Hard-core promises are broken and, in the process, losses reallocated between debtor and creditors and among creditors *inter se*. In fact, in its most fundamental sense, bankruptcy, whether in its liquidation or reorganization mode, represents nothing less than a wholesale and compulsory readjustment of contractual obligations and realignment of property interests. In this mix, the time-honored axioms that "liens pass through bankruptcy" and "bankruptcy respects state law entitlements" are still bandied about with great frequency. Yet they are alone only empty incantations, and even in context they at best represent incomplete and imperfect expressions of reality that take on subtle shadings of different meaning depending on the particular context in which they are raised. . . .

C. *The Multiple Lien Redux*

. . . [T]he assertion that the secured creditor has some form of indefeasible right to postbankruptcy appreciation is a rhetorical position of advocacy, not an eternal legal verity. . . To conflate the matter, once the debtor files bankruptcy, the . . . secured claim in this case is limited. . . .

Not only does postfiling appreciation belong to the debtor, but the prospect of ultimately losing the property to foreclosure, a result often inimical to fresh-start objectives, also is reduced precipitously. Reaching this result, however, requires that we dispatch with the holding and the normative result in *Dewsnup*. That, in turn, requires us to accept the possibility of and to construct an alternative to the conceptualization of security in bankruptcy implicitly endorsed by Justice Blackmun in his *Dewsnup* opinion . . .

V. Legal Concepts and Metaphoric Reasoning
A. *Legal Concepts as Metaphors*

. . . When we speak of reconceptualizing security, we are calling for a fresh consideration of the metaphors by which security has come to be understood. In so doing, we proceed from recent insights from the cognitive sciences that make a compelling case for the proposition that virtually all our concepts, including legal concepts, are metaphoric in nature. . . .

That concepts are metaphoric has important ramifications for legal analysis and law transformation. Traditional legal analysis is deeply grounded in objectivist assumptions that postulate a transcendental, objective reality that exists independent of human concepts. The method of traditional legal analysis is to abstract principles from cases, statutes, and other authority to arrive at transcendent propositions. Inasmuch as the propositions transcend their instantiations in the concrete cases from which they derive, they are assumed to be capable of objective application when brought to bear in subsequent cases. There is a "right answer," and the analyst has only to find it—the decisionmaker need only avoid contaminating the proposition to be applied with subjective impulses.

For example, as discussed in considerable detail above, much of the discourse about the treatment of secured claims in bankruptcy turns on the *nature* of security, whether the rights of secured claimants with security interests or mortgages are property or contract rights. Under an analytic program guided by objectivist assumptions, there is an immutable, correct conception of security—the rights of secured claimants *are* property or they *are* contract rights. The business of legal analysis, rightly understood, is to identify the correct conception.

On acknowledging that our concepts, legal and otherwise, are no more and no less than metaphoric constructs that enable meaning in accordance with our goals and purposes, rather than abstractions of things the way they *really* are, analysis of legal doctrine takes a different turn. . . . [E]xploring alternative metaphors by which the concept of security is structured forces attention upon aspects of security and the fresh start that are otherwise lost to consideration. Moreover, recognizing that our concepts are imaginative devices of cognition, and not symbolic representations of some transcendental state of affairs in experience, frees us to augment, modify, or, where it serves our ends to do so, suspend one concept in favor of others.

B. *Beyond the Bargain, Conveyance, and Property Metaphors*

. . . [T]he undisputed traditional metaphor regards the creation of a security interest as representing the movement of property from the debtor to the creditor. Security is thus understood in terms of property concepts ordinarily associated with absolute transfers. . . .

That a security interest *can* usefully be thought of in terms of a conveyance of possession is irrefutable. That security *must necessarily* be thought of in those terms is not. The creation of a security interest is, in many respects, like a physical transfer of property. . . .

. . . Security . . . represents a conceptual extension beyond the rudimentary notion of a physical transfer. Nothing observable passes from debtor to creditor as the result of the security "transfer." Nevertheless, to think of security *in terms* of a conveyance, and so to think of the security interest *in terms* of property, is to make the concept of security meaningful. The source concept of the conveyance is well understood, and the clearly defined attributes associated with it serve to define the target concept of security when conveyance is mapped onto that concept.

Understanding security in terms of a conveyance of property enables us to reason about security by highlighting those features that we perceive the two concepts to share. As indicated earlier, however, metaphoric reasoning is by hypothesis partial. While similarities between concepts are highlighted, asymmetries are lost to view. It is one thing to say that the creation of a security interest can usefully be understood in terms of a conveyance of property, but quite another to say it *is* a conveyance of property. The former assertion acknowledges that security is in many respects like a conveyance of property, but admits of differences between them. The latter assertion denies those distinctions. . . .

To insist that the creation of security is a conveyance of property rather than a target concept *modeled* on the source concept of the conveyance leads to doctrinal impasse and dysfunctionality. . . . Worse, if discourse about security in bankruptcy is limited by the conviction that there is a single, correct conception of security, meaningful analysis of bankruptcy policy, insofar as it is related to secured claims in consumer cases at least, is foreclosed. . . .

. . . Once it is decided that a lien is the product of a conveyance of property, the secured creditor's claim suddenly enjoys special status because security interest or mortgage is *property*. . . .

. . . [When] we grant a conceptual monopoly to the conveyance and property models, the entailments of the conveyance model—of security as property—tyrannize analysis and suppress penetrating considerations of policy. . . . If we presume security to be property, then of course liens must "pass through" bankruptcy, since they are something within or attached to the collateral. . . .

The *Dewsnup* opinion is completely dominated by the property and conveyance models of security that pervade state law. . . . Given the entailments mapped from that concept to the concept of security, the outcome in the case was inescapable: the secured claimant's "property" cannot be divested through lien stripping. . . .

Dewsnup is therefore dysfunctional. To say that security can only be understood as property leads inexorably to the conclusion reached in that case, but it is not a justification for it. . . .

More important, letting go of the commitment to a single metaphoric system advances discourse by diverting attention from results enjoined by metaphoric entailments to a wide-ranging exploration of bankruptcy policy. Letting go of the property metaphor in bankruptcy focuses attention on the fresh start in a way that, we believe, leads to a very different view of lien stripping. . . . In the next part, we offer an alternative model for security to enable precisely that sort of analysis.

VI. A Reconceptualization of Undersecured Claims in Bankruptcy

A. *In Concept*

. . . [O]ne alternative to a property-based conception of security interests in bankruptcy is a value-based account that recognizes the existence and priority of the secured creditor's interest in the debtor's property up to the value of the collateral as of the moment of filing. . . . [W]e would press . . . that . . . it is appropriate to reassess the character of secured claims with reference to the fundamental underlying nature of a bankruptcy case. We appreciate that this process has ramifications that resonate throughout the fabric of the commercial law. For present purposes, however, we urge such a reconceptualization of secured claims simply as a means for more fairly balancing the rights of secured creditors with the Code's fresh-start policy, a policy that is without analogue in state debt/collection law.

In substance, . . . a bankruptcy case involves nothing less than the complete acceleration and adjudication of all claims against the debtor . . . in a single, expedited proceeding. A pivotal, although frequently unarticulated, premise of bankruptcy policy is that, with a few notable exceptions, pre-filing claims lose their individual identity once a case is commenced. . . .

By and large, courts seem to recognize this principle in reorganization and debt-adjustment cases, but *Dewsnup* stands in the way of a comparable recognition in individual chapter 7 cases. The irony could not be more striking. In the one type of proceeding in which the bankruptcy fresh start is most sharply in focus, the debtor's ability to accomplish a clean break with her past is foreclosed by a determination that the postfiling accrual of value will be burdened by a claim originating in the debtor's prefiling life.

How does this observation inform the question of the proper conceptualization of secured claims in bankruptcy? The *in rem* notion simply superimposes the state-law template onto the bankruptcy landscape while remaining oblivious to the differences in the legal terrain. Under state law, a secured creditor can be said to possess two different sets of rights: rights against the debtor upon default of repossession and foreclosure triggered by default—so-called "default rights"—and rights of exclusivity or priority against other claimants with an interest in the collateral—so-called "priority rights." What is often overlooked in the *Dewsnup* type of analysis is that only one set of rights survives a bankruptcy filing, namely the creditor's priority rights in the collateral. . . .

If the central issue in *Dewsnup* relating to the right to future appreciation in property is framed in these terms instead of using the rhetoric of property law, the picture develops quite differently than the outcome reached by the *Dewsnup* majority. Specifically, in the bankruptcy context, a secured claim must be regarded first and foremost as a "claim," indistinguishable from other claims insofar as the debtor/creditor analysis is concerned. The significance of the secured nature of the claim relates only to the question of priority in particular assets in the ultimate distribution of the estate among the body of creditors as whole—the creditor/creditor analysis. Contrary to Justice Blackmun's suggestion in *Dewsnup*, it is not *property* entitled to protection any more than an unsecured claimant can assert a protectible property interest in its state-law-based contractual rights against the debtor. What was conveyed at the onset was the right to foreclose under state law upon default . . . . Therefore, when a collective procedure is initiated, barring the creditor from unilaterally taking action to foreclose, this right translates into a prior claim to the asset—nothing more and nothing less. This was after all the real *bargain* . . . . [T]here is no defensible basis for recasting the secured claim in a manner that confers an unintended and unwarranted advantage on the secured creditor. This is particularly true when doing so potentially erects an insurmountable obstacle in the way of the debtor's fresh start.

The preceding discussion points to a conceptualization of secured credit in bankruptcy that abandons the inherent subjectivity and ambiguity imbedded in the bargain metaphor and the state-law property entailments that attend that metaphor. In their place, we urge a view that coheres with the bankruptcy notion of a "claim." In effect, a security interest can more accurately be seen as representing a kind of priority claim; it is a priority claim of a different ilk than the statutory priority unsecured claims, but only in that the priority is measured against certain assets of the estate rather than against the unencumbered residue. Thus, . . . the secured creditor's future rights against the debtor are severed by the filing of the petition, including its rights against the debtor's future property interests no less than against the debtor *in personam*. Properly understood, the secured claim is a claim against specific assets that, like any other claim, must be fixed as of the time of filing. . . .

. . . [O]nce we accept this reconceptualization of the meaning of secured claims in bankruptcy, it becomes very easy to let go of the antiquated notions of security in bankruptcy, and the "fairness" kinds of impulses that derive from those notions, that bolstered and may have even accounted for the result in *Dewsnup*. . . .

B. *In Application*

. . . Ultimately . . . the wisdom of the rule and the prospects for its adoption, will be judged in terms of its practical effects on the lending community and the market for consumer credit. Oddly, perhaps, given the furor the issue has generated, we surmise that reversal of *Dewsnup* would cause, at most, a proverbial blip on the screen . . . .

Most home-or other real-property-owning chapter 7 debtors will see their property sold either during the case or very soon after the stay is lifted. In either event, restricting the secured lender to the market value of the property at filing is not prejudicial to the lender because, as a practical matter, there is no, and never will be any, appreciation to be forfeited. A debtor with sufficient postpetition cash flow or resources to carry the property will have chosen, or have been forced into, a chapter 13 debt-adjustment proceeding, or, in rare circumstances, a chapter 11 case. Thus, the fear of cram down in a chapter 7 case—where the debtor can retain the property and modify the underlying obligation—is grossly exaggerated. . . .

CONCLUSION

. . . [J]ustifications for Justice Blackmun's tortured reading of section 506(d) couched in terms of bargain metaphors and nondefeasible property rights are noble sounding, but ultimately empty, rhetorical ruses. In fact, as we have seen, the most articulate defense of *Dewsnup* has forthrightly acknowledged that the real issue is distrust over judicial valuations that are too conservative. . . . [The] issue boils down to a political exercise of balancing fresh-start policy against the competing commercial policies served by maintaining a stable environment for asset-based financing.

Collateral valuations are mere predictions and, as such, are inherently uncertain. Moreover, while it is unclear to us that this uncertainty necessarily produces low valuations—particularly since judicial valuations typically do not factor selling and delay costs into the analysis—even conceding the point does not diminish the case for overruling *Dewsnup*. We make this assertion based on our observation that the fresh-start objectives of the consumer bankruptcy system are attained by recognizing that the filing of the petition changes fundamentally the nature of the debtor's relationships with his creditors, both secured and unsecured. An essential aspect of this closure of the debtor's prepetition life is achieved by liquidating secured creditors' claims in relation to the then-extant value of their collateral. The filing of the petition serves to construct a nearly impenetrable barrier separating the debtor's pre and postpetition lives. A property-based heuristic for understanding security . . . loses its viability, however, as soon as the bankruptcy curtain is drawn. The very act of filing extinguishes the secured creditor's default rights against the debtor and repossessory rights in and to the property. . . .

Despite its interference with the Code's fresh-start policy, *Dewsnup* has proved tenacious. In large measure, we believe that it has been difficult to eradicate because it hangs on a false conception of bankruptcy and, in particular, an appealing but ultimately inaccurate conception of the nature of security in bankruptcy. However, once the misconception is understood, we can finally snip the slender vine from which the rule in *Dewsnup* hangs.

Additional suggested readings

Barry E. Adler, *An Equity-Agency Solution to the Bankruptcy Priority Puzzle*, 22 J. LEGAL STUD. 73 (1993)

Barry E. Adler, *Creditor Rights After* Johnson *and* Dewsnup, 10 BANKR. DEV. J. 1 (1993)

Douglas G. Baird, *Security Interests Reconsidered*, 80 VA. L. REV. 2249 (1994)

Lucian A. Bebchuk & Jesse M. Fried, *A New Approach to Valuing Secured Claims in Bankruptcy*, 114 HARV. L. REV. 2386 (2001)

James W. Bowers, *Whither What Hits the Fan?: Murphy's Law, Bankruptcy Theory, and the Elementary Economics of Loss Distribution*, 26 GA. L. REV. 27 (1991)

Jean Braucher, *Getting it for You Wholesale: Making Sense of Bankruptcy Valuation of Collateral After* Rash, 102 DICKINSON L. REV. 763 (1998)

F.H. Buckley, *The Bankruptcy Priority Puzzle*, 72 VA. L. REV. 1393 (1986)

David Gray Carlson, *Secured Lending as a Zero-Sum Game*, 19 CARDOZO L. REV. 1635 (1998)

David Gray Carlson, *Bifurcation of Undersecured Claims in Bankruptcy*, 70 AM. BANKR. L.J. 1 (1996)

David Gray Carlson, *Car Wars: Valuation Standards in Chapter 13 Bankruptcy Cases*, 13 BANKR. DEV. J. 1 (1996)

David Gray Carlson, *Rents in Bankruptcy*, 46 S.C. L. REV. 1075 (1995)

David Gray Carlson, *On the Efficiency of Secured Lending*, 80 VA. L. REV. 2179 (1994)

David Gray Carlson, *Adequate Protection Payments and the Surrender of Cash Collateral in Chapter 11 Reorganization*, 15 CARDOZO L. REV. 1357 (1994)

David Gray Carlson, *Secured Creditors and Expenses of Bankruptcy Administration*, 70 N.C. L. REV. 417 (1992)

David Gray Carlson, *Time, Value, and the Rights of Secured Creditors in Bankruptcy, or, When Does Adequate Protection Begin?*, 1 J. BANKR. L. & PRAC. 113 (1992)

David Gray Carlson, *Postpetition Interest Under the Bankruptcy Code*, 43 U. MIAMI L. REV. 577 (1989)

David Gray Carlson, *Undersecured Claims Under Bankruptcy Code Sections 506(a) and 1111(b): Second Looks at Judicial Valuations of Collateral*, 6 BANKR. DEV. J. 253 (1989)

Peter F. Coogan, *The New Bankruptcy Code: The Death of Security Interest?*, 14 GA. L. REV. 153 (1980)

Theodore Eisenberg, *The Undersecured Creditor in Reorganizations and the Nature of Security*, 38 VAND. L. REV. 931 (1985)

Chaim Fortgang & Thomas Moers Mayer, *Valuation in Bankruptcy*, 32 UCLA L. REV. 1061 (1985)

Grant Gilmore, *The Good Faith Purchase Idea and the Uniform Commercial Code: Confessions of a Repentant Draftsman*, 15 GA. L. REV. 605 (1981)

Steven L. Harris & Charles W. Mooney, Jr., *Measuring the Social Costs and Benefits and Identifying the Victims of Subordinating Security Interests in Bankruptcy*, 82 CORNELL L. REV. 1349 (1997)

Margaret Howard, *Secured Claims in Bankruptcy: An Essay on Missing the Point*, 23 CAPITAL U. L. REV. 313 (1994)

Margaret Howard, *Dewsnupping the Bankruptcy Code*, 1 J. BANKR. L. & PRAC. 513 (1992)

Thomas H. Jackson, Ch. 7, *Running Bankruptcy's Collective Proceeding*, in THE LOGIC AND LIMITS OF BANKRUPTCY LAW 151-192 (Harvard 1986)

Thomas H. Jackson, *Of Liquidation, Continuation and Delay: An Analysis of Bankruptcy Policy and Nonbankruptcy Rules*, 60 AM. BANKR. L.J. 399 (1986)

Thomas H. Jackson & Anthony T. Kronman, *Secured Financing and Priorities Among Creditors*, 88 YALE L.J. 1143 (1979)

Hideki Kanda & Saul Levmore, *Explaining Creditor Priorities*, 80 VA. L. REV. 2103 (1994)

Frank R. Kennedy, *Secured Creditors Under the Bankruptcy Reform Act*, 15 IND. L. REV. 477 (1982)

Frank R. Kennedy, *Automatic Stays Under the New Bankruptcy Law*, 12 U. MICH. J.L. REF. 3 (1978)

Frank R. Kennedy, *The Automatic Stay in Bankruptcy*, 11 U. MICH. J.L. REF. 175 (1978)

Kenneth N. Klee, *Barbarians at the Trough: Riposte in Defense of the Warren Carve-Out Proposal*, 82 CORNELL L. REV. 1466 (1997)

F. Stephen Knippenberg, *The Unsecured Creditor's Bargain: An Essay in Reply, Reprisal, or Support?*, 80 VA. L. REV. 1967 (1994)

Homer Kripke, *Law and Economics: Measuring the Economic Efficiency of Commercial Law in a Vacuum of Fact*, 133 U. PA. L. REV. 929 (1985)

Saul Levmore, *Monitors and Freeriders in Commercial and Corporate Settings*, 92 YALE L.J. 49 (1982)

Lynn M. LoPucki, *Should the Secured Credit Carve-Out Apply Only in Bankruptcy? A Systems/Strategic Analysis*, 82 CORNELL L. REV. 1483 (1997)

Lynn M. LoPucki, *The Unsecured Creditor's Bargain*, 80 VA. L REV. 1887 (1994)

Ronald J. Mann, *Explaining the Pattern of Secured Credit*, 110 HARV. L. REV. 625 (1997)

Ronald J. Mann, *The Role of Secured Credit in Small-Business Lending*, 86 GEO. L.J. 1 (1997)

Mary Jo Newborn, *Undersecured Creditors in Bankruptcy:* Dewsnup, Nobelman, *and the Decline of Priority*, 25 ARIZ. ST. L.J. 547 (1993)

James F. Queenan, Jr., *Standards for Valuation of Security Interests in Chapter 11*, 92 COM. L.J. 18 (1987)

Steven L. Schwarcz, *The Easy Case for the Priority of Secured Claims in Bankruptcy*, 47 DUKE L.J. 425 (1997)

Alan Schwartz, *Taking the Analysis of Security Seriously*, 80 VA. L. REV. 2073 (1994)

Alan Schwartz, *A Theory of Loan Priorities*, 18 J. LEGAL STUD. 209 (1989)

Alan Schwartz, *Security Interests and Bankruptcy Priorities: A Review of Current Theories*, 10 J. LEGAL STUD. 1 (1981)

Robert E. Scott, *The Truth About Secured Financing*, 82 CORNELL L. REV. 1436 (1997)

Robert E. Scott, *A Relational Theory of Secured Financing*, 86 COLUM. L. REV. 901 (1986)

Paul M. Shupack, *Solving the Puzzle of Secured Transactions*, 41 RUTGERS L. REV. 1067 (1989)

George G. Triantis, *A Free-Cash-Flow Theory of Secured Debt and Creditor Priorities*, 80 VA. L. REV. 2155 (1994)

George G. Triantis, *Secured Debt Under Conditions of Imperfect Information*, 21 J. LEGAL STUD. 225 (1992)

Elizabeth Warren, *Making Policy with Imperfect Information: The Article 9 Full Priority Debates*, 82 CORNELL L. REV. 1373 (1997)

Elizabeth Warren, *An Article 9 Set-Aside for Unsecured Creditors*, 51 CONSUMER FIN. L.Q. REP. 323 (1997)

James J. White, *Efficiency Justifications for Personal Property Security*, 37 Vand. L. Rev. 473 (1984)

William J. Woodward, Jr., *The Realist and Secured Credit: Grant Gilmore, Common-Law Courts, and the Article 9 Reform Process*, 82 Cornell L. Rev. 1511 (1997)

Chapter 9
Unsecured Claims

A. General Principles and the Allocation of Rights

In the last Chapter we examined the status of secured claims in bankruptcy. The most salient fact about secured claims is their full priority over unsecured claims with respect to the encumbered assets. In this Chapter we turn to a more complete inquiry into the status and treatment of unsecured claims. This Chapter contains two parts. The first part looks at general principles regarding unsecured claims in bankruptcy, and how rights are allocated. Part two tackles the specific problem of *involuntary* unsecured claims—those arising out of tort (often mass tort) and environmental liability. Scholars have noted the special problems involved in addressing such claims. In the last Chapter some discussion was included that spoke to the possible subordination of secured claims to these sorts of involuntary claims.

The first part contains excerpts from three articles: Lynn M. LoPucki, *The Death of Liability,* 106 YALE L.J. 1 (1996); Ronald J. Mann, *Bankruptcy and the Entitlements of the Government: Whose Money Is It Anyway?,* 70 N.Y.U. L. REV. 993 (1995); and James W. Bowers, *Whither What Hits the Fan?: Murphy's Law, Bankruptcy Theory, and the Elementary Economics of Loss Distribution,* 26 GA. L. REV. 27 (1991).

Professor LoPucki leads off in *The Death of Liability* with a disturbing analysis of the many ways in which our liability system is being undermined. This problem, of course, transcends the bankruptcy realm, but obviously has enormous implications for bankruptcy. Can you identify all of the ways in which liability is being evaded, according to LoPucki? What solutions does he suggest? Note that his thesis has been controversial: Professor James J. White answered back in *Corporate Judgment Proofing: A Response to Lynn LoPucki's* The Death of Liability, 107 YALE L.J. 1363 (1998), as did Professor Steven Schwarcz in *The Inherent Irrationality of Judgment Proofing,* 52 STAN. L. REV. 1 (1999) and *Judgment Proofing: A Rejoinder,* 52 STAN. L. REV. 77 (1999). LoPucki's surrebuttals can be found at *Virtual Judgment Proofing: A Rejoinder,* 107 YALE L.J. 1413 (1998) (responding to White), and *The Essential Structure of Judgment Proofing,* 51 STAN. L. REV. 147 (1998) and *The Irrefutable Logic of Judgment Proofing: A Reply to Professor Schwarcz,* 52 STAN. L. REV. 55 (1999) (responding to Schwarcz).

Second is Professor Ronald Mann's article, *Bankruptcy and the Entitlements of the Government: Whose Money Is It Anyway?* Mann challenges the "creditors' bargain" theorists and their fundamental premise that creditors presumptively should retain their state-law entitlements, supporting instead the redistributive approach of Warren, Westbrook and other "traditional" theorists. Mann has two main themes. First, he asserts that the government's role in providing the bankruptcy system entitles it to distribute the value created by the bankruptcy system amongst claimants in any way the government sees fit, consonant of course with legitimate governmental interests. This point justifies redistribution in bankruptcy in order to further governmental objectives. Second, Mann argues that the "entitlement" rhetoric of the economic school is flawed because it looks only at the rights of creditors and fails to account for the value added by governmental efforts. Creditors have no necessary claim to that added value.

Professor James Bowers presents a nice counterpoint to Mann in *Whither What Hits the Fan?: Murphy's Law, Bankruptcy Theory, and the Elementary Economics of Loss Distribution*. This article is Bowers's sequel to his seminal work, *Groping and Coping in the Shadow of Murphy's Law: Bankruptcy Theory and the Elementary Economics of Failure*, 88 MICH. L. REV. 2097 (1990), which was excerpted in Chapter 2. In the "Loss Distribution" article, Bowers challenges the fundamental normative premise of bankruptcy distribution that "equality" is at least a desirable goal. Equality is a flawed premise and should be discarded, Bowers asserts. The existence of creditor differences dictates and warrants distributional differences as well. And, Bowers claims, the debtor is the party best positioned to distribute its assets effectively and efficiently, and should be allowed to do so. Bowers calls into question the very need for a bankruptcy system.

Lynn M. LoPucki
The Death of Liability
106 YALE L.J. 1 (1996)[*]

. . . The liability system currently is mired in controversy over who should be liable, for what conduct, and for how much money. Yet this grand debate may be over the arrangement of the deck chairs on the Titanic. To hold a defendant liable is to enter a money judgment against the defendant. Unless that judgment can be enforced, liability is merely symbolic.

The system by which money judgments are enforced is beginning to fail. The immediate cause is the deployment of legal structures that render potential defendants judgment proof. . . .

. . . [T]his Article concludes that currently effective judgment-proofing strategies are fully capable of defeating the liability system. The remaining barriers that constrain use of these strategies—principally expense and cultural resistance—are in decline. . . . The ultimate causes of this system failure are that: (1) the system is unwilling to bar those without wealth from engaging in liability-producing activity; and (2) the system lacks an effective conceptual framework for attributing wealth to those engaged in liability-producing activity. . . .

. . . [I]t should be noted that only tort and statutorily imposed liability are at risk of death. Contract liability can be preserved through private contracting. . . . To return to the poker metaphor, tort liability is confined to the chips in the pot, while contract liability reaches into the players' pockets and may even tap their friends and family. . . .

I. LIABILITY SYSTEM PRINCIPLES

. . .

A. *Enforcement Only Against Property*

Courts will enforce a judgment for civil liability against specific property of the debtor, but not against the person of the debtor. . . .

---

*   Reprinted by permission of The Yale Law Journal Company and Fred B. Rothman & Company from The Yale Law Journal, Vol. 106, pages 1-92.

B. *Property of the Debtor*

The holder of a judgment is entitled to proceed only against property owned by the debtor. . . .

C. *Transferability of Property*

To the extent that property is unencumbered and therefore vulnerable to liability, the owner can sell it or use it to make payment to a favorite creditor. Such a transfer is effective instantly to defeat enforcement against the property. . . .

D. *Exemption*

The legislatures of each of the fifty states have enacted laws exempting specified property from procedures to enforce a judgment for money damages. . . . The laws authorizing such exemptions reflect long-standing, politically vibrant beliefs that debtors' personal lives should not be disrupted because the debtors have failed to pay their debts. . . .

E. *Subordination*

A judgment for civil liability is merely an unsecured debt. The holders of valid security interests, liens, and bankruptcy priorities are entitled to absolute priority over unsecured debts. . . .

F. *Discharge on Demand*

Debtors are entitled to discharge their debts at any time by filing a bankruptcy case. . . .

G. *Productive Use*

During enforcement, bankruptcy courts always stand ready to permit and provide for the continued productive use of the debtor's property. . . .

H. *Enforcement Only After Judgment*

Except in exigent circumstances, obligations for civil liability are enforced only after entry of a judgment. . . .

I. *Territoriality*

As an initial matter, a judgment can be enforced only within the territorial jurisdiction of the court that entered it. . . .

II. JUDGMENT-PROOFING STRATEGIES

The liability system works solely through the entry and enforcement of money judgments. Debtors can defeat it by rendering themselves judgment proof. Judgment-proofing strategies are of four basic types: secured debt, third-party ownership, exemption, and foreign haven.

A. *Secured Debt Strategies*

Secured debt strategies are the most complex and the most common of the judgment-proofing strategies. They are employed primarily by small, relatively uncreditworthy businesses, whose lenders insist on security interests. They are constructed from the three basic principles of subordination, productive use, and discharge on demand. The debtor becomes judgment proof by incurring secured debts in amounts exceeding the liquidation values of the debtor's properties. Money judgments thereafter enforced against the debtor's properties are subordinate to the secured debt. Enforcement is by liquidation of the debtor's property. Pursuant to the principle of subordination, the proceeds of liquidation go first to pay the secured creditors. Because the proceeds are less than the secured debt, no balance remains to be paid to the holder of the money judgment. . . .

The secured debt strategy is a relatively recent phenomenon. It is effective only in a system that permits debtors to encumber all, or substantially all, of their assets. . . .

B. *Ownership Strategies*

Lenders to large, highly creditworthy businesses rarely insist on security interests. Judgment proofing is less common among large businesses. When large businesses do judgment proof, they use different techniques. The two most common are both based on the principle that liability can be enforced only against property of the debtor. Through both these techniques, debtors arrange their affairs so that the liability-generating entity does not own the most valuable property of the business.

1. *Parent-Subsidiary*

In the parent-subsidiary strategy, the debtor isolates the most valuable assets of the business in an entity other than the one that conducts the liability-producing business activity. . . .

This parent-subsidiary ownership strategy is in wide use among the largest companies in America. Most large companies consist of numerous corporate entities. Limiting liability—that is, defeating part of it—is the principal reason for creating those entities. But the parent-subsidiary strategy itself rarely renders companies entirely judgment proof. Alone, it defeats only liability in excess of the value of the assets of the operating company. Nevertheless, . . . [i]ts use in combination with a secured debt strategy can defeat a company's liability entirely.

The parent-subsidiary strategy is vulnerable to legal attack. In theory, at least, courts can disregard a corporate entity if it is being used too aggressively to defeat liability. But the rhetoric of entity disregard far outstrips the reality. . . .

2. *Asset Securitization*

Asset securitization is the issuance of securities representing the ownership of designated assets. In the prototypical asset-securitization transaction, the asset is the accounts receivable of a business. As part of the asset-securitization transaction, the debtor creates a "bankruptcy-remote vehicle," a separate legal entity, and "sells" the accounts to it. The bankruptcy-remote entity obtains the money to buy the assets through a public or private offering of its own securities. The debtor may continue to service the accounts under contract with the bankruptcy-remote entity, processing payments, dunning customers who fail to pay, and filing lawsuits against some of them. All that necessarily changes is that the debtor no longer owns the accounts. . . .

Asset securitization is both a substitute for borrowing and a powerful new strategy for judgment proofing. Like the parent-subsidiary strategy, the asset-securitization strategy puts ownership of the company's valuable assets in an entity separate from the one that is at risk for liability. The advantage of the asset-securitization strategy over the parent-subsidiary strategy is virtual elimination of the risk that the courts will disregard the entity that holds the assets. . . .

Through asset securitization, a company potentially could divest itself of all of its assets, yet continue to use all of those assets in the continued operation of its business. . . .

. . . [T]he courts are unlikely to disregard the asset-securitization transactions. Pursuant to the principle of transferability, the transactions are effective until avoided through litigation so that innocent parties who rely on the transactions in the interim are protected. . . . [Recovery] seems highly unlikely with regard to an arms-length transaction in which the buyer paid the full fair market value of the property. . . .

. . . [T]he fault lies not with fraudulent transfer law but with the more fundamental principle of enforcement only against property of the debtor.

The schemes in the preceding examples show the structure of the future that judgment proofing will produce. There will be entities that own things and entities that do things. Those that own things—the bankruptcy-remote vehicles—will not do anything, lest they expose their assets to liability. Those that do things—the operating companies—will not own anything, lest their judgment creditors have something to attach. . . .

Asset securitization has not been restrained by cultural norms against judgment proofing because it has not been recognized as a judgment-proofing technique. Yet it is. Asset securitization is booming because investors are willing to pay more for securitized assets than for securitized businesses. . . . Asset securitization, unlike business securitization, "eliminat[es] the risk of bankruptcy to investors."

What risk of bankruptcy is eliminated by asset securitization? . . . [A]sset securitization is being substituted principally for unsecured bank lending and unsecured issues of public debt. Such debt is a liability, and in bankruptcy it shares pro rata with other kinds of liability claims. The owners of securitized assets, by contrast, keep their assets when the debtor files bankruptcy; they need not share with the holders of liability. . . .

Asset securitization may be the silver bullet capable of killing liability. . . .

C. Exemption Strategies

. . . [T]he laws of all fifty states and numerous federal statutes exempt various kinds of property from procedures to enforce judgments for money damages. . . .

Employed in conjunction with secured debt strategies, exemption strategies make it possible for individual debtors to retain any property against their judgment creditors, regardless of its value. . . . Once a debtor becomes judgment proof through any of these techniques, the debtor can file bankruptcy. In bankruptcy, the debtor can discharge his or her unsecured debt, including most debt for liability, while keeping the exempt property. . . .

D. Foreign Haven Strategies

Removal of one's assets from the jurisdiction of the court is a time-honored strategy for defeating one's liability. Upon removal, the principle of territoriality takes effect; to recover, the creditor must sue in the foreign legal system where the assets are located. If the foreign legal system will not enforce liability against the assets of the debtor, removal achieves more than hindrance and delay; it bars recovery.

More than a half-dozen nations compete for foreign investment by refusing comity with respect to the enforcement of judgments and providing havens for judgment debtors from their foreign creditors. They implement the latter policy principally by validating self-settled spendthrift trusts under which the settlor is a beneficiary. . . .

. . . [T]he trust, at the [debtor]'s "suggestion," can remove the value of his remaining assets from the United States before litigating the validity of the trust. . . . Once the trust has removed the last of its assets from the United States, the principles of territoriality and enforcement only against property will combine to make enforcement in the United States highly unlikely. . . .

In response to the [debtor]'s deployment of such strategies, it is possible to imagine the U.S. judge abandoning on equitable grounds the principle of enforcement only against property. The court might determine the trust to be invalid and the [debtor] to be the owner of the assets, and then order the [debtor] to surrender them to a sheriff within the jurisdiction of the court. Absent compliance, the U.S. court might order the debtor imprisoned for contempt of court. The [debtor]'s defense would be that he was not in contempt because from the time he was served with the court's order, he lacked the ability to comply with it. . . . [T]he typical asset-protection trust contains a duress provision, barring the trustee from acceding to the settlor's demands for distributions ordered by a court. . . . To continue to live and work in the United States, the [debtor] ultimately would have to comply, to the best of his ability, with any orders issued and upheld by courts in the United States. . . .

. . . [T]he [debtor] might choose to remove himself from the United States to eliminate the possibility of being imprisoned for contempt. . . .

III. Constraints on Judgment Proofing

Any debtor could become judgment proof using the strategies described in the preceding Part. For a large, publicly held company, the most effective strategy would be a combination of secured debt and ownership strategies. The debtor would first reduce its assets through asset securitization, then compartmentalize by incorporating subsidiaries and dividing its assets among them. Finally, it would encumber the assets in those subsidiaries beyond their remaining value. With such redundant judgment proofing in its structure, a company would be beyond the reach of liability. . . .

If judgment-proofing strategies insulate companies from the bane of liability, why doesn't everyone use them? Among small- and medium-sized companies, the answer is that the large majority enjoys most of the benefits of being judgment proof already. They have secured debt that exceeds the liquidation value of their assets. . . .

The mystery is why so few of the largest companies are judgment proof at the time of their bankruptcy reorganizations. . . . [T]he largest companies eschew secured financing. The constraints that might explain why large companies are seldom judgment proof are the subject of the remainder of this Part.

A. *The Self-Immolation Argument*

Some commentators argue that shareholders have nothing to gain by judgment proofing their companies. Bankruptcy sweeps away liability, but when used by large, publicly held companies, it sweeps away shareholdings as well. Thus, in the very situations where judgment proofing actually provides benefits, the shareholders will no longer be around to share in them. One might suppose this would leave shareholders with no incentive to judgment proof their companies in the first place. . . .

. . . But . . . [t]o calculate the value of an investment, one must take account of its potential for profit, its potential for loss, and the likelihood of each. . . . The risks of the investment are reflected in their value *ex ante*. If an investment is structured to externalize liability, it will have a higher value *ex ante* than if it is not. . . . Their shares are worth more than they would be without judgment proofing . . . . The shareholders can cash this value by selling their shares. . . .

B. *The Precarious Position of Managers*

For large companies to remain perpetually judgment proof would put managers in a precarious position. . . .

The interests of the managers are exactly the opposite of those of the investors. To the extent that the managers of large, publicly held companies have power independent of their shareholders, they can benefit themselves by operating their companies with substantial cushions of equity. Their purpose in maintaining these cushions is to protect themselves against creditors and shareholders; the incidental effect of doing so is to expose investments in their companies to liability unnecessarily. Even though their investors are better off with judgment-proof structures that externalize the risk of liability, managers can be expected to resist them.

Once this conflict between the interests of owners and managers over the judgment proofing of investments is generally recognized, it is likely to be resolved in ways that promote judgment proofing. That solution maximizes benefits to the alliance of owners and managers. By contract, owners and managers can then divide between them benefits gained by externalizing liability. . . .

C. *The Marginality of Liability*

To judgment proof a business, managers must finance it differently. . . . To justify the change in method of financing, the savings from the elimination of liability must exceed the additional costs, if any, of the new forms of financing and the occasional bankruptcy reorganizations. For many businesses, judgment proofing is not cost effective for the simple reason that the businesses generate little liability and thus have only low costs to eliminate. . . .

The absence of hard judgment proofing from the largest companies in the U.S. economy may signal any of three things. First, the benefits of such judgment proofing may not be sufficient to exceed the added costs of secured or asset-securitized financing and the occasional bankruptcy. Second, hard judgment proofing may be cost effective for investors in the business, but it may be artificially constrained by managers' conflicts of interest. The third and most likely possibility is that hard judgment proofing is not cost effective for large companies, but only because of cultural and political constraints. . . .

D. *Legal and Clerical Costs*

. . . Strategies such as these depend heavily on computerized recordkeeping and were simply not possible at earlier levels of technology. . . .

Asset securitization also depends heavily on computer translation. . . .

Transactions such as these are cost effective only because of computers. In this sense, they are a direct product of computer technology. Computer technology is generally acknowledged to be a driving force behind asset-securitization and debtor-haven strategies. Not surprisingly, these are the two fastest growing strategies for judgment proofing.

Despite the already high level of computerization in the private sector, judgment-proofing strategies continue to be constrained by transaction costs. . . .

. . . These systems cannot be fixed overnight, but they can become progressively more efficient. As they do, the transaction costs of judgment-proofing strategies will continue to decline. . . .

E. *Culture and Politics*

For Americans to accept the hard judgment proofing of the nation's largest companies would require substantial cultural and political change. Rights enforced through liability are among the most precious we hold. . . . The successful implementation of important social policies—such as those relating to the environment, product safety, pensions, and health care—depend upon liability. If a major American company were caught attempting to deliberately deploy the strategies I described in the preceding Part in order to defeat liability and eliminate the need to pay liability insurance premiums, all hell would break loose.

Judgment-proofing strategists would feel a variety of effects. Adverse publicity might chill the market for the company's products or the company's appeal in the employment market. Judges, juries, legislators, and regulators might retaliate against the company. Activists might boycott a company . . . . Concern about all these effects might discourage investment in the company. In short, the company might develop a reputation for sleaze. . . .

To be culturally and politically acceptable, the process of judgment proofing must appear to be something other than what it is. There is every reason to believe that it will. The reality of asset securitization is that it reduces the financial responsibility of the company while leaving the company's level of liability-generating financial activity constant. The public image of asset securitization is that of the invisible hand of the market, aided by modern technology, generating wealth by forging increasingly sophisticated financial structures. . . . [S]o long as the companies march into this new world in tandem, each objecting that it is forced into its course of action by competitive pressures, it will be difficult for indignation to take hold. The problem will be seen, not entirely incorrectly, as systemic rather than moral. Attention will turn to proposals for reform, which are discussed in Part IV.

IV. Radical System Responses

As the transaction costs of judgment-proofing strategies decline, the fundamental contradiction of the current system for enforcing liability will become increasingly apparent. . . . As the system currently operates, liability is, for wrongdoers, a voluntary system.

To save liability as an involuntary system that implements a wide range of public policy, the system's designers will have to make radical changes in it. The available options fall into three categories. First, if the system designers are willing to abandon the principle of enforcement only against property of the debtor, they can extend liability to the shareholders, affiliates, trading partners, and asset providers of those currently liable. . . .

Second, the designers could subordinate the claims of secured creditors to those of involuntary creditors. Third, the designers could condition the right to do business in the United States on demonstrating financial responsibility.

A. *Shareholder Unlimited Liability*

In recent years, corporate law scholars have vigorously debated a proposal by Professors Henry Hansmann and Reinier Kraakman that shareholders have liability for torts committed by their corporations. That is, if the assets of a corporation are insufficient to satisfy its liabilities, involuntary creditors should be entitled to enforce their judgments against the assets of individual shareholders. . . .

Under the rules of the liability system, modified only by extending liability to shareholders, shareholders who choose to defeat that liability would have little difficulty doing so. . . .

B. *Involuntary Creditor Priority*

. . . [E]conomic efficiency is best served when creditors who did not intend to become creditors of a debtor (involuntary creditors) have priority over those who did (consensual creditors). The argument is simple. As the system currently operates, consensual creditors can contract for security. Once they have done so, they have priority over involuntary creditors. Knowing that they themselves will be paid in any event, the secured creditors have grossly inadequate incentives to limit the debtor's liability-generating activity. As a result of the encumbrance, equity holders may also have grossly inadequate incentives to limit the debtor's liability-generating activity. . . . The immediate solution is to give involuntary creditors priority over consensual creditors, including secured creditors. That rule maximizes the probability that debtors will be forced to pay their involuntary creditors and thus be unable to externalize the risks of their business. Consensual creditors will not be prejudiced. Knowing that they will be subordinate, consensual creditors can protect themselves by selecting and monitoring their debtors and charging a premium for those risks that they cannot eliminate cost effectively.

Large, publicly held companies would probably rely heavily on asset securitization as the means for evading the new rule establishing involuntary creditor priority. The bankruptcy-remote entity used in an asset-securitization transaction is in genuinely separate ownership from the debtor. It is neither a creditor nor an owner of the business. To consolidate it with the debtor would require the disregard of a sale transacted at arms length for market value. Yet through a series of securitizations, a business could divest itself of substantially all of its assets, rendering it judgment proof.

Smaller companies could evade involuntary creditor priority by leasing real property, equipment, and intangibles used in the business, accepting their inventories on consignment, and selling their accounts receivable as they are generated. . . . Today, they are relatively expensive ways of doing business. . . . Under the tort-first regime, small businesses might well find that leasing, consignment, and factoring, which would render them judgment proof, would be more effective than secured borrowing. . . .

C. *Asset-Provider Liability*

The previous Section argued that in a world with unlimited shareholder liability and involuntary creditor priority, strategists could still judgment proof their businesses and defeat liability by operating with assets belonging to others. The system could respond to that strategy either by: (1) giving involuntary creditors priority in the assets used in the business regardless of whether the assets were owned by the business; or (2) imposing liability on the owners of those assets. Under such rules, it would not matter how a business acquired its assets or who owned them; all assets used in the business would be available for the enforcement of judgments for liability. True lessors to the debtor would be treated the same as secured creditors and asset-securitization transactions would no longer be bankruptcy remote.

Even these drastic steps would not provide the system with a permanent victory over strategists seeking to externalize the liability generated by their businesses. Probably the strategists' most effective response would be what Hansmann and Kraakman call "disaggregation." Large businesses would spin off smaller ones and reestablish their structure through contract . . . . Finance theorists long ago reconceptualized the corporation as a web of contracts among participants in the firm. With computerization, the web of contracts may move from concept to reality. . . .

D. *Enterprise Liability*

. . . As entities proliferate in response to the lowered costs of separate incorporation and the wealth available to satisfy particular judgments shrinks correspondingly, the system will be pressed to respond. One response that has already been suggested is to attach liability to *enterprises* rather than *entities.* . . .

Whether this approach could be viable depends on whether there are in fact identifiable, stable boundaries between enterprises. . . . If there are not, the courts would be assigning liability arbitrarily and generating probably intolerable uncertainty for investors. . . .

. . . The most basic problem is that the relationship between liability and entity is so deeply ingrained in our thinking that it is virtually impossible to exorcise. De-entification will deprive the system of a fundamental concept for ordering and specifying liability.

E. *Trading Partner Liability*

. . . Hansmann and Kraakman suggest what may be the strongest response that the system can make to the judgment-proofing strategies discussed in this Article. They posit that "in the case of the oil tankers, for instance, making companies that produce, own, or intend to receive the oil jointly and severally liable for spills may well remove any incentive for inefficient disaggregation." Once liability has been extended in this manner, disaggregation presumably will no longer defeat it. Every fragment of the divided firm will bear the total liability of the unified firm, jointly and severally, with every other fragment. . . .

It is worth noting that this suggestion is contrary to current legislative and academic trends that call for *reductions* in joint and several liability. . . . The principal relevance of this trend toward narrowing liability is not that it demonstrates the worth of the ideas behind it, but that it demonstrates how difficult it will be to persuade the body politic to pursue the opposite course. The real issue is whether, if the system holds *everybody* liable, *anybody* will pay.

The trend does help illustrate the fundamental theoretical problem with the system strategy of casting the net of liability widely. The problem is simply to define its boundary. . . .

. . . For the system to accomplish its goal of enforcing liability, those who have it would have to know they have it. Only then could they insure against it, or protect against the acts of others that might impose it on them. . . . Without a generalizable principle for determining its stopping point, expanded liability might lead to chaos.

F. *Liability Insurance*

Arguments that the liability system will remain viable into the foreseeable future usually rely heavily on the continued existence, if not the expansion, of liability insurance. Typically, the arguments falsely assume that: (1) nearly all liability is of an insurable nature, making liability insurance a functional substitute for solvent debtors; (2) debtors will continue to purchase liability insurance because they have economic incentives to do so; and (3) when economic incentives are insufficient to cause debtors to purchase liability insurance voluntarily, the system can achieve the same result by requiring the purchase of liability insurance. In fact, much, if not most, liability is of an uninsurable nature. The incentives to purchase liability insurance are principally social and cultural rather than economic, and the effectiveness of liability insurance is sharply diminished when the insurance is compulsory. Liability insurance is a valuable adjunct to the working of an otherwise sound liability system, but it can neither save nor replace an unsound one. . . .

G. *Financial Responsibility Requirements*

As an alternative to mandatory insurance, the system might permit would-be entrepreneurs to demonstrate financial responsibility either by posting a bond or by proving their financial condition. . . .

Whatever the method of enforcement, if the system worked, it would bar persons not wealthy enough to demonstrate financial responsibility . . . from engaging in liability-generating economic activity. . . . This frames a central tension in the struggle over liability: Americans do not want judgment-proof businesses to be able to operate, but neither do they want to exclude persons of moderate means from participation in the economy. . . .

V. CONCLUSION

Strategies for defeating liability are readily available. Among individuals and small firms, they already protect the vast bulk of all assets against liability. Not all individuals and small firms are currently judgment proof, but that may be only because they do not need to be. . . . Large firms have only begun to tap the judgment-proofing strategies available to them. For most large firms, the costs of judgment proofing still exceed the benefits. But computerization already has reduced the clerical costs sharply, and cultural deterrents are in decline as well. . . . Trends already established soon will tip the balance of costs in favor of judgment proofing for most large firms and pull down the remaining cultural barriers. . . .

Strategies by which the system can attempt to postpone liability's day of reckoning are plentiful. But they are drastic measures that would require traumatic change. . . .

Sophisticated information systems seem the most likely substitute for liability. It is not difficult to imagine a world in which the only deterrent to nonpayment of debt is a bad credit rating and the only deterrent to medical malpractice is the publication of notice of its occurrence. . . . Because these systems act against persons rather than property, they do not suffer the metaphysical difficulties that plague the future of liability. In part because these system are potentially so powerful, they are tightly constrained by a web of legal and quasi-legal burdens. But in the post-liability world, we might choose to unleash their power. It is not too soon to start thinking about it.

Ronald J. Mann
Bankruptcy and the Entitlements of the Government: Whose Money Is It Anyway?
70 N.Y.U. L. REV. 993 (1995)*

INTRODUCTION

One of the most dominant themes of the criticism of the bankruptcy system under the Code is that the Code's provisions effectively transfer wealth from the creditors of a business—who frequently have bargained for repayment—to the owners and managers of the failed business. . . .

. . . I conclude that the government's role in creating and supervising the bankruptcy system entitles it to use any value created by that system to further any legitimate interests of the government. . . . When the efforts of the government are taken into account, it becomes clear that the entitlements of the creditors cannot by themselves justify a bankruptcy system limited to furthering the goals of the creditors. Any such justification must be gleaned from more particularized consideration of the relevant social policies.

. . . Part III explains why the government's role in creating and operating the bankruptcy system entitles the government to a share of any value that exceeds the value creditors would have obtained if claims against the debtor had been resolved under nonbankruptcy procedures. Because the government has an entitlement to that value, creditors cannot justly complain of unfair treatment if the government chooses not to give all of that value to them. . . .

II
ENTITLEMENTS TO PROPERTY

This Article evaluates the "redistributive" features of the bankruptcy system—the ways in which the system reslices the pie—in light of the ways in which the system might enlarge the pie. The purpose of the project is to determine whether the government's role in any enlargement of the total recovery could justify the effect on creditors of the redistributive features of the system. . . . To answer that question, I must consider whether the creditors or the government have an entitlement to the portion of the proceeds that the government redistributes. Resolution of that issue, in turn, requires analysis of the concept of an entitlement.

. . . [I]t is enough to describe two simple and relatively noncontroversial rules customarily accepted in those theories that emphasize entitlements: (a) individuals have an entitlement to the fruits of their labor; and (b) individuals acquire entitlements in property through a consensual exchange with the prior holder of the entitlements. . . .

III
ENTITLEMENTS IN BANKRUPTCY

The next question to consider is how the bankruptcy system fares under the rules for entitlements . . . . This Part . . . reaches two related conclusions: first, that creditors do not have an entitlement to all of the proceeds of bankruptcy, even if they have bargained with the debtor for an unrestricted promise of payment out of all of the assets of the debtor; and second, that the government is entitled to a portion of the proceeds of bankruptcy because of its role in creating or preserving them.

A. Thesis: The Limited Importance of the Debtor's Promise

The key to any analysis of the entitlement a creditor has to a share of the proceeds of bankruptcy is the creditor's agreement with the debtor. It is the agreement that gives the creditor any claim to a portion of the entitlements of the debtor; absent an agreement, the creditor would have no claim. But whatever the scope of the entitlement the creditor secures by means of a consensual exchange with the debtor, the creditor's entitlement does not extend to include the entire proceeds of bankruptcy. The creditor's entitlement—because it is based on an exchange with the debtor—can be no greater than the entitlement of the debtor. And the entitlement of the debtor cannot extend to all of the proceeds of bankruptcy, for the simple reason that some portion of those proceeds cannot plausibly be attributed to the assets and labor of the debtor, because a portion of the proceeds results from the application of the assets and labor the government has devoted to the bankruptcy system. That portion—the gains from bankruptcy—is subject to a valid claim of entitlement on the part of the government.

. . . Without the commitment of the government personnel and resources that design, enact, implement, and operate the bankruptcy system, the value available for distribution under the bankruptcy system would not exist. The debtor and its creditor would be left to carve up the values that could be recovered in a liquidation under the state-remedies system.

. . . Because the gains from bankruptcy are attributable (at least in part) to application of the resources and efforts of the government, the government has an entitlement (at least in part) to those gains. To the extent that the government is entitled to those gains, neither the debtor nor its creditor can be entitled to them.

For me, the most difficult problem with that thesis is identifying what it is that entitles the government to apply its labor to the debtor's property. . . . [W]e . . . have to find some basis for allowing the interference in the debtor's entitlements. . . . In my view, the solution to that problem lies in the role we have ceded to government in our society. Although political philosophers for thousands of years have debated the proper role of government, the contours of the actual role of government in this society are clear, at least with respect to the relevant question. In this society, the government has the power, and the right, to act on property with or without the consent of the existing owner, and without any claim for compensation by the owner beyond the value of the entitlements as they existed before the government's actions. . . .

B. Application: The Scope of the Government's Entitlement

The next task is to apply my thesis to the bankruptcy system as it exists and, in particular, to consider whether the existing redistributive features of the bankruptcy system can be justified by the entitlements that the government possesses under my thesis. . . . I start with the problem of reorganization . . . .

1. Reorganization

The most direct effect creditors experience from reorganization proceedings comes from the plans courts approve in those proceedings. My analysis strongly supports the propriety of the Code's provisions setting requirements for approving plans. The premise of chapter 11 of the Code is that by keeping businesses alive the bankruptcy system can preserve a going-concern value that could not be obtained absent the reorganization provisions of the Code. The values that could have been obtained without reorganization—the liquidation values—are reserved for the creditors by a provision that bars confirmation of any plan of reorganization without a finding that under the plan each objecting creditor will receive at least as much as it would have received if the enterprise had been liquidated.

. . . [T]he entitlement of the creditor does not extend to the value of the property available for distribution in a reorganization that exceeds the value that would have been available if the debtor had been liquidated. That value—the gains from reorganization—is not attributable to the efforts of the creditor. Rather, it arises from the actions of the debtor's management in continuing to operate the business, together with the effect of the bankruptcy system in preserving the business's chance to survive. . . . Hence, the government is entitled to a say in disposing of that value, which it might exercise in several ways: by taking some portion of the value for itself through taxes or fees, by delivering it to the creditors, or by allowing the management or owners of the debtors to retain it. The key point, however, is that the creditor has no right to complain that it has been treated unjustly solely because the government elects to follow some course other than giving the creditor the entire value of the reorganized enterprise. . . .

That leaves the question of whether the bankruptcy system provides proper compensation to the creditor for the period of delay between the filing of the petition and confirmation of the plan. Here the system is less generous. The Supreme Court has concluded that the Code does not in terms require the payment of interest on secured claims during the pendency of the proceeding . . . .

. . . [T]he creditor's recovery is hindered only if the bankruptcy system takes longer to confirm a plan than the state-remedies system requires for a foreclosure (or other state-law remedy). . . . To the extent that those delays deprive the creditor of the ability to receive what it would have received outside of bankruptcy, the creditor has a serious argument that it has been treated unfairly and is entitled to relief. . . .

My entitlement analysis does not require the choice of any particular remedy, only some system for providing the creditor what it would have recovered in the absence of bankruptcy. . . . To the extent that procedural reforms cannot remove the delay in the creditor's ability to realize on its collateral, however, the creditor should be entitled to compensation at least for the excess of the delay the creditor experienced in bankruptcy over the delay that it would have experienced in the state-remedies system. . . . All that my analysis suggests is that a bankruptcy system that does not provide compensation for that delay has deprived the creditor of something that cannot be justified by the government's role in the bankruptcy system.

The most significant implications of my entitlement analysis for reorganization proceedings relate to the so-called absolute priority rule. . . . The rule rests on the view that the senior creditor has an absolute right to be paid in full before the junior creditor or shareholder receives any payment at all. . . .

My entitlement analysis indicates that principles of distributive justice do not require the absolute priority rule. The funds that the absolute priority rule guarantees to creditors go beyond the baseline entitlement to what the creditors would have received if the enterprise were liquidated. Accordingly, questions about the general propriety and proper extent of the rule are for debate as a matter of social policy; the creditor has no entitlement to the rule in any form.

2. Liquidation

Application of my entitlement analysis to the liquidation process is less determinate, because there is no occasion in the liquidation process to determine what would have happened absent the intervention of the bankruptcy system: whatever would have happened, the court must liquidate the assets. Accordingly, unlike a reorganization proceeding, a liquidation proceeding does not identify and segregate the gains from the proceeding. Hence, it is more difficult to determine whether the intrusions of the system on the interests of creditors cut into preexisting values that the creditors would have secured without the aid of the bankruptcy system. Nevertheless, some tentative conclusions are possible.

For analytical purposes, it is useful to start by following the Code's practice of dividing claims into two groups: secured and unsecured. . . .

a. Secured Claims. The Code's treatment of secured claims in liquidation proceedings is not controversial, because (subject to the problem about compensation for delay discussed above) it generally promises the creditor whatever it would have received under state law. . . .

b. Unsecured Claims. Unsecured claims present much more complex issues. The basic problem, mentioned at the beginning of this section, is that the system does not require the bankruptcy court to determine what creditors would have received in the absence of a bankruptcy proceeding. . . . Because my analysis recognizes a right in the government to control a portion of the proceeds of bankruptcy only when those proceeds exceed the values that would have been obtained outside of bankruptcy, determining the baseline recovery of the creditors is crucial to my analysis.

One way to deal with that problem is to adopt a "bird-in-the-bush" approach, which focuses on the contingency of any particular creditor's enforcement of its unsecured claim under the state-remedies system. If the claim is still unsecured, then whatever the financial position of the debtor, it is possible (perhaps likely) that the creditor would receive nothing under the state-remedies system, because other creditors might pursue their claims more quickly and liquidate (or obtain security interests in) all assets of the debtor. To put it more colloquially, if your claim is still "in the bush," then you really have nothing at all. Under my entitlement analysis, then, unsecured creditors would not have an entitlement to any share of the proceeds of bankruptcy, and the government (subject to the entitlement of the debtor) justly could exercise dominion over any of those proceeds that were not subject to valid entitlements of secured creditors.

An alternative approach focuses on the entitlement of unsecured creditors as a group. Even if it is difficult to predict what—if anything—any individual unsecured creditor would receive under the state-remedies system, it is likely to be true in some cases that at the time the bankruptcy system intervenes the debtor owned some body of assets not dedicated to the claims of secured creditors, which would have been liquidated under the state-remedies system to satisfy the claims of unsecured creditors. Arguably, the unsecured creditors have an entitlement—as a group—to the amount that they would have received if the bankruptcy system had not intervened.

I prefer the latter, broader approach. My effort considers the justice of the bankruptcy system as a whole . . . . I see little to say in favor of a bankruptcy system that could be supported only under a "bird-in-the-bush" approach. . . . A system like that looks less like a just system for dealing with financial distress than it does a shell game, explaining to each unsecured creditor in turn: "There were some assets available for one of you, but you're not the right person, so you take nothing."

The question, then, is whether the current system conforms to the entitlements of unsecured creditors. By contrast to the respectful treatment afforded secured creditors, unsecured creditors fare quite poorly in the bankruptcy system. . . . I will consider three distinct limitations on the rights of unsecured creditors: subordination to administrative expenses; subordination to favored claimants; and limitations on pursuit of the debtor and its assets.

The subordination of the claims of unsecured creditors to administrative expenses is readily explicable under my theory. The premise of the proceeding is that the operation of the proceeding will result in an increased recovery, which will benefit the unsecured creditors. To the extent that those expenses create a value that would not otherwise have been available, the unsecured creditors have no entitlement to the value, and it is only fair for the government to dispose of the value as it sees fit. . . .

The second relevant aspect of the liquidation proceeding is the Code's subordination of the claims of general unsecured creditors to the claims of various specified favored claimants, without regard to whether the federally favored claimants would have had priority under the state-remedies system. . . . Under my entitlement analysis, that action can be justified only if its effects are limited to values created by the bankruptcy system. Given the difficulty of determining precisely what value—if any—would have been available for payment under the state-remedies system, I see no obvious way of determining empirically whether the effects of the priority provisions are appropriately limited. My theory does, however, give some definition to the relevant inquiry: A bankruptcy system can justify provisions elevating favored creditors (other than administrative creditors) to priority status only if those provisions do not depress the recovery of general unsecured creditors below the recovery they would have received as a group in the absence of a bankruptcy system.

Finally, the bankruptcy system limits the creditors' rights of enforcement by allowing the debtor to retain certain assets, exempt from the claims of the creditors, and also by granting a discharge, which protects all future assets of the debtor from the claims of the creditors. To the extent that those provisions limit the creditors' ability to pursue a debtor in a way that decreases the creditors' recovery below what they would have secured under the state-remedies system, this Article's analysis offers no justification for those provisions. That failure of justification, however, in my view does not cast doubt on the propriety of the discharge, which I would justify in a different way. I suggest that the discharge does not rest on a desire to provide economic assistance to those in financial distress, but on deeply felt concerns about the limits our society wishes to place on coercive actions to collect debts. To the extent that those provisions rest on concerns of that sort, they can be supported by analogy to Nozick's "moral side constraints," which absolutely forbid certain types of actions—however just the underlying motivation for those actions—if the actions intrude unacceptably on the liberty of the individual. The application of those constraints to bankruptcy, however, is a topic for another day.

CONCLUSION: LOOKING BACK AND PRESSING ON

The thesis of this Article is a simple one: There is nothing inherently unfair or surprising about the operation of a reorganization system that diverts value from creditors to further other social goals. . . .

The second area for extension of my analysis is to press the analysis onward to consider what types of policies the government should pursue with the entitlements it garners from its creation and operation of the bankruptcy system. The principal issue to be considered on that score would be whether the existing redistributive features of the bankruptcy system increase or decrease the wealth of society as a whole. . . . Furthermore, a complete analysis also would evaluate the effects those redistributive features have on prebankruptcy activity in the economy. . . .

. . . [T]he principal purpose of this Article [is] to present a plausible philosophical basis for the government's use of the bankruptcy system as an instrument of social policy. In light of my analysis, creditors' bargain theorists no longer can proceed on the assumption that creditors have any bargained-for "entitlement" to all the proceeds of bankruptcy. Conversely, those who seek a more inclusive bankruptcy policy have a tool to structure and justify their attempts to remake or explain the system.

James W. Bowers
Whither What Hits the Fan?:
Murphy's Law, Bankruptcy Theory,
and the Elementary Economics of Loss Distribution
26 GA. L. REV. 27 (1991)*

Critical Murphian Studies began with a prediction that losses would occur. The Murphian logic was then refined from the general ("Whatever can go wrong will") to the particular ("Journalists will spell your name right only when reporting your arrests," or "The probability that the toast will fall jam-side up is inversely proportional to the cost of the carpet"). Not until Donovan's Dictum on Dispersion ("What hits the fan will NOT be evenly distributed") did Murphians turn their attention from *how* losses will occur to the related question of *who* will likely suffer them. Bankruptcy law is concerned with the latter question: Upon *whom* should losses be distributed? . . .

The relevance of Murphy's Law to the law of creditors' remedies first became obvious with the formulation of Rafferty's Rule (The First Financial Corollary). . . . The First Financial Corollary . . . states "There are probably more folks out there wanting to get paid than there are other folks eager to pay them." The result is a sort of economic vacuum between demand and supply. Everyone knows nature abhors a vacuum. The question then becomes: How will nature fill it? By simple induction, Murphian philosophers quickly understood why collection law and lawyers exist. . . .

I. THE COMPETING NORMS OF BANKRUPTCY AND FREE CHOICE

The oft-stated goal of bankruptcy law is for creditors to be treated "equally." The logic of the bankruptcy equality norm equates equal treatment with just treatment, from which one can conclude that debtors who do not treat their creditors equally are unfair to the disfavored creditors. Bankruptcy law, therefore, can be justified as a means to prevent such injustices.[10]

The Bankruptcy Code's prescription of pro rata distribution can be, and has been, defended on grounds other than its embodiment of ethical imperatives. Dean Thomas Jackson and Professor Alan Schwartz suggest that it codifies a "what-the-hell-else-you-gonna-do-when-you-don't-have-a-good-reason-for-any-other-formula" position. Equal sharing is what creditors, behind some Rawlsian veil of ignorance, would choose for very much the same reasons that people willingly play the "if-you-cut-the-cake-I-get-first-pick-of-the-pieces" game . . . .

Nevertheless, the Code probably does embody equal distribution as a normative position. . . . The equality formula in the statute governs even in cases that could not be explained on "what-the-hell-we-might-as-well" grounds. Preference law, for example, applies the equality norm *ex post* and thus applies *only* when we *do* have information. . . .

There is a possible competing norm, the ethic of respect for individuals: that each of us should be treated by those with whom we interact in accordance with our individual just deserts, as we can persuade our transacting partners that we are deserving. This norm is accepted when the issue is how creditors and debtors should treat each other generally. . . . [W]e trust debtors to choose their own creditors and the amounts and terms under which they borrow. We also permit creditors to take the

---

    *   This Article was originally published at 26 Ga. L. Rev. 27 (1991) and is reprinted with permission.

    [10]   Equality theories lack precision, however. They cannot distinguish, for example, between schemes that distribute first to the creditor cutting the high card from an honest deck (which equalizes the probability of recovery) from per capita distributional rules.

individual merits of each loan applicant into account in deciding whether and how much credit to extend. . . .

It follows from this "individual respect" norm that, if creditors differ in merit in the eyes of their debtors, treating the more deserving the same as the less deserving is an injustice to the former and a windfall to the latter. Bankruptcy law's default requirement that deserving creditors receive the same distributions as the undeserving can be criticized from this perspective as commanding inequity. The force of that critique depends on whether creditors do differ in meaningful ways. This Article argues that such differences exist and that they relate to the merit of the creditors in the same way that differences in general allow markets to measure merit. Just as markets permit citizens to maximize their overall satisfaction (given resource scarcity), market behavior in the face of misfortune tends to minimize overall losses.

When permitted to choose, debtors are apt to react to the market merits of their creditors. They will distribute their assets to creditors in ways that maximize their gains and minimize their losses. It is thus likely that they will choose to distribute their own assets rather than delegate those decisions to bankruptcy trustees. . . . [W]hen debtors distribute their assets, we are all made better off in the same ways that markets make us better off. It tends to be efficient—to maximize welfare— to permit debtors to distribute their own assets.

II. TAKING EQUALITY SERIOUSLY

Since appeals to "equality" are commonly made to justify the default distributional pattern mandated by the Bankruptcy Code, it is appropriate to begin by imagining a world in which such equality actually exists. . . .

The absolute sameness of the inhabitants of such a world means that everyone would treat everybody else the same. No one would have either the means or incentive to discriminate systematically in favor of or against anyone. They simply could not tell each other apart. So, too, there would never be any problems of debtors making distributions to creditors. Neither debtors nor creditors would exist. People contract with each other in order to exploit prospects for gains available because of *differences* in their preferences, skills, or opportunities. The debtor/creditor relationship arises because people differ from one another in their tastes for present (as opposed to future) investment or consumption and in their relative abilities and opportunities. . . . In the utterly perfect world of our imagining, therefore, there would never be a need for bankruptcy legislation or, for that matter, creditors' remedies or collection law and lawyers. Only in an imperfect (Murphian) universe would they be created.

A. CLASS DIFFERENCES

The minimally perfect world in which bankruptcy law could be relevant, therefore, would contain two classes of clones. Debtors could all be exactly alike, and creditors would be exactly alike, but debtors could have different intertemporal investment and consumption preferences than creditors. . . .

In a world with a single differentiating parameter distinguishing members of two otherwise identical classes, no creditor would have any reason to deal with any specific debtor, and vice versa. Debt obligations would be created in fungible units . . . . Because debtors are all clones, the optimal amount to borrow will be the same for each; they will thus all borrow the same amount. . . .

There is an appealing symmetry to this imagined world: All creditors treat all debtors equally and all debtors treat all creditors equally. In a perfect world, since all creditors and all debtors are, by definition, equally deserving, the operation of the perfect credit market simultaneously achieves the goals of both the "equality" and the "individual respect" ethical norms. (Interestingly, the achievement of the equality norm is also reciprocal: Debtors treat creditors equally, and creditors treat debtors equally too.) . . .

Nevertheless, bankruptcy law remains irrelevant in a world where absolute equality exists, even if only within differing classes. . . . The debtor . . . could . . . costlessly apportion out her completely divisible assets *per capita*. . . .

She could also, however, costlessly distribute her assets at random. . . . [T]he debtor will be indifferent about how her assets are disbursed. *Ex ante*, well-diversified and risk-neutral creditors would also be indifferent as between the certainty of a partial recovery and its actuarial equivalent (an equal probability, *ex ante*, of receiving a random proportion of any loss). Over a number of disasters, aggregate losses to creditors would still tend to be distributed pro rata, *per capita* and would represent equivalent proportions of each losing creditor's total wealth. . . .

In this perfect world, then, debtors would be indifferent about whom to pay, but creditors would likewise be indifferent as between bonds that contained enforceable provisions requiring insolvent debtors to distribute pro rata and those without such provisions. Bankruptcy law, which mandates pro rata sharing, would thus still be unnecessary. In a perfect world in which all creditors were in fact equal, they would probably be treated equally by operation of debtors' decisions to extend such treatment. Even if debtors would not make pro rata payments, creditors still would not care since the operation of chance would result in equal treatment anyway. In a perfect world it does not matter whether the debtor is given the power to decide whom to pay. When all payees are clones it is never necessary for any bankruptcy law to intervene to influence the debtors' decisions.

B. RESPECTING INDIVIDUAL DEBTOR DIFFERENCES

Bankruptcy law thus owes its existence to the grand Murphian premise: Imperfection is pervasive. In a perfect world there would be no debt, and thus no insolvencies, and no bankruptcies either. Even in a world with one imperfection (that creditors are different from debtors), both debtors and creditors would be indifferent to whether or not legal arrangements mandated insolvent debtors to distribute their remaining assets pro rata. . . . [E]ven more imperfections do not justify enacting a bankruptcy code.

Suppose for a moment that the contingency for which bankruptcy law seems to be designed actually occurs: *One* debtor suffers financial reverses. (The assumption of cloned debtors is now relaxed.) . . . The promises of debtors will thereafter no longer be fungible. . . . [C]reditors face no risk because of this development. Each can costlessly distinguish between the bonds offered by the wealthier clones and those offered by their poorer brother. Since the risk of lending to the poorer debtor is more substantial, depending on a number of variables, creditors will charge the singular debtor more interest or buy fewer of his bonds at the same interest rate they charge other debtors. . . . No change is called for to our above conclusions that bankruptcy law is unnecessary, however. Even the singular debtor will distribute his estate to his cloned creditors either pro rata or randomly, and creditors will value each of those options the same.

C. THE LORE OF "LEVERAGE"

It is commonly assumed that debtors will tend to treat creditors unequally by preferring some to others because some creditors manage to obtain something that is loosely called "leverage" over debtors. Equality of distribution can be praised if the techniques for obtaining leverage are somehow contemptible and so should be discouraged. . . . Given our current presumptions, however, there is no reason to believe that any creditor clone will ever have any more or less leverage than will any other. Unequal distributions might occur on account of leverage only when creditors hold different amounts of it. Thus even when illegitimate forms of leverage can be employed, if creditors are in fact equal, there is still no need for bankruptcy law. Just whether and how creditors may come to differ from each other, and what can be profitably made of such differences, is the subject to which I now turn.

III. THE RISE OF CREDITOR DIFFERENCES AND MURPHIAN LOSS DISTRIBUTION THEORY

. . . I showed that as long as creditors are in fact equal to each other, bankruptcy law is unnecessary in order to meet either the equality or the individual respect norm. Bankruptcy thus becomes relevant only in a world in which creditors differ. Only when creditors differ from one another can the two norms conflict. In this part, I explain how such differences come about and what significance may be attached to them. The basic argument is that creditors may *choose* to differentiate themselves from other creditors and may make efficient investments in order to effectuate those choices. To the extent that such investments ought to be encouraged, efficient collection law should honor those choices to become different.

Suppose that the loss of wealth suffered by a debtor clone makes it suboptimal for him to continue to live on the pinhead, so that this debtor now differs from the creditors in two respects: his intertemporal preferences *and* his physical location. Contacts between that debtor and the potential creditors now begin to entail costs because they must occur over nontrivial distances. . . .

A. WHAT A DIFFERENCE A DIFFERENCE MAKES

The existence of the new locational differences, however, creates opportunities for additional gains from further contracting. For example, once the single uncloned debtor moves off of the pinhead, the money bag containing the monthly loan payments must be carried from the debtor's new abode to the creditor in Pinheadville. . . . [M]arginal costs of conducting activities tend to increase, so that while hiking may become easier in the first few warm-up miles, eventually in each additional mile of a ten-mile, round-trip hike, a hiker's feet hurt worse by increasing increments than in the previous mile. It may profit the singular debtor located five miles from the pinhead to deal with one lender who is willing to meet him to collect payments at the two-and-a-half mile mark, cutting his round-trip hike from ten to five miles in length, and *he will be willing to promise a slightly above-market interest rate for his bonds* in exchange for a creditor's agreement to hike out and meet him halfway. . . .

Suppose, however, that along with transaction and information costs, we now endow the world with viable opportunities to achieve gains from making specialized investments. The creditor and the debtor, each with a tendency toward fallen arches, may also consider whether to invest in new high-tech hiking shoes to lower the expected pain (costs) of performing the agreement. . . .

Because hiking shoes have no value to him in his life on the pinhead, such an investment is specialized for the creditor, and because they have no value absent a loan relationship, they are specialized for the debtor as well. The shoes have little value to either party except as they lower the costs of dealing with each other. This story is intended to illustrate the more general point that, even in a world where differentiation offers possibilities to exploit gains from trading, there remain additional gains to be achieved by specializing—investing in means of performing deals that reduce the costs of performance when those same investments have a lesser value in the absence of the deal.

A fundamental problem for the prospective investor, in considering whether to make any specialized investment, is obtaining assurances the promised returns that justify making it will, in fact, be forthcoming. Should the debtor suffer financial reverses, the creditor knows that he is likely to be preferred for two reasons: First, the debtor is likely to want to pay off debt carrying the highest interest rate first, and the creditor's loan carries a higher rate than that of the clones who did not make any specialized contractual arrangements or investments. Second, should the creditor react by pulling out of the arrangement, the debtor's investment in hiking boots is likely to be rendered less valuable, so the debtor's losses in breaking his relationship with the creditor are likely to exceed his losses in deciding to breach his contracts with the remaining creditor clones. These incentives operate to minimize overall bankruptcy losses. Debtors will tend to prefer those creditors who have specialized in dealing with them and whose losses from nonrepayment therefore are likely to be greatest, leaving unpaid those whose losses are relatively less severe. . . .

People distinguish themselves from others by specializing—by making specific investments. We *choose* what we want our comparative advantages to be and create them by investing in skills, information, and specifically tailored and located assets. Legal regimes that do not honor those choices to be different tend to burden those potentially cost-reducing and thus welfare-maximizing sorts of choices and investments. Bankruptcy law's formula, which eliminates (through preference law) the expectation of the lender and borrower that the lender will be paid first, tends to discourage investment by both parties in assets and measures that minimize the total costs of their transactions. One cost of an effective "equality" policy is thus a lot of unnecessary aching arches.

B. A Paean for Preferences: Asset Distributions as Efficient Breaches

Once creditors have chosen to unclone themselves by making specialized investments, the distant debtor no longer faces the same incentives as those prevailing in a perfect (non-Murphian) world. His loans now will be negotiated, *ex ante*, with a series of creditors who have chosen to differ from one another in many ways. Among the ways in which the creditors now may differ are their expectations of the values of their own future opportunities. Any creditor concluding a loan to the debtor must consider what it will cost her should the debtor eventually fail to repay the loan in whole or in part. . . .

Those with excellent opportunities to reinvest payments will lose more than those with poorer opportunities, so if the debtor ceases repaying, some creditors will be more desperate to recover than others. . . . As a result, the creditors acquire differing abilities to impose costs upon the debtor should he decide to breach any of his differing credit contracts, by virtue either of the damage terms of those credit contracts or of other means of making nonpayment costly. . . .

. . . [I]n the slide toward bankruptcy, debtors will be forced to choose to make breaches for which they may or may not eventually be able to compensate their creditors. Frequently the problem arises as a result not of insolvency but rather of illiquidity. . . . If he is rational, the debtor thus will pick and choose whom to pay and which contracts to breach in such a way as to maximize his expected post-breach wealth.

Since creditors differ, their credit contracts are likely to differ. Those creditors whose contractual rights to damages for breach will be especially high will likely get paid first out of the limited bank account. . . . By choosing to pay first those creditors most vulnerable to damage, the debtor minimizes the ratio of claims to remaining wealth so that the debtor's rational choices are also in the best interest of the remaining unpaid creditors whose contracts have been breached by his failure to pay them. He is thus likely to pay in a way that maximizes the remaining wealth against which unpaid the creditors may assert their claims, and he will prefer the same ones whom the creditors, in their joint best interests, would rationally choose to have him pay.

Does the tendency of debtors to prefer the right creditors (looked at from the standpoint of the joint interest of those creditors who remain unpaid) disappear when it later turns out that the debtor was not only illiquid but insolvent as well? Not if our desire is either to maximize the recoveries of the remaining unpaid creditors or to minimize the social costs of bankruptcy. . . . [T]he amount of wealth left to be split among the unpaid creditors still tends to be maximized by such debtor choices, and the most serious losses that stand to be suffered prospectively by creditors are still avoided.

. . . By first paying the insistent creditor, or those who, in the jargon of the trade, are said to have "leverage," the debtor likewise preserves the wealth that remains to be split among the creditors whose contracts he chooses to breach. Such payments avoid the costs that the insistent and leverage-possessing creditors are otherwise able to impose on him and thus extract from that remaining estate.

If the incentives created by nonbankruptcy collection law tend to minimize the impact of financial losses, how can bankruptcy law's disregard of the differences between individuals be justified? Differing creditors may come to possess differing amounts of wealth. The argument sketched above shows that by investing in specialized, cost-minimizing ways to conduct credit relationships, and by investing in post-default collection activity, creditors can distinguish the losses that they will suffer from the losses potentially suffered by competing creditors. . . . [H]owever, it is also true that the wealthier creditors are likely to have more funds with which to make either type of investment than are poorer creditors. . . .

Defenders of bankruptcy law thus may claim that the law's refusal to honor the differences between creditors . . . is justified as a means of leveling the playing field between richer and poorer creditors. Answering just why, in a private property regime, the bankruptcy field is the only field needing leveling would require a lot of theoretical work that defenders have not yet done, however. If it is true that the richer creditors tend to get paid first, those left in bankruptcies under our current and former bankruptcy laws must be the relatively poor. The empirical evidence is that few distributions occur in bankruptcies. Thus, if bankruptcy is intended as a device for redistributing wealth from rich to poor creditors, it has been stunningly unsuccessful.

B. Tort and Environmental Claims

This part of Chapter 9 focuses on the particular issues raised by *involuntary* claimants in bankruptcy—those suffering due to tort or environmental liability. The five selections offered here examine various facets of the involuntary-creditor conundrum and paint a kaleidoscopic portrait of the systemic difficulties encountered. The problems presented by tort and environmental creditors of a financially distressed debtor are not limited to the bankruptcy world, but often are tested in that arena. Perhaps the most overwhelming set of concerns arises in mass tort cases. The environmental pollution cases also present seemingly insoluble issues. Courts and Congress still struggle to make hard choices as to how to deal with these sorts of claims in cases of generalized debtor distress. Identifying the many conflicting policies and finding workable and defensible general principles has proven to be an elusive task. The excerpts offered here are but the tip of the iceberg: few areas in the law since the early 1980s have spawned more academic commentary, much of it excellent. Included here are: Douglas G. Baird & Thomas H. Jackson, Kovacs *and Toxic Wastes in Bankruptcy*, 36 STAN. L. REV. 1199 (1984); Kathryn R. Heidt, *Environmental Obligations in Bankruptcy: A Fundamental Framework*, 44 FLA. L. REV. 153 (1992); Thomas A. Smith, *A Capital Markets Approach to Mass Tort Bankruptcy*, 104 YALE L.J. 367 (1994); David S. Salsburg & Jack F. Williams, *A Statistical Approach to Claims Estimation in Bankruptcy*, 32 WAKE FOREST L. REV. 1119 (1997); and the National Bankruptcy Review Commission Final Report, *Bankruptcy: The Next Twenty Years* (October 20, 1997).

Baird and Jackson begin this part with Kovacs *and Toxic Wastes in Bankruptcy*, using the facts of *Ohio v. Kovacs* as a vehicle for analyzing the proper treatment of environmental clean-up orders in bankruptcy. The year after the article was published the Supreme Court held (at 469 U.S. 274) that debtor William Kovacs' clean-up obligation was a "claim" that could be discharged in bankruptcy. This holding caused considerable consternation. Consistent with their whole approach to bankruptcy theory, Jackson and Baird assert that the proper question to ask is "what state law says about Ohio's right to pursue that obligation against Kovacs' assets relative to the rights of Kovacs' other prepetition creditors." That is, the critical issue is the *priority* of the state's claim against the debtor's property relative to competing claimants, measured under governing non-bankruptcy law. For individual debtors, the distinct "fresh start" policy also needs to be weighed.

The next excerpt is from Professor Katherine Heidt, who has established herself as a leading authority on the treatment of environmental obligations in bankruptcy. In her article entitled *Environmental Obligations in Bankruptcy: A Fundamental Framework,* Heidt presents her analysis and suggested synthesis of the whole question of how environmental obligations should be dealt with in bankruptcy cases. She asserts that the two key questions are whether the environmental obligation is a "claim" and, if so, when that claim "arose," and further explains how these two issues are inter-related. Answering those two questions should determine which obligations will be subjected to bankruptcy and which will be discharged. She breaks down the universe of environmental obligations into three factual situations with four possible remedies, and analyzes how each of those situations should be resolved.

The next article tackles the nettlesome problem of mass-tort bankruptcy. The Manville asbestos fiasco and the A.H. Robins Dalkon Shield bankruptcy are but two of the prominent examples from the 1980s that spawned widespread debate over how to deal with mass torts. Nor is there any reason to think that the mass-tort tide has abated, as indicated by the Dow Corning breast-implant case and the ongoing challenges to the gun and tobacco industries. Here Professor Thomas Smith in *A Capital Markets Approach to Mass Tort Bankruptcy* seeks a finance-based solution to mass-tort bankruptcy. Before finding a solution, though, one must identify the problems to be solved. What does Smith identify as the salient concerns? What is it about mass-tort bankruptcies that make them so intractable? Having isolated the problems, what solutions does Professor Smith suggest? What are the impediments to the implementation of his recommendations?

The last article included in this section, *A Statistical Approach to Claims Estimation in Bankruptcy*, is by David Salsburg and Jack Williams. One of the most critical tasks in any bankruptcy case involving contingent, unmatured, or unmanifested claims is estimating the amount of those claims. Fixing the claims amount is imperative to the bankruptcy process. Salsburg and Williams offer a thoughtful analysis of different claims-estimation techniques, using a variety of statistical methods. They assess the utility, reliability, and difficulty of each alternative model.

The final selection in the Chapter is an excerpt from the 1997 National Bankruptcy Review Commission Report dealing with the topic, "Treatment of Mass Future Claims in Bankruptcy." The Commission recommends: including a definition of "mass future claim" in the Code; providing specific protections for mass future claims, such as the appointment of a representative; estimating those claims; authorizing channeling injunctions; and permitting the discharge of mass future claims.

Douglas G. Baird & Thomas H. Jackson
Kovacs *and Toxic Wastes in Bankruptcy*
36 STAN. L. REV. 1199 (1984)*

During the 1970's, William Lee Kovacs operated Chem-Dyne Corporation, an industrial and hazardous waste disposal business in Hamilton, Ohio. In 1976, Ohio's Environmental Protection Agency and Department of Natural Resources charged Kovacs and Chem-Dyne with polluting Ohio waters with pesticides and industrial wastes. In 1979, a state court enjoined Kovacs from

---

causing further pollution and also required him to remove all industrial wastes from the premises of Chem-Dyne within twelve months. Kovacs did not comply with the injunction and continued to dump wastes on the site. In 1980, Kovacs filed a bankruptcy petition. . . .

A number of businesses that have violated state and federal antipollution statutes by dumping toxic wastes have filed bankruptcy petitions. *Kovacs*, however, is unusual because the debtor is an individual, rather than a corporation. Perhaps because of that fact, the litigants have missed the issues common to both *Kovacs* and other toxic waste cases in bankruptcy. *Kovacs* presents two distinct questions, the first of which applies to every debtor in bankruptcy that has dumped toxic wastes, and the second of which applies only to individuals such as Kovacs. The first question focuses on the status in bankruptcy of any rights that the state or federal government has against a debtor's existing assets to enforce environmental clean-up orders. The second question asks whether an individual's right to a discharge of pre-bankruptcy obligations, and hence to enjoy his future earnings, includes a right to be relieved of a duty to clean up toxic wastes. . . .

Neither question, however, is concerned with whether Kovacs—or Chem-Dyne—must comply with the environmental laws of Ohio with respect to future operations. They, like everyone else in Ohio, must comply with those environmental laws as long as they stay in business. Debtors in bankruptcy have—and should have—no greater license to pollute in violation of a statute than they have to sell cocaine in violation of a statute. At issue in *Kovacs* is the obligation of Kovacs and Chem-Dyne to pay for the clean-up of *pre-bankruptcy* violations of Ohio's environmental laws. The case should not turn on a dispute, which has been dominating the *Kovacs* case, over whether that obligation is a "claim" or a "debt." Ohio has a right to Kovacs' existing assets in bankruptcy if, but only if, it has a "claim" against him within the meaning of the Bankruptcy Code. Because the obligation Kovacs owes Ohio arises out of his past conduct, Ohio should be entitled to share in Kovacs' existing assets, along with other creditors, to satisfy that obligation. The more difficult question, and one that will arise in cases involving both individuals and corporations, concerns the nature and priority of the rights associated with enforcing that obligation against the debtor's assets relative to the rights of other claimants.

To say that a claim is "dischargeable" does not mean that the associated obligation will be "wholly excused." It only means that Ohio may not be able to reach an individual polluter's post-bankruptcy earnings. The failure of all involved in *Kovacs* to comprehend the difference between a right to existing assets and a right, in the case of individuals, to future earnings, suggests that only mischief may result from the Supreme Court's pending decision. . . .

I. State Law and Its Relation to Federal Bankruptcy Law

Before we even look at bankruptcy law, we should understand the state-law consequences of owing an obligation to clean up wastes. To do this, we begin with the simple case of a corporation. Assume that Debtor, a corporation, owns land on which it has dumped toxic wastes in violation of state law. Along with the land, which is worthless, Debtor has $500,000 in assets. At the request of State, a court has previously enjoined Debtor from dumping any more wastes on its land and has required Debtor to file regular reports on the toxic materials that it handles each month. In addition, the court has ordered Debtor to clean up the wastes that are already there. The clean-up will cost $400,000. Debtor also owes $600,000 to a number of general creditors.

A. *Dissolving Under State Law*

The obligation that Debtor owes to State to clean up the toxic wastes that it dumped in the past is always, in a sense, "dischargeable"—not because of anything bankruptcy law says or does, and, indeed, independent of whether the corporation ever resorts to bankruptcy—because corporations have the privilege of dissolving under state law. . . . When the obligations of a corporation exceed its ability to meet them, some of those obligations will not be met. . . . This result is dictated by limited liability, not bankruptcy.

B. *Claims in Bankruptcy*

To counter Kovacs' argument that his obligation is a "claim" that is discharged in bankruptcy, Ohio and the United States are asserting that Kovacs' obligation is not a "claim" within the meaning of the Bankruptcy Code at all, and hence cannot be extinguished. But this argument is perverse. Neither Ohio nor the United States appears to have thought about how its interpretation of the Bankruptcy Code would apply to the more typical case of a corporate polluter. The definition of "claim" in the Bankruptcy Code does not depend on whether the debtor is an individual or a corporation. If Kovacs' obligation to clean up wastes is not a claim for purposes of bankruptcy, neither is the obligation of our Debtor corporation.

If that is so, however, then State will not share in any of Debtor's assets when they are distributed in bankruptcy. . . . Corporations receive no discharge in Chapter 7, but it makes no difference whether they do or not. After the bankruptcy distribution, the obligation of Debtor to clean up the toxic wastes is not enforceable as a practical matter because Debtor will have no assets and, in any event, the obligation will disappear when Debtor dissolves under state law, after the bankruptcy proceeding. Because Debtor's assets will all have been paid out to holders of *claims*, if State has no "claim," it will receive none of Debtor's assets if Debtor runs through bankruptcy before dissolving. This result, we contend, is absurd. Had Debtor dissolved under state law without resorting to bankruptcy, State would have received its share of Debtor's assets on account of Debtor's obligation to clean the toxic waste site. Bankruptcy law should not be interpreted to upset such state entitlements. . . .

There is a distinction that the drafters of the Bankruptcy Code were trying to capture (albeit somewhat inartfully) in their definition of "claim." Excluding some forms of equitable relief from the definition of "claim" makes sense if one considers its role as one of distinguishing two kinds of obligations: those obligations of a debtor that result from activities engaged in before the filing of the petition and whose consequences *continue* to exist even if the debtor goes out of business or dies the moment that the bankruptcy petition is filed, and those obligations that arise because of the debtor's continued existence and that would disappear if the debtor were to cease operations or die.

An order to clean up toxic wastes that already have been deposited is a "claim" because the equitable remedy arises out of a prepetition action by Debtor the consequences of which do not depend upon Debtor's continued existence. By contrast, an injunction to cease polluting, such as State issued against Debtor, is not a claim within the meaning of the Bankruptcy Code because it is directed at Debtor's future operations. If Debtor ceases to exist, the injunction has no meaning because there will be no further pollution by Debtor. . . .

C. *The Status of Obligations Within Bankruptcy Law*

The more difficult question in our example, which has been obscured in *Kovacs* by the focus on the meaning of the word "claim," is the *status* of the obligation that Debtor owes State to clean up the toxic waste site. Again, we must look first at how non-bankruptcy law would treat the right of State to use Debtor's assets to enforce that obligation relative to the rights of other claimants to use those assets to enforce obligations owed to them by Debtor. Holders of claims do not always share equally under non-bankruptcy law, and bankruptcy law, which is largely procedural, generally respects the different attributes of state law claims as long as doing so is not inconsistent with the goals of the bankruptcy process. . . .

For example, if a "claim" is secured, or is the subject of a statutory lien or a statutory trust, that claim is entitled to be paid first in bankruptcy out of the associated assets. If such a claim is not paid in bankruptcy, the "lien" given by statute or the secured contract will "pass through" bankruptcy and be enforceable against the debtor's pre-bankruptcy property, regardless of who now owns that property and notwithstanding that the underlying debt itself was discharged. . . .

Obscured in *Kovacs*, then, is the key issue: the "priority" of State's claim against Debtor's property relative to the claims of holders of other pre-petition obligations. The priority of a claim may result not only from consensual security interests, statutory liens, or statutory trusts—all cases of which are, or should be, uncontroversial—but also from the entitlements of a particular claimant under state law. In other words, the priority of a particular claim may be inherent in restrictions placed by the state on the use of the property in dispute.

The seminal case that shows how bankruptcy law should respond to the attributes of property when evaluating rights among claimants, and not to state (or bankruptcy) labels, is *Chicago Board of Trade v. Johnson*. In that case, the general creditors claimed the right to the proceeds from the sale of the bankrupt's seat on the Chicago Board of Trade. Notwithstanding that, under the Board's by-laws, a member could not sell his seat over the objection of another member unless and until all debts owed by the member to other members were paid in full, the District Court and the Seventh Circuit had concluded that the seat was "property" and passed to the trustee in bankruptcy free of all claims of the members and, accordingly, could be sold for the benefit of the general creditors.

The Supreme Court reversed. . . . The "property" involved—the membership—was defined by the organization granting it, the Chicago Board of Trade, so as to carry with it a limitation on its value to the bankrupt (and his general creditors): Debts to other members had to be satisfied before the membership could be sold and its value could benefit the remaining claimants. . . . [T]he Supreme Court properly noted that the question for purposes of determining what was "property" under federal bankruptcy law was not what Illinois *called* something, but, rather, what its attributes were. The Supreme Court concluded that so viewed, the membership had the attributes of "property" for purposes of bankruptcy. One of those attributes, however, was that a member could not sell the property unless and until all debts to other members were paid. Noting that this right that the other members had was "in some respects similar to the typical lien of the common law," the Court stated that "[t]he lien, if it can be called such, is inherent in the property in its creation, and it can be asserted at any time before actual transfer." For that reason, the Court reversed the Seventh Circuit and held that the claims of the members of the Chicago Board of Trade had to be satisfied before the trustee could include the proceeds of the transfer of the seat in the general estate.

The principle announced in *Chicago Board of Trade* is a fixed feature of bankruptcy law, and complements the admonition in *Butner v. United States* that property rights are created and defined by state law and should be followed in bankruptcy unless the bankruptcy statute clearly directs otherwise. This principle has direct application to *Kovacs*. *If* (and the issue remains unexplored by any of the courts in *Kovacs*) the obligation that Kovacs owes to Ohio is tantamount to a restriction on the value of all (or some) of the property to its owner or to entities that assert claims through that owner, then the case is like *Chicago Board of Trade*. In that instance, the State of Ohio would be entitled to be paid first, in bankruptcy, from Kovacs' assets before Kovacs' other creditors could receive anything. . . .

II. ANALYSIS UNDER BANKRUPTCY AND STATE LAW

A. *The Corporate Debtor*

Returning to the corporate example with which we began, if Debtor's obligation to clean up hazardous wastes were a general claim against assets like those of other creditors, the assets, in a Chapter 7 case, would be sold for $500,000, free of all claims against them, and the proceeds would be distributed pro rata to all the claimants, including State. Since there are $1 million of such claims, State would recover one half of the cost of cleaning up the toxic wastes. Debtor, which would have no remaining assets, could then dissolve under state law. If, instead of liquidating under Chapter 7, Debtor filed a Chapter 11 petition and continued as a going concern, all of its past obligations would be discharged. In the absence of consent to a different arrangement, ownership interests in the reorganized corporation would be divided among the creditors, including State, according to the size of their claims. . . . An injunction against Debtor to stop polluting . . . would remain effective . . . . In its ongoing operations, Debtor would, as always, remain bound to obey all state and federal environmental laws.

If State's claim were a charge upon Debtor's assets analogous to a statutory lien or the restriction in *Chicago Board of Trade*, the analysis would be equally straightforward. If Debtor were to dissolve under state law, without resorting to bankruptcy, the assets would be sold for $500,000. Unlike before, however, State would be entitled to payment on its $400,000 claim first, because of its "lien," and the other creditors would share in the remaining $100,000 of assets pro rata among their $600,000 of unsecured claims. As before, at the conclusion of this process, Debtor would dissolve. . . .

There should be, as a matter of policy, no change in substantive entitlements should Debtor use bankruptcy. In a liquidation under Chapter 7, State, as a secured creditor, must be satisfied in full out of the assets before anyone else is entitled to anything. In a Chapter 11 reorganization, State, unless it agreed to different treatment, must receive a package of rights worth the full $400,000 before anyone else is entitled to anything. After receiving that package of rights, its claim would be discharged.

If for some reason . . . State received nothing in Debtor's bankruptcy, the obligation of Debtor to State would remain the same as under bankruptcy law. In a Chapter 7 proceeding, State would receive nothing in bankruptcy's distribution of assets (since it did not file a claim) but the purchaser of Debtor's assets would continue to be subject to the obligation to State, because that obligation effectively was secured. . . . The effect of this is that State could pursue its collateral, but not Debtor. The same result would occur in a Chapter 11 proceeding. State's claim against Debtor would be discharged whether or not it was listed by Debtor as a creditor or had filed a proof of claim form. But if State, for that reason, received nothing in the Chapter 11 proceeding, State could still pursue Debtor's assets, in an *in rem* action. Although *debts* are discharged in bankruptcy, *liens* are not.

B. *The Individual Debtor*

Up to this point, we have been looking at the issue in *Kovacs* by examining a corporate debtor. Nothing essential to this discussion changes when the debtor is an individual. While corporations enjoy limited liability under state law, individuals have a discharge right only through use of the bankruptcy process. . . .

A corporation must give up all of its assets to creditors when it dissolves, but an individual who receives a bankruptcy discharge is usually entitled to keep one of his most valuable assets: his future earnings. At the end of a liquidation proceeding (and subsequent dissolution), a corporation is stripped of assets and ceases to exist. Hence having an enforceable right—a nondischargeable right—against it following such procedures is meaningless. By contrast, one can talk about nondischargeable debts against an individual, because an individual is allowed to keep an asset and he continues to exist after the bankruptcy proceeding is over.

When a debtor is an individual using bankruptcy, one must ask three questions: first, whether someone has a right against the individual's existing assets; second, what priority that right has relative to others; and, finally, whether, contrary to the general rule, the person with this right can look to the debtor's future earnings. The first question revolves around the question of whether someone has a "claim"; the second around what attributes the claim has under state law; and the third around whether the claim is dischargeable. The first two questions are identical to the ones we must ask in the case of a corporation using bankruptcy. The third question, however, is unique to individuals because an individual debtor retains an asset after the bankruptcy proceeding is over. Whether

Kovacs' obligation to clean up toxic wastes is dischargeable is distinct from whether that obligation gives rise to a "claim" and from whether that claim gives Ohio priority over others to Kovacs' existing assets.

Under current law, whether Kovacs' obligation is dischargeable in a Chapter 7 proceeding is a narrow question of whether that obligation falls within one of the exceptions laid out in section 523 of the Bankruptcy Code. . . . Kovacs' obligations to Ohio are not dischargeable if his actions amounted to "willful and malicious injury . . . to another entity or to the property of another entity." The applicability of this provision to *Kovacs* is uncertain, but this issue, not whether Ohio has a "claim," should be, but has not been, the focus of the bankruptcy litigation. If the obligation does not fall into any of the exemptions from discharge, it should not ultimately matter whether the debtor is an individual or a corporation. If the obligation does not fall within section 523 as it is presently written and if, as a matter of bankruptcy policy, it should, this section of the Bankruptcy Code ought to be amended. Trying to reach the same result by distorting other sections of the Bankruptcy Code will thwart the operation of bankruptcy policy in too many other cases, such as cases in which a polluter is a corporation.

III. CONCLUSION

The threshold question in *Kovacs* should be not whether the obligation to Ohio is a nonexempt claim and thus dischargeable but, rather, what state law says about Ohio's right to pursue that obligation against Kovacs' assets relative to the rights of Kovacs' other prepetition creditors. If, *under Ohio law*, the right is tantamount to an unsecured obligation, then the State of Ohio should share in the property of the estate pro rata with Kovacs' other unsecured creditors in the property of the estate. But if, *under Ohio law*, the right of Ohio to enforce the clean-up order is tantamount to a security interest in Kovacs' assets, then Ohio is entitled to have that obligation satisfied *first* in any bankruptcy distribution of the estate's property. To the extent that it is not satisfied, that obligation attaches to the (nonexempt) assets, whether sold by the trustee or kept by Kovacs, because of the doctrine of lien pass-through. That is true whether state law characterizes the obligation as secured, or the subject of a statutory lien or a statutory trust.

The failure to appreciate these issues in *Kovacs* has led to the erroneous assumption that a reversal of the Sixth Circuit is needed to ensure that a state can make polluters pay for dumping toxic wastes. To the contrary, a reversal of *Kovacs* by the Supreme Court would prevent states from reaching a debtor's assets in the more typical case in which the debtor is a corporation. Freeing Kovacs from financial responsibility for wreaking havoc on the environment may be ill-advised, but one cannot reach this conclusion without first squarely addressing the policies in the "fresh start" policy of the Bankruptcy Code. That issue, as well as the general question of what the status of Ohio's rights relative to competing claimants to Kovacs' assets is (or should be), are properly the subjects of debate. That the obligation to clean up toxic wastes is a "claim" in bankruptcy, however, should not be.

Kathryn R. Heidt
Environmental Obligations in Bankruptcy: A Fundamental Framework
44 FLA. L. REV. 153 (1992)[*]

I. INTRODUCTION

. . . This article examines the problems confronting courts dealing with environmental obligations in bankruptcy. It provides a framework for analyzing these problems. . . . In particular, federal courts hearing these cases have had to address two issues essential to understanding the appropriate treatment of environmental obligations in bankruptcy: (1) Is the particular obligation a "claim" within the meaning of the Bankruptcy Code and, (2) If so, when did the claim "arise"? If a cleanup obligation is held to be a claim that arose before the debtor filed for bankruptcy (a pre-petition claim), then the holder of the obligation may participate in the bankruptcy proceeding and share in any distribution of assets. However, the obligation holder will not be allowed to pursue the debtor post-bankruptcy. On the other hand, if a court holds the cleanup obligation either not to be a claim or not to have arisen pre-petition, then the obligation holder will not be allowed to participate in the bankruptcy proceeding or share in any distribution. However, the obligation holder will be allowed to seek redress from the debtor post-bankruptcy. . . .

III. DEFINITIONS AND TIMING: CLEANUP OBLIGATIONS

The treatment of an obligation in a bankruptcy proceeding ultimately depends on two issues: (1) the definitional issue of whether a particular environmental obligation is a "claim" within the meaning of the Bankruptcy Code and (2) the timing issue of when that obligation arose. . . .

There are three sorts of potential environmental obligations: an obligation to pay money, an obligation to perform a cleanup, and an obligation to refrain from polluting in the future. The following three examples of common situations should help to distinguish these sorts of obligations from each other.

1. The debtor, either an individual or a corporation, is responsible for cleaning up a toxic waste site. The government performed the cleanup and billed the debtor for the expense. The debtor then filed a Chapter 7 or Chapter 11 proceeding.

2a. The debtor, either an individual or a corporation, was ordered to clean up a site. Instead of cleaning up the site, the debtor filed a Chapter 7 or Chapter 11 proceeding. The applicable environmental law provides an alternative remedy of payment to the government instead of cleanup.

2b. Same as #2a above, but the applicable environmental law does not expressly allow the payment of money to be substituted for the actual cleanup.

3. In any of the above situations, an injunction was issued before the bankruptcy filing, prohibiting the debtor from polluting in the future.

A. *Definitions: Is the Obligation a "Claim"?*

The Bankruptcy Code defines "claim" . . . . Subsection (A) includes rights that are legal in nature, meaning those which are for money damages. Subsection (B) includes equitable remedies if the breach of the obligation that gave rise to the equitable remedy also gives rise to a right to pay-

---

ment. Thus, if money may be substituted for the performance of the equitable obligation the obligation is a "claim" under section 101(5)(B). . . .

Examples 1 and 3 above illustrate the claim definition's limits in the environmental context. In example 1, the government cleaned up a site and sought reimbursement from the debtor before the debtor filed bankruptcy. The debtor's only remaining obligation was to reimburse the government. That obligation to pay money is a "right to payment." Therefore, it is within the section 101(5)(A) definition of "claim." . . .

In contrast to the payment obligation of example 1, example 3 involved an injunction prohibiting the debtor from polluting in the future. . . . Such an order generally will be non-dischargeable since the obligation is not a "claim." This order is not a "right to payment" within section 101(5)(A). Nor is the order within section 101(5)(B). If the debtor continues to pollute, the government may be entitled to an injunction prohibiting the debtor from polluting. . . .

On its face, this breach does not give rise to a "right to payment." . . . Although the government might be entitled to damages in the future if the debtor actually does continue to pollute, this does not constitute an alternative right to payment . . . . Since the government cannot substitute money for the injunction before the injunction is violated, the order to stop polluting is not a "claim." It is, therefore, not a "debt" and is not dischargeable.

Examples 2a and 2b from the beginning of this section represent the more difficult case of an order requiring the debtor itself to clean up a contaminated site. The order is not on its face a "right to payment" within section 101(5)(A). A cleanup order often takes the form of an injunction, or is reduced to an injunction when the debtor fails to comply with the order. Therefore, if such an order is within the definition of a "claim," it must fit within the section 101(5)(B) definition of "claim." . . .

. . . [T]he key question is: under what circumstances does an equitable remedy for breach of performance give rise to a right to payment within the section 101(5)(B) definition of "claim?"

Some environmental statutes expressly provide alternatives. For example, the government can order a person to clean up a site, or can perform the cleanup itself and then seek reimbursement from the debtor. This alternative right to payment makes the cleanup obligation a "claim" within section 101(5)(B). Because CERCLA grants the government just this sort of alternative right, a cleanup order issued pursuant to CERCLA is a "claim." . . .

. . . Consider a statute that provides a mechanism to enforce an equitable order, which gives the state control of the debtor's assets. Would this mechanism transform the equitable right into a "right to payment"? Because many states have such enforcement mechanisms for equitable remedies, many otherwise purely equitable remedies ultimately might be deemed "claims" within the meaning of the Bankruptcy Code.

. . . [T]he mere existence of a state law mechanism to enforce an equitable remedy should not be sufficient to transform the obligation into a claim. Rather, the state actually must pursue that alternative, and the court must grant the remedy. In other words, inchoate "rights" must become "actualized" before "claim" status attaches. . . .

In summary, if the environmental statute that requires cleanup creates an alternate right to payment, then the obligation is a "claim" because it fits squarely within the definition of section 101(5)(B). However, if the statute does not create such an alternate right to payment, the obligation nevertheless will be a "claim" if (1) a general mechanism allows the government to pursue the debtor's assets in a way which dispossesses the debtor and renders the debtor unable to perform the cleanup personally *and* (2) the government actually attempts to use that mechanism *and* (3) the court actually grants the government the requested relief. . . .

Professor Baird and Dean Jackson have analyzed environmental obligations more specifically from a timing perspective, distinguishing between past and future claims. They divide environmental claims into two classes: those based on past acts, and those prohibiting certain future acts.

An obligation based on the debtor's past acts is a "claim." However, an obligation to abide by regulatory laws in the future (such as the prohibition against polluting a river) is not a "claim." Thus, in the examples given earlier, all of the cleanup orders would be "claims." Only the last example, enjoining the future pollution of a river, would not be a "claim." . . .

The distinction between past and future acts is good and useful as far as it goes. However, the "past versus future" analysis tends to confuse the definitional issue with the timing issue. The definition of "claim" is independent of time. An obligation can be technically within the definition of "claim" even if it arises after the bankruptcy proceeding was filed. . . .

Although conceptually interesting, the analysis of Baird and Jackson does not track the statute closely enough. Congress eliminated all purely equitable relief from the definition of "claim." There are forms of purely equitable relief other than prohibitions against future acts . . . that have no alternative right to payment. . . .

Even if we accept the past versus future distinction, it fails to classify adequately all environmental obligations. While the analysis identifies the future obligation to refrain from polluting as not a "claim," it fails to identify all of the obligations that are claims. One act in the past can have many effects. . . .

B. *Timing: When Did the Claim Arise?*

The timing issue, like the definitional issue, is easiest to resolve at the extremes. At one extreme, when the government has already cleaned up the site and requested payment before the bankruptcy petition is filed, the claim "arose" pre-petition. This situation is illustrated by example 1 at the beginning of this section. At the other extreme, since an injunction prohibiting pollution in the future is not a "claim," we do not reach the timing issue. This is illustrated by example 3 at the beginning of this section. Further, the obligation not to pollute arises every day and thus continues to arise post-petition. The difficult question between the extremes concerns property that was contaminated pre-petition and has not yet been cleaned up post-petition. . . .

1. Timing: The Relationship Between Government Expenditure and the Timing of the Claim

Assume that all of the acts creating the need for cleanup occurred pre-petition, but the government's action occurred post-petition. CERCLA allows the government to recover for cleanup and related activities, such as investigation, only when the government has "incurred" some response costs. Therefore, the government has argued in several cases that a claim cannot "arise" until the government incurs some cost in connection with the contaminated site. . . .

This argument is rather contrived. The government could manipulate the time a claim "arose" by postponing site cleanup or investigation. If all of the acts giving rise to a need for cleanup occurred pre-petition, there exists pre-petition a fundamental right to relief. This right, under a statute such as CERCLA, carries with it an alternative right to payment, even though it is contingent on the government's expending money. Courts considering this question agreed with this criticism, holding that the incurring of costs is not what triggers liability and not what fixes the time the claim "arose." In this context of foundational right, the timing of government expenditures should not be a factor at all.

This does not mean that all cleanup obligations are pre-petition obligations. The following two sections discuss when cleanup claims can be said to "arise" post-petition.

2. Liability as the Current Owner

Under CERCLA and similar state statutes, the current owner of contaminated property is liable for cleanup. When the bankruptcy petition is filed the debtor's property becomes property of the bankruptcy estate. Therefore, during the bankruptcy proceeding, the bankruptcy estate is responsible for the cleanup because it is the owner of the property. A new cleanup obligation "arises" postpetition every day that the property remains contaminated. Designating the cleanup obligation as post-petition, however, does not determine who will pay for the cleanup. The answer depends on the type of debtor and the type of proceeding involved.

In the case of an individual debtor in Chapter 7, the estate, not the individual debtor, is liable as the current owner of the contaminated property. Because it is often difficult for the estate to "abandon" contaminated property, the estate usually cannot simply return the property with the cleanup liability to the individual debtor by abandoning it. Since the individual debtor's liability *as current owner* is a pre-petition obligation which does not arise anew post-petition, it is generally dischargeable. . . .

If the debtor is a corporation liquidating under Chapter 7, the answer is similar, even though the corporate debtor does not receive a discharge. The contaminated property belongs to the bankruptcy estate and the question becomes one of the trustee's obligation and of the priority to be given to cleanup activity.

In a Chapter 11 reorganization, different factors are relevant. If the reorganization is successful, the reorganized corporation will become the new owner of the property. As the owner, it will have to comply with the environmental laws as it continues its business. However, the debtor may argue that a cleanup obligation is a pre-confirmation obligation since it is based on pre-confirmation acts. . . . But if the reorganized debtor needs to retain the contaminated property as part of the reorganization plan, it nonetheless will be liable as the then-current owner. . . .

3. Other Types of Liability

. . . Even if liability is not based directly on one's status as current owner, the failure to clean up can cause additional post-petition harms, which properly can be viewed as post-petition obligations. The cost of avoiding that harm—cleanup—is arguably a post-petition obligation. Specifically, pre-petition contamination of land and water can create a problem having both pre- and post-petition consequences. . . . The initial contamination sets in motion a chain of events that could cause addtional future harms.

. . . In a sense, the failure to clean up . . . is itself a new harm. This harm arises when the responsible party does not perform needed preventive acts . . . .

. . . [P]ost-petition liability can be based on two theories. First, because any further harm resulting from the current condition creates a post-petition obligation, the cost of avoidance also is a post-petition obligation. Second, the failure to correct the risk is itself a new act on which liability can rest. This act may be the failure to repair or to warn of the danger. Since this act, or failure to act, occurs post-petition, any corresponding liability is a post-petition obligation.

According to either theory, a new obligation has been created. The pre-petition obligation might be dischargeable and subject to the bankruptcy proceeding. However, there is a new obligation in its place. . . .

In other words, a toxic waste site exposes more people, natural resources, plants and animals, to new injury every day it remains contaminated, although the initial need for a cleanup was based on pre-petition acts. In short, environmental contamination creates both past and future harm. The current property owner's continuing obligation to clean up, and the continuing failure of other responsible parties to clean up or to warn of danger, are ongoing acts that create new liabilities. These new liabilities arise post-petition.

Individual Chapter 7 debtors receive a discharge of all pre-petition obligations, and Chapter 11 debtors receive a discharge of pre-confirmation obligations. Thus, it is critical to determine the portions of the liability that "arose" pre- and post-petition. In the toxic waste situation, pre- and post-petition obligations are not necessarily identical. Since the post-petition liability is based on post-petition harms or risk of harms, the portion of the obligation that arises post-petition must be determined. The corrective action required post-petition must correspond to the need to avoid future harm. If, for example, the toxic waste poses no threat of future harm (*i.e.*, waste is contained fully and safely) there is no new obligation. In such a case, the cleanup responsibility is fully pre-petition, and does not "arise" again post-petition. If only a portion of the waste poses a threat, then the extent of the post-petition obligation must be determined. . . .

V. FRAMEWORK FOR CONSIDERING ENVIRONMENTAL CLAIMS

This article suggests examining environmental claims in bankruptcy by asking certain fundamental questions: Is the obligation a "claim" within the meaning of the Bankruptcy Code? If so, when did the claim "arise"? This final section suggests an overall fundamental framework based on the preceding exploration.

All environmental obligations can be divided into three basic categories, with several subcategories. The basic categories are based on three possible *factual* situations: (1) the past act with no future consequence; (2) the past act with future consequences; and (3) the future act of pollution— not simply the failure to clean up. The four subcategories concern the four possible remedies, not all of which are applicable to each factual setting: (1) the obligation which has been reduced to money; (2) the obligation with an express alternative right to money (but which has not been reduced to money); (3) the obligation with no express alternative right to money; and (4) the pure injunction against future pollution. These twelve alternatives encompass the possible combinations of act and remedy. For each combination, we can determine whether the obligation is a "claim" and when it "arose," so as to decide how to treat the obligation during and following bankruptcy.

A. *The Past Act (Pre-petition) with No Future (Post-petition) Consequences*

1. Obligation which has been reduced to a money obligation. Example: (a) Government has already performed a cleanup and sought reimbursement from the polluter; (b) Government has not yet cleaned up but has assessed costs and billed for cleanup.

2. Express mixed remedy. Example: CERCLA system of right to order cleanup or, alternatively, to perform the cleanup and seek reimbursement.

3. Non-express mixed remedy. Example: the government has the right only to order a cleanup, but non-bankruptcy law (usually state law) allows the government to pursue the debtor to enforce the injunction and effectively to control the debtor's assets. This was the situation in the *Kovacs* case.

4. Pure injunction. Example: order to discontinue pollution in the future.

Example "1" is a claim and it arose in the past (pre-petition). Example "2" is a claim also. It fits squarely within section 101(5)(B). . . . Because "1" and "2" are "claims" and arose pre-petition, they are dischargeable. Example "3" is a claim under the *Kovacs* case, at least where the government already has been granted some control over the debtor's assets to enforce the injunction. However, if the government has not been granted some kind of relief to enforce the order, one can distinguish *Kovacs* and argue that this obligation is not a claim. Under *Kovacs*, "3" is a "claim," and is dischargeable. Since there are no future consequences the obligation arose pre-petition. Because "1," "2," and "3" are "claims" that arose pre-petition, they are dischargeable. However, one must look further to the environmental statutes. The "claim" against *the debtor* arose pre-petition and is dischargeable. But we must recognize that if the estate owns the property post-petition, it has a current obligation to clean it up, an obligation that can be enforced by the government. If the estate is not the owner, the estate (or debtor-in-possession) has no continuing liability since this category has no future effects.

Example "4" does not exist since this category is "past act with no future consequences."

B. *The Past Act (Pre-petition) with Future (Post-petition) Consequences*

1. Obligation which has been reduced to a money obligation. Example: (a) Government has already performed a cleanup and has sought reimbursement from the polluter; (b) Government has not yet cleaned up but has assessed costs and billed for cleanup.

2. Express mixed remedy. Example: CERCLA system of right to order cleanup or, alternatively, to perform the cleanup and seek reimbursement.

3. Non-express mixed remedy. Example: the government has the right only to order, but non-bankruptcy law (usually state law) allows the government to pursue the debtor to enforce the injunction and effectively to control the debtor's assets. This was the situation in the *Kovacs* case.

4. Pure injunction. Example: order to discontinue pollution in the future.

Example "1(a)" cannot exist as the property has been cleaned up and has no future consequences. Example "1(b)" is a claim, and it arises pre-petition. Example "2" is a claim . . . .

. . . [T]he clearer view is to consider the obligation a "claim" but determine its status regarding discharge based on the timing issue. That is, if (1) the debtor—now estate—continues to own the property and is liable for cleanup as the *current owner*, or (2) to the extent that future consequences occur as a result of the continued contamination, even if the estate is not the current owner, the obligation arises anew every day. As a post-petition, or post-confirmation claim, its dischargeability is limited. Example "3" is arguably a "claim" under *Kovacs* . . . . As in example "2," the obligation in example "3" can be said to arise every day and is thus post-petition. Example "4," the order prohibiting pollution in the future, does not exist in a category of "past acts" with future consequences.

C. *Future Acts, Future Pollution*

1. This category cannot exist. The types of orders in "1" are divided at *past* acts not future acts.

2. Express mixed remedy. Example: CERCLA system of right to order cleanup or, alternatively, to perform the cleanup and seek reimbursement.

3. Non-express mixed remedy. Example: the government has the right only to order a cleanup, but non-bankruptcy law (usually state law) allows the government to pursue the debtor to enforce the injunction and effectively to control the debtor's assets. This was the situation in the *Kovacs* case.

4. Pure injunction. Example: order to discontinue pollution in the future.

Example "1" does not exist. Examples "2" and "3" arguably do not exist since they concern orders directed to clean up, that is, orders directed to remedy a past act. One could argue, however, that the failure to clean up is itself a future act and an order directing clean up can thus be aimed at a future act. In such a case, the obligation is a claim . . . . However, none of these claims is dischargeable in bankruptcy if the act giving rise to the obligation has not yet occurred. That is, since the act "arises" in the future, it is not governed by the bankruptcy process. Example "4" is not a claim and also has not yet arisen. It too is not subject to the bankruptcy process.

VI. Conclusion

The two key bankruptcy questions of whether a particular environmental obligation is a "claim" and when it "arose" are interrelated. These two questions form the basis for determining which obligations will be subject to in a bankruptcy proceeding and which are dischargeable.

Thomas A. Smith
A Capital Markets Approach to Mass Tort Bankruptcy
104 YALE L.J. 367 (1994)[*]

. . . This Article addresses some of these issues in the context of mass tort bankruptcy: What is a "fair" allocation to future claimants in a mass tort bankruptcy? How can it be achieved? Why are current approaches unfair? . . .

The first Part of this Article describes the general nature of the distributional justice problem in mass tort bankruptcy. Part II analyzes the institutional, psychological, and strategic factors that permit present claimants in mass tort bankruptcy to secure a disproportionate share of the debtor's assets for themselves. Part III proposes a novel structure for mass tort bankruptcy reorganization. This proposal, which I call a "capital markets approach," produces a fair distribution of the value of the debtor's assets among present and future claimants by using the information-processing capabilities of modern capital markets. At the heart of the capital markets approach is a new kind of security—a security designed to be traded on the capital market at a price that reflects a relatively efficient capital market's estimate of how large the total tort liability of a mass tort debtor will be. The fundamental insight of this Article is its proposal to substitute the superior information-processing capabilities of capital markets for the more limited capabilities of administrators. Part IV tentatively suggests how the capital markets approach might be extended to cases where there is substantial uncertainty about whether future tort liability renders a firm insolvent. . . .

I. THE FAIR DISTRIBUTION PROBLEM IN MASS TORT BANKRUPTCY

Mass tort bankruptcies create difficult problems of distributional justice. . . . [C]ourts have suggested that present and future claimants in mass tort bankruptcy should be treated equally in the bankruptcy reorganization process. This principle of equality, however, is easier to state than to implement. Strong forces militate against equal treatment of present and future claimants, causing what I call the "fair distribution problem." . . .

A. *Mass Tort Bankruptcies and Mass Tort Bankruptcy Trusts*

. . . Before explaining why achieving a fair distribution among present and future claimants in mass tort bankruptcy is problematic, however, I must explain why the equal distribution described above is actually fair. . . .

B. *Defining Fair Distribution in the Mass Tort Bankruptcy Setting*

In recent years, legal theorists and others have made frequent use of hypothetical contract analysis when attempting to resolve issues of fairness. The hypothetical contract approach asks whether individuals would have agreed to a given treatment of their claims if their agreement had been solicited in a setting characterized by possession of appropriate information, low transaction costs, and freedom from morally arbitrary influences. . . .

. . . In a hypothetical contract setting, while persons might know that they were exposed to mass tort risk, they would not know whether they would be present or future claimants if a mass tort bankruptcy actually occurred. Under these circumstances, assuming that prospective tort creditors are normally risk averse, prospective tort creditors would not agree to an allocational scheme that

    *   Reprinted by permission of The Yale Law Journal Company and Fred B. Rothman & Company from The Yale Law Journal, Vol. 104, pages 367-434.

paid present claimants more than future claimants; rather, they would select a scheme that treated present and future claimants equally. . . .

Thus, hypothetical contract analysis indicates that, for mass tort bankruptcies that involve serious injuries to at least some claimants, fairness requires equal treatment of claimants regardless of the timing of their claims. This result, I believe, is consistent with the moral intuitions of most people who have reflected on these issues.

II. ORIGINS OF THE FAIR DISTRIBUTION PROBLEM

Even though prospective tort claimants in a hypothetical contract setting would prefer a compensation scheme that treats present and future claimants equally, current mass tort bankruptcy practice favors present claimants over future claimants, distributing to present claimants a disproportionate share of the debtor's assets. This inequality stems from incentives deeply rooted in the institutions of mass tort bankruptcy. . . .

A. *Factors Affecting Allocational Decisions*

Factors that give rise to the fair distribution problem can be placed in several categories. First are psychological factors that operate to favor present over future claimants, quite apart from any self-interested or strategic motives of the parties. Second are incentives of attorneys and judges in the bankruptcy process that encourage the negotiation of plans that favor present over future claimants. Third and most serious is the strategic disadvantage at which future claimants find themselves vis-à-vis present claimants and equity holders.

1. *Psychological Factors*

Present claimants have powerful psychological advantages over future claimants in their battle to maximize their share of the debtor's estate. Present claimants in mass tort bankruptcies are identifiable persons with urgent medical and financial needs, while future claimants are only statistical probabilities. Empirical psychology suggests that decisionmakers give excessive weight to concrete and vivid information before them at the expense of more abstract information that should be given equal weight in a rational decisionmaking process. This phenomenon is called the "vividness effect." . . .

2. *Judicial and Attorney Incentives*

Empirical evidence suggests that bankruptcy courts tend to overvalue reorganized firms, resulting in at least the temporary illusion that the reorganization gives all creditors and interested parties some reasonable value for their claims. Underestimating the value of future claims creates the appearance that all claimants will be reasonably if not fully compensated, an illusion that may last long enough to support judicial confirmation of the plan and the clearing of the court's docket.

Present claimants typically have claims that juries or settlement agreements have already liquidated or will liquidate in the foreseeable future. Future claims, by contrast, are often highly uncertain and likely to remain so for extended periods. . . . Estimating future mass tort liability involves an extremely complex methodology and accords present claimants many opportunities to advance their interests.

When juries determine the damages of present claimants, moreover, they do so independently, without regard to the effect their decisions will have on future claimants. . . . In determining the value of future claims for purposes of a bankruptcy plan, the parties engage in a dependent process that simultaneously decides what will be available for present tort claimants and for other creditors. The dependency tends to distort the valuation decision and invites compromise by the future claimants' representative. . . .

The attorneys who represent present claimants receive a substantial percentage of the settlements they reach with, or the verdicts they obtain against, the debtor. Future claimants, however, are typically represented by a guardian appointed by the bankruptcy court. . . .These guardians are not compensated by a percentage of the debtor's assets that they secure for their clients. They thus lack the economic incentive that plaintiffs' attorneys have to seek the maximum attainable settlement.

3. Strategic Bargaining in the Bankruptcy Process

Perhaps most important, future claimants are at a strategic disadvantage in the bargaining that characterizes the bankruptcy process. The only monitor of the performance of the future claimants' representative is the court itself, whose incentive is less to ensure that future claimants receive the maximum possible or even a fair share, than it is to ensure that the parties reach some agreement. Both present claimants and equity holders of the debtor have a common interest in a reorganization or liquidation plan that undervalues future claims. . . .

Equity holders have a strong incentive to employ dilatory tactics because of the fundamental nature of their financial claim on the firm's assets. Because of its low priority, equity in a bankrupt firm would usually be worthless if the firm were liquidated promptly upon its bankruptcy in order to satisfy creditors. . . . When a firm is bankrupt, therefore, equity holders have everything to gain and nothing to lose from delaying the completion of bankruptcy and the paying off of creditors. . . .

To present tort claimants, by contrast, delay is especially damaging. . . . To avoid delay, tort creditors must deal with equity holders in the reorganization process. . . .

To induce equity holders to consent to a plan, present claimants can offer to agree on a reorganization plan that divides the value of the firm between present claimants and equity holders, but leaves little or nothing for future claimants. . . .

If the reorganization plan adopts fast payout rules for the trust, present claimants will be able to claim, at the extreme, all of the trust funds, leaving nothing for future claimants. . . . Therefore, present claimants are better off entering into a strategic arrangement with equity holders in which present claimants forgo absolute priority in favor of equity holders, but in turn garner a disproportionately large share . . . of a smaller portion . . . of the value of the debtor firm reserved for tort claimants. Essentially, present claimants and equity holders can agree to split among themselves the share that belongs to future claimants under the equal-treatment norm. All that stands in the way of this split is the future claims representative, who is accountable not to the anonymous future claimants, but to the court, an institution with incentives that incline it less to fair allocation than to final agreement on a plan.

B. The Roe Proposal for Mass Tort Reorganization

. . . In an important article that, among other things, proposes a solution to the fair distribution problem, Professor Mark Roe argues for pooling mass tort claims in a manner analogous to a variable annuity fund, which would increase the ability of the trustees to adjust the amounts they award to claimants in light of new information and circumstances.

While an improvement over the current system, the Roe proposal does not remedy the main causes of the fair distribution problem. Under the Roe proposal, the trustees estimate the expected value of future claims. The same institutional, psychological, and strategic pressures that tend to make bankruptcy courts and trust administrators undervalue future claims would also affect the trustees in Roe's scheme. . . . [A]dministrators do not have the benefit of market mechanisms for estimating total tort liability and making allocational decisions accordingly. . . .

Roe's proposal depends on administrative competence and discretion to value future claims. Administrators are not likely to do this job well. . . . Administrative processes are also vulnerable to manipulation by interested parties. . . . [P]resent claimants and equity holders [are] likely to capture mass tort trusts, for the reasons discussed above. Compared to future claimants, present claimants have psychologically more vivid needs, are more zealously represented, have claims that are either liquidated or methodologically more difficult to underestimate, and are better positioned to enter into strategic alliances with equity holders and with the management of the debtor firm.

III. A CAPITAL MARKETS APPROACH TO MASS TORT BANKRUPTCY

What institutional arrangements will solve the fair distribution problem? . . . [T]he capital markets possess powerful information-processing capabilities. When a capital market prices an asset, it takes into account an information set that, for all practical purposes, no one human mind is able to process. . . .

. . . [T]he capital market is the best institutional mechanism for valuing mass tort claims in a manner that takes account of all pertinent information in a timely and accurate manner.

Capital markets can be used to provide a fair distribution between present and future claimants in a mass tort bankruptcy. I explain below how a bankruptcy court could use a capital markets approach to structure a mass tort settlement trust and solve the fair distribution problem. I also show that this solution is consistent with the equal-treatment norm of bankruptcy described above.

A. *Solving the Fair Distribution Problem: Structuring the Trust and Compensation*

. . . [T]he first step under the capital markets approach is for the bankruptcy court to place the entire value of the firm in trust for the tort claimants. The trust will use this trust fund, pursuant to the bankruptcy plan, to compensate both present and future tort creditors. . . .

The next step under the capital markets approach is formulating the payout terms for compensating tort claimants. Determining how the court should formulate these terms is the key to solving the fair distribution problem. Under the capital markets approach, the court would structure the trust as a liquidating trust with a definite term at least as long as, and preferably somewhat longer than, the best available estimate of the time period over which all or virtually all of the injuries caused by the tort would fully manifest themselves. . . .

Under the capital markets approach, the trust would compensate tort claimants with liquidated claims by issuing them shares in the trust fund. . . . The fair distribution problem arises only after claims have been liquidated by some process. . . . I assume here that tort claimants already have their claims liquidated by some process, so they are able to present to the trust a judgment for a certain dollar amount. . . .

The next step under the capital markets approach is the actual compensation of claims. The trust would distribute trust shares to tort claimants so that the face amount of the shares it issued to a given claimant equaled the liquidated value of that person's claim. . . . It is important to note . . . that these shares, like common stock, would be subject to dilution by the subsequent issuance of additional shares. The trust shares would bear interest . . . . In the event that the trust did not have enough funds to pay all claims fully, claimants would be paid pro rata. Since the mass tort firm is insolvent, we can assume that pro rata payment will be the norm.

The function of the trustees under the capital markets approach would be ministerial. . . . Instead, their mandate would be mechanical: Upon presentation of proof of a valid jury verdict, settlement, or other determination of damages in a given amount, the trust would issue the claimant shares with a face value of that amount. The trust would not itself estimate or liquidate the damages of individual claimants or make any estimates regarding expected future claims. The trust would not decide how to allocate its funds among present and future claimants. Hence the factors that tend to make current trusts skew distribution toward present claimants would be neutralized; even if the trust were inclined to favor present claimants, it would be unable to effect its favoritism. Who, then, would make the distributional decision that is the subject of this Article? Under the capital markets approach, the capital markets would "make" this decision.

B. *The Pricing of Trust Shares and the Fair Distribution Problem*

The heart of the capital markets approach is its making the mass tort shares issued by the trust tradeable on capital markets. Because the shares would be subject to dilution by the issuance of additional shares, their market price would express the best estimate of the capital markets as to the number, size, and interest terms of the trust shares that would be issued during the life of the trust.

. . . The court need only determine that the firm's tort liabilities are sufficiently greater than the value of the firm so that, assuming there are no other liabilities, all of the value of the firm should be devoted to satisfying tort claims. The court will then establish a mass tort trust fund and, after the reorganization or liquidation, will fund the trust. . . .

Next, capital market participants who are independent of the bankruptcy process estimate what the total magnitude of liability will be. They are in the business for profit, and if their estimates are poor, they will lose money. These outside participants have every incentive to follow the industry, the particular case, and the relevant science to make their estimates as accurate as possible. . . .

Because the time periods involved in mass tort bankruptcy trusts are significant, a capital markets approach must consider the time value of money. In order to treat claimants fairly . . . the proposed trust shares must include an interest term. . . .

C. *A Capital Markets Approach to Mass Tort Bankruptcy at Work*

The market for trust shares would resemble in many respects the market for stock and debt in publicly traded companies. The markets for these capital assets take account of information much more efficiently than could any administrative process. Prices of trust shares would change rapidly to reflect new information that bears on the value of future tort claims.

1. *Marketable Trust Shares and New Information*

Consider the response speeds of a liquid capital market and an administrative process to new epidemiological information relevant to the value of future claims. Imagine that a scientist discovers evidence suggesting that the damage caused by a toxic tort will be significantly greater than had been previously thought. Under the capital markets approach, prices would adjust quickly to this new information. . . . Efficient capital markets operate in sharp contrast to likely scenarios of administrative price setting. . . . [E]ven estimates of many months may be optimistic. . . .

2. *Capital Markets and Biased Price Determination*

In addition to the problems of delay noted above, the judgment of trust administrators concerning new information would not be impartial. . . . New information that reflected badly on the past judgments of trust administrators would be incorporated especially slowly—or not at all—in payout rates. Price adjustment in efficient or even somewhat efficient capital markets is much less subject to these problems. Indeed, tests of price movements in capital markets indicate that prices have little or no "inertia," suggesting there is little or no commitment to past mistakes and no hesitation by market participants to reevaluate assets on the basis of new information.

In addition, administrators' judgment can sometimes be influenced by politics. . . . The trustees of a large mass tort trust, to the extent they exercised discretionary powers, could easily become enmeshed in political controversy. . . . [P]olitical considerations might influence administrative estimates of the magnitude of future claims. Market pricing of trust shares would be less subject to political influences than would an administrative process. . . .

Market institutions, of course, are not perfectly rational. Capital markets, however, do create powerful incentives to take account of existing information and to respond quickly to new information. Nor in a market system is there any requirement that all market participants follow the same model in determining whether to buy shares (because they think the shares are underpriced) or sell them (because they think the shares are overpriced). Capital markets permit different estimating methodologies to compete against one another, and allow those who subscribe to a given method to risk their own money on its accuracy. Trust administrators would not have such flexibility.

3. *Capital Markets and the Cost of Rent Seeking*

Under the capital markets approach, the trust share pricing process would be decentralized; in an administrative process, it would be centralized. Decentralized processes are more costly for interested parties to manipulate. . . . Rent seeking in the current bankruptcy process involves little risk and promises large gains. . . . Market processes, on the other hand, are not so readily "gamed." . . .

4. *The Liquidation Process and Rational Expectations*

Because the liquidation process is independent of trust administration, the capital markets approach would also tend to defeat bias in favor of present (or other) claimants in the liquidation process. . . . [E]fforts by liquidators to favor present claimants by inflating estimates of their damages will tend to be self-defeating. The market acts as a check on the psychological, political, and other influences that tend to distort the liquidation process away from a fair distribution.

5. *The Market for Trust Shares*

Because the trust shares would be rather exotic securities, trading in trust shares would probably be limited to institutions. Successful trading would require a sophisticated understanding of market dynamics and the scientific and other factors influencing the mass tort. Rival market institutions would likely employ their own analysts with specialized expertise and their own networks of contacts in the relevant scientific and other fields. In contrast to an administrative approach that compensates administrators without regard to the accuracy of their estimates, the capital markets approach would reward these analysts, traders, and financial institutions for successfully estimating the size of future claims. . . .

6. *Risk Sharing Among Participants in the Trust Share Market*

Insurance companies and pension funds seem the most probable participants in the trust share market. These institutions have large portfolios in which trust shares could play a useful diversification role, and they may have a comparative advantage in analyzing the epidemiological and other factors that would bear on trust share value. . . .

D. *The Fairness of the Capital Markets Approach*

Critics of the capital markets approach to mass tort bankruptcy may argue that it is not fair to give claimants a marketable security, which would undoubtedly sell on the market at a substantial discount to its face value, instead of compensation determined by an administrative process. This criticism might be combined with a more general skepticism about the efficiency of the capital market or a more specific criticism about the market's efficiency with respect to the trust shares. . . .

1. *The Role of Government*

No minimally decent society, one might argue, would permit certain basic needs of its citizens, such as the need for medical care, to go unmet. There is no necessary conflict between a capital markets approach to mass tort bankruptcy and this ethical position. It may be that the capital markets approach in a given mass tort bankruptcy would result in claimants receiving only 10 cents on each dollar of proven claims. It is not necessary, however, that these victims endure uncompensated 90% of their losses in order for the capital markets approach to have its desired effects. The general population, acting through the national government, might provide itself with insurance against such shortfalls in compensation. . . .

. . . If undercompensation represents a sufficiently compelling moral and political problem, it can, and should, be addressed directly by legislation.

2. *The Problem of Inefficient Capital Markets*

Some criticism of the capital markets approach is based on skepticism about the efficiency of capital markets. . . . [S]ome commentators have argued . . that capital markets suffer irrationalities that distort prices away from their efficient levels. Significant irrationality in the market for trust shares, if it occurred, could lead to unfair results. If the market priced trust shares at significantly less than their actual liquidation value, claimants and purchasers of trust shares who held their shares until liquidation would receive a windfall.

An adequate response to criticism in this naive form is that it is unlikely that someone will "somehow know" that the implicit market estimate of mass tort damages is wrong, at least not for long. Persons who know that the market has erred in pricing trust shares have valuable knowledge on which they have every incentive to trade. Market mechanisms exist that will propagate this information through the capital market and push the price of trust shares to its appropriate level.

In light of recent work by financial economists, however, more sophisticated criticisms are possible. . . . The criticism of efficient capital markets most pertinent to the capital markets approach, however, has to do with the so-called "closed-end fund anomaly." . . .

It is well established that shares of closed-end funds generally sell at a substantial discount to their actual value. . . . The reasons for this discount are sufficiently mysterious for the phenomenon to merit the moniker of the "closed-end fund anomaly." . . .

If discounts of this kind affected trust shares, distributional problems might arise. The existence of a discount would mean the full value of the debtor's assets was not made available to claimants. . . .

These problems, if they exist, cannot be solved consistently with the capital markets approach by making the trust an open-end rather than a closed-end fund. In an open-end fund, shareholders have the right to redeem their shares with the fund at something close to the net asset value per share. . . . Making a mass tort trust an open-end fund, however, would defeat the solution to the fair distribution problem that the capital markets approach proposes. If present claimants could redeem their shares for the net asset value per share of the trust fund on the basis of the number of shares that had already been issued by that time, they would receive a distribution that would fail to take into account the number and magnitude of future claims that the capital market expected to emerge over the life of the trust fund. Redemption would therefore lead, in all likelihood, to overcompensation of present claimants. . . .

Careful design of the trust fund can probably ameliorate any closed-end fund discount effect. The trust fund under the capital markets approach should not have certain features common to closed-end funds, features that are likely responsible for part of the discount. First, . . . mass tort . . . trust shares . . should embody limited voting powers to enable shareholders to replace incompetent or dishonest management. . . . Second, any closed-end fund discount might be mitigated by specifying a liquidation date in the terms of the trust.

Finally, a large part of the closed-end fund problem could be eliminated by designing the trust so that the trust fund consisted entirely of risk-free investments, such as U.S. Treasury securities. There is some evidence that closed-end bond funds sell not at a discount, but at a small premium to their underlying value. A trust fund composed of U.S. Treasury obligations would presumably behave more like a closed-end bond fund than like a closed-end equity fund. . . .

3. *Administrative and Capital Markets Approaches as Risk Management*

Even with the features suggested above, there is, of course, no absolute guarantee that trust shares will sell at a price that accurately reflects all information, or even all publicly available information, that bears on the ultimate magnitude of the mass tort debtor's liability to present and future claimants. Indeed, critics of ECMH have gathered evidence suggesting that capital markets are not absolutely efficient. Even if capital markets are not perfectly efficient, however, the capital markets approach will still be superior to administrative approaches; and it is the irrationalities inherent in administrative approaches with which capital market irrationalities must be compared. The question, then, is not whether the capital markets approach is absolutely efficient or rational; rather, the question is whether the capital markets approach can allocate available funds to claimants more fairly and with lower transaction costs than can administrative approaches. The intuitive case is strong that while the capital markets approach will not be perfectly efficient, it will be more efficient than any administrative alternative.

The main argument for the relative efficiency of the capital markets approach lies in a comparison of the ability of the two contending approaches to process relevant information. Taking account of both existing and new information by administrative means is quite costly. How costly is difficult to predict, but the administration of mass tort bankruptcy funds historically has involved huge transaction costs. . . .

IV. THE CAPITAL MARKETS APPROACH AND UNCERTAINTY ABOUT INSOLVENCY

Thus far I have assumed that the mass tort firm has incurred so much tort liability that it is certainly insolvent, even if we cannot now know with certainty the total mass tort liability and how it will be distributed among present and future claimants. In this Part, I relax this assumption and consider how the capital markets approach might deal with the more complex setting where substantial uncertainty exists about whether tort liability is so large that the mass tort firm is insolvent.

. . . I offer a tentative application of the capital markets approach to the difficult question of how mass tort bankruptcy should be triggered. The question of when to trigger bankruptcy is especially difficult in the mass tort context because there may be significant uncertainty about whether the mass tort firm is actually insolvent. . . . I propose that a mass tort firm should issue to tort claimants "tort bonds"—securities representing a claim on the assets of a mass tort firm senior to all other claims—at an intermediate stage short of conventional bankruptcy. After this injection of a senior layer of tort claims into the firm's capital structure, the market price of the mass tort firm's equity will provide valuable information about the firm's solvency. A capital markets pricing mechanism will be a more reliable signal for triggering bankruptcy than would a court's estimation that mass tort claims had reached some substantial percentage of the firm's value. . . .

B. *A Capital Markets Approach to Uncertainty Concerning Insolvency*

. . . If there is uncertainty about whether the value of aggregate tort claims exceeds firm value, however, designing appropriate mass tort procedures and institutions becomes more complicated. I provide in this Section a tentative outline of how the capital markets approach might produce a reasonably good solution to this problem. . . .

1. *Tort Bonds*

. . . When insolvency is uncertain, the capital markets approach can mediate uncertainty about both the value of future tort claims and the value of the assets against which tort victims have a claim. . . .

Under the capital markets approach, when the insolvency of the mass tort firm is uncertain, the firm should issue to tort claimants marketable securities that have a claim on the value of the firm that is superior to all classes of equity and all other classes of debt. Because the securities would be a form of debt used for compensating tort claimants, they could be called "tort bonds." . . .

2. *The Pricing of Tort Bonds*

The price of tort bonds should vary, other things being equal, with two magnitudes: the expected value of the firm's assets and the expected value of the tort claims against the firm. . . .

The price of equity in the mass tort firm, because equity represents the residual claim, would depend in part on the anticipated size of tort liability . . . . Thus, if the capital market revised upward its expectation of the magnitude of future tort claims upon the release of a new epidemiological study, the price of equity would decline. . . .

To compensate tort claimants for the riskiness of their involuntary investment in the mass tort firm, tort bonds should bear interest, at a rate commensurate with that of similarly risky instruments. . . .

3. *Operational Costs*

A possible objection to a capital markets approach in the face of uncertainty concerning insolvency is that such an approach would subject the mass tort firm to excessively high operational costs. As the firm issues tort bonds and expectations about the size of tort damages mature, equity in the firm might decrease in value to virtually zero and might cease to be traded at all. My response to the objection is straightforward. This may indeed happen. If it did happen, however, it would merely reflect the judgment of the capital market that expected tort liability equaled or exceeded the value of the firm net of senior obligations. In the mass tort setting, the risk that tort liability will exceed the value of the firm is real. Someone has to bear that risk. It is inefficient and unfair to foist any of this risk upon tort victims, whose relationships with the mass tort firm are involuntary and who would not choose to subsidize their malefactors. . . .

4. *Triggering Bankruptcy*

A difficult problem in devising any mass tort bankruptcy scheme is determining when a firm or its creditors should be able to trigger bankruptcy protections. Roe argues that preserving the viability of a troubled firm requires that bankruptcy be triggered "early," before equity holders, contract creditors, and present tort claimants divert a disproportionate amount of the firm's assets to themselves. In Roe's proposal, a court would determine that tort liabilities had reached a target magnitude, such as 50% of the firm's value, and then place the firm in bankruptcy. More desirable would be a market determination that tort liabilities were sufficiently large to remove control of the firm from the stockholders and place it in trust for creditors.

The capital markets approach goes a greater distance toward providing such a mechanism than does a scheme like Roe's. . . . If equity prices reached virtually zero, . . . this would reflect the capital market's judgment that the firm was either insolvent or on the brink of insolvency. At this point, bankruptcy law could provide that any creditor be able to trigger bankruptcy. . . .

V. CONCLUSION

Mass tort bankruptcy is currently plagued by two related problems. First, because mass torts often inflict damage that becomes evident over a long period of time, it is virtually impossible for administrative procedures to estimate accurately the total magnitude of tort liability. Without such an estimate, courts cannot structure bankruptcy plans that treat tort or other claimants fairly. Second, the process of estimating the magnitude of tort claims and of structuring the mass tort bankruptcy severely disadvantages future claimants. Present claimants evince seemingly more pressing needs. They are better represented and strategically better placed than future claimants to bargain for a reorganization that favors them. Present claimants can reach a bargain with equity holders that essentially excludes future claimants from the reorganization. . . .

In order to counteract the considerable advantages held by present tort claimants, a process of determining liability must take account of all publicly available information that bears on the expected total magnitude of tort claims and remain free from psychological biases and strategic manipulation by participants in the process. The capital market naturally suggests itself. . . . Capital markets, as opposed to courts and administrative bodies, are especially suited to estimate the magnitude of a liability that is a multivariable function. Moreover, markets are far less subject to bias and manipulation than is the current reorganization process or any plausible claims magnitude estimation process that a court might establish.

The capital markets approach to mass tort bankruptcy uses a relatively simple institution—a trust fund that would issue shares to claimants giving them a pro rata interest in the trust fund at a time sufficiently in the future to give all or nearly all tort claims time to emerge. . . . The market price of the trust shares would indicate the capital markets' expectations as to the total magnitude of tort liability over the period during which all or nearly all of that liability was expected to emerge.

A more complicated version of the capital markets approach could handle situations involving uncertainty about whether the mass tort would render a firm insolvent. . . . In this version, a mass tort firm would issue to tort claimants tort bonds that would be superior to the firm's other debt and equity. . . . Imposing a layer of tort bonds upon the capital structure of the mass tort firm would allow the pricing of the firm's equity to reflect the capital markets' valuation of both the value of the firm's assets and the expected total magnitude of its mass tort liability. A decline in the value of the firm's equity to a nontradeable level would provide a more reliable signal for triggering bankruptcy than would a court's estimation that mass tort liability had reached some specified level.

Perhaps most important, using the capital markets approach would assure an allocation of the mass tort firm's value among present and future mass tort claimants that was as fair as possible. The capital markets approach would result in relatively unbiased estimates of total tort liability based on all publicly available information (which is the most for which one can reasonably hope), and would create a distribution process that is difficult for interested parties to manipulate. This approach offers a promising program for the reform of our troubled mass tort bankruptcy process.

David S. Salsburg & Jack F. Williams
A Statistical Approach to Claims Estimation in Bankruptcy
32 WAKE FOREST L. REV. 1119 (1997)[*]

INTRODUCTION

In seventeenth century Europe, the nobility entertained themselves with games of chance. One particular card game was very popular. The problem with this game, however, was that it literally could take days before all hands were played out and scores tallied so that a winner could be identified. The winner would then take the entire pot. The Chevalier de Meré pondered the question whether a ranking of potential winners could be identified before the game was completed based on the hands that had been played, and the pot divided accordingly. The Chevalier de Meré requested his good friends, Pascal and Fermat, to undertake the task. The result was a mathematical formulation of gambling odds and the birth of probability theory.

The estimation of claims in bankruptcy presents many of the same conceptual problems that seventeenth century nobility confronted when playing their card game. A bankruptcy court must end the "game," that is, either the reorganization or liquidation of the debtor, which requires that claims be identified and fixed. However, not all claims are fixed; some claims are unliquidated or contingent. Ideally, a court would like to allow the claims process to play out on its own, but a court is pressed by the Bankruptcy Code itself to end the game prematurely.

A profound assumption lurks in the present model of bankruptcy as framed by the Bankruptcy Reform Act of 1978 (the Bankruptcy Code). This fundamental assumption requires all of a debtor's liabilities existing at the time of the filing of the petition to yield a cash amount. The filing of the petition captures a moment in the bankruptcy process. Yet, our picture of this moment begins to blur when we introduce an additional key variable—time.

Claims administration is at the heart of all bankruptcy systems. . . . As more and more bankruptcies involving mass torts, environmental damage, and products liability arise, the need for a coherent and principled approach to estimating claims in bankruptcy becomes apparent. Present paradigmatic approaches offer little to make sense of the difficult issues presented in estimating contingent or unliquidated claims. The model offered in this article rests on a more coherent and principled approach to the difficult problem. The model uses statistical techniques to estimate claims. A statistical estimator provides a more graceful way to analyze claims estimation issues and to develop an organic estimation model that can "learn" with experience. . . .

I. The Role of Claims in Bankruptcy

The Bankruptcy Code contains within itself a tantalizing contradiction. A claim must yield a cash amount; nonetheless, the definition of "claim" incorporates contingent and unliquidated rights to payment not presently represented by an ascertainable cash value. To muddle the task further, the Bankruptcy Code provides no guidance as to how these claims should be estimated. . . .

C. Traditional Claims Estimation Models

The Bankruptcy Code and Bankruptcy Rules are noticeably silent on what method a court should employ in estimating claims under § 502(c). . . . A bankruptcy court is given wide discretion in estimating the value of a claim and can do so after a cursory proceeding. . . .

Cases provide little insight in identifying what model of estimation a court may use. In fact, a distillation of cases suggests that any reasonable method of estimation is acceptable. Authorities have suggested no less than six different models of estimating future claims in bankruptcy. To add some drama to the exploration of the traditional models used to estimate claims, we suggest three claims scenarios: Anne, Bob, and Jerry. Anne is the holder of a claim against the debtor based on products liability law. The claim arose before the filing of the petition in bankruptcy and is presently contingent and unliquidated. Bob and Jerry are the holders of similar claims. Let us assume that if we had perfect future vision, we would know that a jury would render a verdict on Anne's claim in her favor for $100,000. We would also know that our hypothetical jury would have believed that Anne was entitled to her verdict based on a .51 probability that she was in the right. Further assume that, with the same perfect future vision, a jury would find in favor of Bob for $100,000, believing that Bob proved his case with a probability of .90. Finally, assume that a jury would reject Jerry's claim of $100,000, based on the probability of .49 that Jerry was in the right. As we analyze the paradigmatic models of claims estimation, we will consider the fate of Anne, Bob, and Jerry.

1. Face-Value Model

One model suggested to estimate future claims under § 502(c) is merely to accept the face amount of the claim submitted by a creditor in the proof of a claim filed with the bankruptcy court. . . . Consequently, Anne, Bob, and Jerry are all holders of claims valued at $100,000 under § 502(c).

. . . [T]his is no estimation model. . . . This approach . . . will result in an overvaluation of future claims to the detriment of other unsecured creditors and the debtor.

2. Zero-Value Model

A popular approach to estimating claims in bankruptcy is the zero-value model. Under this approach, courts merely estimate a claim, usually for voting and feasibility purposes, at zero. Courts embracing this approach also suggest that the dischargeability of the claim valued at zero should be waived under § 1141(d). Under this approach, Anne, Bob, and Jerry's claims are valued at zero and are excepted from the discharge provisions under § 1141(d) of the Bankruptcy Code, even though Anne and Bob would have prevailing claims under applicable nonbankruptcy law. Furthermore, Anne, Bob, and Jerry do not possess allowable claims and cannot participate in the reorganization of the debtor or in the distribution of assets of the estate. . . .

A corollary of the zero-value model has been suggested by the court in *Bittner v. Borne Chemical Co.* In *Bittner*, the court affirmed the bankruptcy court's use of an estimation model that resulted in the estimation of creditors' claims at zero. In that case, stockholders argued that for purposes of § 502(c), the court should employ an estimation model considering the present value of the probability that they would be successful in their state court action. Thus, if claimants could show a .40 likelihood of recovery, they should be entitled to forty percent of their claims.

Although unclear, it appears that the bankruptcy court rejected the approach and embraced a model that valued claims at zero if a claimant cannot establish her claim by a preponderance of the evidence. The Third Circuit upheld the estimation model . . . . Under this approach, Anne's and Bob's claims would each be valued at $100,000, and Jerry's claim at zero. . . .

3. Market Theory Model

The market theory model of claims estimation turns to the market, actual or hypothetical, to value claims under § 502(c). The model attempts to identify what the market value of a claim would be if a market existed. The obvious problem is that a market generally does not exist. Thus, courts must conjure up hypothetical markets. One legal fiction builds on another without thought to the internal coherence of the model. Thus, applying the market theory model to the claims of Anne, Bob, and Jerry, we get nowhere. . . .

4. Forced-Settlement Model

A fourth model has strong intuitive and theoretical support. The forced-settlement model provides that a claim should be estimated within a range of amounts that the parties would be willing to accept in a hypothetical settlement of their dispute. . . .

However, the shortcoming of this model lies not in its theoretical construct, but in its application to hard cases and real data. For example, how does one estimate what the range of amounts acceptable to parties in a dispute is and by what method? Lacking an objective rule of decision, the model easily spirals into incoherence. This method provides no direct insight in the actual task of estimating the claims of Anne, Bob, and Jerry. This model, nonetheless, leads directly to the fifth and most often used model of claims estimati on—the discounted value model.

5. Discounted Value Model

The most common model of estimation employed by courts under § 502(c) is the discounted value model. The discounted value model is essentially the forced-settlement model with an actuarial twist. The discounted value model requires that the face amount of the claim be discounted by the probability of prevailing on the claim under applicable nonbankruptcy law. . . .

Applying a crude discounted value model to the hypothetical in this article, Anne's claim is estimated at $51,000 ($100,000 x .51), Bob's claim at $90,000 ($100,000 x .90), and Jerry's claim at $49,000 ($100,000 x .49). Courts typically employ this model for purposes of setting voting rights and determining plan feasibility. Based on our perfect vision, we see that Anne's claim is largely undervalued, Bob's claim is about right, and Jerry's claim is largely overvalued. The model proposed in this article builds on the forced-settlement and discounted value models.

6. Summary Trial Model

The summary trial model, as its name suggests, requires a court to conduct an abbreviated hearing on the validity and extent of the claim. The court then employs common burdens and standards of proof to resolve the estimation issue. . . .

The obvious problem with the summary trial model is that it may use a substantial amount of judicial resources. If a court provides many of the rights litigants expect at trial, . . . then the estimation procedures mire down. . . .

Applying the summary trial model, Anne's claim should be estimated at $100,000, Bob's at $100,000, and Jerry's at zero. The question raised by this model, however, is how much does the procedure take on the character of a trial to insure that all relevant evidence is adduced. By employing streamlined procedures, a court may run the risk of failing to assess the strength of Anne's and Jerry's cases. . . .

II. Using Statistical Techniques in Claims Estimation

. . . [T]he model of estimating claims proposed in this article builds on the forced-settlement and discounted value models as its theoretical construct. However, we go beyond a discussion of theory to address the central claims estimation question by analyzing real case disposition data. We use this data to develop a statistical model based on real experiences with similar claims. We do not stop there, however. By using Empirical Bayes methods, we construct a model that permits a court to adjust a typical value—the claim estimate—by both historical variation and a court's current belief in the credibility of the claim.

A. Statistical Approach: General Discussion

. . . In what follows, we present a sequence of models that were derived from an analysis of 37,355 terminated federal district court cases, . . . wherein the plaintiffs won approximately 50% of the time and the median award for those who won was about 78% of what was demanded. The cases were divided into categories . . . . We chose sixteen of these categories as pertinent to claims estimation in bankruptcy. . . .

The basic idea behind this analysis is that any estimate of the value of a disputed claim can be thought of as an attempt to anticipate what might happen if such a claim had been actually adjudicated before a trier of fact. We assumed that the universe of such court cases will resemble the universe of disputed claims in bankruptcy so closely that the statistical models that fit these cases can be carried over to predict the value of a disputed claim in bankruptcy (or the aggregate of such claims). . . .

B. Statistically Based "One Size Fits All" Model

Both the face-value and the zero-value models described in Part I treat all disputed claims with a single "one size fits all" model of decision. . . . [T]here are many arguments to be made for such an approach. However, both the face-value and the zero-value models are completely arbitrary. The "one size fits all" decision models may be convenient for the court, but they lack any direct relationship to experience.

A statistical "one size fits all" decisional model would draw a single typical value from the 37,355 cases examined that was more realistic. The percentage of times the plaintiff won in those cases is 48.53%. . . . [A] court could allow 48.53% of the face value for all disputed claims. This is typically what courts would do under the discounted value model. . . . [T]he appearance of "fairness" is probably better served by treating each claimant to the same discount. Thus, all claimants "share the loss." Therefore, in the three hypothetical cases, Anne, Bob, and Jerry would each be treated as if they had a claim of $48,530, if the judge decides to stop at this point in the analysis.

However, the statistical analysis of the 37,355 cases yields more information than the percentage of cases in which the plaintiff won. For example, in most cases, plaintiffs were awarded less than they had demanded . . . . Thus, it would be reasonable to consider a typical award/demand ratio and apply that uniformly for all disputed claims. . . .

The typical award/demand ratio across all those cases where the plaintiff won is 0.7804. . . . [A] court may spread the risked award as follows: If we take into account that courts in which the plaintiff lost "awarded" 0% of the claim (that is, plaintiff takes nothing), and combine that information with a typical value of award/demand ratios for cases in which the plaintiff won, we find that the typical award is 37.87% of the demand. Thus, a uniform realistic "one size fits all" approach is to allow 37.87% of the claim in all disputed cases.

Applying the "one size fits all" model, as modified by the use of a typical value of award/demand ratios of 37.87%, results in Anne, Bob, and Jerry having their claims estimated at 37.87% of their face value or $37,870. This result is based on our statistical analysis even though with perfect vision we know that Jerry is receiving more and Anne and Bob are receiving less than they would receive under state law had we allowed the case to play out. This is, however, the nature of the beast when dealing with "one size fits all" decision models.

C. Statistically Based "Off the Shelf" Model

The market theory model and the forced-settlement model attempt to consider the differences among claims in terms of validity and value. This virtue is more consistent with the usual practice under bankruptcy law. These two theories may be thought of as comparing the specific claim at hand with a theoretically similar claim whose outcome is known or can be estimated fairly. Statistical analyses do something similar. A statistical analysis can be used to sub-divide the data into a number of small "bins," where all claims in a single "bin" are somewhat similar. The "bins" in this context are claims categories. The claim at hand is then associated with the "bin" most appropriate to it, and the claim is then assigned the typical values of that "bin." We call this the "off the shelf" model because it is akin to buying a suit of clothes of a given size off the shelf without alterations. . . .

In the hypothetical situations, Anne, Bob, and Jerry all had claims based on product liability. . . . [The data] indicate that there are 7,460 such cases in the analysis, that 30.25% of these cases resulted in judgments for the plaintiff, and that the typical award (taking into account zero awards for judgments in favor of the defendant) was 38.49% of the claim. Thus, using the "off the shelf" model, a court would estimate the value of all three of the claims at $38,490. . . .

D. Statistical "Off the Shelf With Alterations" Model

Whenever an attempt is made to put cases (or people) into a set of pre-defined categories and make conclusions on the basis of those categories, sometimes the conclusions for a specific case are obviously wrong. Such situations are often exploited by adversaries (or newspapers interested in shocking readers) to show how stupid the law is. An example is the "three-strikes and you are out" felon who is sentenced to life imprisonment for grabbing a slice of pizza from the plate of a child in a restaurant.

For a court that seeks to temper justice with mercy (or fairness with common sense), there is a class of sophisticated statistical procedures known as Empirical Bayes, which may be useful in estimating claims. The idea behind Empirical Bayes is that there is an underlying typical value associated with a given category of claims. However, this typical value is subject to "random" perturbation, in the sense that the typical value differs slightly from case to case. A large number of cases are examined to determine both a best estimate of the underlying mean of this typical value and an estimate of the degree of perturbation that is normally seen. A court then examines the disputed claim at issue and tries to determine a reasonable value for the claim along with a measure of the uncertainty that the court has about the "truth" of that reasonable value. Empirical Bayes calculations are used to take into account both the historical variation seen in the typical value and a court's current estimate to produce an estimated value for any given disputed claim. . . .

To illustrate how the Empirical Bayes approach would work, let us apply it to the hypothetical situation that has motivated this discussion. Suppose that in Anne's case, the product liability claim was due to a fire in her kitchen that began in what she claims was a defective appliance produced by the debtor, and that she had been using for a little more than a year. Her claim seems reasonable, but the fact that the toaster had been in use for some time before the fire increases the uncertainty that a jury would decide in her favor. Thus, the judge would think that, in general, this claim would result in an award that was around 90% of the claimed loss, but the uncertainty about the jury's response would put a 50% credibility range to that estimate as lying between 10% and 100%.

. . . [T]he claim would be estimated at $38,720. Note that, although a court thought that Anne's case was quite reasonable (and worth in the judge's mind 90% of the claim), its uncertainty about what a jury would actually decide meant that the Empirical Bayes estimate is closer to the typical value from all such cases.

On the other hand, suppose Bob's claim arose from an appliance that caused a fire the first day it was used. Furthermore, suppose Bob was able to show, from the debtor's own records, that this model appliance had been involved in more than 1,000 other fires. However, his claim for $100,000 includes smoke damages in rooms far removed from the kitchen, and he can show fire related damage of only $85,000. In this case, a court might think that its award would probably be 0.85 times Bob's claim, and the court is quite sure that most juries would make such an award, so a 50% credibility interval would be between 0.845 and 0.855. . . .

. . . Bob's claim would be estimated at $84,040. Note how a small credibility interval (and hence a small variance) associated with the specific case makes the Empirical Bayes estimate very close to the award associated with the specific case. In fact, if a court were so sure of what a jury might award that the 50% credibility interval ran from .85 to .85, then the variance would be zero, and the formula for the Empirical Bayes estimate would result in a judgment exactly equal to the 85% award deemed appropriate in this case.

Suppose Jerry's claim arose from his suing the debtor for perceived slander in some of its advertising. There is little reason to believe that the authors of the advertisement ever knew who Jerry was. He has nothing to support his claim of $100,000 in damages for what he calls the "public shame" he has undergone. And so, while the typical award for such cases . . . is 35.76% of the claim, a court believes that this claim is worth nothing. However, juries are sometimes known to make foolish decisions, and there is a 50% chance that some jury might award Jerry as much as 5% of his claim after taking pity on him. . . . Thus, a court would estimate Jerry's claim at $12,680. Therefore, a court's uncertainty plays out in the final estimate.

CONCLUSION

Estimating claims is no simple task; it is also no sucker's game. No doubt, there is an air of folly dancing about; there is also an air of purpose and determination to do the right thing. Courts must struggle with the task of estimating claims; the nature of the bankruptcy process demands fulfillment of that role. Although announced some forty years ago, courts still may find comfort in the words of Professor MacLachlan: "If the problem be approached with the basic principle in mind that an approximate valuation is much better than none, a reasonable value of some contingencies may be found. . . ." Building on this observation, we suggest a sequence of more coherent and principled statistically based approaches to estimating claims in bankruptcy. We recognize that any estimation model that attempts to depict reality is false; our model, however, strives to be useful. We further recognize that no estimation model is error-free. Nonetheless, by using modern computer intensive robust methods of statistical estimation, we believe that courts can minimize the errors associated with estimations, provide more certainty in the estimation process, and produce fair and reasonable estimates.

NATIONAL BANKRUPTCY REVIEW COMMISSION
FINAL REPORT
BANKRUPTCY: THE NEXT TWENTY YEARS
(OCTOBER 20, 1997)

TREATMENT OF MASS FUTURE CLAIMS IN BANKRUPTCY

Massive tort or contract liabilities can have an enormous impact on otherwise viable enterprises that are vital to the American economy. Parties have found that traditional individual tort or contract litigation for mass torts or mass contract is unwieldy and too expensive for all parties, and has forced them to seek more efficient alternatives. The bankruptcy system offers a structured system to manage multiple liabilities and has provided a forum for companies with massive liabilities to attempt to do so. At least 15 asbestos manufacturers, including UNR, Amatex, Johns-Manville, National Gypsum, Eagle-Picher, Celotex, and Raytech, have reorganized or liquidated in attempts to address massive numbers of known and unknown asbestos claimants using Chapter 11 of the Bankruptcy Code. The fact pattern is not unique to asbestos; manufacturers of other products also must find ways to deal with mass claimants alleging injury or damages from products such as silicone implants, polybutylene pipe, airplanes, and intrauterine devices, and some are resorting to bankruptcy to do so.

Treating massive claims is inherently complicated, partly because of the sheer number of the claims. In addition, a more difficult conceptual issue arises with "future claims" that have not manifested but that are relatively certain to manifest in the future and are based on prior acts of the debtor. A collective process that commences well before the damages or injuries develop might be the only opportunity for future claimants to receive any compensation, both because otherwise early claimants may take all the assets of the company or the company's extraordinary potential liability will dry up access to all capital needed for ongoing business operations. A company may not be able to preserve its going concern value and its work force if it is not able to deal collectively and definitively with all actions arising out of a certain activity. . . .

DISCUSSION

. . . Unlike typical liabilities that are addressed every day in the bankruptcy system and in individualized adjudication, mass tort and mass contract liabilities often have geographically widespread effects and a "long tail;" this means that once a product is distributed, it may take one or several decades for individuals to discover their injuries or property damage caused by that product. As a corollary, widespread damage caused by the product will appear at sporadic times, not all at once. . . .

The bankruptcy system is designed to provide equality of distribution to similar creditors in a collective proceeding while ameliorating the devastating effect that a huge liability may have on the worth of a business and, correspondingly, the compensation available to all victims. Bankruptcy therefore provides an appropriate vehicle to resolve massive liabilities. In theory, incorporating all claimants into the collective bankruptcy process should be workable and universally beneficial: mass future claimants would benefit from the segregation of assets on their behalf, which otherwise will be exhausted long before they would be entitled to collect, while present creditors would benefit by the enhancement in the debtor's going concern value and the company's rejuvenated ability to attract new capital that will accompany a global resolution to the company's massive liability problems.

. . . [N]otwithstanding its inherent advantages, the bankruptcy system has to correct several significant ambiguities and shortcomings if it is to deal with mass future claims fairly and with certainty. In the absence of statutory guidance, courts have reached vastly different determinations of the ability to treat and discharge future claims in bankruptcy. . . .

Recognizing these concerns, Congress enacted amendments in the Bankruptcy Reform Act of 1994 to provide explicit legislative guidance to ensure equitable treatment of mass future asbestos claimants in bankruptcy. Marking an important first step, these amendments introduced a series of additional detailed provisions with limited application to section 524 of the Bankruptcy Code.

As their name suggests, the "asbestos amendments" apply exclusively to demands for payment on account of asbestos injuries. A legislative response to other types of massive future liabilities was specifically reserved for another day. In recent years, it has become even clearer that products other than asbestos give rise to massive liability issues. . . . The Commission's Proposal is not limited to a certain type of liability or industry. Instead, the Proposal focuses on determining the conditions under which it is appropriate to treat mass future claims in the bankruptcy process and the safeguards required in such cases. . . .

. . . Building on the spirit of the 1994 amendments, these Proposals are intended to be the second step in establishing procedures to assure that future claimholders receive fair and equitable treatment in the bankruptcy process by addressing some of the issues left open in 1994. In both reorganizations and liquidations, the Proposals should further the equality of distribution among claimholders, preserve the going concern value of viable businesses, and enhance the likelihood of compensation for parties who might otherwise end up with no compensation. These objectives are applicable in all cases, but the Proposals offer a workable solution for future liabilities in the most pressing and most complex cases, where the claims that are contingent and likely to give rise to future liability are so massive that they warrant special procedures and protections of the type suggested here. Consideration of whether it will be necessary to develop a statutory framework expressly articulating the approach to deal with individual future claims has been reserved for another day. In the meantime, the Commission's Proposals would not change in any way the general handling of obligations that fall within the statutory definition of "claim," including contingent, unmatured, and unliquidated claims, which currently are treated under the Bankruptcy Code.

Chapter 2: Treatment of Mass Future Claims in Bankruptcy

Recommendations

2.1.1 *Definition of Mass Future Claim*
A definition of "mass future claim" should be added as a subset of the definition of "claim" in 11 U.S.C. § 101(5). "Mass future claim" should be defined as a claim arising out of a right to payment, or equitable relief that gives rise to a right to payment that has or has not accrued under nonbankruptcy law that is created by one or more acts or omissions of the debtor if:

1)   the act(s) or omission(s) occurred before or at the time of the order for relief;
2)   the act(s) or omission(s) may be sufficient to establish liability when injuries ultimately are manifested;

3) at the time of the petition, the debtor has been subject to numerous demands for payment for injuries or damages arising from such acts or omissions and is likely to be subject to substantial future demands for payment on similar grounds;

4) the holders of such rights to payments are known or, if unknown, can be identified or described with reasonable certainty; and

5) the amount of such liability is reasonably capable of estimation.

The definition of "claim" in section 101(5) should be amended to add a definition of "holder of a mass future claim," which would be an entity that holds a mass future claim.

2.1.2 *Protecting the Interests of Holders of Mass Future Claims*

The Bankruptcy Code should provide that a party in interest may petition the court for the appointment of a mass future claims representative. When a plan includes a class or classes of mass future claims, the Bankruptcy Code should authorize a court to order the appointment of a representative for each class of holders of mass future claims. A mass future claims representative shall serve until further order of the bankruptcy court.

The Bankruptcy Code should provide that a mass future claims representative shall have the exclusive power to file a claim or claims on behalf of the class of mass future claims (and to determine whether or not to file a claim), to cast votes on behalf of the holders of mass future claims and to exercise all of the powers of a committee appointed pursuant to section 1102. However, a holder of a mass future claim may elect to represent his, her, or its own interests and may opt out of being represented by the mass future claims representative.

The Bankruptcy Code should provide that prior to confirmation of a plan of reorganization, the fees and expenses of a mass future claims representative and his or her agents shall be administrative expenses under section 503. Following the confirmation of a plan of reorganization, and for so long as holders of mass future claims may exist, any continuing fees and expenses of a mass future claims representative and his or her agents shall be an expense of the fund established for the compensation of mass future claims.

The Bankruptcy Code should provide that a mass future claims representative shall serve until further orders of the bankruptcy court declare otherwise, shall serve as a fiduciary for the holders of future claims in such representative's class, and shall be subject to suit only in the district where the representative was appointed.

2.1.3 *Determination of Mass Future Claims*

Section 502 should provide that the court may estimate mass future claims and also may determine the amount of mass future claims prior to confirmation of a plan for purposes of distribution as well as allowance and voting. In addition, 28 U.S.C. § 157(b)(2)(B) should specify that core proceedings include the estimation or determination of the amount of mass future claims.

2.1.4 *Channeling Injunctions*

Section 524 should authorize courts to issue channeling injunctions.

2.1.5 *Plan Confirmation and Discharge; Successor Liability*

Sections 363 and 1123 should provide that the trustee may dispose of property free and clear of mass future claims when the trustee or plan proponent has satisfied the requirements for treating mass future claims. Upon approving the sale, the court could issue, and later enforce, an injunction to preclude holders from suing a successor/good faith purchaser.

Additional suggested readings

Susan Block-Lieb, *The Unsecured Creditor's Bargain: A Reply*, 80 VA. L. REV. 1989 (1994)

David Gray Carlson, *Postpetition Interest Under the Bankruptcy Code*, 43 U. MIAMI L. REV. 577 (1989)

David Gray Carlson, *Successor Liability in Bankruptcy: Some Unifying Themes of Intertemporal Creditor Priorities Created by Running Covenants, Products Liability, and Toxic-waste Cleanup*, 50 LAW & CONTEMP. PROBS. 119 (Spring 1987)

John C. Coffee, Jr., *Class Wars: The Dilemma of the Mass Tort Class Action*, 95 COLUM. L. REV. 1343 (1995)

Jeffrey Davis, *Cramming Down Future Claims in Bankruptcy: Fairness, Bankruptcy Policy, Due Process, and the Lessons of the Piper Reorganization*, 70 AM. BANKR. L.J. 329 (1996)

Richard Epling, *Separate Classification of Future Contingent and Unliquidated Claims in Chapter 11*, 6 BANKR. DEV. J. 173 (1989)

Chaim Fortgang & Thomas Moers Mayer, *Valuation in Bankruptcy*, 32 UCLA L. REV. 1061 (1985)

S. Elizabeth Gibson, CASE STUDIES OF MASS TORT LIMITED FUND CLASS ACTION SETTLEMENTS & BANKRUPTCY REORGANIZATIONS (Federal Judicial Center 2000)

S. Elizabeth Gibson, *A Response to Professor Resnick: Will This Vehicle Pass Inspection?*, 148 U. PA. L. REV. 2095 (2000)

Kathryn R. Heidt, *Products Liability, Mass Torts, and Environmental Obligations in Bankruptcy: Suggestions for Reform*, 3 AM. BANKR. INST. L. REV. 117 (1995)

Kathryn R. Heidt, *Future Claims in Bankruptcy: The NBC Amendments Do Not Go Far Enough*, 69 AM. BANKR. L.J. 515 (1995)

Katherine R. Heidt, *The Changing Paradigm of Debt*, 72 WASH. U. L.Q. 1055 (1994)

Thomas H. Jackson, Chapter 2, *Determining Liabilities and the Basic Role of Nonbankruptcy Law*, *in* THE LOGIC AND LIMITS OF BANKRUPTCY LAW 20-67 (Harvard 1986)

Thomas H. Jackson, *Of Liquidation, Continuation and Delay: An Analysis of Bankruptcy Policy and Nonbankruptcy Rules*, 60 AM. BANKR. L.J. 399 (1986)

Thomas H. Jackson, *Translating Assets and Liabilities to the Bankruptcy Forum*, 14 J. LEGAL STUD. 73 (1985)

Daniel Keating, *The Fruits of Labor: Worker Priorities in Bankruptcy*, 35 ARIZ. L. REV. 905 (1993)

Harvey J. Kesner, *Future Asbestos Related Litigants as Holders of Statutory Claims Under Chapter 11 of the Bankruptcy Code and Their Place in the Johns-Manville Reorganization*, 62 AM. BANKR. L.J. 159 (1988)

David W. Leebron, *Limited Liability, Tort Victims, and Creditors*, 91 COLUM. L. REV. 1565 (1991)

Lynn M. LoPucki, *The Irrefutable Logic of Judgment Proofing: A Reply to Professor Schwarcz*, 52 STAN. L. REV. 55 (1999)

Lynn M. LoPucki, *Virtual Judgment Proofing: A Rejoinder*, 107 YALE L.J. 1413 (1998)

Lynn M. LoPucki, *The Essential Structure of Judgment Proofing*, 51 STAN. L. REV. 147 (1998)

Lynn M. LoPucki & William C. Whitford, *Compensating Unsecured Creditors for Extraordinary Bankruptcy Reorganization Risks*, 72 WASH. U. L.Q. 1133 (1994)

Lynn M. LoPucki, *The Unsecured Creditor's Bargain*, 80 VA. L REV. 1887 (1994)

Ralph R. Mabey & Peter A. Zisser, *Improving Treatment of Future Claims: The Unfinished Business Left by the Manville Amendments*, 69 AM. BANKR. L.J. 487 (1995)

Ralph R. Mabey & Jamie Andra Gavrin, *Constitutional Limitations on the Discharge of Future Claims in Bankruptcy*, 44 S.C. L. REV. 745 (1993)

Ralph R. Mabey & Annette W. Jarvis, *In re Frenville: A Critique by the National Bankruptcy Conference's Committee on Claims and Distributions*, 42 BUS. LAW. 697 (1987)

John C. McCoid, II, *Pendency Interest in Bankruptcy*, 68 AM. BANKR. L.J. 1 (1994)

Charles W. Mooney, Jr., *Judgment Proofing, Bankruptcy Policy, and the Dark Side of Tort Liability*, 52 STAN. L. REV. 73 (1999)

Christopher M.E. Painter, *Tort Creditor Priority in the Secured Credit System: Asbestos Times, The Worst of Times*, 36 STAN. L. REV. 1045 (1984)

William T. Plumb, Jr., *The Federal Priority in Insolvency: Proposals for Reform*, 70 MICH. L. REV. (1971)

Robert K. Rasmussen, *Bankruptcy and the Administrative State*, 42 HASTINGS L.J. 1567 (1991)

Alan N. Resnick, *Bankruptcy as a Vehicle for Resolving Enterprise-Threatening Mass Tort Liability*, 148 U. PA. L. REV. 2045 (2000)

Mark J. Roe, *Corporate Strategic Reaction to Mass Tort*, 72 VA. L. REV. 1 (1986)

Mark J. Roe, *Bankruptcy and Mass Tort*, 84 COLUM. L. REV. 846 (1984)

Steven L. Schwarcz, *Judgment Proofing: A Rejoinder*, 52 STAN. L. REV. 77 (1999)

Steven L. Schwarcz, *The Inherent Irrationality of Judgment Proofing*, 52 STAN. L. REV. 1 (1999)

Alan Schwartz, *Products Liability, Corporate Structure, and Bankruptcy: Toxic Substances and the Remote Risk Relationship*, 14 J. LEGAL STUD. 689 (1985)

William W. Schwarzer, *Settlement of Mass Tort Class Actions: Order Out of Chaos*, 80 CORNELL L. REV. 837 (1995)

Morris Shanker, *Insuring Payment to Contingent and Unidentified Creditors in Bankruptcy*, 92 COM. L.J. 199 (1987)

Morris G. Shanker, *The Worthier Creditors (and a Cheer for the King)*, 1 CAN. BUS. L.J. 340 (1976)

Richard B. Sobol, BENDING THE LAW: THE STORY OF THE DALKON SHIELD BANKRUPTCY (Chicago 1991)

Sheldon S. Toll, *Bankruptcy and Mass Torts: The Commission's Proposals*, 5 AM. BANKR. INST. L. REV. 363 (1997)

Frederick Tung, *Taking Future Claims Seriously: Future Claims and Successor Liability in Bankruptcy*, 49 CASE WESTERN L. REV. 435 (1999)

Georgine M. Vairo, *The Dalkon Shield Claimants Trust: Paradigm Lost (or Found)?*, 61 FORDHAM L. REV. 617 (1992)

James J. White, *Corporate Judgment Proofing: A Response to Lynn LoPucki's* The Death of Liability, 107 YALE L.J. 1363 (1998)

Chapter 10
Executory Contracts

The editor of this anthology has observed that "one of the most confused, difficult, and misunderstood areas in bankruptcy law is that of executory contracts," and further that § 365, the special Code section dealing with that topic, "has mutated into an almost impenetrable legal thicket." Tabb, THE LAW OF BANKRUPTCY, § 8.1, at 575 (Foundation 1997). Given this sorry state of affairs, we are fortunate indeed that some of the best bankruptcy law articles ever written are in the area of executory contracts. The works of Vern Countryman [*Executory Contracts in Bankruptcy* (Part I), 57 MINN. L. REV. 439 (1973), and *Executory Contracts in Bankruptcy* (Part II), 58 MINN. L. REV. 479 (1974)]; Michael Andrew [*Executory Contracts in Bankruptcy: Understanding "Rejection"*, 59 U. COLO. L. REV. 845 (1988)]; and Jay Westbrook [*A Functional Analysis of Executory Contracts*, 74 MINN. L. REV. 227 (1989)], are all giants of scholarship. These works have been extraordinarily influential and have brought much-needed light into the murky darkness of executory contract law. Morris Shanker also has contributed some excellent insight in this field [*A Proposed New Executory Contract Statute*, 1993 ANN. SURV. BANKR. L. 129, and *Bankruptcy Asset Theory and Its Application to Executory Contracts*, 1992 ANN. SURV. BANKR. L. 97]. So too has Thomas Jackson [THE LOGIC AND LIMITS OF BANKRUPTCY LAW, Ch. 5, *Executory Contracts in Bankruptcy: The Combination of Assets and Liabilities* 105-121 (Harvard 1986), and *Translating Assets and Liabilities to the Bankruptcy Forum*, 14 J. LEG. STUD. 73 (1985)].

No study of executory contracts would be complete without inclusion of the "King" in this field—Vern Countryman. Professor Countryman's two-part article, *Executory Contracts in Bankruptcy,* published in 1973 and 1974 in the *Minnesota Law Review,* is a monumental tour dé force that gave coherence to the entire field and shaped the terms of the discussion and debate for the next quarter century and beyond. Countryman's work may be the most-cited (by courts *and* by scholars) bankruptcy law article ever written. In Part I, Countryman undertakes to define an "executory contract." In his analysis, he first excludes contracts already performed by the nonbankrupt, and then excludes contracts performed by the bankrupt (now "debtor"). Why does Countryman exclude each of these categories? By process of elimination, then, Countryman arrives at his famous "material breach" test. What is the logic behind that test?

In Part II, Countryman moves on to examine some of the consequences of his analytic construct. In this excerpt, he first looks at the *effect* of material breach, and considers the distinction between a prebankruptcy breach and a postbankruptcy breach. Countryman next analyzes the "manner and consequence of assumption or rejection," first in straight bankruptcy and then in rehabilitation proceedings.

When Michael Andrew published *Executory Contracts in Bankruptcy: Understanding "Rejection"* in 1988, the courts had thoroughly mucked up the doctrine of "rejection" of an executory contract, and grievously misunderstood and misapplied the law as to the *consequences* of rejection.

Rejection had become a stealth avoidance power. Nondebtor parties to executory contracts endured unfair results (*e.g.*, the loss of an intellectual property license) because the courts did not know what they were doing. Andrew cut through the muck and redefined with astonishing clarity and simplicity what rejection is and what its consequences should be. Rejection, he reminds us, is little more than the estate's decision not to assume the contract; the consequence of rejection is simply that the estate does not obtain the benefit of the contract nor become obligated to perform it—rejection is not a power to avoid, repudiate, or cancel. Courts did listen to Andrew, and the analysis of executory contract rejection was forever changed (for the better).

Published almost contemporaneously with Andrew's path-breaking work was another brilliant reassessment of executory contract doctrine, Professor Jay Westbrook's *A Functional Analysis of Executory Contracts* (in the *Minnesota Law Review*, following in the footsteps of Countryman). Westbrook undertook to "completely reconstruct the fundamentals of bankruptcy contract law"— and he succeeded. Under his "functional analysis," Westbrook recommends discarding the "executory" limitation entirely, and explains that "there is no special bankruptcy 'power' to assume or reject contracts." The only differences from nonbankruptcy contract results that should obtain in bankruptcy are those attributable to bankruptcy avoiding powers, along with some limitations on the remedies available to the non-debtor party attributable to the collective nature of a bankruptcy proceeding. To deal with non-debtor party rights in contract property, he creates the concept of "an 'ITI'—an 'Interest in the Thing Itself.'" An ITI should be honored in bankruptcy unless one of the avoiding powers would apply. Westbrook's analysis, although different in a number of specifics from Andrew's, lent further weight and impetus to the judicial doctrinal revolution of the 1990s in the executory contract field. Westbrook's work also formed the basis of most of the 1997 National Bankruptcy Review Commission's recommendations, which are included at the end of the Chapter.

The final selection in this Chapter is the Review Commission's discussion of, and recommendations regarding, executory contracts. Four significant recommendations are included. As noted, the Commission Report takes its cue from Professor Westbrook's landmark article.

Vern Countryman
Executory Contracts in Bankruptcy (Part I)
57 MINN. L. REV. 439 (1973)[*]

This brings us to a threshold inquiry: what is an executory contract, other than an unexpired lease, which may be assumed or rejected in bankruptcy proceedings?

II. WHAT IS AN EXECUTORY CONTRACT?

As Professor Williston has said, "All contracts to a greater or less extent are executory. When they cease to be so, they cease to be contracts." But that expansive meaning can hardly be given to the term as used in the Bankruptcy Act or even to the Act's occasional alternative reference to contracts "executory in whole or in part." The concept of the "executory contract" in bankruptcy should be defined in light of the purpose for which the trustee is given the option to assume or reject. Similar to his general power to abandon or accept other property, this is an option to be exercised when

---

it will benefit the estate. *A fortiori*, it should not extend to situations where the only effect of its exercise would be to prejudice the other creditors of the estate.

A. Contracts Performed by the Nonbankrupt

Executory contracts, in the sense in which Professor Williston spoke, abound in a bankruptcy proceeding. One example is the contract in which the nonbankrupt party has fully rendered the performance to which the bankrupt is entitled, but which the bankrupt has performed only partially or not at all. Such a contract will give the nonbankrupt party a provable claim in the bankruptcy proceeding, whether it is liquidated or unliquidated and whether it is absolute or contingent as to liability. The trustee's option to assume or reject should not extend to such contracts. The estate has whatever benefit it can obtain from the other party's performance and the trustee's rejection would neither add to nor detract from the creditor's claim or the estate's liability. His assumption, on the other hand, would in no way benefit the estate and would only have the effect of converting the claim into the first priority expense of administration and thus preferring it over all claims not assumed—a prerogative which the Bankruptcy Act has never been supposed to have vested in either the trustee or the court. . . .

It seems clear, therefore, that a contract which is executory only in the sense that it provides the fully performed nonbankrupt party with a claim against the bankrupt estate is not one which may be assumed or rejected. . . . Of course, the nonbankrupt party who has fully performed may have provided an asset which comes into the bankrupt estate and which the trustee will have the option to abandon or accept, quite apart from the bankrupt's liability with respect to it. But if the trustee does accept the property, he accepts it *cum onere*, taking its burdens with its benefits, whether the burden be a liability imposed upon the owner by law solely by virtue of his ownership, a condition to full enjoyment imposed by a contract valid against the trustee, or a lien which the trustee cannot avoid. But the trustee's acceptance of such property should not amount to assumption of a contract of sale so as to elevate an unsecured obligation for the purchase price to the level of a first priority, or even his mistaken attempt to reject the contract of sale, have any effect on a seller's unsecured claim for the price.

Of course, to speak of a contract under which the nonbankrupt party has "fully performed" is to draw an extremely fine line, one which would include among the executory contracts which the trustee can accept or reject some which should be excluded. What of the nonbankrupt building contractor who has fully performed save that he has failed to connect the water or has made a defective connection? Such a failure, even if not cured, would entitle the bankrupt to damages but would not be sufficiently material to permit him to refuse to accept the building or to excuse his performance. The trustee's rejection of such a contract would neither add to nor detract from the estate's benefits or its liabilities; his assumption of it, which likewise would not benefit the estate, should therefore not convert the contractor's claim into a first priority administration expense. Hence, a contract so nearly performed by the nonbankrupt party that failure to complete performance would not be sufficiently material to excuse performance by the bankrupt should not be treated as an executory contract in bankruptcy.

B. Contracts Performed by the Bankrupt

Another example of a contract executory in the Willistonian sense which should not be treated as an executory contract within the meaning of the Bankruptcy Act is a contract which the bankrupt has fully performed, but which the nonbankrupt party has performed only partially or not at all. The bankrupt's claim to further performance under such a contract obviously is an asset which in most instances will pass to the trustee . . . . Obviously, the trustee's assumption of the underlying contract would add nothing to his title to the claim. And it would make no sense to say . . . that the trustee's rejection of a contract fully performed by the bankrupt "shall constitute a breach of such contract."

Nor could the other contracting party, who has received full performance from the debtor, have much of a claim under provisions in the chapters providing that upon rejection of an executory contract any person injured by the rejection shall be deemed a creditor.

Since the bankrupt's claim against the other party is an asset which will pass to the trustee, it is one which the trustee can accept or abandon just as he can accept or abandon noncontractual claims. . . .

Here again, the concept of a nonexecutory contract should accommodate the contract so nearly performed by the bankrupt that his failure to complete performance would not constitute a material breach which would excuse performance by the nonbankrupt party. Rejection of such a contract by the trustee should not be treated as a material breach excusing the other party's performance. Nor should the trustee's assumption of such a contract require that performance of the bankrupt's obligation be completed at the expense of the estate or that the nonbankrupt party's damage claim be elevated to a first priority expense of administration.

C. Contracts Unperformed on Both Sides

Thus, by a process similar to one method of sculpting an elephant,[85] we approach a definition of executory contract within the meaning of the Bankruptcy Act: a contract under which the obligation of both the bankrupt and the other party to the contract are so far unperformed that the failure of either to complete performance would constitute a material breach excusing the performance of the other.

Such a contract, similar to the contract under which the other party has fully performed but the bankrupt has not, represents a claim against the estate. But here that claim may be reduced or totally eliminated if the trustee rejects the contract, because the other party is required to mitigate damages by an amount approximating the value of the performance he is spared by the trustee's rejection. In addition, such a contract, like the one under which the bankrupt has fully performed but the other party has not, represents an asset of the estate to the extent that it carries the unperformed obligation of the other party. But if the trustee elects to assume the contract, . . . he takes it *cum onere* and must render that performance which the bankrupt had contracted to perform as a condition to receive the benefits of the contract. Whether in a given case the trustee will assume or reject depends, presumably, on his comparative appraisal of the value of the remaining performance by the other party and the cost to the estate of the unperformed obligation of the bankrupt, although the Act is silent on that point.

Consistent with this analysis, although often without any extensive analysis of their own, the courts have treated a variety of contracts as executory contracts under the Act where the obligations of both the bankrupt and the other contracting party remained at least partially and materially unperformed at bankruptcy.

---

[85]   Obtain a large piece of stone. Take hammer and chisel and knock off everything that doesn't look like an elephant.

Vern Countryman
Executory Contracts in Bankruptcy (Part II)
58 Minn. L. Rev. 479 (1974)[*]

III. THE EFFECT OF MATERIAL BREACH

Most cases do not deal with all aspects of the effect of a material breach on the bankruptcy trustee's option to assume or reject an executory contract. . . .

A. Prebankruptcy Breach

A material breach by a party to an executory contract before the bankruptcy of either party gives the other party a unilateral option to either treat his own obligations under the contract as discharged and claim damages for the breach or to waive the breach and treat the contract as still in effect. This option of the nondefaulting party is qualified only to the extent that some provision of the contract or some provision of the applicable nonbankruptcy law gives to the defaulting party a right to cure the default.

If the bankrupt party is the party in default, his trustee takes any right of the bankrupt to cure the default. The right to cure the default passes to the trustee . . . . Hence, if the trustee wishes to assume an executory contract, he should be able to cure a default in the contract unless the bankrupt's time for curing the default has expired. . . . If the trustee of the defaulting party does not wish to cure the default, he holds the contract subject to the option of the non-bankrupt party to waive or assert the consequences of the prebankruptcy breach and can assume the contract only if the non-bankrupt party so waives.

If the bankrupt party is not the party in default, his trustee takes the contract subject to any right of the nonbankrupt party to cure the default. If the nonbankrupt party does not cure the default, the trustee has the option either to assert the consequences of the breach (which would rid the estate of the contract without subjecting it to a damage claim for rejection) or to waive the breach (which would enable him to assume the contract). . . .

Several other decisions recognize that where the trustee fails to cure a prebankruptcy default of the bankrupt, waiver of the breach by the nonbankrupt party will preserve the bankruptcy trustee's option to assume or reject the contract. . . .

Absent any waiver of the bankrupt's prebankruptcy breach, the nondefaulting party can successfully assert the consequences of the breach. Sometimes this has been done before the bankruptcy. . . . As often, however, the nonbankrupt party asserts his rights in the bankruptcy court to establish a provable claim for damages without completing his performance. . . .

The nondefaulting party may, however, contract away any right to assert the consequences of the bankrupt's prebankruptcy breach. . . .

B. Postbankruptcy Breach

An analysis of the effect of a material postbankruptcy breach on the bankruptcy trustee's option to assume or reject an executory contract must proceed with little aid from the cases. . . .

Since 1938, section 70b has given the trustee a fixed period, subject to reduction or extension by the court, in which he must decide whether to assume or reject executory contracts. . . . [T]he question then arises how this provision is to be applied where a material postbankruptcy breach in the bankrupt's obligation occurs before that time has expired and before the trustee has either rejected or assumed the contract. When the question does arise, the nonbankrupt party will doubt-

---

less argue both that the right to terminate the contract is unaffected by section 70b and that the contract is no longer executory if it has been so terminated. If that argument prevails, future bankruptcy trustees can preserve their option to assume or reject an executory contract only by making the expenditures necessary to avoid a material postbankruptcy breach.

The acceptance of this argument raises another question. If the trustee uses funds of the estate to avoid a post-bankruptcy breach and ultimately elects to reject the contract, are the expenditures so made to be treated as a first priority expense of administration? After all, the nonbankrupt party's claim for damages based on the rejection of the contract (which claim will be reduced by the prior payments from estate funds) is not entitled to such priority. . . . This conundrum may persuade the courts that the effect of the section is to deprive the nonbankrupt party of the usual right under the state contract law to treat a material breach which occurs during the period prescribed by the section as an excuse of his performance under the contract. Such a conclusion may perhaps compel the concomitant conclusion that where the trustee elects to assume rather than reject the contract he has not only the right but also the obligation to cure the earlier default at the expense of the estate.

The conundrum is even more pronounced where the postpetition breach of the debtor's obligation occurs after the initiation of a chapter proceeding rather than a straight bankruptcy liquidation. The Act provides quite clearly that the chapter proceeding trustee, with court approval, may assume or reject an executory contract at any time before confirmation of a plan and that, if he does not reject, the contract may be assumed or rejected by the terms of the confirmed plan. The time during which a material postbankruptcy breach may occur, that is between the filing of the petition and the exercise of the option to assume or reject, thus may be more prolonged in a chapter proceeding than in a straight bankruptcy case. . . . [T]he courts have been willing to impose restrictions on the contractual rights of individual creditors where the exercise of those rights would jeopardize a rehabilitation. . . .

There are fewer problems where the trustee commits a material postbankruptcy breach after he has assumed an executory contract and before he has disposed of it. If such a breach is not cured, there is no apparent reason why the nonbankrupt party should not have the usual option to assert the consequences of the breach or to waive them. If the nonbankrupt party elects the first alternative, any claim for damages would be entitled to first priority as an administration expense because the trustee has assumed the executory contract. . . .

The effect of a material postbankruptcy breach by the nonbankrupt party is similar to that of a prebankruptcy breach. If the default occurs before the trustee has assumed or rejected the contract and it is not cured, the trustee can either assert the consequences of the breach and thereby rid himself of the contract without a rejection and a resulting claim for damages or can waive the breach and assume the contract. If the default occurs after the trustee has assumed the contract, he can either assert the breach and pursue any damage claim, or waive it.

C. BANKRUPTCY AS BREACH

There remains the possibility that in the absence of an actual default by the bankrupt party to an executory contract the mere fact of his bankruptcy may be treated as a breach of the contract. The treatment of bankruptcy as a breach may spring from the common law doctrine of anticipatory breach, some other provisions of nonbankruptcy law or an express provision in the contract.

1. *Anticipatory Breach*

In the early case of *Central Trust Co. v. Chicago Auditorium Association* the Supreme Court held that, at least where the bankrupt's performance would require some capital, the mere fact of the bankruptcy constituted an anticipatory breach which gave the nonbankrupt party a provable claim for damages. . . .

[T]his court-created doctrine of bankruptcy-as-anticipatory-breach (based, apparently, on state common law contract doctrine) was at its creation inconsistent with the earlier court-created doctrine giving the bankruptcy trustee the option to assume or reject executory contracts. And in 1938 Congress expressly incorporated the trustee's option to assume or reject an executory contract and ignored the doctrine of bankruptcy-as-anticipatory-breach. This congressionally authorized trustee's option should override any inconsistent option that state common law might give to the nonbankrupt party solely because of the fact of bankruptcy.

2. *Other Nonbankruptcy Law*

The only other generally recognized provisions of nonbankruptcy law which might conceivably apply in the bankruptcy of one party to an executory contract are certain provisions of the Uniform Commercial Code applicable to contracts for the sale of goods. Section 2-609 provides that either party to such a contract may, when "reasonable grounds for insecurity arise" with respect to the performance of the other party, make written demand for "adequate assurance of due performance." Failure of the other party to provide such assurance within a reasonable time not exceeding 30 days is treated as a repudiation of the contract. . . .

Clearly, as a matter of fact, the bankruptcy of either the buyer or the seller of goods under an executory contract might provide the "reasonable grounds for insecurity" which would entitle the nonbankrupt party under the provisions of the UCC to demand "adequate assurance of due performance." If the UCC applies, after such a demand the bankruptcy would have only 30 days to provide such assurance—less time than the Bankruptcy Act gives him to decide to assume or reject an executory contract in a straight bankruptcy case and much less time than the Act gives him to decide in a chapter proceeding. This conflict between the UCC and the Act poses the question whether the UCC can compel the bankruptcy trustee to incur the cost of posting adequate assurance as a condition to taking the full time for decision allowed by the Act. . . .

Although interesting, these question are obviated by a recognition of the primacy of the Bankruptcy Act. The provisions of the UCC, like the common law doctrine of anticipatory breach, should not be available to fetter the option, and the time for exercising that option, that the Act gives to the trustee.

IV. MANNER AND CONSEQUENCE OF ASSUMPTION OR REJECTION

The questions remain as to how the trustee assumes or rejects an executory contract and the consequences of his action. In the chapter cases there is the additional question of the consequences when the trustee neither assumes nor rejects. . . .

A. STRAIGHT BANKRUPTCY

For the first 40 years of the administration of straight bankruptcy cases of the Act of 1898, the courts merely applied doctrines which were created earlier and developed contemporaneously in equity receivership cases. . . . [T]he courts also created for themselves the obligation to prescribe how the equity receiver, or the bankruptcy receiver or trustee, must exercise his option and defined the consequences of his action.

In the earliest of its decisions involving the options of a receiver, the Supreme Court . . . said that the receiver of the road "was entitled to a reasonable time to elect whether he would adopt" the lease or would "return the property. . . paying, of course, the stipulated rental for it so long as he used it." . . . In succeeding cases the Court reiterated that railroad receivers had a "reasonable time" to decide whether to assume or reject leases and held that they had not assumed them so as to become liable for the stipulated rentals as first priority administration claims merely by operating the leased lines . . . .

In an attempt to bring some precision to the "reasonable time" within which the receiver must exercise his option, some courts fixed a specific period within which he was to act and then in some instances extended such time at the receiver's request. If the receiver took no action within a reasonable time, however, that inaction did not alone constitute an assumption of the contract, and the receiver could thereafter reject it. . . . Indeed, some of the decisions allowed the receiver to perform under the contract for a time to determine whether it was profitable and then reject it . . . .

Not all the receivers had the temerity to act unilaterally to reject contracts. Some sought court approval of the rejection and obtained it; others were directed to assume the contract. In other instances the application of the nonbankrupt party precipitated the court order to the receiver to reject or assume the contract.

Where the receiver assumed the contract, the cost of the receiver's performance was treated as a first priority administration expense. . . .

Where the receiver rejected the contract, the other contracting party was given a general claim for damages for breach of contract. If the rejected contract was an unexpired lease, the lessor was also given a first priority claim for the reasonable value to the estate of the receiver's use and the occupancy of the leased premises from the time the receiver was appointed until the time the property was surrendered to the lessor. This use of the occupancy value was usually, but not invariably, taken to be the rental rate stipulated in the lease. But the receiver had to *use* the leased property in order to give the lessor such a first priority claim. . . .

A number of decisions established the consequences of a rejection of a lease or contract. Thus it was assumed in a case where the issue was not decided that after rejection of a lease the "leasehold remained the bankrupt's." Where the bankruptcy trustee rejected a contract to sell goods, the buyer was left with a damage claim for breach of contract. The trustee who rejected a lease, however, was liable for the reasonable value (usually but not always the rental price stipulated in the lease) of the use of the premises prior to the rejection and surrender. . . .

The 1938 amendments to the Bankruptcy Act, so far as here relevant, were primarily concerned with making claims for future rent provable and dischargeable but were also directed toward eliminating some of the uncertainty as to whether the trustee has assumed or rejected any executory contract. . . .

Actually, the amendments did little to clarify the manner of the trustee's assumption of rejection of a contract. . . . Only one point seems clear. If the trustee does nothing within the time fixed, . . . he is deemed to have rejected the contract. . . .

The 1938 amendments to the Act have made no change in the rule that a trustee who rejects or is deemed to have rejected a lease is subject to a first priority claim for the value to the estate of his use and occupancy of the premises until they are surrendered to the lessor. . . .

B. REHABILITATION PROCEEDINGS

Chapters X, XI, XII and XIII were adopted in 1938 and contain nearly identical provision which treat executory contracts in a manner now familiar. . . .

These provisions indicate that the court may permit the rejection of executory contracts at any time and that the confirmed plan may also reject such contracts. As either form of rejection requires court approval, moreover, most courts considering the matter have concluded that the 60-day time limit of section 70b and its provision that any contract not assumed within that time shall be deemed rejected are inapplicable in chapter proceedings. As one court has put it, the provisions in Chapter X "clearly indicate Congress intended that before an executory contract should be rejected, a judicial hearing and inquiry, at which interested parties might be heard, should be held, and . . . an executory contract [can] be rejected only with permission of the court . . . ."

That court also concluded that while Chapter X like the other chapters does not expressly impose the same requirements for assumption of executory contracts, "we think by necessary implication it requires judicial approval for such . . . assumption." . . .

Other courts, however, have found without directly addressing the question, that the trustee or debtor in possession has assumed an executory contract in circumstances revealing no court approval . . . .

Where the chapter trustee rejects a contract, the other contracting party has a claim for damages, not a claim for restitution of part of the purchase price paid. The rejection of a lease may give the lessor a first priority claim for use and occupancy of the property, but only to the extent that it was used for the benefit of the estate. . . .

In the absence of very careful advance planning, the latest opportunity for an assumption or rejection of an executory contract, at least in a Chapter XI case, is the time for confirmation. . . .

Because there is no provision in the chapters as there is in straight bankruptcy that an executory contract not assumed within a specified time shall be deemed rejected, there is a possibility as there was under former section 77b that a chapter case may be closed with some such contracts neither assumed nor rejected. It is clear under the chapters, moreover, that the other contracting party is not a "creditor" until his contract is rejected. Thus where there has been no assumption or rejection in a chapter case the claim of the other contracting party is not discharged. . . .

The courts have also concluded that where the contract is neither assumed nor rejected the other contracting party is not entitled to participate in the distribution under the plan.

Michael T. Andrew
Executory Contracts in Bankruptcy: Understanding "Rejection"
59 U. COLO. L. REV. 845 (1988)[*]

INTRODUCTION

Section 365(a) of the Bankruptcy Code provides in seemingly clear and direct language that a bankruptcy trustee, "subject to the court's approval, may assume or reject any executory contract or unexpired lease of the debtor." . . . But that simple prescription has been profoundly troublesome. Much of the trouble surrounds the definition of an "executory" contract, a term which has no statutory definition. More fundamentally, though, the problem in most cases is the concept of "rejection."

"Assumption" rings familiar from general contract law. There it typically refers to the agreement by someone initially a stranger to a pending contract to take on the obligations of one of the contracting parties. . . .

Assumption under section 365 of the Bankruptcy Code is not far removed from that common understanding. There it refers to a bankruptcy *estate's* agreement to take on the obligations of the bankruptcy *debtor* on some pending contract or lease. Assumption permits the estate to obtain the benefits of continued performance by the nondebtor party to the contract. . . .

But what *exactly* does it mean to "reject" a contract? Despite the fact that rejection and assumption are paired in section 365, the term "rejection" suggests no ready contract law analogue. Courts describe the "power" to reject as permitting such things as the release, repeal, reconsideration, discharge, revocation, repudiation, alteration, voiding, cancellation or avoidance of contract or lease obligations. The statute itself provides that rejection "constitutes a breach" of a contract or lease, implying a "power" to breach. Courts frequently use the vehicle of rejection to terminate rights in or to property that are otherwise good in bankruptcy. All of this suggests a radical departure from normal contract law, giving credibility to the notion that "[t]he power of rejection is a valuable weapon . . . in the armory of the trustee."

Viewed as such a special power, rejection seems to demand both a careful definition of the "executory" contracts to which it will apply and standards that will govern its use. . . .

In this article I suggest that much of the jurisprudence of "rejection" is profoundly confused, and that the strikingly simple concept embodied in that term has been all but lost in the confusion. As will be seen, rejection is not the revocation or repudiation or cancellation of a contract or lease, nor does it affect contract or lease liabilities. It is simply a bankruptcy estate's decision not to assume, because the contract or lease does not represent a favorable or appropriate investment of the estate's resources. Rejection does not change the substantive rights of the parties to the contract or lease, but merely means that the bankruptcy estate itself will not become a party to it. Simply put, the election to "assume or reject" is the election to assume or not assume; "rejection" is the name for the latter alternative.

Far from benign, the confusion over rejection has yielded wasteful litigation, absurd results, and dramatic distortions in bankruptcy law. Understanding that rejection does not affect contract liabilities demonstrates, for example, that litigation over whether rejection will be permitted is largely a pointless exercise. That understanding also makes clear that terminating rights in or to property arising under contracts that happen to be "executory" is fundamentally contrary to general bankruptcy principles, to the history and purpose of executory contracts doctrine itself, and to common sense. The most serious consequence of the confusion over rejection is that it has diverted attention away from important questions of bankruptcy policy, focusing it instead on the generally meaningless question of what constitutes an "executory" contract.

The law of executory contracts is in need of a thorough rethinking. . . . [M]y aim in this article is to bring into sharper focus the essentials necessary to an understanding of rejection of contracts and leases.

Any inquiry into executory contracts doctrine must address Professor Vern Countryman's exhaustive 1973-74 analysis of executory contracts in bankruptcy. . . .

In this article I suggest, however, that in several respects Countryman's analysis has clouded rather than clarified the law. . . .

I. FUNDAMENTAL CONCEPTS:
THE DEBTOR, THE CREDITORS, AND THE BANKRUPTCY ESTATE

Liquidation bankruptcy law in the United States . . . always has been built around this basic concept: In some circumstances the property of a debtor—a person who has financial obligations—should be transferred to someone else, to be administered under governmental authority for the benefit of the debtor's creditors. . . . The Bankruptcy Code formally establishes a separate entity, the "estate," to succeed to the debtor's property, and the "trustee" is the fiduciary representative of that estate. As will be seen shortly, understanding that the *estate* succeeds to property of the *debtor*—and that the estate and the debtor are distinct legal entities—is crucial to understanding executory contracts doctrine.

One important consequence of the distinction between the debtor and the estate is that the *debtor's* creditors, like the beneficiaries of an ordinary trust, are not in any direct sense creditors of the bankruptcy *estate*. They merely have a right, ultimately, to a distributive share of the estate . . . .

Because the estate acquires its property from the debtor, the estate's rights in and to the property are in general no greater than were the debtor's. . . .

Bankruptcy law's "avoiding powers" are a significant exception to the recognition of such rights in property. . . .

The rules just summarized relate to the rights of creditors against the bankruptcy *estate*. Bankruptcy law also deals with the rights of creditors against the *debtor*. It provides that, with certain exceptions, debts assertable as claims in the bankruptcy may be "discharged," thereby rendering those debts unenforceable against the debtor. Discharge operates for the benefit of the debtor, not the estate; it does not curtail the assertion of claims in the distribution of the estate, nor does it affect interests in property of the estate.

These principles of bankruptcy liquidation also apply in reorganization cases, with relatively slight modification. The primary difference is that . . . the debtor itself (as "debtor in possession") usually remains in possession of and administers the estate's property in a reorganization. That difference . . . tends to obscure the fundamental principle that ownership of the property has changed hands, but the principle remains applicable. . . . Title to the property has passed to the estate, and the debtor in possession functions as trustee of the estate. . . .

Executory contracts issues arise against that backdrop. Preliminarily, and without focusing on any technical definition, it may be observed that pending contracts and leases potentially embody both an asset for the estate (the debtor's right to the non-debtor party's performance) and a claim in the distribution of the estate (the obligations of the debtor under the contract). Most broadly, the purposes of executory contracts law are to provide for the proper administration of the asset and for the proper placement of the claim in the hierarchy. . . .

II. WHAT IS "REJECTION"?

A. Copeland v. Stephens *and the Basic Assume-or-Reject Election*

The fountainhead of U.S. executory contracts doctrine is largely a single English case, *Copeland v. Stephens*, decided in 1818. Copeland, a lessor of real property, sued to recover rent from Stephens, an assignee of Copeland's original lessee. Stephens had gone into bankruptcy before the rent came due, and argued that the leasehold had passed to his bankruptcy assignees under the general assignment of his property to them under bankruptcy law. Thus, Stephens argued, he no longer was in privity of estate with Copeland and could not be liable for the rent. . . .

The court held that the assignment was "suspended" as to a lease unless and until the assignees accepted, and "the [leasehold] estate must necessarily remain in the bankrupt during the period of suspension; for it cannot be in abeyance, and must exist in some person." Copeland thus prevailed, because the leasehold remained in Stephens, the debtor . . . .

Prior cases . . . likewise had held that the estate in the hands of the bankruptcy assignees should be protected from the continuing liabilities of the debtor that would accompany a leasehold, unless they assented (as they might if the lease were favorable). *Copeland*'s innovation was its explicit conclusion that the proper mode of conceptualizing that rule—"[t]he right to *accept* or *refuse*"—was to treat the leasehold, unlike all other assets, as never passing to the assignees at all unless they affirmatively accepted it. . . .

Copeland's conceptual approach did not endure in England, where contracts and leases now pass to the trustee but . . . may be "disclaimed." . . . However, *Copeland* was imported into the U.S. largely intact, and was applied to both leases and other contracts. Thus, the resulting U.S. doctrine was that the bankruptcy trustee would have to act affirmatively to admit either a contract or lease asset into the estate, and only then would the estate itself become bound to the debtor's contract or lease liabilities. . . .

. . . The courts made repeated reference to the *Copeland* principle in the years before the election to "assume" or "reject" became statutory.

The courts in these pre-statutory cases thus identified contracts and leases as assets having the perceived potential of imposing administrative liabilities *upon the estate* by virtue of its succession to the debtor's ownership. Their doctrinal response was to exclude contracts and leases from the estate. . . . The reasoning was straightforward: If the estate did not succeed to contract and lease assets it certainly could not be obligated on the liabilities that might accompany them.

The doctrine recognized, though, that the trustee could elect to accept a contract or lease into the estate if it appeared desirable or profitable to do so. That election would entitle the estate to the benefits of the other party's performance, at the cost of obligating the estate on the debtor's liabilities as an administrative expense, as if the estate itself had entered into the same contract or lease in the first instance.

Following *Copeland*, then, to "assume" (or "adopt" or "accept") a lease or contract was to admit it to the estate, and consequently to obligate the estate on it. To "reject" (or "repudiate" or "renounce" or "refuse") a lease or contract was simply to elect, expressly or by inaction, *to leave matters as they were*, and neither to admit the lease or contract to the estate nor to obligate the estate on it. *Rejection was nothing more than the label for the decision not to assume*: What the trustee "rejected" was not in any direct sense the contract or lease liabilities; rather, the trustee rejected (*i.e.*, declined to accept) the transfer of title to the contract or lease from the debtor to the estate, which transfer might carry liabilities with it that could become liabilities of the estate. The debtor's obligations were unaffected.

The historical record is quite clear that these were the concepts carried first into the assume-or-reject election of section 70b of the Bankruptcy Act (part of the "Title to Property" section) in 1938, . . . and in turn into section 365 of the Bankruptcy Code. . . .

. . . The important point . . . is that the concept embodied in the term "rejection" simply cannot be understood except in the title-focused context in which it was created: Despite the present widely-held view to the contrary, . . . a trustee or debtor in possession does not "reject" the liability reflected in a contract, but rather rejects—*i.e.*, declines to accept—the transfer of title to the asset. It is that aspect that likens "rejection" of contract and lease assets to "abandonment" of other assets, which do enter the estate initially; in each case, the end result is exclusion of an asset from the estate.

The historical relationship between the assume-or-reject election and the vesting of the estate's title to a contract or lease is rapidly becoming forgotten. . . . Nonetheless, . . . section 365's core concept—the assume-or-reject election—is itself antique. Until section 365 is modernized, its history remains an indispensable guide to its meaning.

What that history demonstrates is that the common portrayal of the rejection of executory contracts—as permitting contract revocation, cancellation, avoidance or the like—is a dramatic misconception. The assume-or-reject election created by the courts and carried forward into the Bankruptcy Code has a clear and fairly modest purpose: to insure that creditors *of the debtor* who are parties to pending contracts and leases do not become administrative creditors *of the estate* merely by virtue of the estate's succession to the debtor's property. The doctrine achieves that goal in simple (though indirect) fashion, by deeming that contract and lease assets do not pass into the estate absent an affirmative decision to accept them; the cost of acceptance is an assumption of the liabilities they entail. "Rejection," at least in the context of the basic assume-or-reject election, is nothing more than the label for the election not to assume a contract or lease.

What, though, of the statute's identification of rejection as a "breach" of a contract or lease? Does that somehow suggest a more powerful role for rejection than its place in the basic assume-or-reject election would indicate? What purpose does rejection-as-breach doctrine serve? I turn next to those questions.

B. The Relationship Between Rejection and "Breach"

1. The Pre-Statutory Era: *Chicago Auditorium*

The basic assume-or-reject election insures that the non-debtor party to a contract that happens to be pending when the debtor's bankruptcy ensues will not be elevated fortuitously to priority over the debtor's other creditors. It does not, however, answer the question whether that party will be entitled to at least some claim in the bankruptcy, so that it is no worse off than other creditors. Courts . . . viewed themselves as confronting this conceptual hurdle: In cases where the debtor is not actually in breach of the contract at the moment of bankruptcy, the time as of which claims are determined, how can the non-debtor be said to have a claim?

. . . At issue was not just the maturity of the claim . . . . Rather, the concern was that neither the debtor's nonperformance nor the other party's performance were *certain* as of the crucial time, the moment of bankruptcy, *because the contract or lease still remained alive outside of the estate.* Would the estate take up the contract? If not, so long as no breach had occurred might not the debtor still perform it? Would the non-debtor render its required performance when due? Viewed as of the moment of bankruptcy, the answers to all such questions are uncertain.

. . . [T]he concern in all these cases was that where no breach had occurred, the *debtor's nonperformance* was not certain at the moment of bankruptcy, and consequently neither was the existence of the other party's damages. . . . [A]n executory contract or lease has two special aspects. First, nonperformance by the non-debtor party (or re-entry by a real property lessor) might terminate or reduce the debtor's liability. Second, under the *Copeland* concept an unassumed contract or lease remains in the debtor; thus, the debtor is left not only with a liability but also with an asset. . . . In short, the relationship between debtor and non-debtor is still *open.*

. . . Lacking . . . direct authority, U.S. courts apparently felt it necessary to address the matter through "breach" concepts that could resolve the open relationship as of the crucial time, the moment of bankruptcy.

In 1916 the Supreme Court approved the "breach" approach, and permitted claims under executory contracts other than leases, in *Central Trust Co. v. Chicago Auditorium Ass'n. Chicago Auditorium*, a much-misunderstood decision, is the precursor of the statutory rule, adopted in 1938 and still present in the Bankruptcy Code, that a rejection constitutes a "breach" of a contract or lease.

In *Chicago Auditorium*, the debtor had contracted for the exclusive right to provide baggage and livery services to a hotel for five years, and agreed to pay a specified amount each month. At the time of the debtor's involuntary bankruptcy, the contract was not in default and had several years yet to run. The trustee did not assume the contract, and the hotel asserted a claim for damages for breach.

The Supreme Court permitted the claim . . . . The Court . . . concluded . . . that "proceedings, whether voluntary or involuntary, resulting in an adjudication of bankruptcy, are the equivalent of an anticipatory breach of an executory agreement." . . .

Chicago Auditorium thus accomplished two goals, one favorable to the non-debtor party and the other favorable to the debtor. First, it gave the non-debtor a claim on its contract, enabling it to participate in the bankruptcy distribution. Second, as a consequence of creating a claim, the case also rendered the contract obligation subject to discharge, enhancing the relief available to the debtor.

Although it labelled *bankruptcy* a breach of contract, the Court in *Chicago Auditorium* expressly recognized the trustee's option to assume the contract, and made clear that it was addressing exclusively the non-assumption situation. . . . The uncertainty problem thus was resolved as of the instant of bankruptcy by holding that, *in rejection (i.e., non-assumption) situations only,* bankruptcy itself would be regarded as a breach for claims purposes; that "breach," however, would have no effect upon the estate's ability to assume.

Chicago Auditorium therefore was not . . . in any sense inconsistent with or preclusive of the election to assume or reject contracts and leases. To the contrary, it provided what may be thought of as the backdrop against which the basic assume-or-reject election would be played out, by explicitly establishing the consequence of a decision not to assume—*i.e.*, to reject—a contract: The non-debtor party participates in the bankruptcy distribution. To say that there is a "breach" is to say, in effect, simply that *for claims allowance purposes in bankruptcy, it will be presumed (conclusively) that a debtor will not perform its pending obligations. . . .*

2. The Statutory Era

. . . [I]n the Chandler Act in 1938, Congress codified the "breach" concept of *Chicago Auditorium* as new section 63c (part of the "Debts Which May Be Proved" provision) . . . .

. . . *Chicago Auditorium* identified bankruptcy as a breach, *but only in circumstances where the trustee elected not to assume—i.e., rejected—a contract*. Hence the rule of section 63c: Rejection constitutes a breach. Section 63c was not inconsistent with *Chicago Auditorium*, it codified it, as was intended. . . .

Section 63c's basic rejection-as-breach rule was carried into the Bankruptcy Code, in section 365(g), essentially unchanged. . . .

Two important lessons emerge from this history of the rejection-as-breach rule. First, the rule provides no more support for the common misconception that a trustee or debtor in possession somehow "rejects" (or revokes or repudiates or cancels) contract liabilities than does the basic assume-or-reject election itself. When an executory contract or lease is not assumed by the *estate*, the "breach" rule simply coordinates the treatment of the non-debtor party with that of all other creditors by creating a presumption, conclusive for claims allowance purposes, that the *debtor* will not perform. The "breach" rule thus is not in any sense designed to diminish the non-debtor's rights vis-à-vis *the estate*, but rather to buttress them. Relief to the *debtor* is correspondingly enhanced, because the debtor's obligation on the contract will be within the scope of discharge.

Second, and relatedly, the "breach" rule is not in any sense itself the essence of rejection. . . . To infer that the section thus creates a special bankruptcy "power to breach" contracts suggests a great deal more than is actually present in the statute or its history, and confuses the inquiry. The *estate* is not obligated on the debtor's contracts in the first place . . . .Thus, the estate does not need any "power to breach" . . . . The "breach" here is the presumed breach *by the debtor*, and its purpose is to insure that the non-debtor party to the contract will have rights equivalent to those of other parties who are otherwise similarly situated. . . .

III. Basic Executory Contracts Doctrine in Operation

A. Restatement and Retrospective

As the foregoing history reflects, by the time the first statutes dealing with the topic of executory contracts appeared in the 1930s, the courts had developed a largely complete executory contracts doctrine. That doctrine had three basic components, designed to accomplish three fairly simple goals.

The first component was the *Copeland* rule, which excluded "executory" contract and lease assets from the bankruptcy estate . . . absent an election by the trustee to accept them. That rule protected the estate from unadvisedly incurring administrative liabilities . . . . "Rejection" (or "repudiation" or "renunciation," among other terms) simply described the estate's decision not to succeed to such an asset. What was rejected was the transfer of the asset to the estate.

The second component was the rule that the estate could elect to succeed to ("assume" or "accept" or "adopt") the debtor's rights in a contract or lease, at the cost of obligating the estate on the debtor's liability as an administrative expense. That rule allowed the estate to realize on the value of a contract or lease asset in circumstances where it seemed desirable to do so.

The third component was the *Chicago Auditorium* rule that, absent assumption, an executory contract would be viewed as having been "breached" as of the instant of bankruptcy. That rule resolved uncertainty over whether the debtor would continue performance on a contract, and thereby permitted a claim by the non-debtor party. Thus, the rule served to counterbalance the first component of the doctrine: The non-debtor party to a contract that happened to be pending when a bankruptcy was commenced would not be elevated over other creditors, but neither would it be demoted below them to the status of non-creditor. Correspondingly, the rule enhanced the debtor's discharge by including within its scope the debtor's contractual obligation. . . .

The three fundamental principles of executory contracts doctrine are not complex, and as a general matter do not seem very controversial. The problem is that they are deployed indirectly. In the modern context the rationale underlying the indirect approach of the cases has been largely forgotten, leaving behind only the cryptic terminology of "rejection" and "breach."

"Assumption" aptly describes what occurs when a bankruptcy estate elects to take on the obligations of a contract or lease as the price of obtaining the benefit of the non-debtor party's performance. By contrast, "rejection" is a particularly inapt term to describe the election not to assume. The reason: it suggests, misleadingly, that the trustee or debtor in possession is somehow rejecting (cancelling? repudiating? renouncing? rescinding?) *liabilities*. In fact, what the estate's representative is rejecting is the contract or lease *asset*, which conceivably could carry continuing obligations with it into the *estate* on an administrative basis. Rejection simply prevents the estate from unadvisedly stepping into such liabilities. The liabilities are not repudiated; to the contrary, as the rejection-as-breach doctrine is designed to insure, the contract or lease liabilities remain intact after rejection and give the non-debtor party a claim in the distribution of the estate.

The doctrinal labelling of rejection as a "breach" is also unfortunate, though, for two reasons. First, it undoubtedly exacerbates the confused view of rejection as a cancellation or repudiation of liabilities. . . .

Second, the use of "breach" terminology . . . suggests that there is some discontinuity between the treatment of "executory" contracts and other liabilities. In fact, "breach" was used as an indirect way of saying that there is no discontinuity: For executory contracts, as for all other obligations, claims will be determined based upon the presumption that the debtor will not perform. . . . Again, it must be emphasized that the "breach" here is a presumed pre-bankruptcy breach *by the debtor*. . . .

B. "Rejection" Confusion

Confusion over "rejection" has been manifested in three primary, overlapping categories of cases, each reflecting the failure to recognize that rejection simply leaves parties to "executory" contracts in the same position as other claimants otherwise similarly situated. The first consists of cases concerned with whether particular contracts are "executory" as a preliminary to determining whether rejection will be permitted. The second consists of cases holding that when a contract is "executory" and is rejected, the contract is somehow destroyed or otherwise altered. The third category, an aggravated derivative of the second, is comprised of cases holding that rejection of a contract somehow destroys a right in or to property created by the contract, even if that right is otherwise good as against all competing claimants and as against the estate itself. . . .

An understanding of the history and purpose of executory contracts doctrine would have greatly simplified the inquiry in . . . the many . . . "rejection" cases that have focused on whether the non-debtor party had any performance remaining. The analysis begins with recognition of two key points. First, rejection does not discharge or revoke contract *obligations*; it is the contract *asset* that is rejected (or, more comprehensibly, declined). Second, the "breach" occasioned by rejection is nothing more than the same presumption of nonperformance *by the debtor* that is used to determine all normal claims in bankruptcy.

Once those points are understood, the struggle over a definition of "executory" contracts is obviated. If the contract is "executory," rejection simply assures the non-debtor party of a right to participate in the distribution or the reorganization plan. If the contract is not "executory," the non-debtor party already has that right, and rejection is unnecessary. *But while unnecessary, rejection is also harmless*: It does not make obligations disappear, and its "breach" consequence . . . is the same as that ordinarily applicable in bankruptcy. Thus, there is no reason to prohibit rejection, or even to litigate the issue, because the case comes out the same either way—[the non-debtor party] has an unsecured claim.

. . . [T]he entire point of rejection doctrine is to assure that there is no discontinuity between the treatment of parties to unassumed "executory" contracts and all other claimants. Thus, properly understood, rejection itself *has* no negative consequence, other than that the non-debtor party will not receive the unique benefit of assumption. . . .

C. What is an "Executory" Contract?

That question—what is an executory contract?—has preoccupied modern executory contracts jurisprudence, particularly under the Bankruptcy Code. But the discussion so far should suggest that more fundamental questions have been overlooked: Does it matter? If so, why?

As has been seen, when rejection is at issue, the definition of an "executory" contract should *not* matter. What a trustee or debtor in possession rejects, on behalf of the estate, is the transfer of the asset represented by a pending contract or lease (*i.e.*, the right to the further performance of the non-debtor party), not the liability. Rejection of an "executory" contract or lease simply places the non-debtor party in the same position as other claimants in bankruptcy. Thus, while rejection of a *non*-"executory" contract is unnecessary, and while it is technically incorrect to refer to "rejection" of such a contract, it is also inconsequential. . . .

By contrast, when *assumption* of a contract is at issue, the definition of an "executory" contract matters significantly. Assumption *is* special. It comes at a price which, unlike rejection, does produce a discontinuity with the normal rules for treatment of creditors: The estate itself becomes obligated on the contract, and the non-debtor party departs the ranks of ordinary creditors and becomes a priority claimant . . . . Because of this by-product of assumption, here it is important that there be a threshold test to prevent prejudice to other creditors.

It is not difficult, though, to describe generally the sort of situation to which assumption should apply: Assumption is proper when the estate, as successor to the debtor, can obtain the benefit of some contract or lease asset . . . only at the cost of taking on the debtor's performance obligations. Any other use of "assumption" confers priority for priority's sake . . . .

Countryman's definition reflects the view that assumption of a liability is proper only when required as the price of capturing an asset, although somewhat indirectly. An executory contract is, in Countryman's formulation, "a contract under which the obligation of both the bankrupt and the other party to the contract are so far unperformed that the failure of either to complete performance would constitute a material breach excusing the performance of the other."

The Countryman definition seems to have, in the assumption context, two elements of significance. First, it requires, with its specification that material performance be due from both parties, that there *be* an asset side and a liability side to the contract or lease. If it is an asset only (because the debtor has fully performed), then that asset will simply pass into the estate without special fanfare; the estate can sue to enforce the non-debtor party's obligations if necessary (or abandon the asset if it chooses). On the other hand if it is a liability only (because the non-debtor party has fully performed), then the non-debtor appropriately has just a non-priority claim against the estate.

Second, the definition apparently was intended to require, through the "material breach" specification, that the non-debtor's remaining performance obligations be conditional on the debtor's. . . .

But while Countryman's definition thus seems at least in part appropriate in the assumption context, it suffers from the same problem that has plagued the executory contracts area for nearly two centuries: It uses conceptual intermediaries to express what surely could be expressed more understandably in direct fashion. If the "material breach" component of the definition is designed to focus the inquiry on whether the non-debtor's duties are conditioned upon the debtor's as a matter of non-bankruptcy law, then why not say so? . . . I wonder whether an "executory" contract might not best be defined simply as a contract under which (a) debtor and non-debtor each have unperformed obligations, and (b) the debtor, if it ceased further performance, would have no right to the other party's continued performance.

The important point here, though, is that in the rejection context it simply should not matter how an "executory" contract is defined, because the definition . . . serves no meaningful purpose. . . . [C]onditioning rejection upon a test of "executoriness" creates pointless confusion because the result should be the same in any event. The very existence of a definitional threshold suggests that there is something important at stake when there is not. . . .

D. Standards Governing the Assume-or-Reject Election

1. The "Business Judgment" Standard

. . . [A]nother element of the basic assume-or-reject election should be understood—the question of what standards are applicable to the choice between assumption and rejection. . . .

The determination whether to assume or reject a contract or lease is not materially different from any other investment decision made by a trustee. The issue is the same: What use or disposition of the assets of the estate is best calculated to maximize the return to creditors? . . .

. . . [T]hat is the sense of the general rule that a "business judgment" standard will apply to court review of the decision to reject ordinary executory contracts. As that label suggests, courts usually will not substitute their judgment for the trustee's or the debtor in possession's on the question whether to assume or to reject a contract or lease.

2. The "Burdensome" Standard

Despite the prevalence of the "business judgment" standard, there has persisted a minority view that, to justify rejection, a contract or lease must be "burdensome" to the estate . . . .

Although invariably based on the kinship between rejection and abandonment, arguments for a "burdensome" standard in fact reflect a superficial view of that relationship. . . . The fact that only worthless or burdensome assets are abandoned hardly suggests that an estate should be compelled to invest other funds in an executory contract or lease that is not otherwise the most favorable or appropriate investment.

But the analogy to ordinary abandonment doctrine is flawed for a more fundamental reason. . . . [I]f a trustee abandons valuable property, the creditors can complain of a breach of the trustee's fiduciary duty to maximize the value of the estate. But in the executory contract or lease context, it is not the creditors who complain when the trustee wishes to reject . . . . Instead, it is the non-debtor party to the contract or lease, who argues not that the trustee should maximize the value of the estate, but that the trustee should maximize the return to that party at the expense of the estate. That argument stands abandonment doctrine on its head.

3. "Balancing"

Even if a "burdensome" standard is rejected in favor of a "business judgment" standard, should the interests of the non-debtor party nonetheless be considered in some fashion? Should there be, as some courts have suggested, a "balancing of interests" . . . ? Should there be a "balancing of equities"?

Again, when rejection is properly understood simply as the estate's decision not to invest in a debtor's contract or lease asset by assuming it, it seems clear that there should be no "balancing" or other special consideration of the interests of the non-debtor contracting party. The reason: applying a balancing test gives the nondebtor party more favorable treatment than that afforded to other claimants, *just because of the "executoriness" of the contract.* . . .

IV. "Avoiding Power" Rejection

Executory contracts doctrine has been confounded by persistent confusion over the term "rejection." . . . [T]hat term has often irresistibly—and incorrectly—suggested to modern courts that the point of the doctrine is the repudiation or cancellation of contract liabilities. . . .

Another more significant result of confusion about "rejection" has been the creation of a distinct doctrine—"avoiding-power" rejection, as I call it—only spuriously related to basic executory contracts doctrine. That separate doctrine, like bankruptcy's explicit avoiding powers, terminates the rights of third parties in or to property in which the debtor had an interest. It does so, however, without any of the justifications of the avoiding powers, but instead only because the third party's rights arise under a contract that happens to be "executory" when the bankruptcy commences.

. . . I begin the examination of avoiding-power rejection by looking first at one context, the bankruptcy of a real property lessor, in which the law has long been clear that rejection properly has no avoiding-power effect.

A. Introduction: The Two-Asset Problem and The Case of Leases

The prototype executory contracts situation . . . is that of the real property lessee in bankruptcy. In a lessor's bankruptcy, however, the basic assume-or-reject election and rejection-as-breach doctrines still apply. . . .

But what of the rule now set out in Bankruptcy Code section 365(h)? That section provides that despite the rejection of a real property lease in a lessor's bankruptcy, the lessee may remain in possession for the term of the lease . . . .

Superficially, the "rule" of section 365(h) seems to produce an asymmetry in the treatment of a lease depending upon whether the lessee or the lessor has filed a bankruptcy case. In the lessee's case there is, after rejection, no continuing relationship between the estate and the lessor. But in the lessor's case the statute contemplates a continuing relationship notwithstanding rejection. Despite the common modern misconception to the contrary, however, that asymmetry is not a creature of the statute itself. It is instead the consequence of an obvious but important difference between a lessee and a lessor.

A lessee has but one basic asset in connection with a lease: the right, under the lease, to occupy the leased premises for the specified term. . . .

By contrast, in a lessor's bankruptcy there are *two* distinct assets at issue. One is the lessor's rights in the lease. That asset . . . raises all of the usual executory contracts issues. Quite apart from the lessor's rights in the *lease*, though, the lessor's estate also includes the lessor's interest in the *underlying* asset, the property which is the subject of the lease. . . .

Focusing on the underlying asset, then, it is clear that the lessor's estate includes, at the moment of bankruptcy, only the lessor's interests in and rights with respect to that asset, which are limited. . . . [A]ll that remains in the lessor at the time of bankruptcy is the reversionary interest. And because only the debtor's interest in property becomes property of the estate, *the reversionary interest is all that is available for the estate to succeed to unless the lessee's rights and interests are somehow terminated*, for example, under one of the avoiding powers.

Thus, while the "rule" that seemingly protects the lessee's interest does resolve certain practical issues, it is fundamentally not a distinct rule at all, and it does not produce the asymmetry in treatment of lessors and lessees. Rather, it simply applies the general principle that the estate succeeds only to the debtor's rights and interests, and reflects, correctly, that there is nothing about rejection of the *lease* asset in the lessor's bankruptcy that terminates the lessee's right to possession of the *underlying* asset. . . .

If the "rule" were otherwise—if the lessor's trustee could, by rejecting the lease, terminate the lessee's right to possession of the property—then rejection would function as an avoiding power. But the "rule" recognizes that there simply is nothing about leases generally, or about the "executoriness" of a lease, that offends some bankruptcy policy, justifying a departure from the general principle of recognizing in bankruptcy rights in and to property that are recognized by non-bankruptcy law. . . .

In the real property lease context, then, the statutes always have recognized that rejection is not an avoiding power. That recognition has led, however, to one of the great ironies of executory contracts law in the U.S.: the notion that, because the statutory recognition referred to real property leases, rejection is an avoiding power in other two-asset contexts. That notion can be traced largely to a single case, *In re New York Investors Mutual Group, Inc.*

B. The Case of Real Property Sales Contracts

1. In re New York Investors Mutual Group, Inc.

New York Investors, decided by a district court in 1956, involved a situation that probably has generated more litigation than any other in the avoiding-power rejection area: a real property vendor in bankruptcy. In *New York Investors*, the debtor had contracted prior to bankruptcy to sell certain real property. A down payment had been made and closing was to occur some months later. The contract, which was recorded, gave the vendee a lien against the property for recovery of the down payment.

. . . [T]he contract was . . . rejected. . . . [U]nder New York law, . . . a vendee is regarded as the equitable owner of the property after entering into a binding contract to purchase it, and is entitled to specific performance of the contract. The vendee argued that it was entitled to specific performance even as against the trustee.

Unpersuaded, the court approved the rejection of the contract and allowed the sale of the property to another party by the estate, although it did enforce the vendee's contractual lien for recovery of its down payment from the sale proceeds. . . . [T]he vendee was left with only a damages claim. . . .

. . . [T]he court in *New York Investors* failed to recognize the two-asset problem before it and the underlying asymmetry in the position of vendors and vendees. The vendor owned two assets of relevance: its rights in the contract for sale, and its residual rights in the real property which was the subject of the contract. The key question was not whether the contract could be rejected—of course it could—but rather the effect of rejection on the second asset. As in the case of leases, nothing about rejection of the *contract* asset—*i.e.*, the estate's decision not to assume it—suggests that the estate should have greater rights in the *underlying* asset than had the debtor. . . .

Remarkably, the court in *New York Investors* showed no real awareness that it was creating, essentially without precedent, a new title-clearing doctrine. . . .

But the court in *New York Investors* ignored the fact that bankruptcy law's treatment of claimants other than parties to "executory" contracts distinguishes among them based upon their differing rights in or to property of the debtor, as in the recognition of security interests. Indeed, bankruptcy law recognizes third parties' equitable interests in property, including interests the essence of which is the right to obtain the specific property. . . .

2. The Bankruptcy Code

Concern with the plight of real property purchasers, particularly consumer vendees in possession under long-term installment contracts, led to the inclusion in the Bankruptcy Code of two protective provisions not contained in the Bankruptcy Act. The first, section 365(i), is very similar to section 365(h) regarding lessees. It provides that . . . a vendee who is in possession may remain in possession, continuing to make payments . . ., and the trustee must deliver title in accordance with the contract.

Section 365(i), then, marks an additional area where avoiding-power rejection is explicitly precluded. . . .

The Code's second new protective provision, section 365(j), takes a different approach. It applies where the vendee is not in possession, and it merely provides that upon rejection the vendee has a lien for recovery of amounts paid on the purchase price. . . .

Many cases under the Code seem to follow the *New York Investors* avoiding-power rejection rule implicitly, still largely without inquiry into reasons that might support it. But a growing number of cases evidence a deep uneasiness with the rule . . . .

3. Retrospective

What conclusion is to be drawn from this three-decade tangle of real property vendor cases? . . . [I]n my view only one important conclusion is very clear. All of this trouble—defining "executory" contracts, determining the effect of state court decrees, applying "balancing" tests and so on—is caused *by trying to apply a rule that has no reason.*

Each of the usual avoiding powers is supported by some articulable policy . . . . But avoiding-power rejection is based upon a supposed policy that does not exist, a policy against "executoriness." . . . To say that rejection serves the goals of enhancing the estate or equalizing treatment of creditors adds nothing; the same goals would support the cancellation of all property-related rights in bankruptcy.

. . . Avoiding-power rejection, purportedly an application of basic executory contracts doctrine, is in fact antithetical to it; with avoiding-power rejection, the happenstance of "executoriness" is the key.

C. The Case of Licenses of Intangible Property

The use of avoiding-power rejection has not been limited to the termination of rights to real property. Recently, its most notorious use has been the cancellation of interests of licensees and franchisees of intangible personal property, such as patents, copyrights, trade secrets and the like, in bankruptcy cases of licensors or franchisors. Precisely the same two-asset issue arises here as in the case of leases and sales contracts: The debtor-licensor or debtor-franchisor has rights in the license or franchise agreement, and also has residual rights in the underlying asset, the intangible property.

Does rejection of the agreement terminate the non-debtor party's right to the licensed or franchised use of the underlying asset? Because the estate succeeds only to the debtor's rights in that asset, the answer should be no. Rejection is not a rescission of the license or franchise, but merely that estate's determination not to assume it. . . .

The case that illustrates perhaps better than any other what is wrong with avoiding-power rejection, and how the Countryman test of an "executory" contract fuels it, is the Fourth Circuit's decision in *Lubrizol Enterprises Inc. v. Richmond Metal Finishers, Inc.* There the debtor had licensed certain technology to Lubrizol non-exclusively, and sought in its chapter 11 case to reject the license and terminate Lubrizol's rights to the technology. The key issue, thought the court, was the hunt for mutual "executoriness."

. . . The court went on to approve rejection of the license and termination of the licensee's interest, relying in part on the absence of any special protection for licensees in section 365.

. . . Lubrizol had what everyone apparently believed was a perfectly valid license. Nothing suggests that the license was in any way subject to termination by any creditor of, or purchaser from, the debtor under non-bankruptcy law, or that it was in any other way avoidable under bankruptcy law. It also seems quite clear that if the license had been found to have been non-"executory," the court would have enforced it. . . .

The court did not pause to ask why the happenstance of "executoriness" should control an issue so important as the licensee's continued ability to use the technology. Its only real attempt at an explanation of the result was to observe that the "clear" purpose of section 365(g), the rejection-as-breach rule, "is to provide only a damages remedy for the non-bankrupt party" . . . .

Concern with the *Lubrizol* result also led in 1987 to the introduction in Congress of the "Intellectual Property Bankruptcy Protection Act" . . . .

D. Avoiding-Power Rejection: The Broad View

. . . *Lubrizol* is but one of many manifestations of the same elephant: avoiding-power rejection and the two-asset problem.

The English statute appears to address the two-asset problem broadly, by recognizing explicitly that "disclaimer" of a contract "does not, except so far as is necessary for the purpose of releasing the bankrupt, the bankrupt's estate and the trustee from any liability, affect the rights or liabilities of any other person." . . .

In the U.S., though, the piecemeal treatment of the issue, and the failure to recognize it as an issue transcending the pieces, has led to the current state of disarray. . . .

Whether the debtor is a licensor, lessor, vendor, or mortgagor, or any other owner of real or personal property in or to which a third party has rights under a contract, the analysis should be the same. Rejection of the contract by the estate—the estate's decision not to assume—is not a rescission or cancellation of the contract. It is merely the estate's decision not to become obligated on it. Thus, rejection of the *contract* does not enhance the estate's rights to the *underlying asset*. The estate acquires that asset, like all other assets, in the "same plight and condition that the debtor himself held it, and subject to all the equities impressed upon it in the hands of the debtor," even though clearly the estate is not itself bound by the contract.

As a starting premise, therefore, the position of the estate is no different from that of any other ordinary transferee acquiring the underlying asset from the debtor without assuming the debtor's contract obligations. The proper inquiry is what the position of such a non-assuming transferee would be vis-à-vis the non-debtor party. To the extent that the non-debtor could enforce its rights as against such a transferee of the underlying asset—by specific performance, other injunctive relief, replevin, or some other remedy—it should be able to do so as against the estate despite the rejection of the contract. . . .

It must be clearly understood, though, that this analysis does not somehow elevate the non-debtor party over other claimants. The non-debtor's right to the property or to some use of it, like any other right in or to property in bankruptcy, is good against the estate only if it survives the true avoiding powers. . . . Thus, the contract right in or to the property is enforced in bankruptcy only to the extent that it was a right *good against other claimants in the first place.*

That point also makes clear the error in arguing that recognition of the non-debtor's rights in or to property will somehow defeat a fundamental purpose of rejection—to insure that parties to executory contracts are treated the same as other claimants. Bankruptcy law distinguishes between *other* claimants on the basis of rights in or to property. . . .

Five arguments contrary to this analysis are common, and should be addressed specifically:

The "Property-Rights-v.-Contract-Rights" Argument.

It is sometimes suggested that the key to whether the non-debtor party's rights to the underlying asset will be recognized after rejection of the contract is whether that party has an interest *in* the asset in the strictest sense. The argument is that "property rights" survive rejection, but "contract rights" do not. . . .

Such arguments . . . are simply an outgrowth of the fundamental misconception of rejection discussed . . . above. . . . The contract is not rescinded by rejection, the estate simply does not become obligated on it. Thus, the estate's rights in the *underlying* asset—the copyright, trade secret, patent, equipment, or other property—still are no greater than the debtor had to give, absent a true avoiding power attack. The estate acquires only the rights to that asset that would be acquired by any other ordinary transferee who declined to assume the debtor's contract obligations. . . .

The important point is that, under whatever label, non-bankruptcy law clearly recognizes the lessee's or licensee's right to a use of the property good as against the owner, any purchaser from or creditor of the owner, and the rest of the world. Since there is no *general* bankruptcy policy against such a right, there is no reason why it should be terminated by executory contracts doctrine. . . .

The "No-Specific-Performance" Argument.

This argument suggests that the entire purpose of rejection is to preclude specific performance, as a way of preventing discriminatory elevation of the non-debtor party to priority over other creditors. . . .

Such observations reflect a partial truth. The purpose of executory contracts doctrine is to insulate the estate from itself becoming unadvisedly obligated on executory contracts of the debtor, thereby elevating the non-debtor parties to administrative priority. . . .

That point does not establish, however, that rejection cuts off all rights to specific performance. Rather, it establishes that rejection cuts off rights against the estate that are dependent upon the estate itself being obligated *on the contract*. And the fact that the estate is not obligated on a contract does not in turn mean that it acquires all-encompassing rights to the underlying asset to which the contract relates. . . .

Nor is that conclusion just a matter of dry logic. The principle behind the "no-specific-performance" argument is that allowing specific performance would prefer one claimant over others similarly situated. But bankruptcy law recognizes that not all claimants are similarly situated; those with rights to property, good as against competing claimants under state law, do not lose those rights. Thus, there is no elevation to priority. The non-debtor party started off differently situated as compared to other claimants, and the analysis simply takes account of and preserves that difference, consonant with the rest of bankruptcy law. Again, the point is that if such a right is good outside and inside bankruptcy as a general matter, its continued existence should not turn on the "executoriness" of a contract, a matter of pure happenstance. To hold otherwise does not preserve equality, it affirmatively demotes the non-debtor.

The "Claims-and-Discharge" Argument.

This argument . . . also focuses on the specific performance remedy. It suggests, in somewhat related fashion, that if the non-debtor's right to specific performance can be fit within the Code's "claim" definition, which also renders it subject to discharge, it does not survive rejection. . . .

The "claims-and-discharge" argument is, I suggest, beside the point altogether. The reason: it focuses on the *debtor's* liability under the contract. . . . The issue here, though, is not the debtor's liability or how that liability translates into a claim. Rather, it is the right of the non-debtor party to enforce its rights in or to property *against the estate* as successor to the debtor's interest in that property. . . .

An issue to which the "claims-and-discharge" argument *is* relevant is whether the non-debtor can specifically enforce a contract *against the debtor* post-bankruptcy. That issue is present in cases where, for example, the non-debtor seeks to enforce a covenant not to compete, or an exclusive performance covenant, typically by negative injunction, against an individual debtor who has filed bankruptcy. Rejection of the contract in which such a covenant is contained should be irrelevant; the determinative issue is the impact of the debtor's discharge.

The "Negative Inference" Argument.

This argument suggests that whatever conclusion might otherwise be dictated by logic, policy or common sense, the negative inference to be drawn from section 365 is that Congress has endorsed avoiding-power rejection in all contexts other than those explicitly carved out by the special provisions of the statute. Many of the principal avoiding-power rejection cases are premised upon this view.

What the legislative record more accurately reflects, however, is that whenever Congress has been confronted with the consequences of the avoiding-power rejection doctrine in a particular context, it has expressed its disapproval of the doctrine with a specific provision. . . . It does not appear that avoiding-power rejection doctrine as a whole ever has received congressional consideration, much less approval.

Avoiding-power rejection is, I suggest, simply more freight than negative inference will bear. It requires that "rejection" be assigned a meaning fundamentally at odds with both the history and purpose of executory contracts doctrine, with no legislative history in support. It requires a corresponding abatement of the general principle, explicit in the statute and its legislative history, that a bankruptcy estate succeeds only to the debtor's rights and interests in property. And it dictates that the result in each case depend not upon some articulable policy or principle, but instead upon the happenstance of "executoriness." That absurdity is not compelled by the statute, and should not be read between its lines.

The "Goal-of-Rehabilitation" Argument.

This final argument probably is the one commonly thought to carry the most weight. It suggests that, while termination of rights to property by rejection of "executory" contracts may be harsh, it is necessary as a way of furthering modern bankruptcy law's goal of promoting financial rehabilitation. . . .

The notion that executory contracts doctrine is somehow uniquely related to rehabilitation rather than liquidation is simply incorrect. . . .

But there are two much more important responses to the "goal-of-rehabilitation" argument. First, that argument, like the argument that rejection is designed to serve the goal of equal distribution, proves far too much. It would support, at a minimum, the termination of all rights in or to property in bankruptcy rehabilitation cases, even where those rights are otherwise good as against the debtor and transferees and creditors of the debtor. But bankruptcy law does not elsewhere purport to accomplish such an end. . . .

The second, related response is this article's most fundamental point. Perhaps the "goal-of-rehabilitation" argument or some other argument might support, say, bankruptcy law's termination of the rights of real property vendees, or cancellation of business franchises, or some other similar consequence in other identified contexts. . . .

But to whatever extent bankruptcy law is to have the effect of terminating rights to property—a matter for considered legislative judgment—the result surely should not depend upon the "executoriness" of a contract. "Executoriness" is happenstance. There is no independent policy against it. Executory contracts doctrine was designed to eliminate any prejudice that might flow from it. That rights to property otherwise good in bankruptcy should turn on it is nonsense, not curable through definitions of "executory" contracts ever more refined (or ever more ad hoc) or "balancing" and "good faith" tests ever more subtle.

V. CONCLUSION

I began by posing this question: What exactly does it mean to "reject" a contract? I have suggested in this article that the answer is vastly simpler than is commonly thought. Rejection is not the power to release, revoke, repudiate, void, avoid, cancel or terminate, or even to breach, contract obligations. Rather, rejection is a bankruptcy estate's election to decline a contract or lease asset. It is the decision not to assume, not to obligate the estate on the contract or lease as the price of obtaining the continuing benefits of the non-debtor party's performance. That decision leaves the non-debtor in the same position as all others who have dealt with the debtor, by giving rise to a presumption that the debtor has "breached"—*i.e.*, will not perform—its obligations. The debtor's obligations are unaffected, and provide the basis for a claim.

Profound and pervasive confusion surrounds those simple principles. . . . Much of the confusion follows from focusing on the question of which contracts are "executory." To ask that question is to suggest irresistibly that rejection must be an important "power" that the "executory" contracts definition serves to limit. . . .

But all of that is aura, not essence. The definition in fact serves the rather pedestrian function of identifying a type of asset that happens to be intertwined with a liability. Executory contracts doctrine simply protects the estate from that liability unless it is knowingly assumed as the price of obtaining the asset. In situations where the liability is not assumed, the doctrine is designed to make the happenstance of "executoriness" irrelevant to the treatment of the non-debtor party. Thus, when the estate wishes to reject, the definition of an "executory" contract is all but meaningless: The non-debtor party to a rejected "executory" contract is in the same position as the non-debtor party to a non-"executory" contract, and the superfluous "rejection" of a non-"executory" contract is a case of harmless error.

The confusion surrounding rejection has led, though, to the mistaken view that rejection of an "executory" contract somehow abates or alters contract liabilities, thereby diminishing the non-debtor's rights. Relatedly, the confusion has yielded the insupportable notion that rejection of a contract also serves as an avoiding power which clears the estate's title to any underlying asset to which the contract relates. . . .

The point here is not that the courts apply a policy with which I disagree. It is that there is no underlying policy. The problem is not that the emperor has no clothes, but that the clothes have no emperor. Much of executory contracts jurisprudence is simply doctrine without meaning.

The understanding of "rejection" set out in this article is consistent with the language, logic and history of section 365. It offers direct answers to a number of otherwise seemingly intractable executory contracts problems, answers that square with other bankruptcy principles and require little ad hoc adjustment. . . .

The conclusion to be drawn from this article, though, is that the core of section 365—10 years young but 170 years old—is itself due for an overhaul. Whatever one may think of the goals to be achieved by rejection in particular, or by executory contracts law in general, no purpose is served by stating them indirectly or obscurely. Present law demonstrates that the costs of doing so—chronic uncertainty and constant litigation—are unacceptable.

Jay L. Westbrook
A Functional Analysis of Executory Contracts
74 MINN. L. REV. 227 (1989)[*]

INTRODUCTION

Bankruptcy is that volume of the law that might have been written by Lewis Carroll, every conventional legal principle refracted through the prism of insolvency. . . . In no chapter of that volume has the law become more psychedelic than in the one titled "executory contracts." . . . Critics express growing concern about decisions that are deeply disruptive of commercial expectations, concerns awkwardly and inadequately addressed by recent congressional patchwork.

Resolution of these difficulties has recently grown more pressing as more bankruptcy cases are filed with rejection of executory contracts as a primary motive. Although these include large and visible proceedings like the *Continental Airlines* case, the greater social and commercial problem lies in thousands of medium sized cases, from the soap opera actress who wants to jump to another network to the Burger King franchisee who wants to shuck its anti-competition covenant. . . . [W]e must completely reconstruct the fundamentals of bankruptcy contract law. My purpose in this Article is to begin that task by proposing a new and relatively simple conceptual framework to replace the bemusing complexity of current case law.

For more than a century, federal courts sitting in bankruptcy have assumed that a pre-bankruptcy contract must be "executory" in order to be assumed or rejected by a trustee in bankruptcy. Because assumption and rejection are merely bankruptcy terms for performance or breach by the trustee, one can say that the courts have required a finding of "executoriness" in a contract before the trustee is permitted to perform or breach it. In the mid-1970s, in two articles in the *Minnesota Law Review*, Professor Countryman took a great muddle of confused and often wrong decisions and made them coherent by developing his famous "material breach" test for determining if a contract satisfied the courts' requirement of executoriness. . . .

I believe we are now ready to build upon Professor Countryman's brilliant accomplishment and to take the necessary further step: abolishing the requirement of executoriness altogether. That is, I suggest that no such threshold finding should be necessary to assume or reject a bankruptcy contract. Instead, I will argue that the estate, as successor to the debtor's pre-bankruptcy contracts, is in exactly the same position as any other contract party under nonbankruptcy law, with just three exceptions: a) pro rata payment of a usually small percentage of the breach of contract claims against the debtor; b) denial of specific performance against the estate of purely contractual covenants; and c) the effect of the avoiding powers. . . .

I call my approach "functional," because it proceeds by working through the problem from first principles. . . .

I. THE PROBLEM

. . .

A. THE FUNDAMENTALS OF BANKRUPTCY CONTRACTS

The question addressed in the bankruptcy courts under the rubric "executory contracts" is the treatment of contracts to which the debtor was a party prior to bankruptcy. Each pre-bankruptcy contract represents a bundle of rights belonging to the estate (the obligations of the other party to the contract) and potential claims against the estate (the obligations of the debtor under the contract). The trustee has the choice of "assuming" a pre-bankruptcy contract or "rejecting" it. These are merely bankruptcy terms for performance or breach. If the trustee assumes a contract, the estate is bound to perform it and the other party to the contract (Other Party) is required to perform as well. If the trustee rejects the contract, the estate has breached and is liable for a damage claim by the Other Party, while the Other Party ordinarily is excused from further performance under normal contract principles. The trustee is given broad discretion to assume or reject, whichever course will maximize the value of the bankruptcy estate and minimize claims against it.

If the trustee rejects the contract, the damage claim is calculated under state contract law, but is treated as a pre-petition debt . . . . By contrast, when a contract is assumed, the estate's obligations are treated as post-petition administration claims . . . .

. . . [T]he trustee's decision to assume or reject can have some fairly remarkable consequences.

. . .

B. Recent History

1. Context

. . . The precedents governing bankruptcy contracts had become a nightmare of confusion and inconsistency by the mid-1970s. Professor Countryman took this doctrine as he found it in the cases and made sense of it. . . .

3. The Material Breach Test

Professor Countryman . . . focused upon the problem as it was actually articulated in the courts: the existence of a pre-bankruptcy contract that could be characterized as executory. From this perspective he developed what has become the standard test for an executory contract:

> [A] contract under which the obligation of both the bankrupt and the other party to the contract are so far unperformed that the failure of either to complete performance would constitute a material breach excusing the performance of the other.

Only a contract that satisfied this test could be assumed by the estate. . . .

The test has been enormously helpful for three reasons. First, it prevents assumption of a contract unless the Other Party owes a material performance. . . . Therefore, this test avoids assumption of contracts when assumption would not be beneficial to the estate.

Second, the "material breach" language focuses the courts' attention on questions of state law. . . .

Finally, and most importantly, the material breach test often serves as a proxy for "finality" in a contractual transaction. . . .

. . . [W]e can now stand on the shoulders of Countryman and see over the wall of "executoriness." When we do so, we can see that the wall should be torn down.

C. The Current Difficulties

Ironically, the most obvious and striking errors in the recent cases have arisen from the greatest benefit of the material breach test, the indirect identification of cases in which the Other Party has acquired a nonrejectable property interest. . . . Unfortunately, this effect of the test leads many courts to infer that executoriness must be found in a contract or it cannot be rejected. The consequence is a contract neither assumable nor rejectable, leaving it in a legal limbo. The absurdity of that idea has been less damaging, however, than the next step taken by a number of courts, positing that obligations owed to the Other Party can be rejected right out of existence. The final, and most serious, complex of errors in this line are the cases that suggest that rejection can void property interests created pre-petition by state law, even though they are not avoidable under the statutory avoiding powers. This last blunder brings the material breach test full circle, compounding the very error that it at first prevented. . . .

II. FUNCTIONAL ANALYSIS

. . . The executoriness requirement is a limitation on assumption or rejection that is not found in the Code. . . . The executoriness requirement has been poured into the word "executory" in section 365(a) by a century of caselaw. . . .

This section presents a functional analysis of the proper treatment of bankruptcy contracts without reference to the caselaw requirement of "executoriness." I argue that general principles of bankruptcy explain why bankruptcy contracts are sometimes treated differently than contracts outside of bankruptcy. . . .

A. The Basics

1. What Makes Contracts Unique in Bankruptcy?

Contracts present unique problems in bankruptcy. The reason is that every contract consists of both rights, which become property of the estate under section 541, and obligations, which become claims under section 502. Furthermore, these rights and obligations often are interdependent, so that realization of a right is dependent upon performance of an obligation. These characteristics of a contract make the trustee's calculation of benefit and cost to the estate far more complicated than for other property and other claims. . . .

2. Nonbankruptcy Law

In the process of maximizing the benefit of the contractual rights the trustee has inherited, and minimizing the burdens of the contractual obligations, the trustee must begin with the central fact that these rights and obligations are completely defined by nonbankruptcy law, usually state contract law.

. . . [T]he contract attaches to the estate without any reference to section 365 and exactly as it existed at state law at the moment of bankruptcy.

Even the trustee's "power" to assume or reject in section 365(a) is not a special rule of bankruptcy law. This option means merely that the trustee may (must) perform or breach any single contract. We know that is what it means because the Code itself says just that. Yet state law gives this option to every party to every contract. . . . [S]tate contract law permits a party to choose between performing or breaching and paying damages . . . . The debtor had that option and so does the trustee.

. . . The contractual rights are property of the estate and, as with any property, the trustee will realize on them or abandon them. The trustee will abandon property if the costs of realizing upon it exceed its value. . . .

. . . The trustee's duty to creditors will be to choose the most profitable alternative, thus maximizing the estate. . . .

3. The Limitation of Remedies In Bankruptcy

Now we introduce the special effect of bankruptcy principles for the first time. . . . [T]he trustee's calculations of benefit and cost will differ greatly from the ordinary contract party because of remedies rules unique to bankruptcy. . . .

The principle that modifies the trustee's position, making it much more favorable than that of the pre-petition debtor, is equality of distribution. . . .

From the equality principle comes the rule of pro rata distribution to pre-petition unsecured creditors. The pro rata rule requires that unsecured creditors share proportionately in distributions, with the result that almost never are they paid in full. Their claims are calculated in full under state law, . . . but their actual relief, the payment of the claims, can be thought of as being in little tiny Bankruptcy Dollars, which may be worth only ten cents in U.S. dollars. In sharp contrast, if the trustee assumes a contract, then it is converted into an estate obligation, a post-petition obligation, and the Other Party becomes entitled to full performance or payment as an administration claim. Because administration claims are paid first in any distribution, they are usually paid in full, 100 cent U.S. dollars.

The resulting change in the trustee's Net Value calculation produces much of the "magic" of executory contract doctrine in bankruptcy. When the trustee calculates the cost of breaching an obligation, it figures the breach claim in full U.S. dollars under state law, but it must calculate real, net costs in light of paying that claim in Bankruptcy Dollars, that is, paying only a percentage of the claim . . . . Conversely, when the trustee calculates the cost of performance, it must figure that cost in 100 cent U.S. dollars, because it must pay for performance as an administration claim. . . .

. . . [T]he breach-claim will be paid in Bankruptcy Dollars, while the performance cost will be paid in full U.S. dollars as a cost of administration. . . . Thus, the trustee often will breach-and-pay when any other contract party in the same position will perform. The dramatic loss of position of the Other Party flows directly from the fundamental bankruptcy rule that all unsecured creditors are paid pro rata and the fundamental bankruptcy fact that such payments often are a tiny percentage of the amount owed under state law. . . .

To summarize, the estate generally should assume only profitable contracts of the debtor, because the severe undercompensation of unsecured creditors in bankruptcy will make it worthwhile to reject (breach) all unprofitable contracts. . . .

B. Specific Performance

. . . Professor Countryman . . . identified the rule that specific performance is not available against the bankruptcy trustee. The reason behind the rule is the principle of equality of distribution. Specific performance is in effect 100% "payment"; that is, performance in full. Giving that remedy to one pre-petition unsecured creditor, the Other Party, would seriously violate the equality principle as to all other unsecured creditors, leaving them with a far smaller distribution. . . .

C. An Interest in the Thing Itself

In general, bankruptcy law enforces what may loosely be called "property rights" existing under nonbankruptcy law. More precisely, bankruptcy will enforce nonbankruptcy remedies on behalf of an Other Party if they are remedies entitling the Other Party to dominion over a specific asset, unless the Other Party's interest is subject to avoidance under the bankruptcy avoiding powers. This "property" principle is central to bankruptcy law because it is by far the most important exception to the principle of equality of distribution. The rule derived from the property principle, payment in full to the Other Party of the proceeds of sale of such an asset, is the most important exception to the rule of pro rata payment. . . .

An interest in a specific asset that entitles the owner of the interest to the asset itself, or to priority payment of the proceeds of its sale, is largely congruent with what is called a property interest. I call it an "Interest in the Thing Itself" (ITI). . . . [A]n ITI is an interest under nonbankruptcy law that entitles its beneficiary to dominion over a specific asset or to priority in the proceeds of the sale of that asset.

. . . [B]ankruptcy law enforces ITIs created under nonbankruptcy law. . . .

The Code further refines the definition of the Other Party's property by reference to the avoiding powers. . . . If the Other Party's claimed interest—its bundle of remedies—survives the avoiding powers, then it is an ITI for bankruptcy purposes.

. . . [I]t is accurate to say that bankruptcy courts will enforce a nonbankruptcy ITI. . . . That fact is crucial to understanding bankruptcy contracts because, as we have seen, the treatment of bankruptcy contracts is governed by the limitations on the Other Party's remedies imposed by the equality principle and the pro rata rule. The enforcement of ITIs is the key exception to those limitations. . . .

D. Step-By-Step Analysis

. . . To summarize, the treatment of bankruptcy contracts is not a function of special bankruptcy rules about executory contracts, but rather a straightforward consequence of the bankruptcy policies limiting the Other Party's remedies in a way that realizes on good pre-petition bargains and minimizes bad ones, all for the benefit of unsecured creditors generally. Nonbankruptcy law often fails to give the Other Party an ITI and therefore relegates it to the poor plight of unsecured creditors generally, an entirely appropriate result and only inequitable in the sense that life is unfair.

The analysis becomes complex in these cases when nonbankruptcy law is unclear about the Other Party's right to an ITI. The complexity introduced by an ITI lies in determining if state law does treat the Other Party's interest as an ITI . . . and, if so, determining if the ITI could survive the trustee's avoiding powers. . . .

E. IMPACT OF THE AVOIDING POWERS

A thorough re-analysis of bankruptcy contract problems is not possible without considering the impact of the avoiding powers. They complete the yin and yang of the equality principle and the property principle in bankruptcy contracts. Although the enforcement of ITIs is an important exception to the equality principle in bankruptcy contracts, as elsewhere in bankruptcy, equality re-emerges as a limitation on the property principle through the operation of the avoiding powers. . . .

The starting point is the proposition that in every bankruptcy contract case where the debtor, as buyer or seller, performed prior to bankruptcy, the debtor's performance (payment or delivery) may be avoidable under the strong-arm clause or as a preference or a fraudulent conveyance. . . .

The impact of the avoiding powers in contract cases is not limited to the debtor's pre-bankruptcy performance. They may operate with respect to the very promise that the debtor made in the contract, if that promise created an ITI under nonbankruptcy law. . . .

F. DISCHARGE

Discharge is almost never the subject of discussions of executory contracts, yet its effect in changing state contract law results is every bit as important as the principles already discussed. . . .

Covenants against competition are good examples of the operation of discharge in bankruptcy contract cases. . . .

. . . The important thing here is that the right to discharge is the correct place to tussle over this issue, rather than it being the offshoot of some special rule about bankruptcy contracts. . . .

The key point about this sort of case is that any felt inequity is solely a function of the discharge. . . .

G. ASSUMPTION AND REJECTION: DECIDING TO PERFORM OR BREACH

. . . Although scholars and practitioners generally agree that assumption means performance and rejection means breach, that usage conceals a semantic hitch. . . .

Assumption is not performance, it is the decision to perform. Rejection is not breach, but the decision to breach. . . .

H. SUMMARY OF THE FUNCTIONAL APPROACH

To summarize briefly the main points of a functional analysis:

1. There is no special bankruptcy "power" to assume or reject contracts. The trustee (or DIP) has the power to perform or breach contracts, just like any other contract party under state law, and it inherits that power from the pre-petition debtor along with the debtor's pending contract rights and obligations.

2. There should be no requirement of a threshold finding that a contract is "executory" as a prerequisite to performance or breach by the trustee. The trustee must abandon or realize upon each contract right in the estate and must perform or breach each contract obligation. When contract law makes certain rights and obligations interdependent, the trustee's right to realize upon the rights will be dependent upon performance of the obligations, as for any other contract party.

3. The only justifiable changes in contract results in bankruptcy are those arising from bankruptcy's limitations on the Other Party's remedies and from the avoiding powers. The principal

provisions involved are the pro rata distribution rules, the corollary rule against specific performance or rescission against the trustee, the avoiding powers, and the bankruptcy discharge.

4. Any apparent inequities in the treatment of the Other Party under the bankruptcy remedy rules fall into one of two categories: a) inequities that are only apparent, because they represent the Other Party's sharing of the losses of insolvency with the other unsecured creditors; and b) inequities that may arise if the debtor benefits from imposing on the Other Party, a question to be addressed under the principles of sections 523 (discharge) and 1129(b) (cramdown and absolute priority).

III. THE PERNICIOUS EFFECTS OF EXECUTORINESS

A. A RULE WITHOUT A REASON

. . . Let me say flatly at the outset that there is nothing to be said for a threshold requirement of executoriness as a precondition to the assumption or rejection of bankruptcy contracts. It is a century-old wrong turning. The material breach test has considerable virtue, but only insofar as it greatly ameliorates the effects of the executoriness requirement.

The discussion just concluded makes the most fundamental case against a threshold requirement of executoriness. It is a requirement with no basis in the Code. If bankruptcy contract problems can be fully understood without reference to that requirement, it is surplusage and has no effect except confusion and obfuscation. . . .

If that requirement never restrains the trustee from proceeding according to the Net Value calculation and maximizing benefits to the estate, then it is irrelevant. If it sometimes prevents the trustee from maximizing the estate on a Net Value analysis, then it is pernicious. . . . [E]xecutoriness is utterly unnecessary to the analysis of bankruptcy contracts. . . .

Because executoriness has no basis in policy or fairness, it is almost infinitely manipulable. That is its central fault. . . . The fact that a threshold requirement of executoriness tacitly assumes some special bankruptcy policy that does not exist is the very reason that it is always capable of giving the right answer—or the wrong one.

The simplest and most fundamental symptom of the weakness of the executoriness requirement is the notion that some contracts cannot be rejected because they are not executory. . . .

The executoriness requirement serves no policy and leads to logically absurd results. Worse still, it obscures the true issues in bankruptcy contract cases, masking the state-law issues that are usually the central difficulty, as well as other bankruptcy issues.

B. TREATING STATE LAW QUESTIONS AS MATTERS OF EXECUTORINESS

The focus of the "executoriness" requirement is on some supposed special rule of bankruptcy law, thus taking the court's attention away from the core question: the parties' rights under state contract law. The hard questions in these cases are usually there, in contract law. . . .

Thus, the threshold requirement of "executoriness" is not merely unnecessary, but leads to error. . . . [T]he executoriness requirement can almost always be manipulated to produce the correct result, but the fact that it deflects the courts from the true problems of state contract law invites— and often produces—error. As a result, bankruptcy contract law conflicts with state contract law without any good federal policy reasons to support the difference.

C. ANCILLARY OBLIGATIONS

The presence of ancillary obligations is an important aspect of executoriness analysis in many of the recent cases. It is frequently encountered in license cases and in cases involving a noncompete covenant. It is another instance of using "executoriness" analysis where state contract law is the real point. . . .

An ancillary obligation (Ancillary) for this purpose is an obligation that is not the central exchange of a contract. An Ancillary may be important, its performance may be a material part of the contract, but it is not the central obligation in a particular single contract. Generally speaking, Ancillaries are important in bankruptcy contract cases when they have the characteristics of being on-going obligations. . . .

. . . Virtually any contract can be called executory if the court is willing to look for Ancillaries to serve the function of "further performance due." . . . Most contracts contain an Ancillary the courts can use as "further material performance," but Ancillaries, being ancillary, are also easy to ignore when courts seek a nonexecutory answer. . . .

D. EXECUTORINESS MASKING AN AVOIDING POWERS PROBLEM

Some significant cases turn on an implicit assumption that bankruptcy law somehow gives the trustee greater contract remedies than the debtor has pre-bankruptcy, in addition to its limits on the remedies of the Other Party. I think courts suppose a special bankruptcy contract power in some cases because another, real bankruptcy policy and power is lurking unidentified. The notion of a special bankruptcy contract "power," coupled with the "magic" of some bankruptcy contract results, leads courts to hold that bankruptcy changes state contract rights in substantive ways, when courts are really responding to the other, unidentified bankruptcy principle. . . .

IV. EXEMPLARY CASES

A. ROVINE

A good place to start discussing exemplary cases is *In re Rovine*, a classic executory contract case. It is one of the cases involving a noncompete covenant. These cases do not involve an ITI . . . .

The facts in *Rovine* are relatively simple. The Rovine Corporation was a Burger King franchisee under a typical franchise contract. . . . Rovine was obligated to pay royalties to Burger King. . . . It also agreed to a covenant not to compete with Burger King. . . . The covenant appeared to be sustainable as reasonable in time and extent under state contract law.

. . . Rovine Corporation filed in Chapter 11 bankruptcy. . . . [I]t decided that the status of Burger King franchisee was more expensive than it was worth. . . .

. . . Rovine decided to go it alone, to purvey its hamburgers under its own name, foregoing Burger King's research and development, but also avoiding the royalty obligation. Thus, in its role as DIP-trustee it rejected the Burger King contract, including the covenant not to compete, and stated an intent to sell its burgers at the same old stand under its own name. Burger King understandably objected. It made its objection under the rubric of executoriness. . . .

The court took the argument on these terms. . . . [T]he problem was to find material performance due from Burger King in order to satisfy the material breach test for executoriness. That task was not easy because Burger King already had done most of the valuable things it promised. Nonetheless, the court found some Ancillaries that did the job. . . .

The result seems entirely correct. . . .

1. The Executoriness Analysis

Although the result in *Rovine* was almost certainly correct as to the release of the noncompete covenant, the inquiry that led to the result seems curiously off the point. The extent of Burger King's additional obligations should not determine the debtor's right to reject. . . . . The further performance due from the Other Party and that party's right to enforce residual covenants are not logically connected. . . .

The Burger King obligations were Ancillaries, unrelated to the underlying economics of the case, yet they had to be found "material" under state contract law if the contract was to be held executory and rejectable. Because it would be easy to find them nonmaterial under contract law, this analysis could produce the wrong result. . . . In this situation, the court's attention is focused on the wrong issue, the central legal point can be manipulated in either direction, and there is every likelihood the court will get the wrong answer. In both situations, the risk of error comes from the fact that the materiality of the Ancillaries is merely incidental. . . .

2. A Functional Analysis

To understand the functional analysis of *Rovine*, consider a hypothetical *Rovine* case, one in which the debtor is a natural person. . . . Now assume that Mr. Rovine, a natural person, was the Burger King franchisee. . . .

Mr. Rovine . . . will be discharged of the covenant and will emerge from bankruptcy free of it. . . . Absent a sustainable claim of fraud by Burger King, or some other basis for objecting to discharge, Mr. Rovine will walk away from his obligations in Chapter 7 like any other Chapter 7 debtor. The noncompete covenant is no different from his promise to pay a promissory note five years from now, and to pay interest in the meantime. Both creditors get stiffed and are relegated to their claims against the estate. It is just that simple. . . .

. . . [T]he Rovine trustee in Chapter 7 . . . will not even consider assumption of the franchise contract. As to the obligations of the contract, it will breach and pay in Bankruptcy Dollars. One of those obligations is the covenant against competition. . . .

The reader may be impatient at this point, feeling that I am just stating the obvious, but nothing in *Rovine* speaks to the discharge and its effect, although it was key to the actual case. . . . Yet the fact that the debtor can walk away from the covenant not to compete, despite having very valuable knowledge and training given to him by Burger King under the contract, is directly the result of the bankruptcy discharge and nothing else. . . .

To this point, the result in this example is perfectly consistent with existing bankruptcy policy. The estate gets the benefit of performance or rejection of the Burger King contract, whichever is best, and Burger King's damage claim will be paid in the same proportions as the other unsecured creditors. Mr. Rovine in Chapter 7 is able to wriggle out of his noncompete promise, but that results, we now see, from the discharge policy. . . .

3. The Shift in Equities in Chapter 11

If functional analysis makes sense in the liquidation context, and the results seem fair within the framework of the principles of equality of distribution and discharge, the situation changes when we put Mr. Rovine, the natural person and Burger King franchisee, into a Chapter 11. . . . The DIP concept conflates debtor and trustee and the consequence is a real risk of inequity, the very inequity that many people feel lurking in the *Rovine* case, but mistakenly attribute to a problem with bankruptcy contract analysis.

Mr. Rovine, as trustee, makes the same economic analysis as the trustee in liquidation, except that the business is to go on. . . . Very plausibly, Mr. Rovine will decide that the business is better off without the franchise contract and will provide for Burger King's breach-damage claim in his plan of reorganization. If the plan is confirmed, then he will be discharged from his debts in Chapter 11, including the covenant not to compete. Here, the risk of inequity in *Rovine* appears. . . . Burger King gets paid some percentage of its damages and is barred by the Chapter 11 discharge from getting the usual injunction against competition in violation of the covenant. That result does not seem fair. And it may not be.

The inequity, however, lies not in the treatment of the contract, but in the step that we have just skipped: confirmation of the plan. . . . [I]f one wishes to keep assets, one promises to pay an amount agreeable to a majority of creditors. Bankruptcy does not permit a debtor to keep assets and stiff creditors over the objection of a majority of them. The cramdown rules, under section 1129(b), preserve and protect these central principles; these rules should prevent the apparent or potential inequity in *Rovine*. . . .

The only remaining transformation required to turn our hypothetical case back into the actual *Rovine* case is to make Mr. Rovine into Rovine Corporation once more. The Chapter 11 analysis is exactly the same, except for two points. One is that the discharge is absolute. . . . Secondly, it is the shareholders who must get the creditors' agreement or forfeit their interests. Otherwise, the analysis is the same.

The rejection of a contract often comes before the court, as it did in *Rovine*, at a time well in advance of confirmation and the application of the cramdown rules. At that stage in the proceeding, the conflation of trustee and debtor seems to create an unaddressed inequity. . . . Yet rejection of the contract and discharge of the covenant not to compete may be crucial to a higher return for unsecured creditors generally. . . .

Rovine, one of the most debated executory contract cases decided under the Code, illustrates the operation of the equality-of-treatment and discharge principles against Burger King's state law rights, as well as revealing the importance of the Chapter 11 requirements for confirmation in protecting against abuse of these bankruptcy principles. Properly understood, none of the policy and fairness factors in *Rovine* has anything to do with the remaining performance Burger King might owe under the contract on the date of bankruptcy. Yet the existence of unperformed obligations is central to a finding of executoriness. The threshold requirement of executoriness is irrelevant to the analysis, to policy, and to fairness.

B. *RICHMOND*

. . . The bankrupt inventor in [*In re*] *Richmond* granted a nonexclusive technology license to Lubrizol, the Other Party, prior to bankruptcy. . . .

Following bankruptcy, the inventor sought to reject the contract and enter into a more profitable arrangement free of Lubrizol's rights. . . . The district court held that Lubrizol could not be deprived of its license, because the contract represented a sale of rights. . . .

The Fourth Circuit reversed. It . . . allowed the inventor to reject it. The effect of the Fourth Circuit decision was to cancel the license. . . .

. . . [T]he result in *Richmond* threatens commercial chaos. . . . So serious were the implications for patents and copyrights that Congress amended the Code to deal with this particular problem. . . . More generally, the *Richmond* approach remains available for application in many other types of contract cases. . . .

The *Richmond* analysis is so dangerous because it provides no requirement of insolvency, limitation of time . . ., or any other limit, except the mirage limit of executoriness. It also leads to the obvious anomaly that the Other Party loses if it has extracted promises of future performance from the debtor, but might win if it has driven a worse bargain, with the debtor promising no future performance. An executoriness analyst stands naked on this bleak, unbounded plain, with all the contract laws struck down, waiting for the Devil to arrive.

1. The Executoriness Analysis

The court found the *Richmond* contract executory because the debtor-inventor had certain contingent, continuing obligations. The *Richmond* inventor's obligations were minimal. . . .

Richmond reveals a second, and more profound, anomaly in the material breach analysis. In that case, it seems highly likely that state law would say that the license contract was final from the perspective of the inventor. In other words, state law would not permit the inventor to terminate the license . . . . [C]ertainly, contract doctrine would not permit the breacher *to benefit from its own breach* by revoking the license. Why should the inventor be able to revoke the license in bankruptcy by rejection? No bankruptcy rule or policy requires that reversal of state law. . . .

2. A Functional Analysis

The functional analyst would find the problem in *Richmond* subject to a coherent, ordered, and clear resolution. The debtor-licensor is in the position of a seller in the functional universe. . . . It is likely that patent-contract law would not permit the debtor-seller to revoke or rescind the license, even if the Other Party breached. . . . Beyond doubt, neither patent-contract law nor Article 2 would permit rescission by the breaching party against a performing Other Party. Absent some special bankruptcy rule granting greater rights to bankruptcy estates, the trustee (or DIP) is equally power-less to revoke the license, especially against a nonbreaching licensee. . . . In short, nonbankruptcy law would say that Lubrizol had an ITI in the license. . . .

3. The Pseudo Avoiding Power

The courts often use executory contract analysis as a type of avoiding power because it serves as a surrogate for one of the statutory avoiding powers. A court uses this surrogate when it perceives equities of the sort traditionally associated with the avoiding powers, but cannot see how to use the powers provided by the statute. . . .

The *Richmond* court was wrong to enforce the equality of treatment principle through the executory contract device. The avoiding powers, including the preference and fraudulent con-veyance provisions, are the method the Code provides for enforcing that principle, not some implied and unbounded contract "power." If the grant of the license was not avoidable under those provi-sions, then the equality of treatment principle did not apply. . . .

A contract approach is unbounded, while an avoiding power analysis is subject to all the con-straints and exceptions imposed by wise policy and compromise. . . .

. . . The equities that concerned the court in *Richmond* could have been properly analyzed, and competing policies given the weight accorded by the Code, by viewing the problem as a possible preference or fraudulent conveyance. . . .

The fact that avoiding power problems are often hidden in a bankruptcy contract case does much to explain why rejection of executory contracts appears to the courts much like an indepen-dent avoiding power. . . .

V. THE EXCLUSIONARY APPROACH

The reader who has studied Michael Andrew's recent article will see that he and I agree on many issues concerning the nature of the present bankruptcy contract dilemma. We also agree about several of the key distinctions in fashioning a better analysis. Yet we disagree in some important respects, conceptually and practically.

The central conceptual disagreement is that Andrew would treat rejected contracts as never becoming property of the estate, and would create special rules to account for the effects of nonas-sumption by granting the Other Party a claim against the estate "as if" the debtor breached the con-tract. This "exclusionary" approach substitutes a new metaphysics of bankruptcy contracts for the old one.

At the core of my suggested analysis is a much simpler idea: the estate inherits the debtor's pre-bankruptcy contracts and is in exactly the same position as any other contract party under non-bankruptcy law, with just two exceptions: a) after rejection (breach), the remedies of the Other Party are limited by the general bankruptcy rules constraining the remedies of unsecured creditors; and b) ITIs of the Other Party may be subject to avoidance under the bankruptcy avoiding powers. . . . [T]he functional approach permits a simple, two-step analysis. What are the rights and obliga-tions of the estate under nonbankruptcy law in case of breach? How are the Other Party's remedies under nonbankruptcy law limited by bankruptcy remedies rules and by the avoiding powers? . . .

The exclusionary analysis requires us to ignore the language and the structure of the Code. Andrew devotes considerable attention to the idea that rejection of a contract is not breach, but the

Code says "the rejection of an executory contract or unexpired lease of the debtor constitutes a breach." . . . [W]hy read this language out of the Code? . . . All this twisting and bending of the language of the Code should be avoided unless some overriding problem of concept and policy compels it.

Even more fundamental are the problems the exclusionary analysis creates under section 541 (Property of the Estate). The estate includes "all legal or equitable interests of the debtor in property." Contract rights undoubtedly are property. . . . Yet the exclusionary analysis requires us to exclude "Unassumed" contracts in section 541. It also requires discovery of a provision in section 541 that admits a bundle of contract rights to the estate after assumption. . . . The exclusionary concept has no foundation in the Code. Worse still, it forces us to evade and distort the whole structure of section 541, creating manifold possibilities for confusion and error.

The difference between the exclusionary and the functional approach is not merely conceptual. Conceptual differences nearly always have concrete and practical consequences. . . .

Andrew is particularly concerned with the locus of an excluded contract, which he says remains in the original debtor. . . . The exclusionary approach, however, leaves open the opportunity for the original debtor to attempt to proceed with the contract after the bankruptcy petition is filed. That consequence of excluding unassumed contracts would create many problems.

The most important difficulty in permitting an original debtor to claim the right to enforce a pre-bankruptcy contract post-petition is that it is unfair to the Other Party, as well as a trap for the unwary. In effect, it creates an assumption-rejection right in the original debtor, requiring the Other Party to continue with a contract after the debtor has been stripped of all of its assets. It establishes a new twilight world of performance and breach. . . .

The principal reason that the exclusionary analysis is so inconsistent with the statutory scheme is that modern bankruptcy law rests upon the fundamental policy of "once and for all," resolving all of the debtor's pre-petition affairs in one proceeding. . . .

VI. PRECEDENT

Even the reader who feels attracted by a functional analysis of bankruptcy contracts may feel that this whole, long, forest-destroying discussion is rather pointy headed, given the firm establishment of executoriness in the precedents and in the Code itself. . . . There are at least two approaches to an answer.

One is that the judge could become a "closet functionalist." Locking the door to chambers, the judge could functionally analyze bankruptcy contracts and then emerge to announce a result in terms of executoriness, leaving precedent safely undisturbed. . . .

The alternative is to abolish the requirement of executoriness as a threshold requirement for performance or breach. This direct approach might seem to fly in the face of the Code. . . . Yet the legislative history does not adopt the material breach test. . . .

Given that position, the courts might decide to look at contract rights and obligations one by one, as functionalism suggests, bundling together those rights that arise from a "single contract" under nonbankruptcy law to the extent that non-bankruptcy law makes realizing some of the rights depend on performance of some of the obligations. . . .

Given the confusion in the courts, it is difficult to claim that commercial expectations would be seriously threatened by this redefinition of executory contracts, or by the proposed new analysis. Instead, the commercial world would be relieved from guarding against unbounded threats to expectations presented by cases like *Richmond*, as well as the dilution of predictability resulting from the present eccentric results throughout the field of bankruptcy contracts.

. . . It is clearly not a good idea, however, to solve our conceptual confusion about bankruptcy contracts by burdening the Code with endless exceptions arising from our confusion rather than from the policies underlying bankruptcy law. Such an approach invites unfair special treatment based on political advantage. It invariably creates a different set of rules for certain kinds of contracts in bankruptcy, without any congressional determination that different bankruptcy treatment is appropriate as a matter of federal commercial policy.

CONCLUSION

After such an arduous journey, a closing summary is the least I can do. The four basic propositions of this article are:

1. There should be no threshold requirement that a contract be "executory" as a prerequisite to assumption or rejection (performance or breach) by the trustee. The trustee may, indeed must, assume or reject every pre-bankruptcy contract of the debtor that is not completely performed or satisfied on Bankruptcy Day.

2. The trustee's contract rights are the same as those of the pre-bankruptcy debtor, except that under the equality of distribution principle, the trustee may pay for breach in tiny Bankruptcy Dollars, which makes breach profitable for the trustee much more often than for a nonbankruptcy party, and the Other Party cannot get specific performance of a purely contractual covenant. . . .

3. The major exception to the equality principle is that bankruptcy courts enforce a state-law interest in a specific asset of the debtor, an ITI. . . .

4. The avoiding powers limit the enforcement of state-law ITIs created by contract. . . .

In a court that adopts a functional approach to bankruptcy contracts, the trustee's analysis proceeds almost backwards through the foregoing propositions in analyzing each pre-bankruptcy contract that is not fully performed or satisfied before Bankruptcy Day:

1. Does this contract create a state-law ITI?

2. If the contract gives rise to a state-law ITI, is the ITI avoidable?

3. A) If there is no ITI, or only an avoidable one, will the estate profit more from performance of this contract, or from breach and payment in Bankruptcy Dollars?

B) If the ITI is unavoidable and therefore enforceable, will the estate profit more from performance or breach, given that any breaches of the other covenants in the contract will be payable only in Bankruptcy Dollars?

NATIONAL BANKRUPTCY REVIEW COMMISSION
FINAL REPORT
BANKRUPTCY: THE NEXT TWENTY YEARS
(October 20, 1997)

GENERAL ISSUES IN CHAPTER 11
DISCUSSION

I. Issues Arising During a Chapter 11 Case

Section 365

The filing of a bankruptcy petition triggers the creation of an estate encompassing all of the debtor's property interests, including contractual rights. Unlike many other types of property that come into the estate, contracts involve both rights and duties. Therefore, the treatment of contracts in bankruptcy raises more complicated questions. . . .

The countless types of contracts and number of circumstances have complicated attainment of the goal of establishing clear and uniform rules. In an attempt to address discrete situations, section 365 has been amended repeatedly over the past twenty years and now spans over thirteen pages in a typical version of the Bankruptcy Code. These additions to section 365 may have abrogated questionable case law interpretations, and have offered pockets of certainty for some industries or types of contracts, but they have not resolved fundamental ambiguities that should be addressed generically. Therefore, instead of undertaking a piecemeal analysis of each subsection of section 365, the Commission reviewed the larger conceptual issues inherent in section 365 to eliminate confusion on a more global basis.

2.4.1 *Clarifying the Meaning of "Rejection"*
The concept of "rejection" in Section 365 should be replaced with "election to breach."

Section 365 should provide that a trustee's ability to elect to breach a contract of the debtor is not an avoiding power.

Section 502(g) should be amended to provide that a claim arising from the election to breach shall be allowed or disallowed the same as if such claim had arisen before the date of the filing of the petition.

Section 365 permits a debtor in possession or trustee to elect to "reject" a contract entered prepetition, subject to court approval. The term "rejection" has no obvious state contract law counterpart. Although the Bankruptcy Code provides that rejection should be treated as a breach, the Code does not state expressly that rejection is synonymous with breach, nor does it fully delineate the consequences of a trustee's decision to reject. Not surprisingly, the concept of rejection has been applied inconsistently by the courts, and has led to the numerous special interest amendments to section 365.

The Commission recommends a common-sense clarification of the term "rejection" by replacing it with "election to breach." The Commission further recommends that the Bankruptcy Code delineate the consequences of electing to breach to correct on a generic basis the contrary results reached by some courts. The bankruptcy trustee's election not to perform a contract is nothing more or less than a breach of the contract and should be treated accordingly. Rejection does not "nullify," "rescind," or "vaporize" the contract or terminate the rights of the parties; it does not serve as an avoiding power separate and apart from the express avoiding powers already provided in the Bankruptcy Code. . . . Under most circumstances, this means that the nondebtor party would be entitled to a claim for money damages, and the contract obligations themselves would be discharged. The claim would be paid in the bankruptcy *pro rata* with other unsecured creditors.

With a few important exceptions, bankruptcy law accepts the nonbankruptcy substantive law applicable to a contract, but bankruptcy adjusts the form of the remedies available upon breach. Damages may be calculated under state law, but they are paid out according to bankruptcy priorities and principles. Specific performance may be available under state law, but it is rarely permitted against the trustee. Thus, state contract law generally defines a party's rights, while federal bankruptcy law determines how those rights are enforced in a bankruptcy case. . . .

Competing Considerations. Some would argue that a trustee or debtor in possession should be able to avoid or rescind a contract in bankruptcy whenever it would be helpful to a reorganization to do so. . . . However, this would enable the debtor in bankruptcy to make contracts disappear—a power that is very different from a simple breach of contract for which the debtor would incur damages. . . . To permit the trustee or debtor in possession to undo valid contracts whenever the estate might benefit would introduce a great deal of uncertainty into private bargaining and might lead to abuse. . . .

2.4.2 *Clarifying the Option of "Assumption"*
"Assumption" should be replaced with "election to perform" in Section 365.

Court approval of a trustee's request to assume a contract is a significant event. Once a debtor in possession or trustee has assumed a contract, the bankruptcy estate becomes obligated to perform or to find an adequate replacement to perform through its right to assign. Any failure to do so will result in an administrative priority claim for damages that must be paid ahead of all other general creditors, as opposed to the *pro rata* distribution that is received by a party to a breached contract. . . . The trustee should elect to commit the estate to perform and receive performance or transfer the contract only if such actions are likely to yield a net benefit to the estate. . . .

Due to the confusion already inherent in section 365, the Commission believes that it is sensible to use more comprehensible terms that characterize the events they represent. By using the words "election to perform," this Proposal would introduce a concept parallel to "election to breach" and would replace problematic language with clear language. . . .

2.4.3 *Interim Protection and Obligations of Nondebtor Parties*

A court should be authorized to grant an order governing temporary performance and/or providing protection of the interests of the nondebtor party until the court approves a decision to perform or breach a contract.

Section 503(b) should include as an administrative expense losses reasonably and unavoidably sustained by a nondebtor party to a contract, a standard based on nonbankruptcy contract principles, pending court approval of an election to perform or breach a contract if such nondebtor party was acting in accordance with a court order governing temporary performance.

. . .

2.4.4 *Contracts Subject to Section 365; Eliminating the "Executory" Requirement*

Title 11 should be amended to delete all references to "executory" in section 365 and related provisions, and "executoriness" should be eliminated as a prerequisite to the trustee's election to assume or breach a contract.

As the previous discussions have explored, section 365 of the Bankruptcy Code governs the "assumption" (performance), "rejection" (breach), and "assignment" (transfer) of contracts and leases in bankruptcy. Because section 365 currently refers to *executory* contracts and not to all contracts, commencing the inquiry on the appropriate disposition of a contract depends on whether the parties believe and the court determines that the contract is "executory."

Development of the Bankruptcy Term "Executory." Under nonbankruptcy law, the term "executory" is a broad modifier, referring to all contracts not fully performed. Bankruptcy law has developed a different interpretation of the term starting well before the enactment of the Bankruptcy Code of 1978. Section 365 is derived from section 70b of the Bankruptcy Act of 1898. . . . The Bankruptcy Act offered very little additional guidance for dealing with executory contracts. . . . [C]ourts developed a more restrictive interpretation of the term "executory" for bankruptcy purposes to ensure contracts would be assumed only if economically beneficial for the estate. However, by many accounts, those approaches were not always consistent. To ameliorate some of this confusion, Professor Vern Countryman articulated the following "material breach" analysis to identify an "executory" contract that could be assumed or rejected:

> A contract under which the obligation of both the bankrupt and the other party to the contract are so far unperformed that the failure of either to complete performance would constitute a material breach excusing the performance of the other.

Using the material breach test, courts gauged remaining future performance of both the debtor and the nondebtor to determine whether the estate would benefit by becoming administratively obligated to perform. . . . Congress declined to define "executory contract" when it enacted section 365 of the Bankruptcy Code. . . .

It seems clear that the requirement of executoriness was developed in large part to prevent unwise or inadvertent assumptions or rejections by trustees, because under the Bankruptcy Act of 1898 there was no requirement of court approval and notice to creditors for those actions. The Bankruptcy Reform Act of 1978 closed that gap by requiring court approval for assumption or rejection, largely eliminating the underlying reason for the constraining concept. . . . The goal to be served by the executoriness test is now met directly by court review.

A growing case law trend de-emphasizes a strict analysis of the term "executory" in favor of a "functional" analysis, an approach articulated by Professor Jay Westbrook, Michael Andrew, and others. Using a functional analysis, a court does not consider remaining mutual material performance but instead considers the goals that assumption or rejection were expected to accomplish: enhancement of the estate. Under this approach, the term "executory" ultimately serves no purpose. . . .

The term "executory" is not merely harmless surplusage. First, . . . a functional analysis of contracts . . . would appear to depart from the statutory guidelines. To use an arguably more efficient approach, a statutory amendment is advisable to assure that shift and to cause all courts to follow the same route. Second, few would dispute the persistent inconsistencies and difficulties in identifying an executory contract for bankruptcy purposes. . . . Finally, the traditional strict interpretation of the executory requirement leads some courts to results that contravene the initial purpose of the restriction because it does not isolate valuable contracts and does not preclude improvident elections to perform or breach. Some very valuable contracts may be unassumable on account of a strict executory test. An executoriness analysis therefore can hamper the process of permitting the bankruptcy estate to elect to perform contracts that will be highly beneficial.

So long as the term "executory" remains in the statute, this issue will continue to incite debate and to increase litigation costs without an evident corresponding advantage. Therefore, the Commission recommends the elimination of all references to the term "executory." . . . [T]he Proposal would streamline the analysis of the debtor's contracts and provide a directive to courts to analyze the relevant considerations guiding one's decision to perform, breach, or transfer a contract, just as a contracting party would do outside of bankruptcy. . . .

Competing Considerations. Notwithstanding recent case law developments that de-emphasize the executory requirement, some might be concerned that eliminating any term already in use, including "executory," could have an unsettling effect on case law and thereby encourage new litigation. However, this Proposal would not introduce a foreign concept, but rather would streamline the analysis so that courts can focus on the critical issue of the benefit to the estate, which originally was the intended goal of the executoriness requirement.

No proposal in this area of the law can eliminate all litigation because court approval is a crucial component and the review of the perform-or-breach-election is an assessment based on the facts and circumstances of each case and each contract. The removal of the threshold executory requirement would permit courts to focus on pertinent case- and estate-related factors and would curtail litigation on tangential issues relating to the term "executory." By eliminating this source of confusion, costs and unnecessary delays should be minimized.

Additional suggested readings

Michael T. Andrew, *Executory Contracts Revisited: A Reply to Professor Westbrook,* 62 U. Colo. L. Rev. 1 (1991)

Douglas W. Bordewieck, *The Postpetition, Pre-Rejection, Pre-Assumption Status of an Executory Contract,* 59 Am. Bankr. L.J. 197 (1985)

Daniel J. Bussel & Edward A. Friedler, *The Limits on Assuming and Assigning Executory Contracts*, 74 AM. BANKR. L.J. 321 (2000)

Jesse M. Fried, *Executory Contracts and Performance Decisions,* 46 DUKE L.J. 517 (1996)

Thomas H. Jackson, Chapter 5, *Executory Contracts in Bankruptcy: The Combination of Assets and Liabilities, in* THE LOGIC AND LIMITS OF BANKRUPTCY LAW, 105-121 (Harvard 1986)

Thomas H. Jackson, *Translating Assets and Liabilities to the Bankruptcy Forum*, 14 J. LEG. STUD. 73 (1985)

Daniel L. Keating, *The Continuing Puzzle of Collective Bargaining Agreements in Bankruptcy*, 35 WM. & MARY L. REV. 503 (1994)

Daniel L. Keating, *Good Intentions, Bad Economics: Retiree Insurance Benefits in Bankruptcy*, 43 VAND. L. REV. 161 (1990)

Brett W. King, *Assuming and Assigning Executory Contracts: A History of Indeterminate "Applicable Law,"* 70 AM. BANKR. L.J. 95 (1996)

James A. McLaughlin, *Amendment of the Bankruptcy Act*, 40 HARV. L. REV. 583 (1927)

Raymond T. Nimmer, *Executory Contracts in Bankruptcy: Protecting the Fundamental Terms of the Bargain*, 54 U. COLO. L. REV. 507 (1983)

Alan Schwartz, *A Contract Theory Approach to Business Bankruptcy*, 107 YALE L.J. 1807 (1998)

Morris G. Shanker, *A Proposed New Executory Contract Statute*, 1993 ANN. SURV. BANKR. L. 129

Morris G. Shanker, *Bankruptcy Asset Theory and Its Application to Executory Contracts*, 1992 ANN. SURV. BANKR. L. 97

Jay Lawrence Westbrook, *The Commission's Recommendations Concerning the Treatment of Bankruptcy Contracts*, 5 AM. BANKR. INST. L. REV. 463 (1997)

Chapter 11

Consumer Bankruptcy: Discharge, Exemptions, and the Fresh Start

A. Prologue

Consumer bankruptcy carries at its core the notion of a financial "fresh start" in life for individual debtors. That "fresh start" policy has two core components: the discharge of debts, which enables a debtor to keep her future earnings, free from the grasp of her pre-bankruptcy creditors; and exemptions, which allow an individual debtor to retain certain current assets. This Chapter examines these parameters of consumer bankruptcy. After a Prologue, which sets the stage, the Chapter follows with sections devoted to detailed examinations, in turn, of the discharge and exemptions. Chapter 12 will examine in more depth a variety of proposals to reform the consumer bankruptcy system. Before considering reform, though, it is important to examine the essence of the current regime as constituted.

The Prologue begins with a brief excerpt from the House Report that accompanied the reform legislation of the 1970s. That Report highlighted the basic nature of and reasons for the consumer bankruptcy system. Next is a presentation of some fascinating statistical information developed by Professor Robert Lawless. Lawless shows how the incidence of consumer bankruptcy filings is closely related to certain measures of debt. Finally, selections are taken from the path-breaking book by Sullivan, Warren & Westbrook, As We Forgive Our Debtors: Bankruptcy and Consumer Credit in America, published in 1989. The excerpts included here paint a financial portrait of people in bankruptcy. The picture is not a pretty one, as the real financial distress of most bankruptcy debtors is vividly revealed. While the study was done in the early 1980s, subsequent empirical work has reinforced the basic findings of that earlier study. As you read the next two chapters, keep those findings in mind.

H.R. Rep. No. 95-595
95th Cong., 1st Sess. (1977)

Chapter 3. Consumer Debtors

Since World War II, the incidence of consumer credit has grown enormously. Consumer finance has become a major industry . . . . As we have become a consumer society, we have also become a credit society. . . .

The result of the increase in consumer credit has been a corresponding increase in the number of consumers who have overburdened themselves with debt. Often, these consumers are able to keep up with their obligations in normal times, but have saved very little for emergencies or unexpected events. When a family member takes seriously ill or when the breadwinner is laid off from his job, a financial crisis ensues. . . .

The vast majority of consumer financial crises are of these kinds. Aggressive advertising and sales techniques by the consumer credit industry . . . add to the problems . . . . When the crises finally erupt, the experience of the industry in collecting from overburdened debtors allows it an enormous advantage against the inexperienced and generally distraught consumer. Harsh collection practices heaped on top of already serious financial problems often result in ill health, family strain and divorce, and loss of jobs for many overextended consumer debtors. Bankruptcy often provides the only remedy. . . .

. . . The premises of the bill with respect to consumer bankruptcy are that the use of the bankruptcy law should be a last resort; that if it is used, debtors should attempt repayment under chapter 13 . . .; and finally, . . . bankruptcy relief should be effective, and should provide the debtor with a fresh start.

I. Adjustment of Debts of an Individual With Regular Income

. . . The purpose of chapter 13 is to enable an individual, under court supervision and protection, to develop and perform under a plan for the repayment of his debts over an extended period. . . .

The benefit to the debtor . . . is that it permits the debtor to protect his assets. . . . Chapter 13 also protects a debtor's credit standing far better than a straight bankruptcy . . . . In addition, it satisfies many debtors' desire to avoid the stigma attached to straight bankruptcy and to retain the pride attendant on being able to meet one's obligations. The benefit to creditors is self-evident: their losses will be significantly less than if their debtors opt for straight bankruptcy. . . .

II. Liquidation

Some consumer debtors are unable to avail themselves of the relief provided under chapter 13. For these debtors, straight bankruptcy is the only remedy that will enable them to get out from under the debilitating effects of too much debt. The purpose of straight bankruptcy for them is to obtain a fresh start, free from creditor harassment and free from the worries and pressures of too much debt. . . .

The two most important aspects of the fresh start available under the Bankruptcy laws are the provision of adequate property for a return to normal life, and the discharge, with the release from creditor collection attempts.

Robert M. Lawless
The Relationship Between Nonbusiness Bankruptcy Filings and Various Basic Measures of Consumer Debt
http://www.law.missouri.edu/lawless/bus_bkr/filings.htm
(Version 1.1, last updated July 18, 2001)[*]

	U.S. Nonbusiness Bankruptcy Filings, Calendar-Year Basis Table 1 Source: AOUSC			
Year	Chapter 7	Chapter 11	Chapter 13	Total
1980	213,988	460	73,122	287,570
1981	226,604	1,110	88,104	315,818
1982	212,664	2,187	96,100	310,951
1983	196,214	3,032	87,198	286,444
1984	195,834	2,472	86,211	284,517
1985	237,653	2,975	100,605	341,233
1986	324,082	3,376	121,745	449,203
1987	362,599	2,779	130,189	495,567
1988	399,134	2,140	148,338	549,612
1989	439,636	1,978	175,139	616,753
1990	506,940	2,501	208,666	718,107
1991	617,359	3,195	251,883	872,438
1992	643,538	3,198	254,138	900,874
1993	568,415	3,018	241,464	812,898
1994	537,551	2,265	240,639	780,455
1995	597,048	1,369	276,225	874,642
1996	779,741	1,173	344,092	1,125,006
1997	957,117	1,071	391,930	1,350,118
1998	1,007,922	862	389,398	1,398,182
1999	904,564	706	376,311	1,281,581
2000	838,885	687	378,400	1,217,972

Revolving Consumer Debt Outstanding and Nonbusiniess Bankruptcy Filings

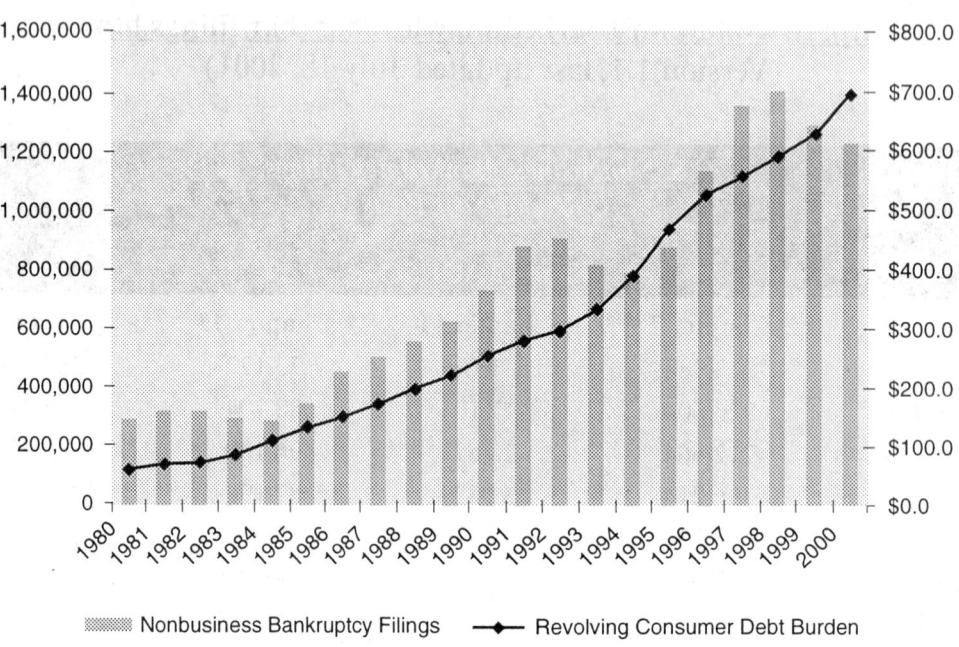

Nonbusiness Bankruptcy Filings   ◆ Revolving Consumer Debt Burden

Total Consumer Debt Outstanding and Nonbusiniess Bankruptcy Filings

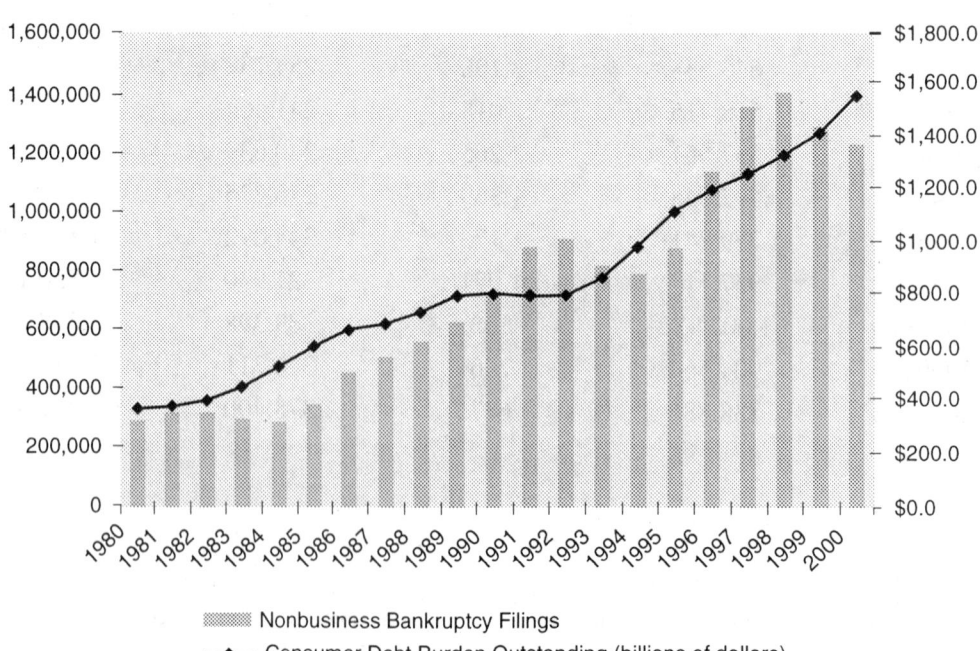

Nonbusiness Bankruptcy Filings
◆ Consumer Debt Burden Outstanding (billions of dollars)

Personal Sector Nonfarm Mortgage Debt and Nonbusiniess Bankruptcy Filings

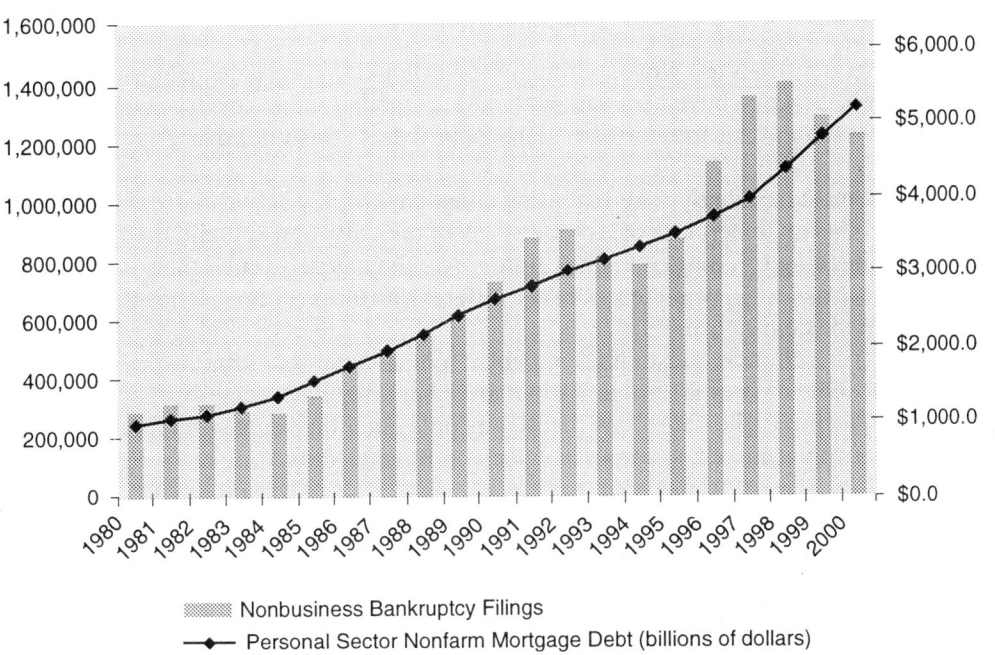

Nonbusiness Bankruptcy Filings
Personal Sector Nonfarm Mortgage Debt (billions of dollars)

Sullivan, Warren & Westbrook
AS WE FORGIVE OUR DEBTORS:
BANKRUPTCY AND CONSUMER CREDIT IN AMERICA (1989)[*]

1
Introduction

Bankrupt. The single word is a body blow, like "Dead." . . .

Bankruptcy is a remarkable phenomenon. It is financial death and financial rebirth. Bankruptcy laws literally make debts vanish. When a judge signs a paper titled "Discharge," debts legally disappear. This is the fate of billions of dollars of debt discharged in bankruptcy every year. Hundreds of thousands of debtors are released from their obligations, free to earn and spend as they choose.

Bankruptcy is a powerful phenomenon. But curiously enough, given our information-hungry society, it is one about which we have little hard information. . . .

This book is based on the Consumer Bankruptcy Project, the largest study of consumer bankruptcy ever undertaken. It required collection of more than a quarter of a million pieces of information from a sample of 2400 bankruptcy petitioners whose cases began in 1981 and for the most

---

part ended by 1985. . . . We wrote this book to shed light on a bankruptcy system that is largely unknown to the public. . . .

. . . We try not to let the statistics about debtors and creditors obscure the very real pain, anger, deceit, fear, and relief that color each bankruptcy file. . . .

Framing the Issues

Three central questions are woven throughout this book. Who are the debtors and the creditors in bankruptcy? What factors have contributed to the spectacular increases in consumer bankruptcy? How should these data affect the normative and policy decisions underlying the consumer bankruptcy laws? . . .

Perhaps the most frequently asked question about bankruptcy is "Who goes into bankruptcy?" Are bankrupt debtors an underclass of Americans, economically and socially marginal, hanging on the edge until something tips them into bankruptcy? Are they largely blue-collar workers or a broad mix of the middle class? . . . [W]e present many different pictures of those who step up to the bankruptcy counter in the courthouse.

The next most common question is probably "What causes bankruptcy?" This is a far more treacherous issue. One answer is simple: Debt causes bankruptcy, especially debt that is very high in comparison to income. The data show that few people enter bankruptcy without fairly spectacular debts that dwarf their incomes, and in that sense debt is the culprit. . . .

The Moral Dimension

We have no illusion that bankruptcy policy is a function merely of facts. Bankruptcy raises profound moral issues as well as financial ones. It is a concept and an experience surrounded by moral ambiguity and filled with paradox.

People see bankruptcy through a lens of fault. Most people would be moved by the plight of a steelworker laid off after years of service, depleted of savings, unable to find a job, and worried to distraction about feeding a family. Few people would shed a tear for the family who charged vacations, waterbeds, and dinners at Antoine's, and then skipped off to bankruptcy court. The result is a pervasive ambivalence about bankruptcy. Rebirth and a fresh start lie at the heart of our national mystique and many of our religious beliefs. But we do not admire broken promises, and we fear those who would avoid hard work by taking advantage of our compassion. Most people envision one or the other stereotype of the typical bankrupt . . . and their visceral reaction to the idea of bankruptcy is largely a function of the stereotype they hold.

The cases in our files suggest endless combinations of irresponsibility, misfortune, and fault. . . . The question of fault is not limited to the debtors. Once again, people's reactions to bankruptcy's treatment of creditors is largely a function of stereotypes. If we think of a huge finance company that enticed the debtor with frequent letters about "the $2,000 that is waiting for you," we are apt to be unsympathetic to its bankruptcy losses. If we think of the accident victim or the family doctor or the defrauded widow as the typical creditor, we may be ready to lean on debtors very hard. Even among professional creditors, we feel differently about careful lenders than careless and greedy ones.

The question when the law says "let go" to the creditor and when it says "pay" to the debtor is the central issue in consumer bankruptcy. Ultimately, this is a moral decision. Will we collectively permit a creditor to take a debtor's last crust of bread? Will we permit a debtor to live high and avoid legal obligations? The answer to both is no, but it is hard to find a line between the two that can be easily administered, cheaply enforced, and collectively endorsed. . . .

Viewing the data as a whole, we come to some conclusions about the reasons for the startling increases in consumer bankruptcy filings in the 1980s. Although there are many contributing factors, we find that the two primary systemic factors have been the burgeoning of consumer credit that has arisen from the changing attitudes of both consumers and the credit industry, and increased volatility in the American economy.

   . . .

4
A Financial Portrait of People in Bankruptcy

Most people have a general notion that debtors in bankruptcy face economic trouble, but little information is available to document their situations. As a result, completely contradictory assumptions about the financial circumstances of debtors flourish side-by-side. In the rhetoric of policymaking debates, some speakers implicitly assume that all debtors are a poverty-stricken, chronically unemployed segment of the lower class . . . . Others argue that debtors in bankruptcy are not really so financially different from those who struggle to pay their bills, but they have made the clever decision to manipulate bankruptcy to avoid payment. What we found is that neither stereotype describes debtors of the 1980s. . . .

Financial Profile

. . . There is enormous variation in the financial circumstances of our CDS debtors. Most have jobs of some kind, but many are unemployed. Most are wage earners, at least by the time they file bankruptcy, but a substantial proportion ran small businesses that had failed. Most have crushing burdens of debt in comparison with their incomes, but a few have debts that appear small compared with their incomes. In general, these people are far below the general population financially, but their financial profiles vary greatly. . . .

Income

TABLE 4.1. Distribution of Income, Assets, and Debts for Bankruptcy Petitioners

Distribution	Family Income	Total Assets	Total Debt	Secured Debt	Unsecured Debt
Mean	$15,779	$29,355	$38,599	$23,034	$15,498
s.d.	9,609	40,034	54,815	38,566	31,268
25th percentile	9,448	2,988	9,737	1,600	3,826
Median	14,974	14,025	20,956	9,601	7,052
75th percentile	21,329	44,334	44,480	30,460	13,935
N	1,289	1,490	1496	1,501	1,495
Missing	213	12	6	1	7

. . . In 1981, the year our cases were filed, national median (middle) family income was $22,400 . . . . National mean incomes were higher, at $25,800 . . . . By contrast, both the mean and the median incomes of the bankrupt debtors were less than two-thirds of the national figures. . . .

The lower incomes of the debtors help explain their financial stress. But another piece of information puts the income data into context. The family income of bankrupt debtors is also spread among more people. In the United States in 1981, mean household size was 2.7. Mean family size among debtors in our sample was about 3.4, or nearly one person more. Thus the already low incomes must stretch further. Because expenses rise with the number of people to be supported, the bankrupt debtors are in the worst possible squeeze: lower incomes supporting higher costs.

Assets

. . . Table 4.1 shows the overall mean assets for the debtors in bankruptcy. The mean is $29,400; the median is far lower at $14,000. The dollar amounts represent everything the debtors own, from their homes to their toothbrushes, with no deductions for outstanding mortgages or liens. . . .

Of the families surveyed nationally, mean financial assets were $27,365, and mean home values were $56,133. Thus a homeowning family (60% of all families surveyed) with mean financial and home assets would have total assets over $83,000. . . . [T]he bankrupt debtors had considerably lower asset value. The debtors' mean assets on the same basis, including homes, were far lower, at $24,700. . . .

. . . The asset data show the debtors once again falling below most Americans, with assets typically about two-thirds lower than those reported for most families.

Debts

While debtors' incomes are low and their assets are even lower relative to other Americans, the debtors in bankruptcy show some extraordinary debt figures. Their debts are summarized in the third column of Table 4.1. These data show debtors with median total debts of nearly $21,000 and mean total debts nearly twice as high at $38,600. . . .

. . . These data show that bankrupt homeowners carry mortgages of roughly the same size as those of most homeowning Americans.

It is nonmortgage consumer debt that shows vast differences between people generally and debtors in bankruptcy. Families across the nation had average nonmortgage consumer debts of $5,400, whereas the debtors in this sample averaged $20,600 per family . . . .

Although unsecured debts are a smaller portion of the total debt load, they are remarkable because they indicate how much money debtors can borrow with a smile and a signature. The average bankrupt debtor had $15,500 of unsecured debt, about equal to the average debtors' yearly income. . . .

An Interim Summary

. . . The most consistent pattern is the relationship between total debts on the one hand and income and assets on the other: At the mean, the 25th percentile, the median, and the 75th percentile, total debts exceed annual income. Similarly, debt dramatically exceeds assets—except at the top quartile, where they nearly match.

The aggregate description in Table 4.1 shows that few bankrupt debtors are affluent and many are poor. They earn about one-third less than most Americans. They support larger families, and they report two-thirds fewer assets than the general population. But they owe far more, nearly four times more in nonmortgage debt alone.

Analysis of Individuals' Circumstances

Net Worth

. . . Net worth is usually taken to mean what is left when a person's liabilities are subtracted from the total value of all assets. . . .

The national data show that a substantial portion of the general population has a small net worth. One-third of all the families surveyed showed a net worth of less than $5,000. . . .

More than three-quarters of the bankrupt debtors are insolvent; that is, they have a net worth of less than zero because their debts exceed the total value of their assets. . . . Another 5% of the debtors could sell everything right down to the skin and have less than $5,000 after they paid their debts. . . . [A]bout one-third of the general population has a net worth of less than $5,000, while 84% of the debtors are worth less than that amount.

The mean net worth of bankrupt debtors is –$13,900, which is a long way from the mean net worth of $66,100 for the general population. . . . The median bankrupt debtors has a negative net worth, –$8,100, while the median person in the general population has a positive net worth of $24,600.

But not all debtors are under water. . . . 16% of the debtors have a positive net worth over $5,000. The asset that produces net worth for debtors in either Chapter 7 or Chapter 13 is almost always the family home. Homeowners represent 94% of the debtors with a positive net worth greater than $5,000. . . .

The net worth data give one more comparison in which the debtors in bankruptcy divide sharply from the general population. When assets and debts are matched for each family, as they are in the net worth calculation, we find most debtors are in terrible shape, but a few, mostly Chapter 13 debtors, look much better off. . . .

A Comparison of Debts with Income

In contemporary society, the relationship of income to debts is the most critical measure of financial condition. . . . Income compared with debt is particularly important in the context of financial collapse.

. . . We compute the ratios by dividing each debtor's reported debt by reported annual income. . . . A ratio of 1.0 means the debtor owes debts equal to one year's income; a ratio of 1.5 describes a debtor who owes debts equal to a year and a half's worth of income. A fraction less than 1.0 indicates that the debts equal less than one year's income, so that 0.5 would mean the debtor owes half a year's income in debts.

. . . The mean total debt/income ratio is 3.2. At the mean, a family in our bankruptcy sample owed debts greater than three years and two months' worth of income. Once again, the mean is considerably larger than the median, suggesting that some extreme cases raise the report of the "typical" case. The median is 1.4, meaning that the middle family owes debts equal to almost one year and five months' worth of income. . . .

Debt/Income Ratios for the General Population

. . . Only 5% of the general population has a consumer debt burden of 20% of income or worse, but the average (mean) burden of debt for the bankrupt debtors is 145% of their incomes—more than seven times greater. . . . This is one of the largest differences between the debtors in bankruptcy and the general population. . . .

Policy Implications

. . . By all economic measures, when bankrupt debtors as a group are compared to the general population, their situations are grim. The debtors in bankruptcy earn much less and owe much more than most Americans. They have staggering debts in relation to their incomes. Their net worth, on average, is many thousands of dollars below zero. With incomes one-third lower, assets two-thirds lower, and consumer debts four times higher, the debtors in bankruptcy are those at the tail end of the financial curves for all Americans. The data show a segment of America in financial collapse. . . .

. . . In the context of debates about the extraordinary rise in the use of bankruptcy and whether bankruptcy laws should be "tightened" and debtor protections withdrawn to prevent debtors from seeking the shelter of bankruptcy, the findings take on practical significance.

. . . [T]his chapter shows that the central tendency is a group of people who are broke. The bankruptcy laws are generally serving the people they are designed to serve: people in serious, even hopeless financial trouble, who need either a fresh-start discharge from their debts or at least some protection from their creditors and a breathing spell while they try to repay. . . .

. . .

18
Conclusion: Bankruptcy and the Consumer Credit System

Like death, a bankruptcy is a dramatic event. . . . Our data show that it is . . . generally used by people in very serious financial difficulty. . . .

Who Is in Bankruptcy?

Bankrupt debtors are a cross section of America. . . . [B]ankrupt debtors are not an identifiable class. They are not all—or mostly—day laborers and household maids dwelling in squalid apartments on the wrong side of the tracks. More than half are homeowners, and they work at pretty much the same jobs as everyone else. . . . The financial trouble that leads to bankruptcy can be found in any community and no social or economic group is immune from it.

. . . In our . . . investigation of bankruptcy, we found that most people in our sample were very sick financially, weighed down with debts far beyond their capacity to repay. A small group, perhaps 5% of all bankrupt debtors, might be abusing the system. . . .

Finding a small group of potential abusers raises the same question in any system: What should be done to identify and deal with them, and how much cost should be borne to support that effort? But the key finding in our data is that abuse should be dealt with as an aberration, not as the guiding issue in restructuring the system. Overwhelmingly, this system treats those who need it. . . .

Other groups in bankruptcy may be more notable for their absence than their presence. A few debtors used bankruptcy to deal with crushing medical debts, a few others seemed unable to resist the lure of their credit cards, and a very few waltzed through the bankruptcy courts more than once. But their numbers were small. . . . The reality is the far more ordinary story of middle-class people drowning in debt.

Causes of Bankruptcy

Debt

. . . [I]n one sense the cause of bankruptcy is self-evident. Bankruptcy is caused by debt. If there were no debt, there would be no bankruptcy. This simplistic formulation is not as silly as it seems, because it starts the inquiry with the central proposition that bankruptcy is a function of debt. Our data confirm the perspective, showing that people in bankruptcy are typical Americans in many ways, but they have debts far out of proportion to their incomes.

This central fact emphasizes the distinction between an increase in bankruptcy as a response to financial trouble and an increase in financial trouble itself. . . . The rise in bankruptcy has, in a general sense, been coincident with the rise in consumer debt.

Even more significant has been the increase in consumer debt as a proportion of income. The debt/income ratio for consumers in America has steadily risen. . . . Our data show that the most distinguishing characteristic of bankrupt debtors is their high debts in relation to their incomes. The constant increase in debt helps to drive the American economy and therefore the world economy, but it has also made more American consumers candidates for bankruptcy. . . .

Irresponsibility and Volatility

The bankruptcies in our sample seem to stem from two intertwined explanations. One is the increased volatility and instability of economic life, an accelerating change to which both consumers and their creditors have failed to adjust. The other is the irresponsibility of particular debtor-creditor dyads, reflected in credit far beyond any reasonable prospect of repayment. In some cases economic disaster preceded bankruptcy: the failed business, job layoff, or serious medical debt. Other cases offer no apparent explanation for the bankruptcy except that spending outstripped income until the balance was no longer supportable—reflecting debtor and creditor irresponsibility.

We cannot know if increased debtor or creditor irresponsibility has led to increased bankruptcy. . . .

Debtors who save little and charge to the limits of prudence are making a wager with Providence, betting that they can never get sick or be fired, or that they can quickly find new jobs if they lose the ones they have. And their creditors have matched the wager. The twin evils of economic volatility and irresponsibility haunt increasing numbers of debtors and creditors.

Bankruptcy Within a Broader Social Context

Bankruptcy must be understood within a broad range of social support systems. . . . Bankruptcy is not just about debtors and creditors; it is a link in a network of legal structures of far-reaching social significance. To examine bankruptcy laws only within the abstraction of debt discharge, without the context of its other social implications, is to miss a large part of how bankruptcy functions. . . .

Ultimately bankruptcy has profound political implications, in the largest sense of the word political. Debt is social dynamite and always has been. . . . In the modern setting, bankruptcy is one of the safety valves that sophisticated capitalism keeps in place to release the pressures of fear and greed that accompany free market incentives. Every machine must have give in the joints or it will destroy itself, and bankruptcy is part of the give in a free market society. . . .

To indenture the unemployed steelworker and the others to their creditors would also create a serious problem of externalities. Taxpayers would be forced to assume the burden of supporting their families while the family income satisfied old debts and their attendant high rates of interest. In effect, tax dollars would be subsidizing creditors, many of whom were equally culpable players in the credit game.

The bankruptcy discharge is not the only approach to these problems. American law is by far the most generous in the world in granting discharges. . . . Other countries address in different way the social problems that are ameliorated in the United States by bankruptcy discharge. . . . [T]he apparent toughness of bankruptcy law in other industrial societies is usually balanced by unemployment and social welfare benefits substantially more generous than our own. Taxpayers in those societies have in effect agreed to subsidize the losses of creditors and to accept the externalities just discussed.

Our bankruptcy discharge is a free market solution to the pathologies of borrowing and lending. Creditors are free to extend credit as they like and debtors to accept it. Both face the prospect of bankruptcy if they are foolish or unlucky. The system places the losses on the debtors and creditors who accepted the benefits and took the risks of credit transactions. So understood, bankruptcy is likely to remain the preferred solution for Americans.

Professors Sullivan, Warren, and Westbrook did another empirical study of individual consumer debtors based on cases filed in 1991. Their findings are reported in Teresa A. Sullivan, Elizabeth Warren & Jay Lawrence Westbrook, *Consumer Debtors Ten Years Later: A Financial*

Comparison of Consumer Bankrupts 1981-1991, 68 AM. BANKR. L.J. 121 (1994). The bottom line is that the 1991 debtors were every bit as financially distressed as their 1981 counterparts, if not more so. The mean family income for 1991 debtors was $20,535—actually 13% *less* than the 1981 figure (as adjusted to 1991 dollars). The median income in 1991 was $18,000—a full 20% less than the adjusted 1981 median. And the mean of total debts for 1991 debtors was $50,783, over 2¹/₂ times the debtor's annual income. The debt median in 1991 was $31,077, which was 1.79 times annual income. The debtors' asset picture was no rosier, with a 1991 mean of $38,553 (12% less than in 1981, as adjusted), and a median asset value of a paltry $16,765 (20% less than 1981). *See* 68 AM. BANKR. L.J. at 129-34. Even though consumer (non-business) bankruptcy filings had gone from 315,818 in 1981 to 872,438 in 1991, the debtors were just as bad off as before.

B.   Discharge and the "Fresh Start"

The central fact of consumer bankruptcy is the discharge. An individual debtor who receives a discharge is legally excused from ever having to pay the discharged debt. How did the law come to embrace such a radical doctrine? And how can that doctrine be justified? Those are the questions considered by the following extensive selection of works.

The first two articles, by Professors McCoid and Tabb, deal with the historical issue. McCoid, in *Discharge: The Most Important Development in Bankruptcy History*, delves into how the first discharge provision came to be included in the Statute of Anne in 1706. As the title indicates, the introduction of the discharge could well be considered the single most important event in bankruptcy history. This work is worth reading purely for the fascinating historical record it reveals. Furthermore, though, McCoid convincingly demonstrates that the seeds for the development of the discharge were planted over an extended time period; the discharge did not spring up like spontaneous combustion. In addition, he shows that the discharge marked the culmination of the transformation of bankruptcy in concept from a pure collection device for the benefit of creditors alone to a mandatory composition procedure designed to benefit creditors *and* the debtor. Viewing the discharge in this light has many ramifications for our conception of bankruptcy.

In *The Historical Evolution of the Bankruptcy Discharge*, Tabb surveys the development of discharge over a more extended period. He traces debtor relief from the earliest English laws in the late Middle Ages, to the watershed of the Statute of Anne, and then on to the uneven path of the sporadic discharge laws in the United States in the nineteenth century, ending with the introduction of permanent federal bankruptcy relief in the Bankruptcy Act of 1898. By that point, the general shape and substance of United States discharge policy had been fairly well settled.

The remaining articles in this part of Chapter 11 seek to answer the *why* questions: (1) why does United States law offers individual debtors a discharge at all?; (2) why does that law exclude some debtors and some types of debts from the discharge?; and (3) why is the discharge unwaivable by the debtor in advance? How do Professors Jackson, Howard, Tabb, and Hirsch approach these problems? In what ways do they agree? How do they differ? On what grounds does Professor Carlson critique Jackson? Catalogue all of the different justifications offered for the discharge. Which are the most persuasive? Do you think that the scope of the discharge should be broader? Narrower? Should debtors be permitted to waive the discharge *ex ante*? And finally—does it matter?

For a recent superb theoretical examination of consumer bankruptcy, justifying that institution from an economic perspective, see Barry Adler, Ben Polak & Alan Schwartz, *Regulating Consumer*

Bankruptcy: A Theoretical Inquiry, 29 J. LEGAL STUD. 585 (2000). That work surely will be included in the next edition of this Anthology.

John C. McCoid, II
Discharge: The Most Important Development in Bankruptcy History
70 AM. BANKR. L.J. 163 (1996)[*]

On March 19, 1706, during the reign of Queen Anne, Parliament passed a bankruptcy act containing a provision for the discharge of the debtor from prebankruptcy debts as a feature. . . . [T]here has been occasional speculation about what prompted it. Some have suggested that it can be attributed to a belated recognition that not all debtors are scoundrels and that the discharge was designed to benefit the honest ones. Others, pointing to the fact that a discharge was available only in bankruptcy, which in turn, was limited to traders and merchants and could only be initiated by creditors, have argued that the discharge was simply a carrot to induce those in trade who became insolvent to cooperate in supplying information about assets and dealings for the benefit of their creditors. Arguably, the true explanation might lie in a combination of these claims. A bankruptcy proceeding which includes a discharge could be mutually beneficial to both debtors and creditors.

. . . Attempting to uncover what it was that led to the discharge provision, a development which, it seems, ranks ahead in importance of all others in Anglo-American bankruptcy history, has led to the conclusion that it was probably not generally seen at the time as being as momentous as we might today be tempted to regard it. The discharge was not very significant at the time because it followed quite naturally from steps already taken, though perhaps in hesitant fashion, in the sixteenth and seventeenth centuries and was itself apparently an experiment. . . .

However it was regarded at the beginning of the eighteenth century, the discharge dramatically transformed bankruptcy. Before 1706, bankruptcy had been a narrowly focused *creditor's collection remedy* pure and simple, differing from other collection remedies because of its collective character and the corollary principle of ratable distribution. After that date, in England and later in this country, it was a *statutorily mandated composition*; an exchange of the collection and distribution of assets to the creditors in which the debtor cooperated in return for a release from further obligation on prebankruptcy debts. . . .

I. THE HISTORY

. . . [S]eventeenth century English history . . . was also a period during which commerce grew, and grew, and grew some more. . . . Trade expanded enormously both at home and abroad. . . .

With the combination of new wealth and troubled times, financial failure often had a ripple effect. The ruin of one could trigger disaster for others as well.

A. THE STATUTE

What we know about the statute is to be gleaned from its text, the Journal of the House of Commons for the period leading up to passage, and the essentially contemporaneous commentary of Daniel Defoe, himself a famous bankrupt and advocate of the idea of a discharge.

---

1. *The Text*

The statute was not a full-blown bankruptcy act covering all aspects of the subject. Rather, it built on existing legislation. Although the statute contained twenty sections, it really dealt with only three subjects. It elaborately dealt with what is of concern here, *i.e.*, what was expected of the bankrupt and certain third parties after issuance of the commission and what would follow from their behavior. . . . [T]he act's coverage, its benefits and sanctions, and the conditions it attached to the enjoyment of benefits were the important features. . . .

The act's benefits were threefold. Under § VII, bankrupts who surrendered to the commissioners and conformed to the directions of the act or who were apprehended within thirty days of issuance of the commission and then conformed "shall be discharged from all debts by him, her, or them due at the time he, she, or they did become bankrupt." Here, then, was what has turned out to be the central provision. There was, however, more. If arrested, prosecuted, or impleaded on such a debt, the bankrupt was entitled to a discharge on common bail and to the recovery of costs if able to prevail by pleading the act in a cause or suit accruing before bankruptcy. Finally, the act called for an allowance to the bankrupt, not exceeding two hundred pounds, of five pounds per hundred of the net estate revealed by the bankrupt and recovered, so long as creditors received eight shillings per pound owed. . . .

To receive these benefits, the opening section of the act required that the bankrupt surrender to the commissioners within thirty days (sixty days if the appropriate official granted an enlargement) after notice of issue of the commission was left at the bankrupt's abode and given in the *Gazette*. The bankrupt was then obliged to submit to examination under oath and there to disclose any disposition of assets (and writings related thereto) in which the bankrupt had an interest at any time before or after issuance of the commission. Lastly, the bankrupt was required to turn over assets (and writings related thereto), necessary wearing apparel excepted, in the bankrupt's possession at the time of the examination. In effect, what was demanded was total cooperation with the commissioners. The statute did more than confer benefits on a debtor who complied with its terms, however. It also contained a sanction for noncompliance. For a failure to meet the statutory requirements, the bankrupt was to "suffer as a felon, without benefit of clergy," language at that time used to prescribe the death penalty.

There were additional conditions to receipt of the benefits described above. Section XIX required the bankrupt to obtain a certificate in writing signed by at least a majority of the commissioners and addressed to the Lord Chancellor, the Lord Keeper, or commissioners entrusted with the seal. The certificate had to certify that the bankrupt made the requisite discovery and conformed to the act, as well as that the commissioners were satisfied that the discovery was both full and true. As a further prerequisite, the certificate had to be confirmed by the Lord Chancellor, the Lord Keeper, the commissioners entrusted with the seal, or by two judges of Queen's Bench, Common Pleas, or Exchequer. Creditors were allowed to be heard in opposition to both the making and confirmation of the certificate.

Moreover, certain prebankruptcy behavior of the debtor was disqualifying. Those who had lost more than five pounds in one day or one hundred pounds in the year before becoming bankrupt by gaming in specified ways were excluded. And, one who had given more than one hundred pounds on the marriage of a child without retaining assets sufficient to pay all debts then owing was also ineligible for benefits.

Thus, the principal focus of the act was to prescribe the appropriate behavior of certain bankrupts and to set rewards for conforming to its requirements and sanctions for noncompliance. The statute's title, however, was "An act to prevent frauds frequently committed by bankrupts." And the preamble recited that "many persons have and do daily become bankrupt, not so much by reason of losses and unavoidable misfortunes, as to the intent to defraud and hinder their creditors of their just debts and duties to them due and owing." . . . The condemnatory nature of this wording, however, may be explained by the fact . . . that the benefits of the discharge and allowance were not a part of the original bill but were added by amendment without any alteration of the preamble.

2. *The House Journal*

The House of Commons Journal adds only modestly to the account. Essentially, its value lies in its report of the chronology of enactment, beginning with the first reading on October 31, 1705, and ending with the passing of the act in both Houses on March 19, 1706, *and* in its identification of the locus of new ideas. . . .

. . . [I]t seems apparent that the discharge provision came into the bill on February 27 or March 5 as a result of committee action in response to the February 4 instruction. The bill passed the House of Commons by a 54-53 vote on March 6, 1706, after still further modification of the provision extending benefits to those already bankrupt. It was in the House of Lords that the idea of conditioning the discharge on a certificate and its confirmation emerged. The House of Commons assented to this addition on March 19, and the deed was done.

3. *Defoe's Commentary*

A bankrupt in 1692, Daniel Defoe had experienced imprisonment at the behest of his creditors.
. . .

From February 12, 1706, to March 27, in his thrice-weekly newspaper, "*A Review of the State of the English Nation,*" Defoe authored a series reporting on the bill and providing his own commentary. Thus, the series overlapped the activity in Parliament. . . .

In his beginning comments, Defoe dealt with fraudulent bankrupts. On Tuesday, February 26, he turned to the plight of honest debtors. Here, Defoe emphasized the importance of encouraging traders in financial difficulty to "come in fairly to their Creditors, and resign their effects:"

> [W]hen men know, that if they *stop in time*, they shall be well Treated, that on a fair Surrender, they shall be us'd like Honest Men, and *pitty'd as Men of Misfortune*; they then have no Temptation, no Excuse to run on, *to all manner of lengths*; he that does so *then*, Declares himself a *Profess'd Thief*, deserves no Pity, and ought to be handled *like himself*, no Law can be too Severe with him. . . . Experience tells us, that Present Advantage has a greater Influence on Mens Minds, than future Apprehension; Men are rather *Drawn* than *Driven*, and Fear has not half the Effect in Cases of Crime, as Profit. . . .

Quite clearly, Defoe thought a carrot would be more effective in achieving the debtor's cooperation than a stick. He argued that the promise of a discharge would deter fraudulent behavior by a trader in trouble more effectively than would the assurance of punishment for fraud if committed. This was an idea, he opined, that had not been a part of the original bill, which had only required the bankrupt to surrender on pain of punishment.

Returning to the issue of benefits on February 28, Defoe's language again suggested that the provisions of the bill providing benefits to a cooperating bankrupt were not in the original draft:

> I Debated in the last Paper, the Injustice *of a Law*, to oblige the Debtor or Bankrupt-Trader, to Surrender his Books and Effects to his Creditors, or to the Commissioners, while at the same time, the Creditors *are not at all oblig'd to come in and accept of it*, and Discharge him.

> I Presume, the undeniable force of this Argument, prevail'd upon the Gentlemen, who have *this Law* under Consideration *to receive a Clause*, to encourage all such bankrupts, or Insolvent Debtors, as are under the Hands of their Creditors, to make an Honest Surrender, of all their Effects and Estate, for the Use of their creditors, and by obliging the Creditors *to accept* of such Surrender, and Discharge the Creditor.

A comparison of the Journal's chronology of the legislative process and the dates of Defoe's commentary in the *Review* seems to confirm that the proposal for discharge was the committee's response to the instruction of the House of Commons of February 4 . . . .

On March 2, Defoe suggested that punishment only drove merchants to leave the country . . . . On March 7, he argued that the cruelty of some creditors drove debtors to misbehavior.

On March 16, after the bill had gone from the House of Commons to the House of Lords, Defoe complained that "this Law has the Misfortune to be now alter'd, *for I cannot call it Amended*," by the provision requiring the commissioners' certificate as a condition of discharge and allowance. Yet, on March 23, Defoe reported the passage of "one of the best Bills that ever was produc'd in Parliament, since the *Habeas Corpus* Act, for Securing the Liberty of the Subject." He was not entirely approving. Defoe continued to criticize so much of the bill as allowed the commissioners to decline to issue a certificate *"without showing Cause*—Why they refuse it."

Defoe had already suggested, on March 12, that he could see no reason to limit the bill's beneficiaries to future bankrupts . . . . Later, in light of the enacted extension, he revived his own, earlier bankruptcy with the apparent aim of obtaining a discharge. Defoe was examined several times by the commissioners, but opposition by his creditors and a necessary trip to Scotland on Crown business delayed his obtaining a certificate. By the time he returned, the law had been amended to require the consent of four-fifths of his creditors as a condition of discharge. This he was unable to manage.

Defoe's separate essay, entitled *"Remarks on the Bill to Prevent Frauds Committed by Bankrupts,"* was apparently written sometime after the bill was passed by Parliament. Losses at sea, because of war with the French, and because of fierce storms, especially one on November 27, 1703, he said, were the underlying causes of many failures. Defoe thought that the bill was more immediately precipitated, however, by the failure of one Thomas Pitkin, a linen draper who had broken "for a very great Sum of Money, and that with all the dark Circumstances of a designed Fraud." Willing to take some credit for the amendment introducing the discharge, Defoe argued that the bill in its initial form had been an "absurdity," *conducive* to fraud because it required the debtor to surrender all, left him vulnerable to creditors, and preferred some creditors at the expense of others. This weakness in the initial draft, he believed, was what had prompted the motion in the House of Commons that the committee be empowered "to receive a Clause for the Encouragement of such Bankrupts as shall voluntarily surrender their Effects to the use of their Creditors." . . .

B. The Earlier History

. . . Acts of the Privy Council from about the middle of the sixteenth century to the middle of the seventeenth, bills of conformity in Chancery used for a longer period but coming to an end a little earlier, an Interregnum ordinance dealing with imprisoned debtors, and later efforts in Parliament dealing with composition agreements were aimed at resolving the conflict between an insolvent debtor and his or her creditors in a way that avoided permanent ruin of the debtor. . . .

1. *Privy Council*

During the Tudor and Stuart reigns, the Privy Council was active in both public and private matters, so that English government was significantly conciliar. . . .

Whether at the instance of a majority of creditors or of the debtor, the Council acted in various ways, ordinarily through appointees called commissions. Typically the focus was on the plight of a named debtor or debtors, usually merchants, but protection of groups of debtors also occurred. . . .

If persuasion was more frequently the tool than coercion, the latter was nonetheless in evidence. Recalcitrant creditors were routinely required by the appointees to post bonds to secure appearance before the Council to justify any manifested obduracy. Though it was usually left unclear how non-assenting creditors would be treated, threats of serious sanction for noncooperation by creditors were sometimes only thinly veiled . . . . There was an iron fist in the velvet glove. Even imprisonment was a possibility for a truly obstinate creditor.

Inevitably perhaps, this activity of the Council came into conflict with the jurisdiction of the common law courts. The judges first formally protested in 1591, and Coke repeated the complaint some twenty years later. As a consequence, the Council's jurisdiction ultimately was abolished by the "Long Parliament" in 1641.

2. *Chancery*

Chancery protection of debtors began even earlier. . . . Chancery's involvement was interrelated with the Council's efforts. . . . Treiman documented debtor relief through Chancery occurring as early as the fourteenth century. According to his account, the practice began in the form of "bills of protection" awarded debtors by the Chancellor. As the Privy Council came to grant similar relief, these bills disappeared, but Chancery supported the Council's protections with subpoenas and injunctions. . . . Still later, there were suits by creditors based on protections granted a debtor to restrain other, recalcitrant creditors from collection actions. In a further development, majority creditors brought suits in Chancery to enforce a composition or extension agreement against a dissenting minority even in the absence of any preexisting protection. Ultimately, these "bills of conformity" came to be used by debtors themselves.

. . . [T]he underlying procedure was ill-defined and resulted in abuses. These, in turn, first led to regulation of the bills by the Lord Chancellor, Francis Bacon. Among his requirements was that assenting creditors must represent at least three-fourths of the amount of the insolvent's debt. Finally, in the wake of Bacon's resignation in disgrace, bills of conformity were abolished by royal proclamation in 1621. In 1623, the very filing by a debtor of such a bill was made an act of bankruptcy.

Ritchie's Reports of Francis Bacon's decisions as Lord Chancellor reveal both extensions and compositions ordered by him against a dissenting minority in the period between 1617 and 1620, just before the abolition of bills of conformity. These orders might be accompanied by injunctions against further actions at law and were enforced, if necessary, by the imprisonment of holdouts. . . .

3. *The Interregnum*

With the Privy Council and Chancery both barred from providing aid to debtors and creditors, the problem of insolvent-but-honest debtors fell to Parliament. . . . [L]egislative action on the subject was taken during the Interregnum in mid-century.

In October, 1653, provision already having been made by the "Long Parliament" for the release from prison of debtors who would take an oath that they owned an estate worth no more than five pounds, the "Little Parliament" passed an act providing for relief of creditors and poor prisoners. This act, which was to be in force for only a year, called for the payment of the debts out of the sale of the estates of debtors imprisoned on or before October 20, 1653. . . . Covering imprisoned debtors of any description, not just merchants and traders, it provided that they should be treated as bankrupts if they did not pay their debts before April 1, 1654.

The judges appointed to act were also authorized to "discharge, abate, or give respite to any Prisoner . . . according to the circumstances of each particular case. . . ." An additional provision, "nevertheless, the Estate of any such Prisoner is to remain subject to the Creditors satisfaction, according to Law," makes clear that discharge of obligations as well as from prison was not contemplated.

There was outcry against the act, particularly from the prisoners themselves, partly based on their objection to being treated as bankrupts. . . . [A]n ordinance issuing from the Lord Protector and his Council on June 9, 1654, supplied the necessary direction.

The ordinance similarly provided for payment of creditors from the revenues generated from sale of the estates of their debtors and for the release from custody of the debtors, but it conditioned payment of creditors in the following terms:

> Provided also, That no Creditor shall have advantage or benefit of any sale as aforesaid, made for or towards satisfaction of the Debt, unless he give a legal Discharge of the whole or part of his said Debt, as the Case requires, to be ordered by the said Judges.

. . . [F]ull payment would result in discharge without the necessity of a statutory provision. The provision was more than likely intended to authorize the judges to grant a full or partial discharge based on other considerations, such as how the debtor fell into financial difficulty or how well he cooperated in the liquidation of his estate.

Here, then, was a statutory provision for discharge a half-century earlier than its better-known successor. . . . Operation of the ordinance was modestly extended to December, 1654. Although it, along with others, was declared null and void on June 26, 1657, by the Second Parliament of the Protectorate, acts done by virtue of it were nonetheless validated by the same act.

4. *Parliament*

The Crown restored, much of the effort of Parliament similarly had to do with discharge from custody of imprisoned debtors. A scheme for accomplishing this was finally passed in initial form in 1670-71 . . . . But freedom from the gaol, however important, still was an incomplete solution, for under these acts a creditor might continue to seek collection from a debtor discharged from custody.

Composition offered an avenue of relief. Pursuing this possibility in 1679, the House of Commons drew up, but ultimately dropped, a bill to prevent a minority of the creditors of a bankrupt from obstructing a composition to which the majority assented. . . . A more expansive House of Lords, 1694 bill, covering all insolvent debtors, finally led to enactment in 1696-97 of a composition statute binding on a minority where two-thirds in number and value were agreed. This statute was repealed the following year, however, because of "pretended agreements with persons who were not real creditors, and for greater advantages than what were expressed in such compositions." . . .

D. The Aftermath

Designed from the outset for a limited time period, the 1706 act was in operation for less than a year before claims of misuse prompted its amendment. Noting the fraudulent behavior allegedly growing out of the discharge provision, Parliament in 1707 provided that the consent of four-fifths, in both number and value, of a bankrupt's creditors was to be an additional condition of the discharge, a condition that apparently blocked Defoe's attempt to get one.

. . . Not until the codification and revision of 1732 did discharge become a permanent feature of English bankruptcy law. Creditor consent continued to be a prerequisite in England until 1842. . . .

II. THE MEANING OF HISTORY

What is one to make of the events preceding and immediately following the 1706 enactment of the bankruptcy discharge provision? This much, at least, appears certain. The discharge was not an invention of the Parliament sitting in 1705-1706. Neither did it originate in the fruitful mind of Daniel Defoe in the 1690s. The discharge provision of the Interregnum ordinance, although the ordinance dealt only with imprisoned debtors and applied only to creditors who participated in the distribution of the debtor's estate, refutes those possibilities beyond question. The concept of discharge of an insolvent from debt by *rule of law* clearly had existed as early as the middle of the seventeenth century.

. . . The bankruptcy discharge provision of 1706 seems to have been one in a series of experiments, largely centered in the seventeenth century, in the use of composition as the remedy for the insolvency of honest, but unfortunate, debtors. Ultimately, what began as an experiment permanently transformed bankruptcy from an instrument of *collective debt collection* to a *statutorily mandated composition*, a final settlement of an insolvent's relations with his creditors.

The introduction of the discharge is described as initially an experiment because the limitation from the outset on the duration and coverage of the 1706 act strongly suggests that it was meant to be tentative in character. . . . Moreover, the idea of an experiment fits comfortably in the pattern formed by the sporadic efforts to deal with the problem of insolvency made previously by the Privy Council, Chancery, Interregnum Council, and Parliament. . . .

. . . [A]ll the efforts to deal with insolvencies in the century preceding the 1706 enactment . . . had the same basic goal, a resolution of the debtor's relations with creditors. Taken together, they reveal a natural progression from *agreement* to *persuasion* to *coercion* to *statute*, an evolution from bargain to rule that is familiar in other contexts as well as here. . . .

It is not surprising that the various authorities saw composition as an appropriate solution to the insolvency of honest debtors. It is socially desirable because it makes possible the debtor's return to productivity, which is beneficial to others as well as to himself. It is easy to see why it was and remains regarded as an outcome superior to debtor impoverishment which is the consequence of a system looking only to collection, whether or not that system includes imprisonment. . . .

What is important about the bankruptcy discharge is, thus, *not* that it involved the *invention* of a new concept. Rather, what is truly significant is the *transformation* of bankruptcy from a collection device to a scheme of statutorily mandated composition designed to salvage the debtor from insolvency to the general advantage of all. Thinking of bankruptcy as having a composition, rather than a debt collection, goal may significantly affect one's view as to its proper structure. . . .

CONCLUSION

Seen in historical context, the discharge was the ultimate instrument of the transformation of bankruptcy from a creditors' collection remedy to a system of statutorily mandated composition mutually beneficial to debtors and creditors. Just as the composition solution to the problem of insolvency of honest debtors was not a sudden invention, this change in underlying theory was not made explicit in legislation.

. . . More than changes in the law, recognition by judges and litigators, as well as by debtors and their creditors, that the insolvencies of honest debtors are best addressed with a view to composition can do much to improve our treatment of financial failures.

Charles Jordan Tabb
The Historical Evolution of the Bankruptcy Discharge
65 AM. BANKR. L.J. 325 (1991)[*]

I. INTRODUCTION

Bankruptcy has permeated our national consciousness and conscience. A federal bankruptcy law has been on the books for as long as any but the oldest among us has been alive. To most Americans, bankruptcy probably is synonymous with the idea of a discharge from one's debts. . . . The idea of a bankruptcy law without a freely available discharge seems unimaginable.

Yet, the unimaginable is the historical norm. Bankruptcy has been around for almost half a millennium in Anglo-American jurisprudence, yet the discharge as we know it in the United States did not exist until the turn of this century. . . . Even England, the source of our own bankruptcy law, offers debtors a much less generous discharge than the United States.

This article traces how the discharge in the United States became such a central part of our bankruptcy scheme. Specifically, the article examines the evolution of the bankruptcy discharge from the inception of the Anglo-American bankruptcy laws in 1542 until the first part of this century, by which time the fundamental shape of our current discharge laws had been formed. . . .

II. THE DEVELOPMENT OF ENGLISH DISCHARGE LAWS PRIOR TO 1800

A. LAW PRIOR TO THE STATUTE OF 4 ANNE: THE ORIGINS OF ENGLISH BANKRUPTCY

. . . [I]n 1542 Parliament enacted the first English bankruptcy law, 34 & 35 Henry 8, chapter 4, entitled "An act against such persons as do make bankrupts." As the title indicates, the act was not passed with any heed for the interests of the debtor. Instead, it was intended to give creditors a further collection remedy. . . . This act, along with all of the early bankruptcy laws, was quasi-criminal in nature . . . . The right to commence a bankruptcy proceeding rested solely in the hands of the *creditors* of the debtor. This limitation was perfectly consistent with the rationale of the act, which was to protect creditors and thus facilitate commerce. . . .

Of particular relevance for this article is the fact that the 1542 Act of 34 & 35 Henry 8, chapter 4, did *not* provide for a discharge of debts of the "offender." Indeed, a discharge provision would have been fundamentally inconsistent with the act's entire premise. . . .

The century and a half following the 1542 act saw episodic English legislation on the subject of bankruptcies, in 1570, 1604, 1623, and 1662. Each law focused in considerable part on means to improve the lot of creditors vis-à-vis the offending debtor . . . . One senses in the statutes a growing frustration of creditors unable to stem the tide of bankruptcies. . . . No discharge was available under any circumstances. . . .

B. THE STATUTE OF 4 ANNE: THE ORIGINS OF THE DISCHARGE

The first watershed event in the Anglo-American history of the bankruptcy discharge occurred in 1705 when Parliament, in the Statute of 4 Anne, enacted the first provision enabling an honest and cooperative bankrupt to obtain a discharge from prebankruptcy debts. Paradoxically, given its historical importance in the evolution of a more humane treatment of distressed debtors, the statute probably was motivated largely by concerns for creditors' welfare, and may have had only a limited beneficial effect for most debtors. . . .

The discharge language is found in the seventh section of the act:

> And be it further enacted by the authority aforesaid, That all and every person and persons so becoming bankrupt, as aforesaid, who shall, within the time limited by this act, surrender him, her, or themselves to the major part of the commissioners therein named, and in all things conform as in and by this act is directed . . . shall be discharged from all debts by him, her, or them due and owing at the time that he, she, or they did become bankrupt.

The discharge was not self-executing, however. For the bankrupt to receive a discharge, a majority of the bankruptcy commissioners had to certify to the Chancellor that the bankrupt had in fact "conformed" to the act. Thus, the operative document that the bankrupt needed to enforce a discharge came to be called a "certificate of conformity." "Conformity" required the bankrupt voluntarily to surrender to the commissioners for examination as to his or her financial affairs, full disclosure of those affairs, and delivery of all of his or her assets to the commissioners. These acts, obviously, facilitated the recovery of the most assets for the benefit of the creditors. . . .

The conforming debtor also received a monetary allowance out of the estate. The allowance could be as much as five per cent of the estate, up to a maximum of £200. If, however, the creditors did not receive a dividend from the bankruptcy estate in the amount of "eight shillings in the pound," *i.e.*, 40 per cent, net of administrative expenses, then the size of the bankrupt's allowance rested in the commissioner's discretion. Thus, the idea of a minimum percentage dividend to creditors as a prerequisite to a debtor's entitlement to a full fresh start, an idea which persisted in this country until the dawn of the twentieth century, is found in the very first statutory embodiment of the fresh start.

Two very important limitations on the scope of the first discharge law must be noted. First, only "traders" were eligible for treatment under the bankruptcy laws. Since a discharge of debts was available only in bankruptcy, non-trader insolvents had no opportunity to receive a discharge. . . .

The second limitation on the reach of the discharge was that bankruptcy remained a purely involuntary remedy. A debtor desiring a discharge could not simply file bankruptcy and receive a discharge, as the overwhelming percentage of modern-day debtors do. Only creditors could put the debtor into bankruptcy, if the debtor had committed an "act of bankruptcy." . . . [C]lever debtors contrived ways to put themselves in with the assistance of friendly creditors, but Parliament tried to stop such practices. Voluntary bankruptcy per se did not exist until the middle of the nineteenth century.

While the Statute of 4 Anne on the one hand introduced provisions for the relief of honest and cooperative debtors, as just described, on the other hand it struck with especial severity against "fraudulent bankrupts." . . . [I]n the Statute of 4 Anne, Parliament went to the final extreme, providing that persons convicted as fraudulent bankrupts "shall suffer as a felon, without benefit of clergy." In the legal lexicon of the time, that meant the death penalty. The discharge was the "carrot" offered to induce debtors to cooperate in disclosing and turning over their estates; the death penalty was the "stick." . . .

What motivated this landmark statute? . . .

Certainly the primary purpose of the act was to facilitate creditors' recoveries; the title of and preamble to the statute make that abundantly clear. . . . The prerequisite to the debtor receiving a discharge—"conforming" to the act—shows the fundamentally creditor-oriented basis of the law, since the required conforming activities were designed to enlarge and ease the creditors' recoveries. Furthermore, the very rapid retreat taken by Parliament, which soon required creditor consent to the discharge, indicates that the interests of the creditor were paramount. Finally, the predominance of the creditors' interests is shown by the limitation to traders, and the reservation to creditors of the right to institute bankruptcy proceedings.

It would be a mistake, however, the ascribe to Parliament no concern for the debtor's interests. The century preceding the passage of the Statute of 4 Anne had seen considerable agitation regarding the plight of honest insolvents . . . . As the "Age of Reason" moved into full bloom, thoughtful persons began to recognize a moral distinction between fraudulent debtors and honest but unfortunate traders . . . . The importance of commercial credit to the growth of commerce, the possibility of honest losses suffered solely because of the uncertainties of trade, and the corresponding need for merchants to be able to limit their liability, were all recognized. . . .

C. DEVELOPMENTS AFTER THE STATUTE OF 4 ANNE: RETRENCHMENT AND RECODIFICATION

1. Prior to the Statute of 5 George 2

The generosity of the 1705 Statute of 4 Anne to compliant bankrupts was extremely short-lived. The very next year, 1706, Parliament passed an act which introduced creditor consent as a prerequisite to obtaining a discharge. From that point forward, creditor control over the discharge persisted until almost the twentieth century. . . . Under the new law the bankrupt's prebankruptcy debts were not discharged unless the certificate of conformity was signed by four-fifths in number and value of the creditors proving their debts in the bankruptcy proceeding. . . .

2. The Statute of 5 George 2, Chapter 30

In 1732, in the fifth year of the reign of King George 2, Parliament passed "An act to prevent the committing of frauds by bankrupts," a comprehensive codification and revision of the bankruptcy law of Great Britain. . . . It was the law in effect at the time of the American Revolution, the Constitutional Convention of 1787, and the enactment of the first United States bankruptcy law in 1800. It thus was the bankruptcy model envisioned by the drafters of the bankruptcy clause of the Constitution and which was followed in material part in the first United States law.

The essential features of prior discharge laws were maintained in the Statute of 5 George, and no major innovations were made. . . .

The carrot and stick approach of the Statute of 4 Anne was continued. On the one hand, nonconforming bankrupts continued to be subject to treatment as "felons without benefit of clergy," i.e., the death penalty. Conforming bankrupts, on the other hand, were eligible for a discharge from prebankruptcy debts. They also were entitled to a graduated allowance, depending on the percentage dividend paid to creditors, and were permitted to retain certain property as exempt. . . .

Other sections of the act specified how the discharge was to be enforced. Basically, the certificate of conformity was a shield that the bankrupt could use to defend postbankruptcy efforts to collect prebankruptcy debts. It did not operate automatically to forestall such efforts, however, but had to be invoked by the bankrupt. . . . This system of the discharge as an affirmative defense was copied in the United States, where it lasted until 1970. . . .

III. THE EVOLUTION OF UNITED STATES DISCHARGE LAWS

A. THE BANKRUPTCY ACT OF 1800

Thus matters stood in England in 1787 when the bankruptcy clause was included in the United States Constitution. . . .

Finally, in 1800, the first federal bankruptcy law was enacted. . . . [T]he Bankruptcy Act of 1800 closely followed the 1732 English Statute of 5 George 2. . . . Some of the more debtor-oriented colonial bankruptcy laws were not followed in the 1800 Act. The 1800 Act thus contributed very little to the evolution of the bankruptcy discharge. Like its English forebears, it was principally designed to assist creditors. . . .

The salient features of the 1800 act for the purposes of this article are that: only merchants were eligible debtors; only involuntary bankruptcy was allowed, on proof of an act of bankruptcy; and the act provided for a discharge of the debts as well as the person of a cooperative debtor. It granted a graduated allowance to the conforming bankrupt, depending on the size of the dividend paid to creditors. Furthermore, the bankrupt was allowed limited property exemptions: the "necessary wearing apparel" and "necessary bed and bedding" of the bankrupt and his wife and children.

. . .

As under the English system, discharge was not a matter of right, but could only be obtained with the approval of the bankruptcy commissioners and the creditors. The operative document evidencing the bankrupt's entitlement to a discharge from debts and from prison was called a "certificate of discharge." . . . The certificate also had to be signed by two-thirds in number and in value of creditors holding proved debts of at least $50. . . .

Proof by a creditor of one of a few specified grounds prevented the bankrupt from receiving a discharge. These grounds were (1) failure of the bankrupt to disclose a fictitious claim, or (2) loss of $50 at one time or $300 total in the year preceding bankruptcy "by any manner of gaming or wagering whatever." In addition, discharges in successive cases were restricted: the discharge in the second case was denied, no matter how much time had elapsed since the first discharge, unless a 75% dividend was paid to creditors in that case. The coverage of the discharge was broad: only debts owing to the United States or any of the States were excepted.

Once the certificate of discharge was allowed and entered of record in the district clerk's office, the burden of invoking its benefits fell upon the bankrupt. . . . [T]he bankrupt had to raise the discharge as an affirmative defense if sued on or arrested for any such debts. . . .

The 38 years following the repeal of the 1800 Act saw a return to piece-meal state legislation on bankruptcy and insolvency. The inadequacies of such laws . . . were confirmed in two famous Supreme Court cases, *Sturges v. Crowninshield* and *Ogden v. Saunders*. *Sturges*, decided in 1819, held that a state law which allowed the discharge of *preexisting* debts unconstitutionally impaired the obligation of contracts. *Ogden* held in 1827 that a discharge under one state's law could not constitutionally discharge a debt due to a citizen of *another* state. However, the *Ogden* court also held that a state law discharging *prospective* debts was valid against citizens of the *same* state. This latter aspect of Ogden provided opponents of federal bankruptcy legislation with an argument that state insolvency laws were not wholly powerless to deal with debt crises. . . .

B. The Bankruptcy Act of 1841

While the Bankruptcy Act of 1800 broke little new ground, the next United States bankruptcy law, the Bankruptcy Act of 1841, stands as the second watershed event, along with the Statute of 4 Anne, in the evolution of the bankruptcy discharge. The 1841 law introduced a completely new focus and purpose to a bankruptcy proceeding. Before, bankruptcy had been a creditors' remedy available only on an involuntary basis and only against merchants and traders. . . . The Panic of 1837 established the ineffectiveness of state laws to deal with a national economic crisis, and led to the Bankruptcy Act of 1841.

The Bankruptcy Act of 1841 sought to protect debtors directly. For the first time in Anglo-American jurisprudence *voluntary* bankruptcy was allowed. A debtor desiring the benefit of a bankruptcy discharge could simply file a petition in bankruptcy, comply with the provisions of the act, and, if the creditors consented, receive a discharge.

The second major innovation of the 1841 act was the elimination of the limitation of the class of eligible bankruptcy debtors to merchants. Eligibility was extended to "all persons whatsoever . . . owing debts." The act did retain involuntary bankruptcy, against merchants only. In its very simplicity this law fundamentally transformed the underlying assumptions regarding the nature of bankruptcy.

Not surprisingly, the radical nature of the 1841 law precipitated a firestorm of controversy involving the leading political figures of the day. Many alleged that such a law was not only bad policy but also unconstitutional. . . . Although never tested directly in the Supreme Court, the constitutionality of the 1841 law was upheld at the circuit level by Justice Catron. Even though widespread discontent with the 1841 act led to its repeal just over a year later, the issue of the permissible scope of the federal bankruptcy power had been settled as including voluntary bankruptcy for non-merchants. The issue was not even raised during the debates over the next bankruptcy bill in 1867.

Another important provision of the 1841 act was the attempt to clamp down on the prevalent practice of preferring some creditors over others. . . . The 1841 act thus denied a debtor a discharge if the debtor had made a preference in the two months preceding bankruptcy, unless a majority of the non-preferred creditors consented to the discharge.

. . . The basic requirement for receiving the discharge followed previous discharge laws: the debtor had to make a "bona fide" surrender of the nonexempt property for the benefit of creditors, obey all court orders, and generally "conform" to the provisions of the act.

The creditor consent requirement was softened from the 1800 act provisions in a legislative compromise. First, the burden was shifted to creditors to take the initiative to file a written dissent, instead of being on the bankrupt to gain their affirmative consent. Second, the percentage of consenting (actually non-dissenting) creditors required was reduced from the two-thirds required by the 1800 act to a majority in number and value. . . .

The statutory grounds for denying a discharge were, however, expanded considerably beyond those contained in the 1800 law. . . . The grounds for denying discharge were fraud, wilful concealment of property, making a preference, wilful failure to comply with court orders, wilful failure to conform to the requirements of the act, admitting a false or fictitious debt, or applying trust funds to the debtor's own use. Merchants were required also as a condition of their discharge to keep proper books of account. The limitation on discharges in successive cases was copied from the 1800 act: no discharge was granted in the second case unless a 75% dividend was paid to creditors in that second case. As with the 1800 act, this was the only use of a minimum dividend requirement.

Also like the 1800 act, few debts were excepted from the operation of the general discharge. The statute itself only excepted debts arising from "defalcation as a public officer" and fiduciary obligations. The courts created an exception found in the 1800 law, for debts due to the United States or any of the states. . . .

As under all prior discharge laws, the benefits of the discharge once granted had to be raised by the bankrupt as an affirmative defense. . . .

The law proved a boon for debtors, 33,739 of whom took advantage of the act, and of whom only 765 were denied a discharge. Creditors shocked by the "deluge" of debtors seeking relief sought to repeal the law almost immediately after its passage. Very small dividends were paid, and administrative expenses were high. The act was repealed in March 1843. Despite its short life, however, the Bankruptcy Act of 1841 represented a significant milestone in the evolution of the bankruptcy discharge.

C. THE BANKRUPTCY ACT OF 1867

After the repeal of the 1841 act the United States went almost a quarter of a century without a national bankruptcy law, until the enactment of the Bankruptcy Act of 1867. . . .

. . . [T]he economic disaster wrought first by the Panic of 1857 and then by the Civil War revived serious agitation for a federal bankruptcy act. Perhaps the most telling reason a *federal* law was needed (as opposed to state law coverage only) was to offer debtors a more complete discharge. A number of states did not have any discharge laws. Even those that did could afford only partial relief because of *Sturges* and *Ogden,* Supreme Court cases which precluded the discharge under state laws of prior debts and debts of nonresident creditors.

. . . Major points of debate relating to the fresh start included (1) whether to allow debtors to invoke the exemption law of their domiciliary state in a federal bankruptcy proceeding; (2) whether a creditor consent limitation on the debtor's discharge should be included; and, (3) related to the creditor consent question, whether a minimum dividend percentage payment to creditors should be required as a condition of receiving a discharge, and if so, what that percentage should be. . . .

The exemption question was resolved squarely in favor of the debtors. Many state exemption laws, typically quite beneficial to debtors, had been passed in the middle part of the nineteenth century. . . .

The 1867 act did include state exemption laws, in addition to federal exemptions similar to those found in the 1841 act. . . .

Whether to include the state exemption laws was not the only issue, however; it also was critical to decide as of *when*. The 1867 act incorporated the state exemption laws as of *1864*, which of course excluded the Southern states. After the war in the late 1860s the Southern states and many of the Western states adopted new constitutions and statutes providing for very generous exemptions to debtors. In response to pressure from those regions the 1867 law was amended in 1872 to change the incorporation date to 1871, which was much more favorable to debtors. . . .

The related issues of creditor consent to discharge and a minimum dividend to creditors as a condition to discharge similarly produced a fascinating display of legislative legerdemain. Again the pro-debtor forces claimed victory. In an apparent concession to pro-creditor factions, the 1867 act required the debtor to pay a 50% dividend to obtain a discharge unless a majority in number and value of creditors holding proved claims consented to the discharge. . . .

The supposed creditor victory on the issue was even more chimerical, however. The bigger victory for the pro-debtor group was the legislative postponement of the effective date of the consent/dividend provision for a year. In 1868 Congress again extended the effective date of the creditor consent provision, this time to January 1, 1869. These delays allowed the many thousands of extant debtors whose very existence largely precipitated passage of the bankruptcy law a substantial grace period within which to file bankruptcy and apply for a discharge without being subject at all to the minimum dividend/creditor consent requirement. . . .

These legislative victories for the pro-debtor forces did not, however, ultimately carry the day in terms of accomplishing the fundamental goal of affording a ready discharge to those who needed it. Indeed, one of the principal shortcomings of the 1867 act proved to be the difficulty of obtaining a discharge. Fewer than one-third of the bankrupts ultimately received a discharge. Initial access to the bankruptcy forum was not the problem. . . .

Rather, the chief difficulty in obtaining a discharge was presented by the extremely long list of grounds for denying the discharge contained in section 29 of the act. The harshness of this section may have been a reaction to the widely-stated criticism that the 1841 law had been too favorable to debtors. . . .

Like the acts of 1800 and 1841, the 1867 act did not except many debts from the operation of the discharge once granted. The only statutorily excepted debts were those "created by the fraud or embezzlement of the bankrupt, or by his defalcation as a public officer, or while acting in any fiduciary capacity." . . .

The discharge released the debtor from all provable claims other than those specifically excepted. However, as was the case previously and until 1970, the bankrupt had the burden of pleading the certificate of discharge as an affirmative defense. . . .

A new concept in debtor relief, the composition agreement, was introduced for the first time into American bankruptcy law by the 1874 amendments. . . . The debtor thus would propose to pay a stated percentage of his or her debts in full satisfaction thereof, a meeting would be called to consider the proposed composition, and the creditors would vote on whether to accept that proposal. An affirmative vote of a majority in number and three-fourths in value of the creditors was required. If the proposal was passed, and the court approved, the debtor could retain his or her property and discharge the debts by paying the amounts provided for by the composition. This innovative approach to debtor relief provided "the first escape in American legislation from the stigma attaching to bankruptcy."

Importantly, *all* creditors listed on the debtor's statement of debts, even those who dissented from the proposed composition, were bound by its provisions. . . .

The rights of the minority creditors were protected by the requirement that the court confirm that the composition was "for the best interest of all concerned." . . . [C]reditors were entitled to be paid at least as much in the composition as they would be in an immediate bankruptcy liquidation. . . .

The composition provision did not offer a refuge for dishonest debtors more favorable than that available in straight bankruptcy cases. In the 1881 case of *Wilmot v. Mudge*, the Supreme Court held that a debt based on fraud could not be discharged in a composition when the defrauded creditor did not assent. . . .

The composition provisions died along with the rest of the 1867 act and its accretions in the 1878 repeal. Apparently the sentiment to repeal the bankruptcy law was overwhelming, even though the United States had not yet emerged from the economic devastation wrought by the Panic of 1873. Creditors were fed up with the familiar problems: small dividends, exorbitant fees and expenses, and interminable delays. For the next twenty years, and the third time in the nineteenth century, but probably for the last time in our nation's history, beleaguered debtors (and creditors, for that matter) were relegated to the uncertain and incomplete relief afforded by state insolvent laws.

D. THE BANKRUPTCY ACT OF 1898

. . . The 1898 act marked another significant step in the evolution of the bankruptcy discharge. It brought the country much closer to the basic type of system still in effect today. Some of the features of earlier laws were reenacted. . . . Voluntary bankruptcy was made available on demand to "[a]ny person who owes debts, except a corporation." With the increased availability of the corporate form to limit liability for entrepreneurs, discharge in bankruptcy now was principally important only for non-merchant individuals. . . . The only exemptions available to debtors were those of their state of domicile; no separate federal bankruptcy exemptions were provided. Compositions were offered by section 12, and the confirmation of the proposed composition served as the discharge.

The 1898 act signaled a clear . . . parting of the ways between England and the United States regarding the discharge. For the most part the major English reforms of 1883, which established the general model of English bankruptcy and discharge still in effect today, were not followed in the 1898 legislation. Under the 1883 English law control over the discharge was removed once and for all from creditors. Instead the English court was given a broad discretion to grant or deny discharges, to condition them on making certain payments to creditors, or to suspend them for a period of time. Such discretion was not given to United States bankruptcy judges in 1898 or thereafter; rather, the discharge rules have been fixed by the Congress. With few exceptions the role of the court has been to rule on whether the statutory grounds for denial of or exception to the discharge have been proven, and no more.

The United States Congress in 1898 did not just decline to give the bankruptcy court control over the discharge. At the same time, that control was taken away from creditors. The long-standing requirement of either creditor consent or a minimum dividend as a prerequisite to obtaining a discharge was eliminated. No check on discharges other than the statutory limitations remained. This innovation marked as much as anything else the arrival of the "modern" American pro-debtor discharge policy. . . .

Thus, the notion that the debtor's entitlement to a discharge rests solely on the impact on the interests of the immediately affected creditors was rejected in 1898. No longer was the discharge to be viewed as primarily an inducement to debtors to cooperate in the collection of assets in the bankruptcy case for the benefit of the creditor body. Instead, the 1898 law recognized formally for the first time the overriding public interest in granting a discharge to "honest but unfortunate" debtors. The theory is that society as a whole benefits when an overburdened debtor is freed from the oppressive weight of accumulated debt. That debtor then is able to resume his or her place as a productive member of society. Furthermore, societal forgiveness of the debts of the honest unfortunate is considered to be humane.

The pro-debtor orientation of the 1898 act with respect to the discharge also was manifested in a drastic curtailment in the number of statutory grounds for denying the discharge. In section 29 of the 1867 act Congress, reacting to the pro-debtor bias of the 1841 law, had provided an extremely long list of such grounds. Accordingly a large percentage of debtors did not receive a discharge. The pendulum swung back sharply the other way in the 1898 act, which provided very few grounds for denying a discharge. . . .

. . . A bankruptcy referee writing shortly after the 1898 act went into effect commented, "[t]he principal object of the law appears to be to make discharges easy, inexpensive and certain." Section 14b only allowed a discharge to be refused by the court on proof (1) that the debtor had committed a bankruptcy crime, or (2) that the debtor had "with fraudulent intent to conceal his true financial condition and in contemplation of bankruptcy, destroyed, concealed, or failed to keep books of account or records from which his true condition might be ascertained." . . .

The narrow scope of section 14b was, however, quite short-lived. Many believed that Congress had gone too far to help the debtor. One contemporary commentator lamented that "bankruptcy has come to be regarded as a sort of poor-debtor law," and attacked the "fallacious and superficial view that bankruptcy legislation should partake of the nature of a 'Hebrew Jubilee.'" Another stated, "Our law of 1898 is philanthropic to a degree, but as a discourager of commercial dishonesty it is like a peace officer without a warrant, or policeman with unloaded revolver." . . .

Accordingly, just five years later, in 1903, four new grounds upon which a court could refuse a discharge were added to section 14b. The new grounds were: (1) obtaining credit by a materially false writing; (2) making a fraudulent transfer within four months of the bankruptcy case; (3) refusing to obey a bankruptcy court order or answer a material question in the bankruptcy case; and (4) obtaining a discharge in a prior voluntary case within six years. . . . With these additional grounds section 14 assumed the essential form that it would carry for the next 75 years . . . .

The limitation on receiving discharges in successive cases presents an interesting example of the new discharge approach. In previous bankruptcy acts the limitation had been keyed to the amount of the dividend or creditor assent in the second case. That type of scheme was abandoned in 1903 in favor of an absolute six-year bar, irrespective of the dividend paid in the second case. Such a system was more consistent in theory with the rigid treatment of discharge limitations in the 1898 law.

Unlike the discharge denial section, which retracted severely from the 1867 law, the 1898 act in section 17a provided *more* grounds upon which a particular debt might be *excepted* from the discharge of all of the bankrupt's provable debts. Excepted debts were those based on: taxes; fraud, or obtaining property by false pretenses; wilful and malicious injuries; unscheduled claims . . . ; and fiduciary misconduct. . . . What the 1898 scheme did attempt was to draw more carefully and precisely the rules and sanctions implementing the "honesty" limitation on discharges. This more tailored approach continues today.

Even with more numerous discharge exceptions in the 1898 act, some agitation persisted to tighten the rules for particular types of debts. Accordingly, in the 1903 amendments Congress added a clarifying exception for alimony, maintenance or support. . . . Congress also added exceptions "for seduction of an unmarried female, or for criminal conversation." These exceptions, which typify the Victorian era from which they sprang, . . . eventually disappeared from the bankruptcy laws.

The procedure for obtaining a discharge followed in some respects the practice under the 1867 act. The debtor had to make special application for a discharge . . . . A noticed hearing on the merits of the application then was held before the judge . . . and the judge then granted the discharge unless one of the few disqualifying grounds was proven. No longer did the creditors vote on the application, and the statute did not require the bankrupt to make an oath of conformity. The requirement that the bankrupt specially apply for a discharge was not abandoned until 1938.

Unlike the prior American bankruptcy acts, the 1898 law was silent as to the effect of a discharge once granted. This omission did not, however, lead to a change in practice; the bankrupt still had the burden of pleading the discharge as an affirmative defense. It is in this area that discharge law and practice after the 1898 act (as amended in 1903) most differed from the approach to discharge today. In virtually all other significant respects, however, the evolutionary development of the bankruptcy discharge in the United States had, by 1903, reached a stage almost identical to that still in practice today.

IV. CONCLUSION

Few legal relations evoke more visceral emotions than that of debtor and creditor. The creditor's rage over unpaid debts has led to severe sanctions. Noel notes, "Extreme cases are recorded in which a debt was satisfied by the creditor violating with impunity the chastity of the debtor's wife." Even in less primitive societies, including most of the commercial European countries, an anti-debtor philosophy prevails. In the United States, however, a strong pro-debtor policy has been a linchpin of the national bankruptcy laws for more than ninety years. . . .

This article has examined how this "evolution of beneficent principles" has taken place, beginning tentatively in England in the early eighteenth century and then accelerating in the middle to late nineteenth century. The evolutionary process has not always been in a straight line. The pro-creditor 1800 Bankruptcy Act was followed by the pro-debtor 1841 Bankruptcy Act, after which came the more restrictive 1867 law, which in turn was followed by the exceedingly liberal 1898 act, which then was ameliorated in 1903, leaving us roughly where we still are today.

One fascinating aspect of this historical development has been how the rationale has changed to justify the remedy. In the present time the bankruptcy discharge is viewed primarily as a debtor relief mechanism. As the article has explained, however, the discharge began in 1705 as another tool to help creditors collect their debts. The transformation in the discharge's *raison d'être* did not begin in earnest until 1841, with the introduction of voluntary bankruptcy for non-merchants, and was not complete until the debtor-oriented bankruptcy law became permanent in 1898.

The war over the proper treatment of bankrupt debtors continues. . . . In fighting the ever-present modern skirmishes over the nature and extent of the discharge in bankruptcy, we need to bear in mind the lessons of 450 years of historical experience.

Thomas H. Jackson
The Fresh-Start Policy in Bankruptcy
98 HARV. L. REV. 1393 (1985)[*]

The principal advantage bankruptcy offers an individual lies in the benefits associated with discharge. Unless he has violated some norm of behavior specified in the bankruptcy laws, an individual who resorts to bankruptcy can obtain a discharge from most of his existing debts in exchange for surrendering either his existing nonexempt assets or, more recently, a portion of his future earnings. Discharge not only releases the debtor from past financial obligations, but also protects him

---

from some of the adverse consequences that might otherwise result from his release. For these reasons, discharge is viewed as granting the debtor a financial "fresh start."

The availability of discharge raises a series of critical normative questions. For example, why does the "honest but unfortunate debtor" enjoy a right of discharge at all? Why cannot an individual, confident in his knowledge of his own best interest, expressly waive the right when he seeks to obtain credit? Why does discharge, while allowing an individual to keep human capital and its proceeds as well as certain other assets, generally require him to surrender other forms of his wealth? Why, if we assume the appropriateness of a financial fresh start, is an individual freed of only some and not all adverse consequences of exercising his right of discharge? Why, finally, is discharge denied to an individual who has defrauded his creditors, but not to others, such as murderers or arsonists, who are morally reprehensible in other ways?

. . . [T]he Article develops two principal hypotheses to account for the nonwaivability of discharge. The first is that most people would choose to retain a nonwaivable right of discharge if they knew of the psychological factors that tempt them to overconsume credit. This hypothesis consists of two distinct, though related, concepts. The first of these—"impulse control"—is the notion that individuals would willingly take steps (such as the creation of a discharge rule) to control impulsive tendencies that tempt them to "mortgage" the future in favor of present consumption. The other concept—"incomplete heuristics"—posits that, in assessing courses of action, people unwittingly use tools for aiding their judgment that systematically induce them to overconsume credit. The second hypothesis is that individuals tend to ignore the full costs that their credit decisions impose on others. Society is accordingly justified, quite apart from any solicitude for individual preferences, in making discharge inalienable in order to reduce such externalities. . . .

II. TWO PARTIAL JUSTIFICATIONS FOR THE NONWAIVABLE RIGHT OF DISCHARGE: RISK ALLOCATION AND SOCIAL SAFETY NETS

. . .

A. *Superior Risk Allocation*

. . . [R]ecent scholarly treatments of discharge law have focused on whether the debtor or the creditor is the superior risk bearer and whether discharge should be presumptively available. For example, . . . Theodore Eisenberg . . . suggests that risk bearing is the main issue underlying the right of discharge. . . . Although he concludes that the superior insurer cannot be determined *a priori*, Professor Eisenberg suggests that the debtor should be presumed to be the superior risk bearer because he is in "greater control of [his] financial activities than any particular lender" and thus better able to judge when he is taking on too much credit.

Yet the conclusion that the debtor is likely to be the superior risk bearer is by no means beyond question. Discharge may be viewed as a form of limited liability for individuals—a legal construct that stems from the same desire, and serves the same purposes, as does limited liability for corporations. . . .

. . . [T]he creditors of an individual, having gained experience through dealing with many debtors, may be more adept than the individual at monitoring his borrowing. This argument squarely questions Professor Eisenberg's analysis. Moreover, . . . to the extent that individuals can invest their capital in securities and various other income-producing assets, they can further their desire to avoid risk by diversifying their holdings. . . .

Even if we could determine whether the debtor or his creditor is more likely to be the superior risk bearer in any particular situation, risk-allocation analysis of this sort can yield no more than a presumption subject to alteration by contract. Such an analysis cannot explain why the presumption should be frozen into a nonwaivable right of discharge. . . .

B. *Discharge and Other Social Safety Nets*

The nonwaivability of the right of discharge may also be justified—albeit only partially—by the existence of various social insurance programs, such as unemployment insurance, medicare, and social security. By this, . . . I mean only that, against the background of general social programs, bankruptcy's fresh-start policy may be justified in part because it reduces "moral hazard" that those social programs create.

The existence of social welfare programs leads individuals to undervalue the costs of engaging in risky activities today because they can depend on society to bear a portion of the costs that may arise tomorrow. . . . [W]e may view such programs as a form of social insurance. . . . But because the "rate" that any individual pays for the insurance is not geared to the probability that he will engage in a risky activity, such insurance creates what is commonly referred to as a "moral hazard": a situation in which individuals systematically—and rationally—underestimate the real costs of engaging in a risky activity because those costs are borne by someone else.

If there were no right of discharge, an individual who lost his assets to creditors might rely instead on social welfare programs. The existence of those programs might induce him to underestimate the true costs of his decisions to borrow. In contrast, discharge imposes much of the risk of ill-advised credit decisions not on social insurance programs but on creditors. The availability of a limited, nonwaivable right of discharge in bankruptcy therefore encourages creditors to police extensions of credit and thus minimizes the moral hazard created by safety-net programs. Because creditors can monitor debtors and are free to grant or withhold credit, the discharge system contains a built-in checking mechanism. . . .

. . . [T]o justify the discharge rule's restriction on autonomy by stressing the need to minimize the costs of safety-net programs is to leave a more basic question unanswered. Because safety nets themselves may be viewed as a form of a fresh-start policy, . . . we need to ask what justifies such a policy in the first place. Since both the discharge and the safety net can be seen as incarnations of a fresh-start policy, we should not be surprised to learn that the normative underpinnings of discharge largely reflect the justifications for maintaining social insurance programs within a system that takes individual autonomy as a fundamental premise.

III. THE NORMATIVE UNDERPINNINGS OF THE FRESH-START POLICY

Not only the American law of contracts, but also much of American society in general, is structured around the premise that individuals should for the most part have the freedom to order their own affairs as they please, because rational, self-interested actors will tend to make decisions that maximize their own utility. In the context of such a presumption, making discharge nonwaivable raises troubling implications: such a prohibition on contractual waiver both contravenes the principle of contractual freedom and increases the cost of credit.

But this neoclassical model, along with its presumption in favor of contractual freedom, depends on at least two key assumptions: first, that the individual acts rationally out of free will and is capable of discerning his best interests; and second, that no costs are imposed on noncontracting parties. If either of these assumptions fails in a particular case, so might the presumption in favor of contractual freedom. . . .

The question raised by bankruptcy discharge is whether the non-waivability of the right of discharge, although facially inhibiting a borrower's individual autonomy, does not in fact faithfully protect his own interests and those of noncontracting parties. To my mind, the answer is a qualified yes. I will argue in this Section that available evidence suggests that many people systematically fail to pursue their own long-term interests when making decisions about whether to spend today or save for tomorrow. . . . [I]n order to justify nonwaivability, it must be shown that individuals systematically misjudge (or ignore) their own interests and that this bias leads them to consume too much and save too little. I will also argue that societal intervention in the decisions of individuals to consume credit may be justified by the negative effects that those decisions may have on third parties.

A. *Protecting the Individual: Volitional and Cognitive Justifications for the Fresh-Start Policy*

1. *Paternalism and the Notion of Regret*—Several theories suggest that our decisions about how to allocate our wealth over our lifetimes are systematically biased in favor of present consumption. . . . But this justification fails to justify a general right to a fresh start. . . . [O]ne would have to identify the volitional or cognitive weaknesses that lead individuals systematically to ignore or overdiscount the uncertainties of the future. The question is whether we can demonstrate such weaknesses.

. . . Over time, the argument runs, changes in the way an individual evaluates his opportunities, desires, and risks lead him to experience regret. In order to shield the individual from such regret, and from the unfortunate consequences of his regretted decisions, we impose "paternalistic" restrictions on the individual's freedom of contract, among them, the nonwaivability of discharge.

. . . [T]his theory, by itself, seems inadequate as an explanatory tool. . . . [T]he theory of regret does not satisfactorily explain why individuals, in making decisions about the future, cannot adequately take into account the possibility that their ideas and values will change. . . .

2. *Impulse Control: A Volitional Justification.*—The theory of regret, then, does not explain why society should honor the preference of the future self at the expense of the present one. The concept of "impulse" provides at least a partial answer. When presented with an either-or choice, people, like animals, exhibit a tendency to choose current gratification over postponed gratification, even if they know that the latter holds in store a greater measure of benefits. Although, by itself, this predilection might be explained by the rational tendency to discount the value of deferred benefits, such an explanation does not account for this further observation: the same individuals who prefer current to postponed gratification will nevertheless favor a rule that requires them to defer gratification.

This tendency of individuals to desire external restraints on their impulses provides a basis for deciding which of an individual's personalities to favor. One personality is the rational planner; it carefully assesses the relative merits of current versus future consumption. The "impulse" personality, in contrast, approaches life like an addict, unable to consider or plan for the future. . . .

The control of impulsive behavior, then, may provide a key to justifying discharge policy. If unrestrained individuals would generally choose to consume today rather than save for tomorrow, and if this tendency stems in part from impulse, they may opt for a way of removing or at least restricting that choice. If individuals cannot control the impulse themselves, they may want the assistance of a socially imposed rule, one that will simply enforce the hypothesized decisions of their fully rational selves. . . .

. . . [A] social rule discouraging the extension of credit might be the best means to assist individuals in controlling impulsive credit decisions. A nonwaivable right of discharge controls impulsive credit decisions by encouraging creditors to monitor borrowing. . . .

. . . [A]lthough the law might respond to the problem of impulsive credit behavior by letting individuals choose whether or not to waive the right of discharge, the problem may be better handled by means of a legal rule that uniformly disallows waiver. This kind of legal rule is justified by a hypothesized Rawlsian original position: if the members of society had gathered together before the fact and had anticipated the human tendency toward impulsive behavior, they would have devised a rule that denied them the opportunity to behave impulsively in the future.

3. *Incomplete Heuristics: A Cognitive Justification.*—Whereas impulsive behavior is volitional, there is a closely related cognitive feature of decisionmaking that makes the need for a legal rule perhaps more evident: because of systematic failures in their cognitive processes, individuals appear to make choices in which they consistently underestimate future risks. This problem—which

I shall call the problem of "incomplete heuristics"—provides a powerful argument that most individuals . . . would favor a legal rule making discharge nonwaivable. Like impulsiveness, incomplete heuristics may lead the individual to favor present consumption in a way that does not give due regard to his long-term desires and goals. Likewise, incomplete heuristics would justify the decision to adopt a universal, nonwaivable right of discharge on a ground similar to that cited in the case of impulsive behavior: if individuals in the "original position" had recognized that they would face informational constraints when making credit decisions, they would probably have chosen a system that would make some of the consequences of their borrowing avoidable.

. . . [T]he term "heuristics" refers to tools that individuals employ in processing and assessing information. These tools aid us in digesting immense quantities of diverse information by breaking it down into familiar groupings. . . . Although reliance on these heuristic "rules of thumb" enables us to make decisions quickly, evidence suggests it also causes us to make systematic cognitive errors . . . . Much evidence indicates that . . . these heuristics apparently tend to lead individuals in one direction: toward underestimating the risks that their current consumption imposes on their future well-being. . . .

If these solutions are not promising, and if individuals are not likely to develop corrective devices on their own, the underlying problem remains: how do we free the individual from the adverse effects of incomplete heuristics and ensure that his decisions adequately reflect both his present and future wants and needs? The problem is not one of "pure" irrationality but one of incomplete information—an incompleteness unknown to the individual. . . . In light of evidence that the phenomenon of incomplete heuristics makes individuals overly optimistic about the future, the need to redress this problem offers a second normative justification for a nonwaivable right of discharge, one that complements the need for impulse control.

4. *The Justification for a Socially Mandated Rule.*—The preceding discussion suggests that what seems initially to be a paternalistic justification for discharge may in fact be consistent with society's preference for individual autonomy, because the nonwaivable right of discharge accords with the result of a hypothetical initial deliberation behind a Rawlsian "veil of ignorance." If people in the "original position" had known about the problems of incomplete heuristics and impulsive behavior, and about the difficulty of adjusting for these problems in making credit decisions, they presumably would have opted for a legal rule designed to avert those problems in advance. . . .

A nonwaivable right of discharge may be desirable even if some individuals do not need its protection, as long as (1) a substantial number of people are likely to experience unanticipated regret as a result of impulsive behavior or unwitting reliance on incomplete heuristics and (2) it is either impossible or extremely expensive to distinguish those who will experience such regret from those who will not. To justify a nonwaivable general rule, one need not show that all people require its protection; it is enough to show that the rule promises to be less intrusive, or less costly, than one that attempts to discriminate between people who are likely to experience regret because of impulsive behavior or the use of incomplete heuristics and those who are not. . . .

B. *Protecting Others: Rational Behavior and the Notion of Externalities*

The above justifications for societal intervention in individuals' credit decisions rest on the claim that most people would agree in advance to protect against the distortions caused by defects in their volitional and cognitive processes and that creating a nonwaivable right of discharge is one way to achieve that protection. Another justification for a uniform, nonwaivable discharge rule derives from the possibility that waiver of the right of discharge will generate externalities. Put simply, the cost to the debtor of waiving that right might not reflect the costs to third parties of such a decision. To avoid these externalities, which individuals might systematically ignore if permitted to do so, it may be appropriate to impose a nonwaivable discharge rule. Such a rule helps curtail the costs otherwise imposed on a wide range of people—from family and friends, to business associates, to "society" in general. . . .

Requiring debts to be paid out of future income may lead an indebted individual to devote more of his energies and resources to leisure, a consumption item that his creditors cannot reach. By doing less work and enjoying more leisure, the individual undoubtedly decreases his productive contributions to society. . . .

. . . [T]here may be several reasons to believe that a negative externality exists. First, in an extreme case, an individual may shift from work to leisure at no personal cost at all. . . . Faced with a world in which he can either work—only to have Creditor garnish his wages—or enjoy leisure, Debtor's choice seems clear: because Creditor, not Debtor, bears the cost of the substitution of leisure for work, Debtor will make the substitution. In such a case, the social cost of lost productivity exceeds Debtor's personal loss in shifting to leisure. . . .

Moreover, in many professions, an individual's wages systematically underrepresent the marginal social value of his labor. Many jobs have a social utility that wage rates do not fully reflect; the costs to the worker in such a job of substituting leisure for work are less than the costs to society. Consider the case of a law professor. . . . [L]aw professors pass up the prospect of significantly higher wages in order to remain law professors. . . . [L]aw professors must regard those nonpecuniary benefits as worth the wage differential, because they remain academics. . . . But because wages can be reached by creditors whereas the other job benefits cannot, a law professor faced with a lifetime of wage garnishment might switch to a job with a lower wage level but similar amounts of leisure and nonpecuniary benefits. Even though the lower absolute level of entitlements (wages plus leisure and non-pecuniary benefits) reflects a socially less productive job, the switch would be less costly to the law professor than it would be to society. . . .

The fact that negative externalities may follow from certain behavior does not automatically justify a societal prohibition of such behavior. Society, after all, does not require us to become lawyers rather than law professors just because externalities may result. . . . But when the preference for leisure stems from an overconsumption of credit, a nonwaivable right to discharge might be justified in spite of the constraints it sets on an individual's freedom to choose his own course. . . . [W]e must balance the social costs of allowing borrowing—that is, the risks of overindulgence due to impulsiveness, incomplete heuristics, and the failure to account for externalities—against the need for credit in our economic system. . . .

IV. APPLICATION OF THE NORMATIVE THEORY: DEFINING THE CONTOURS OF THE FRESH START IN A MARKET ECONOMY

. . .

D. *Limits on the Right of Discharge Itself: Denying Access to Discharge in Order To Enforce Social Norms*

Discharge is principally a device for freeing up a debtor's human capital. . . . It is therefore in the context of human capital that we must ask when discharge should be granted or withheld. Most explanations of bankruptcy law insist that discharge should be available only to the "honest but unfortunate" debtor. But if notions of impulsive behavior, incomplete heuristics, or externalities do justify the right of an individual to free up his future income stream in the first place, why should an individual be denied discharge because of "mistakes," of whatever sort, he made in the past? To what extent should an individual's commission of certain acts deprive him of a fresh start, either in toto or with respect to a particular debt?

1. *Section 727 and Denial of Discharge.*—One commonly asserted reason for denying discharge to those who have engaged in certain undesirable activities is that denial will help deter such conduct. The activities listed in section 727 of the Bankruptcy Code . . . have one attribute in com-

mon: they all concern fraud or similar misbehavior against creditors. . . . [T]he prohibitions on fraud and similar conduct may be viewed as designed to deter various activities regardless of whether they are products of impulsiveness, incomplete heuristics, or the disregard of externalities.

The question is therefore whether denying a debtor the right of discharge is an appropriate means of preventing fraudulent conduct. . . .

. . . The relation between the activities covered by section 727 and creditors' collection efforts may be so close as to justify presumptively denying discharge to a debtor who engages in such activities. . . . Section 727 proscribes behavior directed at foiling creditors' collection efforts during the individual debtor's insolvency, behavior that is likely to occur in connection with a bankruptcy proceeding. . . .

Even if a socially disfavored activity is so closely linked with bankruptcy or creditor collection efforts that some restriction of the debtor's financial fresh-start is justified, a complete denial of discharge is not necessarily an appropriate response. In determining the proper penalty, one must weigh the benefits of the fresh-start policy against the effectiveness of using denial of discharge as a lever to enforce behavioral norms. . . .

V. CONCLUSION

. . . A principled basis does exist for a fresh-start policy. The nonwaivability of the right of discharge is justified even in light of society's general commitment to individual autonomy: a nonwaivable right of discharge protects the individual from his own impulsive or biased decisions that lead him to overconsume credit, and it protects others from the externalities produced by these decisions. This normative theory of discharge sheds light on the trade-offs that must be made in order to implement that right while still preserving the availability of credit. This Article has concluded that exercise of the discharge right should carry some costs if our system of credit is to be preserved. It has also suggested that human capital may deserve special protection under the fresh-start policy.

In the following excerpt, Professor David Gray Carlson of the Benjamin N. Cardozo School of Law challenges Professor Jackson's discharge theories. Back in Chapter 2, we saw Carlson's rebuttal to Jackson's "creditors' bargain" theory in the same article excerpted here. While Carlson refers to Jackson's discharge theories as published in his 1986 book, THE LOGIC AND LIMITS OF BANKRUPTCY LAW, that portion of Jackson's book was taken directly from his *Harvard Law Review* article, *The Fresh-Start Policy in Bankruptcy*, excerpted just above.

Carlson attacks what he calls "Jackson's Theory of Personality," which supposedly justifies the discharge. In turn Carlson assails the two main pillars of Jackson's debtor personality theory, namely, "impulse buying" and "incomplete heuristics." What are Carlson's arguments? Are they convincing?

In the final section, Professor Carlson challenges Professor Jackson's "noncontractarian" justifications for the discharge. These focus first on the "externalities" that would flow from any system other than a nonwaivable discharge (which might be no discharge at all, a limited or conditional discharge, or a waivable discharge). Carlson doubts whether Jackson has proven the existence of such externalities. Finally, he scorns Jackson's suggestion that a bankruptcy discharge helps keep debtors off of welfare.

David Gray Carlson
Philosophy in Bankruptcy
85 MICH. L. REV. 1341 (1987)*

B. *Discharge of Debt*

. . .

2. *Jackson's Theory of Personality*

. . . Jackson's theory of the personality that prefers bankruptcy discharge is most unconvincing. Jackson starts off by promising to expose a universal human trait that renders the bankruptcy discharge desirable to all people (although he ends up not delivering). He identifies two departures from the rational calculator that supposedly justify equal priority in bankruptcy: (1) the impulsive, noncalculating desire to go on a buying binge, and (2) incomplete information about the future. Careful reading of Jackson's book will reveal that Jackson does not intend these to be universal traits, however. It turns out that only some of us suffer from these traits, so that there is no "systematic" human failure after all. I don't think Jackson is close to making his case for these predicates, in either the universal or nonuniversal versions. . . .

a. *Impulse buying.* Jackson claims that *some* (all?) people have "impulse" personalities. Jackson is not completely insensitive to the charge that what we call a person's "impulse" the person might call her own "rational" preference for present consumption over future consumption. . . .

The difference between the sovereign consumer and the impulsive individual is defined by the impulsive person himself, according to Jackson. The impulsive person wants protection against the impulse and hence wants the bankruptcy discharge. The discharge (Jackson claims) has the effect of making credit unavailable today, thereby removing a person from danger. Thus, anyone who wants the bankruptcy discharge *for himself* shows himself to be an impulse buyer. Indeed, this declaration is, apparently, the only evidence available to distinguish rational from irrational behavior.

That *some* people want bankruptcy discharges for themselves does not answer (and is not intended to answer) why we all must take or not take the discharge as a group. Why should the great majority suffer the "loss" of credit opportunities because a few addictive personalities will abuse the privilege? Jackson's response is to fall back on Rawls:

> This kind of rule is justified by [a] hypothesized Rawlsian original position . . . : if the members of society had gathered together before the fact and had anticipated the human tendency toward impulsive behavior, they would have devised a rule that *denied them the opportunity* to behave impulsively in the future.

This leap from "some people want self-protection from their contracts" to "we all want self-protection" is presumably based on Rawls' convention that, behind the veil of ignorance, each person does not know whether she will be dealt the defective binge-buying personality and must therefore bargain as if she will be the binge-buyer.

. . . This Rawlsian argument is a complete self-contradiction, unless Jackson abandons the claim that we each have an uncontrollable impulse within us. How can contract be the basis of society when human beings are systematically too incompetent to contract? Instead, the binge-buying impulse must be in the nature of learned behavior, or perhaps a disease. Otherwise, Jackson could not practice his contractarianism at all.

Be that as it may, Jackson's argument that binge-buyers want the discharge *for themselves* is also rendered confusing by his false assumptions about the effect of the bankruptcy discharge. Jackson assumes that the discharge will "control" the binge-buying impulse "by encouraging creditors to monitor borrowing." Here Jackson implies that creditors will withhold credit altogether as a result of monitoring.

This does not follow for at least two reasons. First, Jackson's dichotomy between "rational" *creditors* and potentially irrational *borrowers* is a false one. Why are all creditors rational, while all irrational people end up as debtors? Extending bad loans can be a form of binge-buying, as any bank failure will demonstrate. In short, Jackson fails to account for the fact that perhaps creditors will make mistakes in controlling debtors' credit habits.

Second, Jackson is quite unrealistic in imagining that rational creditors will withhold credit from binge-buyers. Creditors may be unable to recognize the good borrowers from the binge-buying maniacs. They may choose to increase the cost of credit to everyone, collecting the lost principal from the interest charged to the "rational" buyers and the irrational-but-lucky bingers. . . . "[M]onitoring" must consist of creditors asking prospective borrowers whether they are uncontrollable binge-buying maniacs. Now what do you suppose the typical binge-buyer is going to say (having already succumbed to the dark forces of unreason and asked for a loan)? I think it is fair to assume that at least *some* of the irrational binge-buyers are going to lie and say that they are not bingers at all. As a result, monitoring will fail to identify the bingers. They will be lumped in with everyone else. That means everyone gets credit, but at a higher price. So long as credit remains available at a higher price, the discharge, if anything, worsens the short-term effect of the binge-buying impulse by driving the debtor into bankruptcy earlier than if interest rates were lower. Therefore, it is wrong to premise the argument on discharge as "controlling" the impulse, unless Jackson is serious that the creditors will withdraw credit altogether. Rather, the discharge protects a person from *long-term* suffering because the impulse is in fact uncontrolled.

Another thing that must be said about this alleged binge-buying impulse is that Jackson obviously views it as a type of insanity that cannot be controlled. That is, no type of incentive will cause the rational side of the personality to increase its strength against the irrational side. This claim is central to Jackson's entire analysis; if punishments succeed in strengthening the resolve of the rational personality to squelch the irrational personality, then the bankruptcy discharge is counterproductive. . . .

Now, *if* there are really uncontrollable spendthrifts out there, Jackson can go ahead and make his Rawlsian argument on their behalf. But he cannot make his efficiency argument without adding in another important factor. One thing Jackson completely leaves out is that the discharge itself transforms binge-buying from irrational to rational behavior. Or to put it another way, the discharge itself might in fact encourage the very behavior that Jackson supposes the discharge squelches. Surely the diseconomies of strategic binge-buying in anticipation of bankruptcy must be added to Jackson's cost-benefit analysis.

Here Jackson faces a serious circularity problem. Are people binge-buyers and hence there's a discharge, or are people binge-buyers because there's a discharge? In fact, it is impossible to determine whether law is a product of human desire or whether human desire is a product of law. . . .

To summarize, Jackson attempts to isolate a phenomenon of uncontrollable impulsive behavior and then connect it to the existence of the bankruptcy discharge. The attempt, however, is completely botched. His method of isolating those with a propensity to binge from rational calculators depends entirely upon self-identification. Yet the mode of self-identification—wanting the discharge for protection against impulse—is said to be a universal Rawlsian desire. This universal desire to destroy freedom of contract defeats Jackson's contractarianism generally and his justification of the discharge in particular. Finally, his explanation of discharges ignores the possibility that people can be influenced by the incentives of the law and that binge-buying might itself be a strategic reaction to the existence of the discharge.

b. *Incomplete·heuristics.* In addition to binge-buying, Jackson also offers up a second flaw in the human personality—incomplete heuristics—that justifies the bankruptcy discharge. As with impulsive behavior, Jackson is evasive on whether this flaw is systematically present in human beings. . . .

Whatever Jackson's theory of incomplete heuristics is, it seems to stem from two anecdotes told by psychologists. These anecdotes are supposed to prove that all (some?) human beings are too incompetent to manage their futures when the facts are held constant. . . .

Now I will concede that if you give the public pop quizzes in statistics, untrained individuals will make mistakes and will not give the answers that the statisticians want. But can we deduce from this general statistical naivete that each and every person in the world is likely to overmortgage the future? Statistical expertise is a learnable skill. It is possible to teach people how to pass pop quizzes (or so undergraduate professors assume). This kind of knowledge has nothing to do with the innate, genetic flaw in the human psyche that Jackson claims exists. I don't know beans about the odds of picking blue or red poker chips out of a sack, but I am pretty confident that I can live within my means. These two threadbare little anecdotes about statistical ignorance in no sense prove that some or all people are too incompetent to plan their lives.

Now even if it were true that "most people" cannot rationally figure out how to match future income and future outflow, there are several other obstacles between this fact and the successful justification of the bankruptcy discharge. Since the Bankruptcy Code includes no distinction between good and bad calculators, Jackson must at a minimum show that bad calculators end up in bankruptcy more often than good calculators (for the mere fact of rational risk implies some rational failures). How can we distinguish between good and bad calculation? All we know is that (a) the credit transaction took place, and (b) repayment did or did not occur. These data do not prove whether the borrower calculated correctly or miscalculated. A person who repaid might have miscalculated and still have been lucky. A person who defaulted might have calculated correctly and been unlucky. Therefore, Jackson has given us a theory of bankruptcy behavior that is completely unverifiable. . . .

3. *Noncontractarian Justifications of Bankruptcy Discharge: Externalities and "Welfare" Economics*

. . . Jackson has two other "explanations" of the bankruptcy discharge that I cannot resist commenting on. One is based on bad economics and the other is based on even worse sociology. The economic claim is that the bankruptcy discharge prevents externalities. The sociological claim is that the bankruptcy discharge might help relieve the welfare rolls of deadbeat debtors (a claim that Jackson tentatively rejects after lengthy commentary).

a. *Externalities.* . . . Jackson's theory of externalities produced by the bankruptcy discharge goes like this: (a) Even with garnishment protection, workers at the margin will quit their jobs if twenty-five percent of their wages is garnished for the foreseeable future. (b) Workers usually produce a surplus beyond their wages, which belongs to the employers. (c) This surplus guarantees that the public cost of garnishment (the cause of quitting) exceeds the private cost to the debtor.

There is something very wrong with this account. Why does Jackson assume that workers in debt will obviously quit their jobs? A lot of workers might take *second* jobs to keep up with their debts. And even if they do quit, where does this employer's surplus come from? Usually, it comes from competition on the wage front. If there is no competition, there may be no surplus, because the worker is a monopolist who will have extracted the surplus for herself. On the other hand, if there is wage competition between workers, there is no loss of surplus as Jackson supposes, because the employer will simply go out and hire someone else.

Jackson's argument about social loss is quite incomprehensible, but it is so much fun that I think we should look it over rather carefully. Jackson writes:

> Consider the case of a law professor. Assume that all law professors are suited equally to either teaching or practice and that the prevailing wage rates are set at a level that will attract the necessary number of law professors. . . . Assuming the prevailing salary of law professors to be $75,000 a year and that of practicing lawyers to be $150,000, the law professor at the margin will be enjoying $75,000 of nonpecuniary benefits from his job. Because of the assumption of full substitutability of law professors for lawyers, the social benefit of the two jobs will be equal, notwithstanding the wage differential. But because wages can be reached by creditors whereas the other job benefit[s] cannot, a law professor faced with a lifetime of wage garnishment might switch to a job with a lower wage level but similar amounts of leisure and nonpecuniary benefits. Even though the lower absolute level of entitlements (wages plus leisure and nonpecuniary benefits) reflects a socially less productive job, the switch would be less costly to the law professor than it would be to society.

Although the above analysis is truly rotten economics, it is anthropologically fascinating. First, . . . [t]he thought that a tenured professor would quit such a job is truly fantastic. Many a dean wishes Jackson were right.

But look at Jackson's assumption! A tenured professor who has 25% of her wages garnished is going to switch to a new job with the *same* leisure and prestige and *less* wages? Where's the sense in that? For one thing, the new job will presumably be garnishable just like the old one. But even if it were not, what incentive does the professor have to take the dead loss that Jackson suggests? Putting aside a desire to spite the creditor, it seems to me that the professor is much better off staying put than taking the same leisure and less money elsewhere.

Finally, the thought that society suffers a deadweight loss because a tenured law professor quits is just laughable. The dean at the Harvard Law School needs to put Professor Jackson on the faculty appointments committee for a semester. I think Jackson would find it a revelation how many people are willing to fill a vacated professorship for a good deal less than $75,000. I don't see the social loss if some tenured professor heads for the hills. Quite the opposite. If repealing the bankruptcy discharge could get rid of overpaid, underproductive, tenured law professors, then, far from proving the rationality of the discharge, Jackson has made the strongest conceivable argument for getting rid of it!

I don't think Jackson has shown that the social loss of an employee quitting his job is higher than the private loss to the employee. But even if this were so, Jackson has once again forgotten the Coase Theorem, which says that, absent transaction costs, the affected parties will simply bargain for an efficient solution. . . .

b. *Debtors on the dole.* If Jackson's economic display fails badly, so does his suggestion that the discharge helps keep the welfare rolls clear. Admittedly, Jackson concludes (on inadequate reasoning) that this rationale is "incomplete." But Jackson gives it considerable credence: "If there were no right of discharge, an individual who lost his assets to creditors might rely instead on social welfare programs. The existence of those programs might induce him to underestimate the true costs of his decisions to borrow."

Such a thesis shows a fantastic ignorance of the American welfare system. In the United States, federally funded welfare programs are limited to the aged, blind, disabled, or single parents with dependent children. . . . It is safe to say, then, that the debtor who could work but refuses will find it hard to get welfare from the government.

Margaret Howard
A Theory of Discharge in Consumer Bankruptcy
48 OHIO ST. L.J. 1047 (1987)[*]

I. INTRODUCTION

The purpose of the consumer bankruptcy system, effectuated by discharge, is to give a fresh start to the "honest but unfortunate debtor." . . .

The appropriate scope of the "fresh start" and thus of the discharge that implements it, however, is far from settled. Discharge of legal obligations is an extraordinary exception to the usual obligation orientation of the law and it must have equally extraordinary justification. To describe the goal of bankruptcy as providing a "fresh start" for certain debtors is inadequate. That formulation does not specify the goals of bankruptcy sufficiently to distinguish debts and debtors that should be discharged from those that should not. . . .

. . . [A] number of different, sometimes mutually inconsistent, policies have developed to justify isolated aspects of the Bankruptcy Code's discharge rules. Five of these policy threads weave through the Code. First, bankruptcy is a collection device by which a debtor's assets can be discovered and made available for creditors. Second, bankruptcy is intended to reward only an honest or worthy debtor with discharge. Third, bankruptcy should protect the interests of creditors who are particularly worthy. Fourth, bankruptcy is designed to rehabilitate the debtor. . . . Finally, bankruptcy may be designed to achieve economic efficiency in its allocation of the risk of loss, connected with nonpayment, between debtor and creditor.

. . . After tracing existing discharge policies, the Article advocates a new functional economic theory of discharge: that discharge should be broadly available in order to restore the debtor to participation in the open credit economy, limited only as is necessary to prevent the skewing of economic decisions, whether to lend or to borrow, by the intrusion of irrelevant noneconomic factors. . . .

II. GOALS OF BANKRUPTCY—TRACING THE THREADS

A. *Collection Mechanism*

. . . Bankruptcy began in England as a response to inadequate collection remedies. . . .

England introduced discharge from debt in 1705, but not purely out of the belief that the "honest but unfortunate" debtor should, as a normative matter, be relieved of oppressive debt. Rather, discharge was intended to encourage and reward cooperation by the debtor in the discovery and distribution of his assets—a distinctive collection function.

B. *The Worthy Debtor*

A second goal of bankruptcy is to reward only the honest debtor with a fresh start. Policymakers have long been concerned that bankruptcy not be a haven for the dishonest. . . .

Debate centers around the question of what conduct is so dishonest or unworthy that discharge is appropriately jeopardized. . . .

The policy against granting discharge to a dishonest debtor is firmly rooted in the normative proposition that debts should be paid. . . . [M]orality-based philosophies of bankruptcy must be con-

---

* Originally published in 48:4 Ohio St. L.J. 1047 (1987). Reprinted by permission of the Ohio State Law Journal and the author.

cerned, in general, about the effects of bankruptcy on the moral fiber and, in particular, must reflect the social consensus that debts should be paid.

. . . There is an impasse indeed and formulations turning on ethical considerations or on quantifying the debtor's honesty are helpless to guide.

C. *Creditor Worthiness*

An additional, albeit fairly weak, policy in current bankruptcy law recognizes that some characteristics of the claim or the claimant entitle that claim to special treatment in bankruptcy. This policy . . . focuses on the nature of the debt or of the creditor to whom the obligation is owed.

Two provisions of current bankruptcy law reflect the policy that certain claims—specifically, those for family support and tax obligations—should not be discharged in bankruptcy because of the deservingness of the creditor. . . .

D. *Rehabilitation*

A House Judiciary Committee report states that the second purpose of bankruptcy, after equitable distribution of the debtor's assets to creditors, is "the effective rehabilitation of the bankrupt." The term "rehabilitation," however, is "particularly elusive." . . .

Subsumed under the concept of rehabilitation are at least three analytically separate policy threads: 1) that discharge should (whether or not it does) serve a consumer education function; 2) that discharge constitutes an emotional and psychological purgative for the debtor; and 3) that discharge allows the debtor to resume active participation in the open credit economy. . . .

1. *Consumer Education*

A view of bankruptcy as an educational experience for debtors carries an assumption that something inherent in the experience itself equips the debtor to go forth and sin no more. Conceivably, a debtor discharged in Chapter 7 may have learned something in the process that will assist him in avoiding future financial catastrophe, but nothing in the current structure is designed to provide training in financial management. Any such lesson will be a fortuitous and ancillary benefit. . . .

2. *Psychological Goals*

Debt is demoralizing, we are told, and "a hopeless, unbelievable financial situation leads to a very costly social situation with its resulting relief costs, suicides, and criminality concomitant to financial despair." Discharge of debt in bankruptcy, however, "liberates the bankrupt psychologically." The newly freed debtor has renewed confidence in his ability to control his future and newly-resurrected self-respect.

The problem is, of course, that we have little empirical support for conclusions about the psychological or emotional impacts of debt and discharge. These effects are difficult to measure. . . .

Given these difficulties, any notion of bankruptcy policy as it relates to the debtor's psychological and emotional state is not helpful to explain the bankruptcy statute as it is drafted or to guide discussions of how the system should be modified.

3. *Economic Rehabilitation*

The last bankruptcy policy subsumed under the concept of rehabilitation is economic rehabilitation—that discharge enables the debtor to resume economic participation in the open credit economy.

E. *Economic Analysis and Efficiency Purposes*

Inevitably, discussion of participation in the open credit economy raises questions of the impact of bankruptcy discharge on the economic efficiency of the credit market. Professor Eisenberg's analysis posits that the "risk of financial distress of bankruptcy" should be placed on the party better able to bear the risk. That, in turn, depends on two factors: which party is better able to prevent the risk from occurring; and which party is the "superior insurer" against the risk. . . .

Assume . . . that default is the risk of concern. Professor Eisenberg asserts that generally "borrowers know more about themselves and have greater control of their affairs than lenders do." That may be true of individual debtors, but the knowledge needed to assess the risk of default is actuarial, not individual. As between consumer debtors and commercial lenders, who constitute the majority of bankruptcy claimants, the latter are clearly better able "to assess the likelihood" of default. They know, statistically, what percentage of loans will result in default for a particular set of credit standards. Thus, lenders are better able to control the incidence of default by manipulation of credit standards and by more thorough credit investigations. . . .

The second inquiry of the economic approach is which party is the "superior insurer" against the risk. That party is the commercial lender rather than the consumer borrower, whether by "superior insurer" one means the party more aware of the need for insurance or the party who can purchase insurance more cheaply. The commercial lender knows that a determinable proportion of consumer borrowers will default and that bad-debt insurance is available. Undoubtedly, such a lender can purchase bad-debt insurance more cheaply than its borrowers can. . . .

Given that most bankrupts are consumer debtors and that most of their creditors are commercial lenders, economic analysis leads to the conclusion that discharge should be freely given. Professor Eisenberg comes out differently: "If bankruptcy law is going to reach a single conclusion with respect to discharge, the single economic answer would most likely be to limit the discharge." This difference derives from his focus on the individual rather than the actuarial. . . .

Economic inquiry is more useful when the focus is actuarial and looks not at who controls the risk that default will occur, but at who can better bear the risk of the loss that necessarily will flow from the default. This is a simple inquiry into who is the least-cost insurer, free from complex and judgmental conclusions about fault. . . .

Before tinkering with bankruptcy rules in the name of economic efficiency, we should admit our limitations. First, if costs are passed along when creditors bear the risk, so that paying debtors subsidize nonpayers, this pass-along will occur without regard to the rules in bankruptcy. Those who pay subsidize those who *default*, not just those who default and obtain a discharge in bankruptcy. . . . Second, economic analysis requires a great many assumptions. Before we make major changes in the scope of bankruptcy in order to benefit commercial lenders and sellers, we need substantially more empirical data.

III. A THEORY OF DISCHARGE

These competing policies leave the impression that bankruptcy is expected to serve entirely too many masters. Rather than attempting to serve this range of policies, discharge in the context of non-tort claims should have only one goal—to restore the debtor to economic productivity and viable participation in the open credit economy. This standard calls for making discharge broadly available, since viable economic participation is restored by lifting the burden of impossible debt. No one advocates discharge on demand, however. Thus, some limitation is necessary. This single goal of discharge should be limited only as necessary to prevent skewing of economic decisions, including decisions both to lend and to borrow, by the intrusion of factors irrelevant to economic decisions.

Asking whether a debtor's conduct has skewed economic decisions avoids the difficulties of normatively-based discharge policy. . . .

The educational and psychological portions of the rehabilitative goal of bankruptcy play no part under the functional economic approach. . . .

Once the normative, ethical, and psychological factors are set aside, only the rehabilitative purpose of restored participation in the open credit economy remains as a meaningful goal of discharge. . . .

A. *Issues Related To Debtor's Conduct*

A debtor aware of the potential availability of a discharge in bankruptcy might be more inclined to incur debts than would an individual who is making a decision to borrow on the basis of purely economic factors, such as current ability to repay and expected future income. Because this inclination would skew the economic decision by introducing non-economic factors, some limitation on discharge is necessary to control the debtor's conduct. Thus, discharge should be barred for a debtor who has knowingly hindered the bankruptcy proceedings in ways currently covered by the bankruptcy statute. In addition, discharge of particular debts should be barred if the debtor engaged in disfavored kinds of conduct, such as dishonesty, in connection with that particular debt. This limitation, too, is part of current law. These provisions are appropriate not because we dislike dishonesty and want to discourage it. . . . Provisions discouraging dishonesty are appropriate in bankruptcy because discharge for debts affected by such conduct would introduce noneconomic factors into the decisions to lend and borrow. . . .

D. *Chapter 13*

Two issues surrounding Chapter 13 currently provoke, perhaps, the hottest bankruptcy policy debates—the scope of the Chapter 13 discharge and whether consumer debtors should be mandated to file under Chapter 13 rather than Chapter 7. The functional economic approach helps shed light on both of these issues.

1. *Scope of Chapter 13 Discharge*

. . . The very availability of the "better discharge" could alter a debtor's economic decision-making, rendering his actions more reckless, if not downright malicious and fraudulent. Moreover, a debtor who did not factor in the availability of a broader bankruptcy discharge in the first instance still might, after an obligation has been incurred and bankruptcy looms, decide to choose a Chapter 13 payment plan rather than a Chapter 7 liquidation on the basis of factors other than economic feasibility. His own ability to repay, in light of his future economic obligations and prospects, may become less important than the opportunity to avoid the economic consequences of his noneconomic conduct. Thus, the bankruptcy process is misused. For this reason, rather than for reasons turning on evaluation of the moral worthiness of a debtor's conduct, the discharge provisions of Chapter 13 should be more carefully coordinated with those of Chapter 7 to eliminate the internal inconsistencies now present.

2. *Mandatory 13*

. . . However mandatory 13 is defended, mandating 13 comes down to a diminution of the goal of economic productivity. This is true because, during the pendency of the plan, the debtor's assets beyond those required for minimal support are devoted to repayment of creditors. The availability of a debtor's earning capacity as an asset free from the reach of creditors is what gives the debtor a new start. Discharge of old obligations is what makes the start a fresh one. Mandatory 13, therefore, is not a fresh start at all, at least during the pendency of the plan, and does nothing to return the debtor to economic productivity. The debtor is, rather, held in economic limbo while tied to past obligations. Under the functional economic approach, therefore, Chapter 13 should not be mandatory. . . .

IV. CONCLUSION

Strong theoretical justifications should be offered for discharging in bankruptcy obligations that are otherwise enforceable. . . .

None of the policy goals of bankruptcy, reviewed above, provide a reason to abandon the principle of renewed economic vigor of the debtor as the goal of bankruptcy. This is the goal stated in the functional economic approach under which discharge would be structured to enhanced return of the debtor to productive economic participation, limited only as necessary to prevent skewing of economic decisions by the intrusion of noneconomic factors. This approach focuses on the economic impact on society as a whole that is the appropriate concern of those who structure the bankruptcy system.

Charles Jordan Tabb
The Scope of the Fresh Start in Bankruptcy:
Collateral Conversions and the Dischargeability Debate
59 Geo. Wash. L. Rev. 56 (1990)[*]

IV. Normative Underpinnings of the Discharge and the Willful and Malicious
Injury Exception

A number of different justifications have been offered over the centuries for the bankruptcy discharge and for the conditions and exceptions to its general operation. Sir William Blackstone explained in the eighteenth century that the discharge enabled the bankrupt to again "become a u[s]eful member of the commonwealth." Earlier in this century Harold Remington, a leading bankruptcy commentator, identified three rationales for the discharge:

> [1] that it was just and humane to the debtor himself, [2] that it aided creditors in discovering and recovering assets, and [3] that it was in the interest of a sound public policy not to keep the debtor forever in bondage to his debts, but to restore his energies to the business community.

Recent scholars have explored new justifications. . . .

A. The Debtor Cooperation Theory

The debtor cooperation theory justifies the discharge as a carrot dangled in front of debtors to induce them to cooperate with the trustee and the creditors in the bankruptcy case in the location, collection, and liquidation of the debtor's assets. If the debtor cooperates, the discharge is granted; if not, it is denied. Debtor compliance arguably benefits creditors by increasing the size of the asset pie available for distribution and by decreasing the administrative costs necessary to effect that distribution. In short, creditors essentially forego the possibility of postbankruptcy recovery tomorrow in the hope of reaping larger bankruptcy dividends today.

This theory was the principal justification first offered for the earliest discharge law in England and for the United States Bankruptcy Act of 1800. . . .

The debtor cooperation theory continues to thrive under the current United States bankruptcy law. Most of the grounds for complete denial of discharge in section 727 of the Bankruptcy Code are predicated on debtor noncooperation in connection with the bankruptcy case.

Although the debtor cooperation theory may justify granting the discharge only to a compliant debtor, it does not really support the concept of exceptions to discharge. Indeed, allowing creditors to prove exceptions to the general discharge arguably creates a disincentive for debtors to cooperate. After all, if the bulk of the debtor's debt is not going to be discharged, why should the debtor cooperate? The prudent, amoral debtor who believes that significant debts will be excepted

---

from the discharge under section 523 rationally might attempt to shield assets from the bankruptcy trustee so that those assets could be used to pay the nondischarged debts after bankruptcy.

A dilemma is thus presented. Offering a discharge to a cooperative debtor provides one sort of incentive. Many of the exceptions, however, including the willful and malicious injury exception, also have incentive-based (or, viewed conversely, deterrence-based) rationales of an entirely different sort. The incentive behind many exceptions is not to perform the "bad" act, be it fraud, a willful and malicious injury, or embezzlement, on threat of later losing the discharge for the affected debt. If debtors are allowed to get away with such behavior via a bankruptcy discharge, it could be argued that their initial decision whether to engage in the behavior might be skewed in favor of committing the fraud or other bad act.

This justification for exceptions does not mesh well with the debtor cooperation theory underlying the general discharge where the goal is to encourage debtors who already have committed various financial sins to cooperate in the bankruptcy proceeding now. An analogous situation is that of a prosecutor who agrees to a reduced sentence for a criminal who agrees to "sing." Although society's preference is that the criminal not commit the crime in the first place, a preference supported by criminal sentences designed in part to deter criminal activity, we still attempt to make the best of the situation after the commission of the crime is a fait accompli.

Normatively, the tension between incentives for the discharge and exceptions thereto must be faced head-on. Do we favor the creditor group at the expense of the single victimized creditor, or vice versa? Given that a larger class—the entire creditor body—is affected by the debtor's "bankruptcy compliance" behavior, compared with a single creditor in the case of an exception, a straightforward utilitarian case can be made for giving priority to those incentives supporting the general discharge, and eliminating or cutting back on exceptions. This conclusion must be tempered, however, with the observation that in advance of the debtor's actions that could lead to an exception, a large class of potential victims exists, with the specific victim still unknown. The entire class of potential victims may therefore agree to create incentives in advance for the debtor not to engage in "bad" behavior. . . .

. . . [A] distinction can be drawn based on the degree of control the victimized creditor has over its own fate, in terms of acting to prevent the debtor's bad behavior from impacting negatively on the creditor. A person who is viciously stabbed in the back presents a more appealing discharge exception candidate than a creditor who voluntarily lends money to a dubious debtor and then is lax in monitoring the debtor's maintenance of a collateral account. We might conclude that the interests of the entire body of creditors in inducing the debtor's compliance must give way to the interests of the stabbing victim but not the lax secured creditor. Yet it must be borne in mind that not all tort victims are protected from their tortfeasor's discharge; dischargeability depends upon the culpability of the debtor's conduct.

B. The Social Utility Theory and the Concept of Externalities

An additional justification for the discharge points out that granting a discharge to hopelessly indebted individuals benefits society generally, not just the body of creditors in a given case. The nonwaivable aspect of the discharge can be explained by this theory, in that waiver might generate externalities, which debtors might systematically ignore. The social utility theory has several facets.

First is the notion that freeing the debtor from past debts encourages the debtor to become (or resume being) a productive member of the commercial society. Conversely, under the weight of debt, the debtor supposedly has less incentive to work because his creditors can take away the benefits of that work through collection efforts such as garnishment. This notion has persisted since Blackstone's day. Campaigning for the passage of the 1841 Bankruptcy Act, President John Tyler stated: "The distress incident to the derangements of some years past has visited large numbers of our fellow-citizens with hopeless insolvency, whose energies, both mental and physical, by reason of the load of debt pressing upon them, are lost to the country." In more modern jargon, if the entire decrease in productivity is not internalized by the debtor in the form of lost wages, a negative externality may result.

A second and related facet of the social utility theory could be called the "fabric of society" argument. In times of widespread financial ruin and calamity, the very "fabric of society" is weakened by the existence of a large class of hopeless insolvents. The existence of this large debtor class causes social and political unrest and financial hardship for the rest of society, which somehow has to support these debtors and their families. The simplest solution to this scenario is to wipe out the essential problem afflicting the debtor class—their debts.

Historically, substantial support can be found for this aspect of the social utility theory as a motivation for the discharge in the bankruptcy laws. Until the Bankruptcy Reform Act of 1978, every major bankruptcy law passed in United States history came in the aftermath of a major financial panic. Troubled times have often generated political pressures for a general discharge.

The two facets of the social utility theory, like the debtor cooperation theory, do not readily support having exceptions to the discharge. If we want to provide an incentive for people to work, the discharge needs to be complete and not partial. Similarly, if an impoverished debtor class is causing social dislocation, keeping them impoverished because they were "bad" debtors in the way they generated their debts will not cure the larger social problem. As a society, we must weigh the importance of realizing these social-utility goals against the importance of deterring or punishing certain types of debt-creation behavior.

C. The Humanitarian Theory and Moral Problems

A third major justification for the bankruptcy discharge is that it is humane to free hopelessly indebted individuals from their debts. This theory also has several facets. The first focuses on the need to recognize and facilitate the intrinsic self-worth of the individual debtor, a self-worth severely undermined by oppressive debt obligations. Freeing the debtor from those debts helps restore the debtor's sense of self-worth.

The second facet of the humanitarian theory focuses on how society benefits from restoring the debtor's self-worth. Society supposedly benefits through the promotion of humanitarian values, which "makes us all better people," and through the reintroduction into the community of more "worthy" people. As Shakespeare's Portia noted in discussing Antonio's credit problems with Shylock:

> The quality of mercy is not strained;
> It droppeth as the gentle rain from heaven
> Upon the place beneath. It is twice blest;
> It blesseth him that gives and him that takes.

Of course, discharged creditors might ask why they have to bear the brunt of this form of charity relief; they might prefer the opportunity to collect money to being "blesseth." They are always free to choose to be humane (and thus blessed) in any particular case, but, under the discharge, their dispensation of mercy is compelled.

One reply is that by unchecked overlending creditors may contribute to the debt problem in the first place. Furthermore, creditors can better avoid their debtor's default crisis if they are selective in granting credit initially. It also can be argued that the creditors themselves are morally tainted by encouraging overuse of credit. If a creditor sends a complimentary credit card to a prime candidate for Debtors Anonymous, should the creditor really be considered guiltless?

It can be argued, of course, that surely not all creditors are blameworthy. Many creditors are no doubt quite careful in extending credit and are in fact taken advantage of by dishonest debtors. . . .

Attempting to specify the proper scope of the discharge under the humanitarian theory requires addressing some difficult questions. First, should the creditor's consent (or lack thereof) to participate in this societal forgiveness scheme be considered at all in the equation? Second, should the debtor have to be deserving in some fashion to be able to appropriate for himself society's discharge gift?

The answers to these two lines of inquiry are of direct relevance in determining the scope of the discharge and the extent of discharge exceptions. If the creditor's consent is not considered relevant, and no limitation to "good" debtors is imposed, then the justification for discharge exceptions disappears in the context of the humanitarian theory.

If, however, only "good" debtors are entitled to humane treatment, then we can pick and choose what forms of "bad" behavior will be disentitling. Further, if nonconsenting creditors are not bound by the societal forgiveness scheme, then many of the existing discharge exceptions retain their vitality. For instance, the collateral conversion exception could be justified on the ground that the creditor only consented to be a part of the system if it had collateral on which to fall back.

To some extent the question of what is the best approach is purely theoretical. The historical evidence suggests that most people do not want a totally humanitarian or merciful system that allows all debtors to walk free, no matter what their moral worthiness. On the contrary, there has historically been a steady increase in the number of discharge exceptions. Although some of these exceptions focus on the creditor's "worthiness," many are directed against debtors who have committed intentional misdeeds causing financial or other injury.

Aside from the moral view that debts created by intentional wrongdoing should not be discharged, a major concern with the system of complete forgiveness is that bad debtors will intentionally abuse the system. A discharge system with no exceptions could provide incentives for debtors to take advantage of creditors. Yet the argument that exceptions are essential is not necessarily conclusive.

On the one hand, there is little doubt that some debtors will take advantage of a more lenient discharge law. . . . How many debtors would do so is impossible to say, but most would acknowledge that the number is greater than zero.

On the other hand, who cares if debtors take advantage of the discharge law? If letting people who are hopelessly in debt regain their sense of self-worth and identity through debt forgiveness is justifiable on a humanitarian basis, the justification remains valid whether the debtor is a commercial Mother Theresa or Saddam Hussein. Indeed, it is a greater expression of society's mercy to forgive the debts of a debtor whose commercial sins are great. Furthermore, one suspects that, although the number of likely abusers in a complete discharge system—one with no exceptions—almost certainly is positive, that number probably is quite low. Historically the concern that "going easy" on debtors, for instance, by discontinuing the remedy of imprisonment for debt, would encourage sloth and abuse, has generally proven to be overstated.

The moral question is not beyond argument. The obligation to repay debt itself is typically viewed as a moral obligation of the debtor. One could argue, therefore, that creating the opportunity to discharge debts through bankruptcy without payment actually works to the moral detriment of debtors, by tempting them to follow the amoral course of nonpayment.

Ultimately the humanitarian and moral arguments prove somewhat elusive and in some respects contradictory. The conclusions to be drawn from a consideration of these arguments do not follow clearly and inexorably in the way that adding two plus two dictates a total of four. Nevertheless, the response to this uncertainty should not be to throw up one's hands and ignore the humanitarian side of the equation entirely. The bankruptcy discharge implicates moral issues. A full and informed discharge policy of necessity must take those issues into account.

D. The Systematic Overborrowing Theory: Impulse Control and Incomplete Heuristics

Dean Jackson recently attempted to explain why the right of discharge exists at all, and why it is nonwaivable in advance. Although he recognizes the externalities argument discussed above, and the risk allocation theory discussed below, Dean Jackson focuses on volitional and cognitive justifications for the nonwaivable discharge right. Nonwaivability, according to Dean Jackson, can best be justified as a necessary corrective to a systematic overborrowing problem. Such systematic overborrowing may occur, he posits, due to a lack of volitional control by debtors, who cannot effectively prevent themselves from taking on too much debt. A nonwaivable discharge right curtails this problem by shifting to the creditor—who will lose money if credit is extended to a debtor who later takes advantage of a bankruptcy discharge without paying—the incentive to monitor borrowing.

According to Dean Jackson, a cognitive justification, called "incomplete heuristics," may also exist for the nonwaivable discharge right. The argument is that many individuals systematically underestimate the risk that they will be unable to pay for their current level of credit consumption in the future. Recognizing this fact, members of society rationally restrict the adverse consequences of informationally defective behavior by agreeing to discharge certain debts. This prophylactic rule must be applied uniformly because of the extreme difficulty of sorting out those individuals who are likely to experience unanticipated regret, and those who are not.

Dean Jackson's volitional and cognitive arguments, as with most of the justifications for the discharge, do not readily account for the discharge exceptions. If we concede that certain individuals cannot control their impulses to engage in systematic overborrowing, the argument that creating a discharge exception might deter such behavior, is inherently flawed. For example, a compulsive gambler who is embezzling from his employer to pay his gambling debts (and to avoid the very unpleasant collection tactics of some unpaid bookies) is unlikely to give significant weight to the possibility of losing a bankruptcy discharge, in deciding whether to continue embezzling. The same person is also likely to have serious cognitive deficiencies that lead him to underestimate the likelihood of going bankrupt at all and of having his embezzlement detected, and to overestimate the chances of correcting his financial troubles by making a few winning bets. Although society may decide that such a person still should not be discharged from his debts in order to punish that sort of criminal activity (in addition to any criminal sanctions), it is important to be clear about why the discharge is being denied.

E. The Limited Liability and Economic Efficiency Theory

The discharge also may be justified as a form of limited liability for individuals. Foreknowledge of the discharge encourages entrepreneurial risk-taking, which is assumed to be beneficial to the economic health of the nation. Individuals are willing to take chances on new business ventures because they know they will not have to live forever with negative results. For individuals acting as consumers, the argument is that the availability of the discharge encourages participation in an open credit economy.

One might question whether this justification is necessary today and if so, whether it is efficient. The discharge developed before limited liability via the corporate form was commonplace. Today, however, the corporate form can be used to limit liability for a business debtor and therefore the discharge loses part of its justification in the individual business debtor case. The counter argument is that limited liability for individuals running small businesses is a myth because the individual principals almost always have to guarantee personally the corporate debts.

Even if limited liability can only be achieved effectively through a bankruptcy discharge, it might not be efficient to encourage entrepreneurs to take chances with other people's money where the risk of failure is effectively discounted by the discharge escape hatch. For example, consider a hypothetical individual entrepreneur who is trying to decide whether to undertake a new business venture requiring $100,000 in capital. Assume that the venture has a fifty per cent chance of making a total of $150,000 (*i.e.*, returning the initial $100,000 investment, plus a profit of $50,000) and a fifty per cent chance of failing completely, resulting in the loss of the $100,000. Economically, this venture should not be undertaken. Its value, in advance, is a negative $25,000. If the venturer has to invest his own money, or will remain liable for the $100,000 debt if he borrows the money (that is, if no discharge is available), he will not go forward if acting rationally. If, however, the entrepreneur can escape personal liability for the $100,000 loan via a bankruptcy discharge, he will proceed with the venture. Now the venture has, to the entrepreneur, a positive value of $25,000.

Nevertheless, creditors may be able to regulate risk taking through more effective monitoring, both before and after loans are made. In the hypothetical just discussed, a creditor who can make the assumed projections should not make the loan. If the creditor is in fact better able than the debtor to assess the risk of default and to insure against that risk, as some commentators have concluded, then limited liability for individuals may be justified.

Professor Eisenberg disagrees with this proposition. He argues that usually the debtor is better able than the creditor to determine if he is taking on excessive credit obligations and to insure against the default risk. Accordingly, in his view, which has generated controversy, the general presumption should be one of nondischargeability.

The risk-bearer approach better justifies having some exceptions to the discharge. Under this theory, debtors should be discharged only from those risks that their creditor voluntarily agreed to finance. For example, the defrauded creditor does not knowingly consent to the risk actually being taken, and should not have to assume unknown risks. As to collateral conversions, the creditor only consents in advance to risks being taken with their money if they have collateral to fall back on in the event of default. No consent at all is involved in embezzlement or larceny, or with regard to most tort creditors. . . .

The discharge and its exceptions seem driven, in differing degrees, by a variety of normative policies, some of which conflict. To develop a coherent discharge policy requires a thoughtful and balanced consideration of these different policies. Ultimately these policies must be implemented in the bankruptcy law as it is written and applied. Bankruptcy and discharge are not mere abstract notions; real cases involving real people are implicated. . . .

Conclusion

It has been observed that "[a] bankrupt law, which is founded on public policy, has for its object the advancement of justice and mercy." This statement, made over 170 years ago by an anonymous author urging the passage of a national bankruptcy law, continues to ring true today. The rub, of course, is how to reconcile the conflicting demands of justice and mercy. Justice says that a debtor should be compelled to pay his debts whenever possible. . . . Mercy says that the debtor should be relieved of his debts.

Adam J. Hirsch
Inheritance and Bankruptcy: The Meaning of the "Fresh Start"
45 HASTINGS L.J. 175 (1994)[*]

B. Discharge Theory

. . . [W]e must first address a more fundamental question: *viz.*, what is the discharge supposed to accomplish for society? Only after we pin down (if that is possible) the policies underlying the discharge can we proceed to consider whether inclusion of expectancies in the bankruptcy estate conforms or conflicts with those policies.

The discharge has given rise to a lively debate in recent years, a debate made all the more intriguing by the subject's many-sidedness. The idea of the fresh start can be probed from half a hundred different pedagogical angles, including history,[87] political theory,[88] contract theory,[89] natural law,[90] libertarian philosophy[91] (and its mirror image, paternalism[92]), moral philosophy, distrib-

---

[*]   Copyright © 1994 by University of California, Hastings College of the Law. Reprinted from Hastings Law Journal Vol. 45, No. 1, pp. 175 et. seq., by permission, and with the approval of the author.

[87]   The discharge was originally developed in Great Britain primarily as a device to encourage debtors to disclose assets they had fraudulently concealed. . . .

[88]   Early republican theorists feared that debt threatened the survival of a republic because, as a lure to luxury and extravagance, it debased the "virtue" of its citizens and made them subservient to creditors who were potential tyrants. In addition, some theorists feared that a vibrant market for credit would push the United States toward commercialization and away from the agrarian economy they considered essential ballast for a republic. Thomas Jefferson (who never got out of debt himself) thus urged legal reforms to make credit less attractive, and he stood opposed to federal bankruptcy legislation. . . .

In another variation on this theme, some theorists feared that debtors facing stringent debtor-creditor laws would be driven to revolt against the state, a prophecy fulfilled in post-revolutionary Massachusetts. . . . From this political perspective, however, the discharge appears double-edged. On the one hand, it encourages persons to get into debt and thus tends to promote commercial speculation. On the other hand, the discharge provides an escape route from debt and therefore could be viewed as a means of defusing the political threat of widespread debtor subservience or unrest. The continued relevance of these early political concerns is, at any rate, dubious in the latter-day republic, with its stronger state apparatus. One modern bankruptcy court has offered a different political rationale for the discharge, turning agrarian republicanism on its head: Were each citizen restricted to "only one economic life," then the threat of a single economic failure "would frustrate and still the creative spirit which lies at the heart of our democratic society." . . .

[89]   The discharge has been conceived as equivalent to a doctrine of impossibility covering contracts for credit. This is not the whole story of the discharge, since it—unlike doctrines of contract excuse—cannot be waived or modified by the parties. But, were the discharge simply conceived as a default rule built into the contract for credit, its utility as a means of efficiently assigning risk of impossibility would be unclear. Pertinent considerations include: (1) the relative ability of debtor and creditor to bear (or insure against) the risk, (2) the relative abilities of the parties to control the risk, (3) the assignee of risk most bargaining parties would agree upon (which, if presumed, can avoid transaction costs), and (4) the relative knowledge (or cost of information) of the parties concerning the extent of the risk. . . .

[90]   Were the debtor to remain indefinitely in bankruptcy without a discharge, she would lose her right to enjoy income or to sue for personal wrongs, except for the benefit of the bankruptcy estate. Some have suggested that this state of affairs would leave the debtor "an outlaw, a mere slave to the trustee," which is contrary to natural justice. . . .

[91]   Denying debtors the right to waive the discharge *ex ante* arguably violates their autonomy. Such autonomy may be grounded on utilitarian ideology (assuming that individuals are the best judges of their own interests), on transcendental philosophy (assuming that self-reliance and individual responsibility are morally compelled), or on existential philosophy (assuming that the making of choices is an essential aspect of the human condition). . . .

[92]   Making the discharge nonwaivable could be justified as a paternalistic move: protecting those persons who are prone to reckless borrowing from their own poor judgment and the subsequent "regret" they would otherwise experience.

utive ethics,[94] cultural anthropology,[95] behavioral psychology,[96] even cognition and sociobiology.[97] But the conventional justification for the discharge, articulated most famously (though hardly originally) in the *Local Loan* case, [292 U.S. 234 (1934)] proceeds from the direction of economics. Put

---

That a significant class of irrational borrowers exists is evident. Though denying the equation of insolvency and slavery, Professor Jackson argues that a nonwaivable right of discharge can still be reconciled with libertarianism—that is, can be conceptualized as *not* paternalistic—if we find that debtors (like Ulysses) recognize in themselves a susceptibility to some irrational temptation (here, to waive the discharge) and *wish* to prevent themselves *ex ante* from succumbing to it. Such an act of "self-paternalism," since it is self-imposed, accords with individual autonomy. . . . There is, however, no reported empirical evidence of such a recognition and widespread political preference in connection with contracts for credit. Thus, characterization of the nonwaivable right of discharge as self-paternalistic is problematic. . . .

Professor Jackson also argues that nonwaivability is not paternal because, irrespective of current popular preferences, awareness of the temptation to waive the discharge and a consequent move for nonwaivability "accords with the result of a hypothetical initial deliberation behind a Rawlsian 'veil of ignorance.'" This argument appears too clever by half. To suggest that persons who *fail* to perceive what is in their interest *could* perceive it if they engaged in a Rawlsian *gedanken* experiment does not alter the fact that they do *not* perceive it, and that others are accordingly acting on their behalf. Indeed, that is part and parcel of the concept of paternalism! If subjects *would not* perceive outside intervention to be in their best interest if in possession of hypothetically perfect information, then the central moral justification for paternalistic intervention—namely, that the paternalist spares the subject from regret—would disappear. Rawlsian theory provides a justification for the division of rights, by asking what rights persons would create before they knew their status (as, say, a debtor or a creditor). It does not offer a way around the dilemma of paternalism.

[94]   Because creditors demand an interest rate that will allow them to profit in the aggregate, despite incidental debtor bankruptcies, the discharge produces a wealth transfer from those debtors who avoid bankruptcy to those who succumb to it. Richard Posner has described this transfer as a subsidy from the "prudent" to the "feckless," "a curious basis on which to redistribute wealth!" . . . But the discharge can also be viewed as a form of insurance against insolvency, in which capacity it redistributes wealth from the fortunate to the unlucky—a less ethically troubling proposition. Part of the cost of the discharge may also be borne by creditors and by society at large.

[95]   Bankruptcy, and the discharge that culminates it, can be viewed as classic sort of ostracism-*cum*-reinstatement ritual. . . . The breaking of the bench was the original cultural ritual signaling the debtor's ostracism (and giving bankruptcy its name). . . .

[96]   The discharge arguably functions to relieve the psychological trauma of financial calamity, along with its common symptoms (depression, alcohol abuse, marital difficulty, etc.). . . . But the psychological impact of a bankruptcy proceeding (which by tradition incorporates no psychological counseling) may not be unambiguously salutary. . . .

[97]   Professor Jackson has argued that certain cognitive processes predispose persons to act impulsively and to underestimate risk, thereby leading them "systematically" to overconsume credit. These disabilities can serve to justify state intervention to prevent persons from irrationally waiving their right to a discharge. . . . A number of responses are in order. First, processes of cognition may operate systematically, but they do not tend *uniformly* toward the overconsumption of credit: For example, the empirically verified phenomenon of *risk aversion* also affects social behavior. This psychological cross-current could just as easily incline persons toward *conservative* borrowing. . . .

Second, to the extent that some persons today are prone to over-borrow, this proneness may well be partly (I dare say, largely) *cultural* in nature—a sequela to the rise of a consumerist ethic that cherishes material possessions and encourages persons to favor present over future consumption, coupled with the concurrent development of modern marketing. These cultural attributes are notorious. . . .

Third, whatever its organic and/or environmental origins, the existence of an identifiable class of "credit card junkies" has now been confirmed empirically. . . . But if the discharge does function to protect these persons from their own bad judgment, one may observe that it is merely a palliative remedy, for it makes no effort to cure their behavioral tendencies. Debtor education has long been urged by other commentators, and Jackson's analysis could be applied to underscore its importance, but it has never been incorporated into formal bankruptcy process. . . .

Finally, a mandatory rule overriding irrational undervaluation of the discharge, standing alone, will not work unequivocally to the advantage of debtors, because that same undervaluation may irrationally drive down demand for credit once its price is adjusted to reflect the actual cost of the discharge. . . .

simply, the discharge functions to avoid the social costs of insolvency. Without the discharge, a hopelessly insolvent debtor would lose her incentive to produce, preferring instead to consume leisure, and administratively costly welfare benefits.[99] By restoring the debtor to solvency, the discharge simultaneously removes the debtor's incentive to rely on inefficient state aid and renews her incentive to contribute to the gross national product. In this respect, the utility of the discharge is not unequivocal, for it has a second economic edge.[101] As a form of insurance against insolvency, the discharge creates incentives for individuals to risk higher loads of debt. But the marginal significance of this "moral hazard" is probably small, for absent the discharge insolvent debtors would *still* be substantially judgment-proof (and potentially eligible for state welfare), a circumstance creating similar incentives for reckless borrowing.[104]

The bar on *ex ante* waivers of the right of discharge also follows from this economic theory. Because the social costs of insolvency are external to the contract for credit, the bargaining parties would not bear the full cost of an agreement to foreclose the fresh start. At the same time, the parties are not significantly injured by the loss of this opportunity, for an *ex ante* waiver is of marginal value to lenders: If prevented from seeking a discharge, an insolvent debtor could still stymie her creditors by ceasing to produce property against which they could levy. Hence, by mandating an unwaivable right of discharge, lawmakers avoid external costs *without* significantly distorting the cost of credit.

---

[99]   . . . An analogy can be drawn here to the economic theory of taxation. Like taxes, indebtedness reduces one's net return from labor, though the consequence of that reduction is unclear. One may be stimulated to *greater* labor to make up for the tax (the "wealth effect"), or one may be stimulated to substitute leisure for labor because, as a valuable good, leisure is now relatively less costly (the "price effect"). In the case of hopeless insolvency—like confiscatory taxation—the price effect swamps the wealth effect. . . . Still, to the extent persons *enjoy* their jobs, or are simply *habituated* to a work routine, their productivity may not suffer (or suffer as badly as we would expect) in the event of insolvency. . . .

[101]   And a third one: for one must also consider the impact of the discharge on creditors, who are thereby denied satisfaction of their debts. Such denial may render some creditors dependent on state support, which again entails social costs. The Bankruptcy Code operates to blunt this edge of the discharge, however, by excepting from its coverage certain creditors who would otherwise likely fall into this category. Thus, alimony and child support obligations are not discharged in bankruptcy. 11 U.S.C. § 523(a)(5) (1988). On the other hand, *all* creditors who suffer bad debt losses as a result of the discharge pass part of them on to society, *inter alia,* by deducting them from their taxable income. . . .

[104]   . . . The incentive to recklessness created by stringent insolvency laws was noticed early. . . . Compare Professor Jackson's argument that a right of discharge operates to *mitigate* the moral hazard of borrowing. According to Jackson, the discharge shifts "the risk of ill-advised credit decisions" from social insurance to creditors, who are better able to monitor debtors and thereby to check their propensities to over-consume credit. The difficulty with this analysis is that, even in the absence of a discharge, creditors still bear the *private cost* of a default. It is only the *social cost* of default (cessation of labor, etc.) that falls on society, and this does not shift to creditors if the discharge is available—it simply disappears, given the debtor's renewed incentive to productivity. Because creditors must suffer the private cost of a default irrespective of whether the right to a discharge exists, they will monitor debtors to avoid over-borrowing under *either* hypothetical legal regime. And if a discharge raises incentives to over-borrowing above the level that would exist without it, as it is bound marginally to do, then private costs (in terms of monitoring plus defaults not efficiently preventable) must accordingly rise. Of course, social costs will simultaneously fall—that is the cutting edge of this legal sword—but not as a result of a shift in the risk of default.

C. Exemptions

A cornerstone of the bankruptcy law's "fresh start" policy for individual consumer debtors is the allowance of exemptions. Exempt property is that portion of the debtor's assets that the debtor may retain, free from the claims of her creditors. That is, even if a debtor's creditors are not paid in full, they may not collect out of the debtor's exempt property. The allowance of exemptions to a consumer debtor dovetails with the bankruptcy discharge: the discharge protects a debtor's future earnings, while exemptions shield from creditors certain portions of a debtor's existing assets as of the time of bankruptcy, which assets the debtor may need or use to generate future earnings. Exemption laws, however, are not solely a creature of the bankruptcy fresh start policy; exemptions also exist outside of bankruptcy, under the law of each state.

Several interesting and important questions arise with regard to exemptions in bankruptcy. The passages excerpted in this Part address some of those questions. The first and most fundamental exemption issue is, why allow exemptions at all? By definition, exempt property is property that the debtor is permitted to keep even while her creditors remain unpaid. Why should a debtor's creditors be compelled to subsidize the debtor in this manner? What answers are given to this threshold question by the commentators in this Part?

Whether an individual debtor should be allowed to retain *some* property as exempt is fairly well settled in favor of debtors at this juncture. Much more significant as a practical matter is the second exemption question: what property, and how much property, should be exempt? It is one thing for everyone to agree that a debtor should be allowed some exemptions; it is quite another to fix the level of exemptions. An abiding aspect of the American exemption scene has been the fact of enormous disparities between states regarding the generosity of exemptions.

In the context of bankruptcy exemption policy, this second question leads inexorably to a third and related question, which is the subject of much of the commentary in this Part: *who* decides what exemptions should be allowed? In a federal bankruptcy case, the choice is between the federal government on the one hand and the fifty states on the other. As noted above, a central fact of exemption law in America is that all fifty states have their own exemption laws, which vary widely. Should a debtor in a federal bankruptcy case be afforded exemptions set by the federal government, which would then be uniform across the country, or should the debtor be limited to the exemptions provided by her home state? Or should the debtor be given a choice between the two exemptions systems?

The federal bankruptcy law has vacillated over the resolution of this critical question. The early Bankruptcy Acts of 1800 and 1841 used uniform federal exemptions; the Act of 1867 allowed a debtor both state *and* federal exemptions; and the Act of 1898 granted a debtor *only* state exemptions. In 1902, the Supreme Court held in *Hanover National Bank v. Moyses*, 186 U.S. 181, that the use of state exemptions in bankruptcy did not violate the constitutional requirement that any federal bankruptcy law be "uniform," reasoning that the exemption laws would be applied uniformly on a geographic basis within each state, which would suffice. In the first article, *Limitations of Exemptions in Bankruptcy*, 45 Iowa L. Rev. 445 (1960), Professor Frank Kennedy argues that deference to the states in setting exemptions was a wise choice. What reasons does Kennedy offer in support of the state scheme then in effect? Are those reasons still relevant today?

In the debates leading up to the passage of the 1978 Bankruptcy Reform Act, the question of whether states or the federal government would set bankruptcy exemptions was a central issue. The House of Representatives favored allowing debtors a choice between state and federal exemptions, as the excerpt from the 1977 House Report reveals. The Senate, though, preferred the then-existing system under which states set exemptions for resident debtors, as shown by the included portion of the 1978 Senate Report. The compromise between these two positions reached in the enacted bill is described by Senator DeConcini in the excerpt from the *Congressional Record*: debtors could choose between the federal and state exemptions *unless* the debtor's state elected not to allow their debtors this choice and instead limited domiciliary debtors to state exemptions. This bizarre solution has become known as "opt out" (a state may "opt out" of the federal exemptions), and nearly three-fourths of the states have decided to avail themselves of the opt-out privilege. The next two selections address aspects of the opt-out compromise.

First, Professor Eric Posner discusses the political machinations and motivations for the opt-out compromise, in *The Political Economy of the Bankruptcy Reform Act of 1978*, 96 MICH. L. REV. 47 (1997). How does Posner explain what happened?

Second, Professor Judith Koffler, in *The Bankruptcy Clause and Exemption Laws: A Reexamination of the Doctrine of Geographic Uniformity*, 58 N.Y.U. L. REV. 22 (1983), questions the constitutionality of delegating the setting of federal bankruptcy exemption levels to the states. After an exhaustive and thoughtful historical analysis, she argues that *Moyses* was wrongly decided and that deference to state exemptions violates the constitutional uniformity requirement.

The final major exemption issue addressed in this Part is the thorny problem of exemption "planning": what should be done with debtors who anticipate filing bankruptcy and studiously and intentionally convert non-exempt assets to exempt assets on the eve of bankruptcy? Is this a terrible fraud practiced on creditors, which should be answered with denial of exemptions or even of the discharge? Or is this a responsible, prudent action that should be encouraged? Attorneys advising debtors need to have some guidelines, but the courts have failed miserably to offer much beyond tired cliches that are honored in the breach.

Back in the very first article in this Part, Professor Kennedy offers a thoughtful assessment of the problem, and argues against a policy that would treat exemption planning as fraudulent per se. He asserts that it is "indefensible" to reward a debtor who plans his exemptions well in advance while penalizing a debtor who does not: "If the exemption idea is sound at all, however, it is stultifying to withhold exemptions from those whose need for their protection is the greatest because they did not have the foresight to get their quota of exemptions early." Kennedy also decries the "incongruity of predicating a fraud on the debtor's seeking the sanctuary provided by law for his family when their need becomes desperately clear to him." Professor Kennedy's arguments resonate with much force today, and courts should heed his admonitions.

Professor Alan Resnick addressed the exemption planning question on the cusp of enactment of the 1978 Code in *Prudent Planning or Fraudulent Transfer? The Use of Nonexempt Assets to Purchase or Improve Exempt Property on the Eve of Bankruptcy*, 31 RUTGERS L. REV. 615 (1978). Resnick examined the justifications for allowing exemptions in the first place, and found that most of those justifications are consistent with allowing a debtor to acquire exempt property on the eve of bankruptcy. He argued that the need for certainty in planning is great, and thus recommended an immunity from invalidation for exempt assets acquired more than 90 days before bankruptcy. Within the 90-day period, he suggested limiting acquired exemptions to the debtor's reasonable needs. Resnick would not use debtor intent as a determinant. Finally, he would eliminate the threat of loss of discharge for exemption planning.

The final article dealing with the exemption conversion issue is Lawrence Ponoroff & F. Stephen Knippenberg, *Debtors Who Convert Their Assets on the Eve of Bankruptcy: Villains or Vic-*

tims of the Fresh Start?, 70 N.Y.U. L. REV. 235 (1995). Professors Ponoroff and Knippenberg examine the problem from a fresh perspective. After suggesting that the prevailing characterization of asset conversion as a "transfer" is flawed, they urge adoption instead of a "property" metaphor to analyze the question. Applying their model, they conclude that the judiciary should abandon efforts to police the pre-bankruptcy conversion of non-exempt property to exempt property. Viewed from the "property" perspective, Ponoroff and Knippenberg argue "that to deny exemptions is to take property from the debtor and confer it upon unsecured creditors who did not bargain for it."

Those pondering the merits of the exemption planning debate also might profit from consulting an exchange of articles in the *UCLA Law Review*, which are highly recommended but not included here. The creditors' best friend in the exemption planning debate is Professor Theodore Eisenberg. In *Bankruptcy Law in Perspective*, 28 UCLA L. REV. 953 (1981), Eisenberg took the position that pre-bankruptcy exemption planning is an illegitimate "manipulation" or "frustration" of the bankruptcy law by "clever debtors," which needs to be dealt with by a limiting federal rule. Indeed, he even suggests that Congress might consider imposing sanctions on debtors beyond disallowance of the exemption, and questions whether actual fraud should have to be established.

Eisenberg's strident position provoked a heated response from Professor Steven Harris in *A Reply to Theodore Eisenberg's "Bankruptcy Law in Perspective,"* 30 UCLA L. REV. 327 (1982). Harris pointed out that Eisenberg's approach would undermine both the deference to state exemptions in bankruptcy *and* the bankruptcy "fresh start" policy. Drawing on an argument made by Professor Kennedy, Harris also took Eisenberg to task for being unsympathetic to the problem of the differential treatment of sophisticated and unsophisticated debtors that would occur if eve-of-bankruptcy exemptions were upset.

The final selection in the Chapter is from the National Bankruptcy Review Commission Report. That Report makes several significant recommendations, including: first, that "opt out" be eliminated; second, that homestead exemptions allowed under state laws be cabined by a dollar floor and ceiling; and third, that a lump-sum dollar exemption be allowed for non-homestead property.

Frank Kennedy
Limitations of Exemptions in Bankruptcy
45 IOWA L. REV. 445 (1960)[*]

There has been a curiously developing concern in recent years over the fairness and adequacy of the panoply of laws that establish exemptions for debtors' property. Since existing exemption laws of the states typically reflect their nineteenth century origins and are exceedingly diverse in scope and pattern, the conclusions are almost automatically reached that the laws are generally antiquated, that some are excessively generous to debtors and correspondingly prejudicial to the legitimate interests of their creditors, and that others fail to give adequate consideration to the social and economic advantages of provisions permitting debtors to retain reasonable minima of their property free from their creditors' claims. Since the Bankruptcy Act extends to bankrupts whatever is prescribed by the exemption laws of their domiciliary states, the criticism leads to a plea for a long overdue revision of federal as well as state exemption legislation. It is an argument of this Article that

---

notwithstanding the great variety and the deficiencies of the state exemption laws, Congress has wisely deferred in its bankruptcy legislation to the states' resolution of the conflicting interests of debtors and creditors embodied in their exemption laws. . . .

I. THE STATE LAW OF EXEMPTIONS

It has been remarked elsewhere how the common law of creditors' rights, once incredibly harsh toward the delinquent debtor,[4] has felt the impact of the developing social conscience during the nineteenth century. The yield of this humanitarianism included drastic restriction of the role of imprisonment for debt, the award of discharge from unpaid indebtedness after liquidation of the debtors' estate, and the grant of exemptions of certain property from legal process by creditors. This latter development, of principal concern in this paper, is entirely statutory, or practically so, and the variety of legislation encountered in American jurisdictions almost defies classification. While variety characterizes even the objectives of exemption legislation, a persistent theme is the protection of the family of the debtor from penury.[11] Exemption legislation embodies a deliberate choice of policy to prefer the social interest in providing a minimum of economic security and other benefits to debtors and their families over the economic interest to be served by assuring creditors the maximum availability of their debtors' property for the satisfaction of their claims.

The classifications of property and debtors embraced by the exemption laws often carry a whimsical quality and conspicuous evidence of the quite different conditions that prevailed in the society contemporaneous with their enactment. The statutes are thus easily vulnerable to attack as anachronistic and ill-adapted to serve their original purposes. . . . The fact that legislatures have largely ignored the increasing obsolescence of their exemption laws seems not to be an entirely inexplicable phenomenon, however. . . . Finally, there has been increasing recognition that family security and rehabilitation ought not to be achieved solely at the expense of creditors but on the contrary are public responsibilities that ought to be widely shared. . . .

II. DEFERENCE IN BANKRUPTCY TO STATE EXEMPTION LAWS

Although the Constitution empowers Congress to enact only uniform laws of bankruptcy, the tenor of the present act is to allow every bankrupt whatever exemptions are prescribed by the law of the state of his domicile.[18] While the result appears to be decidedly unfavorable to bankrupts

---

[4] Consider, *e.g.,* the following dire dictum of Mr. Justice Hyde in Manby v. Scott, 1 Mod. 124, 132, 86 Eng. Rep. 781, 786 (Ex. Chamb. 1663): "If a man be taken in execution and lie in prison for debt, neither the plaintiff at whose suit he is arrested, nor the sheriff who took him, is bound to find him meat, drink, or clothes; but he must live on his own, or on the charity of others: and if no man will relieve him, let him die in the name of God, says the law; and so say I."

[11] The purpose of most exemption statutes to sustain a minimum level of family security is evident from the usual limitation of the availability of the exemption to heads of families. Exemption of the homestead, family wearing apparel, household furniture, and provisions for the family contributes quite obviously to this main purpose. Protection of the financial security of the family unit serves such public welfare objectives as relieving the community of the burden of supporting paupers and preserving the social values of family life. The generosity of some homestead statutes suggests that legislatures have sought in addition to encourage settlement by immigrants within the state, development of the state's agricultural potentialities, and home ownership as a means of stabilizing community growth. Exemption of tools of the trade and other personalty having particular value in vocational pursuits is related to family security by providing the means for debtor rehabilitation. Exemption of such items as private libraries, family Bibles, portraits, pictures, musical instruments, paintings not kept for sale, and seats or pews in places of worship indicates a legislative concern that no family should be denied the benefits of a cultural and spiritual upbringing by a creditor's levy. Exemption of a burying ground exhibits a legislative sensitivity to the need for personal dignity of even the lowliest debtor. . . .

[18] Constitutional doubts as to the power of Congress to import the diversity of state exemption laws into bankruptcy were resolved in Hanover Nat'l Bank v. Moyses, 186 U.S. 181 (1902).

residing in states in the northeastern sector when they are compared with bankrupts living elsewhere in the country, the discrimination is attributable to a difference in the appraisal of the relevant interests by the legislatures of the states where they live. Congress could surely deny exemptions in bankruptcy altogether, or it could set up a federal catalogue of exemptions allowable in bankruptcy without reference to state law. It is at least an understandable choice for Congress to seek to conform bankruptcy policy to that of the state. ·

If a state legislature is exceedingly liberal in its grant of exemptions to debtors, creditors are entitled, and may be expected, to take the exaggerated risk into account in their dealings with debtors. If the legislative choice is unwise, it is likely that the impact will be felt within the state in the form of decreasing availability of credit and financial hardship accruing to lenders and sellers of goods and services on credit. . . . If the state legislature remains unresponsive to demands of creditor groups for relief against extravagant exemptions, there is at best only a tenuous national interest in a reappraisal of the interests of creditors and debtors which disregards the state's policy.

. . . [T]he use of the bankruptcy power to level the privileges and immunities conferred by local law on debtors *vis-à-vis* their creditors would run counter to the current of history. This opinion finds confirmation in the history of the treatment of exemptions in American bankruptcy legislation: The first two acts contained provisions uniformly applicable across the country; the Act of 1867 recognized state bankruptcy laws but supplemented the state legislation with a federal grant; the Act of 1898 defers to the state exemption laws. . . . It is to be remembered that the concern here is with debtors who are individuals and usually heads of families. The state's interest in preserving the family unit and in averting poverty and dependence on public support is entitled to careful consideration when weighed against the national interest in the improved effectiveness and uniformity in debt collection attainable by superimposing federal designation or limitation on exemptions allowable to its domiciliaries. The overriding bankruptcy theme of equality of distribution is of course not at stake here.

. . . It is of course to be anticipated that the existence of any federal exemption allowance will exert a powerful pressure to bring state exemptions up to the federal figure. A federally established figure for exemptions allowable in bankruptcy is, on the other hand, bound to be substantially lower than allowable by the law of many states. A result to be anticipated is a reduction of the number of voluntary petitions filed in such states and some increase in the number of involuntary petitions; for here a new incentive is given to the creditors to put debtors into bankruptcy. . . . If a more realistic figure is arrived at, however, . . . there will be many, particularly from the creditor-conscious states of the northeast, who will say that it is better to leave the Bankruptcy Act unchanged than to fix a uniform exemption allowance at such an extravagant figure.

Reservations may thus be legitimately entertained regarding the wisdom as well as the political feasibility of a uniform law of exemptions in bankruptcy. . . . It may be assumed, however, . . . that neither creditor nor debtor interests are so disproportionately represented in state legislatures as to require federal intervention to protect their interests for the sake of a sound national economy.

III. THE RIGHT OF THE TRUSTEE IN BANKRUPTCY TO EXEMPT PROPERTY . . .

G. Fraudulent Acquisition of Exempt Property

It goes without saying that no debtor should be allowed to make use of the exemption laws for the purpose of defrauding his creditors. While the basis for the result has not always been clear, the trustee in bankruptcy has successfully defeated claims to exemptions on such grounds. The statutory support for the result should be made more clear, particularly where the fraud is of the kind assertable by one of some but not all of the creditors of the bankrupt. A proposal . . . to invalidate exemptions acquired by the conversion of nonexempt property on the eve of bankruptcy as a fraud on the act, is objectionable, however, as an unwise federal interference with the availability of exemptions provided by state law for improvident debtors.

What constitutes an intent or purpose to defraud creditors in the acquisition of exempt property? Acquisition during insolvency? Generally the courts reject such a suggestion. . . .

What of the exchange of nonexempt property in contemplation of the eventuality of bankruptcy? Most lawyers, and laymen too, are offended by the spectacle of a man who, having some means but more debt, systematically canvasses the exemption statutes of his state, converts his leviable assets into the forms of property protected by those statutes, and then comes into the bankruptcy court for an award of his exemptions and of an order of discharge. It is understandable that a majority of the members of the National Bankruptcy Conference should resolve at a recent annual meeting that if such a thing is possible, as it appears to be,[144] the law ought to be changed.[145]

If the exemption idea is sound at all,[146] however, it is stultifying to withhold exemptions from those whose need for their protection is the greatest because they did not have the foresight to get their quota of exemptions early. It is indefensible to take away a $1,000 homestead, or a $500 tractor needed for his work, exempted by a cautious state to the head of a large family, because he acquired his interest on the eve of bankruptcy, but to leave intact the mansion and Cadillac of a man and wife because acquired in time and in a state without a ceiling on the value of the homestead or exempt motor vehicle. A man of some sophistication can be expected to maneuver his dispositions with sufficient perspicacity to be prepared for bankruptcy when it eventually comes, if a sufficient premium is placed on advance preparations.[151] A debtor of little forethought or aptitude in managing his affairs can be expected to neglect the taking of precautions for his family's financial security until desperate prospects force him to contemplate liquidation. While it is meet enough ordinarily for the law to encourage diligence and prudence, it is suggested that a restriction on the allowance of exemptions in bankruptcy to those acquired well before the filing of the petition puts an inordinate premium on advance planning for the eventuality and runs counter to the policy of American exemption laws. A finding of intent to defraud from the circumstance of the proximity of the acquisition to the subsequent bankruptcy that occurs involves the incongruity of predicating a fraud on the debtor's seeking the sanctuary provided by law for his family when their need became desperately clear to him. To make the mere contemplation of bankruptcy the test without reference

---

[144] Generally the conversion of nonexempt property into exempt property on the eve of bankruptcy is not itself such fraud as will deprive the bankrupt of his right to exemptions. Forsberg v. Security State Bank, 15 F.2d 499, (8th Cir. 1926) . . . .

[145] Summary of Proceedings of 1958 Ann. Meeting, p. 7. The resolution as adopted read as follows:

RESOLVED, that the National Bankruptcy Conference approves the proposal to amend the Bankruptcy Act to make the purchase on the eve of bankruptcy of exempt property with non-exempt funds and the conversion on the eve of bankruptcy of non-exempt property into exempt property a fraudulent transfer and a possible bar to a discharge in bankruptcy, except as to the creation of homestead rights with respect to homes in which the bankrupt has lived within four months prior to bankruptcy . . . .

To categorize a conversion of nonexempt funds into exempt property as a fraudulent transfer is a questionable legislative technique, even if such action is regarded as a fraud on creditors. The only transfer in the case is presumably for a fair exchange, and the fraud, if any, could be frustrated by denying the exemption without touching the transfer. . . .

[146] Cf. MacLachlan § 162, at 161: "In general, exemption laws may be recognized as legalized frauds on creditors, in the sense that they declare a public policy in favor of having debtors retain certain essential aids to their support in preference to the satisfaction of creditors' claims."

[151] The problem of developing a law of creditors' rights that deals adequately and fairly with both the honest debtor who is a victim of circumstances, including his own ineptitude, and the scheming debtor whose financial difficulties are largely of his own making is an ancient one. Holdsworth, in discussing the emergence of bankruptcy laws in England, refers to debtors who in anticipation of insolvency would conceal their ill-gotten gains for later use to ease the discomforts of imprisonment and to gain concessions from their creditors. . . .

to its imminence, however, is to jeopardize the exemption for the man who is aware enough to realize his plight. . . . At its last meeting the National Bankruptcy Conference rescinded its prior approval of the proposal to make acquisition of exempt property on the eve of bankruptcy a fraudulent transfer under the Bankruptcy Act. This conclusion reflects an appreciation of the difficulties of formulating a national solution for a problem exhibiting many aspects in the more than half a hundred different jurisdictions where the law must be applied. . . .

IV. Conclusion

For all the antiquarianism, diversity, and inadequacies of state exemption legislation, there seems to be no impelling need to impress a federal mold on the exemptions recognizable in bankruptcy. Certainly it would be a dubious approach to the problem of modernizing such legislation for Congress to confer exemptions beyond those recognized by state law. A new incentive for entering the gates of voluntary bankruptcy would be afforded. Any proposal increasing the spate of wage-earner bankruptcies will be viewed askance. On the other hand, imposition of a federal limitation on exemptions allowable in bankruptcy would require Congress to assume the responsibility for determining the minima for reasonable security of debtors and their families in the more than fifty jurisdictions where the Bankruptcy Act applies. The process of striking the right balance between debtors' and creditors' rights would not be essentially different when engaged in by Congress rather than by the state legislatures. State legislatures have reached exceedingly diverse results in accommodating the competing interests in exemption legislation, and the result in each state is a complex which affects and is affected by patterns of credit extension and economic activity. It is not to be anticipated that the competence of Congress is sufficient to enable it, by imposing a single uniform ceiling or standard on a national scale, to achieve as wise and satisfactory a solution of the exemption problem in any jurisdiction as that previously evolved by its own lawmakers. The advantages of permitting the prevailing diversity continue to appear to stand off the advantages of an enforced uniformity. This conclusion moreover is believed to conform to political realities.

H.R. Rep. No. 95-595
95th Cong., 1st Sess. (1977)

Chapter 3. Consumer Debtors . . .

II. Liquidation . . .

B. EXEMPTIONS

Under current law, what property is exempt is determined under State law. However, some State exemption laws have not been revised in this century. Most are outmoded, designed for more rural times, and hopelessly inadequate to serve the needs of and provide a fresh start for modern urban debtors. The historical purpose of these exemption laws has been to protect a debtor from his creditors, to provide him with the basic necessities of life, so that even if his creditors levy on all of his nonexempt property, the debtor will not be left destitute and a public charge. The purpose has not changed, but neither have the level of exemptions in many States. Thus, the purpose has largely been defeated.

Though exemption laws have been considered within the province of State law under the current Bankruptcy Act, H.R. 8200 adopts the position that there is a Federal interest in seeing that a debtor that goes through bankruptcy comes out with adequate possessions to begin his fresh start. Recognizing, however, that circumstances do vary in different parts of the country, the bill permits the States to set exemption levels appropriate to the locale, and allows debtors to choose between the State exemptions and the Federal exemptions provided in the bill. Thus, the bill continues to recognize the States' interest in regulating credit within the States, but enunciates a bankruptcy policy favoring a fresh start.

SECTION-BY-SECTION ANALYSIS

§ 522. Exemptions

. . . Subsection (b), the operative subsection of this section, is a significant departure from present law. It permits an individual debtor in a bankruptcy case a choice between exemption systems. The debtor may choose the Federal exemptions . . ., or he may choose the exemptions to which he is entitled under . . . the law of the State of his domicile. . . .

As under current law, the debtor will be permitted to convert non-exempt property into exempt property before filing a bankruptcy petition. . . . The practice is not fraudulent as to creditors, and permits the debtor to make full use of the exemptions to which he is entitled under the law. . . .

Subsection (d) specifies the Federal exemptions to which the debtor is entitled. They are derived in large part from the Uniform Exemption Act, promulgated by the Commissioners on Uniform State Laws in August 1976.

S. Rep. No. 95-989
95th Cong., 2d Sess. (1978)

CHAPTER 5—CREDITORS, DEBTOR, AND THE ESTATE

Current law is retained in the area of exempt property, which is property that the debtor may retain after bankruptcy for a fresh start. For this purpose, current law adopts the exemption law of the State in which the debtor is a resident. . . . The committee feels that the policy of the bankruptcy law is to provide a fresh start, but not instant affluence, as would be possible under the provisions of H.R. 8200. Moreover, current law has allowed the several State legislatures flexibility to meet the needs and fresh-start requirements of the debtors of their particular States.

SECTION-BY-SECTION ANALYSIS

§ 522. Exemptions

Subsection (b) tracks current law. It permits a debtor the exemptions to which he is entitled under . . . the law of the State of his domicile. . . .

As under current law, the debtor will be permitted to convert non-exempt property into exempt property before filing a bankruptcy petition. The practice is not fraudulent as to creditors, and permits the debtor to make full use of the exemptions to which he is entitled under the law.

124 CONGRESSIONAL RECORD S17404 (October 6, 1978)

Mr. Deconcini: In the area of exemptions, it was agreed that a Federal exemption standard will be codified but that the States could at any time reject them in which case the State exemption laws would continue to prevail.

Eric A. Posner
The Political Economy of the Bankruptcy Reform Act of 1978
96 Mich. L. Rev. 47 (1997)[*]

2. Exemptions

The 1898 Act incorporated state exemptions by reference. State exemptions were rules that prevented creditors in state actions from collecting debts from debtors by seizing and selling off the exempt assets. These laws exhibited striking diversity in their generosity and in the kind of property protected. . . . Many exemption statutes were archaic, singling out bibles, guns, crops, or farm animals. They reflected the rural origins of states that had since become highly urbanized. . . . The lack of uniformity among the statutes, the obsolescence of many of them, and the unintelligibility of some of them led commentators to call for the creation of a uniform system of federal exemptions.

. . .

VI. Exemptions

Federal and state interests divided even more sharply over exemption policy than they did over administrative structure. States had controlled exemption policy since the United States had come into existence. On the eve of the 1978 Act, federal bankruptcy law incorporated state exemptions. . . . The legislative history of the 1978 Act displays an effort by federal authorities once again to wrest control of exemption policy from the states. . . .

These observations raise the question whether the politicians involved in bankruptcy reform during the 1960s and 1970s actually believed that having control over exemption law was valuable. At first sight, one might think not. . . . The dominant view of commentators writing before the enactment of the Bankruptcy Code was that state legislatures did not care about exemption law.

This view, however, was wrong. Control over exemption policy had proved its value to state politicians in many ways. First, control over exemption law had allowed state authorities to respond to the demands of newly powerful classes of overburdened debtors during times of economic depression. Again and again during the nineteenth and twentieth centuries, states increased the generosity of exemption laws when an economic downturn caused default by debtors in large numbers. . . . The enactment of such laws must have been a straightforward and effective way for politicians to earn the gratitude of a large number of highly interested voters, the overburdened debtors, without alienating continuing debtors, who were probably sympathetic to the plight of overburdened debtors, and without risking much retaliation from the creditors, whose political power ebbed during economic downturns. Second, a glance at the current state exemption laws reveals the fingerprints of traditional interest groups. The exemption laws of virtually every state single out for favorable treatment groups of well-known political influence, such as insurance companies, farmers, teachers, veterans, and charitable organizations. Third, at least one state (Texas) and possibly others that sought to expand their population in the nineteenth century used exemption laws to encourage immigration from other states. . . .

If control over exemption policy was valuable to state politicians, then it must have appeared valuable to federal politicians as well. Control over exemption policy would have given federal authorities the power to provide relief to debtors in times of economic distress. More immediately,

---

Congress would have the power to create exemptions that benefited insurance companies, banks, farmers, and other groups that could provide the greatest political support. . . .

The normative case for federal control of exemption policy, however, was weak. The academic critics in the 1950s and 1960s argued that Congress should enact a system of uniform federal exemptions on the grounds that the state exemptions were too often archaic, too variable, and too generous or too mean; but they never explained why control of exemption policy should lie with the federal government rather than with the states. The variability of exemption law suggested, if anything, that tastes about credit risk and protection against default differed greatly from locality to locality and that therefore uniformity imposed at the national level would have served no purpose.

The strongest case for uniform federal exemptions arises from the problem of spillovers. When states enact inconsistent laws, there sometimes results a "race to the bottom," in which all states become worse off as a result of their competition for resources. . . .

One analogy with respect to exemption laws concerns their effect on migration. As noted above, Texas originally created generous exemption laws to encourage migration from other states. Texas may correctly have calculated that the benefits of an increased population would exceed the higher cost of credit incurred by its citizens; but if all states had enacted generous exemption laws for this purpose, the migration gains would have disappeared while the cost of credit would have remained high everywhere. By preventing states from competing for migrants through exemptions, a uniform federal exemption law would prevent the race to the bottom. . . .

Another possible source of spillovers might be efforts by states to externalize the cost of default. If one state's exemption regime is more generous than those of other states, perhaps national creditors would spread the increased cost of collection in the high-exemption state among debtors in all the other states. All debtors would pay the same higher interest rate, but debtors in the high-exemption state would, in effect, pay less in interest charges for their right to keep more assets in case of default. But if the other states responded by increasing their exemptions, this benefit would be lost, while debtors in all states would pay the high interest rates—in effect, paying for more protection in case of default than they want. . . .

If spillovers caused significant losses, one would expect efforts by the states to produce a uniform law, because the reciprocity of the supposed harm means that uniformity would have produced mutual gains. Yet the uniform exemptions law recommended in 1976 by the National Conference of Commissioners on Uniform State Laws was enacted by just one state!

Despite the shaky normative foundations for nationalizing exemption law, that idea made it onto the agenda of bankruptcy reform in the 1970s. The Commission endorsed the idea of uniform federal exemptions without justifying its position. It simply referred to the great diversity of state exemption laws. . . .

It may seem facile to argue that the Commission favored uniform federal exemptions because they would transfer power over exemption policy from the states to the federal government. But recall that four of the nine members were members of Congress . . . and three were presidential appointees. . . . The entire membership of the Commission comprised people whose position, influence, and interest were connected with the federal government; seven of the nine members either would directly benefit from a transfer of the power over exemption law from the states to the federal government or were appointed to the Commission by someone who would benefit from such a transfer. As agents of the federal government, they sought an expansion of its power. . . .

Although bankruptcy judges were officials of the federal government, their power was local. Unlike the Commission members, they did not have an interest in transferring power over exemption law from the states to the federal government. . . . Because the bankruptcy judges did not share the Commission members' interest in federalizing exemption policy, they preferred to leave some of exemption policy under local control.

Rather than choosing between the CB [Commission Bill] and the JB [Judge's Bill], House Bill 8200 established a set of federal exemptions but gave the debtor the right to choose between the federal exemptions and the state exemptions. This approach effectively meant that the federal exemptions provided a floor. . . . Senate Bill 2266 followed the 1898 Act and left exemption policy to the states. . . .

Why did the House retreat from uniformity and propose instead a federal floor? . . . One conjecture is that state officials made their influence felt behind the scenes. . . .

Another conjecture emerges from the conflicting behavior of creditors. One might believe that creditors would, as a group, prefer a federal ceiling to a federal floor and that House Bill 8200 represented a defeat. In fact, the story is more complicated. . . . To explain this distribution of positions, observe that creditor groups whose members were locally powerful—banks, insurance companies, and local businesses—preferred either complete state control or some state control. Creditor groups whose members were not locally powerful—credit unions, finance companies—preferred more federal control. Because their power was greater at the federal than at the local level, the credit unions and finance companies believed that their influence could ensure that only federal, not local, exemptions would be sufficiently low. Whatever the content of exemption law, creditors likely preferred authority over exemption policy at that level of government over which they had the most influence.

Creditors may also have tried to use the opportunity of exemption reform to gain competitive advantages in the credit market. . . .

We can summarize the argument so far in the following way. Consider the biggest winners and losers from the federal exemption floor. In the stingy states the continuing debtors and creditors as a group would lose, but the lawyers, the overburdened debtors, and possibly certain powerful classes of creditors, such as the banks, would win. The losers had less political power at the national level than the winners did, especially because, as we saw, the creditors were divided by their interests. In the generous states a federal exemption floor would have had no effect.

Now consider the winners and losers from uniform federal exemptions. The story is the same for the stingy states, but in the generous states, now the lawyers, possibly the overburdened debtors, and certain creditors would lose, while the continuing debtors and creditors as a group would gain. In other words, the politically weak would prevail.

Minimum federal exemptions benefited some politically powerful groups without offending any other politically powerful groups, so they were preferred to uniform federal exemptions, which offended the politically powerful groups in the more generous states.

This argument raises the question why the Senate sought to leave exemption policy to the states. If the House would have gained from enacting a minimum exemption law because it would transfer payoffs from the state governments to the federal government, why wouldn't the Senate have gained as well? . . . First, senators owed more of their political power to state political organizations than representatives did. Exemption policy does not interest people at the district level; it does at the state level, since the state, not the district, is the source of state law. Second, the Senate was disproportionately influenced by the less populous, more rural states. The powerful farming lobbies in those states care deeply about a transfer of control over exemption policy from the states, where their influence is strong, to the federal government, where their influence is diluted. Since their influence at the federal level is stronger in the Senate than in the House, however, they can use their national influence to block the transfer. . . .

The compromise bill in Stage 3 provided still another variation on exemption law: a set of uniform federal exemptions, including the power to avoid certain liens, with a state right to opt out. The compromise meant that a state could, by legislative direction, force debtors to use exemptions that are lower than the federal exemptions; or it could force debtors to use exemptions that are higher than the federal exemptions; or it could leave the debtor the choice of using federal or state exemptions. The opt-out idea ingeniously gave the federal government control over exemption policy in all the states for which the interest in exemption policy was low, but not from the states that had a powerful interest in control of exemption policy. As a result, the federal government picked up some power without offending those with the most to lose. Most states did, in fact, opt out, showing again that the states did care about controlling exemption policy. Nevertheless, Congress gained some control over exemption policy.

Judith S. Koffler
The Bankruptcy Clause and Exemption Laws: A Reexamination of the Doctrine of Geographic Uniformity
58 N.Y.U. L. REV. 22 (1983)[*]

INTRODUCTION

The interpretation of the constitutional provision empowering Congress to make *"uniform* Laws . . . on the subject of Bankruptcies" has defied principled interpretation since its adoption and continues to be a source of analytical confusion, particularly in the area of bankruptcy exemptions. This Article analyzes the early roots of the "uniformity" provision and its historical development, concluding that its present interpretation is at odds with the broad purposes of the uniformity clause. . . . The Article . . . closely analyzes *Hanover National Bank v. Moyses*, the seminal case in this area, demonstrating its weaknesses as well as discussing the curious stranglehold it has exerted over subsequent bankruptcy adjudication. . . . [C]haos . . . has arisen under the illusory uniformity provided under the Bankruptcy Reform Act. . . . [T]he author suggest[s] . . . rejecting the *Moyses* doctrine, which sacrifices federal policy to the parochial concerns of the states, and . . . reviving the spirit of the clause as understood by the Framers.

I
THE CONSTITUTIONAL MANDATE OF UNIFORMITY

A. The Moyses Doctrine

The bankruptcy clause has stood as the authority for the five major bankruptcy statutes which Congress has enacted in the past two centuries. Each Act has provided that certain property may be set aside, or exempted from claims of creditors, to help the hopeless debtor avoid utter destitution and return to economic self-sufficiency—the proverbial "fresh start." One topic keenly debated in the past century, and prematurely buried in our own, is the meaning of the constitutional mandate of "uniformity" as applied to bankruptcy exemptions. Although the first two Acts, the Bankruptcy Act of 1800 and the Bankruptcy Act of 1841, prescribed uniform federal exemptions for necessities such as wearing apparel and bedding, the next two statutes, the Bankruptcy Act of 1867 and the Bankruptcy Act of 1898, incorporated the disuniform exemptions specified by the laws of the states. The Bankruptcy Act of 1867 set forth a list of federal bankruptcy exemptions and then supplemented it with whatever property was exempt under state laws. Although the 1867 Act allowed for a variety of bankruptcy exemptions, the prescribed federal minimum nevertheless imposed a measure of uniformity. In the Act of 1898, however, uniformity of bankruptcy exemptions was abandoned altogether. . . .

As one might expect, such diversity of bankruptcy exemptions in the face of the constitutional language of "uniformity" raised questions concerning the constitutionality of the Acts of 1867 and 1898 that ultimately reached the Supreme Court. In a 1902 decision, *Hanover National Bank v. Moyses*, the Court, faced with a challenge to section 6 of the Act of 1898, upheld the constitutionality of the disuniform scheme of exemptions. Articulating a doctrine of "geographic, not personal, uniformity," Chief Justice Fuller declared "that the system is, in the constitutional sense, uniform throughout the United States, when the trustee takes in each State whatever would have been available to the creditors if the bankrupt law had not been passed."

The *Moyses* decision approved as constitutional a bankruptcy law in which the determination of a debtor's federal bankruptcy exemptions—and thus the size of the bankruptcy estate available to creditors—did not embody a uniform specification of bankruptcy exemptions. Instead, the *Moyses* Court purported to discover "uniformity" in the fact that Congress had evenhandedly abdicated its power to prescribe bankruptcy exemptions to each state. . . .

Under the recently enacted Bankruptcy Reform Act of 1978, a uniform scheme of specific federal exemptions is once again available but in such circumstances as to make uniformity illusory. Section 522(d) spells out a very generous and elaborate list of items for the bankruptcy debtor to claim as exempt. But this uniformity can be defeated in two ways. First, the Act permits debtors to elect the exemptions specified by state law instead of the federal package. Second, the states are specifically authorized to deny their bankruptcy debtors the opportunity to choose the federal bankruptcy exemption package. This provision of section 522(b)(1) has come to be known as the "opt-out" provision . . . . [T]he issue of geographic uniformity of bankruptcy exemptions merits reexamination. . . .

C. The Distinct Nature of Bankruptcy Exemptions: Federal Versus Local Policy

It is important at the outset of a discussion of bankruptcy exemptions to distinguish them from state insolvency exemption laws and to articulate the vital role that bankruptcy exemptions play in formulating national policy governing the relations between debtor and creditor and in fostering a sound national consumer credit system.

At first glance, exemptions appear to play a role in state insolvency law no different from the role they play in federal bankruptcy proceedings. On the local level, exemption laws operate to protect debtors from overreaching creditors . . . . Typically, state exemptions . . . are motivated by the economic and social welfare policies of the state as well as by concern for the welfare of the individual debtor. . . .

Bankruptcy exemption policy embodies many of the same concerns for the debtor and his rehabilitation as does state exemption policy. There are, however, several elementary differences. In the first place, state exemptions laws are enacted with a view to local public purposes and reflect the concerns of the particular state legislature. By contrast, federal bankruptcy exemptions are enacted with a view to general national purposes. Only federal law can fashion a national policy of debtor rehabilitation and creditors' rights. . . .

Second, state exemption laws typically contemplate the debtor's eventual satisfaction of unpaid debts because . . . the state has the independent concern of observing the constitutional prohibition against the impairment of contracts. In contrast, since Congress has the exclusive power to discharge retrospective debts in bankruptcy, federal bankruptcy exemptions typically contemplate the debtor's discharge from those debts. Thus, . . . Congress . . . seeks to ensure that the unfortunate bankruptcy debtor will retain sufficient property for a fresh start in the national economic system of production and consumption. . . .

Third, state exemption law normally contemplates a system of piecemeal—as opposed to wholesale—liquidation whereby the individual creditor executes and realizes upon whatever property she may locate. State exemption laws thus do not ordinarily contemplate creditors as a class in competition for a scarce resource. In contrast, the bankruptcy system entails the orderly appropriation and liquidation of all the debtor's nonexempt property for distribution to all creditors according to a general scheme of equality. . . . It follows, therefore, that the existence and size of the bankruptcy exemption directly determines the existence and size of the estate available to bankruptcy creditors *as a class*. National policy, therefore, differs from local policy in looking toward the creation of a bankruptcy estate with which to satisfy creditors on a pro rata basis, on the one hand, and in protecting the bankrupt debtor as a significant actor in the national economic system on the other. Federal bankruptcy exemption policy also is concerned with adjusting the economic needs of creditors, a goal fundamental to the very existence of a national system of commerce and credit. . . .

II
UNIFORMITY IN HISTORICAL CONTEXT: WHAT DID THE FRAMERS INTEND?

There is a dearth of direct historical evidence to show what the Framers intended by authorizing "uniform Laws on the subject of Bankruptcies." The purpose behind the Framers' vision of a national system of uniform bankruptcy laws may be understood by reference to the mischiefs that the bankruptcy power was designed to cure . . . .

A. *Historical Evidence*

1. The Framing of the Bankruptcy Clause

Prior to the framing of the Constitution, the individual states had exercised bankruptcy powers as an incident to their sovereignty. Pennsylvania, for example, had enacted a bankruptcy statute in 1785 that provided merchants and traders with a discharge from debts, as well as an insolvency system that released debtors from prison. . . . The Framers did not consider the subject of bankruptcy until late in the Constitutional Convention . . . .

The only recorded discussion of the bankruptcy power consists of a colloquy between Roger Sherman of Connecticut and Gouverneur Morris. Sherman remarked that he was reluctant to confer a bankruptcy power upon Congress because, in England, some bankrupts were sentenced to death. Morris did not share Sherman's concern. Assenting to the power, he said that he saw no danger of congressional abuse of the bankruptcy power. . . .

2. Uniformity in Other Constitutional Clauses

During the Constitutional Convention, debates occurred over three proposed "uniformity" clauses to be included in the same article of the Constitution. At the time of the Convention, there were compelling reasons for circumscribing some of Congress' powers with a requirement of uniformity. The fears and jealousies among the states and the apprehensions that the general legislature might discriminate in favor of one state or region to the economic detriment of another were among the most strident themes of the Convention. The imposition of uniformity requirements on certain federal legislation quelled these concerns, ensuring that no invidious distinctions would be made among states or regions and that the legislation would indeed be general. . . .

While no conclusive statement regarding the meaning of the word "uniform" in the bankruptcy clause can be derived from its use in these three instances, significant inferences provide clues. Uniformity of taxes and duties served to assure the states that Congress would not discriminate in favor of or against a particular locality. Uniformity in establishing naturalization rules, although it did not deprive the states of authority to legislate on the subject, clearly was intended to encourage preemptive congressional action to foster important national interests in a coherent manner. The companion clauses suggest concerns that the Framers may have had regarding bankruptcy laws and a unique concept implicit in the uniformity provisions. It is instructive to compare the rejection of such a requirement in the militia clause, in which the Framers apparently recognized a need for state diversity and independent control. Its history indicates that the Framers well knew how to allow for disuniformity when they wanted to and throws the uniformity provisions of the remaining clauses into relief. Although the precise meaning of the term "uniform" in the bankruptcy clause remains indeterminate, it demonstrably has independent significance, a significance which must be sought in other quarters.

3. The Federalist Papers

Madison wrote:

> The power of establishing uniform laws of bankruptcy is so intimately connected with the regulation of commerce, and will prevent so many frauds where the parties or their property may lie or be removed into different States that the expediency of it seems not likely to be drawn into question.

. . . Madison thus promoted the bankruptcy clause as a grant of power to safeguard the nation's interest in establishing and maintaining a single market for the extension of credit without interference from parochial or otherwise obstreperous action on the part of the states.

4. Uniformity Reflected in Early Bankruptcy Legislation: 1792 to 1841

An examination of the contemporaneous legislative debate over the adoption of a national bankruptcy bill adds to our understanding of the Framers' concept of uniformity in bankruptcy law. . . . After [a] financial crash in 1797, an extensive bankruptcy bill was proposed and finally enacted as the Bankruptcy Act of 1800.

Throughout this period, Thomas Jefferson opposed broad federal power to execute against a bankrupt's land. In Jefferson's bucolic Virginia, freehold land was exempt from execution, as it had been under medieval law, so that Virginia debtors with land were largely immunized from claims of northern commercial creditors. Jefferson adopted an extreme states-rights attitude with respect to exempt property. . . .

But this very power—the power of the central government to defeat the parochial, anticommercial policies of the agrarian states—was precisely what the advocates of the bankruptcy bill intended. This intention is evident in debates over the proposed bankruptcy bill and its successor, which was enacted as the Bankruptcy Act of 1800. James Bayard, one of the Act's main proponents, attacked Jefferson's narrow view of federal power . . . . Other advocates of the bill agreed with Bayard that creditors should be given "a control over the property of their debtors." The objections of Jefferson and other Virginians to a federal law permitting the creditors to seize debtors' land established a tradition of fierce opposition to federal bankruptcy legislation.

Despite Jefferson's agrarian idealism, the Bankruptcy Act of 1800 ultimately did impose a uniform rule governing property exemptions. The uniformity imposed by the Act was very different from that contemplated by the *Moyses* Court: the bankruptcy act categorically replaced the variant exemption policies of the states with a uniform federal rule. . . . All creditors—foreign and domestic—would enjoy the same right to reach the bankrupt's property notwithstanding local agrarian sentiment or parochial prejudice toward commerce. . . .

The Panic of 1837 revived the struggle for national regulation of bankruptcy. Webster and Story emerged as the champions of a new bankruptcy bill, and, due largely to Webster's eloquence, the bill became the Bankruptcy Act of 1841. This second national Bankruptcy Act retained the predecessor act's uniform treatment of exempt property. . . .

Thus legislative activity contemporaneous with and immediately succeeding the framing of the Constitution discloses a concept of uniformity inconsistent with the *Moyses* view that the constitutional stricture only requires a form of geographic uniformity that permits distinctions based upon state boundaries. National bankruptcy policy was designed to defeat individual state practices that favored local interest at the expense of a uniform commercial policy especially in the area of exempt property. If the *Moyses* view advocating federal adoption of individual state policies had been entertained, that view did not express itself in any of the early statutes and seems to have been explicitly repudiated by the proponents of national bankruptcy legislation. Only in the private writings of Jefferson, who seems to have stood as the sworn enemy of a bankruptcy law, do we find the view that federal recognition of multiform local exemption laws might meet the constitutional stricture of uniformity. . . .

B. The Ebbing of the Framers' Influence: The Bankruptcy Acts of the Later Nineteenth Century

The first two bankruptcy acts, that of 1800 and that of 1841, prescribed a uniform federal definition of exempt property. Twenty-five years after having repealed the Act of 1841, Congress again enacted a bankruptcy act, this time in the face of the disastrous economic consequences of the Panic of 1857 and the Civil War, which saw an estimated 300 million dollars owed to northern creditors repudiated by their southern debtors. This third act, the Bankruptcy Act of 1867, marked a drastic shift in federal exemption policy. For although section 14 of the Act prescribed a uniform federal exemption of wearing apparel, together with necessary household items up to an amount of $500, the bankrupt was also allowed to claim property exempted by his state's exemption laws or immune from execution thereunder. Thus, for the first time under a federal bankruptcy act, the bankruptcy estate available to creditors would be determined in large part by state law.

The historical and political causes behind this treatment in the Act of 1867 are colorfully explained by historian Charles Warren. To pass the proposed bill, concessions had to be made to conflicting factions in Congress: those who opposed any bankruptcy law, those who endorsed a bill favoring creditors, those who advocated a bill for both debtor and creditor, and those who opposed involuntary bankruptcy per se. According to Warren, debtors had not pressed for a national bankruptcy law after repeal of the Act of 1841 since many states had exempted generous amounts for a homestead and other property. . . . In order to appease the debtors, the bill's advocates reluctantly accepted the incorporation of all state property exemptions by the Act, voicing grave misgivings regarding its constitutionality. . . .

. . . This exemption scheme of the Bankruptcy Act of 1867 received varying responses among the lower courts, but, unfortunately, the Supreme Court never had occasion to pass on the uniformity question it posed.

From the repeal of the 1867 Act in 1878 until 1898, the country was again without a federal bankruptcy law. By the time the Bankruptcy Act of 1898 came into being, the country had been accustomed to the dominant influence of state exemption laws for over fifty years. When one considers this tradition of state control in addition to the legislative precedent of the Act of 1867 and the support for state exemption laws prevailing at the time, it is not surprising that section 6 of the Bankruptcy Act of 1898 deferred the matter of bankruptcy exemptions entirely to state law. Since the enactment of the Bankruptcy Act of 1898, bankruptcy has become a permanent aspect of our national jurisprudence, and as a result of the incorporation by the federal bankruptcy law of state exemption laws, the tradition of state domination in the area of exempt property continued unabated from 1843 until the present day. In our time, however, Congress' neglect of constitutional principle has become so firmly entrenched, and its tradition of ignoring the Framers' intent so encrusted, that a legislative return to the bankruptcy clause's vital origins seems unlikely. . . .

III
THE *MOYSES* DOCTRINE OF "GEOGRAPHIC UNIFORMITY"
A. The Moyses *Decision*

Hanover National Bank v. Moyses arose out of a dispute between a judgment creditor, Hanover National Bank, and a bankrupt debtor, Max Moyses. The bank sought to enforce its judgment against Moyses, despite the fact that Moyses had received a discharge in bankruptcy subsequent to the judgment. The bank argued that the Act of 1898 violated the bankruptcy clause of the Constitution in that it failed to provide "uniform laws on the subject of bankruptcies throughout the United States." Specifically, counsel for the bank pointed out that, by the terms of the Act, a debtor could contract debts in Rhode Island, which had no homestead provision, thereafter move his residence to Texas, and, before filing his bankruptcy petition, invest a million dollars in a Texas homestead that bankruptcy creditors could not reach. . . .

The Supreme Court . . . addressed the constitutional problem of uniformity with disarming simplicity. Noting that bankruptcy laws must be uniform throughout the United States, the Court remarked "that uniformity is geographical and not personal." . . .

Chief Justice Fuller rested the doctrine of geographic uniformity on *In re Beckerford* and *In re Deckert*, two circuit court opinions which had arisen not under the Act of 1898 but under the earlier Bankruptcy Act of 1867. These decisions did not, therefore, present the precise constitutional issue posed by the 1898 Act. The Act of 1867 provided for minimum uniform federal exemptions in addition to whatever property was exempt under state law. The Act of 1898 contained no uniform federal exemption at all. Chief Justice Fuller ignored this difference, however, and relied heavily on the two decisions . . . . Chief Justice Fuller simply noted his agreement with the *Deckert* decision, holding that the system was constitutionally "uniform throughout the United States, when the trustee takes in each state whatever would have been available to the creditors if the bankrupt law had not been passed. The general operation of the law is uniform, although it may result in certain particulars differently in different States."

The *Moyses* Court did not inquire into the Framers' purpose or intent in imposing the uniformity requirement. . . . The historical survey . . . indicates that the *Moyses* conception of uniform laws of bankruptcy had strayed far from the intent of the Framers. . . .

C. Doctrine into Dogma: The Persistence of Geographic Uniformity

The Supreme Court has had occasion to reconsider the *Moyses* doctrine of geographic uniformity. In every instance, however, that decision has been perfunctorily invoked, with the result that, through a process of incantation and accretion, the *Moyses* doctrine appears to enjoy an unassailable finality. . . .

V
The Nemesis of *Moyses*: Constitutional Chaos Under the Bankruptcy Reform Act

The logical, legal, and historical analyses set forth above indicate that the *Moyses* doctrine of geographic uniformity was a departure from principle. . . . [T]his Section will discuss how the Reform Act's chaotic exemption scheme leaves the Court with little choice but to pronounce a new doctrine of uniformity.

A. Disuniformity Redoubled

The Bankruptcy Reform Act takes the concept of multiform uniformity beyond the *Moyses* doctrine and into utter incoherence. Section 522 expresses Congress' aim to provide the debtor with exemptions sufficient for a fresh start by permitting the debtor a choice between the federal exemptions contained in section 522(d), on the one hand, and the exemption scheme established by his state on the other. But the same section simultaneously empowers a state to reject the federal exemptions and confine debtors within its jurisdiction to its own scheme. This statutory authorization for states to opt out appears to carry with it the license to defeat or to exalt the debtor's fresh start, to affect the size of the creditor's dividend, and to dictate the terms upon which bankruptcy will be an acceptable alternative to state proceedings for both creditor and debtor.

It is questionable whether the exemption provisions of the Reform Act could be deemed uniform even under the *Moyses* doctrine. . . .

Given the opt-out provision, it appears that the standard for bankruptcy exemptions differs not only according to locality but also according to whether the state exemption scheme encourages a particular class of debtors to elect the federal scheme instead of the state's. It appears that the states, and not Congress, control vital national questions such as the nature and extent of a debtor's assets that should be available to distribute to bankruptcy creditors and the nature and extent of assets requisite to the debtor's rehabilitation. The opt-out provision, which is virtually unprecedented, can only be understood by considering the legislative history of section 522.

B. Moyses' *Ghost at Work in Congress*

The legislative history of section 522 reveals an overly deferential attitude to state power and a confused notion of uniformity that beclouded the deliberations of the legislators. . . .

The legislative history of section 522 reveals that Congress once again misconceived the bankruptcy exemption issue as one of states' rights. Since the days of the Framers, the controversy surrounding the proper exercise of the bankruptcy power has spawned disingenuous states' rights arguments, such as the defense by Jefferson and other Virginians asserting Virginia's right to keep freehold land beyond the reach of creditors. . . .

In light of the Framers' concerns, the legislative debate over section 522 appears misguided. History leaves little doubt that the parochial interests enshrined in state exemption laws were among the precise evils impeding national commerce and credit addressed by the Framers and are better viewed as the intended victims of an exercise of the bankruptcy power than as its beneficiaries. Yet enactment of section 522 appears to have turned the tide in Jefferson's hitherto losing battle against exercises of the bankruptcy power. That battle, which the Jeffersonians lost in the Act of 1800 and again in the Act of 1841, has been refought with increasing success in the Acts of 1867, 1898, and 1978. In the din of legislative skirmish, the true intent of the Framers has receded beyond Congress' vision. National control of the bankruptcy power now suffers from undue deference to local interests and enjoys legislative entrenchment. . . .

D. *Avoiding* Moyses: *Detour or Destruction*

From the discussion above, it appears that one possible exit from this chaos lies through the door of history. The earliest bankruptcy acts avoided the uniformity problem by declaring, entirely without reference to state law, what the federal bankruptcy exemptions should be. . . . If the history of the past century is any indication, it is unlikely that the Court will abandon the *Moyses* doctrine. . . .

In the spirit of a Latin maxim, now rarely invoked, doctrines long settled may nonetheless warrant acquiescence in the interest of finality. It appears that the *Moyses* doctrine is so entrenched in our tradition of constitutional adjudication by means of political happenstance and judicial habit that it may never be dislodged. Nonetheless, the Bankruptcy Reform Act reveals that the tautological reasoning of *Moyses* has been extended to the limit, abandoning even the *Moyses* understanding of geographic uniformity, vindicating chaos in the name of uniformity. The Court's opportunity to draw order out of chaos—for the Greeks, a divine act—may require that it exercise that Olympian prerogative by which alone constitutional principles may be preserved.

CONCLUSION

. . . [B]ankruptcy exemptions may play a critical role in the preservation of a healthy economy and a stable society. They should also aid us in seeing how a well-regulated political and economic order may be undermined if replaced with fifty different exemption schemes. Such disuniformity would be the bane of effective central control as indeed it threatens to be under present law.

The . . . relationship between bankruptcy, exemption laws, and a stable economic order may not have been in the minds of the Framers of the Constitution. But their espoused principles of national control and uniformity in the establishment of federal bankruptcy laws surely envisioned a national policy, not a hydra-headed beast of fifty different rules. As we have seen, the *Moyses* doctrine has effectively obliterated judicial memory of that principle and has helped to destroy the impetus for national legislative control over bankruptcy exemptions.

Alan N. Resnick
Prudent Planning or Fraudulent Transfer?
The Use of Nonexempt Assets to Purchase or Improve Exempt Property on the Eve of Bankruptcy
31 RUTGERS L. REV. 615 (1978)[*]

It is an economic necessity for creditors to have an efficient collection mechanism which gives them maximum protection in the event of default by the debtor. Nonetheless, all states shield the debtor from complete destitution by keeping certain property . . . beyond the reach of creditors. By permitting the debtor to keep those assets necessary for his economic survival, state exemption laws fulfill important social policies which must be balanced against the need for creditor protection. . . .

A debtor who faces bankruptcy is naturally tempted to salvage as much of his property as possible to protect himself and his family. In order to maximize the benefits available under exemption statutes, such a debtor might purchase or improve exempt property on the eve of bankruptcy.

This article will address the question of whether an insolvent debtor should be permitted to use nonexempt assets to acquire or improve exempt property in contemplation of bankruptcy. . . .

II. ORIGIN AND DEVELOPMENT OF EXEMPTION LAWS

Various historical factors influenced the adoption of state exemption laws in the Untied States. Many of the northeastern states adopted restrictive exemptions similar to those then in effect in England. The English law, based on the notion of affording all debtors a degree of human dignity and decency, were limited to such necessities for survival as clothing, bedding, and tools of the trade. Economic depressions in the United States during the eighteenth and nineteenth centuries, however, demonstrated that anyone could be economically victimized by fortuitous events. As a result, legislators became willing to grant more generous exemptions to protect debtors from poverty. More liberal exemption laws were passed in response to widespread impoverishment following the Civil War. In some western and southern states, liberal exemption laws were enacted to attract settlers who were permitted to keep their homesteads and other property free from creditors' claims. It has also been suggested that generous exemption laws resulted from hostility in rural areas toward creditors who were concentrated in urban centers.

In addition to historical forces, lobbying efforts by various interest groups undoubtedly had an impact on state exemption laws. . . .

These historical and political influences resulted in wide disparity among exemption laws from state to state and region to region. These factors also make it difficult to generalize about the original legislative purposes underlying particular exemption laws. Nonetheless, in order to deal with the question whether a debtor should be permitted to purchase exempt property in contempla-

---

tion of bankruptcy, it is necessary to identify the justifications, if any, for maintaining exemption laws in modern society.

Current state and federal exemption laws promote five distinct social policies. Each specific exemption should further one or more of the following policies:

(1) To provide the debtor with property necessary for his physical survival;

(2) To protect the dignity and the cultural and religious identity of the debtor;

(3) To enable the debtor to rehabilitate himself financially and earn income in the future;

(4) To protect the debtor's family from the adverse consequences of impoverishment;

(5) To shift the burden of providing the debtor and his family with minimal financial support from the society to the debtor's creditors.

A. *Providing the Debtor with Property Needed for Survival*

Providing the debtor with assets needed for basic survival is an important purpose of debtor exemption laws. The most common exemptions which serve this purpose are those for food, clothing, and household furniture. . . .

The homestead exemption . . . also serves the purpose of providing necessities of life by permitting the debtor to keep his home. The debtor is thus assured of a place to live, as well as the food, household items, and clothing contained therein. . . .

Exemption laws which protect various forms of income also assist the debtor is purchasing necessities in the future. . . .

Since both state and federal legislatures have chosen to keep certain items needed to maintain a minimal standard of living beyond the reach of creditors, the acquisition of such property by the debtor in contemplation of financial disaster should not affect the exemption. It is incongruous for the law to discourage the intentional acquisition of property which the legislature considers necessary for basic living if it is acquired when the debtor is faced with immediate loss of his assets in bankruptcy or by operation of state law. In fact, encouraging the purchase of this type of property would further the goal of providing the debtor and his family with the items necessary for their basic survival and financial support. . . .

B. *Protecting the Dignity, Culture, and Religious Identity of the Debtor*

Most people have property which has significant sentimental value greatly outweighing its monetary worth. If an item has important subjective value to the debtor and would realize a relatively small amount of money on liquidation, respect for the item's personal worth to the debtor should dictate that the property be exempt from the creditor's grasp.

This rationale justifies many of the exemption laws today, including those for Bibles, family pictures, wedding rings and other jewelry, books, cemetery plots, seats occupied in places of worship, and domestic pets. The importance of these items is not their monetary value nor the physical survival of the debtor; they relate instead to the cultural, religious, and moral aspects of life which should be preserved despite the debtor's financial hardship. . . .

. . . [E]xemptions designed to serve this social policy should not be applied to property purchased in contemplation of bankruptcy for the purpose of maximizing the benefits of the exemption laws; a debtor should not be permitted to stock up on wedding rings and domestic pets in order to defeat creditors' claims.

C. *Enabling the Debtor to Rehabilitate*

It is in the best interest of both the debtor and the creditor to assist the debtor to earn more income in the future in the absence of bankruptcy. Permitting the debtor to earn income increases the probability that future creditors will be paid. To allow the first-grabbing creditors to take items that aid in the production of income, however, leaves other creditors with little likelihood that the debtor will be able to replenish his assets. . . . [W]hether or not the debtor becomes bankrupt, the need for his financial rehabilitation justifies certain exemptions under state law, the most common of which are tools of the trade and machinery, books used in business, and farming implements.

If the debtor's ability to continue in his trade depends in part on his tools, it makes sense to permit him to purchase such tools in contemplation of bankruptcy. . . . Such purchases on the eve of bankruptcy will assist the debtor in making a fresh start.

D. *Protecting the Debtor's Family*

Many courts have identified the protection of the debtor's family and dependents as a primary justification for exemption laws. . . . Many exemptions will apply only when the debtor is the head of a household. . . .

Exemption laws also protect debtors' families by helping to preserve family stability. Economic hardship is a significant cause of family breakdown and increases the likelihood of divorce. Permitting the family to keep property necessary for basic living minimizes extreme impoverishment and helps the family unit to remain intact. . . .

E. *Shifting the Burden of Welfare from Society to Creditors*

Assuming that exemptions are necessary and effective in the financial rehabilitation of debtors, if state and federal governments did not grant any exemptions, society would have to support debtors in the form of welfare payments. Therefore, another policy furthered by exemption laws is to shift the cost of the debtor's survival from society to his creditors. The wisdom of this policy aside, it is consistent to permit the debtor to make improvements in his exempt assets or to purchase new exempt property on the eve of bankruptcy, so long as the items improved or purchased will at least partially relieve the debtor of the need for governmental assistance.

III. THE PROBLEMS

Although consistent with most of the policies furthered by exemption laws, several problems may result if courts uphold the acquisition or improvement of exempt property on the eve of bankruptcy. First, many exemptions are no longer relevant to the social policies which justify exemption laws and serve no useful function in modern society. State exemption statutes have been criticized for being seriously obsolete . . . .

[Second], many exemption laws either have no value or quantity limits at all, or have extremely high limits. The most notable example of the latter is the homestead law of Texas, which exempts a rural ranch of two-hundred acres regardless of worth. . . .

The obsolescence and open-endedness of many state exemption laws enable debtors to keep property beyond the reach of creditors when no justifiable social policy is served and when creditors are thereby unduly restricted in their attempts to obtain payment of their claims. The problems resulting from this obsolescence and open-endedness would be compounded were debtors encouraged, or even permitted, to purchase exempt property on the eve of bankruptcy. . . . These problems have not been resolved by the Bankruptcy Reform Act. Because the debtor retains the right to elect state exemption laws as an alternative to the federal bankruptcy exemptions, the potential for abuse of state law continues. . . .

VI. RECOMMENDATIONS

It is consistent with most of the modern justifications for exemption laws to permit a debtor to acquire exempt assets in contemplation of bankruptcy. Allowing exemptions for such property is also consistent with the federal bankruptcy policy of affording the debtor a fresh start in life. Property necessary for the physical and financial survival of the debtor and his family, as well as property necessary for the debtor's dignity and his moral, religious, and cultural identity, should be available to him regardless of his financial condition when he acquired these essential items. The policies behind exemption laws must be balanced, however, against the possibility of abuse of the laws, which would unfairly burden creditors and permit the debtor to keep property unrelated to his actual needs. Judicial approval of conversions of nonexempt to exempt property prior to bankruptcy, without regard for the amount of property acquired so long as there is an absence of extrinsic fraud, is unfair to creditors. Further, lawyers are handicapped in advising clients properly prior to bankruptcy because of the lack of uniformity among states, the inability to predict accurately a court's decision in a particular case, and the serious consequences of a possible fraud on creditors.

The ideal solution to the problem of abuse would be to reevaluate and modernize state exemption laws, carefully defining the limits on the necessities that the debtor may keep and permitting debtors to acquire exempt property at any time and under any financial conditions. This solution would permit a debtor to plan for bankruptcy by acquiring property reasonably related to his actual needs and would avoid the problems of abuse. There is no reason to continue to have open-ended exemptions which allow a debtor to protect an excessively large portion of his estate by buying an unreasonable amount of otherwise necessary items. Calls for modernization of state exemption laws have been largely unheeded, however, and it is unrealistic to expect such changes in the near future. Creating appropriate federal exemptions to replace state exemptions in all bankruptcy cases would be another possible solution. The Bankruptcy Reform Act, however, continues to permit debtors who so desire to take advantage of existing state exemption laws. Nevertheless, conversion of nonexempt to exempt assets prior to bankruptcy should be governed by federal law. First, uniformity facilitates certainty and there is a serious need for certainty on this issue. . . . [D]ebtors and their counsel should not have to guess what standards a court will apply when ruling on the propriety of the acquisition of exempt property. Clarity is especially important because of the serious danger of unwittingly crossing the murky line that separates prudent planning for a bankruptcy from actual fraud. It is unfair to deprive a debtor of a discharge of debts when he is unable to determine in advance whether his conduct will be judged proper.

Another reason for treating this issue as a federal question is that, in order to arrive at a rational approach, bankruptcy courts should be permitted to give appropriate weight to the purposes and policies behind the federal bankruptcy laws. . . . [I]t is a more serious deprivation of creditor's rights to sanction the purchase of exempt property when the debtor files or intends to file a bankruptcy petition. On the other hand, it can be argued that the federal policy of affording the debtor a fresh start following bankruptcy by permitting him to keep exempt property is so important that it should apply whether or not the property is purchased in contemplation of bankruptcy. . . . For these reasons, it would be advisable for bankruptcy courts to apply uniform federal standards for recognition of exemptions purchased on the eve of bankruptcy, which give appropriate weight to the subsequent discharge of debts and to the federal policy of giving the debtor a fresh start.

Recognition of state exemption laws in bankruptcy, subject to a uniform federal rule governing the acquisition or improvement of exempt property on the eve of bankruptcy, would not be a novel approach. Bankruptcy in the United States is characterized by a deliberate recognition of state property rights, as limited by the federal principles designed to further dominant bankruptcy policies. . . .

Encouraging financially distressed debtors to plan for bankruptcy by permitting them to acquire or improve exempt property will prevent prejudice against those debtors who do not have the foresight to predict financial disaster or the sophistication to purchase their exemptions early. The items and quantity to which the debtor is entitled must be carefully limited, however, to prevent abuse and to protect the rights of creditors. The limitations imposed must depend on the particular needs and circumstances of the individual debtor. . . .

The need for certainty with regard to the propriety of acquiring exempt property prior to bankruptcy makes it appropriate for federal bankruptcy legislation to deal expressly with the issue. . . .

VII. Conclusion

Debtors and their attorneys should be permitted, and even encouraged, to plan actively for bankruptcy by acquiring or improving exempt property which the debtor reasonably needs to make a fresh start. The present law discourages such planning because it has produced uncertainty concerning the propriety of converting nonexempt to exempt property in contemplation of bankruptcy and because it threatens to impose severe sanctions in the event that the conversion is declared improper. The mere possibility of a denial of a discharge of debts is enough to chill efforts to make even modest acquisitions of the most essential property. . . .

This article does not purport to suggest that absolute certainly and uniformity of treatment can be attained simply by statutory change. Balancing the rights of creditors against the needs of debtors to acquire property necessary for a fresh start must be left to the courts for factual analysis on a case-by-case basis. It is suggested, however, that the Bankruptcy Reform Act be amended to establish a uniform standard to guide the courts in reaching their decisions, based on the reasonable needs of the debtor and his dependents. . . .

Mere approval of reasonable purchases or improvements of exempt property on the eve of bankruptcy may not suffice, however, to overcome the reluctance of debtors and their attorneys to plan such purchases or improvements. The indefiniteness of the reasonableness standard will continue to discourage conversion unless the possible penalty for exceeding the bounds of reasonableness is mitigated. Accordingly, this Article also recommends that the Bankruptcy Reform Act be amended so that even an unreasonable purchase of exempt property in contemplation of bankruptcy will not act to deprive the debtor of a discharge of his debts. A denial of the exemption when a purchase or improvement is found to have been unreasonable is sufficient to protect the interests of creditors and deter abuse by debtors.

Lawrence Ponoroff & F. Stephen Knippenberg
Debtors Who Convert Their Assets on the Eve of Bankruptcy: Villains or Victims of the Fresh Start?
70 N.Y.U. L. Rev. 235 (1995)[*]

Introduction

. . . The scope of [the] two core constituents of the fresh start policy—discharge and exemptions—is put to the test when the debtor, while insolvent and anticipating a bankruptcy filing, converts what were nonexempt assets to exempt assets for the purpose of taking maximum advantage of available exemptions. On the one hand, there is something instinctively unsettling in abiding a debtor with significant unencumbered assets who purposefully converts those assets into exempt form, thereby placing them beyond the reach of creditors, and then seeks absolution from her unpaid debts by means of the bankruptcy discharge. On the other hand, the very existence of statutory exemptions reflects a deliberate policy choice to tolerate this type of "legal fraud" in order to further even more important social interests. . . .

The practical and policy questions created by this interplay of related doctrines are obvious. First, does the debtor's urge to exempt as much property as possible from liquidation in bankruptcy, if indulged, at some point cross the line into conduct sufficient to sustain an objection to discharge

---

under § 727(a)(2)? Second, should the trustee be permitted to recoup for the estate's benefit exempt property acquired by the debtor on the eve of bankruptcy? . . .

Convinced that the contemporary discussion about asset conversion and bankruptcy has become locked into a single analytical framework that has failed either to advance our understanding of the practice or our ability to respond to it in a principled way, we propose that this form of prebankruptcy planning needs to be approached from an entirely fresh perspective. Accordingly . . . we discuss metaphorical reasoning as an alternative way of both appreciating the limitations of the transfer metaphor, which has dominated the dialogue to date, and freeing ourselves from those limitations in order to bring new insight to bear on the issue.

. . . [W]e . . . reach the conclusion that judicial attempts at regulating the prebankruptcy conversion of nonexempt property to exempt property ought to be abandoned as unwarranted. Without necessarily contending that debtors should be free to convert assets with impunity, we do assert that to deprive a debtor of a discharge or of her exemptions on the ground that an eve-of-bankruptcy conversion constitutes a "transfer," is to avoid, rather than to undertake, reasoned analysis. . . . In fashioning any such response, however, we urge explicit recognition that any limitation imposed on a debtor's ability to change the form in which her assets are held can be regarded plausibly as a taking of property. This recognition, in turn, derives from the alternative conceptualization of asset conversion . . ., a conceptualization that views the right to convert assets as a property interest forming an essential component in the debtor's fresh start. . . .

IV. Conceptualizing Asset Conversion: The Transfer Metaphor

. . .

A. Asset Conversion Understood as Preferential Transfer

If state law does not abhor a preference, bankruptcy law does, as reflected in § 547 of the Code.

. . .

This conception invites modeling the practice of converting assets in anticipation of bankruptcy as a preferential transfer. Asset conversions can be understood as a transfer—a journey from the land of nonexempt to the land of exempt. Value otherwise destined to become property of the estate is diverted from its natural course and the estate is correspondingly reduced. . . . As with preferential transfers to creditors, there is an attendant distributional advantage, seemingly in violation of bankruptcy norms. However, in the case of a prebankruptcy conversion of assets, the advantage belongs to the debtor. There is no change in the relationship inter se among creditors. In short, the debtor who converts assets prefers herself to her creditors, usually with that intention, but always with that consequence.

Proposals for law reform in the area of prebankruptcy asset conversion have seized on this apparent similarity in technique, deploying the metaphor that conversion of nonexempt assets in the shadow of a bankruptcy filing is a preferential transfer. . . .

The conflation, however, of the two phenomena—asset conversion and preferences—elevates the necessary consequences of transfers out of a fixed estate to the status of preeminent normative principle. . . . To treat asset conversion as a preferential transfer, in other words, requires two steps. First, the conversion of nonexempt assets to exempt assets must be understood as an estate-reducing transfer. Next, the debtor must be thought of as a creditor. . . .

Where a first principle of bankruptcy is presumed to be maximization of estate value for distribution to creditors, and where the principle is extended to preference law, there seems to be no compelling reason to distinguish debtor from creditor in this context. But the wealth-maximization view leaves no room for that which differentiates the two—the fresh start as implemented through the bankruptcy discharge and the exemptions. . . . [W]e think it is inappropriate, not to mention dangerous, to use preference law as the source concept for developing an approach to the dilemma of asset conversion. . . . Ultimately, however, if the prebankruptcy conversion of assets is to be regulated at all, it must be done in a manner that accommodates all of the policy considerations implicated by the practice, including, in particular, the bankruptcy fresh start policy.

B. Asset Conversion Understood as Fraudulent Transfer

. . . Once conversion of assets is understood or perceived as a transfer by the debtor to herself, it is a short conceptual step to § 548(a)(1) avoidance provided that the requisite intent can be established. Nevertheless, it is a conceptual step rarely taken overtly. . . . [T]he cases invariably begin by reciting the dogma that the transformation of assets from one form to another in anticipation of bankruptcy is not itself a fraudulent transfer.

The influence of fraudulent conveyance doctrine in this area, however, is clear from the remedial responses that have been employed by the courts. First, and most defensible, is the line of discharge cases. Since § 727(a)(2) tracks the language of § 548(a)(1) in making prebankruptcy conduct that amounts to actual fraud grounds for global denial of discharge, the nexus between asset conversion and fraudulent disposition law is clear. But this assumes that a prebankruptcy asset conversion, when undertaken with intent to deprive creditors of property that would otherwise be available for distribution, is properly analogized as a fraudulent transfer. The consequences of indulging that assumption are not inconsiderable. . . .

. . . The conception of asset conversion as a transfer—one that may at times be perceived as a fraud on creditors or as preferential—is, therefore, quietly at work in the case law. However, just as the preference analogy is an imperfect one, the similarities of asset conversion to fraudulent transfer begin and end with the impact of those forms of prebankruptcy activity on the estate, namely, a reduction in net assets to which all claimants are entitled upon liquidation. . . .

Whether the conversion of assets from nonexempt to exempt form in contemplation of bankruptcy is more like secreting assets away in a concealed location or more like engaging in extravagant spending may be debatable. However, the transfer metaphor, which has dominated the case law analysis, forecloses fair consideration of both alternatives. Upon reconceptualizing asset conversion . . ., the most significant differences between this form of prebankruptcy planning, on the one hand, and fraud, on the other, become readily apparent. . . .

C. The Dysfunctional Consequences of Conceptualizing Asset Conversions as Avoidable Third-Party Transfers

Defining asset conversions with reference to preference and fraudulent disposition law highlights a salient dimension shared by all three concepts, namely, diversion of assets from the estate. At the same time, however, it eclipses the differences between prebankruptcy transfers to creditors or other third parties and prebankruptcy "transfers" (conversion) to the debtor herself. But such is the power and the threat of metaphoric reasoning. To understand a target concept, such as asset conversion, in terms of a source concept, such as the concept of the preference or fraudulent conveyance, is to bring into bold relief similarities between them. The metaphor thereby creates a useful system of analogies that make otherwise undefined concepts intelligible and manageable. At the same time, in highlighting similarities between source and target concepts, metaphor hides differences between them. It is our claim that the hiding power of metaphor has led, if not to dysfunctional analysis, then at least to theoretical impasse in the case of prebankruptcy conversions of nonexempt assets to exempt form.

. . . [W]e offer a discussion of new insights from the cognitive sciences on the nature and importance of metaphoric reasoning. These insights form the basis for our claim that the traditional analysis of asset conversion has been heretofore dysfunctional; that the dialogue has become hopelessly locked into an unresolvable conflict between the policy of debtor relief from oppressive debt, on the one hand, and creditor protection from fraudulent prebankruptcy conflict, on the other. The object of the discussion is to pave the way in Part VI for reconceptualizing asset conversion free of the transfer metaphor and, in the process, free from the "honest but unfortunate debtor" platitude. Once we eliminate, once and for all, the shadow cast by these concepts, we can see prebankruptcy asset conversions in an entirely new and different light. . . .

In the final Part of this Article, we make the claim that the transfer metaphor in the context of asset conversion has created an analytical impasse. On abandoning the metaphor, important considerations heretofore unexplored come to light on the basis of which analysis might be advanced beyond present levels. Specifically, reconceptualizing conversion outside the prevailing metaphors of the transfer reveals important dimensions of a debtor's property in nonexempt assets that we do not believe have received explicit consideration in the literature to this point. . . .

VI. Reconceptualizing Asset Conversion: From "Transfer" to "Property"

. . . How, then, should the conversion of assets be conceptualized, if not in terms of fraudulent or preferential transfers, and what is achieved on reconceptualizing asset conversion? Setting aside the transfer metaphor, with its emphasis on the effects of conversion on the estate and, therefore, claimholders, invites consideration of the matter from another perspective, namely, that of the debtor. Specifically, we perceive in a debtor's ability to exchange nonexempt assets for exempt assets the salient dimensions of the concepts of property and ownership. In this final Part we explore the implications of conceptualizing asset conversion in terms of a property interest belonging to debtors, a thought experiment that cannot be undertaken while the transfer metaphor monopolizes analysis.

Exemption of certain species of assets under state law can be understood usefully as creating a set of property interests in the debtor, which we shall refer to here collectively as "Exemption Property." An important attribute of property is that, to one extent or another, it may be alienated, voluntarily or involuntarily, absolutely or for security. State law, where Exemption Property originates, qualifies the extent of property in exempt assets both by defining the exemptions themselves and by stating limits on the ability to transfer rights embodied in Exemption Property.

. . . For the most part . . . Exemption Property is not subject to involuntary alienation, as by the execution process, with the result that unsecured creditors cannot be transferees of Exemption Property. . . . That dimension of Exemption Property—freedom from the claims of attaching creditors— may also be understood as a restraint on alienation imposed by the state that created the property interest. . . .

The creation of security effectively forecloses the possibility of conversion of assets. In conceptualizing the right to convert as one of the property interests embraced by Exemption Property, the grant of security can therefore be understood in part as an alienation of that interest. . . .

Conversely, unsecured creditors suffer the risk that a debtor will alienate her assets and the risk that the debtor will substitute exempt assets for nonexempt assets and so frustrate the collection process under state law. . . .

Mapping the concept of containment onto the concept by which we understand a debtor's assets entails that a lien or other property interest remains in that asset notwithstanding its subsequent transfer. Inasmuch as the unsecured creditor has, prior to the execution process, no property interest in a debtor's assets, it follows from the consequences entailed by the governing metaphors that a debtor is free to alienate those assets. It entails, in other words, that the debtor is free to convert assets from one kind, nonexempt, to another, exempt. The result coheres with the metaphor here proposed, Exemption Property, which under our definition includes the right to convert as a kind of special form of alienation. As a property interest belonging to the debtor, the right to convert is a thing of value that may be voluntarily transferred or traded away. Where credit is extended unsecured, the creditor has declined to bargain for Exemption Property. The debtor, therefore, retains the Exemption Property and all of the attributes of ownership, including the right of conversion. Unlike the secured creditor, the general creditor chooses the larger return in the form of higher interest (risk of nonpayment notwithstanding), preferring not to buy out the debtor's Exemption Property.

Consider now that a debtor has petitioned for chapter 7 relief owing unsecured debt, and that prior to bankruptcy she has substituted exempt assets for nonexempt assets. . . . The transfer metaphor (whereby asset conversion is understood as a debtor's transfer of property to herself) paves the way for modeling asset conversion on the concepts of preference and fraudulent conveyance. The result entailed is avoidance.

Reconceptualizing asset conversion in the manner we have proposed—specifically, as one of a set of interests that comprise a debtor's Exemption Property—casts a very different light on avoidance indeed. To permit unsecured creditors to undo exemptions in property is to grant to those creditors an interest unavailable to them outside bankruptcy. In bankruptcy the ability to avoid the exemption on the grounds that asset conversion is a fraudulent conveyance is the right to reach Exemption Property. . . .

Where exemptions or discharge are denied as a result of asset conversion, unsecured creditors thereby acquire an interest that attaches to specific property of the debtor. In effect, unsecured creditors acquire an involuntary lien on Exemption Property in bankruptcy that they could not acquire outside bankruptcy without bargaining for security. . . .

Given one of the central premises of this Article—that no single source concept can bring complete meaning to a target concept—it would be fair to observe that the conception of asset conversion as an aspect of Exemption Property is no less a metaphor than the conception of conversion as fraudulent conveyance or preferential transfer. . . . Why, therefore, reconceptualize asset conversion along the lines we have suggested?

The answer is found in a feature inherent in metaphoric reasoning alluded to earlier. Metaphoric reasoning is by hypothesis partial, the meaning it brings to concepts necessarily incomplete. . . .

The most significant difference between fraudulent transfers and asset conversions is revealed on conceiving of asset conversion as a right associated with Exemption Property, the metaphor we urge herein to augment and enrich, not supplant, existing conceptualizations. A characteristic that asset conversions seem to share with fraudulent conveyances is the resulting impact of both actions on the bankruptcy estate. The fraudulent transfer and asset conversion alike appear to reduce assets otherwise available for distribution to unsecured creditors. The Exemption Property metaphor, however, highlights an important distinction, a distinction that is unavailable when asset conversion is understood exclusively in terms of the transfer metaphor.

Understood as property, the right to convert may be the object of bargaining, an interest the debtor may contract away voluntarily to procure more favorable terms from her creditor. The possibility that debtors can substitute exempt for nonexempt assets, thereby placing them beyond the reach of state law creditors' remedies, is a risk reasonably within the parties' contemplation at the time of bargaining. . . . In contrast, a debtor's fraudulent treatment of her assets, by spiriting them away or destroying them, is something creditors cannot meaningfully bargain to avoid. That is to say, the risk of fraud is outside the contemplation of the parties at the time of bargaining. . . .

The distinction between the risk of nonpayment which can be alleviated by contract (the risk of alienation by transfer or conversion) and that which cannot (the risk of fraudulent transfer or concealment) demonstrates the difference in impact on the bankruptcy estate from asset conversion, on the one hand, and fraudulent transfers to third parties, on the other. A debtor's Exemption Property, if not traded to a creditor for some contractual advantage, simply remains with the debtor, and would follow her assets into bankruptcy to prevent their distribution to general creditors. The debtor's right to convert is simply a pre-existing condition that limits property that will find its way into the bankruptcy estate. Understood in that way, the substitution of exempt for nonexempt assets in advance of bankruptcy is simply the exercise of a right originating in Exemption Property.

By contrast, a debtor has no property interest that would entitle her to destroy or fraudulently convey assets, the risk of which, as has been noted, a creditor cannot ameliorate through the bargaining process. . . .

If we come to regard the right to convert assets in advance of bankruptcy as property, is that to say there can be no limitations on its exercise? No property interest known to the law is absolute. . . .

Under the new analysis, with its view of the right to convert as a separate property right, denial of exemptions based on asset conversion would be understood as a taking of that property in bankruptcy. . . . What is called for is an analysis, a test, the substantive components of which manifest due regard for the property interests implicated. The analysis would therefore no longer be about avoiding exemptions in bankruptcy after the fashion of fraudulent conveyances or preferential transfers. Instead, the analysis would consist of deciding whether some normative policy, some first principle of bankruptcy, is so far contradicted by eve-of-bankruptcy asset conversions as to justify depriving the converting debtor of Exemption Property.

In weighing whether such a policy exists, we offer this admonishment as a point of departure for further dialogue and analysis. The exemption concept in bankruptcy is central to the fresh start, making that first principle the most promising source of normative policy in the light of which asset conversions might be evaluated. The question thus becomes formulated in the following manner: Does a debtor's right to convert nonexempt assets, exercised on the eve of bankruptcy, exceed the scope of the fresh start in bankruptcy such that the debtor should be deprived of that property? If it is concluded that it does, then on the conceptualization of asset conversion as property, it would appear that bankruptcy actually contracts a debtor's property rights under state law. . . .

. . . [U]nder the analysis proposed, the decision to divest a debtor of Exemption Property turns not on perceived analogies between asset conversions and the concept of transfers to third parties; instead, the decision turns on the scope of the fresh start. Whether asset conversion exceeds the scope of the fresh start is not, however, a question susceptible to answer under law or policy as they have so far evolved. There is . . . no consensus on what the scope of the fresh start is or ought to be.

. . . Until such time as there is consensus on the concept of the fresh start, its objective, and its limits, no principled determination about the effect of bankruptcy on asset conversions, and so a debtor's right associated with Exemption Property, can be made. Moreover, we believe that the development of such a consensus can only be achieved as the end-product of the kind of pluralistic process—where conflicting views can be voiced and competing interests accommodated—that characterizes lawmaking in the legislative rather than the judicial branch of government. . . . Therefore, if there is a need to respond to the practice, we think that the response should be a legislative one. . . .

CONCLUSION

It may be that a debtor's ability to substitute exempt assets for nonexempt assets should be curtailed, but in our view a principled determination that it should or should not cannot depend exclusively on the metaphors that currently structure the concept of asset conversion. Where analysis proceeds entirely from the transfer metaphor, there is no opportunity to value that which is being deprived the debtor by denying exemptions or discharge.

In this Article, we have attempted to show that the paralysis, and consequent frustration, that seems to plague analysis of prebankruptcy asset conversions in both the case law and the scholarly literature is a product of the tendency to conceive of the debtor's actions as involving a "transfer" of her assets. The effect of this characterization is not an insignificant one. . . . [T]he concept of "transfer" evokes a powerful stereotypical image in bankruptcy law. And yet, there is nothing inherent in the practice of adjusting assets to maximize exemption values in bankruptcy (or out) that compromises an individual's right to claim any of the entitlements that together establish the limits on a debtor's eligibility for bankruptcy relief in chapter 7. We have suggested, therefore, that it might be profitable to reconceptualize asset conversion as a property right, not simply for the new insights revealed upon viewing the practice from this perspective (although that surely is a benefit), but also because this perspective may offer a more defensible normative model than the one that has dominated the discussion to date.

On reconceptualizing ability to convert assets as state-created property, we are forced to acknowledge that to deny exemptions is to take property from the debtor and confer it upon unsecured creditors who did not bargain for it. This is not to argue, *a fortiori*, that it should never occur. However, before taking that step, we must first make the case that some weighty normative policy is offended by asset substitution. If it is to be found anywhere, we believe that such normative parameters must reside in the policy of fresh start, a concept that, notwithstanding its centrality in consumer bankruptcy cases, still awaits precise and accepted definition.

NATIONAL BANKRUPTCY REVIEW COMMISSION
FINAL REPORT
BANKRUPTCY: THE NEXT TWENTY YEARS
(October 20, 1997)

Chapter 1: Consumer Bankruptcy—Property Exemptions

1.2.1 *Elimination of Opt Out*
A consumer debtor who has filed a petition for relief under the Bankruptcy Code should be allowed to exempt property as provided in section 522 of the Code. Subsection (b)(1) and (2) of section 522 should be repealed.

1.2.2 *Homestead Property*
The debtor should be able to exempt the debtor's aggregate interest as a fee owner, a joint tenant, or a tenant by the entirety, in real property or personal property that the debtor or a dependent of the debtor uses as a residence in the amount determined by the laws of the state in which the debtor resides, but not less than $20,000 and not more than $100,000.

Subsection (m) of section 522 should be revised to reflect that all exemptions except for the homestead exemption shall apply separately to each debtor in a joint case.

1.2.3 *Nonhomestead Lump Sum Exemption*
With respect to property of the estate not otherwise exempt by other provisions, a debtor should be permitted to retain up to $20,000 in value in any form. A debtor who claims no homestead exemption should be permitted to exempt an additional $15,000 of property in any form.

1.2.4 All professionally-prescribed medical devices and health aids necessary for the health and maintenance of the debtor or a dependent of the debtor should be exempt.

1.2.5 *Rights to Receive Benefits and Payments*
All funds held directly or indirectly in a trust that is exempt from federal income tax pursuant to sections 408 or 501(a) of the Internal Revenue Code should be exempt.

1.2.6 *Rights to Payments*
Rights to receive future payments (*e.g.*, social security benefits, life insurance) should be exempt, and the debtor's right to receive an award under a crime victim's reparations law or

payment for a personal bodily injury claim of the debtor or the debtor's dependent should be exempt.

Chapter 1: Consumer Bankruptcy—
Reaffirmation Agreements and the Treatment of Secured Debt

1.3.4 *Security Interests in Household Goods*
Household Goods Worth Less Than $500
Section 522(f) should provide that a creditor claiming a purchase money security interest in exempt property held for personal or household use of the debtor or a dependent of the debtor in household furnishings, wearing apparel, appliances, books, animals, crops, musical instruments, jewelry, implements, professional books, tools of the trade or professionally prescribed health aids for the debtor or a member of the debtor's household must petition the bankruptcy court for continued recognition of the security interest. The court shall hold a hearing to value each item covered by the creditor's petition. If the value of the item is less than $500, the petition shall not be granted; if the value is $500 or greater, the security interest would be recognized and treated as a secured loan in Chapter 7 or Chapter 13.

Additional suggested readings

On Discharge and the Fresh Start

Barry Adler, Ben Polak & Alan Schwartz, *Regulating Consumer Bankruptcy: A Theoretical Inquiry*, 29 J. LEGAL STUD. 585 (2000)

Peter C. Alexander, *With Apologies to C.S. Lewis: An Essay on Discharge and Forgiveness*, 9 J. BANKR. L. & PRAC. 601 (2000)

Lawrence M. Ausubel, *Credit Card Defaults, Credit Card Profits, and Bankruptcy*, 71 AM. BANKR. L.J. 249 (1997)

Paul M. Black & Michael J. Herbert, *Bankcard's Revenge: A Critique of the 1984 Consumer Credit Amendments to the Bankruptcy Code*, 19 U. RICH. L. REV. 845 (1985)

Douglass G. Boshkoff, *Fresh Start, False Start, or Head Start*, 70 IND. L.J. 549 (1995)

Douglass G. Boshkoff, *Bankruptcy-Based Discrimination*, 66 AM. BANKR. L.J. 387 (1992)

Douglass G. Boshkoff, *Limited, Conditional, and Suspended Discharges in Anglo-American Bankruptcy Proceedings,* 131 U. PA. L. REV. 69 (1982)

Douglass G. Boshkoff, *The Bankrupt's Moral Obligation to Pay His Discharged Debts: A Conflict Between Contract Theory and Bankruptcy Policy*, 47 IND. L.J. 36 (1971)

Richard E. Coulson, *Substantial Abuse of Bankruptcy Code Section 707(b): An Evolving Philosophy of Debtor Need*, 52 CONS. FIN. L.Q. REP. 261 (1998)

Vern Countryman, *Bankruptcy and the Individual Debtor—And a Modest Proposal to Return to the Seventeenth Century*, 32 CATH. U. L. REV. 809 (1983)

Rafael Efrat, *The Evolution of the Fresh-Start Policy in Israeli Bankruptcy Law*, 32 VAND. J. TRANSNATL. L. 49 (1999)

Rafael Efrat, *The Moral Appeal of Personal Bankruptcy*, 20 WHITTIER L. REV. 141 (1998)

Theodore Eisenberg, *Bankruptcy Law in Perspective*, 28 UCLA L. REV. 953 (1981)

Karen Gross, *As We Fleece Our Debtors*, 102 DICK. L. REV. 747 (1998)

Karen Gross, *The Debtor as Modern Day Peon: A Problem of Unconstitutional Conditions*, 65 NOTRE DAME L. REV. (1990)

Karen Gross, *Preserving a Fresh Start for the Individual Debtor: The Case for Narrow Construction of the Consumer Credit Amendments*, 135 U. PA. L. REV. 59 (1986)

Charles G. Hallinan, *The "Fresh Start" Policy in Consumer Bankruptcy: A Historical Inventory and an Interpretive Theory*, 21 U. RICH. L. REV. 49 (1986)

Michael J. Herbert & Domenic E. Pacitti, *Down and Out in Richmond, Virginia: The Distribution of Assets in Chapter 7 Bankruptcy Proceedings Closed in 1984-1987*, 22 U. RICH. L. REV. 303 (1988)

Robert A. Hillman, *Contract Excuse and Bankruptcy Discharge*, 43 STAN. L. REV. 99 (1990)

Thomas H. Jackson, Chapter 10, *The Fresh-Start Policy in Bankruptcy Law*, 225-252, and Chapter 11, *The Scope of Discharge and Exempt Property*, 253-279, *in* THE LOGIC AND LIMITS OF BANKRUPTCY LAW (Harvard 1986)

Frank R. Kennedy, *Reflections on the Bankruptcy Laws of the United States: The Debtor's Fresh Start*, 76 W. VA. L. REV. 427 (1974)

Anthony Kronman, *Paternalism and the Law of Contracts*, 92 YALE L.J. 763 (1983)

Jeffrey W. Morris, *The Continuing Development of Consumer Bankruptcy*, 23 CAP. U. L. REV. 395 (1994)

Jeffrey W. Morris, *Substantive Consumer Bankruptcy Reform in the Bankruptcy Amendments Act of 1984*, 27 WM. & MARY L. REV. 91 (1985)

Raymond T. Nimmer, *Consumer Bankruptcy Abuse*, 50 LAW & CONTEMP. PROBS. 89 (Spring 1987)

Lawrence Ponoroff, *Vicarious Thrills: The Case for Application of Agency Rules in Bankruptcy Dischargeabiltiy Litigation*, 70 TUL. L. REV. 2515 (1996)

Doug Rendleman, *The Bankruptcy Discharge: Toward a Fresher Start*, 58 N.C. L. REV. 723 (1980)

Steven H. Resnicoff, *Is It Morally Wrong to Depend on the Honesty of Your Partner or Spouse? Bankruptcy Dischargeability of Vicarious Debt*, 42 CASE W. L. REV. 147 (1992)

Steven H. Resnicoff, *Barring Bankruptcy Banditry: Revision of Section 523(a)(2)(C)*, 7 BANKR. DEV. J. 427 (1990)

Richard Sauer, *Bankruptcy Law and the Maturing of American Capitalism*, 55 OHIO ST. L.J. 291 (1994)

Philip Shuchman, *An Attempt at a "Philosophy of Bankruptcy,"* 21 UCLA L. REV. 403 (1973)

Philip Shuchman, *The Fraud Exception in Consumer Bankruptcy*, 23 STAN. L. REV. 735 (1971)

Teresa A. Sullivan, Elizabeth Warren & Jay Lawrence Westbrook, THE FRAGILE MIDDLE CLASS (Yale 2000)

Teresa A. Sullivan, Elizabeth Warren & Jay Lawrence Westbrook, *Consumer Debtors Ten Years Later: A Financial Comparison of Consumer Bankrupts 1981-1991*, 68 AM. BANKR. L.J. 121 (1994)

John A. Weistart, *The Costs of Bankruptcy*, 41 LAW & CONTEMP. PROBS. 107 (1977)

Michelle J. White, *Personal Bankruptcy Under the 1978 Bankruptcy Code: An Economic Analysis*, 63 IND. L.J. 29 (1987)

Barry Zaretsky, *The Fraud Exception to Discharge Under the New Bankruptcy Code*, 53 AM. BANKR. L.J. 253 (1979)

On Exemptions

William Houston Brown, *Political and Ethical Considerations of Bankruptcy Limitations: The "Opt-Out" as a Child of the First and Parent of the Second*, 71 AM. BANKR. L.J. 149 (1997)

David Gray Carlson, *Security Interests on Exempt Property After the 1994 Amendments to the Bankruptcy Code*, 4 AM. BANKR. INST. L. REV. 57 (1996)

Vern Countryman, *For a New Exemption Policy in Bankruptcy*, 14 RUTGERS L. REV. 678 (1960)

Margaret Howard, *Avoiding Powers and the 1994 Amendments to the Bankruptcy Code*, 69 AM. BANKR. L.J. 259 (1995)

Margaret Howard, *Multiple Judicial Liens in Bankruptcy: Section 522(f)(1) Simplified*, 67 AM. BANKR. L.J. 151 (1993)

Thomas H. Jackson, Chapter 11, *The Scope of Discharge and Exempt Property, in* THE LOGIC AND LIMITS OF BANKRUPTCY LAW 253-279 (Harvard 1986)

C. Robert Morris, *Bankrupt Fantasy: The Site of Missing Words and the Order of Illusory Events*, 45 ARK. L. REV. 265 (1992)

William T. Plumb, Jr., *The Recommendations of the Commission on the Bankruptcy Laws—Exempt and Immune Property*, 61 VA. L. REV. 1 (1975)

Lawrence Ponoroff, *Exemption Limitations: A Tale of Two Solutions*, 71 AM. BANKR. L.J. 221 (1996)

William T. Vukowich, *Debtors' Exemption Rights Under the Bankruptcy Reform Act of 1978*, 58 N.C. L. REV. 769 (1980)

William T. Vukowich, *The Bankruptcy Commission's Proposals Regarding Bankrupt's Exemption Rights*, 63 CALIF. L. REV. (1975)

William T. Vukowich, *Debtors' Exemption Rights*, 62 GEO. L.J. 779 (1974)

William J. Woodward, Jr. & Richard S. Woodward, *Exemptions as an Incentive to Voluntary Bankruptcy: An Empirical Study*, 57 AM. BANKR. L.J. 53 (1983)

William J. Woodward, Jr., *Exemptions, Opting Out, and Bankruptcy Reform*, 43 OHIO ST. L.J. 335 (1982)

Chapter 12

Consumer Bankruptcy: Reform

The shape of the consumer bankruptcy system as enacted in the 1978 Bankruptcy Code has been the subject of unremitting cries for reform. No area of bankruptcy law has received the sort of continued agitation for fundamental reorientation as consumer bankruptcy. The recurring plea is that individual consumer debtors should be forced to repay their creditors what they can out of future income. This Chapter airs that debate. First is the House Report that accompanied the 1978 Code. That Report concluded that repayment plans (under chapter 13) should be purely voluntary with the debtor, thereby rejecting the argument for compulsory repayment plans. What are the grounds that influenced the House?

H.R. REP. NO. 95-595
95TH CONG., 1ST SESS. (1977)

Chapter 3. Consumer Debtors

I. ADJUSTMENT OF DEBTS OF AN INDIVIDUAL WITH REGULAR INCOME

. . . The purpose of chapter XIII is to enable an individual, under court supervision and protection, to develop and perform under a plan for the repayment of his debts over an extended period.
. . .

The benefit to the debtor . . . is that it permits the debtor to protect his assets. . . . Chapter XIII also protects a debtor's credit standing far better than a straight bankruptcy . . . . In addition, it satisfies many debtors' desire to avoid the stigma attached to straight bankruptcy and to retain the pride attendant on being able to meet one's obligations. The benefit to creditors is self-evident: their losses will be significantly less than if their debtors opt for straight bankruptcy. . . .

B. VOLUNTARINESS

As under current law, chapter XIII is completely voluntary. This Committee firmly rejected the idea of mandatory or involuntary chapter XIII in the 90th Congress. The thirteenth amendment prohibits involuntary servitude. Though it has never been tested in the wage earner plan context, it has been suggested that a mandatory chapter XIII, by forcing an individual to work for creditors, would violate this prohibition. On policy grounds, it would be unwise to allow creditors to force a debtor into a repayment plan. An unwilling debtor is less likely to retain his job or to cooperate in the repayment plan, and more often than not, the plan would be preordained to fail. Therefore, the bill prohibits involuntary cases under chapter XIII, and forbids the conversion of a case from chapter VII, liquidation, to chapter XIII, unless the debtor requests.

The Bankruptcy Commission also considered proposals that would permit an individual to file straight bankruptcy only if he were unable to obtain adequate relief under chapter XIII. The Commission rejected the proposals, and stated their reasons as follows:

. . . [F]ulfillment of a debtor's commitment made pursuant to a Chapter XIII plan requires not merely a debtor's consent but a positive determination by him and his family to live within the constraints imposed by the plan during its entire term and a will to persevere with the plan to the end. Imposition of a Chapter XIII plan on an unwilling debtor, it was said, would be almost bound to encourage the debtor to change employment and, if necessary, to move to another area to escape the importuning calls and correspondence of his creditors. . . . To force unwilling wage earners to devote their future earnings to payment of past debts smacked to some of debt peonage . . . .

The Commission has considered the arguments made for conditioning the availability of bankruptcy relief, including discharge, on a showing by the debtor that he cannot obtain adequate relief from his condition of financial distress by proposing a plan for payment of his debts out of his future earnings. The Commission has concluded that forced participation by a debtor in a plan requiring contributions out of future income has so little prospect for success that it should not be adopted as a feature of the bankruptcy system.

The first chink in the legislative armor pertaining to a future income test occurred in 1984, when Congress adopted the "Consumer Credit Amendments." Of importance for the present debate were two key provisions: first, the "substantial abuse" test of § 707(b), whereby a court could dismiss a chapter 7 individual consumer debtor's case if it found that filing to be a "substantial abuse"; and second, the "disposable income" test in § 1325(b) for confirming chapter 13 plans, mandating that a chapter 13 debtor commit all of her disposable income for three years to plan payments. In an excellent article, *Preserving a Fresh Start for the Individual Debtor: The Case for Narrow Construction of the Consumer Credit Amendments*, 135 U. PA. L. REV. 59 (1986), Professor Karen Gross argued for a "narrow construction" of the 1984 Amendments, arguing that doing otherwise would undermine the debtor's fresh start.

In the following passage from that article, Professor Gross sets out four hypothetical cases, which serve as a springboard for assessing the appropriate breadth of interpretation of the relevant amendments. As you proceed through the ensuing articles, refer back to Gross's four hypotheticals and assess how you think they should be resolved, and why. As a normative matter, how should our bankruptcy system deal with these paradigmatic cases?

Karen Gross
Preserving a Fresh Start for the Individual Debtor:
The Case for Narrow Construction of the Consumer Credit Amendments
135 U. PA. L. REV. 59 (1986)*

Consider a physician who is just completing her residency at a major teaching hospital and who is contemplating entry into a lucrative private practice. Assume that in all of the following hypotheticals the doctor would be able to repay her creditors in full in a Chapter 13 case but that she

---

does not, at present, have sufficient non-exempt assets to do so. As such, her creditors would get only a meager distribution in a Chapter 7 case.

Hypothetical One: The doctor has several unsecured trade creditors to whom she is paying minimum monthly installments as required. The doctor also owes money to a secured creditor who has sold an automobile to the debtor. The doctor is behind in these payments, and the creditor is threatening foreclosure. Assume that the automobile is the debtor's second car. The doctor seeks relief under Chapter 7 merely to postpone the foreclosure on the second car. Assume that the debtor has determined that she wants the second car sold but that she wants to sell it at a time and in a manner of her choosing. By filing, the doctor believes that she will gain, in addition to time, leverage in terms of persuading the secured creditor to wait to foreclose.

Hypothetical Two: The doctor incurs substantial, unsecured indebtedness from a variety of lenders for personal use. Assume that there is no fraud on the debtor's part in obtaining these loans and, hence, they would be dischargeable under applicable Code provisions. Assume also that the doctor spent the loan proceeds on speculative ventures in the stock market and that all of the monies were lost due to poor investments. In addition to these debts, the doctor owes other creditors for goods and services provided. She has paid the latter group of creditors in the ordinary course on an installment basis. The doctor seeks relief under Chapter 7 principally to obtain relief from the losses in the stock market.

Hypothetical Three: The doctor has incurred unsecured debt in the ordinary course. Some of this indebtedness is for "non-luxury" items such as food, clothing, furniture, books, and other day-to-day expenses, including cash advances. The doctor has also purchased several "luxury" items, including a fur coat, a stereo, a hot-tub, and a vacation in the Caribbean. She seeks relief from all of this indebtedness, because she cannot satisfy the minimum monthly debt service.

Hypothetical Four: The doctor has incurred unsecured credit in the ordinary course and is unable, at her present earning level, to meet the requisite debt service payments. The doctor did not purchase any "luxury" items but rather purchased clothing, furniture, books, food, and other day-to-day expenses. She seeks relief under Chapter 7 to get out from under excessive debts . . .

. . . [U]nder the expansive interpretation of section 707(b) . . ., courts would be likely to dismiss the Chapter 7 cases presented in each of the hypotheticals because the debtor in each could repay her creditors out of future earnings. The availability of future income would be the key factor in determining whether there was substantial abuse. Such an expansive interpretation would permit dismissal even in the situation presented in Hypothetical Four, where the debtor's only "wrong" was being in debt above her present means while having the earning power to allow for eventual repayment of such debt.

Under a narrow interpretation of section 707(b), a court still would be likely to dismiss the cases presented in Hypotheticals One and Two, although these results would be reached for very different reasons than those suggested by an expansive interpretation. The situations in Hypotheticals Three and Four, however, would not warrant dismissal, although the "luxury" debts in Hypothetical Three would be nondischargeable. This result achieves a better balance between the needs of both debtors and creditors.

The ink was hardly dry on the 1978 Code when agitation for reform of the consumer provisions began in earnest. An early and influential critic was Professor Theodore Eisenberg. In the following excerpt, Eisenberg argues that Congress should have given more serious consideration to providing for involuntary chapter 13 cases, in which debtors would be compelled to pay creditors out of future income. He dismisses the standard justifications for declining to adopt a forced payment regime. Eisenberg's proposal then was rebutted by Professor Steven Harris. Harris looked closely at the many implications that would flow from a compulsory chapter 13 system. Identify the arguments Eisenberg makes and note how Harris answers.

Theodore Eisenberg
Bankruptcy Law in Perspective
28 UCLA L. REV. 953 (1981)[*]

C.   *Will Involuntary Chapter 13 Plans Work?*

. . . [M]any empirical studies suggest that many bankruptcy debtors could afford to pay their debts in full over a reasonable period of time. . . . If the empirical studies are accurate, even greater numbers of debtors could be characterized as able to fulfill Chapter 13 plans. If the studies understate the debtor's burden, the reduced burden a modified Chapter 13 composition plan would impose offsets at least some of that understatement.

Requiring the court to pass upon Chapter 13's possible use in each case would overcome one other problem that has limited Chapter 13's effectiveness. Testimony at Congress's bankruptcy reform hearings suggested that many debtors who might have wished to use Chapter 13 did not do so for the simple reason that they were never made aware of it. Neither lawyers nor judges called it to their attention. If the court or creditors may raise the possibility of a Chapter 13 plan, the information problem would greatly decrease.

D.   *The Uneasy Case for the Status Quo*

. . . Requiring greater efforts from debtors who can repay was and is, however, a possibility worth studying. . . . Yet modification of Chapter 13 to allow involuntary proceedings and to require consideration of a debtor's future earnings in assessing the minimum he is able to pay received no serious consideration. . . . Bankruptcy experts abruptly dismissed the possibility.

The growing isolation of bankruptcy law partly explains this inadequate consideration. Plausible modifications of Chapter 13 were not considered in part because of bankruptcy reformer's misinformed and unchallenged views of constitutional limitations on the bankruptcy process . . . . The roots of the problem precede the recent reform movement. In 1932, and again in 1967, Congress conducted hearings on proposals to allow involuntary Chapter 13 plans. The arguments made against these proposals are worth exploring because some of those arguments helped foreclose any serious efforts to include involuntary Chapter 13 plans in the 1978 act.

As summarized in 1967, there are three arguments against involuntary Chapter 13 plans. First, society has progressed away from peonage, other forms of involuntary servitude, and imprisonment for debt. Involuntary Chapter 13 plans are a step backwards. . . . Second, involuntary bankruptcy proceedings just will not work. The debtor who does not wish to be in bankruptcy will not make the

---

effort necessary for a successful Chapter 13 plan. Third, involuntary Chapter 13 plans discriminate against noncorporate debtors. . . .

Although these arguments have preempted serious debate about involuntary Chapter 13 plans, none of them is persuasive. The first reason roughly equates involuntary Chapter 13 plans with peonage and involuntary servitude. . . .

An involuntary Chapter 13 plan, despite the presence of the word "involuntary" in its label, bears none of the offensive attributes of involuntary servitude or peonage. Such a plan does not require the debtor to work under the threat of imprisonment. Unlike involuntary servitude, it involves no physical compulsion to work. Like many other conditions to a discharge, an involuntary Chapter 13 plan deprives certain uncooperative debtors of what would otherwise be their right to a discharge in bankruptcy. Over the years the bankruptcy act has imposed many other conditions upon the availability of a discharge. . . .

Equating deprivation of discharge with involuntary servitude and peonage suggests that debtors have a right to a discharge. . . . [T]he argument ignores the numerous periods in this country's history when there has been no federal bankruptcy law. At those times, except in states with insolvency laws, no debtor could avoid creditor collection efforts through discharge or any other provision of a bankruptcy act. One cannot seriously argue that such debtors were in a condition of involuntary servitude or peonage. . . . A promising, sensitive route for balancing debtor-creditor relationships in bankruptcy received no serious consideration in part because of the ignorance of constitutional law.

Skepticism over debtor cooperation forms the second objection to widespread use of involuntary Chapter 13 plans. Even if the law mandates the Chapter 13-type plan as the preferred route in bankruptcy, a debtor may frustrate the system by refusing to work. But if a debtor is allowed to keep significant portions of his future wages, it is difficult to conceive of many debtors refusing to work just to frustrate a Chapter 13 plan. Those so inclined might be persuaded to cooperate by a rule authorizing the court to deny any such debtors any discharge if they frustrate what would otherwise be a successful plan. In any event, creditors ought to be able to judge for themselves whether a debtor will cooperate. If they do not believe a Chapter 13 proceeding will yield more than a straight bankruptcy, they will not invoke Chapter 13.

The third objection asserts that involuntary Chapter 13 plans unfairly give individual debtors a worse deal than corporate debtors receive. . . . State laws limiting shareholder liability for corporate debts, rather than bankruptcy law, assure corporations of the functional equivalent of discharge. . . .

One can imagine other, more serious objections to using a new Chapter 13-type plan as the basic bankruptcy prototype in lieu of traditional liquidation proceedings or Chapter 13 in it current form. Courts must make some judgment as to the prospects of successful participation by each debtor. This requires detailed scrutiny of likely future earnings and some assessment of the debtor's minimal needs. There will be marginal questions about what percentage or fixed amount of the debtor's wage should go to creditors and how far into the future to reach. A mechanism more sophisticated than the existing one would be required for determining which plans must be approved. Proceedings before the bankruptcy court would remain open for years while payments under the Chapter 13-type plan are being made, and this may increase the administrative burden placed on bankruptcy courts.

Whatever increased administrative burden might result from widespread use of wage earner plans, many of the necessary determinations already must be made in Chapter 13 plans. . . . The administrative burdens on bankruptcy courts may increase but they will not be qualitatively different from those already imposed on bankruptcy courts.

Steven L. Harris
A Reply to Theodore Eisenberg's "Bankruptcy Law in Perspective"
30 UCLA L. REV. 327 (1982)*

INTRODUCTION

. . . Professor Eisenberg's first sentence is his thesis: "The new bankruptcy act is a failure." . . . Professor Eisenberg . . . argues . . . that the Code should permit creditors to compel a debtor to pay, or attempt to pay, whatever portion of pre-petition debts he can afford, as a condition of receiving a bankruptcy discharge.

In my view, Professor Eisenberg's article is the failure. . . .

IV. DISCHARGE OF DEBTS

Professor Eisenberg's orientation in favor of creditors also explains his views on discharge. He favors modification of chapter 13 to allow involuntary proceedings and to require consideration of a debtor's future earnings in assessing the minimum the debtor must pay for any discharge. . . . I will suggest that the apparently minimal attention that Congress devoted to mandatory conditional discharges was wholly appropriate given the implications of a mandatory conditional discharge system and the goals Congress sought to achieve. . . .

B. *The Implications of Professor Eisenberg's Discharge Proposal*

Professor Eisenberg also fails to make a persuasive case for mandatory conditional discharge, in large part because he ignores a number of his proposal's potentially serious ramifications and inadequately analyzes those that he mentions. He does not acknowledge the truly radical nature of his proposal; instead he minimizes the severe differences between the goals and effects of a mandatory conditional discharge system and those of the present system. . . .

I am prepared to accept *arguendo* that a conditional discharge system will probably force some debtors to pay more in bankruptcy than they now pay under the Code. Professor Eisenberg seems to conclude that greater payments to creditors *ipso facto* establish the desirability of conditional discharges. Unable to accept creditor satisfaction as the primary goal of bankruptcy law, I am not persuaded that the system he proposes is preferable to the existing one, or even that it "can be no worse." My skepticism derives from my understanding of the relationship between the surrender of assets and the availability of a discharge. Historically, the requirement that a debtor surrender his nonexempt assets for liquidation and distribution to his creditors was not intended to force every debtor to "sacrifice something" as the price of obtaining a discharge. . . .

. . . Modern bankruptcy law . . . has become much more than an aid to the collection of debts; it has developed into a debtors' relief measure as well. One product of this development is a change in the purpose of the discharge. Discharge is no longer primarily the means to achieve greater payments to creditors. It has become the principal means of achieving a goal of equal or greater importance—the opportunity for the debtor to recommence his economic life free from past debts.

One of the most important ways in which Congress implemented the fresh start policy was by permitting debtors alone to decide whether and to what extent they will surrender post-petition earnings to pre-petition creditors. Congress made chapter 13 wholly voluntary: creditors may not force a debtor into chapter 13, nor may they compel him to continue a chapter 13 case that he

---

started. . . . By freeing up post-petition income, the present Code, like its predecessors, enables the debtor to begin anew—to be relieved of the pressures of overwhelming indebtedness, to apply his income to his needs and those of his family, and perhaps to become a successfully functioning economic unit. . . .

The system that Professor Eisenberg favors would deprive the debtor of control over the proceeds of his post-petition labor. In that way it would change considerably more than the measure of what a debtor can afford to pay; it would work a fundamental change in the basic philosophy of the fresh start policy. Under Professor Eisenberg's proposal, the debtor would continue to be encumbered by his pre-petition debts; he would continue to work largely for the benefit of creditors; and he may have great difficulty obtaining new credit—all despite his desire for a fresh start. More importantly, the debtor may be worse off as a practical matter under Professor Eisenberg's proposal than under nonbankruptcy law; *i.e.*, the proposal may provide some debtors no relief at all. Although a mandatory chapter 13 may permit the debtor to retain more property, it simultaneously may deprive him of a greater portion of his income than would nonbankruptcy law. By enabling creditors to compel the turnover of a substantial part of the debtor's post-petition earnings, Professor Eisenberg's proposal in some cases would transform bankruptcy into a creditors' remedy more powerful than any available nonbankruptcy remedy, and generally would be more intrusive than any remedy that American bankruptcy law has ever known.

Just as Professor Eisenberg's proposal removes from debtors the decision whether to forego a complete fresh start and subject future earnings to pre-petition claims, so it prevents debtors from determining how much of their future earnings to devote to the payment of those debts. Instead, Professor Eisenberg proposes that bankruptcy judges determine the extent to which bankruptcy affords relief to each individual debtor. American judges rarely are permitted to decide the difficult and sensitive question of what portion of his own earnings a person may keep and what portion he must surrender to his creditors. The law permits judges to determine what a person can afford in cases of alimony and child support; however, those cases are unique. . . .

The ordinary creditor's claim is not viewed with the same societal concern that accompanies familial support debts; thus, compelling payment of the former may not justify the same intrusion into the debtor's life. As difficult as it is for a judge to determine how a person ought to allocate his income between himself and his dependent children, it is immeasurably more difficult to do so when the normative choice involves contract creditors. . . .

On what basis will the judges determine how much each particular debtor must pay in order to receive a discharge? Professor Eisenberg offers no standards, other than to suggest that the judge scrutinize the debtor's "likely future earnings and [make] some assessment of the debtor's minimal needs." I question the desirability of delegating to a group of federal judges the responsibility of deciding which of his "needs" a debtor may fulfill and the extent to which he may fulfill them. That task is better left to the members of Congress, whose values typically are subject to greater public scrutiny. Unfortunately, Congress is most unlikely to promulgate detailed schedules of debtors' permissible expenditures and of amounts that debtors may retain. Absent clear legislative guidance, judges no doubt would rely to some extent on their own predilections. . . . Judges can be expected to differ significantly in their approval of the debtor's expenditures, even when those expenditures are for "necessities." (How much spent on housing is too much? Is a particular medical treatment really necessary? How much may a debtor spend on food or education for himself and his family?) The availability of relief can be expected to differ from judge to judge. . . .

Professor Eisenberg's proposed solution . . . rejects making discharges more readily available to the more "deserving" debtors, preferring instead to link discharge solely to the debtor's effort to repay. Regardless of a debtor's moral or financial turpitude, he will pay only what he can "afford." The wholly innocent debtor beset by unavoidable insolvency may pay considerably more for his discharge than the "unappealing discharge candidate" does. . . .

The cost of such inquiries into the debtor's present and past financial affairs is likely to be significant. . . . I think his proposal frequently may require bankruptcy judges to make decisions that are costly and that the judges are called upon to make only infrequently under current law. . . .

We have no way of knowing the precise costs of Professor Eisenberg's proposal. . . . [T]here is a significant possibility that Professor Eisenberg's system would increase greatly the burden on the bankruptcy courts. . . .

One potential cause of additional costs, which Professor Eisenberg overlooks, is the debtor's refusal to cooperate with a creditor-initiated chapter 13 proceeding. . . . If a debtor works at a low paying job or is unemployed, the court may need to determine whether the debtor is able to secure a higher paying job or any job at all, as the case may be, in order to decide whether the debtor is frustrating a plan. That determination may be costly.

Professor Eisenberg does not elaborate on the effect of denying a discharge on the ground that the debtor failed to cooperate. I presume that he intends that the court dismiss the case, leaving the creditors to their nonbankruptcy remedies and the debtor to his own devices, which may include fleeing the jurisdiction. The debtor will not receive a fresh start; he will not begin a new economic life, free from the burdens and pressures of past debt. The fresh start is not the only value that Professor Eisenberg's proposal affects adversely. By requiring as preconditions for bankruptcy relief that the debtor work at employment he otherwise would forego and that he turn over a part of his income to his creditors, the proposal runs counter to the values that underlie the thirteenth amendment. Those values are threatened to an even greater extent if the case proceeds and the court is empowered to authorize a plan notwithstanding the debtor's refusal to cooperate.

An important practical question dogs the involuntary payment debate, namely, will it work? That is, do a significant number of debtors have the means to repay creditors, even if forced to do so? If not, it might seem foolish to try to compel the impossible. The tremendous empirical study conducted in the 1980s by Professors Sullivan, Warren, and Westbrook sheds light on the "can pay" question, and suggests that debtor repayment capacity is quite limited. Indeed, their data reveals that even voluntary chapter 13 cases have a very poor success rate. Would involuntary chapter 13 cases fare better? Unlikely. Their findings follow.

Teresa A. Sullivan, Elizabeth Warren & Jay Lawrence Westbrook
AS WE FORGIVE OUR DEBTORS:
BANKRUPTCY AND CONSUMER CREDIT IN AMERICA (1989)[*]

12
Can These Debtors Pay?

The generous willingness of Americans to help those in trouble is balanced by a demand that only the truly needy be helped. Ultimately, the central question most people pose about bankruptcy is whether those who file could have repaid their debts if bankruptcy had not been available. Is the process one of humane discharge or sanctioned abuse?

No single question has a more profound and direct influence on bankruptcy policy. If it is the needy who use bankruptcy, the bankruptcy system can focus on efficiency and fairness. The present system has a number of provisions directed at abuse and there will always be concern with abuse, but it would be a peripheral issue in a system perceived to serve the truly deserving. On the other hand, if the system is shot through with slick manipulation, bankruptcy should be structured around protections to weed out abusers even at greater cost to everyone, including the needy.

. . . In 1984 Congress passed amendments to the Bankruptcy Code that imposed substantial new restrictions on a consumer bankruptcy. These amendments were adopted in response to a perceived problem of abuse. . . .

Our data show that consumers in bankruptcy look very much like the rest of America in their work, but very different in their financial circumstances. The data for the debtors show that, on average, they are at the extreme end of the financial spectrum—earning less and owing more than most Americans, so that their overall financial condition makes them worse off than most of the population. But being at the bottom of the credit heap does not necessarily mean these debtors could not pay. If a substantial portion of debtors could repay, then bankruptcy policy must account for them. On the other hand, if the abusers are rare, the system may have braced for an onslaught that is not coming.

The Moral Definition of "Can Pay"

"How many debtors can pay?" is in part a normative question: the answer depends on moral and social value judgments. . . . A debtor's ability to pay is a function of the level of sacrifice demanded . . . .Where to draw the line—how much sacrifice to require of people in debt—is a key question in bankruptcy. . . .

The Costs of Finding Abusers and Policing Repayment

. . . Abuse in a particular case cannot be determined from the cold numbers alone. . . .

. . . [I]dentifying abuse requires individualized inquiry. In the real world this means a judge must call in the alleged abusers and question them carefully about their particular circumstances.

Another reason that identifying abuse may require information outside the files is that our normative judgments about abuse may not depend solely on the difficulty of repayment. We might want to impose different levels of sacrifice on different debtors. For example, we might like to show why the debtor got into financial trouble. . . .

Because of the need for particularized inquiry, identifying abusers is costly. . . . [T]he ultimate question for us is whether abuse is both widespread and subject to systematic detection. . . .

Testing Ability to Repay

Debtors might repay by selling their assets and giving the cash to their creditors, or they might repay by committing a portion of their future income to repayment. We examine both possibilities to see if our debtors in Chapter 7, those who said in effect they could not or would not pay, would have had a reasonable likelihood of repaying their debts. Because all reform proposals to date stress that debtors who could repay should file in Chapter 13, we also examine the Chapter 13 debtors. We test first to determine how many of them seem able to pay and then to see if they are in fact repaying, as policy debates assume. . . .

Paying from Assets

. . . [W]e separate asset sales into two categories: the home and everything else. . . .

Nonhome Assets

. . . To determine whether the sale of debtors' assets would produce much for their unsecured creditors, we computed the proportion of debt that a debtor family could repay if they sold all their assets, paid 10% in trustee and sales costs, and kept a minimum exemption . . . .

Over 87% of the debtors could pay nothing at all; only 86 could pay anything. Most of those who could manage some repayment could pay relatively little. . . . That is, 2% of the wage-earning debtors could have paid all their unsecured debts by selling off their nonhome assets and less than 4% could have paid even half. A separate calculation shows that the mean amount of unsecured debt Chapter 7 debtors could pay if they sold everything above a $5,000 exemption would be 5 cents on the dollar. Selling nonhome assets is not a potential source of meaningful repayment for creditors. . . .

Selling Homes

Over half those in the bankruptcy sample own their homes. If unsecured creditors could insist that the debtors sell their homes and distribute what remains after the mortgage is paid off, how much would they get?

. . . Over 90% of the Chapter 7 homeowner debtors could pay nothing. . . . [D]ebtors who could pay something cover a wide range of repayment. . . . The average amount realized for unsecured creditors from the sale of . . . homes would be $13,500. The median would be $8,140. Once again, we find debtors who could repay their unsecured debts from assets, but they are a tiny fraction of the wage-earning debtors in Chapter 7.

Selling All Assets

. . . [W]e can combine the two to see what payments could be obtained by forcing debtors to sell *all* their assets. . . . That calculation showed that . . . 3% of the total could pay all their unsecured debts by selling all assets. . . . We conclude that selling debtors' assets—even down to minimal exemption levels—is unlikely to yield more than trivial repayments for most creditors.

Paying from Future Income

If we move away from assets and focus instead on income to see whether the debtors in bankruptcy could repay, we bring our analysis more closely into line with the credit industry's lending practices. This section considers whether bankrupt debtors might be able to repay their debts from their incomes. . . .

Hypothetical Chapter 13 Plans for Chapter 7 Debtors

. . . [W]e constructed for each of our Chapter 7 debtors a hypothetical payment plan in Chapter 13, to see how many of them could have paid had they tried. If the debtor could pay according to this plan, then we speculated that here we had someone who might have abused the bankruptcy system by filing Chapter 7.

OUR ASSUMPTIONS

First we decided how long the hypothetical plan would run. We settled on a three-year payment period, in part because the Bankruptcy Code presumes this to be the period of a Chapter 13 payout plan. . . .

For most calculations we use 100% repayment as the only meaningful standard. . . .

CALCULATING THE PAYMENT PLAN

To find which debtors could repay their nonmortgage debt in full in three years, we calculated each family's capacity to pay by figuring how much money it would take to meet a Chapter 13 plan that repaid debts in full and subtracting that amount the debtor would be expected to live on, an amount we could evaluate according to normative conclusions about the appropriate degree of sacrifice . . . .

For each debtor we calculated what would be required in a Chapter 13 repayment plan. We calculated each debtor's income, less federal income taxes. . . . We then deducted payment to the home mortgagee, payments to the secured creditors, and a statutory fee to the Chapter 13 trustee. Finally, we deducted a household budget for each debtor. When the required Chapter 13 payments and the budget were subtracted from the after-tax income, the remainder was applied against the unsecured debt under the hypothetical Chapter 13.

The hardest issue we addressed was the budget question: how much the debtor needs to live, to have an incentive to continue getting up for a job, to feed the kids and have lunch money, to pay a doctor bill, and so on. . . . [W]e used budgets published by the Bureau of Labor Statistics. The Bureau published three budgets each year, low, moderate, and high. . . .

. . . The pretax low budget for 1981 was $15,323, the moderate was $25,407, and the high was $38,060. All in all, these budgets represent the government's best estimate of the personal expenses of each third of Americans by income. . . .

. . . There were 721 wage-earner households in the Chapter 7 sample who gave enough data to make this calculation. The first number . . . reveals that 75—about 10%—of these households could have paid all their debts in three years while living on the Labor Department's low budget. Only 15 of these households, about 2%, would have had the moderate budget after full payment, and 4 households could have paid and still enjoyed the high-budget existence—not affluent, but not brutal either. . . .

. . . Should the law require a family earning $35,000 a year to live on $15,000? Policymakers have to decide if it is fair, socially desirable, and economically sensible to have this family living so dramatically below their income for three years. It may also be difficult to maintain these income levels on an involuntary basis. Will a debtor work overtime, will a spouse keep a part-time job, when only the creditors profit? . . .

CONCLUSIONS: PAYING IN HYPOTHETICAL CHAPTER 13'S

These data reveal some extreme findings. The overwhelming majority of Chapter 7 debtors—90% by any measure—could not pay their debts in Chapter 13 and maintain even the barest standard of living. But we might want to examine even these few debtors more closely. The debtors who could pay all if they gave up 40% of their income are merely suspects. Some have already lost their jobs or they may be saddled with continuing medical or other expenses. . .

The ultimate question for policymakers is whether the abusers are worth finding. Some would not hesitate to say that if 3%, or 7%, or 9% of these deadbeats are able to pay, we should track them down. We count ourselves among those who are not convinced. A complex statistical analysis yields about 3-9% of the debtors who are suspect for further, more extensive investigation. By law, these debtors are already paying some substantial portion of their secured debt. . . . A new bankruptcy regime that invested more time to find and to investigate the potential can-pay debtors would prompt only a small amount of new repayment. This is the classic case in which a policymaker asks if the game is worth the candle.

Already Trying to Pay—Chapter 13 Debtors

In the bankruptcy debates, the Chapter 13 debtors are frequently idealized as the family in financial trouble struggling to regain financial responsibility and to pay their debts. Virtually all debate has been premised on this view of Chapter 13 and the corollary proposition that if more Chapter 7 debtors would simply file Chapter 13 instead, abuse would be a thing of the past.

The Purdue University Study argued for putting more debtors in Chapter 13, but this study considered Chapter 7 debtors only. Evidently the researchers thought it was axiomatic that the Chapter 13 debtors must be paying. After all, no one can force a debtor to declare Chapter 13, so those who attempt to repay are the volunteers, declaring themselves in effect to be "can-pay" debtors. Given the terrible financial circumstances of most bankrupt debtors, we were skeptical about whether Chapter 13 debtors in fact enjoyed such successes. . . .

Chapter 13 Debtors and Hypothetical Chapter 13's

For our hypothetical test, we use exactly the same criteria we used to find "can-pay" Chapter 7 debtors, including the proposition that the debtor is making a 100% repayment. In fact, many Chapter 13 debtors propose to pay only a small percentage of their debts, and many Chapter 13 debtors fail to pay whatever percentage they promised. . . . To determine, however, whether the Chapter 13 debtor is in fact paying anything more than the Chapter 7 debtor who settles up with his secured creditors and perhaps even reaffirms an unsecured debt or two, the only meaningful comparison comes from putting the Chapter 13 debtor through a full, hypothetical repayment plan . . . .

. . . About 18%—79 current Chapter 13 debtors—can pay all their debts and maintain at least a low budget. Less than 5%—21 debtors—could maintain a moderate budget, and 2 debtors could maintain a high budget. These proportions are higher than among Chapter 7 debtors, but they are not much higher. . . .

How can it be that we find so few Chapter 13 debtors able to pay 100%, when these debtors have declared themselves "can-pay" debtors? There are two reasons. One is that many of these debtors are undertaking to pay much less than 100% and therefore may not be paying more than many Chapter 7 debtors actually pay. The second reason is that most of these Chapter 13 cases are failing.

Actual Outcomes in Chapter 13 . . .

Our Data

. . . Overall, 32% of the cases for which we had usable data had already failed by the time we looked at the files. Another 31% of the cases were troubled, leaving about 32% still paying at the time of our sample. About 4% of the cases were missing. For a rough comparison, if we assume that as many troubled cases revived as still paying cases later failed, then about one-third of the Chapter 13 cases made it through the payment process to the end; two-thirds of them failed. . . .

Possible Explanations for the Chapter 13 Failures

. . . [T]he Chapter 13 failure rate is extraordinarily high. Several factors may contribute to that outcome, but the overriding fact may be the simplest one. Almost none of the debtors in either chapter can pay, except at the price of enormous sacrifice and on the very shaky premise that they will not again suffer the income interruptions and high expenses so many of them have suffered in the past. These data indicate that those who choose Chapter 13 are doing so not because of some careful calculation of their ability to pay, but for other reasons—and the financial realities they face often spell failure. . . .

Policy Implications

To most people, abuse of the bankruptcy system means use of bankruptcy by those who could pay if they were willing to give up those assets that they had bought and now want to keep without paying. In the more sophisticated debates that have taken place in Congress, the assumed source of repayment is the debtor's future income, which would be ample to pay creditors if the debtor had a truly moral view of the obligation to keep promises. Because these concerns are powerful, we devoted this chapter to a careful analysis of our debtors' capacity to repay from asset sales or from future income. We found very little capacity to repay in either way, although some will feel that the little we found justifies expending considerable resources to ferret out "can-pay" debtors and make them pay. We have sympathy with this point. But we also have great reservations. . . .

The point of our complicated financial scrutiny had been to test the level of abuse, to see whether the system requires tightening. We scrutinized the Chapter 7 debtors, forcing them into repayment plans that kept them on the government's "low budget" regardless of what they really earned.

After an exhaustive (and exhausting) search for a sizable group of can-pay debtors, we find so few likely prospects for repayment that we conclude the effort to keep can-pay debtors out of bankruptcy or force them into Chapter 13 is a wasteful misdirection of energy. . . . Of course, our conclusion is laden with normative assumptions. A policymaker who would demand great sacrifice would put more debtors in the can-pay category than we would. Nonetheless, these data should be useful and interesting to that policymaker. These data give some idea of the general range of repayment capacity. One observer might say 3% of the Chapter 7 debtors could repay; another might say 9%. What these data show is that it is not true that 70% of the debtors abuse the system. Or 40%. Or even 20%.

We conclude that bankruptcy laws should not be shaped around the can-pay question. When Congress responded to allegations of widespread abuse in 1984, it wrote a law to correct a problem that did not exist. The "solution" was costly to debtors who later used the system even though the changes would have little appreciable affect on actual abuse. . . .

On balance, we think that the mitigation of a relatively small level of clear abuse is not worth idiosyncratic, luck-of-the-draw justice. . . .

The other major conclusion of this chapter is that Chapter 13 has not turned out to be what was promised. For years participants in bankruptcy policy debates have talked about Chapter 13 as if it were a panacea, as if getting a debtor into Chapter 13 were virtually the same thing as getting all or most debts paid. . . .

Our data show the contrary. Debtors in Chapter 13 fail at extraordinary rates, with fewer than a third still making payments an average of two years after confirmation. On average, those who are paying have proposed plans that promise to pay only about half their debts. This is not surprising, considering how little they have. . . . A Chapter 13 family may be doing for their creditors as little— and possibly considerably less—than many Chapter 7 debtors.

The implications of these findings for establishing policy are far reaching. In 1981 choosing Chapter 13 was an entirely voluntary act, with no legal bar to a Chapter 7 nor any creditor leverage to force a Chapter 13, which makes the failure rate in Chapter 13 all the more noteworthy. High failure rate among volunteers raises serious questions about the efficacy of proposals to force debtors into Chapter 13. If success eludes most debtors who evaluate their own finances and their own desire to pay their debts, and choose to try to pay, how much payment can we expect from those who are coerced into payment plans? . . .

The larger question is whether we have done debtors any service by promoting Chapter 13. Debtors have filed Chapter 13 in record numbers since the adoption the 1978 Code. Would Chapter 13 be so attractive if the debtors knew that two-thirds of them would either be in Chapter 7 or out from under bankruptcy protection altogether in a short time?

Drawing on the above findings of Sullivan, Warren, and Westbrook, Professor William Whitford turns the consumer bankruptcy debate around and asks, not whether debtors should be forced into chapter 13, but whether chapter 13 simply should be repealed. In the political climate of the times Whitford's suggestion has fallen on deaf ears. But does it make sense? What grounds does Whitford put forth to support his proposal?

William C. Whitford
Has the Time Come to Repeal Chapter 13?
65 IND. L.J. 85 (1989)[*]

The wonderful book by Sullivan, Warren and Westbrook [AS WE FORGIVE OUR DEBTORS (1989)—Ed.] sheds light on many questions about consumer bankruptcy that have been long-debated. It also raises a new one—has the time come to repeal Chapter 13? . . .

The case for repeal is based on the data showing that what Sullivan, Warren and Westbrook call the "economic model" can account for only a small part of debtor choice between Chapter 13 and Chapter 7. . . . Sullivan, Warren and Westbrook believe that what they call "local legal culture" accounts for a much greater part of debtor choice. By local legal culture they mean essentially that actors in the legal system "steer" debtors towards one chapter or the other. . . .

I. THE CASE FOR PROTECTING THE UNINFORMED FROM CHAPTER 13

The importance of local legal culture in determining a locality's Chapter 13 filing rate raises the fundamental question of whether the Bankruptcy Code should continue to provide consumer debtors with a choice between Chapters 7 and 13. In a great many circumstances, this choice is being made for petitioners, as they are "steered" to one chapter or the other. In a culture that has traditionally emphasized consumer sovereignty, the ideal solution would be adoption of reforms to insure that most consumer bankrupts make an informed choice between chapters. I will argue subsequently, however, that such a system cannot practically be devised. If consumer choice is not possible, in my view the selection of a bankruptcy procedure should be one that informed persons would agree best serves the material interests of the petitioner concerned. I believe that in a great many circumstances where Chapter 13 is selected for a consumer debtor, this standard is not met. Though selection of Chapter 13 is sometimes in a debtor's material best interests, in this section I will argue that we will serve the best interests of the greatest number of debtors by eliminating the Chapter 13 option, thereby compelling all consumer debtors to use the Chapter 7 procedure.

The argument for repealing Chapter 13 rests on the assumption that it is not practical to alter existing bankruptcy practice so that most consumers make an informed and self-interested choice between Chapters 7 and 13. This is an assumption that is easily defended. . . .

. . . [I]t seems to me that if choice of chapter procedure is to be made for consumers, it should be based on objective material grounds rather than on moral grounds. It is not acceptable for one per-

---

son (*e.g.*, the debtor's attorney) to decide that a debtor should file under Chapter 13 because she can afford to pay debts and that is the moral thing to do, if Chapter 7 is a statutorily available procedure and would better serve the debtor's material interests. . . .

The data gathered and reported by Sullivan, Warren and Westbrook indicate that the determiners of local legal culture are not in many cases acting in accordance with the material interests of petitioners when influencing the Chapter 7/13 choice. If they were, we would not find the variance in Chapter 13 filing rates that are reported. . . .

Suppose consumer debtors were uniformly compelled to choose Chapter 7, instead of acting in accordance with the value preferences of local bankruptcy elites. Would bankruptcy proceedings better serve the material interests of consumer bankrupts as a whole than they do today? Although there are circumstances in which Chapter 13 is in a consumer debtor's material interest, there is overwhelming evidence that many debtors elect Chapter 13 contrary to their personal material interests. This evidence is the high failure rate for Chapter 13 plans. . . .

When a plan fails, the debtor usually loses the most significant material benefits of Chapter 13. The superdischarge is not available . . . . The debtor is likely to lose collateral after the plan fails, unless perchance she has paid off the debt before dismissal or conversion of the proceeding. . . . What is the point of living under the regimen of a Chapter 13 plan for a few months, if in the end benefits such as these will be denied when the proceeding is converted to a Chapter 7? . . .

In sum, the argument for repeal of Chapter 13 rests on the finding of Sullivan, Warren and Westbrook that a great many debtors electing Chapter 13, perhaps most of them, do not do so as a result of an informed and self-interested choice, but because they are steered to that alternative by local bankruptcy elite, most likely their attorney. . . . [F]or most debtors directed to Chapter 13, the election of Chapter 7 would have better served their material interests. . . . [T]he many less-than-voluntary Chapter 13s must be viewed as a cost of maintaining the Chapter 13 option, and I have argued that it is probably not practical to reduce these costs by better educating consumer debtors to make their own decisions about bankruptcy chapter. There are circumstances in which a consumer debtor can serve her material interests by electing Chapter 13, as will be discussed in depth in the next section. Nonetheless, any reasonable effort to calculate the greatest good for the greatest number of consumer bankrupts is likely to come down on the side of repeal of Chapter 13. The costs most likely exceed the benefits.

II. Is Chapter 13 Needed for the Informed Debtor?

To many, repeal of Chapter 13 will seem like an extreme response to the problem identified by Sullivan, Warren and Westbrook. Some individual debtors do make an informed and self-interested choice in favor of Chapter 13. Many will feel it is better to preserve a choice for those who inform themselves sufficiently to exercise the choice than it is to deny it for the benefit of those who for whatever reason do not. Because our society worships freedom, it may be appropriate to sacrifice the material interests of the majority in order to preserve choice for the few who can exercise it in an informed manner.

In the balance of this article, my intent is to lessen the force of this argument for preserving Chapter 13 by demonstrating that many of the principal benefits that an informed consumer debtor might seek to achieve through Chapter 13 can be substantially achieved in other ways, either outside bankruptcy or through a Chapter 7. To the extent that material benefits of a Chapter 13 election cannot otherwise be obtained, I will argue that they are benefits that, for policy reasons, either should not be available in Chapter 13 or should be available under both Chapters 7 and 13. While this is not necessarily an argument for repeal of Chapter 13 in the present circumstance, it does support repeal once desirable reforms in Chapter 7 are enacted.

The principal benefits from choosing Chapter 13 are: (1) the debtor wishes to repay some debts, for reasons of personal morality or in order to sustain continuing relations with some creditors, and Chapter 13 provides a mechanism for doing so; (2) the debtor wants to avoid the stigma of bankruptcy; (3) the debtor needs the superdischarge to avoid a burdensome liability not otherwise dischargeable; (4) the debtor cannot receive another Chapter 7 discharge because of the six-year bar, but is still eligible for a discharge in Chapter 13; (5) the debtor needs to avoid repossession of a necessary asset (other than a home) and can avoid default only by stretching out payments to secured creditors; (6) the debtor needs to cure late payments on a home mortgage while avoiding foreclosure; (7) the debtor wants to keep non-exempt property; and (8) the debtor wants to protect cosigners from execution until she can pay. . . .

Moral Desires to Repay Debt

It is a common misassumption that only Chapter 13 debtors repay unsecured debts. However, we know that reaffirmations have been a common feature of Chapter 7 practice . . . . It is not as often recognized that after discharge Chapter 7 debtors can and often do repay discharged creditors . . . .

For the debtor who wishes to repay only some creditors—probably the situation of most debtors—Chapter 7 will often be a preferable procedure to Chapter 13. There is no legal impediment preventing a Chapter 7 debtor from preferring those creditors deemed deserving of repayment, while avoiding payment to other creditors. . . .

Avoiding the Stigma of Bankruptcy

It is sometimes argued that a debtor who completes a Chapter 13 plan and receives a discharge is less stigmatized than a debtor who receives a Chapter 7 discharge. That may be true in some localities, and it may be a reason to retain Chapter 13. But it is unlikely that the difference in stigma is large, and in most communities it is probably non-existent. . . .

The Superdischarge

There is no doubt that the availability of the superdischarge is a sensible reason for some debtors to choose Chapter 13 under the current statutory scheme. . . .

Although the superdischarge is a distinctive feature of Chapter 13, its existence may not represent good policy. Commentators usually state that the legislative purpose in adopting the superdischarge was to provide an incentive for debtors to elect Chapter 13. . . . What is lacking in this justification of the superdischarge, however, is any rationale for sacrificing the interest of creditors holding claims that would be excepted from a Chapter 7 discharge. . . .

I suspect that Congress chose the superdischarge as a method for providing an incentive to elect Chapter 13, because it believed that many of the exceptions to discharge were not proper ones in any event. . . . But this rationale for the superdischarge suggests that Congress should also eliminate the questionable exceptions from a Chapter 7 discharge. . . .

Relief from the Six-Year Bar

. . . The more substantial question is whether Chapter 13 should provide the only avenue for relief from the six-year bar. The rationale for the six-year bar is to retard bankruptcy abuse—to make it more difficult for the debtor to repeatedly run up debts in anticipation of discharging them in bankruptcy. The data collected by Sullivan, Warren and Westbrook raises questions about whether this kind of debtor behavior occurs frequently enough to justify the six-year bar, which deprives debtors of a Chapter 7 discharge even in situations of real hardship. If the bar is not to be repealed entirely, at least a case can be made for a hardship discharge within Chapter 7 for debtors under the six-year bar. . . .

Stretching Out Secured Creditors

Under Chapter 7, the only way to prevent foreclosure of property subject to a security interest in default, absent the consent of the creditor to a revised payment plan, is to redeem the collateral by paying the secured creditor the value of the property in a lump sum. Debtors in financial distress typically have difficulty raising substantial amounts of cash for this purpose. Consequently, an informed debtor might choose Chapter 13, which permits retention of collateral . . . . In effect, it is possible to redeem collateral by installments in Chapter 13.

There is no complete substitute for this use of Chapter 13. Collateral frequently has its highest use-value in the hands of the consumer rather than some other possessor. . . . In the absence of regulation, a secured creditor would have an incentive to expropriate this extra use-value by threatening foreclosure unless the consumer paid the creditor in excess of the benefits of repossession. . . .

What is hard to justify is restricting the right to redeem by installments to debtors in Chapter 13. Under the present scheme, if a debtor fails to choose Chapter 13, a secured creditor in effect receives a windfall, by being able to exploit the lost value phenomenon in its subsequent negotiations with the debtor about redemption payments. . . .

My conclusion with respect to stretching out payments to secured creditors is very similar to my analysis with respect to the superdischarge. The right to redeem by installments is indisputably a reason for an informed debtor to select Chapter 13. But either this benefit of Chapter 13 should not be available at all or it should be available to both Chapter 7 and Chapter 13 debtors. If either of these policy alternatives were adopted, then it would not matter if Chapter 13 were repealed.

Curing Home Mortgage Defaults

. . . The provisions on home mortgage arrearages are very similar to the provisions discussed above permitting a Chapter 13 debtor to stretch out payments to redeem collateral. The policy analysis is also similar. If the purpose of treating the Chapter 13 debtor specially with regard to home mortgage arrearages is to provide incentives to file Chapter 13, it is difficult to justify sacrificing the rights of some creditors (mortgagees), for the benefit of others who will collect more under Chapter 13. If on the other hand, Congress believes that debtors should be able to forestall foreclosure while making up arrearages over time, then it is difficult to justify granting a windfall to the real estate creditor where Chapter 7 is chosen. Any disincentive to election of Chapter 7 should take some other form.

Preserving Non-Exempt Property

The ability to keep non-exempt property has traditionally been cited as a primary reason why an informed debtor might choose Chapter 13. Under Chapter 13, if a debtor completes a plan, unpaid debts are discharged, freeing unencumbered, non-exempt property from the claims of past creditors. Under Chapter 7, on the other hand, unencumbered, non-exempt property is an asset for the benefit of unsecured creditors. . . .

. . . In some circumstances, therefore, Chapter 13 is a desirable refuge for debtors with property of the type under consideration . . . . But a better solution than continuation of Chapter 13 would be amendment of the exemption laws to insure that all debtors, including those choosing Chapter 7, could protect such property from execution.

Protecting Cosigners

A creditor can be restrained from proceeding against a cosigner of the debt if a Chapter 13 plan provides for full payment to the creditor concerned. Since cosigners are commonly friends, relatives, co-workers or even employers—all persons with whom the debtor desires to maintain relationships—this ability to forestall action against the cosigner provides a strong incentive for some debtors to elect Chapter 13. No equivalent provision exists for Chapter 7 debtors. . . .

In practice, even without the formal authority to restrain action against co-debtors, a Chapter 7 debtor will frequently be able to achieve that result. . . . [S]he can offer the creditor with rights against a cosigner a reaffirmation, conditioned on agreement to postpone collection against the cosigner. . . .

In those instances in which the cosigner can only be protected in Chapter 13, is this a feature of Chapter 13 whose uniqueness to that procedure can be justified on policy grounds and thus serve as a rationale for maintaining that procedure? My analysis here is similar to that advanced with respect to stretching out payments to secured creditors. . . . [I]f the conclusion is that . . . protection should be available to the debtor, it is difficult to justify limiting protection to debtors who devise a confirmable Chapter 13 plan promising full payment to the creditor concerned and typically at least some payment to other creditors. . . . At a minimum, Chapter 7 should be amended to restrain creditors from proceeding against cosigners in consumer cases if they have been offered reasonable reaffirmation agreements by the debtor. But if that happened, there would be no need to maintain Chapter 13 in order to provide the informed debtor an opportunity to restrain action against cosigners.

Conclusion

I have attempted to make the case that even if debtors all made informed choices between Chapters 7 and 13, Chapter 13 should be repealed. I have done so by trying to show that no legitimate interest of debtors would be sacrificed by such action. To be sure, there are special benefits debtors can achieve through resort to Chapter 13. Some of these, I have argued, can be achieved or mostly achieved in other ways. As to the others, my analysis has turned on whether the benefits are to provide debtors with an incentive to choose Chapter 13 or whether they are viewed as needed debtor protections in the collection process. Where the reason is the first of these alternatives, I have argued that there is little justification for sacrificing the interests of one creditor for the benefit of others. If there are to be special rewards for choosing Chapter 13, they ought to be provided by creditors who benefit from that choice, or from the general purse. Alternatively, where the benefits to the debtor from choosing Chapter 13 are needed debtor protections, I have argued that mostly they are protections that should be available in Chapter 7 as well as Chapter 13. . . .

We live in a second or third best world. Although sound arguments may exist for amending Chapter 7 to provide greater debtor protections, in the absence of such amendment a case can be made for retaining Chapter 13 so that debtors have at least one avenue of access to desirable debtor protections. Before jumping to that conclusion, however, account has to be taken of the startling data collected by Sullivan, Warren and Westbrook. This data supports the inference that many, probably most, debtors electing Chapter 13 do not do so as a result of an informed and self-interested choice, but rather because they are led to that alternative by local bankruptcy elite. Moreover, there is reason to believe that most of these debtors have elected Chapter 13 even though election of Chapter 7 would have better served their material interests. These less-than-voluntary Chapter 13s must be viewed as a cost of maintaining the Chapter 13 option. Any reasonable utilitarian calculus emphasizing the greatest good for the greatest number of debtors is likely to come down on the side of repeal.

The 1994 Bankruptcy Reform Act created a National Bankruptcy Review Commission. Unsurprisingly, the Commission proved to be a lightning rod for consumer bankruptcy reform proposals. In particular, the consumer credit industry vigorously pushed their idea that supposed "can-pay" debtors—those with some projected disposable future income—should be barred from chapter 7. In the jargon used, a "means test" should be invoked to screen debtors—those with the "means" to repay creditors should not be allowed into the hallowed halls of chapter 7. While the credit industry stopped short of advocating a compulsory chapter 13, their proposal would leave debtors with "means" the options of forgoing bankruptcy relief altogether or "voluntarily" filing for chapter 13 relief.

In the following three selections, the Commission debate is put on the table. First is an excerpt from the Commission Report itself, including the bulk of the Commission's Recommendations. The Commission voted against means testing and recommended instead a series of targeted reforms designed to improve the consumer bankruptcy system. Professor Elizabeth Warren, who served as the very able Reporter for the Commission, then explains the Commission's conclusions and recommendations in her article *A Principled Approach to Consumer Bankruptcy*. She also addresses why the Commission majority did not adopt means testing.

The opposition is given the floor next. The vigorous dissent to the Commission Report written by Judge Edith Jones and James Shepard makes a spirited case for means testing. Judge Jones followed up her dissent in an article coauthored with Professor Todd Zywicki, *It's Time for Means-Testing*, 1999 BYU L. Rev. 177.

Following the Commission Dissent is an article by economist Michelle White, *Why it Pays to File for Bankruptcy: A Critical Look at the Incentives Under U.S. Personal Bankruptcy Law and a Proposal for Change*. Professor White demonstrates how our legal system contains various financial incentives for individuals to file personal bankruptcy. She focuses particularly on the role of property exemptions. White also shows how debtors could adopt specific strategies that would make filing bankruptcy even more financially beneficial to them. If debtors nationwide were to utilize the tactics identified, more than half could profit from filing. White suggests as a solution a unified personal bankruptcy chapter which requires debtors to attempt repayment out of both current assets and future income, with appropriate exemptions levels in place.

Means testing may sound like a good idea (or not) in theory. But how would a means test play out in the real world? Are there a significant number of "can pay " debtors abusing the system? Those are the questions addressed by Professors Marianne Culhane and Michaela White in *Taking the New Consumer Bankruptcy Model for a Test Drive: Means-Testing Real Chapter 7 Debtors*. Culhane and White run the numbers on a substantial database of real debtors assuming one of the proposed "means testing" congressional bills was in place. Their findings suggest that "abuse" in the form of can-pay debtors is occurring in only about 3% of the cases. Furthermore, Professors Culhane and White report that means-testing would result in only marginal amounts being repaid to creditors on a macroeconomic basis—perhaps as little as a tenth of what credit industry advocates assert. If Culhane and White are correct in their findings, the case for means-testing loses much of its appeal.

NATIONAL BANKRUPTCY REVIEW COMMISSION
FINAL REPORT
BANKRUPTCY: THE NEXT TWENTY YEARS
(October 20, 1997)

CHAPTER 1: CONSUMER BANKRUPTCY

INTRODUCTION

. . . Consumer bankruptcy has become part of America's economic landscape. Once regarded as an unlikely legal alternative chosen by only a few desperate families, bankruptcy had become a refuge for one in every 96 American families . . . .

As bankruptcy filings increase, creditors justifiably worry whether a promise to repay has any meaning, while consumer advocates express concern that the financial distress of more than a million American families each year foreshadows a larger economic problem. The inherent conflict between the twin goals of bankruptcy—appropriate relief for those in trouble and equitable treatment for their creditors—ensures that it always will be an area of contention. To deal with financial loss, the bankruptcy system necessarily embraces competing interests. Recommendations fully endorsed by either debtors or by creditors would not maintain the balance essential to any consumer bankruptcy system. Bankruptcy is a system born of conflict and competing values. To function well, it must remain unpopular and controversial. . . .

The Proposals

. . . The recommendations embrace three goals:

- Enhancing integrity and fairness in the system
- Reducing abuse by both debtors and creditors
- Increasing operational efficiency

Notwithstanding the vigorous debates, multiple proposals and votes, the Commission's final report reflects remarkably consistent positions on a significant number of issues. The Commission almost without dissent supported the principle of uniform federal exemptions to end debtor abuse made possible by unlimited exemptions and to provide minimal exemptions for all debtors. . . . Among the recommendations with broad Commission support:

Restrictions on serial filings
Restrictions on reaffirmation of unsecured debt
Random audits of bankruptcy schedules
A statutory standard for valuation of property
A national filing system
Clearer rules for the treatment of secured debt following a Chapter 7
In rem orders to stop abusive filings
Credit rehabilitation programs to increase Chapter 13 filings
Increased plan completion with secured debt payments in Chapter 13
Specified payments to unsecured creditors in Chapter 13 plans
Automatic review and modification of Chapter 13 plans
Uniform treatment of attorneys' fees
Clarified rules governing the discharge of credit card debt
Strengthened nondischargeability of family support obligations
Amplified rules for objections to discharge
Limitations on application of vicarious liability . . .

The Rise in Bankruptcy Filings

The most visible and disturbing fact about consumer bankruptcy has been the extraordinary increase in filings in less than two decades. Since 1980, the rate of consumer bankruptcy filings has risen nearly three-fold. . . .

Who is "at fault" for the rise in consumer bankruptcies? The Commission struggled with this question but never reached a resolution. . . . [T]he Commission can make no final pronouncement on why more families have financial problems that lead to more bankruptcy filings. It can only catalogue the surveys for Congress and note the enduring correlation between consumer debt and consumer bankruptcy.

In considering a variety of recommendations, however, the Commission tried to develop an appreciation for why bankruptcy filings have increased. If the higher number of consumer bankruptcy filings reflects an influx of debtors not in financial distress, then the system has lost its way by serving those who would take advantage of their creditors and, correspondingly, of everyone who pays their bills. But the statistical evidence suggests that consumers who file for bankruptcy today, as a group, are experiencing a financial crisis similar to the crisis faced by families when filing rates were only a fraction of their present levels.

In 1981, two years after the 1978 Bankruptcy Code went into effect, Americans who filed for bankruptcy listed in their schedules short-term, nonmortgage debts that were, on average, slightly more than twice their annual income. . . . For a family making $26,000 a year, average short-term debts amounted to more than $56,000, leaving an impossible choice between current expenses and interest payments on outstanding loans. If this family did not file for bankruptcy or reach some agreement with creditors, it simply would owe more the next day.

The statistics suggest that the picture has not changed appreciably since the early 1980s. Families filing for bankruptcy in 1997 apparently have incomes, assets, and debts little different from those of their counterparts nearly two decades earlier when bankruptcy filing rates were far less alarming. The sharp rise in bankruptcies, these data suggest, cannot be attributed primarily to a group of "well-off" debtors who have decided that filing bankruptcy is somehow easier than paying the monthly bills. While some debtors in bankruptcy no doubt file for reasons that are illegitimate, most families come to the bankruptcy courts as they have for many years—seeking relief from debts they have virtually no hope of repaying.

Measured by bankruptcy filings, nearly four times as many American families are in serious financial trouble today as at the beginning of the last decade. Despite low unemployment, low inflation, low mortgage rates, and a long period of economic expansion, a growing number of American families no longer can make it from one paycheck to the next. . . .

Why are so many Americans in financial trouble? The question haunts the economic prosperity of the 1990s. . . .

Americans in the 1990s have unprecedented access to consumer credit, and the American economy has benefitted from that access. . . . Greater access to credit has improved the quality of life for millions of American families. But the benefits of credit are not free. Between 1977 and 1997, consumer debt has grown nearly 700%. For generations, Americans have experienced divorces, illnesses and uninsured medical costs, and job layoffs. However, never before have so many families faced these setbacks with so much consumer debt. The ordinary and not-so-ordinary troubles that families weathered a generation ago can become unmanageable for a family that already has committed several paychecks to meet monthly bills. . . .

. . . After a comprehensive analysis, the Congressional Budget Office told Congress that "non-business bankruptcy filings move with measures of household indebtedness." In another detailed statistical study, economists Jagdeep Bhandari and Lawrence Weiss reached a similar conclusion: "Our evidence indicates that the increase in the number of bankruptcy filings is primarily due to the increased level of debt as a percentage of income." Economist Lawrence Ausubel, focusing particularly on credit card debt, noted that the rate of consumer bankruptcies is "astonishingly highly correlated with the rise in credit card defaults." These studies offer a reminder that talking about the rise in consumer bankruptcy filings without talking about the rise in consumer credit probably misses the point. Bankruptcy is largely a function of debt.

Why Bankruptcy?

Although the correlation between debt and consumer bankruptcy is clear, in some sense it still begs the real question: why are so many families taking on so much debt and filing for bankruptcy? Bankruptcy and debt may be related, but that does not explain why some families fail and others do not. . . . It is unlikely, however, that any one explanation will ever capture the variety of reasons that families fail.

The research presented to the Commission from the consumer credit industry concluded that "social factors," rather than a rise in consumer debt, have caused the sharp increase in consumer bankruptcy filings. The study, funded by Visa, USA, said, "Such factors include changes in the bankruptcy laws, the reduced stigma associated with filing for personal bankruptcy and broader advertising of legal assistance with bankruptcy filings." A chief analyst at the Congressional Budget Office reviewed the Visa study and other analyses submitted to the Commission [and] conclude[d]: "Visa's conclusion about the importance of social factors [on the bankruptcy filing rate] is unfounded."

A number of factors may influence the decision to file bankruptcy, and changing attitudes undoubtedly affect a family's decision to seek legal help in the face of financial distress. As more families amass overwhelming debts, attitudes toward bankruptcy well may change. . . . But the empirical studies seem to indicate that the sharp rises in consumer bankruptcy—27% last year alone—may be more a function of a changing debt picture than of a sudden willingness to take advantage of the bankruptcy system.

Free Market Solutions

Independent economists have been almost uniform in their conclusions that changes to the bankruptcy laws by themselves do little to change the overall picture of debt and credit industry losses. For example, Ian Domowitz and Elie Tamer of Northwestern University examined nearly 100 years of bankruptcy filings. They concluded that changes in the law to restrict access to consumer bankruptcy would have no substantial effect on filings. In separate assessments of the data, Professors Domowitz and Eovaldi, Professors Bhandari and Weiss, and a government analyst also conclude that changes in the bankruptcy laws have had little effect on consumer bankruptcy filing rates.

While economists generally agree that any statutory change is unlikely to have a significant effect on family decisions to file for bankruptcy, some have cautioned that tightening the bankruptcy laws could have an unanticipated effect: Two research economists have warned that new restrictions could encourage more lending to customers who are not creditworthy. That, in turn, could increase the number of defaults generally with the potential for more bankruptcies. . . .

Changes in credit practices may have more powerful effects. The private market can have a significant influence on debt, default and, for some, bankruptcy. George Salem, a securities analyst with an investment research firm, testified . . . that changes in underwriting standards, rather than changes in law, will address the problem more effectively. Other industry analysts agree that the better use of credit scoring would cut both delinquencies and bankruptcies. One industry consulting firm, August, Fair, Isaac & Co., released a new bankruptcy predictor that it says can eliminate 54% of bankruptcies by eliminating potential nonpayers from the bottom 10% of credit card holders. The solution to the bankruptcy problem, say some market analysts, lies within the credit industry—not in federal regulation. . . .

Other possible private market solutions, such as consumer financial counseling, are often underwritten by the credit industry as an alternative to deal with family finances that are out of control. Creditors help support such agencies financially as they provide both debt restructuring and credit education for their clients without the need for bankruptcy. Credit counseling cannot solve all problems, but it is an important part of the solution for debt problems and debt collection problems without involving the courts.

Alternative Approaches

The Commission received a series of submissions from the credit industry advocating the general proposition that the bankruptcy system should be dramatically changed to require debtor-by-debtor scrutiny before permitting debtors to file for Chapter 7. The consumer bankruptcy debates never lacked a discussion of whether debtors are receiving "more relief than they need," although the cost and implementation of a "means testing" system were not developed in specific detail. These features are now detailed in the "means test" legislation recently proposed . . . .

A study funded by the credit industry supports the contention that substantial numbers of debtors who file for bankruptcy could repay some of their debts. The Purdue Study, conducted by Dr. Michael Staten, was presented repeatedly to the Commission in support of the credit industry's call for a means test for consumer bankruptcy. The study has been criticized by researchers, and the General Accounting Office is completing an audit of the data presented. A chief analyst of the Congressional Budget Office reviewed the Staten study, questioning the reliability of its findings and characterizing the study as "misleading." He concluded that the defects in the study may "contribute to an overstatement of [the debtors'] capacity to repay."

Some witnesses concluded that using a means test to establish Chapter 7 eligibility would fall hardest on families already financially pressed past the breaking point, with little provable benefit. Others expressed their concern that, with a completion rate of only 32% for *voluntary* Chapter 13 plans today, forcing unwilling debtors into Chapter 13 would only burden the system, decreasing both the overall repayment to creditors and the successful rehabilitation of debtors. . . . In a time of increasing strain on judicial resources, questions also have arisen about the number of judges, clerks, and other staff needed to administer a means test to hundreds of thousands of debtors annually. The credit industry has sought means testing consistently for at least 30 years, but Congress has consistently refused to change the basic structure of the consumer bankruptcy laws.

There is no dispute on one point: bankruptcy should be used only by the needy and not by others. The bankruptcy laws should *never* invite abuse. When Congress charged the Commission with its duties, it cautioned that there was no evidence that the bankruptcy system needed radical reform. It characterized the system as "generally satisfactory," and directed the Commission to review, improve and update the Code "in ways which do not disturb the fundamental tenets and balance of current law." The Commission conducted an intensive review of consumer bankruptcy that resulted in a full set of recommendations, but the proposals contemplate no change in the basic structure of consumer bankruptcy. Access to Chapter 7 and to Chapter 13, the central feature of the consumer bankruptcy system for nearly 60 years, should be preserved.

. . .

RECOMMENDATIONS TO CONGRESS

Chapter 1: Consumer Bankruptcy—System Administration

1.1.1 *National Filing System*
A national filing system should be established and maintained that would identify bankruptcy filings using social security numbers or other unique identifying numbers.

1.1.2 *Heightened Requirements for Accurate Information*
The Bankruptcy Code should direct trustees to perform random audits of debtors' schedules to verify the accuracy of the information listed. Cases would be selected for audit according to guidelines developed by the Executive Office for United States Trustees.

1.1.3 *False Claims*
Courts should be authorized to order creditors who file and fail to correct materially false claims in bankruptcy to pay costs and the debtors' attorneys' fees involved in correcting the claim. If a creditor knowingly filed a false claim, the court could impose appropriate additional sanctions.

1.1.4 *Rule 9011*
The Commission endorses the amended Rule 9011 of the Federal Rules of Bankruptcy Procedure, to become effective on December 1, 1997, which will make an attorney's presentation to the court of any petition, pleading, written motion, or other paper a certification that the attorney made a reasonable inquiry into the accuracy of that information, and thus will help ensure that attorneys take responsibility for the information that they and their clients provide.

1.1.5 *Financial Education*
All debtors in both Chapter 7 and in Chapter 13 should have the opportunity to participate in a financial education program.

Chapter 1: Consumer Bankruptcy—Property Exemptions . . .

[*The recommendations regarding property exemptions are found in Chapter 11—Ed.*]

Chapter 1: Consumer Bankruptcy— Reaffirmation Agreements and the Treatment of Secured Debt

1.3.1 11 U.S.C. § 524(c) should be amended to provide that a reaffirmation agreement is permitted, with court approval, only if the amount of the debt that the debtor seeks to reaffirm does not exceed the allowed secured claim, the lien is not avoidable under the provisions of title 11, no attorney fees, costs, or expenses have been added to the principal amount of the debt to be reaffirmed, the motion for approval of the agreement is accompanied by underlying contractual documents and all related security agreements or liens, together with evidence of their perfection, the debtor has provided all information requested in the motion for approval of the agreement, and the agreement conforms with all other requirements of subsection (c).

Section 524(d) should be amended to delineate the circumstances under which a hearing is not required as a prerequisite to a court approving an agreement of the kind specified in section 524(c): a hearing will not be required when the debtor was represented by counsel in negotiations on the agreement and the debtor's attorney has signed the affidavit as provided in section 524(c), and a party in interest has not requested a judicial valuation of the collateral that is the subject of the agreement. If one or more of the foregoing requirements is not met, or in the court's discretion, the court shall conduct a hearing to determine whether an agreement that meets all of the requirements of subsection (c) should be approved. Court approval of an agreement signifies that the court has determined that the agreement is in the best interest of the debtor and the debtor's dependents and does not impose undue hardship on the debtor and the debtor's dependents in light of the debtor's income and expenses.

The Commission recommends that the Advisory Committee on Bankruptcy Rules of the Judicial Conference prescribe a form motion for approval of reaffirmation agreements that contains information enabling the court and the parties to determine the propriety of the agreement. Approval of the motion would not entail a separate order of the court.

1.3.2 An additional subsection should be added to section 524 to provide that the court shall grant judgment in favor of an individual who has received a discharge under section 727, 1141, 1228, or 1328 of this title for costs and attorneys fees, plus treble damages, from a creditor who threatens, files suit, or otherwise seeks to collect any debt that was discharged in bankruptcy and was not the subject of an agreement in accordance with subsections (c) and (d) of section 524.

1.3.3 *No Ride-Through*

Section 521(2) should be amended to clarify that a debtor with consumer debts that are secured, as determined by the provisions of title 11, by property of the estate must redeem the property or obtain court approval of an agreement under section 524(c) of title 11 in order to retain the property postdischarge, except for a security interest in real or personal property that is the debtor's principal residence.

1.3.4 *Security Interests in Household Goods*
Household Goods Worth Less Than $500

Section 522(f) should provide that a creditor claiming a purchase money security interest in exempt property held for personal or household use of the debtor or a dependent of the debtor in household furnishings, wearing apparel, appliances, books, animals, crops, musical instruments, jewelry, implements, professional books, tools of the trade or professionally prescribed health aids for the debtor or a member of the debtor's household must petition the bankruptcy court for continued recognition of the security interest. The court shall hold a hearing to value each item covered by the creditor's petition. If the value of the item is less than $500, the petition shall not be granted; if the value is $500 or greater, the security interest would be recognized and treated as a secured loan in Chapter 7 or Chapter 13.

1.3.5 *Characterization of Rent-to-Own Transactions*

Consumer rent-to-own transactions should be characterized in bankruptcy as installment sales contracts.

Chapter 1: Consumer Bankruptcy—
Discharge, Exceptions to Discharge and Objections to Discharge

1.4.1 *Credit Card Debt*

Except for credit card debts that are excepted from discharge under section 523(a)(2)(B) (for materially false written statements respecting the debtor's financial condition) and section 523(a)(14), (debts incurred to pay nondischargeable taxes to the United States), debts incurred on a credit card issued to the debtor that did not exceed the debtor's credit limit should be dischargeable unless they were incurred within 30 days before the order for relief under title 11.

1.4.2 *Debts Incurred to Pay Nondischargeable Federal Tax Obligations*

Section 523(a)(14) should remain unchanged to except from discharge debts incurred for federal taxes that would be nondischargeable under section 523(a)(1).

1.4.3 *Criminal Restitution Orders*
Section 523(a)(13) should be expanded to apply to all criminal restitution orders.

1.4.4 *Family Support Obligations*
Sections 523(a)(5), (a)(15), and (a)(18) should be combined. The revised 523(a)(5) should provide that all debts actually in the nature of support, whether they have been denominated in a prior court order as alimony, maintenance, support, property settlements, or otherwise, are nondischargeable. In addition, debts owed under state law to a state or municipality in the nature of support would be nondischargeable in all chapters.

1.4.5 *Dischargeability of Student Loans*
Section 523(a)(8) should be repealed.

1.4.6 *Issue Preclusive Effect of True Defaults*
For complaints to establish nondischargeability on grounds set forth in section 523(c), the Bankruptcy Code should clarify that issues that were not actually litigated and necessary to a prior judgment shall not be given preclusive effect.

1.4.7 *Vicarious Liability*
Section 523(c) should be amended such that intentional action by a wrongdoer who is not the debtor cannot be imputed to the debtor.

1.4.8 *Effect of Lack of Notice on Time to Bring Objection to Discharge*
Creditors that did not receive notice of a bankruptcy should get an extension of time to file an objection to or seek revocation of a discharge.

1.4.9 *Settlement and Dismissal of Objections to Discharge*
Section 727 should be amended to provide that (a) any complaint objecting to discharge may be dismissed on motion of the plaintiff only after giving notice to the United States trustee, the case trustee and all creditors entitled to notice, advising them of an opportunity to substitute as plaintiff in the action; (b) any motion to dismiss a complaint objecting to discharge must be accompanied by an affidavit of the moving party disclosing all consideration given or promised to be given by the debtor in connection with dismissal of the complaint; and (c) if the debtor has given or promised to give consideration in connection with dismissal of the complaint, the complaint may not be dismissed unless the consideration benefits the estate generally.

Chapter 1: Consumer Bankruptcy—
Chapter 13 Repayment Plans

1.5.1 *Home Mortgages*
A Chapter 13 plan could not modify obligations on first mortgages and refinanced first mortgages, except to the extent currently permitted by the Bankruptcy Code. Section 1322(b)(2) should be amended to provide that the rights of a holder of a claim secured only by a junior security interest in real property that is the debtor's principal residence may not be modified to reduce the secured claim to less than the appraised value of the property at the time the security interest was made.

1.5.2 *Valuation of Collateral*
A creditor's secured claim in personal property should be determined by the property's wholesale price.

A creditor's secured claim in real property should be determined by the property's fair market value, minus hypothetical costs of sale.

1.5.3 Payments on secured debts that are subject to modification should be spread over the life of the plan, according to fixed criteria for interest rates.

1.5.4 *Unsecured Debt*

Payments on unsecured debt should be determined by guidelines based on a graduated percentage of the debtor's income, subject to upward adjustment to meet the section 1325(a)(4) requirement that creditors receive at least the present value of whatever they would have received in a Chapter 7. The trustee or an unsecured creditor should be authorized to file an objection to any plan that deviates from the guidelines, and a court would determine whether the deviation was appropriate in light of all the circumstances.

1.5.5 *Consequences of Incomplete Payment Plans*

The Bankruptcy Code should provide that a case under Chapter 13 that otherwise meets the standards for dismissal shall be converted to Chapter 7 after notice and a hearing unless a party in interest objects on the basis that the debtor had been granted a discharge in a Chapter 7 case commenced within six years of the date on which the conversion would take place, in which case the Chapter 13 case will be dismissed. In addition, the debtor may object to conversion without grounds, in which case the Chapter 13 case will be dismissed. The standards for modification, dismissal, and discharge in Chapter 13 would not otherwise change.

Section 362 should be amended to provide that the filing of a petition by an individual does not operate as a stay if the individual has filed two or more petitions for relief under title 11 within six years of filing the instant petition for relief and if the individual has been a debtor in a bankruptcy case within 180 days prior to the instant petition for relief. On the request of the debtor, after notice and a hearing, the court may impose a stay for cause shown, subject to such conditions and modifications as the court may impose.

1.5.6 *In Rem Orders*

Section 362 should be amended to provide that the filing of a petition by an individual does not operate as a stay with respect to property of the estate transferred by that individual to another individual who was a debtor under title 11 within 180 days of the filing of the instant petition, unless the court grants a stay with respect to such property after notice and a hearing on request of the debtor.

After notice and a hearing, a bankruptcy court should be empowered to issue *in rem* orders barring the application of a future automatic stay to identified property of the estate for a period of up to six years when a party could show that the debtor had transferred such real property or leasehold interests or fractional shares of property or leasehold interests to avoid creditor foreclosure or eviction. A subsequent owner of the property or tenant of the leasehold who files for bankruptcy (or the same owner or holder in a subsequent filing) should be permitted to petition the bankruptcy court for the imposition of a stay to protect property of the estate, which the court would be required to grant to protect innocent parties who were not a part of a scheme to transfer the property to hinder foreclosure or eviction.

1.5.7 *Retention of the "Superdischarge"*

Congress should retain 11 U.S.C. § 1328(a), which permits a debtor who completes all payments under the plan to discharge all debts provided for by the plan or disallowed under section 502 of title 11 except for those listed in section 1328(a)(1) - (3).

1.5.8 Debtors who choose Chapter 13 repayment plans should have their bankruptcy filings reported differently from those who do not. Debtors who complete voluntary debtor education programs should have that fact noted on their credit reports.

1.5.9 Trustees should be encouraged to establish credit rehabilitation programs to help provide better, cheaper access to credit for those who participate in repayment plans.

Elizabeth Warren
A Principled Approach to Consumer Bankruptcy
71 AM. BANKR. L.J. 483 (1997)[*]

III. MAKING THE SYSTEM BETTER: THE NRBC PROPOSALS . . .

A. THE GOALS: MEET THE DEBTOR'S NEEDS AND DISCOURAGE ABUSE

There is no need to reiterate the familiar discussion ground for consumer bankruptcy reform: encourage Chapter 13s, cut fraud and abuse, increase equality among creditors, and offer the kind of "fresh start" Congress has supported since at least 1898 for families in financial trouble. . . .

During the course of the Working Group sessions, the dual nature of consumer bankruptcy became increasingly clear. Americans need a safety valve to deal with the financial consequences of the misfortunes they may encounter. They need a way to declare a halt to creditor collection actions when they have no reasonable possibility of repaying. They need the chance to remain productive members of society, not driven underground or into joblessness by unpayable debt. But Americans are rightly suspicious of those who may avail themselves of help too quickly, those who may take advantage of a system of debt forgiveness when a little self-sacrifice would suffice. . . .

. . . [T]he role of debtor abuse in shaping the national dialogue over consumer bankruptcy should not be overlooked. . . . The million-mark on bankruptcy filings raised warning flags around the country. . . .

Academicians have an obligation to be clear on one point: there are no data showing that the consumer bankruptcy system is shot through with abuse. Indeed, most data, including the consumer credit industry's own studies, show that the system is generally used by American families in desperate financial circumstances. Without bankruptcy, most of the debtors would be hopelessly trapped with debts on which they could never even pay the annual interest; they would face a future of increasing debt loads until they died.

While the level of abuse may be low, it is nonetheless important to recognize that public confidence is undermined . . . . Regardless of its accuracy, when the idea takes hold that some people are taking bankruptcy as an easy out for large, but not impossible, debt loads, one event is certain: the system itself will be headed for fundamental change.

Anyone who is serious about making consumer bankruptcy a shelter for families in real financial trouble must understand that the laws will provide sanctuary only if the public believes the system is used only by those who really need it. Whether abuse is rare or widespread, it imposes a cost on the consumer bankruptcy system. One task of the Commission was to make recommendations to deal effectively with abuse. By doing so, the Commission could strengthen a system that would be called on to deal with increasing financial failure among American families, and it could serve to increase public confidence that the system would function as it should. . . .

B. The NRBC Approach: Exemptions, Reaffirmations, Refilings

The challenge facing the Commission was how to make certain that the consumer bankruptcy system is sound in its basic structure. . . . The primary question facing the Commission was how could the system accommodate different family financial problems while it provided that an honest person struggling for financial survival could find debt relief? The Commission also needed to satisfy itself that public confidence was well-placed in the consumer bankruptcy system, ensuring that abuse is the rare exception rather than an ordinary occurrence among clever debtors.

There were two functional approaches available to accomplish this task: reduce some options available to debtors to make the system less susceptible to abuse and easier to use without detailed guidance, or add another layer of complexity by directly means testing each debtor to see if bankruptcy is an appropriate remedy. The credit industry strongly supported the second alternative; the Commission adopted the first.

The credit industry approach seemed easily defensible. Like many reform proposals, it stated its vision of the problem—that too many people are using the system who do not need it—and it argued for reform based on adding another layer of rules, review, supervision, verification, and bureaucracy overtly aimed at pressing people into Chapter 13 or out of the system altogether. . . . The credit industry approach had the advantage of "sound-bite." . . .

. . . The Commission took the much harder path to reform. It took the one, however, that was more likely to produce long-term success as measured by reducing strategic uses of bankruptcy without increasing the burden on debtors who barely survive the current system.

1. Exemptions

The floor-and-ceiling approach of the newly-proposed uniform federal exemptions illustrates this point. The exemption proposal follows the principle of maintaining protection for low-end debtors while squeezing high-end debtors. It would curtail bankruptcy relief for high-end debtors because it would take away the bankruptcy benefits of moving to a state with unlimited exemptions or converting assets from nonexempt to exempt on the eve of bankruptcy. . . .

At the same time the Commission's exemption proposal would reign in high-end debtors, it would extend protection for debtors at the very bottom of the economic scale by eliminating the unrealistically low exemptions of some states. . . .

2. Reaffirmations

The proposal to restrict reaffirmations illustrates the same principle, although somewhat more subtly. Proposals to limit access to reaffirmations have been hotly contested by creditors who profit from such arrangements with their debtors. Creditors testified repeatedly at Commission meetings that reaffirmations were a great deal for "their" debtors. . . .

Many reaffirmation "deals" make little financial sense, however. . . .

Notwithstanding the economic irrationality of many reaffirmation agreements, more than forty percent of the debtors have been willing to sign on. If the "deals" are not in the debtor's best financial interest, it is fair to infer that well-advised debtors avoid them. . . . Sophisticated debtors and debtors with strong, careful lawyers are least likely to sign reaffirmation agreements that would give so little to the debtors.

But some high-end debtors reaffirm debts as part of a sophisticated plan to "work the system." Debtors with adequate resources to commit a portion of their future income to debt repayment can pick a few creditors to receive special treatment, thereby ameliorating any negative consequences from bankruptcy. . . .

By recommending a ban on all unsecured reaffirmations, the Commission simplifies the consumer bankruptcy system: no more filed reaffirmation agreements, attorney affidavits, court review, creditor contacts, statements of intention, and hallway negotiations for some debts. A whole bureau-cratic morass now affecting hundreds of thousands of debtors would disappear from the consumer bankruptcy system. For secured debt the rules would be clearly spelled out: a debtor could reaffirm the debt only up to the value of the collateral. . . .

But the principal impact of the reaffirmation recommendation would be its effect on two different kinds of debtors. First, the consumer bankruptcy system would give better protection for the debtors who need help. The debtors who have little or no legal guidance as they run the gauntlet of demands for debt reaffirmation would see a significant change. Those low-end debtors who currently leave bankruptcy having reaffirmed debts equal to more than half their annual income would not face these post-bankruptcy burdens. Discharged debt would remain discharged, whether or not the debtor had a good lawyer who took the time to give careful advice. . . . The fresh start would not be reserved for sophisticated debtors with more elaborate legal advice.

At the same time, the reaffirmation recommendation would reduce the strong advantage of people who currently have the resources to "work the system." . . .

3. Refilings

The Commission's recommendation to place a restriction on refiling for Chapter 13 follows the same principle of trying to provide adequate help for struggling debtors while trying to cut off strategic maneuvering by more sophisticated debtors. . . .

IV. REJECTION OF THE CREDIT INDUSTRY'S MEANS TEST

Rather than putting much effort into responding to the Working Group on Consumer Bankruptcy's specific proposals, the credit industry focused its energy on pushing the means test as a way to force repayment from debtors who could repay. . . .

. . . With the addition of a means test to the present system, the consumer bankruptcy system would continue to be hospitable to well-advised debtors with substantial assets. No one has suggested that means tests can do anything more than force some debtors into Chapter 13. Under the current rules, many of those debtors can avoid making any repayments in Chapter 13. They can drop out and refile repeatedly. Many of the clearest abuses in the consumer bankruptcy system . . . would remain equally possible.

Not only may the worst debtor practices continue with a means tested system, new abuses may arise, accentuating the differences among debtors. Debtors with resources do not passively accept their fate in bankruptcy; they hire counsel to work the system to their maximum advantage. They may, with newly developed legal expertise, find ways to survive any means test devised by the credit industry or anyone else. A means test based on annual income, for example, may require some debtors to "retire" for a few months before their filings, while a means test based on disposable income may encourage some debtors to load up on secured debt obligations to diminish the income available for general distribution. A means test that is triggered when a debtor can pay a specific percentage of debt, such as twenty percent of all unsecured debt, encourages the well-advised debtor to incur more debt before filing for bankruptcy. A means test may increase the demand for pre-planning and good legal advice, but it is unlikely to deter the abusive cases.

The effects of a means test would be felt throughout the system. . . . [S]omeone would have to pay for means testing. . . . An increase in filing fees would likely be the smallest problem low-end debtors would face in a means-tested system. . . . [T]he debtors with the least resources to hire counsel would find themselves facing the same dilemmas they now face—a complex system with significant legal consequences for decisions they make with little or no legal advice. . . . While debtors with adequate resources would respond to the challenges imposed by means tests, their less sophisticated counterparts would simply be less likely to get a "fresh start."

Professor Jean Braucher . . . concludes that sorting through can-pay and can't-pay debtors is a process fraught with the kinds of judgments on which no group of policymakers can agree. This raises the concern that means tests would create one more form of local legal culture, with practices and outcomes differing widely across the country. Like cases would be even less likely to be treated alike than they are today. . . .

. . . With a means test in place, either the system would have to commit vastly more resources to reviewing the circumstances of each failing debtor in Chapter 13 or it would make bankruptcy relief unavailable for people who could not repay their creditors, regardless of what some necessarily arbitrary chart said they could repay. In the latter case, the safety valve that keeps consumer debt burdens in check would be lost. The consumer bankruptcy system would not be strengthened; it would be destroyed.

CONCLUSION: COMPLEXITY AND STRATEGY

An improved consumer bankruptcy system is one that strengthens protection for the neediest debtors while it defends against abuse by debtors who do not need its help. The key to accomplishing these improvements is not to add another layer of bureaucracy, but to understand the implications of the complex system that has evolved over the past one hundred years. Complexity may have created the opportunity to craft better-fitting solutions to diverse family situations, but it also opened new doors for well-advised debtors with the resources and willingness to pre-plan to work the system in unimagined ways.

With consumer debt loads rising and loan default rates near historic highs, everyone would like a magic bullet. The consumer credit industry offered one: means test the debtors and be sure that only those who really need help will get it. The problem is that a means test adds a layer of complexity without eliminating even one clearly abusive practice. There would be less protection for debtors with few assets and little representation, while the planning challenges would be only slightly increased for the debtors determined to take advantage of the system.

The Commission's approach to exemptions, reaffirmations and refilings illustrates the principle of trying to provide sufficient protection for those who need help and to constrain the availability of bankruptcy for those who do not. . . . [T]he principle is clear in these recommendations: some debtors need help, and their access to effective help should be carefully preserved; some debtors have the resources to use a complex system to their advantage in ways that are not consonant with a fresh start, and their use of the current system should be deterred.

The Commission faced an important policy question about the way it would recommend improving the consumer bankruptcy system. The approach it employed is principled, based on the twin assumptions that the system must accommodate diverse participants dealing with a variety of different circumstances, but that complexity often benefits the least deserving debtors and creditors in the system.

Hon. Edith H. Jones & James I. Shepard
Additional Dissent to Recommendations for
Reform of Consumer Bankruptcy Law
NATIONAL BANKRUPTCY REVIEW COMMISSION
FINAL REPORT
(October 20, 1997)

I. General Observations

The consumer bankruptcy recommendations of a five-four majority of the Commission speak volumes about the error of entrusting reform to defenders of the institution that needs reforming. Many of these recommendations are not only unrealistic, they are simply deaf to the public debate over and frustration with this nation's bankruptcy system. And in conspicuous areas, the majority recommendations are also mute. It is foolish not to view with alarm the fact that 1.2 million people filed for bankruptcy relief in 1996, nearly 30% more than in the previous year, and that a similar proportional increase appears to be happening during 1997. When filings rise dramatically while unemployment is declining, it is inevitable that the next economic downturn will produce a cataclysm of filings. When the cataclysm occurs, the stability of our credit-driven economy could be shaken.

The Commission's response to this reality, novel in our history, is silence. The reporter's introduction to consumer bankruptcy purports to conclude that the cause of the high rate of bankruptcy filings is debt. That controversial conclusion is about like saying that the cause of the high rate of divorce is marriage. . . .

There remains a normative question which is very much within our competence to evaluate: whether a bankruptcy law that permits well over one million people a year to break their contracts and discharge debts—during "good times"—is functioning correctly. In this respect, the five-member majority tome on consumer bankruptcy is silent. . . .

. . . The Framework is silent on any notion of personal responsibility for one's debts. . . .

II. Means-Testing Bankruptcy Relief

In 1980, just after the Bankruptcy Code was passed and amid an economic recession, annual filings stood at slightly over 330,000. Sixteen years later, following a sustained period of economic growth, the number of filings has risen suddenly and dramatically from just under a million to 1.2 million consumer bankruptcies in 1996. The disproportionate increase has continued in the first part of 1997.

We now have an anomalous situation in which unemployment is falling but bankruptcy is rising. Moreover, it has been estimated that Americans pay a hidden bankruptcy tax of $300-400 per household as the losses occasioned by higher bankruptcies are redistributed through higher-priced goods and services.

This is not the place to speculate on all of the causes of increased filings. But no one suggests that the filings are any longer demographically confined to the lowest socioeconomic groups or those who have irrevocably lost their jobs or have become physically disabled—seeking bankruptcy protection has become more and more common among fully employed middle- and upper-class people. . . .

In part, the bankruptcy boom springs from the intention of the 1978 Code. The drafters of the Code, many of whom have actively influenced this Commission's work, consciously sought to remove the social stigma from filing bankruptcy. The Code, for instance, replaced the term bankrupt with "debtor" and described a case filing as seeking an "order for relief." If you craft a social welfare statute, people soon learn to appreciate the benefits of seeking welfare.

Social and moral changes have also accelerated the trend to accepting bankruptcy as a feature of "normal" life. Movie stars, governors and "famed heart surgeons" have taken advantage of the process to discharge their debts, so why shouldn't ordinary Americans? To take just one example from the wealth of bankruptcy-promoting advertising and literature a book titled *Debt Free!* offers "Your Guide to Personal Bankruptcy without Shame."

A prominent bankruptcy judge once commented to me that when he graduated from law school around 1950, there were two things that "people never did: divorce and bankruptcy." This comment captures an insight often overlooked by those who make their living from the bankruptcy process. Declaring bankruptcy has a moral dimension. To declare bankruptcy is to break one's contracts and agreements. Our society cannot function if it becomes widely acceptable to do this. . . .

Beyond contracts and mere transactional effects are the distrust, disaffection and misunderstanding that erupt in a society which broadly permits such promise-breaking as occurs in bankruptcy. . . . No doubt, bankruptcy is a necessary feature of Judeo-Christian capitalist societies, but to advance the equally moral goals of protecting social cohesion and general welfare, it cannot become more than an act of grace available to those who are truly and seriously needy. . . .

Finally, bankruptcy has a macroeconomic effect on the cost and availability of credit. . . . The rising number of bankruptcies will increase interest rates for all consumers and will cause businesses to scrutinize credit more closely and discriminate among borrowers. The real losers as the supply of consumer credit tightens are those at the bottom of the ladder. In the final analysis, bankruptcy "reforms" that favor bankrupts do not favor bill-paying customers. Without further belaboring what should be an obvious point, bankruptcy as a social welfare program is subsidized by creditors and, through them, by the vast majority of Americans who struggle and succeed to make ends meet financially.

In light of these considerations, it is hard to justify why the Commission has not formally considered means-testing for bankruptcy relief, as a device to limit the adverse consequences of the filing explosion. . . .

If the Commission had engaged in this important debate, we might have considered at least five different options for means-testing. It appears that the primary considerations in setting up such a program are fairness and ease of administration together with the maximum feasible simplicity. The point of means-testing is to permit Chapter 7 discharge and liquidation of debt only to those debtors who are truly unable to repay their debts in the future. Those debtors who are income-earning, however, should not receive the benefits of the full discharge and the automatic stay to the extent that they are able to repay creditors the secured and a portion of the unsecured debts they have incurred. Each of the following proposals, listed in no particular order of importance, has the potential to accomplish the objective of means-testing within the noted constraints.

1. Section 707(b) could be amended to require that the court dismiss or convert the case of a debtor who has filed for Chapter 7 if, on the motion of a party in interest or the U.S. Trustee, it is found that the debtor has the ability to repay a portion of his debts in Chapter 13. . . . The provision might set as a threshold the debtor's ability to pay back 10% of unsecured debt within five years, or any other amount chosen by Congress.

2. Any debtor whose family income exceeded $35,000 or $40,000 per year, a solid middle-class income, might be permitted to file for Chapter 7 liquidation relief only by agreeing to pay for and submit to a full bankruptcy audit conducted by the panel trustee.

3. A presumptive income ceiling for the availability of Chapter 7 relief could be defined. Thus, any debtor whose family income exceeded an average middle-class income, say $35-40,000 per year, would presumptively be required to seek Chapter 13 repayment plan relief unless the debtor could establish extraordinary and compelling circumstances justifying Chapter 7 liquidation. . . .

4. A "least-common-denominator" means test would automatically channel any debtor seeking bankruptcy relief into a Chapter 13 proceeding if she is able to repay a minimum level of unsecured debt within five years. This proposal is administratively feasible, because it uses the information now recorded on the debtor's bankruptcy Schedules I and J, reflecting income and monthly expenditures, and derives the debtor's "disposable income" from those charts. . . .

5. The needs-based test suggested by some creditors derives from the assumption that all debtors should be directed into a Chapter 13 repayment plan to the extent their family income exceeds average costs of living in their area, as determined by statistics from the Bureau of Labor Statistics. Immediate questions are raised about the complexity and fairness of this proposal, but those objections may be allayed in various ways. First, BLS statistics are already in use in one form or another by Chapter 13 trustees as a gauge against excessive expenditures claimed by Chapter 13 debtors. Second, if BLS statistics are fair geographically, they can be administratively disseminated to bankruptcy courts, trustees and debtors' attorneys and promptly updated. Third, the use of similar measures by family courts and tax collection agencies in working out debtor payment plans suggests their feasibility for bankruptcy plans. Fourth, the statute could except debtors from this standard under circumstances in which its application would be clearly unjust. . . .

Three vehement objections to means-testing bankruptcy relief, and requiring many income-earning debtors to pay back some portion of their debts, have been frequently voiced. The first is that, given the current high failure rate of cases in Chapter 13, it can hardly be expected that when debtors are forced into debt payment plans, they will be more likely to complete their court-ordered obligations. While this is certainly a possibility, it is mitigated by the alternative that such debtors would face. If they did not complete their Chapter 13 plans, their cases would be dismissed, and they would again be at the mercy of creditors. The option of converting to Chapter 7 liquidation in a means-testing regime would necessarily be limited for those debtors who originally qualified only for Chapter 13 payment plans. It should also be noted that none of the presently-conceived means-testing proposals requires a particularly draconian level of debt repayment. Moreover, once debtors become well aware that their earning capacity will limit the debt relief to which they may be entitled, they can plan their lives accordingly. It is patronizing and short-sighted to assert that debtors are too stupid and undisciplined to adjust their expenditures to the default standards that society will maintain.

Second, it is often cavalierly asserted by bankruptcy professionals that requiring people to repay some portion of their debts amounts to unconstitutional "involuntary servitude." One court appropriately dismissed this odd notion as follows:

> . . . The 13th Amendment proscribes slavery or its functional equivalents, *e.g.,* peonage, *U.S. v. Kozminski*, 487 U.S. 931, 941-42, 108 S. Ct. 2751, 2759, 101 L.Ed.2d 788, 804ff. (1988). As noted above, § 707(b) is intended to prevent debtors who are capable of paying their just debts from discharging them by misuse of an extraordinary privilege to which they are not properly entitled. If this violates the 13th Amendment, then it would seem that having to pay one's just debts is "slavery" or "peonage"—put another way, debtors would read the 13th Amendment as if it provided a *Constitutional right* to a Chapter 7 discharge! . . . Judicial review of voluntarily-filed Chapter 7 cases for abuse does not force anyone to work and does not force debtors to divert any part of their income to payment of debts. Such judicial review merely requires debtors who already work and have enough income to pay their debts to "take their chances" under State law if they refuse to meet their obligations.

In re Tony Ray Higginbotham, 111 B.R. 955, 966-97 (Bankruptcy N.D. Oklahoma 1990) . . . .

A third complaint by those who resist means-testing is that debtors cannot pay back anything, according to some empirical studies, or alternatively, there is no good proof that they can repay a portion of unsecured debts. I am not an economist or statistician and will not debate these hypotheses, although they are strongly controverted. Having been a member of the Commission's Consumer Bankruptcy Working Group, however, and having read the thousands of pages submitted to us on consumer bankruptcy, I draw two firm conclusions. First, too many letters from lenders and news articles depict instances of filings by people with steady jobs whose lifestyles got out of control or who gambled (sometimes literally) with their finances and lost. . . . If they have steady income, and no exceptional problems such as physical disability, it does not seem unfair for society to ask them to repay some of their unsecured debts. Second, if by some chance it is true that no debtor can afford to repay some unsecured debts, then the critics of means-testing will be vindicated by that very program. No means-testing proposal I have seen would impoverish anyone with an impossible level of debt repayment. On the contrary, if all debtors are so needy as the means-testing critics contend, none of them will qualify for debt repayments, and all will receive a Chapter 7 discharge.

The arguments for means-testing are clear and are also consistent with accepted public policy for similar situations. Means-testing is not a radical idea. We already use it to determine child care benefits, Medicaid benefits, social security benefits, supplemental security income, food stamp benefits and student aid benefits at the federal level alone. . . .

The Commission has in my view neglected its duty to investigate alternatives to the present-day reality of excessive bankruptcy filings. I hope that Congress will take up the challenge.

Michelle J. White
Why It Pays to File for Bankruptcy:
A Critical Look at the Incentives Under U.S. Personal Bankruptcy Law and a Proposal for Change
65 U. CHI. L. REV. 685 (1998)[*]

. . . This Article considers why consumer bankruptcy is so common in the United States, focusing particularly on the role of property exemptions and how strategic behavior can make filing for bankruptcy attractive even to high-income households. To avoid such pathologies, this Article proposes changes to the bankruptcy system that would appropriately limit the attractiveness of the bankruptcy process. . . . Part II examines the economic justification for having a personal bankruptcy procedure at all and argues that having such a system improves economic efficiency. However, the costs of the procedure rise more quickly than the benefits as the amount of assets exempt from the bankruptcy process increases. Thus, while exemptions from bankruptcy may sometimes be appropriate, the level should not be set too high. Part III then explores various strategies that households can use to increase their financial benefit from bankruptcy. This Part calculates the proportion of households that have a financial incentive to file for bankruptcy when they use these strategies. These calculations show that current U.S. bankruptcy laws are manipulated so easily that a majority of households can benefit financially from bankruptcy if they plan in advance. . . . Finally, Part IV proposes a reform of the personal bankruptcy system under which debtors in bankruptcy would be required to use both their current wealth and their future earnings to repay debt, with appropri-

---

ate exemptions for both. The proposed reform would end the anomaly under the current system whereby some debtors obtain discharge of their debts in bankruptcy even though they have high incomes and, often, high wealth. Under the proposed reform, fewer households would have an incentive to file for bankruptcy, and debtors with a high ability to repay their debts would be deterred from filing. Households that have low wealth and low income, however, would still benefit from the discharge of debt in bankruptcy and receive a "fresh start." . . .

II. WHY HAVE BANKRUPTCY?

The basic economic argument for having a personal bankruptcy procedure is that it provides risk-averse borrowers with insurance against the possibility that their income or wealth might fall before they have to repay their loans. As a result, borrowers and creditors share the risk of a fall in borrowers' income or wealth. However, the cost of having a personal bankruptcy procedure is that it encourages some borrowers to take advantage of the system. Their behavior makes the rest of the borrowing population worse off. . . .

Assume that there are two types of households, Type A and Type B. Type A households would only file for bankruptcy if some misfortune occurs that causes them to become financially distressed. Events such as job loss, serious illness, or divorce would be examples. Type As do not "plan for" bankruptcy, and they are assumed to be risk averse. Type B households, in contrast, plan in advance to take advantage of the possibility of bankruptcy in the same way that many households plan in advance to reduce their tax liability. Type Bs are more likely to file for bankruptcy as the financial benefit from filing increases. . . .

. . . [R]aising the exemption level in bankruptcy makes Type As better off by insuring them in both the worst and the intermediate outcomes, rather than just in the worst outcome. However, it makes them worse off in the best outcome, because they must pay much higher interest rates to compensate lenders for the increase in the number of Type Bs (adverse selection) and for the higher default rates of both types (moral hazard). This is the basic tradeoff in bankruptcy. . . .

To summarize, the United States bankruptcy system provides what it was intended to provide—insurance for risk averse Type A borrowers that makes them better off when financial setbacks occur. However, it also provides something unintended—a subsidy from Type A to Type B borrowers who take advantage of bankruptcy by filing even when they are not in financial distress. The system also reduces borrowers' access to credit relative to a system without a bankruptcy procedure, particularly in those states that have the highest exemption levels. Thus, while there is a strong economic argument for having a bankruptcy system, the gain from raising the exemption level diminishes and the costs rise as the exemption level gets higher. The best exemption level is greater than zero, but not too high.

III. WHAT PROPORTION OF HOUSEHOLDS WOULD BENEFIT FROM BANKRUPTCY?

This Part analyzes the actual system of bankruptcy exemptions in the United States and the incentives it gives households both to file for bankruptcy and to shift from Type A to Type B behavior. When households file for bankruptcy under Chapter 7, their immediate financial benefit is the value of debt that is discharged, and their immediate cost is the value of nonexempt assets, if any, that they must turn over to the bankruptcy court plus the costs of filing. The net financial benefit of bankruptcy is the difference between these two. . . .

. . . [T]he proportion of households that would benefit financially if they filed for bankruptcy . . . for the United States is .17. In general, the more generous the state's bankruptcy exemptions, the higher the proportion of households that would benefit financially from bankruptcy.

. . . The results show that when the costs of filing for bankruptcy are taken into account, the overall proportion of households that would benefit financially from bankruptcy drops from .17 to .15, or about two percentage points. . . .

C. Strategic Behavior

Part II assumed that Type B households planned in advance for bankruptcy and followed strategies that would increase their financial benefit if they filed. How is this done in practice? One method . . . is to shift assets from nonexempt to exempt categories. . . . [D]ebtors often can increase their financial benefit by selling nonexempt assets such as financial accounts and vacation homes and using the proceeds to reduce the mortgages on their principal residences. Call this "Strategy I." . . . The largest increases relative to the base case occur in states that have high or unlimited homestead exemptions. In Texas, the proportion of households that would benefit from bankruptcy rises from .32 in the base case to .36 when households follow Strategy I. For the United States overall, the increase is from .17 to .20.

Even if debtors paid off their mortgages completely, some of them still would have nonexempt property and home equity less than the homestead exemption. These debtors can benefit further by using their nonexempt assets to pay for improvements to their principal residences or by buying and moving to more valuable principal residences in the same state. Under "Strategy II," debtors are assumed to sell nonexempt assets until they exhaust these assets or have used up their homestead exemptions. . . . [U]sing Strategy II, the proportion of households that benefit from bankruptcy under the Texas exemption is .42 and the proportion that benefit under the Mississippi exemption is .41. For the United States overall, the figure is .24.

Another strategy involves debtors borrowing more on an unsecured basis and using the proceeds to purchase goods for immediate consumption (such as vacations and clothing) or to reduce their nondischargeable debt. When debtors file for bankruptcy, the new debt will be discharged along with older unsecured debt. . . . "Strategy III" assumes that debtors borrow the maximum amount on all their unsecured lines of credit before filing for bankruptcy, but do not obtain new lines of credit and do not engage in the other types of strategic behavior already discussed. . . . The largest increase occurs in Texas, because it has a high exemption for personal property. The proportion of households that benefit from filing for bankruptcy under the Texas exemption rises from .32 in the base case to .44 under Strategy III. For the United States overall, the increase is from .17 to .24. These figures would be even higher if they included loans obtained from new sources, such as new credit cards.

Households also might pursue all of these strategies simultaneously. . . . [I]n this case, the proportion of households that would benefit financially from filing for bankruptcy using the Texas exemption is .61, and over half would benefit using the Mississippi exemption. The overall figure for the United States is .34. . . . In a low exemption state such as Ohio, the median benefit figure increases from $1,585 in the base case to $2,770, or by about 75 percent. In states with generous exemptions, such as Florida, Mississippi, and Texas, the median benefit figures increase three- to four-fold. In Texas, for example, the median benefit increases from $1,680 in the base case to $5,900 when all strategies are used. Finally, households might both move to high exemption states such as Texas and pursue all of the strategies discussed here before filing for bankruptcy. In this case the overall proportion of households that would benefit from bankruptcy would be .61. . . .

The [data] clearly show that the proportion of households that would benefit financially from bankruptcy is much higher than the proportion of households that actually file for bankruptcy. While more than half of households could benefit from bankruptcy if they behaved strategically, in fact only about 8 percent of United States households actually filed for bankruptcy during the entire last decade.

. . . These factors suggest that the bankruptcy filing rate will continue to rise.

D. Equity Effects of Bankruptcy

Not only is the bankruptcy system manipulable, it is manipulable in a distributionally troublesome way. . . .

. . . These results show that when households behave strategically and the bankruptcy exemption is generous, well-off households benefit far more from bankruptcy than households with a low ability to pay. . . .

Several conclusions can be drawn from these figures. First, virtually any creditworthy household can benefit from filing for bankruptcy if it plans in advance and uses strategies such as those discussed here to increase its financial benefit. Because so many strategies are so effective, the bankruptcy system gives too many households an incentive to file. Second, the bankruptcy system produces inequitable results, because well-off households get much higher financial benefit from filing than those in true financial distress. The higher the bankruptcy exemption level, the more the distribution of benefit from filing for bankruptcy favors those with higher abilities to pay. Bankruptcy therefore provides the greatest "relief" to those in the least need. Third, the various strategies discussed here for increasing the financial benefit of bankruptcy have the practical effect of making the bankruptcy exemption nearly unlimited, because households can benefit from bankruptcy even though they are high up in the wealth distribution. . . .

IV. BANKRUPTCY REFORMS

Combining the current Chapters 7 and 13 into a single personal bankruptcy procedure would solve many of the problems discussed above. Debtors filing for bankruptcy would be obliged to repay part or all of their debt using both wealth and future earnings, but there would be exemptions for both. The proposed reform is based on the principle that ability to repay debt depends on both wealth and future earnings, rather than only on wealth (as under Chapter 7) or only on future earnings (as under Chapter 13). Under the proposal, bankruptcy would be both more equitable and more efficient.

. . . [M]y proposed bankruptcy reform exempts all of debtors' post-bankruptcy earnings that are below a minimum dollar amount from the obligation to repay debt, but requires that debtors use a proportion of their post-bankruptcy earnings above the minimum dollar amount to repay debt. . . .

Requiring that debtors use a fraction of their future earnings to repay their debt is more workable than the current Chapter 13 provision, under which all of debtors' "disposable income" for three years must be used to repay debt if unsecured creditors object to confirmation of a repayment plan. The current formula is clearly impractical. . . . This standard is not merely difficult to implement, but doing so would be extremely inefficient, because the 100 percent tax on disposable income would give debtors an incentive to reduce their income to the point where none of it is disposable. In contrast, the proposed approach of requiring that a fixed fraction of future earnings be used to repay debt slightly reduces, but does not eliminate, debtors' incentives to earn. It also would be much easier to administer, because only income needs to be verified, and this can be done using tax returns.

In addition to providing a fractional wage exemption, this proposal incorporates asset exemptions. Two different reforms of asset exemptions in bankruptcy are analyzed. Reform I involves retaining the actual state-specific asset exemptions in bankruptcy that prevailed in 1992, but will include the higher federal exemptions that Congress enacted in 1994. . . .

Under Reform II, everything remains the same except that a uniform asset exemption in bankruptcy of $30,000 replaces the state-specific exemptions. . . . The main advantage of adopting a single bankruptcy exemption for most assets is that it sharply reduces households' incentives to engage in the types of strategic behavior discussed in the previous Parts. . . .

. . . [U]nder Reform I, . . . [r]equiring that households use part of their future earnings to repay debt in bankruptcy sharply reduces the pool of households that would benefit from filing for bankruptcy, from .185 to .08 of all United States households. The largest reduction occurs in Texas, where the proportion of households that would benefit from bankruptcy falls from .33 to .12, and in Mississippi, where the reduction is from .30 to .11. The median net benefit also falls sharply for the United States, from $1,650 when the federal exemption is doubled to $1,280 under Reform I. This is because those households that previously received the largest benefit from bankruptcy tend to have a relatively high ability to repay and therefore are less likely to find bankruptcy worthwhile if future wages are not fully exempt. The results suggest that even a moderate obligation to repay debt from future earnings substantially reduces the proportion of households that would benefit from filing for bankruptcy.

Reform II . . . substitutes a uniform asset exemption of $30,000 for the state-specific asset exemptions in bankruptcy . . . . Because the results do not vary across states, only the figure for the United States overall is given. The proportion of households that benefit financially from bankruptcy is similar under Reforms I and II: .08 versus .09, respectively. The median dollar benefit figures are also very similar: $1,280 for the United States overall under Reform I compared to $1,200 under Reform II. Although the uniform asset exemption eliminates the most favorable exemptions currently in effect, it increases the value of the bankruptcy exemption for households in low exemption states and also allows households to utilize the exemption more fully. . . .

Thus both Reform I and Reform II improve efficiency by reducing the overall proportion of households that have an incentive to file for bankruptcy, and also improve equity by reducing the number of households that benefit financially from bankruptcy despite having a high ability to repay their debts. A striking aspect of the Reforms is that even a relatively low requirement to repay debt from future income—10 percent of gross future earnings over three years—causes a very substantial reduction in the proportion of households in the middle and upper deciles of the ability to pay distribution who find it worthwhile to file for bankruptcy. Reform II has the additional advantage of being strategy-proof, because households cannot increase their financial benefit from bankruptcy by using "asset shuffling" strategies.

CONCLUSION

This Article has demonstrated that United States bankruptcy procedures can be reformed in a way that increases both efficiency and equity. Combining Chapters 7 and 13 and reforming the asset exemptions would reduce the overall proportion of households that benefit financially from bankruptcy, but would accomplish this mainly by reducing the proportion of high ability to pay households that have an incentive to file. If the Reforms were adopted, bankruptcy still would be available to provide debt relief to households that have low ability to pay, but it would no longer give well-off households with high earnings and/or high assets an incentive to file for bankruptcy. . . . [E]ven with higher exemption levels, the proposed reform of combining Chapters 7 and 13 would still improve equity by concentrating more of the benefit from bankruptcy on the least well-off households. The proposed reforms better align bankruptcy law with debtors' ability to repay, and also eliminate the perverse incentive structure that currently allows the households with the highest ability to repay to obtain the largest benefit from bankruptcy.

Marianne B. Culhane & Michaela M. White
Taking the New Consumer Bankruptcy Model for a Test Drive:
Means-Testing Real Chapter 7 Debtors
7 AM. BANKR. INST. L. REV. 27 (1999)[*]

INTRODUCTION

. . . The debate about bankruptcy abuse has been accompanied by bankruptcy reform bills in both houses of Congress. Several of these bills include means-testing for chapter 7 debtors—a concept long advanced by the consumer credit industry. Means-testing would develop a mathematical model to predict which chapter 7 debtors have substantial ability to repay unsecured debt and require those "can-pay debtors" either to repay in chapter 13 over five to seven years, or to forego a discharge. Means-testing would deny such debtors the relatively quick chapter 7 fresh start, which does not require use of post-petition income to repay most debts. . . .

VISA/U.S.A. Inc., a preeminent unsecured creditor and vigorous advocate of means-testing, has commissioned a series of empirical studies of the repayment capacity of chapter 7 debtors. The most recent of these, by the accounting firm of Ernst & Young in March, 1998, followed the means-testing formula of House of Representatives bill number 3150 ("H.R. 3150"), the bill which appeared to have the greatest prospect for passage in the 105th Congress. Ernst & Young initially concluded that 15% of a national proportional sample of 2,200 chapter 7 filers were "can-pays" under that bill. They further asserted that H.R. 3150's means-testing would have allowed unsecured creditors, on a national basis, to collect $4 billion more than did the current system. Ernst & Young later reduced the can-pay estimate to 11%. . . .

The VISA-funded studies were highly criticized by academics as well as by the General Accounting Office ("GAO"). The GAO's chief criticisms were that these studies ignored chapter 13 administrative expenses and based their projections on two unrealistic assumptions: first, that for the next five years, each affected debtor's income would rise as quickly as debts and expenses; and second, that 100% of these debtors would complete a 60-month chapter 13 plan. The GAO noted that current voluntary chapter 13 plans have only a 30% completion rate.

It appeared to us that one more study was needed—one that was not funded or controlled by creditors with a financial stake in the outcome. . . . [W]e applied for a grant from the non-profit American Bankruptcy Institute ("ABI") Endowment to support an empirical investigation of means-testing. . . .

. . . [T]he ABI agreed to fund the project. [W]e decided to apply the version of means-testing in H.R. 3150, passed by the House of Representatives in June, 1998. We also decided to follow many of the steps used by Ernst & Young in order to facilitate a comparison of results. . . .

I. OUR RESULTS, ERNST & YOUNG'S RESULTS AND WHY THE TWO DO NOT MEET

Our test drive has led us to the following conclusions:

First, abuse of chapter 7, in the form of filings by debtors who could repay under H.R. 3150's formula, appears minimal. Only 3.6% of sample debtors emerged as apparent can-pays. Ninety-six and four-tenths percent of the sample debtors were rightly in chapter 7.

Second, sophisticated debtors could avoid can-pay status by taking on more debt or increasing charitable contributions. The 3.6% could drop once debtors adjusted to the new rules.

Third, even under the overly optimistic assumptions of the VISA studies, H.R. 3150 would allow nonpriority unsecured creditors to collect at most an additional $930 million from can-pay debtors across the nation. If our sample results held for the nation as a whole, a more realistic estimate would be $450 million, less than one-eighth of VISA's estimate.

Fourth, in operation, the necessary analysis will be costly and labor-intensive when applied to a million or more chapter 7 cases a year. . . .

We did not attempt to assess the cost to taxpayers of H.R. 3150's means-testing. The Congressional Budget Office ("CBO"), however, estimated that H.R. 3150's provisions as a whole would have cost $214 million in the first five years, plus another $8-16 million for the additional judges needed for means-testing.

All the empirical studies to date agree on one point; the vast majority of chapter 7 debtors belong in that chapter. They have too little income after necessary expenses to repay unsecured debt. It is vital, therefore, that no undue burdens be thrust on that needy majority in order to flush out a small minority of abusers. . . .

We conclude that only 3.6% of our sample are can-pays under H.R. 3150. Ernst & Young put 11% of their sample into the can-pay category. Both studies assumed, unrealistically, no avoidance behavior by debtors likely to be impacted. If many debtors chose to increase debt or charitable contributions, these percentages would fall. This dramatic difference is due to a variety of factors. First, we interpreted H.R. 3150's car ownership expense allowance more broadly than did Ernst & Young. Ernst & Young allowed debt retirement only, while we added major repairs, replacement and leasing costs. Second, we estimated chapter 13 administrative expenses and deducted these priority claims from amounts available to creditors. Ernst & Young, like previous creditor studies, ignored these real world costs. Third, we charged interest on secured claims for five years rather than just two years. . . .

III. PROJECTED NET GAIN AND THE IMPOSSIBLE DREAMS

How much more might unsecured creditors collect under means-testing? VISA estimated that number at "over $4 billion," then qualified that estimate by stating "[t]his assumes that income remained unchanged relative to expenses and liabilities during the 60 month repayment period."

In 1997, some 926,000 nonbusiness chapter 7 cases were filed. If we assume that our sample holds for the nation as a whole, then 3.55% or 32,873 would be can-pays, each with nonpriority unsecured debt of $35,303, and each could repay 75% or $26,477 of that unsecured debt. If all 32,873 debtors repaid $26,477 apiece, it would total about $870 million, nowhere close to VISA's estimate. However, even that $870 million is based on at least five unrealistic assumptions:

• First, that well-counseled debtors will not evade can-pay status by increasing debt or charitable contributions;

• Second, that the debtors' incomes, expenses and debts will remain relatively unchanged for five years;

• Third, that 100% of the can-pays will file and complete five-year chapter 13 plans;

• Fourth, that unsecured creditors will bear no part of the cost to sort all chapter 7 cases for means-testing and to monitor the 30,000 + can-pays over five years in chapter 13; and

• Fifth, that unsecured creditors collect nothing from chapter 7 debtors at present.

None of these assumptions is well-founded. The first four are impossible dreams and the last is simply untrue. . . .

CONCLUSION

Our intent in this article is to assess, by means of a test drive of sorts, whether one suggested legislative response to perceived bankruptcy abuse would fulfill its apparent aims. That is, would H.R. 3150's formula find debtors with the ability to repay and divert them into chapter 13 plans that would produce a net gain to unsecured creditors without undue cost to other debtors and taxpayers?

As we have shown, H.R. 3150's formula produces relatively few apparent abusers for diversion into chapter 13. Second, because the sample cases were filed in 1995, when the only sanction for abuse was section 707(b) dismissal, debtors and their attorneys had less reason to make evasive maneuvers. At this writing, of course, the Religious Liberty and Charitable Donation Protection Act of 1998 is in force, providing an escape route for all but the wealthiest few. Further, incentives to load up on secured debt, especially by purchasing a new car shortly before filing, are substantially increased. Thus, there is reason to believe that the number of can-pays in our sample is substantially higher than would be found today if means-testing were adopted. Third, the assumed benefits to unsecured creditors from means-testing depend very substantially on whether those can-pay debtors in fact convert to and complete lengthy chapter 13 plans. Chapter 13's recent history provides little reason to believe that even a bare majority of the debtors would in fact complete their plans. The net gains to unsecured creditors, in sum, appear small relative to the costs likely to be imposed on the great majority of chapter 7 debtors, as well as trustees, judges and taxpayers. In sum, we conclude that means-testing as enshrined in H.R. 3150 will not go the distance.

Local Legal Culture

The wisdom of reforming the consumer bankruptcy system by tinkering with the law "on the books" may be tempered by how much of an impact statutory revision can have in the real world inhabited by consumers, attorneys, trustees, and judges. Professor Jean Braucher's article, *Lawyers and Consumer Bankruptcy: One Code, Many Cultures*, 67 AM. BANKR. L.J. 501 (1993), examines the importance of "local legal culture" and the habits and practices of the bankruptcy bar in shaping consumer bankruptcy. Braucher reports the findings of an empirical study of consumer bankruptcy practice in four cities in two states. She shows that chapter choice and many other aspects of consumer bankruptcy are driven much more by "who your lawyer is" and by where you live than by the substantive laws on the books. Variances in practice in these four localities are quite dramatic. Her "socio-economic" model of "consumer bankruptcy law in action" offers a cautionary tale to lawmakers who mistakenly believe that they can readily affect outcomes in consumer bankruptcy by tinkering with enacted legislation.

If Professor Braucher's study of the importance of "local legal culture" somehow does not fully persuade the skeptical reader, despite the overwhelming evidence she presents, then perhaps that skeptic will be satisfied after examining the data presented in *The Persistence of Local Legal Culture: Twenty Years of Evidence From the Federal Bankruptcy Courts*, 17 HARV. J.L. & PUB. POL'Y 801 (1994), by Professors Sullivan, Warren, and Westbrook. In that article Sullivan, Warren and Westbrook examine variations from state to state and judicial district to district in bankruptcy filing rates and in chapter choices over twenty years, from 1970 to 1990. They conclude that the most plausible explanation for the dramatic differences they find lies in the distinct legal cultures in each locality. Like Braucher, they see in these results a cautionary note for lawmakers.

Jean Braucher
Lawyers and Consumer Bankruptcy: One Code, Many Cultures
67 AM. BANKR. L.J. 501 (1993)[*]

I. INTRODUCTION

The Bankruptcy Code is federal law, but consumer bankruptcy law in action is local. Each bankruptcy court has its own official and unofficial practices. In each city with a court, there is a distinctive legal culture concerning the most appropriate uses of bankruptcy for consumers. Individual lawyers assimilate this local culture to varying degrees. In a sense, there is a consumer bankruptcy law of each city, even of each law office.

This article reports the findings in an empirical study of the attitudes and practices of lawyers who represent consumer debtors in bankruptcy cases in four cities in two states. The lawyers practice in Austin and San Antonio, Texas, and Cincinnati and Dayton, Ohio. . . . The focus of the study was to identify the factors that affect the choice between chapter 7 and chapter 13 in consumer bankruptcy cases, and particularly the nature of the influence of lawyers' attitudes.

The "simple" thesis of this article is that debtors' lawyers pursue different mixes of four goals in consumer bankruptcy practice. They seek to serve their clients' and their own financial interests, and they also attempt to fulfill some version of appropriate social role playing on the part of their clients and themselves. Lawyers face a complex task of balancing, compromising and reconciling these sometimes conflicting financial interests and social concerns. It is not surprising that they come to greatly varying conclusions about how to do this job.

These findings are consistent with a socio-economic, as opposed to a purely economic, model of consumer bankruptcy law in action. The socio-economic paradigm of human behavior . . . makes two assumptions . . . . One is that people pursue at least two utilities: pleasure *and* morality. The other is that individuals *and* social groups are prime decision-making units; individuals' decisions reflect collective values and are significantly influenced by social context. . . .

The study suggests that local administrative practices and legal culture have more effect on choices in consumer bankruptcy than do features of the law conventionally thought to be important to chapter choice, such as available exemptions, the substantial abuse test in chapter 7 and the broader discharge in chapter 13. One of the objectives of the study was to investigate the influence of "local legal culture" on chapter choice. Local administrative practices of judges and trustees, and prevailing professional attitudes vary dramatically in the four cities. The context created by these practices and attitudes is what I mean by local legal culture. There is a predominant culture in each of the cities studied. But equally significant, the reaction of lawyers to local culture is not monolithic in any of the four. In each city, despite the differences in local legal culture, there are two very different patterns of lawyer use of the two chapters. Some lawyers in each city use both chapters 7 and 13 frequently, and other lawyers use chapter 13 infrequently or not at all, and file at least 90% of their consumer cases under chapter 7. In short, the attitudes of each individual lawyer play a central role in how consumer bankruptcy law is used on behalf of each lawyer's clients. . . . The chapter 13 standing trustee in San Antonio made the point bluntly: "the biggest factor in chapter choice is who your lawyer is." . . .

III. DESCRIPTION OF METHODOLOGY

A. General Approach

. . . I did not aim primarily for statistical information, but rather for pictures of the different ways lawyers see and do their jobs. In keeping with this purpose, I conducted the interviews in this project using non-directive, open-ended questions . . . .

B. The Sample

I interviewed 45 consumer debtor lawyers: 12 in Austin, 11 in San Antonio, 12 in Dayton and 10 in Cincinnati. I also interviewed 12 other persons involved directly or indirectly in the bankruptcy system—the four chapter 13 standing trustees (one in each of the four cities studied), one chapter 7 trustee who was not an active consumer bankruptcy lawyer . . ., the director of a credit counseling agency, five business bankruptcy lawyers not then actively engaged in consumer debtor work . . ., and a legal aid attorney. . . .

The four cities in the study are in two bankruptcy districts. Austin and San Antonio are 80 miles apart in the western district of Texas, and Cincinnati and Dayton are 50 miles apart in the southern district of Ohio.

A comparison of the rates of use of chapter 7 and chapter 13 in the two particular districts, one in Texas and one in Ohio, defies neoclassical economic predictions about chapter choice based on differences in exemptions. An economic approach predicts that the lower the exemptions allowed in chapter 7, the more debtors will use chapter 13 to hold on to property. . . . Texas has very generous exemptions, while Ohio has moderate ones. A simple neoclassical economic model would predict that chapter 13 would be used in a higher proportion of bankruptcy cases in Ohio than in Texas, yet the statistics are the reverse. In the Ohio district, the rate of use of chapter 13 in nonbusiness cases in 1991 was 27%, while the rate of chapter 13 use in the Texas district was 45%. These two districts are thus a good pair for comparative investigation of the influence of local legal culture. The simplest explanation of why differences in exemption levels do not control the rate of chapter use is that, in the overwhelming majority of cases in both chapters in both states, debtors have no property subject to liquidation. In most instances, the chapter 7 cases are no asset, and the chapter 13 cases would be no asset if filed in chapter 7.

. . . [T]he intradistrict comparisons in the study also prove interesting. Each of the four cities studied has its own court and its own bankruptcy judges and trustees. The practices in Austin are very different from those in San Antonio, and those in Cincinnati are very different from those in Dayton. The patterns of chapter use reported by the subject lawyers in Austin and San Antonio . . . also defy neoclassical predictions. More repayment is required in chapter 13 in San Antonio than in Austin, yet the rate of use of chapter 13 is higher in San Antonio. On the other hand, the Cincinnati-Dayton comparison of chapter use patterns is compatible with a neoclassical economic model: chapter 13 is used more in Dayton, where the repayment requirements are lower than in Cincinnati. . . .

IV. THE LAWYERS AND PATTERNS IN THEIR PRACTICES

. . .

B. Categorizing Lawyers by Case Volume and Chapter Use

I asked all 45 active consumer debtor lawyers what volume of bankruptcy filings they handled and how much of that volume was in chapter 7 and how much in chapter 13. . . .

The figures on volume and chapter use suggest two types of classification that are useful to describe the patterns of consumer debtor lawyers. One classification is whether the lawyers are high-volume or low-volume filers. I classify as high-volume any lawyer who files 15 or more cases per month. Using this division, there were 17 high-volume and 28 low-volume filers in the study. . . .

The other classification is by chapter use. I classify as "two-chapter lawyers" those who use chapter 13 more than 10% of the time, and as "chapter 7 lawyers" those who use chapter 13 in 10% or less of the cases they file. In the study there were 30 two-chapter lawyers and 15 chapter 7 lawyers. . . .

The most striking pattern is that all of the high-volume lawyers in the study are two-chapter lawyers. This pattern, along with what a number of lawyers said about how it is easier to get more clients using chapter 13, suggests that it is difficult or maybe even impossible to be a high-volume lawyer in these cities without being willing to use chapter 13 a substantial percentage of the time. Some low-volume lawyers also use chapter 13 frequently (such as a third or half the time), so willingness to use chapter 13 does not necessarily result in a high-volume practice, although it seems to be necessary.

V. HOW THE LAWYERS SERVE FOUR INTERESTS OR CONCERNS

Lawyers representing consumer debtors in bankruptcy seek to serve some mix of four interests and concerns—their clients' and their own financial interests as well as their clients' and their own social concerns. . . .

A. CLIENTS' FINANCIAL INTERESTS

Clients' major financial goals, in typical order of priority to the clients, are:

1. stopping creditors' collection efforts (foreclosure, repossession, suit, garnishment, phone calls, letters, home visits);
2. keeping property, often serving as collateral, such as homes, cars and household belongings;
3. reducing and stretching out debt;
4. having future access to credit. . . .

1. To File or Not to File

The first decision in a consumer bankruptcy case is whether to file at all. Any bankruptcy filing will achieve the first client goal—stopping collection activities. . . . In the unanimous view of the lawyers, filing is usually the most effective and cheapest way to stop collections against the debtors. . . .

A few lawyers said that they counsel some debtors to consider evasion, such as moving and changing telephone numbers, to avoid heavy-handed collection. They give this advice to debtors who have small amounts of debt that they cannot afford to pay, no assets subject to execution and no other concern such as possibility of garnishment or desire to retain collateral. Alternatively, a few lawyers counsel defiant refusal to pay as the best way to discourage debt collectors. . . .

The most common nonbankruptcy solution that lawyers suggest to clients with a manageable load of multiple debts is to go to a consumer credit counseling agency to arrange a repayment plan. Although most of the lawyers said that they make occasional referrals to these agencies, it was far more common for them to see debtors who had already been to such agencies and who had learned that they could not afford a repayment plan under the terms that these agencies arrange. . . .

2. Chapter 7 or Chapter 13

Assuming bankruptcy is chosen as the means to stop collection and provide the proverbial "breathing space" of the automatic stay, the next question is which chapter to use—chapter 7 or 13. Clients' major financial considerations in chapter choice are keeping property (including collateral), reducing payments, and being able to obtain credit in the future. Another factor . . . is the comparative cost of legal services. . . .

a. Keeping Property

The overwhelming majority of chapter 7 consumer bankruptcies filed by the lawyers studied are "no asset" cases, meaning that, after exemptions, an insufficient amount of non-exempt property remains to make it worthwhile for a trustee to conduct a liquidation. In addition, consumers in both chapters frequently keep collateral by continuing to make payments, and some end up returning collateral because they cannot afford the payments. . . .

Lawyers and chapter 7 trustees overwhelmingly agree that liquidation of household items—appliances, furniture and other household goods—is virtually unheard of in chapter 7 in all four cities studied. Occasionally a chapter 7 trustee sells a gun collection or valuable jewelry, antiques or art, but few debtors have personal property of this sort. In addition, it is uncommon for debtors to have significant savings or investments, and even debtors who do have some savings often can engage in prebankruptcy planning to convert nonexempt property to exempt property.

The infrequency of cases where debtors have nonexempt property helps to explain why chapter 13 filing rates in the districts studied do not follow the neoclassical economic model, which predicts more chapter 13 cases as exemptions become less generous. . . . The lawyers in all four cities described protecting nonexempt property as an infrequent concern in consumer bankruptcy practice. . . . [T]he facially quite different state statutes of Texas and Ohio do not produce substantially different results on consumers' ability to keep property.

If debtors in the four cities are not for the most part filing under chapter 13 to avoid the liquidation of assets under chapter 7, why do they use chapter 13? The major reason is to retain collateral, particularly where the debtor is in arrears on the debt. Here again, however, practice belies common scholarly assumptions about the ways the two chapters are used: it turns out that debtors can frequently keep collateral under chapter 7 by keeping payments current. . . . Debtors who accomplish reaffirmation at collateral value in chapter 7 are in better shape than chapter 13 debtors because they get an immediate discharge of their unsecured debts . . . .

Debtors often keep collateral by continuing to pay after a chapter 7 filing, but there are three major reasons that they sometimes need chapter 13. In Ohio, sometimes creditors refuse to reaffirm a debt, even though the debtor's payments are current and the debtor proposes to pay the entire debt. Another reason to use chapter 13, in both Ohio and Texas, is that a debtor may wish to reduce the secured debt on items such as cars or appliances to the collateral value, but the creditor refuses to do that voluntarily: chapter 13 allows a cramdown of secured debts to collateral value.

By far the most frequently cited reason to use chapter 13 in both states is that the debtor is *not* current in payments on one or more secured debts and has a substantial arrearage to cure. Arrearages on home mortgages and other secured debts can be made up in chapter 13 without creditors' consent. . . .

In sum, those who are behind on secured and unsecured debts frequently use chapter 13 in a last ditch effort to keep collateral such as homes and cars. Those who are not behind in payments on secured debt, by contrast, can frequently keep collateral under chapter 7, while discharging unsecured debt. These uses of the two chapters add up to one big reason that bankruptcy law is *not* succeeding in sorting "can pay" debtors into chapter 13 and "can't pay" into chapter 7. Many chapter 13 debtors really cannot afford the collateral they seek to keep—they agree to pay under a plan, but they are really "can't pay" debtors who eventually fail with their plans.

b. Repayment

. . . [M]any chapter 13 bankruptcies involve little or no repayment to unsecured creditors because of use of low percentage repayment plans. On the acceptability of low percentage plans, the four cities vary dramatically: low percentage plans are common in Austin and Dayton and uncommon in San Antonio and Cincinnati. These variations are primarily a result of informal practices rather than formal legal decisions.

... On one reading of the Bankruptcy Code, if the case would be no-asset under chapter 7 and the debtor is committing all disposable income for at least three years in order to pay secured creditors, then nothing need be paid to unsecured creditors—a "0%" plan would be permissible.

The reality is that chapter 13 trustees and judges in the four cities effectively deter 0% plans and keep most plans above a floor percent that is known to local practitioners. The lawyers then respond by rarely or never submitting plans with less than the specified percentage. . . . [I]n all four cities, lawyers can sometimes get plans confirmed below the floor, if they convincingly establish inability of the debtor to pay more.

According to the chapter 13 standing trustees, the floor percentages for routine confirmation are as follows:

Austin	25 to 33 percent
Dayton	10 percent
Cincinnati	70 percent
San Antonio	100 percent

According to San Antonio practice, if a plan is not for 100% repayment, it must extend for five years. . . .

According to the chapter 13 trustees in the three cities other than San Antonio, lawyers either tend to submit plans clustered at the floor percentage for routine approval or at 100%. This is because most lawyers do not frequently challenge the floor, and most will only design a plan for greater repayment for three reasons—(1) when necessary to meet the best interest test, (2) because there is adequate disposable income to do so, or (3) because the client wants to make 100% repayment even though less could be justified. Some lawyers routinely submit all chapter 13 plans at 100%, either out of the desire to avoid resistance or because they believe this is best for clients.

A neoclassical economic model would predict that there would be a higher percentage of chapter 7 filings the more repayment is demanded in chapter 13. Yet, chapter 13 is used more frequently by the subject San Antonio lawyers, who are under strong pressure to file 100% plans, than by the subject lawyers in Austin, where low percentage plans are common. San Antonio's local legal culture embraces repayment in chapter 13 as the preferred type of consumer bankruptcy. On the other hand, the higher rates of use of chapter 13 by the subject lawyers in Dayton compared to Cincinnati are consistent with neoclassical predictions. The Dayton lawyers use chapter 13 more under the 10% repayment rule than the Cincinnati lawyers under the 70% rule.

In addition to low percentage plans, another reason that repayment under chapter 13 does not necessarily mean greater repayment than under chapter 7 is that chapter 13 debtors do not always pay what they plan to pay. In fact, noncompletions are common (half or more in two of the cities). According to the chapter 13 trustees, the noncompletion rates in each city . . . were as follows:

Austin	about 80% (of filings)
San Antonio	35-40% (of confirmed cases)
Cincinnati	about 40-45% (of filings)
Dayton	about 55% (of filings) or about 50% (of confirmed cases)

. . . Many people who file under chapter 13 are really "can't pay" debtors who inevitably fail to complete their plans. The converse does not appear to hold—that many "can pay" debtors are filing under chapter 7. The reality seems to be that both groups lack resources to pay their debts. . . .

Many chapter 7 debtors repay secured debts on homes and cars to keep the collateral. One indication that most chapter 7 debtors cannot pay more than that is the infrequency of "substantial abuse" challenges in chapter 7 based on ability to pay unsecured creditors in chapter 13. Lawyers and chapter 7 trustees in all four cities agreed that such challenges are rare. The chapter 7 trustees interviewed said that they do look for excess income over expenses in debtor's schedules, but they rarely find it. They also give some attention to the reasonableness of expenses, but again they rarely spot abuses. Experienced lawyers have little difficulty accounting for all or most debtors' income in expenses that are not lavish. . . .

c. Credit Availability

Most debtors who consult bankruptcy lawyers are concerned about future access to credit . . . .

Most of the lawyers are convinced that there is faster access to credit after filing under chapter 7 than after a chapter 13 case. Many had anecdotes about chapter 7 clients who were offered new credit immediately after filing (before discharge), in some cases *because* of the filing. A discharge in chapter 7 releases debtors from legal obligation for nearly all debts, and suddenly makes the debtor more capable of repaying new debt, if the debtor has income. Also, the debtor discharged in chapter 7 cannot file another chapter 7 for six years. By contrast, a debtor who has filed under chapter 13 is at high risk to convert to chapter 7 before the three-to five-year plan is completed and thus to discharge postpetition as well as prepetition debt. Many lawyers said that it is common for debtors to obtain credit within a year or two of a chapter 7 filing. "It's too easy to get new credit," said one lawyer. Another said, "the credit industry is recycling people." Car loans and credit cards can often be obtained quickly after filing a chapter 7 case . . . .

Why does chapter 13 not lead to new credit as quickly as chapter 7? The lawyers' main explanation is that debtors are struggling to repay old debts under their plans, and they do not obtain a discharge until the plan is completed. . . . [I]f they convert to chapter 7, any new debt will be discharged along with prepetition debts. . . .

B. Clients' Social Concerns

Bankruptcy has strong social, psychological and moral implications for many debtors, concerns which I will refer to collectively as "social" ones. To describe clients' feelings and attitudes, the subject lawyers used words such as these—dejected, ashamed, humiliated, so tired, seeking face-saving solutions. The lawyers also said that their clients are influenced by moral values and religious beliefs. Many lawyers said the sense of social stigma about bankruptcy has been waning in recent years, but clients are still often embarrassed or ashamed. Clients also struggle with loss of self-esteem. . . .

One point made by most of the lawyers is that clients usually *say* they want to pay their debts. Some lawyers take such statements at face value and put the clients who make them into chapter 13, if they have regular income, without any serious effort to force clients to think through the alternatives. Some lawyers admit that they use declarations of desire to pay to funnel clients into chapter 13 quickly, in the lawyers' own financial interest. In contrast, others make efforts to probe and reconcile clients' needs and wants. Some of these lawyers see their clients as sincere in their desire to repay, but as not having adequately thought through how difficult it can be to complete a chapter 13 plan and how little financial reward there probably is for doing so. . . .

Clients' social and financial concerns are frequently intertwined. The best example of this interrelationship is the question of whether to save the family home. Lawyers say that the number one reason to use chapter 13 is the need to save the home by paying arrearages on a home mortgage. This can be seen as a financial reason, but it also reflects social concerns. . . . It makes economic sense to pay an arrearage if it is not too great, and in that way a family can also avoid dislocation and retain a piece of the American dream.

On the other hand, financial considerations and social concerns can conflict on the question of whether to keep the home. . . . [F]or many debtors, their homes were worth less than the mortgage debt. Also, mortgage payments for some debtors in both the Texas and Ohio cities far exceeded what they would have to pay to rent. However, people resist giving up homes. . . .

Homes are central to status and self-esteem. . . .

Status considerations also play into a debtor's desire to keep a late model car rather than get a cheap used one. "Cars are important to people," said one lawyer. . . .

C. LAWYERS' FINANCIAL INTERESTS

In addition to the interaction between clients' financial and social concerns, there is an interaction between clients' and lawyers' concerns. Clients' social concerns affect how lawyers practice consumer bankruptcy law to serve the lawyers' own financial interests and their sense of appropriate professional role playing.

As in many areas of law practice, getting clients and getting paid are obsessions for consumer bankruptcy lawyers. In addition, standardization of services makes the most of a scarce resource, time, and is particularly important in high-volume practices.

. . . The fees in consumer bankruptcy are relatively low. Thus, a lawyer who wishes to make a good living needs a steady stream of new clients. Advertising is essential . . . and attractive fee terms are crucial . . . . In addition, standardization and control of clients are frequent components of a financially successful practice. . . .

2. Fees

. . . In all four cities, the fees of the subject lawyers for a chapter 13 case were substantially higher than for a chapter 7 case, and chapter 7 fees varied more within each city than chapter 13 fees. The fees for both chapters were higher for the Texas lawyers than for the Ohio lawyers. . . .

a. Total Fee Charged

In each of the four cities, there was a maximum fee that an attorney could charge in a chapter 13 case without needing special justification or time records. In some cases, this amount was set by a judge, and in others it was set by the chapter 13 standing trustee and was backed up by the judges. These "maximums" have essentially become minimums for the vast majority of cases. Two-thirds of the subject lawyers who handled chapter 13 cases charged the maximum to all but a few clients . . . . At the time of the study, the fees charged to most chapter 13 clients in the four cities were these "maximums":

Austin	$1500
San Antonio	$1300
Cincinnati	$650
Dayton	$650

. . . Chapter 7 fees charged by the subject lawyers were lower and more variable than chapter 13 fees, particularly in the two Texas cities. Each lawyer was asked the fee charged to most chapter 7 clients, and the median of this figure and its range in each city was as follows:

	Median	Range
Austin	$700-750	$500-1800
San Antonio	$700-750	$500-1100
Cincinnati	$450-500	$400-600
Dayton	$300-350	$250-600

The chapter 7 trustees and the bankruptcy judges in the four cities have not set standard fees like those in chapter 13. The primary reason seems to be that competition keeps the fees low. . . .

Fees charged by the Texas subject lawyers were higher in both chapters than for the Ohio lawyers. The difference was most pronounced for chapter 13 fees . . . . There is no obvious explanation based on higher overhead costs in Texas . . . that would justify judges and chapter 13 trustees in setting chapter 13 fees this much higher in the Texas cities . . . . The more obvious explanation of the differences is that the chapter 13 trustees and judges in the Texas cities are giving lawyers a big incentive to use chapter 13. The higher rate of chapter 13 use in the Texas bankruptcy district in question may be attributable in significant part to this difference. . . .

c. Comparing Fees under the Two Chapters

Median chapter 13 fees were higher than median chapter 7 fees for the subject lawyers in all four cities. The differential between total fee amount for chapter 7 cases as opposed to chapter 13 cases was widest in Austin and Dayton, where the median chapter 7 fees were about half the standard chapter 13 fees. . . . In absolute dollar amounts, the subject lawyers typically charged this much more for chapter 13 than for chapter 7: Austin ($775), San Antonio ($525), Dayton ($325), Cincinnati ($175). . . .

In sum, it is not easy to determine whether the subject lawyers make more from chapter 13 or chapter 7 cases. Although fees are higher in chapter 13 cases, lawyers almost always give more credit for a longer time in chapter 13 than in chapter 7 cases . . . . Also, there is somewhat more work in chapter 13 cases, and doing a high volume of chapter 13 cases usually involves having a computer system and more staff to handle them. . . .

My best estimate is that, in a majority of chapter 13 cases, lawyers collect at least as much or more as in most chapter 7 cases, and that the increased time and overhead is not significant for many lawyers, so that on average a chapter 13 case is more lucrative than a chapter 7 case. Thus lawyers have a financial incentive to use chapter 13 to collect higher fees, although some eschew higher profitability for lower risk and less stress . . . . Many lawyers in the study confirmed this view that chapter 13 is more profitable. . . .

VI. CONCLUSION

This empirical study presents a picture of dramatic variations in the way that consumer bankruptcy law is put into action by the lawyers in four cities. The study reveals at least two causes of the variations—differences in local legal culture and differences in the attitudes of individual lawyers. Each city has its own culture, to which lawyers react differently: some assimilate and others resist it.

In San Antonio and Dayton, there are strong local cultures favoring chapter 13, but these two cities have very different versions of chapter 13 in place. In San Antonio the expectation is for high-percentage plans . . . . Attitudes back up these high repayment expectations. . . .

In Dayton, in contrast, 10% plans are routinely confirmed. The local culture emphasizes use of chapter 13 for financial, not moral reasons. The most common reason given for using chapter 13 is to pay arrearages on home and car loans. . . .

The cultures of Cincinnati and Austin are more mixed. Lawyers in these cities are divided in their practices and attitudes, and fewer among them are enthusiastic about chapter 13. Cincinnati has a repayment expectation of 70% in chapter 13, and this is not backed up by moral fervor. As a result, lawyers view chapter 13 as infeasible for many. In Austin low percentage plans are common. There are two opposing views among the Austin lawyers interviewed: high-volume lawyers are much more willing to use chapter 13, primarily for financial reasons, while the low-volume lawyers tend to think that chapter 13 is a bad deal for clients, and is peddled by the high-volume lawyers for their own financial gain.

The consumer bankruptcy system gives great potential power to local officials, particularly chapter 13 standing trustees. Chapter 13 trustees and bankruptcy judges can and do administer the law in ways that create incentives and disincentives not apparent in the Bankruptcy Code or reported court decisions. Apart from the minimum repayment expectations in chapter 13, the most glaring incentive determined locally is directed at lawyers' financial interests, not clients. Some local officials set standard attorneys' fees for chapter 13 much higher than the local median fee for chapter 7. . . .

In a large, far-flung, locally administered system such as consumer bankruptcy it is inevitable that there will be local variation in practices and attitudes. But the current state of consumer bankruptcy is very far from the constitutional ideal of uniformity, and takes more the form of a network of fiefdoms with significantly different customs. . . .

The study supports both the fairness and consumer protection critiques of the consumer bankruptcy system. A central feature of the governing law is that it provides two options to consumer debtors, most of whom could justify using either one. Debtors in similar financial circumstances routinely end up with different legal treatment: some get an immediate discharge under chapter 7; and others struggle under three- to five-year plans in chapter 13, in an attempt to make partial or full payment to creditors, and often fail. . . .

The first major question is: do we care about fairness? Is it acceptable, even desirable, to have a system that can be used differently by debtors in the same circumstances? If so, other questions follow: can greater consumer understanding of the two options be achieved? Must the law be simplified to achieve better understanding? Also, in a two-option system, do we want local administrative officials (primarily chapter 13 standing trustees) empowered to act as cheerleaders for one option, and to use discretionary power to set up local variations in incentives and disincentives for choice of one chapter or the other?

One type of incentive currently in use should be eliminated—much higher attorneys' fees in chapter 13, set in excess of what is needed to compensate lawyers adequately for any greater costs and risks. By setting much higher fees in chapter 13, bankruptcy officials reward lawyers for acting as hucksters. Giving financial incentives to lawyers is an inappropriate way to get more debtors to file under chapter 13.

The second major question is, if fairness *should* be a goal of consumer bankruptcy law, can this be achieved without jeopardizing the central purpose of the law, debtor relief? The type of reform that would most effectively lead to greater fairness among similarly-situated debtors and at the same time reduce complexity (so as to facilitate consumer understanding) would be to offer only one form of bankruptcy to consumers. Then the difficult question would be whether the one form should look more like chapter 7 or chapter 13.

The study reveals that the primary financial reasons that debtors use chapter 13 are to cure defaults on secured debts and to redeem collateral on an installment basis. Chapter 7 could be enhanced to permit debtors to achieve these goals while also discharging unsecured debt. But the credit industry lobby would undoubtedly vigorously oppose such a reform of the Bankruptcy Code.

A more politically acceptable unitary form of consumer bankruptcy would include an expectation of repayment out of income by all consumer debtors to the extent that they are reasonably capable. This would essentially mean making chapter 13 the only choice. . . . A unitary chapter 13 option would likely mean more debtor failure to complete plans and less debtor relief.

In short, there is no easy, politically feasible solution to the fairness concern that would not jeopardize the goal of giving consumers relief from unmanageable debt. At a minimum, the study reported in this article should add volume to the chorus of concern that chapter 13 is currently being oversold by some lawyers, encouraged by some local officials. Pushing more debtors who are marginal into payment plans that fail is not a promising solution to the fairness and consumer protection problems in the consumer bankruptcy system. The study also provides dramatic evidence for the proposition that law in action is very different from either law on the books or law according to elegant theory. Arm-chair policy analysis in this field, as in many others, is doomed to be wrong.

Teresa A. Sullivan, Elizabeth Warren & Jay Lawrence Westbrook
The Persistence of Local Legal Culture:
Twenty Years of Evidence From the Federal Bankruptcy Courts
17 Harv. J.L. & Pub. Pol'y 801 (1994)[*]

III. Measurable Variations in Debtor Choices

. . .

B. *Local Variations*

1. *Bankruptcy Rates*

The crucial decision to file for bankruptcy is made in nearly all cases by the individual debtors. That decision is made by dramatically different proportions of debtors in different states. Table 1 shows the rate of nonbusiness bankruptcy filings per 100,000 population filing for bankruptcy in 1970, 1980 and 1990.

Table 1
Bankruptcy Filings (Chapters 7 & 13) per 100,000 Population
(By State and District, 1970 - 1990).

	1970	1980	1990
National Total	94.78	128.21	266.09
Alabama	280.82	242.23	584.59
Northern	316.44	283.95	692.12
Middle	213.75	219.62	487.10
Southern	253.01	137.06	360.63
Alaska	61.22	58.23	186.53
Arizona	167.05	119.71	420.08
Arkansas	58.29	101.25	273.83
Eastern	76.30	124.72	295.49
Western	29.30	65.99	239.77
California	172.36	168.99	324.63
Northern	166.70	202.41	257.51
Eastern	186.96	175.65	313.31
Central	171.79	151.14	347.98
Southern	164.35	167.15	382.27
Colorado	182.13	176.37	443.48
Connecticut	42.87	59.98	121.57
Delaware	21.16	74.70	124.89
District of Columbia	13.20	86.48	150.60
Florida	22.81	51.18	216.17
Northern	11.64	36.63	155.92
Middle	29.86	63.28	282.84

Southern	16.61	38.79	140.84
Georgia	**156.75**	**180.26**	**568.30**
Northern	161.58	188.60	602.35
Middle	164.53	184.77	478.85
Southern	132.37	150.43	583.28
Hawaii	**48.19**	**63.65**	**72.46**
Idaho	**151.89**	**189.00**	**376.26**
Illinois	**117.12**	**216.66**	**296.13**
Northern	113.72	231.03	301.13
Central	56.39	229.49	314.12
Southern	247.81	103.97	232.55
Indiana	**143.12**	**218.57**	**381.86**
Northern	108.29	204.07	316.54
Southern	168.18	228.85	428.63
Iowa	**92.71**	**99.87**	**163.86**
Northern	91.53	76.82	130.80
Southern	93.82	120.90	192.18
Kansas	**217.29**	**160.30**	**306.59**
Kentucky	**163.54**	**196.11**	**341.17**
Eastern	102.71	120.53	319.84
Western	216.57	268.19	361.83
Louisiana	**160.94**	**100.43**	**277.40**
Eastern	159.95	112.55	289.92
Middle	N/A	77.95	246.85
Western	161.94	97.19	276.77
Maine	**179.24**	**68.91**	**100.66**
Maryland	**11.96**	**84.44**	**175.47**
Massachusetts	**24.91**	**46.14**	**99.71**
Michigan	**75.27**	**139.01**	**186.14**
Eastern	75.94	142.00	196.22
Western	73.61	132.32	165.11
Minnesota	**72.27**	**96.44**	**288.43**
Mississippi	**57.38**	**175.04**	**400.12**
Northern	38.47	101.71	341.28
Southern	70.04	220.94	435.73
Missouri	**121.58**	**130.62**	**239.77**
Eastern	105.19	110.27	254.81
Western	141.10	153.18	223.65
Montana	**130.04**	**107.92**	**199.11**
Nebraska	**95.70**	**154.60**	**216.11**
Nevada	**252.69**	**233.86**	**483.59**
New Hampshire	**68.73**	**61.70**	**133.06**
New Jersey	**19.63**	**63.67**	**149.03**
New Mexico	**150.59**	**98.55**	**241.18**
New York	**31.65**	**104.49**	**145.68**
Northern	70.99	129.35	170.12
Eastern	11.09	88.77	126.18
Southern	14.05	67.25	116.08
Western	73.36	172.00	213.96

North Carolina	15.29	117.21	147.80
Eastern	8.69	122.11	130.02
Middle	29.64	145.19	166.33
Western	7.16	82.50	151.47
North Dakota	43.38	56.53	132.44
Ohio	160.53	222.95	323.95
Northern	140.42	214.66	281.08
Southern	186.28	232.98	372.68
Oklahoma	133.63	138.80	408.76
Northern	204.02	175.74	433.63
Eastern	37.86	56.86	219.37
Western	136.37	152.69	468.88
Oregon	217.94	157.53	376.73
Pennsylvania	12.63	54.44	120.89
Eastern	12.50	61.36	141.26
Middle	10.47	48.01	106.33
Western	14.03	50.23	104.33
Rhode Island	47.91	86.15	147.99
South Carolina	7.99	31.07	128.40
South Dakota	27.77	59.93	150.43
Tennessee	225.32	262.88	693.47
Eastern	195.02	197.09	510.92
Middle	239.52	258.63	662.94
Western	253.29	363.42	994.12
Texas	13.88	44.52	215.00
Northern	19.00	37.05	264.23
Eastern	6.16	13.37	109.84
Southern	8.36	40.81	183.95
Western	18.10	76.59	253.86
Utah	128.58	139.83	432.60
Vermont	68.58	34.61	58.64
Virginia	120.25	150.65	274.35
Eastern	109.68	154.76	288.85
Western	141.20	142.57	240.82
Washington	135.99	154.47	312.86
Eastern	120.17	166.08	324.18
Western	141.15	150.65	309.60
West Virginia	96.89	73.86	172.79
Northern	81.98	66.22	123.09
Southern	108.87	80.02	210.20
Wisconsin	80.85	91.87	182.98
Eastern	83.71	91.07	209.62
Western	76.06	93.10	142.27
Wyoming	181.10	85.19	294.54

Source: Administrative Office of the Courts, Annual Reports and unpublished data.

The rate at which people choose bankruptcy as a solution to their perceived financial problems varies dramatically, both over time and by geographic region. The data show that bankruptcy filing rates nearly tripled over the past two decades, from a national average of about ninety-five in 1970 to 266 in 1990. . . . In the largest sense, these data confirm that bankruptcy is a national phenomenon and that debtors have come to the system with increasing frequency.

Yet Table 1 also shows great variations in filing rates, both among the states and among the districts within those states. In 1990, for example, we observe variations in filing rates of more than one hundred percent among districts within Texas, Florida, and Oklahoma. Of the twenty-four states that have more than one district, nine had variations of more than sixty percent and thirteen had variations of more than thirty percent. . . . In sum, the data show that powerful variation in the decision to file for bankruptcy takes place locally, a phenomenon unexplained by variations in formal debtor-creditor laws.

2. Chapter Choices

At the second stage in the bankruptcy process, the debtor must choose between filing a Chapter 7 liquidation and a Chapter 13 payment plan. In this section, we use data regarding this choice in two ways. First, we reexamine the filing rates per 100,000 of the population, this time separating the debtors by chapter to produce filing rates for Chapter 7 and filing rates for Chapter 13, as shown in Table 2. Second, we look at the relative proportions of filings within a district that are filed in Chapter 7 or Chapter 13. Although consumers occasionally file in other chapters, we have eliminated these chapters from our table, so that the sum of the proportions is 1.00. Table 3 presents the proportion of filings that are in Chapter 7 and in Chapter 13.

TABLE 2
BANKRUPTCY FILING RATES PER 100,000 POPULATION
(BY CHAPTER, STATE, AND DISTRICT, 1970-1990).

	1970 Chapter 7	1970 Chapter 13	1980 Chapter 7	1980 Chapter 13	1990 Chapter 7	1990 Chapter 13
National Total	79.68	15.10	95.09	33.12	187.45	78.65
Alabama	76.22	204.61	78.76	163.46	247.19	337.40
Northern	89.69	226.76	92.98	190.97	265.88	426.25
Middle	59.92	153.84	53.35	166.28	168.09	319.01
Southern	54.23	198.78	65.84	71.22	289.86	70.77
Alaska	59.90	1.32	46.29	11.94	159.99	26.54
Arizona	159.21	7.84	112.57	7.14	322.87	97.21
Arkansas	27.71	30.57	27.77	73.48	152.38	121.45
Eastern	30.52	45.78	27.54	97.19	136.40	159.09
Western	23.20	6.10	28.12	37.86	177.50	62.27
California	149.54	22.83	133.03	35.96	248.89	75.74
Northern	131.12	35.59	139.06	63.35	180.85	76.66
Eastern	156.77	30.19	132.07	43.58	250.44	62.87
Central	159.28	12.51	133.97	17.17	279.15	68.84
Southern	128.04	36.30	111.77	55.37	241.86	140.41
Colorado	165.23	16.90	93.53	82.84	320.73	122.75
Connecticut	42.38	0.49	54.77	5.21	106.02	15.55
Delaware	21.16	0.00	67.47	7.23	96.67	28.22
District of Columbia	12.81	0.40	86.48	0.00	79.58	71.02

Florida	22.40	0.41	48.33	2.85	191.88	24.29
Northern	11.39	0.25	32.54	4.09	145.60	10.31
Middle	29.37	0.49	60.36	2.93	248.72	34.12
Southern	16.25	0.36	36.40	2.40	126.41	14.43
Georgia	100.68	56.06	116.11	64.16	249.33	318.98
Northern	126.13	35.44	131.56	57.04	271.03	331.32
Middle	88.49	76.04	121.06	63.71	239.74	239.12
Southern	53.19	79.18	65.79	84.64	193.39	389.88
Hawaii	41.82	6.36	28.20	35.45	64.07	8.39
Idaho	122.86	29.03	124.06	64.94	249.32	126.94
Illinois	106.01	11.11	154.19	62.47	224.74	71.40
Northern	104.73	8.99	149.12	81.91	215.30	85.83
Central	51.57	4.82	208.26	21.24	280.33	33.80
Southern	211.89	35.92	88.16	15.81	189.06	43.48
Indiana	141.87	1.25	208.33	10.24	346.26	35.61
Northern	108.20	0.09	189.88	14.19	276.95	39.59
Southern	166.10	2.09	221.41	7.44	395.89	32.75
Iowa	85.59	7.11	89.40	10.47	148.70	15.16
Northern	88.92	2.61	63.73	13.09	124.09	6.71
Southern	82.42	11.40	112.83	8.07	169.78	22.40
Kansas	151.40	65.89	114.91	45.40	247.50	59.09
Kentucky	127.82	35.72	157.62	38.49	264.81	76.36
Eastern	77.24	25.48	97.42	23.11	245.08	74.76
Western	171.92	44.65	215.03	53.16	283.93	77.90
Louisiana	134.09	6.34	81.22	19.21	199.24	78.15
Eastern	145.19	14.75	94.92	17.63	222.93	66.99
Middle	N/A	N/A	71.19	6.76	177.45	69.41
Western	160.69	1.25	72.98	24.21	186.71	90.06
Maine	95.61	83.63	40.01	28.90	74.76	25.90
Maryland	11.91	0.05	79.75	4.70	114.61	60.86
Massachusetts	23.68	1.23	37.16	8.98	80.08	19.63
Michigan	66.62	8.64	105.68	33.33	140.12	46.01
Eastern	64.58	11.36	123.24	18.76	153.04	43.18
Western	71.63	1.98	66.39	65.93	113.18	51.93
Minnesota	62.63	9.65	80.72	15.73	203.40	85.03
Mississippi	56.79	0.59	116.20	58.83	251.86	148.26
Northern	38.47	0.00	97.28	4.43	223.36	117.92
Southern	69.06	0.98	128.05	92.89	269.11	166.62
Missouri	116.37	5.22	115.85	14.77	176.47	63.30
Eastern	105.03	0.16	102.77	7.50	165.09	89.72
Western	129.86	1.24	130.36	22.82	188.67	34.98
Montana	129.32	0.72	105.63	2.29	179.84	19.27
Nebraska	90.44	5.26	121.29	33.32	145.78	70.33
Nevada	247.99	4.71	220.24	13.62	344.31	139.29
New Hampshire	68.32	0.41	60.39	1.30	117.20	15.87
New Jersey	18.57	1.06	47.28	16.39	105.34	43.69
New Mexico	131.10	19.49	91.64	6.91	216.43	24.75
New York	31.31	0.34	84.51	19.99	116.78	28.90
Northern	70.85	0.14	119.84	9.51	141.17	28.95

Eastern	11.05	0.04	64.49	24.28	102.24	23.93
Southern	13.99	0.06	58.64	8.60	102.90	13.18
Western	71.60	1.76	133.43	38.57	147.24	66.72
North Carolina	7.08	8.21	33.99	83.22	53.12	94.68
Eastern	7.86	0.83	45.64	76.47	71.47	58.55
Middle	6.27	23.37	26.34	118.85	33.71	132.61
Western	7.02	0.14	27.43	55.07	49.60	101.87
North Dakota	41.76	1.62	54.54	1.99	124.92	7.51
Ohio	143.55	16.98	163.14	59.81	245.07	78.88
Northern	132.09	8.33	159.18	55.48	223.57	57.52
Southern	158.22	28.06	167.93	65.05	269.51	103.16
Oklahoma	130.00	3.63	133.67	5.12	369.31	39.45
Northern	196.38	7.64	168.06	7.68	406.63	27.00
Eastern	37.86	0.00	56.06	0.79	203.25	16.12
Western	133.26	3.11	147.14	5.56	414.19	54.69
Oregon	210.29	7.65	136.08	21.46	270.62	106.11
Pennsylvania	12.57	0.07	41.97	12.47	81.46	39.43
Eastern	12.38	0.12	34.45	26.91	72.87	68.39
Middle	10.43	0.04	46.49	1.52	87.85	18.48
Western	14.00	0.02	48.09	2.14	88.27	16.06
Rhode Island	47.70	0.21	66.41	19.74	136.73	11.26
South Carolina	7.84	0.15	23.06	8.01	66.31	62.09
South Dakota	27.77	0.00	50.96	8.98	137.07	13.36
Tennessee	148.26	77.06	141.97	20.91	268.88	424.59
Eastern	137.36	57.66	111.90	85.19	264.00	246.92
Middle	203.18	36.35	191.22	67.41	280.17	382.77
Western	112.65	140.64	135.75	227.67	263.50	730.61
Texas	12.89	0.99	25.66	18.86	131.40	83.60
Northern	18.67	0.33	28.25	8.80	152.56	111.67
Eastern	6.16	0.00	11.62	1.74	77.85	31.99
Southern	8.36	0.00	22.14	18.67	119.06	64.89
Western	14.38	3.73	35.13	41.47	151.21	102.65
Utah	125.94	2.64	125.53	14.30	298.98	133.62
Vermont	68.58	0.00	33.83	0.78	46.20	12.44
Virginia	102.29	17.96	126.47	24.18	214.78	59.57
Eastern	108.16	1.52	138.62	16.14	220.81	68.04
Western	90.67	50.53	102.57	40.00	200.83	39.99
Washington	113.40	22.59	106.00	48.47	242.34	70.52
Eastern	110.28	9.90	131.08	34.99	262.15	62.03
Western	114.42	26.73	97.74	52.91	236.63	72.97
West Virginia	94.31	2.58	70.06	3.80	157.01	15.78
Northern	81.59	0.39	63.92	2.30	111.54	11.56
Southern	104.53	4.34	75.02	5.00	191.24	18.96
Wisconsin	69.58	11.27	73.65	18.21	156.16	26.82
Eastern	69.94	13.76	77.34	13.72	181.82	27.80
Western	68.97	7.09	67.96	25.14	116.95	25.32
Wyoming	178.39	2.71	75.60	9.58	266.32	28.22

Source: Administrative Office of the Courts, Annual Reports and unpublished data.
Note: Nonbusiness cases.

TABLE 3
PROPORTION OF BANKRUPTCY FILINGS THAT ARE
CHAPTER 7 AND CHAPTER 13 (BY STATE AND DISTRICT, 1970-1990).

	1970 Chapter 7	1970 Chapter 13	1980 Chapter 7	1980 Chapter 13	1990 Chapter 7	1990 Chapter 13
National Total	0.841	0.159	0.742	0.258	0.704	0.296
Alabama	0.271	0.729	0.325	0.675	0.423	0.577
Northern	0.283	0.717	0.327	0.673	0.384	0.616
Middle	0.280	0.720	0.243	0.757	0.345	0.655
Southern	0.214	0.786	0.480	0.520	0.804	0.196
Alaska	0.978	0.022	0.795	0.205	0.858	0.142
Arizona	0.953	0.047	0.940	0.060	0.769	0.231
Arkansas	0.475	0.525	0.274	0.726	0.556	0.444
Eastern	0.400	0.600	0.221	0.779	0.462	0.538
Western	0.792	0.208	0.426	0.574	0.740	0.260
California	0.868	0.132	0.787	0.213	0.767	0.233
Northern	0.787	0.213	0.687	0.313	0.702	0.298
Eastern	0.839	0.161	0.752	0.248	0.799	0.201
Central	0.927	0.073	0.886	0.114	0.802	0.198
Southern	0.779	0.221	0.669	0.331	0.633	0.367
Colorado	0.907	0.093	0.530	0.470	0.723	0.277
Connecticut	0.988	0.012	0.913	0.087	0.872	0.128
Delaware	1.000	0.000	0.903	0.097	0.774	0.226
District of Columbia	0.970	0.030	1.000	0.000	0.528	0.472
Florida	0.982	0.018	0.944	0.056	0.888	0.112
Northern	0.979	0.021	0.888	0.112	0.934	0.066
Middle	0.984	0.016	0.954	0.046	0.879	0.121
Southern	0.978	0.022	0.938	0.062	0.898	0.102
Georgia	0.642	0.358	0.644	0.356	0.439	0.561
Northern	0.781	0.219	0.698	0.302	0.450	0.550
Middle	0.538	0.462	0.655	0.345	0.501	0.499
Southern	0.402	0.598	0.437	0.563	0.332	0.668
Hawaii	0.868	0.132	0.443	0.557	0.884	0.116
Idaho	0.809	0.191	0.656	0.344	0.663	0.337
Illinois	0.905	0.095	0.712	0.288	0.759	0.241
Northern	0.921	0.079	0.645	0.355	0.715	0.285
Central	0.915	0.085	0.907	0.093	0.892	0.108
Southern	0.855	0.145	0.848	0.152	0.813	0.187
Indiana	0.991	0.009	0.953	0.047	0.907	0.093
Northern	0.999	0.001	0.930	0.070	0.875	0.125
Southern	0.988	0.012	0.968	0.032	0.924	0.076
Iowa	0.923	0.077	0.895	0.105	0.907	0.093
Northern	0.971	0.029	0.830	0.170	0.949	0.051
Southern	0.878	0.122	0.933	0.067	0.883	0.117
Kansas	0.697	0.303	0.717	0.283	0.807	0.193
Kentucky	0.782	0.218	0.804	0.196	0.776	0.224
Eastern	0.752	0.248	0.808	0.192	0.766	0.234

Western	0.794	0.206	0.802	0.198	0.785	0.215
Louisiana	0.955	0.045	0.809	0.191	0.718	0.282
Eastern	0.908	0.092	0.843	0.157	0.769	0.231
Middle	N/A	N/A	0.913	0.087	0.719	0.281
Western	0.992	0.008	0.751	0.249	0.675	0.325
Maine	0.533	0.467	0.581	0.419	0.743	0.257
Maryland	0.996	0.004	0.944	0.056	0.653	0.347
Massachusetts	0.951	0.049	0.805	0.195	0.803	0.197
Michigan	0.885	0.115	0.760	0.240	0.753	0.247
Eastern	0.850	0.150	0.868	0.132	0.780	0.220
Western	0.973	0.027	0.502	0.498	0.686	0.314
Minnesota	0.867	0.133	0.837	0.163	0.705	0.295
Mississippi	0.990	0.010	0.664	0.336	0.629	0.371
Northern	1.000	0.000	0.956	0.044	0.654	0.346
Southern	0.986	0.014	0.580	0.420	0.618	0.382
Missouri	0.957	0.043	0.887	0.113	0.736	0.264
Eastern	0.999	0.001	0.932	0.068	0.648	0.352
Western	0.920	0.080	0.851	0.149	0.844	0.156
Montana	0.994	0.006	0.979	0.021	0.903	0.097
Nebraska	0.945	0.055	0.785	0.215	0.675	0.325
Nevada	0.981	0.019	0.942	0.058	0.712	0.288
New Hampshire	0.994	0.006	0.979	0.021	0.881	0.119
New Jersey	0.946	0.054	0.743	0.257	0.707	0.293
New Mexico	0.871	0.129	0.930	0.070	0.897	0.103
New York	0.989	0.011	0.809	0.191	0.802	0.198
Northern	0.998	0.002	0.927	0.073	0.830	0.170
Eastern	0.996	0.004	0.726	0.274	0.810	0.190
Southern	0.996	0.004	0.872	0.128	0.886	0.114
Western	0.976	0.024	0.776	0.224	0.688	0.312
North Carolina	0.463	0.537	0.290	0.710	0.359	0.641
Eastern	0.904	0.096	0.374	0.626	0.550	0.450
Middle	0.211	0.789	0.181	0.819	0.203	0.797
Western	0.981	0.019	0.332	0.668	0.327	0.673
North Dakota	0.963	0.037	0.965	0.035	0.943	0.057
Ohio	0.894	0.106	0.732	0.268	0.757	0.243
Northern	0.941	0.059	0.742	0.258	0.795	0.205
Southern	0.849	0.151	0.721	0.279	0.723	0.277
Oklahoma	0.973	0.027	0.963	0.037	0.903	0.097
Northern	0.963	0.037	0.956	0.044	0.938	0.062
Eastern	1.000	0.000	0.986	0.014	0.927	0.073
Western	0.977	0.023	0.964	0.036	0.883	0.117
Oregon	0.965	0.035	0.864	0.136	0.718	0.282
Pennsylvania	0.995	0.005	0.771	0.229	0.674	0.326
Eastern	0.991	0.009	0.561	0.439	0.516	0.484
Middle	0.996	0.004	0.968	0.032	0.826	0.174
Western	0.998	0.002	0.957	0.043	0.846	0.154
Rhode Island	0.996	0.004	0.771	0.229	0.924	0.076
South Carolina	0.981	0.019	0.742	0.258	0.516	0.484
South Dakota	1.000	0.000	0.850	0.150	0.911	0.089

Tennessee..............................0.658	0.342	0.540	0.460	0.388	0.612
Eastern..............................0.704	0.296	0.568	0.432	0.517	0.483
Middle...............................0.848	0.152	0.739	0.261	0.423	0.577
Western.............................0.445	0.555	0.374	0.626	0.265	0.735
Texas....................................0.929	0.071	0.576	0.424	0.611	0.389
Northern............................0.983	0.017	0.762	0.238	0.577	0.423
Eastern..............................1.000	0.000	0.870	0.130	0.709	0.291
Southern............................1.000	0.000	0.543	0.457	0.647	0.353
Western.............................0.794	0.206	0.459	0.541	0.596	0.404
Utah.....................................0.979	0.021	0.898	0.102	0.691	0.309
Vermont...............................1.000	0.000	0.977	0.023	0.788	0.212
Virginia................................0.851	0.149	0.839	0.161	0.783	0.217
Eastern..............................0.986	0.014	0.896	0.104	0.764	0.236
Western.............................0.642	0.358	0.719	0.281	0.834	0.166
Washington..........................0.834	0.166	0.686	0.314	0.775	0.225
Eastern..............................0.918	0.082	0.789	0.211	0.809	0.191
Western.............................0.811	0.189	0.649	0.351	0.764	0.236
West Virginia.......................0.973	0.027	0.949	0.051	0.909	0.091
Northern............................0.995	0.005	0.965	0.035	0.906	0.094
Southern............................0.960	0.040	0.938	0.062	0.910	0.090
Wisconsin.............................0.861	0.139	0.802	0.198	0.853	0.147
Eastern..............................0.836	0.164	0.849	0.151	0.867	0.133
Western.............................0.907	0.903	0.730	0.270	0.822	0.178
Wyoming.............................0.985	0.015	0.888	0.112	0.904	0.096

Source: Administrative Office of the Courts, Annual Reports and unpublished data.
Note: Nonbusiness cases.

a. *National Changes*

Once again, the data demonstrate a national trend: since 1970, Chapter 13 has become an increasingly important part of the bankruptcy picture. In 1970, the national Chapter 7 filing rate was eighty, and eighty-four percent of all filings were in Chapter 7. By 1990, the Chapter 7 filing rate had more than doubled to 187, but the proportion of Chapter 7 filings had shrunk to seventy percent. For Chapter 13, the filing rates more than quintupled from fifteen in 1970 to seventy-nine in 1990; the proportions nearly doubled from about sixteen percent to about thirty percent of all filings. . . . The proportion of Chapter 13 filings seems to have reached a rough equilibrium, with about one in four bankrupt debtors now filing in Chapter 13.

b. *Local Variation*

Despite a clear national trend to more Chapter 13 filings, the data show great variation in chapter choice among the districts and among the states. Local Chapter 13 filing rates in 1990 varied by a factor of one hundred, from seven in the Northern District of Iowa to 731 in the Eastern District of Tennessee. Six districts had rates over 300, and ten districts were below fifteen. Chapter 13 filings as a proportion of all bankruptcy filings in 1990 ranged from a high of eighty percent in the Middle District of North Carolina to a low of five percent in the Northern District of Iowa.

Once again, the key point for present purposes is that the variation *within* states was quite pronounced. For example, in the Southern District of Alabama, only twenty percent of 1990 filings were in Chapter 13, versus sixty-six percent in the adjacent Middle District of Alabama. In the Western District of Missouri, the proportion of Chapter 13 filings was sixteen percent; it was over twice as high in the Eastern District, with thirty-five percent. In New York, the proportions ranged from eleven percent in the Southern District to thirty-one percent in the Western District. In the Western District of Pennsylvania, fifteen percent of bankrupcies were in Chapter 13, versus almost half of bankrupcies in the Eastern District of Pennsylvania. In six of twenty-four multi-district states, the percentage of Chapter 13 cases varied between districts by more than one hundred percent. These intrastate variations cannot be explained by variations in formal laws, as the laws were the same in Manhattan and Buffalo, in Philadelphia and Pittsburgh.

As with Bankruptcy Rates, these differences among districts have persisted over decades. . . .

The data concerning Chapter Choices reinforces the inferences drawn from the Bankruptcy Rates. While there are national trends regarding consumer debtors' choices in bankruptcy, there is a great deal of persistent local variation. That variation suggests that something other than national and state laws may affect the proportion of debtors who try to resolve their debt problems with liquidation in Chapter 7 and those who may attempt a repayment in Chapter 13. Indeed, districts and states tend to replicate predictable patterns in their relative balance of Chapter 7 versus Chapter 13 filings; that is, their preferences as between the two procedures persist over time. . . .

The data reported here demonstrate enormous local variation at all three decision points for debtors in bankruptcy. Local variation will almost inevitably produce variation among states as well, but the intrastate data make it clear that the most powerful variation in the three key bankruptcy choices is at the local level and is a product of local differences.

Additional suggested readings

Peter C. Alexander, *With Apologies to C.S. Lewis: An Essay on Discharge and Forgiveness*, 9 J. BANKR. L. & PRAC. 601 (2000)

Jean Braucher, *Increasing Uniformity in Consumer Bankruptcy: Means Testing as a Distraction and the National Bankruptcy Review Commission's Proposals as a Starting Point*, 6 AM. BANKR. INST. L. REV. 1 (1998)

Jean Braucher, *Counseling Consumer Debtors to Make Their Own Informed Choices: A Question of Professional Responsibility*, 5 AM. BANKR. INST. L. REV. 165 (1997)

Vern Countryman, *Bankruptcy and the Individual Debtor—And a Modest Proposal to Return to the Seventeenth Century*, 32 CATH. U. L. REV. 809 (1983)

Theodore Eisenberg, *"Bankruptcy Law in Perspective": A Rejoinder*, 30 UCLA L. REV. 617 (1983)

Carl Felsenfeld, *Denial of Discharge for Substantial Abuse: Refining—Not Changing—Bankruptcy Law*, 67 FORDHAM L. REV. 1369 (1999)

Marjorie L. Girth, *The Role of Empirical Data in Developing Bankruptcy Legislation for Individuals*, 65 IND. L. REV. 17 (1989)

Karen Gross, FAILURE AND FORGIVENESS: REBALANCING THE BANKRUPTCY SYSTEM (Yale 1997)

Edith H. Jones & Todd J. Zywicki, *It's Time for Means-Testing*, 1999 BYU L. REV. 177

Kenneth N. Klee, *Restructuring Individual Debts*, 71 AM. BANKR. L.J. 431 (1997)

Gary Klein, *Means Tested Bankruptcy: What Would It Mean?*, 28 U. MEM. L. REV. 711 (1998)

Lynn M. LoPucki, *Common Sense Consumer Bankruptcy*, 71 AM. BANKR. L.J. 461 (1997)

Lynn M. LoPucki, *"Encouraging" Repayment Under Chapter 13 of the Bankruptcy Code*, 18 HARV. J. ON LEGIS. 347 (1981)

Hon. Robert D. Martin, *A Riposte to Klee*, 71 AM. BANKR. L.J. 453 (1997)

Teresa A. Sullivan, Elizabeth Warren & Jay Lawrence Westbrook, *The Use of Empirical Data in Formulating Bankruptcy Policy*, 50 LAW & CONTEMP PROBS. 195 (Spring 1987)

Teresa A. Sullivan, Elizabeth Warren & Jay Lawrence Westbrook, *Limiting Access to Bankruptcy Discharge: An Analysis of the Creditors' Data*, 1983 WIS. L. REV. 1091

William T. Vukowich, *Reforming the Bankruptcy Reform Act of 1978: An Alternative Approach*, 71 GEO. L.J. 1129 (1983)

Elizabeth Warren, *The Bankruptcy Crisis*, 73 IND. L.J. 1079 (1998)

William C. Whitford, *The Ideal of Individualized Justice: Consumer Bankruptcy as Consumer Protection, and Consumer Protection in Consumer Bankruptcy*, 68 AM. BANKR. L.J. 397 (1994)

Todd J. Zywicki, *With Apologies to Screwtape: A Response to Professor Alexander*, 9 J. Bankr. L. & Prac. 613 (2000)

Chapter 13

Introduction to Chapter 11 Reorganizations

Chapter 11 of the Bankruptcy Code permits firms to attempt to "reorganize" their financial affairs under court supervision. While some form of court-directed corporate reorganization has been possible for over a century, in recent years chapter 11 has become the focus of immense criticism and debate. This chapter introduces some of the basic notions and pirnciples underlying chapter 11. In the first selection Professor Tabb highlights the "first principles" of chapter 11.

Charles Jordan Tabb
The Future of Chapter 11
44 S.C. L. Rev. 791 (1993)[*]

II. First Principles: Why Chapter 11?

In assessing "the future of Chapter 11," it is important initially to focus on first principles. . . . Why do we have Chapter 11 at all?

It would be an understatement to note that not everyone agrees on what the fundamental purposes of the corporate reorganization chapter of the Bankruptcy Code are or should be. Having said that, until fairly recently there was a relatively strong consensus as to why we have Chapter 11. The 1977 House Report summarizes the essence of that consensus:

> The purpose of a business reorganization case, unlike a liquidation case, is to restructure a business's finances so that it may continue to operate, provide its employees with jobs, pay its creditors, and produce a return for its stockholders. The premise of a business reorganization is that assets that are used for production in the industry for which they were designed are more valuable than those same assets sold for scrap.

Professors LoPucki and Whitford have observed that "[t]he existence of bankruptcy reorganization procedures is commonly premised on the existence of a difference between the going concern value of the firm and its liquidation value." Professor Warren has summarized the so-called "traditionalist" theory of corporate reorganization, finding that four primary goals dominate: "(1) to enhance the value of the failing debtor; (2) to distribute value according to multiple normative principles; (3) to internalize the costs of the business failure to the parties dealing with the debtor; and (4) to create reliance on private monitoring."

This idea that the preservation of a business as a going concern is better for everyone—creditors, stockholders, bondholders, employees, and the public generally—is not a new one. It has been around for at least a century, really ever since the Industrial Revolution reached full flower. Reorganizations were first developed in earnest in the late nineteenth century as a way of keeping the railroads running. The mechanism used was the equity receivership. . . .

. . . [V]oices from the past serve as useful rejoinders to some of the more radical suggestions now being made that Chapter 11 should be sacrificed on the altar of perfect markets. If we forget the past, are we doomed to repeat it? To give one example, John Gerdes, a noted corporate reorganization lawyer and lecturer on corporate reorganizations at NYU, observed in 1936:

> The solvency or insolvency of a "big" corporation, having thousands of stockholders, owning and operating property throughout the world, and employing a veritable army of workers, is a matter of importance to the entire nation. The well-being of such a corporation makes its mark upon the prosperity of the country; the closing of its plants is a major catastrophe in the lives of hundreds, often thousands, of employees; its continuation in business is an item of public concern.

> . . .

Point one, then, is that a business is worth more alive than dead—*i.e.*, it is worth more as a going concern than in a forced sale liquidation; and that all affected parties, defined broadly, benefit if that going concern is maintained. Along these lines, it is worth remembering that more than just the private rights of the creditors and debtor may be implicated; the greater good of the community at large has always been considered, and rightly so, relevant to the formulation of bankruptcy policy.

It should be borne in mind that the foregoing conclusion is not a result of purely academic conjecture. Indeed, the truth is quite the opposite; it is what parties in fact do. When a business becomes financially distressed, the first order of business for the company and its creditors and stockholders is to try to put together a consensual workout. Studies have shown that about half of the business reorganizations effectuated today are done out of court, by voluntary agreement. Thus, it is only when an out-of-court workout cannot be achieved that the need for some other means of business reorganization presents itself. When a company gets into financial difficulties, the first thought is not, "let's auction off the assets"; rather, the first thought is, "let's make a deal."

Point two concerns the means to achieve the end of maintaining the business as a going concern when voluntary arrangements cannot be effected out of court. In thinking about what those means should be, it is helpful to focus on the reasons why voluntary workouts fail. One of the biggest problems is dealing with dissenting or recalcitrant creditors. Outside of some form of court-supervised model, creditors are free to pursue their own individual collection remedies—execution or garnishment by unsecured creditors, repossession and foreclosure by secured creditors, and so forth. This piecemeal seizure and sale of corporate assets has the potential to destroy the debtor's business. . . .

If some creditors are able to pursue collection in their own interest, a holdout problem appears. Even if a proposed workout would be better for the entire group of creditors than a liquidation, each creditor acting selfishly has an incentive to "hold out" and not sign on to the workout agreement. The holdout creditor can threaten to pursue individual collection activities that might irreparably damage the workout unless paid in full.

Two principal remedies are needed to counter the holdout dissenter problem. One is a stay or injunction against all creditors preventing them from pursuing their own claims during the pendency of the reorganization discussions and negotiations. Such a stay preserves the status quo. Under our current Bankruptcy Code section 362 serves this function. . . .

The second essential ingredient required to counter the holdout problem is the ability to bind dissenting creditors to the plan agreed to by the majority of creditors. Such a provision allows the reorganization plan to work once agreed to by the majority. Dissenters are permanently enjoined from pursuing their own prior claims after the requisite majority of creditors agree to a deal. The only claim the dissenter is left with is that provided for in the reorganization agreement itself. Once such a majority-rule provision is in effect, the incentive to hold out in the first place is largely eliminated, and meaningful negotiations can be carried out. Under our current law, section 1141 implements this policy of binding recalcitrant creditors. At the same time, other provisions in Chapter 11 attempt to provide for fair treatment of the dissenters' claims.

Any reform proposal that does not contain these two provisions—a stay of individual collection actions during plan negotiations and a subjugation of minority wishes to those of majority—is doomed to fail and is unworkable. Again, this is not a matter of conjecture; it is simply a recognition of the way the world works. Chapter 11 is the product of experience. . . .

Adopting the two provisions just referred to does not dictate any answers to the question of the extent to which a business reorganization law should reallocate or redistribute losses between different groups of creditors and equity holders. So far all I am stating is that asset value maximization, through proper deployment of the debtor's property in a going business, is to be preferred to the diminished returns available in a forced liquidation sale. At a minimum, collective action in the interests of the group as a whole should be mandated.

Law and Language

The following article is timeless in its thoughtful analysis of the basic principles underlying a system of court-supervised reorganization of corporations. Professor Walter Blum of the University of Chicago Law School was a leading scholar in the field of corporate reorganizations in the era from the end of World War II to the enactment of the 1978 Bankruptcy Code. Almost everything in the following article written in 1950 is of relevance today, even though the statutory particulars in some instances may be different. But the fundamental problems and issues have not changed.

As you read Professor Blum's seminal work, consider the following dozen questions:

1. What are the "two main principles" that form the framework for the corporate reorganization system?
2. What explanations support bypassing "the market" in favor of a court-supervised reorganization process? Are these persuasive?
3. What are the nature of and reasons for the political compromise that led to our system of court-supervised corporate reorganizations?
4. What are the essential doctrinal parts of the reorganization system?
5. What is "reorganization value" and why is it important? How is it computed? How does reorganization value differ from market value?
6. What is the "absolute priority" standard and why is it important? How does it relate to the requirements (i) that a plan be "fair"; (ii) that a plan be "feasible"; and (iii) the concept of "reorganization value"? How is the absolute priority standard applied?
7. How do the concepts of fairness and feasibility interrelate?
8. What is "cram-down" and why is it important? How does the absolute priority standard bear on cram-down?
9. What are the conflicting interests of different classes of creditors? How are the differences in classes mediated in a reorganization system? What voice do these groups have in the process? What voice should the supervising court have?

10.   What is the fundamental choice facing the creditors of a financially distressed company and the court that is supervising the reorganization proceeding?
11.   Why is the attitude of the reorganization judge significant?
12.   What is the "ultimate question" in a reorganization system? What approaches does Professor Blum explore in answering that question? Which answers and approaches do you find most convincing? Why?

Walter A. Blum
The Law and Language of Corporate Reorganization
17 U. Chi. L. Rev. 565 (1950)*

I.

Corporate reorganization under the National Bankruptcy Act is a process of dealing with the rights of those having financial commitments in distressed corporations. It is primarily concerned with the rights of investors—shareholders and bondholders and other lenders. . . .

. . . [T]wo main principles . . . constitute the framework for our existing system of reorganization. One is that the assets of a distressed business are not to be disposed of until there has been a reasonable opportunity to determine what disposition will be most advantageous. This principle is so clearly sound that elaboration is unnecessary. The other is that the market value of a distressed business or its assets is not to govern the rights of those financially interested in the company. More particularly the creditors are not to foreclose and force a sale or valuation of assets at prevailing market prices. Instead junior interests are to be protected from forced sales and the impact of unfavorable market conditions. It is the fulfillment of this principle which has produced the primary substantive content of our reorganization system.

Abandonment or avoidance of the market in reorganizations has been explained in a number of ways. The most general explanation is that ordinarily no pertinent market exists. . . .

It is obvious that a distressed enterprise or its assets can be sold at *some* price. . . . But the effective sale price might be very low as judged by those who already have a jeopardized financial commitment in the company. This judgment is at the bottom of another explanation for by-passing the market: Even if there is a market for distressed corporations it is too thin to be meaningful and in times of economic slump it is too chaotic to be fair. . . .

Another explanation for shelving the market in reorganizations builds upon the previous one. Senior investors whose claims are in default ordinarily will not be satisfied, it is said, with the prices obtainable through a sale of the business to outsiders in a thin market. Instead they will usually prefer to bid in their claims and thereby take over the distressed enterprise. In practice few defaulting large corporations have been sold to outsiders for new money; they have been reorganized by invalidating some or all of the rights of junior investors and distributing equivalent rights to the old senior claimants. Under such an arrangement the market price of the company or its property is said to have little significance because no real sale is involved or contemplated. . . .

The explanations advanced for ignoring market values of distressed companies are useful in understanding our reorganization system, but their soundness was not the decisive factor in molding that system. The prevailing pressure was to relieve junior corporate investors from those senior contracts which had turned out disastrously for them. This pressure was only a single facet of the

---

broader drive to relax strict enforcement of all bargains which sympathetic bystanders felt were harsh. . . . Seasoning the combination was the recurringly popular notion that economic slumps are temporary and therefore the settlement of rights at depressed prices which exist during them is unfair to junior interests. . . .

The pressure to undo security contracts was met by a counterforce. Direct resistance was offered by many senior groups seeking to secure the advantages of their bargains. In addition law-makers and courts generally recognized that in a credit economy financial pacts cannot be disturbed too much without seriously impairing the entire credit structure. Constitutional limitations moreover seemed to coincide with the demands for honoring security contracts. The impact of the various competing forces called for a political compromise. The result was an almost self-contained system of corporate reorganization.

The essential parts of the system perhaps might easily have been foreseen. Since market value was ruled out, a substitute standard of measurement had to be devised. For psychological and constitutional reasons the new gauge would be named to convey the impression that it measures "value." Probably the first appropriate name that comes to mind is "reorganization value." The quantity represented by this label is that which is to be apportioned among possible claimants. But the allocation must not seem arbitrary and accordingly canons of fairness for a plan of distribution are needed. These ought to stress upholding contractual priorities among classes of security contracts in order to emphasize that contracts are being enforced and not ignored. Obviously it would be embarrassing if the rehabilitated company soon ran into distress again. To prevent that from happening reorganization plans must be workable; the synonym "feasible" suggests itself as a label for this idea because it pairs better with "fair" and sounds less mundane. The entire reorganization process should appear to remain democratic in a democratic society. Accordingly those having a financial stake in the distressed company ought to vote on the important questions that arise during the proceedings. However, there may be some irreconcilable differences between investor groups having conflicting interests. To avoid everlasting stalemates someone must have power to resolve the issues by cramming a plan down the pockets of one side or the other. This is a task naturally cut out for a judge. Finally the whole process should seem to be predicated on principles and not on arbitrary actions. . . .

The compromise between enforcing and relaxing security contracts of course did become embodied in such a reorganization system. It now may be looked upon, for analytical convenience, as having three key doctrinal aspects: reorganization value; the fair and feasible plan; and the cramdown power. . . . Their products currently comprise the basic law and language of corporate reorganization.

II.

Reorganization value is the substitute for market value in reorganization. . . . Basically it purports to determine what classes of claimants are entitled to be satisfied in whole or part out of the assets of the distressed company. This it does by seeming to measure what classes are to participate in the reorganized entity and what ones are to be left out. . . .

The difference between market value and reorganization value is a touchstone for analyzing the reorganization system. Market value is a real value in that it not only is expressible in dollar terms but is realizable in dollars. Property can always be exchanged for cash at market price because that price is made by those who are ready and willing to back up their own estimates of value with money. For the same reason market value can always be ascertained objectively by noting the highest bid. In marked contrast, reorganization value has the opposite characteristics. It is a fictional value which cannot command real money dollar for dollar. It is set by the estimates of persons who are not standing back of them with a willingness to invest their own funds. Accordingly it can never be objectively ascertained or verified but always remains in the realm of opinion or belief. . . .

The imitation of investor practices resulted in crystallizing the calculation of reorganization value into an approved procedure that formally involves making three guesses. The first is an estimate of the annual income which the business hereafter most probably will earn. . . . The crystal gazing of course must be bottomed on facts, and therefore it is to be a projection of the company's past and present, rather than mere fancy about its future. The facts however are likely to be slippery and plastic. . . .

The second guess pertains to the probable life of the business as a going concern after reorganization. . . . A guess about continuation of the business under these circumstances necessarily involves assumptions as to replacement costs, the rate of technical change in the industry, the replacement program of competitive firms, and other factors of a similar nature. On these matters agreement among the technicians is neither likely nor very persuasive.

The third guess, which generally is most consequential, consists of picking a proper rate at which to capitalize the projected earnings. This endeavor presents a double puzzler. On the one hand *the* rate cannot be obtained from a review of the capitalization rates for the distressed enterprise itself which are implicit in the ratio between its earnings and the evaluation of the company (or its securities) by investors. Its current rate (that is, its earnings-valuation ratio) is fixed by the current market and that institution has been cast aside as a standard for measuring values in reorganizations. . . . On the other hand the spread of capitalization rates (again meaning earnings-valuation ratios) for similar or competing businesses during these various time periods seems to afford equally little data upon which to base selection of *the* rate. Most businesses do not have twins. Similar or competing firms may range from highly successful concerns to others undergoing the reorganization treatment. . . . At best the guessers can fall back only on average long-run capitalization rates for each of the corporations which they feel is more or less comparable to the one being rehabilitated.

This cursory review of the guesses which go into reorganization value indicates that all three have similar characteristics. Being guesses they of course cannot possess certainty. . . .

Accompanying the three-part estimate there is a one-part necessary assumption in calculating reorganization value which the authorized guides do not mention. It deals with the future state of our economy and in the cases it is usually implied rather than expressed. Because reorganization value concerns future conditions, something must be assumed as to the future general level of economic activity and the future real worth of the monetary unit. . . . The solution evidently is to wrap up the critical assumption in vagueness and bury it. In most reorganization cases it probably is assumed that the economic future will be much like the economic past . . . .

A troublesome but central question doubtless has been intruding. The guiding formula for finding reorganization value is a copy of that used by careful and informed investors. Presumably the copywork was accurate. Why then should anyone duplicate the valuation work which is independently and simultaneously being undertaken anyway by numerous investors with sharp pencils? . . . The correct answer is not so simple and it lies nearer the core of the reorganization process. . . .

. . . The essence of reorganization value can now be restated in other terms: Reorganization value is what some appraisers believe the current market value of the distressed company ought to be if the present were like the future they foresee. . . .

These . . . observations concerning reorganization value should not obscure the main point about the concept. Not only is it different from valuation by the market, but it can be understood fully only when contrasted with market value. . . . To assign a higher amount as reorganization value is to assume that the company's officers will manage its assets more profitably than investors believe these or similar assets will or can be managed. . . . [D]oing so nevertheless assumes that the debtor's officers will perform better, or that general economic conditions will be better, than is believed likely by those who make the market.

III.

Apart from the over-all valuation issue, questions of fairness about a reorganization plan arise principally because there is an uncertain ratio between reorganization value and market value, and so between a dollar of reorganization currency and a real dollar. If reorganizations were predicated on real dollars, presumably cash or its equivalent in securities would be allocated to claimants in the amounts and order of their contractual priorities. With claims being satisfied in this manner the fair allocation could be worked out mechanically. However no objectively gauged allocation is possible when the medium of distribution is reorganization currency of unknown dollar value. . . . Unless contractual priorities are to be dismissed entirely someone has to decide whether in his opinion a proposed allocation of reorganization currency is fair to the classes of claimants. Such a subjective judgment cannot be avoided; at best an effort can be made to hedge it about by formulating additional official guides for making an allocation. These, along with the guides for determining reorganization value, become the standard for a fair and equitable plan. . . .

The prevailing allocation guides collectively are designated the absolute priority standard. They purport to call for strict enforcement of security contracts as qualified by the premises contained in the reorganization value concept. In theory the contractual priorities affecting the rights of creditors and shareholders are to be recognized in full. Senior claimants are supposed to be completely compensated, which includes being given equitable compensation for loss of any valuable rights, before junior claimants are permitted to receive anything of value. Compensation to the seniors may be incorporated in the new securities or take some other form. In any case the new bundle of rights and claims allocated to them are supposed to be the equitable equivalent of their old packet. The worth of the new securities is not to be tested by reference to market quotations because that yardstick is patently inconsistent with predicating the plan on reorganization values. Instead their worth presumably is to be gauged by assuming that the corporation's market value has come up to its reorganization value or soon will do so. The stage for formulating a fair plan thus has a complex backdrop. The seniors are supposed to be compensated in full, but only in terms of reorganization currency which generally is not immediately convertible into dollars except at large discounts. The juniors are supposedly entitled to the excess, if any, of reorganization value over and above the amount needed to satisfy claims of the seniors. Interaction between these two guides is at the core of our absolute priority standard.

The main source of friction in this interaction is not difficult to locate. Reorganization value by hypothesis should equal the new capitalization of the rehabilitated enterprise. The new capitalization by definition equals the aggregate of nominal values assigned to the new securities. . . . Superficially it might seem that the juniors should receive the difference between the total nominal amount of senior claims and the reorganization value. But this formula assumes that the seniors receive new paper thought to be equivalent in quality, as well as in nominal quantity, to their old holdings. In most situations that arrangement would undermine the rehabilitation operation. . . . The statutory requirement that a plan be feasible as well as fair usually necessitates a more or less drastic scaling down of such obligations and this ordinarily can be accomplished only by reducing the quality of paper allocated to the seniors. Compensation for the deterioration usually can be provided only by giving the seniors a sum of reorganization currency greater than the aggregate nominal amount of their old claims. When this is done the balance of reorganization currency left for the juniors is concomitantly decreased.

. . . [T]he conflict among the sparring classes of security holders runs into what is considered to be an overriding public interest that the rehabilitation of distressed companies be soundly executed. The standard of feasibility for a plan is supposed to protect this public interest. . . . One might speculate whether our standard of fairness could not itself be stretched to impose comparable limitations so that there would be no need for a separate requirement of feasibility. There surely seems to be an element of unfairness in awarding seniors new securities which are unsound. But such doubts about fairness are likely to be associated with a distrust of the valuation for reorganization purposes. It would be awkward to accept a certain value as fair and then label an allocation of securities unfair on the ground that they are unsound though within the permissible capitalization. The feasibility requirement at least seems to avoid what might appear to be double-talk about fairness. . . .

. . . [A] strong argument can be made that the theory of reorganization dictates that there can be only a single fair allocation for any particular situation. In large measure the reorganization process was designed to preserve for juniors the greatest possible amount of value consistent with both full compensation for seniors and adequate protection of the public interest as reflected in the canons of feasibility. To accomplish this objective, the fair allocation must be that arrangement which gives juniors maximum participation within such limits. It must therefore be the plan which compensates seniors qualitatively to the fullest extent practicable in order to minimize the need for compensating them quantitatively and thereby increasing their nominal interests in the company. . . .

This approach to fairness also highlights the role that feasibility guides can be made to play. The single fair plan idea means, in effect, that *the* plan should push to the limits of feasibility whenever necessary to protect the juniors. . . . A two-directional relationship between fairness and feasibility is brought into focus. As a plan is thought to exceed the limits of feasibility it tends to seem unfair to seniors. As a plan is thought to fall short of the limits of feasibility it tends to seem unfair to juniors. In this sense it might be said that in reorganization doctrine fairness and feasibility are merely two different impressions of the same panorama.

. . . The absolute priority standard consists of guides for distributing reorganization currency among classes participating in a reorganization. Would adoption of another set of allocation guides, appropriately named, make any appreciable difference in the reorganization process? A change of guides would not lessen the need for making subjective judgments about the fairness of proposed allocations. Pressure and negotiation accordingly would continue to shape reorganization plans. Any change wrought by the new guides would simply be a shift in the permissible range for negotiation resulting from a changed effectiveness of the guides in confining official discretion about the fairness of plans. . . .

IV.

Financial distress of an industrial enterprise always focuses attention on what should be done with the business. Should it be continued in operation, sold as a going concern, scrapped, or disposed of in some other way? Even without the intervention of our reorganization system this question often is attended by many complications. There may be differences of opinion among those who have invested in the company. Fights for control are apt to develop. Sometimes the group in the saddle may have no equity in the entity under existing market values, and therefore it struggles to keep the company going. . . .

None of the complications disappears when our reorganization system is introduced into the affairs of a company in trouble. On the contrary the goal of a fair plan based on reorganization value adds a new dimension of complexities in deciding whether the business is to be sold or reorganized and, if the company is to be reorganized, in deciding what plan of reorganization is to be adopted. To protect their own interests the creditors and shareholders who continue to have a financial stake in the company will want to make these determinations. . . .

The determination of which classes of creditors and shareholders shall have a voice in formulating the program of rehabilitation is treated under reorganization doctrine as a function of reorganization value. All classes whose claims, taken in the order of their priority and at their nominal amounts, fit within the reorganization value are considered as having a stake in the business. Accordingly these groups are allowed to participate through appropriate representation in drawing up the program and to vote upon it. The classes that are wholly eliminated by reorganization value are given more limited rights. . . .

More difficult is the problem of settling differences between classes of participants as to disposition of the business or as to reorganization plans. In many situations a number of plans can meet the fairness and feasibility standards as presently construed. Where one such plan is championed by senior security holders and another by juniors the reorganization might be stymied unless one of the groups could be forced to yield. Similarly there might be an impasse where one group favors a given plan and the other class opposes it without coming forward with an alternative fair and feasible plan. . . . [A] more direct and flexible approach is needed. That need is filled by the explicit or implicit power of the reorganization court to cram down a fair and feasible plan upon a dissenting class of claimants. It is this power which is at the root of judicial control over the ultimate disposition of a company undergoing reorganization. . . .

. . . Where reorganization value cuts out all but one class of security holders, a disagreement among that class whether to sell or reorganize is like a family fight in which a minimum of judicial intervention is needed. . . . [I]t seems reasonable to rest the decision with the investors. . . . [I]n dealing with an industrial company no consideration appears paramount to permitting those who have capital already committed to decide whether to liquidate or reorganize.

Where the controversy over sale or reorganization is not within a single class but is between two classes, both of whose claims are or may be accommodated within the reorganization value, the essence of the problem under reorganization doctrine is different. Presumably the seniors favor immediate liquidation at the prevailing market price while the juniors insist upon either reorganization at a higher reorganization value or a sale at not less than that value. Such a dispute between classes best exposes the basic antagonism between the enforcement and renegotiation pressures surrounding our corporate rehabilitation system. The dispute neatly frames the question whether seniors can deprive juniors of their "rights" under a fair plan built on reorganization value by bringing about a sale at a lesser amount. It is a question which goes to the nucleus of our reorganization system. Obviously it is one which must be answered by the court and not by the contending parties. . . .

The sale-versus-reorganization issue also offers an opportunity for exploring further the relationship between reorganization value and market value. . . .

In looking into the relationship between market value and reorganization value we have noted how it might be thought to bear on deciding whether a distressed business is to be sold or reorganized. To an extent largely unknown, courts may consider the relationship in exercising their ultimate control over disposition of the business where participating classes are in disagreement. It has been suggested . . . that courts are motivated by a simpler line of reasoning: Reorganization value is someone's guess as to what the value of the business will be during "good times." The court adopts it to prevent the juniors from being squeezed out at a lesser valuation. Thus reorganization value is always a kind of upset price; it is an upset price used when reorganization rather than sale is to be the solution of the distress. When courts believe we are at a low stage in the "business cycle" they will approve of reorganization values and upset prices which are substantially above prevailing market price levels. When they believe we are at a fairly high stage in the cycle, courts will refuse to endorse such differentials. Under this explanation the critical factor in the reorganization process is the optimism or pessimism of the judge regarding the economic future. He will permit a sale at market value if he believes that conditions are not likely to improve markedly, but bar a sale, through fixing a comparatively high upset price, if he feels that prosperity is not gone forever.

This simple explanation no doubt contains a significant element of realism. Judges surely are influenced by their intuition concerning the economic future just as all the expert guessers are so affected. But to offer this as an adequate analysis of reorganization value and the upset price is to assume that the whole procedure of reorganization is a sham. . . . Reorganizations might be based on fictitious values and subjective judgments; but those who operate the process and accept its doctrines do not think they are playing a game or acting under false pretenses. . . .

V.

. . . Using reorganization value is a way of inflating the putative value of a company beyond its market value. This *extra* value is allocated among participants by means of a plan which must be fair and feasible. . . . The end result fulfills the basic objective of reorganization: Junior interests receive something of value, out of the extra value, which would have been denied them under a market-place regime. The value conferred on juniors must be withdrawn or withheld from seniors. . . .

VI.

There remains for consideration the ultimate question about our reorganization system: Is a fair plan a just plan? One approach to this problem has already been explored in part. It consists of explaining why the market apparatus is inadequate in reorganization and then arguing that a fair plan based on reorganization value simulates the results an adequate market would reach. . . .

In our society it may not be manifestly just to allow or compel renegotiation of security contracts but it may be more unjust to enforce such contracts strictly and thereby let widely fluctuating market values govern the rights of the parties. Renegotiation through reorganization under a fair plan based on reorganization value may be the least unsatisfactory adjustment to economic instability. This perhaps is the most persuasive justification for our system of corporate reorganization. But the effects and accomplishments of the system should not be overstated. At most the system results in what is thought by many to be a more equitable way of adjusting rights among those who have a financial interest in distressed companies. Beyond this its demonstrable reach is almost negligible. . . . [T]he net effect of the reorganization system on economic instability is unlikely to be significant and the system cannot reasonably be rated as an important instrument for maintaining stability. Likewise the system has an indeterminate, but certainly a very slight, effect on the composition of the capital structures of enterprises. . . . In the end its most significant aspect for society as a whole may be a negative one: The junior interests who are relieved by it from the judgments of the market are rescued without the direct disbursement of public funds for their benefit.

Ayer's "Field Guide"

Professor Jack Ayer of the University of California at Davis has written numerous wonderful articles on bankruptcy. With his wickedly funny sense of humor and unflinchingly incisive assessments, Professor Ayer is always a delight to read. The following article, *Through Chapter 11 With Gun or Camera, But Probably Not Both: A Field Guide*, was presented in 1994 as part of a symposium on bankruptcy at Washington University. This article should be required preliminary reading for any student of chapter 11. Ayer offers a "typology" of chapter 11, hoping "to show some of the various tasks that bankruptcy is called upon to perform, and how it undertakes to perform them." Using a series of hypothetical cases, he analyzes what functions a bankruptcy case might serve. Ultimately Ayer concludes that bankruptcy is richer and more complex than any simple model, and serves a variety of purposes. There is no "essence" to chapter 11, Professor Ayer assays, but he does not find that to be a cause for concern; indeed, such ambiguity may have been precisely what Congress intended.

John D. Ayer
Through Chapter 11 With Gun or Camera,
But Probably Not Both: A Field Guide
72 WASH. U. L.Q. 883 (1994)[*]

If I have not seen farther than I do,
It is because giants were standing
on my shoulders.

I. INTRODUCTION

. . . The purpose of this paper is to offer some clarification in the interest of complication. As much as I admire some of the law and economics scholarship, my sympathies are with those who believe that bankruptcy is, in the end, richer than its models. I think that the way to make this point is to try to specify some of the numberless tasks that bankruptcy is called upon to perform, coupled with some suggestions of their complications and ambiguities. What I offer here, then, is a typology—a field guide, of sorts—to show some of the various tasks that bankruptcy is called upon to perform, and how it undertakes to perform them. By clarifying things in this way, I hope to make it less clear that bankruptcy will reduce itself to a simple model. . . .

II. THE "NATURE" OF BANKRUPTCY

As a preliminary matter, let me say a few words about what bankruptcy (as distinct from Chapter 11) "is." At the risk of repeating myself too often, my ultimate point is that bankruptcy "isn't" in any internally self-contained sense. But in order to make that point, I need to suggest some of the various overlapping meanings that the term may denote. To understand this point, consider these cases:

CASE 1A: Guillemot, an individual, owes $800,000 to unsecured creditors. All debts were incurred at a time when he sincerely expected to pay them, and had good reason for this expectation. He has no prospect of any future earnings.

CASE 1B: Auklet is a corporation, formerly a manufacturer and distributor of widgets. Auklet has ceased operation and has no prospect of beginning anew. It has $5 million in debts and perhaps $1 million in assets—leftover inventory, forklift trucks, an unexpired, valuable long-term leasehold, customer lists, and so forth.

CASE 1C: Vireo, an individual, operated as a broker. Over the years, he handled large quantities of money in a variety of complex transactions. Those who did business with him believe that he kept most of his accounts in his head. Lately he has not been meeting his obligations as they come due. Evidence (and rumors) about his difficulties abound. It appears that he is reducing inventory and turning his hard assets into cash. Some say that he has been concealing money via sham transactions. There is reason to believe that he is favoring some creditors over others.

CASE 1D: Flycatcher is a corporation actively engaged in the manufacture and sale of widgets. It owes $5 million to creditors, all unsecured. It would be worth $4 million if it

---

could be sold as a going concern. The individual components would yield a total of only $1.5 million in liquidation.

All four of these examples bear the marks of familiar bankruptcy cases. Yet their relationship to the bankruptcy process is more complex than may appear at first blush. Taking them in turn, Guillemot's case seems to represent the most typical case of all: an individual with debts beyond his capacity to repay, who will seek bankruptcy relief in order to get the bankruptcy discharge. Probably the vast majority of bankruptcy cases represent no more than this. . . .

Auklet suggests a more traditional use of the bankruptcy power: a mechanism for the "orderly" (whatever that means) collection and disposition of assets. It is readily conceivable that the managers (or the creditors) will decide that the best thing to do with the assets of Auklet is to put the firm under the control of the court, so that an independent trustee may collect the assets and distribute them to the creditors as their interests may appear. Yet such a result is not inevitable, either from the standpoint of the creditor or from that of the debtor. It is entirely conceivable, in principle, that the old managers will simply undertake the collection and distribution on their own initiative. . . .

So, a bankruptcy is not a necessary precondition for an orderly distribution. As for the discharge aspect—with respect to Auklet, a discharge is neither necessary nor possible. It is not possible because the Bankruptcy Code prohibits a discharge for a liquidating corporation. It is not necessary because a corporation is a limited liability entity that receives its own "discharge" when it is wound up.

An added complication is that even if Auklet goes into bankruptcy, the creditors may prefer to leave existing management intact (so as to minimize expense) rather than to suffer the appointment of a trustee. They may be able to do so, but only under the pretense that the business is "reorganizing" rather than liquidating. This is so because the Code permits the debtor (i.e., the former managers) to remain in possession with the powers and obligations of a trustee—but only if the case is administered under Chapter 11, the reorganization chapter of the Code.

The relevance of Vireo's case to the bankruptcy process is easy to demonstrate. On its face, this is precisely the case where creditors (and the sovereign) might want to deploy an independent officer to take charge of the debtor's affairs. Such an officer might be given the power to prevent the dissipation or concealment of assets, and to serve some principle of "equity" in distribution. In short, the officer would fulfill precisely the mandate of the traditional bankruptcy trustee. Yet it is worth noting that some or all of these processes may occur even if bankruptcy never intervenes. Many nonbankruptcy laws are designed to prevent the dissipation of assets. . . .

Conceding that nonbankruptcy devices may be sufficient to police against dissipation or wrongdoing, it is still commonly thought that the bankruptcy process is necessary to set aside preferences in the interest of "equitable distribution." Apparently, this is not quite right. California confers the power to avoid a preference on a state-law assignee. No court has held that a nonbankruptcy preference avoidance law is impermissible in the face of the constitutional bankruptcy power.

If the going-concern value exceeds the value in liquidation, as in Flycatcher's case, a somewhat more subtle problem is presented. At first blush, it would seem that all parties should agree that there are good reasons to preserve the going-concern value, even though the old residual owners will receive nothing. On the other hand, it is likely that individual creditors, left to their own devices, will be motivated to collect their claims piecemeal—and entirely possible that piecemeal liquidation by some creditors will destroy the going-concern values otherwise available to all. This is commonly supposed to be a good reason for filing a Chapter 11 case—that is, to get the protection of the automatic stay, preventing unilateral creditor action pending sale. This is indeed a good reason for filing a bankruptcy, but it does not follow that the case must be filed in Chapter 11.

All of these cases, then, make plausible claims on a system of bankruptcy administration, although none makes a really convincing claim to be the "essence" of bankruptcy. The plot thickens when one recognizes that these various purposes may overlap, interweave, and sometimes conflict. . . .

III. CHAPTER 11

A. *The Paradigm Case*

Consider, first, what may be the model of a Chapter 11 bankruptcy.

CASE 2: Veery, Inc. is the world's largest maker of mandolin picks. It owes $2.7 million to OldBank, secured by Blackacre, on which its factory is located. It owes $4 million to LoanCo, secured by inventory and receivables. It owes $2 million to a variety of unsecured trade creditors. Blackacre would sell for $3.5 million. The inventory and receivables carry a book value of $3.5 million. Veery always kept current on all of its claims until last year, when a series of calamities caused its operating cash flow to fall. Cash flow has since risen to historic levels, but the episode left Veery with an extraordinary backlog of debt. Veery engaged in several ad hoc devices to continue operating under the burden. It slowed payment on trade debt (from 30 days to 45 days, then to 60 days). On occasion it paid particularly importunate creditors to preserve the continuation of necessary supply lines, or to prevent levy on critical assets. In a few cases, it was able to make deals with individual creditors, scaling down old obligations in exchange for ready cash.

Veery's contract with LoanCo provides that LoanCo will lend no more than eighty percent of the book value of the inventory and receivables. Veery has been out of ratio for months. LoanCo let things slide at first, knowing that it had to show some flexibility if it intended to preserve the customer relationship, and if it expected to get full value out of the collateral (see below). Veery is certain, however, that LoanCo will call the loan soon. About two months ago, Veery called an informal meeting of creditors and proposed a compromise: for all outstanding unsecured debt, it would pay forty cents on the dollar now with the balance paid in three annual installments of twenty cents on the dollar per year. To all appearances, a large number of Veery's creditors want to take the deal, but there is some vigorous dissent.

This case, if any, bears the earmarks of an old-fashioned "paradigm Chapter 11 bankruptcy." The debtor is a moderate-sized firm. In terms of current cash flow, the debtor seems able to operate without difficulty. The problem arises because of an (allegedly) isolated episode of misfortune. The burden seems to have fallen most harshly on "the trade"—unsecured creditors, typically suppliers.[11]

To understand this case, it is useful to begin by understanding that everyone has motivations that may not be obvious to the untutored eye. For example, the debtor's strongest card is the threat of suicide—the threat of going down with guns blazing and flags flying, taking the loot with it to Davey Jones' locker.[12] The business is almost certainly worth more as a going concern than in liquidation. Unsecured creditors may thus regard it as worth their while to accept a partial settlement

---

[11]   A lawyer I know, with more compassion than may be apparent at first blush, calls them "the poor bums in polyester." His point is helpful in understanding bankruptcy negotiation. The point is that the trade creditors are typically far less likely to be arriving in Porsches, wearing Brooks Brothers or Gucci, and far less likely to be sending their kids to fancy Eastern colleges, than anyone else in the room—their own lawyers, their adversaries' lawyers, the bankers, or even, as if adding insult to injury, the representatives of the debtor itself. Yet, it is the trade creditors who are being invited to make a large voluntary surrender of their legal rights.

[12]   I have heard Elizabeth Warren describe it as a case where the creditor is trying to push the debtor off a twenty-story building while the debtor is threatening to jump.

rather than to force termination of the business. The same reasoning may also apply to LoanCo, even though LoanCo is nominally secured: inventory and receivables evaporate fastest in the liquidation of a business of this sort. Indeed, LoanCo may stand not only as the largest secured creditor of the business, but also as the largest unsecured creditor. LoanCo may even find it in its interest to "lend into the problem"—seemingly throwing good money after bad—in order to salvage its position. OldBank, on the other hand, appears to be fully secured and indeed may not even be pressing hard for payment, because it knows that there is enough collateral to satisfy its claim.

Veery's case makes a particularly appealing argument in favor of Chapter 11, for two over-lapping reasons. First, the facts suggest the kind of case in which "reasonable people" (whoever they are) might well want to reach agreement to preserve going-concern values in any event. Second, there is no specific suggestion of moral culpability here—the kind of culpability that might argue in favor of liquidation as a kind of "punishment." Taken together, these facts argue strongly for some sort of collective settlement, whereby the debts are reduced and the business continues under the old residual equity ownership.

The motivations for a collective settlement are so powerful that it may be possible to reach a settlement out of court. Yet, there are many factors that impel the case towards bankruptcy juris-diction. Most, if not all, involve the so-called "holdout problem." That is, out of court, there are any number of ways in which a dissenting minority can scotch the wishes of a unified majority. Chap-ter 11 provides the structure to impose an allocation that state law does not afford. The most obvi-ous example may be the mandate to impose "equity of distribution" on unsecured creditors, supplanting the "grab law" of state collection procedures. Although this might be the most obvious motive, it is far from the most important. Far more interesting, perhaps, are the cases where the dis-senter, by unilateral action, can scotch the entire effort (as, for example, by levying on the hypo-thetical essential device that the factory needs to make the firm go), or the cases where the holdout, by virtue of being a holdout, can put herself in a position to be bought off by the debtor.

The Bankruptcy Code provides devices, not normally available at state law, to deal with hold-out problems of this sort. For example, the automatic stay of § 362 embargoes unilateral action, while the confirmation provisions of Chapter 11 provide for imposing the plan on a dissenting minority. . . .

But there is a greater difficulty with this "paradigm case," and that is whether any lawyer now living has ever actually seen it. Perhaps some have. There are certainly no precise records classify-ing Chapter 11 bankruptcies on principles like those set down here. However, anecdotal evidence suggests that the paradigm case is not only rare but may well be entirely nonexistent. To get a bet-ter fix on Chapter 11, it is necessary to review a number of other cases, beginning with the next set.

B. The Meaning of "Reorganization"

A central difficulty in devising a core meaning for Chapter 11 concerns the concept of "reor-ganization." The drafters do not define it. Their failure to do so seems to be intentional, and that may have been a wise decision. Compare these two cases:

> CASE 3A: Bobolink is a retail clothing dealer whose products have gone out of fashion. He is not able to cover ordinary operating expenses, to say nothing of debt service. Easter is approaching and creditors generally concede that they would get more money if the business continues to operate at retail through the upcoming Easter season. A sub-stantial body of creditors agree that present management, though it has lost its fashion touch, is otherwise neither incompetent nor dishonest. A substantial majority of creditors agree to advance new credit to permit the debtor to operate through the Easter season. The creditors intend that the debtor will collect as much as it can through retail sales and liquidate the remaining assets by any means possible thereafter.

CASE 3B: Meadowlark is a seemingly prosperous retailer of health foods. One day a delivery person arrives to find the store padlocked. Inquiry discloses that existing owners have simply abandoned the property and disappeared. Nonetheless, suppliers, who know each other and establish contact easily, determine that Meadowlark is a viable business that will yield more in operation than in liquidation. They therefore agree to seek a means to continue the operations with creditors enjoying their ordinary priority and the equity interest, if any, remaining in the old equity owners.

Each of these cases has a good claim on the jurisdiction of the bankruptcy court, yet their positions seem almost the opposite of what the drafters envisioned. Bobolink clearly offers an opportunity for a "going-concern liquidation." Bankruptcy will provide a mechanism for keeping creditors at bay while the liquidation goes forward. . . .

Meadowlark is, in a sense, just the reverse: a case where the old equity owners seem to have abandoned their position, even though they may have an interest in the continued operation of the business. Ordinarily, in a business of this sort, if there were any need for a bankruptcy, the DIP would continue to operate the business pending its sale as a going concern. Here, a DIP is impossible, yet a going-concern sale seems to make the most sense. Thus, the appropriate course seems to be to appoint a trustee and to let her sell the property as is, distributing proceeds to claimants as their interests may appear. Such a scenario is possible under Chapter 11—indeed, Chapter 11 pretty clearly foresees it. Yet on the facts of this case, it will perhaps be easier in Chapter 7.

Thus, the distinction between Chapters 7 and 11 seems to be a blur. We think of Chapter 7 as the "liquidation" chapter, and Chapter 11 as the chapter for the preservation of the going concern. But liquidation is possible in Chapter 11, and there is no barrier against using Chapter 7 to preserve the values of the going concern. . . .

C. Some Variations

This sketch merely begins to suggest the possibilities for Chapter 11, of course. Without any pretense of being exhaustive, here are a few others:

CASE 4A: Turnstone, Inc. is the world's best-known maker of cheeseburger-shaped nightlights. Although the field is competitive, Turnstone controls a dominant market share. Sales and earnings grew briskly for several years, but about a year ago Bufflehead, a competitor, developed a new version that threatened to strip away Turnstone's market lead. Since then, Turnstone's inventory has begun to pile up on the shelves, and Turnstone has started to lose money on current operations. As its cash supply shrinks, it has tried harder and harder to hang onto money for research and development. About three weeks ago, Turnstone quit paying all but its most importunate trade creditors. Turnstone is current on its inventory and receivables line to LoanCo, but LoanCo has declared the collateral insufficient and has indicated that it will call the loan. Management is convinced that it can get back into the game if it receives a six-month grace period and a slug of new cash. Goshawk, an investor who has never been involved with Turnstone, is willing to lend the money if she can get the right security.

Turnstone bears a superficial resemblance to Veery in Case 2. In both cases, the going-concern values probably exceed the liquidation values, and in each case there may be a need for creditor coordination. The big difference is that in Turnstone, the debtor's troubles are not the result of some exogenous past event. On the contrary, Turnstone's success, if any, depends on its getting new money for the future. The most important contribution of the Bankruptcy Code will be the power it confers on the court to authorize "super priority" lending. Thus, with the court's approval, the debtor may be able to acquire new capital from Goshawk in exchange for a claim equal or superior to all existing debt.

CASE 4B: Titmouse runs a small factory in which it makes silk purses out of sows' ears. It owes $3 million to LoanCo, secured by inventory and receivables. It owes $500,000 to unsecured creditors. It conducts its business on leased premises; the lease is "at the market," *i.e.*, neither a benefit nor a burden to the estate. It purchased all of its operating equipment from vendors who secured their sales with purchase money security interests. In all such cases, the value of the collateral equals the value of the loan. Titmouse would sell for about $2.5 million as a going concern, but the liquidation value is no more than $1 million.

Titmouse is another case where the solution is obvious—sell the business as a going concern. Once again, this is a deal that might be consummated outside of bankruptcy. But again, it is possible that bankruptcy will provide for a "cleaner deal"—staying unilateral creditor action while the deal is progressing, and providing for a full accounting of the disposition of proceeds. As with the earlier cases, there is no inherent reason why the bankruptcy has to be a Chapter 11, although Chapter 11 does make it easy to continue the business and permits the debtor to continue in possession, saving the expense of a trustee. . . .

Variants of this case may arise when the bankruptcy forum provides a more convenient arena than state law for secured creditors seeking to liquidate their claims. For example, the pervasive jurisdiction of the bankruptcy court may make it easier to collect accounts receivable than do ordinary state processes.

CASE 4C: Greenshank is a limited partnership. The general partner is a corporation. The limited partners bought their interests under pre-1986 tax law, through which they acquired the right to deductions that would shield other income. The only asset is an apartment house, Blackacre. Greenshank acquired the apartment house for $4.2 million with $600,000 down and a mortgage for twenty years at ten percent. When it was no longer able to meet payments out of cash flow, Greenshank filed for relief under Chapter 11. The principal balance remaining on the mortgage was $3.8 million. An independent appraiser says that the parties might be able to sell the property for $3.2 million if they aggressively market it for six months.

In the past year or so, this type of case may have generated the most discussion and (in terms of court and attorney time) perhaps also the most litigation of all Chapter 11 cases. Although the property is obviously insolvent, the real problem may not be apparent to the untutored eye. That is, if the property goes to foreclosure, the investors lose not only their residual claim, but also the substantial tax deductions they have enjoyed over the years. They also face the prospect of "rollup liability": they have to raise the money to pay taxes after the asset is gone.

Although it is easy to understand why the limited partners want protection in this case, the fact is that these debtors have perhaps the least persuasive claim on the jurisdiction of the bankruptcy court. . . . [T]hese facts present none of the traditional justifications for a bankruptcy filing. Thus, there is no need for a discharge (the limited partnership cannot get a discharge in any event); there is no need for creditor orchestration (the senior secured claim alone exceeds the asset value); and there is no need to preserve a going-concern value (the apartment house will be an apartment house in any event). Indeed, one of the principal embarrassments to debtor-proponents in cases of this sort is their difficulty in creating enough of a semblance of creditor grievance to create the appearance of a bankruptcy case.

D. The Ambiguity of the "Personal"

Even taking all of this into account, there is still greater difficulty in giving a core meaning to "reorganization." This difficulty is specifically evident in the case of the closely held family corporation. Consider this case:

CASE 5: Assume the facts in any of the preceding cases and add the fact that the company president is Prez, who also owns sixty percent of the stock, with the balance being held by members of his immediate family. Prez personally guaranteed the debt of the lead secured creditor, and he is responsible by statute for certain back taxes and unpaid wages.

Even though everything else remains the same, the presence of an owner-manager almost certainly changes the dynamics of the case from the standpoint of both debtor and creditor. It is inevitable that the interests of Prez (and perhaps the interests of other insider-shareholders) will conflict with the interests of ordinary unsecured creditors in the case. Prez wants to make sure that the secured claim gets paid, along with the back taxes and unpaid wages (because he is personally liable for those claims), but he does not have nearly the same motivation to protect the unsecureds (because he is protected by the corporate veil). Under the circumstances, it seems that the inevitable course would be to make sure that Prez had nothing to do with the case after filing.

Remarkably, just the opposite seems to be the case. Again, it is hard to find precise data. But there is every reason to believe that most closely held corporate bankruptcies involve "differential debt" of some sort. Yet, the appointment of a trustee is not even remotely typical in bankruptcy cases: far more commonly, the "debtor" (which is to say, Prez) remains in position with the obligations (as the statute provides) of a trustee. It is easy to get a discussion going regarding whether this modality is within the "spirit" of bankruptcy law.

A case can easily be made for either side. . . .

IV. OPERATING IN CHAPTER 11

A. The Polycentricity of the "Plan"

The foregoing suggests some of the limitations of trying to develop a core definition for Chapter 11. It is possible to throw more light on the problem by considering just how a "reorganization" might work itself out. Consider this case:

CASE 6A: Ptarmigan makes widgets, which it sells for $100 per unit. Variable costs (supplies, wages, etc.) are $60 per unit. There is a mortgage on its factory for $40 million at ten percent interest. Ptarmigan has been selling 80,000 units per year. Ptarmigan estimates that it needs $5 million for deferred maintenance, product upgrade, and the like. With the extra money, it believes that it could increase production to 115,000 units per year.

Although some things are clear from this brief statement, the case is more important for what it leaves out rather than for what it says. As it stands, Ptarmigan is losing money on every sale: the firm needs $4 million per year for debt service alone. At the current price, it would need to sell 100,000 units per year just to break even. Add another $5 million in debt and the break-even point rises to 112,500 units per year. At this level of production, the project would seem to be modestly profitable.

This is clear enough, but everything else is open to question. Will the lender—any lender—be willing to provide the $5 million capital infusion? That depends on the lender's appraisal of the probable outcomes, which are never as certain as they appear in this kind of hypothetical. If there is no infusion of new capital, something has to give. Three choices present themselves: (1) raise prices (to $125 per unit); (2) lower variable costs; or (3) reduce debt service. Price policy is within the unilateral control of Ptarmigan, so it does not normally become a part of the bankruptcy negotiation. That leaves only two choices—reduce variable costs and/or reduce debt service. In practice, a battle often arises between "the employees" and "the banks," each fighting for a share of a necessarily limited cash flow. Stated this starkly, it may appear that the banks have a natural (if perhaps unfair) advantage, because their claims are "on the balance sheet," while the employees, however much they may depend on the debtor for continuing sustenance, hold claims that appear—transitorily—only "on the income statement."

There may be something to this for rhetorical purposes, but I think there is less to it than meets the eye. What counts for both employees and banks is a term that does not appear anywhere in the accounting documents—the "opportunity cost," the question of what the parties could do with their inputs if they did not have the present project. Thus, suppose that the bank could not liquidate the plant at foreclosure for more than $30 million. Then it makes sense to continue with the present project, even if it means scaling down the implied capital value, as long as the resultant value exceeds $30 million. Similarly, the employees' attitude may well depend on what other alternatives they have if this business fails.

The preceding observation is readily apparent if one reflects on some of the major bankruptcies of the 1980s. Some cases—*Campeau* is perhaps the most obvious example—seem to have been the result of nothing more than absurd overleveraging, where a balance sheet adjustment left behind a functional, solvent business. Other cases—*Continental I* is the paradigm—were driven by the income statement, where the case was resolved on the backs of the employees. Still other cases—*Wheeling Pitt* is perhaps notorious here—seem to have presented an instance of a state-of-the-art plant (with attendant balance sheet liabilities) and a costly, inefficient labor force, both of which had to be scaled down in order for the business to survive. . . .

B. "More Time"

As judge's jobs go, there is good reason to believe that the bankruptcy judge's job, taken day for day, is one of the most interesting. . . .

In an important paper, Richard Levin put his finger on one good reason why this is so. Levin pointed out that the core job of the bankruptcy judge is prospective, not retrospective. . . .

Why is the bankruptcy judge so involved in the future? The answer is straightforward: the debtor always gains from more time. If the value of the assets goes down, she only loses what she has. If they go up, her return is potentially infinite. It is easy to formalize this point. As many observers have noted, the position of the residuary equity owners in a leveraged corporation is a call option, with the payoff value of the debt serving as the strike price. A corollary point, also demonstrable as a matter of option theory, is that the call option holder also gains value from an increase in volatility. The combined teaching of these points is that the debtor always has a motivation to take the assets and run another risk. The basics of this intuition are clear to anyone who spends much time around the bankruptcy court. The conventional formulation is that to let the debtor continue in business after bankruptcy is, in effect, "gambling with other people's money." I think that there is an element of truth in this formulation, but it is sufficiently limited so as to be substantially misleading. To explore the point, consider the following example:

CASE 6B: Towhee, Inc. is a debtor in a Chapter 11 case. The only asset is $10 in the bank. The trustee can invest the money in any one of three projects (A, B, and C), each of which has two possible returns, with a fifty percent chance of each return. The probability-weighted expected returns (gross present values) are as follows:

Project A = 0.5($45) + 0.5($55) = $50;
Project B = 0.5(0) + 0.5($120) = $60;
Project C = 0.5($10) + 0.5($80) = $45.

Suppose that the debts equal $75. As a matter of total probability-weighting, the debtor is insolvent in any event, which would suggest that the assets "belong to" the creditors. But until the hammer has fallen, making the transfer final, the picture appears more complicated. To see how this can be, consider the differential payouts for each of the two parties, equity and debt. First, here are the probability-weighted values of the prospective returns to debt:

Project A = $50 (just as in the earlier case);
Project B = 0.5(0) + 0.5($75) = $37.50;
Project C = 0.5($10) + 0.5($75) = $42.50.

And now, to equity:

Project A = 0;
Project B = 0.5(0) + 0.5($45) = $22.50;
Project C = 0.5(0) + 0.5($5) = $2.50.

To understand the implications of these numbers, first consider the case where the only available choices are A and C. Debt will clearly prefer A over C because it has the higher probability-weighted value, measured either from the standpoint of debt alone ($50 over $42.50), or from the standpoint of the assets of the firm taken as a whole ($50 over $45). Equity, of course, will favor C over A, because that is the only project under which it has any chance of recovery.

In a conventional Chapter 11 scenario, chances are that the court will side with debt rather than equity, ruling that equity's rights will be cut off, and this might well be the right decision. But it is one thing to identify the decision, and quite another to name the reason. If the court decides that equity has no rights because (as is so often the grounds of decision) equity has no "property," or because (identically) the property "belongs" to debt, then it is being circular: the plaintiff wins because he has property, and has property because he wins. Equity does have a definable interest—the contingent upside. Whether it will be permitted to assert or vindicate that interest is a separate matter. If the court decides that creditors win because, *e.g.*, a contractual or statutory termination has expired, then the court may or may not be correct, but at least it is being coherent.

But suppose that, instead of being presented with A and C, the court is presented with A and B. It seems to me that these facts present quite a different problem. Once again, of course, debt will favor Project A, the less volatile alternative and the one offering the creditors the higher return. Meanwhile, equity, as the holder of an out-of-the-money option, will readily prefer the more volatile B, which is the only one that gives it any chance of recovery.

The difficulty is that this time, the more volatile project is the more valuable one, not merely from the standpoint of equity but also from the standpoint of the assets taken as a whole. If the court decides for creditors in this case, it must recognize that it is doing so to satisfy the creditors' taste for risk aversion at the expense of the values of the asset pool as a whole.

If this instance seems trivial or uninteresting, consider the case where the debts are not $75, but $55. In this case, the relevant payoffs are as follows, first for debt:

Project A = 0.5($45) + 0.5($55) = $50;
Project B = 0.5(0) + 0.5($55) = $27.50;
Project C = 0.5($10) + 0.5($60) = $35.

And for equity:

Project A = $0;
Project B = 0.5(0) + 0.5($65) = $32.50;
Project C = 0.5(0) + 0.5($20) = $10.

As between A and C, creditors will prefer A, and the court is likely to go along with them, for all the same reasons. As between A and B, creditors will again favor A and equity will favor B, but with a difficulty—if the choice is B, then the company is solvent in the balance sheet sense (assets > liabilities). Under standard rhetoric, if the court favors A over B, it is, in effect, permitting the creditors to gamble with the debtor's money, rather than the other way around. The difficulty here may lie in the definition of solvency: we treat solvency as if it were a "snapshot"; either the debtor is solvent, or she is not. Numbers like those in this example make it clear that solvency is perhaps better understood as a continuum, although nothing in the law allows this kind of choice.

V. CONCLUSION

. . . This paper is, to repeat: there is no "essence" to Chapter 11. Rather, Chapter 11 serves a variety of purposes, overlapping and superficially similar, yet often in tension. But it does not follow that one must lament this kind of ambiguity. Rather, there is good reason to believe that the drafters intended just this sort of thing.

Warren on Bankruptcy Policymaking

Elizabeth Warren has proven time and again to be one of the most pragmatic, honest, and unpretentious appraisers of the bankruptcy system. She denies being able to hypothesize adroit academic solutions for complex, tough, real-world problems. But she knows what the problems are, and what questions need to be asked, and what the paramount goals of bankruptcy should be. Her approach is aptly captured by the title of the following article: *Bankruptcy Policymaking in an Imperfect World*. In that article she focuses on policymaking in the realm of business bankruptcy, recognizing that consumer bankruptcy imports critical personal "fresh start" issues that affect the analysis.

As you read Warren's clear exposition of the role of the business bankruptcy regime, consider:

1. What does Warren identify as the four functions or goals of the business bankruptcy system?
2. What are the four devices Congress used to enhance value?
3. What economic assumptions underlie the value-preservation goal?
4. How does the bankruptcy system differ from non-bankruptcy law in distributing scarce value?
5. What distributional principles are at work in business bankruptcy?
6. How does the system restrict externalization of costs?
7. What is the meaning and significance of private monitoring?
8. What are the most significant constraints on bankruptcy policymaking?

Elizabeth Warren
Bankruptcy Policymaking in an Imperfect World
92 MICH. L. REV. 336 (1993)[*]

INTRODUCTION

Why have a bankruptcy system? What function is it designed to serve? To argue whether it is costly, whether it is failing, or whether it should be reshaped, amended, or scrapped, some joinder over what the system is designed to do is essential. A success by one normative measure may be a failure by another. . . .

This essay is about bankruptcy policy. It attempts to articulate a comprehensive statement about the various and competing goals that underlie the bankruptcy system. The essay offers both a positive observation, drawn from the Code and its operation, and a normative evaluation, designed to outline the difficult value judgments that comprise the bankruptcy system. It also serves warning: before commentators propose any sweeping changes or policymakers take seriously any suggestions to scrap the system, they must consider the impact of such proposals on a number of competing normative goals. . . .

The list of policy goals I offer is deliberately open textured. . . . The statement of goals this essay presents is intended to be a direct challenge to everyone who worries about the bankruptcy system . . . . I hope at least for joinder of issue in our continuing debates. . . .

II. The Functions of the Business Bankruptcy System

This description of the functions of the business bankruptcy system begins with a factual observation: when a business fails, there is a substantial risk that it will not have sufficient resources to meet all its outstanding obligations. To complicate this problem, businesses rarely fail after neatly wrapping up all their outstanding obligations. Instead, they tend to falter during active, sometimes frantic, operations, leaving contracts in various states of performance and nonperformance; owing past-due bills along with contingent future obligations; and disappointing legions of suppliers, employees, customers, creditors, and others who fear that they will not get all they had expected from their dealings with the debtor. Some entity or group of entities will likely bear the losses of the business' inability to meet its obligations.

It is possible to have a legal regime with no formal bankruptcy system, but it is not possible to avoid legal rules that deal with the consequences of business failure. Some rules must determine the rights of the contract claimants and tort victims, banks and employees, or suppliers and customers when the pool of the debtor's assets rapidly diminishes and the claimants clamor for satisfaction. We might integrate such rules into a single system or scatter them throughout the collection system. We may construct them deliberately or inadvertently. We may also call them "bankruptcy" or "rutabaga" or any other fanciful word. Regardless of these elements, the rules will create a collection system that determines the value of a failing business, how to distribute that value among parties whom the failure affects, and the extent to which affected parties can externalize the costs of failure to others who did not deal with the debtor.

In bankruptcy a single federal system that supersedes state law collection priority rules brings together the collection rules. This system aims, with greater or lesser efficacy, toward four principal goals: (1) to enhance the value of the failing debtor; (2) to distribute value according to multiple normative principles; (3) to internalize the costs of the business failure to the parties dealing with the debtor; and (4) to create reliance on private monitoring. In this section, I consider each of these functions in turn, exploring both the normative values at stake and the ways in which the current bankruptcy system implements these goals.

A. A System To Enhance Value

. . . One of the principal functions of bankruptcy law is to enhance the value of a failing firm. The normative analysis is fairly straightforward: if the rule can increase the value of the failing firm, it will reduce the total costs imposed on the parties dealing with the failing debtor. If the cost of producing the increase in value is less than the value obtained, then the rule has increased net values, which is the desired result.

This goal, which focuses on the allocative efficiency of the bankruptcy system, is implemented through reduction in collection costs and retention of value that a state collection action would otherwise dissipate. The positive analysis is equally straightforward: key elements of the bankruptcy system were created to accomplish this cost savings and value conservation. Congress used four principle devices: (1) development of specialized collection rules; (2) implementation of collective creditor action; (3) reduction in the strategic behavior of debtors and creditors; and (4) preservation of the business' going-concern value.

1. *Creating Specialized Collection Rules*

Because legal obligations are rarely self-executing, collection rules emerge that define the rights of parties to extract payment when others fail to meet their obligations. These rules define how one party forces another to pay, as they also—deliberately or inadvertently—order the priority of repayment among different creditors who have collection rights. Both federal bankruptcy law and state debtor-creditor law define the rules of debt collection, but the goals of the two systems differ markedly, resulting in very different applicable rules in each system.

The principal objective of state collection law is to provide a single creditor with an avenue to pursue the collection of an unpaid obligation. . . .

The issues at stake in a typical business failure, however, are substantively different from those in routine state law collection suits. When a debtor faces failure, the possibility of default on a number of outstanding obligations or of a complete cessation of business activities transforms collection issues. Any single collection effort against a failing debtor necessarily affects the likelihood of collection by all other creditors. . . .

While state law deals with routine single-debt collections, bankruptcy laws deal specifically with the more complex issues raised in the context of impending multiple default. When the debtor faces failure, questions of the priority of repayment and discharge from debt become central to the collection process. Bankruptcy laws are developed explicitly to order priority of repayment. . . .

2. *Enhancing Collective Action*

The Bankruptcy Code reduces the costs of collection from a troubled debtor by collectivizing creditor activities. By replacing the competitive state law collection systems, in which each creditor engages in separate monitoring and collection activities, with a collective-action system, the bankruptcy mechanism attempts to achieve significant cost savings. The primary collective device in the Bankruptcy Code is the creditors' committee. . . .

In addition, the interests of the creditors are represented by officials paid by the debtor's estate but who are responsible to the creditors as a group. In chapter 7 cases, a trustee is appointed to act on behalf of all the creditors. The U.S. Trustee, a representative of the Justice Department, has both general supervisory responsibility for these appointed trustees and the power to enter a case if there is reason to believe that they are not adequately representing the creditors' interests. In a chapter 11 case, the debtor's management team is left in place unless a party makes an affirmative showing that a trustee is needed to protect creditors' interests. . . .

To further the collective interests of the creditors, the Bankruptcy Code operates directly to reduce the costs of coping with a business failure. A number of provisions are designed to increase collection efficiency in a bankruptcy action; quick decisions, abbreviated trials, estimation of claims, elimination of duplicate efforts, restricted notification requirements, reduced waiting periods, minimal paperwork, automatic stays from collection, stipulated valuations, and emergency orders are all bankruptcy devices intended to capture value for the estate under the adverse conditions that multiparty litigation and a failing business present. Perhaps no part of the legal system is more cognizant of the transaction costs of collection and dispute resolution than the bankruptcy system, and surely no system is so conspicuously directed toward cost reduction.

3. *Reducing Strategic Behavior*

Strategic, and often wasteful, action is a persistent problem in collection systems. Under any system, both debtors and creditors can be counted on to press whatever advantages they may have. . . .

The debtor most likely to engage in wasteful strategic behavior is the one facing business failure. This debtor has the least to lose and the most to gain from such strategies. Developing a uniform federal bankruptcy law that stretches across the nation—and has some international reach—can better control the circumstances most fraught with the potential for waste. A single bankruptcy filing creates an estate that nets all the debtor's property, wherever located, and covers all the debtor's economic relationships, in whatever stage of performance or breach. To resolve their claims, all creditors must come to a single forum where they are assured of notice and an opportunity to be heard before the debtor's assets are distributed. . . . The reach and uniformity of bankruptcy law sharply reduce the opportunities for strategic behavior. . . .

4. *Retaining Value in the Failing Business*

The rationale commentators most often cite for a bankruptcy system is its ability to capture the going-concern value of a business; for many analysts, the function of bankruptcy—and hence the measure of its viability—begins and ends here. This feature is undoubtedly a significant part of the bankruptcy scheme, but the opportunity to preserve the full value of the business has broader implications than simply the capture of going-concern rather than liquidation valuations.

Two empirically based economic assumptions underlie the attempt to preserve the value of a failing company: (1) orderly liquidation is likely to produce more value—or to avoid more loss—than piecemeal liquidation; and (2) going-concern value is likely to be higher than liquidation value. Chapter 7 implements the first premise by requiring an organized liquidation, monitored by all the creditors and supervised by the bankruptcy court, that presumably produces greater value than the chaotic mix of self-help repossession and judicial execution available at state law. The chapter 11 reorganization alternative implements the second premise, explicitly attempting to capture the going-concern value of a business that would likely be lost in any liquidation. . . .

To make liquidations orderly and to attempt to capture a going-concern premium, the bankruptcy system embodies overtly utilitarian principles. A creditor with a state law right to repossess collateral, for example, may be forced to relinquish that right in bankruptcy if the debtor business is more valuable when the property remains in place. The individual creditor loses something by forgoing immediate liquidation and waiting for continuing payments. Yet, the business—and all those who rely on the business—gains from the opportunity to liquidate in a more orderly fashion, to sell itself as a going-concern, or to reorganize itself into a viable enterprise.

Bankruptcy laws also enhance the value of the failing company by reducing creditors' incentives to dismantle it. . . . State law rewards creditors for racing to grab assets and thereby encourages behavior that dismantles debtors in distress and precipitates business failures that might have been averted if the creditors had been more patient. The state system distributes benefits to aggressive creditors rather than cooperative ones; it thus tends to raise business failure rates generally. The bankruptcy system denies creditors access to more aggressive collection methods, such as immediate foreclosure, and ends the race to dismantle the debtor. Moreover, because the collection rules of bankruptcy have some retroactive application—for example, the return of preferential payments received within three months of a bankruptcy filing—bankruptcy laws may serve not only to enhance the value of a business that has filed bankruptcy, but also to improve the value of a business that is foundering on the brink of a bankruptcy filing. . . .

The most frequently discussed policy rationale for the bankruptcy system is its stated goal to enhance the value of the failing business, thereby reducing the collective losses suffered by the parties who have dealt with the debtor. The bankruptcy laws create a specialized collection system that uses a number of different devices to maintain the value of the failing firm. The Code actively promotes collective action for the creditors while it hems in the strategic behavior of the debtor that can dissipate the estate assets. By giving the business an opportunity for organized liquidation or for reorganization as a going concern, the laws also help retain the value of the debtor business.

B. *A System To Distribute Value*

Any collection system necessarily has significant distributional implications because it fixes legal rights and creates priorities of repayment that represent the basis for participation in any renegotiation effort. Imbedded within state collection law is a straightforward scheme of distribution: secured creditors get cash or take their collateral; the first judgment creditor collects in full from what remains; the next judgment creditor takes in full from what still remains; and so on, until all the assets are gone. . . . When there are insufficient assets to satisfy all claims against the debtor, however, the state collection scheme permits some creditors to receive payment in full while other creditors bear all the costs of a debtor's failure. . . . [T]he state law system has a powerful distributional impact when the debtor fails.

The bankruptcy system reflects a deliberate decision to pursue different distributional objectives from those that the de facto scheme of general collection law embodies. Rejecting the "race of the diligent" that characterizes state law, the bankruptcy system substitutes a different normative principle: "equity is equality." The Bankruptcy Code begins with the premise that all similarly situated creditors should be treated alike. The fact that general creditors—the last residual class of creditors, for whom much of the bankruptcy operation is run—share assets or participate in payments on a pro rata basis most directly embodies this premise.

. . . [W]hen bankruptcy law deviates from a strict equality principle, it does so for self-consciously redistributive ends. Every distribution that benefits a particular creditor at the expense of the collective estate represents a considered judgment to depart from the norm in a particular instance. Equality—and deliberate deviations from equality—stand at the center of bankruptcy policy.

1. *Parties with Different Legal Rights*

The framework of the bankruptcy system embodies the principle of equality. Within a single bankruptcy case, the consequences of debtor default can be determined for a large number of diverse parties, far more than could be heard in any state collection suit. . . .

Bankruptcy law . . . bring[s] all the competing creditors into a single forum, where their competing claims can be resolved. Claimants with matured claims and those with contingent claims, those with liquidated claims and those with unliquidated claims, and those with negotiated rights and those with rights found elsewhere in law are all heard in a single bankruptcy case. Assets and losses can be distributed among them on a principled basis, replacing the differing treatment they would have received under state law.

2. *Parties with No Formal Legal Rights*

Bankruptcy policy also takes into account the distributional impact of a business failure on parties who are not creditors and who have no formal legal rights to the assets of the business. Business closings affect employees who will lose jobs, taxing authorities that will lose ratable property, suppliers that will lose customers, nearby property owners who will lose beneficial neighbors, and current customers who must go elsewhere. Congress was acutely aware of the wider effect of a business failure on the surrounding community, and it adopted the 1978 Bankruptcy Code specifically to ameliorate those harmful effects. . . .

The Code accounts for the rights of other parties that a business failure affects by giving a failing company an opportunity to sell itself as a going concern in chapter 7 or to reorganize in chapter 11. . . .

To be sure, the protection the Code gives to parties without formal legal rights is derivative in nature and limited in scope. These groups have no specific right to be heard in the bankruptcy case, nor can they exercise any rights either to support or to oppose a proposal for the disposition of the failing business. The Code leaves those decisions to the parties more immediately affected—the debtor and the parties with formal rights against the debtor. . . .

3. *Other Distributional Principles*

. . . A number of principles are applied to justify deviations from the baseline equity-is-equality principle and to implement a preference for orderly sale and reorganization. . . . The following list may not be exclusive, but it identifies a number of the key factors:

a. *Relative ability to spread the risks of default.* Some creditors and parties affected by business failure are unlikely to have anticipated the risk that a business will cease to function, while others may face especially acute difficulties in spreading the risks of a debtor's default. Employees, for example, may be particularly ill-suited for the task of assessing and spreading risk in order to shield themselves from the effects of their employer's misfortunes. . . . Priority of repayment for past due wages gives employees preferential treatment, reducing their costs when a business fails and permitting some correction for costs that market imperfections imposed on them. . . .

b. *Encourage investment risk taking.* If investors perceived that businesses in some financial trouble faced immediate liquidation, they would likely have two responses: they would not invest their money to start businesses, or they would direct their business investments toward less risky enterprises. . . . At the margins, any law permitting reorganization of a business increases the likelihood of survival of companies through troubled times, which makes risk-taking behavior more attractive.

c. *Incentive effects on prebankruptcy debtor-creditor transactions.* A number of Code provisions are created with a view toward their ex ante incentive effects, with a particular focus on the period that precedes the business' collapse. To encourage creditors to work with a failing debtor and to avoid the state law asset grab that wastes assets and pushes many debtors into bankruptcy, bankruptcy laws are designed to negate the benefits a creditor gains by dismantling a troubled debtor. . . .

d. *Similarity over time.* The bankruptcy system equalizes the treatment of creditors and parties affected by business failure when timing variations leave them with very different formal rights. For example, those who have been injured by a debtor's product, such as workers who have been exposed to asbestos, can bring state law actions only after their injuries are manifest. . . . Bankruptcy law, however, may resolve both present and future claims at once, giving comparable outcomes to those with similar legal rights, but different timetables for reaching the courthouse. . . .

e. *Owners bear the primary costs of business failure.* Residual owners of the business have the least protected status in bankruptcy. This situation mirrors the principle outside bankruptcy that those who take the largest gains if the business succeeds also assume the risk of loss if the business fails. Accordingly, the Code permits the owner to retain ownership of the postbankruptcy business only if the creditors collectively consent or the business is able to pay all the creditors in full.

f. *Minimize disruption of established economic patterns.* While bankruptcy necessarily reorders the rights of all parties with claims against the estate, the Code gives powerful residual protection to the most established forms of transactions, thereby reducing the impact of a bankruptcy filing on ordinary commercial expectations. Secured creditors provide a case in point. . . .

. . . The point of this analysis is that bankruptcy is a forum in which everyone parts with some rights in order to participate in a process that works for the collective good.

C. A System To Internalize the Costs of Failure to the Parties Dealing with the Debtor

The third normative function the bankruptcy system serves is to constrain externalization of business losses to parties not dealing with the debtor. . . . [T]he bankruptcy laws are organized to minimize losses to the general public when a business fails and to force parties dealing with the failing debtor to bear the burden of the failure.

The benefits of such a policy are obvious. Creditors' ability to externalize losses significantly blunts their incentives to make carefully considered lending decisions or to monitor the debtor to assure repayment. . . .

Bankruptcy restricts externalization of costs in three key ways: (1) it provides priority repayment of debt to the public fisc ahead of most other creditors; (2) it maintains a largely self-supporting implementation system; and (3) it insulates Congress from pressure to fund bailouts for individual business failures.

1. Priority Repayments to the Public Fisc

Bankruptcy policy minimizes losses to the public fisc in an obvious way: it requires payment first and in full to government taxing authorities. . . .

2. A Self-Supporting System

The bankruptcy system offers significant services to the parties involved with a failing company: it provides courts and associated personnel to hear parties' disputes, but it also requires those courts to deal with an extensive list of uncontested matters that arise in the course of a liquidation or reorganization. . . . Notwithstanding the far greater expenditure of resources than most civil actions require, these special bankruptcy features are largely self-supporting. . . .

Private trustees, appointed in all chapter 7 and chapter 13 cases, receive a fee from the receipts of the case. A large proportion of chapter 7 cases yields no fees, so that the trustee collects only a portion of the filing fee as compensation. An informal compensation system exists, nonetheless, in which trustees can count on occasional big cases that will yield substantial fees, in part to make up for carrying a number of small cases which are not cost effective. . . . In no case, however, does the public at large bear these fees. . . .

3. Political Insulation

The bankruptcy system also forces greater internalization of costs by providing a mechanism to deal with failing companies and the enormous claims against them in a manner that discourages the parties from demanding a public bailout. . . .

Thus, bankruptcy laws give large companies the opportunity to reorganize. . . . The opportunity for the business to reorganize and its accompanying hope of success allow Congress greater leeway to withstand the pleading of all those who will be injured by the failure of the business. This process, in turn, tends to block the development of an ever-growing number of specialized government programs that externalize the costs of business failure to the taxpaying public.

D. A Privately Monitored System

. . . A crucial feature of the bankruptcy system—and one that is essential to implement the other normative goals of the system—is that an effective means exists to bring the system into play at the appropriate time.

Both privately and publicly initiated systems are used throughout the world to deal with failing businesses. In countries throughout Asia and Europe, government or regulatory intervention is the standard means to cope with insolvent corporations. The American bankruptcy system relies on a different mechanism: recourse to the bankruptcy courts is a private affair, available only when the parties more directly affected by its operation initiate it. No public resources are allocated to monitor debtors' financial conditions or to bring debtors in danger of collapse under court supervision. There are no "debt police" to scrutinize the likelihood that a debtor will not pay, nor are there state-authorized trustees to impose bankruptcy protection upon those at risk. The law leaves debt-collection and asset-distribution costs to the private parties who stand to lose or gain as the debtor suffers or prospers. The state merely provides the forum and the procedures to regulate the parties' efforts.

. . . A properly constructed bankruptcy system places the bankruptcy decision in the hands of the parties who have superior information about the finances and the likely future of the business, and who will not expend resources to dispute the appropriateness of the filing.

In most businesses, the debtor best fits the description of the well-informed decisionmaker. The debtor is typically the only party with access to full information about its outstanding obligations, future business plans, and income projections. . . .

While a debtor may have the information to make the best decision about entering bankruptcy, there are substantial reasons for a debtor to resist a bankruptcy filing. The normative rationalization for bankruptcy often favors the interests of the creditors at the expense of either the shareholders or the managers of the business. . . . Even if the business survives, the distributive norms of the Bankruptcy Code are nearly always contrary to the interests of the business owners, whom it places at the end of the payment line that forms outside the debtor's door in bankruptcy. . . .

In order to stimulate the debtor to initiate bankruptcy proceedings at an appropriate point when the business risks economic failure, there must be some incentive to attract the business into the bankruptcy process. The Bankruptcy Code offers one powerful incentive: the opportunity to save a failing business. . . .

One of the key reasons for the adoption of the 1978 Code was the widespread perception that the old Code was unworkable. . . . The new Code—chapter 11 in particular—was designed with an avowed intention to make bankruptcy more attractive to businesses in trouble. . . . By creating an opportunity for a business to survive its immediate financial crisis, the system serves several normative goals, including the objective goal of encouraging voluntary submission. . . .

IV. Constraints on Bankruptcy Policymaking

. . . Ultimately, bankruptcy policymaking is not an academic exercise. . . . This policy debate is about real provisions in real laws that have a real impact on millions of debtors, creditors, and others who are affected by economic failure.

Before I end this essay, I want to touch on two elements that limit a meaningful policy debate about bankruptcy: bankruptcy laws operate in imperfect markets, and bankruptcy operates against a background of state collection laws that create strategic opportunities for resistant debtors. These circumstances shape both the actual forms bankruptcy laws can take as well as the aspirational goals bankruptcy may embody. . . . [T]he policy discussion of this essay takes its cue from the tradition of legal realism, asserting that real-world constraints necessarily—and properly—bind bankruptcy policy, and that only in a specified factual context does a policy discussion become meaningful.

A. *An Imperfect World*

We must consider bankruptcy policies in light of their application to cases that arise in the real world. It is therefore critical to note that the markets bankruptcy affects are not perfect and that they contain substantial transaction costs, information asymmetries, and ambiguities about the property rights of the parties. While one might make this blanket warning to constrain any policy debate, it is a particularly pertinent limitation in the bankruptcy area for two reasons: bankruptcy policy is itself grounded in market imperfections, and critics have ignored market imperfections in constructing a hypothetical system that is superior to the current bankruptcy system. . . .

B. *A Dual Collection System*

Another restraint on bankruptcy policymaking is that bankruptcy necessarily displaces an alternative collection system. There exists an intricate, well-developed collection system, based primarily on state laws that govern the collection of debt. The unspoken assumption of many commentators that the collection alternatives are either bankruptcy or payment is not true. Nor is it the case that, absent bankruptcy, defaulting debtors would be forced immediately and costlessly to hand the business over to their creditors. Instead, the state collection system and the bankruptcy system provide alternative, formal rules for dealing with the collection of debt. Each creates the bases for informal leverage and negotiated settlements. Whenever commentators explore either the direct or indirect costs of bankruptcy, it is important to consider the concomitant costs of resolution through the state collection system. . . .

It is good to criticize any system; constant vigilance in the form of vigorous debate is useful to maintain or improve the efficacy of a legal regime. The criticism is more meaningful, however, if it takes account of the circumstances that constrain the operation of the system. . . . To model improved systems that operate only in perfect markets, or to ignore the high costs of collection outside the bankruptcy system when critiquing the high costs of collection in bankruptcy, is to design an airplane that carries no payload, flies only in a gravity-free environment, and consumes no fuel. The exercise may be great fun, but it yields little that is useful for those who need to build planes that fly. It is important to separate debates about bankruptcy fancy from debates about bankruptcy policy.

Conclusion

. . . The bankruptcy system is designed to serve critical functions to preserve the value of failing businesses, to distribute that value according to deliberately defined policies, and to internalize the costs of business failure. The system assists a variety of businesses, more than ninety-nine percent of which are not traded publicly traded. It also serves literally millions of different creditors and other interested parties affected by the bankruptcy laws. Because the functions of the bankruptcy system are deeply intertwined, a single change has the potential to create multiple effects throughout the system. Moreover, changes pursued for one end may simultaneously move the system further away from a number of other objectives.

It is appropriate to end this essay by repeating the initial call for caution. Debates about bankruptcy policy must be more carefully framed to expose their policy presumptions, and any proposal for reform should be accompanied by a thoughtful evaluation of its impact on the competing policy concerns.

Additional suggested readings

Bruce G. Carruthers & Terence C. Halliday, Rescuing Business: The Making of Corporate Bankruptcy Law in England and the United States (Oxford 1998)

Julian R. Franks & Walter Torous, *An Empirical Investigation of U.S. Firms in Reorganization*, 44 J. Fin. 747 (1989)

Laurence H. Kallen, Corporate Welfare: The Megabankruptcies of the 80s and 90s (Carol Publishing 1991)

Lynn M. LoPucki, *The Debtor in Full Control—Systems Failure Under Chapter 11 of the Bankruptcy Code?*, 57 Am. Bankr. L.J. 99 (1983)

Eric A. Posner, *The Political Economy of the Bankruptcy Reform Act of 1978*, 96 MICH. L. REV. 47 (1997)

Richard B. Sobol, BENDING THE LAW: THE STORY OF THE DALKON SHIELD BANKRUPTCY (Chicago 1991)

Sol Stein, A FEAST FOR LAWYERS—INSIDE CHAPTER 11: AN EXPOSÉ (Evans 1989)

Elizabeth Warren & Jay Lawrence Westbrook, *Financial Characteristics of Businesses in Bankruptcy*, 73 AM. BANKR. L.J. 499 (1999)

Chapter 14

Reorganizations in Operation

A. Portraits of Chapter 11

Professor Blum in his article *The Law and Language of Corporate Reorganization* (see Chapter 13) ably identified the legal and theoretical issues that underlie business reorganizations. But what actually happens in the real world of chapter 11 reorganizations? For a very interesting and revealing study, see Elizabeth Warren & Jay Lawrence Westbrook, *Financial Characteristics of Businesses in Bankruptcy*, 73 AM. BANKR. L.J. 499 (1999). Here three excerpts are included. The first is from an unpublished but still quite well-known paper written in 1989 by Ed Flynn for the Administrative Office of United States Courts. That paper examined the results of a study of over 2400 cases during the first decade that the Bankruptcy Code was in effect. Perhaps the most publicized statistics from this paper—and which served as fodder for critics of chapter 11—were that only 17% of all cases resulted in a confirmed plan and only 10% to 12% of all cases resulted in a successful reorganization of the debtor's business. Also of concern was the revelation that the average time from filing to confirmation was over two years (740 days). The paper also contains interesting information about the characteristics of businesses in chapter 11 (*e.g.*, asset size, debts, payment ratios).

The second excerpt is from the study of large business bankruptcies by Professors William Whitford and Lynn LoPucki. LoPucki and Whitford scrutinized the details of what transpired in the 43 chapter 11 bankruptcies during the Code's first decade involving publicly held companies with at least $100 million in assets. The article included here, *Patterns in the Bankruptcy Reorganization of Large, Publicly Held Companies*, 78 CORNELL L. REV. 597 (1993), reveals many fascinating facts about those large reorganizations. For example, in these giant cases, LoPucki and Whitford find a much higher confirmation rate (96%) than Flynn found for the broader universe of all chapter 11 cases (only 17%). Other articles that came out of that study include: *Venue Choice and Forum Shopping in the Bankruptcy Reorganization of Large, Publicly Held Companies*, 1991 WIS. L. REV. 11; *Corporate Governance in the Bankruptcy Reorganization of Large, Publicly Held Companies*, 141 U. PA. L. REV. 669 (1993); and *Bargaining Over Equity's Share in the Bankruptcy Reorganization of Large, Publicly Held Companies*, 139 U. PA. L. REV. 125 (1990).

The third and final selection in this section is by Susan Jensen-Conklin, entitled *Do Confirmed Chapter 11 Plans Consummate? The Results of a Study and Analysis of the Law*, 97 COM. L.J. 297 (1992). Professor Jensen-Conklin reports her findings from a decade-long empirical study of actual chapter 11 case results in a particular judicial district. That district did not have any of the "megacases" of the sort that comprised the LoPucki-Whitford study. Her findings mirror those of Flynn closely, reflecting a confirmation rate of 17% and an average confirmation time of 22 months. Additional interesting information about real chapter 11 case outcomes is revealed.

Ed Flynn
Bankruptcy Division, Administrative Office of United States Courts
Statistical Analysis of Chapter 11
(October 1989)
(unpublished paper)

INTRODUCTION

In the first ten years under the Bankruptcy Code (October 1, 1979 through September 30, 1989) there were about 176,500 chapter 11 cases initiated nationwide. To date little summary information has been available on the outcomes or current status of these chapter 11 cases. . . .

Recently the Administrative Office retained Ernst & Young, Inc., to conduct a study of confirmed chapter 11 cases. Their accountants reviewed nearly 2,400 confirmed cases in the 15 districts included in the study. . . .

This paper is an attempt to provide a clearer picture of the results of chapter 11 filings. . . .

SUMMARY OF FINDINGS . . .

IV. CONFIRMATION RATES:

—It is estimated that approximately 17% of chapter 11 cases filed nationwide prior to 1987 have been or will be confirmed. . . .

—The Ernst & Young employees who reviewed the most cases estimated that 20-30% of the cases they reviewed contained liquidating plans rather than reorganization plans.

—The author estimates that 10 to 12 percent of chapter 11 cases result in a successful reorganization of the debtor's business. . . .

VI. CASE SIZE:

. . .

—The overall average confirmed case reviewed by Ernst & Young had $4.75 million in assets, $5.02 million in debts, and proposed plan payments of $2.62 million. . . .

—The average case size was heavily influenced by a few large cases. In more than one-half the cases reviewed, asset, debt, and proposed payment amounts were under $1 million. . . .

VII. TIME FROM FILING TO PLAN CONFIRMATION:

—Nearly two-thirds of confirmations occur in the second and third years after filing. Very few cases are confirmed more than five years after filing.

—The average time from filing to confirmation was 740 days; The median (age of the middle case at confirmation) time from filing to confirmation was 656 days. . . .

—There seems to be little relationship between filing to confirmation intervals and debt levels . . . .

—There seems to be little relationship between filing to confirmation intervals and asset levels . . . .

—Cases where the debtor was relatively solvent took slightly longer to confirm than cases where the debtor was rather insolvent.

Lynn M. LoPucki & William C. Whitford
Patterns in the Bankruptcy Reorganization of Large, Publicly Held Companies
78 CORNELL L. REV. 597 (1993)[*]

. . . We recently completed an extensive empirical study of forty-three Chapter 11 cases involving large, publicly held firms. . . . These cases constitute the universe of cases filed under the Bankruptcy Code by publicly held companies reporting at least $100 million in assets at filing in which a plan of reorganization was confirmed before March 15, 1988. In this Article we report what has happened to the corporations and businesses involved in these cases, both during reorganization and thereafter. . . .

I. CONFIRMATION RATE

Confirmation of a reorganization plan was a requirement met by all of the cases included in our principal study. . . . [W]e can document confirmation of a plan in sixty-nine of the seventy-two (96%) cases filed by large, publicly held companies within the eight and one-half year study period. Clearly, confirmation of a reorganization plan is commonplace in Chapter 11 cases involving large, publicly held companies.

These findings contrast with the conventional wisdom that in the large majority of Chapter 11 cases, generally involving smaller companies, plans are not confirmed. Practices with respect to confirmation in the large cases sharply diverge from that pattern. This was not noted by some of the commentators advocating the repeal of Chapter 11 for large firms, causing them to advance some misleading arguments.

II. ENTITY SURVIVAL

A reorganization plan can provide for the elimination of the filing entity. Typically, in such cases, all assets of the filing company are sold during the proceeding, with the proceeds of the sale distributed to claimants under the reorganization plan. After consummation of the reorganization plan, the company has no assets and ceases to exist. In five of the forty-three (12%) cases that we studied that is precisely what happened.

In the thirty-eight remaining cases, some form of entity survived the Chapter 11 case. In six instances, an entity with few tangible assets was preserved primarily in order to take advantage of Net Operating Loss Carryovers (NOLs). . . . Absent tax considerations, it is likely that only thirty-two of forty-three (74%) cases would have produced a surviving entity.

When a debtor entity survives through confirmation, the plan distributes shares in the surviving entity to holders of claims or interests. An expeditious auction of all assets is one of the most prominent of the currently proposed radical reforms of Chapter 11. If this reform were accomplished by requiring a Chapter 7 type of liquidation, there would be no shares in a surviving entity available for distribution. In this respect, the reform would change the current practice.

III. BUSINESS SURVIVAL

. . . [W]e consider a business to have survived only if the core business at filing remained intact in a single entity through confirmation. We considered the core business at filing to have remained intact if a major portion of the assets remained under common ownership and were fundamentally committed to the same business purpose, whether that ownership was maintained by the same entity or not.

The alternative to business survival is what we call "shattering." Shattering means that a large portion of the company as it existed at filing was sold off in discrete units to different buyers. . . .

The principal criterion we used in deciding whether a core business survived was reduction in asset size during the case. If, without sale of the core business, a company's assets fell by more than 50% during the period of the case, we usually considered the company to have shattered.

In twenty-two of the forty-three (51%) cases studied, we judged that the core business survived. In fifteen of these twenty-two (68%) cases the core business survived within the same entity structure. In the other seven cases the core business was transferred as a unit to a third party.

In three cases the company emerged from bankruptcy with its core business intact, but a decision had been reached to shatter the company . . . . However, it was thought more efficient to conduct the asset sales outside of bankruptcy. In eighteen other cases, we determined that the shattering occurred while the company was in bankruptcy. Thus, in nearly half (twenty-one of forty-three) of the cases studied, the company either shattered before confirmation or was expected to shatter shortly thereafter. . . .

IV. REDUCTION IN ASSET SIZE

The total value of the company's assets commonly declined during Chapter 11, even when the core business survived. . . .

. . . [R]eduction in asset size is almost a universal feature of Chapter 11 cases involving large, publicly held corporations. Bankruptcy analysts often characterize particular bankruptcy cases as reorganizations or liquidations. This distinction is of limited usefulness with respect to large, publicly held companies. Nearly all of them liquidate some assets and a few liquidate all assets. Most of the companies . . . cut their size by more than half. The meaningful distinction is among various degrees of liquidation, not between liquidation and reorganization as discrete categories.

V. FINANCIAL SUCCESS

A bankruptcy reorganization may be able to resolve two distinct kinds of financial problems for a troubled company. First, a company may be incurring substantial operating losses that are not merely the product of temporary market conditions. In these cases, the company normally considers selling losing parts of its overall business and cutting costs through the adoption of more efficient methods. Second, the company may have incurred too much debt and become unable to meet its obligations at any reasonably foreseeable level of operating revenue. One solution is to reduce the amount of debt through bankruptcy discharge.

. . . [W]e worked from the amounts of debt and equity shown on the emerging companies' annual financial reports for the first reporting dates after confirmation. From these statistics we calculated debt/equity ratios for twenty-six of the forty-three companies in our study. From a published source, we found the average debt/equity ratio for companies of comparable size in the same businesses as each of these twenty-six debtors. We refer to this industry average as the "benchmark" ratio for each of our emerging companies

For nineteen of the twenty-six companies (76%) in our study, the actual debt/equity ratio exceeds the benchmark ratio. . . . From this, we conclude that some factor or factors caused some of these companies to have above average debt/equity ratios at the time of their first post-confirmation financial statement. . . .

We have other data suggesting a tendency for companies to emerge from Chapter 11 with too much debt. A surviving entity remained after confirmation in thirty-eight of the forty-three companies in our study. In twelve of those thirty-eight cases (32%), the emerging entity filed another bankruptcy petition . . . . This is a strikingly high refiling rate. Moreover, a review of contemporary news accounts indicates that at least four of the twelve refilings were significantly caused by financial problems still existing at the time of confirmation. . . .

We were able to collect information about the post-confirmation financial performance of twenty of the twenty-six surviving companies that did not refile for bankruptcy. Of the twenty companies, exactly half suffered net operating losses in the year before filing. Six of these ten companies experienced significant increases in asset size and operating income in the three years after confirmation. Two of the other four companies experienced steady financial performance during these years. From this information we conclude that Chapter 11 has sometimes been useful in dealing with the first of the financial problems identified above—the failure to earn operating profits.

In summary, evidence about the ability of large, publicly held companies to resolve their financial problems in Chapter 11 is mixed. Shortly after confirmation, a statistically significant majority of the companies we studied had greater indebtedness than is customary for their industry. In some cases that extra indebtedness led to a future bankruptcy filing. Moreover, the general refiling rate for companies that have emerged from Chapter 11 is extraordinarily high. On the other hand, while in Chapter 11, a number of companies were able to correct whatever problems were causing their net operating losses and conduct successful business after confirmation. In terms of the financial rehabilitation objective with which it is commonly identified, Chapter 11 has had some successes.

VI. Changes in Control

Some commentators assert that managers or controlling shareholders use Chapter 11 to maintain control of corporations. . . .

We have reported elsewhere that a significant number of managers were not able to stay in office throughout the Chapter 11 process in those cases that we studied. In thirty-one of the forty-three cases (70%) there was at least one change in CEO either during the pendency of the Chapter 11 case or in contemplation under the reorganization plan. . . . For the managers of publicly held companies, Chapter 11 is not the safe harbor that some have assumed.

The ownership of shares also usually changes dramatically because of the terms of the reorganization plan. . . . As might be expected, reorganization plans were much more likely to permit existing shareholders to retain their shares when the company was solvent at confirmation. For insolvent companies, however, it was rare for existing shareholders to retain a majority of the reorganization shares.

We conclude that Chapter 11 has not been a vehicle by which insiders have retained control of large, publicly held companies. Changes in control are regular occurrences in the Chapter 11 reorganizations of these companies.

Conclusion

This account presents a mixed picture of what happens to large, publicly held firms in Chapter 11. There are "successes," regardless of which definition of success is used. Most significantly, there are companies that retain their core businesses in Chapter 11 and become financially successful after confirmation. These Chapter 11 experiences confirm the popular conception of Chapter 11 as a place where the company with remediable financial problems has an opportunity to make necessary changes. Chapter 11 is not a complete failure.

Nonetheless, there are problems with Chapter 11. Particularly disturbing is the evidence that many large, publicly held companies emerge from Chapter 11 with too much debt and refile for bankruptcy at a strikingly high rate.

Two consistent patterns emerge from the forty-three cases we studied. First, a reduction in asset size is an almost uniform feature of the Chapter 11 experience when a large, publicly held company is involved. Though few companies cease to exist entirely, nearly all engage in some form of liquidation. The distinction commonly drawn between reorganizations and liquidations is misleading. Second, those formerly in control of a corporation ordinarily lose their position during a Chapter 11 case. Commentators who assume that Chapter 11 provides an easy way for managers or shareholders to maintain control of large, publicly held companies should re-evaluate their positions.

Apart from these consistencies, the data suggests that the chief characteristic of Chapter 11 is variety. There is no stereotypical pattern for a Chapter 11 case involving a large, publicly held company. In about half of the cases studied, the core business survived intact within a single entity. . . .

Proposals for reform of Chapter 11 should take this multiplicity of uses into account. Proposals designed to enhance some uses may hinder other uses. For example, in some circumstances Chapter 11 may be a better vehicle for liquidating a large, publicly held company than Chapter 7. . . . A requirement that a company be auctioned shortly after filing—a commonly made reform proposal—may prevent some financially unwise reorganizations, but it may also foreclose liquidation in the most efficient manner. It is far from clear that bankruptcy would be a better institution if all cases were forced into a single mold.

Susan Jensen-Conklin
Do Confirmed Chapter 11 Plans Consummate?
The Results of a Study and Analysis of the Law
97 COM. L.J. 297 (1992)[*]

INTRODUCTION

. . . This article focuses on the extent to which the feasibility prediction of Code Section 1129(a)(11) for confirmed cases bears out in reality. Specifically, it reports on and analyzes the results of a Study conducted by the author into the consummation of confirmed Chapter 11 plans filed over a ten-year period at a particular bankruptcy court. In addition to determining the consummation rate of these cases, the Study attempted to identify factors indicative of successful consummation. . . .

II. THE STUDY

. . .

B. PURPOSE AND NATURE OF THE STUDY

With these concerns in mind, the following Study was undertaken by the author. Spanning the ten years between 1980 to 1989, the Study was based on all Chapter 11 cases filed in the U.S. Bankruptcy Court for the Southern District of New York located at Poughkeepsie.

The purpose of the Study was twofold. First, the Study sought to discover what percentage of confirmed Chapter 11 plans were fully consummated. . . . Second, the Study sought to identify any parameters that would indicate whether a confirmed plan was more likely than not to be successfully consummated. . . .

C. STATISTICAL RELEVANCE OF THE STUDY

Admittedly, the statistical relevance of a study based on cases filed only at one court is suspect. Nevertheless, several analyses were conducted to test the case base of this court in comparison with the case base utilized in a national study referred to here as the "Flynn Study." Surprisingly, the

---

cases comprising the Poughkeepsie Study comport nearly exactly with the cases reported in the national Flynn Study . . . . This result may support a conclusion that the Poughkeepsie Study, although based on cases filed at a single court, is representative of national trends and developments. . . .

Concerning the overall Chapter 11 filing percentage, confirmation rate, percentage of liquidating plans, median time to confirm, and debtor profile, the case base of the Poughkeepsie Study is virtually identical to that of the Flynn Study in each of these five areas. First, whereas nationwide Chapter 11 cases represent roughly four percent of all bankruptcy filings, the percentage of Chapter 11 cases filed at the Poughkeepsie bankruptcy court over the ten-year period of the study, *i.e.*, from 1980 to 1989, was 3.84 percent.

Second, the confirmation rates were nearly identical. Over the ten-year period of the Poughkeepsie Study, a total of 260 Chapter 11 cases were filed. Of these, 45 Chapter 11 cases were confirmed, representing a 17.31 percent confirmation rate. This confirmation rate closely comports with the 17 percent national confirmation rate estimated by the Flynn Study.

Third, the percentage of liquidating plans comprising the confirmed plans were similar. Of the 42 cases in which the nature of the confirmed plan could be determined in the Poughkeepsie Study, 11 were liquidating plans or about 26 percent. Similarly, the Flynn Study estimated that approximately 25 percent of the confirmed cases had liquidating plans.

Fourth, as to the median time expended between filing and confirmation, the Flynn Study reported that the period was approximately 22 months. Likewise, the average time for confirmation of the 45 cases comprising the Poughkeepsie Study was 22.04 months. . . .

Fifth, the Poughkeepsie debtor profile is not unlike that reported in the Flynn Study. The Flynn Study stated that more than one-half of the cases reviewed had debt levels of less than $1 million. Of the 45 Poughkeepsie cases, 30 of them, or 66 percent fell into this category. Whereas the Flynn Study reported that less than 15 percent of the cases studied had liabilities in excess of $5 million, approximately 9 percent of the Poughkeepsie cases exceeded this debt level. . . .

E. RESULTS OF THE POUGHKEEPSIE STUDY

In general, the Study data can be broken down into two categories: general and consummation-oriented.

1. General Data

The general data primarily serves to identify the debtor-body making up the Study, the type of plan confirmed, the average time required to confirm a plan, and whether a post-confirmation monitor was to have shepherded the plan post-confirmation.

a. Nature of the Debtor

Of the 45 confirmed cases comprising the Study, 44 cases were voluntarily commenced as original Chapter 11 cases. One case was commenced involuntarily under Chapter 7 and subsequently converted to Chapter 11. Thirty-eight of these debtors were corporations and six were sole proprietorships. One was a partnership.

None of the 45 debtors in the Study would qualify as a "mega" Chapter 11 case. The bulk of the cases, that is 22 debtors or 49 percent, had liabilities under $500,000. Eight debtors or 18 percent had liabilities between $500,000 and $1 million. Eleven or 24 percent had liabilities between $1 million and $5 million, while four debtors or approximately 9 percent had more than $5 million in liabilities.

The businesses of the debtors comprising the Study were diverse. . . .

b. Postpetition Events

Each of the 45 debtors were represented by counsel. Creditors' committees existed in roughly half of the cases. In none of the 45 confirmed cases was a Chapter 11 trustee appointed.

Regarding the plan formulation process, only debtor-proposed plans were confirmed in each of the 45 cases. As noted previously, the average period between the time the case was filed and the plan was confirmed was 22.04 months, ranging from a minimum of 12 months to a maximum of 33 months.

. . . Of the 42 cases for which this information could be derived, there were 11 liquidating plans, 24 plans funded solely from the debtor's operations, and seven combination-type plans. . . .

In 42 of the cases, the confirmed plans were examined to determine the treatment to unsecured creditors. Seven plans proposed payments to general unsecured creditors of less than ten percent. The bulk of the plans proposed payments in the ten to 30 percent range. Of the 26 plans within this group, nine plans offered general unsecureds ten percent, six plans offered 11 to 15 percent, while another 11 plans promised between 16 to 30 percent. The average distribution in this category was 17.3 percent. There were two plans that respectively offered a 53 and 75 percent distribution. The remaining seven plans promised a 100 percent distribution to unsecured creditors.

Of the 41 plans in which the duration of the payout to unsecured creditors could be determined, the range varied from immediately upon confirmation to approximately nine years from confirmation. Those plans projecting a payout in one year or less numbered 22 or approximately 54 percent. . . .

2. Consummation Data

a. In General

Out of the 45-case study, nine cases were converted post-confirmation to Chapter 7. . . . In addition, one case was dismissed post-confirmation for the debtor's inability to comply with the plan. Thus, ten out of 45 confirmed cases, or 22 percent, were either converted to Chapter 7 for liquidation or dismissed. . . .

b. Results

The status of the 45 debtors and their compliance with their plans was determined . . . .
The results are characterized into the following four categories:

Definitely Consummated:	21 cases
Probably Consummated:	5 cases
Definitely Did Not Consummate:	11 cases
Probably Did Not Consummate:	8 cases

. . .

3. Analysis

a. In General

Grouping the definitely consummated plans with those that probably consummated, it appears that 26 cases or 58 percent of the 45 cases constitute this group. By multiplying the previously determined 17.3 percent confirmation rate by the 58 percent consummation rate, we can determine the percentage of cases that actually confirmed and resulted in consummated plans in the Poughkeepsie Study. That figure is approximately *ten percent*.

As the number of liquidating plans that comprise the consummated plans is a known number (nine), we can also determine the percentage of cases that confirmed and resulted in consummated plans which contemplated the debtor's continuation in business. That figure is *6.5 percent*, based on the Poughkeepsie Study.

From the debtor's perspective, this means that a Chapter 11 debtor has a *6.5 percent* chance of confirming and consummating a plan as well as surviving as a rehabilitated entity post-confirmation. From the creditor's perspective, the liquidation of the debtor is less of an issue. Thus, as among all Chapter 11 cases filed, a creditor has a *ten percent* chance of receiving the distribution promised in a confirmed Chapter 11 plan, according to the Poughkeepsie Study.

b. Trends

In addition to analyzing the raw consummation data, the Poughkeepsie Study sought to determine the existence of any indicia regarding the likelihood of a plan's potential for full consummation. To this end, a number of factors were tested.

i. Funding of the Plan

One unequivocal, though perhaps obvious, conclusion from the Poughkeepsie Study is that a liquidating plan, as among the other plan types, will most likely be consummated. Of the 11 liquidating plans confirmed, nine or 82 percent were successfully consummated. In contrast, only 42 percent of all confirmed operating plans were consummated. Five out of seven combination plans or 71 percent were consummated and these five comprised 21 percent of the consummated plans. . . .

ii. Term and Payout of the Plan

A plan with a term of one year or less appears to be a more likely candidate for consummation than one of longer duration. Fifty-four percent of those confirmed cases in which the plans could be analyzed were premised on distributions of one year or less. They, in turn, comprised 67 percent of the consummated cases, but accounted for only 35 percent of the plans that failed to consummate.

As to the percentage of the plan's payout where such payout is less than 100 percent, it generally appears that the lower this figure is, the probability is greater that the plan will be consummated. Six out of the seven plans promising less than a ten percent distribution or 86 percent consummated. As to plans offering between ten to 30 percent return to unsecured creditors, half of these consummated. Interestingly, 57 percent of the 100 percent plans were consummated.

iii. Creditors' Committees

It was anticipated that the presence of a creditors' committee in a case would increase the likelihood that the plan would be consummated. The results of the Poughkeepsie Study appear to confirm this.

Creditors' committees were appointed in approximately 49 percent of the 45 Chapter 11 cases that confirmed. Of the consummated cases, committees existed in 58 percent of these cases. On the other hand, creditors' committees were appointed in 37 percent of the cases that did not consummate. Thus, . . . there appears to be a significant difference between the presence of creditors' committees in consummated plan cases and in cases where the plan was not consummated.

iv. Size of the Case

The relative size of the case, based on the amount of liabilities, appears to correlate to the potential for consummation. Cases with less than $500,000 of liabilities made up 49 percent of the confirmed cases and accounted for 42 percent of the consummated cases. Nevertheless, only 11 out of 22 cases that confirmed in this category or 50 percent of these consummated. At the opposite extreme, cases with liabilities exceeding $5 million constituted nine percent of the confirmed cases and comprised 15 percent of the consummated cases. Still, 100 percent of these cases resulted in consummated plans.

Those cases falling between these two extremes had less dramatic trends. Of the eight confirmed cases with liabilities exceeding $500,000, but less than $1 million, five yielded consummated plans, that is 63 percent of these cases consummated. Out of the 11 cases with liabilities in excess of $1 million, but less than $5 million, six or 55 percent consummated.

v. Months to Confirmation

There appears to be little correlation between the average number of months to confirm a case and the likelihood that the confirmed plan will be consummated. As among all the confirmed cases, the average time expended to reach confirmation was 22.04 months. As for cases that resulted in consummated plans as compared to those that did not, the average time was respectively 21.96 months and 22.15 months, a difference of a few days. . . .

III. OBSERVATIONS

Several broad conclusions are evident from the Poughkeepsie Study. . . .

First, confirmation of a plan does not equate to consummation of the plan, notwithstanding the feasibility finding that must be made as a condition of the plan's confirmation. To begin with, the chances of a Chapter 11 case being confirmed are slim; only 17 percent even make it to confirmation. Of those that are confirmed, a quarter may be converted or dismissed for failure to comply with the plan. Out of the remaining survivors, 60 percent will ultimately yield consummated plans. And of these, approximately 25 percent will liquidate pursuant to their plans. Thus, the net end result is that out of all Chapter 11 cases filed, only 6.5 percent of these cases will culminate in a consummated plan and a rehabilitated debtor. Clearly, Chapter 11 is not a panacea and consummation is not guaranteed.

Second, factors associated with a plan that will likely consummate include a plan calling for the liquidation of the debtor, the presence of a creditors' committee in the case, and a plan payout of one year or less. It also appears that the larger debtors will more likely consummate a plan. . . .

IV. CONCLUSION

. . . Certainly, one factor that should be considered in the "private ordering" that occurs in a Chapter 11 case is what will happen post-confirmation, beyond the promised distribution. . . . The Poughkeepsie Study indicates that confirmation of a plan may not necessarily lead to consummation, but there are factors and plan drafting provisions that may make this a more likely possibility.

B.   Venue Choice

Debtors in large chapter 11 cases often demonstrate a desire to choose a forum that they believe will be more beneficial to them. The forum chosen may be one in which the debtor has little or no physical presence. Through the decade of the 1980s, the venue of choice for large chapter 11 cases was New York City—the Southern District of New York. This phenomenon was discussed by Professors LoPucki and Whitford in *Venue Choice and Forum Shopping in the Bankruptcy Reorganization of Large, Publicly Held Companies*, 1991 WIS. L. REV. 11. Around 1990, the preferred "big-case" forum suddenly shifted to Delaware. That occurrence is examined in the following article by Professors Eisenberg and LoPucki.

Professor LoPucki co-authored a follow-up article in which the Delaware venue choice syndrome is shown to be highly problematic. *See* Lynn M. LoPucki & Sara D. Kalin, *The Failure of Public Company Bankruptcies in Delaware and New York: Empirical Evidence of a "Race to the Bottom,"* 54 VAND. L. REV. 231 (2001). Other scholars, though, have applauded the forum shopping idea, at least in some circumstances. *See* Robert K. Rasmussen & Randall S. Thomas, *Whither the Race: A Comment on the Delawarization of Corporate Reorganizations*, 54 VAND. L. REV. 283 (2001); Robert K. Rasmussen & Randall S. Thomas, *Timing Matters: Promoting Forum Shopping by Insolvent Corporations*, 94 NW. U. L. REV. 1357 (2000); David A. Skeel, Jr., *What's So Bad About Delaware?*, 54 VAND. L. REV. 309 (2001); David A. Skeel, Jr., *Bankruptcy Judges and Bankruptcy Venue: Some Thoughts on Delaware*, 1 DELAWARE L. REV. 1 (1998).

The second excerpt in this section is from the National Bankruptcy Review Commission's 1997 Report. After much debate, the Commission decided that forum shopping was a bad thing, and recommended tightening up the rules regarding corporate venue choice. In particular, the Commission suggested eliminating state of incorporation as a basis for venue, which, if adopted by Congress, would end the Delaware phenomenon.

Theodore Eisenberg & Lynn M. LoPucki
Shopping for Judges:
An Empirical Analysis of Venue Choice in Large Chapter 11 Reorganizations
84 CORNELL L. REV. 967 (1999)[*]

INTRODUCTION

For almost two decades, an embarrassing pattern of forum shopping has been developing in the highly visible world of big-case bankruptcy reorganization. Forum shopping—defined here as the act of filing in a court that does not serve the geographical area of the debtor's corporate headquarters—now occurs in more than half of all big-case bankruptcies. . . .

In response to widespread concern and the "troubling specter of courts competing for big-case bankruptcy business," the National Bankruptcy Review Commission recommended in the fall of 1997 that Congress amend the bankruptcy venue statute to prevent forum shoppers from filing in Delaware. . . .

This Article reports the results of a comprehensive study of big-case bankruptcy forum shopping from 1980 to 1997. A description of what has occurred helps explain both the causes of Delaware's rise as the preferred Chapter 11 forum and why embarrassment forced the system to take extraordinary countermeasures. . . .

This Article casts doubt on the two common explanations for forum shoppers' attraction to Delaware: (1) that Delaware resolves bankruptcy cases more quickly, and (2) that Delaware has developed expertise in prepackaged cases. No statistically significant evidence exists that Delaware processes large Chapter 11 cases more quickly than other districts. . . .

Forum-shopping debtors must believe that the benefits of filing in Delaware outweigh the costs. The Delaware Bankruptcy Court requires that local counsel represent each party, adding an expense that the debtor usually would not incur when filing elsewhere. Because debtors who file in Delaware also incur travel expenses for nonlocal professionals and company personnel, the direct costs of forum shopping to Delaware are not trivial. Forum-shopping debtors must believe that the benefits of filing in Delaware are substantial. . . .

Delaware's replacement of New York in 1990 as the forum shopper's destination of choice makes sense only in light of the political context in which it occurred. Changes in New York's

---

judge-assignment mechanisms and a bankruptcy venue decision in Delaware, in combination with Delaware's recognized tradition of providing pro-corporate legal structures, may have triggered this shift to Delaware. Once Delaware gained a reputation as a shopping destination, this reputation probably persisted in part because the state had become a safe choice for bankruptcy lawyers and their clients. . . .

I

WHY FORUM SHOPPING IN CHAPTER 11 CASES EMBARRASSES THE SYSTEM

. . . One type of forum shopping . . . has received uniform condemnation . . .—shopping for judges. Observers seem to agree that judge shopping "breeds disrespect for and threatens the integrity of our judicial system" and undermines the aphorism that "ours is a government of laws, not men."

. . . Convenience cannot explain the forum shopping that this Article explores because this shopping has focused successively on two courts, New York and Delaware, neither of which is convenient to the filers. Nor can a search for friendly juries explain Chapter 11 forum shopping. Juries play no significant role in bankruptcy cases. Differences in law and procedure cannot drive the shopping because the governing law and procedure are federal. Theoretically, every significant aspect of Chapter 11 reorganization is uniform throughout the United States. Significant, persistent differences among bankruptcy courts that would make forum shopping the norm should be impossible. Contrary to these implausible explanations, the persistence of forum shopping demonstrates the importance of judges to litigants and, implicitly, the relative unimportance of law. . . .

II

METHODOLOGY

A. Case Selection

This study includes all Chapter 11 bankruptcy cases in the United States by or against companies that were, at the time of filing, publicly held with assets worth at least $100 million in 1980 dollars. . . .

B. Variable Definitions and Data Sources

1. Defining Forum Shopping

The key variable studied is forum shopping. We define a "forum shop" or "shop" as the filing of a case in a court other than that which serves the location of the debtor's chief executive office. . . .

2. Measuring Case-Processing Time

To measure case-processing time, we use the time between the bankruptcy filing and the entry of an order confirming the plan or otherwise disposing of the case. . . . The principal difference that affects case-processing time is "prepackaging." In a prepackaged case, the debtor proposes the plan and obtains the agreement of creditors before filing the reorganization case. Cases with prepackaged plans, on average, proceed to confirmation more quickly and more surely than other cases. . . .

3. Categorizing Case Outcomes

To explore whether forum affects case outcomes, this study divides case outcomes into five categories: (1) "confirmed" if the court confirmed a plan; (2) "dismissed" if the court dismissed the case without confirmation of a plan; (3) "converted" if the court converted to Chapter 7 for liquidation without confirming a plan; (4) "§ 363 sale" if the debtor sold all or substantially all of the assets during the Chapter 11 case without the prior confirmation of a plan; and (5) "pending" if the court did not confirm any plan and the case remained under Chapter 11 as of August 27, 1998. . . .

III

DESCRIBING TRENDS IN FORUM SHOPPING,
CHAPTER 11 CASE-PROCESSING TIMES, AND PREPACKAGED CASES

. . .

A. The Level and Time Trend of Forum Shopping

By any reasonable measure, the rate at which large corporations file Chapter 11 cases at locations distant from their headquarters is high. One hundred twenty-two of the 284 cases studied (43.0%) were filed in a court located in a jurisdiction different from the jurisdiction where the company maintained its chief executive office at the time of filing.

Forum shopping is not only prevalent, it has been increasing. . . .

The already low rate of forum shopping declined from 1980 to 1984. The rate jumped in 1985 to about 40% of large Chapter 11 fillings and remained at that level through 1993, despite large changes in the number of filings from year to year. From 1994 to 1996, the rate climbed sharply to 86%. The rate fell in 1997, but remains at historically high levels. Forum shopping in large cases has reached the point at which it is the rule rather than the exception.

Strong geographical tendencies exist. . . . The historical pattern of forum shopping exhibits three phases. From 1980 to 1989, the cumulative number of shopped cases split almost evenly between New York with thirteen (46.4%) and all other cites with fifteen (53.6%). From 1990 to 1993, the shopped cases split almost evenly between Delaware and New York, with a combined total of twenty-eight cases (52.8%), and all other cities, with twenty-five cases (47.2%). Between Delaware and New York, Delaware led slightly with fifteen filings to New York's thirteen. In the third phase, from 1994 to the present, Delaware has been the dominant destination for forum shopping with thirty-three cases (82.5%). New York has had four (10.0%), and all other cities have had only three (7.5%). Thus, Delaware currently dominates forum shopping to a degree that New York never has. . . .

B. Decreasing Case-Processing Times, Increasing Prepackaged Bankruptcies

The increase in forum shopping occurred against a background of changing case-processing times. . . . The trend, especially since 1989, is toward faster case processing. . . .

. . . Two debtors filed prepackaged plans in 1986, but the next prepackaged filing did not take place until November 1990. Since 1992, 28.3% (34 of 120) of the filings have been prepackaged. . . .

. . . Prepackaged and prenegotiated cases exhibited higher forum-shopping rates than unnegotiated cases. Among the fifty-eight prepackaged or prenegotiated cases in the study, thirty-three filings occurred in bankruptcy courts that did not serve the cities of the debtors' chief executive offices—a forum-shopping rate of 56.9%. Among the 226 other cases, eighty-nine (39.4%) were filed in a court other than that serving the city in which the corporation's chief executive office was located. . . .

IV

EXPLAINING FORUM-SHOPPING TRENDS

Several trends in large Chapter 11 cases—the increase in forum shopping, the increase in Delaware filings, the reduction in case-processing times, and the increase in prepackaged bankruptcy filings—have coincided. The coincidence of these trends makes it difficult to identify separate causes for Delaware's ascension as the forum of choice. Some scholars have attempted to explain the shift to Delaware as a response to what they perceive as Delaware's greater efficiency in handling prepackaged bankruptcies or large Chapter 11 cases in general. The true story is in some ways simpler and in other ways more complex.

Delaware may not have attracted forum shoppers so much as the changing situation in New York repelled them. Once forum-shopping debtors began filing in Delaware, more followed. Something about Delaware attracts forum shoppers, but identifying that something is not easy. In contrast to explanations of the Delaware Bar and some academics, this study finds no robust evidence in the pattern of filings or processing times that suggests Delaware offers a more efficient forum for resolving large Chapter 11 cases, whether or not they are prepackaged.

A. The Shift from New York to Delaware

. . . New York was the principal destination for big-case forum shopping through the 1980s. Two events in 1988 appear to have contributed to the shift to Delaware. Despite the existence of a random draw in the bankruptcy clerk's office, large New York bankruptcy reorganizations in the early 1980s tended to gravitate to Bankruptcy Judge Burton R. Lifland. Debtors may have viewed an assignment to Judge Lifland as desirable both because he had more experience than any other judge in bankruptcy reorganizations of large, public companies and because he had a reputation for being pro-debtor and pro-reorganization. In January 1988, the New York court changed its random assignment system so that the Administrative Office of the United States Courts in Washington would generate the random element.

In that same year, Judge Helen S. Balick, the only bankruptcy judge in the District of Delaware, ruled that a corporation's "residence or domicile" for venue purposes was at its place of incorporation. The decision might have encouraged large, corporate debtors to file in Delaware. . . . Judge Balick's ruling confirmed that Delaware was a proper venue for all these companies. Under a contrary ruling, Delaware would have been a proper venue for fewer than 1% of them.

The shift to Delaware as the preferred destination for big-case forum shopping began in the last two months of 1990 . . . . Delaware's proportion of filings grew swiftly. . . . From 1994 to 1996, the proportion of cases involving forum shopping increased sharply, and Delaware assumed dominance. In 1996, twelve of fourteen large, public companies that filed for bankruptcy reorganization (85.7%) did so in Delaware.

The clearest evidence that forum shopping into Delaware had reached disturbing levels came from Chief Judge Joseph J. Farnan, Jr. of the Delaware District Court. Effective February 3, 1997, Chief Judge Farnan took the unprecedented step of withdrawing the automatic reference of Delaware bankruptcy cases to the bankruptcy court and personally taking over the assignment of Chapter 11 case filings in Delaware. . . . [L]ikely, Judge Farnan's purpose was to reduce concerns regarding the significant shift of forum shopping to Delaware. . . .

B. Delaware's Comparative Speed in Processing Cases

The argument that Delaware more efficiently processes large bankruptcies rests heavily on its allegedly faster case-processing time. Differences in case-processing times do influence forum choice. If efficiency attracts debtors, then the shift of forum shopping to Delaware indicates convenience shopping rather than judge shopping.

. . . If Delaware offers reliably faster reorganization, this speed could explain its attractiveness to debtors and creditors.

To explore the relation between case-processing time and forum, we compare processing times in New York, Delaware, and other locales. . . . The data show meaningful differences in processing time between Delaware and New York. The mean unnegotiated case took 510 days in Delaware and 765 days in New York. . . . Their medians also differ: New York cases have a median elapsed time of 582 days, and Delaware cases have a median elapsed time of 463 days. . . .

[A]lso[,] . . . processing times in Delaware are somewhat faster than processing times in all districts other than New York, but . . . the differences are not statistically significant in either the means or the medians. Statistically, one cannot reject the hypothesis that there is no difference between elapsed times in Delaware and non-New York districts . . . .

. . . Delaware cases terminate more quickly than cases in other states, but the effect is not statistically significant except in comparison to New York. . . .

C. Delaware's Expertise in Prepackaged Bankruptcies

Since 1990, when debtors began filing prepackaged cases in significant numbers, Delaware has received a disproportionate share of these cases. Nineteen of the forty-nine filings in Delaware (38.8%) were prepackaged, while only twenty of the 140 cases in other districts (14.3%) were prepackaged. . . .

2. Delaware as the Efficient Chapter 11 Forum

. . . Rasmussen and Thomas, along with Skeel, suggest that allowing continued shopping to Delaware will maximize social welfare. The Delaware Bankruptcy Court, they argue, has developed expertise in handling prepackaged bankruptcies that "allows the managers (with the cooperation of the majority of creditors) to implement a value-increasing plan of reorganization quickly and without holdout problems from rent-seeking dissenting creditors." Perceiving that Delaware cases are faster and assuming that prepackaged bankruptcies benefit both debtors and their creditors, Rasmussen and Thomas conclude that disabling Delaware from specializing in prepackaged bankruptcies without permitting any other court to assume a similarly dominant position would cause "a decrease in social welfare." . . . [T]wo key factual assumptions are questionable.

First, these commentators assume that the Delaware Bankruptcy Court handles prepackaged cases more quickly and with greater certainty of outcome than other courts. The data, however, provide thin support for their assumption. Of the forty-one prepackaged cases in our study, nineteen proceeded in Delaware, and the other twenty-two proceeded in eighteen different cities. Courts confirmed plans in all forty-one cases; thus there was no difference in this measure of success. . . . [T]he average number of days in Chapter 11 was fifty-two for the Delaware prepackaged cases and fifty-nine for cases in other cities. The median time in Chapter 11 was thirty-eight days in Delaware and forty-six days in other cities. Neither of these differences approaches statistical significance. . . . Although Delaware processed cases more quickly than courts in other cities, the time difference is small enough to qualify as immaterial. Indeed, . . . prepackaged cases may even proceed more quickly in New York than in Delaware.

Second, Rasmussen and Thomas assume that confirming a prepackaged plan is *always* in the interests of both the debtor and its creditors. This assumption is also questionable. . . . Delaware is not efficient if it attracts prepackaged reorganization cases by assuring a confirmation so quick that dissenting creditors or United States Trustees cannot participate effectively. . . .

Other commentators argue that forum shoppers select Delaware because its bankruptcy court has adopted better case-processing procedures and more efficient methods of administration. . . .

Although these conveniences undoubtedly make a lawyer's job easier, it is hard to believe that they could counterbalance the expense of traveling to Delaware and the required retention, in every case, of local counsel. . . . The decision to file in Delaware rather than New York is, for all practical purposes, the decision to incur the expense of another law firm's fee.

D. More Complete Explanations of Forum Shopping

For the reasons described above, we doubt that Delaware's efficiency or expertise drove Chapter 11 debtors to file in Delaware. Other considerations cast further doubt on this explanation.

1. *The Inadequacy of Processing-Speed Explanations of Forum Shopping*

. . . [S]tatistical analysis suggests that New York is significantly slower than other districts in processing unnegotiated cases. This result undermines the conclusion that faster case-processing times in Delaware prove Delaware's greater efficiency. The underlying premise—that fast is efficient—would suggest that New York's case processing was inefficient during the period when New York was the venue of choice. To endorse forum shoppers' successive choices of both New York and Delaware as efficient, one must conclude that slow case processing was efficient until 1990, but became inefficient by 1994. . . .

A more plausible explanation for the shift is a change in the perception—probably around 1988—that filings in New York had an excellent chance of being assigned to Judge Lifland. This judge-oriented explanation is consistent with Delaware's rise because the rise occurred when only one bankruptcy judge served in Delaware. One could no longer be so confident in the chances of assignment to Judge Lifland in New York, but one could be sure of assignment to Judge Balick in Delaware. . . .

This judge-oriented explanation also is consistent with the system's embarrassed reactions to the forum shopping. . . .

2. *Flight from Source Districts as an Explanation*

Explanations of the forum-shopping pattern tend to focus solely on the characteristics of the selected court while ignoring the characteristics of the rejected courts. But forum shopping does not result solely from the attractiveness of the destination court. Forum shopping always involves a choice among courts. The home forum usually has the advantage of physical proximity to the debtor's senior management. Debtors from other jurisdictions will not go to the trouble of filing in Delaware or New York unless these districts provide benefits the home districts lack.

To explore the source-district side of the forum-shopping equation, we examine the rate of shopping from each jurisdiction that contained the chief executive office of six or more of the debtors in the study. . . . [S]ignificant city-level effects exist. . . . [M]ost cities with six or more potential large Chapter 11 filings have extreme shopping rates. Either a surprisingly large percentage of cases leave or a surprisingly large number stay. Only Chicago has a rate that approximates the average rate for all cities. . . . [C]haracteristics of the home courts, rather than simply the attractiveness of Delaware or New York, have affected the level of forum-shopping rates.

The relationship between case-processing times and shopping rates for particular cities is relevant to the claim that forum shoppers seek greater efficiency by filing in jurisdictions with faster case-processing times. If Skeel, Rasmussen, and Thomas are correct in stating that speedy case-processing times attract forum shoppers to Delaware, then home courts that process cases the slowest should have the highest rates of debtors seeking other venues. Once again, however, the data belie a processing-time explanation: slow case-processing times do not correlate with high outbound shopping rates. . . . [C]ase-processing times are not significantly lower in shopped cases. . . .

E. Transfer's Inadequacy as a Venue Correction Mechanism

The court to which a case is shopped has discretion to transfer the case to a more appropriate venue "in the interest of justice or for the convenience of the parties." The Delaware Bar Association has argued that transfer effectively counters shopping into Delaware.

The data, however, do not support its argument. Transfer is rare in voluntary cases, though common in involuntary cases. . . .

CONCLUSION

The data establish New York as the primary destination for forum shoppers in the 1980s. Around 1990, the destination shifted abruptly to Delaware. The benign reasons offered for forum shopping—efficiency and convenience—do not find support in the data. Efficiency based arguments fail to explain New York's initial popularity because New York is a slow case-processing district. Moreover, there is no evidence that cases shopped conclude significantly faster than cases filed in the debtors' home districts. Efficiency explanations remain unproven as a basis for Delaware's current popularity.

Convenience, the principal reason why many legislatures give plaintiffs a choice of venue, is also not a plausible explanation for Chapter 11 forum shopping. In every debtor-initiated case involving forum shopping, the debtor's executives decided to file in a city other than their home city. The abrupt shift in the principal destination of forum shopping from New York to Delaware also undermines a convenience-based explanation. Prior to the shift, some had argued that forum shoppers filed in New York for the convenience of prominent New York lawyers who would have been the debtor's choice of counsel regardless of venue. Given that those same lawyers are now riding the Metroliner from New York to Wilmington, the convenience argument seems implausible.

Explanations of the forum-shopping pattern as a form of judge shopping, on the other hand, are consistent with New York's and Delaware's popularity. The message of this forum-shopping pattern is troubling. Although bankruptcy law and procedure are uniform throughout the United States, the perception that case processing is different across cities induces forum shopping. Thus, the system's worst fears about the reasons for shopping are likely correct: debtors shopped to New York and now shop to Delaware in large part to secure particular judges or to avoid judges in their home districts. . . .

Closing Delaware, the most visible manifestation of the nonuniformity that breeds forum shopping, would provide the system with a fig leaf. . . . [T]his study's findings that Chapter 11 forum shopping is in significant part driven by judge shopping and by source-district conditions suggest that, even without Delaware, forum shopping would continue.

NATIONAL BANKRUPTCY REVIEW COMMISSION
FINAL REPORT
BANKRUPTCY: THE NEXT TWENTY YEARS
(October 20, 1997)

Chapter 3: Jurisdiction

The 1978 Bankruptcy Reform Act changed the venue standards for commencing a case under the Bankruptcy Code. For a corporate debtor, the major change was to permit the filing in the state of incorporation in addition to the location of its principal place of business or principal assets. Some corporations have used the opportunity to choose a forum that they believe will be friendlier to the debtor—a practice that is, at the least, unseemly. Some debtors go to their state of incorporation, which may have no bearing on the actual location of any of the relevant parties including the creditors, shareholders, officers, and employees of the business. . . .

The Recommendations also would limit the ability of one corporate debtor to follow an affiliate into the venue used by the affiliate. The limitation would permit a subsidiary to follow a parent corporation, but it would not permit other forms of selection of venue based on following a related entity. The Commission recognized the importance of keeping parent and subsidiary filings in the same jurisdiction to aid in the reorganization, but it recognized that affiliate venue also creates opportunities for inappropriate forum shopping.

3.1.5 *Venue Provisions under 28 U.S.C. § 1408*

28 U.S.C. § 1408(1) should be amended to prohibit corporate debtors from filing for relief in a district based solely on the debtor's incorporation in the state where that district is located.

The affiliate rule contained in 28 U.S.C. § 1408(2) should be amended to prohibit a corporate filing in an improper venue unless such debtor's corporate parent is a debtor in a case under the Bankruptcy Code in that forum. Section 1408(2) should be amended as follows:

> (2) in which there is pending a case under title 11 concerning such person's affiliate, as defined in section 101(2)(A) of title 11, general partner, partnership, or a partnership controlled by the same general partner.

The court's discretionary power to transfer venue in the interest of justice and for the convenience of the parties should not be restricted.

C. Extraordinary Orders and the Limits of Judicial Power

The congressional mandate favoring the reorganization of firms has been taken (too?) seriously by bankruptcy courts. Eager to effectuate a successful chapter 11 reorganization, courts often are unable to resist the temptation to test the outer boundaries of their equitable powers by entering extraordinary orders that they justify by invoking the pro-reorganization mantra. In their enthusiasm to promote the supposed "greater good" of reorganization nirvana, however, these courts may exceed their powers, trample illegally and unjustifiably on the rights of certain interested parties, and invade the domain of the Congress via quasi-legislative directives. This section explores this general problem in two specific contexts.

First, in *A Critical Reappraisal of Cross-Collateralization in Bankruptcy*, 60 S. CAL. L. REV. 109 (1986), Professor Charles Tabb attacks the practice of granting a *post*-petition lender new collateral to secure its *pre*-petition unsecured claim. He argues that such a "cross-collateralization" order exceeds the bankruptcy court's powers and is bad policy to boot, and critiques the justifications commonly offered in support of those orders.

Second, Professor Ralph Brubaker, in *Bankruptcy Injunctions and Complex Litigation: A Critical Reappraisal of Non-Debtor Releases in Chapter 11 Reorganizations*, 1997 U. ILL. L. REV. 959, criticizes the use of "non-debtor releases" in complex chapter 11 reorganizations. Under such a release, a party who is *not* a debtor is granted immunity from suit for pre-bankruptcy liabilities pursuant to the confirmed plan of reorganization. The non-debtor in effect gains the equivalent of a bankruptcy discharge without having to go through the bankruptcy process. Brubaker explodes the myths supposedly justifying such releases and explains why they are impermissible except in the narrow context of a consensual release. He demonstrates why non-debtor releases are both bad policy and beyond the jurisdiction of the bankruptcy courts.

Charles Jordan Tabb
A Critical Reappraisal of Cross-Collateralization in Bankruptcy
60 S. CAL. L. REV. 109 (1986)[*]

I. THE SETTING

The setting in which cross-collateralization operates and the nature and extent of the preferential treatment involved can be illustrated by a simple hypothetical case. The curtain opens to reveal a financially distressed debtor ("Debtor") contemplating filing for reorganization under chapter 11 of the Bankruptcy Code. Prior to bankruptcy, Debtor has been financing its operations with a financial institution ("Lender"). Lender has a lien on all or virtually all of Debtor's assets to secure a $10 million loan debt. The collateral securing this debt, however, is valued at only $9 million. Thus, if Debtor files a chapter 11 case, Lender will have a secured claim of $9 million and an unsecured claim of $1 million against Debtor's estate. Cross-collateralization has a preferential impact only in this situation, where the prepetition Lender has an unsecured prepetition claim, *i.e.*, is undersecured. If Lender were fully secured on its prepetition claim, the prepetition collateral (or its bankruptcy equivalent in value) would be used to satisfy that claim, without the need to resort to postpetition assets.

Before filing the chapter 11 case, however, Debtor wants and needs to arrange for financing during the case. Without such financing a successful reorganization probably would not be possible. . . . [F]or several reasons, obtaining voluntary financing in the chapter 11 case from someone other than Lender may be difficult. Typically, Debtor will go before filing to its prepetition Lender with its plea for postpetition financing. Lender then agrees to finance the Debtor in the reorganization, hoping in the chapter 11 case, (1) to realize the going-concern value of its prepetition collateral, and (2) to recover some or all of the $1 million unsecured portion of the debt.

In addition to requiring liens on all of Debtor's prepetition and postpetition assets to secure the new postpetition advances and superpriority status for those advances, Lender insists that a cross-collateralization clause be included in the financing package. The cross-collateralization clause grants Lender a lien on all of Debtor's *post*petition assets to secure Lender's *pre*petition debt. The bankruptcy court then approves this financing package. During the chapter 11 case, Lender advances $2 million to Debtor, and $3 million in postpetition assets is generated. As so commonly occurs, however, the reorganization fails, and the case is converted to a chapter 7 liquidation case. The trustee then proceeds to liquidate Debtor's assets and distribute those assets to Debtor's creditors.

What distribution is made? First, of course, Lender's $2 million in postpetition advances is repaid out of the $3 million in postpetition collateral. Second, Lender's $9 million prepetition secured claim is satisfied out of Lender's prepetition collateral or its proceeds. The trustee now has $1 million remaining to distribute. Lender has a $1 million prepetition claim remaining. Assume that allowed prepetition unsecured claims of other creditors total $1 million and allowed priority expenses total $500,000. Without the cross-collateralization clause, the $1 million of estate assets will be distributed (1) $500,000 to repay the priority claims in full, and then (2) $500,000 pro rata to the $2 million in unsecured claims (Lender's $1 million plus the other $1 million), *i.e.*, a twenty-five percent payment.

With the cross-collateralization clause, however, the entire $1 million goes to Lender. Nothing goes to the priority creditors. Nothing goes to the other unsecured creditors. The cross-collateral-

---

ization clause has effectively transformed Lender's $1 million claim from an unsecured claim that shares pro rata with all other unsecured claims and comes behind priority claims into a secured claim which is preferred over all other claims. . . .

II. THE STATE OF THE LAW: *TEXLON* AND ITS AFTERMATH

A. *TEXLON*

. . . [I]n the leading Second Circuit case of *Otte v. Manufacturers Hanover Commercial Corp. (In re Texlon Corp.)* . . . [t]he Second Circuit affirmed the district court's order deleting the cross-collateralization clause. Although finding no specific provision of the Act which the clause violated, the Second Circuit denounced cross-collateralization clauses as "a post-adjudication preference," and "contrary to the spirit of the Bankruptcy Act.". . .

B. THE AFTERMATH OF *TEXLON*

Since *Texlon* was decided, . . . [t]he more prevalent view . . . recognizes substantive objections to the practice, but, assuming procedural safeguards are met, approves cross-collateralization after a consideration of various factors. . . .

The leading case for this view is *In re Vanguard Diversified, Inc.* The court first noted that under *Texlon* cross-collateralization is "a disfavored means of financing which may only be authorized after its necessity has been established at a hearing held on notice to creditors." Judge Parente then formulated a four-part test for approval of cross-collateralization provisions:

(1) Absent the proposed financing, its [the debtor-in-possession's] business operations will not survive . . . ; (2) It is unable to obtain alternative financing on acceptable terms . . . ; (3) The proposed lender will not accede to less preferential terms; and (4) The proposed financing is in the best interests of the general creditor body. . . .

III. THE ARGUMENTS FOR AND AGAINST CROSS-COLLATERALIZATION

A. THE EXCLUSIVITY OF SECTION 364

In analyzing the substantive validity of cross-collateralization, the critical first step is determining whether section 364 contains the exclusive list of permissible financing arrangements. If section 364 is exclusive, then those provisions which section 364 does not expressly authorize, including cross-collateralization, are not valid under any circumstances. Suprisingly, this crucial issue of section 364's exclusivity has been largely ignored. An examination of the legislative history, structure, derivation, and language of section 364 lends strong support to the conclusion that section 364 was intended by Congress to be exclusive. Thus, the approval of a financing order containing cross-collateralization, an extra-statutory financing term, is improper. . . .

The detailed and comprehensive nature of section 364, and the historical antecedents of the respective subsections of section 364, strengthen the argument for exclusivity. A consideration of these matters shows that section 364 specifically authorizes and states the prerequisites for granting every type of inducement to a prospective lender to the bankruptcy estate—whether a lien, priority, or both—that was accepted and approved generally under the Act. The comprehensive treatment of financing in section 364 suggests, both as a matter of logic and as an accepted principle of statutory construction, that section 364 contains the exclusive list of acceptable inducements to prospective lenders.

. . . [T]he important point is not just what powers the court now has in the financing context, but where the authorization for the exercise of these powers is found. The bankruptcy court under the Code has the power to provide for all of the permissible financing techniques accepted under the Act—pursuant to section 364. Thus section 364 attempts to bring together in one place all accepted prior financing practices. . . .

Another statutory argument supporting the exclusivity view is derived from the presence of the language "under this section" in section 364(e), the "safe-harbor" provision of section 364. Section 364(e) protects good faith lenders from a reversal or modification of a financing order on appeal unless that order was stayed pending appeal. However, this safe harbor extends only to authorizations to obtain credit or incur debt "under this section," and to the granting of a priority or lien "under this section," meaning, obviously, section 364. . . .

Thus, absent a clear direction to the contrary by Congress, the policies and purposes behind section 364(e) argue for its application to all financing orders, and thus the limitation of permissible financing orders to "this section," *i.e.*, section 364. This reading is consistent with the construction of section 364 as exclusive based upon its history and structure, as discussed earlier.

B. THE INDUCEMENT RATIONALE

Even if section 364 is not read to be exclusive and thus to negate even the possibility of cross-collateralization, several additional statutory and policy arguments dictate against the allowability of the practice. The first such argument could be labeled the "inducement" rationale. In section 364 and elsewhere in the Code, special priority or lien status is given to induce third persons to do business with the debtor-in-possession in the postpetition period. Such provisions are considered necessary to overcome the typical hesitancy of creditors to extend credit or loan money to debtors in reorganization.

Thus, sections 364(a) through (d) are drafted specifically with postpetition inducement in mind. Those sections on their face clearly apply only to postpetition credit extensions. . . .

This refusal to award some special priority status absent evidence of postpetition inducement has been followed in contexts other than section 364 credit extensions. . . .

Cross-collateralization, however, by definition awards lien status to credit extended by the lender to the debtor prior to the filing of the case. This prepetition credit extension is not in any way induced by the promise of postpetition collateral. Giving lien status to this prepetition credit extension thus is inconsistent with the inducement rationale.

The lender's response, of course, is that the preference for the prepetition portion of the loan induces the postpetition loan and thus is not inconsistent with the inducement principle. This argument characterizes cross-collateralization as a form of compensation for the postpetition loan, similar to interest. Several replies to this argument may be made. First, the lender's characterization blurs the line between the prepetition and postpetition loans. The cross-collateralization lender itself has chosen to seek compensation which by definition will be applied to the prepetition debt. As such, that compensation does not fit within the inducement principle. If the lender in fact wants additional compensation for the postpetition loan, it should have to admit as much. The court in deciding whether to approve the requested financing then could more clearly assess the fairness of the amount of compensation sought for the postpetition loan. The court could compare the requested amount with market rates for loans of similar risk. In short, the lender should have to live with its own characterization.

Second, aside from this characterization problem, the assumption that the grant of cross-collateralization is necessary to induce the postpetition loan will not always be true. In many cases the decision to lend postpetition turns primarily on the lender's desire to recover and the lender's assessment of the likelihood of recovering: (1) the going-concern value of existing collateral, and (2) an increased dividend on its unsecured claim in the reorganization case. . . . [T]he presence or absence of a cross-collateralization clause may not alter this decision.

Even if the lender can show that the promise of cross-collateralization induced it to make the postpetition loan, this showing does not answer whether (1) that promise was one that properly could be made, and (2) reneging on such a promise constitutes any real prejudice to the lender that the lender should not be permitted to suffer. The lender would argue that it obviously is prejudiced by not getting what it bargained for. *Texlon* holds, however, that reconsidering a promised cross-collateralization order does not constitute impermissible prejudice to the lender. . . . This holding is proper since the postpetition loan—*i.e.*, the money actually advanced in reliance on the financing order—will be paid back first. The presence or absence of a cross-collateralization clause has no bearing on whether this postpetition loan will be repaid.

The lender still may argue that it is not getting the full compensation for the postpetition loan that it was promised. The first answer to this argument is that the lender itself chose to characterize the promised benefit as a payment on its prepetition debt and not as compensation for the postpetition loan, and it should not be heard later to complain about its own characterization. Furthermore, even if the lender is permitted to recast the nature of the compensation requested, the court would be acting properly in refusing to enforce the promise of extra compensation. This extra compensation is in effect a monopoly profit, and would not have been available to the lender elsewhere.

C. THE PRINCIPLE OF EQUAL DISTRIBUTION

Granting a lien on postpetition estate assets for a lender's unsecured prepetition claim thus is inconsistent with the inducement rationale. Cross-collateralization, by giving this lien status to an unsecured prepetition claim, also conflicts directly with one of the fundamental principles of bankruptcy law, that of equality of distribution to similarly situated claims. . . .

The primacy of the concept of equal treatment is seen most clearly in the bankruptcy distribution scheme. Secured claims are paid first. All other claims—*i.e.*, those without security—are then considered. As to these claims, the initial premise is equal, pro rata treatment.

Some of these unsecured claims are then given priority, pursuant to section 507, to further various policy objectives. . . .

Priorities—those claims elevated above others for policy reasons—are purely statutory under section 507. . . . Furthermore, this statutory priority scheme may not be varied by a court on equitable principles. . . .

While cross-collateralization does not involve a "priority" in the technical section 507 sense, it does involve in effect a priority, since the lender is granted a lien on assets which otherwise would be available for distribution to other general unsecured creditors. This "priority" is not contained in the Code. Thus in spirit cross-collateralization violates the basic Code premise of equal treatment unless specifically stated otherwise in the statute. . . .

D. EQUITY

The bankruptcy court is a court of equity, possessing the standard panoply of powers available to an equity court. This status of the bankruptcy court has been seized upon as a justification for granting cross-collateralization clauses. The argument is that no Code provision expressly prohibits cross-collateralization, that entry of a cross-collateralization order may promote the general Code policy favoring rehabilitation, and that the equitable powers of the court thus may be invoked to support the entry of such an order. . . .

The issue of the bankruptcy court's *power* to authorize such clauses must be answered in the affirmative before even asking of such a clause *should* be authorized. Courts have not focused on this distinction, and generally have assumed without discussion that they have the power to enter a cross-collateralization order. . . . While equity is an elastic concept, the better view is that the bankruptcy court's equitable powers do not stretch so far as to permit cross-collateralization clauses. Even if the bankruptcy court is considered to have the power to authorize cross-collateralization, policy considerations dictate that this power should not be exercised.

Equity is not without limits. The specific limitations on the power of an equity court relevant to the bankruptcy court's power to approve cross-collateralization clauses are three: (1) new substantive rights may not be created; (2) actions inconsistent with the Code are forbidden; and (3) the distributive scheme of the Code may not be altered to fit the court's notion of equity. . . .

The better conclusion . . . is that cross-collateralization is inconsistent with the Code. If section 364 is construed to contain the exclusive list of permissible financing arrangements, then any non-section 364 financing terms, including cross-collateralization, would be directly inconsistent with section 364 and, thus, the Code. It follows that the equity court would have no power to approve such a clause. Even if section 364 were not construed to be exclusive, cross-collateralization still directly contradicts the Code's pervasive equality principle, and thus is inconsistent with the Code within the meaning of the equity limitation. An express Code provision saying "no cross-collateralization" is not required. . . .

The third limitation is that the bankruptcy court as a court of equity lacks the power to reorder the statutory priority and distribution schemes. In a sense, this limitation is simply a more specific statement of the "inconsistency" limitation. Cross-collateralization also violates this restriction by securing the lender's otherwise unsecured prepetition claim with a lien on estate assets that the Code otherwise would require to be distributed to all unsecured creditors pro rata. . . .

The existence of the bankruptcy court's equitable power to subordinate claims does not support assertion of a corollary power to elevate other claims, the result in cross-collateralization. . . . [S]ubordination is predicated on "bad" conduct of the subordinated party, the operative principle being that in equity a wrongdoer should not be allowed to profit from his misdeeds. In the absence of any inequitable conduct, subordination will be denied. "Good" conduct, on the other hand, does not entitle a creditor to preferential treatment, except as specifically granted in the statute. Even if it did, the lender seeking cross-collateralization would not qualify since, as will be seen, the lender basically is engaging in extortion. Nor can it be said that *all* the other creditors should be subordinated (which obviously would have the same effect as elevation of one creditor), since they have not engaged in any inequitable conduct. . . .

The status and applicability of the Necessity of Payment Rule under the Code is not as clear. . . . The underlying rationale of the Necessity of Payment Rule, however, is that in cases involving the public interest a creditor with a stranglehold on the debtor may be permitted to extort payment of his prepetition debt, despite the violence this does to established principles of bankruptcy law such as equality of distribution. This extortion premise similarly underlies cross-collateralization. . . . Therefore it is not surprising that the Necessity of Payment Rule has been advanced as a justification for cross-collateralization.

The issue, then, is whether extortion should ever be recognized as a ground for allowing cross-collateralization. . . . [T]his analysis will follow the terms of the *Vanguard Diversified* test. This analysis leads to these conclusions: (1) the *Vanguard Diversified* test is not very meaningful and will be satisfied in virtually all cases where the issue arises; (2) a case-by-case approach is unwise, since it gives preferential treatment when unnecessary, and possibly causes otherwise deserving cases to fail; and (3) the potential cost attributable to a flat rule denying cross-collateralization in all cases is probably small, and does not justify the countervailing detriments of the practice.

The first part of the *Vanguard Diversified* test requires that "[a]bsent the proposed financing, its [debtor's] business operations will not survive." This is simply a "need" test. In the cross-collateralization cases this test is always answered in the affirmative—a result which is not surprising.
. . .

The second element of the *Vanguard Diversified* test requires that the debtor-in-possession "is unable to obtain alternative financing on acceptable terms." This element in effect recognizes the monopoly position of the prepetition lender which is so essential to the lender's ability to extort favorable financing terms, and this element is surely correct to the extent it says that attempted extortion by a non-monopolist will be ignored. . . .

The third part of the *Vanguard Diversified* test is that "[t]he proposed lender will not accede to less preferential terms." This is the extortionate demand. It is not very meaningful, beyond saying the obvious: that the bankruptcy court will not grant extraordinary benefits to someone who does not really insist on them. The difficulty is in determining if this particular lender in fact insists on the clause. Approaching the issue of approval of cross-collateralization orders on a case-by-case basis dictates that the decision virtually always will be to approve the requested order, whether or not this particular lender actually would have refused to lend postpetition without cross-collateralization. . . .

. . . Experience has shown that cross-collateralization is becoming a standard clause on sophisticated lenders' forms, with virtually all lenders "insisting" on this preferential term, even though it is very doubtful that all lenders would decide not to finance if cross-collateralization were never available.

If a flat rule prohibiting cross-collateralization is in effect, however, lenders are forced to decide in advance of the financing hearing whether to finance or not without cross-collateralization. While saying that the unavailability of cross-collateralization would never affect this decision probably would be an overstatement, certainly in many cases financing would be forthcoming anyway. . . .

One might argue, however, that prohibiting cross-collateralization would merely cause the lender to recoup the benefits currently received under cross-collateralization through a higher interest charge on the postpetition loan. Thus, the argument goes, nothing is accomplished by eliminating cross-collateralization. On the contrary, making the lender identify in advance of approval of the postpetition loan the total compensation sought for that loan in terms of the loan interest rate would be a significant improvement over the current system.

The most obvious advantage of requiring postpetition loan compensation to be stated in terms of an interest rate is that the court and the other creditors would then be able to appraise more accurately whether the lender's projected compensation is fair and acceptable, considering the risk to the lender and the potential benefit to the estate. Market rates for loans of similar risk could be compared, and a proposed loan bearing a disproportionately high interest rate might not be approved. . . .

With a cross-collateralization clause, however, the court has no idea what the lender's potential return might be, and cannot make an intelligent decision on whether to approve the clause. Cross-collateralization might be approved even though such approval would result in the lender receiving an enormous profit, unsupported by even a generous assessment of the lender's risk. This possibility exists since the only theoretical limit on the amount of the lender's return is the amount of the lender's prepetition unsecured claim.

The facts of *Texlon* strikingly illustrate this point. The lender in that case advanced $667,000 over two months, and in return would have received from the cross-collateralization provision a return of $267,000 plus repayment of the principal. This recovery represents a return of forty percent in two months, or 240 percent per year. . . .

Another argument that can be made for cross-collateralization in this context is that the prepetition lender might be willing to accept a lower interest rate on the postpetition loan in return for a cross-collateralization clause. If the cross-collateralization clause proves to be worth less than the interest forfeited in return for the clause, then the estate is benefitted by allowing cross-collateralization. A problem with this argument is the cynical suspicion that a prepetition lender in a monopoly position with regard to making a postpetition loan is not giving up anything for the cross-collateralization clause, but instead is taking everything that the court will allow. . . .

A related problem is the difficulty of policing the fairness of the "trade" of interest for cross-collateralization, since the court lacks the information to value the cross-collateralization clause with any accuracy. A cynic might wonder why the party with the most information, the lender, is willing to make the trade. . . .

The decision, then, between the flat rule approach and the case-by-case approach can be reduced to the following issue: should some cases be allowed to fail where the lender will not finance without cross-collateralization (with the lender having time in advance rationally to make and act upon the financing decision)? Or instead, should the reorganization always be tried, even at the cost of almost always preferring the lender via a cross-collateralization clause, including those cases where the lender would have decided to finance even without cross-collateralization? At this juncture the fourth part of the test must be considered. An analysis of the issues raised by this test suggests that the better approach is a flat rule against cross-collateralization.

Under *Vanguard Diversified*, the fourth part of the test is whether "[t]he proposed financing is in the best interests of the general creditor body." The theory is that the other unsecured creditors are the ones being harmed by cross-collateralization, and if they would do no better absent the cross-collateralization financing, then no reason exists to deny the financing. Accordingly, this test is found to be satisfied if the court believes that this "protected" class of creditors would receive nothing in a present liquidation. Others have urged that this test should be satisfied if the creditors "consent" to the order.

Even taking these proposed criteria at face value, severe shortcomings appear which vitiate the usefulness of this test. The court's judgments (1) that liquidation would ensue without financing, and (2) that the liquidation dividend for unsecured creditors would be less than the dividend in a reorganization with cross-collateralization financing, are speculative at best. This concern is heightened by the fact that the court's decision comes at the inception of the case, with little time to develop facts and little experience in the case by which to judge the prospects for reorganizing successfully. The timing of the financing decision limits the ability of the creditors to object meaningfully. Also, bankruptcy courts have a strong bias in favor of attempting the reorganization, which could color their assessment of the issues under this fourth element.

Nor is creditor "consent" a viable theory. . . . [C]reditors often do not have the information necessary to make informed judgments. . . . Furthermore, even if the creditors were able to make an informed choice, they are not actually given a "vote." The consent approach considers failure to object a positive vote. This result is unfair to creditors. . . . In addition, even if the creditors did object, the bankruptcy court might very well approve the financing anyway.

An even more fundamental objection is that the basic orientation of the fourth *Vanguard Diversified* element is flawed. The creditors are put to the Hobson's choice of liquidation versus cross-collateralization only because cross-collateralization is allowed in the first place. Neither cross-collateralization nor liquidation is in the creditors' "best interests." To characterize the issue as such begs the ultimate question. . . . The issue is when extortion will be allowed; to answer that it will be allowed when those extorted give in to the extortion is absurd. Instead, the answer given was that extortion only would be allowed if required to protect the *public* interest. . . .

. . . Despite the unattractiveness of the prospect of a business failing, the hard fact is that businesses do fail, and lenders cannot always be urged to pour more money into a sinking ship. The bankruptcy court should not override basic principles of the bankruptcy laws in a desperate attempt to forestall such an eventuality—an eventuality which very well may occur anyway. No one wants the reorganization to succeed more than the prepetition lender who already has large sums invested in the debtor and who wants to realize the maximum return on its prepetition collateral. If that lender lacks sufficient confidence in the reorganization to loan new money to support that reorganization without demanding extraordinary benefits such as cross-collateralization, is that not a good indication that this case is one of those cases with a high risk of failure?

Assume that such a lender under a flat rule approach is denied cross-collateralization, refuses to finance, and the reorganization fails—the "worst case" scenario. Does not this prospect argue for cross-collateralization? No. The flaw in the argument is the assumption that the cause of the failed reorganization was the refusal to grant cross-collateralization. Instead, the cause of failure in our hypothetical case is probably attributable to deeper problems. In our case, the underlying business problems facing the company—the same problems that motivate the lender to agree to finance only with cross-collateralization—are the true causes of failure. Thus, the actual "costs" *fairly* attributable to a flat rule denying cross-collateralization probably are very low.

These low costs are overshadowed by the costs associated with allowing cross-collateralization. . . .

In addition, if cross-collateralization is allowed based on the *Vanguard Diversified* rationale, courts will have trouble drawing the line against further extortionate demands by lenders and by other parties who deal with the estate both before and after the bankruptcy filing. . . .

Thus, the better approach is to refuse to allow cross-collateralization in all cases. Lenders then will have to make realistic decisions about financing the debtor in possession—decisions which, because of the lender's interest in the debtor's success, are likely to be tilted in favor of continued lending except in extremely doubtful cases. In these doubtful cases, it is questionable whether the futile attempt to reorganize should be made at all.

Ralph Brubaker
Bankruptcy Injunctions and Complex Litigation:
A Critical Reappraisal of Non-Debtor Releases in Chapter 11 Reorganizations
1997 U. ILL. L. REV. 959[*]

I. INTRODUCTION

A rather disturbing development . . . is a growing judicial acceptance of reorganization plan provisions that not only provide for discharge of the obligations of the Chapter 11 debtor, but that also release non-debtor third parties from liability to the debtor's creditors—often supplemented by injunctions that permanently restrain creditors from pursuing the released non-debtors. . . .

This article sets forth the long-overdue challenge to non-debtor releases by questioning policy justifications and judicial authority, both of which prove illusory. The issue is a pressing one, as the bankruptcy court is quickly becoming the forum for resolution of many of the largest and most complex mass litigations. . . .

. . . [P]olicy study counsels against any judicial discretion to approve non-debtor releases. Quite apart from these policy considerations is the question of whether bankruptcy courts presently possess any authority to approve non-debtor releases. Careful historical analysis reveals that non-debtor releases overstep the bounds of limited bankruptcy jurisdiction; bankruptcy judges have *no* jurisdictional authority to approve non-debtor releases, in the absence of express congressional authorization.

. . . Non-debtor releases use a Chapter 11 reorganization, designed to restructure creditor claims against a bankruptcy debtor, to discharge creditor claims against others, and in the process, pervert both nonbankruptcy and bankruptcy conceptions regarding appropriate treatment of such claims. The generic desire to promote settlement tells us little about non-debtor releases, other than highlighting the fact that they permit an extraordinary nonconsensual settlement, unheard of in any other context. Unique bankruptcy policies provide no separate justification for such an exceptional "settlement." Non-debtor releases violate fundamental creditor equality norms embodied in the Bankruptcy Code and dismantle a series of procedural and substantive protections designed to safeguard the value of creditor distributions. As a result, the released non-debtor, as well as the debtor's other creditors and shareholders, are allowed to walk away with value rightfully belonging to creditors whose viable non-debtor rights are extinguished.

. . . [T]he reorganization policy . . . ultimately fails to substantiate non-debtor releases, because they appear to serve a redistribution end more than one of reorganization. Any reorganization potential that non-debtor releases might possess falls victim to intractable screening difficulties, engendered by the fact that non-debtor releases purchase benefits at no cost to the reorganized debtor. . . .

. . . Even more startling, though, is the fact that the jurisdictional disarray has caused the courts to completely ignore binding Supreme Court precedent prohibiting a permanent non-debtor injunction. Therefore, part IV concludes that non-debtor releases are not an appropriate use of a bankruptcy court's injunctive powers, and bankruptcy courts are without authority to approve non-debtor releases, in the absence of express congressional authorization.

II. BANKRUPTCY INJUNCTIONS AND THE EXTANT STATUTORY DEBATE . . .

B. Supplementary Equitable Injunctions and Section 524(e)

. . . Although this article contends that a bankruptcy court does, indeed, lack the authority to approve a nonconsensual release of creditors' non-debtor claims, courts' and commentators' reliance upon section 524(e) as a statutory prohibition is misguided and unfortunate. Section 524(e) is necessary, as a matter of mere mechanics, to prevent the debtor's discharge from automatically discharging co-debtors and guarantors, through the operation of common-law suretyship rules that release secondary obligors upon release of the primary obligor. . . . [T]he literal terms of section 524(e) say only that the debtor's discharge does not, by its own force, affect the liability of others. Nothing in section 524(e) can be read to affirmatively prohibit a bankruptcy court from using its equitable injunctive powers in furtherance of a successful reorganization by the debtor. . . .

III. NON-DEBTOR RELEASES AND BANKRUPTCY POLICY . . .

A. Facilitating Compromise and Settlement

Policy justifications for non-debtor releases often begin with the worthy and seemingly benign objective of encouraging negotiated settlement of disputes. Bankruptcy law, however, holds no monopoly on the general policy of encouraging and facilitating settlement over litigation, and the settlement analogy is incomplete and misleading. . . .

1. Mandatory Settlement Through Non-Debtor Release

. . . As a matter of general principles, though, the assent of the debtor, statutory committees, and the contributing non-debtor would appear to be insufficient to compromise the non-debtor claims of an objecting creditor. The general policy favoring settlement operates within the confines of the accepted notion that a settlement is a voluntary undertaking that a court cannot impose upon an unwilling litigant. . . . Indeed, the only nonbankruptcy context in which a court can impose a settlement upon a nonconsenting claimant is through a court-approved settlement of a mandatory, non-opt-out class action. . . .

2. Mandatory Settlement Through Class Action

. . . Class action doctrine . . . tempers aggregation and consolidation impulses with various devices designed to assure that class procedures protect individual claimants' interests . . . . The total absence of any similar protections as a prerequisite to a bankruptcy court's approval of non-debtor releases suggests that non-debtor releases are not a legitimate means to foster equitable settlements. . . .

Most importantly, the so-called settlement effected by a non-debtor release is not a consensual endeavor; it is imposed by judicial fiat. . . .

The fact that the Chapter 11 debtor's resources may constitute a limited fund from which to satisfy creditors' claims does not justify limited-fund treatment of creditors' claims against non-debtors, whose resources may not constitute a limited fund. The use of non-debtor releases in bankruptcy, in effect, imposes a non-opt-out settlement of creditors' non-debtor rights, without regard to whether such a mandatory settlement is necessitated by limited fund principles, and without any other general indicia of an appropriate settlement. Unless non-debtor releases and injunctions are to be used as an end run around such inveterate precepts, the practice must rest upon policy considerations unique to the bankruptcy context in which it is employed. . . .

B. Creditor Equality

One of the most enduring bankruptcy policies is that favoring equal treatment of similarly situated creditors. . . . Courts approving non-debtor releases liberally invoke a creditor equality rationale for support—characterizing the possibility of enhanced recoveries from non-debtors by some claimants as "inequitable" and "unfair." However, by injecting discharge of creditors' non-debtor claims into a process constructed for treatment of creditors' claims against the debtor, non-debtor releases actually upset the Bankruptcy Code's design for creditor equality and permit creditors without valuable non-debtor rights to take value away from creditors with valuable non-debtor rights.

1. Substantial Similarity and Equal Treatment

. . . [T]he Bankruptcy Code does not adopt absolute creditor equality. Rather, the prevailing norm is equal treatment for those *similarly situated.* . . .

With respect to non-debtor releases, the simple response to the creditor equality argument is that creditors that have recourse against non-debtors are *not* similarly situated with creditors that have no such rights; therefore, permitting creditors to pursue non-debtors in no way violates the policy of equal treatment for similarly situated creditors. In fact, a plan of reorganization that classifies together, for equal treatment, creditors both with and without non-debtor recourse, while eliminating the rights of those with non-debtor recourse, actually undermines the Bankruptcy Code's classification and treatment scheme. . . .

2. Class Voting and Impairment

. . . Ignoring the classification and treatment implications of non-debtor releases inevitably weakens the creditor protections underlying a class voting scheme. . . . We can only place confidence in the assent of a class if the class has uniform rights and treatment. By their nature, non-debtor releases only affect class members with valuable non-debtor rights. If destruction of those creditors' non-debtor rights is ignored in constructing classes, the integrity of the class voting process is corrupted. In fact, machinations of the process can go so far as to completely disenfranchise impaired creditors. . . .

3. Distribution Value Protections

The ultimate injury non-debtor releases visit upon creditors is distributional. Creditors without valuable non-debtor rights can take value away from creditors whose valuable non-debtor rights are extinguished through non-debtor releases. . . .

a. Cram Down

. . . To the extent that non-debtor releases infect the soundness of the classification system, they dilute the voting power of those creditors with valuable non-debtor rights, and as a consequence, they also weaken those creditors' ability, by class vote, to block distributions that depart from their baseline priority rights. And that is the nub of the nefarious nature of non-debtor releases: they permit improper redistributions of value amongst the debtors' creditors. . . .

b. Best Interests of Creditors

. . . [G]iving at least liquidation value to each creditor requires protection of the Chapter 7 right to pursue non-debtor actions. The lopsided view of creditor equality, which sanctions confiscation of these non-debtor rights in Chapter 11 through non-debtor releases, ignores the creditors' Chapter 7 right to seek full satisfaction from non-debtors in gauging satisfaction of the best interests test—comparing a creditor's Chapter 11 distribution with a hypothetical Chapter 7 distribution, from the debtor *only*. Yet, the best interests equation also properly mandates consideration of creditors' comparative recoveries on non-debtor claims, to the extent the plan is treating those non-debtor claims by release.

Proponents of non-debtor releases are quick to point out that released parties often make contributions to the debtor that enhance the reorganization surplus—contributions that would not be forthcoming in a Chapter 7 liquidation. These contributions, however, do not fully compensate for the released claims. . . .

. . . [N]othing in the process by which releases are approved requires contributions by released non-debtors to approximate the value of the released claims . . . . Even if the released party were to contribute to the reorganization the full value of the released claims (or more), there is still no assurance that creditors whose non-debtor claims are extinguished will receive as much as they would under a Chapter 7 liquidation scenario. This is because the non-debtor's contribution to the reorganization is not necessarily earmarked for those creditors whose non-debtor claims are released. The contribution goes into the reorganization pot, for distribution amongst all of the debtor's creditors and shareholders, regardless of whether they have valuable non-debtor claims.

The driving force behind non-debtor releases seems to be a relentless desire to steadfastly avoid articulating and valuing what and whose claims are being released. As a result, non-debtor releases present an opportunity for those without viable non-debtor claims to take value away from those with such claims. Contributions by released non-debtors, made in the name of the debtor's reorganization effort, simply obscure the underlying value redistributions inherent in non-debtor releases. . . .

4. The Non-Debtor's "Discharge"

Non-debtor releases systematically dismantle the Bankruptcy Code's attempt to carefully protect the relative payment rights of creditors of a Chapter 11 debtor . . . . Furthermore, the perverse effects of non-debtor releases go beyond the relative rights of the debtor's creditors; they also do violence to the rights of the permanently enjoined creditor vis-à-vis (1) other creditors of the released non-debtor and (2) the released non-debtor. A non-debtor release is a discriminatory discharge of only certain debts of the non-debtor, in violation of basic creditor equality norms. This discharge comes without giving released creditors recourse to the non-debtor's full repayment resources—violating another basic tenet of distribution and discharge principles. Worse yet, the non-debtor's discharge can extinguish debts that would *not* be dischargeable in an individual bankruptcy case.

a. Equitable Treatment of the Non-Debtor's Creditors

. . . A non-debtor release is a discriminatory discharge, discharging some, but not all of the debts of the released non-debtor. . . . Creditors subject to the release are restricted to their diminished recovery rights under the Chapter 11 debtor's plan of reorganization, while others with similar payment rights against the released non-debtor retain the right to seek full payment from the non-debtor. . . . Among the *released non-debtor's* creditors, . . . non-debtor releases bring unequal treatment for equal creditors.

This aspect of creditor inequality—amongst the *non-debtor's* creditors—is easily overlooked. Yet, this inequality points out why it is particularly misguided to attach significance, as many courts do, to creditor approval percentages in voting on the Chapter 11 debtor's plan of reorganization, as somehow sanctioning the worth of a non-debtor release. . . . [C]lass voting by creditors of the *Chapter 11 debtor* says nothing about an appropriate distribution of the assets of the *released non-debtor*. . . . Mere voting approval by the *Chapter 11 debtor's* creditors and shareholders cannot even begin to approximate this process for a fair distribution of the value of the *released non-debtor's* assets.

The equitable distribution contemplated by the Bankruptcy Code also requires a debtor to submit all assets and affairs to the jurisdiction of the federal bankruptcy court. . . . Through non-debtor releases, however, many non-debtors are released without making any contribution whatsoever toward satisfaction of the released claims. Even in those cases in which released non-debtors do make contributions in exchange for the release, the contribution, as discussed above, bears no necessary relationship to the non-debtor's liability on the released claims. In fact, the non-debtor's contribution has nothing at all to do with satisfying the obligations of the non-debtor. . . . Thus, released non-debtors can receive a discharge of indebtedness, while retaining substantial wealth. . . .

b. The Non-Debtor's Super Fresh Start

. . . Non-debtor releases blunt the sharp edge of fresh start policy, because they do not contain discriminating exceptions that deny discharge of the obligations of the knavish non-debtor. In fact, non-debtor releases have been used to grant many individuals discharge from debts that could not, or at least arguably could not, be discharged through an actual bankruptcy filing by the non-debtor. . . .

C. Debtor Rehabilitation

The debtor rehabilitation arguments for non-debtor releases are of two distinct types. One is a discharge-related argument, misleadingly characterized as protecting the debtor's "fresh start." . . . In reality, the fresh start argument seems to be yet another attempt to legitimize non-debtor releases' redistributional effects.

The more substantial debtor rehabilitation concern is the one underlying the very existence of Chapter 11—preservation of an operating business otherwise destined for piecemeal liquidation. In many cases, however, non-debtor releases do not save the debtor's business, and the reorganization policy is simply another smoke screen for non-debtor releases' redistributional consequences. Because non-debtor releases can bring the reorganized debtor various benefits at no cost, any effort to restrict the practice to the rare non-debtor release actually necessary to reorganization is doomed to failure. . . .

2. In Pursuit of the Elusive Reorganization Policy

. . . Ultimately, non-debtor releases must stand or fall depending upon the strength of their primary raison d'être: promoting successful reorganization of the Chapter 11 debtor. . . . Overlooking the numerous statutory and theoretical deficiencies of non-debtor releases in order to assure a debtor's reorganization has a very tempting visceral appeal, but it is a dangerous practice that should not be permitted.

Initially, as a policy matter, there is substantial disagreement about whether pursuit of reorganization for the sake of reorganization is ever an appropriate independent goal of the Chapter 11 process. Even if one accepts reorganization . . . as an acceptable policy objective, vindicating that policy through non-debtor releases presents insuperable practical and instrumental problems. Many factors contribute to a substantial risk that, in most cases, non-debtor releases do not, in fact, promote successful reorganization. . . . Quite apart from these practical problems is a more fundamental difficulty. Implicit in the idea that a non-debtor release is appropriate where necessary to the debtor's successful reorganization is the assumption that the reorganization policy is supreme, and in furtherance thereof, a bankruptcy judge can unilaterally override legitimate policies embodied in nonbankruptcy law that would place liability upon the released non-debtors. Such a notion is hard to square with the inherent limitations of the judicial process and Congress' primary role in making such policy determinations in the bankruptcy context.

a. Efficiency and the Reorganization Policy

. . . [F]or a bankruptcy court to use its general equitable powers in an attempt to give the reorganization policy affirmative, substantive content, independent of any express provision of the Bankruptcy Code is of dubious validity, especially given the Supreme Court's admonition that equitable powers are confined by the provisions of the Bankruptcy Code. This reasoning applies with special force to non-debtor releases, which are inconsistent with numerous principles and provisions of the Code . . .

b. What Is a "Reorganization"?

. . . [T]he reorganization policy often adds very little to the debate concerning non-debtor releases and, at its worst, seems to be a vacuous and pretextual cover for the redistributional effects of non-debtor releases. Such abuse, though, seems endemic to any effort to transform the reorganization policy itself into an extra-statutory power. The success of a reorganization is (like beauty) in the eyes of the beholder. The reorganization policy, therefore, simply cannot place any realistic limits on the use of non-debtor releases.

c. Screening for Releases Necessary to Reorganization

Even if non-debtor releases and the reorganization policy could be restricted to reorganization in its conventional sense of preservation of an operating business, there are still good reasons to believe that non-debtor releases, in most cases, are immaterial to the debtor's ability to reorganize. . . . [I]mportantly, . . . even the most stringent requirement of necessity has not and cannot confine non-debtor releases to those cases in which the debtor's business will fail without such relief. . . .

The other threat to a debtor's reorganization cited as necessitating non-debtor releases is the potential loss of contributions the released non-debtors are making to the debtor's reorganization effort. Obtaining contributions necessary to the debtor's survival that would not be forthcoming in the absence of non-debtor releases would appear to advance the reorganization policy directly. To approve non-debtor releases on this basis, however, assumes an ability to determine that the proffered contribution is, in fact, necessary for the debtor's continued operations *and* that this necessary contribution can be procured only through release of creditor claims against the contributing non-debtor party. . . .

One could certainly imagine an instance in which a non-debtor seeking the protection of a release could make a contribution to the debtor's operations that could not be obtained elsewhere and that could mean the difference between continuing and discontinuing operations. For example, . . . many smaller, closely-held businesses are highly dependent upon the efforts and skills of the owner-manager. . . . If that key manager insists on a non-debtor release as a condition to continued participation in the business, then why should the bankruptcy court be denied the authority to approve the non-debtor release in order to save the debtor's business?

To begin with, the key manager's demand for a non-debtor release can be usefully recharacterized as a demand for more compensation for providing future managerial services to the reorganized debtor. . . .

In point of fact, the non-debtor release will serve the reorganization policy and save the debtor's business from liquidation only if (1) the key manager would not accept, in lieu of the non-debtor release, monetary or another form of compensation of equivalent value, paid directly by the reorganized debtor, *or* (2) the debtor's continuing business operations simply could not underwrite the full cost of this additional compensation for the key manager. Scenario (1) seems unlikely enough that scenario (2) appears to capture the essence of necessity. If the debtor's business *can* afford to pay the key manager this additional compensation directly, the debtor's desire for the non-debtor release is the common desire of any business for cost-free management compensation. Necessity only attaches if the prospect of fully compensating the key manager means the business is not worth continuing, and creditors and shareholders will fare better through liquidation.

When the bankruptcy court faces a request to approve a non-debtor release for the key manager, the judge must decide the knotty question of whether the request flows from the universal desire for cost-free compensation or is a true case of necessity. The bankruptcy judge will have little to rely on in this regard, other than the self-serving and vague statements of the debtor, statutory committees, or the key manager. . . . [T]rue necessity—in the sense of meaning the difference between continuing economic viability and inevitable liquidation—is nearly impossible to either verify *or* disprove in any reliable manner. To ask a bankruptcy judge to make this determination is to ask the court to engage in unbridled speculation. . . .

d. Congress, the Courts, and the Reorganization Policy

Discretionary equitable approval of non-debtor releases would be a fundamentally objectionable practice, even if it were possible to overcome the innate screening problems associated with non-debtor releases and approve only those non-debtor releases absolutely necessary to preserve a business operation otherwise destined for liquidation. . . .

A non-debtor release, though, is cost-free only from the standpoint of the reorganized debtor's business operations; the cost of this additional compensation is extracted involuntarily from those creditors with valuable non-debtor claims against the key manager. Nonbankruptcy law would place liability upon the key manager. . . . [T]he propriety of a necessary non-debtor release directly pits the reorganization policy against these legitimate nonbankruptcy policies underlying non-debtor liability.

Given these conflicting policies, then, approval of a non-debtor release is a unilateral determination by a bankruptcy judge that the reorganization policy alone, without any further statutory directive from Congress, is sufficient to override *both* fundamental distributional policies and provisions of the Bankruptcy Code *and* the nonbankruptcy law and policy of non-debtor liability. Yet, the Supreme Court's most recent pronouncements on the scope of a bankruptcy court's equitable powers emphasized that they may not be used to reorder distributional priorities in a manner that arrogates to the courts the policy-making functions that Congress exercises in enacting specific provisions of the Bankruptcy Code. Moreover, the Court has never gone so far as to sanction a use of general equity powers that would so directly contravene nonbankruptcy law and policy. Indeed, *Callaway v. Benton*, striking down a permanent non-debtor injunction under the 1898 Act, was premised on legislative supremacy in making such cardinal policy choices: "We do not believe that Congress intended to leave to individual judges the question of whether state laws should be accepted or disregarded, or to make the criterion to be applied the effect of the law upon the [reorganized debtor's operations]."

The case for withholding such policy-making judgments from the bankruptcy courts is compelling in the context of non-debtor releases. . . . By what means . . . is a bankruptcy judge to determine that the indirect "benefits" of reorganization are more important than the indirect benefits produced by non-debtor liability, and outweigh the direct costs imposed on creditors whose valuable non-debtor rights are extinguished?

. . . The adjudicative process through which bankruptcy reorganizations are effected is ill-suited for engaging in an appropriate case-by-case analysis of such far-reaching consequences. . . . [A] discretionary case-by-case assessment of the ultimate public interest in reorganization, versus the public interest in non-debtor liability, is simply beyond the ken of the adjudicative process. . . . Any attempt to give the judiciary such a function with respect to non-debtor releases will be fraught with inconsistency and arbitrariness . . . .

Ultimately, then, not even the reorganization policy will support the practice of approving non-debtor releases. Strictly in terms of policy considerations, the courts should flatly prohibit non-debtor releases. . . .

IV. BANKRUPTCY JURISDICTION TO ENJOIN NON-DEBTOR ACTIONS

Perhaps the most complicated and confusing aspect of the controversy surrounding non-debtor releases and injunctions is the preliminary inquiry for any exercise of judicial power—jurisdiction. Without regard to the advisability of a non-debtor release in any particular case, is there bankruptcy jurisdiction to release non-debtors from liability to creditors and permanently enjoin creditors' actions against them? Most of the cases approving or disapproving non-debtor releases contain little, if any, discussion of the jurisdictional issue, and what little discussion appears is woefully cryptic and conclusory. Courts that have approved non-debtor releases have done so pursuant to the equitable injunctive powers of bankruptcy courts under section 105 of the Bankruptcy Code. Section 105, however, is not an independent source of jurisdiction . . . .

The traditional powers of a federal court to enjoin collateral litigation that would interfere with the court's jurisdiction, frequently relied upon as support for permanent non-debtor releases and injunctions, cannot sustain this exceptional exercise of injunctive powers. It can only be defended based upon the unique character of jurisdiction over bankruptcy reorganization proceedings. . . .

. . . History reveals that wide-ranging status quo injunctions have always been integral to the administration of bankruptcy estates, especially in bankruptcy reorganization proceedings. . . . Permanent non-debtor releases and injunctions . . . go well beyond the traditional status quo injunction; in the name of promoting the debtor's successful reorganization, they extinguish obligations of non-debtors that historically have been completely beyond the reach of bankruptcy jurisdiction.

. . . [C]onfusion concerning jurisdiction to enjoin non-debtor actions has led the courts to overlook Supreme Court precedent under the 1898 Act striking down a permanent non-debtor injunction. A proper understanding of the reach of bankruptcy courts' jurisdiction and accompanying injunctive powers leads to the conclusion that non-debtor releases are not an appropriate extension of the historical injunctive powers of federal bankruptcy courts. The courts have no jurisdictional authority to approve nonconsensual non-debtor releases in the absence of express congressional authorization. . . .

D. Temporary Non-Debtor Stays Under the Bankruptcy Reform Act of 1978

The Bankruptcy Reform Act of 1978 . . . brought sweeping changes to bankruptcy law . . . . Undoubtedly the most significant changes came through an expansive grant of federal bankruptcy jurisdiction. The courts promptly seized upon this enlarged bankruptcy jurisdiction to find jurisdiction to enjoin non-debtor actions, and the Supreme Court recently held that the courts do have bankruptcy jurisdiction to temporarily stay non-debtor actions.

. . . The courts quickly concluded that section 105 of the Bankruptcy Code, in conjunction with the broad jurisdictional grant, gave bankruptcy courts jurisdiction to enjoin an action between non-debtors if the action was, in the words of the jurisdictional grant, "related to" the pending bankruptcy case. In Chapter 11 reorganization cases, the courts have held that jurisdiction to enjoin attaches if prosecution of the non-debtor action would interfere with the debtor's prospects for a successful reorganization. Of course, this approach to jurisdiction to stay non-debtor actions is precisely in accord with the Supreme Court's view of the role of injunctions in reorganization cases, as originally articulated in the *Continental Illinois* case: a tool to protect and promote the debtor's reorganization effort. Moreover, the Supreme Court recently held this to be a proper jurisdictional foundation for temporary non-debtor stays in the case of *Celotex Corp. v. Edwards*. . . .

G. Jurisdiction to Permanently Release Non-Debtors

For purposes of jurisdiction and the historical distinction between jurisdiction to enjoin and jurisdiction to adjudicate, temporary non-debtor stays must be distinguished from permanent non-debtor releases. While there is bankruptcy jurisdiction to temporarily stay a non-debtor action, there is *no* jurisdiction to permanently release a non-debtor action.

Courts disapproving non-debtor releases only occasionally assert lack of jurisdiction as a basis. . . . Most courts, without regard to their view of the propriety of non-debtor releases, simply have applied to non-debtor releases the same jurisdictional framework used in temporary non-debtor stay cases: jurisdiction depends on whether the non-debtor action is "related to" the debtor's reorganization case—"related to" meaning that continuation of the non-debtor action will make the debtor's reorganization more difficult in some way—and the non-debtor release is a core proceeding respecting administration of the debtor's estate and confirmation of the debtor's plan of reorganization.

. . . This approach, however, is fundamentally flawed, as it permits an oblique enlargement of courts' bankruptcy jurisdiction. It abuses the historical distinction between jurisdiction to enjoin and jurisdiction to adjudicate, and it improperly assumes that facilitation of the debtor's reorganization effort is an independent basis on which to adjudicate a non-debtor action. Most importantly, it ignores the Supreme Court case of *Callaway v. Benton*, which refused to take the *Continental Illinois* reasoning beyond status quo injunctions to permanent non-debtor injunctions.

1. The Indirect Jurisdictional Enlargement

Jurisdiction to permanently release a non-debtor action is *not* the equivalent of jurisdiction to temporarily stay a non-debtor action. The error in equating the two concepts is that it unthinkingly incorporates the historical distinction between jurisdiction to enjoin and jurisdiction to adjudicate. . . . In the case of a permanent non-debtor release and injunction, however, the distinction between jurisdiction to enjoin and jurisdiction to adjudicate disappears, because the injunction *does* adjudicate. A non-debtor release is not a mere status quo injunction; a non-debtor release effectively adjudicates the released non-debtor action. The release operates as an adjudication on the merits, fully binding for res judicata/preclusion purposes. . . .

2. Facility in Reorganization and the Forgotten Callaway v. Benton Case

The dominant approach to jurisdiction to permanently release and enjoin non-debtor actions, with its focus on interference with the debtor's reorganization, not only ignores the fact that this permits an indirect "adjudication by release" of non-debtor actions that could not be adjudicated directly, it also implicitly assumes that facilitation of the debtor's reorganization effort is an independent basis on which to adjudicate matters that are otherwise beyond the jurisdiction of the court. This takes the *Continental Illinois* notion of a general jurisdiction to protect and promote the debtor's reorganization, beyond status quo injunctions, to binding alterations of nonbankruptcy rights and obligations between non-debtors. . . . [T]he Court subsequently refused to extend *Continental Illinois* to permanent alterations of non-debtor rights in *Callaway v. Benton*. . . .

a. Jurisdiction to Adjudicate a Non-Debtor Action

. . . In response to the assertion that the reorganization court could adjudicate the non-debtor dispute because its resolution was important to the debtor's reorganization, the Court rejected the idea that the *Continental Illinois* line of cases supported jurisdiction to adjudicate this non-debtor dispute . . . .

If facilitation of the debtor's reorganization does not supply jurisdiction to adjudicate a non-debtor action, then the courts are "adjudicating by release" many non-debtor actions they have held to be outside the scope of "related to" jurisdiction to adjudicate. More importantly, though, the *Callaway* opinion speaks to the direct and ultimate jurisdictional issue posed by non-debtor releases and holds that jurisdiction to release and permanently enjoin a non-debtor action is wanting without regard to jurisdiction to adjudicate the non-debtor action.

b. Jurisdiction to Release a Non-Debtor Action

Even assuming that the importance of a non-debtor dispute to a debtor's reorganization effort might give a federal court bankruptcy jurisdiction to actually hear and adjudicate that dispute using governing nonbankruptcy law, can that jurisdiction to protect and promote reorganization be taken even further—can a federal court permanently extinguish the non-debtor action, without even purporting to address the merits of the underlying dispute, all in the interests of aiding the debtor's reorganization? . . . [T]he *Callaway* opinion, rather unambiguously, disapproved such an injunction. . . . [T]he reorganization court could not permanently release and enjoin enforcement of these non-debtor rights and obligations in order to facilitate the debtor's reorganization efforts. . . .

. . . *Callaway*'s prohibition on permanent non-debtor releases has been completely ignored. Subsequent expansion of bankruptcy jurisdiction in no way denigrates the continuing vitality of the *Callaway* holding. In fact, this aspect of the *Callaway* opinion precedes any discussion of bankruptcy jurisdiction and is not premised upon presence or absence of jurisdiction to adjudicate the non-debtor dispute. Rather, *Callaway* disapproved the permanent non-debtor release and injunction because there was no explicit statutory authority for displacing and extinguishing the non-debtor rights and obligations.

In the end, then, the jurisdictional infirmity of permanent non-debtor releases and injunctions is that suggested by general "in aid of jurisdiction" jurisprudence. . . . The courts' procedural power to protect the integrity of the reorganization process, through channeling and status quo injunctions, cannot be converted into a substantive power to extinguish non-debtor rights and obligations, independent of any explicit statutory authorization. It is not a matter of determining whether Bankruptcy Code section 524(e) prohibits non-debtor releases; it is a matter of finding statutory authorization for non-debtor releases.

Section 105 alone . . . certainly cannot be the sole source of this new substantive power. . . .

V. CONCLUSION

This article has argued that the bankruptcy courts' practice of discharging creditor actions against non-debtors is an abusive one, with no redeeming theoretical merit. Policy concerns advanced by proponents of non-debtor releases seem designed primarily to obfuscate the redistributional consequences of these liability releases. Most bewildering, though, is the fact that authority to issue these exceptional injunctions has been manufactured out of whole cloth, and in disregard of Supreme Court precedent prohibiting them. Given both the weight of this issue in complex reorganizations and the circuit split regarding authority to approve non-debtor releases, the matter seems ripe for resolution by the Supreme Court—again.

D.   Corporate Governance and Chapter 11 Control

One of the most difficult problems afflicting the reorganization process concerns identifying which of the multiple interested parties is entitled to exercise *control* over the reorganization. The question of control arises at virtually every stage of the reorganization and affects almost all of the important decisions. Outside of bankruptcy, normal corporate governance processes operate, with the familiar interaction of shareholder control, a governing board of directors, and managerial operation. But in bankruptcy, the process is complicated enormously by the uncertainty over who the "residual" claimants are; is there sufficient value to reach all interested parties? If that question is in doubt, for whom does management govern? Indeed, should management even be permitted to continue? And how should "reorganization value" be allocated? Who decides? And how? The conflicts between different classes of claimants is well-known; lower ranking claimants are more than happy to gamble with the money that otherwise would go to senior claimants.

Many superb articles have been written concerning some of these knotty problems of corporate governance. A partial list of highly recommended articles includes: Christopher W. Frost, *The Theory, Reality and Pragmatism of Corporate Governance in Bankruptcy Reorganizations*, 72 AM. BANKR. L.J. 103 (1998); Christopher W. Frost, *Running the Asylum: Governance Problems in Bankruptcy Reorganizations*, 34 Ariz. L. Rev. 89 (1992); Edward S. Adams, *Governance in Chapter 11 Reorganizations: Reducing Costs, Improving Results,* 73 B.U. L. REV. 581 (1993); Daniel B. Bogart, *Liability of Directors of Chapter 11 Debtors in Possession: "Don't Look Back—Something May be Gaining on You,"* 68 AM. BANKR. L.J. 155 (1994); Mark E. Budnitz, *Chapter 11 Business Reorganizations and Shareholder Meetings: Will the Meeting Please Come to Order, or Should the Meeting be Cancelled Altogether?*, 58 GEO. WASH. L. REV. 1214 (1990); Anna Y. Chou, *Corporate Governance in Chapter 11: Electing a New Board*, 65 AM. BANKR. L.J. 559 (1991); Barry L. Zaretsky, *Trustees and Examiners in Chapter 11*, 44 S.C. L. REV. 907 (1993); Kenneth N. Klee & K. John Shaffer, *Creditors' Committees Under Chapter 11 of the Bankruptcy Code*, 44 S.C. L. REV. 995 (1993); Stuart C. Gilson & Michael R. Vetsuypens, *Creditor Control in Financially Distressed Firms: Empirical Evidence*, 72 WASH. U. L.Q. 1005 (1994); Stuart C. Gilson, *Bankruptcy, Boards, Banks, and Blockholders*, 27 J. FIN. ECON. 355 (1990); Stuart C. Gilson, *Management Turnover and Financial Distress*, 25 J. FIN. ECON. 241 (1989); Thomas G. Kelch, *Shareholder Control Rights in Bankruptcy: Disassembling the Withering Mirage of Corporate Democracy*, 52 MD. L. REV. 264 (1993); Thomas G. Kelch, *The Phantom Fiduciary: The Debtor in Possession in Chapter 11*, 38 WAYNE L. REV. 1323 (1992); Raymond T. Nimmer & Richard B. Feinberg, *Chapter 11 Business Governance: Fiduciary Duties, Business Judgment, Trustees and Exclusivity*, 6 BANKR. DEV. J. 1 (1989); Lawrence Ponoroff, *Enlarging the Bargaining Table: Some Implications of the Corporate Stakeholder Model for Federal Bankruptcy Proceedings*, 23 CAP. U. L. REV. 441 (1994); Susan Rose-Ackerman, *Risk-Taking and Ruin: Bankruptcy and Investment Choice*, 20 J. LEGAL STUD. 277 (1991); and Gerald K. Smith, *Conflicts of Interest in Workouts and Bankruptcy Reorganization Cases*, 48 S.C. L. REV. 793 (1997).

Included here are three pieces: Lynn M. LoPucki & William C. Whitford, *Corporate Governance in the Bankruptcy Reorganization of Large, Publicly Held Companies*, 141 U. PA. L. REV. 669 (1993); Daniel J. Bussel, *Coalition-Building Through Bankruptcy Creditors' Committees,* 43 UCLA L. REV. 1547 (1996); and David A. Skeel, Jr., *The Nature and Effect of Corporate Voting in Chapter 11 Reorganization Cases*, 78 VA. L. REV. 461 (1992).

First is an installment of LoPucki and Whitford's empirical study of "megacases" of the 1980s. They examine a series of critical governance issues: What are the basic conflicts in a reorganization? What are the foundations of management power? To what extent do creditors and shareholders have the ability to control management? How much power does management actually enjoy? For whose benefit does management govern? And, for whose benefit *should* management govern? What conclusions do LoPucki and Whitford draw?

The second excerpt is from an article by Professor Dan Bussel of UCLA. Bussel focuses on a key player in the reorganization drama: the creditors' committee. He examines in depth the role the creditors' committee and its counsel play in negotiating the conflicts inherent in a reorganization case, with a view to building consensus. Any experienced chapter 11 participant will vouch for the practical necessity of achieving a consensual resolution to the case; Bussel explains how the creditors' committee can contribute positively to that end. He urges that creditors' committees, in terms of their selection, structure, and duties, should be viewed with an eye avowedly to their coalition-building role.

Finally, Professor David Skeel examines the final and ultimate means of exercising control over a chapter 11 reorganization: voting on a plan of reorganization. In the process Skeel also analyzes many of the control problems that might arise prior to the confirmation stage, such as major asset sales, compelling shareholder meetings, and acquiring blocking claims. During the pendency of the case negotiations are carried on, management may put forward possible plans, and disputes are aired, sometimes before the court, but in the end the fruit of the negotiations and what went before is put to the test: financially interested parties must vote on the plan. While the confirmation rules do not always require every class to accept the plan (cram down of a dissenting class might be possible), obtaining the affirmative vote of affected classes usually is a paramount goal of the plan proponent. Skeel offers a useful insight into the difficulties and nuances of corporate voting problems in chapter 11. In the end he recommends sticking as closely as possible to the norms underlying voting outside of bankruptcy under state law.

<h1 style="text-align:center">Lynn M. LoPucki & William C. Whitford</h1>
<h2 style="text-align:center">Corporate Governance in the Bankruptcy Reorganization of Large, Publicly Held Companies
141 U. PA. L. REV. 669 (1993)[*]</h2>

In the decade of the 1980s, the bankruptcy reorganization of companies worth hundreds of millions or even billions of dollars became commonplace. The companies that sought the protection of the bankruptcy courts were usually in tremendous upheaval. Under bankruptcy law, it fell to the incumbent managers to decide how to respond to these problems. Their decisions were often between courses of action that would serve either the interests of their shareholders or the interests of their creditors, one at the expense of the other. . . .

Decisions such as these raise two important questions in stark relief. The first is who the management of a reorganizing company is normatively supposed to represent. . . . The second is who these managers in fact represent. . . .

---

[*]   Copyright © 1993 University of Pennsylvania Law Review. Reprinted with permission.

We address both questions in this Article. We show empirically that neither the assumption of shareholder control nor the assumption of creditor control is correct. The process by which the behavior of managements of insolvent, reorganizing companies is influenced and controlled is complex and in many ways haphazard. It differs from case to case. The results are often troubling from a normative perspective. We also show that creditor and shareholder influence over management frequently prevents companies from maximizing their value.

In recent years it has become fashionable to argue in the strongest terms that management has too much power in chapter 11 proceedings and that they exercise it in a self-serving manner. . . .

. . . Our conclusions on this point are less certain. We have found that managements are often able to exploit power for their own benefit. But we have also found that management is highly vulnerable to the power of others. That vulnerability is perhaps best demonstrated by the high rate of turnover of both the managements that presided over the companies' declines and the managements that replaced them.

This Article is based on an empirical study of the forty-three largest publicly held companies to file and complete a bankruptcy reorganization between 1979, when the new Code became effective, and 1988. We have attempted to discover the actual practices with respect to corporate governance in these kinds of cases. . . .

I. The Bankruptcy Context

. . .

B. *The Basic Conflicts in a Reorganization*

The process of corporate governance is, among other things, a process of conflict resolution. . . . Three issues tend to predominate: (1) what levels of investment risk should the company seek while it determines whether or how to reorganize; (2) to what degree should the assets of the company be liquidated rather than reorganized; and (3) what mix of cash, debt and equity should be distributed and to whom?

1. Level of Risk in Investment Policy

Senior interests are often in sharp conflict with juniors as to the level of risk an insolvent company should accept in its investment policy. . . . [W]hen a marginally solvent company engages in high risk investment, the risks are borne primarily by creditors while the benefits accrue primarily to shareholders.

This splitting of the risk of loss and the prospect of gain has profound implications for corporate governance of insolvent and marginally solvent companies. . . . [T]he holders of junior interests will have reason to prefer that the company engage in high risk investments while the holders of senior claims have reason to prefer the opposite policy. . . .

2. Reorganization Versus Liquidation

Management often has a career interest in preserving the company. . . . Reorganization under their continued management is sometimes the managers' only means of salvaging their reputations and careers. . . .

The holders of underwater claims and interests often have reason to oppose liquidation until the distributions to them under a reorganization plan have been fixed. Such holders derive at least part of their bargaining leverage in plan negotiations from their ability to dispute the value of the assets continued in their current use. . . . But this leverage disappears to the extent that the values of assets are fixed through their liquidation during the case. Reflecting this change in leverage, in interviews we encountered the adage that "cash goes to creditors; only equity goes to equity." . . .

3. Nature and Beneficiaries of the Distributions

The most evident conflict of interest between different classes of creditors and shareholders concerns how much value each should receive in the distribution under the plan. In addition, there can be conflicts about whether the distributions that are made should consist of cash, debt, or equity. . . .

The various classes often differ as to the type of property they prefer to receive. Creditor classes tend to prefer distributions in cash or debt. . . . [T]hat preference appears to be especially strong among trade creditors. The holders of underwater equity may believe they can win a bigger distribution if they accept equity.

Most managements can be expected to prefer that substantial portions of the distributions be made in equity. Cash distributions immediately deprive the company of liquidity. . . . [D]ebt distributions . . . fix a claim against the company that may later threaten the managers' jobs.

II. The Foundations of Management Power

. . .

D. *Summary*

. . . To summarize, the fundamental source of management's power is its ability to remain in office after the filing of the reorganization case and to initiate the business and reorganization plans. Shareholders may be able to vote the managers out of office and creditors may be able to oust them through the appointment of a trustee, but neither of these events is likely. The automatic stay relieves the debtor of the necessity to repay already outstanding debt.

Individually or through their committees, creditors and shareholders can resist management's implementation of the business plan in court, but this direct approach is unlikely to be successful. Their leverage against management is much greater with regard to the plan of reorganization, where the consent of creditors is considered to be a virtual necessity and the consent of organized equity holders only somewhat less so. The perceived need for creditor consent to the reorganization plan may give creditors sufficient leverage to affect or control the business plan. If the debtor must seek additional credit from existing creditors, it may also fall under their hegemony.

Neither creditors nor shareholders are likely to take formal legal action against managers for perceived breaches of the managers' fiduciary duty of loyalty. Prepetition employment incentive contracts are unlikely to motivate management to serve the interests of shareholders once the reorganization case has been filed. But contracts entered into postpetition may motivate management to serve particular interests, most likely those of creditors. Finally, the market for management services may provide important incentives for management behavior during reorganization, but the effect is uncertain as to both its magnitude and direction.

. . . The most prominent attribute of this system is its complexity. . . . [A]ny one of these sources of power may become predominant in a particular case. But it is more likely that several influences over management power will operate in a particular case, and each will pull management in a somewhat different direction. Because these influences work in such a conflicted environment, it is difficult to predict how management will view their incentives in a particular case, let alone in a population of cases.

III. The Applications of Management Power

In this Part we present empirical evidence about how much power management had in the cases studied and for whose benefit they exercised it. . . .

B. *How Much Power Does Management Have?*

1. Management Turnover as an Index of Power

We have already reported several empirical indications that management's power was extensive in the cases studied. Trustees were rarely appointed. Shareholders tried to discipline management by electing new directors in only four instances; in two of the four the court enjoined the attempt. Management retained the exclusive authority to propose a plan of reorganization for the duration of all but nine of the forty-three cases we studied.

One finding conflicts dramatically with this image of management power during reorganization. The turnover rate for the CEOs of these distressed companies was much higher than the turnover rate for CEOs of most large, publicly held companies. In the period starting eighteen months before filing and ending six months after confirmation, there was at least one change in CEO in thirty-nine of forty-three cases (91% of the total number of cases).

In thirty-one of these cases (72% of the total number of cases) there was at least one change in CEO during the pendency of the chapter 11 case, or contemplated by the plan of reorganization. The changes were concentrated around the two critical dates in a reorganization case, filing and confirmation. . . . Other studies have found a "normal" CEO turnover rate of approximately 10% annually for large, publicly held firms. . . . For the CEOs of the companies we studied, the comparable annualized turnover rate during the first concentration period (around filing) was 167% per year. For the second concentration period (the month after confirmation) the annualized turnover rate was 307%.

Surprising as these statistics are, they are consistent with two other recent studies of CEO turnover during bankruptcy reorganizations. Gilson reported that only 29% of "senior managers"—defined as the CEO, the chairman of the board, and the president—remained with the firm over a four year period beginning two years before filing. Betker found that only 9% (18 of 202) of the top managers who held office two years before default still held office one year after confirmation.

. . . Management autonomy is limited. Chapter 11 is not a safe haven for incumbent management, as it is sometimes described. . . .

C. *For Whose Benefit Did They Manage?*

. . . In an effort to bring some order to the massive amount of information we collected, we invented four distinct models of management behavior during reorganization. . . .

The models that we invented are as follows:

1. *Aligned with creditor interests.* By "aligned," we mean that management generally took the side of creditors in the exercise of its discretion during the case. . . .

2. *Aligned with shareholder interests.* Management advocated what they considered to be the interests of shareholders, or some class of shareholders. . . .

3. *Maximize the estate.* Management was not aligned with either creditors or shareholders. Instead, management sought to maximize the value that could be distributed under the reorganization plan. . . . These managements did not play an active role in negotiating about the strictly distributional issues that are covered in a reorganization plan.

4. *Preserve the company.* Management was not aligned with either creditors or shareholders. Instead, management was committed to preserving some part of the traditional business as a going concern under the same corporate structure. . . . [W]e were able to classify the managements of twenty-five of our forty-three cases. . . .

TABLE VII
MANAGEMENT ORIENTATIONS

	Aligned with creditors	Maximize the estate	Preserve the company	Aligned with equity
Solvent	None	[1]	[3]	[3]
Insolvent	[9]	[3]	[4]	[2]
TOTAL	9	4	7	5

Several implications can be drawn from this table. First, management does not consistently favor or represent either creditor or shareholder interests. . . .

Second, the alignment of management is clearly a function of solvency. The managements of solvent companies never aligned with creditors; the managements of insolvent companies aligned with creditors far more frequently than they aligned with shareholders. . . .

Third, management aligned with shareholders in only five cases. It is interesting to note that in all five cases large shareholders held seats on the board of directors. . . . Among the thirty-two cases of insolvent debtors, management aligned with shareholders only twice, and in both of those cases a shareholder owning a controlling block of shares was personally involved in management.

. . . [S]everal other findings from our study buttress the conclusion that creditors dominate many of the managements of insolvent, reorganizing companies. First, recall that creditors frequently participated in CEO turnover . . . .

Second, . . . [i]n an earlier article, we documented that while there were systematic deviations from the absolute priority rule among the cases of the clearly insolvent debtors studied, those deviations were usually small. . . .

Finally, substantial creditor influence over management can be inferred from the frequency with which significant corporate assets were liquidated. We found that in thirty of the forty-three cases in our study there was extensive liquidation of assets. . . . Liquidation of assets is in general, though not without exception, a reorganization strategy that favors creditor interests. . . .

D. *The Lack of Corporate Expansion*

. . . [T]he making of high risk investments that might sharply increase the value of the company during a reorganization case is generally in the interests of shareholders or junior creditors whose interests are underwater. Such investments were relatively rare among the cases studied. Generally, these companies did not start new businesses, make acquisitions not integrally related to the company's existing business, expand significantly the existing business, or engage in other high risk activity. There seemed to be a cultural norm that such investments were inappropriate for a company in reorganization. . . .

E. *Summary and Assessment*

. . . Our most dramatic empirical finding concerns the fragile tenure of CEOs of large, publicly held companies that reorganize. Tenure is especially fragile for CEOs we have labeled as tainted, virtually all of whom were replaced. . . .

. . . One would expect that self-serving managements would ordinarily make preservation of their own jobs their first objective. Yet the CEOs in the companies studied were generally unable to accomplish even that. Nor were we able to detect any sizeable number of cases in which reorganization managers were able to convert their power as such into personal compensation, what we have called management "grabs." On the other hand, tainted managers often had enough leverage to negotiate releases from personal liability for possibly wrongful acts.

As to whose interests management did serve, our basic conclusion is that management orientations were diverse. . . .

We have made two findings of significance in this respect. First, shareholder interests were more likely to command the loyalties of management when an active shareholder held a controlling block of shares. Second, management's orientation was clearly a function of the company's solvency. The managements of solvent companies never aligned with creditors, while the managements of insolvent companies did so frequently. These alignments may partly account for the tendency for managements of insolvent companies to avoid risky investment policies and for deviations from the absolute priority rule to be limited.

We see two reasons to be concerned with the present state of affairs. First, there is tremendous uncertainty about how management is supposed to orient when it exercises the considerable authority extended to it by the Bankruptcy Code. . . .

Second, and more important, we are concerned that many managements are not acting to maximize the values of their firms. The problem is most obvious with respect to the decisions concerning the business plan. The tendency to avoid high risk investments generally serves the interests of senior creditors. The tendency to avoid quick liquidations generally serves junior interests. Neither necessarily serves the whole by maximizing the value of the firm. . . .

V. FOR WHOSE BENEFIT SHOULD MANAGEMENT GOVERN?

. . . In this Part we consider for whose benefit management should govern and also discuss what mechanisms could insure that management behaves in desired ways.

. . . We believe that management has greater influence over investment policy than they do over the reorganization plan. . . .

A. *Management as Representative of Shareholders*

Some commentators have asserted that insolvent, reorganizing companies should be governed for the benefit of their shareholders. We disagree. Because shareholders bear little of the risks of loss in the context of insolvency, they have a bias in favor of high risk investments. In bankruptcy, the bias is especially strong because the shareholders face cancellation of their interests at confirmation. . . . Even a modicum of commitment to wealth maximization as a normative principle should make one uncomfortable with leaving the management of an insolvent corporation in the control of shareholders with such incentives.

When insolvent companies make risky investments in the interests of shareholders, creditors bear the losses. So long as those companies are not in chapter 11, it is possible to argue that through contract provisions defining default, the creditors can protect themselves and society from wasteful investments intended to serve only shareholder interests. . . . In chapter 11, exercise of those contractual rights is inhibited by the automatic stay, making it unacceptable to allow management to continue to exercise their discretion solely in the interest of shareholders. . . .

While there is no doubt that shareholder bargaining leverage and ability to discipline management will be reduced if shareholder elections are enjoined, we believe the greater danger is that shareholders will use the threat of elections to induce management to adopt corporate policies that are wasteful and inconsistent with a public policy favoring resource allocation efficiency. . . .

We believe it is "clear abuse" for shareholders to use the election process to influence management to hold out for better treatment for shareholders in the business and reorganization plans of an insolvent company and that this practice can and should be enjoined. The more difficult issue is whether there are *any* circumstances in which the shareholders of an insolvent, reorganizing company should be permitted to elect directors. . . .

Our reasons for opposing shareholder elections apply most strongly to the insolvent corporation. But if the equity of a solvent company is so thin that the risks of loss created by managerial decisions are borne largely by creditors rather than shareholders, shareholders will not have the correct incentives to control investment policy. . . . Consequently, in this circumstance as well, shareholders should not have the unfettered right to call meetings of shareholders for the purpose of electing managers who will prefer their interests over those of creditors. . . .

B. *Collapsed Residual Ownership*

From an economic perspective, an accepted approach for ensuring that a corporation acts in accordance with wealth maximization norms is to vest the power to govern the corporation in the "residual owners"—that is, those who stand to gain from profits and suffer from losses. . . . We do not doubt that placing control of the reorganizing firm in the hands of parties who have both the risk of loss and the possibility of gain can be an effective way to promote wealth maximizing behavior. The primary problem—often unrecognized—is that there will commonly be more than one class of claims or interests that qualify simultaneously as the "residual owner" of an insolvent firm. The prescription that control should lie with the residual owners does not tell us how control should be apportioned among those classes. . . .

Under Baird and Jackson's concept, creditors would be the "collapsed residual owners" of any insolvent firm. Yet these collapsed residual owners, while bearing most of the risk of decreases in value, stand to reap only a small part of increases in value. They would not be as interested as they should be, from a wealth-maximization perspective, in a business plan that maximized the value of the company through high risks fully warranted by correspondingly high returns.

It is important to realize that this problem of inappropriate incentives is likely to exist even though the firm is substantially insolvent and certain to remain so. . . . [G]iven the number of layers of claims in large, publicly held companies, there is likely to be a creditor class immediately junior to the collapsed residual ownership class that stands to benefit from any significant increase in the collapsed value of the firm.

To provide the collapsed residual owners with the appropriate incentives to manage the reorganizing company would require radical change in the reorganization process.

C. *The Principle of Prudent Investment*

. . . While prudent investment seems to be the principle governing investment policy in many reorganizations, there is reason to think it is not the best one. This policy means that during the often extensive period of a chapter 11 proceeding management is not investing company resources in a manner that maximizes their value. . . . The result may be to lock the company into an inefficient "holding pattern" because any change in investment policy would have distributional consequences adverse to particular classes of creditors and shareholders. . . .

E. *Maximize the Estate*

One possible solution to the problem of corporate governance would be to postulate that management's objective should be to maximize the value of the bankrupt company, without regard to how this might affect the relative distributions to creditors and shareholders. Management would decide between alternative courses of action by deciding which yielded expected returns with the higher market value. . . . The purely distributional issues dealt with in the reorganization plan would be most appropriately negotiated among the creditors and shareholders. . . .

The most obvious difficulty with the maximization principle . . . is that it requires management to take whatever level of risk will maximize the value of the estate. When management chooses between investments with different levels of risk, its choice has distributional effects. . . . The magnitude of those distributional effects can far exceed the increase in the value of the estate achieved by maximizing. . . .

The existence of potentially huge distributional effects from the investment policies pursued by management casts doubt on management's ability to remain unbiased while determining what course of action will maximize the estate. . . .

. . . Nevertheless, until concrete evidence to the contrary is produced, we suggest that attempting to maximize the value of chapter 11 estates offers the best possibility for minimizing deadweight losses. . . .

CONCLUSION

. . . [W]e found much reason to doubt the currently fashionable view that chapter 11 leaves tainted managers with virtually unbridled power. The strongest reason for doubt is the fragile tenure of CEOs in the cases studied. Nearly all of the CEOs tainted by the firm's failure were out of office by the time a plan was confirmed. . . . If management has extensive ability to determine the outcome of reorganization proceedings, we would expect that they would also have the ability to retain their own jobs.

We conclude instead that the power equation in the reorganization of large, publicly held companies is far more complex than is reflected in current scholarship. We hope this Article will lay to rest two false but common assumptions that have plagued the economic modeling of bankruptcy reorganization. The first is that management represents the interests of shareholders in these proceedings. The data show that direct alignment of management with shareholder interests in insolvent, reorganizing companies is relatively rare. Equally false, however, is the second assumption sometimes made that once a company becomes insolvent, management thereafter represents creditor interests. We observed a diversity of management behaviors. . . .

In reporting this diversity of management behaviors, we do not mean to imply that management orientation results from random processes about which no generalizations can be drawn. First, . . . we conclude that management orientation is to some degree a function of solvency.

Second, with respect to the conduct of the business during reorganization, we conclude that it is common practice for managements to follow a principle we call "prudence." In essence, managers put the company in a holding pattern until the parties reach agreement. . . . [T]hey avoid risky new business initiatives that could lead to major gains or losses. . . . [M]anagements are systematically avoiding actions necessary to maximize the value of the firm.

The most difficult question is the normative one. For whose benefit *should* management govern in a chapter 11 reorganization? The problem is acute for insolvent or marginally solvent companies, because the risk of future loss is likely to be borne by different parties than enjoy the prospect of future gain. . . .

We conclude that the best proposal for maximizing the value of the company's assets is the most direct: adopt a rule requiring that management do so. . . . The pursuit of wealth maximization by a reorganizing debtor can have important distributional effects. . . .

To lessen the creditors' incentives to oppose management efforts to maximize the value of the firm, we have advanced a novel proposal that bankruptcy courts order payments from the groups who stand to benefit from maximization to compensate the creditors who are required to bear the risk. These "risk compensation payments" would consist of a transfer of an appropriate portion of the interests of junior classes who stand to benefit from the business initiative, to the senior classes who will be disadvantaged by it. . . .

. . . In the absence of this reform, we anticipate that most managements will continue the current practice of avoiding both early liquidation and high risk business expansions or acquisitions while in reorganization. In following what we have called the principle of prudent investment, they will be insuring that the social costs of bankruptcy remain unnecessarily high.

Daniel J. Bussel
Coalition-Building Through Bankruptcy Creditors' Committees
43 UCLA L. REV. 1547 (1996)[*]

INTRODUCTION

Creditors' committees in bankruptcy reorganization cases perform a "representative" function—mediating conflict among constituents with differing stakes in the proceeding—that bears a family resemblance to that of a legislature. In this way, the committees can facilitate the formulation and confirmation of consensual reorganization plans. Unfortunately, . . . the authorities that structure and regulate these committees implicitly view the committees as representatives of creditors in another sense, more akin to the "representativeness" of a fiduciary or attorney-in-fact. This Article attempts to refocus the U.S. Trustee and the federal bankruptcy courts on the mediative and coalition-building function. This changed focus should enable these authorities to structure better functioning committees. . . .

Existing doctrine generally considers committee members to be "fiduciaries" to all unsecured creditors and assumes that the committee's primary function is to represent a constituency. But all along, committees have "represented" multiple constituencies with conflicting interests. The committee itself can be a means of mediating this conflict as well as a champion of a particular interest. This ambivalence is reflected in the peculiar history of creditors' committees and is consistent with ambiguities in the concept of representativeness.

This Article makes explicit this tension in the role of the creditors' committee and argues that the mediative function of the committee should be openly celebrated and fostered, not hidden away and ignored as if it were the dark secret of bankruptcy reorganization law. Within reasonably broad constraints, reorganization law prefers consensus solutions to business problems. A well-functioning creditors' committee can contribute to building consensus around sound and fair solutions to business problems more effectively through its mediative power than as an advocate for a particular interest. Maximizing the consensus-building power of the committee should lead to more efficient and consistent resolution of bankruptcy reorganization cases. Moreover, those resolutions may well be more congruent with the parties' underlying legal entitlements. Seen in this light, conflicting interests among committee members are the raw material out of which a solution to the common problem must emerge, not a cause for concern about the committee's ability to fairly represent its constituency. . . .

I. SOME HISTORY, SOME DOCTRINE, AND SOME REPRESENTATION THEORY

. . .

E. Representativeness

. . . Section 1102 sets as the standard that the committee structure in a Chapter 11 case ensures "adequate representation of creditors." But this statutory standard is ambiguous because at least two distinct types of representativeness seem relevant: the fiduciary and the quasi-legislative.

Statutory ambiguity suggests that the statute's meaning should be derived from a thoughtful inquiry into its purposes. Moreover, in this particular case the statutory language cries out for a functional interpretation: "Adequate" to what end? I contend that if the primary objective is to control

   *   Originally published in 43 UCLA L. Rev. 1547. Copyright 1996, The Regents of the University of California. All Rights Reserved. Reprinted by permission of the UCLA Law Review, Fred B. Rothman & Co., and the author.

insider abuse, the historic fiduciary model is appropriate. On the other hand, if the primary objective is to promote consensus around a confirmable reorganization plan, the quasi-legislative model makes more sense.

1. The Fiduciary Model

. . . The fiduciary principle makes eminently good sense in the context of the classic, narrowly focused, self-appointed, insider-controlled, proxy-wielding "protective" committee. The risk under that structure was of a coerced or false consensus seducing the court into approving a fundamentally unfair plan. The fiduciary principle's salutary effect was to restrain the committee in its effort to promote an apparent consensus around the insiders' self-interested plan, presumably making any consensus that nevertheless emerged genuine.

I should think it obvious, however, that the potential for insider abuse of the statutory multi-constituency committee under Chapter 11 is substantially less than for the old-style protective committee. The kinds of abuses that characterized the protective committee are unlikely under the current system. . . . The force of the abuse-curbing rationale for the fiduciary principle is substantially diminished under the current structure. The fiduciary shoe cobbled by Justice Douglas for the old-style protective committee simply does not fit our new-fangled statutory committee. . . .

Far better, then, to describe the committee member's role consistently with that of businessmen generally in arms-length business negotiations—that of an interested party who accepts obligations of confidentiality and good faith in return for a seat at the negotiating table.

2. The Quasi-Legislative Model

Viewing representative bodies as consensus-building mechanisms is hardly novel. Republican government is grounded in this notion. At least one function of legislatures is to compromise among conflicting interests in order to solve problems. . . .

Legislators are expected to engage in deliberation and compromise. They are free to advance and then compromise parochial interests, and pick and choose among such interests. . . .

I do not want to be understood as suggesting that the members of a creditors' committee are "just like" legislators. There are obvious, highly salient differences between them. On the one hand, committee members' powers are less threatening to those they represent than the powers of legislators. . . . On the other hand, committee members are not accountable to constituents in the exercise of these lesser powers in the ways that legislators are. . . .

Still, at their cores, both the legislative process and the committee process are deliberative and function by compromising conflicting interests in light of practical realities and the general interest.
. . .

The structure of the Bankruptcy Code suggests that the central role of the modern statutory committee is to facilitate the formulation of a confirmable, consensual plan of reorganization. . . . The Code establishes a process and provides incentives to encourage the parties to resolve cases through the development of consensus around one of many plausible plans and specifically assigns the task of participating in plan formulation to the committee. . . .

Creditors' committees play a crucial role in the process by which this consensus is brought about. The negotiation of a consensual plan is an exercise in multi-layered coalitional bargaining. . . .

The formation of an unsecured creditors' committee is a critical juncture in forging a coherent negotiating bloc of unsecured creditors—generally a collection of the least organized and most poorly focused constituencies at the beginning of the case. The task of the appointing authority is to attempt to anticipate and stimulate a natural coalition among as broad a group as feasible under the circumstances. . . . The broader the coalition that can be provoked among unsecured creditors early in the case, the easier it should be to build the grand coalition that is necessary to resolve the case.

True protection for nonmember creditors is not in appointing and holding other creditors to a position of trust, but in the balance of power created by: (i) the appointment of a committee that consists of members from the key constituencies and that employs competent professionals to advise it; (ii) the general supervisory role of the bankruptcy court over administration of the estate; (iii) creditors' rights to obtain relevant information and to vote their claims before confirmation of a plan that impairs their legal rights; and (iv) court review of the plan to ensure it meets with the substantive requirements of the Bankruptcy Code. . . .

III. STRUCTURING CONSENSUS-BUILDING COMMITTEES

A. Nurturing Consensus

I start from the premise that the creditors' committee should principally be thought of, structured, and regulated so as to foster the development of consensus around one particular reorganization plan out of the many that might otherwise meet the legal requirements of Chapter 11. The key operational questions then become the following:

(1)   Among which constituencies must this consensus be developed?
(2)   What committee structure maximizes the likelihood of achieving that degree of consensus?
(3)   How can the consensus-building power of a properly structured committee best be harnessed to advance successful resolution of the bankruptcy case?
(4)   What protection should there be for interests not represented on the committee?

. . . [S]ome generalizations are useful as starting points. With respect to the first and second points, the U.S. Trustee (in the first instance) and the bankruptcy court should seek to appoint a single committee that includes members from all key unsecured constituencies, particularly when those constituencies have somewhat adverse economic interests. Key constituencies are those whose consent will be necessary to confirm a plan without resorting to nonconsensual confirmation procedures. . . .

With respect to the third and fourth points, less rather than more direct regulation of the committee process is the answer. The basic protection for parties not on the committee is their legal rights, created by the Bankruptcy Code, which limit the ability of the committee (or anyone else) to impose unfair plans upon them.

1. Of Coalitions

Given conflicting interests, absent intervention by the court, successful reorganization depends upon bargaining. Bargains fix the terms by which the reorganization plan reconciles conflicting interests. . . . Success in complex multi-party plan negotiations generally involves the process of coalition building. Coalitions are interim agreements among some subset of parties to a negotiation to combine forces in order to achieve desired outcomes from the bargaining process. Coalitions are most likely to form among parties with congruent interests. Identifying and broadening such natural coalitions as a step towards global resolution should be the primary object in structuring and regulating creditors' committees. . . .

4. Some Insights

. . . [T]hose who have studied coalition building have generated at least seven interesting observations that may have some operational significance when cautiously considered, in the light of our experience in Chapter 11 reorganization.

First, . . . coalitions are highly likely to form when the circumstances require direct communication—and considerably less likely to form when direct communications are prohibited or restricted. . . .

Second, audience presence and negotiator accountability can be serious obstacles to coalition formation. . . .

Third, the number of parties to a negotiation (party arithmetic) may have significant strategic implications. Parties may seek to shift the bargaining range in their favor by recruiting allies or excluding opponents. In general, increasing the number greatly complicates the process of coalition formation.

Fourth, "natural coalitions" between relatively weak parties with shared interests have a tendency to form easily. The terms of coalition formation are highly sensitive to the power differences among the parties. . . .

. . . Parties with similar interests are likely to find themselves in a natural coalition. . . . Once a winning coalition preliminarily forms it is likely to attract new partners—the "bandwagoning effect." When some parties trust others, "patterns of deference" can be identified and exploited to simplify and facilitate bargaining.

Fifth, neutrals play a valuable role in creating coalitions and mediating conflict within them.

Sixth, there are marked differences between intra-coalition and inter-coalition bargaining. Intra-coalition bargaining tends to be cooperative rather than competitive. Coalitions are subject to a type of inertia—once formed they tend to be rather stable.

Seventh, collegial decision-making bodies tend to be conservative, that is, risk averse. It is something of a natural tendency to compromise towards the less risky course of action. This tendency, however, may be overwhelmed in certain instances by the groupthink phenomenon: Members of a highly cohesive collective body sharing common views and a common "enemy" may reinforce each other, exaggerate extreme tendencies, and exclude or fail to consider countervailing factors—even ethical considerations.

B. Some Principles for Structuring Committees

. . . Assuming the point of the statutory committee is to facilitate the consensus-building process, ready access to court review, that is, real accountability for the U.S. Trustee when it exercises its discretion regarding committee appointments, seems appropriately calculated to keep the process working. . . .

One striking finding from the study of the history of reorganization law, and all the empirical and case study data available, is that, somehow, if we do place people in a room together and make them discuss a problem, usually, but not always, bargains will be struck. People have a powerful tendency to draw towards consensus where gains from trade exist—and experience suggests that this tendency manifests itself in bankruptcy crises as it does elsewhere. So, putting people together in one room is usually a good idea: Multiple committees should be avoided. . . .

The proper size of the creditors' committee is as few as possible without excluding constituencies that can reasonably be expected to find themselves in an unsecured creditors' coalition. The difficulty of building consensus grows with each additional party. . . . There appears to be a psychological cost in expanding much beyond seven members . . . .

If the proper size is as few as necessary, how many are necessary? All the key constituencies in a natural coalition of unsecured creditors should be represented on the committee, with allocations of votes that roughly parallel actual power differences among constituents. . . .

Parties essential to the formation of a coalition of unsecured creditors should be included. Constituencies likely to form a coalition, but not essential to its success, should generally be included if this can be done without making the committee unduly cumbersome. Trade creditors are almost always attractive coalition members. . . .

It is important to avoid burdening potential committee members with onerous duties, restrictions, or liabilities. One great service would be to avoid the inapt and discouraging pretense of fiduciary obligation. Committee members should be instructed simply to work together in good faith. . . . As a further means of promoting committee service, committee members should be broadly immunized from suit for liability arising out of committee service.

. . . [C]onstituencies highly unlikely to make it into a coalition with other unsecured creditors should be excluded—their protection is in the substantive and procedural protections of the Bankruptcy Code, not representation on a committee composed of adverse parties. . . .

Debtor "insiders" frequently raise the same problem—being "insiders," they are naturally in coalition with the debtor, not creditor constituencies. They too belong on the other side of the table.

Nor are government creditors likely to be appropriate committee members. For one thing, a government committee member is likely to be both accountable to and playing to an audience, an audience that probably has little formal role in the bankruptcy case. . . .

. . . Considerable deference ought to be paid to a request from the committee to expand its membership in order to broaden its constituency. Such coalition broadening requests should generally be encouraged.

On the other hand, fragmentation into multiple committees, or exclusion of a member whom the appointing authority views as a part of a natural unsecured creditors coalition, should generally be resisted. Given the substantial success of skilled neutrals in mediating such conflicts, formal mediation should be considered before authorizing such a change in committee make-up and structure. . . .

Principals rather than representatives seem to be better at forging consensus. A committee member ought to be discouraged from designating its lawyer as its representative. . . .

V. AN IDEALIZED MODEL OF THE COMMITTEE PROCESS AND SOME OBJECTIONS

A. The Model

. . . I want to briefly describe my idealized model of the committee process. . . .

Direct participation in the committee process from major creditors from the various constituencies should be unambiguously encouraged. Imposing vague and conflicting fiduciary duties, limiting immunity, or unnecessarily restricting securities trading should be avoided. The point of the committee process should be to bring the diverse real parties in interest together and encourage them to freely and in good faith work out a solution that is consistent with their various perceptions of their economic self-interests.

Individuals, preferably businesspersons, designated by the committee members, should very early in the case meet face-to-face, to take each other's measure, hire legal counsel experienced in bankruptcy matters that has the confidence of the committee, and deal with immediate crises. . . . Continuity of individual representatives should be encouraged. Counsel and these individual representatives should meet face-to-face with some frequency early on in the case in an effort to build rapport. . . . When differences of opinion occur, the committee should try to work through them by consensus.

. . . A coherent but tentative consensus on the ultimate disposition of the case should be reached in committee, and then should evolve through interactions with other constituencies such as the debtor, equity holders, and secured creditors, all in light of the changing circumstances of the reorganization case. Finally, a grand coalition of all the constituencies should emerge around a confirmable reorganization plan. . . .

B. The Regulatory Objection

The open and free-wheeling coalition-building process I envision assumes that, operating under the framework of the Bankruptcy Code, interested businesspersons and their bankruptcy lawyers can, with a minimum of supervision, privately negotiate a consensual solution to the reorganization problem at hand. . . .

The history of reorganization law gives one some pause before embracing this assumption. In the 1930s, a broad political consensus emerged that the then-existing, free-wheeling, and unsupervised process had become a shield for self-dealing and abuse by debtor management and their investment banking allies. It is possible that history will repeat itself. . . . [M]ore optimistically, we can assume that we learn from the past and that, through successive refinements, we can modulate the swing of the pendulum, bringing it closer to equipoise at a point where the opportunity for insider abuse is minimal, yet the flexibility to creatively address complex cooperative and distributional issues through free negotiations remains great.

. . . The "deregulation" of the committee process that I envision does not touch this fundamental point: Plans must still be ratified by the entire creditor body only after full disclosure. Moreover, the plan process will still operate under the general supervision of the bankruptcy court. . . . Finally, the professional fees and the "emoluments of control" over the plan process and the reorganized debtor that were targeted by Justice Douglas as the incentives driving insider abuse remain under the statutory control of the bankruptcy court.

In this context, a loosening of restraints on committee members through explicit toleration of what are, after all, inherently conflicting interests, done with an eye towards facilitating the consensus-building process that lies at the core of Chapter 11, is reasonable. . . .

C. Reinforcing the Power of Large Claim Holders

Under the model of committee process suggested here, those with large claims that have present economic value will do well. Crafting the committee to reflect the actual distribution of economic power in the case favors those with economic power. . . .

I do not wish to defend the actual distribution of wealth and power even in the limited context of bankruptcy reorganization law. I do wish to assert, however, that that distribution of power exists regardless of what the committee looks like. Power based on legal entitlement and economic resources ultimately prevails in most reorganizations. Substantially mismatching the committee to the actual distribution of power will obstruct rather than facilitate resolution of the reorganization case consistently with those entitlements. It will encourage deadlock and litigation. . . .

E. The Investigatory and Supervisory Functions

I have focused on the coalition-building, mediating, and negotiating functions of the committee. But the statute also explicitly assigns the creditors' committee investigatory and supervisory functions. Surely, as to such matters, doesn't the committee owe the creditor body some general duty of prudence? How do these powers fit into the coalition-building model of the committee's role?

I suggest that the most sensible way to view these powers is as powers, not responsibilities. Their use, in the hands of a creditors' committee, is, with apologies to von Clausewitz, the carrying on of plan negotiations by other means. In the context of a contested Chapter 11 case, the power to investigate and the right to consult on case administration is used strategically by the committee to advance its objectives in the plan formulation and confirmation processes. Investigation and supervision for its own sake, apart from the plan process, may be necessary, but if they are, then the functions are more appropriately carried out by individuals acting as true fiduciaries—the statutory trustees and examiners that the court may appoint under the Code. Viewed in this way, these statutory functions should play a minimal role in shaping the structure and regulation of the committee.

CONCLUSION

. . . The institution of the creditors' committee has evolved over time, for peculiar historical reasons. The legal framework governing the institution has failed to keep up with the changes in the institution. Meanwhile, in practical operation, we have discovered that the committee can be an effective device for building the consensus necessary to the successful resolution of reorganization cases. The next step is to embrace the goal of consensus building, and, with that goal in mind, continue to evolve the institution so it can become even more effective.

David A. Skeel, Jr.
The Nature and Effect of Corporate Voting in Chapter 11 Reorganization Cases
78 VA. L. REV. 461 (1992)[*]

INTRODUCTION

... [B]argaining is only a part of the reorganization process; chapter 11 points toward, and culminates in, a vote among the various constituencies of the debtor. A complete understanding of the chapter 11 reorganization process requires an evaluation of its voting provisions. ...

A logical first place to look for help in understanding the chapter 11 voting rules is to the voting regime that is displaced when a firm files its bankruptcy petition. On first inspection, the two sets of voting rules appear quite different. Outside of bankruptcy, corporate voting is governed by state corporation law. ...

After a chapter 11 petition has been filed, corporate voting is governed by a federally imposed bankruptcy system. Unlike state corporation law, chapter 11 provides only for a single, all-encompassing vote on whether to approve or reject a reorganization plan. Also unlike state corporation law, which limits the franchise to the firm's shareholders, chapter 11 permits every holder of a claim or interest to cast a ballot on the plan, except those who will be compensated in full or who will receive nothing under a given plan of reorganization.

This Article attempts to demonstrate that, despite striking superficial differences, chapter 11 voting can and should be seen as an extension of the state corporate law voting rules. ... [C]hapter 11's voting rules are responsive to precisely the same normative concerns that explain shareholder suffrage outside of bankruptcy. ...

... I apply my analysis to several particularly troublesome chapter 11 voting issues—including sales of most or all of a firm's assets, directorial elections, and the supermajority requirement for plan approval. The analysis suggests that once in bankruptcy, sales of most or all of a firm's assets should be approved by a majority of the firm's unsecured creditors, rather than by a court. The analysis also suggests that unsecured creditors, rather than shareholders, should be the voters in any directorial election. Finally, Part III argues for replacing chapter 11's current supermajority voting standard with simple majority voting to reduce the threat of a creditor's acquiring a blocking position and using this veto power improperly. ...

II. AFTER DISASTER: CORPORATE VOTING IN CHAPTER 11 REORGANIZATION CASES

Sections 1121 to 1129 of the Bankruptcy Code provide an elaborate network of voting rules for the purpose of regulating the chapter 11 franchise. ... My inquiry shows that, despite their major superficial differences, state corporate law voting rules and the chapter 11 voting framework are largely consistent from a normative perspective. The voting regime is not perfect, however. ...

A. An Overview of Corporate Voting in Chapter 11

Chapter 11 provides a voting framework remarkably different from corporate voting outside of bankruptcy. The crucial distinction lies in section 1126(a), which states that any "holder of a claim or interest allowed under [section] 502 of this title . . . may accept or reject a plan." Simply put,

---

whereas shareholders enjoy a monopoly of the franchise before the corporation files its petition, section 1126(a) establishes universal suffrage as the norm in chapter 11. . . .

. . . Section 1126 establishes a system of classified voting on the plan. Under section 1126(c), acceptance by creditors requires the approval of two-thirds in amount and a majority in number of the claims in each class of creditors. . . . Thus, the emphasis of section 1126 rests on whether the class as a whole votes for or against the plan. . . .

B. A Normative Assessment of the (Nearly) Universal Suffrage of Chapter 11 . . .

1. Applying the Residual Ownership Prong to Chapter 11 Suffrage

At first blush, the chapter 11 voting regime seems wholly inconsistent with the residual ownership perspective on corporate voting. . . . In affording every constituency access to the voting process, chapter 11 abandons the goal of limiting suffrage to the single constituency with the best decisionmaking incentives. The true residual owners vote, but so do numerous classes whose decisionmaking incentives are less desirable.

The analysis is not so simple as this characterization suggests. Consider first the fact that because chapter 11 not only effects a sale of the firm's assets, either to its current claimants and interest holders or to a third party, but also compromises the claims of most or all classes of claimants, multiple constituency voting is inevitable. . . . [R]ealistically the drafters of the Code could not have meant to give a single class of claims the authority to determine whether and how to compromise the claims of another class. . . .

More important, despite the inevitability of multiple constituency voting, the Bankruptcy Code still seems to focus voting authority on the residual class. The residual class is the first class that will be impaired if the plan proponent seeks to compensate as many classes in full as the firm's assets will allow. Because unimpaired classes of claims or interests are deemed to accept a reorganization plan, full compensation eliminates the ability of a class to vote against the plan. Therefore, the residual class will vote in nearly every chapter 11 case . . ., and its vote frequently will prove pivotal.

. . . [T]he residual class is the highest priority class whose vote the plan proponent *must* get, given that the residual class invariably will be impaired. . . .

C. Shareholders' Role in the Chapter 11 Voting Process

Although chapter 11's voting rules focus attention on the residual class, the rules cannot completely eliminate the multiple peak problem that arises whenever parties with divergent and often conflicting interests make decisions. The presence of the shareholder constituency in particular most distorts decisionmaking in chapter 11. . . . [S]hareholders usually have lost their residual owner status by the time a corporation enters chapter 11. Because chapter 11 debtors typically are insolvent . . ., the new residual owners of a publicly held firm are likely instead to be its unsecured creditors. . . .

In contrast to the shareholders of a flourishing business, whose incentives further the firm's wealth-maximization goal, shareholders of an insolvent corporation pursue a separate agenda because they will receive nothing upon an immediate liquidation. First, shareholders may wish to prolong the chapter 11 case as long as possible in the hope that the firm's fortunes will improve. Second, they will encourage gambling with the assets of the firm because they have nothing to lose, and everything to gain, if the firm takes extraordinary business risks. . . .

The question that emerges is whether chapter 11 should eliminate shareholders' voting rights if the firm is insolvent. Withholding the franchise from shareholders would further focus decisionmaking authority on the true residual class. . . .

At least two arguments can be made in support of the current voting regime, however. First, were an insolvent firm liquidated today, shareholders would have no financial interest in the proceeds, but so long as the firm continues to operate there is a chance that its fortunes will improve dramatically and again give value to the shareholders' ownership interest. . . .

Second, permitting shareholders to participate in the chapter 11 process may be necessary to create the proper incentives to enter bankruptcy. . . .

. . . The important point for present purposes is that because chapter 11 permits shareholders to vote even in contexts where their incentives are skewed, and because the parties seldom resort to cramdown, shareholder suffrage often undermines the efficiency of the chapter 11 franchise.

D. The Majority in Number/Two-Thirds in Amount Voting Requirement

. . . [T]he one-share, one-vote requirement for shareholder voting outside of bankruptcy is explained by the direct relationship between the number of shares owned and the financial stake in the firm. Accounting for creditors' interests proves more difficult, for their claims differ vastly in origin and amount. As a result, chapter 11 requires not only that a majority in number of the claims in a class approve a reorganization plan, but also that two-thirds of the total amount vote in favor. The voting standard thus includes aspects both of a majority and of a supermajority standard. . . .

Whatever the rationale, the drafters' adoption of a supermajority standard is misguided. . . . Supermajority voting standards protect the minority shareholders. . . .

Minority protection comes at a price, however. A minority shareholder may also use her veto power strategically, as a weapon designed to extract concessions from the remaining shareholders. This cost is justified, and supermajority voting is thus desirable, if the actions taken by majority shareholders could have a disproportionate effect on the minority, as in a close corporation. The franchise operates very differently in chapter 11, however. . . . If the class votes in favor of a plan, and the plan is confirmed, every member of the class receives exactly the same distribution. . . . Because each member of the class is affected in the same way by the outcome of the vote, there is no need to impose supermajority voting as a protective device. . . .

III. An Analysis of Chapter 11 Voting Issues

. . . We now are ready to apply the analysis . . . to three controversial chapter 11 issues: sales of most or all of a firm's assets prior to confirmation, the shareholders' right to compel a shareholders' meeting, and the acquisition and exercise of a blocking position in a class (or classes) of claims. Understanding these issues as voting issues helps clarify some of the confusion. . . .

A. Sales of Substantial Assets Prior to Confirmation

Section 363(b)(1) of the Bankruptcy Code authorizes the bankruptcy trustee, after notice and a hearing, to sell assets of the firm outside of the ordinary course of business. . . . What is less clear is whether section 363(b)(1) also gives the trustee the power to sell all or substantially all of the assets of the firm.

1. Judicial Analysis: A Description and a Critique

. . . Consider that outside of bankruptcy, sales of most or all of a firm's assets constitute a fundamental change. . . . [S]tate corporation statutes require that such sales be submitted to a shareholder vote. . . . [T]he cases correctly recognize a similar problem in chapter 11. But the solution cannot be for courts to step in and more closely scrutinize the reasons for proposing the sale. Unfortunately, judges have even worse decisionmaking incentives than managers: because judges have no financial interest in the enterprise and are immune from the market forces . . . .

This reasoning suggests that sales of substantial assets should be decided by a vote, rather than by a judge. Because chapter 11 locates the franchise in the plan process, one could argue that such sales should not be permitted prior to the plan's confirmation. . . .

Proponents of the current regime point out that requiring all asset sales to take place in connection with the plan process ignores the fact that an earlier sale sometimes is in the best interests of everyone, as when the firm's assets could decline in value. Recognizing that in some cases all interested parties will prefer a preconfirmation sale does not mean that enhanced judicial scrutiny under section 363 is the best way to effect such sales, however. . . .

A better solution would permit preconfirmation sales of substantial assets in chapter 11 but transfer authority to a more effective decisionmaker. One way to achieve this goal might be to amend the Bankruptcy Code to compel a vote by all claimants and shareholders prior to approval of any preconfirmation sale of most or all of a firm's assets. . . . [T]his framework would probably prove unworkable. . . .

Alternatively, the ultimate decision could be entrusted to the single class of creditors who are identified as the true residual owners of the firm, just as outside of bankruptcy firms give the vote to a single class of common shareholders to reflect their status as residual owners of a solvent firm. . . . The most obvious difficulty with importing this strategy into the bankruptcy context is determining who the residual owners are. . . .

Finally, the law could designate a particular class as the sole voting class. Adopting a blanket rule would eliminate the need for a costly valuation. Moreover, by defining the voting class relatively broadly, by vesting the vote in unsecured creditors generally, for example, . . . the danger of choosing the wrong class as voters, as well as the danger that the residual class could change while the case is pending, could be minimized. . . . Notwithstanding its limitations, however, the benefits of a clear rule outweigh the costs of attempting to determine precisely the firm's residual owners. The analysis clearly suggests that it is preferable that a majority of the firm's unsecured creditors, rather than a court, approve any preconfirmation sale of substantial assets. . . .

B. Shareholders' Right to Compel a Shareholders' Meeting

1. Judicial and Academic Treatment of Shareholders' Meeting Requests

. . . [T]he most important of the chapter 11 voting issues may be shareholders' right to compel a shareholders' meeting. . . .

. . . [C]ourts continue, in bankruptcy, to recognize shareholders' state law right to hold a meeting. Nonetheless, courts will interfere with shareholders' efforts to replace and elect directors if . . . the shareholders clearly have overstepped their bounds. . . .

Neither the case law nor the commentary, however, provides a persuasive response to the question of why shareholders should retain the right to hold a meeting if the corporation is insolvent, as most chapter 11 debtors are. Both courts and commentators suggest that shareholders need this privilege as leverage in the negotiation process, regardless of whether the firm is insolvent; this is costly, however, especially considering that the shareholders' interest is much more attenuated in an insolvent firm.

One cost is that shareholders may (and do) call shareholders' meetings opportunistically. . . .

The "clear abuse" test relied on by the courts is an insufficient response to this problem because shareholders' incentives are systematically, not just occasionally, flawed. Moreover, any directors elected by shareholders also will have suspect decisionmaking incentives. Thus, the effect of permitting a shareholders' meeting would be to put decisionmaking authority in the hands of directors who do not represent the best interests of the corporation as a whole. . . .

2. Who Should the Voters Be and When Should Elections Be Held?

If shareholders should not be permitted to compel a meeting, who should hold this right? Again there are two possible answers: either all constituents or the true residual owners of the firm. . . .

. . . [L]imiting the franchise to the firm's true residual owners—presumably its unsecured creditors—emerges once again as the better choice. As before, the chief virtue of such a rule is its effect on decisionmaking incentives. . . .

Selecting unsecured creditors as the appropriate voters still leaves the question of when elections should be held. . . . One could plausibly argue . . . that the firm's directors should be replaced, or at the least an election held, at the commencement of every chapter 11 case in order to ensure that directors have proper decisionmaking incentives.

But holding an election and replacing the firm's directors at the start of every bankruptcy would be both cumbersome and expensive. . . .

The same concerns also suggest that the firm's residual owners should not have an automatic right to compel a meeting. The Bankruptcy Code should provide some opportunity for the replacement of directors, however, because at times mismanagement or stalemate will make an election desirable.

One possibility that could effectively balance these concerns would be to adopt the "for cause" standard. . . .

C. Buying a Blocking Position Within a Class of Claims

. . . A two-thirds voting requirement gives any claimant who acquires claims totaling just over one-third in amount veto power over the vote of the class in question. Courts already have begun to struggle with the question of what limitations (if any) should be imposed on parties' exercise of this veto power. The dramatic increase in the trading of bankruptcy claims suggests that the issue will play a crucial role in future bankruptcies. . . .

. . . [A]mending section 1126 of the Bankruptcy Code to provide for simple majority rather than supermajority voting might diminish the threat of creditors' acquiring a blocking position and wielding their influence improperly. . . .

IV. Collective Action Problems and the Role of Committees in Chapter 11

. . . In this Part, I address what appears at first to be a major practical problem with the conclusions of Part III: although unsecured creditors might, in the abstract, be the firm's best decisionmakers in chapter 11, the *real* unsecured creditors of *real* publicly held chapter 11 debtors are numerous and highly dispersed. Unsecured creditors therefore are likely to face the same obstacles to effective voting—rational apathy and the incentive for individual creditors to free ride—that undermine shareholder voting outside of bankruptcy. If this is true, amending the Bankruptcy Code to give them the franchise in these contexts would be pointless.

I argue in this Part that the game is in fact worth the candle. . . . I show . . how chapter 11 committees help the parties to surmount their collective action problems, but I also note the limitations of the committee solution. Finally, I conclude that unsecured creditors should, as I originally argued, be given voting authority. . . .

C. The Impact of Chapter 11 Committees on Collective Action Problems

Collective action theorists have posited that highly latent groups, such as the shareholders and unsecured creditors of a publicly held chapter 11 debtor, will succeed in supplying a collective good only through coercion or selective incentives. Government intervention presents a third option. The government may provide the collective good itself or may compel the members of a group to contribute to the provision of the collective good. Chapter 11 committees are a classic example of the latter approach. Chapter 11 committees enable the parties to overcome their collective action problems in two related ways. First, committees centralize all of the functions necessary to effective monitoring-and-contesting by the class or classes of claims in question. . . .

Second, the Bankruptcy Code provides for the costs of committees to be paid as an administrative expense from the bankruptcy estate. . . . This arrangement spreads the costs of committees across all claimants. . . . As a result, chapter 11 committees are likely to be more effective than their counterparts outside of bankruptcy at solving collective action problems, perhaps even causing overmonitoring because of the independence of payment and success.

. . . Nevertheless, the committee solution suffers from several significant shortcomings.

The first stems from agency costs that arise from the committee's acting in essence as an agent for the class. . . .

A second problem with chapter 11 committees stems from the breadth of their coverage. . . . The unsecured creditors of large corporations comprise distinct and potentially conflicting classes, yet the Bankruptcy Code contemplates that a single committee will represent them all. . . . [C]ollective action problems will reemerge: a single committee cannot possibly effectively represent each of three or four different classes with frequently divergent interests in the parties' negotiations on division of the reorganization pie. . . .

E. Are Unsecured Creditors Still the Right Voters?

The suggestion that chapter 11 committees resolve the collective action problems of unsecured creditors and shareholders in only an imperfect way returns us to the question with which this Part began: should the Bankruptcy Code be amended to give unsecured creditors voting control over preconfirmation sales of substantial assets and directorial elections?

With respect to choosing directors in chapter 11, the change clearly would be an improvement over the current regime. Although committees provide only an imperfect solution to unsecured creditors' collective action problems, shareholders face precisely the same obstacles. Given unsecured creditors' better decisionmaking incentives, it is more appropriate that they be the voters in the event of an election.

The question of whether unsecured creditors or bankruptcy judges are likely to make better decisions on preconfirmation sales is somewhat closer. Again, however, amending the Bankruptcy Code appears to be the preferable choice. Despite their imperfectly resolved collective action problems, unsecured creditors have much more at stake and can therefore be expected to wield their influence more effectively.

CONCLUSION

This Article recommends several changes to the way bankruptcy courts and the Bankruptcy Code currently treat corporate voting in the chapter 11 context. Each proposal is at bottom a suggestion that courts and the Bankruptcy Code should stick more closely to the normative principles reflected in state law corporate voting provisions.

E.   Cram Down

Bankruptcy reorganizations are in many respects formalized settings in which negotiations over the allocation of value in the enterprise among competing claimants can take place. But some rules must guide this negotiation. One of the cornerstone principles of reorganization doctrine has been that the priority entitlements of various classes of creditors normally should be respected in a reorganization plan. Under the current Bankruptcy Code classes of creditors may waive this privilege. Still, the idea that a plan must be "fair and equitable" to dissenters (now a dissenting class) has been an article of reorganization faith for over a century. In particular, this principle has been interpreted to implement the "absolute priority" standard, meaning that senior creditors must be paid in full before junior creditors can share in the reorganized enterprise. However, the doctrine of "absolute" or "strict" priority, while longstanding, has been the subject of much debate and criticism.

This section examines "cram down" and the absolute priority rule. Some of the best bankruptcy articles ever written concern this critical topic. Not all of them could be included here. Some of those articles that are recommended highly include: Charles W. Adams, *New Capital for Bankruptcy Reorganizations: It's the Amount that Counts*, 89 Nw. U. L. REV. 411 (1995); Douglas G. Baird & Robert K. Rasmussen, *Boyd's Legacy and Blackstone's Ghost*, 1999 SUP. CT. REV. 393; David Gray Carlson, *The Truth About the New Value Exception to Bankruptcy's Absolute Priority Rule*, 21 CARDOZO L. REV. 1303 (2000); Allen C. Eberhart et. al., *Security Pricing and Deviations from the Absolute Priority Rule in Bankruptcy Proceedings*, 45 J. FIN. 1457 (1990); Kenneth N. Klee, *Cram Down II*, 64 AM. BANKR. L.J. 229 (1990); Kenneth N. Klee, *All You Ever Wanted to Know About Cram Down Under the New Bankruptcy Code*, 53 AM. BANKR. L.J. 133 (1979); Lynn M. LoPucki & William C. Whitford, *Preemptive Cram Down*, 65 AM. BANKR. L.J. 625 (1991); Bruce A. Markell, *A New Perspective on Unfair Discrimination in Chapter 11*, 72 AM. BANKR. L.J. 227 (1998); Raymond T. Nimmer, *Negotiated Bankruptcy Reorganization Plans: Absolute Priority and New Value Contributions*, 36 EMORY L.J. 1009 (1987); Isaac M. Pachulski, *The Cram Down and Valuation Under Chapter 11 of the Bankruptcy Code*, 58 N.C. L. REV. (1980); Lawrence Ponoroff, *Enlarging the Bargaining Table: Some Implications of the Corporate Stakeholder Model for Federal Bankruptcy Proceedings*, 23 CAP. U. L. REV. 441 (1994); David A. Skeel, Jr., *The Uncertain State of an Unstated Rule: Bankruptcy Contribution Rule After Ahlers*, 63 AM. BANKR. L.J. 221 (1989); Elizabeth Warren, *A Theory of Absolute Priority*, 1991 ANN. SURV. AM. L. 9; Lawrence A. Weiss, *Bankruptcy Resolution: Direct Costs and Violation of Priority of Claims*, 27 J. FIN. ECON. 285 (1990); and Robert M. Zinman, *New Value and the Commission: How Bizarre!*, 5 AM. BANKR. INST. L. REV. 477 (1997).

Excerpts from six articles are included: Walter J. Blum & Stanley A. Kaplan, *The Absolute Priority Doctrine in Corporate Reorganizations*, 41 U. CHI. L. REV. 651 (1974); Chaim Fortgang & Thomas Moers Mayer, *Valuation in Bankruptcy*, 32 UCLA L. REV. 1061 (1985); Lynn M. LoPucki & William C. Whitford, *Bargaining Over Equity's Share in the Bankruptcy Reorganization of Large, Publicly Held Companies*, 139 U. PA. L. REV. 125 (1990); Douglas G. Baird & Thomas H. Jackson, *Bargaining After the Fall and the Contours of the Absolute Priority Rule*, 55 U. CHI. L. REV. 738 (1988); John D. Ayer, *Rethinking Absolute Priority After Ahlers*, 87 MICH. L. REV. 963 (1989); and Bruce A. Markell, *Owners, Auctions, and Absolute Priority in Bankruptcy Reorganizations*, 44 STAN. L. REV. 69 (1991). In addition, short excerpts from the 1977 House Report and the 1997 National Bankruptcy Review Commission Report are included.

The article by Professors Walter Blum and Stanley Kaplan is a good place to begin consideration of the absolute priority debate. They wrote their article in 1974, in the heat of the reform discussions that led to the substantial revision of the bankruptcy law in 1978. In their work, they consider many of the charges leveled against the absolute priority rule and the then-pending proposals for change. In many respects their analysis provides a useful backdrop to the timeless issues involving the relative rights of conflicting creditor groups.

As you read Blum and Kaplan (as well as the ensuing articles), consider these questions:

1. What is the doctrine of "absolute" (or "strict") priority?
2. What functions does the doctrine serve?
3. What are the essential components of and assumptions underlying the absolute priority doctrine?

4. What is the leading basis for attacking the doctrine? Is it convincing? If so, what should be done?
5. How is the value of a company in reorganization computed?
6. What other criticisms of the absolute priority doctrine may be made?
7. What possible changes to or modifications of the fairness standard of strict priority might be made? What are the primary concerns?
8. How did the historical fact of and dissatisfaction with a bifurcated reorganization system under the old Act influence demands for reformation of the absolute priority doctrine? What difficulties arose?
9. How does the "best interests of creditors" test differ from the absolute priority rule? Is it a preferable way of dealing with the fairness issue?
10. In its 1978 reforms, to which criticisms of the absolute priority rule did Congress accord the most weight, and what changes did Congress make?
11. Is a strict or relaxed fairness standard preferable? Why?

Walter J. Blum & Stanley A. Kaplan
The Absolute Priority Doctrine in Corporate Reorganizations
41 U. CHI. L. REV. 651 (1974)[*]

The absolute or strict priority doctrine in corporate reorganizations under the Bankruptcy Act has never been comfortable for practitioners or theorists to live with. . . . Despite the fact that discussion of the doctrine has been ongoing, the framing of the issues in controversy has generally been troublesome. . . .

The . . . difficulty in firming up the issues concerns the nature of the doctrine itself. In a sense, the absolute priority doctrine does prescribe a general rule: before a class of investors can participate in a reorganization, all more senior classes must be compensated in full for their claims, measured on the basis of their priorities upon involuntary liquidation, unless the junior class contributes to the reorganized enterprise something that is reasonably compensatory and is measurable. Reorganizers have always understood, however, that this general formulation does not dictate a specific pattern of adjusting rights among classes of investors. Reorganization plans are the result of a process in which representatives of the investors "negotiate" . . . . The function of the absolute priority doctrine has in essence been to set guidelines for carrying on these negotiations . . . .

This perspective on the doctrine helps to explain why so many questions of fairness remain unresolved. It may also explain why any proposal to relax the hold of the absolute priority doctrine might be seen as an attack on the doctrine itself. Since the doctrine is really a loose mold for controlling negotiations, it is understandably taken in some quarters as a symbol of the position that any plan of adjusting rights must be structured so that it is governable by courts. . . . The fear is that a back track from the absoluteness of strict priority will make it easier for reorganization courts to approve deals under an illusory "rule" that permits unjustifiable allocation of securities while precluding effective complaint by an objecting member of a senior class.

I

. . . The early railroad reorganizations, predating the landmark case of *Northern Pacific Railway Co. v. Boyd*, might have tolerated resolution of the problems in either of two ways. The first approach involved a general scaling down of various competing claims of creditors and equity investors through relative reduction of their claims. The second approach involved allocating all or substantially all of the value of the enterprise to the top level or levels of creditors and also allowing a share to any class of equity investors that might be in a position to provide a special future benefit or might be able to obstruct or delay consummation of the reorganization. The first procedure was commonly followed in railroad and industrial reorganizations. The second procedure was typical of the real estate mortgage foreclosure reorganizations of the late 1920s and early 1930s. . . .

The *Boyd* case was generally understood to require that a class of juniors could not participate in the reorganized corporation (absent a contribution of new value) if a more senior class of claimants lacked proper participation. In 1939 the Supreme Court held in *Case v. Los Angeles Lumber Products Co.* that the *Boyd* doctrine was mandatory in section 77B proceedings (the predecessor of Chapter X). That decision necessarily implied that: (1) the value of the debtor's property and business first had to be ascertained; (2) the classes of claimants had to be arranged in proper order of priority, so that participation in the reorganized enterprise could be distributed to claimants in descending order of priority; and (3) all claimants below the level of available reorganization value would be excluded from participation in the reorganized enterprise.

II

The leading basis for attack upon the strict priority doctrine is that its premise of a valid and reliable valuation is specious or inflexible or illusory. In order to distribute the value of an enterprise among the various claimants, it is first necessary to fix the precise dollar value as of a given time. The usual valuation process involves making a projection of earnings (based upon past performance, foreseeable capital needs, and estimated revenues and costs) and then capitalizing earnings at an appropriate rate. Capitalization establishes the relationship between projected earnings and total present value. That value can be viewed as being 100 percent, and a level earnings stream can then be taken as a percentage of that total. For example, if the annual earnings of the business are deemed to constitute 20 percent of its worth, the earnings would be said to be capitalized at a 20 percent rate or on a five times earnings basis.

The relationship between total present value and estimated earnings is necessarily a matter of judgment. Some guidance may be found in comparisons with rules of thumb frequently used in the valuation of businesses and in the price-earnings ratios of securities traded in the public market. These determinations entail many uncertainties, assumptions, and conjectures. Any choice of capitalization rate necessarily involves many judgments concerning hazards, business stability, and future developments. It is difficult to adduce convincing "proof" to justify applying, say, a 5 percent rather than a 6 percent capitalization rate—or vice versa. Nevertheless, a 5 percent capitalization rate could result in a total value that would include a particular class of creditors as participants in the reorganization plan, whereas a 6 percent rate would result in a lower value that could exclude those creditors.

The valuation procedure always produces a dollars and cents figure. Although that figure looks mathematically exact, it actually reflects in a single number a whole series of highly conjectural and even speculative judgments concerning long-range business expectations and hazards as well as future social and general economic conditions. To exclude a class of creditors or investors from participation in a reorganization plan based upon so illusory a figure is criticized as capricious. The process is said to deceive by treating "soft" information as if it were "hard" and by cloaking predictions in the guise of mathematical certainty, under circumstances where consequences are drastic and final.

Dependency of the valuation process upon the future outlook as of a particular moment adds to this dissatisfaction. The resultant value figure is inextricably related to the then accepted set of expectations and assumptions. If the situation improves shortly after the reorganization proceedings have been terminated (so that the risk factor used in determining valuation may appear to have been too high and the valuation too low), the elimination of certain investors from participation in the plan might be regarded as having been unwarranted and unduly harsh. . . . [V]aluation is always subject to attack as evanescent . . . .

The imprecision of the valuation process has also led to the argument that valuation is so malleable that the entire process is perverse—that, in actuality, it is the reverse of what it seems to be. On this view, valuation is not an objective process by which projected earnings are capitalized to reach an ultimate figure under a procedure that has admitted infirmities. Instead, these critics assert, the trustees or the courts first determine the classes of claimants that should participate in the reorganization plan—on the basis of rough judgment or visceral reactions or other unexpressed or even unexpressible criteria—and then select the projection of earnings or the capitalization ratio necessary to reach a valuation figure that will include the preselected groups. The valuation process is not viewed as unduly harsh or rigid, but rather as so flexible that it is subject to abuse.

A second major criticism of the strict priority rule is that it frequently eliminates common stockholders from participation in the reorganized enterprise and thereby excludes the class of investments usually owned by management. . . . [M]anagement personnel may be unwilling to remain with the reorganized firm as employees if the common stock interest is wiped out in the reorganization. This is alleged to have an adverse effect upon operation of the reorganized enterprise, at least where management has something in the way of unique characteristics, specialized know-how, or other particular abilities important to the enterprise. . . .

A third but related criticism is that the strict priority doctrine unnecessarily fetters the court and the parties. Reorganization planners, it is said, should have greater freedom in negotiating an imaginative adjustment of various interests and should not be limited to determining participations pursuant to the strict priority doctrine. . . .

A fourth criticism is that the strict priority doctrine introduces unreasonable delay in the reorganization process by extending litigation over its proper application. . . .

The extension of litigation increases the cost of reorganization. . . .

In connection with its criticism of the strict priority doctrine, both the report of the Bankruptcy Commission and a recent article by one of its consultants regard the fundamental issue in a reorganization proceeding as the determination of who shall receive the difference between the enterprise's liquidation value and its higher reorganization value. Under the strict priority doctrine the total valuation of the enterprise goes to the claimants in order of their involuntary liquidation priorities. The Bankruptcy Commission and its consultant apparently agree that the liquidation value of the enterprise should be distributed to claimants in order of strict priority, but they submit that the difference between liquidation value and any higher reorganization value could be more properly handled in a different manner. . . .

One might ask why liquidation value should be discussed at all in a specialized proceeding in which liquidation is not contemplated. . . . By introducing the liquidation value concept as a separable item in the reorganization process and pursuing the analysis by asking how this segment of incremental value should be allocated, the central question of fairness is begged: a dubious assumption is treated as if it were an unassailable axiom. The assumption that the courts should not apportion the entire reorganization value among the interested parties in order of contractual priority implicitly attacks the core of the present concept of fairness in a reorganization. . . .

III

These criticisms of the absolute priority doctrine have given rise to a variety of suggested changes in the standard of fairness to govern reorganizations in bankruptcy. . . .

One type of proposal for relaxing the absolute priority doctrine seeks to adjust the weight given involuntary liquidation rights in a bankruptcy reorganization. . . .

Strict adherence to this liquidation standard would take into account only liquidation features of securities in measuring claims in reorganizations . . .

In reorganizations brought on by financial difficulties a standard that disregards liquidation claims is manifestly unfair in that it defeats important expectations: it in effect gives senior security holders, who bargained for specific protection in case of financial distress, smaller claims as the enterprise moves into a more precarious position. Once one retreats from this sweeping but unfair position, however, there is no obvious way to prescribe which rights should be measured by the liquidation standard and which by a going concern standard.

IV

Another type of proposal for relaxing the absolute priority doctrine would give the reorganization judge wide discretion to depart from it if he found that strict adherence would not be in the best interests of those it is intended to benefit. These suggestions generally stem from the complaint that reorganization proceedings are longer and more costly than necessary. . . .

The trouble with conferring this wide discretion on the reorganization judge is patent. A chief concern behind the adoption of the absolute priority doctrine was to prevent junior investors from gaining participation in a reorganized entity by trading on the nuisance value of otherwise worthless claims. Explicit authorization of judicial discretion would again legitimate and encourage that technique. . . .

The ultimate weakness in permitting this exercise of discretion relates to valuation. Although one might be able to value the nuisance participation given to juniors (and thus the cost to seniors), there is no way to value the benefit to seniors that derives from expediting the reorganization proceedings through a compromise. The value of an uncalled bluff or an unfulfilled threat is never ascertainable. . . .

. . . [T]he reorganization system cannot do without the ability to articulate why a deal is fair or reasonable from a business point of view. The potential for that exposition is a great strength of the absolute priority doctrine; its absence is a great weakness of any nebulous test based on a doctrine of "it looks all right to me." . . .

There is an obvious explanation for the recent coolness of the Bankruptcy Commission and certain commentators towards the absolute priority doctrine. Their main dissatisfaction may not be with the doctrine itself, but with the fact that rigid adherence to the doctrine is a major impediment in the path of another innovation: the development of a single procedural framework for handling all corporate readjustments under the Bankruptcy Act, merging Chapters X and XI into a unified new chapter. The real preference appears to be not so much a relaxation of the fairness standard as it is the replacement of the present bifurcated system. . . .

V

Another type of proposal for relaxing the absolute priority rule focuses on the interests of stockholders who are also managers of the company undergoing reorganization. . . . [T]hese proposals grow out of the historical relationship between Chapter X and Chapter XI. Both chapters originally contained the requirement that a plan of reorganization be "fair and equitable." The courts . . . were presented with the question of how compositions could be acceptable under the "fair and equitable" language of Chapter XI. . . .

The answer to the question was not long in arriving, and on the whole it has been both sound in theory and workable in practice. Chapter XI compositions between debtor and creditors can survive the fair and equitable test, even where the debtor is clearly insolvent, because the usual Chapter XI composition preserves values for the debtor that are not accessible to the creditors anyway. In the typical situation, the debtor is an owner-operator of the enterprise and the creditors are businessmen or financiers who can fend for themselves in negotiating compositions. According to the theory, something of value—whether it be called good will, know-how, or trade connections—inheres in the owner-operators of the distressed business, and this value would disappear if they were forced out of the firm or if the business were liquidated. Since that value cannot be captured for creditors, fairness is not violated if an arrangement under Chapter XI leaves that value in the hands of the owner-operators. . . . The corollary is that creditors are entitled to not less than they could realize through an immediate liquidation of the enterprise. This standard of protection has come to be regarded as reflecting the best interest of the creditors; in time the "fair and equitable" language in Chapter XI was replaced with an explicit "best interest of the creditors" test.

The answer does have one weakness and it has not gone unnoticed. . . . In some corporations undergoing Chapter XI reorganization, overlap between the shareholders and the operators of the business is not complete, and some of the creditors are not of the "fend for themselves" type. When there is substantial variance between stock ownership and management, a Chapter XI arrangement . . . would always seem to fail the absolute priority test. By and large this difficulty has been glossed over. . . . It would no longer be possible to disregard the underlying problem if Chapters X and XI were telescoped into a single framework.

To meet the problem, it has been proposed that shareholders be entitled to participation in a reorganized firm whenever they contribute value to the enterprise as managers. . . . On initial impression this proposed change seems to be a logical extension of the old Chapter XI notion that value inhering exclusively in the owner-operators of a corporation cannot be considered as value available to creditors. The extrapolation is, however, not free of difficulty. . . .

The approach also requires measuring the "non-monetary" contribution that specific shareholders make to the enterprise. . . . The "best interest of the creditors" test circumvented this difficulty: in a "proper" case, part or all of the value in excess of liquidation value could (at least in theory) be claimed by the shareholders through a composition. . . . But this is not the case when the "going concern" value inheres in only some of the shareholder-managers. . . .

It was noted earlier that the Bankruptcy Commission and certain commentators have argued that, as a general principle, distribution of the going concern differential (reflecting the difference between immediate liquidation value and value as a reorganized concern) should be a proper subject for negotiation and division between shareholders and debt-holders in reorganizations. The weakness of this argument now emerges. When reorganization value falls short of total creditor claims, shareholders should have no equity in the firm and should be cut out unless the going concern differential inheres in the particular shareholders as irreplaceable operators of the business and not merely as holders of common shares. . . .

One might appropriately ask whether there are situations in which stockholders make special contributions to a corporation as owners rather than as managers. . . . [I]n all cases the special equities urged by these stockholders should be ignored. Contributions of this kind are impossible to quantify; their existence is likely to be tenuous or debatable; and they are least deserving of compensation in terms of sound notions of fairness. All the vices of nuisance claims can accompany their recognition as a legitimate ground for participation in reorganizations. . . .

It has also been repeatedly urged that one good reason to include old shareholders in a reorganization is that they may constitute the only available source of additional capital for the enterprise. This contention may have had a basis in fact at an earlier date. Current data do not support the belief that old shareholders are a fruitful source of additional funds when the public capital markets are unlikely to provide funds. . . .

VI

The most common type of proposal to modify the absolute priority doctrine is to relax the finality of the reorganization valuation. These suggestions rely on a deceptively simple argument. Valuation determines the classes of claimants that can participate in the reorganized entity. The process of arriving at a valuation by capitalizing estimated earnings involves prediction founded on much guesswork. . . . The contention is that it is only fair to arrange at the outset for a squeezed-out class to come back into the enterprise if the future is markedly better than predicted in arriving at the initial reorganization valuation.

By now the shortcoming in this line of thought is quite familiar: the future just might be worse than predicted. Proper valuation takes into account the probabilities of falling short of predictions as well as of exceeding them. The participating classes that receive equity interests in the reorganized corporation or debt securities with fixed interest rates take the risk in both directions. To require them to share good fortune with an excluded class while demanding that they bear the full burden of bad fortune would provide them with less than full compensation for their claims. . . .

VII

The starting point for a summary assessment of proposals to modify the absolute priority doctrine is the proposition that the doctrine serves primarily to (1) set limits on direct and indirect negotiations among those who have invested in an enterprise, and (2) structure those negotiations within a framework that facilitates judicial review of the results. All proposals to alter the doctrine can be assessed in terms of their potential impact on these functions.

Proposals to base the measurement of claims on the going concern value of securities instead of on their liquidation priorities need not affect the process of valuing the enterprise, the pace of the reorganization proceedings or the reviewability of the reorganization plan. . . . The major and decisive infirmity is that this change would undermine a crucial aspect of the bargain embodied in the senior securities: as corporate financial conditions worsened and the seniors were most in need of the default protection for which they had bargained, the change would reduce the magnitude of their claims and hence their participation in the reorganized enterprise.

Proposals to authorize judicial discretion to approve "good business deals" or to recognize nuisance claims, so that reorganizations may be expedited, would undercut the very essence of the absolute priority doctrine. They would give junior classes playing cards they now lack and to which they are not now entitled . . . .

Proposals to allocate to the shareholder-manager group all or some of the going concern value—meaning the excess of reorganization value over liquidation value—could greatly expand the permissible limits of negotiation. Old shareholders, especially those associated with operation of the enterprise, would be encouraged to dredge up a large variety of benefits they arguably could confer on the firm. . . .

Proposals to authorize contingent participations for junior classes wholly or partially excluded from unconditional participation in the reorganized enterprise would likewise expand the boundaries of permissible negotiations and further reduce the possibility of effective control through judicial review. It seems most unlikely that a rational system could be developed for determining the proper magnitudes for contingent participations. In practice conditional participations would probably reflect rough compromises, producing results similar to arrangements that recognize the nuisance value of worthless junior claims.

Taken together, these observations suggest that there is no persuasive case for relaxing the doctrine under the existing structure of Chapter X. The doctrine as it now stands and operates, however, would not be fully compatible with a statutory change of the type proposed by the Bankruptcy Commission, replacing Chapters X and XI with a single framework for both corporate reorganizations and compositions. . . .

A unified framework requires a basic choice in its design: a determination whether the strict priority doctrine or a composition standard is to apply has to be made near the beginning of each reorganization; or, in order to preserve a function for the strict priority rule, one or more of the modifying proposals has to be adopted, even though doing so may seriously weaken the doctrine. . . . The total impact of unification on strict priority should be a major factor in determining whether the procedural advantages of unification outweigh its substantive costs.

The following excerpt from 1977 House Report briefly explains the modification to the absolute priority rule effected in the 1978 Bankruptcy Code. Under the new law, absolute priority as to full reorganization value could be waived by senior classes. The baseline entitlement for every creditor (irrespective of class vote) was to receive at least liquidation value (under the "best interests" test of § 1129(a)(7)). But the spread between that liquidation value and going-concern value was open to negotiation between classes, and absolute priority would not be enforced in a fully consensual plan. Only if a senior class dissented would absolute priority be enforced.

H.R. Rep. No. 95-595
95th Cong., 1st Sess. (1977)

Chapter 5. Reorganizations

II. THE FINANCIAL STANDARD

The premise of the bill's financial standard for confirmation is the same as the premise of the securities law: parties should be given adequate disclosure or relevant information, and they should make their own decision on the acceptability of the proposed plan or reorganization. The bill does not impose a rigid financial rule for the plan. The parties are left to their own to negotiate a fair settlement. The question of whether creditors are entitled to the going-concern or liquidation value of the business is impossible to answer. . . . [N]egotiation among the parties after full disclosure will govern how the value of the reorganizing company will be distributed among creditors and stockholders. The bill only sets the outer limits on the outcome: it must be somewhere between the going-concern value and the liquidation value.

Only when the parties are unable to agree on a proper distribution of the value of the company does the bill establish a financial standard. . . . [T]he bill requires that the plan pay any dissenting class in full before any class junior to the dissenter may be paid at all. The rule is a partial application of the absolute priority rule now applied under chapter X and requires a full valuation of the debtor as the absolute priority rule does under current law. The important difference is that the bill permits senior creditors to take less than full payment, in order to expedite or insure the success of the reorganization.

Valuation is at the heart of any dispute over the division of reorganization value under the absolute priority rule. But making such a valuation is fraught with uncertainty. In the following passage from an excellent article dealing with a myriad of bankruptcy valuation issues, Fortgang and Mayer quote a federal judge who neatly highlighted the impossibility of making a precise valuation.

Chaim Fortgang & Thomas Moers Mayer
Valuation in Bankruptcy
32 UCLA L. REV. 1061 (1985)[*]

The SEC used to begin its Chapter X valuations with a quote from *Consolidated Rock Products Co. v. Dubois* to the effect that valuation of a business in bankruptcy "requires a prediction as to what will occur in the future, an estimate, as distinguished from mathematical certitude, is all that can be made." This cautionary note can be applied to most valuations in bankruptcy. We leave the last word to Fred M. Winner, the recently retired district court judge whose unreported valuation of King Resources Company in Chapter X remains something of a landmark in valuation analysis. . . . Judge Winner rendered a decision in the spirit of *Consolidated Rock Products*. He concluded:

> With all of these things, to say that you can forecast—that you can appraise the values in the Canadian Arctic is to say that you can attend the County Fair with your crystal ball, because that is absolutely the only possible way you can come up with a result.
> . . .

> My final conclusion ... is that it is worth somewhere between $90 million and $100 million as a going concern, and to satisfy the people who want precision on the value, I fix the exact value of the company at the average of those, $96,856,850, which of course is a total absurdity that anybody could fix a value with that degree of precision, but for the lawyers who want me to make that fool estimate, I have just made it.

The Tenth Circuit affirmed.

Professors LoPucki and Whitford made a monumental contribution to bankruptcy scholarship with their massive study of megacases. Of great interest and significance is their analysis of the extent to which the absolute priority rule is not adhered to in those large cases. They report a systematic deviation from absolute priority, but only in relatively small amounts. Under the 1978 Code, Congress empowered senior claimants to give up value to juniors, and at least in large cases it appears that invitation has been accepted. Standard practice is to throw equity a bone, even when it is plainly out of the money. Insistence on strict compliance with absolute priority is quite rare in these monster cases. Similar findings were reported in Lawrence A. Weiss, *Bankruptcy Resolution: Direct Costs and Violation of Priority of Claims*, 27 J. FIN. ECON. 285 (1990), and Allen C. Eberhart et. al., *Security Pricing and Deviations from the Absolute Priority Rule in Bankruptcy Proceedings*, 45 J. FIN. 1457 (1990). In another thoughtful article, *Preemptive Cram Down*, 65 AM. BANKR. L.J. 625 (1991), Professors LoPucki and Whitford suggest that equity's unwarranted leverage should and could be eliminated in obvious insolvency situations via a "preemptive" cram down order.

Lynn M. LoPucki & William C. Whitford
Bargaining Over Equity's Share in the Bankruptcy Reorganization of Large, Publicly Held Companies
139 U. PA. L. REV. 125 (1990)[*]

This Article reports some of the results of an empirical study of the bankruptcy reorganization of large, publicly held companies. We present data relevant to what many consider to be the central issue of reorganization theory—how the value of the reorganizing enterprise should be divided among the various claims and interests. We demonstrate that there is indeed systematic deviation from the absolute priority rule in favor of junior interests; but, with respect to large, publicly held corporations, the debate about how to prevent these deviations is, for the most part, a tempest in a teapot—the difference between absolute priority and the actual outcomes of these cases is relatively small. . . .

V. THE TERMS OF SETTLEMENT: INSOLVENT DEBTORS

Our primary focus in this Article has been on distributions to unsecured creditors and shareholders. We were able to calculate a dollar value for these distributions for all but two of the cases in our study . . . . Table III reports these figures for the thirty companies that were insolvent at the time of plan confirmation. We classified a company as "insolvent" if the total value of the distributions to unsecured creditors and shareholders was less than the estimated claims of the unsecured creditors. Table III orders the cases by the percentage of claims paid to unsecured creditors.

Table III
Insolvent[a] Debtors: Adherence to the Absolute
Priority Rule

(1) Name of Case	(2) Percentage Paid on Unsecured Claims	(3) Distribution to Equity (in Millions)	(4) Total Distribution Unsecureds and Equity (in millions)	(5) (3) as% of (4)	(6) Equity Committee Appointed
Seatrain Lines	0.5%	$ 0	$ 1.4	0	No
MGF	1.1%	0	2.0	0	No
Towner	2.5%	0	3.2	0	No
Air Florida	3.1%	0	6.0	0	No
Braniff	4.9%	1.7	35.4	4.9%	Yes
Amarex	7.8%	0	18.5	0	No
Oxoco	9.5%	0.4	11.2	4.0%	No
Technical Equities	11.0%	0	6.6	0	No
Sambo's	11.0%	0	unknown	0	No

---

(1)	(2)	(3)	(4)	(5)	(6)
	Percentage Paid on Unsecured	Distribution to Equity	Total Distribution Unsecureds and Equity	(3) as%	Equity Committee
Name of Case	Claims	(in Millions)	(in millions)	of (4)	Appointed
Dreco	11.7%	6.5	11.2	57.7%	Yes
NuCorp	13.4%	0	39.2	0	No
McLouth	18.2%	1.4	27.2	5.1%	No
Pizza Time Theatre	20.0%	0.5	23.0	2.2%	No
Crystal Oil	23.9%	3.9	52.7	7.5%	No
Evans Products	26.5%	0	2.4	0	Yes
Combustion Equip	27.7%	0.4	37.4	1.0%	Yes
Energetics	29.9%	3.0	14.5	20.8%	No
Tacoma Boat	29.6%	2.5	40.7	6.1%	No
Towle	35.6%	1.0	20.4	5.0%	Yes
FSC	37.6%	1.9	40.2	4.8%	Yes
Cook United	38.7%	2.3	28.1	8.1%	Yes
Marion	40.4%	0.9	60.9	1.5%	Yes
Saxon	41.2%	8.2	140.2	5.8%	Yes
Baldwin-United	54.3%	20.0	259.1	4.8%	Yes
White Motor	60.9%	4.7	178.4	2.6%	Yes
KDT	62.6%	3.2	42.6	7.4%	No
Anglo Energy	64.6%	4.6	99.5	4.6%	Yes
Itel	64.9%	18.2	652.8	2.8%	No
HRT	68.5%	5.7	84.9	6.7%	Yes
Wickes	81.6%	63.0	1,100.4	5.7%	Yes

. . . Three observations are apparent from Table III. First, though each of these companies was insolvent, in twenty-one of the thirty cases, creditors agreed to allow shareholder recoveries ranging from $400,000 to $63 million.

Second, of the nine cases in which equity received nothing, eight were cases in which unsecured creditors recovered less than 14% of their claims. . . .

Third, in the cases in which creditors received more than 14% of their claims, there was no obvious relationship between the percentage of claims recovered by creditors and the size of the distribution to equity. . . . Certainly it is not possible to conclude that as the size of the distribution to unsecured creditors increased, the proportionate distribution to equity increased as well. . . .

VI. THE TERMS OF SETTLEMENT: SOLVENT DEBTORS

Table IV(A) shows the values distributed to creditors and shareholders in the cases of solvent debtors. The second column of Table IV(A) shows the value available for distribution to unsecured creditors and shareholders as a percentage of the allowed claims owing to unsecured creditors at the time of the filing of the petition. . . .

. . . The third and fourth columns show how the value available actually was apportioned between shareholders and creditors. Comparison of columns 2, 3, and 4 shows that when a company was only marginally solvent, equity holders were able to capture a substantial portion of the creditors' entitlements. Column 5 indicates the dollar amount of "shortfall" to creditors resulting from lack of enforcement of the absolute priority rule. Column 6 shows the total dollar value recovered by equity holders.

Table IV (A)
Solvent Debtors: Deviation From The Absolute Priority Rule

(1) Case Name	(2) Cents per Dollar of Unsecured Claims Available	(3) Cents per Dollar Paid to Unsecured Creditors	(4) Cents Captured by Equity	(5) Unsecured Creditor Shortfall (in millions)	(6) Equity Holder Recovery (in millions)	(7) Equity Committee?
Am Int'l	100.3	86.1	14.2	$37.4	$38.5	No
Charter	104.1	86.3	17.8	58.2	91.2	Yes
Lionel	112.5	85.6	26.9	20.7	38.6	Yes
Manville	131.0	125.3	5.7		132.9	Yes/No
Penn-Dixie	134.6	96.8	37.8	.6	7.5	Yes
Revere	136.6	92.7	43.9	11.1	83.7	Yes
Storage Tek	145.6	130.5	15.1		117.2	No
Smith Int'l	151.1	107.1	44.0		159.7	Yes
Salant	157.0	96.5	60.5	2.2	37.5	Yes
Wilson Foods	205.9	104.7	101.2		59.6	No
Continental	262.1	114.3	147.8		441.7	No

CONCLUSION

. . . The data reported here bear on what many consider to be the central issue of reorganization theory: how the value of the reorganizing enterprise should be divided among the various claims and interests. . . .

First, bargaining and settlement rather than adjudication determined the outcomes of the cases in our study. . . . [A] contested cram down against shareholders was a rare event. . . .

Second, shareholders of insolvent companies nearly always shared in the distribution under the plan. . . . With one exception, equity was "zeroed out" only in cases in which creditors were receiving less than fourteen cents on the dollar. Though equity regularly shared in the distribution in these cases, equity's share almost invariably was small when measured as a percentage of the total distribution. . . . [T]he relative size of equity's recovery appeared to be not so much a product of the financial conditions of the company as it was a product of the quality and aggressiveness of equity's representation.

Third, in the cases of insolvent debtors, the observed deviations from absolute priority were not to any significant degree the product of difficulties in valuation. In nearly every case, the negotiators knew the company was insolvent and that equity would be entitled to nothing in an adjudication. Equity was allowed to share in the distribution for a wide variety of reasons. Central among them was a generalized desire to have a consensual plan—one supported by the debtor, the official committees, and major creditors. Part of the reason for seeking such a plan was a concern that equity might make trouble if there was an attempt to exclude it. Yielding to such a fear was easier for creditors because the cost of a distribution to equity was spread among so many creditors that the portion borne by each one was too small to justify resistance. To a large degree, however, the preference for a consensual plan rather than an adjudication was a matter of legal culture. Although these cases were spread throughout the United States, most of the lawyers who played key roles in them were members of the same legal community. They could expect to be involved in future cases with their current adversaries and were to various degrees dependent on those adversaries for professional respect and advancement They were not entirely free to ignore the conventional wisdom that consensual plans were the responsible, appropriate means for accomplishing reorganization and that despite the absolute priority rule, everyone at the bargaining table was entitled to a share.

Fourth, in the cases in which the debtor was marginally solvent, there were substantial deviations from the absolute priority rule, leading to a kind of "equitable sharing" between creditors and equity holders. In part, this sharing was a product of perceived difficulties with valuation. . . . [A]ggressive representation seemed to yield big rewards for equity holders.

Fifth, in the cases of clearly solvent debtors, claims for pendency interest highlight an important ambiguity in the absolute priority rule: does the rule require that creditors have absolute priority over shareholders only for the face amounts of their claims or should the time value of the creditors' money also be protected? . . . If we assume that creditors are entitled to pendency interest at full market rates, then in only one of our solvency cases did creditors receive full payment. In that sense, it truly can be said that the overall pattern in the cases of both solvent and insolvent debtors was an "equitable sharing" of the loss between creditors and shareholders.

. . . With regard to the bargain over equity's share in the distribution, while the dollar amounts of the deviations in favor of equity are large, for the most part they are only a small percentage of the overall distribution in these cases. Many perceive these deviations as the "grease" that permits complex and otherwise unwieldy cases to reach relatively expeditious conclusion. . . . [P]articipation in these cases by junior claims and interests clearly not entitled to a share under the absolute priority rule may generate unnecessary complexity and expense and encourage obstructionist tactics. The "preemptive cram down" that we propose should permit the bankruptcy courts to limit these deleterious effects.

Professors Douglas Baird and Tom Jackson have been among the leading analysts of the bankruptcy scene since the enactment of the Code. The following article is a superb critique of the essence of and practical and conceptual problems connected with the absolute priority rule. In this short excerpt, they explain how the core problem is one of bargaining. The best approach, they posit, is to identify the residual owner, and, while limiting agency problems in representing the residual owner, to ensure that the negotiations are controlled by the residual owner. Baird and Jackson suggest that the "freeze-out" scenario in which an intermediate class is eliminated by a senior class relinquishing value to equity is not obviously problematic, and they question whether the strict prohibitory rule against such a freeze-out enunciated in the *Boyd* case is defensible.

Douglas G. Baird & Thomas H. Jackson
Bargaining After the Fall and the Contours of the Absolute Priority Rule
55 U. CHI. L. REV. 738 (1988)[*]

. . . We focus on a narrow category of firms in economic trouble. Many cases do not present difficult bargaining problems. . . .

. . . Harder cases, however, arise when the firm, although insolvent, is worth keeping intact as a going concern and an existing owner is a peculiarly well-positioned source of capital, supplies, or expertise to the firm or otherwise has the ability to strike a deal that gives it a better position than its preexisting position in the ownership hierarchy entitles it to. The problem is most stark when the firm is worth less than what the most senior creditor is owed and the senior creditor has reason to recombine with the old shareholder. The effect of the recombination would be to freeze out an intermediate creditor.

It might seem that the intermediate creditor has little to complain about. The senior creditor is entitled to exercise its default rights. . . . If . . . the remaining assets of the firm prove to be worth less than what is owed the senior creditor, the effect of the original deal the firm struck with its creditors is that the senior creditor gets those assets, and the intermediate creditor gets nothing. One can argue that intermediate creditors have lost nothing when the senior creditor exercises those rights and then decides to share the assets it thereby acquires with the old shareholder.

Under this view, the senior creditor, having the exclusive right to the firm's assets following foreclosure, should be able to convey an interest in them to anyone it pleases. That it is willing to share those assets with the old shareholder suggests that it sees advantage in doing so. Perhaps the shareholder will bring new capital when no one else will. Perhaps the shareholder has firm-specific skills that the senior creditor wants to preserve. The old shareholder is acquiring an interest because the senior creditor has concluded doing so is in its interest, not because of the old shareholder's pre-existing status. . . .

In *Northern Pacific Railway v. Boyd* [228 U.S. 482 (1913)], however, a sharply divided Supreme Court struck down a transaction that froze out an intermediate class of owners while granting some ownership rights to former shareholders. The Court held that any restructuring of the firm must take note of the intermediate creditors. . . . The basic lesson of *Boyd* . . . is that leaping over an intermediate class triggers special scrutiny. This is the crucial feature of the absolute priority rule that we want to focus on because it is central to the problem of renegotiations in bankruptcy.

Given our characterization of this problem, it is not at all clear why passing over an intermediate class is objectionable. We have described any recombination of a senior creditor with the old shareholder as consisting of two separate steps: a foreclosure on the assets by the senior party that is followed by a recombination of those assets with the old shareholder for a reason of the senior creditor's choosing. *Boyd*, however, rests on a different description of the transaction: The old shareholder starts with an ownership interest in the firm that is subject to the claims of its general creditors. She then strikes a deal with the senior creditor, and immediately finds herself with an ownership interest in the same firm that is free of those claims.

Sharply different initial conclusions follow from this vision of the transaction. The general creditors may not have been entitled to anything if all the firm's assets were converted to cash today, but a recapitalization is occurring, not a dismemberment of the firm. Where the firm contin-

---

ues, the general creditors, but for the restructuring, might have something of value that the restructuring takes away and gives to the shareholder. Even though the firm will likely not be able to pay off the secured creditor, the possibility that the firm will do much better than expected makes the general creditors' right to reach the assets of the firm before the shareholders worth something.

The general creditors' objection is not to the senior creditor's right to foreclose and sell the firm as a going concern. . . . Their objection instead goes to the shareholder's recapture of an interest in the firm. Under this argument, the general creditors should be able to object if the old shareholder recovers something over which the general creditors have a prior claim and does so by means of a transaction in which the general creditors have no voice.

Viewed this way, the general creditors should be able to prevent the old shareholder from engaging in a transaction that freezes out the interests of the general creditors while leaving something for the old shareholder. It is not enough for the shareholder to strike a deal with the senior creditor in order to keep an interest in the firm. The shareholder must also strike a deal with the general creditors, as they have the right to enjoy the firm's potential revenues before the shareholder. . . .

An understanding of the absolute priority rule, then, must turn on choosing between two radically different ways of viewing the same transaction. From one perspective, the transaction is viewed as a proper foreclosure, followed by a recombination between the senior creditor (or other buyer of assets) and the old shareholder (who is making some contribution to the firm that entices the senior creditor, or other buyer, to share its assets with the old shareholders). From the other perspective, the transaction is viewed as a conveyance that, by preferring holders of equity interests over creditors, violates the payout norms implicit in the debtor-creditor relation. . . .

II. THE RESIDUAL OWNER AND THE FREEZE-OUT PROBLEM

. . . As a general matter, the residual owner of the firm is entitled to negotiate on behalf of the firm. The residual owner is given the power to bind the firm because the residual owner stands to have the right set of incentives. The dollar that is won or lost because of good or bad negotiating by definition is felt by the residual owner. In a solvent firm, the shareholders are the residual owners, and the managers of the firm typically act with their interests in mind.

Identifying the residual owner, however, is more difficult in the cases in which the *Boyd* rule is likely to be invoked. The firm that is reorganizing is typically insolvent. In the case that we focus on throughout this paper, if all future possibilities were collapsed to present values, the senior creditor would be entitled to the entire firm. In this sense, the senior creditor is the residual owner of the firm. But, in the absence of a default, everyone's ownership interest has value. There is always a possibility that the firm's assets will be worth more—and its liabilities less—than expected. That possibility makes the reorganization case different from the typical solvent firm in which the residual owners are the shareholders and the shareholders are the decision makers.

Bargaining after the fall should be conducted by the residual owner of the firm, even if in the original capital structure others are junior to it. Even if the freeze-out problem were a genuine one—that junior owners were able because of valuation problems or any other reason to retain their ownership interests at the expense of those senior to them—the rule in *Boyd* is exceedingly unlikely to be worth the costs that necessarily accompany it. The solution to bankruptcy's bargaining problems lies elsewhere. . . .

We would argue that the only difficulty peculiar to bankruptcy in any of these cases lies in the problems associated with identifying the residual owner and establishing a mechanism that allows the residual owner to bargain effectively. In many cases, the residual owner may be not a single senior owner, but rather a large group of general creditors, not all of whom can be identified. The trustee in bankruptcy acts on their behalf, but like any other agent the trustee represents the interests of the principal imperfectly. Moreover, under existing Chapter 11, the interests of the residual owners continue to be represented by the old managers. The agency cost problems are apt to be especially acute.

To the extent that our critique of *Boyd* is right, the law of corporate reorganizations should focus on identifying the residual owner, limiting agency problems in representing the residual owner, and making sure that the residual owner has control over the negotiations that the firm must make while it is restructuring. Except for the changes in residual ownership that are themselves the occasion for the restructuring, the rules governing these negotiations should be the same as those that exist even when a financial restructuring is not taking place.

One of the best law review articles ever written on bankruptcy came from the pen of Professor Jack Ayer. One leading academic told the editor of this Anthology that "the one law review article I wished I had written" was Ayer's *Michigan Law Review* article on absolute priority and new value, which follows. Ayer wrote in the wake of the Supreme Court's decision in the *Ahlers* case [485 U.S. 197 (1988)], in which the Court held that a farmer's proposed contribution of labor did not suffice as "new value" sufficient to satisfy the "new value exception" to the absolute priority rule—*if* such an exception existed at all, which the Court questioned in passing! Professor Ayer engages in an extensive historical assessment of the development of the absolute priority doctrine, and identifies two distinct strands—one statutory, and one constitutional. One of Ayer's core insights is to link the two lines. Ayer then proceeds to explicate the origins, nature, and meaning of the "new value" doctrine. In doing so Ayer questions whether there even can *be* a new value rule—or indeed ever *was*. In sum, he concludes that "the new value doctrine . . . is highly evanescent." His masterful work also points to institutional confusion and hesitation at work in both the Congress and the Supreme Court. In the final analysis, he suggests a lack of any "controlling theory" and states the ultimate "rule" as follows: "Congress can give the debtor leeway, but not too much." Perhaps that is as good a rule as any, he concludes.

John D. Ayer
Rethinking Absolute Priority After Ahlers
87 MICH. L. REV. 963 (1989)[*]

I. INTRODUCTION

There was no evident reason why the Supreme Court granted *certiorari* in *Norwest Bank Worthington v. Ahlers*. It can be conceded that the issue was important: in the midst of an agricultural depression, a farmer was trying to hang onto his farm without paying the full amount of his bank debt. The farmer argued that he ought to be able to do so because he was offering to contribute "new value" beyond what he was obliged to contribute—specifically, his efforts as a farmer.

The Eighth Circuit held, in effect, that he could do so and the Supreme Court (as became apparent) thought the Eighth Circuit was wrong. But these facts alone hardly justify Supreme Court intervention. By common understanding, the Eighth Circuit decision was a maverick. The issue was,

---

on its face, statutory only. If the Supreme Court had any role, the obvious choice was simply to order summary reversal. The Court chose instead to address the issue head-on.

Now, the decision having been rendered, it is still not obvious just what the Court had in mind. The Court did reverse the Eighth Circuit—just as it might have in summary reversal. . . . [B]y all appearances, the Court rendered judgment with an opinion which purports to add nothing to the law as it has been understood for fifty years. One is necessarily led to speculate as to just what the fuss was all about. It could be that the justices made a mistake: that they thought they saw an issue where in fact there turned out to be none. It could be that they wanted to head off a spasm of judicial sympathy for debtors in the farm belt.

Or it could be anything. Speculation of this sort, in the absence of hard evidence, is necessarily futile. What is not futile, however, is an effort to understand the *Ahlers* opinion itself, which remains a force to contend with in Supreme Court bankruptcy jurisprudence. And the opinion is important in at least two ways. First, the opinion offers a striking insight into the way the Court approaches bankruptcy law—which conceptual tools it chooses to use, and which it chooses to ignore. Specifically, it is remarkable just how narrowly the justices defined the issue before them— how completely they chose to make it an issue of statutory construction only, resisting or ignoring any possible constitutional tincture.

Of greater practical interest is the Court's handling of the problem of new value. . . . [I]t appears that the Court, advertently or otherwise, at least sharply restricted the use of the new value rule in future cases. Even more intriguing, a review of *Ahlers* in context raises a question as to whether there ever was a conceptual basis for the new value rule, at least as conventionally understood.

Both of these points require a fairly extensive sojourn into history. For *Ahlers* is a case with a past, as well as a future. Thus, in Part II, I sketch the history of the absolute priority doctrine. I undertake to show also how the Supreme Court had available two very different paths to its result—one constitutional, one statutory. And I offer a few thoughts on the relationship between the two. In Part III, I address myself directly to the new value rule. I try to show that it is a rule whose parentage is at best questionable. I also try to give an account of what a new value rule might look like. In that context, I suggest that Justice White may have invalidated any new value rule that did exist, and indeed, that there may never have been any adequate basis for such a principle.

II. ABSOLUTE PRIORITY

A. Ahlers *on Absolute Priority*

On its face, *Ahlers* is simply a case of a farmer struggling to keep his farm. . . .

FLB and Norwest objected to confirmation, relying on the so called absolute priority rule. . . .

. . . The Eighth Circuit . . . reasoned that there is a "modification" to the absolute priority rule that would allow the Ahlerses to participate in the plan. Specifically, the Ahlerses might participate if they contributed something to the reorganized enterprise "that is reasonably compensatory and is measurable"—the so-called new value principle. In a 2-1 decision, the court held that the Ahlerses' "farm operation and management skills" constituted new value. . . .

The Supreme Court granted *certiorari*, on the absolute priority question only. A unanimous Supreme Court, Justice White writing, reversed. Justice White's opinion can be tightly summarized. He held that the Ahlerses' promise of future labor did not justify an exception to the absolute priority rule. But for a fuller appreciation of his rationale, it is useful to identify four separate points in the opinion, as follows:

First: Justice White accepted as binding the principle of absolute priority as codified in the Bankruptcy Code. . . .

Second: Justice White accepted, for purposes of analysis, that there is a new value exception to the absolute priority rule. . . .

Third: Justice White found that the Ahlerses' "labor, experience and expertise" were not a sufficient contribution to permit them to keep their farm. . . . Justice White thus treated the case as "analogous" to *Case v. Los Angeles Lumber Products Co.* . . .

Finally, Justice White rejected one more of the Ahlerses' arguments. . . . [T]he Ahlerses argued that the Bank wasn't being deprived of anything because the Bank was getting all it could have gotten for the farm in liquidation. Thus, the interest they wished to retain had no value to the Bank. Justice White identified and rejected this "no value" theory, as he called it. . . .

B. *Our Two Laws of Absolute Priority*

The first remarkable fact about *Ahlers* is its doctrinal posture. The court . . . treated it as a problem under the absolute priority rule, developed in a well-known series of cases and crystallized in Bankruptcy Code section 1129(b)(2)(B). I shall label this the "statutory" line of cases. While this is a perfectly legitimate way to approach the issue, there is a wholly separate body of doctrine . . . . This separate body of doctrine treats the problem as involving the taking of property, governed by the due process clause of the fifth amendment to the Constitution; I shall label this the "constitutional" line of cases.

The Court in *Ahlers* never even considered this constitutional line . . . . Additionally, the courts (and the commentators with them) have always kept these two lines of authority in separate, watertight compartments with only trifling seepage between the two. Trifling as it is, this seepage links these divergent principles.

1. *The Statutory Line*

The first point to be understood about the "statutory line" is that it is not "statutory"—or at best, is statutory only incidentally and belatedly. To Justice White, the issue in *Ahlers* turned on the language of the Bankruptcy Code. But the Code's language must be read under layers of case law that run back more than 100 years.

The early history of the absolute priority rule has been told before and can be quickly recapitulated here. The rule arose in the context of the equity receivership. The equity receivership, in turn, is bound up with the building of the railroads. From the Civil War until World War II, investors repeatedly built railroads that could not generate operating revenues sufficient to service their debt. . . .

This *modus vivendi* collapsed during the Great Depression under the weight of the investor protective legislation implemented by the New Deal. Those regulatory changes have become so pervasive that they are almost part of the air we breathe. To understand the absolute priority rule, it is necessary to recognize that it emerged first as a primitive pre-statutory effort to regulate receiverships in the judicial process.

In the chronicle of case law, the critical juncture is *Northern Pacific Railway Co. v. Boyd*, decided 5-4 by the Supreme Court in 1913. Boyd was a general creditor of the Northern Pacific Rail*road*. The "Road" asserted that it was not liable, in that all of its property had been transferred (via receivership) to the Northern Pacific Rail*way*. Boyd then sued the Railway, which, of course, claimed that it was insulated in that it had purchased the assets via a bona fide receivership. But by the Court's account, the receivership sale was in fact a transfer engineered by the old bondholders and stockholders from themselves and to themselves, "squeezing out" the intermediate unsecured debt. The Court held that such a sale cannot defeat the claim of a nonassenting creditor. As against him the sale is void in equity, regardless of the motive with which it is made. . . .

The decision sent chills of terror down the spines of the corporate reorganization bar. . . .

In any event, absolute priority thereafter passed into the language and lore of the corporate lawyer. But ingrained practice seems to have proved stronger than writ, as reorganization lawyers developed elaborate schemes to circumvent or emasculate the rule. Thus, counsel developed the practice of getting the reorganization court to bless the deal, with the intent of barring later objections. . . .

That was the situation as it stood when the Supreme Court decided *Case v. Los Angeles Lumber Products Co.* in 1939. The facts of *Case* are simple: the debtor holding company had liabilities of $3.8 million and held a subsidiary that owned the Los Angeles Shipyard and Drydock—an asset valued at $830,000. The plan was to cancel old securities and issue new ones in their place. Some twenty-three percent of the new securities would go to the former stockholders. Both lower courts confirmed the plan, but a unanimous Supreme Court reversed.

The case is both historically and doctrinally important. In terms of political history, the case marks a milestone in the career of Justice William O. Douglas, who wrote the opinion for the unanimous Court. Douglas had served on the Court less than a year at the time of the decision, having come from the chairmanship of the Securities and Exchange Commission. At the SEC, he was one of the principal architects of the New Deal corporate law reforms, and one of the authors of Chapter X of the Bankruptcy Act. His opinion adopts much of the substance of an *amicus* brief filed by the SEC.

As an instance of decisionmaking strategy, the case is noteworthy because it is the first major absolute priority case in which the Court interprets a statute. And indeed, Justice Douglas' interpretation has become so rooted in the culture of the law that it is a surprise to note just how attenuated it is. For the statute—Bankruptcy Act, Section 77B, the precursor of Chapter X—nowhere states that claims must be paid by a principle of absolute priority. Instead, Justice Douglas deploys a provision in subsection (f), which provides that a plan must be "fair and equitable." These words, Justice Douglas writes, "are words of art which prior to the advent of Section 77B had acquired a fixed meaning through judicial interpretations in the field of equity receivership reorganizations." Strictly speaking, this is poppycock, and Justice Douglas knew it. None of the Supreme Court's absolute priority cases used that particular phrase in that particular way. . . . On the other hand, the question was at least open, and it was reasonable to infer that the drafters intended to import at least some kind of absolute priority rule into Section 77B.

But what kind of rule? Substantively, the remarkable fact about *Case* is that over ninety percent of all bondholders had accepted the plan. Justice Douglas held that this fact was "immaterial on the basic issue of its fairness." The only possible inference was that this time, the Supreme Court meant business.

. . . [T]he Court soon made clear that the "fair and equitable" language also applied under the superseding Chapter X. The Court also articulated one further principle necessary to make the absolute priority rule work in practice. Thus, in *Consolidated Rock Products Co. v. Du Bois*, the Court held that in order to apply the absolute priority rule, a finding as to the value of the reorganized enterprise must be made. . . .

The Court thus established absolute priority as the ruling principle in Chapter X. That would have finished the story (until the coming of the Bankruptcy Act of 1978) except that Chapter X was not the only pre-1978 source of reorganization law. Rather, there were—indeed there long had been—two separate strains of reorganization law, existing side-by-side in uneasy harness. One evolved from the law of equity receivership and crystallized in Chapter X, as just described. The other grew out of the common law remedy of composition, whereby creditors and debtor together agree to "compose"—or scale down—the debtor's debts. A common law composition might be binding on all creditors who agreed to it, but it was not binding on dissenters. . . . In 1938, Congress acknowledged this tradition by embodying it in Chapter XI of the Chandler Act.

The line between "compositions" and equity receiverships had never been clear, but a vulgar oversimplification, adequate for present purposes, is that the composition cases involved small businesses and face-to-face dealings between owner-managers, on the one hand, and vendor-creditors, on the other. The receivership cases, by contrast, involved publicly-traded, mortgage-backed debt and limited-liability corporations. Perhaps more important, the cases emerged from different cultures, each habituated to its own way of going about its task. No one can be certain of the influence that the competing principles of equity receivership and common law composition had upon the development of absolute priority doctrine. It is safe to conclude, however, that each laid an independent foundation for the ultimate bankruptcy structure.

. . . For our purposes, the important point is this: This absolute priority rule had never been a principle of composition law. Quite the contrary, the point was that a creditor might be bound to anything he agreed to in a composition. . . .

The difficulty was that Chapter XI as drafted included the "fair and equitable" standard which Justice Douglas, construing Chapter X in *Case*, read to mean absolute priority. It took an amendment to the Bankruptcy Act, striking the phrase "fair and equitable" from Chapter XI, to solve that problem. . . .

Against this background, Congress adopted the Bankruptcy Code of 1978. The Code clearly adopted a modified absolute priority rule, but it is crucial here to grasp not only what Congress did, but what it chose not to do. The fountainhead of learning that underlay the 1978 Code was the *Report of the Bankruptcy Commission*, filed in 1973. The Report proposed to emasculate substantially the absolute priority rule. Specifically, it would have given broad powers to the reorganization court to leave a stake with the old equity owners even though claims were not paid in full and it would have invited the court to fudge the question of value. . . . Additionally, it would have permitted individual debtors or shareholders to participate in any event, if the court found that they would make an "important" contribution to the reorganized enterprise.

The Commission proposal met with adverse criticism in the law reviews, and in due course Congress abandoned it in favor of the present scheme. That present scheme, in effect, adopts the absolute priority rule as a "default" or "off-the-rack" standard, but permits waiver by consent. It provides that any individual may block confirmation unless he gets at least what he would get in liquidation. Subject to this limitation, it provides that a plan may be binding on any class of creditors if it is accepted by more than half in number, and at least two thirds in amount, of that class.

That is the state of the "statutory" branch of absolute priority doctrine at the adoption of the Bankruptcy Reform Act of 1978. . . .

2. *The Constitutional Line*

a. Radford *and the* Wrights. The following discussion traces the constitutional history of the absolute priority rule from the time of its birth to its apparent demise during the New Deal, and its reputed reappearance six years ago. Central to the discussion is the relation of absolute priority to the takings clause of the fifth amendment. . . .

. . . This branch is rooted in the recurrent war between the Supreme Court on the one hand and Congress or the states on the other, with the Court policing supposedly undesirable economic legislation. "Debtor relief" legislation, however defined, intensifies this conflict; witness the repeated challenges to the constitutionality of debtor relief laws during the Great Depression.

The central episode is the case of *Louisville Joint Stock Land Bank v. Radford*. The Court had to consider the Frazier-Lemke Act, a farm mortgage relief bill passed by Congress in 1934. Frazier-Lemke offered farm debtors a five-year moratorium on foreclosure, with the power to buy the farm property at its "appraised" value—*i.e.*, below the debt. . . .

. . . Speaking for a unanimous court, Justice Brandeis held the Act unconstitutional as a denial of the creditor's property right, guaranteed under the fifth amendment. . . .

Complicating the political dynamic was the fact that *Radford* was announced on "Black Monday"—May 27, 1935, the day that also saw the invalidation of two other initiatives, both central to the New Deal. In this charged climate, Congress almost immediately undertook to revise Frazier-Lemke; a new version won approval just three months later, on August 28. . . .

This time in *Wright v. Vinton Branch of Mountain Trust Bank* ("*Wright I*") the Court, again speaking through Justice Brandeis, unanimously upheld the Act. *Wright I*'s facts were distressingly familiar. Wright mortgaged his farm to the bank. The bank undertook to foreclose, and he filed for relief under Frazier-Lemke II. . . . But early on, Justice Brandeis carved out some room to maneuver in evaluating the revised Act. "It was not held," he declared, "that the deprivation of any one of these rights would have rendered the Act invalid, but that the effect of the statute in its entirety was to deprive the mortgagee of his property without due process of law." Translated, this means: Frazier-Lemke II does violate at least one of the five rights enumerated in *Radford*, but we are going to uphold it anyway. . . .

. . . There is undoubtedly room for argument over the clarity and consistency of the doctrine created by *Radford* and *Wright I*. But there can be no doubt that the opinion is a Brandeis tour de force. Frazier-Lemke II was different from Frazier-Lemke I, particularly insofar as it gave the creditor the power to demand a sale. But the fact is that, under both versions, the creditor was barred from foreclosure for long periods of time, during which the debtor remained in possession, obliged to pay over no more than what the property, after necessary expenses, would yield.

The suspicion is that the Court had not so much seen the light as felt the heat. This was, by any measure, one of the most explicitly "political" periods in the history of the Court. Two relevant events intervened between *Radford* and *Wright I*. One was President Roosevelt's landslide reelection in 1936, where he carried all but two states. The other was the advent of President Roosevelt's campaign to finesse a hostile judiciary by enlarging membership on the Supreme Court, memorialized in history books as the "court-packing plan."

Roosevelt began the campaign with his message to Congress on February 5, 1937, recommending the reorganization of the judicial branch. The Supreme Court decided *Wright I* less than two months later, on "White Monday," March 29, 1937. For the Court it was a period of repentance on many fronts.

Further decisions undercut *Radford* still more. In *Wright v. Union Central Life Insurance Co.* ("*Wright II*") the Court had occasion to speak on the constitutionality of the "extension" aspect of Frazier-Lemke II; it found the extension provision was constitutional. . . .

Finally, one year later, in *Wright v. Union Central Life Insurance Co.* ("*Wright III*"), the debtor sought to purchase the property at its appraised value; the secured creditor sought to insist on his right of sale. . . . Justice Brandeis had made it clear that the presence of the right of sale was a critical distinction between (constitutional) Frazier-Lemke II and its (unconstitutional) predecessor. The Court in *Wright III*, this time speaking through Justice Douglas, conceded that there was a right of sale in Frazier-Lemke II. But Justice Douglas pointed out that the right of sale and the right of redemption appeared to trump each other. In that event, Justice Douglas said, the debtor wins. He said Frazier-Lemke II provided "safeguards" to protect the value of the secured creditor's interest in the property. He stated: "There is no constitutional claim of the creditor to more than that."

b. *The constitutional doctrine of absolute priority today.* In *Wright III*, Justice Douglas drew the teeth from Justice Brandeis's analysis; when the dust settled, debtors and creditors found themselves pretty much where they were before the Court decided *Radford*, given that one would have concluded in 1940 that the *Wrights* overruled it

Today, can we conclude that because *Ahlers* was entirely "statutory," lacking any trace of *Radford*-based constitutional doctrine, that the constitutional branch is dead? The answer seems to be "no": The constitutional branch is not dead; it is only sleeping—and sleeping rather fitfully, at that. . . .

Constitutional doctrine? Who needs it! All it brings is trouble and strife. This analysis gains plausibility from the insight that the facts of *Ahlers* are, after all, far closer to *Radford* than they are to *Case*. . . . [S]ilence alone does nothing to justify constitutional agnosticism. In fact, there are good reasons for believing that constitutional absolute priority doctrine is alive and ready to rise again. . . .

Radford, however emasculated, has never been expressly overruled. Quite the contrary; just recently *Radford*, in the hands of then Justice Rehnquist, has proven to have an extraordinary vitality. Justice Rehnquist used *Radford* to build his argument. . . . [I]n . . . *United States v. Security Industrial Bank*, decided just seven years ago, *Radford* played a critical motivational role, like the ghost of old King Hamlet, who makes a sinister entry to get the action going and then remains as a haunting presence throughout the rest of the drama. . . .

This is all very well as far as it goes, but it ignores the fact that this is essentially the same process the Court later validated in the two *Wright* cases. The only obvious difference is that the "nominal" moratorium term was five years in *Radford* but only three years in *Wright I*. Justice Rehnquist doesn't mention that fact. Indeed, he doesn't cite any *Wright* case, or give any hint that *Radford* has been substantially defanged. . . .

c. *The demise of property as possession.* Aside from its significance in its own right, the *Radford-Wright* group of cases stands as a chapter in a larger chronicle concerning the Supreme Court's treatment of "property rights" in debtor-creditor cases. . . . The history of Supreme Court bankruptcy doctrine discloses a trajectory, however halting, toward "monetizing" the claim of the secured creditor. This involved, first, breaking the nexus between "property" and "possession," and, second, establishing that what the secured creditor "owned" was not a particular piece of property but a claim to a particular sum of money, however defined.

Wright III is the keystone of this arch, holding that the secured creditor has a right to no more than payment of his claim or the value of his collateral, whichever is less. . . .

Insofar as these cases break the nexus between possession and property, they find their modern exemplar in *United States v. Whiting Pools*, where the Court ordered the Internal Revenue Service, as a repossessing creditor, to return collateral to the bankruptcy estate. Insofar as they represent the idea of "monetizing" the secured claim, the logic of these cases is woven into the fabric of the present Bankruptcy Code.

d. *Other constitutional strategies.* . . . [T]he Court encountered a variety of debtor-relief problems employing an almost embarrassing array of strategies. . . .

. . . There must be some constitutional limitation under the bankruptcy clause, however, as a matter of logical necessity; else Congress could do anything it wished, simply by purported to invoke the bankruptcy power. On the other hand, the Court was never successful in finding any important limitation in the bankruptcy clause, and it has been no more so lately. . . .

. . . In any event, taken together, the Court's Depression-era bankruptcy cases represent a striking variety of efforts to articulate a theory to control debtor-creditor law. Today, the scope of bankruptcy clause powers remains a mystery; there must be some constitutional fences around the bankruptcy clause terrain, but they lie beyond current judicial horizons. Nevertheless, Congress certainly cannot do whatever it pleases under the rubric of the bankruptcy clause. . . . The foregoing discussion of the various other constitutional constraints dramatizes the morass created by constitutional judicial review of bankruptcy legislation. Under the circumstances, it is perfectly understandable that the Court would wish to steer safely clear of the Constitution and decide cases on statutory grounds; witness *Ahlers*.

3. *Summary—The Two Lines*

It requires no extensive analysis to recognize that the "statutory" doctrine of absolute priority, whose centerpiece is *Case v. Los Angeles Lumber Products*, addresses the same problem as the "constitutional" line, where *Radford* is the centerpiece. In each case, the ultimate question is whether the equity owner can retain the collateral without discharging all of his debts. *Case* and *Radford* are alike, of course, insofar as they answer that question negatively. But it surely is a matter worthy of remark that they do it with so little recognition of each other. *Case*, in particular, reveals no hint that there is any "constitutional" overtone to its doctrine. . . .

. . . [W]hy did the "statutory" and the "constitutional" approaches proceed as if in separate universes? What accounts for this discontinuity, whereby the Court creates two parallel bodies of law on the same topic? Several possibilities present themselves. Perhaps they are simply different cases that require different strategies. . . . This cannot be rejected completely, but there is less merit to the proposition than might appear at first glance. Justice Douglas presents *Case* as being statutory only, but, as argued above, this is done largely with smoke and mirrors. . . . A second and more intriguing possibility is timing. *Radford* was decided in 1936, *Case* in 1939. By conventional understanding, 1937 is the year of the great doctrinal watershed in Supreme Court thinking—the year of the Roosevelt Court-packing bill, the year of Justice Roberts' apparent retreat, the year the Court ultimately abandoned its commitment to economic due process. By this reading *Radford* stands on one side, and *Case* on the other, of the great divide.

The retreat from economic due process might explain why Justice Douglas in *Case* insisted on a narrow statutory result for what was, after all, an ambitious intrusion into bankruptcy law: he could have all the satisfaction of economic interference with none of the doctrinal embarrassment. . . .

Focusing on these decisions in terms of doctrinal history has a surprising bonus, in that it explains why Justice Brandeis laid such stress on the ideology of property rights in *Radford*. At first glance, this is surprising because virtually every prior inquiry into the limits of the bankruptcy power had turned on the bankruptcy clause. . . .

. . . [T]here is at least one additional, perhaps even more plausible, explanation for the discontinuity between *Radford* and *Case*. That is, the two bodies of doctrine grew up in two separate legal cultures: two different sets of lawyers who dealt with two different kinds of clients. They didn't attend the same summer camps or play on the same volleyball teams, and no one told them that they were addressing what was, economically, the same kind of case.

III. The New-Value Rule

A. *Stating the "Rule"*—Case *Reprised*

Questions as to the existence of a new value rule and its form make sense only insofar as there is an absolute priority rule—after all, if there is no such rule, there is no need for a new value corollary because junior interests that would normally be precluded from participating in the organization could do so without the need to contribute new value. Therefore, the place to begin the search for a new value rule is in the lore of the absolute priority rule—particularly in the opinions of Justice Douglas . . . . Justice Douglas in these cases did more than just reaffirm (or declare) the absolute priority doctrine. He also went a long way toward setting out its contours and limits. Thus, for example, in *Case v. Los Angeles Lumber Products Co.*, Justice Douglas held that the absolute priority rule of Section 77B could not be overridden by a mere majority vote of creditors. In *Consolidated Rock Products Co. v. Du Bois* he articulated the Court's holding that in order to implement the absolute priority rule, the reorganization court must make a finding as to value. More important for present purposes, in *Consolidated Rock*, expanding on *Case*, he spelled out just how that valuation should be made. Specifically, he stated that valuation for purposes of the absolute priority rule should be made on the basis of the normally higher "going concern" value rather than the normally lower liquidation value. . . .

The full import of this rule becomes apparent in *Marine Harbor Properties, Inc. v. Manufacturers Trust Co.*, another opinion by Justice Douglas. . . . It was conceded that the property was worth less than the amount necessary to satisfy the first mortgage debt. The creditor started a state court foreclosure proceeding, and the debtor filed a Chapter X case. The court of appeals ordered dismissal . . . . The Supreme Court affirmed the dismissal. . . . [I]n this case, the debtor was unable to show sufficient "need for relief." Justice Douglas based this analysis squarely on the absolute priority rule. Only mildly restated, his reasoning was that because the property was worth less than the senior debt, there would never, under the absolute priority rule, be anything left for juniors. The same result would obtain in state foreclosure anyway, so there was no reason for the reorganization court to take jurisdiction. Under this logic, the equity owners of the debtor can never keep anything in a reorganization unless they pay the prior claims in full. For debtors, this considerably reduces the attractiveness of a statute like Chapter X. And that would explain why Justice Douglas, going back to *Case,* was so insistent on trying to make room for the new value rule.

B. *Articulating the New Value Rule*—Kansas City Terminal

This analysis provides a basis for understanding why Justice Douglas, in *Case,* embraced the new value principle so enthusiastically. . . . The old shareholders sought to justify their continued participation by offering "their familiarity with the operation" of the business and their "financial standing and influence in the community," together with "continuity of management." This contribution, they argued, justified their continued participation.

Conceivably Justice Douglas, in rejecting this plea, might simply have shown that there was no new value rule under the absolute priority standard of Chapter X. Or he might have left the issue open, arguing that whether there was a new value rule or not, it didn't fit this case. But he did neither. Quite the contrary, he embraced the new value principle with seeming enthusiasm and undertook to spell it out in some detail. . . .

Justice Douglas relied for this proposition on one previous case from which he quoted liberally, *Kansas City Terminal Railway Co. v. Central Union Trust Co. of New York.* To understand fully what Justice Douglas was up to in *Case, Kansas City Terminal* deserves a careful reading, for, in fact, it stands for less than Justice Douglas made of it.

Kansas City Terminal was a classic equity railroad reorganization. . . .

. . . The point is to make clear why it is not surprising that Justice McReynolds gave a muddled answer to the new value issue. The point is that he started with a muddled question, or questions. Given this muddle, Justice McReynolds repeatedly contradicted himself in his analysis. . . . [H]e took away with one hand what he gave with the other.

Thus, as part of his general discussion, Justice McReynolds offered language which seemed to acknowledge the absolute priority rule. . . . But Justice McReynolds didn't stop there. Instead he asserted that reasonable adjustments should be encouraged. . . .

But what was there to cooperate about or adjust? Either absolute priority is the rule, or it is not. . . .

The gist of this analysis is that Justice McReynolds' opinion in *Kansas City Terminal,* while it does indeed contain intimations of an absolute priority rule and also of a new value exception, is equivocal at best, and can be read as supporting something quite different. All this is captious or fanciful in the absence of evidence that the opinion was actually (mis)read this way. . . .

The point of all this is that neither of the cases taken as seminal for the new value doctrine can be read as an application of the new value doctrine. *Kansas City Terminal* "states" it, but in a self-contradictory manner, and accepts the ruling of the lower court when that court chose not to apply it. *Case* "states" it well enough (indeed, one is tempted to say that Justice Douglas understood Justice McReynolds' opinion far better than Justice McReynolds understood it himself) but then refuses to apply it on the particular facts. One gets the distinct impression that the real purpose of "restating" *Kansas City Terminal* with such force in *Case* was to take the sting out of what was otherwise a fairly radical interpretation. Only Justice White's opinion in *Ahlers* subsequently recognized the new value rule. But to assert that Justice White recognized the rule stretches a point, because he specifically refused to commit himself on whether any new value rule remains in the Code. On the other hand, *Case* and *Kansas City Terminal,* which Justice White recognized as the fountainheads of new value doctrine, didn't apply it either. . . .

C. Ahlers *on New Value*

Ahlers poses a two-fold issue: (1) whether there is a new value exception and, if the answer is "yes," then (2) whether the Ahlerses' farming efforts constitute sufficient new value to protect them from the absolute priority rule. For the moment, it is useful to restrict ourselves to the first of these questions—whether there is a new value rule.

1. *New Value After the 1978 Bankruptcy Code*

. . . The Supreme Court refused to find that the new value rule has been abolished, ruling instead that Ahlers' efforts would not in any event constitute sufficient new value under the rule. Justice White wrote that "our decision . . . should not be taken as any comment on the continuing vitality of the [new value rule]." . . .

2. *New Value Case Law in the Lower Courts* . . .

3. *New Value and the Going Concern*

Later in the opinion, Justice White addressed another argument which he treated as separate from the new value analysis, but which, as we shall see, may be closely related to it. The debtors argued that "the property which the [debtors] wish to retain has no value to the senior unsecured creditors." . . . According to this view, the debtors' retained equity interest in the farm would have value only in their hands, and thus their interest could never detract from the value properly accorded to senior claims.

Justice White rejected the argument. . . .

Justice White joined "with the overwhelming consensus of authority" in rejecting the "no value" argument. For the moment, it is probably useful to note that the "no-value" argument seems to involve two separate issues: one is the question of who may enjoy the "going concern premium" in a Chapter XI case; the other is whether one can ever impute different "values" to the property in the hands of different parties. Just about everyone talked about the new value issue as if it involved the going concern premium. It is better understood as involving the second, more abstract, question. Thus, the court of appeals explicitly treated the matter as a controversy over "going concern" and "liquidation" values. . . .

This may be attractive as a pragmatic matter, but the court of appeals was simply wrong. In fact, this issue was vigorously debated in the development of the current Bankruptcy Code. . . . [T]he act adopted contains no such provision.

The difficulty with this "going concern premium" approach is that it is, as a matter of history at least, conceptually irrelevant to the new value argument. Justice Douglas, who insisted that there was indeed a new value exception to the absolute priority rule, also formulated the principle that the creditor in an old Chapter X case had the right to the entire going concern premium.

D. *Can There Be a New Value Rule?*

Recall that in *Ahlers*, the Solicitor General argued that the new value rule had been "repealed" by the adoption of the new Chapter XI, but the Court refused to rule on the issue. But close scrutiny of the opinion yields two surprising inferences. First, Justice White may indeed have "overruled" the new value exception, whether he intended to or not. And second, new value may have been an illusion all along—or less dramatically, there may never have been an adequate doctrinal basis for the new value rule, as articulated by Justice Douglas. . . . But a careful reading of *Ahlers* together with *Case* and its kin, suggests that they may never have been well founded.

Consider the following example. John Debtor is president and majority shareholder of Debtorco, a closely-held corporation. . . . The balance sheet of Debtorco thus looks like this:

Assets	Liabilities	Shareholders' Equity
$85	$100 (Loanco secured debt)	(-$ 65)
	$ 50 (trade creditors)	

In behalf of Debtorco, John Debtor proposes the following plan: Debtorco will give Loanco a note with a present value of $85 secured by all the assets of Debtorco, satisfying Loanco's secured claim. The $15 deficiency on Loanco's secured claim will be grouped with the $50 worth of trade debt into a single class of unsecured claims. Debtorco proposes to satisfy the claim of this class by a single cash payment of $10. The $10 payment for unsecured creditors will come from John Debtor, who will make the payment in exchange for new shares. All old Debtorco shares will be canceled, and all creditors holding unsecured claims vote on the plan. All except Loanco vote in favor; Loanco votes against. May the plan be confirmed? On the information given, the answer would appear to be clearly "yes," except for a question over the $10 payment, which I shall address below. . . .

Thus, on all points discussed here, the plan would appear to be confirmable. And so we turn to the presence of new value—the contribution from the shareholder. But here is the problem: What is it that the shareholder purports to be "buying" with his $10? The obvious answer has to be the residual equity in the company. But the balance sheet after confirmation, and before the $10 contribution, looks like this:

Assets	Liabilities	Shareholders' Equity
$85	$85	$ -0-

Given that no one would pay $10 for a company with a net worth of zero, then the offer of a $10 payment has to be taken as an "admission" that the company is worth more than $85. But if it is worth more than $85, then Loanco's secured claim is undervalued, and Loanco is not being fully compensated on that secured claim. That being the case, cram-down is not available, and the plan may not be confirmed.

The same logic forbids confirmation at any valuation until Loanco either (a) consents or (b) receives full value for its claim. . . .

In the abstract, it might be possible to argue that there is more than one "value" that may be relevant to a bankruptcy case, and that a court might, without inconsistency, impute one "value" to the creditor's interest and another to the debtor's interest in the same property. From the standpoint of doctrine, however, there is a difficulty in that this is precisely the argument that Justice White seems to have rejected in *Ahlers*—specifically, when he rejected the so-called "no value" argument, summarized above. To recall, the Ahlerses had argued that they should be permitted to retain their farm because the creditor had been deprived of nothing of value. Justice White roundly rejected this argument . . . . Restated, this seems to mean that anything retained by the debtor must be "value" for purposes of Section 1129(b). If that is the case, then there is no basis for letting the shareholder participate on the basis of new value. If this is true, then at least it is the case that the new value strategy is impermissible under the new Code. But it seems that under the same theory, new value was impermissible under Chapter X as well. The difficulty is that in applying the absolute priority rule under Chapter X, it is clear that creditors had the right to the entire "going concern value" of the business. We have this on the authority of no less an arbiter than Justice Douglas himself. . . . But if the going concern value belongs to the creditor and not to the equity owners, then it is impossible to imagine what there can be for the equity owners to "buy." And if there is nothing for the equity owners to buy, then the new value rule, just as it does not exist under Chapter XI, did not exist under Chapter X. At first blush, the point may seem frivolous: after all, Justice Douglas, who insisted that the creditors owned the going concern value, also insisted on the new value rule. But recall: Justice Douglas in *Case* did not implement the rule, nor did he in *Marine Harbor Properties*, nor did he ever implement the new value rule, at least not under Chapter X. What he did in *Case* was to take an older, well-nigh unintelligible decision, handed down before the absolute priority rule had truly crystallized, and dress it up in respectable garments, where it served to dignify the absolute priority pronouncement. In order to understand this, it is desirable to take one more look at the cases, and to identify those instances where the new value principle has in fact been applied.

E. *Applying the Rule*

1. *Pre-1978, Under Chapter X*

The courts apparently applied the new value rule under old Chapter X. There appears to be no reported case in the entire period in which the court expressly permitted the "debtor," or former equity owners, to retain assets on the strength of a new value contribution and for no other reason. But the fact is that Justice Douglas' supposed "exception," born of the confusion of the *Kansas City Terminal* opinion and matured in *Case v. Los Angeles Lumber*, is nowhere present as a rule of decision in Chapter X cases. New value under Chapter X, then, is an illusion.

2. *Post-1978, Under Chapter XI*

Under Chapter XI, unlike Chapter X, a handful of cases purports to apply the new value principle, but they are instructive in their own way. In particular, the genesis of new value doctrine under the 1978 Code represents a remarkable instance of doctrinal circularity, where law was created out of nearly nothing. . . .

3. *Some Comparisons*

Lest the point be forgotten, it is important to emphasize again that Justice White in *Ahlers* treated the issue as statutory only, rejecting any suggestion of a constitutional taint. . . .

. . . [W]hile there may be no clear support for the new value principle in old Chapter X, it seems clear that it was available under Frazier-Lemke, as interpreted by the Supreme Court in *Wright III.* . . .

The same can be said about both Chapter XII and Chapter XIII of the present Bankruptcy Code. In each case, the Code permits the debtor to retain property that might otherwise go to creditors, even where creditors are not paid in full. . . .

F. *What Is New Value?*

There remains one issue central to *Ahlers* not directly addressed in this article so far. In a way, it is the most visible issue of all: Should the Ahlerses' "contribution" of their efforts constitute new value? Discussion of the issue in the context of this article is somewhat unreal, of course, because if there is no new value at all, it makes no sense to ask whether a thing does, or does not, constitute new value. Nevertheless, a discussion of the Court's approach to the new value problem may help to explain just why the concept is so elusive.

The court of appeals enthusiastically embraced the idea that the Ahlerses' work constituted new value sufficient to let them keep the land. . . .

Justice White, refusing to recognize the contribution as value, put the case within the ambit of *Case v. Los Angeles Lumber Products*. . . . But the "differences" between *Case* and *Ahlers* are more than trivial. . . . Although Justice Douglas did not articulate it, the tenor of his opinion indicates that he did not believe that this constituted any "contribution" at all, either of new value or otherwise. . . .

By rejecting the "labor" argument, Justice White thought he was bringing himself within an unbroken tradition. . . .

He was following the lead of counsel here, but, strictly speaking, he was wrong. . . .

However, saying that *Ahlers* is different from *Case* is not the same as saying that *Ahlers* was wrongly decided. In saying the "value" in *Ahlers* was not sufficient, there were at least two approaches available to the Court. One . . . is to question whether the Ahlerses were bound to anything or whether, by contrast, they were undertaking to buy an option. To understand this point, consider what would have happened if the plan had been confirmed and the Ahlerses had decided not to follow through. What sort of remedy would the creditors have had against them? It is hard to identify a situation where any meaningful remedy would have been available. . . . This fact obviously impressed Justice White when he spoke of the contribution of future services as "intangible, inalienable, and, in all likelihood, unenforceable."

The second approach is to try to identify just what the Ahlerses' "contribution" might be . . . . Both the court of appeals and the Supreme Court seem to have assumed that there was some sort of "going concern" value that would not be realized in "liquidation." But it is not clear that this is so. Quite the contrary, it would seem that there is every reason to assume that another farmer could operate the farm as well as *Ahlers*. If that is the case, then whatever "value" a farmer's efforts might have is already reflected in the value of the farm. If this is true, then what is the point of discussing new value at all? An answer could be that the "value" in *Ahlers*, is the product of human capital, exempt from bankruptcy administration, except when explicitly included. . . .

IV. Conclusion: The Meaning of *Ahlers*

In this article I have tried to put *Ahlers* in the context of history and doctrine, showing that the new value doctrine, tested in *Ahlers* is, at best, highly evanescent. I have also shown how the Court, while skirting constitutional doctrine, has characteristically avoided putting the problem in any such framework, and Congress seems to have felt comfortable imposing results that are at least superficially inconsistent. Thus I have suggested a lack of controlling "theory" in this realm. On the other hand, I have not tried to supply any such theory, nor do I lament the possible absence of one. The effort to articulate "theory" for bankruptcy and kindred subjects is certainly alive and well, but theorizing requires theoretical justification. And at least in this realm, Congress and the courts have proven uniquely resistant to pressures to organize their work under any grand design. Their reasons for resistance may be better than our instincts might first suggest: once burnt, twice shy, might do for starters. Or more generously, the work product of both the courts and Congress may bespeak a conviction that bankruptcy law is too complex for facile categorization. Taken in context, the teaching of *Ahlers* may be: Congress can give the debtor leeway, but not too much. Properly understood, that may be a good enough rule until a better one comes along.

Professor Bruce Markell published an insightful analysis of the absolute priority rule and the new value doctrine in the following article in the *Stanford Law Review*. In the excerpt included here, Markell proves that the new value principle and the absolute priority rule as traditionally understood are in fact *equivalents*. Thus, the supposed new value "exception" is an "ephemeral exception"—*i.e.*, no exception at all. How does Markell show this equivalence? Having established equivalency, Markell then explains the most important consequences that flow from that recognition. He then moves to a reconsideration of owner participation in light of absolute priority and new value, drawing on auction theory. He visualizes an owner bid as one possible bid in an auction process. Necessarily, to have meaningful bidding, the owner's exclusive right to terminate a plan must terminate once the owner proposes a new value plan. Importantly, Markell's insights and suggestions formed much of the conceptual basis for the National Bankruptcy Review Commission's recommendation on absolute priority, which follows. His inspiration also is seen in the approach taken by the Supreme Court in *Bank of America National Trust and Savings Association v. 203 North LaSalle Street Partnership*, 526 U.S. 434 (1999), where the Court turned away a new value plan that was had not been subjected to a market test or independent bidding, but was propounded while the debtor retained exclusivity.

Bruce A. Markell
Owners, Auctions, and Absolute Priority in Bankruptcy Reorganizations
44 STAN. L. REV. 69 (1991)[*]

III. THE EPHEMERAL EXCEPTION: NECESSARY NEW VALUE . . .

B. *The Ephemeral Exception*

1. *The equivalence of new value and absolute priority.*

Confusion over the absolute priority rule is deplorable, especially when the rule is fundamental to reorganization. The basic problem is that the use of the term "exception" to describe new value principles is a catachresis. The conditions required to satisfy the new value "exception" also satisfy the absolute priority rule.

Recall the requirements for the new value "exception" as set forth in *Case*: "[W]here the debtor is insolvent, the stockholder's participation must be based on a contribution in money or money's worth, reasonably equivalent in view of all the circumstances to the participation of the stockholder." . . .

. . . The court's inquiry under *Case* is disarmingly simple. First, the court measures the owners' proffered contribution against a quality scale. If the contribution possesses the requisite quality, that is, if it is equivalent to money or money's worth, then *Case* requires a second and more interesting inquiry. Will the "old stockholders . . . receive in return a participation reasonably equivalent to their contribution"? This test appears to require two simple valuations: that of the proffered contribution and that of the interest received. The application of the test then consists of comparing the two to see if they are reasonably equivalent. This comparison, however, also requires the valuation of at least one more item: the debtor itself. . . . This introduction of the debtor's value, however, leads to the realization that application of *Case*'s dicta yields the same result in all cases as does application of the absolute priority rule to the same facts. For all practical purposes, the two are equivalent.

This can be seen from a simple example. *Case*'s dicta requires that an owner's contribution be reasonably equivalent to the interest retained. In the most common example, this means that if an owner seeks to retain a 100% interest in the debtor, then she must contribute property reasonably equivalent to the debtor's postconfirmation value.

But postconfirmation value is not the price that a third party would pay for a debt-free company. Although this is the starting point, such value must reflect reductions from that debt-free value equal to the amount of obligations incurred or continued in the reorganization plan. For example, if a company which is otherwise worth $200 incurs $150 of debt in its plan of reorganization, then its postconfirmation value will reduce to $50.

Case would seem to require the owner in this example to pay $50 for the debtor's equity. But if creditors receive nothing more than the $150 in reorganization debt, the reasonable equivalence requirement is not met. The contribution of $50 raises the post-confirmation value to $100.[179] If no further value is given to creditors, the owner will have purchased the debtor for $50 less than its

---

[179]   This number is derived by adding the original $200 in reorganization value to the $50 cash contribution, and then subtracting the $150 of reorganization debt. The sequence assumes that the owner will contribute only if her plan is confirmed, which, given the uncertainties of confirmation, is probably reflective of actual practice.

post-confirmation value. The only way to balance the equation, and achieve reasonable equivalence, is to force the transfer of the $50 contribution, directly or indirectly, to the creditors.

If creditors receive the extra $50, then they will have received $200, or the amount of pre-confirmation reorganization value. At one level, this is only fair. Postconfirmation value in an insolvent debtor exists only to the extent that creditors' claims are discharged. Cast a different way, creditors participate in a reorganization based upon their antecedent debt, but owners participate only on the basis of new value.

At a more important level, using *Case* to force creditors to receive an amount equal to reorganization value is trivial. The absolute priority rule itself requires that creditors participate in a reorganization in an amount equal to the lesser of their claims or the debtor's reorganization value. In an insolvent debtor, this means that creditors of an insolvent debtor are entitled to property equal to reorganization value. . . . *Case*'s new value standard yields the identical result.

The interplay of these relationships means that any contribution of money or money's worth permits owners to retain ownership so long as creditors receive property equal to the debtor's reorganization value. This result obtains, regardless of whether the inquiry starts with the absolute priority rule or *Case*'s dicta. In one sense, this is all the creditors could expect. . . . Moreover, this value probably represents the maximum amount a third party would pay for the debt-free reorganized company. Regardless of expectations, however, creditors will receive the same amount under the absolute priority rule as under the new value principles.

2. The consequences of equivalence.

Recognizing the equivalence between absolute priority and new value principles has critical implications for the relative roles of owners and creditors in business reorganizations. First, owners of an insolvent debtor need not contribute anything to the reorganization if their plan allocates all reorganization value to creditors. This means that once their plan allocates all reorganization value to creditors, owners are not at risk for anything other than their original risk capital. Their obligations as owners end. To require otherwise would violate the nonbankruptcy concept of limited liability. . . . As a corollary, owners who do not wish to bid for their debtor may simply walk away, leaving the remains of the debtor to creditors. . . .

Equivalence also has harsh consequences for owners. Allocation of all reorganization value to creditors in the form of reorganization debt leaves a truly valueless residual equity interest. In such circumstances if owners retain the equity interest, confirmation of the reorganization plan may be difficult, if not impossible, without some contribution of additional value. The owner . . . must show that the postconfirmation debtor will not need "further financial reorganization." . . . In short, business needs, not creditor claims, dictate the need for owner contributions.

Equivalence highlights a deeper problem: defining and determining value. If absolute priority is satisfied, creditors will receive all reorganization value, leaving a valueless entity. If an owner nonetheless desires to contribute more, then the owner appears irrational. A rational owner would not invest in a worthless company. But if owners are acting rationally then there must be *some* value they hope to capture by their contribution. If so, *Boyd* requires that this value be allocated to the creditors, not purchased by the owners in a transaction in which the creditors do not participate.

The apparent irrationality arises only if we believe that there is one fixed value upon which all parties agree. The setting of value is not so precise. Reorganizations do not have the benefit of a fluid and functioning market. As a consequence, in valuing the debtor, participants—including courts—rely upon educated guesses. . . .

Owners, if they are risk-taking entrepreneurs, may perceive a debtor's value differently than risk averse creditors. Nonoperational reasons, such as tax incidents of ownership or sentimentality, which increase the allure of continued ownership, may also shape owners' perceptions of value. In any of these situations, owners may be willing to risk additional personal capital to preserve their preferences and perceptions and thus rationally buy a debtor at a price which others believe exceeds the debtor's net worth.

Owners who have higher private values, and who act upon them, either seek to preserve values irrelevant to creditors, or simply choose a value higher than that acceptable to creditors for the creditors' continued participation. In neither situation is it necessarily the case that owners are arrogating to themselves value that could be transferred to creditors if creditors simply extinguished their debt in exchange for all of the equity interests in the debtor.

If owners as a group do have different perceptions of value, they may be willing to bid for the debtor when others will not. This consequence carries with it the possibility of abuse. Owners can bid low and seek to bluff creditors as to reorganization value. If creditors fail to call this bluff, then owners walk away with value that does not rightfully belong to them. Although owners may be able to set the initial reorganization value, their use of that value should be subject to inspection and overbid by creditors or others whose own valuations may be influenced by owners' initial positions. As a result, the procedural protections developed in *Boyd* and *Case* become relevant. . . .

IV. Owner Participation Under the Code . . .

B. *New Wine in Old Bottles: A Proposal for Fair Owner Participation* . . .

3. *The preservation of new value concepts.*

. . . Viewing plan confirmation as an auction provides the first step in analyzing the role of the owner, and a basis for rethinking *Case*. A new value plan is simply a bid in the auction for control of the reorganized debtor, proposed by holders of prepetition interests, which leaves some class paid less than in full, and which does not require creditor consent. Any other plan is simply another bid.

The best bid should win the auction. This still leaves undetermined exactly what the best bid is, or should be. Two means of evaluation exist. As in *Case*, a court can make the decision, taking into account, but not being bound by, creditor preferences. Alternatively, creditor preferences alone can control. The Code answers this question. It requires courts to defer to creditor preferences when more than one competing plan qualifies for confirmation. Given this background, methods and procedures which provide incentives for the promulgation of competing creditor plans accomplish two goals: they increase the number and amount of bids; and they provide creditors with alternatives beyond those offered by the debtor.

With this in mind, I offer the following standard for owner participation. It is consistent with both the Code and, except for the necessity requirement, with *Case*. A holder of a prepetition equity interest satisfies the fair and equitable requirement if it proposes a plan in which it retains or receives an equity interest in the reorganized debtor, without payment in full of all creditors, only if it sustains the burden of showing that: (1) it will contribute money or money's worth to the debtor; and (2) the value of the interest retained or received in the reorganized debtor will be no greater than the value of the contribution.

In addition, this standard needs to be augmented by revised procedural rules to equalize the bargaining positions of the parties. If owners submit a new value plan, exclusivity terminates. Second, a competing plan proponent will not be required to prove reorganization value to eliminate the class proposing the new value plan. Finally, if any creditor or class of creditors thereafter proposes a plan that gains creditor acceptance, then that creditor plan will be confirmed. . . .

These requirements for owner participation flow from basic rules for the conduct of an auction. An owner must support its bid with consideration; and the contribution of money or money's worth satisfies that requirement. Further, the buyer must pay the consideration to the seller; the requirement of reasonable equivalence fills this bill. Auction theory, however, enables us to go beyond this position. It permits the construction of rules that promote the conduct of a fair auction, in which the seller receives maximum revenue. The final portion of the owner participation test incorporates procedural safeguards against unfair exploitation by owners of their special position.

NATIONAL BANKRUPTCY REVIEW COMMISSION
FINAL REPORT
BANKRUPTCY: THE NEXT TWENTY YEARS
(October 20, 1997)

Chapter 2: General Issues in Chapter 11

2.4.15 *Absolute Priority and Exclusivity*

11 U.S.C. § 1129(b)(2)(B)(ii) should be amended to provide that the court may find a plan to be fair and equitable that provides for members of a junior class of claims or interests to purchase new interests in the reorganized debtor.

11 U.S.C. § 1121 should be amended to provide that on the request of a party in interest, the court will terminate exclusivity if a debtor moves to confirm a non-consensual plan that provides for the participation of a holder of a junior claim or interest under 1129(b)(2)(B) but does not satisfy the condition set forth in section 1129(b)(2)(B)(i).

. . .

Chapter 2: Single Asset Proposals

2.6.3 *Require Substantial Equity in order to Confirm a Lien-Stripping Plan Using the New Value Exception*

In cases where the secured creditor has not made the election under section 1111(b)(1)(a)(i), a plan must satisfy the following requirements to be confirmed under the new-value exception following rejection by a class that includes the unsecured portion of a claim secured by real property: (1) The new value contribution must pay down the secured portion of the claim on the effective date of the plan so that, giving effect to the confirmation of the plan, sufficient cash payments on the secured portion of the claim shall have been made so that the principal amount of debt secured by the property is no more than 80 percent of the court-determined fair market value of the property as of the confirmation date; (2) the payment terms for the secured portion of the claim must both (i) satisfy all applicable requirements of section 1129 of the Code, and (ii) satisfy then-prevailing market terms in the same locality regarding maturity date, amortization, interest rate, fixed-charge coverage and loan documentation; and (3) the new value contribution must be treated as an equity interest that is not convertible to or exchangeable for debt.

Additional suggested readings

Charles W. Adams, *New Capital for Bankruptcy Reorganizations: It's the Amount that Counts*, 89 Nw. U. L. Rev. 411 (1995)

Edward S. Adams, *Governance in Chapter 11 Reorganizations: Reducing Costs, Improving Results*, 73 B.U. L. Rev. 581 (1993)

Barry E. Adler & Ian Ayres, *A Dilution Mechanism for Valuing Corporations in Bankruptcy*, 111 Yale L.J. 83 (2001)

John C. Anderson, *Classification of Claims and Interests in Reorganization Cases Under the New Bankruptcy Code*, 58 AM. BANKR. L.J. 99 (1984)

John D. Ayer, *Bankruptcy as an Essentially Contested Concept: The Case of the One-Asset Case*, 44 S.C. L. REV. 863 (1993)

Douglas G. Baird & Robert K. Rasmussen, *Boyd's Legacy and Blackstone's Ghost*, 1999 SUP. CT. REV. 393

Cynthia A. Baker, *Other People's Money: The Problem of Professional Fees in Bankruptcy*, 38 ARIZ. L. REV. 35 (1996)

William Blair, *Classification of Unsecured Claims in Chapter 11 Reorganizations*, 58 AM. BANKR. L.J. 197 (1984)

Daniel B. Bogart, *Games Lawyers Play: Waivers of the Automatic Stay in Bankruptcy and the Single Asset Loan Workout*, 43 UCLA L. REV. 1117 (1996)

Daniel B. Bogart, *Liability of Directors of Chapter 11 Debtors in Possession: "Don't Look Back—Something May be Gaining on You,"* 68 AM. BANKR. L.J. 155 (1994)

Richard L. Broude, *Cramdown and Chapter 11 of the Bankruptcy Code: The Settlement Imperative*, 39 BUS. LAW. 441 (1984)

Ralph Brubaker, *Nondebtor Releases and Injunctions in Chapter 11: Revisiting Jurisdictional Precepts and the Forgotten* Callaway v. Benton *Case*, 72 AM. BANKR. L.J. 1 (1998)

F.H. Buckley, *The Termination Decision*, 61 UMKC L. REV. 243 (1992)

Mark E. Budnitz, *Chapter 11 Business Reorganizations and Shareholder Meetings: Will the Meeting Please Come to Order, or Should the Meeting be Cancelled Altogether?*, 58 GEO. WASH. L. REV. 1214 (1990)

Jeremy L. Bulow & John B. Shoven, *The Bankruptcy Decision*, 9 BELL J. ECON. 437 (1978)

David Gray Carlson, *The Truth About the New Value Exception to Bankruptcy's Absolute Priority Rule*, 21 CARDOZO L. REV. 1303 (2000)

David Gray Carlson, *Artificial Impairment and the Single Asset Chapter 11 Case*, 23 CAP. U. L. REV. 339 (1994)

David Gray Carlson, *The Classification Veto in Single-Asset Cases Under Bankruptcy Code Section 1129(a)(10)*, 44 S.C. L. REV. 565 (1993)

Anna Y. Chou, *Corporate Governance in Chapter 11: Electing a New Board*, 65 AM. BANKR. L.J. 559 (1991)

Allen C. Eberhart et al., *Security Pricing and Deviations from the Absolute Priority Rule in Bankruptcy Proceedings*, 45 J. FIN. 1457 (1990)

Richard Epling & Terence W. Thompson, *Securities Disclosure in Bankruptcy*, 39 BUS. LAW. 855 (1984)

Chaim J. Fortgang & Thomas Moers Mayer, *Trading Claims and Taking Control of Corporations in Chapter 11*, 12 CARDOZO L. REV. 1 (1990)

Julian R. Franks & Walter Torous, *An Empirical Investigation of U.S. Firms in Reorganization*, 44 J. FIN. 747 (1989)

Christopher W. Frost, *The Theory, Reality and Pragmatism of Corporate Governance in Bankruptcy Reorganizations*, 72 AM. BANKR. L.J. 103 (1998)

Christopher W. Frost, *Running the Asylum: Governance Problems in Bankruptcy Reorganizations*, 34 ARIZ. L. REV. 89 (1992)

Michael A. Gerber, *The Election of Directors and Chapter 11: The Second Circuit Tells Shareholders to Walk Softly and Carry a Big Lever*, 53 BROOK. L. REV. 295 (1987)

Stuart C. Gilson & Michael R. Vetsuypens, *Creditor Control in Financially Distressed Firms: Empirical Evidence*, 72 WASH. U. L.Q. 1005 (1994)

Stuart C. Gilson, *Bankruptcy, Boards, Banks, and Blockholders*, 27 J. FIN. ECON. 355 (1990)

Stuart C. Gilson, *Management Turnover and Financial Distress*, 25 J. FIN. ECON. 241 (1989)

Edith S. Hotchkiss, *Post-Bankruptcy Performance and Management Turnover*, 50 J. FIN. 3 (1995)

Thomas H. Jackson, Chapter 7, *Running Bankruptcy's Collective Proceeding*, in THE LOGIC AND LIMITS OF BANKRUPTCY LAW 151-192 (Harvard 1986)

Gregory K. Jones, *The Classification and Cram Down Controversy in Single Asset Bankruptcy Cases: A Need for the Repeal of Bankruptcy Code Section 1129(a)(10)*, 42 UCLA L. REV. 623 (1994)

Steven N. Kaplan, *Federated's Acquisition and Bankruptcy: Lessons and Implications*, 72 WASH. U. L.Q. 1103 (1994)

Thomas G. Kelch, *Shareholder Control Rights in Bankruptcy: Disassembling the Withering Mirage of Corporate Democracy*, 52 MD. L. REV. 264 (1993)

Thomas G. Kelch, *The Phantom Fiduciary: The Debtor in Possession in Chapter 11*, 38 WAYNE L. REV. 1323 (1992)

Frank R. Kennedy & Gerald K. Smith, *Postconfirmation Issues: The Effects of Confirmation and Postconfirmation Proceedings*, 44 S.C. L. REV. 621 (1993)

Kenneth N. Klee, *Adjusting Chapter 11: Fine Tuning the Plan Process*, 69 AM. BANKR. L.J. 551 (1995)

Kenneth N. Klee & K. John Shaffer, *Creditors' Committees Under Chapter 11 of the Bankruptcy Code*, 44 S.C. L. REV. 995 (1993)

Kenneth N. Klee, *Cram Down II*, 64 AM. BANKR. L.J. 229 (1990)

Kenneth N. Klee, *All You Ever Wanted to Know About Cram Down Under the New Bankruptcy Code*, 53 AM. BANKR. L.J. 133 (1979)

Robert M. Lawless & Stephen P. Ferris, *The Expenses of Financial Distress: The Direct Costs of Chapter 11*, 61 U. PITT. L. REV. 629 (2000)

Lynn M. LoPucki & Sara D. Kalin, *The Failure of Public Company Bankruptcies in Delaware and New York: Empirical Evidence of a "Race to the Bottom,"* 54 VAND. L. REV. 231 (2001)

Lynn M. LoPucki & William C. Whitford, *Venue Choice and Forum Shopping in the Bankruptcy Reorganization of Large, Publicly Held Companies*, 1991 WIS. L. REV. 11

Lynn M. LoPucki & William C. Whitford, *Preemptive Cram Down*, 65 AM. BANKR. L.J. 625 (1991)

Lynn M. LoPucki, *The Debtor in Full Control—Systems Failure Under Chapter 11 of the Bankruptcy Code?*, 57 AM. BANKR. L.J. 99, 247 (1983)

Bruce A. Markell, *A New Perspective on Unfair Discrimination in Chapter 11*, 72 AM. BANKR. L.J. 227 (1998)

Bruce A. Markell, *The Case Against Breakup Fees in Bankruptcy*, 66 AM. BANKR. L.J. 349 (1992)

Peter E. Meltzer, *Getting Out of Jail Free: Can the Bankruptcy Plan Process Be Used to Release Nondebtor Third Parties?*, 71 AM. BANKR. L.J. 1 (1997)

Peter E. Meltzer, *Disenfranchising the Dissenting Creditor Through Artificial Classification or Artificial Impairment*, 66 AM. BANKR. L.J. 281 (1992)

Richard E. Mendales, *Looking Under the Rock: Disclosure of Bankruptcy Issues Under the Securities Laws,* 57 OHIO ST. L.J. 731 (1996)

Herbert P. Minkel, Jr. & Cynthia A. Baker, *Claims and Control in Chapter 11 Cases: A Call for Neutrality*, 13 CARDOZO L. REV. 35 (1991)

Raymond T. Nimmer & Richard B. Feinberg, *Chapter 11 Business Governance: Fiduciary Duties, Business Judgment, Trustees and Exclusivity*, 6 BANKR. DEV. J. 1 (1989)

Raymond T. Nimmer, *Negotiated Bankruptcy Reorganization Plans: Absolute Priority and New Value Contributions*, 36 EMORY L.J. 1009 (1987)

Isaac M. Pachulski, *The Cram Down and Valuation Under Chapter 11 of the Bankruptcy Code*, 58 N.C. L. REV. (1980)

Lawrence Ponoroff, *Enlarging the Bargaining Table: Some Implications of the Corporate Stakeholder Model for Federal Bankruptcy Proceedings,* 23 CAP. U. L. REV. 441 (1994)

Robert K. Rasmussen & Randall S. Thomas, *Whither the Race: A Comment on the Delawarization of Corporate Reorganizations*, 54 VAND. L. REV. 283 (2001)

Robert K. Rasmussen & Randall S. Thomas, *Timing Matters: Promoting Forum Shopping by Insolvent Corporations*, 94 NW. U. L. REV. 1357 (2000)

Stefan A. Riesenfeld, *Classification of Claims and Interests in Chapter 11 and 13 Cases*, 75 CAL. L. REV. 391 (1987)

Susan Rose-Ackerman, *Risk-Taking and Ruin: Bankruptcy and Investment Choice*, 20 J. LEGAL STUD. 277 (1991)

Linda J. Rusch, *Single Asset Cases and Chapter 11: The Classification Quandary*, 1 AM. BANKR. INST. L. REV. 43 (1993)

Linda J. Rusch, *Gerrymandering the Classification Issue in Chapter Eleven Reorganization*, 63 U. COLO. L. REV. 163 (1992)

Steven L. Schwarcz, *Rethinking a Corporation's Obligations to Creditors*, 17 CARDOZO L. REV. 647 (1996)

David A. Skeel, Jr., *What's So Bad About Delaware?*, 54 VAND. L. REV. 309 (2001)

David A. Skeel, Jr., *Bankruptcy Judges and Bankruptcy Venue: Some Thoughts on Delaware*, 1 DELAWARE L. REV. 1 (1998)

David A. Skeel, Jr., *The Uncertain State of an Unstated Rule: Bankruptcy Contribution Rule After Ahlers*, 63 AM. BANKR. L.J. 221 (1989)

Gerald K. Smith, *Conflicts of Interest in Workouts and Bankruptcy Reorganization Cases*, 48 S.C. L. REV. 793 (1997)

Charles Jordan Tabb, *Emergency Preferential Orders in Bankruptcy Reorganizations*, 65 AM. BANKR. L.J. 75 (1991)

Marshall E. Tracht, *Contractual Bankruptcy Waivers: Reconciling Theory, Practice, and Law*, 82 CORNELL L. REV. 301 (1997)

George G. Triantis, *A Theory of the Regulation of Debtor-in-Possession Financing*, 46 VAND. L. REV. 901 (1993)

Frederick Tung, *Confirmation and Claims Trading*, 90 Nw. U. L. REV. 1684 (1996)

Elizabeth Warren & Jay Lawrence Westbrook, *Financial Characteristics of Businesses in Bankruptcy*, 73 AM. BANKR. L.J. 499 (1999)

Elizabeth Warren, *A Theory of Absolute Priority*, 1991 ANN. SURV. AM. L. 9

Lawrence A. Weiss, *Bankruptcy Resolution: Direct Costs and Violation of Priority of Claims*, 27 J. FIN. ECON. 285 (1990)

Michelle J. White, *The Corporate Bankruptcy Decision*, 3 J. ECON. PERSP. 129 (1989)

Barry L. Zaretsky, *Trustees and Examiners in Chapter 11*, 44 S.C. L. REV. 907 (1993)

Barry L. Zaretsky, *Co-Debtor Stays in Chapter 11 Bankruptcy*, 73 CORNELL L. REV. 213 (1988)

Robert M. Zinman, *New Value and the Commission: How Bizarre!*, 5 AM. BANKR. INST. L. REV. 477 (1997)

Chapter 15
Chapter 11 Reorganizations: Reform

A. The *"Untenable Case"* Debate

One of the most famous academic debates on bankruptcy occurred in 1992. Michael Bradley and Michael Rosenzweig created a firestorm of controversy when they published the following article in the *Yale Law Journal* in which they concluded that chapter 11 was "untenable" and should be repealed. *See The Untenable Case for Chapter 11*, 101 YALE L.J. 1043 (1992). They drew inspiration for both their title and their idea from an article written six years before by Professor Douglas Baird, *The Uneasy Case for Corporate Reorganizations*, 15 J. LEGAL STUD. 127 (1986). Professor Jackson expressed similar skepticism in 1986 in a chapter (*"Reconsidering Reorganizations"*) in his landmark book, THE LOGIC AND LIMITS OF BANKRUPTCY LAW. Bradley and Rosenzweig went on in their article to propose a "contingent equity" scheme for handling corporate defaults that would replace chapter 11.

Professor Barry Adler proposed a somewhat similar "chameleon equity" scheme in an article that is excerpted in the second part of this chapter, *Financial and Political Theories of American Corporate Bankruptcy*, 45 STAN. L. REV. 311 (1993). Adler wrote several sequels addressing different aspects of the business bankruptcy conundrum, including *A Theory of Corporate Insolvency*, 72 N.Y.U. L. REV. 343 (1997); *Finance's Theoretical Divide and the Proper Role of Insolvency Rules*, 68 S. CAL. L. REV. 401 (1994); and *A World Without Debt*, 72 WASH. U. L.Q. 811 (1994).

The response to Bradley and Rosenzweig's article was swift and pointed. Professor Elizabeth Warren answered in *The Untenable Case for Repeal of Chapter 11*, 102 YALE L.J. 437 (1992). The two articles most requested by bankruptcy law professors for inclusion in this Anthology were those by Bradley and Rosenzweig and by Warren. Another prominent rebuttal was made by Professor Lynn M. LoPucki, in *Strange Visions in a Strange World: A Reply to Professors Bradley and Rosenzweig*, 91 MICH. L. REV. 79 (1992). Excerpts from Warren and LoPucki follow the Bradley and Rosenzweig article. Theirs were hardly the only responses, though; other thoughtful replies to Bradley and Rosenzweig include Jagdeep S. Bhandari & Lawrence A. Weiss, *The Untenable Case for Chapter 11: A Review of the Evidence*, 67 AM. BANKR. L.J. 131 (1993), and Donald R. Korobkin, *The Unwarranted Case Against Corporate Reorganization: A Reply to Bradley and Rosenzweig*, 78 IOWA L. REV. 669 (1993).

Warren and LoPucki were answered in turn the next year by Professor James Bowers in *The Fantastic Wisconsylvania Zero-Bureaucratic-Cost School of Bankruptcy Theory: A Comment*, 91 MICH. L. REV. 1773 (1993). [For those readers curious about the derivation of "Wisconsylvania," Bowers was referring to the fact that LoPucki then was at *Wiscon*sin and Warren at Penn*sylvania*; since then they have moved on to UCLA and Harvard]. Baird restated some of his ideas proposing auctions in Douglas G. Baird, *Revisiting Auctions in Chapter 11*, 36 J.L. & ECON. 633 (1993). Neither Bradley nor Rosenzweig, to the knowledge of the anthology's editor, ever bothered to answer Warren and LoPucki.

As you read those portions of the heated "untenable case" debate excerpted in the ensuing four articles, consider the following questions:

1. When Bradley & Rosensweig (B & R) talk about "endogenous" causes as contrasted with "exogenous" causes, what are they talking about?
2. What is the "chapter 11 dilemma"?
3. What are "near-default costs" and why are they important?
4. What evidence do B & R present against chapter 11? What are their principal findings?
5. Why do Warren & LoPucki (W & L) argue that the B & R data do not support their conclusion that chapter 11 should be repealed? What are the major problems W & L identify with the B & R data?
6. What alternative hypotheses do W & L suggest to explain the B & R data?
7. Whom do B & R identify as the "winners" in chapter 11 as presently constituted? Why? What incentives do they claim managers enjoy? What is the meaning of the supposed "soft landing" for managers, and how do B & R assert that it affects chapter 11 usage?
8. According to W & L, is the "soft landing" theory supported by the facts? On what bases do W & L dispute B & R's assertions about management incentives?
9. How would the B & R "contingent equity" scheme work? What do they advertise as its chief virtues?
10. Does the B & R contingent equity proposal necessarily follow from their empirical findings?
11. What assumptions underlie the contingent equity scheme? Do W & L believe that these assumptions are valid and supportable?
12. According to W & L, what policies do B & R overlook? What consequences do B & R ignore?
13. Does the Coase Theorem have anything of importance to say to this debate?
14. How do W & L answer the question, "why not repeal chapter 11?"
15. What is the essence of Bowers' criticism of W & L's approach?
16. What solution does Bowers propose?

Michael Bradley & Michael Rosenzweig
The Untenable Case for Chapter 11
101 YALE L.J. 1043 (1992)[*]

I. INTRODUCTION

Corporate bankruptcy law scholars generally view financial distress as an exogenous development. These scholars see bankruptcy, or "financial distress" or "insolvency," as a condition created by extrinsic factors that have rendered the firm unable to meet current obligations to creditors out of liquid assets.

Congress embraced this view in its adoption of the Bankruptcy Reform Act of 1978 and, more specifically, determined to push managers of financially troubled firms toward reorganization rather than liquidation. Simply stated, Congress believed that assets would be more highly valued if utilized in the industry for which they were designed, rather than scrapped, that "it is more economically efficient to reorganize than liquidate, because it preserves jobs and assets." Put differently, Congress was concerned that liquidations destroy valuable firm-specific assets and impose substantial costs on corporate stakeholders such as security holders, employees, suppliers, customers, and communities, and therefore concluded that the law must afford managers of financially troubled companies the *preferred* alternative of court-supervised reorganization. In Congress' view, easier access to the protections of Chapter 11 would enhance social welfare by preventing the inefficient liquidation of financially viable firms. . . .

This presumption favoring management's continued control, when combined with other provisions of Chapter 11 affording the corporate debtor considerable latitude regarding its treatment of creditors, effectively gave managers powerful incentives to pursue bankruptcy reorganization. Managers are more likely to keep their jobs by reorganizing rather than liquidating their firm, and during reorganization they can operate without the constraints ordinarily imposed by creditors. As we show below, one result of these incentives has been to increase the endogeneity of the corporate bankruptcy decision.

Even commentators who embrace bankruptcy law's implicit starting point—that the corporate bankruptcy decision is exogenous—have found much in the law to criticize. . . . [M]any of these scholars have argued that bankruptcy law is inefficient because it impedes the flow of corporate assets to higher-valued uses[, and] . . . may permit managers to effect wealth transfers from creditors (and perhaps other stakeholders) to equity holders.

These commentators have offered a variety of proposals for improving the existing bankruptcy system. . . . All of these proposals share a common empirical assertion and a common perspective. The common assertion is that market-determined prices are better indicators of value than judicially-determined estimates. The common perspective is that "financial troubles" or "failures" are exogenous events. . . .

Different starting points, of course, often lead to different ways of looking at a problem. Our starting point is quite different from that of others, and as a result our critique of the law of corporate bankruptcy reorganization is also somewhat different. While we agree with the assertion that markets are more efficient than courts in determining values, we disagree with the notion that "financial distress" or "insolvency" is purely an exogenous event. We therefore embrace an alternative explanation for the cause of "bankruptcy," an explanation whose public policy implications

---

    *   Reprinted by permission of the Yale Law Journal Company and Fred B. Rothman & Company from The Yale Law Journal, Vol. 101, pages 1043-1095.

differ from the implications of both the congressional view of bankruptcy and the view of other bankruptcy law scholars.

If we think of "financial distress" or "insolvency" as the inability to meet current obligations to creditors out of liquid assets, then in a real sense, firms can *choose* to become "insolvent" by not maintaining a sufficient balance of such assets. As long as there is a possibility of court-supervised reorganization, corporate managers have no real incentive to maintain an "adequate" balance. More fundamentally, fashioning a firm's capital structure obviously involves certain choices regarding the use of debt financing. To the extent that managers, influenced by the availability of bankruptcy protection, *choose* to burden their firms with "too much" debt or "impossible" debt-payment obligations, financial distress is hardly an entirely exogenous event. On this view, corporate bankruptcy frequently is significantly *endogenous*, chosen by, rather than imposed upon, corporate managers.

Viewing corporate bankruptcy as endogenous in some measure raises important issues of public policy, some of which have quite interesting empirical implications. Did the 1978 Act really enhance social welfare by promoting more efficient asset allocations? Or is Chapter 11 more appropriately viewed as a mechanism that permits managers to abridge contractual agreements with creditors and other stakeholders in order to enhance their own welfare? If the latter view is correct, then Chapter 11 almost certainly reduces social welfare. . . .

. . . Generally speaking, the theory we develop regarding such reorganizations derives from the view that the 1978 Act significantly changed the law of corporate bankruptcy. . . . [T]he changes in the law of bankruptcy reorganization effected by the 1978 Act provide us with an indirect means of testing empirically the validity of our views . . . . By studying findings from corporate bankruptcies before and after the effective date of the 1978 Act, we can indirectly determine whether empirical evidence supports or refutes certain suppositions. Thus, if our starting point is correct, one should be able to observe tangible evidence of the increased endogeneity of the corporate bankruptcy decision following the effective date of the 1978 Act. Similarly, if, as Congress hoped, the Act enhanced social welfare by making it easier for managers to preserve valuable corporate assets, then the security holders of bankrupt firms should fare better in the post-Act environment that before.

. . . In brief, our findings and their implications are as follows. First, the evidence supports our view that corporate bankruptcy is more endogenous in the post-Act environment. We find that in the wake of the 1978 Act the frequency of corporate bankruptcy filings has increased dramatically, the relationship between the number of bankruptcy filings and general economic conditions has become more attenuated, a smaller fraction of bankrupt firms are delisted from the major exchanges in the year before their bankruptcy filing than in the pre-Act period, and bankrupt firms are generally in better financial condition than firms filing before the 1978 Act.

Second, we find that stockholders of bankrupt firms lose significantly greater wealth in the post-Act environment than before the Act. Specifically, we compare the experiences of the stockholders of bankrupt firms before and after the Act became effective and find that, while stockholders of bankrupt firms lose significant wealth in both periods, the loss to stockholders is significantly greater in the later period. We also find that under the Act, corporate insiders of such firms sell significantly more of their stockholdings in the two years surrounding the bankruptcy filing.

Third, we find, just as we do with stockholders, that bondholders of bankrupt firms also lose significantly more wealth in the post-Act period than previously. Consistent with this finding, we also observe a dramatic increase in default premiums on corporate debt under the Act.

In sum, our empirical results indicate that both stockholders and bondholders of bankrupt firms suffer dramatically greater losses under the 1978 Act than previously. These results not only challenge the theory of corporate bankruptcy advanced by proponents of the 1978 Act—that reorganization enhances social welfare and should therefore be facilitated and promoted—but also raise an important and intriguing question regarding bankruptcy law and policy: If stockholders and bondholders, the only corporate stakeholders with readily measurable claims, are both losers under Chapter 11, then who are the winners?

We believe that, insofar as corporate bankruptcies are concerned, the principal beneficiaries of Chapter 11 (excluding the legions of lawyers, accountants and financial advisors who earn substantial fees from bankruptcy reorganizations) are corporate managers. Chapter 11, in other words, may be seen as a kind of management defensive tactic against corporate debtholders which, like certain antitakeover defensive measures, enhances management's wealth at the expense of corporate security holders. . . . [T]he data show that Chapter 11 preserves and protects the jobs of corporate managers, not corporate assets.

. . . [W]e offer a proposal for refining the law of corporate bankruptcy to address the problem that we have identified. Our proposal . . . is quite simply to *repeal* Chapter 11 of the Bankruptcy Code . . . and thereby abolish court-supervised corporate reorganizations, effectively reassigning a "failing" firm's property rights to those with the best incentive to allocate the firm's resources efficiently. This proposal, in a sense, may be viewed as the extreme version of a "market-based" solution to corporate bankruptcy.

Under our proposal, firms would never reach a state of "insolvency"; obligations owed to creditors would be financed through the sale of new residual claims, and if such claims could not be sold, the firm's residual claimants would relinquish their claims to the firm's net cash flows. In such a regime, there would never come a day of reckoning when all claims to the corporation would have to be valued and cashed out. This reform, we argue, would improve the efficiency of the corporate bankruptcy system while significantly reducing the deadweight costs of bankruptcy itself.

II. An Economic Analysis of Court-Supervised Corporate Reorganizations

A. *Overview*

. . . Most economists examine corporate bankruptcy from the perspective of a bankruptcy judge, who is confronted with the choice of either liquidating the firm to pay its creditors or reorganizing it while scaling back creditor claims and (usually) leaving the firm's managers in control. We refer to the choice between liquidation and reorganization as the Chapter 11 dilemma.

The economic analysis of the Chapter 11 dilemma treats the firm's financial condition as having been determined by some prior exogenous event(s). . . . Viewing the Chapter 11 dilemma in this setting, economists typically weigh the consequences of liquidating a firm that has greater value as a going concern against the possibility that reorganization may permit managers to make suboptimal managerial decisions. . . .

The related literature in financial economics has expanded this inquiry to consider welfare-reducing activities that managers of a financially troubled firm undertake in order to expropriate wealth from the firm's stakeholders. This literature focuses on the conflicts of interest that naturally arise in resolving the Chapter 11 dilemma: the conflict between managers and security holders and the conflicts among different classes of security holders. Typically, this literature assumes that the firm's management is an efficient agent for the firm's stockholders, using its control of the firm to protect stockholder interests. Consequently, the discussion generally centers on the conflict between stockholders and bondholders.

Our empirical findings regarding the impact of bankruptcy reorganization on stockholder wealth . . . suggest that, in fact, managers are not efficient agents of stockholders in Chapter 11 proceedings. If, however, we view corporate management as the ultimate residual claimant, which it arguably is in a Chapter 11 proceeding, then the analysis of the management/bondholder conflict in the financial economics literature is nevertheless quite pertinent to our finding suggesting a management/security holder clash in Chapter 11. That is, while financial economists may have mis-specified the conflict that in fact arises in corporate bankruptcy reorganizations, the means by which they imagine that managers extract wealth from bondholders for the benefit of stockholders may well be utilized by managers to expropriate for *themselves* the wealth of both bondholders *and* stockholders.

B. *The Costs of Court-Supervised Corporate Reorganizations*

The social costs of Chapter 11 proceedings are well known. Bankruptcy law encourages corporate managers to reorganize their firms under court supervision, which effectively invites them to create a net equity position for stockholders by overstating expected net cash flows and understating risk. While creditors may complain loudly in response, the Chapter 11 presumption in favor of reposing control of the debtor-in-possession in the hands of pre-bankruptcy management leaves creditors with too little influence over the reorganization process to protect themselves adequately against such tendencies. The costs of these suboptimal managerial decisions are a major component of the social costs of court-supervised corporate reorganizations.

Students of financial economics have long recognized the incentives of corporate managers (equity holders) to effect wealth transfers from bondholders by embracing value-decreasing operating strategies. . . . The costs largely result from one of two suboptimal managerial decisions: the acceptance of negative net present value projects or the rejection of positive net present value projects. In either case, social welfare is compromised.

Under certain circumstances corporate managers, assumed to be acting on behalf of equity holders, have an incentive to adopt increasingly risky investment/production strategies, leading, at the extreme, to the adoption of strategies having a negative net present value. . . .

If we think of "default" as the act by which equity holders relinquish all claims to their firm's net cash flow, it is clear that equity holders have an incentive to generate the social costs discussed above only when they perceive that the firm is near default. Accordingly, we refer to these costs as "near-default" costs, by which we mean the social costs generated by suboptimal operating strategies that cause wealth transfers from bondholders and other corporate stakeholders and, ultimately, reduce social welfare.

C. *The Perfect Markets Solution to the Chapter 11 Dilemma*

Clearly the Chapter 11 dilemma evaporates in a world of perfect markets. If the capital market is perfect, and property rights are well defined, then the market value of a firm's securities will precisely and accurately reflect the discounted net cash flows of its current and future investment/production decisions. Under such conditions, a creditor can easily write (and enforce) a contract with the debtor that permits the creditor to invoke default remedies should the firm's value fall below the face value of its debt. As long as the value of the firm exceeds the face value of the debt, equity holders can always issue additional equity to forestall default. If the firm's market value were to fall below that amount, bondholders could step in, take control of the firm, and then sell it to capital market participants. This "perfect markets solution" thus obviates the need for judicial intervention in the affairs of financially troubled corporations. . . .

In this hypothetical world of perfect markets, valuable firm-specific capital could never be destroyed. If there were firm-specific assets with value in excess of the next-best alternative allocation, which might be piecemeal liquidation, the firm could raise money by issuing claims (securities) and thereby retain control of these assets. . . .

From the opposite perspective, the only way in which firm-specific assets may be lost is if the firm is unable to convince the capital market of its true (higher) intrinsic value, which is an impossibility in a perfect-markets environment. Only then would there perhaps be an economic justification for a court to intervene and force a reorganization of the firm's capital structure, although even in a world of imperfect markets, it seems doubtful that courts have a comparative advantage over capital market agents in determining the intrinsic value of corporations and their equity claims.

. . . Judicial intervention is warranted only if there are significant information asymmetries, transactions costs, or ambiguous property rights.

We now attempt to test certain empirical implications of the foregoing theoretical analysis. As we demonstrate in Part III, and as our discussion here would predict, the current corporate bankruptcy regime is indeed difficult to justify economically.

III. An Empirical Inquiry into the Social Costs of Court-Supervised Corporate Reorganizations: An Analysis of the Economic Effects of the Bankruptcy Reform Act of 1978

A. *Overview*

. . . [T]he 1978 Act made it significantly easier for firms to obtain court protection from creditors. Indeed, to many of its proponents, a principal purpose of the legislation was to curtail the inefficient liquidation of viable corporations and thereby preserve jobs and valuable firm-specific assets. Implicitly, the Act's proponents must also have believed that the benefits inherent in preserving such assets generally exceed the costs engendered by court-supervised reorganizations.

If these proponents were correct, or alternatively, if the 1978 Act improved the efficiency of the reorganization process, we would expect to observe relative wealth increases for both bondholders and stockholders under the 1978 Act. Thus, by comparing the experiences of security holders of firms in bankruptcy reorganization before and after the 1978 Act became effective, we can draw certain inferences regarding the welfare effects of court-supervised reorganizations. In this way, we can examine empirically the validity of the theoretical analysis of court-supervised reorganizations that we offered. . . .

In this part, we attempt to measure empirically the social costs of the 1978 Act by examining the economic effects of that legislation. Our analysis proceeds in three stages, each of which compares data from two periods, pre-1980 and post-1979. We first examine the frequency of voluntary corporate bankruptcy filings before and after the Act to test our hypothesis that the Act made it easier to secure bankruptcy protection. Next we try to gauge the extent to which the financial conditions of bankrupt firms differ in the two periods, investigating whether, as our analysis suggests, the relaxed standards of the Act afforded to financially stronger firms the advantages of court-supervised reorganization. Finally, we examine directly (through several empirical tests) the experiences of security holders of firms filing bankruptcy petitions in the two periods, which allows us to determine whether bondholders and stockholders of bankrupt firms have fared better under the Act. . . .

Our tests and findings may be summarized as follows. The frequency of bankruptcy filings has increased significantly since the passage of the 1978 Act. . . .

. . . Taken together, these results suggest that the potential earnings of firms filing bankruptcy petitions in the post-Act period were significantly greater than those of firms filing in the earlier period . . . . More generally, under the 1978 Act, bankruptcy filings apparently are less a function of exogenous economic factors and are more a function of firm-specific factors, such as management discretion, than during the pre-Act era.

. . . [W]e directly examine the effect of the Act on security holder wealth. We find that both bondholders and stockholders have suffered significantly greater losses in the post-Act environment. We also find that bond ratings of firms about to file bankruptcy petitions are significantly lower and that default premiums on the debt of such firms are significantly higher in the post-Act period. Finally, we find that post-Act insiders sell significantly more of their holdings than do their pre-Act counterparts in the two years surrounding the filing of a bankruptcy petition. . . .

In sum . . . our empirical tests and findings show that in the post-Act environment the frequency of bankruptcy filings has increased . . ., the potential earnings of filing firms have increased . . ., and the market value of the financial claims of filing firms has decreased . . . . We therefore conclude that the social costs of bankruptcy . . . have increased under the 1978 Act. Our empirical findings, in other words, cast strong doubt on the proposition that the more liberal use of bankruptcy reorganization occasioned by the Act has enhanced social welfare by preserving firm-specific capital and security holder wealth. . . .

I. *Summary and Interpretation of Empirical Results*

In this part we have examined the empirical effects of the Bankruptcy Reform Act of 1978. Our findings indicate that there has been an overwhelming increase in the number of bankruptcy filings since this legislation became effective. Moreover, we find that this phenomenon cannot be attributed to a weakening of the economy or an increase in the number of financially troubled corporations. The financial condition of the typical firm filing a bankruptcy petition in the post-Act environment is significantly stronger than that of the typical firm filing before the Act. We conclude that under the Act, managerial discretion is more significant, and poor financial performance less significant, in determining whether a firm is likely to seek bankruptcy protection. Finally, we find that the probability of being delisted before a bankruptcy filing is three times greater in the pre-Act period. This is further evidence that the decision to file a bankruptcy petition has become more endogenous under the 1978 Act.

Our empirical results suggest that corporate security holders have *not* benefited from the provisions of the 1978 Act. Prior to the Act, stockholders of firms that filed bankruptcy petitions typically lost fifty cents on the dollar, risk-adjusted. Under the Act, stockholders lose almost *all* of their investments. This is a surprising finding, if a principal purpose of the Act was to preserve corporate assets by more effectively preventing the liquidation of economically viable corporations.

As might be expected, the Act has not helped corporate bondholders either. The default premium . . . is almost a third greater in the post-Act period, reflecting the higher probability of a bankruptcy filing and the greater bondholder losses that are likely should one occur. . . .

The fact that both stockholders and bondholders have suffered under the 1978 Act leads us to conjecture that the Act's principal beneficiaries have been corporate managers. We believe that Chapter 11 has increased the latitude of corporate managers to abridge contracts and effectively breach their duties (be they fiduciary or contractual) to security holders while their firms are in reorganization. Chapter 11 allows, indeed encourages, managers to place their interests ahead of the interests of their security holders and to take actions that they could not take without court protection from creditor scrutiny. The 1978 Act thus provides managers with what amounts to a kind of defensive tactic against corporate debtholders. Filing a Chapter 11 petition, in effect, is a way to keep control of the firm free from the intrusive monitoring of creditors, thereby permitting management to extract wealth from the firm's various security holders.[77]

---

[77]   Professor Gilson reports that on average only 46% of incumbent directors remain in office following a bankruptcy or debt restructuring, and concludes that corporate default leads to significant change in the allocation of control rights over corporate assets. Stuart C. Gilson, *Bankruptcy, Boards, Banks, and Blockholders*, 27 J. FIN. ECON. 355 (1990). While Gilson's findings appear at first blush to contradict our theory, we would argue that what matters is not the particular identity of the managers running the firm in bankruptcy reorganization, but rather the latitude (and incentive) these managers have under Chapter 11 to pursue suboptimal strategies. As we argue in Part II, the principal deficiency of the existing law of corporate bankruptcy is that it leaves corporate control for *some period* in the hands of actors who do not suffer the economic consequences of their actions. Professor Gilson's findings do not suggest otherwise.

Judge Easterbrook has argued, contrary to our claim, that corporate bankruptcy is efficient. Frank H. Easterbrook, *Is Corporate Bankruptcy Efficient?*, 27 J. FIN. ECON. 411 (1990). He argues that corporate bankruptcy law survives as an "[e]nduring legal institution," and that such institutions "endure either because they are efficient or because they redistribute wealth to concentrated, politically effective interest groups." *Id.* at 413. Finding no redistributive effect, Judge Easterbrook asserts that efficiency is the likely explanation for the survival of the current bankruptcy regime. *Id.* at 413-14. In this part, however, we have documented that wealth transfers from stockholders and bondholders occur under Chapter 11, thereby challenging Judge Easterbrook's efficiency claim.

Recall that in our discussion of the Chapter 11 dilemma, in Part II, we noted that judicial intervention in the affairs of a financially troubled firm seems appropriate only if there are significant inefficiencies in the relevant markets for labor, capital, information, and corporate control. Our empirical findings indicate that a greater reliance on court-supervised reorganizations under the 1978 Act has not resulted in the preservation of valuable corporate assets. Rather, in view of our findings, it would appear, as noted above, that the Chapter 11 process effectively renders ambiguous the claims of corporate security holders, thereby allowing managers to abridge contractual agreements and violate their fiduciary duties. We believe, however, that one can fashion a proposal for reforming the law of corporate bankruptcy that would facilitate the preservation of valuable corporate assets by building on the perfect markets solution to the Chapter 11 dilemma. We conclude by presenting such a proposal.

IV. A Proposal for Reform

A. *Overview*

. . . [N]obody nobody has yet embraced what we regard as the logical conclusion to which these observations and our claim regarding the increased endogeneity of the Chapter 11 decision lead: *Chapter 11 should be repealed, abolishing court-supervised corporate reorganizations and, in effect, precluding residual claimants from participating in any reorganization of the firm.* More technically, we propose a federal law repealing Chapter 11 (insofar as it applies to corporate reorganizations) and providing for automatic cancellation of residual claims in the event of default. This law would leave the relative rankings of claims and the definition of default to contracts (including provisions in the company's charter specifying the rights and priorities of its capital stock) between the company and its claimholders. This repeal of Chapter 11 would permit corporate claimants to enforce these contracts strictly in the event of default, since the law would no longer provide for a stay of enforcement actions in that event. We would expect companies and their claimants to tailor their agreements to this world of strictly enforceable, default-contingent contracts. . . .

B. *A Proposed Model for a World Without Corporate Bankruptcy Reorganization*

Consider a firm with three classes of securities outstanding: senior debt, junior debt, and common equity. The terms of the securities stipulate that in the event of liquidation, absolute priority will be maintained in that senior creditors will be paid in full before junior creditors receive anything. Likewise, the firm's junior creditors must be paid in full before equity holders receive any payment.

. . . [W]e assume that when the two debt instruments were created, each class received what we term "contingent equity shares."

. . . [W]e assume that in the current period, the firm owes senior creditors an interest payment of I. Under existing law, the firm's managers have the option of defaulting on the firm's promise to pay senior creditors and seeking court-supervised reorganization under Chapter 11 of the Bankruptcy Code. . . . Under our proposal, however, if the firm defaults rather than pay the I owed to senior creditors, the equity holders will relinquish their status as residual claimants and therefore *lose all claims to the firm's assets*, including the next period's net cash flow.

The immediate problem confronting management under our proposal is to determine the value of the firm's equity. Modern finance theory offers a number of techniques for valuing the equity position in a leveraged firm. . . .

. . . [E]quity holders receive payment only if the terminal value of the firm exceeds the aggregate amount owed to the junior and senior debtholders . . . . We refer to E as the value of the equity holders' residual claim.

Assuming an efficient capital market, it follows that the firm's managers can and will issue additional equity to pay the senior creditors if $E > I$. Alternatively, if $E < I$, the managers will default, and under our proposal the equity holders will relinquish all claims to the terminal value of the firm. . . .

In effect, the managers (whom we assume to be acting on behalf of the company's equity holders) of a leveraged firm have an "option" to pay the firm's senior creditors today for a residual claim to the firm's terminal value. The managers will "exercise" this option only if the present value of the residual claim exceeds the amount owed to the firm's senior creditors in the current period (I). In terms of our model, managers will make the current debt payment only when the following condition is satisfied:

$$I < E \quad (8)$$

Put simply, equity holders (or, more precisely, the managers who represent them) will default unless the amount currently due (I) is less than the value of the residual claim (E), which is equal to the expected terminal value of the firm (V) less the amount promised creditors. . . .

Expression (8) defines the firm's equity position. If the condition stated in Expression (8) holds, then there is positive net equity in the firm and, assuming an efficient capital market, managers could issue new equity shares to finance the debt payments that are currently due. If Expression (8) does not hold, then there is no equity in the firm, and managers could not sell new equity to finance the current debt payments since, under these circumstances, no investor would pay a positive price for an additional residual claim to the firm's terminal value. The firm would therefore default on its senior debt obligation as a result of the *market's assessment* that there is no longer a net equity position in the firm. Thus, under our proposal the market rather than a bankruptcy court would determine whether there is a net equity position in the firm.

Suppose that the firm's management is unable to sell new equity in the market. Under such circumstances, management will have no choice but to default on its obligation to senior creditors, in which case the common stockholders will *lose all claims to the firm's assets*; for all intents and purposes, the firm's equity securities will "evaporate."

Under our proposal, the firm's junior debt will also "evaporate" in the event of default. In its place, the contingent equity owned by the junior debtholders will be "transformed" into the firm's new common equity securities. Put differently, default will oust the firm's equity holders from their position as residual claimants to the firm's cash flows and, in effect, substitute the junior debtholders as the new common stockholders.

The firm's junior bondholders would now face the problem of valuing the firm's new equity claims. . . .

. . . Like the equity holders before them, junior creditors maintain their claims to the firm's terminal value only if they pay senior creditors I today. . . .

Once the firm's junior debtholders effectively become the firm's new residual claimants, they will face the same choice that confronted the old common stockholders: they must either pay the obligation owed to the firm's senior creditors or default. Once again, the choice between these two alternatives will be made by capital market participants rather than by the new residual claimants, since financing a payment to the senior creditors will require the issuance of new equity securities.

We can generalize our model to contemplate a capital structure with several classes of securities outstanding, each with its own contingent equity shares. Under this system, when debt payments come due, management has the option of making the payment or defaulting. If the firm defaults, then the existing residual claimants give up all claims to the terminal value of the firm. Their claims would be extinguished and their residual claim status would pass to the next-higher priority security class. The contingent equity shares, for which we would expect claimholders to contract, would provide the mechanism by which this transfer of residual claim status would be accomplished.

This process of "passing" common equity rights "up through" the priority of the firm's securities would continue until one of two things happens: either the rights are passed up to the firm's senior creditors, or a class of security holders with lower priority is able to issue sufficient new equity to meet the obligations owed to the senior creditors. . . .

Recall that in our discrete-time model, we assume that the distribution of terminal values becomes known to market participants at the beginning of the current period. Based on this distribution, the firm's equity holders, and then its junior bondholders, can assess the value of their claims. However, our development of the model suggests, artificially, a step-by-step process for these value assessments, starting with the firm's equity holders and moving up the priority structure of the firm's securities. In reality, of course, this process would be continuous. Thus, at every point in time, capital market agents would be evaluating the firm's securities in light of the promised payments and the distribution of terminal values. . . .

An important feature of our proposal, distinct from others, is that it *completely avoids* judicial intervention. Under our proposal, there would be no "day of reckoning" and no need for a court-supervised sale or recapitalization of the firm. Rather, as the market learned more about the distribution of terminal values, the values of the firm's securities and its contingent securities would adjust accordingly. Thus, the elimination of firm's equity holders and the erosion of their holdings would be a slow, orderly process.

In addition, our proposal would ensure adherence to the rule of absolute priority by precluding payments to junior claimants when senior claims are not fully paid. This would eliminate uncertainties currently associated with the reorganization process and thereby increase the utility of risk-averse investors, who would be willing to pay a premium for the certainty afforded by strict application of the absolute priority rule.

Our proposal would plainly reduce the inefficiencies associated with court-supervised corporate reorganizations. Most notably, the incentive that managers have under existing law to abandon value-maximizing operating strategies and generate near-default costs would be eliminated, since the common equity holders would be ousted from control of the firm *immediately* upon the firm's default on its obligation to pay senior creditors. In addition, the costs of reorganization itself (*i.e.,* judicial resources and legal, accounting, and financial advisory fees) obviously would be avoided.

C. *The Problem of Near-Default Costs*

We should discuss . . . one possible objection to our proposal. While we claim that repeal of Chapter 11 would drastically reduce near-default costs, some might argue that the impact would be precisely the opposite, since disabling equity holders from participating in court-supervised reorganizations could induce managers to abandon optimal operating strategies (thereby generating near-default costs) well before any debt payment is actually due. . . .

We believe, upon reflection, that the increase in near-default costs that might be occasioned by our proposal is more apparent than real and that, as a consequence, there is no inevitable trade-off between improving allocative efficiency and reducing near-default costs. More specifically, we imagine that a market solution to this potential problem would evolve were our proposal adopted. . . . [W]e would expect creditors to bargain for covenants pursuant to which debt obligations would be payable only from certain sources, and drastic changes in the firm's operating strategy would require creditor approval. . . .

Recent developments in the credit markets strongly suggest that creditors are perfectly capable of bargaining for such protections. . . . In a world without corporate bankruptcy reorganization, one could expect creditors to demand such provisions with even greater urgency; the flexibility of corporate managers would, as a result, be severely limited.

V. Conclusion

We have argued that under the 1978 Act the corporate bankruptcy decision is increasingly endogenous, and that operation or reorganization of a company under court supervision permits managers to effect wealth transfers through the pursuit of suboptimal strategies, thereby generating net social costs. Managers, we have argued, effectively invoke Chapter 11 as a defense unwelcome interference by creditors and as a mechanism for extracting significant wealth from the firm's various security holders. We have also presented empirical evidence supporting our claims.

Having suggested a theoretical analysis that reveals no economic benefits from court-supervised corporate reorganizations, and having identified the significant social costs that such reorganizations engender, we conclude that Chapter 11 should be repealed and replaced by the mechanism we describe for dealing with "financially distressed" corporations. Our model would produce more efficient allocations of the assets of such firms by effectively assigning control of those assets to individuals having powerful incentives to achieve such allocations. As a consequence, social welfare would be enhanced.

Elizabeth Warren
The Untenable Case for Repeal of Chapter 11
102 Yale L.J. 437 (1992)[*]

. . . Michael Bradley and Michael Rosenzweig [made] an extensive analysis of the behavior of certain companies in Chapter 11. . . . On the basis of the evidence they present, they propose the repeal of Chapter 11. In this Article I argue that Bradley and Rosenzweig's study does not support their conclusion that Chapter 11 should be repealed. . . .

. . . I conclude that the data they present do not demonstrate the validity of the hypothesis they claim to have substantiated. . . .

II. What the Data Show

The difficulties with Bradley and Rosenzweig's data are numerous, but one problem appears throughout their article: the data do not demonstrate what Bradley and Rosenzweig claim they do. In this section, I examine five major problems with the data: 1) the applicability of the data is limited to the cases they studied; 2) the filing data contradict the management incentives hypothesis; 3) other available data contradict the management incentives hypothesis; 4) flaws in the collection of the data bias the sample; and 5) plausible alternative hypotheses may explain many of their statistical findings.

A. *Applicability of the Data*

To understand how Chapter 11 has operated under the Code, Bradley and Rosenzweig look at only 162 post-Code Chapter 11 cases—about 16 cases per year. . . . [T]he Bradley and Rosenzweig sample is not random. It restricts itself to publicly traded companies, and, moreover, to only those companies for which certain data were available through public sources. The sample contains *none* of the private companies that declared bankruptcy.

---

   *   Reprinted by permission of The Yale Law Journal Company and Fred B. Rothman & Company from The Yale Law Journal, Vol. 102, pages 437-479.

The impact of this bias in sample selection is significant. In the post-Code period surveyed by Bradley and Rosenzweig, there were 173,108 Chapter 11 filings. Publicly traded companies represent less than one-tenth of 1% of all the Chapter 11 cases during that time period . . . . Bradley and Rosenzweig thus diagnose a problem and propose a solution that purports to be applicable to all Chapter 11 cases based on their analysis of a highly selective sample.

Bradley and Rosenzweig are not unaware of this difficulty. . . . [T]hey acknowledge the problem in a footnote: ". . . We therefore make no empirical case against Chapter 11 insofar at it applies to nonpublic corporations. . . . [O]ne might conclude that our proposal to abolish court-supervised corporate reorganization should be limited to public companies. . . ." In the same footnote, however, Bradley and Rosenzweig go on to defend their sweeping indictment of Chapter 11, maintaining that their "theoretical analysis of corporate reorganization, particularly [the] discussion of management-creditor conflicts, arguably applies with equal force to private companies."

There are a number of reasons why the management strategies of a mom-and-pop grocery, a separately incorporated apartment complex, a four-state trucking concern, a family owned construction company, a tax-driven real estate investment trust, a single employee professional corporation, and a manufacturing subsidiary of a large lumber mill might differ from the management strategies of Johns Manville, LTV Steel, or Eastern Airlines. The close link between residual ownership and management in smaller businesses sets managerial decisionmaking in that context apart from decisionmaking in larger cases where management often has little in common with shareholders. This makes Bradley and Rosenzweig's assertion that bankruptcy "enhances management's wealth at the expense of corporate security holders" nonsensical in most Chapter 11's, since managers and shareholders are often the same people.

Not only do management incentives differ, but the dynamics of reorganization of large publicly traded companies may differ from those of their smaller, private counterparts, and these differences may influence the decision to file for bankruptcy. . . .

Even in the absence of these structural distinctions, the data suggest a critical difference between the bankruptcy experiences of private and public corporations. Over the past two decades, the filing rates for all corporate bankruptcies have risen by 2,000%, while the filing rates for publicly traded companies have remained steady. The fate of these cases once they are in Chapter 11 also differs markedly. Only about 17% of all Chapter 11 cases manage to confirm a plan of reorganization, while nearly 90% of publicly traded companies survive to confirm a plan. . . . Chapter 11 repayments also differ as a function of size, with larger cases paying a proportionately larger share of their outstanding debts. By every statistical measure available, then, the experience of large, publicly traded companies in bankruptcy differs sharply from that of smaller, private companies, and this casts serious doubt on Bradley and Rosenzweig's claim that their data apply with equal force to all corporations choosing Chapter 11.

B. *Analysis of the Filing Data*

Despite the fact that Bradley and Rosenzweig do not produce data that permit valid inferences to be drawn about Chapter 11 cases generally, their study would still be useful if it produced reliable data about the bankruptcies of publicly traded companies. They could, in this case, simply limit their conclusions to publicly traded companies. . . .

1. *The Rise in Bankruptcy Filings*

Bradley and Rosenzweig begin their argument for the hypothesis of managerial misbehavior by documenting a precipitous rise in post-Code corporate filings. . . .

Bradley and Rosenzweig report that the filing rates for publicly traded companies rose during the period in which the total number of Chapter 11 filings rose precipitously. . . . [T]he only reason Bradley and Rosenzweig are able to report a statistically significant difference between the period "before 1979" and the "ten years thereafter" is that the former period reaches back to include data from the 1960's, when the filing rates were quite low. When the number of filings by publicly traded companies in the 1970's alone is compared with the number during the "ten years thereafter," there is no statistically significant difference. . . .

The distinction is critical. Bradley and Rosenzweig use the rise in filing rates after the enactment of the 1978 Code as the first step in their argument, but a comparison of the decade before the Code was enacted with the decade after the Code was enacted shows no difference in filing behavior. These data, therefore, do not support their claim that "the decision to file a bankruptcy petition has become more endogenous under the 1978 Act." Instead, the data support the opposite conclusion: passage of the 1978 Code had no discernible effect on the bankruptcy filings of publicly traded companies.

2. *Testing the Effects of Management Replacement Laws*

Bradley and Rosenzweig's data furnish other indications that their management control hypothesis is incorrect, even with respect to the publicly traded corporations for which they have gathered data. . . .

. . . [F]ilings for publicly traded companies show a rise ten years *before* the Code was enacted and virtually *no* change from the decade before enactment to the decade after enactment. These data demonstrate that the rise in bankruptcy filings for public companies bears no discernible relationship to changes in the law concerning managerial control.

C. *The Management Incentives Hypothesis*

A number of scholars have inquired into the question of incentives and the potential for management misbehavior when a company is in financial distress. Most researchers observe that managers try to avoid financial trouble for their firms, and that bankruptcy is a particularly unwelcome event.[40]

Bradley and Rosenzweig explain their radically different model of managerial decisionmaking:

[F]irms can *choose* to become "insolvent" by not maintaining a sufficient balance of [liquid] assets. . . . [C]orporate bankruptcy frequently is significantly *endogenous*, chosen by, rather than imposed upon, corporate managers.

The Bradley and Rosenzweig model pictures managers around the country reading the newly passed 1978 Code, swiveling back in their chairs, and giggling with delight: "Now that we have bankruptcy laws that will leave us in charge, we're gonna get wild with this business. If it flops, we'll just take it out of the hide of the creditors and the shareholders, and Chapter 11 will save us!"[43]

Given some of the high risk decisions that corporate managers made during the 1980's, the model is not without some superficial appeal. On further examination, however, it proves less than satisfactory. It hypothesizes a managerial cohort that combines uncanny sensitivity to the nuances of legal change with astonishing myopia about what really happens when companies file for bankruptcy.

---

[40]   *See, e.g.,* Susan Rose-Ackerman, *Risk Taking and Ruin: Bankruptcy and Investment Choice*, 22 J. LEGAL STUD. 277 (1991) ("Managers seek to avoid leading their firms into financial difficulties. Bankruptcy is particularly to be avoided.").

[43]   Interestingly, Bradley and Rosenzweig never explain why management would want to begin high risk operations in the first place. As they present it, the model simply presumes that if management could reduce the cost to itself of high risk strategies it would adopt them. But they do not explain what the benefit to management of such high risk strategies would be. This is a troubling omission in light of other research that supports a contrary conclusion. . . .

For the argument from incentives to succeed, it would have to be the case that the allure of court-supervised reorganization is so powerful that it encourages managers to make risky business decisions they would otherwise not make and to choose bankruptcy filings over nonbankruptcy alternatives once that risk materializes. Bradley and Rosenzweig advance no direct evidence to support such a hypothesis . . . . At the same time, they ignore a wealth of data that bear directly on management incentives, data that are inconsistent with their hypothesis.

1. Managerial Control After the Code

Bradley and Rosenzweig assert that "Chapter 11, far from preserving valuable assets, in fact serves mainly to protect managers' jobs." This hypothesis has been tested by Stuart Gilson, who conducted a careful study of 409 of the most financially troubled publicly traded companies from 1979 through 1984. In the companies that filed for bankruptcy, managers lost their jobs within two years following filing in 71% of the cases. Managers who arranged out-of-bankruptcy debt restructuring for their troubled companies did somewhat better, but 60% had been replaced within two years of the restructuring. The replacement rates of management for companies not in financial distress for a comparable two-year period was about 6-10%.

LoPucki and Whitford studied a somewhat different sample of companies in bankruptcy, focusing on those publicly traded companies that were successful in confirming a plan of reorganization under Chapter 11. They found even higher turnover rates, at least among these companies' CEO's. During the two-year period beginning eighteen months before the bankruptcy filing and ending six months after the plan confirmations, 91% of these companies changed CEO's at least once. . . .

Yet another study confirms the gloomy prospect for managers of distressed companies. Brian Betker examined management turnover for 202 publicly traded companies that filed for Chapter 11, and discovered that only 8% of the top managers who held office two years before filing retained their positions one year after confirmation of the reorganization plan.

The replaced managers in the financially troubled companies were young enough to look forward to many years of occupying the chief corporate office, but they did not simply hop to greener pastures when their companies began to fail. Not one manager in Gilson's sample was employed in another exchange-listed company any time during the three years following the manager's departure. The loss in personal earnings, Gilson speculates, amounted to a present value of about $1.3 million for each manager.

The loss to self-esteem is harder to quantify . . . . [E]arlier work demonstrat[es] that managers suffer substantial losses in reputation and self-esteem when their companies fail . . . . Other studies have documented management's aversion to filing bankruptcy, even when a company is in serious trouble.

Bradley and Rosenzweig in fact provide data that tend to support the findings of the above-mentioned studies. They note that in the cases they studied, 16.7% of the publicly traded companies that filed for bankruptcy after the Code was adopted had been delisted from their exchanges within two years of filing, and that 38.3% had been delisted within four years of filing. These failure rates would have come as no surprise to management. . . . Management has had over thirty years to learn that Chapter 11 is a high risk proposition. The point should be clear enough to any manager who is not in a coma: managers that operate a company in a way that risks a Chapter 11 filing also run a substantial risk that within a few years of filing there will be no firm for them to manage, and that, even if the firm survives, they will no longer be carrying the keys to the executive washroom. . . .

In a footnote, Bradley and Rosenzweig acknowledge some of the contradictory evidence . . . . They argue instead that data of this sort are irrelevant to their model: "[W]hat matters is not the particular identity of the managers running the firm in bankruptcy reorganization, but rather the latitude (and incentive) these managers have under Chapter 11 to pursue suboptimal strategies." This remark, however, presupposes an improbable model of human behavior. The data show that managers of public companies that file for Chapter 11 face the loss of their jobs, their reputations, their self-esteem, and their incomes. . . . Bradley and Rosenzweig seem to suggest that incentive structures are primarily abstract and that individuals do not take their personal well-being into account when they decide how to behave. Moreover, the claim that such factors are irrelevant contradicts their repeated assertion that Chapter 11 "serves mainly to protect managers' jobs."

2. Managerial Control Before the Code

As I noted in the last section, the high management replacement rates for bankrupt companies since the adoption of the Code contradicts the hypothesis that Chapter 11 saves management jobs. It is still possible, however, that the point about changing incentives is valid: if pre-Code replacement rates were even higher, so that the adoption of the 1978 Code lowered the rate of management job loss, then the claim that the increase in filings is due to increased management control is still open for consideration. But the converse must also be true: if management turnover rates were lower before 1978 and rose with the adoption of the new Code, then the hypothesis that the new laws increased incentives for managers to misbehave is directly contradicted. . . .

These data show that the kind of pre-Code/post-Code changes in the control of publicly traded companies that Bradley and Rosenzweig assume simply do not exist. Indeed, the data suggest that managers in the post-Code environment face a substantially higher risk of job loss than did their pre-Code counterparts—70 to 90% two year turnover rates post-Code versus about 16 to 41% two year rates pre-Code. . . .

D. *Data Biases*

Bradley and Rosenzweig report that their data are based on a study of all publicly traded companies that filed for bankruptcy after the new Code went into effect, which they count as 162, and on all the pre-Code filings of publicly traded companies from 1964 through 1979, which they also count as 162. There are, however, some unfortunate difficulties with the data base as constructed. First, they miss key groups of cases that could have altered the reported findings. Second, they use nonrepresentative subsets of their data to report stock and bond price changes. And third, they report valuation changes over selected times that may not be representative of overall changes. Because their data base is very small, the problems of data collection and analysis are particularly acute: errors that involve only a few cases can skew the reported results significantly. . . .

. . . [T]heir sample does not contain any firms that filed initially in Chapter X. Firms that filed in Chapter X differed significantly from those that filed initially in Chapter XI. This omission produces a potentially significant bias, and it also raises questions about the overall care with which the data were collected.

. . . In either case, they eliminated roughly half of the publicly traded companies that filed pre-Code from an already small data base.

The post-Code Chapter 11 data have similar deficiencies. Smaller publicly traded companies were also eliminated from the sample if their filings were not covered in the *WSJ Index* . . . . Morse and Shaw studied fifty publicly traded cases filed between 1980 and 1982 for which they have adequate financial data to compute shareholder losses before and after bankruptcy, but Bradley and Rosenzweig have only thirty-three publicly traded cases from the same time period in their sample. LoPucki and Whitford studied forty-three companies with assets greater than $100 million at the time of filing that filed and confirmed a plan of reorganization between 1979 and 1988, but fifteen of their cases fail to appear in the Bradley and Rosenzweig list. . . .

The data base contains more serious errors. Four of the companies listed by Bradley and Rosenzweig in their bond sample (8% of the total) were not in Chapter 11. . . .

. . . [T]he omission for any reason of a substantial number of other publicly traded cases coupled with the inclusion of companies not in bankruptcy is deeply troubling. With a sample size as small as Bradley and Rosenzweig's, the observed errors alone reduce the reliability of their data to an unacceptable level.

The data problems are exacerbated as Bradley and Rosenzweig progress through their financial analysis. Their claim that shareholders and bondholders lost more in post-Code cases is based on the analysis of financial data from only a subset of their data base. This subset analysis drops the data base precipitously. . . .

There are two serious problems with the sharp declines in the size of the data base. The first is that a sampling bias may be at work. Some other factor—such as size, success, or trading activity—might cause some companies to continue trading while others suspend trading, so that the resulting analysis is based on a subset that differs from the larger groups . . . . The second problem is that when the samples are very small, as the stock and bond samples are in this study, the possibility that a tiny handful of aberrational cases skewed the overall report for the group is very high.

Finally, the Bradley and Rosenzweig data suffer from the possibility that biases are introduced by the time periods covered by the reported data. . . .

E. *Multiple Causation*

Even if the Bradley and Rosenzweig data were reliable and were not contradicted by other data, their findings would not confirm their hypothesis of management misbehavior unless they had eliminated alternative explanations for the results they present. If other events of the period under consideration could account both for a rise in bankruptcy filings by publicly traded companies and for increased losses to their shareholders and bondholders, the idea that there is a causal link between the data they report and the hypothesis they wish to test remains unsubstantiated. There are two sorts of alternative explanations Bradley and Rosenzweig should have considered. First, a number of other important factors outside the bankruptcy system could plausibly have produced the reported results. Second, managers of troubled companies made different filing decisions in the 1980's than they had in earlier decades for reasons other than that suggested by Bradley and Rosenzweig.

The economic environment for companies operating during the 1980's was substantially different from the environment of the preceding two decades. During the 1980's, inflation rates reached record levels and then subsided, causing wild gyrations in the costs of corporate debt. Closely related to the extraordinary changes in inflation rates were the changes in interest rates, which also rose sharply, then declined. . . .

The leveraged buyout phenomenon provides perhaps the best example of the changing business environment of the 1980's. . . . To finance these acquisitions—or to avoid becoming a target themselves—companies loaded up on debt. . . . The resulting debt-laden companies had a much lower tolerance for fluctuations in the business environment . . . . This put these companies at risk for default and, eventually, bankruptcy. Not surprisingly, the Bradley and Rosenzweig post-Code bond data are filled with companies issuing junk bonds. . . .

Some industries took especially hard hits during the 1980's, and their problems are reflected in the Bradley and Rosenzweig data. . . . Considering the numerous problems companies of these types confronted during this period, it seems unlikely that the critical factor in their failure was that management faced a kinder, gentler Bankruptcy Code.

The problem of multiple causation appears in yet another form. The Bradley and Rosenzweig data are consistent with a hypothesis directly counter to their own. If the number and magnitude of business failures remained constant while the attitude of debtors about the usefulness of bankruptcy shifted, we would predict data such as those Bradley and Rosenzweig report. These data may reflect changes in the bankruptcy decisions made by debtors themselves, rather than indicating more frequent and larger failures. During the 1980's, debtors might have decided to file earlier in the decline of a business or to file bankruptcy rather than simply to close the company down or hand it over to the toughest creditor. If they made such decisions, the reported declines in the value of Chapter 11 companies during the 1980's may mean only that more failing companies are now liquidated through bankruptcy than privately and that debtor self-selection alters the mix of businesses in bankruptcy.

A great deal of anecdotal evidence suggests that some debtors who would simply have liquidated or sold their businesses to other companies in the pre-Code environment now see bankruptcy as a viable means of financial restructuring. The large, publicly traded companies that filed for bankruptcy in the 1980's differed substantially from those that filed in earlier periods. . . .

Another indication that different businesses may now be using bankruptcy is the increased willingness of very large companies to seek bankruptcy protection. . . .

If the data established that greater losses were imposed on bondholders and shareholders in the months immediately surrounding the bankruptcy filing, it does not necessarily follow that total losses are greater because of the new laws, as Bradley and Rosenzweig assert. The correct inference may be instead that more business failures are being handled in bankruptcy than ever before. . . . The data do not compare the pre- and post-Code total returns from all failing businesses, as Bradley and Rosenzweig imply. Instead, they only show that different debtors now deal with their failures through bankruptcy than did in the past.

It is also possible that businesses in distress are now filing at a different stage of financial collapse. . . .

The data collected by Bradley and Rosenzweig suggest that Chapter 11 is working better than it did a decade ago. The data show that the relative strength of the post-Code companies filing for bankruptcy is greater at the date of filing and that the relative short-term survival rate of the post-Code companies has risen somewhat. Companies that delayed filing until the business was at death's door, as so many did in the 1960's and 1970's, may have been near their lowest valuations for a substantial period of time before they filed. Other companies may have simply collapsed without ever filing for bankruptcy. By contrast, companies that filed earlier in the process may have had more value to lose. And by filing earlier, more companies that might have failed without filing in the pre-Code era may now show up as "bankruptcy failures" in the post-Code era. The data offered support the working hypothesis that managers are taking failing firms into bankruptcy at an earlier stage and, perhaps as a result, are saving more of them.

The presence of a plausible alternative hypothesis consistent with Bradley and Rosenzweig's reported results leaves open two conflicting explanations for their findings. This is like discovering that the results of a medical test are consistent with two diagnoses: the patient is ill and the patient is healthy. Bradley and Rosenzweig conclude the patient is so ill that the entire Chapter 11 system should be scrapped. I argue that it is equally plausible that the patient is healthy, and that there is some evidence to suggest that the system is working as it should—encouraging more troubled businesses to deal with their problems earlier and consequently saving more of those businesses. At a minimum, it would seem prudent to run more tests before we run the risk of burying the patient alive. . . .

III. Losing Value Or Redistributing Value?

Bradley and Rosenzweig's work rests on the premise that bankruptcy has a single goal: preservation of value for public shareholders and bondholders. If this assumption had not been among their unstated premises, they could not have recommended the repeal of Chapter 11 on the basis of their results.

Bankruptcy functions to preserve value in faltering businesses and to enhance the return to all those who have an interest in the business, but it also serves to redistribute value. Even if redistributional goals are inadequate to justify an extremely inefficient system, I would argue that they are sufficiently important to justify slight inefficiencies. Moreover, the data presented by Bradley and Rosenzweig do not illustrate system inefficiencies. . . .

A. *Redistributional Goals of Bankruptcy*

Bankruptcy law is deliberately designed to distribute assets—and losses—when a business cannot meet its outstanding obligations. When Congress passed the Bankruptcy Code, it made a great number of distributional decisions. . . .

The Code is thus designed not only to enhance the value of the failing business, but also to distribute that value among interested parties in specified ways. . . .

Even if Bradley and Rosenzweig had been able to produce data incorporating the full range of redistribution, and thus overall preservation of value could have been estimated, the inquiry would be incomplete. If the value enhancement goal and the redistributive goals conflict—as would be the case if it turned out that bankruptcy reduced total value but allocated a larger portion of the remaining value to certain preferred creditors who would not receive such protection without bankruptcy—it would remain an open question whether Chapter 11 should be dismantled. The question would present itself in cost-benefit terms: policymakers would have to decide whether the costs of the overall losses are so large that they outweigh the benefits of redistribution. . . .

1. *Distribution Away From Public Bondholders and Shareholders*

Tracing redistributive consequences is extraordinarily difficult, but there is substantial evidence that Congress intended public bondholders and shareholders to bear a greater share of the losses of failing companies. . . .

. . . Congress actively pursued redistributional strategies vis-à-vis public bondholders and shareholders of bankrupt companies through changes in the role of the Securities and Exchange Commission. . . . [T]he new Code sharply reduced the influence of the SEC. . . .

2. *Distribution to Other Affected Parties*

The experience of stockholders and bondholders is only one part of the collapse of a company, often a relatively small part. Mortgage lenders, equipment financers, inventory financers, receivable financers, trade creditors, factors, employees, taxing authorities, pensioners, customers, landlords, tenants, warranty claimants, tort victims—the list goes on and on—all stand to profit from any enhancement of the value of troubled firms. Bradley and Rosenzweig make no effort to collect data on any of the other parties who might be affected by a bankruptcy filing. . . .

Bradley and Rosenzweig excuse the narrowness of their focus by noting that it would be difficult to measure claims by constituents other than bondholders and shareholders because "they do not hold claims that trade in organized markets." . . . [T]he observation that it is too hard to measure the total value distributed to all interested parties when a business reorganizes or liquidates in bankruptcy, while data on the value received by public securities holders are easier to acquire, does not justify a research design that ignores most of what takes place in Chapter 11.

I am unaware of any comparative data on the distributions to all parties pre- and post-Code, but the data on distributions to creditors in the largest post-Code cases lend some credence to the idea that Chapter 11 is working to encourage creditor repayment ahead of payments to public security holders. . . .

B. *Redistribution in the Perfect Markets Solution*

Bradley and Rosenzweig offer what they call a "perfect markets solution" as a substitute for Chapter 11. . . . They fail, however, to reflect on the distributional consequences of their proposed scheme.

Eliminating Chapter 11 and substituting a contract-based priority system would obviously disadvantage claimants who have no contract. This means that those injured by a debtor, such as tort victims, discrimination and harassment complainants, or antitrust plaintiffs, would be left out of the scheme. It is not simply that these claimants have the lowest collection priorities when a business fails in a perfect markets world; rather, it is not clear that the perfect markets mechanism would permit them to enforce those rights at all. Consider the plight of claimants against Dalkon Shield manufacturer A.H. Robins, in a hypothetical situation in which Robins had defaulted on a senior debt obligation of $100 million. Would the thousands of women who were injured by the Dalkon Shield receive phone calls requiring them to come up with a $100 million dollar debt payment by sundown or face the loss of their claims? . . .

A number of other creditors also suffer in the contract-only paradigm. Government collectors, for example . . . are omitted. . . . Would they continue to enjoy priorities by operation of law? Would their priorities be superior to contract priorities? Would nongovernmental claimants with collection priorities, such as material-men and mechanics, enjoy priorities ahead of or behind contract and government priorities? Would we simply recreate a bankruptcy priority scheme through non-bankruptcy law?

Even among contract-based claimants, some classes would persistently win out over others. Can rank-and-file employees be expected to negotiate for stronger repayment rights more effectively than commercial lenders? Can pensioners be expected to bargain for collection rights ahead of public bondholders? Can trade creditors be expected to collect on a par with secured creditors? A contract-based scheme is overtly distributional in a regressive sense; it redistributes wealth away from those parties currently receiving—and who deserve to receive—protection under the Code.

The parties who have been left out of the perfect markets solution serve as a reminder that a key goal of bankruptcy is to determine precisely what Bradley and Rosenzweig claim will be obvious in the parties' contracts: the relative priorities of the collecting parties. Currently, priorities are established by a combination of contract and the operation of law. To change to a priority system determined entirely by contract would involve a significant reordering of the rights of many who are owed obligations by large corporations. . . .

C. Comparing Costs of Bankruptcy and "Perfect Markets"

. . . Bradley and Rosenzweig describe their proposal as an "extreme version of a 'market based' solution to corporate bankruptcy," noting that their perfect markets solution works in a perfect world. But what happens in an imperfect world? . . . Unfortunately, we live in an imperfect world. Economists have long recognized that solutions proposed for perfect markets may not work in imperfect markets. Using a theory of the second best, economists note that a device that works well within the constraints of a perfect market may, in fact, aggravate, rather than solve, problems in an imperfect market.

If we had perfect markets, Bradley and Rosenzweig might be right that we would have no need for Chapter 11. But if we had perfect markets with perfect information, perfectly understood and undisputed property rights, and zero transaction costs, it is not clear that we would have defaults or business failures. . . .

There is thus a curious asymmetry in Bradley and Rosenzweig's proposal: they assume a sufficiently imperfect market for businesses to fail, but a sufficiently perfect market for their "extreme version of a 'market based' solution" to be effective in dealing with those failures. I have difficulty envisioning that market.

Bradley and Rosenzweig argue that bankruptcy is justifiable only if there are problems generated by "significant information asymmetries, transactions costs, or ambiguous property rights." In my view, Chapter 11 was specifically designed to respond to such problems. Chapter 11 creates the conditions for collective creditor action, reducing the costs of individual creditor collection activities. . . . All of these functions help to reduce transaction costs, correct information asymmetries, and resolve legal disputes that exist in the real world between a troubled company and the thousands of entities with which it conducts business. . . .

Would the perfect markets solution be less costly? . . .

The perfect markets solution may work in a perfect market, where it is unlikely ever to be needed. But in the markets in which business failures occur, there is no evidence that the costs would be lower or that the system would be fairer than the current Chapter 11 system.

IV. Conclusion

... [W]hy not repeal Chapter 11? Because thus far, no one has come up with a good substitute. By the time we invent a system that establishes priorities among creditors, supervises defaulting debtors, provides notice and a hearing to creditors whose rights need to be determined, preserves going-concern value, and provides a collective forum to determine the rights of multiple parties, we have created another reorganization system. The details may differ, and reasonable people may disagree about what those details ought to be. We may call the system something other than "Chapter 11." There remains, however, a compelling need for some centralized procedure to deal with business failure. ...

The bankruptcy system matters. It mattered to a $10 billion business like Federated, and it mattered to their 80,000 employees who stayed on the job. The system also matters to every borrower, lender, potential victim, and warranty claimant, as well as to every person who may some day have to consider the consequences of nonpayment of a debt she owes or is owed. ...

Facts also matter. They have a powerful virtue: once they are known, policy makers and academics alike must adjust their arguments to accommodate them. Credible empirical data, more than anything else scholars bring to the table, can drastically change the terms of a debate. Bankruptcy policymaking should proceed with as much factual information as possible. ... But all those potentially affected by the system have a right to demand that the debates proceed on the basis of reliable information. Because empirical research is extraordinarily difficult to review, the researcher bears a unique burden to conduct the work with care and to present the results cautiously and accurately. The data produced by Bradley and Rosenzweig are unsound, too unsound to earn a place in the Chapter 11 debate.

Lynn M. LoPucki
Strange Visions in a Strange World: A Reply to Professors Bradley and Rosenzweig
91 Mich. L. Rev. 79 (1992)*

The same amount of smoke would be released from the factory's chimney whether the factory owner or the householder was legally responsible for the smoke damage. If this proposition strikes you as incredible on first hearing, join the club. The world of zero transaction costs turns out to be as strange as the physical world would be with zero friction.

—George J. Stigler

Introduction

The beating of the drums grows louder. In academia, they beat for a market-based solution to the problem of bankruptcy reorganization. ... Outside academia, the drums sound a different message: chapter 11 poorly serves the public by holding creditors at bay and thereby protecting incompetent managers against the natural consequences of their own mismanagement. In their provocative call for the repeal of chapter 11, Michael Bradley and Michael Rosenzweig have fused these highly resonant themes with data that purport to show the virtually complete failure of chapter 11 to serve the interests of either creditors or shareholders. . . .

Much about chapter 11 is in need of improvement. But, as is so often the case, the resonant themes are not the right ones. All three legs of Bradley and Rosenzweig's argument for repeal are seriously flawed. The heart of their empirical argument is their claim to have shown that financially stronger companies reorganizing under chapter 11 have been paying less to both their creditors and their shareholders than did weaker companies reorganizing under prior law. In Part I below, I present several more plausible explanations for the stock and bond price phenomena they observed. In all likelihood, their data reflect not a difference in the efficiency of the Act and Code regimes, as they claim, but merely the arrival of the junk bond era. Chapter 11 is processing more highly leveraged companies.

Bradley and Rosenzweig's provocative assertion that chapter 11 shields managers from creditors while they expropriate for themselves the wealth of both bondholders and stockholders in no way follows from their empirical findings, nor is it true. In Part II, I present empirical evidence from several studies to show that during the reorganization of large, publicly held companies, managers are rarely the powerful actors that Bradley and Rosenzweig make them out to be. . . .

The third leg of Bradley and Rosenzweig's argument for repeal of chapter 11 is their assertion that, in its absence, the conflicts between failing companies and their creditors could be regulated through contracts and markets. In Part III, I argue that their analysis depends so heavily on the twin assumptions of perfect capital markets and zero transaction costs that it is not helpful in evaluating the usefulness of chapter 11. Their strange visions of debtor-creditor relations after repeal of chapter 11 are the unique product of the strange world in which they conduct their analyses. In Part IV, I generalize from the critique of Bradley and Rosenzweig's proposal to a more general critique of the use of perfect market zero transaction cost models in the evaluation of procedures for bankruptcy reorganization and perhaps other legal regimes as well.

I. Are Social Costs Higher Under Chapter 11?

The empirical leg of Bradley and Rosenzweig's argument rests on an apparent anomaly. They show that the companies filing for bankruptcy reorganization since October 1, 1979 (the Code-filing companies) were, by several measures, financially stronger as they approached bankruptcy than were the companies filing before October 1, 1979 (the Act-filing companies). The apparent anomaly is that, as the companies approached bankruptcy, the equity and debt securities of the still stronger Code-filing companies lost a larger proportion of their value than did the debt and equity securities of the weaker Act-filing companies.

The difference in the losses was dramatic. Over the two-year period preceding bankruptcy, stockholders of the Act-filing companies lost only a little more than $.50 per dollar of investment, while stockholders of the Code-filing companies lost nearly all of their investment. In the period beginning twelve months before filing and ending six months after filing, bondholders of the Act-filing companies lost only 42% of their investment while bondholders of the Code-filing companies lost 70% of their investment. From these data, Bradley and Rosenzweig reach their direct empirical conclusion that financially stronger Code-filing companies were making smaller distributions to both shareholders and bondholders than financially weaker Act-filing companies. . . .

. . . [T]he central flaw in their empirical analysis is in their implicit assumption that, by showing that the *bondholders* of Code-filing companies fared worse, they had shown that the *creditors* of Code-filing companies fared worse. . . .

Unfortunately, in determining that the value of the *debt* of filing companies had declined, Bradley and Rosenzweig made a classic error in methodology. Its nature is best captured in a joke that empirical researchers like to tell. A Samaritan offers to help in the search for a valuable item on a generally dark sidewalk. Noting that the Searcher is looking only in the small area lighted by a street lamp, the Samaritan asks whether that area is where the Searcher lost the item. "No," the Searcher replies, "but the light is better here." In gathering their data on change in the value of debt claims against the reorganizing companies, Bradley and Rosenzweig looked only where the light was good. That is, they considered only publicly traded debt (bonds). Undoubtedly, their reason for doing so was that market values for the publicly traded debt were published, while market values for other kinds of debt were not readily available. The data Bradley and Rosenzweig collected showed that the market values of the traded debt had decreased; they assumed without commenting that the market values of the nontraded debt had done the same.

Substantial reason exists to believe that, if Bradley and Rosenzweig had looked beyond the light of the published trading data, their findings would have compelled them to reach a different conclusion. . . .

The summary shows that bonds, the only kind of debt examined by Bradley and Rosenzweig, constituted only 11% of the total debt of these companies as they approached bankruptcy. Most of the balance of the debt of these reorganizing companies was in the form of loans from financial institutions such as banks and insurance companies (hereinafter *bank debt*). The summary also shows that most of the bond debt (68%) was contractually subordinated to the bank debt. That is, at the time the bonds were issued, the purchasers contracted that they would forgo payment during any period the bank debt was in default until the bank debt was paid in full. Thus, the bonds that Bradley and Rosenzweig examined were not only a small portion of the total debt, but a highly atypical portion. Their atypical nature provides the basis for several explanations of the bond value decline observed by Bradley and Rosenzweig that do not support their conclusion of a debt value decline.

The most likely explanation for the sharper decline in bond values in companies approaching Code filing than in companies approaching Act filing is that the bonds of code-filing companies had more leverage working against them. The 1980s were not only the decade of the Code; they were also the decade of the junk bond. Between the Act and Code periods studied by Bradley and Rosenzweig, there was a sharp increase in corporate debt. . . . [T]he debt-to-equity ratios of Code-filing companies during the 1980s must have been considerably higher than the debt-to-equity ratios of Act-filing companies.

Other factors remaining constant, the effect of higher debt-to-equity ratios will be exactly what Bradley and Rosenzweig observed among Code-filing companies: a faster decline in the value of the subordinated debt and equity as financial problems set in. That is what makes a junk bond junk. . . .

Another way of understanding this effect is to realize that subordinated debt is like equity. It carries high risk; it represents only the right to what is left after others are paid; and its value depends heavily on the amount of debt to which it has been subordinated. When Bradley and Rosenzweig measured the decline in value of stocks and bonds, they were essentially taking two measures of the fate of equity and leaving the typical debt unexamined.

Greater leverage also explains the apparently more rapid decline in the value of the equity of Code-filing companies. Bradley and Rosenzweig did not measure the decline in the values of the companies, but only in their equities. Because equity was thinner in Code-filing companies, it seemed to be disappearing more rapidly. . . .

Bradley and Rosenzweig's complex empirical design implicitly assumed that the variables they considered were the only ones that changed from the Act era to the Code era. Yet there were probably several other systematic changes that contributed to the observed decline in the distributions to bondholders under the Code. . . . Some reason also exists to believe that deviations from the absolute priority rule in favor of shareholders and bondholders have declined between the Act era and the Code era. . . .

That effects such as these *could* account for Bradley and Rosenzweig's observations does not mean that they *do*. The returns to creditors from financially stronger companies reorganizing under the Code may have been lower than the returns to creditors from weaker Act companies reorganizing under the Act. But Bradley and Rosenzweig's assertion that they have proved it is a gross exaggeration. I have shown at least three more plausible explanations for the sharper decline in stock and bond values in Code-filing cases:

1. Code-filing companies were more highly leveraged.
2. The bonds of Code-filing companies were more likely to be subordinated.
3. Deviations from the absolute priority rule were greater in Act era reorganizations.

In addition, I have shown that the comparability of their samples of Code- and Act-filing companies is suspect because the former includes liquidating companies while the latter does not. Until Bradley and Rosenzweig can establish that creditors, not just bondholders, got less in Code-filing cases, their startling assertion that the Total Social Costs of Voluntary Bankruptcy increased with adoption of the Code simply remains unproved.

II. ARE MANAGERS THE PRIMARY BENEFICIARIES OF CHAPTER 11?

Having satisfied themselves that both shareholders and creditors got less in reorganizations under the Code, Bradley and Rosenzweig turned to the obvious next question: Where *did* the money go? While they equivocate as to whether the money was lost in operations, was pocketed by the managers themselves, or disappeared in some ill-defined combination of the two, they are consistent in asserting that management are the culprits. They "conjecture that the [Code's] principal beneficiaries have been corporate managers."

. . . They assert that managers benefit from the reduction in the recoveries of stockholders and bondholders. They reach their conclusion based on the implicit assumption of only three players in the chapter 11 game: stockholders, bondholders, and managers. If stockholders and bondholders did worse, managers must have done better.

To the extent that Bradley and Rosenzweig assert that managers extract wealth for themselves, numerous studies contradict them. Gilson was the first to publish findings that the supposedly omnipotent managers of companies in chapter 11 were highly likely to lose their jobs during the case. . . . Contrary to Bradley and Rosenzweig's assertion that the reorganization managers are "actors who do not suffer the economic consequences of their actions," the managers of reorganizing companies appear considerably more vulnerable to their constituencies than the managers of healthy companies. . . .

Bradley and Rosenzweig offer no explanation as to *how* managers "expropriate for themselves the wealth of both bondholders and stockholders." During our study of the bankruptcy reorganization of large, publicly held companies, however, Whitford and I examined the compensation and other benefits that managers extracted from their companies. . . . We specifically searched for the kinds of self-serving behavior that Bradley and Rosenzweig imagine. While we found several incidents in which managers held up their companies . . ., the amounts involved were only a tiny fraction of the amounts that Bradley and Rosenzweig report missing. If the managers are expropriating for themselves the wealth of bondholders and stockholders, they are doing it by means that neither we nor the financial writers who covered these forty-three cases were able to detect. . . .

III. CAN THE "MARKET" SUBSTITUTE FOR CHAPTER 11?

Bradley and Rosenzweig do not purport to base their provocative call for the repeal of chapter 11 on their empirical findings. They acknowledge that the direct implication of their finding that reorganization under the Act was more efficient than reorganization under the Code is that Congress should repeal chapter 11 in favor of the former law. It is on the basis of their nonempirical economic analysis that they conclude that court-supervised bankruptcy reorganization should be eliminated entirely.

The heart of that analysis lies in the concluding section, appropriately entitled "The Perfect Markets Solution to the Chapter 11 Dilemma." There the authors demonstrate that in the "hypothetical world of perfect markets" the problems of bankruptcy reorganization disappear, and "there is no economic justification for judicial interference in the contractual relationship between corporate creditors and debtors." Though the section seems on its face to have been written facetiously, the authors never crack a written smile. Instead, "building on the perfect markets solution to the Chapter 11 dilemma," they propose the repeal not only of chapter 11 but of all other forms of court-supervised reorganization.

According to Bradley and Rosenzweig, in the world that would follow, the financially distressed company would face no day of reckoning. Instead, when the company needed money to pay its debts, it would sell additional stock. Unless the firm was insolvent someone would always buy the stock. If the firm was insolvent, it would default, and the existing residual claimants (shareholders) would give up all claims to its value. They would be ousted from control of the firm immediately, without judicial intervention. Control would pass to next higher priority class, who would become the new shareholders.

To those not already familiar with the economist's hypothetical world of perfect markets and zero transaction costs (hereinafter the *PM-ZTC World*), this description must seem strange. But Bradley and Rosenzweig's strange visions do in fact follow from the strange assumptions upon which the PM-ZTC World is based. In their attack on chapter 11, Bradley and Rosenzweig have pushed those assumptions to their limits and demonstrated again how great are the differences between the world in which we live and the world in which so many economists do their thinking. A comparison of four problems addressed by chapter 11 and Bradley and Rosenzweig's PM-ZTC solutions to those problems will illustrate my point.

1. *Illiquidity*. In traditional bankruptcy theory, an asset is said to be "illiquid" when its value cannot easily be converted to cash. If the owner is forced to sell an illiquid asset under pressure of time, in a market in which there are too few buyers, or to buyers who must make major expenditures to evaluate the asset, the sale price may be considerably less than the actual value of the asset. . . . Chapter 11 addresses the deficiencies of the marketplace by offering the owners, and more importantly the creditors, an alternative to putting the debtor's assets on the auction block. . . . [T]he debtor and creditors may be able to avoid the necessity for a costly sale at a depressed price.

In the PM-ZTC world, the problem of illiquidity does not exist. Because the markets are assumed to be perfect, anything that has value can be sold for that value, immediately and costlessly. A corollary to that proposition is that, if an asset cannot be sold for its putative value of X, it does not have that value. . . . The assumption of perfect markets enables Bradley and Rosenzweig to reach the conclusion that, in the PM-ZTC World, when management can no longer raise capital through the sale of stock, the debts of the company exceed the value of its assets.

2. *Communication and coordination*. During the bankruptcy reorganization of large, publicly held companies, a great deal of time and effort goes into coordinating the activities of the thousands of stakeholders. . . . Communication is difficult. . . . Direct negotiations among so many parties are unthinkable.

Under the assumptions of the PM-ZTC World, these problems also disappear, enabling thousands of corporate stakeholders to act virtually as one. Without transaction costs, both communications and negotiations are free and instantaneous. . . . [T]he PM-ZTC World . . . assumes that parties always accept proposals that are in their interests. . . .

3. *Relief from contractual default provisions.* Another important function of chapter 11 is to relieve debtors from the sometimes draconian provisions of loan agreements that specify the effects of default. Bradley and Rosenzweig tell us that, under their proposal, enforcement of the creditor's bargain would occur automatically upon default. . . . They apparently mean that if any contract with a creditor goes into default, the common stock of the company will, to use their word, "evaporate." Readers who fall into the trap of analogizing to the world in which they live might be concerned about the possibility that a PM-ZTC World debtor might default on a single, small debt, thereby converting the remainder of the company's debt to stock, perhaps to the great distress of the latter's owners. In the PM-ZTC World, however, that could not happen. . . .

4. *Soft landings for managers and shareholders.* In the world of imperfect markets and transaction costs, extricating the productive resources of a failed business from the managers and owners who presided over the failure can be difficult. . . . Whitford and I have argued elsewhere that chapter 11 plays a crucial role in removing failed management and shifting ownership and control of large, publicly held companies to their true residual owners. . . . Tainted managers are nearly certain to be removed; control of an insolvent company almost invariably changes hands.

Bradley and Rosenzweig assert that, under their proposal, the ouster of management from control of the failed company would occur immediately on default, without the need for judicial intervention, leaving the sacked managers without the leverage needed to negotiate a deviation from the absolute priority rule. . . .

Chapter 11 exists solely to deal with transaction costs. It should be apparent by now that Bradley and Rosenzweig are correct in their conclusion that there is no need for court-supervised reorganization in a world without transaction costs. A perfect market would be a perfect substitute for chapter 11; in a PM-ZTC world, chapter 11 *should* be repealed. The issue is what significance should be accorded conclusions from the PM-ZTC World in evaluating proposals for reform of the world in which we live.

IV. MOVING BETWEEN WORLDS

Bradley and Rosenzweig's economic analysis of bankruptcy reorganization tells us more about economic analysis than about bankruptcy reorganization. The way problems melt away in this PM-ZTC World seems at first elegant, then suspicious, and finally boring. Every new proposal seems to maximize societal wealth.

The reason is simple. In this strange PM-ZTC World, every new proposal *does* maximize societal wealth. The explanation is captured most concisely in the Coase Theorem: In the absence of transaction costs, parties will reach an agreement that maximizes joint wealth. From this Theorem is derived the invariance thesis: The parties involved in a particular legal system (imaginary world) will reach the same efficient result regardless of initial legal entitlements. . . . No matter what rule or structure is legislated, when the deal making is over, that rule or structure maximizes societal wealth just as well as any other.

Unfortunately for Bradley and Rosenzweig in their call for repeal of chapter 11, the Theorem means not only that the same amount of smoke would be released from the factory's chimney whether the factory owner or the householder were legally responsible for the smoke damage, but also that the most efficient course will be taken to reorganize a company, whether the law entitles managers to hide themselves and their companies from creditors in chapter 11 or not. Answers to complex social and economic problems flow so easily in a world without transaction costs that anybody who proposes doing *anything* about a perceived problem can easily be bested. Whatever is (or can be imagined), is efficient.

The proof for the besting of Bradley and Rosenzweig proceeds as follows. If, in the PM-ZTC World, chapter 11 imposed large social costs on creditors through inefficient operation of the business and looting by management, the debt collection *system* would still operate with perfect efficiency. Creditors would simply bribe shareholders or managers . . . not to file the chapter 11 case. . . . In the PM-ZTC World, no one can do anything that does not maximize his own utility, and with it the utility of society. An unused chapter 11 is harmless, so its repeal is unnecessary.

As the simplistic nature of this slippery World comes into focus, the limited value of its study becomes clear. That the primary use of the Coase Theorem has been as a tool for economists to study the PM-ZTC World is ironic. Consistent with the view presented here, Coase himself saw his Theorem as a kind of *reductio ad absurdum* of PM-ZTC reasoning—proof that the PM-ZTC World was getting too much attention. . . .

To date, legal scholarship has generally accorded conclusions based on the assumptions of perfect markets or zero transaction costs a kind of presumptive validity until they can be disproved empirically. . . .

As yet, no one has demonstrated that any relationship at all exists between the way things work in the PM-ZTC World and the way things work in the world in which we live. No basis exists for assuming that, because a proposition is entirely true in the former world, it is even a little bit true in the latter. To prove that a necessary premise of an argument is false is to defeat the argument. By that standard, all arguments that depend on PM-ZTC assumptions fail, as do all attempts to import conclusions from the PM-ZTC World. The assumptions of perfect markets and zero transaction costs are not "theoretical." They are false. . . .

. . . Now that we have seen what is possible in the PM-ZTC World, perhaps we are ready to consider that it may have little to teach us.

James W. Bowers
The Fantastic Wisconsylvania Zero-Bureaucratic-Cost School of Bankruptcy Theory: A Comment
91 MICH. L. REV. 1773 (1993)[*]

In two recently published articles, Wisconsin Law Professor Lynn LoPucki and Pennsylvania Law Professor Elizabeth Warren, nearly simultaneously, fired the latest shots in one of academia's hottest ongoing debates: whether any good reason for having bankruptcy law exists. . . .

I write to highlight what one might easily overlook in LoPucki's and Warren's pieces. As they assail the usefulness of economic analysis, particularly analysis that begins by assuming zero transaction costs, they simultaneously inaugurate a new analytic tradition: the Fantastic Wisconsylvania School of Zero-Bureaucratic-Costs. They use their new theory to argue that markets are costly and thus are of limited or no use to people who want to take businesses apart or to reconfigure them. Corporate reorganizations, they urge, require the costless and perfectly functioning political appointee, the bankruptcy judge. The birth of this jurisprudential school is too significant to be permitted to pass unheralded.

I. THE BANKRUPTCY DEBATE: THEORY AND DATA

The bankruptcy debate . . . is over whether chapter 11 of the Bankruptcy Code is justifiable. . . .

LoPucki and Warren make three principal theoretical criticisms of the Bradley and Rosenzweig analysis which *do* invoke their new theory:

---

1. The first, argued by LoPucki alone, is that the Bradley and Rosenzweig data, strictly speaking, only justify replacing chapter 11 with chapters X and XI of the Chandler Act;
2. The second, advocated by both, is that a showing of increased bankruptcy losses for publicly listed firms does not justify a repeal of the statute insofar as it applies to unlisted companies; and
3. Third, both argue that there are possible corporate stakeholders whose gains might outweigh the losses chapter 11 imposes on stockholders and bondholders. . . .

A. The Pull of Positivism

The Bradley and Rosenzweig study shows that a regime in which bankruptcy relief is easy to obtain creates more losses than a regime in which such relief is harder to obtain. Technically, Bradley and Rosenzweig admit, the direct conclusion to be drawn from this finding is that the current law ought to be repealed in favor of the former law. However, making bankruptcy relief easier to obtain seems to increase bankruptcy losses, a fact from which one might also infer that chapter 11 ought to be repealed entirely. The process of inference employed to arrive at this last conclusion is not, at least obviously, based on any economic analysis. It is as simple as drawing the following common sense conclusions:

1. *Premise*: Less unpleasant states of the world are preferable to more unpleasant states.
2. *Data*: I hate a regime in which you stick needles into my body for ten minutes more than one in which you stick them in for only two minutes.
3. *Strict Empirical Observation*: The two-minute needle state of the world is better than the ten-minute state.
4. *Extended Inference*: The best of all worlds is probably neither the two- nor the ten-minute state, but instead a third one in which you do not stick needles into me at all.

LoPucki's first argument relies on the proposition that by itself data supports only a strict empirical observation but will not support any extended inferences so that, if you draw them, their source has to be some entirely extraneous theory. . . .

It is very difficult to obtain data which support strict empirical observations about prospective future states of affairs that have never existed. To demand that legal conclusions be based only on what can be proven by strict empirical observation, as LoPucki apparently does, is to carry the demands of positivistic methodology to an untenable extreme. . . .

Not so "strictly speaking," we can draw the inference that Bradley and Rosenzweig drew without resort to any theory other than one which holds that regimes in which costs are low are preferable to regimes in which costs are high. Indeed, I show below that the Fantastic Wisconsylvania Zero-Bureaucratic-Cost Model that drives the LoPucki and Warren critiques relies on this same preference hypothesis. . . .

B. Stakeholders and Close Corporations

The second and third arguments that both Warren and LoPucki make are especially curious in light of LoPucki's first one. If one may not form valid conclusions from anything other than strict empirical observations of facts, LoPucki cannot know anything about the market values of closely held corporations because nobody has reliable data about the value of claims to the assets of such firms. It follows that he can say to Bradley and Rosenzweig, "you do not know." He cannot say, "you are wrong." . . .

The difficulty is not only in the extent of our present knowledge, however. It is apparently LoPucki's position that whether chapter 11 is justifiable is inevitably unknowable. . . . It will thus never be possible either to justify the application of bankruptcy or to justify its repeal as it applies to such corporations or stakeholders unless either justification comes from a *theory*. This realization, when combined with LoPucki's succeeding argument in favor of having chapter 11 apply to close corporations and other stakeholders, leads to the insight that he is ignoring his own strict empirical observation restriction by employing a theory based on extended inference himself. That insight prompts this attempt to unearth the principles of his theory.

II. MARKETS AND BUREAUCRACIES

A. Aspirations and Economic Models

The meat of the Warren and LoPucki commentary on the Bradley and Rosenzweig study is their attack on economic theory . . . . The problem, LoPucki asserts, is "the economist's hypothetical world of perfect markets and zero transaction costs . . . *the PM-ZTC World*." LoPucki and Warren both argue that the distance between this assumed world and the real world in which we live is so great that conclusions about the former are simply irrelevant to the lives of people living in the latter. This argument flies in the face of a long human tradition of insisting that good can come from contemplating heaven, if for no other reason than to better the odds that we can get there.

. . . The Coase Theorem, application of which inaugurated the use of ZTC models, posits the ZTC world as one of aspiration. The ZTC world is the one in which the most is made out of the world's scarce resources. . . . In their model Bradley and Rosenzweig propose that the law be altered to mimic more closely the outcomes in a ZTC world. LoPucki and Warren, however, reject as nonsensical the use of a ZTC world even as an aspiration. This is particularly ironic because it appears that, upon close examination of their argument, LoPucki and Warren seem devoted to the lowering of transaction costs as justification for their own legal arguments. . . .

B. The Transaction Costs Avoided by Bankruptcies

The heart of LoPucki's argument is not a systematic attempt to discredit economic reasoning, but rather an argument by example. . . . LoPucki never even asks whether, in order to defend bankruptcy law, one must do anything more than assert that the world has transaction costs. Rather than face the question of whether bankruptcy has costs of its own that might exceed the market's transaction costs, he has taken the easier route of assuming that command structures entail zero bureaucratic costs. Thus, if one can demonstrate that markets impose transaction costs on people, one can easily justify chapter 11 because, unlike markets, it operates perfectly and costlessly. *Voilá* ZBC!

Warren's view may not be quite as extreme. She only suggests that bankruptcy provides certain functions at lower cost than state courts or markets. She gives us nothing except her own unvarnished opinion to support her suggestions, however. Analytically, an undefended assumption of low bureaucratic costs is so nearly the equivalent of a zero-bureaucratic-cost assumption that Warren deserves credit as codiscoverer of ZBC analysis.[43]

---

[43] If either Warren or LoPucki had less disdain for economic theory, they might not have overlooked an obvious and simple *theoretical* argument for the assumption that chapter 11 involves lower transaction costs than market activity would. Debtors always have the option of trying to work out and solve their problems in markets. To the extent that markets are cheaper than chapter 11, then, profit-maximizing debtors will avail themselves of market solutions. Assuming, as is typical in economic argument, that for any input like market restructuring activity the marginal costs are increasing, one might predict that debtors will use markets to solve their illiquidity problems until the marginal cost of additional efforts in the market exceed the marginal costs of employing chapter 11. Thus, voluntary chapter 11s will occur only when they are cheaper than alternative market-based solutions to the debtor's problems. Because the market is always available as a choice for management, the chapter 11s that actually occur will only be in cases in which command techniques cost less than market techniques; the world should never be troubled with chapter 11s in which the contrary is the case.

The Bradley and Rosenzweig study is so troubling to LoPucki and Warren because Bradley and Rosenzweig's empirical data tend to call the ZBC assumption into question. . . .

1. *The Problem of Illiquidity*

The market-based alternative to chapter 11 proposed by Bradley and Rosenzweig assumes that debtors in financial trouble can raise new capital in the market either by selling equity claims or by liquidating assets. LoPucki points out that it is costly to identify and assemble all the world's potential buyers, who are ready to make their best deals, at one place and one time . . . . Instead, it is cheaper to permit bidders to present themselves and assess potential deals with the debtor serially, over time, until a satisfactory bid is received. A market-based alternative, then, will fail because, in the real world, debtors will not have enough time between default and foreclosure to access the serially appearing buyer market. . . . LoPucki argues that chapter 11 buys time, thus overcoming this market failure, and is therefore economically justifiable. The argument is valid, however, only if one assumes that the command structure proceedings which replace these otherwise costly market transactions are themselves costless, or, as Warren is more explicit in suggesting, less costly than the market alternative. . . .

. . . In Bradley and Rosenzweig's view, on the other hand, financial distress is endogenous—chosen by management. It would be avoidable if management constantly accessed the market, perhaps years in advance of any financial downturn in the firm's fortunes, so that fire-sale time constraints would never have to be faced. If corporate managers carry out that function, they could buy and hold puts covering the firm's assets years before any financial crisis created illiquidity. . . .

Nevertheless, LoPucki would undoubtedly say, the investment in puts would divert corporate resources from their current uses, and thus would not be costless, transactionally speaking. He would, of course, be correct, but the argument would not end there. The issue then would be: Is chapter 11 cheaper than the cost of buying the puts? If it were, then management would not buy them, opting instead for chapter 11. The key defect in the current Bankruptcy Code is that, if the converse is true, the debtor cannot contract out of the chapter 11 method of dealing with the timing problem and into the cheaper put-buying technique for doing so. Of course, this is not a serious argument to a believer in the Fantastic Wisconsylvania School, which assumes that chapter 11 is *always* the low-cost alternative.

The point here is that both Bradley and Rosenzweig *and* Warren and LoPucki can be right. They differ only in their estimation of the costs of reorganizing businesses. To the extent that neither markets nor bureaucracies function costlessly, both Bradley and Rosenzweig and Warren and LoPucki carry their arguments too far. In cases of doubt, probably the best solution is to permit firms to choose which regime they feel is least costly. Firms that believe LoPucki and Warren will then opt for bankruptcies; firms that believe Bradley and Rosenzweig will choose the market-based solution. LoPucki and Warren are thus right that there is no need to adopt Bradley and Rosenzweig's solution of repealing chapter 11. All that is necessary is to amend chapter 11 so that debtors can contract out of its provisions.

2. *Communication and Coordination*

a. Communications among a multitude of parties. LoPucki's second identified market failure is that, because there are likely to be many thousands of claimants with rights against the firm, transaction costs to adjust the affairs of all these claimants are likely to be high unless one assumes them away by positing a zero-transaction-cost world. . . . To avoid these difficulties, chapter 11 is justifiable, LoPucki argues.

It is a common belief at the bar that one purpose of chapter 11 is to force negotiations among the throngs of people in a doomsday setting. It is not obvious, however, why suddenly placing all this bargaining under the mantle of chapter 11 suddenly renders it costless. If management remained liquid enough, which could be done in markets as suggested above, the hundreds of simultaneous negotiations would not have to take place in the expensive fashion that LoPucki suggests the market imposes. Everybody's property rights would not have to be redetermined at once. Instead, only the property rights of those involved in the lowest priority at any time need be involved in the renegotiations.

There are additional reasons to believe that the market offers managements techniques for lowering coordination costs. For example, lender syndicates who offer to deal through a single representative would offer competitive advantages to syndicate members over other lenders who insisted on dealing individually. . . .

In a world that still has a nonwaivable chapter 11, however, the competitive advantage of lenders who join in syndicates is nullified. . . .

3. Relief from Contractual Default Provisions

Unlike the problem of serially time-accessed markets and the problem of coordination and negotiation, this function supposedly served by chapter 11 does not involve avoidance of transaction costs. Rather, the blurring of rights that occurs when courts do not decide in advance which contract clauses to enforce and which not to enforce *creates* transaction costs. However, . . . the solution is not to add to the number of preexisting transaction costs out there in the world. Rather, it is to propose and adopt a federal law of contract that will override the inefficient state doctrines that enforce those draconian clauses. Achieving this solution, however, requires a theory to distinguish between worthwhile default clauses and objectionable ones.

It is questionable whether bankruptcy law is a rational response to an imperfection in a small part of the common law of contract that permits objectionable default clauses to be enforced. . . .

4. Soft Landings for Managers and Shareholders

LoPucki's final apology for chapter 11 is that it is needed to eliminate managers who are unwilling to be fired and shareholders who will not admit that their interest in bankrupt firms has evaporated. . . . Because LoPucki does not indicate the particular transaction costs that dictate a bureaucratic rather than a market-based solution to these problems, it is hard to believe that he offers this argument seriously.

III. SEARCHING UNDER THE STREETLAMP

. . . If I am right, the issue between those of us who rely on economic analysis to criticize bankruptcy law and those who, like LoPucki, think our work is screwball is . . . a question of how well our real markets actually work. The symmetrical question would be, "Well, how well do those bureaucrats really function?" That is the question Bradley and Rosenzweig sought to answer, and their answer is that the bureaucrats impose a lot of costs on corporate investors.

Is there any reason to believe that real market costs are sufficiently low to make them an attractive solution to the creditors' remedy problem? I believe there is. . . .

My empirical hunch is that the claimholders of the firms who chose to cope with difficulty by using the market are better off than the claimholders of the firms that did not. I defend this hunch by observing that even believers in the ZBC hypothesis like LoPucki and Warren are not yet advocating a bureaucratic alternative to the problems of those businesses that face the same transaction costs faced by declining businesses. People who put businesses together and make them grow, for example, have to enter the same serially accessed markets LoPucki and Warren decry as expensive in order to build their businesses. How much better would be a costlessly operating central planning agency that forced all resources to be registered in a central data bank so that the planners could direct, by fiat, those possessing assets to deliver them to the business-builders! . . . If bureaucratic solutions are costless, it is surprising that there is no apparent demand that they be used to replace the costly markets people use for *building* businesses. . . .

During the past seventy-five years, the efficiency of bureaucratic solutions to the problems posed by transaction costs was extensively experimented with throughout Eastern Europe. That experience validates hunches like mine: bureaucratic solutions are far from costless. Markets seem to work well enough, despite their imperfections, to put businesses together. That, it seems to me, is enough to justify my belief that markets also ought to be permitted to take them apart.

B.   Proposals for Reform

Market-Based Theories

Apart from repeal, which was discussed in the preceding section, one of the first and most commonly proposed radical reforms of chapter 11 has been to move to a *market*-based model. The idea is to use the market to value financially troubled firms, rather than relying on a judicial estimate of valuation. Recall from Professor Blum's seminal works that a key component of the theoretical justification for chapter 11 is that the market systematically fails in the case of distressed companies, necessitating a supposedly fairer and more accurate valuation method, *viz.*, judicial appraisal. In the 1980s, a number of leading free-market theorists questioned this assumption of systematic and pervasive market failure. Regardless, those theorists doubted whether judicial estimation was any more accurate; indeed, they suspected the contrary. Furthermore, those analysts suspected that the current chapter 11 judicially-supervised process led not only to mis-valuations, but also generated *redistributive* effects. That is, with the judge possibly "in their corner," junior interests had the potentiality to hold up senior interests for a cut of the pie that they did not really deserve. The two leading recommendations to rely on the market in order to achieve more accurate valuations and to avoid unwarranted redistribution have been Mark J. Roe, *Bankruptcy and Debt: A New Model for Corporate Reorganization*, 83 COLUM. L. REV. 527 (1983), and Lucian A. Bebchuk, *A New Approach to Corporate Reorganizations*, 101 HARV. L. REV. 775 (1988). Excerpts from those important works follow.

As you read Roe and Bebchuk, consider:

1.   How would their theories operate?
2.   How do their theories differ?
3.   What assumptions are necessary to support their theories?
4.   Why do they believe their theories would generate results superior to current chapter 11?
5.   If a market solution is better, why don't financially interested parties voluntarily pursue a market sale?
6.   Given their preference for the market, why not just repeal chapter 11? In short, what role is left for the reorganization court under their proposals?
7.   What limitations constrain the utility of their theories?

Mark J. Roe
Bankruptcy and Debt: A New Model for Corporate Reorganization
83 COLUM. L. REV. 527 (1983)[*]

Three general mechanisms might be considered to accomplish reorganization: (1) the bargain among creditors and stakeholders, *i.e.*, a "workout" that occurs outside the bankruptcy court or after the filing of a bankruptcy petition, but even then with minimal court supervision; (2) litigation in which the court imposes a solution and capital structure; and (3) although rarely even noted as a serious possibility, use of the market. Congress preferred that the parties first attempt a bargained-for solution, and if the bargain failed, that a judicial solution be imposed. Congress and the courts have assumed that marketplace valuation for bankrupts is too inaccurate, principally because of a lack of adequately informed buyers, to be a viable alternative. If, however, the bargain fails, courts in the ensuing litigation often hear investment bankers and other experts on the crucial questions of valuation and capital structure. The judicial solution thereby mimics the market, attempting to reach an idealized value of the bankrupt that the court believes would arise if a perfect market were at work. Both the bankruptcy bargain and the litigation mechanisms are slow, costly, and often unpredictable. Could a more direct market-based mechanism be better?

This Article examines the intertwined propositions that (1) the goal of a speedy and inexpensive reorganization for the large public firm whose stock is widely traded could best be attained by a general rule requiring that reorganization courts confirm only plans with simplified all-common-stock capital structures; and (2) the reorganization value of the public firm could be found by selling a slice, say 10%, of new common stock into the market, and extrapolating enterprise value from the sale price. Once the corporation were so valued by the market and given an all-common-stock capital structure, claimants and interests would fall into place according to the Bankruptcy Code's absolute priority rule, under which senior claimants are paid in full before juniors receive anything. If this proposal could be successfully implemented, two major tasks of reorganization—valuation and restructuring—could take place not as now occurs over the course of years, but over a much shorter period. . . .

I. CURRENT DOCTRINE, CURRENT PRACTICE, AND THE PROBLEM OF DEBT

. . .

C. *The Reorganization Bargain and Cram Down: The Best Method of Reorganization?*

The principal reorganization mechanism, in which courts loosely oversee a bargain among the claimants and owners, does not seem well equipped to resolve problems of valuation and capital structure. The available evidence regarding the bankruptcy bargain, although speculative, impressionistic, or anecdotal, indicates that the bankruptcy bargaining process is likely to be a time-consuming effort to break an initial deadlock and could result in inferior, high-debt capital structures that help resolve the deadlock, preserve tax advantages, or resolve claim-valuation tensions. . . .

2. Cram Down and the Independent Judicial Finding of Viability. The bankruptcy court is unlikely to make an astute independent determination of either the firm's value or the impact on firm viability of a questionable level of debt. Bankruptcy courts lack substantial financial expertise; they are judges, not investment bankers. . . .

. . . [B]ecause of a lack of judicial expertise, a potential need to rely on the parties, and the ease with which bankruptcy litigation problems can be resolved by using complex capital structures, there

---

[*] This article originally appeared at 83 Colum. L. Rev. 527 (1983). Reprinted by permission.

is a substantial basis for concluding that action in the reorganization court seems unlikely to lead to a capital structure as sound as those ordinarily derived from marketplace bargains. More important, the reorganization court seems unlikely to lead to quick resolution of the problem of recapitalization. . . .

II. Efficient Capital Markets and a New Reorganization Paradigm

A. *Outline of a Market-Based Solution*

If the reorganized firm can market its securities reasonably effectively, there would (at first) seem to be little justification for a bankruptcy court to take on the burden of determining the value of the bankrupt or the appropriate level of its debt. The market could, better than a court, accurately and quickly determine the enterprise value of an all-common-equity structure. To illustrate this point we will use a simple example, with no priority creditors, secured creditors, holding company structure, or other complicating features. Assume that a bankrupt firm has a capital structure consisting of $5 million of senior debt, $5 million of junior debt, and (old) common stock. There are no other creditors. Seniors argue the corporation is worth $5 million, juniors argue $10 million, (old) common argue $20 million. The court recapitalizes with a structure of 1,000,000 new common shares held for the parties, with the distribution of these shares to be specified later. Uncertain as to the ease of quickly marketing all 1,000,000 shares, it has an underwriter sell 100,000 of these shares to the public. The underwriter obtains $10 per share, indicating an extrapolated enterprise value (with the proceeds of the offering) of $10 million. The $9 million in residual value ($10 million in total enterprise value minus $1 million owned by the purchasers of the 100,000 shares) is allocated among the seniors and juniors; the old common shareholders receive nothing. The remaining 900,000 shares are then distributed: 500,000 to the seniors, 400,000 to the juniors.

Such an approach would slash through the tangled bankruptcy knots of valuation, distributional conflicts, and recapitalization. The wisdom of replacing the current means of valuation in bankruptcy with this market-based approach is initially dependent on the relative accuracy, speed, and cost of market valuation when compared to the current mechanisms.

B. *Efficient Capital Markets*

1. *The Concept of an Efficient Market.* In an efficient capital market, the price of a security will soundly reflect an informed estimate of the security's expected value. . . . [T]he critical variables are information, analysis, and breadth of the market. Is the market for a bankrupt firm's securities efficient? More to the point, is a court better equipped than the capital market to value the public bankrupt and determine its capital structure?

2. *Data with Implications as to the Efficiency of the Post-Reorganization Market.* . . . [T]he available empirical evidence seems to dispel any notion that the stigma of bankruptcy is so severe that the market will usually demand an extremely high return that is out of proportion with the long-run value of the bankrupt enterprise. . . .

C. *Judicial Doctrine Examined*

Bankruptcy institutions have frequently assumed that a reorganized firm's securities and assets are systematically undervalued (in economic jargon, that the market is imperfect), despite the evidence just cited that indicates no systematic undervaluation for public firms. . . .

. . . Only a few, generally impressionistic, bases—informational biases, monitoring problems, and stigma—could justify a court's conclusion that it can significantly improve upon the public market in valuing publicly traded securities of bankrupt enterprises. Use of these bases to reach such a conclusion does not, however, withstand analysis. . . .

1. *Informational Impediments.* The publicly available information concerning bankrupts might be insufficient to allow many investors to gauge value accurately. As such, it might be argued, the court is better able than the market to search out and evaluate information that is not publicly dispersed and then use this information to value the firm. . . . One might thus argue that either judicial intervention or valuation by those closest to the scene (claimants on, and stakeholders in, the bankrupt) would therefore be warranted.

Such an argument is unsound. The institution seeking the information need not also evaluate and act upon it. Efficient-capital-market theory asserts that the market consensus represents the best guess as to value, other than the guess of insiders. To the extent the "buried" information is especially significant for bankrupts, the proper role of the court would then be to uncover it and make it public. . . .

2. *Monitoring Impediments.* The divergence of goals among creditors, equity-holders, and management motivates the creditor to monitor management and supervise some corporate actions. The extra costs of monitoring bankrupts could make the market for the bankrupt's securities inefficient. . . .

This consideration is, however, principally applicable to the question of whether the bankrupt can raise new funds at an appropriate cost. It has little relevance to the question of undervaluation of funds already sunk into the enterprise. For funds already sunk, judicial valuation does not displace the need for monitoring. Furthermore, neither the bargaining parties nor the court can monitor well. . . .

3. *Uncertainty and Institutional Considerations.* The *Equity Funding* court attempted to justify its assumption of an inadequate stock of informed buyers: "[B]ecause of uncertainties associated with a company emerging from [reorganization] proceedings [and] possible initial selling pressure . . . individual shares of stock of [the reorganized company] may trade in the near future at less than reorganization value." The error in the first part of the justification is obvious. The economic uncertainties *are* a source of lower value. The emerging reorganized company that might not survive is worth less than its highest potential value precisely because of the uncertainties. The reorganization value is a bet on, or a best guess of, the value if operational, discounted by the chance that the reorganization will not work. . . .

The court also views initial selling pressure as an unwarranted drag on immediate market value. This view is problematic . . . because it begs the question: short-term selling "pressure" may be the result of the market's correctly valuing the firm at a value lower than did the bankruptcy court. . . . [T]o the extent dumping is a real, not an imagined, concern, the problem could be resolved by making a portion of each holding of stock nontransferable for a year or two. . . .

4. *Resolution as to Basic Impediments.* The post-reorganization market cannot provide a perfect valuation or perfectly fit the risk preferences of the claimants. But . . . the market mechanism appears to offer an accuracy no rougher than the current one.

As to the question of informational and monitoring barriers, the problem at hand cannot be resolved by protestations that some bankrupts might face these barriers. Bankruptcy institutions must decide whether their wards, individually or as a class, are likely to face them, and, if so, whether these barriers are sufficiently crippling so as to impair effective marketability. Evidence and theory of adequate marketability suggest that many of their wards probably are not crippled. . . .

D. *Efficient-Capital-Market Theory Further Considered*

. . . The efficient-capital-market hypothesis leads to the question of why judicial reorganization is necessary at all. That is, why does the firm prior to bankruptcy fail either to sell its business and then distribute the proceeds in priority fashion, or to recapitalize? As to the former, the legal deadlock between creditors and shareholders that often prevents a sale of the firm outside of bankruptcy is by now familiar to students of corporate finance. . . . Similarly, in regard to recapitalization, shareholders would not agree to a plan that left them with little or nothing. . . .

The reorganization court can be seen as necessary to break this deadlock created by statute and contract. Even so, the efficient-capital-market hypothesis would initially suggest a limited role for the reorganization court, since the court could conceivably sell the entire enterprise intact as a going concern and then distribute the proceeds, according to the hierarchical absolute priority rules, to the creditors and shareholders. . . .

The basic objection to such a course of action is the bankruptcy institutions' cherished, but overinclusive, notion that the market persistently undervalues bankrupt public firms, their piecemeal operations, and their securities. This notion is surely often correct as it applies to the sale of a large firm in its entirety. Therefore, a better basis for objection than the overinclusive notion of unmarketability is that although the market may be efficient for the handful of a firm's securities actually traded, it is likely to be ineffective for the immediate sale of an entire enterprise. . . .

Even if efficient-capital-market theory does not necessarily always cover the sale of the entire firm, such a sale could play some role in a market-based mechanism for reorganization. The court could place the firm (i.e., its assets and operations, but not its liabilities) up for bids shortly after the bankruptcy petition is filed. The highest of those bids could act as a floor for the slice-of-capital sale. . . .

The intermediate solution we are examining would employ the comparatively efficient capital market for trading securities representing a slice of the enterprise, irrespective of the marketability of the entire firm, to establish a fair market value of the entire firm. . . .

If the market is more effective than the court in valuing the firm, then one must wonder why the parties do not soon after the filing of the bankruptcy petition agree among themselves to use it in place of the court. Even if permissible under the statute the reason is apparent. Those owning the capital layer or layers in the firm likely to be damaged by use of the market will resist it. . . .

Prior to reorganization, parties would similarly be unlikely to agree among themselves to the use of a market system. . . . When bankruptcy is looming on the horizon, any effort on the part of claimants and stakeholders to agree contractually to market-based valuation will be resisted by those who would expect to do better in a bargained-for result. . . .

5. *Summary.* Thus, there is a substantial basis to believe that although the post-reorganization market might be better than a court, and quicker than the bargaining parties, in valuing the firm, bringing the market into an ongoing reorganization could introduce several distortions. As such, the proposals of finance economists, that a simple market sale and extrapolation of value is about all that is necessary to an effective reorganization, must be treated with skepticism. An administrative apparatus to control or assess the significance of the distortions would be necessary; the relevant choice is not simply among market, bargain, and judicial administration, but also among judicial administration of different matters. Since no one has tested either the severity of the market distortions or the capacity of legal institutions to control them during a reorganization, the question of the superiority of a market-based reorganization on this score is one of judgment, not economic deduction or statistical observation. . . .

CONCLUSION

. . . Bankruptcy courts oversee a rambling bargain that implicitly assigns a value to bankrupt public firms and then provides a capital structure that often is high in debt. If the bargain fails, litigation results. Both these processes are lengthy, costly, and, if a rapid, objective basis to value the firm is available, unnecessary. Since the post-reorganization market seems likely to value the firm more accurately than does the court, the reasons offered by bankruptcy institutions for rejection of the market in favor of judicial valuation (when bargaining fails)—incomplete information, stigma, and insufficient buyers—seem unpersuasive. Similarly, if the firm could effectively issue new debt into the market, there is little reason arising from a goal of firm viability for the bankruptcy court to attempt to ascertain the appropriate level and terms of debt for the bankrupt firm. . . . [W]hatever the relative accuracy of the mechanisms, a market-based valuation and recapitalization via the slice-of-common-stock sale begins with the potential to be quicker and cheaper than the alternatives, without undermining the legitimacy or predictability of the process.

Lucian A. Bebchuk
A New Approach to Corporate Reorganizations
101 HARV. L. REV. 775 (1988)[*]

I. INTRODUCTION

The concern of this Article is the way in which corporate reorganizations divide the reorganization pie. The Article puts forward a new method for making the necessary division. This method can address some major efficiency and fairness problems long thought to be inherent in corporate reorganizations. . . .

Reorganization, which is governed by chapter 11 of the Bankruptcy Code, is an alternative to liquidation. Reorganization is essentially a sale of a company to the existing "participants"—all those who hold claims against or interests in the company. This "sale" is of course a hypothetical one. The participants pay for the company with their existing claims and interests; in exchange, they receive "tickets" in the reorganized company—that is, claims against or interests in this new entity.

Why is the reorganization alternative necessary? The rationale commonly offered is that a reorganization may enable the participants to capture a greater value than they can obtain in a liquidation. In particular, reorganization is thought to be especially valuable when (i) the company's assets are worth much more as a going concern than if sold piecemeal, and (ii) there are few or even no outside buyers with both accurate information about the company and sufficient resources to acquire it. In such situations, liquidation might well leave the participants with less than the going-concern value of the company's assets; consequently, the participants will have more value to split if they retain the enterprise and divide it among themselves. . . .

II. THE DIVISION PROBLEM IN CORPORATE REORGANIZATION

The division problem in corporate reorganization, on which this Article focuses, may be stated briefly as follows. Given the set of all claims by participants, each claim defined by its size and relative priority, how should the reorganization pie (that is, the value of the reorganized company) be divided among the participants? . . .

As explained below, the existing reorganization process resolves the problem of division in a way that suffers from substantial imperfections. These imperfections are all rooted in a problem of valuation. It is generally impossible to place an objective and indisputable figure on the value that the reorganized company will have (the "reorganization value"). If such a figure were available, the distribution of tickets in the reorganized company would be easy to determine. Without such a figure, however, it is difficult to decide where, down the rank of creditors and preferred shareholders, it is necessary to stop issuing tickets in the newly reorganized entity. . . .

In contrast to liquidation, the sale of the company's assets in a reorganization is fictional. Consequently, no objective figure is available for the total monetary value to be distributed or, as a result, for the monetary value of the various tickets in the reorganized company. . . . It is of course possible to ask courts to estimate the reorganization value, and courts indeed sometimes must make such estimates. But no one suggests that we can rely on such judicial estimates to be generally accurate.

The law has always dealt with this valuation problem by leaving the division of tickets in the reorganized company to a process of bargaining among the participants. . . . The rules constrain the bargaining process by prescribing the limits within which the classes may bargain. . . .

This process of bargaining and litigation is quite imperfect. First, and most importantly, the reorganization process often produces a division that substantially deviates from the participants' entitlements. . . .

Second, the reorganization process often results in the choice of an inefficient capital structure for the reorganized company. . . .

Third, putting aside the severe shortcomings of the outcome of the division process, the process itself has substantial costs. . . .

III. The Proposed method
A. *The Example*

To describe and assess the proposed method, it will be useful to consider it in the context of a concrete and simple example. Consider a publicly traded company that has three classes of participants. Class A includes 100 senior creditors, each owed $1. Class B includes 100 junior creditors, each owed $1. Class C includes 100 equityholders, each holding one unit of equity.

The company is now in bankruptcy proceedings and is to be reorganized. The Reorganized Company, which I will call RC, is going to have a capital structure that for now I will assume to be given. For any chosen capital structure, it is of course possible to divide the securities of RC into 100 equal units. For example, if RC will have 100 shares of common stock and 50 shares of preferred stock, then each of the 100 RC units will consist of 1 common share and $1/2$ preferred share. The question for the reorganization process is how to divide the 100 units of RC among the three classes of participants.

B. *Dividing the Pie Supposing its Size is Known*

Let us denote the value of the reorganized company RC as V per unit. Thus, $100V$ is the total size of the pie to be distributed. As already noted, the division of the pie would be a straightforward matter if we could measure its size exactly (that is, if we could estimate V with precision). In such a case, we would simply proceed according to the ranking of the various classes involved.

Consider first the case in which the figure placed on V is no higher than $1. In this case, the total pie is no greater than $100, which is the full value of class A's claims. Therefore, all the 100 units of RC should be given to the senior creditors (and divided among them pro rata).

Consider next the case in which the figure placed on V is greater than $1 but no greater than $2. In this case, the total pie is no greater than $200, which is the full value of the claims of the senior and junior creditors, and it thus should be divided only among the creditors. Because there is enough to pay the senior creditors in full, they should receive a value of $100, which can be accomplished by giving them $100/V$ units. Dividing these units among senior creditors pro rata, each senior creditor would receive $1/V$ units worth $1. The junior creditors should receive the remaining value of $100V - \$100$, which can be accomplished by giving them the remaining $100-(100/V)$ units. Dividing these units among the junior creditors, each would end up with $1- (1/V)$ units.

Finally, consider the case in which the figure placed on V is higher than $2. In this case, there is more than enough to pay both class A and class B in full. To be paid in full, the senior creditors as a class should receive 100/V units, with each senior creditor getting 1/V units. The junior creditors, also paid in full, should also receive 100/V units total, or 1/V units each. And the equityholders should receive the remaining value of 100V - $200. This would be accomplished by giving them—and dividing among them pro rata—the remaining 100 - (200/V) units (that is, 1 - (2/V) units for each equityholder). . . .

C. *Participants' Entitlements as a Function of Reorganization Value*

The question of division thus would pose no problem if we could measure V with precision. As already emphasized, however, the value of V—and thus also the monetary value to which each participant is entitled—cannot be determined with indisputable accuracy. But even though we cannot identify precisely the value to which each participant is entitled, we can precisely express this value as a function of V, the reorganized company's per unit value.

Consider first the senior creditors. As the analysis above has shown, a senior creditor is entitled to a value of V if $V < 1 and a value of $1 if $V > 1. Alternatively put, a senior creditor is entitled to a value of $1 unless the reorganization value is less than $100, in which case the senior creditor is entitled to his pro rata share of the reorganization value (that is, to one unit of RC).

Consider next the junior creditors. A junior creditor, we have seen, is entitled to nothing if $V < 1, is entitled to V - $1 if $1 < V < 2, and is entitled to $1 if $V > 2. Alternatively put, a junior creditor is entitled to a value of $1 unless the reorganization value is less than $200, in which case he is entitled to his pro rata share of the value that is left, if any, after the senior creditors are paid in full.

Finally, an equityholder is entitled to nothing if $V < 2, and to V - $2 if $V > 2. Alternatively put, an equityholder is entitled to his pro rata share of the value that is left, if any, after the senior and junior creditors are paid in full. . . .

D. *The Proposed Approach*

The idea underlying the proposed method is simple. Even though we do not know V and consequently do not know the value of participants' entitlements in terms of dollars or RC units, we do know precisely what participants are entitled to as a function of V (that is, for any value that V might take). With this knowledge, it is possible to design and to distribute to the participants a set of rights concerning RC's units such that, for any value that V might take, these rights would provide participants with values perfectly consistent with their entitlements.

. . . [E]ach of the rights distributed to participants will have an "option" component. In principle, the options should be for immediate exercise. However, because the participants might need a little bit of time to understand the terms of the options given to them, it might well be desirable to provide them with such time. The exercise date of the options, then, will be shortly after the distribution of the rights. For concreteness, I will assume below that the reorganized company will start its life and distribute the rights to participants on January 1; and that the exercise date for all the rights distributed will be four days later, on January 5.

. . . Instead of receiving RC units, on January 1 the participants will get the following rights with respect to RC units.

1. *Senior Creditors.*—Each senior creditor will receive one type-A right. A type-A right may be redeemed by the company on January 5 for $1. If the right is not redeemed, its holder on January 5 will be entitled to receive one unit of RC.

To get some sense at this stage of the value to senior creditors of receiving type-A rights, consider a creditor that holds his type-A right until January 5. If the right is redeemed, then the creditor will be paid in full. If the right is not redeemed, then the creditor will receive a value of V. And indeed, the senior creditor is never entitled to receive more than either $1 or V.

2. *Junior Creditors.*—Each junior creditor will receive a type-*B* right. The company may redeem a type-*B* right on January 5 for $1. If the right is not redeemed, its holder will have the option on January 5 to purchase one unit of *RC* for $1. To exercise this option, the holder of the right must submit it to the company by January 5 accompanied by a payment of the $1 exercise price.

Again, it might be worthwhile to describe briefly how receiving a type-*B* right will provide a junior creditor with the value to which he is entitled. If the creditor holds on to the type-*B* right and the right is redeemed, then the creditor will be paid in full. If the right is not redeemed, exercising it will provide the creditor with a value of *V* - $1. And indeed, the creditor is never entitled to receive a value higher than both $1 and *V* - $1. . . .

3. *Equityholders.*—Each equityholder will receive one type-*C* right. A type-*C* right may not be redeemed by the company. The holder of a type-*C* right will have the option to purchase one *RC* unit on January 5 for $2. To exercise this option, the holder must submit the right to the company by January 5 accompanied by a payment of the $2 exercise price.

Note that if an equityholder holds on to his right until January 5 and then chooses to exercise it, he will get a value *V* - $2. And indeed, the equityholder is never entitled to a positive value exceeding *V* - $2.

These three types of rights will all be transferable. Thus, between January 1 and January 5, there will presumably be public trading in the rights. A participant that is given any one of the rights may thus either sell it on the market or retain it until the exercise date of January 5.

E. *The Exercise of Rights*

Adding up the obligations that *RC* will have toward the holders of type-*A*, type-*B*, and type-*C* rights shows that the net obligation of *RC* is to distribute 100 *RC* units on January 5, which is exactly what is available for distribution. Thus, *RC* should have no problem meeting all its obligations toward the holders of the three types of rights. . . .

Suppose first that all of the holders of type-*C* rights wish to exercise their options to buy *RC* units and that they submit a total of $200 to the company. *RC* then will provide them with all 100 units of *RC* (one unit for each right submitted), and it will use the $200 received from them to redeem all of the type-*A* and type-*B* rights.

Suppose now that no type-*C* rights are submitted for exercise, but that all holders of type-*B* rights wish to exercise their options to buy *RC* units at $1 and therefore submit a total of $100 to the company. In this case, *RC* will give all of the *RC* units to the holders of these type-*B* rights, and it will use the $100 received from them to redeem all of the type-*A* rights.

Next, suppose that no type-*B* or type-*C* rights are submitted for exercise. The mechanics of this case will be simpler still: the 100 units of *RC* will be distributed to the holders of type-*A* rights (one *RC* unit per right). . . .

IV. Consistency With Participants' Entitlements

This Part demonstrates that the outcome of the proposed method of division will be perfectly consistent with the entitlements of the participants. As emphasized earlier, the problems of the division process arise from the difficulties involved in determining the monetary value of the reorganized company. The proposed method, however, makes no attempt to estimate this monetary value, nor does it require even a rough sense of the monetary value of the rights that the participants will receive. Although we may not know how much these rights are worth, we can be confident that whatever their worth is, they will provide the receiving participants with no less than the value to which they are entitled.

A. *The Significance of Not Relying on Accurate Market Pricing*

The rights given to the participants will be traded on the market in the brief period between the issue date and the exercise date. As the analysis below will indicate, if the market does not underestimate the reorganized company's value, then the market price of any type of right will be no less than the value to which the participants receiving the right are entitled; consequently, the participants will be able to capture the value of their entitlement by immediately selling their rights on the market. . . . [H]owever, such an assumption is not necessary to reach this conclusion: the method's effectiveness does not hinge on the market's not undervaluing the rights or even on the presence of market trading in the rights.

This feature of the method is very important. . . . [O]ne must recognize that many public officials and commentators believe that the market often errs (and usually in the direction of undervaluation) in appraising the value of companies that emerge out of reorganization. . . .

This feature of the method is the main reason why it is superior to the method of division put forward by Professor Roe five years ago. . . . He proposed to estimate the value of the reorganized company by selling ten percent of the reorganized company's securities on the market and then extrapolating the company's value from the sale price for these securities. . . . [T]he method's reliance on market pricing makes it, as Roe himself recognized, substantially imperfect.

. . . [I]t is worth stating briefly why accurate market pricing of the rights is not essential for the proposed method's effectiveness. Although participants may sell their rights on the market, they can always choose to retain them until the exercise date. If they do so, then, as is shown below, they will not end up with less than the value to which they are entitled. Consequently, even assuming that a given participant does not have, or attaches no value to, the opportunity to sell his rights on the market, the participant will have no basis for complaining about the method's outcome.

B. *The Outcome in the Example*

To demonstrate the method's effectiveness, I wish first to show that, in the example used in Part III, no participant has any basis for complaining about the method's outcome. Consider first the senior creditors. If they retain the type-*A* rights given to them, they will end up in one of two positions. First, their rights may be redeemed for $100 (if the holders of the type-*B* or type-*C* rights choose to exercise them). In this case, the senior creditors surely cannot complain about the outcome, as their claims will be paid in full. Alternatively, the senior creditors' rights may not be redeemed, in which case the creditors will end up holding all 100 units of *RC*. Again, they will have no basis for complaining, for they will be getting the whole reorganization pie: there is nothing more that could be given to them. . . .

Consider now the junior creditors. If the junior creditors do not sell their type-*B* rights, they can end up in one of two positions. First, their rights may be redeemed by the company at $1 per right (if the type-*C* rights are submitted for exercise). In this case, the junior creditors will be paid in full and clearly have no reason to complain. Alternatively, the junior creditors may end up with options to purchase *RC* units at $1 per unit. The value of these options is by definition not lower than the value to which the creditors are entitled—for the junior creditors are entitled to no more than the value that is left, if any, after the senior creditors are paid in full. And having the option to receive all of the reorganization pie by paying the senior creditors' prior $100 claim makes the above value accessible to the junior creditors. . . .

Finally, consider the equityholders. If they do not sell their type-*C* rights, they will on the exercise date have options to purchase *RC* units at $2. These options will make accessible to them the very value to which they are entitled—which is all that is left, if anything, after the claims of the senior and junior creditors are paid in full. . . .

VII. Conclusion

This Article has put forward a new method of division for corporate reorganizations. This method can eliminate certain efficiency and fairness problems that have been long viewed as inherent to the reorganization process. Under the method, once the size and relative priority of the participants' claims are determined, the division of the reorganization pie will be resolved quickly and efficiently—and in perfect consistency with the entitlements of all the participants. The method is put forward as a basis for law reform: the optimal reorganization regime is one that requires and facilitates the application of the proposed method in every reorganization case. Furthermore, the method can be used even under the existing legal rules, as a basis for reorganization plans that participants may want to file. It is hoped that the method will indeed prove useful to public officials overseeing corporate reorganizations and to participants in such reorganizations.

Contract-Based Theories

The market theorists of the 1980s were skeptical about the accuracy and fairness of judicial valuation, but they stopped short of proposing complete contractual autonomy as a means of resolving financial distress. What problems might infect contract-based solutions to corporate insolvency?

In the decade of the 1990s corporate bankruptcy reform theorists centered the terms of the debate on the possibility of *contract* as a means of resolving business financial distress problems. Under these "contract" approaches the key players in the debtor-creditor regime would determine *ex ante* via contract how to handle any ensuing financial problems. Note that these contract theories rely heavily on efficient markets, theorizing that the markets will make necessary adjustments once the terms of the parties' default contracts are known. The contract theories differ from the market theories of Roe, Bebchuk and others, though, by insisting on the wisdom of permitting *ex ante* contracts to fix the terms of *ex post* financial distress resolution. The market proponents would not take that step, using the market only in the *ex post* world after default occurred.

Recall that Bradley and Rosenzweig proposed a form of contract-based resolution in 1992 by suggesting use of "contingent equity" in *The Untenable Case for Chapter 11*. The watershed article that put contract bankruptcy at the heart of the debate was the first that follows, Professor Robert Rasmussen's provocative work, *Debtor's Choice: A Menu Approach to Corporate Bankruptcy*, 71 Tex. L. Rev. 51 (1992). Rasmussen further elaborated his views on corporate bankruptcy in Robert K. Rasmussen & David A. Skeel, Jr. *The Economic Analysis of Corporate Bankruptcy Law*, 3 Am. Bankr. Inst. L. Rev. 85 (1995), and Robert K. Rasmussen, *The Ex Ante Effects of Bankruptcy Reform on Investment Incentives*, 72 Wash. U. L.Q. 1159 (1994).

What is Rasmussen's proposal in his *Debtor's Choice* article? What problems does he claim his proposal will solve? How? What concerns does he recognize with his proposal, and why does he not believe they are fatal? What are the limitations of his idea? How would he deal with nonconsensual creditors?

As noted in the first part of this chapter, Professor Barry Adler has also written many insightful works about corporate bankruptcy. Among his excellent articles not included here on corporate bankruptcy reform are *A Theory of Corporate Insolvency*, 72 N.Y.U. L. Rev. 343 (1997); *Finance's Theoretical Divide and the Proper Role of Insolvency Rules*, 68 S. Cal. L. Rev. 401 (1994); and *A World Without Debt*, 72 Wash. U. L.Q. 811 (1994). He recently published an article on valuation of firms in bankruptcy with Professor Ian Ayres, *A Dilution Mechanism for Valuing Corporations in Bankruptcy*, 111 Yale L.J. 83 (2001). The article excerpted here is *Financial and Political Theories of American Corporate Bankruptcy*, 45 STAN. L. REV. 311 (1993). In that work, Professor Adler recommends adoption of a contractual scheme of "chameleon equity," which is similar to but—as he vociferously emphasizes—*not* identical with Bradley and Rosenzweig's "contingent equity" schema. Adler also explains what changes would have to be made in other laws to accommodate his proposal. Furthermore, he examines political choice theory to assess the practical obstacles to adoption of his idea.

Perhaps the most eloquent and persistent proponent of contract-based corporate bankruptcy theories in recent years has been Professor Alan Schwartz. Schwartz first explored this concept in *Bankruptcy Workouts and Debt Contracts*, 36 J.L. & ECON. 595 (1993), and pursued his thinking further in *Contracting About Bankruptcy*, 13 J.L. ECON. & ORG. 127 (1997). The culmination of his theories on this subject came with the publication of the article included here, *A Contract Theory Approach to Business Bankruptcy*, 107 YALE L.J. 1807 (1998). Schwartz's views have been hotly contested, notably by Professor Lynn LoPucki, in *Contract Bankruptcy: A Reply to Alan Schwartz*, 109 YALE L.J. 317 (1999). Schwartz answered LoPucki's challenge in *Bankruptcy Contracting Reviewed*, 109 YALE L.J. 343 (1999). LoPucki rejoined in *Bankruptcy Contracting Revised: A Reply to Alan Schwartz's New Model*, 109 YALE L.J. 365 (1999). Others who have weighed in on the contract bankruptcy debate include Steven L. Schwarcz, *Rethinking Freedom of Contract: A Bankruptcy Paradigm*, 77 TEX. L. REV. 515 (1999), and Susan Block-Lieb, *The Logic and Limits of Contract Bankruptcy*, 2001 U. ILL. L. REV. 503.

Robert K. Rasmussen
Debtor's Choice: A Menu Approach to Corporate Bankruptcy
71 TEX. L. REV. 51 (1992)*

The first Part of this Article argues that a firm's ability to file for bankruptcy reorganization should be determined by the firm's investors rather than by the government. This conclusion flows from the realization that a creditor's treatment in bankruptcy is nothing more than a term of the contract that a firm makes with that creditor. Bankruptcy law simply specifies the payoff that the creditor will receive if a given contingency arises; namely, that the firm files a bankruptcy petition. Bankruptcy law thus is part of the bargain between the investors of a firm and its creditors; it is not a bargain amongst the creditors themselves.

Before specifying what content this contract term should take, this Article examines whether this term should be a default rule or a mandatory rule. Contrary to the prevailing wisdom, this Article argues that bankruptcy law should be treated as a default rule. There is no reason to think that a single bankruptcy regime would be appropriate for all firms or that those affected by the bankruptcy term of the credit contract should not be able to select the term of their choosing. This does not mean, however, that the crafting of a bankruptcy regime should be left totally to private contract. The rights of nonconsensual creditors should be set by a mandatory rule. Moreover, to decrease transaction costs, Congress should create a menu bankruptcy system. Under this system, a firm upon formation would be required to select one of the alternatives from the menu, thereby specifying the firm's available bankruptcy option. . . .

I. A Default Rule Approach to Corporate Reorganization

. . . A creditor's treatment in a bankruptcy proceeding is not something that the creditor considers only after it has extended credit to the firm. Similarly, bankruptcy is not an unknown disease that the affected parties must confront only after the firm's financial difficulties have become apparent. The fact of the matter is that the possibility of bankruptcy hangs over every decision to lend money to a firm. It is a contingency of which both parties are aware. Asking how the law should sort out rights either after the firm finds itself in a bankruptcy proceeding or after the creditors' initial lending decisions have been made ignores the fact that firm failure is an event that the contracting parties take into account at the beginning of the contractual relationship. . . . To the extent that bankruptcy theory attempts to justify bankruptcy law from any point in time after a party becomes a creditor of a firm, it begins the inquiry in the wrong place.

Any attempt to justify bankruptcy law from a normative perspective should begin with the observation that bankruptcy law is a term of the contract between the firm and those who extend credit to it. . . .

. . . So long as a creditor can anticipate its treatment in bankruptcy, it can ensure that it receives a market-based rate of return on its loan. . . .

From this perspective, it is clear that bankruptcy law is an implied term of the contract between a creditor and the firm. It specifies the creditor's return in those situations where the financially beleaguered firm files a bankruptcy petition. . . .

The realization that bankruptcy is part of the initial contract a creditor makes with the firm calls into question the assumed mandatory availability of Chapter 11. Legal rules implicitly determine the content of much of the contract between two parties. Contract scholars identify two types of rules: mandatory rules and default rules. . . . [I]t is clear that the current option afforded to all firms to file for corporate reorganization under Chapter 11 is a mandatory rule. In other words, a firm cannot contract around its provisions; it cannot make a legally enforceable contract not to file for bankruptcy. Those who advocate maintaining the current universal access to bankruptcy in essence suggest that access to bankruptcy should be fixed by a mandatory rule. All firms have the right to file for Chapter 11, and these advocates of the status quo do not recognize any reason for denying a firm the ability to file for Chapter 11. Indeed, these theorists generally advocate preventing a firm from waiving its right to file for bankruptcy.

. . . [T]his assumption is an anomaly. Many, if not most, rules in contract law are default rules; they apply only if the parties fail to contract around them. . . .

The standard justification for having default rules is that a default rule, by giving the parties freedom to specify what they actually want, leads to improved returns to the contracting parties. If the default rule is the most efficient one for the parties, they will not, as a general matter, bargain to a different result. . . .

The case for default rules becomes stronger as the types of parties or situations covered by a given rule become more diverse. The greater the diversity of parties or situations covered by a rule, the less likely will it be that one size fits all. . . . Given that current bankruptcy law provides only one standard bankruptcy term for all firms, and that firms vary greatly in size and complexity, it is hard to imagine that such law maximizes the contracting surplus for all parties. Indeed, it is hard to imagine that any one bankruptcy rule, whatever it may be, would be the optimal rule for all firms. There thus is strong reason to suspect that treating bankruptcy as a default rule would increase the overall welfare of the contracting parties. . . . This strongly suggests that a default-rule approach is superior to the law's current prescription of a mandatory rule.

To be sure, mandatory contract rules do exist. . . . However, mandatory rules are generally viewed as the exception rather than the norm. As such, one must provide a justification for invoking mandatory rules. Contract theorists generally agree that mandatory rules can be justified either by society wanting to protect the contracting parties themselves (paternalism) or by society wanting to protect third parties (externalities). In other words, the burden is on those advocating a mandatory rule to demonstrate the necessity for its existence.

In light of these potential gains from shifting to some sort of default rule, the premise that the ability to file for bankruptcy should be a mandatory rule, while at times noted in passing, cannot be justified. To be sure, some have defended the mandatory nature of bankruptcy. . . .

A[n] argument raised in defense of the mandatory nature of bankruptcy is the need for standardization. In short, some argue that having a mandatory bankruptcy scheme makes it easy for all players to know the rules of the game. This argument has two aspects. First, standardization saves the parties the cost of creating an entire bankruptcy regime from scratch. If each firm were required to draft its own set of bankruptcy procedures, it may very well be that for many firms the cost of drafting such procedures would outweigh the gain that the firm would realize through the introduction of the efficient bankruptcy term. Added to this drafting cost is the cost of communicating the bankruptcy term to all subsequent creditors. . . .

A second aspect of the standardization argument is that the mandatory nature of bankruptcy guards against strategic behavior. If one creditor could contract out of bankruptcy, all creditors would have to be on guard and learn about such efforts. The firm cannot contract with all creditors at once. The first creditor contracting with the firm, in light of the potential problem of the firm reaching a different contract with subsequent creditors, might adopt a maximin approach. In other words, a creditor would attempt to maximize its return assuming that the other creditors were attempting to minimize its return. The motivation of the creditor would be as follows. If the firm cannot credibly commit itself to offering only one bankruptcy term, the creditors may not agree to the optimal bankruptcy term for fear that other creditors would not be bound to the same term. Instead, the creditor would agree only to a bankruptcy term that protected the creditor from future expropriation. In other words, while there might be potential gains from contracting out of Chapter 11, the costs of trying to implement such a regime would outweigh the potential benefits. According to its proponents, the benefits of standardization outweigh the benefits of customizing.

The solution to both the transaction-cost problem and the strategic-action problem is to have a menu of bankruptcy options available. When a firm is formed, it would be required to select what courses of action it wishes to have available if it runs into financial difficulties down the road. The virtue of standardized options is that they reduce transactions costs and make communication to third parties easy. One can still allow parties to write their own contract if none of the options available suit their needs . . . . The existence of a known menu of bankruptcy choices thus answers the transaction-cost argument for treating bankruptcy as a mandatory rule.

A menu approach can handle the strategic-manipulation problem as well. An approach that limits the firm's ability to change its selection after it has incurred debt ensures that the threat of the firm amending its bankruptcy choice so as to transfer wealth from the creditors to the equity holders is eliminated . . . . [T]he important point is that these limitations ensure that a firm can publicly announce what bankruptcy option it would choose, and all future creditors would be able to rely on the option that the firm specifies.

A menu approach to corporate bankruptcy law creates another benefit as well; it would aid the owners of a firm in deciding which option they should choose. By offering a discrete set of choices, the menu would enable banks and other creditors to anticipate the interest-rate adjustments that would be made for each option. They could then communicate to those establishing the firm the true cost of selecting one bankruptcy provision over another. . . .

It is thus clear that as far as those who choose to deal with a firm are concerned, the law of corporate reorganization should be a default rule. However, involuntary creditors should be subject to a mandatory rule. Persons such as tort creditors have in no meaningful sense contracted with the firm. If their rights could be set by the investors of the firm, their rights would most likely be nonexistent. Since the firm does not need their consent, the equity holders have an incentive to foist on them the harshest terms possible. Stated differently, given the inability of nonconsensual creditors to contract with the firm ex ante, a default-rule approach would encourage consensual creditors to shift the costs of insolvency onto nonconsensual creditors. If the firm could assign the lowest possible priority to nonconsensual claimants, it could thus increase the return to consensual claimants, thereby lowering the firm's cost of credit.

This problem is easily remedied. It is beyond peradventure that mandatory rules can be justified as protecting third parties. It is clear that nonconsensual creditors need such protection. They do not, however, need the protection of a mandatory bankruptcy regime. . . . [O]nce policymakers decide the optimal treatment of nonconsensual creditors, this treatment should be unalterable by any debt contract. In other words, the priority status of tort claimants should not depend on which bankruptcy option a firm selects. Thus, a bankruptcy regime consisting primarily of default rules can readily accommodate the existence of nonconsensual claimants. . . .

III. The Menu

A. The Selections on the Menu

Drafting a menu of bankruptcy options requires a balance between specifying the optimal rule for each different type of firm and the information costs associated with learning the contours of a number of different bankruptcy terms. At some point the marginal gain of another option is outweighed by the cost of learning the details of that option. . . .

The first alternative on the bankruptcy menu would enable the firm to commit to never filing a petition under federal bankruptcy law. This would be the "no-bankruptcy" option. . . .

Equity holders may find it in their interest to select this no-bankruptcy option where the firm is comprised of a single asset, the equity holders contribute no firm-specific value, and there is a financing secured creditor whose claim exceeds the asset's value. In this situation, creditors might offer the firm a lower interest rate than they would if the firm could choose to file either Chapter 11 or Chapter 7. . . .

A second option on the menu would enable the firm to file a Chapter 7 petition only. The current version of Chapter 7 would be modified to provide expressly that firms filing under its provisions are to be auctioned off to the highest bidder. Such an option would be preferable for those equity holders who would prefer the possibility of an actual sale to a hypothetical sale provided by Chapter 11. Equity holders in public companies would probably prefer such an option because if assured that an actual sale would take place in the event of insolvency, creditors would offer lower interest rates. Under this modified Chapter 7 option the creditors would be assured that bankruptcy would be relatively short, thus promising a quicker payout than under most Chapter 11 proceedings, and that all proceeds from the firm's assets would go to them rather than to equity holders. Creditors in such a situation would thus offer lower interest rates to a firm whose only option is a Chapter 7 auction as opposed to a firm that could file for Chapter 11 protection. . . .

. . . [I]t may be the case that the equity holders at the time of contracting would prefer a bankruptcy term that provides for some sort of Chapter 11 proceeding. To accommodate these diverging preferences, the menu also needs a version of the current Chapter 11. With the competing selections of a real and a hypothetical sale available, the menu approach will allow banks to tell the equity holders the exact cost of their choice. Whether or not the cost of Chapter 11 is worth its benefits will be a decision that each firm will have to make on its own.

The next selection on the menu would be one for a type of bankruptcy proceeding that does not yet exist. It would stay all creditors except for the financing creditor. The motivation for this type of bankruptcy provision is as follows: There are two types of risk—those over which the firm has control and those over which it does not. Lenders know that courts may have trouble distinguishing between these two types of risk. In situations where the financier can distinguish which type of risk is responsible for a particular business failure (in other words, the risks are observable but not verifiable), the efficient solution may be to give the bank the power to call the loan on demand. When such a provision is in place, the manager has the incentive to work hard because she bears all the downside risk. . . . This selective-stay model of bankruptcy may leave the bank with the liquidation value of its collateral while giving the manager the full value of her human capital.

The final choice on the menu is to allow the firm to create its own bankruptcy regime, subject to the restraint that it must treat nonconsensual creditors according to the rule that the state selects. . . . It may be that those in control of the firm would desire a system bearing little resemblance to current law. To be sure, the gain over any of the choices on the menu would have to exceed the drafting and communication costs that a custom-designed system would entail. . . .

C. Strategic Considerations

. . . This leaves the problem of changes in the firm's original choice. Firms evolve. Most companies do not start out as publicly held entities; most of today's large corporations were yesterday's start-up companies. Any scheme that seeks to optimize the value of the firm based on the nature of the firm's investors has to recognize that the type of investor in any given firm may change over time. . . . Thus, firms need a mechanism by which they can change the type of reorganization for which they are eligible. Just as one bankruptcy procedure is not optimal for all firms, one bankruptcy procedure may not be optimal for the same firm throughout all of its existence. Locking firms into their original choice will undoubtedly lead to inefficient results.

The obvious answer to the problem of firm evolution, letting firms change their bankruptcy option as their needs change, cannot be adopted. Firms cannot be allowed unlimited freedom to amend their chosen menu option. Such freedom to change the corporate charter would rob the menu regime of many of its benefits. The benefit that a firm receives from committing to a bankruptcy option that gives the equity holders less ex post than does the current Chapter 11 would evaporate because the commitment would not be credible. . . . The gains from the menu system would be lost.

The problem, however, is not insolvable. What is needed are sensible restraints on the amendment process to ensure that a firm cannot reallocate its value from the debt holders to the equity holders. There should thus be no prohibition on a firm that had originally contracted for Chapter 11 amending its charter to allow for Chapter 7. . . . Since the change from a Chapter 11 selection to a Chapter 7-only selection cannot transfer wealth from the debt holders to the shareholders, such amendments should be allowed without legal constraints.

Other changes in the bankruptcy term would be more problematic. As described above, a firm should not have complete freedom to change from a Chapter 7-only selection to a Chapter 11 selection. Yet at times such a change may be necessary given the change in the nature of the firm. . . . In this situation, change in the corporate charter should be allowed only with the consent of all of the creditors. . . .

One more amendment problem remains, and that is how to handle a firm's desire to move either to or away from the no-bankruptcy option. . . . The main difference that would be caused by a move from any bankruptcy selection to the no-bankruptcy selection would be a change from the pro rata sharing among general creditors mandated by bankruptcy to the nonbankruptcy rule of first come, first served. The potential danger of allowing unrestrained moves to the latter regime is that the change in bankruptcy option may be done simply to give a particular creditor a preference. . . .

There are two ways in which this opportunistic switch could be prevented. The first, as in the case of the switch to a Chapter 11 selection, would be to require creditor approval of the change. . . . The second way to handle the problem of opportunistic switching would be that, absent creditor approval, the firm could change its charter, but would have to wait a set period of time, say one year, before the change became effective. . . .

Equity holders might strategically amend away from the no-bankruptcy option, when that rule is the traditional state-law remedy, in two other ways. The first is simply to stay the collection efforts of its creditor. . . . For this reason, changes from no-bankruptcy to bankruptcy should require creditor consent. . . .

The second possible manipulation by the managers may be to reallocate assets to themselves, just as in the case of the potential switch from Chapter 7 to Chapter 11. Thus, for the same reasons that the switch from Chapter 7 to Chapter 11 must be conditioned on creditor consent, so must the switch from no-bankruptcy to Chapter 11. . . .

The final amendment problem that should be considered is one involving the selective stay. The move from a selective stay to another form of bankruptcy law should require the consent of the financing lender. It is the party that could potentially lose out if such an amendment is made opportunistically. . . . Similarly, a move from a selective stay to the no-bankruptcy option should require the approval of all creditors. . . .

Potential amendment to the selective-stay option also requires legal constraints. Allowing freedom of movement from a bankruptcy option to the selective-stay situation creates the possibility of using the change to prefer the financing lender. Thus, such a change would require creditor approval. . . .

The above analysis also answers a practical problem with the proposed menu approach; namely, what we should do about firms that already exist. While a menu approach may be superior for firms formed after the menu has been put into place, one may ask what should be done with the many firms that never had the choice to select their bankruptcy term because of the law's current insistence on treating bankruptcy law as a mandatory rule. The answer to this problem is simple: all current firms have contracted based on the assumption that the firm could file for Chapter 11. In other words, all firms have been paying premiums for reorganization insurance. . . . Thus, all existing firms should be presumed to have selected the Chapter 11 option. . . . If a firm desires a different option, it should have to follow the amendment procedures detailed above.

IV. Conclusion

For too long bankruptcy scholars have failed to realize that bankruptcy law is really part of contract law. The reorganization proceeding offered by federal bankruptcy law is simply a term in the fully contingent contract between a firm and each of its creditors. When the focus shifts from a firm in trouble to the contract that the firm would offer those deciding whether or not to extend credit to the firm in the first instance, many of our previously held conceptions about the nature of bankruptcy shift as well. One prominent shift is the assumption that the availability of Chapter 11 is a mandatory rule. A world with a menu of bankruptcy options is certainly no worse, and indeed may be quite better, than the world as it exists today.

Barry E. Adler
Financial and Political Theories of American Corporate Bankruptcy
45 STAN. L. REV. 311 (1993)[*]

I. INTRODUCTION

What explains American corporate bankruptcy, with its time-consuming and expensive reorganization process? . . .

I argue here that the willingness of creditors and other investors to accept the corporate bankruptcy process is as much a political adaptation as an economic decision. . . . In a legal environment hospitable to all forms of contract, investors could agree efficiently to preserve a firm's value without the aid of the costly, rule-based bankruptcy process. We do not observe such agreements in the United States because political compromises have produced a legal regime that discourages optimal contracts. . . .

Part V proposes a "Chameleon Equity" firm as a hypothetical contractual arrangement that could, in theory, eliminate the need for reorganization, and without the risk that creditors would dismantle a viable firm. A Chameleon Equity firm would issue no traditional debt, and would structure its capital in a hierarchy with common equity investors at the bottom and preferred investors owed fixed obligations stacked in classes above. No investor would have the right individually to collect a fixed obligation from the firm. Should a Chameleon Equity firm become insolvent and default on its obligations, the common equity class would vanish as would the fixed claims of the next lowest investor class, which would then become the new common equity class. All other claims would survive unchanged. Such a firm could pass through insolvency at lower cost than a similar traditional firm that passes through bankruptcy. The absence of conventional debt distinguishes the Chameleon Equity firm from existing and proposed firms and provides the key to understanding why we do not observe Chameleon Equity in practice. . . .

Part VII uses public choice theory to explain the perseverance of these inefficient laws despite potential gains from reform. Those who would benefit from an efficient insolvency process include dispersed investors with diversified interests, dispersed tort victims, and the plaintiffs' bar—all but the last relatively poor candidates for effective organization. In contrast, the beneficiaries of the current regime include business lawyers, corporate managers, and politicians, who are relatively concentrated holders of relatively undiversified interests. Business lawyers and their clients, corporate managers, form effective lobbying groups that would oppose limitations on managerial discretion to control the bankruptcy process or to issue traditional debt. Politicians may use the corporate income tax as a bargaining tool in their discussions with corporate lobbying groups. The politicians would be unlikely to sacrifice this tool in the name of efficiency. Thus, the small benefits derived by a few from the current legal regime may, on a political scale, be sufficiently concentrated to outweigh the potentially larger benefits of reform.

In sum, I conclude in this article that a legal system hospitable to Chameleon Equity would have no use for bankruptcy. The political reality, however, is that the needed reforms are impractical. Society as a whole suffers the consequences. . . .

IV. PARTIAL SOLUTIONS

One might expect that the expense of the current bankruptcy process would prompt proposals for reform. It has. Some proposals present market solutions to bankruptcy valuation problems. Starting with the assumption that both the relationships among creditors and those between creditors and equity investors are fixed, each market-based proposal offers amendments to the bankruptcy process that intervene only after insolvency threatens those relationships. By contrast, *ex ante* proposals reach back before insolvency and suggest how investors might structure their claims initially to minimize potential insolvency costs. While each market-based or *ex ante* structuring proposal may offer some improvement over current bankruptcy law, each could leave investors with substantial costs of reorganization, risk of dismemberment, or restrictions on capital structure. Thus, these proposals do not provide a conclusive reason to expect that investors given the choice would adopt an alternative to bankruptcy law. . . .

V. CHAMELEON EQUITY

While no insolvency process is completely costless, a better solution to the problem of expensive insolvency exists. This solution, "Chameleon Equity," would not require an auction or a separate postinsolvency capital structure. Rather, it would give a firm the flexibility to issue a single set of unbundled residual and fixed obligations. A Chameleon Equity firm would closely resemble a traditional firm, except that fixed-obligation Chameleon Equity holders would replace creditors. Such a Chameleon Equity holder would possess the same right as a creditor to set payments from the firm, but it would not be permitted to collect individually on an obligation in default. Instead, if the firm defaulted and remained in default on a fixed Chameleon Equity claim, the holder would gain a portion of the firm's residual claim and of voting control over the firm. Unpaid Chameleon Equity holders could then collectively decide to continue or to liquidate the firm, which would remain subject to any fixed claim not in default. In essence, a Chameleon Equity firm would retain the benefits of fixed obligations but would bear neither the costs that accompany a race to assets nor, in many instances, the costs of reintroducing fixed claims after insolvency.

To maintain investor certainty about the firm's structure and internal insolvency resolution system, the investors would adopt the Chameleon Equity structure at the firm's outset or, if a traditional firm wished to convert, immediately upon the creditors' exchange of debt for Chameleon Equity interests. . . .

A. *Tiered Structure*

To avoid restructuring costs, a Chameleon Equity firm would establish a multi-tiered priority hierarchy by issuing claims in tranches. Traditional equity would comprise the initial residual class, subject to the fixed obligations of any higher-priority Chameleon Equity class. Should a Chameleon Equity firm be unable to meet all of its fixed obligations, it would retain, unaltered, obligations to any higher-priority class of investors with claims the firm could satisfy, convert to traditional equity the highest-priority class whose obligations the firm could not fully pay on time, and extinguish the claims of all lower-priority classes. No asset valuation would be necessary. The new traditional equity class could either retain predefault management, or replace it, at will or in accordance with any prior contractual agreements. After such a transformation, the firm would continue as before with at least one less tranche, but without any change in the surviving fixed obligations or immediate need for further alteration of its capital structure. . . .

As an illustration, assume that a traditional firm with equity, unsecured debt, and secured debt assumes a Chameleon Equity structure, then becomes insolvent and defaults on its obligations. The equity investors will lose their interest in the firm, while the unsecured claimants will gain control of the firm and have the residual claim against its assets. The firm will remain subject to the secured claims under their original terms, including the obligations to cure any current payment default and to comply with any continuing conditions of the credit contracts. If the firm later defaults on the secured obligations, the secured claimants will become the sole claimants. Thus, the firm will lose its fixed obligations only when the insolvency reaches the highest-priority class. This ensures that insolvency or a desire for some debt in the firm's capital structure will not easily force a sale or court valuation of the firm.

Moreover, the potential benefit of Chameleon Equity extends beyond the traditional three-tiered firm in this illustration. To forestall the day on which the highest-priority class could become the residual class, investors could initially establish numerous classes, making the highest-priority investor class sufficiently "thin" so that by the time it ever held the residual claim, the firm would probably have become unworthy of any restructuring and a candidate for piecemeal liquidation. Such a firm could conceivably continue to exist subject to fixed obligations and free from the need to issue new debt despite repeated insolvencies.

B. *Secured Finance*

The Chameleon Equity structure could easily accommodate incidental arrangements such as secured finance. A Chameleon Equity firm would offer collateral only to its highest-priority consensual claimants. So long as these claimants never became the residual class, secured claimants would receive payment in full, and collateral would prove unnecessary. If the highest-priority class ever became the residual class, then any secured claimant in that class would have the right to foreclose on its collateral unless the investors agreed otherwise. . . .

C. *Subsequent Capital*

The adoption of a Chameleon Equity structure need not restrict the firm's ability to raise capital. Just as a traditional firm may issue new obligations subject to any restrictions agreed on by existing investors, a Chameleon Equity firm could issue new obligations subject to contractual restrictions. Initial investors could permit subsequent issuances of obligations in all, some, or no classes, and could provide the terms by which their initial decision could be amended.

Even financially unsophisticated trade creditors could fit easily into this structure by signing a standard form contract placing them either entirely in one priority class or partially in multiple classes. Although such creditors might often find themselves in the lowest-priority class, this fact does not distinguish a Chameleon Equity firm from a traditional firm. In a traditional firm, creditors whose lack of sophistication leads them to accept a firm's terms at face value similarly end up with the low-priority status of a general creditor. . . .

Investors in a Chameleon Equity firm could . . . sensibly authorize management to issue high-priority claims despite financial distress and lack of court supervision if the issue were conditioned on a Chameleon Equity transformation. After a transformation—Chameleon Equity's counterpart to a bankruptcy petition—the new equity class would likely have a substantial stake in the firm that management as equity's agent would be reluctant to gamble and would have the authority to invest only as limited by prior contract. Thus, Chameleon Equity could easily solve in advance the new capital problem that bankruptcy solves only through the laborious process of regulation and oversight.

D. *Capital Retention*

Firms in financial distress can find retaining capital to be as difficult as raising new capital. . . . Chameleon Equity contracts could provide that a nonpriority, nonratable payment would constitute a transformation default. The prospect of such a transformation and the termination of equity could well dissuade equity's agent, management, from having the firm make preferential transfers while insolvent. . . .

E. *Agency Costs*

Although Chameleon Equity would significantly reduce the expense of insolvency, it would not cure all conflicts among investors or between investors and managers. . . . [A] firm's equity investors like the firm to take risks that claimants with fixed obligations prefer it avoid. This is particularly true when the firm is at or near insolvency and the residual claimants face a complete loss of their investment unless they can enhance the firm's value. . . . The conflict cannot be fully eliminated, however, and it would exist in a Chameleon Equity firm as it does in a traditional firm.

Management discretion creates another agency problem common to all firms that separate ownership and control. When making business decisions, managers' personal incentives may conflict with the goal of maximizing firm value. . . .

A Chameleon Equity firm's susceptibility to these agency problems is not, however, a valid criticism of Chameleon Equity as an insolvency process. Each of these problems would be *no greater* in a Chameleon Equity firm than in a traditional firm of similar structure. Moreover, assuming that firms separate debt and equity interests, neither current bankruptcy law nor any proposal for reform of the insolvency process better addresses these problems than does Chameleon Equity. Therefore, a Chameleon Equity structure would save insolvency expenses without imposing any additional agency costs.

F. *A New Look at Preferred Stock*

For all the emphasis on Chameleon Equity's advantages over traditional firm structure, Chameleon Equity is, in essence, an old idea. It is merely a variant of preferred stock, one with a contingent right to common equity and control of the firm if the firm fails to pay dividends or to repurchase the stock after a specified period. . . .

In essence, a Chameleon Equity firm differs from a traditional firm that issues preferred stock with contingent control rights only in that a Chameleon Equity firm would replace *all* traditional debt with preferred stock. The novelty of Chameleon Equity is not its postdefault method of passing control and the residual claim up through its tiered structure. Instead, the novelty lies in the Chameleon Equity firm's complete prohibition of both traditional debt and the fixed claimant's individual collection right.

This insight, while important, is not obvious. It was, for example, overlooked by Michael Bradley and Michael Rosenzweig who, in a paper prepared contemporaneously with this one, suggest that a firm could eliminate the need for bankruptcy by issuing contingent equity shares to its creditors. Under their proposal, default would trigger the contingency, allowing the lowest-priority creditors to replace equity as the residual claimants in control of the firm. The residual claim would pass up the class hierarchy as with Chameleon Equity. But this is where the similarity ends. Bradley and Rosenzweig would not have creditors give up their traditional rights of individual debt collection. Instead, they posit that creditors would have little incentive to race to the courthouse and the debtor's assets once the residual claim passed from equity. On this point, Bradley and Rosenzweig are wrong. It is true that creditors would have nothing to gain from equity, which would vanish. But each creditor could have much to gain from the other creditors. Thus, competition for firm assets would threaten any going-concern surplus and the Bradley-Rosenzweig proposal would not serve an insolvency process' primary function-avoiding a common pool problem. Moreover, because this proposal, like others, countenances traditional debt, it fails to focus on the salient feature of a pure preferred stock firm—the absence of traditional debt. And failure to focus on the prospect of a firm without debt diverts attention from a critical question: Why don't we see such firms?

VI. An Inhospitable Legal Environment

Investors prefer traditional firms and bankruptcy to Chameleon Equity because legal rules create incentives that make the latter untenable. Most prominent among these rules is the provision of a nonwaivable bankruptcy option. But the importance of such an option is dubious. Other rules include the corporate income tax, commercial and corporate law limitations on free contracting, and insufficient priority for tort victims. Standardization of the bankruptcy process presents an additional obstacle. . . .

A. *Waiver of Bankruptcy*

. . . Alan Schwartz argues that bankruptcy law forbids bankruptcy option waivers such as those that would be required in a Chameleon Equity firm. . . . But Schwartz misplaces his focus on the nonwaivability of the bankruptcy option. Whether management could initiate a bankruptcy case is unimportant. What matters is whether management could sustain the bankruptcy process. In the case of a Chameleon Equity firm, a court would quite likely dismiss a bankruptcy case filed by management contrary to prior agreement because contractual insolvency procedures would leave no issue for the court to resolve. . . .

B. *Corporate Income Tax*

The corporate income tax is probably the greatest single impediment to Chameleon Equity. The Internal Revenue Code permits a firm to deduct interest but not dividends from taxable income. Because a Chameleon Equity firm would grant holders of fixed obligations a contingent right to control the firm—subject to any higher-priority obligations—rather than a right to collect, the Internal Revenue Service would likely classify even fixed Chameleon Equity obligations as equity interests. As a result, if investors adopted a Chameleon Equity structure, they would likely sacrifice the tax advantage of traditional debt. . . .

C. *Commercial and Corporate Law Limitations*

. . . Uncertainties in commercial and corporate law also limit investors' ability to structure a Chameleon Equity firm. At its core, Chameleon Equity is an agreement among all investors that an individual investor will have the right to collect a debt from the firm only to the extent provided by the firm's initial contracts. . . .

In practice, however, investors have no effective way to bind future third parties who might purchase traditional debt from a firm. Consequently, management could have a Chameleon Equity firm issue traditional debt. If the firm then became insolvent, any traditional creditor would hold an absolute right to payment and the legal authority to individually enforce that right. Chameleon Equity investors, who would at all priority levels lack an individual collection right, could find themselves in the subordinate position of preferred stockholders. . . .

D. *Nonconsensual Claimants*

The status of nonconsensual claimants under existing law is another impediment to Chameleon Equity. Every nonconsensual claimant has an individual right to collect from a debtor. A Chameleon Equity contract could not alter this right because, by definition, nonconsensual claimants are not parties to such contracts. Consider a Chameleon Equity firm unable to fully satisfy its nonconsensual and consensual fixed obligations. The nonconsensual claimants could exercise their collection right and receive full payment to the extent possible out of firm value that would otherwise be available to consensual claimants with unsecured fixed obligations. . . .

In contrast to fixed obligation Chameleon Equity investors, ordinary creditors possess from the outset the same right as tort victims to collect on obligations in default and do not possess even a contingent right to general control of the debtor. As a result, they face little risk of subordination. . . . The risk of tort liability and investor subordination may not be large for many firms, and may not, therefore, be a substantial determinant of corporate structure. But firms overwhelmed by tort claims are not extraordinary. Whatever the size, the risk is a factor that guides investors away from Chameleon Equity.

Ideally, nonconsensual claimants would have highest priority in any sort of firm. This change in the law would both encourage efficient project choices that minimize external risk and eliminate the existing bias against Chameleon Equity or a similar alternative insolvency process.

Apart from the affirmative disincentive to adopt Chameleon Equity that tort law's inferior priority scheme creates, the tort victim's collection right itself limits Chameleon Equity's potential usefulness. Tort victims acting individually can compete with one another as well as with any traditional creditors, and might, but for bankruptcy, dismember an insolvent but viable firm. Therefore, to permit protection of potential going-concern surplus without bankruptcy, tort law should provide that victims of a Chameleon Equity firm could not exercise individual collection rights. Tort claimants would not lose a right to compensation or the advantage of their status—if the law so granted—as highest-priority claimants. The law would permit nonconsensual Chameleon Equity claimants rights similar to those of consensual Chameleon Equity claimants. . . .

E. *The Power of an Entrenched Standard*

Reinforcing external impediments, the very presence and common use of the bankruptcy option may dissuade investors from adopting a more efficient alternative such as Chameleon Equity. . . .

This is not an argument of inefficiency but of entrenchment. . . . [E]ven if we removed the government subsidy of the bankruptcy process and all bias against Chameleon Equity, bankruptcy might survive by the power of inertia. Thus, to spur effective reform, it may be necessary to eliminate bankruptcy entirely or, at a minimum, make it a less convenient option.

VII. PUBLIC CHOICE

Bankruptcy's predominance is likely an accident largely of tax, commercial, corporate, and tort laws that dissuade investors from adopting a more efficient insolvency process. Standard public choice theory offers an explanation of why these laws exist. Public choice theory posits that organized groups can persuade politicians—with campaign contributions, honoraria, and in-kind benefits—to adopt or retain rules the groups prefer, even if the rules impose great costs on others who are unable or unwilling to effectively organize in opposition. Corporate bankruptcy survives because its costs are too dispersed to overcome the concentrated interests of those who benefit from the bankruptcy process or the laws that preserve it.

A. *Diffuse Costs and Diversified Investment*

Investors bear most of bankruptcy's costs and would be the primary beneficiaries of an insolvency process like Chameleon Equity. However, investors are ill-suited to be effective lobbyists on this issue. . . . [W]hile investors wish to minimize the costs of insolvency, an investor with diversified interests is not at great risk that those costs will seriously impair its own wealth or viability. This lack of urgency will dampen investors' willingness to fund reform efforts. Compounding this dampened interest is entrenchment of the current bankruptcy process. . . .

As claimants, tort victims also suffer from current bankruptcy law. However, potential tort victims by nature have difficulty organizing as a group. Actual tort victims are scattered and not identifiable in advance. . . .

Another potential difficulty is the prospect that investors and potential tort victims would be at odds in any reform effort. . . .

B. *Concentrated Benefits*

Opposite the dispersed reform interests of investors and potential tort victims stands an impressive array of status quo beneficiaries. These beneficiaries include the bankruptcy and corporate bars, incumbent corporate managers, and politicians.

1. *Attorneys.*

Members of the bankruptcy and corporate bars are direct beneficiaries of the current bankruptcy regime and the commercial and corporate laws supporting it. These attorneys possess substantial sunk investments in knowledge of the current bankruptcy and corporate systems and benefit from the complexity and uncertainty of the current laws. Consequently, the well-organized bankruptcy and corporate bars can be expected to oppose any reform proposal—whether in bankruptcy law or the underlying tax, commercial, corporate, or tort law—that threatens members' investments in human capital.

Reform that would permit Chameleon Equity would threaten the lawyers' sunk investments. By eliminating bankruptcy and simplifying the insolvency process, Chameleon Equity would eliminate the bankruptcy lawyer's specialty without providing a substitute field. Hence it is easy to predict that bankruptcy lawyers would oppose reform. Similarly, corporate lawyers, though perhaps not as directly interested in the bankruptcy law, are also likely to oppose any underlying changes in commercial and corporate law needed to facilitate Chameleon Equity. . . .

2. *Managers.*

Incumbent corporate managers also benefit from the status quo. They are almost certain to oppose any reform that threatens their discretion. Therefore, managers—like bankruptcy and corporate lawyers—may oppose not only reform of the bankruptcy system, which currently gives them discretion to direct an insolvent firm and delay the insolvency process, but also reform of tax, commercial, corporate, and tort laws that directly or indirectly prevent investors from tying management's hands.

Managers are well organized and effective lobbyists . . . . Reform proposals that would permit Chameleon Equity would implicate managers' vital interests. . . . [A] manager could lose much if the firm she manages becomes insolvent. . . . Bankruptcy offers a manager an opportunity to save herself from personal disaster. This opportunity may be more valuable to managers and their lawyers than the dispersed savings of Chameleon Equity would be to investors and the plaintiffs' bar. Thus, the intensity of management interest in controlling the insolvency process helps explain the existence of current bankruptcy law and its survival in the face of potential reform.

3. *Politicians.*

Legal and managerial lobbies benefit not only lawyers and managers, but the lobbied politicians as well. . . . In this context, Chameleon Equity's chief impediment, the corporate income tax, is an ideal vehicle through which politicians barter with interest groups. . . .

VIII. CONCLUSION

Without existing legal and political disincentives, investors would agree to avoid many of the costs associated with the current bankruptcy system. In principle, contract can solve the fabled common pool problem that is the primary justification for bankruptcy law, and can do so without bankruptcy's sometimes staggering costs. Yet we do not observe contractual alternatives to bankruptcy, likely because the most effective of these alternatives, such as the "Chameleon Equity" structure proposed in this article, face an array of tax, commercial, corporate, and tort law impediments and limitations. Potential efforts to reform those impediments and limitations face, in turn, a powerful concentration of political interests that prefer and preserve the status quo, inefficient though it may be.

Alan Schwartz
A Contract Theory Approach to Business Bankruptcy
107 Yale L.J. 1807 (1998)[*]

II. Contracting for Bankruptcy Systems

A. *A Methodological Introduction*

. . . In the real world, the contract theory problem is not trivial for two reasons. First, investors may be unable to observe at reasonable cost how the firm is spending their money—*i.e.*, there may be hidden action. Second, it may be very costly to write contracts that proscribe certain ex post actions and require others. . . . In addition, proving in court that an action is suboptimal . . . would be difficult and costly. When the investment contract cannot expressly require the firm to behave optimally, the contract theory problem is to identify the contract, if any, that will induce optimal actions.

This Essay asks whether parties can contract to use the bankruptcy system that is optimal in their situation. A contracting problem exists because an insolvent firm and its creditors may disagree ex post about which bankruptcy system to use. Conditional on insolvency's having occurred, the firm's managers or owners will prefer the bankruptcy system that is more likely to permit the firm to survive or to enable them to enjoy control privileges for a longer time if it ultimately fails. The creditors will prefer the system that maximizes the firm's net expected insolvency return because creditors can recover only monetary returns.

If parties can choose bankruptcy systems, and a particular firm and its creditors expect a certain system always to be optimal for them, then the contract theory problem is trivial. These parties would write a contract requiring the firm to use the efficient bankruptcy system upon insolvency. The contract theory problem is serious, however, because the optimality of a bankruptcy system is state-dependent: Under some values of the *ex post* economic parameters, it would be efficient to liquidate the firm, while under other values, reorganization would be best. Thus, a lending agreement that required the firm to use a bankruptcy system that commonly chooses reorganization might turn out to yield a suboptimal result. . . . Describing all of the possible facts and their implications in the lending agreement would be costly.

Bankruptcy contracting, therefore, poses a difficult contract theory problem. In consequence, the model described below assumes that parties can contract over bankruptcy systems but cannot write contracts of the form: "Choose system *A* in the following circumstances; otherwise, choose system *B*." This model supports two claims. First, a set of contracts that will induce optimal bankruptcy choices exists. Second, prohibiting parties from writing these contracts produces the bad effects described above. Firms could finance more projects if they had more freedom to contract, and they would have better incentives to maximize value.

---

    *   Reprinted by permission of The Yale Law Journal Company and Fred B. Rothman & Company from The Yale Law Journal, Vol. 107, pages 1807-1851.

B. *The Model*

There are three obstacles to the making of bankruptcy contracts: A firm may have numerous creditors; these creditors may lend at different times; and they may have different preferences about bankruptcy systems. The analysis begins by assuming that all of a firm's creditors lend at the same time and have the same preferences respecting bankruptcy. On these assumptions, the obstacle of numerous creditors dissolves because the firm can offer the same contract to everyone. This part initially takes up the question of whether parties would contract about bankruptcy systems under the assumed conditions, and what the effects of banning the contracts that parties might write would be. Later, this part argues that the conclusions reached initially do not change when sequential credit extensions and heterogeneous preferences are taken into account.

A firm has a project to pursue. At a time denoted t^0, the firm attempts to borrow the project's cost in a competitive capital market. The project will begin at t^1 and the firm will repay its creditors at t^2 if the project is successful. If the firm is insolvent at t^2, it will choose a bankruptcy system to use at t^3. The project continues to run during the course of the system the firm chooses, and creditors are paid their bankruptcy return at t^4. Two bankruptcy systems are assumed to exist. One, denoted R, is the current Chapter 11 reorganization regime with two exceptions: Unlike the current regime, system R strictly follows absolute priority. Also, parties are free to contract in the lending agreement for system R or the other system. This system, denoted L, auctions insolvent firms, or the assets of those firms, to the market, distributing the proceeds strictly according to absolute priority.

The monetary return the firm earns during bankruptcy is a function of the bankruptcy system the firm chose and the circumstances obtaining when the firm made the choice. Under some circumstances, it will be optimal for the firm to use the system R, and under other circumstances, L will be best. . . .

The parties may also choose not to contract about bankruptcy in the lending agreement. In this event, the firm will either choose the system it prefers given the circumstances obtaining when it becomes insolvent, or the parties may renegotiate after insolvency. . . .

To understand when parties will write contracts about bankruptcy, rely on renegotiation to induce an optimal bankruptcy choice, or let the firm choose unimpeded, it is necessary to make the conflict between an insolvent firm and its creditors more precise. Firms generate monetary returns, and their owners or managers can consume private benefits. . . . [P]rivate benefits are assumed to be unverifiable. . . . As a consequence, the lending agreements here . . . cannot ban or regulate private benefits by contract. These benefits are the principal source of conflict between the firm and its creditors.

In particular, because creditors are legally entitled to the monetary return when the firm becomes insolvent, creditors want the firm to choose the bankruptcy system that maximizes monetary returns. In contrast, since after insolvency the firm legally has no claim to monetary returns, the firm prefers the bankruptcy system that permits it to consume the most private benefits. The firm makes an optimal bankruptcy choice when it picks the system that maximizes the sum of monetary returns and private benefits.

When a certain state of the world obtains *ex post* that is denoted $_L$, it is assumed to be optimal for the parties to use the bankruptcy system L; this system would maximize the sum of monetary returns and private benefits for these parties. When the second possible state of the world obtains *ex post*, denoted $_R$, it will be optimal to use system R. Thus, a firm that makes optimal bankruptcy choices will choose system L when state $_L$ obtains, and will choose system R when state $_R$ obtains. The parties know the probability that one or the other of these *ex post* states will materialize.

The private benefits that the firm can obtain derive from continuing with its project. These benefits are likely to be greater under bankruptcy system R because this system prefers reorganization and thus permits the firm to survive intact for a longer period. It is assumed that the firm derives greater private benefits from system R whichever state of the world obtains *ex post*—i.e., the firm will always choose system R unless it is constrained by *ex ante* contract or by *ex post* renegotiation.

Recall that choosing system L when state 0_L obtains maximizes the sum of monetary returns and private benefits. If the firm nevertheless obtains greater private benefits from choosing system R even when the circumstances summarized by 0_L obtain, it must follow that monetary returns are maximized by system L given 0_L. As a consequence, when state 0_L does obtain *ex post*, the insolvent firm and its creditors will be in conflict: The firm will prefer system R—i.e., want to reorganize— but the creditors will prefer system L—i.e., want to liquidate. Moreover, if the firm is unconstrained, it will inefficiently choose system R. In contrast, the parties' preferences are in harmony when state 0_R obtains. The firm will prefer to choose system R then, and because R in this case generates greater monetary returns than L, the creditors will prefer R as well. The parties' contracting problem thus is to induce the firm to choose bankruptcy system L when the *ex post* state of the world 0_L obtains.

. . . . The timing of the game is illustrated in Figure 1.

Figure 1

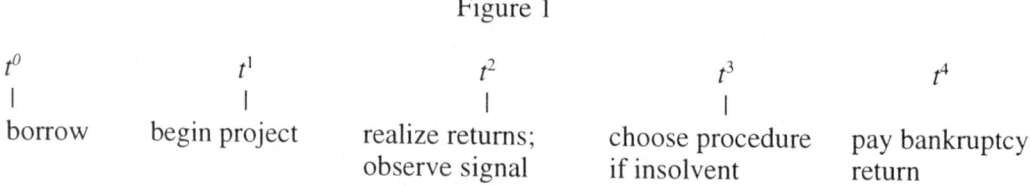

In this model, firms bear the consequences of choosing inefficient bankruptcy systems. . . . Firms have an incentive to offer lending agreements to creditors that minimize the moral hazard risk. A firm, however, cannot simply promise to use the efficient bankruptcy system (to choose system L when *ex post* state 0_L obtains) because the circumstances that make a system optimal cannot be described in a contract. Can the firm otherwise make a credible commitment to choose optimally?

C. Bankruptcy Contracts

A firm has three contractual choices in the situation modeled here. First, it can offer creditors a "renegotiation-proof" contract that will induce the firm to choose the optimal bankruptcy system in the event of insolvency. . . . Second, the firm can offer creditors a contract that does not deal with bankruptcy. In this case, the parties rely on renegotiation to induce the optimal bankruptcy choice. Third, the firm can offer a contract that conditions the bankruptcy choice on a signal that correlates with the firm's *ex post* circumstances. . . . [T]his contract is called "partially renegotiation proof." The firm will offer creditors the contract that maximizes the creditors' expected insolvency return because this will maximize the amount the firm can borrow.

1. Renegotiation-Proof Contracts

The firm must be bribed to choose optimally because it cannot be required to choose optimally. A renegotiation-proof contract bribes the firm by permitting it to keep $s\%$ of the insolvency mone- tary return no matter which bankruptcy system the firm chooses. The firm does better monetarily if it chooses the system that maximizes monetary returns, but the firm also wants to consume private benefits. Hence, the percentage s must be high enough so that the firm will do better all in all when it makes the optimal choice of a system.

To see how the percentage s is set, recall that the object is to induce the firm to choose bank- ruptcy system L when insolvency state 0_L obtains. Denote the firm's monetary return when it does choose L in this case as y_{LL} and the firm's monetary return when it inefficiently chooses system R as y_{LR}. Also, denote the firm's private benefits when it chooses system L in state 0_L as b_{LL}, and its private benefits when it inefficiently chooses system R as $b_{L,R}$. If the firm must do better all in all choosing system L when 0_L obtains, the following inequality must be satisfied:

$$sy_{L,L} + b_{L,L} \geq sy_{L,R} + b_{L,R}$$

Recall that s is the percentage share of the insolvency monetary return that the contract permits the firm to keep. The first term on the left-hand side of this inequality is the firm's monetary payoff from choosing the optimal bankruptcy system L in state 0_L, and the first term on the right-hand side is the firm's monetary payoff if it chooses suboptimally. The second term on the left-hand side represents the private benefits the firm realizes if it chooses the efficient system L in state 0_L, and the second term on the right-hand side represents the larger private benefits the firm would obtain from choosing the suboptimal system. The left-hand side of the inequality will exceed the right-hand side if the firm's share of the relatively high monetary return from choosing optimally makes up for the lower private benefits of accepting liquidation.

Solving this inequality for s^*, the optimal bribe, yields

$$s^* = \frac{b_{L,R} - b_{L,L}}{y_{L,L} - y_{L,R}}$$

This equation shows that the optimal bribe is lower when the firm cannot realize significantly greater private benefits from choosing wrongly ($b_{L,R} - b_{L,L}$ is small), and when the marginal monetary return from choosing correctly is large ($y_{L,L} - y_{L,R}$ is big). The reasoning underlying the former result should be obvious. As for the latter, when the marginal return from choosing optimally is large, the firm needs to be given a smaller share of it to induce good behavior.

An immediate implication of this analysis is that the possibility of moral hazard can prevent the firm from financing some projects. If the firm must be given a share of the bankruptcy return to induce optimal behavior, the firm can credibly promise to repay less money when insolvent than it could promise to repay if the firm always behaved optimally. The lower the creditors' insolvency payoff, the less they will lend and some positive value projects that would be funded if creditors could directly control the firm will not be funded when the firm must be bribed. The extent of the inability of a firm to fund good projects and the contribution of bankruptcy contracts to reducing it is best shown by illustration.

The examples that follow assume that the firm has available to it a project that will return $260 if it succeeds. If the project fails, and if reorganization would be optimal, the monetary reorganization return would be $180; if liquidation would be optimal upon project failure, the liquidation return would be $120. The probability that the project succeeds is .8. In the event of failure, the probability that reorganization will be optimal is .3. The reorganization probability is chosen to be relatively low because it is often efficient to liquidate failed firms. If the firm always voluntarily chose the optimal bankruptcy procedure without being bribed, the project would have an expected value of

$$E(R) = .8 \times \$260 + .2 \times (.3 \times \$180 + .7 \times \$120) = \$235.60.$$

. . . To see how a bankruptcy contract could respond to this problem, let the firm obtain private benefits of $40 if state 0_L were to obtain and the firm were to choose bankruptcy system L, and let the firm obtain private benefits of $70 if it were to choose system R instead. . . . [T]he firm would have to be paid one-third of the bankruptcy return in order to induce an optimal bankruptcy choice. This bribe reduces the amount available to creditors in the insolvency state, with the result that the firm can promise to repay creditors at most $226.49. Hence, if the firm's project costs between $226.50 and $235.59, it could not be financed.

This example teaches two lessons. First, a renegotiation-proof contract exists that will induce the firm to choose the efficient bankruptcy system. The contract is renegotiation-proof because the firm does better choosing efficiently and being bribed than choosing inefficiently. Because the contract always induces the firm to choose optimally, the creditors' return is maximized as well and no one has an incentive to renegotiate. . . . The second lesson is that there can be underinvestment even with free contracting: The firm may be unable to finance a positive value project because of moral hazard.

2. Renegotiation Contracts

The firm also could offer creditors a contract that does not deal with bankruptcy. Such a contract would not pay the firm a bribe to choose the optimal bankruptcy system (*i.e.*, $s* = 0$). If state 0_R obtains upon insolvency, the firm would choose system R voluntarily for the reasons given. Because the bribe then is zero, creditors could keep the full monetary return that using the optimal system would generate. On the other hand, if state 0_L were to obtain, the firm would also choose system R unless the creditors bribed it in a renegotiation to choose the optimal system L. It is assumed here that the firm has all the bargaining power and so could capture the entire marginal return from making an efficient bankruptcy choice. In the example here, that would be the difference between the optimal-state 0_L liquidation return and the suboptimal-state 0_L reorganization return ($120-$30 = $90). On the values for the parameters here, such a renegotiation contract would produce an expected gain for creditors of

$$E(R) = .8 \times \$260 + .2(.3 \times \$180 + .7 \times \$30) = \$223.00.$$

. . .

3. Partially Renegotiation-Proof Contracts

A partially renegotiation-proof contract would condition on a signal that correlates with the firm's insolvency-state circumstances. Denote this signal v and assume that a high value for v signals an increasing probability that the firm is in state 0_R, in which the firm would choose the optimal bankruptcy system voluntarily, while a low value for v signals an increasing probability that the firm is in 0_L, in which it would have to be bribed to choose optimally. A partially renegotiation-proof contract would pay a bribe of zero if a high value for v is observed when the firm becomes insolvent and a bribe of $s*_v > 0$ if a low value for v is observed. The parties will renegotiate this contract only if a high value for v is observed, but 0_L surprisingly occurs. In this case, because the contract pays no bribe, the creditors must renegotiate to induce the firm to choose the efficient bankruptcy system.

Partially renegotiation-proof contracts do best when the signal is highly informative. In this event, the parties will seldom have to renegotiate in the state (0_L) when renegotiation would maximally disadvantage creditors. To see how such a contract would work, retain all of the values set out above, and let $_R$ be the probability that the firm is in state 0_R when v_{high} is observed, and $_L$ be the probability that the firm is in state 0_R when v_{low} is observed. Assume that the signal is highly informative: $_R = .9$ and $_L = .1$. Then, using the values in the examples above, the creditors' return under a partially renegotiation proof contract is $235.30. . . .

4. The Effect of Preventing Parties from Writing Bankruptcy Contracts

The legal prohibition on contracting for bankruptcy systems is inefficient because the ban requires parties always to use "renegotiation contracts" even when other contracts would generate higher expected values for creditors. Table 1 illustrates the maximum value that the firm could promise to creditors if it could always voluntarily commit to choosing optimally and under the three contracts considered above.

Table 1

Voluntary Optimal Choice	$235.60
Partially Renegotiation-Proof Contract	$235.30
Renegotiation-Proof Contract	$226.49
Renegotiation Contract	$223.00

Current law will not enforce the first two contracts, which pay bribes to induce firms to make optimal bankruptcy choices. The law forces parties to use the renegotiation contract, which is silent about bankruptcy, relying instead on ex post renegotiation to achieve efficient choice. The table above shows that parties would sometimes eschew renegotiation contracts in favor of one or the other bankruptcy contract if they had a choice. The legal ban on free contracting exacerbates the underinvestment problem: Firms today cannot finance projects that they would be able to finance if the ban were repealed.

The ban additionally worsens firms' incentive to maximize project value. Because firms cannot contract for bankruptcy procedures, they sometimes cannot offer contracts to creditors that maximize the creditors' insolvency payoffs. Consequently, firms must pay too much for debt capital when projects are funded. When firms must share part of the upside return with creditors, they will not invest effort until marginal cost equals marginal gain.

5. *The Choice Between Renegotiation and Contract*

Despite the numerical comparison above, parties will sometimes prefer the renegotiation contract. This preference exists when the expected value of choosing reorganization—system *R*—in the "reorganization state" is high. Reorganization will have a high expected value when there is a high probability that the reorganization state will occur or when the payoff in it will be high relative to the liquidation return. A renegotiation contract maximizes the creditors' expected insolvency return when these conditions obtain because the firm will choose reorganization voluntarily; it need not be bribed. Consequently, creditors could appropriate the entire (high) reorganization return, and this is better for them than a contract that would pay the firm a bribe to choose optimally no matter which *ex post* state occurred. Conversely, when the probability that the firm will be in the "liquidation state" is high, or that the liquidation return will be high relative to the reorganization return, creditors do better under a contract that bribes the firm to choose the liquidation system *L*. Such a contract reserves to creditors some fraction of the liquidation return, while if the parties had to renegotiate to system *L ex post*, creditors would get none of this return. Hence, the current ban on bankruptcy contracts bites only in some cases.

D. *Barriers to Bankruptcy Contracts*

The conclusion that it is inefficient to ban contracting for bankruptcy systems would have only theoretical interest if practical obstacles prevented parties from writing bankruptcy contracts. One possible obstacle to writing these contracts is that a firm may have many creditors. This obstacle is not serious, however, because the firm can offer contracts to creditors, and it would offer to all creditors the efficient contract with respect to bankruptcy. A possibly more serious obstacle is an intertemporal coordination problem because creditors sometimes lend at different times while the parameters that determine which contract would be optimal can be time variant. Another possibly serious obstacle is that a firm's creditors may have inconsistent preferences concerning bankruptcy systems. If so, there is no contract to which everyone will agree. This section argues that parties could overcome these barriers with some help from the law. . . .

1. Intertemporal Coordination

A set of contracts exists that will achieve the results described above even though creditors lend at different times. To describe these contracts, let a firm have two creditors, with the first arriving at t^0 as in the model in Section II.B. Assume that it is optimal at t^0 to use a renegotiation-proof contract that would pay the firm s^* of the bankruptcy return to choose the optimal bankruptcy system. The initial creditor has an incentive to sign this contract . . . . The firm can ensure the initial creditor's consent to the renegotiation-proof contract by offering two "conversion terms" that will update the creditor's contract as later creditors arrive.

To see how these conversion terms would work, assume that a second creditor arrives at t^1 and that it remains optimal to use a renegotiation-proof contract. . . . The first conversion term in the contract with the initial creditor will provide that if the bribe that the time t^1 parameters imply differs from the bribe that the t^0 parameters implied, the bribe in the first contract will convert to the bribe in the second contract. The first creditor would agree to a contract with this feature because the optimal bribe for it will not vary in expectation, and also because the initial creditor always wants the firm to make an optimal bankruptcy choice. The conversion term also ensures that the firm's contracts will be consistent: As of bankruptcy, all contracts will have the same bribe.

There may seem to be more cause for concern if the type of lending agreement that turned out to be optimal at t^1 differed from the contract that initially was optimal. For example, suppose that the parameters at t^0 imply a renegotiation contract rather than the renegotiation-proof contract that the first creditor signed. The firm wants to offer its second creditor the currently optimal contract. Consistency among the firm's contracts can be achieved with a second conversion term, which provides that the initial creditor's contract will convert (only as regards bankruptcy) to the contract type that is currently optimal for the firm. If it becomes optimal for the firm to offer the second creditor a renegotiation contract, the initial creditor's contract will convert to a renegotiation contract as well. The initial creditor would agree to a contract with this conversion term because the firm would switch contracts only if the new contract would give creditors a greater expected return than the old. The firm would offer the conversion term because it benefits from the flexibility to switch contracts as economic conditions change.

A possible objection to these results is that, as regards the renegotiation-proof contract, the firm would strategically not lower the optimal bribe s^* in a contract with the later creditor, though circumstances made a lower bribe efficient. . . . As a consequence, s^* would be systematically biased upward, but in a magnitude that would be hard to anticipate. A creditor that expected the bribe to rise unpredictably might be reluctant to sign a bankruptcy contract.

This form of strategic behavior would be rare for two reasons. First, the optimal bribe typically would not change with time. . . . The optimal bribe would change if the firm would consume relatively more or fewer benefits in an inefficient reorganization than originally thought . . . , or the relative monetary attractiveness of liquidation over reorganization, conditional on liquidation being efficient, unexpectedly varies . . . .

The optimal bribe would also fall if the relative financial attractiveness of liquidation increased, but it is hard to see how that would happen. . . . Firms, therefore, would seldom have an incentive to engage in the strategic behavior described above because the optimal bribe is unlikely to fall materially in the period while the initial credit extension remains unpaid and the firm borrows more money.

The firm would also probably not behave strategically because the behavior can be unprofitable. . . . [T]he expected costs to the firm of offering later creditors inefficient contracts apparently would often outweigh the gains.

To summarize, the presence of numerous creditors that lend at different times would not preclude bankruptcy contracting. The large number-coordination barrier would fall because the firm deals with everyone and so can coordinate bankruptcy contracting. The intertemporal coordination barrier would fall because a set of sequentially efficient contracts respecting bankruptcy exists. This set of contracts would be strategy-proof in the usual case.

2. Creditor Conflict

Creditors care only about monetary returns and so would be able to agree upon contracts that induce firms to choose bankruptcy systems that maximize monetary returns. Such agreement seldom could be achieved today, however, because the current U.S. bankruptcy system does not respect absolute priority. Instead, the liquidation system (Chapter 7) respects absolute priority much more than the reorganization system (Chapter 11) does. . . . As a consequence, senior creditors today commonly prefer firms to use Chapter 7, whether liquidation would be efficient or not, while junior creditors commonly prefer firms to use Chapter 11, whether reorganization would be efficient or not. The creditors in the model here would have similarly conflicting preferences over systems L and R if they expected the two systems to vary in the order in which they paid claims, and this conflict would make bankruptcy contracts hard to write. The model assumes this conflict away by supposing that systems R and L both pay claims strictly in order of priority. . . .

There may be two other sources of creditor conflict. . . . [W]hen creditors are paid pro rata, there is no creditor conflict: Every creditor wants the firm to choose the bankruptcy system that maximizes the monetary return.

This preference would continue to exist in most cases if the firm's creditors ranked unequally. If absolute priority is respected, junior creditors would prefer the firm to choose the system that maximizes the monetary return, because they are paid nothing until claims senior to theirs are paid in full. Turning to senior claimants, a senior claimant would also prefer the firm to choose the optimal procedure if it would be paid less than in full under either system (L or R). A senior claimant would be indifferent to the firm's bankruptcy choice if it would be paid in full under both procedures. Such a creditor would be unwilling to incur the cost of a bankruptcy bribe to induce the firm to choose optimally. A senior creditor who expected to be paid in full regardless of the bankruptcy system the insolvent firm chose, however, would hold riskless debt, and this is unusual. On the analysis so far, then, if systems L and R both respect absolute priority, creditor conflict would seldom exist: Every creditor would be willing to bribe the firm to choose the optimal system except senior creditors who held riskless debt.

Trade creditors, however, would sometimes share the firm's preference for system R, even when R is inefficient, because the firm can operate for a longer time under a reorganization system. A trade creditor may prefer R if the firm would be liquidated piecemeal under system L and the firm would be hard for the creditor to replace. The creditor, perhaps, could earn more in new transactions with the firm during the pendency of a wasteful reorganization attempt than it would lose by having its prebankruptcy debt collected under an inefficient system. Trade creditors who anticipated preferring system R in all cases would be unwilling to bribe the firm to choose system L when L turned out to be optimal for creditors as a group. Too many such holdouts could preclude bankruptcy contracting.

The current Bankruptcy Code binds minority dissenters in a reorganization proceeding to the deal a majority prefer in order to avoid inefficient holdout behavior. For similar reasons, a trade creditor who prefers an inefficient bankruptcy contract should also be bound to the bankruptcy bargain that the *ex ante* majority prefer. The freedom to contract should not be used to prevent efficient contracting.

In sum, if the ban on contracting for bankruptcy systems were repealed and majority rule were to govern the contracting process, the current U.S. system would make a better contribution to the maximization of social wealth. . . .

IV. CONCLUSION

Bankruptcy analysis traditionally has focused on the problems that exist after insolvency has occurred. Scholars agree that a bankruptcy system should attempt to maximize the value of the insolvent estate for the benefit of creditors. High coalition costs prevent creditors from performing this task themselves by coordinating on jointly maximizing debt collection strategies. . . . Most participants in bankruptcy debates do agree, however, that the problems that prevent creditors from coordinating strategies after insolvency would also be present ex ante, when the firm borrows money. Apparently because contracting about bankruptcy is thought to be impractical, few scholars have analyzed the mandatory nature of the U.S. bankruptcy systems. Parties are required to use the bankruptcy system the state supplies, and they cannot contract out of many of the rules in the monopoly system.

. . . Requiring parties to use a single, state-supplied bankruptcy system does not maximize the value of bankrupt estates, because the optimality of a bankruptcy system is state-dependent: No system, however well constructed, is best for parties in all states of the world. Thus requring parties always to use the same system impairs the ability of firms to raise debt capital. In the world of bankruptcy, one size cannot fit all. . . .

Viewing bankruptcy through the lens of contract theory reveals bankruptcy's anachronistic character: Bankruptcy is a government enterprise. The state runs the postal system and the bankruptcy system, and restricts competition with both by law. This Essay's central claim is captured in a variation on a trendy slogan: Privatize bankruptcy.

Skeel's Response

Many proposals have been made to radically restructure corporate bankruptcy. Some of those ideas have been included in the preceding parts of this chapter. The final say goes to Professor David Skeel, who wrote the following article in 1993. In it he examines critically the merits and demerits of many of the most prominent reform ideas. His critique is intriguing both because Skeel is sympathetic to economic analysis as a legitimate method of approaching bankruptcy reform theory, *see, e.g., The Economic Analysis of Corporate Bankruptcy Law*, 3 AM. BANKR. INST. L. REV. 85 (1995) (with Rasmussen), and because he is open to "thinking outside the box" and considering radically new ideas, *see, e.g., Rethinking the Line Between Corporate Law and Corporate Bankruptcy*, 72 TEX. L. REV. 471 (1994). Skeel's careful assessment fittingly concludes this presentation of the debate. But the debate goes on—and it should.

David A. Skeel, Jr.
Markets, Courts, and the Brave New World of Bankruptcy Theory
1993 WIS. L. REV. 465[*]

I. BANKRUPTCY THEORY AND THE EMERGING NEW ORDER . . .

B. *The New Proposals to Replace Chapter 11*

. . . Two central concerns help explain why Chapter 11 is suddenly more out of fashion than Nero. The first, and most obvious, issue is the tremendous costs of Chapter 11. . . . Second, Chap-

---

ter 11 may also have negative effects even before a firm files for bankruptcy relief. Commentators have focused in particular on managers' incentives. Because it limits the downside of any business disaster, they reason, Chapter 11 encourages managers to issue excessive debt and otherwise take excessive risks.

What should be done if we conclude that Chapter 11 has failed of its essential purposes? Almost all of the recent literature argues for the adoption of one or more of four general alternatives in place of the current regime: 1) auctions; 2) implementation of a predetermined bankruptcy capital structure; 3) automatic cancellation of shareholders' interests; and 4) elimination of bankruptcy altogether. I devote the remainder of this part to a brief discussion of the various proposals and of the advantages they appear to offer over Chapter 11.

1. The Bankruptcy Auction

In its current form, Chapter 11 combines the decisions as to how a firm's assets should be deployed—*i.e.*, should the firm be liquidated or reorganized, and if reorganized, in what form—with those concerning the parties' claims and their priorities vis-à-vis one another. This intertwining of the asset deployment and claimant entitlement issues creates two significant and related costs. First, parties' views about entitlement may color their perceptions concerning asset deployment. For instance, unsecured creditors may support an inferior reorganization plan if it offers them a larger piece of the overall pie. Second, inability to resolve asset deployment issues until heterogeneous groups of claimants thrash out their entitlement disputes is costly and can all but paralyze a firm for the duration of a Chapter 11 case. . . .

Douglas Baird was perhaps the first to suggest that Chapter 11 might profitably be jettisoned in favor of an auction, at least if the debtor is a large, publicly held firm. The chief virtue of a mandatory bankruptcy auction is that it would separate the deployment and entitlement decisions. . . . Replacing the hypothetical sale of Chapter 11 with an actual sale might therefore both improve the quality of the asset deployment decision and decrease the deadweight costs of bankruptcy.

2. Implementation of a Preplanned Capital Structure

Both Alan Schwartz and Robert Rasmussen have recently suggested that firms should be permitted to opt out of bankruptcy if they so choose. If Chapter 11 were optional, rather than being a firm's only choice of insolvency regime, debtors might devise their own alternatives to bankruptcy; firms might, for instance, provide for a special "bankruptcy capital structure" in their debt contracts or their charter. . . .

Use of a predetermined capital structure would ideally simplify both the asset deployment and the claimant entitlement decisions, since the parties would make these decisions in advance, at a time when their interests are more likely to be congruent. The strategy also seems largely to obviate the need for judicial involvement in the insolvency process.

3. Automatic Cancellation of Shareholders' Interests:
The Contingent/Chameleon Equity Proposal

The Bradley and Rosenzweig proposal, which has been modified and refined by Barry Adler as a "chameleon equity" approach . . ., boasts similar virtues. These commentators argue for automatic cancellation of shareholders' interests in the event of a default. Upon cancellation of shareholders' interests, the next highest class of claimants would replace them as the firm's shareholders.

Bradley and Rosenzweig envision that a firm in danger of defaulting on its obligations will raise money by issuing equity. Only when the firm's liabilities exceed its assets, and its stock has therefore become worthless, will the firm be unable to sell equity. The firm's subsequent default will reflect true insolvency, thus justifying the elimination of its current stockholders' interests.

One potential benefit of automatic cancellation is its effect on managers' incentives. Because managers cannot look forward to the "soft landing" provided by Chapter 11 in its current form, they will be less inclined to gamble excessively with the firm's assets. Like the implementation of a pre-determined capital structure alternative discussed above, automatic cancellation also dramatically simplifies the asset deployment and claimant entitlement questions by resolving them in advance, and all but eliminates the role of the court.

4. ELIMINATION OF CHAPTER 11 ALTOGETHER

Some commentators have at least tentatively suggested that Chapter 11 should be eliminated altogether and that creditors and their debtors should simply be left to the state law collection regime. James Bowers . . . argues that . . . the debtor [is] the most efficient liquidator of its estate. In his view, bankruptcy[] may interfere with debtors' efforts efficiently to distinguish among their creditors in responding to financial crises. Thus, abolishing Chapter 11 not only would save the direct and indirect costs of a bankruptcy proceeding, it might also facilitate more efficient adjustments by debtors in the event that disaster strikes.

II. WHAT A WONDERFUL WORLD IT WOULD BE?

In this part, I take a closer and more critical look at each of the proposals described in Part I. My aim throughout is to present a fuller picture of the consequences the proposals would have and implicitly to ask, with respect to each, whether it offers an improvement over current Chapter 11. . . .

A. Chinks in the Case for Mandatory Auctions

1. A WORLD THAT ONLY ALLOWED AUCTIONS

Mandatory auctions intuitively seem to offer tremendous savings in comparison with the cost of a protracted Chapter 11 case. An auction can move the assets of a financially troubled firm to the highest valuing user much more quickly, and can prevent asset deployment decisions from bogging down in the parties' negotiations over their respective entitlements. But on closer inspection the promise of mandatory auctions is far less clear.

The chief problem with the mandatory auction proposal—one which largely renders moot the question whether auctions would be any less costly than Chapter 11—is that it simply would not work as intended in the insolvency context. First, auctions are likely to be plagued by an absence of potential bidders. At least with respect to publicly held debtors, few bidders could raise financing sufficiently quickly to participate actively in an auction market. . . . [T]he likelihood of a truly competitive market seems remote. This dilemma is exacerbated by the fact that the most likely bidders for a corporation frequently are firms in the same industry. If the problems that led to the debtor's demise were industry-wide, few or none of these firms would be able to bid. . . .

Second, even in an otherwise competitive market, the potentially enormous costs of gathering and analyzing information, of choosing an appropriate capital structure for the firm, and of the bidding process itself would deter many bidders. Each bidder knows that these costs will be lost for all except the winning bidder and that, if the auction is hotly contested, every bidder may end up with losses. . . .

Because small and medium-sized firms tend to be local or regional in scope, do not regularly supply financial information to the markets, and are most effective if their owners also manage the firm, the limitations of an auction regime would be exacerbated in this context. Moreover, bidders' realizations that the success of a close corporation usually depends upon the continued involvement of its current managers, and that the managers would refuse to stay on board unless they retained their ownership interest, would significantly dampen their incentive to bid. In short, mandatory auctions are problematic even for publicly held corporations and seem wholly implausible as an alternative to Chapter 11 for smaller corporations.

2. Aghion, Hart, and Moore: The Options Alternative

Aghion, Hart, and Moore have recently proposed a modified version of the mandatory auction proposal, one which uses an options scheme originally proposed by Lucian Bebchuk, in an effort to remedy several defects of a pure auction regime. In an options regime, the bankruptcy judge or other official would begin by determining the amounts and respective priorities of all of the claims and interests in the financially troubled firm. The court would distribute all of the firm's stock (subject to redemption) to its senior creditors in lieu of their claims, and members of each lower class would be given options to purchase a pro rata share of the stock temporarily held by senior creditors. . . . The proposal contemplates that lower priority creditors and shareholders would exercise their options only if they felt the firm was worth more than the sum of all superior claims. Thus, the process would ideally put stock in the hands of the true residual claimants of the firm, and provide for payment in full of the firm's higher priority creditors. . . .

The principal advantage of the options alternative lies in its opening up of the bidding process.

. . .

The most obvious problem with the options approach, as with the Bebchuk proposal upon which it is based, is that the distribution and exercise of options that the scheme envisions would only work effectively in a perfectly efficient market. Even if claimants could accurately predict the value of the firm (an extremely problematic assumption, particularly in the insolvency context) and, based on their prediction, make informed decisions as to whether to exercise, the proposal forces them to contribute new cash to the firm if they wish to receive stock. Many claimants may have difficulty raising the necessary cash. . . .

Moreover, a court could not begin distributing stock options to the parties until *after* it had resolved the parties' entitlement disputes; nor could it open the bidding process prior to this point . . ., since shareholder and creditor bidders could not bid until they knew their status within the firm. Untangling the parties' entitlements would significantly delay the auction . . . .

Finally, although the options approach does expand the bidding process, its auctions still would suffer from a serious lack of outside bidders, since industry-wide financial difficulties would create the same problems in this context as they would for the traditional auction approach. In addition, other potential bidders might decline to participate for fear that, because the firm's managers also are likely to be bidders, the managers may and probably would stonewall outsiders who sought to acquire detailed information about the firm.

In short, the options approach offers a valuable twist on the mandatory auction regime, but it is far from a perfect solution to the ills of Chapter 11.

B. A Closer Look at Preplanned Adjustments to the Capital Structure

Preplanned adjustments represent an important departure from the auction-based proposals discussed in the previous section. By deciding its response to financial crisis in advance, the firm eliminates almost all of the direct costs of bankruptcy. Such a regime obviates both the need for an ex post judicial (as in current Chapter 11) or market (as with an auction) valuation, and the need for costly ex post bargaining among the parties. In effect, we shift with this proposal from a partially market-based alternative, to an entirely market-based one.

Two related defects raise serious questions about the proposal, however. First, the costs of negotiating a capital structure in advance could outweigh, and at the least would reduce, the ex post benefits. A debtor would incur these costs even if shifting to the special capital structure never became necessary. Only if insolvency were relatively likely, or the costs of negotiation low, would preplanned adjustments seem a promising solution to the inefficiencies of current Chapter 11. . . .

Second, choosing an insolvency capital structure in advance requires the parties to predict the future. If the firm guessed wrong about the likely source of financial difficulties, changed significantly between its inception and the time it encountered trouble, or both, the special insolvency structure could prove wholly ineffective. To be sure, the parties could attempt to adjust their pre-arranged structure midstream in an effort to address changed conditions, but negotiations of this sort would be costly and frequently unsuccessful. . . .

C. *Another Look at Contingent/Chameleon Equity*

The contingent/chameleon equity proposal proffered by Bradley and Rosenzweig, and by Adler, can be seen as an off-the-rack version of prearranged capital structure. Simply committing to cancel current equity in the event of default, as these commentators propose, saves the parties the costs of negotiating a firm-specific insolvency capital structure and appears to address the twin goals of disciplining management and avoiding the expense of a prolonged bankruptcy proceeding. The proposal also would introduce significant costs, however. . . .

1. THE LIQUIDITY PROBLEM

Initial criticism has focused upon Bradley and Rosenzweig's suggestion that the cancellation of equity would rarely be triggered by premature defaults, as one might fear. So long as the firm is solvent, its managers could solve any cash flow problems by issuing additional equity. Critics have pointed out that this proposal, like the options alternative discussed above, assumes that markets function with perfect efficiency: Managers must be able to raise money quickly and cheaply, in an equity market that assesses accurately the value of the firm.

In the context of publicly held firms, it is at least remotely possible that the market would function somewhat as Bradley and Rosenzweig imagine. To assess the cost of a contingent/chameleon equity regime, one would need to consider the very significant costs of raising equity. One must also take into account the lagtime between the decision to issue equity and actual receipt of the funds. Only if firms could predict a cash crunch sufficiently far in advance, would the equity solution prove effective. A final concern is the risk that cash-strapped firms might be forced to sell equity at artificially low, "fire sale" prices. . . . On the other hand, many large firms *do* look to the equity markets for help with their cash flow problems. . . . To the extent it might force managers to be more judicious in their use of debt, and to the extent the option of issuing equity is available to address temporary crises, contingent/chameleon equity has some initial appeal for a publicly held firm.

Closely held and other small and medium-sized firms are an entirely different story. Issuance of equity is not a viable response to financial difficulties for many of these firms, since the transaction costs alone of a new public issue are likely to be prohibitive. Moreover, investors may hesitate to acquire a minority interest in a close corporation, and dilution of control would undermine many of the virtues of a closely held firm. Downsizing, or sales of nonessential assets, would be equally unavailable as alternatives for firms whose value is tied up in crucial equipment. In short, the liquidity problem alone raises serious doubts about contingent/chameleon equity for all but a narrow slice of publicly held firms. . . .

2. STRATEGIC BEHAVIOR IN PUBLICLY HELD CORPORATIONS

A recurring problem with forfeiture rules—rules that eliminate one party's interest if a specified triggering event occurs—is that they create enormous incentives for strategic behavior. . . .

Both Bradley and Rosenzweig, and Adler neglect this problem; yet, in publicly held firms, contingent equity would create a serious risk of similar opportunism. First, . . . the unsecured creditors of a publicly held firm could use the equity cancellation rule to divert value from shareholders to themselves. . . .

The parties might attempt to curb the threat of strategic behavior by adjusting the default provisions in their debt contracts. One might expect to see fewer "early warning signal" default provisions, and a greater reliance on default provisions (such as payment terms and prohibitions on the sale of essential assets) likely to be triggered only in the event of true, nontemporary financial reverses, as well as more widespread use of cure provisions. Unfortunately, while restricting the breadth of debt contract default terms in this fashion might reduce strategic behavior somewhat, it also would seriously increase the indirect costs of financial difficulties. . . .

The second strategic behavior problem arises from the uncertainty as to who will manage the firm in the event of an equity cancellation. Adler suggests that the firm's new shareholders, its current unsecured creditors, should vote on the managers. The vote he envisions would entail significant expense, including both the direct costs of holding an election and the indirect costs of forgone opportunities during the time before a management team is firmly in place. The prospect of these costs, together with the prospect of substantial indirect costs prior to default, would give unsecured creditors an incentive to strike a deal with the firm's current managers. . . .

In short, in a contingent/chameleon equity regime, unsecured creditors could divert value from shareholders to themselves by either strategically invoking default provisions in their debt contract or colluding with management, or both.

3. MONITORING GONE AMOK: THE COST OF CREDIT IN CLOSELY HELD CONTINGENT/CHAMELEON FIRMS

. . . Liquidity is not the only problem in this context, however. The proposal would also undermine the use of secured credit and, as a result, significantly increase monitoring and thus overall credit costs. . . .

a. *Monitoring and the choice of capital structure*

. . . The most persuasive explanations for secured credit emphasize the bonding effect of security and the monitoring role that secured creditors perform, arguing that secured credit offers efficiencies in policing the debtor that reduce the overall cost of credit. . . .

b. *The cost of the contingent/chameleon*

The problem with contingent/chameleon equity in this context is that it would impair a secured creditor's ability to actively monitor closely held debtors in the fashion described above. Because default has such draconian consequences in a contingent/chameleon equity regime, and because they are unlikely to find alternative financing if they encounter even temporary financial problems, closely held debtors would be even more concerned with narrowing the scope of default terms, or including cure provisions, than the publicly held debtors discussed earlier. Yet loss of the leverage afforded by the current panoply of default terms would significantly limit a secured creditor's ability to actively monitor, particularly with respect to intangible problems such as shirking or underperformance. . . .

In effect, contingent/chameleon equity shifts authority to a firm's unsecured creditors, because they, rather than the secured creditor, will decide the firm's fate in the first instance in the event of a default. Unsecured creditors' newfound authority would force them to take a much more active role in the monitoring process. . . .

Contingent/chameleon equity thus substitutes a regime with many active monitors for one with a single active monitor and numerous passive ones. Moreover, many of these monitors—trade creditors in particular—are particularly unlikely to shoulder this responsibility effectively. By undermining the role of secured credit, and reinjecting unsecured creditors into the process, contingent/chameleon equity would significantly increase the overall cost of credit in closely held firms. . . .

D. A World with No Bankruptcy

Eliminating bankruptcy and relegating the parties to the state law collection regime, as Bowers suggests, holds promise in cases involving a debtor and a secured creditor that is likely to be undersecured in the event of a default. In these cases, bankruptcy often simply postpones an inevitable liquidation and, in doing so, generates significant deadweight costs. . . .

Bowers does not limit his critique of Chapter 11 to this context, however. His view of the debtor as the best liquidator argues for abolition of bankruptcy in a much broader array of cases. The first problem with his proposal is that its predictions conflict with observed reality. Bowers posits that debtors will use security as a means of insuring optimal liquidation in the event of loss. . . . In practice, however, debtors who use secured credit frequently give blanket security interests to their financing lender. One rarely observes the subtle apportioning of security interests that Bowers's analysis has in mind.

More importantly, the proposal would lead to the dismemberment of many corporations that are more valuable as going concerns. Medium-sized and large firms would be particularly vulnerable in this respect. Given their fixed upside return, many creditors would have little incentive to wait patiently as the debtor sought either to renegotiate or to arrange a sale of the firm. . . .

History suggests an additional problem . . . . Critics of the equity receivership process were particularly concerned that management and senior creditors conspired to squeeze out bondholders and other widely dispersed investors.

While investors are probably less vulnerable now than they were in the early decades of the century, one suspects that strategic behavior might once again become a more pressing problem in the absence of bankruptcy. This threat, together with the risk of undesirable and unnecessary dismemberment, makes elimination of bankruptcy a particularly unattractive alternative for all but a limited class of closely held firms.

E. *Summary*

Each of the new proposals to replace Chapter 11 is problematic in important respects. Both the auction proposals and contingent/chameleon equity hold promise only for publicly held corporations. Even in that context, mandatory auctions would suffer from a lack of bidders; and contingent/chameleon equity assumes the existence of smoothly functioning markets for the equity of an insolvent debtor, and would give rise to significant strategic behavior problems even if the assumption held true. In contrast to auctions and contingent/chameleon equity, eliminating bankruptcy makes no sense for a publicly held corporation, although it does seem attractive for some closely held firms.

Additional suggested readings

Charles W. Adams, *An Economic Justification for Corporate Reorganizations*, 20 HOFSTRA L. REV. 117 (1991)

Barry E. Adler, *A Theory of Corporate Insolvency*, 72 N.Y.U. L. REV. 343 (1997)

Barry E. Adler, *Finance's Theoretical Divide and the Proper Role of Insolvency Rules*, 68 S. CAL. L. REV. 401 (1994)

Barry E. Adler, *A World Without Debt*, 72 WASH. U. L.Q. 811 (1994)

Philippe Aghion et. al., *The Economics of Bankruptcy Reform*, 8 J.L. ECON. & ORG. 523 (1992)

Edward A. Altman, *Evaluating the Chapter 11 Bankruptcy Reorganization Process*, 1993 COLUM. BUS. L. REV. 1

John D. Ayer, *Chapter 11: Uses and Consequences*, 4 AM. BANKR. INST. L. REV. 493 (1996)

John D. Ayer, *Bankruptcy as an Essentially Contested Concept: The Case of the One-Asset Case*, 44 S.C. L. REV. 863 (1993)

Douglas G. Baird, *Revisiting Auctions in Chapter 11*, 36 J.L. & ECON. 633 (1993)

Douglas G. Baird & Randal C. Picker, *A Simple Noncooperative Bargaining Model of Corporate Reorganizations*, 20 J. LEGAL STUD. 311 (1991)

Douglas G. Baird, *The Uneasy Case for Corporate Reorganizations*, 15 J. LEGAL STUD. 127 (1986)

Jagdeep S. Bhandari & Lawrence A. Weiss, *The Untenable Case for Chapter 11: A Review of the Evidence*, 67 AM. BANKR. L.J. 131 (1993)

Susan Block-Lieb, *The Logic and Limits of Contract Bankruptcy*, 2001 U. ILL. L. REV. 503

James W. Bowers, *Rehabilitation, Redistribution, or Dissipation: The Evidence for Choosing Among Bankruptcy Hypotheses*, 72 WASH. U. L.Q. 955 (1994)

Jean Braucher, *Bankruptcy Reorganization and Economic Development*, 23 CAP. U. L. REV. 499 (1994)

Frank H. Easterbrook, *Is Corporate Bankruptcy Efficient?*, 27 J. FIN. ECON. 411 (1990)

Theodore Eisenberg & Stefan Sundgren, *Is Chapter 11 Too Favorable to Debtors? Evidence From Abroad*, 82 CORNELL L. REV. 1532 (1997)

Theodore Eisenberg & Shoichi Tagashira, *Should We Abolish Chapter 11? The Evidence From Japan*, 23 J. LEGAL STUD. 111 (1994)

Lisa H. Fenning, *The Future of Chapter 11: One View from the Bench*, 1993-1994 ANN. SURV. BANKR. L. 113

Thomas H. Jackson, Chapter 9, *Reconsidering Reorganizations, in* THE LOGIC AND LIMITS OF BANK- RUPTCY LAW 209-224 (Harvard 1986)

J. Bradley Johnston, *The Bankruptcy Bargain*, 65 AM. BANKR. L.J. 213 (1991)

Edith A. Jones, *Chapter 11: A Death Penalty for Debtor and Creditor Interests*, 77 CORNELL L. REV. 1088 (1992)

Kenneth N. Klee, *Adjusting Chapter 11: Fine Tuning the Plan Process*, 69 AM. BANKR. L.J. 551 (1995)

Donald R. Korobkin, *Vulnerability, Survival, and the Problem of Small Business Bankruptcy*, 23 CAP. U. L. REV. 413 (1994)

Donald R. Korobkin, *The Unwarranted Case Against Corporate Reorganization: A Reply to Bradley and Rosenzweig*, 78 IOWA L. REV. 669 (1993)

Lynn M. LoPucki, *Bankruptcy Contracting Revised: A Reply to Alan Schwartz's New Model*, 109 YALE L.J. 365 (1999)

Lynn M. LoPucki, *Contract Bankruptcy: A Reply to Alan Schwartz*, 109 YALE L.J. 317 (1999)

Lynn M. LoPucki, *Chapter 11: An Agenda for Basic Reform*, 69 AM. BANKR. L.J. 573 (1995)

Lynn M. LoPucki, *Stakeholders in Bankruptcy: Some Comments*, 43 U. TORONTO L.J. 711 (1993)

Lynn M. LoPucki, *The Trouble With Chapter 11*, 1993 WIS. L. REV. 729

Frank R. Kennedy, *Creative Bankruptcy? Uses and Abuses of the Bankruptcy Law—Reflection on Some Recent Cases*, 71 IOWA L. REV. 199 (1985)

Mark E. MacDonald et al., *Chapter 11 as a Dynamic Evolutionary Learning Process in a Market with Fuzzy Values*, 1993-1994 ANN. SURV. BANKR. L. 1

Lawrence Ponoroff, *Enlarging the Bargaining Table: Some Implications of the Corporate Stakeholder Model for Federal Bankruptcy Proceedings*, 23 CAP. U. L. REV. 441 (1994)

Robert K. Rasmussen & David A. Skeel, Jr. *The Economic Analysis of Corporate Bankruptcy Law*, 3 AM. BANKR. INST. L. REV. 85 (1995)

Robert K. Rasmussen, *The Ex Ante Effects of Bankruptcy Reform on Investment Incentives*, 72 WASH. U. L.Q. 1159 (1994)

Linda J. Rusch, *Bankruptcy Reorganization Jurisprudence: Matters of Belief, Faith, and Hope—Stepping into the Fourth Dimension*, 55 MONT. L. REV. 9 (1994)

Steven L. Schwarcz, *Rethinking Freedom of Contract: A Bankruptcy Paradigm*, 77 TEX. L. REV. 515 (1999)

Alan Schwartz, *Bankruptcy Contracting Reviewed*, 109 YALE L.J. 343 (1999)

Alan Schwartz, *Contracting About Bankruptcy*, 13 J.L. ECON. & ORG. 127 (1997)

Alan Schwartz, *Bankruptcy Workouts and Debt Contracts*, 36 J.L. & ECON. 595 (1993)

David A. Skeel, Jr., *An Evolutionary Theory of Corporate Law and Corporate Bankruptcy*, 51 VAND. L. REV. 1325 (1998)

David A. Skeel, Jr., *Rethinking the Line Between Corporate Law and Corporate Bankruptcy*, 72 TEX. L. REV. 471 (1994)

Charles Jordan Tabb, *The Future of Chapter 11*, 44 S.C. L. REV. 791 (1993)

Michelle J. White, *Does Chapter 11 Save Economically Inefficient Firms?*, 72 WASH. U. L.Q. 1319 (1994)

Michelle J. White, *Corporate Bankruptcy as a Filtering Device: Chapter 11 Reorganizations and Out-of-Court Debt Restructurings*, 10 J.L. ECON. & ORG. 268 (1994)

Michelle J. White, *The Corporate Bankruptcy Decision*, 3 J. ECON. PERSP. 129 (1989)

William C. Whitford, *What's Right About Chapter 11*, 72 WASH. U. L.Q. 1379 (1994)